Carmichael's
MANUAL OF CHILD PSYCHOLOGY

Carmichael's

MANUAL OF CHILD PSYCHOLOGY

Third Edition

PAUL H. MUSSEN, *Editor*

VOLUME II

JOHN WILEY & SONS, INC.   New York · London · Sydney · Toronto

Library of Congress Catalogue Card Number: 69–16127

SBN 471   62696   1

Printed in the United States of America

Contributors to Volume II

E. James Anthony
Seymour Feshbach
William Goldfarb
Willard W. Hartup
Robert D. Hess
Martin L. Hoffman
Robert A. LeVine
Eleanor Maccoby
Walter Mischel
H. B. Robinson
N. Robinson

Preface

This is the third edition of the *Manual of Child Psychology*. The first and second editions, edited by Leonard Carmichael, were published in 1946 and 1954 respectively. It should be clear from the outset, however, that the present volumes are not, in any real sense, a *revision* of the earlier editions; this is a completely new *Manual*.

The general purpose of this edition, like that of the previous ones, is to provide a comprehensive and accurate picture of the current state of knowledge—the major systematic thinking and research—in the most important research areas of the psychology of human development. But developmental psychology has been radically transformed, in numerous and complex ways, in the last two decades. While some features of the discipline—its goals, approaches, and research foci—have not changed much, its overall "look" in 1970 is vastly different from what it was in 1950. Complete specifications and analyses of all the changes, which are intimately connected with one another, and of the reasons for them, would require a long essay on the history of the field and the social forces that shaped it. However, a brief survey of some of the enduring characteristics and major shifts may help to provide a broader perspective and to clarify the contrasts between the 1954 edition and the present one.

Many crucial contemporary problems were apparent even in antiquity and have recurred repeatedly throughout the history of developmental psychology; however, they remain unresolved and continue to be the impetus for much research. An example is the problem of whether the individual's development and attainments are primarily determined by his genetic makeup or by environmental conditions, by nature or by nurture? Generally speaking, the basic objectives or tasks of present-day developmental psychology, which are interrelated, are the same ones that characterized the field 20 years ago—description of the genesis of behavior and of age changes; explanation of these (the mechanisms, processes, and determinants of change); delineation of the relationships between early and later behavior. But the distribution of scientific resources and publications devoted to the various goals has changed markedly. Until approximately 25 years ago, developmental psychologists were primarily concerned with precise descriptions of children's capabilities at various ages and reliable determination of age changes in psychological functions such as psychomotor performance, problem solving, and aggressive reactions. And there are continuing needs for more accurate, detailed descriptions of the transformations, continuities, stages, and discontinuities in many aspects of development, particularly in cognitive functions and in social and emotional behavior.

The major contemporary empirical and theoretical emphases in the field of developmental psychology, however, seem to be on *explanations* of the psychological changes that occur, the mechanisms and processes accounting for growth and development. Hypotheses dealing with the beginnings of behavior, and with the determinants of change have been tested experimentally and in naturalistic settings. Investigations of factors correlated with individual differences in psychological functions, traits, and abilities as well as longitudinal research, also yield valuable data bearing on the problems of stability and continuities in development and the mechanisms of change. Compared with the last edition, this one includes many more accounts of studies of these kinds.

Increased interest in mechanisms of change stimulated more theory-building and, consequently, theory seems to be generally more prominent in the literature of developmental psychology today than it was in 1950, often playing a much more critical role in determining the direction of empirical research. This is particularly true in the area of cognitive development, where the theories of Piaget and of Werner have been major sources of research hypotheses and further conceptualizations relating to the nature of perception, thought, and problem solving.

The 1954 edition of this *Manual* had only one theoretical chapter and that was concerned with Levinian theory which, so far as we can see, has not had a significant lasting impact on developmental psychology. Volume I of the present edition includes four chapters exclusively devoted to theory and, in addition, relevant theoretical issues are discussed in some detail in most of the substantive chapters. Psychoanalytic theory is probably not as powerful an intellectual force in child psychology today as it was 20 years ago but it is still important in stimulating and guiding research in personality and social development. Unfortunately, the chapter on psychoanalysis as a developmental theory, originally planned for this edition, was not completed. However, a number of chapters in this volume discuss aspects of this theory and two recent books offer excellent discussions and critiques of psychoanalytic developmental theory.[1]

Like all scientific fields, developmental psychology has experienced its own "knowledge explosion." The sheer number of revelant articles and books has increased, and continues to increase, at an awe-inspiring rate, and the newer literature is broader in scope and more varied in content than that of 20 years ago. Theoretical and empirical analyses of fundamental problems have become more penetrating, refined, and sophisticated. At the same time, the invention of ingenious new methods and techniques of investigation in

developmental psychology and related fields, together with modifications and improvements in older ones, paved the way for more adequate, reliable, and meaningful research into complex problems of long standing (or variations of these) and into more recently formulated questions. As a result of these advances, many new facts have been accumulated and many previously "accepted" findings have been reconsidered and discarded. Some established theories have been revised and abandoned while alternative theoretical approaches have been proposed and systematized. Whole areas of research and theory such as behavior genetics, ethology, and large segments of developmental physiology, hardly existed 20 years ago but, by 1970, they have achieved scientific maturity and contribute substantially to the field of developmental psychology. Largely because of this kind of knowledge explosion and its consequences, this edition of the *Manual* is in two volumes, rather than the one-volume previous edition, and has twice as many pages.

Recent social and historical events have also generated more active concern with the potential practical contributions of the systematic study of developmental psychology. Responding to critical social needs, many developmental and educational psychologists have turned their research attention to applied problems such as promoting cognitive abilities, improving teaching techniques, raising the educational and intellectual status of the culturally disadvantaged, understanding the etiology and treatment of mental retardation and psychopathology, and preventing juvenile delinquency. The findings of empirical investigations in these problem areas have both practical and theoretical significance, as several of the chapters in this volume demonstrate. (See, for example, the chapters in Volumes I and II on early experience, creativity, implications of cognitive development for education, social class and ethnic group influences on socialization, moral values and behavior, mental retardation, behavior disorders, and psychosis in childhood.)

Inevitably, the knowledge explosion and the continuous, if modest, advance in theory and application in developmental psychology have resulted in greater specialization within the field. The organization of the present volume and the contents of the chapters are

[1] See Baldwin, Alfred L., *Theories of child development.* New York: Wiley, 1967, and Langer, Jonas, *Theories of development.* New York: Holt, Rinehart, and Winston, 1969.

testimony of this. While the 1954 edition of the *Manual* had only one chapter on emotional development and another on social psychology, Volume I of the present edition has a major section on socialization, consisting of seven chapters. These deal with the following topics: sex typing and identification, affiliative behavior and dependency, aggression, moral values and behavior, peer interaction, and social organization. Two chapters of the second edition were devoted to mental growth and development, and one dealt with psychopathology. The present edition contains ten chapters on cognitive development (Volume I), and three on abnormal behavior in children (Volume II).

The enormous growth in quantity of relevant literature, the high degree of specialization, and the changing tone of developmental psychology make it exceedingly difficult to produce a full, balanced, accurate, and up-to-date representation of the state of the discipline. In trying to achieve this, I was most fortunate to have the help of five distinguished developmental psychologists who served as an Advisory Committee: Professors Jerome Kagan of Harvard University, William Kessen of Yale University, Eleanor Maccoby of Stanford University, Harold Stevenson of the University of Minnesota, and Sheldon White of Harvard University. We worked together in every phase of planning and organizing this *Manual*, from original conceptualization to final editing.

As we conceived it, the *Manual* is a comprehensive textbook or sourcebook for advanced undergraduate and graduate students as well as for specialists in many areas of psychology and in related fields such as ed-ucation, psychiatry, and pediatrics. Hence, it must represent, as far as possible and in abbreviated form, all the established and influential theories, as well as the reliable accumulated knowledge, in developmental psychology. But it should not consist simply of organized summaries of the literature. Instead, great stress should be given to critical analyses and evaluations; major gaps in theory and data should be illuminated. In brief, the *Manual* should foster the development of new perspectives and insights and, ultimately, it may stimulate some readers to formulate hypotheses and to conduct research.

With this in mind, we made many difficult, critical decisions about the table of contents, essentially pooling our judgments about the areas that are currently most productive of theory and investigation. Obviously, specialized areas of interest could not be fully covered. We collaborated in selecting and inviting recognized authorities who could write stimulating, comprehensive, and integrated chapters, and fortunately, almost all our invitations were enthusiastically accepted. Every "working outline" and final manuscript was reviewed by the editor and at least one member of the Advisory Committee who made suggestions for revisions.

Without the diligent and painstaking work of the authors and the invaluable assistance of the members of the Advisory Committee, this book could not have been completed. I gratefully acknowledge my vast indebtedness to all of them. Whatever success these volumes achieve is due as much to their efforts as to my own.

Paul Mussen

Berkeley, California, January, 1970

Contents

VOLUME II

Carmichael's
MANUAL OF CHILD PSYCHOLOGY

PART IV

SOCIALIZATION

20. Sex-Typing and Socialization[*]

WALTER MISCHEL

This chapter examines some of the processes through which children become psychological males or females. The study of this genesis illustrates many of the chief theoretical, methodological, and empirical problems that arise in investigations of virtually every other aspect of personality development and socialization. An analysis of the development of sex differences in social behavior (rather than in sexual behavior itself) should serve to highlight some of the most basic issues that one must face in efforts to understand socialization in general.

This chapter thus is intended to serve two main purposes. It is an introduction to the area of socialization, and as such raises some fundamental points and problems about personality research that will recur repeatedly in the chapters that follow in this section of the present volume. Simultaneously, this chapter also tries to illustrate the range and meaning of psychological sex differences in social behavior and examines the development of these differences.

The biological differences between the sexes obviously may play an important part in the development of their psychological characteristics (e.g., Broverman et al., 1968). A good deal of research, chiefly conducted with lower animals, tentatively suggests some provocative links between hormonal conditions, brain functions, and behavior (e.g., Hamburg and Lunde, 1966). Likewise, observational studies of human neonatal behavior indicate sex differences in activity level and in reactivity to a variety of stimuli (e.g., Bell and Darling, 1965; Weller and Bell, 1965). This chapter is restricted, however, to a psychological analysis of sex differences in social behavior. It does not deal with either biological antecedents or physical characteristics, concentrating instead on socialization and hence on social and psychological determinants.

The enormous importance of socialization processes in the development of gender roles is vividly illustrated by the investigations of Money and his associates (1957, 1965a, 1965 b). These researchers conducted extensive clinical studies with hermaphrodites. The results suggested that the development of normal sexual behavior requires that the individual be labeled and raised in accord with one sex before he reaches the age of 3 or 4 years. When hermaphrodites were reassigned after that age to the other sex (in order to be more consistent with their internal sex characteristics) severe maladjustment seemed to result. In contrast, children who were reassigned earlier seemed ultimately to develop normal sexual adjustments (Money, Hampson, and Hampson, 1957). The importance of the sexual role to which the child is assigned is also dramatically evident from other data. Money (1965a, 1965b) studied genetic males (with internal male genitalia) who had been reared consistently as females in accord with their external genitalia. He found that these people maintained a feminine psychosexual and gender role throughout life, consistent with the roles in which they had been socialized. Results of this type point to the critical role of socialization

[*]Completion of this chapter was facilitated by Research Grant M 6830 from the National Institutes of Health, United States Public Health Service.

processes in the development and maintenance of sex differences in social behavior (Hampson, 1965). They leave unanswered, of course, the relevant specifics of the socialization process that determine psychological sex differences. Some of these specifics will be considered in this chapter.

The following sections summarize some of the main psychological differences between the sexes. Some of these findings have been based on directly observed differences in the frequency with which the sexes display particular behavior patterns. Many other widely accepted ideas about males and females rest instead on stereotypes about sex differences in broad dispositions inferred more globally. Studies that seek to infer such broad sex-linked dispositions point up some of the complex relations between observed behavioral differences and the stereotypes and personality constructs generated about those differences. It will become evident that inferences about sex differences on such broad traits as "masculinity" and "femininity" entail the same methodological problems, and raise the same basic issues, found in personality research in any other domain of individual differences. Some of the most important of these methodological problems will be illustrated to show the complexity of inferring underlying personality dispositions from behavior. After considering some of the personality correlates found in sex-typing research, the causes of psychological sex differences will be examined closely. Both the concepts and the evidence pertinent to major approaches to the development of psychological differences will be analyzed in detail.

ILLUSTRATIVE SEX DIFFERENCES

Sex-Typed Behavior

The psychological differences between the sexes have been approached in several ways. One of the most direct strategies has been to search for those social behavior patterns that seem to be most clearly "sex-typed." Sex-typed behaviors may be defined as those that are less expected and sanctioned when performed by one sex, and, in contrast, are considered to be more appropriate when manifested by the other sex. Behaviors differ greatly, of course, in the degree to which their value, and their consequences for the

person who engaged in them, are affected by his sex. During socialization many behaviors become sex-typed and acquire different value and meaning for boys and girls.

Many researchers have tried to establish differences in the frequency or in the amount of particular sex-typed behavior syndromes typically displayed by males and females. In our culture the two sex-typed behavior patterns that have received most research attention are behaviors aimed at inflicting injury on others (*aggression*) and at eliciting attention and help from others (*dependency*). Some of the main sex differences found for aggression and for dependency are reviewed briefly in the following paragraphs.

Beginning at the age of about 3 years sex differences in aggression have been noted. Indeed, aggression has become one of the key variables in defining masculine and feminine role behavior (Sears, 1963, 1965). Consistently, boys are more physically aggressive and show more "negativistic" behavior; negative attention getting, antisocial aggression, and physical aggression all characterize boys more than girls. Even in nursery school, boys already participate more in physical quarrels (e.g., Dawe, 1934; Jersild and Markey, 1935). Young boys also have more aggressive contacts with their peers (Walters, Pearce, and Dahms, 1957), and they initiate more fights and conflicts, as well as resisting attack more often (McCandless, Bilous, and Bennett, 1961). These results are based mainly on direct observation of youngsters and they appear to have considerable generality across cultures; for instance, Whiting and Whiting (1962) report more physical aggression by boys in six different cultures.

Similar findings also come from rating studies; judges consistently rate boys as more negativistic and as generally more hyperaggressive than girls. Even when as young as 2 to 5 years, boys are rated as more negativistic (Beller, 1962; Beller and Neubauer, 1963; Beller and Turner, 1962; Hattwick, 1937). Ratings of older children also yield similar results; at ages 5 to 8 boys are rated as more aggressive, negativistic, and noisy than girls by their teachers (e.g., Digman, 1963; Feshbach, 1956). Sanford et al. (1943) likewise reported that teachers judged boys aged 5 to 14 as more aggressive than girls. Moreover, ratings by peers attribute more aggressiveness to 8 year-old boys (Toigo et al., 1962) and to boys in the age range 8 to 10 (Tuddenham, 1952).

The belief that boys are more directly aggressive than girls is shared by the youngsters themselves. As expected, males rate themselves as more physically and antisocially aggressive than do females (e.g., Gill and Spilka, 1962; Sears, 1961). These findings extend to adults; college men rate themselves as more directly and overtly aggressive, especially after their hostility has been aroused experimentally (e.g., Rothaus and Worchel, 1964; Wyer, Weatherley, and Terrell, 1965). Greater self-reported overt aggressiveness by males holds for a wide age range, having been found for people aged from 15 to 64 (Bennett and Cohen, 1959).

With some exceptions (e.g., Lindzey and Goldberg, 1953), projective tests further corroborate more direct aggression and hostility expressed by men. To illustrate, on a sentence completion test college men tend to form more hostile (rather than neutral) sentences (Sarason et al., 1965), and among young adults men recognize more tachistoscopically presented pictures of aggression (Kagan and Moss, 1962). In general, more direct physical aggression and more hostile and aggressive acts also tend to be found in the doll play of young boys as compared to preschool girls (e.g., Bach, 1945; Durrett, 1959; Gordon and Smith, 1965; Sears, 1951; Sears, Rau, and Alpert, 1965).

Sex differences in self-reported daydreams and fantasies are consistent with those found in other forms of behavior. In particular, college men exceeded women in their reports of aggressive, assertive, sexual, heroic, and self-aggrandizing themes in daydreams. Women more frequently reported content dealing with "fantasies of a passive, narcissistic, affiliative, and physical attractiveness type" (Wagman, 1967, p. 331).

Experimental studies also have convincingly indicated greater overt physical aggressiveness by boys than by girls. In one experiment, nursery school youngsters observed adult models displaying distinctively aggressive behavior toward a Bobo doll—for example, pummelling and kicking the doll vigorously (Bandura, Ross, and Ross, 1961). After a short delay the child was escorted to a new setting in which toys and another Bobo doll were available. The child was left alone to play freely while an observer recorded through a one-way mirror the frequency of the child's physical and verbal aggressiveness. As expected, youngsters who had been exposed to an aggressive model now showed more imitative and nonimitative aggressiveness than did those who had observed nonaggressiveness modeled. Of main interest here is the fact that boys imitated the model's physical aggressiveness more than did girls; however, they did not differ in verbal aggression. Similar findings, showing more imitative and nonimitative physical aggression by boys, come from several other studies investigating modeling phenomena (e.g., Bandura, Ross, and Ross, 1963a, 1963b; Bandura, 1965; Hicks, 1965).

After frustration males generally seem to show more direct aggression than females. For example, after a brief period of social isolation nursery school boys are more aggressive in doll play than are girls (Hartup and Himeno, 1959); they also show more direct aggression after frustration (Jegard and Walters, 1960; Moore and Updergraff, 1964), as evidenced by such behaviors as hitting a punch toy. These sex differences in children are found as well in adults. In one study (Buss, 1963) college students were told that their own rewards would depend on how quickly their "victim" would learn in a concept-learning task. To ostensibly guide the victim's learning process the subjects were told to administer electric shocks to him, being free to select the strength of the shock. The subjects were deliberately frustrated by having their bogus victims learning too slowly to earn the rewards for them. In this situation men used more shock than women and they shocked male victims more than female victims.

Dependency is a second behavior domain in which sex differences have been studied thoroughly. Few major sex differences in dependency have been observed at early ages (e.g., in nursery school). A possible exception is the greater incidence of "negative attention" in males (Sears, 1963), which, however, is probably a reflection of the greater physical aggression of boys. At later phases in development (teens and college) girls generally are judged to be more dependent than boys. This finding rests to a large degree on rating measures and self-reports (e.g., Beller and Turner, 1962; Beller and Neubauer, 1963; Lynn and Sawrey, 1959; Sanford et al., 1943; Sears et al., 1953). On the whole, the sex differences in dependency are less clear than those for physical aggressiveness. Nevertheless, more studies indicate greater dependency, social passivity, and conformity in females than in males (e.g., Hovland and Janis, 1959; Kagan and Moss, 1962; Lindzey and Goldberg, 1953; Sears et al., 1953; Siegel et al., 1959). Affiliative and nurturant behaviors also tend to occur more often in females than in males both overtly and in more indirect measures such as themes in storytelling (e.g., Goodenough, 1957; Honzik, 1951; Lansky et al., 1961; Terman and Miles, 1936; Whitehouse, 1949).

Most research on sex differences has dwelt on aggression and dependency, but other dimensions have not been neglected. In addition to studying differences on numerous personality variables, investigators also have explored sex differences in cognitive and intellectual functioning (e.g., Maccoby, 1966). An excellent and comprehensive survey and review of these differences is provided by Oetzel (1966).

Psychological studies of the development of sex-typed behavior have been confined largely to the young child (usually under age 7). Yet some of the most important aspects of distinctively male and female behavior occur at later ages, at and after puberty, when the individual practices adult sex role behavior, not during dress-up play in his parents' shoes, but in actuality and in his own right. It is during adolescence, for example, that sex differences in many character processes, in the cultivation of skills, and in the expression of sexual feelings become evident (Douvan and Kaye, 1957; Harris, 1959). It is in early adulthood, rather than in childhood, that sex-typed expectations become pertinent for a host of interpersonal and sexual behaviors (e.g., Bennett and Cohen, 1959; Harris, 1959). It is also in adolescence that important interactions between physical sexual maturation and psychological socialization may occur. Mussen and Jones (1957, 1958) report, for example, that adolescent boys whose physical development is retarded are more likely to develop personality difficulties, presumably because they cannot engage as successfully in many prestigeful sex-typed activities, such as athletics. Although some of the dramatic differences in sex-typed behaviors commence in adolescence, they do not end there. Throughout peoples' lives the role expectations and the role behaviors of the sexes differ in numerous critical respects. These patterns are not static. They continue to change and to come under new influences as appropriate role demands and role models shift, and as the consequences for particular forms of sex-typed behavior change, in accord with alterations throughout the individual's life and in the larger society (e.g., Brim and Wheeler, 1966).

Sex-Role Stereotypes

Psychologists of course are not the only ones who recognize and study the differences between the sexes; an outstanding characteristic of all people (regardless of vocation) is that they observe and interpret their own behavior and formulate constructs and stereotypes about it. Hence, in addition to actual average differences in the frequency of particular behavior patterns enacted in specific situations, the sexes are also characterized by broad stereotypes they generate about the traits they are expected to have.

Stereotypes involve expectations about the dispositions and typical behaviors supposedly displayed by members of a category. Consider, for example, the characteristics of Cadillac owners versus those of Ford owners. Obviously there are enormous differences within each category, and millions of all kinds of people drive each kind of car. Nevertheless, when asked to assess the attributes of the owners of different makes of cars, clear and consistent stereotypes emerged (Wells, Goi, and Seader, 1958). Ford owners, for example, were described as virile, youthful, and adventurous; owners of the Plymouth were sensible but stodgy; and Chevrolet owners were cheap. More important categories, like masculinity, femininity, and even the self, are also constructions and abstractions which individuals endow with consistent attributes and motivations. Such stereotypes are generated most readily when people try to describe and infer psychological dispositions in themselves or in others and use such global trait terms as "masculine," "feminine," "friendly," "aggressive," or "introverted" to summarize their complex behaviors (Mischel, 1968).

Much of the research on sex-typing has measured such stereotypes. Inferences about masculinity or femininity in research on sex-typing have relied mainly on people's own verbal self-reports about their attributes, attitudes, interests, values, and preferences, or on ratings made by their parents or peers. On the paper-and-pencil Terman-Miles masculinity-femininity (M-F) test, for example, adolescents and adults are asked to report their interests, emotional attitudes, and so on (Terman and Miles, 1936). The Gough Test is another paper-and-pencil inventory that asks for self-descriptions in a dichotomous-choice format (Gough, 1952). Other tests have avoided asking the subject to characterize his own traits and instead require him to indicate the kinds of toys, games, and activities (all shown on pictures) that he would prefer. Examples of these techniques are the IT Scale (Brown, 1957), the Toy Preference Test, and the Pictures Test (Sears, Rau, and Alpert, 1965). All of these measures ask the subject to indicate his preferences for stereotypically masculine or feminine objects or activities. On the IT Scale, for example, the child is presented with a drawing of "IT," an ambiguous child-figure, and has to choose what IT would like in a series of objects or picture cards associated with either masculine or feminine sex roles. The resulting scores, ranging from 6 to 84, are intended to reflect the degree of masculinity-femininity in the child's sex-role preferences.

Masculinity-femininity measures for the most part have been constructed so that on each item the response scored "masculine" is the one that is endorsed by most males, whereas the one scored "feminine" is the one favored verbally by the majority of females. Any individual's masculinity-femininity score therefore serves as an index of how closely his self-reports, self-descriptions, and preferences correspond with those of the majority in his sex. Similarly, when observers rate the attributes of others on a masculinity-femininity dimension the score is intended to reflect the rater's judgment of how closely the ratee matches the attributes supposedly displayed by most males (or females). It is self-evident that these "majority attributes" involve a stereotype about modal or typical characteristics rather than a precise behavior description.

Sex-role stereotypes are pervasive and widely shared within particular cultures, and to some extent across cultures (e.g., D'Andrade, 1966; Whiting and Whiting, 1962). These stereotypes about the actual and expected attributes of each sex tend to be correlated with the average differences actually found between the sexes in the frequency of particular behavior patterns, but the correlation is probably far from perfect. Kagan (1964, p. 143) summarized the cluster of dispositions attributed differentially to males and females in our culture this way:

In sum, females are supposed to inhibit aggression and open display of sexual urges, to be passive with men, to be nurturant to others, to cultivate attractiveness, and to maintain an affective, socially poised, and friendly posture with others. Males are urged to be aggressive in face of attack, independent in problem situations, sexually aggressive, in control of regressive urges, and suppressive of strong emotions, especially anxiety.

To emphasize that in their extreme forms sex-role stereotypes become almost caricatures, Roger Brown draws this portrait (1965, p. 161):

In the United States a *real* boy climbs trees, disdains girls, dirties his knees, plays with soldiers, and takes blue for his favorite color. A real girl dresses dolls, jumps rope, plays hopscotch, and takes pink for her favorite color. When they go to school, real girls like English and music and "auditorium"; real boys prefer manual training, gym, and arithmetic. In college the boys smoke pipes, drink beer, and major in engineering or physics; the girls chew Juicy Fruit gum, drink cherry Cokes, and major in fine arts. The real boy matures into a "man's man" who plays poker, goes hunting, drinks brandy, and dies in the war; the real girl becomes a "feminine" woman who loves children, embroiders handkerchiefs, drinks weak tea, and "succumbs" to consumption.

When impressions about the psychological attributes of a category (e.g., males, females, the self, Cadillac-owners) are formed by laymen they usually are called "stereotypes"; when they are offered by scientists they are given the more formidable name of "constructs." In fact, both stereotypes and constructs are abstractions about events, about people, and about oneself. Sometimes "stereotypes" are attacked because they are generalizations that lump diverse phenomena and many individual differences into a broad category. That is not an appropriate objection, however, because people (and animals) do generalize and categorize events pervasively, and it is hard to imagine life without this ability to group and subsume many events into fewer units. Rather than objecting to categories, it is important to assess their value for particular purposes. The stereotypes generated when the individual (regardless of his formal credentials as a scientist) construes events in terms of traits and dispositions may or may not correspond well with other evidence about the events. The scientist interested in dispositions must assess the accuracy and utility of his trait stereotypes and a great deal of research on socialization and personality development has done just that, seeking to demonstrate the construct validity of such hypothesized dispositions as "masculinity" and "dependency" or "ego strength" and "aggression."

In one popular research strategy personality dispositions are inferred mainly by having judges rate the attributes of people. The results then are submitted to various analyses intended to discover the dimensions reflected by these ratings. These ratings, however, may hinge on the concepts and stereotypes of the judge rather than necessarily reflecting the attributes of the ratee.

The important role of the observer's concepts is illustrated in a study in which boys and girls gave free verbal descriptions of each other. Their descriptions were reliably coded into dispositional categories (Dornbusch et al., 1965). There were several conditions: either one child described two others, or two children described the same child, or two children described two different other children. Descriptions with a common *perceiver* had the highest overlap of categories. The next highest catagory overlap was found for

descriptions with a common perceived person, and was "followed, surprisingly closely, by description with only a common culture" (p. 434). Description with "only a common culture" refers to the category overlap obtained between descriptions made by different persons of other *different* persons, with no overlap between perceiver and perceived. *A* thus described *B* and *C* described *D*. The only commonality in this paradigm is that all persons are members of the same culture —in this case a summer camp. The category overlap between this situation and one in which different perceivers describe the *same* individual was increased only about 7%. The investigators concluded that:

. . . the small difference introduced by specifying a common social object reinforces our finding of the greater impact of the perceiver (1965, p. 440).

In the foregoing study the judges were children; it might be expected that adults could transcend their own categories more readily and achieve ratings that primarily reflect the ratee's traits. Many sophisticated efforts have been made to achieve that aim. One major psychometric strategy started by collecting all "trait names" in a standard English dictionary and found some 18,000 dispositional terms (Allport and Odbert, 1936). Cattell (1947, 1957) selected from this list 4504 terms which Allport (1937) had characterized as:

. . . most clearly "real" traits of personality. They designate generalized and personalized determining tendencies—consistent and stable modes of an individual's adjustment to his environment . . . these terms do not imply merely temporary and specific behavior . . . (p. 366).

Cattell (1957) then used judgments of "just distinguishable" differences in semantic meaning to reduce these items to smaller groups spanning the "personality sphere." Ratings for these "trait elements" then were correlated and submitted to cluster analyses, producing 36 clusters. In turn, these clusters were converted into bipolar descriptions, called the "standard reduced personality sphere" rating scales. Using scales of this kind several extensive and sophisticated factor analytic studies subsequently investigated the factors obtained for samples of people rated by their peers (e.g., Norman, 1963; Tupes and Christal, 1961).

The same set of five relatively independent or orthogonal factors appeared consistently, and led to the conclusion that a "highly stable structure of personal characteristics has been identified" (Norman, 1963, p. 581), and that:

The structure obtained reflected the organization of these attributes in the ratees (Passini and Norman, 1966, p. 44).

However, when *complete strangers* were rated the factor structure obtained was highly similar to the five-factor structure from ratings of subjects that raters knew well (Passini and Norman, 1966). In this study judges rated fellow college students whom they had not known before. Their contact with the ratees in the rating situation was limited to being in the same room for less than 15 minutes and there was no possibility for verbal communication. The rating task was made plausible by requesting the judge to rate the subjects as "you would imagine" them to be. Since the raters were strangers they could not possibly have had direct knowledge of the ratee's attributes on dimensions like "cooperative-negativistic," or "responsible-undependable." The results nevertheless yielded factors very similar to those obtained from ratings by groups of close acquaintances in earlier studies. As the investigators recognized, the main information available to the raters "was whatever they carried in their heads."

In another approach, college students rated the similarity *in meaning* between all the possible pairs of words that described each of the poles on Norman's (1963) 20 bipolar trait scales. These similarity ratings for words were then factor analyzed by D'Andrade (1965). His analysis of ratings of meaning similarity produced a five-factor structure virtually identical with Norman's structure for ratings of people. The unities found in ratings of words alone thus corresponded with those yielded by ratings of people. As D'Andrade noted, this convergence suggests that traits at least in part exist as components of the verbal terms used to describe the external world; they do not necessarily mirror the external world itself. D'Andrade also found similar results from studies based on rating scales of interpersonal behavior (1965).

Mulaik (1964) in three separate factor analytic studies investigated the degree to which ratings may reveal personality factors in the subjects as opposed to the rater's conceptual or semantic factors. Judges in one study rated real persons such as family members, close acquaintances, and themselves on many trait-rating scales. Another group of judges in a second study rated such stereotyped persons as "Suburban Housewife," "Mental Patient," or "Air Force General" on the same scales. In the third study still another sample of judges rated the "meaning" of selected trait words on the scales. The match between the trait factors from the three studies was compared. The results revealed great overlap between the factors found for real people and those from ratings of stereotype persons and led Mulaik to note that " 'personality factors' based upon trait ratings of persons can be interpreted as distinct concepts implied by trait words rather than internal structural features of persons" (Mulaik, 1964, p. 506).

Commenting on the factor patterns replicated from rating studies, Vernon reached a similar conclusion: "It seems best to regard ratings, not so much as summaries of objectively observed behavior, as rationalizations abstracted from the rater's overall picture (his homunculus) of the subject" (Vernon, 1964, p. 59).

Stereotypes, Constructs, and Behavior

Broad cognitions and stereotypes about dispositions help to simplify the enormously large informational inputs that face the perceiver in the process of impression-formation and person-perception. These inputs about events, about people, and about oneself are channelized and restricted by the categories and the organizational limits available to the perceiver. Categorizations of perceptions into fewer and simpler units places them within the limited scope of memory (e.g., Bruner, 1958). Incoming data are coded and simplified by assigning labels to them and sorting them into categories. Without such information processing it would be impossible to deal with the continuous flood of perceptions that impinge from the environment (Miller, 1956). Thus the construction of consistent stereotypes, by assigning diverse events into a broader category that subsumes them, may be highly adaptive for many purposes and may be dictated by the limitations in the observer's organizing capacity.

Almost regardless of the content that is being rated, there is considerable consistency in the two or three main rating factors found over and over again in research on trait judgments (e.g., Mulaik, 1964; Vernon, 1964). As Vernon has noted:

Thus there is usually a prominent good vs. bad factor including such traits as emotional stability and reliability, and an extravert-introvert dichotomy, or some variant of active-potent vs. passive-weak (1964, p. 59).

This same set of factors found in ratings of people also tends to be found in ratings of concepts and words (D'Andrade, 1965). In semantic differential research, for example, the meaning of diverse words, phrases, and concepts was rated on many scales (Osgood, Suci, and Tannenbaum, 1957). The rater is supplied with a stimulus word like "feather," or "me," or a phrase like "my ideal self," and he has to rate each stimulus on a graphic seven-point bipolar scale. Polar adjectives like rough-smooth or fair-unfair are the extremes of each scale. The rater is instructed to mark the point that shows how closely the stimulus concept is related to the points on the scale. The results from diverse samples of stimulus content and raters repeatedly have produced three main dichotomous semantic response factors. A primary *evaluative* (good-bad) factor accounted for approximately half to three-quarters of the extractable variance. The two other major factors were *potency* (potent-impotent), represented by scale items like hard-soft, masculine-feminine, strong-weak; and an *activity* factor (active-passive), tapped by scales like active-passive, excitable-calm, and hot-cold.

Note that the "potency" and "activity" dimensions seem pertinent also to some of the main characteristics of the sexes in the sex-role stereotypes summarized by Kagan and Brown. Indeed, the activity and potency dimensions seem to be defined, to a consider-

able extent, by the stereotypes of masculine and feminine traits. Male sex-typed adjectives implying aggressiveness such as large, loud, rough, rugged, and strong load most heavily on the potency factor. Similarly, adjectives such as active, agitated, angular, fast, ferocious, and hot load heavily on the activity factor. Males tend to be characterized most often by the foregoing adjectives, whereas females are endowed with the opposite characteristics.

Stereotypes and other categories not only play an important part in the organization of information; they also may influence the person's further observations. After an individual categorizes or groups stimuli he often tends to retain his category even when faced with contradictory evidence. Having formed his category, he may pay less attention to new information and may focus instead on information that confirms his category. This constraining effect of a category has been shown in such diverse contexts as impression formation in person perception (e.g., Asch, 1946; Anderson, 1965; Wishner, 1960); hypothesis testing in problem-solving (Davison, 1964; Wyatt and Campbell, 1951); and clinical diagnosis (e.g., Rubin and Shontz, 1960; Sines, 1959). In all these contexts people often categorize events and each other rapidly even on the basis of little information and then adhere to their categories. For example, psychotherapists develop fairly stable images of their clients within the first four hours of psychotherapy. These categories may be retained more or less unchanged and do not differ much from those found after 24 therapy sessions (Meehl, 1960).

Similar constraining effects of categories have been shown in several ways. In one familiar approach, studies exposed subjects to a series of decreasingly ambiguous stimuli in the form of out-of-focus slide pictures. On successive presentations, the focus became increasingly clear and after each presentation the subject stated what he thought the picture was. The findings indicated that the hypotheses the subject forms during the early stages of inaccurate guessing constrain and retard the development of more veridical perceptions of the stimulus (e.g., Blake and Vanderplas, 1950; Davison, 1964; Wyatt and Campbell, 1951).

Sex-role stereotypes, like other global con-

structs and stereotypes about broad and se-
mantically ambiguous dispositions, may be
hard to test and difficult to disconfirm, are
widely generalized to diverse events, and tend
to be tenaciously retained. Nevertheless, these
concepts are not impervious to cultural
changes. To illustrate, expectations concerning work outside the home for women,
women's rights to be sexually provocative
and responsive, and even the physical appearance and fashions permissable for men
and women, all seem to undergo alterations.
These shifts, interestingly, often seem to be
construed as consistent with the more traditional sex-role standards. For example, increased work by women outside the home
often tends to be interpreted as reflecting the
woman's nurturant role in the family and as
motivated by the desire to help her children
through the additional material advantages
that her income can provide for them (Hartley, 1960).

Some dispositional constructs have such
broad and ambiguous semantic meanings,
and such diverse behavioral referents, that
they may be almost impossible to disconfirm
definitively. The construct that a particular
man is, for example, "very masculine," may
be potentially supported by almost any kind
of evidence about his behavior. Since the
construct about what constitutes "real" masculinity may be modified and progressively
elaborated as new evidence becomes available, it can be stretched so that all sorts of diverse behaviors are taken as confirmation. Just
as with any *post hoc* hypothesis, almost any
data can be made to fit the hypothesis. Consistent with the preceding considerations,
many verbal constructions or interpretations
about behavior tend to be quite stable over
time. For example, ratings of traits in people, and ratings of the semantic meanings
of words and concepts, evoked by paper-and-
pencil tests, tend to be enduring (Mischel,
1968).

Thus people label and categorize behavior
(their own as well as other people's) pervasively, and although the label may not fit the
condition to which it refers, the label itself
generates consequences. For example, sex-
typing labels may have highly aversive effects, as in "homosexual," "queer," or "sissy,"
both when one applies these terms to oneself privately and when one employs them

as public descriptions. Application of such
potent labels can have powerful emotional
consequences regardless of their objective
representational accuracy (Mischel, 1968).

DISPOSITIONAL CONSTRUCTS

Assessing the Validity of Dispositional Constructs

Of course, observers do not categorize an
empty world and there are congruences between their stereotypes and the people and
events that they construe. But because trait
ratings by themselves may reflect the biased
cognitive system of the judge, it becomes
necessary to pursue a more complex strategy that looks for *external* validity data to
justify the dispositional constructs hypothesized by observers. To talk validly, for example, about another person's "masculinity"
or "femininity," one has to establish associations between one's intended measure of that
disposition and other independent data
sources. The chief objective of one of the
main approaches to personality has been to
establish the existence and meaning of such
dispositions. The constructs that have been
generated range from masculinity-femininity
and sex-role identity to such dimensions
as introversion-extraversion, ego strength,
achievement motivation, anxiety, rigidity, and
so on. Researchers in this vein have investigated the consistency of personality
traits, their organization, and their antecedents. To understand these efforts properly
it is necessary to examine the meaning of
"disposition" and the assumptions of this approach to personality.

"Disposition" or "trait" has become an ambiguous term because it is used in a number
of quite different ways. Most simply, a trait
merely refers to the differences between two
or more persons on some dimension. As Guilford (1959, p. 6) says, "A trait is any distinguishable, relatively enduring way in
which one individual varies from others." As
such, a trait is just a term for some observed
differences among people in specified behavior. In its more complex meaning as a personality construct, however, a trait or disposition is an abstraction invoked to explain
enduring behavioral consistencies and differences among individuals. Most personality
theorists have conceptualized traits as under-

lying attributes or processes that exist in persons and determine their behavior (Allport, 1937, 1966; Cattell, 1950). As Gordon Allport put it: "A trait has more than nominal existence . . . and is dynamic, or at least determinative, in behavior" (1966, p. 1). In the context of sex-typed traits, one might thus posit that such attributes as one's masculinity, or one's aggressiveness, in turn exert pervasive influences on one's behavior.

The dispositional or trait approach to personality rests on several widely shared assumptions. It is assumed that particular dispositions are common to many people, vary in amount, and can be inferred by measuring their behavioral indicators (e.g., Cattell, 1957; Guilford, 1959). Perhaps most important are the additional assumptions that these traits are relatively stable and enduring and that they exert fairly generalized effects on behavior (Allport, 1966).

Most investigations of personality dispositions have been guided by a cumulative quantitative measurement model. The chief characteristic of that model is that trait indicators are related *additively* to the inferred underlying disposition (Loevinger, 1957). For example, the more "masculine" behavior the person shows, say, by endorsing more masculine terms on an inventory, the stronger the underlying trait of masculinity. Psychodynamic theories, in contrast, often posit highly *indirect,* nonadditive relations between behaviors and the hypothesized dispositions that supposedly underlie them. "Masculine" behavior thus sometimes may be interpreted as a sign of underlying femininity or of deeply passive homosexual trends or conflicts. This indirect inference process is a main difference between psychodynamic theory and cumulative trait theories. In spite of that difference, and many others, psychodynamic theory shares with most trait theories the basic assumption that although behavior may vary, personality is more or less consistent and stable across many situations.

Much of the work on sex-typing—and on socialization—has pursued a correlational strategy to assess dispositions. This kind of research seeks correlations among a person's response patterns to different standardized tests or experimental conditions. For this purpose test batteries are administered, and the obtained empirical associations between responses to these tests indicate how strongly the measured behaviors converge across situations. A typical question here might be how do boys and girls who have high scores on a dependency scale differ in their reactions to success and failure from those children who have low dependency scores, and what is the nature of the sex differences and sex interactions.

If investigators restrict themselves to operational descriptions of the test results and their empirical interrelations, there are no problems of interpretation. Both personality and developmental psychologists, however, usually have not been interested in merely describing test responses and their patterns of correlation; instead, a "sign" approach has been followed in which test behaviors are used as signs of the broader dispositions that supposedly underlie them (Loevinger, 1957). In research of this kind it is necessary to establish the reliability and validity of behavior samples as indicators of the dispositions hypothesized by the investigator. The researcher guided by constructs about sex-typing and identificatory processes, for example, must demonstrate through correlational and experimental studies how his measures and results illuminate his constructs about the meaning of the sampled behavior.

A great deal of correlational research on dispositions has relied on data from personality questionnaires. As in most research on individual differences, the resulting findings hinge on differences found between people in what they say on paper-and-pencil inventories and questionnaires. These questionnaires generally either evoke the respondent's concepts and stereotypes about his own dispositions or ask him to rate the attributes of other people. Usually the focus is on fairly global, higher-order inferences about dispositions rather than on specific descriptions of behavior in particular situations. Sex differences on these personality tests have been described often; in addition, individual differences on these tests have been correlated with responses to other paper-and-pencil tests and ratings, and much less often with behavior elicited by nonquestionnaire techniques. Before one can consider the results, however, it is necessary to face some methodological issues.

The interpretation of the meaning of these

questionnaire findings involves some special problems found repeatedly in research on socialization. These problems occur because what a person says about his attributes does not necessarily reflect accurately either the trait that he has or the things that he does outside the test. Sex differences on questionnaires thus may reflect differences between the sexes in their self-reports that may or may not be closely related to other indices of their nontest behavior. For example, the sexes may give different self-reports in part because the *admission* of particular attributes or behaviors may have different value and may lead to different consequences as a function of the individual's sex. Extreme self-reports about test anxiety, for example, probably are less likely to be acceptable for schoolboys than for schoolgirls. Sex stereotypes suggest that admitting anxiety, especially about school matters, is not considered "manly" for boys. Consistent with this is the finding (by Sarason et al., 1960) that boys have persistently lower scores on self-report anxiety measures. Boys probably tend to believe that they are not supposed to report anxiety about schoolwork. Girls, in contrast, may either do so or not do so and neither pattern leads to more negative consequences for them. The finding that boys report less anxiety than girls therefore cannot be taken as automatic evidence that boys "have" less anxiety than girls: the results merely show that girls will say they are more anxious than boys.

Sex differences thus may exist on self-reports where there are none in nontest behavior, and vice versa. For example, on a self-report measure involving hypothetical choices between immediate but less valued rewards as opposed to larger but delayed rewards girls report significantly greater willingness to wait for larger rewards. However, in concrete choices between immediate, smaller as opposed to delayed, larger rewards in a real choice situation, in which the child had to make actual choices between one or the other, no sex differences were found (Mischel, 1962).

Bronfenbrenner (1960b) obtained teachers' ratings of leadership and responsibility for almost 200 boys and girls in the tenth grade. The youngsters themselves reported on the child-rearing practices that their parents had used with them. The results revealed different patterns for boys and girls. Boys who themselves were rated as irresponsible reported their fathers had been more neglecting, rejecting, and lacking in discipline toward them. Moderately strong discipline, especially from the father, and warmth and nurturance, especially from the mother, were correlated with high ratings of responsibility in boys. Reports of extremely high discipline, however, tended to be negatively associated with responsible behavior. The patterns obtained for girls, in contrast, were somewhat different. Just as with boys, rejection and neglect were associated with low responsibility. However, the presence of strong discipline by the father was much more negatively correlated with responsibility ratings in girls than in boys. The highest ratings of responsibility were obtained by those girls who rated their fathers as exerting a low-moderate level of discipline rather than the higher to moderate level of paternal discipline that seemed to be optimal for boys.

These findings rely on the children's own reports of child-rearing practices and therefore are hard to interpret definitively. It is possible, for example, that the children who were rated more favorably by their teachers tended to be the ones who reported about their families and parental practices in more stereotypically desirable ways. Thus conventionally "good" children may also be the ones more likely to say they have nice fathers rather than fathers who are severely rejecting and extremely neglectful. It would also seem consistent with culturally sanctioned stereotypes that girls who are favored by their teachers are especially unlikely to describe their fathers as brutes, whereas "good boys" report that their fathers are solid disciplinarians and their mothers are warm.

A more complicated manifestation of the same phenomenon may be involved in a study by Crandall, Katkowsky, and Preston (1962). Expectancy statements about intellectual ability were found to be highly positively correlated with measures of intelligence for boys but negatively for girls. As Crandall and his colleagues suggested, boys and girls may be differentially rewarded for *stating* intellectual achievement expectations and standards. Boys may be rewarded for stating expectations and standards that are accurate (e.g., they are taught to "face the facts"), whereas intellectually proficient girls may be criticized for "unfeminine boasting" when stating high (albeit realistic) expectations. As a result they may learn to verbalize differently about their intellectual strengths.

In light of these results it would be interesting to assess the extent to which sex differences in conformity, dependency, and so on, may hinge on differences in sex-role appropriateness of specific items contained in the measures. At any rate, it is clear that personality inferences based on relationships found with self-report personality questionnaires require special interpretative cautions, and these cautions must be taken especially seriously because so many conclusions about personality structure hinge largely on such tests. To illustrate further, on the Ego Strength (Es) scale of the MMPI it has been found consistently that men obtain higher scores than do women (e.g., Distler, May, and Tuma, 1964; Hathaway and Briggs, 1957; Korchin and Heath, 1961). This result has been especially intriguing theoretically because it seems relevant to Freud's belief that women develop a weaker superego than do men. A plausible consequence of the weaker superego of women may also be deficiencies in their ego strength and character structure as reflected in their lower Es scores.

One possible interpretation offered for the Es sex difference is in terms of perceived sex roles. Men and women in our culture may not differ in ego strength but rather in their willingness to admit pathology and socially undesirable behaviors. It has been shown repeatedly that the tendency to categorize oneself in socially undesirable terms may account for much of the variance on self-report inventories similar to the Es scale (e.g., Edwards, 1957, 1959, 1961). On psychiatric inventories and tests like the MMPI, scores on scales depend on the respondent's willingness to endorse socially undesirable statements such as confessions about strange and deviant behavior, peculiar thoughts, and body changes. The individual's scores therefore may reflect the degree to which he endorses socially desirable items rather than either autobiographical events or underlying traits. This argument seems tenable because correlations between the social desirability of items and the tendency to endorse them on personality questionnaires is quite high, often

exceeding .80 and sometimes even .90 (Edwards, 1957). Moreover, correlations between scores on many personality scales and on measures of the tendency to endorse desirable items also tend to be high (Byrne, 1966). It is difficult to choose between the social desirability interpretation and the characterological or trait interpretation of self-report scores on psychiatric inventories. The choice among interpretations is complicated because even an accurate self-report of problematic, idiosyncratic, or debilitating behavior invariably requires endorsing a socially undesirable item (Block, 1965).

Recognizing the important role of the tendency to admit undesirable attributes and pathology in determining scores on inventories like the Es scale, Distler, May, and Tuma (1964) have tried to explain the obtained sex differences (especially in Es scores) as reflecting sex differences in the acceptability of admitting deviant behavior. Referring to clinical groups, they comment:

For patients from a predominantly lower-middle, and lower socio-economic background, the perceived female role permits a disintegrated admission of symptoms and bid for dependency and care, whereas the perceived male role demands the maintenance of a facade of strength and control even in the face of the obviously upsetting circumstances of hospitalization (p. 175).

To test some of these possibilities, Holmes (1967) tried to determine the extent to which Es sex differences could be due to sex differences in the tendency to admit pathology as opposed to differences in ego strength. A close examination of the Es scale revealed that it also contained items from the Masculinity-Femininity (MF) scale of the MMPI. Holmes administered the MMPI to a sample of psychiatric subjects and found that the men were significantly higher than women in both MF and Es scores. He also found that the sexes did not differ in admitting pathology in general and in overall defensiveness. An item analysis on the Es scale revealed that several of the items on which men responded significantly more in the Es direction overlapped with MF scale items. In each case the overlapping items were scored so that a response that indicated greater masculinity also increased the person's ego strength score. If, for example, an individual indicated that he did not like to cook, or did not want to paint flowers, his Es score was automatically increased. Since men endorsed such male-inappropriate items less often than did women, their ego strength scores of course were higher—this result reflecting an artifact in the scales rather than the initially hypothesized dispositional sex difference. When the items on the Es scale that overlapped with those on the MF scale were removed, the previously obtained significant sex difference in ego strength was no longer found (Holmes, 1967).

As these results suggest, the relationships found in correlational personality research may be due in part to redundancies among measures. Inventory constructors have regularly borrowed items from earlier questionnaires, producing much repetition among scales. Even within the same multiscale tests, the items overlap considerably. For example, Shure and Rogers (1965) have noted that the basic 13 scales of the MMPI consist of items which overlap 69% on the average with items on one or more other scales of the test.

Similarities in the format of measuring techniques, called "method factors" or "apparatus factors" (Campbell and Fiske, 1959), thus may contribute to the personality correlations found in research on sex differences and all other aspects of socialization. In other words, the correlations obtained among measures intended to tap various dispositions in part may reflect similarities between the measuring methods. Campbell and Fiske (1959) have noted that analyses of the correlations among personality measures indeed do show that much of their common variance is attributable to overlap between the methods employed to elicit responses on them. For example, when questionnaires are used to measure traits, the obtained relations sometimes seem to be more attributable to the questionnaires than to the dispositions they intend to elicit (Campbell, 1960; Campbell and Fiske, 1959).

Recognizing that correlations may be due to method similarities among the measures, Campbell and Fiske have urged that the relative contributions of method as opposed to trait variance must be estimated. To accomplish this one must employ more than one method as well as more than one trait in the validation process. When several ostensible traits are elicited by several techniques a multitrait-multimethod matrix results, containing all of the intercorrelations found when each of several traits is measured by each of several methods.

Thus validity research has to demonstrate not only convergence among similar methods (e.g., questionnaires) intended to investigate a response pattern representing a trait but also among *dissimilar* methods studying the same trait indicators. In this fashion, it is possible to separate the degree to which obtained correlations reflect convergence due to common stimulus conditions, as opposed to convergence of a trait across diverse evoking conditions. Such methodological cautions are now essential, because trait judgments from the same data source may be as highly correlated for ostensibly *diverse* traits as for the same trait when it is evoked by different methods (e.g., Campbell and Fiske, 1959; Goldberg and Werts, 1966).

One popular technique for inferring identification consists of psychometric ratings of parent-child similarity. These indices of identification have tried to assess the similarity in the rated or self-rated attributes of the child and of the same-sex parent (e.g., Helper, 1955; Lazowick, 1955; Sopchak, 1952). Some of the special interpretative difficulties and rating biases in person perception that arise from such procedures have been discussed thoroughly by Bronfenbrenner (1958) and by Cronbach (1955). In light of their criticisms, more recent psychometric studies of the correlates of identification have made sophisticated efforts to avoid the confounding effects of response sets and of other systematic rating biases (e.g., Heilbrun, 1965).

Apart from systematic biases in ratings of similarity, numerous other "response sets" also have been found to play a significant role in personality questionnaires. The tendency to either agree or disagree consistently with ambiguous statements regardless of their content may be especially important. On inventories like the California F scale or the Minnesota Multiphasic Personality Inventory, the total scores are a direct function of the number of times that one agrees with or says "yes" to the items. That is, the questions are worded so that agreement increases the trait score. The more often the person answers "yes" on the California *F* scale, for example, the higher his "authoritarian" score will be. It is therefore difficult to separate the role of scale content from the effects of any tendency for subjects to say "yes" to items regardless of their content. Some surveys have claimed that the principal variance on self-report inventories is attributable to such response styles (e.g., Couch and Keniston, 1960; Jackson and Messick, 1958; Messick and Jackson, 1961; Wiggins, 1962). But some careful studies suggest these styles may be less important (e.g., Block, 1965; Rorer, 1965). Other closely related response sets or styles include the tendency to check extremes on rating scales, to give cautiously "doubtful" or "don't know" answers, to falsify responses, and to be consistent or inconsistent (Vernon, 1964). It is therefore important to assess the extent to which differences between the sexes on personality measures, and differences in the patterning of these relationships, may be due to possible sex differences in the strength of particular rating response sets.

Most test and construct validation efforts have been directed at demonstrating that scores on a measure relate to scores on another measure. However, *discriminant* validation as well as convergent validation is required to demonstrate that a test measures something novel (Campbell, 1960; Campbell and Fiske, 1959). It is important to determine the relationship between any dispositional measure and other indices which are known to account for large variance in test responses; high correlations with other tests may tend to invalidate a test supposedly measuring something different. The necessity for establishing the discriminant validity of dispositional measures becomes especially obvious if one considers the correlations between personality indices and measures of intelligence.

Many indices of personality are correlated substantially with intelligence. For example, intelligence is negatively associated with measures of authoritarianism and prejudice and positively associated with certain cognitive styles, with honesty, with indices of impulse control, with tests of creativity, and so on

(Mischel, 1968). These correlations are quite variable in strength, but not infrequently they may be as large as the associations between the personality variable and the other external measures that serve to define it. Moreover, recent work on children's sex-role attitudes (Kohlberg and Zigler, 1967) reveals that IQ is closely related to the development of these attitudes. Their overall results suggest that brighter children generally express more advanced sex-role attitudes in terms of the age trends found among average subjects.

In particular, Kohlberg and Zigler (1967), in their extensive study, found that IQ has a highly significant effect on certain aspects of sex-typing. In doll play, for example, bright children tended to choose father dolls more than did children of average IQ. Intelligence had a particularly strong influence on sex-typed preferences on the IT Scale and the Pictures Test. On these measures brighter children tended to be much more same-sex oriented in their sex-typed preferences than were children of average intelligence. Kohlberg and Zigler interpreted their overall findings as evidence for the important role of mental maturation in the development of children's sex-role attitudes. Most of their results, however, also seem consistent with the view that brighter children more readily learn and display the sex-role stereotypes that they are expected to have in the culture. The authors favored a cognitive-developmental interpretation, noting many suggestive parallels between the sex-typing patterns of brighter children and those of older children of average intelligence. They construed these trends as indicative of correlations between mental age and rate of development in sex-role attitudes. Regardless of specific interpretation, the results make it plain that intelligence has an important part in sex-role attitudes and preferences.

Correlations between measures of intelligence and personality indices raise important theoretical and methodological issues. Intelligence may be especially important in self-report inventories and other paper-and-pencil personality questionnaires. One obtains high scores on indices of adjustment, such as neuroticism and anxiety questionnaires, for example, to the degree that one expresses complaints and admits socially undesirable behavior. If brighter people respond more perceptively and discriminatively to the negative consequences of self-derogatory reports, they would be less likely to describe their own behavior in undesirable terms. A tendency for more intelligent persons to express more socially appropriate and stereotypically normative responses on questionnaires may be reflected, for instance, in the fact that more educated individuals tend to express less "authoritarian" and antidemocratic beliefs on attitude questionnaires such as the California F scale (Brown, 1965; Christie, 1954). Hartshorne and May (1928) also found that the correlation between IQ and honesty was .344; that correlation is about as high as the average consistency of honest behavior itself. Thus the correlations between personality tests and intelligence tests sometimes may be as great as those between the personality tests and their intended criterion referents. In light of these findings, Campbell and Fiske (1959) have urged, appropriately, that personality research must include correlations between the disposition being studied and standard measures of intelligence.

One stream of research has studied the relations between indices of personality adjustment and sex-typing. In efforts of this kind one can circumvent the previously described hazards of correlational research on socialization to a large extent by a converging strategy utilizing many different data sources. Such a strategy was employed by Mussen (1961) to study the correlates of masculinity-femininity. He found that adolescent boys who had highly masculine interests on the Strong Vocational Interest Test when compared to those with highly feminine interests had more positive self-concepts and more self-confidence on the TAT. The children with more masculine interests also were rated by peers as showing more masculine behavior. Since these results were based not only on self-reports but also on inferences from projective data and on independent ratings by others, one can be confident that the obtained patterns do not simply reflect consistent self-descriptions or redundancies among overlapping measures. Moreover, the masculine and feminine groups were shown not to differ in either intelligence or social class status, thus ruling out the possibility that the differences between them were due to either generalized ability or education.

The preceding findings are supported by those of many other investigators. Studies in a similar vein in general repeatedly have found positive correlations between indices of the appropriateness of the child's sex-typed preferences and concurrent measures of his personal and social adjustment (e.g., Cava and Rausch, 1952; Gray, 1959; Heilbrun, 1965; Payne and Mussen, 1956; Sopchak, 1952). Anastasiow (1965), for example, selected groups of fifth- and sixth-grade boys differing in their degree of masculinity (high, median, and low) as inferred from their toy and activity preferences. The most masculine boys were found to have higher reading scores than the median boys but did not differ from them in arithmetic. The most feminine boys did not differ significantly from the most masculine in either reading or arithmetic. On ratings by their teachers, however, the most masculine boys tended to be rated somewhat more favorably on several dimensions.

Mussen also took the rare step of following up the adolescents in his studies and reexamined their later adjustment when they reached their late thirties (Mussen, 1962). On the basis of extensive personality ratings and of scores on self-report personality tests Mussen was able to compare the men who as adolescents had expressed more traditionally masculine interests with those who had reported more feminine interests. He summarized the findings this way:

Comparison of the ratings assigned to the two groups showed that in adulthood, as during adolescence, those who had relatively feminine interest patterns manifested more of the "emotional-expressive" role characteristics, e.g., they are rated as more dependent but more social in orientation. In contrast, those with highly masculine adolescent interest patterns possessed, in their late teens and in their late thirties, more active, "instrumental" characteristics: greater self-sufficiency, less social orientation and, in adulthood, less introspectiveness. There was little congruence between the adolescent and adult statuses of the two groups with respect to several other characteristics, however. During adolescence, highly masculine subjects possessed more self-confidence and greater feelings of adequacy than the other group, but as adults, they were relatively lacking in qualities of leadership, dominance, self-confidence, and self-acceptance (Mussen, 1962, p. 440).

Mussen's results indicate that sex-appropriate identification, inferred from sex-typed interests, even as late as in adolescence, cannot be taken as a sign of an overall enduring adjustment pattern. Adolescents with stereotyped masculine interests may obtain more positive experiences during adolescence and are rated more positively at that time. Presumably in the middle-class adolescent subculture youngsters who profess stereotypically masculine interests, attitudes, and values would fare better, especially with their peers, than would boys who have markedly feminine interests. These stereotyped masculine preferences, however, do not assure a generalized adjustment pattern.

On the contrary, Mussen (1962, p. 440) noted that:

In general there seems to have been a shift in the self-concepts of the two groups in adulthood, the originally highly masculine boys apparently feeling less positive about themselves after adolescence, and, correlatively, the less masculine groups changing in a favorable direction.

To understand psychological sex differences properly it is necessary to consider the psychological processes that lead to them and to evaluate their significance for other aspects of the individual's personality. The very extensive investigations available on the development of sex roles are often grouped under the rubric of research on "sex-typing." *Sex-typing* is the process whereby the individual comes to acquire, to value, and to adopt for himself sex-typed behavior patterns. The psychological constructs and principles invoked to understand sex-typing depend on the more general approach that one takes to issues of socialization and personality. Some approaches view sex-typing phenomena simply as the products of social learning processes. As such, "identification" would not require special constructs and would instead be subsumed under broader principles of observational learning and reinforcement, as discussed in later sec-

tions. In more traditional formulations sex-typing is viewed as one aspect of the far broader process of identification, as described in the next section.

Unitary Identification Theory

Identification often has been the mechanism invoked to explain how children develop attributes and behavior patterns similar to those of their parents and of other social models. As in most areas of socialization, the theorizing of Sigmund Freud has had an enduring impact on formulations about identification. Freud's ideas about identification shifted considerably in the course of his writings, and, as Bronfenbrenner (1960a) has noted, the concept of identification has had at least three distinct meanings in Freud's thinking and in the elaborations provided by most of his more recent followers.

First, according to Bronfenbrenner's analysis, identification refers to *behavior*, as when one person behaves like another. It should be noted that behavioral similarity between two people does not by itself demonstrate that one of them has identified with the other. The behavioral similarity between them may be caused by some other variables that independently exert the same effects on both people. A mother and her daughter may both, for example, be unhappy at the same time, but each for entirely different reasons, and each without knowing the other's state.

Identification often also refers to a *motive*, in the form of a generalized disposition to act or to be like another. Most often this motive refers to the tendency to emulate idealized standards and behaviors of the parent. In some recent formulations this motive is invoked to deal with the child's desires to have the attributes of a category—such as "masculinity." For example, Kohlberg (1966, p. 165) says: "Desire to be masculine leads to the desire to imitate a masculine model, which leads to a deeper emotional attachment to the model." Another definition of identification (Kagen, 1958, 1964) emphasizes the child's *belief* that some of the attributes of a model belong to the self. Kagan says:

If a six-year-old boy is identified with his father, he necessarily regards himself as possessing some of his father's characteristics, one of which is maleness or masculinity. Moreover, if a child is identified with a model, he will behave, to some extent, as if events that occur to the model are occurring to him. If a child identifies with his father, he shares vicariously in the latter's victories and defeats, in his happiness and in his sorrow; in his strengths and in his weaknesses (1964, p. 146).

This definition of identification would seem to refer to any closely empathetic relationship and might characterize the feelings of a father toward his son just as much as those of the son toward his father.

Finally, identification refers to a *process* —to the mechanisms through which the child comes to emulate a model. A variety of such mechanisms has been posited by different theorists, beginning with Freud. Freud's account of the identification process has been carefully explicated elsewhere (e.g., Bronfenbrenner, 1960a) and a brief summary suffices here.

In his formulations Freud distinguished two main types of identificatory mechanisms. According to him, "anaclitic identification" is based on the intense dependency of a child on his mother, beginning early in development. For girls, identification is based mainly on this love or dependency relation with the mother. In contrast, for boys dependency or anaclitic identification with the mother is supplemented later by "identification with the aggressor," in the form of the potentially castrating father, during the resolution of the Oedipus complex. As a result of this additional process of identification with the aggressor, boys were believed by Freud to develop a harsher superego. Identification with the aggressor was seen as motivated by fear of harm and castration from the punitive father in retribution for the son's Oedipal fantasies and his libidinal wishes toward the mother.

Both forms of identification presuppose a strong relationship with each parent as the precursor of identification. In anaclitic identification the child must first have developed a dependent love relationship with his caretaker (usually the mother). Later, when the mother begins to withdraw some of her nurturant attention from the dyadic relation with the child, he becomes motivated to recapture her, as it were, by imitating and reproducing her in actions and fantasy. Identification with the aggressor requires that the boy must have a strong (but ambivalent) relation with the father, in which his love for him is mixed with hostility for possessing his mother and for interfering with his own libidinal urges. The hostile feelings that the boy experiences in the Oedipal situation engender great anxiety in him; he desires the mother but fears castration from the father. To defend against the resulting anxiety he resolves the Oedipal dilemma, repressing his aggressive wishes toward the father and trying to become more like him.

R. R. Sears and his colleagues have conducted extensive empirical studies that are most relevant to Freud's theorizing on identification. As Sears has noted, his investigations, like those of other researchers in this area, generally have assumed that a broad cluster of seemingly related behaviors are subsumed under the effects of a single process of identification (Sears, Rau, and Alpert, 1965, p. 1). In particular, the syndrome of patterns believed to be the products of a unitary identification process include "sex typing, adult role formation, self-control, self-recrimination, prosocial forms of aggression, guilt feelings, and other expressions of conscience" (Sears, Rau, and Alpert, 1965, p. 1). These behaviors, it will be seen, seem to be referents for even broader concepts such as Freud's construct of superego and ego-ideal (Freud, 1949). According to the view of identification as a unitary process, all these seemingly diverse components of socialization should cluster together as the highly correlated products of identification with the like-sex parent.

The most appealing theoretical virtue of a unitary theory of identification is that it tries to explain many important features of social development under one set of concepts. It would certainly be elegant if one unitary identification process could be shown to account for the development of such seemingly diverse behavioral manifestations as conscience and self-control, for the formation of enduring sex roles and sex-typing patterns, and for the acquisition by the child of appropriate adult role behavior. Such a unitary underlying process would be especially attractive because the relations between parental behavior and the subsequent developmental patterns of their children tend to be extremely complex.

Consistency and Specificity in Sex-Typed Behavior

Sears and his associates began by noting that if a more or less unitary process of identification regulates the many traits that have been interpreted to result from identification, then those traits should themselves be closely related. As Sears, Rau, and Alpert put it:

. . . if there is a single mediating process governing the various hypothesized behavioral products of identification, there should be high positive correlations among the measures of the several so-called identification behaviors (1965, p. 2).

Earlier sections indicated that dependency and aggression are dimensions on which the sexes are thought to differ most strikingly. Therefore these dispositions often serve as key referents for sex-typing, and evidence for their consistency becomes important to justify theorizing about the unity of the identification process and of its broad consequences. If diverse behaviors are to be viewed as mediated by identification, then it becomes necessary to show that these behaviors are components of generalized consistent traits or dispositions that characterize the individual stably in many situations.

For this purpose, Sears (1963) and Sears, Rau, and Alpert (1965) studied the intercorrelations among identification-mediated behaviors in preschool girls and boys. Recognizing the kinds of methodological problems that complicate the meaning of broad, global trait ratings (as discussed in earlier sections), Sears and his colleagues have been careful to include objective and detailed observational measures of the child's actual behavior in clearly delineated situations.

For dependency, Sears' (1963) five categories of observed dependency behavior were: *negative attention seeking*, that is, attention getting by disruption or aggressive activity; *positive attention seeking*, as in seeking praise; nonaggressive *touching or holding*; *being near*, for example, following a child or teacher; and *seeking reassurance*. The children were observed carefully at nursery

school and their behavior was scored reliably with an extensive time-sampling procedure. In free play each child was observed for a total of 7 to 10 hours. The intercorrelations among the five dependency categories reached statistical significance in only one of the twenty consistency coefficients that were computed.

Additional research on dependency (reviewed in Maccoby's chapter in this book) indicate some statistically significant but generally small correlations in observational studies sampling dependency in closely related situations. For example, Mann (1959) obtained ratings of 55 2-minute observations of 41 nursery school children in free play on six kinds of dependency behavior. Only one of fifteen intercorrelations among these components turned out to be significant. Likewise, Heathers' (1953) observations of nursery school children showed no relation between the frequencies of their "affection-seeking" and "approval seeking." Factor analyses also yield multiple factors for what appear to be similar behavior. Gewirtz (1956), for instance, did a factor analysis of nine observational measures of attention-seeking and showed that even this one dependency component may be at least two-dimensional. One factor seemed to involve direct, active verbal attempts to maintain the attention of the adult; the other included nonverbal, passive actions.

As would be expected, the correlations tend to be much higher when broad trait judgments about dependency are made by raters. For example, Beller (1955) reported correlations that ranged from .48 to .83 for teacher ratings of five dependency components in nursery school children. Although the correlations from such broad trait ratings often are impressively large, the high likelihood of halo effects and stereotyped impressions in such judgments makes them hard to interpret, except as indices of consistent stereotyping (e.g., Mischel, 1968).

The consistency or specificity of dependency is of special importance because of the critical place given to dependency motivation in Sears' formulation of anaclitic identification. Sears, Rau, and Alpert (1965), after reviewing their own empirical evidence, concluded this way:

The original formulation of the theory assumed that a dependency motivational system would provide the reinforcement of the imitative responses that constituted the new repertoire of actions composing more mature and more adultlike roles. There was no evidence in the data, however, that any unitary concept of dependency was justified (p. 260).

In light of these considerations, the authors abandoned the "notion of a dependency drive as the source of reinforcement for imitation or modeling . . ." (p. 260). They suggest, instead, that the most valuable next research steps would be to examine the conditions that determine attachment in early infancy and those that facilitate or inhibit imitation.

Sears, Rau, and Alpert (1965) also studied the consistency of aggression in the same sample of nursery school children. A total of 132 consistency coefficients (half for boys and half for girls) was computed among a dozen independent aggression measures. Of this overall total, twelve intercorrelations reached statistical significance for the boys and six were significant for the girls. These correlations suggested some clustering of aggressive behaviors that exceeds sheer chance, especially in boys. Considering the large number of coefficients computed, and the generally modest magnitude of even those relations that did reach significance, the evidence for a broadly consistent aggressive trait was not impressive. This relative lack of consistency is understandable when one considers the heterogeneous behaviors subsumed under such a broad category as "aggression." If such diverse behaviors as prosocial aggressive verbalizations, as in "tattling," and antisocial physical aggressive acts, such as injury to objects, all are grouped together into one dispositional category of "aggression," it should not be too surprising that relatively few high correlations are found among them. Indeed, it would be difficult to understand such consistencies considering that, as discussed earlier, girls show more prosocial verbal aggression than boys, whereas boys are more physically aggressive than girls.

There is some correlational support for meaningful sex differences in the consistency of patterns of sex-typed behaviors. In particular, more (and somewhat stronger) intercor-relations were found for girls than boys on Sears' (1963) five observation measures of dependency, whereas the reverse held for aggression. For aggressive behaviors more significant intercorrelations among aggression components seem to be found for boys than for girls (Lansky et al., 1961; Sears, 1961; Sears, Rau, and Alpert, 1965). Consistent with these trends, Kagan and Moss (1962) also have found greater stability over time in sex-appropriate behaviors as compared to sex-inappropriate patterns. In this longitudinal study girls showed significant temporal stability in dependency, while boys did not; conversely, male-appropriate behaviors such as aggressiveness tended to be more temporally consistent throughout the development of males than of females, as discussed later.

To support the idea of a unitary identification process it would be most important to show that people are highly consistent in their sex-role behaviors. The relations among measures of sex role were studied carefully by Sears, Rau, and Alpert (1965). Their work illustrates both the kinds of measures most often used to study gender role in children and the level of consistency generally found among these indices. They included several tests in which children chose among objects, toys, and activities that differed in their sex-appropriateness. In one pair of the "Pictures Test," for example, the youngster must indicate whether he prefers a picture showing a child walking a doll in a buggy or one playing cowboy. Other measures included real and symbolic play area and activity preferences, as well as an extensive series of observations by adults. These observers then rated each child on a five-point scale of sex-typing. In addition, the children's doll play was scored for sex-typing. Their willingness to adopt the opposite sex role in a game while interacting with their mothers also was recorded. On the whole, agreement among raters was adequate and scoring reliability was good. The expected mean differences between the sexes also were found quite strongly on most of the sex-role measures.

The correlations among the sex-role measures themselves are of main interest. For the small sample of subjects used (21 boys and 19 girls) correlations exceeding about .40 would have been required to reach statistical significance for either sex. The findings revealed a median correlation among five assessments of .36 for girls; for boys the median correlation was .15. The IT Scale, one of the most popular measures of sex-role identification, was virtually unrelated to other indices of sex-typing. When IT Scale results were disregarded there was some indication of consistency among measures for girls. For boys there was almost no sign of consistency. Generally the relations were modest and complex, and therefore hard to interpret. For example, while girls showed some consistency in certain sex-typed preference measures and boys did not, in the context of doll play these trends were reversed. In doll play the girls were not consistent in their tendencies to perform male or female adult work, whereas there was a trend for boys. The instability of these indices of sex roles becomes evident when one realizes that even within a fairly narrow subset of gender role measures, such as different aspects of doll play, the youngsters' behavior was far from consistent.

The relationships obtained by the Sears group seem fairly representative. Other researchers generally also have found only modest consistency among diverse direct measures of sex role and sex-typing in children (e.g., Borstelmann, 1961; Hetherington, 1965). To illustrate, Hetherington (1965) computed correlations among several measures of sex-typing (IT Scale, imitation of same-sex parent, and rated similarity between parent and same-sex child). The results indicated significant correlations among these measures only for older girls from father-dominant homes. Apart from this subgroup, few systematic or meaningful correlations were found among the identification measures. For boys, no significant correlations were found between the IT Scale and any other measure. Although more substantial correlations may be found among masculinity-femininity self-reports and global ratings, consistency among indices of sex-typing tends to be limited when more direct and more diverse observational measures are used. This general finding is highly congruent with results on the consistency of other personality dimensions (Campbell and Fiske, 1959; Mischel, 1968; Vernon, 1964).

In addition to sex-typing, conscience and moral behavior also have been assumed to be fairly consistent, enduring products of the identification process. A great deal of research has inquired into the consistency of moral behavior. The very extensive Character Education Inquiry more than 40 years ago exposed thousands of children to a host of situations in which they could cheat, lie, and steal. These deviations were made possible in many settings, including the home, party games, and athletic contexts (Hartshorne and May, 1928). The children were substantially consistent in their self-reported thoughts and opinions about moral issues when questioned about them in their classrooms. The correlations among various forms of these paper-and-pencil tests also tended to be high. But when the forms of these tests were administered in diverse social settings (such as at home, in Sunday school, at club meetings, as well as in the classroom), the correlations were reduced to about .40.

The more the situation was changed, the more specific the youngsters' moral behavior became. For example, copying from a key on one test correlated .696 with copying from a key on another test, and cheating by adding on scores from a speed test correlated .440 with adding on scores on another speed test. Copying from a key on one test, however, correlated only .292 with adding on scores. The average intercorrelations among four classroom tests was .256 (Hartshorne and May, 1928, p. 383). Moreover, the average correlation between four classroom tests and two out-of-classroom tests (contests and stealing) was only .167. The lying test given in the classroom averaged .234 with the other classroom tests but only .064 with the two out-of-classroom deception tests.

A reanalysis of some of the Hartshorne and May data (Burton, 1963) submitted findings from some of their most reliable tests to a factor analysis. The results indicated more than random consistency in the children's moral behavior but, as Burton (p. 492) put it, led to a conclusion "not greatly different from that made by Hartshorne and May." Their basic conclusion was: "as we progressively change the situation we progressively lower the correlations between the tests" (Hartshorne and May, 1928, p. 384).

Essentially similar conclusions have been reached about the relative specificity of moral guilt from studies employing responses to projective tests. To illustrate, in one study

(Allinsmith, 1960) moral feelings were inferred from the projective story-completions given by adolescent boys in response to descriptions of various immoral actions. Allinsmith concluded from the resulting data that a person with a truly generalized conscience is a statistical rarity.

Most research on moral behavior has concentrated on three areas: moral judgment and verbal standards of right and wrong (e.g., Kohlberg, 1964); resistance to temptation in the absence of external constraint (e.g., Aronfreed, 1969; Aronfreed and Reber, 1965; Grinder, 1962; MacKinnon, 1938; Mischel and Gilligan, 1964); and post-transgression indices of remorse and guilt (e.g., Allinsmith, 1960; Aronfreed, 1964; Sears, Maccoby, and Levin, 1957; Whiting, 1959). Correlations among measures sampling these three areas of moral behavior indicate that they are either virtually independent or at best only minimally interrelated domains (Becker, 1964; Hoffman, 1963; Kohlberg, 1964). Even within each of these subtypes of morality, specificity also tends to be high. An extensive survey of diverse reactions to transgression, for example, yielded no predictable relationships among specific types of reactions (Aronfreed, 1961). Sears, Rau, and Alpert (1965) also failed to find very consistent relations among their various indices of reactions to transgression.

It might be argued that consistency in the trait products of identification does not manifest itself clearly until much later in the course of development. Therefore it might be more profitable to study the consistency of identification-mediated traits in adults. One belief shared by many theoreticians of diverse orientation is that as a consequence of identification people develop enduring and highly generalized attitudes toward authority. Freud, Piaget, and Rogers, as well as many others, all posit that reactions toward authority originate in the family situation and manifest themselves later throughout life as broadly generalized attitudes expressed in many situations toward superiors. This belief is seen in the widespread assumption that attitudes toward parental figures are mirrored in reactions to such diverse authority figures as teachers, policemen, and work supervisors throughout life. As Piaget put it:

Day to day observation and psychoanalytic experience show that the first personal schemas are afterward generalized and applied to many people. According as the first inter-individual experiences of the child who is just learning to speak are connected with a father who is understanding or dominating, loving or cruel, etc., the child will tend (even throughout life if these relationships have influenced his whole youth) to assimilate all other individuals to this father schema (Piaget, 1951, p. 207).

To study this assumption, Burwen and Campbell (1957) tested a large sample of Air Force personnel. Their assessments included interviews, TAT, description of self and others, judgments of photos, and autobiographical inventories, as well as an attitude survey and sociometric questionnaire. Where possible, they scored attitudes toward father, symbolic authority (e.g., in responses to pictures of older persons on the TAT), and immediate boss through each of their techniques. Attitudes toward real and symbolic peers also were scored with similar measures. The interjudge reliability of all ratings on each instrument was sufficiently high. To their surprise, the investigators found that atttitudes toward father, symbolic authority, and boss were not more highly correlated with each other than they were with attitudes toward real or symbolic peers, and all correlations tended to be low. When method-produced correlations were disregarded, there was little evidence for generality of attitudes toward either authority or peers. The authors were compelled to conclude the following:

Evidence for a generalized attitude toward authority which encompasses attitudes toward father, symbolic authority, and boss is totally negative, suggesting the need for reconsideration of the applicability of commonly held theory in this area (Burwen and Campbell, 1957, p. 31).

Specificity also has been found repeatedly with adult subjects when their consistency is assessed on character traits like "rigidity" or on sex-typed traits like social conformity, or on virtually any other nonintellective personality dimension (Mischel, 1968; Vernon,

1964). Results of this kind present a fundamental problem not only for unitary theories
of identification but for all approaches to
socialization that assume the existence of relatively situation-free broad dispositional syndromes. Considering the fact that specificity
tends to be high among the components of
traits like dependency or self-control, it should
not be surprising that the correlations between such traits tend to be modest at best
for adults as well as for children (e.g., Byrne,
1966; Mischel, 1968; Sears, Rau, and Alpert, 1965; Vernon, 1964).

The interpretation of all data on behavioral
consistency depends of course on the criteria
chosen to evaluate them. Consistency coefficients averaging from about .20 to .40, such
as those found by Hartshorne and May, can
be construed either as evidence for the relative specificity of the particular behaviors or
as support for the presence of some generality
(Burton, 1963). In correlational research one
has to distinguish clearly between "statistically significant" associations and equivalence.
When the sample of subjects is large a correlation of .30 or even .20 easily may reach
significance and suggests an association that
is not likely on the basis of chance. The
same coefficient, while reassuring us that
behavior is neither random nor capricious,
accounts, however, for less than 10% of the
relevant variance and therefore has limited
value for understanding and predicting individual behavior.

The meaning of any correlation coefficient
and its interpretation depends on many considerations, such as the reliability and the
length of the tests on which it is based, and
the homogeneity in the tested behavior range
of the sample of subjects. Statistical considerations of this kind (Cronbach, 1960) caution
one to interpret the meaning of particular
coefficients carefully. In spite of such methodological reservations, however, the behaviors
which traditionally have been construed as
stable personality trait indicators often turn
out to actually be highly specific. Although
broad traits may be excessively gross categories for the analysis of personality, the
reader should not construe the evidence on
trait specificity as suggestive of psychological
anarchy in place of personality. A person's
past behavior often can serve to predict his
future behavior in similar situations, and

many syndromes show considerable stability
over long periods of time, especially when
relevant stimulus conditions remain stable
(Mischel, 1968). Cognitive consistencies tend
to be especially strong, as later sections discuss, and the subjective impressions of
constancy in oneself and in the personality of
others is not an illusion (Mischel, 1968; Vernon, 1964). The findings on trait consistency
and specificity do imply that the organization of personality is far more subtle, and is
moderated by much more complex variables,
than the notion of broad unitary traits would
suggest.

Traits, of course, can be inferred only
from behavioral measurements and these involve "errors of measurement." Gradually,
however, psychometricians are acknowledging that behavioral fluctuations reflect more
than imperfections in our measuring instruments (Loevinger, 1957). The modest and
even zero intercorrelations obtained between
different measures used as referents for sex-
typed behaviors, such as dependency or
aggression, emphasize the importance of considering more specific antecedents, more specific contingencies, and more circumscribed
units in the analysis of these syndromes. In
light of the empirical data the utility of
describing behavior with molar trait units
(e.g., dependency) is being questioned increasingly (e.g., Brim, 1960; Hartup, 1963;
Wallace, 1966) and the theoretical implications are pursued in later sections of this
chapter.

If the components of the behaviors construed to be the generalized products of
identification are actually only marginally intercorrelated, there cannot be much support
for the belief that socialization is a relatively
homogeneous product of a unitary identification process. Consider once more the main
data relevant to the hypothesis of positive
intercorrelations among the products of identification in the Sears, Rau, and Alpert
(1965) study. These data yielded a median
intercorrelation of .25 (not statistically significant), which suggests a trend for beyond-
chance consistency among identification
measures in girls; virtually no evidence was
found for strong positive intercorrelations in
these data for boys (Sears, Rau, and Alpert,
1965). Clearly the hypothesis of close relations among traits hypothesized to be medi-

ated by identification cannot fare very well if the traits themselves turn out not to be highly consistent.

Cognitive Consistency Strivings

Although behavior may change even across seemingly similar situations, it is not capricious. Persons do construe themselves as consistent and they also attribute enduring personality dispositions to others, as was discussed earlier in regard to categorizing behavior. We noted that people generate broad categories that subsume great behavioral diversity, as is illustrated in the pervasive stereotypes that exist about sex roles. In some formulations these categorizations are considered to be especially important (e.g., Kagan, 1964).

Kagan (1964) has emphasized the close link between sex-role stereotypes and sex-role standards. Empirically, stereotypes about the nature of sex differences tend to be closely linked with "sex-role standards" or expectations about how the sexes *ought to* differ. Rothbart and Maccoby (1966), for example, gave parents questionnaires asking them about differences they felt actually existed between boys and girls on such behaviors as their degree of obedience. The parents' opinions about these differences between the actual frequency of sex differences correlated significantly with their self-reported attitudes about the differences that *should* exist between boys and girls.

The stereotypes that define appropriate sex-role behaviors may serve as sex-role *standards,* as Kagan (1964, p. 138) puts it, which summarize the "culturally approved characteristics for males and females." According to his conceptualization, sex-role stereotypes serve as standards that are used by the person to guide and to evaluate his behavior. Sex-role *identity,* in turn, usually refers to the "degree to which an individual regards himself as masculine or feminine" (Kagan, 1964, p. 144). In Kagan's view sex-role identity significantly influences many critical aspects of behavior. He posits the existence of a fundamental "motive to match one's behavior to an internal standard" (p. 137). One of the most important of these standards involves culturally shared sex-role expectations about masculinity and femininity. There is little doubt about the existence

of culturally shared sex-role stereotypes and standards and there is wide agreement about their content (e.g., Brown, 1965). The place of these sex-role stereotypes and standards in personality functioning is less clear, however. Kagan's formulation of sex-role identity stresses the person's global concept of his own overall masculinity or femininity. As he puts it:

> The degree of match or mismatch between the sex-role standards of the culture and the individual's assessment of his own overt and covert attributes provides him with a partial answer to the question, "How masculine (or feminine) am I?" (1964, p. 144).

Some conceptualizations of identification attach the greatest importance to cognitive strivings for consistency and make consistency motivation the crux of sex-role development. In particular, Kohlberg (1966) has noted that cognitive self-categorizations as "boy" or "girl" are made as simple reality judgments early in development and, once formed, tend to be fairly irreversible, being maintained by the physical reality of one's sex. In Kohlberg's cognitive-developmental formulations this direct self-categorization of gender is given central importance as the fundamental organizer of sex-role attitudes and values. As Kohlberg says:

> Basic self-categorizations determine basic valuings. Once the boy has stably categorized himself as male he then values positively those objects and acts consistent with his gender identity (1966, p. 89).

Or, in other words:

> The child's sexual identity is maintained by a motivated adaptation to physical social reality and by the need to preserve a stable and positive self-image (p. 88).

Such theorizing rests on the assumption that strong tendencies or strivings toward cognitive consistency exist and lead the person to acquire values consistent with his cognitive judgments about himself. As Kohlberg points out, many conceptualizations and research findings on self-consistency and on dissonance reduction or cognitive balance (e.g., Abelson and Rosenberg, 1958; Festinger, 1957) support the view that people tend to seek cognitive consistency.

Consistency theories lead one to expect that people should retain important cognitions about themselves fairly stably. Consistency over time does seem to be high for the self-concepts and for the descriptive categories, personality labels, and attitudes and values which individuals attribute to themselves on trait-rating scales. E. L. Kelly (1955) compared trait self-descriptions obtained on questionnaires answered almost 20 years apart. During the years 1935 to 1938 several personality questionnaires were administered to 300 engaged couples. Most of these people were retested with the same measures in 1954. The questionnaires included the Allport-Vernon values test, the Bernreuter personality questionnaire, and the Strong Vocational Interest Blank, among others. Self-reports of attitudes about marriage were highly unstable ($r < .10$). However, the stability coefficients for ratings of self-confidence and sociability and for self-descriptions of interests and of economic and political values were high. For these self-reported traits the consistency coefficients ranged from about .45 to slightly over .60, indicating very considerable stability, considering the long temporal delay between measurements. Similar results have come from other sources. For example, the test-retest correlations on the California Psychological Inventory scales for high school students retested after 1 year and for a sample of prisoners retested after 7 to 21 days were also high (Gough, 1957). In general, self-descriptions on many personality questionnaires seem to show a good deal of stability (Byrne, 1966; Mischel, 1968).

Personal constructs as measured by Kelly's Role Construct Repertory Test (Reptest) also show much consistency over time (Bonarius, 1965). A retest correlation of .79, for example, was found for constructs after a 2-week interval (Landfield, Stern, and Fjeld, 1961). Moreover, factor analyses of the Reptest indicate that the first factor extracted is stable, the average retest correlation being .83 (Pedersen, 1958). People thus seem to construe many events—and themselves—with stable concepts and to view their own dispositions as consistent.

Apart from the foregoing correlational data, voluminous experimental research and theorizing on cognitive incongruity, on cognitive dissonance, and on cognitive balance also indicates that persons generally reduce inconsistencies between incompatible cognitions (e.g., Abelson and Rosenberg, 1958; Festinger, 1957; Glass, 1968; Heider, 1958; Osgood, Suci, and Tannenbaum, 1957). People do minimize and avoid discrepant cognitions about themselves and others and reconstrue discrepant events to impose compatibility upon them.

Although there may be strong tendencies to reduce cognitive inconsistencies, the relations between such cognitive consistency strivings and behavior are not clear. Tendencies to reduce cognitive dissonance cannot be taken as automatic evidence that the individual's noncognitive behaviors—the things that he actually does—are necessarily under the control of such cognitive consistency strivings. The complexity of these causal relations between cognitions and actions becomes most evident when one considers, as Festinger (1964) has noted, studies of the effects of cognitive or attitudinal changes upon subsequent behavior changes. Festinger pointed out in his review of the literature that, surprisingly, there is little evidence that alterations in attitudes or beliefs produce changes in relevant behavior. On the other hand, there are data suggesting that cognitive and value changes may *follow* after new behaviors have been performed, rather than being the antecedents or prerequisites for these new actions (e.g., Brehm and Cohen, 1962; Festinger, 1957). Cognitions and values thus often may be realigned to make them consistent with behavior changes and may be used to justify the altered behavior rather than being the causes of the new behavior.

Although Festinger (1964) correctly noted that evidence showing that attitudinal changes lead to behavior change is limited, certainly such effects can occur. The fact that affective and cognitive changes can lead to altered overt behavior has been illustrated often. For example, it has been shown that cognitive desensitization of a fear may facilitate actual approach behavior toward the feared object. Thus subjects who learned to relax calmly to snakes in imagination later were more able to handle the snakes physically (Davison,

1968). The preceding considerations suggest that while a person's attitudes and his cognitions are a critical part of the chain of behavior, they do not necessarily have singular, unidirectional causal powers. Changes in what a person does can lead to cognitive reorganization, just as cognitive changes can lead to behavior modification (e.g., Mischel, 1968). The multiplicity of the conditions that jointly determine the degree of consistency—or of inconsistency—among cognitions, affects, and actions is being recognized increasingly (e.g., Insko and Schopler, 1967).

The links between attitudes and cognitions on the one hand and overt behavior on the other are illustrated by the empirical associations found among their measures. An extremely extensive survey of the numerous correlations obtained among many kinds of motivational imagery (TAT themes) and behavior ratings in longitudinal research was presented by Skolnick (1966a, 1966b). The survey tabulated the associations between cognitions and fantasies, as measured by projective and storytelling techniques, and indices of the person's overt behavior in the same content area. The results indicated that cognitions and thoughts sometimes were positively related to relevant actions, less often negatively, but most frequently not at all. For example, achievement concerns and ideations measured from imagery in TAT stories were found to relate in highly limited ways to other indices of achievement. The findings were similar for other content areas, such as the associations between aggression imagery and aggression-relevant behavior. McClelland (1966), reviewing this elaborate survey, pointed out that while the total number of associations significant at the $p < .10$ level exceeded chance the relationship was not close. The predicted relationships were found only about 25% of the time and generally at low magnitudes.

Often there is some significant association between attitudes and measures of the relevant overt behavior, but the correlations are small (e.g., Becker, 1960; Harding et al., 1954). Brody's (1965) study of the relations between maternal attitudes and mother's actual behavior toward her child is fairly representative. Brody administered the Parental Attitude Research Instrument (PARI) and other measures to the mothers of preschool children. Afterward independent direct observations were obtained of interactions between the mothers and their children in a play setting. These interactions were scored reliably on dimensions relevant to those sampled verbally in the attitude scale (e.g., authoritarian-controlling, hostility-rejection). Of 15 behavioral indices only 7 were statistically significantly related to maternal attitude scores. Even the significant relations were of moderate magnitude. The total findings led the author to conclude that there was no support for a strong relationship between expressed maternal attitudes toward child rearing and the direct observation measures of the mother's behavior toward her child.

As another example, Grinder (1964) studied the associations between cognitive moral judgments (moral realism and immanent justice) inferred from story completions and the children's actual resistance to temptation. No important sex differences were found and conscience strength generally seemed to increase with age. However, the correlations between the cognitive and behavioral measures of conscience were, on the whole, nonsignificant. The associations led the author to conclude that the "behavioral and cognitive dimensions of conscience develop independently" (p. 881). After an extensive review of research on moral values, Pittel and Mendelsohn (1966) also noted the frequent independence of values and behavior in this domain.

Taken collectively, the results on the relations between cognition and behavior suggest that whereas people may construe their diverse behaviors as congruent, and perceive themselves and others as consistent, the bridge between such constructed cognitive consistencies and other relevant aspects of their behavior may be quite complex and indirect. Cognitive consistency strivings may help to account for *cognitive* consistency but they cannot be invoked as the automatic causes of the individual's actions, especially when those actions turn out to have relatively little cross-situational generality. Even if one assumes the existence of powerful strivings for cognitive consistency, as posited by consistency theories of sex-role development, one must consider the processes through which the individual adopts his specific values and behaviors from among the many possibilities that could be consistent with his gender. It may be, as Kohlberg (1966, p. 89) suggests, that after the boy has "categorized himself as male he then values positively those objects and acts consistent with his gender identity." That hypothesis, however, cannot by itself account for how the boy now learns and selects the particular sets of sex-typed behaviors that he adopts from the vast array that could be "consistent with his gender." As the study of individual differences shows, there are many different acceptable ways of being a boy or girl, and even more diverse ways of being a man or woman. A comprehensive approach to sex-typing must account for individual differences in sex-typed behaviors within each sex and not just for modal sex differences. Children of each sex are exposed to a great variety of potentially appropriate sex-typed behaviors by same-sex models, yet they select and choose discriminatively from this array of gender-consistent possibilities. A comprehensive approach to sex-role development and socialization must deal with the total processes through which personality develops, and some of these are explored further in the following sections.

THE ACQUISITION OF SEX-TYPED BEHAVIOR

Sex-Role Learning through Identification or Observation?

Traditionally, identification has been singled out as a special process requiring concepts different from those necessary to account for other forms of social learning. More recent social learning formulations, however, call attention to the functional equivalence of the concepts of identification and imitation and subsume both of them under more general principles of social learning (e.g., Bandura, 1969; Gewirtz and Stingle, 1968; Hill, 1960; Mischel, 1968). In this latter view, the principles needed to explain the development of sex-typing are the same ones that must be invoked to understand how any other complex socialization occurs. Viewed from social learning theory, the acquisition and performance of sex-typed behaviors can be described by the same principles used to analyze any other aspects of an individual's behavior (e.g., Bandura and Walters, 1963; Mischel, 1966a; Rotter, 1954). In addition to

discrimination, generalization, and observational learning, such principles include the patterning of reward, nonreward, and punishment under specific contingencies, and the principles of direct and vicarious conditioning.

Most of the research on the development of sex differences has been guided by such Freudian-derived concepts as "identification," "incorporation," "internalization," and "introjection." These terms received much discussion in the literature and the many confusions and inconsistencies in their use have been criticized repeatedly (e.g., Bandura and Walters, 1963; Hill, 1960; Rotter, 1954; Sanford, 1955). It has been pointed out (Bandura and Walters, 1963) that observational learning is generally labeled "imitation" in experimental psychology but "identification" in personality theories, and although numerous distinctions have been proposed, the same behavioral phenomena are encompassed by these terms. Both imitation and identification refer to the tendency for a person to reproduce the actions, attitudes, or emotional responses exhibited by real-life or symbolized models (Bandura and Walters, 1963). After reviewing some of the many attempts that have been made to differentiate identification from imitation, Bandura (1969) points out that although there is little agreement about differentiating criteria, some theorists argue that imitation causes identification, whereas others assume that identification produces imitation. Because the same basic learning processes appear to be involved, Bandura argues that, for the sake of clarity and parsimony, the terms "identification," "imitation," and "observational learning" may be used as synonyms to refer to behavioral modifications that result from exposure to modeling stimuli.

Early attempts to apply concepts from learning theories to problems of socialization relied heavily on S-R formulations that had emerged from laboratory research on simple learning with lower animals. The concepts that figured most importantly in these formulations were contingent reinforcement, in the form of direct rewards and punishments for the animals' behaviors; primary and learned drives (whose reductions were believed to have reinforcing effects); and conflict in such situations as the approach-avoidance or avoidance-avoidance paradigms (e.g., Miller and Dollard, 1941). More recent social learning formulations, however, instead have emphasized concepts that deal with observational and cognitive processes in the learning of complex social and interpersonal behaviors, as the following sections will illustrate (e.g., Bandura and Walters, 1963; Mischel, 1966a, 1966b, 1968; Rotter, 1954). The term "learning theories" often is applied to all these positions, sometimes resulting in confusion. It should be clear, for example, that social learning theories which use the concept of observational learning obviously do not restrict themselves to simple reinforcement principles to account for the acquisition of such behaviors as sex-typing. Although it has been contended repeatedly (e.g., by Kohlberg, 1966) that contemporary social learning formulations neglect cognitive processes, in fact they rely on them in their account of the development of all complex social behaviors, as the next section shows.

Observational Learning

Sex-typed behaviors, like all other social behaviors, depend to a large extent on observational learning and cognitive processes. Such learning can occur without any direct reinforcement to the learner (e.g., Bandura and Walters, 1963; Campbell, 1961; Hebb, 1966; Mischel, 1966a, 1966b). People learn sex roles through their eyes and ears by observing other persons and events and not merely from the consequences they get directly for their own overt behavior. Learning without direct reinforcement sometimes is called "cognitive," sometimes "vicarious," and sometimes "observational" or "modeling." These labels all refer to an individual's acquiring new knowledge and potential behavior through observation without any direct external reinforcement for his own acts. Observational learning may result from watching what others (models) do, or from attending to the physical environment, to events, and to symbols such as words and pictures. Much human learning is mediated by perceptual-cognitive processes and hinges on observation of environmental contiguities rather than on direct reinforcement for the individual's own behavior; even lower animals can learn without making any overt response during the observational learning experience (Deutsch and Deutsch, 1966).

Individuals learn through observation about the structure of the environment and the behavior of others. They learn not only what people do, but also about the characteristics of the physical and social environment (Bruner, Olver, and Greenfield, 1966). By simply observing behavioral sequences the observer can learn entirely novel response patterns that previously were unavailable to him (Bandura and Walters, 1963). The acquisition of these new response patterns through observational processes seems most apparent in language learning (e.g., Bandura and Harris, 1966), although the exact nature of such learning may depend on many variables (Odom, Liebert, and Hill, 1968).

Through observational and cognitive processes the young child soon comes to recognize his sexual identity or gender. He rapidly develops a conception of his permanent sexual identity through the same cognitive processes that permit him to understand the invariable identity of physical objects in the environment (Kohlberg, 1966). These concepts appear to occur early in development, generally before the age of 5 years. By the time children reach school age they clearly have learned the concepts "male" and "female" (Hartup and Zook, 1960; Kagan, Hosken, and Watson, 1961). During the course of early socialization they also rapidly acquire knowledge of the stereotypes about masculinity and femininity prevalent in their subculture.

As Kohlberg (1966) has stressed, these concepts and stereotypes probably arise in part from children's observations of sex differences in bodily structure and capacities. At around age 4 to 5 children become distinctly aware of adult sex differences in size and strength. These perceived differences may in turn be linked with stereotypes about sex differences in power (Horowitz, 1943; Kohlberg, 1966). Observation of extrafamilial roles also helps children to learn about sex differences in social power and in other dimensions. Many of these sex-role differences and stereotypes seem to be found across diverse cultures and may emerge with considerable regularity in the course of the child's development (e.g., D'Andrade, 1966; Kohlberg, 1966). Cross-cultural consistencies in sex roles probably reflect differences in the role of men and women within the family and in the economic institutions of the society. These roles, in turn, are linked to biological sex differences and the woman's child-bearing. Most sex differences in social behavior, however, depend on the specific response patterns which are sex-typed in a particular culture and are not universal entities. This fact is illustrated by the failure to replicate in Holland (Houwink, 1950) more than a few of the M-F (masculinity-femininity) items which differentiated the sexes in the United States, reported by Terman and Miles (1936).

Observational learning not only leads to the acquisition of new concepts and potential behavior; it also may have eliciting or inhibiting effects on the observer's present performance of previously learned behaviors. To illustrate some of the motivational effects of exposure to models a study on the vicarious transmission of delay-of-reward behavior in children will be described in detail (Bandura and Mischel, 1965). This study investigated how self-imposed delay of reward is influenced by the delay patterns displayed by real-life and symbolic models. In the initial phase of this experiment elementary school children from the fourth and fifth grades were administered a series of paired rewards presented as real choices. In each of these pairs they were asked to select either a small reward that could be obtained immediately or a more valued item contingent on a delay period ranging from 1 to 4 weeks. The children chose, for example, between a smaller, immediately available candy bar and a larger one that required waiting for several days. From the total pool of subjects, those with extremely high or very low delay-score totals were selected for the succeeding phases of the experiment. Youngsters in these extreme groups then were assigned to one of three treatment conditions. In one group the children observed live adult models who exhibited delay-of-reward responses counter to the group's self-gratification pattern; those in a second group were exposed to a model who displayed the opposite delay-of-reward behavior, but the modeling cues were presented only symbolically in written form. Children in the third group had no exposure to any models. After this experimental procedure the children's delay-of-reward responses were measured with different choice items. To further assess the generality and stability of changes in delay behavior, the children were retested by a different experimenter in a new social setting approximately 1 month after completion of the experimental phase of the study.

As predicted, the modeling procedures altered the children's delay-of-reward behavior in the direction of their model's choice patterns. Youngsters who initially had a predominantly delayed-reward pattern now displayed a substantially increased preference for immediate and less valued rewards as a result of watching models favoring immediate gratification. Conversely, children who had exhibited a strong preference for immediate rewards now increased and maintained their willingness to wait for more highly valued delayed outcomes following exposure to high-delay models. Most interesting, basically similar results were found whether the modeling cues were symbolic or whether they were conveyed by live adults, although cues presented by live adults produced somewhat more stable generalization effects.

Many similar experiments have demonstrated that a variety of complex verbal, emotional, and motoric behaviors may be learned, elicited, inhibited, maintained, and modified, at least in part, by modeling cues. Behaviors affected by exposure to models include such sex-typed patterns as physical aggression, as well as prosocial responses, psychotic syndromes, fears, and even linguistic and judgmental styles (e.g., Bandura, Grusec, and Menlove, 1966; Bandura and Walters, 1963; Chittenden, 1942; Lovaas et al., 1966). By attending to the verbal and nonverbal behavior of live or symbolic models the observer also can change his own language, his standards, and his social judgments. For example, observational learning has been shown to influence the standards people use privately for their own self-reward and self-evaluation (e.g., Bandura and Whalen, 1966; Carlin, 1965; Mischel and Liebert, 1966; Staub, 1965), their broad moral judgments about behavior (Bandura and McDonald, 1963), and the language categories they employ in speech (Bandura and Harris, 1966).

The potent and diverse modeling effects demonstrated in laboratory studies have major implications for theories of socialization and the development of sex roles. Traditional reinforcement learning theories of socialization have relied heavily on the belief that direct rewards and punishments from the parents mold the child's personality. In particular, some important attempts to reconcile Freud's ideas with the concepts of learning theories have put the greatest emphasis on the role of the rewards and punishments administered directly to the child by his parents (e.g., Miller and Dollard, 1941). But as Sears, Rau, and Alpert (1965, p. 2) point out, one of the striking features of such behaviors as efforts at self-control or prosocial aggression is that although they begin fairly early in the child's life, they often seem to develop independent of direct tuition by the parents. Referring to sex-typed behaviors, they say:

A pervasive quality such as masculinity (or femininity) receives at least some intentional reinforcement by parents and peers, of course, but the training task required for creating this kind of role conformity seems too great to permit an explanation in terms of the direct reinforcement of each of the components that compose the roles (1965, p. 2).

The findings from research on observational processes suggest that it is indeed unnecessary for social learning theories to depend on the concept of specific reinforcement provided for discrete acts, and on the laborious "shaping" or "training" of each minuscule role component by external reinforcements administered by the parent. On the contrary, it now has been demonstrated repeatedly that children may rapidly learn large and complex sequences through cognitive-perceptual processes that hinge on their observing events rather than on their being reinforced for performing acts.

It also has become evident that when exposed to many models—as is always true under normal life conditions—children imitate in varying degrees the behavior of many of these models rather than simply mirroring one. When exposed to several models the child may adopt components from the behavior displayed by each one, and his own later behavior reflects a synthesis and novel recombination of elements rather than being a robotlike replica of a single model (Bandura, Ross, and Ross, 1963a). Therefore children's sex-typed patterns and preferences are

not merely a child-sized version of those displayed by the same-sex parent. In some areas, such as toys and activity preferences, parental patterns may have virtually no influence on the child, and the youngster's values may be influenced chiefly by peers rather than by the personality of the parent. Mussen and Rutherford (1963), for example, studied the correlates of masculinity (inferred from preferences on the IT Scale) in a sample of first-grade boys. They found that the sex-typed preferences of boys were unrelated to the masculinity-femininity scores of their fathers. Indeed, in regard to the IT Scale preferences of boys these authors found that "there is no evidence that his parents' personality structures, particularly degree of sex-typing and self-confidence, have any significant influence" (1963, p. 596). The parents also answered a questionnaire intended to assess how strongly they encouraged their children to engage in traditionally sex-appropriate play, games, and activities. No significant relations were found between this measure and the children's sex-typed preferences, suggesting that children's game and activity choices may be relatively independent of parental tuition and more influenced by their peer culture than by hypothesized identification processes with adults.

These findings are congruent with results from extensive family studies by Rosenberg, Sutton-Smith, and their colleagues (e.g., 1968) and also by Brim (1958). The naturalistic field studies of these researchers have investigated the relationship between sex-typing and the family structure in the home. For example, they have compared the masculinity-femininity scores on self-report measures of people who came from two-child families in which both siblings were girls to those from families in which one sibling was a boy and the other was a girl. In general, the results reveal some complex interactions between the sex of the siblings and the patterning of masculinity-femininity scores among all the family members. A main theoretical point made by these studies is that the child's sex-role learning is not based merely on the like-sex parent but is also influenced substantially by other children (e.g., Brim, 1958; Rosenberg and Sutton-Smith, 1968). For example, cross-sex behavior is increased by exposure to the opposite sex behavior of older children as well as adults, as is reflected in the greater frequency of such cross-sex behavior in children who have older opposite sex siblings (Brim, 1958). Moreover, Rosenberg and Sutton-Smith (1968) found that the sex-role scores of the parents seem to be influenced by their children, as well as the reverse! Modeling thus is not a one-way process; children may serve as models for the sex-role patterns of their parents as well as emulating them and their own peers and siblings. Rosenberg and Sutton-Smith, discussing these results, have noted that they undermine the traditional assumption that sex roles are learned chiefly or exclusively through the child's identification with the like-sex parent (Kagan, 1964).

Characteristics of the Model Influencing Observational Learning

Although socialization usually involves numerous models, children obviously do not emulate the behaviors of everyone they see, nor do they imitate in equal degrees all the people they know. It is therefore important to understand the variables that determine the extent to which the child adopts for himself the attributes and behaviors displayed by different models. In recent years many studies have tried to clarify how the characteristics of a model affect the extent to which his behavior is adopted by observers. The results bear directly on theories of identification, since several different hypotheses have been advanced in these theories about the conditions most conducive to modeling effects.

Extensions of Freud's identification theory have put the greatest emphasis on anaclitic identification and hence on the nurturant and rewarding qualities of the model. Mowrer (1960), for example, conceptualized "developmental identification" (a process very similar to Freud's anaclitic identification) as based on the child's dependence upon his adult caretaker. Mowrer points out that the mother (or other principal caretaker) regulates the social and biological gratifications of the young, dependent child. Therefore during the course of her caretaking her characteristics and her behaviors increasingly acquire secondary reinforcement value. Through stimulus generalization, according to Mowrer, behaviors similar to the mother's also become reinforcing. Thus by closely emulating the

mother (or other caretaker) the child can provide himself with positively valenced conditioned reinforcers.

Similarly, the formulations of Robert Sears and his colleagues have focused on the nurturant relationship between the caretaking mother and her child as the bases for identification. According to Sears (1957) the mother becomes valuable for the child through her nurturance and the child therefore develops a strong dependency drive for her early in his life. When later frustrated by the mother's absence or unavailability, the child can engage in the nurturant acts himself through fantasy or by role-playing them, imitating the mother's behaviors.

Empirical studies have shown that the model's nurturance and rewardingness do facilitate the tendency of observers to emulate him. Mussen (1961) studied adolescent boys who were either highly masculine or highly feminine in their vocational interests as measured by their masculinity-femininity score on the Strong Vocational Interest Blank. These boys also were given personality tests (such as the TAT and the CPI) and, in addition, their behavior was rated by others. The obtained correlations suggested that boys with more masculine interests tended to portray their relationships with their fathers (inferred from TAT stories) as more positive and rewarding. On the TAT they also less often told stories in which fathers were punitive or restrictive to their sons. Moreover, boys whose fathers were affectionate and warm tended to show greater preference for the male role (Mussen and Distler, 1959) and were more similar to their fathers on a personality inventory (Payne and Mussen, 1956). Young boys whose fathers were nurturant also tended to assume the father role more frequently in doll play (P. S. Sears, 1953).

Another study investigated the antecedents of sex-role preferences in kindergarten boys (Mussen and Distler, 1960). On the basis of sex-typed preferences on the IT Scale, two extreme groups were selected, containing children with the highest and lowest masculinity scores. The mothers of these youngsters then were interviewed carefully about a host of familial child-rearing variables. Differences between the masculine and feminine boys were found especially in reports of the affectional bond between father and son. Compared to the feminine boys, the masculine boys were described as having more affectionate and warm relations with their fathers. The results also provided some discriminant validity evidence for the role of paternal nurturance in the development of masculinity since it was also found that *maternal* warmth was unrelated to the son's masculinity. These results were basically replicated in a later study. Mussen and Rutherford (1963, p. 602) found that in general "the boy who sees his father as a highly salient person in his life— instrumental in both rewarding and punishing him" is more likely to develop sex-appropriate patterns than the one who perceives his father as having little salience. In addition, they found that girls who were more appropriately sex-typed (on the IT Scale) perceived their mothers to be more warm, gratifying, and important (inferred from the stories told by the girls in a doll-play situation) than did girls who were less feminine in their IT Scale preferences. The more feminine girls also had mothers who were more self-accepting.

The facilitating effect of a model's nurturance on the observer's tendency to emulate him is further supported by experimental studies. Thus Bandura and Huston (1961) engaged nursery-school children in a highly nurturant and rewarding encounter with a female adult model. Children in a second group were exposed to the same model but her behavior toward them was distant and non-nurturant. After these interactions all the children saw the model display a series of novel aggressive, verbal, and motoric behaviors during the course of a game. Aggressive responses were imitated readily by most children regardless of their initial relationship with the model. The model's nonaggressive behaviors, however, were substantially more adopted by youngsters toward whom she had been more rewarding than by those toward whom she had been aloof.

The preceding research indicates that whereas nurturance may enhance the tendency to emulate a model, it is not necessarily an essential prerequisite for the occurrence of imitation. A model's nurturance, permissiveness, and warmth, for example, depending on the particular circumstances, can even serve to elicit less stringent and less self-control-ling behavior on the part of observers. Consider a model who displays a stringent pattern of self-gratification in her own behavior but permits the child to indulge himself more liberally. In this condition youngsters later showed far greater self-indulgence than did children who had been exposed initially to an adult who was equally self-stringent but less permissive toward them (Mischel and Liebert, 1966). Similarly, Bandura, Grusec, and Menlove (1966) found that high nurturance by a model led the child to engage later in more self-gratification rather than adopting the high standards displayed by the model herself. In particular, children who had undergone a brief nurturant and rewarding relation with an adult model subsequently tended to adopt the low standards set by peers more than did youngsters who had interacted with a less gratifying adult in the first place.

Burton, Allinsmith, and Maccoby (1966) investigated resistance to temptation in preschool children. In accord with theories of identification that emphasize nurturance-withdrawal (e.g., Hartup, 1958; Sears, Maccoby, and Levin, 1957), the authors had predicted that attention-withdrawal by the experimenter would enhance dependency arousal in the children and thus would increase identification with—and consequently conformity to —the experimenter's standards. In fact, withdrawal of attention had an effect only on boys and in a direction opposite to the prediction. In this instance, then, arousal of "dependency drive" had the same effect as nurturance in the two studies just cited—it increased self-indulgence.

Our discussion thus far has focused on the model's rewardingness. Other theorists have attached great significance to the parent's power over important outcomes in the child's life (e.g., Maccoby, 1959; Mussen and Distler, 1959; Parsons, 1955). These conceptualizations emphasize the model's control over the child's resources, in the form of both rewards and punishments, as chief determinants of the youngster's tendency to adopt the model's behaviors and to be influenced by him.

Anecdotally and in clinical observation it often has been noted that individuals rehearse and transmit to others behaviors which had aversive consequences for them. Parents claim, for example, that they unwillingly behave toward their children in ways similar to those that produced pain for them when performed by their own parents. The variables governing the reproduction of a model's novel behaviors which were painful to the individual in his prior interactions with that model have remained ambiguous. Several theories (e.g., Maccoby, 1959; Sears, 1957; Whiting and Child, 1953), including the well-known theory of "identification with the aggressor" (Bettelheim, 1943; A. Freud, 1946), have been invoked to account for this reproduction and transmission of social punishments, and the difficulties of a secondary reinforcement interpretation have been noted (e.g., Aronfreed, 1964). Data relevant to this issue have been primarily clinical and informal and even the occurrence of the phenomenon itself has been rarely demonstrated in experimental research. A study by Mischel and Grusec (1966) therefore investigated how the characteristics of a model influence the reproduction of social punishments, such as imposed delay of reward, which the individual not only observed but also directly received from the model.

Mischel and Grusec (1966) exposed preschool children to an adult female whose noncontingent rewardingness (nurturance) and future control over the child were varied. To manipulate rewardingness they varied the degree to which the model provided the child with both material and social noncontingent reward (e.g., attention, games, treats, praise) in a pre-experimental interaction. Power or control over both rewards and punishments was manipulated cognitively by varying the model's role. For some children the model was introduced as a visiting out-of-town teacher who would never reappear, whereas for the others she was introduced as the child's new schoolteacher. In the next phase, the children participated with the model in a "special game" involving a cash register and other toys in a play store setting. The model was aversive to the child in novel ways ("aversive" behaviors) during this interaction, and she also exhibited novel behaviors with no direct reinforcement consequences for the child ("neutral" behaviors). In particular, her aversive acts consisted of making the child wait for rewards, removing rewards from him, and sharp criticism. Her neutral be-

haviors consisted of distinctive verbal and motor behaviors (e.g., marching around the room while saying "March! March! March!"). The aversive behaviors were intended to have direct negative consequences for the child, whereas the neutral behaviors were merely displayed without any direct reinforcement consequences for him. In the former instances the child was the object of the behaviors, whereas in the latter he was only the observer of the modeled behaviors.

After the child had a chance to play the game with the model he was left alone briefly but was observed through a one-way mirror. Any of the model's neutral or aversive behaviors reproduced by the child, either in the model's presence or while alone, were scored as "rehearsals." In the final phase the subject's task was to show another person (a confederate dressed as a clown) how to play the game in the model's absence. The transmission of the modeled neutral and aversive behaviors to the "clown" in the model's absence was also assessed.

The effects of the model's attributes were quite specific. For example, the results showed that significantly more children *rehearsed* both the model's aversive and neutral behaviors when the model was both highly rewarding and had future control than when her rewardingness and control were low. The model's rewardingness significantly affected the rehearsal of neutral but not aversive behaviors; aversive behaviors were rehearsed only when the model had high control. The model's rewardingness also led to greater *transmission* by the children of her aversive behaviors to the clown, but it did not influence the transmission of her neutral behaviors. Children imposed upon others the painful behaviors that had been imposed on them initially by rewarding models, rather than by models with high control. This finding seems to contradict the expectations of defensive identification theory, which holds that the punitive behaviors of potentially threatening models (high future control) should be transmitted most (e.g. Bettelheim, 1943).

The overall results demonstrated that observed behaviors may be reproduced and transmitted to others without external reinforcement for their performance, even when the observer was the object of the modeled behaviors (and not just their witness) and received aversive consequences from the model. Indeed, the percentage of aversive behaviors transmitted exceeded the percentage of neutral behaviors transmitted. In addition, the extent to which the model's behaviors were reproduced was affected by her rewardingness, i.e., use of noncontingent reinforcement, and her future control over the subject. The total findings support the view that the model's rewardingness and his power may determine in part the extent to which his behavior is adopted. The results indicated, however, that these two variables have different effects as a function of the type of behavior (neutral or aversive) shown by the model and of the stimulus situation in which the subject reproduces it (rehearsal or transmission). These findings once more highlight the specificity of the determinants controlling behavior and show that the effects of the model's attributes depend on the particular behavior and situation involved, rather than exerting a unitary influence regardless of subjects and conditions.

A study by Grusec (1966) investigated how the model's attributes interact with her direct training procedures to influence the acquisition of self-criticism in young children. In the first phase of this study children interacted with a female model who was either high or low in rewardingness. Thereafter the children played a game with her during which she criticized and punished them for their performance either by withdrawal of love or by withdrawal of material reward. The termination of this punishment was made either contingent or noncontingent on the child's verbalization of the self-critical response. Grusec found that models who were high in rewardingness were more effective than those low in rewardingness, regardless of the kind of punishment they used, in establishing the initial self-critical response in the child. After the initial response, the subsequent course of self-criticism was affected substantially by the model's rewardingness and contingent reinforcement only when these procedures were combined with withdrawal of love. As this study shows, the model's attributes may interact with her direct training procedures to influence the child's learning experiences.

An experiment by Mischel and Liebert (1967) investigated how a model's power affects children's adoption of self-reward patterns which the model had displayed or imposed previously. All subjects were exposed to an adult model who exhibited a lenient self-reward pattern but imposed a stringent pattern on the child. More specifically, each child participated individually with a male adult model in a task that seemingly required skill but on which scores were experimentally controlled. A generous supply of small rewards (candies) was available to both the model and the subject. The model always rewarded himself for certain low performances but led the subject to reward himself only for higher achievements. The independent variable was the model's power, in the form of his ostensible ability to dispense valuable rewards to them in the future. Children in the control group experienced the identical manipulations but from a model who did not have the explicit power to dispense future rewards to them. As predicted, children who had interacted with a potentially rewarding model showed greater stringency in their own self-reward when subsequently performing alone than did control subjects.

The obtained results suggest that an agent's potential rewardingness increases his influence over others in the direction of greater obedience and generates more stringent adherence to his imposed reward standards and greater inhibition in self-reward for poor performances. Less powerful agents, in contrast, may be more likely to generate disobedience. It is especially interesting that greater stringency or inhibition was displayed by children in the potential reward group, although attainment of the reward controlled by the agent was not contingent on the child's self-reward behavior. The results thus suggest that subjective contingencies, or expectancies, presumably based on prior learning in which obedience to an agent's rules and attainment of rewards from him were correlated, may affect self-reward behaviors.

In this design, the model's own self-reward behavior was less stringent than the pattern he tried to impose on the child. Since children exposed to the less powerful or less potentially rewarding model became less stringent, their self-reward behavior of course resembled the model's own self-reward pattern more than did the behavior of youngsters exposed to the potentially rewarding model. This situation illustrates the seemingly paradoxical situation in which the behavior of the child may resemble the model's own behavior *less* when the model is powerful than when he is nonpowerful. Such an outcome would be expected only when adherence to the model's demands requires the person to perform in a way dissimilar to the model. Thus the effects that a model's attributes, such as rewardingness and power, have on the socialization of children exposed to that model depend on the particular behaviors displayed by the model and on numerous other conditions. Although the model's powerful resources and his nurturance often may facilitate identification, they by no means necessarily lead to the development of a more stringent superego and to more rigorous patterns of self-control.

Whiting (1959, 1960) has been one of the few contemporary theorists who have expanded Freud's concept of defensive identification. Whiting focused on the rivalry between child and parent. He posited this competition not merely in the sexual context of the Oedipal situation, but more broadly as involving competition over a variety of valuable resources in the form of both social and material gratifications. The child, Whiting assumes, envies the parental status and resources of his parents. Usually the child cannot compete successfully with his parents for their status and resources directly; he can attain them only through fantasy and identification with the high-status parent-consumer. His identification is thus motivated by the desire to have the envied resources consumed by the parents.

An experiment by Bandura, Ross, and Ross (1963b) is directly relevant to Whiting's conceptualization. In this experiment nursery school boys and girls participated with two adults in triadic relations designed as analogies to various types of nuclear families. In one condition, for example, an adult male controlled the positive resources while an adult female received and consumed them and the ignored child was the passive onlooker. In another condition the child was the recipient of the resources while one adult dispensed them and the second adult was the powerless subordinate. Each triad contained an adult male and female, and the design systematically tested the effects of having the male or the female be the dominant figure who controlled the resources. After these relationships were established, the children were assessed for their tendency to imitate the attributes of these adult models in their absence.

The results showed that the children identified much more with the controller of rewards than with the competitor who consumed the rewards. The findings therefore support the power, rather than the status-envy, hypothesis. When the male adult had greater control over resources than the female, both boys and girls imitated him to a greater degree. If the female adult had greater power than the male, her behaviors tended to be imitated more often, particularly by girls. This experiment demonstrated that cross-sex imitation occurs and is facilitated when the opposite-sex model has greater power than the same-sex model. Girls showed a greater tendency than boys to imitate the cross-sex model. When females have markedly less control over potent rewards than males, as they do in our culture, it is not surprising if they emulate male behavior to the degree that such cross-sex behavior is tolerated.

An additional finding in the foregoing experiment merits special attention because it illustrates how sex-role relationships and stereotypes may influence the effectiveness of social models. Although the powerful adult was generally greatly preferred to the noncontrolling adult, there were some notable exceptions. In particular, when the boy was the recipient of reinforcement but the same-sex adult was ignored by the controller of resources there was a tendency for the boy to prefer the noncontrolling male and to reject the powerful female. In part this tendency may have reflected the strong stereotype shared by many children that only a male can control potent resources. For example (p. 533): "He's the man and it's all his because he's a daddy. Mommy never really has things belong to her. . . ." A closer inquiry revealed that several of the youngsters indeed had attributed rewarding power to the ignored male adult in spite of the experimental efforts to render him powerless.

More naturalistic studies in which parents are the models (e.g., Hetherington, 1965; Hetherington and Frankie, 1967) also document the importance of the model's power and dominance as determinants of identification. A series of recent studies by Hetherington has relied on a variety of measures in efforts to relate parental attributes to child behavior. One study (Hetherington, 1965) investigated how the sex of the dominant parent in the home influences the child's identification. The subjects were children ranging in age from 4 to 11 years. The measurement of parental dominance was based on Farina's (1960) Structured Family Interaction Test. Each parent was presented individually with a set of hypothetical problem situations involving the parental handling of children. After the answers were obtained from each parent alone they were both brought together and asked to reach a compatible solution in handling each of these problems with children. The parents continued their discussion until both gave the terminating signal "agreed." These discussions were tape recorded and later scored for a number of dominance indices, such as percent of total talk, yielding, initiation and termination of talk. The resulting total parental dominance score was then correlated with the child's scores on each of the following measures.

One measure consisted of sex-typed preferences on the IT Scale. A second index of identification was the degree to which the child imitated paternal versus maternal behavior. To measure these modeling effects each child was tested on an esthetic preference test in two sessions conducted about 1 month apart. In one session the father chose the picture he preferred in each of 20 pairs of pictures; after the child observed his father's preferences his own choices were elicited. The second session followed the same procedure except that the mother rather than the father was the model. The imitation measure involved the number of similar choices in father-child and mother-child pairs. A third identification measure was based on the rated similarity between the nonsextyped personality traits of each parent and of his child. A checklist of 40 adjectives, selected as descriptive of both child and adult nonsex-typed personality traits, was used for this task. On these traits each parent was rated by a friend and each child was rated by his teacher; the extent of parent-child similarity

in these attribute ratings then was scored.

Hetherington (1965) found that parental dominance facilitated imitation in both boys and girls. Moreover, in families in which the mother was the dominant figure there was some disruption in the development of appropriate masculine sex-role preferences in boys. Under conditions of maternal dominance boys also tended to be rated as less similar to their fathers. According to Hetherington, parental dominance had little relation to sex-role preferences in girls or to their rated similarity to their mothers. As expected, girls in mother-dominant homes identified much more with mother than with father. In father-dominant homes, however, girls showed more rated similarity to their fathers than they did in mother-dominant homes, again documenting the role of the model's power in facilitating cross-sex imitation in girls. There is also some evidence to suggest that paternal dominance may be especially important for appropriate identification in boys, whereas for girls the mother's warmth seems helpful in facilitating their tendency to imitate her (Hetherington and Frankie, 1967).

Similarity between Model and Observer

In an ingenious experiment Maccoby and Wilson (1957) examined how similarity between the observer and the model influence observational learning. In this study seventh-grade students watched films in which a variety of interpersonal behaviors were displayed by the heroes. In one film the main characters were two boys, one obviously from an upper-middle-class background and the other from the lower socioeconomic class. In a second study seventh-grade children watched a film featuring an adolescent boy and an adolescent girl as the primary characters. A week after they had observed each film each sample of children was assessed to determine how well the children had learned the behaviors displayed by the model who was more similar to themselves compared to the behaviors of the hero who was less similar to them. In addition to measuring the children's recall of the movie content for each hero, they also were questioned about the role attractiveness of each of the primary characters. They were asked, for example, to indicate the character who was most like them, and the one that they would wish to be like in real life. Their answers to these questions were summed into an "identification index."

The results showed that viewers did identify themselves more with the same-sex leading character. Most interesting, the children tended to recall somewhat better the actions and verbalizations of the model of their own sex. Moreover, this tendency to learn more closely the behaviors of the same-sex model, rather than being widely generalized, was highly discriminative and depended on the sex-typed nature of the behavior that was being modeled. Maccoby and Wilson summarized their data this way:

For boy viewers, aggressive content appears to be particularly relevant, for they remember aggressive content better than girls, *provided* its agent is the boy hero. For girls, boy-girl interactive content appears most relevant, and they remember this content better than boys whenever the girl heroine is the agent of the action (1957, p. 86).

These findings are most interesting, yet one cannot be sure that the differences in recall assessed differences in learning (or merely differences in performance and willingness to report) since no incentives were offered to assure that children would be motivated to remember as much as they possibly could from the repertoires of both sexes. The memory measures relied heavily on open-ended techniques in which the richness of the subject's answers might well have been influenced by motivational considerations.

With regard to similarity in socioeconomic levels, observers in the study by Maccoby and Wilson were more likely to prefer (and to recall) the model whose social class matched the one to which the observer aspired (as assessed independently) rather than the one to which the observer currently belonged. Thus the results for social class similarity and those for sex similarity were different. In part this difference may reflect the fact that people can change their social class identity much more readily than their sexual gender! For many children there exists a major discrepancy between the social class to which they aspire and their actual socio-economic level. In contrast, children generally report overwhelmingly that they prefer adults of their own sex (e.g., Stevenson et al., 1967), and that they do not want to change their own sex, preferring it whether it be male or female (e.g., Hartley and Hardesty, 1964; Kagan and Lemkin, 1960; Kohlberg, 1966; Minuchin, 1965). Young children also tend to prefer same-sex youngsters in sociometric choices. Moore and Updergraff (1964), for example, found that nursery school children tended to make same-sex peers their positive sociometric choices, while giving their negative choices to opposite-sex peers.

To summarize, in the Maccoby and Wilson study children tended to recall better the behaviors of the same-sex model, especially when he was displaying appropriately sex-typed behaviors (e.g., aggression for boys, and boy-girl relations featuring female heroines for girls). This finding supports the hypothesis that people attend more closely to same-sex models. A later study by Maccoby and her colleagues measured the eye movements of young adults while they were viewing an entertainment film. Evidence for differential attention by the sexes was found again. The men spent more time looking at the male lead and the women spent proportionately more time watching the female lead (Maccoby, Wilson, and Burton, 1958). Greater observational learning from same-sex models was also reported more recently by Hetherington and Frankie (1967). They found that boys tend to imitate their father more than their mother, while girls imitated their mother more than their father.

From the viewpoint of social learning theory, the greater attentiveness to same-sex models, especially when they are displaying appropriately sex-typed behavior, probably reflects that people generally are reinforced throughout their histories more for learning the sex-typed behaviors of same-sex models than those of cross-sex models. It certainly seems likely that children are much more frequently rewarded for watching and imitating same-sex models (rather than cross-sex models), especially when the models display sex-typed behaviors. Boys do not learn baseball by watching girls and girls do not learn about fashions from observing boys. Especially when subjects have little information they tend to match the behavior of another person to a greater extent when they are led to believe that the other person is more similar, rather than dissimilar, to them (e.g., Burnstein, Stotland, and Zander, 1961; Stotland, Zander and Natsoulas, 1961). For example, if subjects are led to believe that they have musical preferences similar to those of a confederate, they match his choice of nonsense syllables more than if they believe his tastes to be dissimilar to their own (Stotland, Zander, and Natsoulas, 1961). Studies by Rosekrans (1967) and by Tannenbaum and Gaer (1965) also indicate that a model's actions influence the observer more when he perceives himself to be similar, as opposed to dissimilar to the hero. Thus Rosekrans (1967) found preadolescent boys imitated a filmed hero more when they were told he had interests and attributes similar to theirs (e.g., scouting) than when he was described as living far away and being highly different from them (e.g., not liking to scout and hike). Similarity enhanced the youngsters' learning of the model's repertoire as well as their willingness to perform it spontaneously. These results support the role of perceived similarity as a determinant of imitation. The operations to induce perceived similarity, however, also may have enhanced the perceived valence or attractiveness of the model. It therefore would be important to assess independently the effects on imitation of similarity between model and observer in undesirable traits as well as in more positive attributes.

The overall results on the effects of similarity between observer and model indicate that similarity often does enhance imitation, consistent with Kohlberg's (1966) results. However, similarity obviously is not the only basis for identificatory learning, as the preceding sections have illustrated. Moreover, if cognitive similarity were the main basis of attachment and identification, as Kohlberg suggests it is, one also would expect children to identify more strongly with same-sex peers than with same-sex adult strangers because peers presumably share more similar characteristics with the child than do adults. But it has been shown repeatedly that children may imitate adult models more than peer models (Bandura and Kupers, 1964; Hicks, 1965; Jakubszak and Walters, 1959). It was

also seen that children identify with models from the social class to which they *aspire*, rather than from the class to which they belong (Maccoby and Wilson, 1957), indicating that identification may be more with models who have *desired* attributes and resources rather than with models who have attributes *similar* to those possessed by the observer himself.

Social Structure and Socialization

Naturalistic studies of identification processes have focused on the child's immediate family, and especially on the parents, as main models. Identification theories have given a central place to the father as the chief model for the development of appropriate sex-typing in boys. Freudian formulations, for example, imply that if the father is absent the child remains mother-identified and is more likely to develop latent or even overt homosexual tendencies and feminine attributes (e.g., Fenichel, 1945). Consequently there has been much interest in the effects of father absence on personality development. In general, studies on this question have suggested a tendency for father-absent children to show less appropriate sex-typing (e.g., Bach, 1946; Lynn and Sawrey, 1959; Sears, Pintler, and Sears, 1946).

Father-absent children may be less adequately socialized than comparable father-present children in nonsex-typed behaviors and not just in sex-linked attributes. Mischel (1958b, 1961c) investigated the relation of father-absence and voluntary delay of gratification in several different Negro and East Indian cultures in the Caribbean islands of Trinidad and Grenada. For this purpose many children were extensively sampled for their actual preferences of immediate, smaller as opposed to delayed but more valuable gratifications in real choice situations. For young children (ages 8 to 9 years) a clear and significant relation was found between father-absence and preference for immediate gratification. The father-absent youngsters were less willing to wait for delayed rewards than were those who had come from father-present homes. Interestingly, this relationship held *regardless of the child's sex* and it was replicated consistently. This result suggests that father-absence may be an index of an overall inadequate home environment (one not conducive to trust, to voluntary delay-of-reward, and to other characteristics of appropriate socialization for both boys and girls), rather than being a debilitating influence restricted only to the identification and sex-typing of boys. Most previous studies on father-absence have been confined mainly to very young children. The present study also included samples of older children, ages 11 to 14. For these youngsters the relationship between father-absence and preference for immediate gratification was not found. This finding was interpreted to suggest that as youngsters gain more experiences outside the confines of their immediate families their behavior becomes increasingly influenced by extrafamilial sources. They then become less dependent upon the expectations and response patterns modeled and condoned in the home, and their behaviors become more dependent upon social reinforcement from peers (e.g., Patterson and Anderson, 1964) and on sociological variables (e.g., Brim and Wheeler, 1966).

A study by Greenstein (1966) provided a rare inquiry into the relationship between prolonged father-absence and direct measures of sex-typed behavior in adolescent delinquent boys. Contrary to the expectations of most identification theories, the father-absent boys did not differ from those from father-present homes on any measures of overt or covert sex-typing (as inferred from a variety of masculinity-femininity inventories and projective tests). An unusual and interesting feature of this study was that it included a direct measure of homosexuality, in the form of the subject's answers under sodium amytal medication to carefully structured questions about homosexual encounters. Again there were no differences in homosexual behavior for father-present as compared to father-absent boys. These results seem congruent with the previously described finding (Mischel, 1958b, 1961c) that father-absence seems to have less effect (or even no effect) when children are older since their behavior then may be regulated by numerous extrafamilial variables.

Greenstein's (1966) study also included ratings by social workers of the dominance of the father in the home and his closeness to his son for the adolescents who came from father-present homes. None of the relations between father-dominance and son's sex-typing approached significance. Ratings of father-closeness indicated *more* overt homosexuality by sons whose fathers were rated as "close" to them. This result is difficult to interpret without detailed knowledge both of the possible homosexual propensities of the fathers who were rated as closer to their sons and also of their tolerance for, or even provocation of, homosexual behavior in their sons. On the basis of case histories Greenstein favors the latter interpretation, and he believes that the fathers who were rated closer to their sons may have been more seductive toward them. His reports suggest, for example, that some of the fathers rated as being closest to their sons may have actively encouraged and reinforced homosexual tendencies in them. On the other hand, if these "warmer" fathers were themselves more homosexually inclined, then the greater homosexuality of their sons may be taken as a sign of closer father-son identification! This seemingly paradoxical possibility—in which paternal nurturance enhances the son's identification with the father but also results in a more homosexual son—points up a peculiar feature of identification theory that must be discussed more fully.

Most traditional theories of identification generally assume that the development of sex-appropriate social behaviors (and other indices of identification) in the boy depends on his adopting the characteristics of his father; for the girl normative sex-typing and socialization supposedly hinges on her adopting behaviors modeled by her mother. These assumptions may seem plausible when one considers sex-role stereotypes according to which fathers personify masculinity while mothers are the embodiments of femininity. If one goes beyond stereotypes to a closer examination of individual lives, some greater complexities become evident. First, it seems apparent that enormous individual differences exist among fathers in their "masculinity" (no matter how it is defined), just as among millions of mothers there surely exist great differences in "femininity." Consequently, a boy who closely identifies with or emulates his father actually may through this identification acquire "feminine" characteristics to the degree that his father displays feminine attributes, just as a girl who identifies closely with a "masculine" and dominating mother would herself become correspondingly masculine. In light of these considerations it becomes hazardous to assume that the extent to which a child shows socially normative behaviors— such as appropriate sex-typing or conformity to social standards of honesty and self-control —serves as a reliable index of his identification. Would the son of a habitual criminal, for example, show more identification if, unlike his father, he became a pillar of society, or would he be more identified if he followed closely in his father's path?

The view that the amount of normative behavior (in sex roles, conscience, self-control, or other hypothesized products of identification) displayed by the offspring is an index of the degree to which the child has identified with the parents seems to be rooted in Freud's belief that the parents are the sources of the superego and the transmitters of social sanctions, norms, and restrictions. However, when the parents themselves deviate substantially from social norms their role as superego models conveying societal standards becomes dubious.

An account of modeling influences on socialization, and especially on the development of psychological sex differences, could not even begin to be complete without recognizing the role of the social system in which the individual functions. Psychology's emphasis on the person sometimes obscures the intimate dependence of personality on environment—and the enormous role of social forces, institutions, large organizations, and groups in shaping that environment (e.g., D'Andrade, 1966).

Even within the same relatively homogeneous culture there are important differences among the component subcultures. The degree to which children develop traditional sex-role concepts and sex-typing, for example, depends on the extent to which they participate in a subculture that shares, models, and encourages those traditional attitudes and values. Thus youngsters from "modern" middle-class homes and schools in which individualized development was stressed tended to depart more from conventional sex-role standards than did those from more traditional backgrounds (Minuchin, 1965). These findings were particularly strong for girls.

Influenced by the belief that a stable personality is formed by the time a child reaches age 5 or 6, most studies of identificatory processes have focused on the role of the immediate family, especially the same-sex parent, in the socialization of preschool youngsters. Yet some of the most significant aspects of sex-typing and socialization are influenced by extrafamilial variables and societal influences that occur outside the immediate family and throughout the life cycle (e.g., Brim and Wheeler, 1966). The kinds of behaviors that are sex-typed, the consequences for appropriate and inappropriate sex-typing, the sex-role models that are esteemed and those that are disparaged, all shift significantly and repeatedly in the course of the individual's life and hinge on variables that go much beyond one's mother and father.

Longitudinal studies of personality development corroborate the intuitive conviction that there are significant continuities in many aspects of personality functioning (E. L. Kelly, 1955; Kagan and Moss, 1962). At the same time such longitudinal data also reveal the great changes that occur in the characteristics, and even in the basic adequacy, of the same individual as the conditions of his life change (Livson and Peskin, 1967; Mussen, 1962). These truly dynamic alterations in personality indicate that theories of socialization must attend to the conditions that regulate important behavior changes and not merely to static consistencies. That task, discussed in the following sections, requires a consideration of the variables that influence what people choose to do as well as an analysis of the conditions that determine their behavioral capacities.

THE PERFORMANCE OF SEX-TYPED BEHAVIOR

Distinction between Acquisition and Performance

It is helpful to distinguish between the processes through which a person learns sex-typed behaviors and those that regulate his selection of particular sex-typed behaviors from the repertoire that is already available to him. Obviously people do not perform all the behaviors that they have learned and that they are able to enact. For example, both sexes are capable of many cross-sexed behaviors even if they more frequently perform sex-appropriate acts. In our culture both men and women know how to curse, or to fight, or use cosmetics, or primp in front of mirrors, although they differ in the frequency with which they perform these activities. The acquisitional phases of sex-typing to a large extent involve cognitive and observational processes through which concepts and potential behaviors are learned. On the other hand, the individual's choice or selection of sex-typed behaviors from the available array that he already has learned and knows how to execute depends on motivational considerations. This distinction between acquisition and response selection is not restricted to sex-typing. It is also made for all other aspects of social behavior by most current social learning theories. According to these formulations the acquisition of novel responses is regulated by sensory, attentional, and cognitive processes; learning may be facilitated by reinforcement but does not depend upon it (e.g., Bandura, 1969; Bandura and Walters, 1963; Hebb, 1966). Direct and vicarious reinforcement is, however, an important determinant of response selection in *performance*.

The potential discrepancy between what persons have learned and what they do is illustrated in a study in which preschool children watched a film of an adult who displayed novel aggressive responses (Bandura, 1965). The consequences produced by the adult's aggressive behavior were manipulated experimentally in the film. The film sequence in one condition showed the adult's agressive behavior punished; in a second it was rewarded; and in a third it was left without consequences. As expected, children who had watched the model's aggressive behaviors punished in the film later imitated them less than those who had observed her aggressiveness either rewarded or left without consequences. It was also found, as expected, that boys tended to perform more imitative physical aggression than did girls, replicating the sex differences obtained earlier (Bandura and Walters, 1963). The next phase of the experiment was of greatest interest for understanding the role of response consequences in sex-typing. Children in all three treatment conditions now were offered attractive reinforcers (pretty sticker pictures and additional juice treats) for aggressive behavior. The

introduction of these positive incentives for performance of aggressive behaviors practically wiped out the prior performance disparity between the sexes. When appropriately motivated the girls as well as the boys could show physical aggression.

As these results indicate, boys and girls may be similar in their knowledge of aggressive responses, but they usually differ in their willingness to perform such responses. These differences presumably reflect differences in the sex-determined response-consequences that boys and girls obtained and observed for such behavior in the past and that they therefore expect in the future. Commenting on his findings in the foregoing experiment, Bandura (1965, p. 594) suggests that "The inhibitory effects of differing reinforcement histories for aggression were clearly reflected in the observation that boys were more easily disinhibited than girls in the reward phase of the experiment."

The psychological attributes of the model, such as his rewardingness and power, may also influence the attention, and hence the learning, of observers who watch him. Grusec and Mischel (1966) varied the model's rewardingness and control over resources before preschool children observed her display a novel sequence of behaviors. In a postexposure test in which the children were offered incentives contingent on reproducing her behavior children recalled the behaviors of the rewarding and powerful model better, in addition to imitating her more. Thus the model's manipulated attributes not only affected the children's subsequent willingness to adopt and perform her behaviors, but also the degree to which they learned them.

Probably males and females attend differentially to male and female models and therefore may learn their behaviors (as well as perform them) differentially. Some evidence that persons may attend more closely to behaviors displayed by people who are similar to them was found in the previously cited studies by Maccoby and her colleagues showing that attention tends to be greater to sex-typed behaviors displayed by same-sex models (e.g., Maccoby and Wilson, 1957). In addition to attending differentially to males and females, the sexes probably are exposed more to models of their own sex (e.g., in school, in play situations) and this segregation and differential exposure leads them to master modeled sex-appropriate behaviors to a greater extent since they see them more often.

Sex differences in the frequency of social behaviors in part reflect the fact that in the course of socialization boys and girls rapidly discover that the consequences for many of the things that they try are affected by their sex. Indeed, that is exactly the meaning of "sex-typed behaviors": their appropriateness depends on the sex of the person who displays them. From the viewpoint of social learning theory, sex-typed behaviors may be defined as those that are typically more expected and approved for one sex than for the other and that lead to different consequences when performed by males as opposed to females in the particular community. As a result of their differential consequences for males and females, these sex-typed behaviors come to be performed with different frequency by the sexes and to have different value for them.

Reinforcers, in spite of many popular misconceptions, are not limited to simple hedonic pleasures, to mundane material outcomes such as candy, food pellets, or smiles and sounds of social approval. Such cognitive gratifications as information (Jones, 1966), or the attainment of competence and the mastery of sex-typed skills, or doing what is expected of one, may be included among the almost infinite events that can be identified as reinforcers. Whether or not an event is reinforcing depends on numerous factors. One of the most important of these factors is the sex of the subject. Many events which, through processes of direct, vicarious, and higher-order conditioning, become positively reinforcing for men may be neutral or even aversive for females, and of course the reverse also occurs. Similarly, behavior patterns that may be prized when shown by one sex come to be despised when displayed by members of the wrong sex. Whereas clinging dependency may be viewed as a virtue in a young woman, it is likely to be detested when shown by an able-bodied young man; whereas physical aggressiveness may be taken as a sign of virile courage in the male, it is apt to be seen as the mark of the shrew in a woman. We next consider some of the ways in which the consequences produced by sex-typed behaviors alter the performance of these behaviors by males and females.

Response-Reinforcement Relations

According to most learning formulations, the reinforcing outcomes or consequences produced by an individual's behavior change the likelihood that he will show similar behavior subsequently in related situations (e.g., Bandura and Walters, 1963; Rotter, 1954). Any conditions that alter the reinforcers to which a response pattern leads also change the probability that similar behavior will occur. If, for example, parents give prompt and solicitous attention to loud whining requests for attention from their child, the probability that the child will become similarly dependent in the future increases. On the other hand, if the behavior is ignored and unrewarded, its future likelihood decreases.

In the previously discussed study by Greenstein (1966), for instance, the father of one homosexual delinquent boy reportedly hugged and kissed his adolescent son and called him "darling." When he talked about his son's childhood he spoke "with great delight about how he enjoyed washing his son and ministering to him" (p. 276). Such data imply that the fathers of the homosexual boys in part may have been directly encouraging and stimulating them to develop in homosexual directions.

Demonstrations that the consequences obtained by the child for the sex-typed (and sex-irrelevant) behaviors that he tries to enact influence his subsequent behaviors have come repeatedly from experimental studies. Davitz (1952), for example, working with 10 small groups of children rewarded half the groups with praise and approval for making aggressive and competitive responses during a series of brief training sessions. Children in the remaining groups were rewarded for cooperative and constructive behavior during the training periods. Subsequently all children were frustrated by being exposed to a film which was interrupted just as it approached its climax. The children at this point also were forced to return a candy which had been given to them earlier. Their reactions to these frustrations were recorded immediately on motion picture film in a free play situation. Analyses of the filmed behavior revealed that children who had been rewarded previously for constructive behavior responded more constructively to the frustration. In contrast, those children who had been rewarded for aggression in competitive games during the training sessions now were more aggressive when frustrated.

The effects of the consequences obtained by the individual for his behavior on his subsequent responses in similar situations are perhaps most clearly demonstrated in efforts to change behavior therapeutically. Some of the main points are illustrated in a study designed to reduce the maladaptive dependency of Ann, a nursery school girl (Allen et al., 1964). Ann was a bright 4-year-old girl from an upper-middle-class background who increasingly isolated herself from children in her nursery school. At the same time she developed many techniques to gain the prolonged attention of adults, and she became more and more dependent upon them. At first her bids for attention from teachers were successful and she gained much warm recognition from them. Her efforts to maintain adult attention, however, led to great isolation from other children and her dependency on adults became increasingly problematic and extreme.

A careful assessment of how Ann spent her time during nursery school showed that most of the attention that adults were giving her was contingent, unintentionally and inadvertently, upon behaviors from Ann that were incompatible with her playing with peers. Unwittingly her teachers were reinforcing precisely those activities that led Ann away from children; the more isolated she became from her peers, the more attentive and warmly concerned adults became toward her. In order to end this vicious circle a plan was formed to give Ann minimum adult attention for her isolate behavior and for her efforts at solitary interactions with adults; simultaneously she would get maximum attention from adults contingent on her play with other children. Now whenever Ann began to interact with children an adult quickly attended to her as a participating member of the group. Attention was withdrawn promptly as soon as Ann began to leave the group or attempted solitary adult contacts. These deliberate changes in the consequences to Ann for isolate behavior versus social behavior with her peers swiftly and dramatically changed her interactions with children. Before the new response-reinforcement contingencies were instituted Ann was spending only about 10% of her school time interacting with children. She was entirely solitary for about half the time and spent about 40% of the time with adults. When the contingencies were changed and warm attention from adults was given only when Ann was near children or interacting directly with them, she soon started to spend almost 60% of her time with peers. Similarly when her solitary interactions with adults were no longer followed by attention they quickly diminished. The speed with which Ann was able to change when contingencies changed, even without direct tuition, indicated that Ann apparently had the skills necessary both for play with children and for isolated dependency on adults. Although she knew how to engage in both patterns, the one she chose depended on the probable outcomes or incentives available in the situation.

In later stages the teachers deliberately phased out their intervention and started to give less frequent, intermittent, nonsystematic attention for interactions with children. The schedule of nonreinforcement for adult contacts also was gradually relaxed as Ann's play behavior with her peers became increasingly rewarding for its own sake apart from the adult attention to which it had led initially. Follow-up checks of Ann's behavior after termination of systematic reinforcement by adult attention showed Ann continuing to maintain her new social behavior with children. Her new play patterns with her peers now presumably were being maintained by the gratifying consequences produced by the play behavior itself.

Studies of this type also have demonstrated that behavior depends on the consequences it yields by showing that when the response-reinforcement contingencies are reversed back to the conditions that held during the pretherapeutic period, the original behavior is restored; later, when the more prosocial contingencies are reinstated once more, the therapeutic changes are regained. These demonstrations have shown repeatedly that even seemingly deeply ingrained patterns, including many severe social deviations, can be changed rapidly in accord with the new contingencies. Similar therapeutic studies have demonstrated that systematic alterations in response consequences predictably alter a wide range of behaviors, from psychotic talk, criminal delinquency, and maladaptive sexual behavior to nursery school interactions of the kind just described (see Ayllon and Azrin, 1965; Bandura, 1969; Bijou, 1965; Mischel, 1968). Such studies also illustrate that predictions about individual behavior can be substantially facilitated by knowledge of the environments in which the behavior occurs. Ann's dependent behavior at nursery school, for example, could be predicted by knowledge of her *teachers'* behavior on any particular day without any inferences about her own dependency traits or other dispositions.

Vicarious and Symbolic Response Consequences

Although learning studies with animals have emphasized direct, experimenter-dispensed reinforcement, reinforcement does not have to be administered directly in order to alter the individual's choice behaviors. Information about the reinforcing consequences of sex-typed behavior can be acquired vicariously by observing the differential behavior of male and female models, and not merely by the consequences that the child encounters directly when he himself tries out overt behaviors. As the previously discussed studies of observational learning suggested, observing outcomes to others for such sex-typed activities as aggression can potently influence the observer's tendency to perform the behavior. Performance thus often may be determined by vicarious and inferred response consequences rather than through direct "trial and error" learning. In human learning, information conveyed through verbal or other symbols can short-cut to zero the number of trials needed for errorless performance (Bandura, 1965). A boy does not have to be laughed at by his peers in order to learn the consequences of trying feminine behavior. Observation of positive reinforcing consequences for a response pattern tends to disinhibit the observer and to increase the probability that he will engage in similar behavior. Observing encouragement and praise encountered by people who display a certain pattern of behavior increases the observer's own tendency to behave in simi-

lar ways. Conversely, when social models are punished for their behavior, those who watched them will later tend to show greater inhibition of similar behavior (Bandura, 1965; Bandura, Ross, and Ross, 1963a; Walters, Parke, and Cane, 1965).

It also has been found repeatedly in social psychological research that high-status models are more influential and more readily emulated than those who are less successful or prestigeful (e.g., Hovland, Janis, and Kelley, 1953; Lefkowitz, Blake, and Mouton, 1955). Presumably such enviable models are more potent influences because of the more desirable resources that they control, and the more reinforcing outcomes that they supposedly obtain, resulting in more vicarious reinforcement for those who watch them or fantasize about them.

Any information that alters the person's anticipations about the probable outcomes to which a behavior will lead should change the likelihood that he will engage in the behavior. This information about response consequences can be mediated by symbolic and cognitive processes that do not depend upon actual observation of the model's behavior. For example, individuals may change their attitudes and preferences after either reading or hearing about the relevant behavior of others (e.g., Bandura and Mischel, 1965; Duncker, 1938). These symbolically produced effects may be strikingly potent. In one study (Duncker, 1938) preschool children were told an exciting, vivid story in which the hero, Eaglefeather, violently abhorred a pleasant-tasting food while he supposedly relished a more noxious food. After listening to the exploits and emotional reactions of the hero, the children tended to adopt his food preferences. These dramatic changes in the children's subsequent food preferences, moreover, were not merely momentary but remained fairly stable over time. Undoubtedly, television, movies, books and stories, and other symbolic media play an important part in the transmission of information about sex-typed behaviors and the diverse consequences to which they may lead when displayed by males and females.

Self-Reactions

A notable attribute of people is that they judge and evaluate themselves, rewarding and punishing their own behavior, and not merely passively receiving reinforcement from others. People compare their own achievements and attributes with standards, and the sexes may differ in the criteria they set in assessing many aspects of their behavior. As previously noted, in this regard Kagan (1964) has emphasized an overall, global self-evaluation of one's masculinity or femininity in relation to stereotyped sex-role standards. Social learning approaches to self-evaluations also pay much attention to how people react to themselves, not only in regard to their masculinity or femininity in general, but also more discriminatingly (e.g., Bandura, 1969; Mischel, 1968).

From the viewpoint of social learning theory, during the course of development sex differences in the value and acquired meaning of stimuli become increasingly independent of external reinforcement and are regulated to a large extent by the person's own self-reactions and relatively enduring standards. Much research (e.g., Bandura and Kupers, 1964; Kanfer and Marston, 1963; Liebert and Ora, 1968; Mischel and Liebert, 1966, 1967; McMains and Liebert, 1968) has studied how people set standards and learn to monitor their own behavior. These self-evaluative processes are seen, for example, in an individual's reactions to his own accomplishments, such as his test results, his creative achievements, or his sexual prowess. The person's standards determine, in part, the conditions under which he self-administers or withholds the numerous gratifications and self-punishments that are readily available to him. Failure to meet one's own self-imposed performance standards often results in self-denial or even harsher self-punishments. Attainment of difficult criteria, in contrast, usually leads to positive feelings about oneself and warm self-congratulations (e.g., Bandura and Whalen, 1966; Mischel, Coates, and Raskoff, 1968).

The same objective performance may be a signal for joy in one person but for self-flagellation in another. There are, of course, wide individual differences in the kinds of standards and the levels on which persons make their own self-reward contingent, and these criteria influence their behavior in many contexts. There also are many differences between the sexes in the kinds and levels of standards that they impose on themselves. Highly skillful baseball pitching, for example, is likely to be an important achievement for boys but is much less likely to be relevant for self-evaluation in girls. Similarly, whereas the ability to tolerate high levels of physical pain may be a salient concern for men, it is less significant for women (Lambert, Amon, and Goyeche, 1967).

Although stereotypes and gross verbal reports about standards may be global and fairly situation-free, the actual standards that people employ to evaluate their own behavior and the stringency or leniency with which they subsequently reward themselves all are influenced by highly situational considerations (e.g., Mischel, 1966b). Just as with behavior that is controlled by externally administered direct and vicarious reinforcement, self-evaluative reactions also depend on specific stimulus variables. It has been demonstrated, for example, that a variety of performance standards and self-evaluative patterns can be transmitted by the same basic observational and reinforcement processes that regulate other forms of behavior (Bandura and Kupers, 1964; Bandura and Whalen, 1966; Mischel and Liebert, 1966). Experiments by Bandura and Whalen (1966) and by Bandura, Grusec, and Menlove (1967), for example, have illustrated some of the social comparison processes that influence the individual's selection of modeled performance standards. In accord with social comparison theory, children tend to reject models who set excessively high, superior standards. Experiments of this type document the subtlety of the social comparison processes that regulate self-reactions. Findings from experiments on self-evaluation also indicate that individuals tend to make their own self-rewards highly contingent on very specific situational considerations (see Mischel and Liebert, 1966). Social comparisons, for example, often may be based on highly select special reference groups (Schachter, 1959) rather than on people "in general" or "males" and "females." It may be, however, that for some sex-linked attributes, such as sexual potency, the reference group for self-evaluation is both broad and vague and is heavily influenced by diffuse stereotypes. But even standards of sexual and physical attractiveness may vary considerably, depending on such factors as one's socioeconomic position in the culture.

Child-Rearing Practices and Sex-Typing

Laboratory and therapeutic demonstrations of the effects of manipulated direct and vicarious reinforcement often are impressive, but they do not illuminate the reinforcement patterns that occur under naturalistic conditions. Not surprisingly, results relevant to reinforcement practices obtained from field studies are much less clear and much more difficult to interpret. These greater complications have many causes.

First, under naturalistic conditions any particular behavior pattern may be subjected to extremely complex reinforcement schedules, being reinforced on some occasions by some people (but not by others) in highly irregular ways. Reinforcement even from the same source (e.g., the father) is likely to be moderated by numerous considerations that interact with a host of variables. Further, and often neglected, is the role of vicarious and symbolically mediated reinforcement under uncontrolled conditions. Such vicarious reinforcement may counteract and undermine the effects of direct reinforcement as happens when parents, in full view of their children, enact, enjoy, and are amply reinforced for the very practices that they deny their children and for which they even punish them. The effects of reinforcement under naturalistic conditions are especially complicated because socializing agents such as the mother and father inevitably have a multiple role: they not only encourage and discourage or "shape" the child's behavior through direct tuition, but they also model relevant behavior. Often the information conveyed through these diverse modes may be inconsistent, producing additional complexities in the behavior that is ultimately generated by the child under the uncontrolled conditions of life.

Consider, for example, the mother who tries to instill self-control in her child while she herself models self-indulgence. When researchers refer to "consistency" in child-rearing practices they usually mean consistency in direct training techniques across different situations; almost no attention has been given to the effects of consistency or discrepancy between direct training and modeling procedures. Therefore the previously cited study by Mischel and Liebert (1966) investigated the effects of discrepancies in the stringency of the self-reward standards used by an adult and the critera he imposed on a child.

In this study children participated with a female adult model in a task that seemingly required skill but on which scores were experimentally controlled. Both the model and subject had free access to a large supply of tokens which could be exchanged later for attractive rewards. The model in one condition rewarded herself for high performances only but guided the subject to reward himself for lower achievements; in a second condition the model rewarded herself for low performances but led the subject to reward himself for high achievements only; in the third group the model rewarded herself for high performances only and guided the child to reward himself for equally high achievements only. After exposure to these experimental procedures the children's self-reward patterns displayed in the model's absence were observed and scored through a one-way mirror.

The results showed that when the observed and imposed criteria were consistent they later were adopted and maintained readily by all children. However, when the observed and imposed criteria were discrepant, and the criterion leading to more reward was the one that subjects were directly trained to adopt, they subsequently rewarded themselves generously in the model's absence. Children who had been trained to be stringent but had observed a more lenient model afterward rewarded themselves more liberally than did those children who had been trained on a stringent criterion by a model who was similarly stringent with herself. Children adopted and transmitted more stringent reward criteria when their model was stringent than did those who received the identical direct training but from a model who had exhibited greater leniency in her own self-reward. In a posttest the children demonstrated the game to another, younger child, still in the absence of external constraints and of the experimenter herself. The children consistently imposed on their peers the same standards that they had adopted for themselves, hence transmitting their own learned self-reward criteria.

This experiment illustrated how self-reactions are affected jointly by the criteria displayed by social models and the standards directly imposed on the child, the child's resultant behavior being determined by a predictable interaction of both observational and direct training processes. Many apparent paradoxes in the relationships between child training practices and the child's subsequent behavior may reflect insufficient attention to the discrepancies between the behaviors the child observes used by powerful and successful models and those he is directly trained or guided to perform. It should not be surprising, for example, if a mother who tries to train her daughter to become "feminine," while she herself behaves in a "masculine" fashion, rears a girl whose scores show conflict on masculinity-femininity measures. In light of these considerations one should not expect high correlations between indices of child training and the child's behavior unless the rearing variables take account of both modeling and direct training influences.

Theories of sex-typing that rely primarily on the concept of reinforcement would lead one to expect that parents and other significant social agents treat boys and girls in sharply different ways. Reinforcement theory would suggest that parents positively reinforce sex-appropriate behaviors while punishing or extinguishing sex-inappropriate responses. Data relevant to this expectation come from studies that ask children about the rearing practices employed by their parents and also from investigations that assess the socialization techniques of parents more directly.

It does seem that children quickly learn that their parents and their peers expect boys and girls to behave differently, at least in some ways, beginning at a fairly early age. Fauls and Smith (1956), for example, exposed 5-year-olds to a series of paired pictures depicting a sex-appropriate and sex-inappropriate activity. Their personal preferences and their beliefs about the activity which Mother and Father would prefer for boys and girls were elicited (e.g., "Which does Mother want the boy to do?"). Boys chose "masculine" activities more often than did girls, and children of both sexes indicated that the parents preferred the activities appropriate to the child's sex more often than the sex-inappropriate activities.

Boys and girls also report that their parents treat them differently and display different attitudes toward them. Droppleman and Schaefer (1961) obtained separate ratings of fathers and mothers from seventh-grade boys and girls on a number of rearing variables. The authors found that "girls as contrasted to boys report both mother and father to be more affectionate and less rejecting, hostile and ignoring" (1961, p. 5). They summarize their data as suggesting that "females report that they received more affection as children than do males, and both sexes report that the female parent gives more affection than does the male parent" (1961, p. 5).

Children also develop consistent stereotyped perceptions about parental attributes (e.g., Emmerich, 1959; Finch, 1955; Kagan, 1956; Kagan and Lemkin, 1960). In general these studies show children from the preschool years to adolescence tend to label the mother as more nurturant than the father. The father, in contrast, is construed as more competent and powerful, but also as more punitive and fear-arousing. Consistent with other studies, Kagan and Lemkin (1960) also found that children overwhelmingly indicated they wanted to be most like the same-sex parent, and "liked" the same-sex parent best. According to the children it was the opposite-sex parent who "kissed the most." Children tend to see women as more nurturant than men, and adult women also view themselves as being more nurturant than their male counterparts (Bennett and Cohen, 1959).

Studies like the foregoing suggest that the sexes differ in their perception of parental attitudes and attributes and that they rapidly learn about sex-linked parental expectations. Attitudes and rearing practices in relation to each sex also have been studied more directly in many field investigations (e.g., Carlson, 1963). From the viewpoint of reinforcement theory one would expect parents to treat boys and girls most differently in such strongly sex-typed behavior domains as aggression and dependency. Parental practices toward each sex in these two domains therefore have been investigated with special interest.

Sears, Maccoby, and Levin (1957) found that parents made the sharpest distinctions in the rearing of boys and girls in the area of aggression. A significantly larger proportion of boys were given high freedom in the expression of aggression toward the parents. Boys also were allowed more aggression in relation to other children and they were more frequently encouraged to fight back if another child started a fight. Girls obtained somewhat more praise for "good" behavior and were somewhat more often subjected to withdrawal of love for "bad" behavior, which seems consistent with their developing greater "prosocial" aggression than boys. That is, girls tend to verbalize more about the goodness or badness of behavior, and to make verbal threats for bad behavior. The correlational findings, although not strong, generally seem consistent with the view that physical or antisocial aggression is less sanctioned for girls than for boys in our culture. Physical aggression seems to be expected and rewarded for boys more than for girls; "prosocial" aggression, in contrast, when displayed by boys is probably labeled "sissy stuff," whereas such verbal righteousness is more acceptable when it is manifested by girls. These results are entirely consistent with the greater frequency of physical aggression in boys and the greater incidence of prosocial and verbal aggression in girls at least in some settings, as discussed previously.

In regard to dependency, the average differences between the sexes described in earlier sections seem consistent with the widely assumed greater permissiveness for dependency by females as opposed to males in our culture. It has been demonstrated in laboratory studies that permissiveness for dependency, and reward for dependency, increased children's dependency behavior. In a study by Heathers (1953), for example, 6- to 12-year-old children were blindfolded and then walked an unstable and narrow plank elevated 8 inches from the floor. Children who accepted help from the experimenter at the starting point tended to have parents who encouraged them to depend on others rather than to take care of themselves.

An observational study of infants playing with their mothers revealed that at the age of 13 months girls already were more dependent and less exploratory than boys in their play (Goldberg and Lewis, 1969). Most interesting, these sex differences seemed to be related to the mothers' differential responses to boys and girls in the first 6 months of life. Earlier observation of the mothers' behavior toward their infants at age 6 months showed that the mothers talked to, handled, and touched their daughters more than their sons; when observed 7 months later the daughters, in turn, talked to and touched their mothers more than the sons did. The overall results strongly suggested that mothers behave differently toward young boys and girls, reinforcing sex-appropriate behavior even in infancy.

Field studies also have reported positive relations between parental demonstrativeness and warmth and the dependency of their children. For example, Sears, Maccoby, and Levin (1957) found that mothers who were affectionately demonstrative responded positively to their children's dependent behavior and also described their children as high in dependency. Moreover, a correlational analysis of field data from families of aggressive and inhibited children indicated that parents who were warm, affectionate, rewarded dependency, and had spent a good deal of time in caring for their sons had children who tended to display a high degree of dependency behavior (Bandura, 1960).

Mussen and Rutherford (1963) found some evidence that more feminine girls have *fathers* who actively encouraged them to engage in sex-appropriate behaviors and to become feminine. In the Sears, Rau, and Alpert (1965) study, however, the fathers of "masculinized" girls were found to be more "warm, interactive, permissive, and understanding in their attitudes toward their daughters." In the study by the Sears group, moveover, interview-based ratings of the children's probable perception of the relative power and nurturance of each parent revealed no significant correlations with any of the numerous measures of sex-typing and gender role (Sears, Rau, and Alpert, 1965). This picture did not change even when only the more extreme cases were examined, nor when the "warmth" of each parent was assessed independently.

Considering the differences in the consequences produced by sex-typed behaviors when displayed by men and women, one also should expect sex-typed behaviors to have different correlates for each sex. Take, for example, extensive dependency in a 10-year-old boy and in a girl of the same age. In the girl dependency is more likely to have been consistently permitted and rewarded, whereas similar dependency in the boy may reflect that he is not adequately performing alternative new and more age-appropriate responses. Dependent boys and girls may even get opposite consequences from parents and peers for highly similar behaviors. Dependent behavior by the girl may reflect an acceptable and even prized outcome; for the boy it may mean a failure to learn new adequate age-appropriate responses. In one sex the behavior may thus be correlated with indices of parental warmth and satisfaction, adjustment, and many signs of age-appropriate behaviors, whereas the opposite correlates may characterize the child of the wrong sex.

Thus Sears (1963) reports that for preschool girls dependency is correlated with indices of maternal permissiveness for dependency (and sex). In contrast, for boys various forms of dependent behaviors (none of which are significantly intercorrelated) seem to be associated with "coldness in the mother, slackness of standards, and a rejection of intimacy by the father" (Sears, 1963, p. 60). For girls "dependency seems to be acceptable or even desired, and mothers who encourage intimacy achieve their aims." "Positive attention seeking," for example, appears to be associated with the mother's satisfaction with her daughter. Referring to dependency antecedents in boys, Sears indicated "an inhibited and ineffectual mother—and to some extent father, too—who provides little freedom for the boy, and little incentive for maturing" (Sears, 1963, p. 62). It is possible that dependency may be directly reinforced in girls, whereas dependency in little boys may indicate a failure to acquire independent behavior and would thus be correlated with other indices of poor adjustment.

Most correlational studies of sex-typing have obtained global measures of the parents' personality, and of their broad child-rearing qualities (such as "warmth" or "permissiveness") and have tried to relate them to indices of sex-typing in their children. In the Sears, Rau, and Alpert (1965) study, for example, hundreds of correlations were computed between children's behavior and possible rearing antecedents. The results were enormously complicated and generally of low magnitude,

especially if one considers the number of correlations that could be expected by chance when large matrices are involved. These authors theorize about the possible meaning of their overall findings on the correlates of sex-typing thus:

> The major child-rearing correlates of gender role are the clusters of parental sex-permissiveness scales and punishment for aggression. A closed, anxious, non-permissive attitude on the part of either or both parents was conducive to femininity in both sexes of children, as were the use of physical punishment and severe control of aggression (Sears, Rau and Alpert, 1965, p. 198).

Other studies that have tried to correlate parental child-rearing practices with the child's sex-role learning indicate similar tentative conclusions. Permissiveness (as opposed to restrictiveness) by parents tends to be related to such "masculine" attributes as aggression, assertiveness, achievement, and independence in their children (Baldwin, 1949; Sears, 1961; Watson, 1957). In contrast, parents who are restrictive may tend to have children who are somewhat more dependent, compliant, conforming, fearful, and polite (Levy, 1943; Watson, 1957; Sears, 1961).

Such relations between parental practices and attributes and their children's sex-typed characteristics, while often highly suggestive, usually are of modest magnitude, and generally are difficult to replicate firmly. These limited associations should not be unexpected when one recalls the previously discussed specificity of sex-typing itself. Moreover, as the preceding field studies illustrate, most investigations of naturalistic antecedents of sex-typing have tended to focus on broadly generalized parental variables such as affection, child-centeredness, indulgence, and acceptance. Much less attention has been given to the concrete contingencies employed by parents for reinforcing specific sex-typed behaviors and simultaneously to the sex-typed patterns modeled by parents and peers. As Kagan and Moss (1962, p. 209) have suggested: "It is possible that girls and boys receive different patterns of maternal treatment during the childhood years, and a more rigorous, microscopic examination of the mother-child interaction might reveal the details of these differences." Such microscopic scrutiny would have to focus on differences in paternal and maternal behavior for boys as opposed to girls at different phases during socialization. It would have to be highly specific with respect to the type of behaviors reinforced and the exact situations in which they occur. Such an examination would have to explore differences in the ways in which similar behaviors are differentially evaluated and labeled as a function of the performer's sex, and would have to take account of vicarious reinforcement and observational learning effects as well as of direct reinforcement practices. It would have to extend beyond parental modeling and parental practices to include the relevant behaviors of peers and other significant social agents. A more "microscopic examination" probably also would reveal the enormously subtle discriminations, as well as generalizations, that children learn to make in their selection among sex-typed behaviors, as discussed in the following section.

Generalization and Discrimination in Sex-Typed Behaviors

According to the learning principles of stimulus generalization and discrimination, behavior patterns become widely generalized only if they are reinforced uniformly across many stimulus conditions. One should not expect a person to react consistently across situations if he gets discrepant consequences for the same behavior pattern in different situations. Specificity in behavior occurs when the consequences of behavior differ drastically across situations, as they usually do in the uncontrolled conditions of real life. Consider, for example, the differences in the typical outcomes to an American adolescent girl for verbal aggressiveness against her best friend privately at home and against her high school principal in public. To the extent that verbal aggressiveness is sanctioned in one context, but not in the other, cross-situational consistency should not occur. The object at which behavior is directed, and numerous other characteristics of the situation, all may influence the consequences of the behavior and hence the probability for its future occurrence.

Subtle discriminations also are made among the specific forms and subtypes of behavior that are differentially reinforced for the sexes. As the summary at the beginning of this chapter indicated, males clearly tend to be more antisocially and physically aggressive than females as measured in many response media and situations and over a wide age range. These differences, however, do not extend to forms of aggressiveness beyond the physical and directly antisocial. For example, fewer differences have been found between the sexes in amount of verbal disapproval and tattling shown by nursery school children (Sears, Rau, and Alpert, 1965). Other studies also yielded either no sex differences in verbal and indirect aggression (e.g., Sears, 1961) or found more verbal aggression on the part of girls (Durrett, 1959). Occasionally girls may be more verbally aggressive than boys and they may tend to show more "prosocial" aggression. For example, at age 12 girls may state rules and threaten punishments for breaking rules more often than do boys (Sears, 1961). Presumably these patterns reflect less stringent and less uniform sex-linked sanctions with regard to verbal forms of aggression than with regard to physical and antisocial aggresion.

The specificity of the consequences yielded by behavior in natural situations is illustrated by the complex interactions found between the sex of parents and the sex of their child in determining reinforcement practices (Rothbart and Maccoby, 1966). Mothers and fathers of preschool children were asked to listen to a tape recording of a child's voice. The voice made 12 statements whose content ranged from seeking help (e.g., Daddy [or Mommy] help me) to aggression (e.g., "I don't like this game—I'm gonna break it!). The parents were asked to imagine that the voice belonged to a child of their own. In half the cases, the parents were told that the voice was that of a son; in the other cases the voice was depicted as that of a daughter. The parents were asked to indicate their immediate reactions by recording what they would say or do if a son (or daughter) of their own made such a statement. The parents' written answers later were reliably scored for their permissiveness toward the child's expressions of dependency, aggression, help-seeking, and so on.

There were almost no major overall average differences in the reactions of mothers and fathers. There were, however, several interactions between the sex of the parent and the sex of the child. In general, mothers tended to be more permissive toward their daughters than their sons. In particular, these interactions were statistically significant when the child expressed pain, and also when he complained that the baby had stepped on his hand. A similar trend $(p < .10)$ was found for dependency. There were no effects for aggression, with one exception. Namely, when the child expressed anger directly at the parent ("I don't like this game. It's a stupid game. You're stupid, Daddy [Mommy].") then mothers were significantly more tolerant toward sons than toward daughters while fathers were more permissive toward daughters than toward sons. Discussing their total results, Rothbart and Maccoby concluded:

Rather than consistent reinforcement of sex-typed behavior by both parents, inconsistency between parents seems to be the rule, and while a parent may treat his child in a manner consistent with the cultural stereotype in one area of behavior, in another he may not (1966, p. 242).

These findings illustrate that the consequences produced by even seemingly similar types of behavior—such as several forms of aggression—are far from uniform and depend on a host of moderating conditions. Different instances of these behaviors lead to quite different outcomes depending, for example, on the exact form of the behavior, as well as on the sex of the parent who reacts to it and the sex of the child who performs it. In light of such results, the situational specificity found for personality indices, reviewed in earlier sections, becomes more understandable. These findings also imply that concepts like parental "permissiveness" have limited value to the degree that broad reactions such as permissiveness hinge on a host of situational variables rather than being fairly stimulus-free attributes of the parent. Wallach (1962) and Kogan and Wallach (1964) have noted that many such "moderator variables" may influence the correlations found in research on behavioral consistency. By moderator variables Wallach and Kogan

mean interactions among several variables that influence the correlations obtained between any one of the variables and other data. For instance, correlations between two response patterns may be found for males, but not for females, or may even be negative for one sex but positive for the other. If the correlations between two response patterns thus are analyzed for both sexes combined, the different relations that might be obtained if each sex were taken into account separately could become obscured. Similarly, relations between two measures might be positive for children with low IQ but negative for those who are highly intelligent. In other words, there are complex interactions so that the relations between any two variables depend on several other variables.

A study by Taylor and Epstein (1967) illustrates how sex roles influence behavior; at the same time it shows the discriminations people make as a function of situational moderating conditions. Taylor and Epstein exposed male and female college students in a competitive situation to fictitious opponents described as either male or female. The relative aggressiveness of each sex when provoked increasingly by an allegedly male or female opponent was assessed by permitting subjects to set the amount of electric shock they wished their opponent to receive on each trial. The fictitious opponent's provocativeness was manipulated by giving subjects increasing amounts of shock as the trials progressed.

Both sexes were much less aggressive toward opponents whom they believed were females than toward those they thought were males. Even when the female opponent became increasingly provocative both sexes remained reluctant to use strong electric shock against her. These findings are consistent with the widespread cultural sanctions restricting physical aggression against women. Even when subjects became infuriated against their increasingly sadistic female opponent, and lashed out verbally, they continued to inhibit their physical aggression. One male, for example, after being severely shocked, yelled a curse and threatened that "I'll kill her"— although he actually continued to use the lowest shock level against his alleged opponent. Asked why he never tried to hurt his opponent, another young man simply said "because she was a girl." The cultural taboos against hurting females physically are obviously familiar to the females themselves; as one young lady anxiously remarked, "I hope he knows I'm a girl."

Most interesting are the findings regarding the reactions of females to highly aggressive fictitious male opponents. As Taylor and Epstein noted, it is broadly assumed that females are expected to be generally unaggressive, especially physically. This assumption has been widely held, and usually implies a generalized inhibition of physical aggression by women in their relations to both sexes. In fact, when girls were faced by ostensible male opponents who shocked them increasingly, they themselves became extraordinarily aggressive. In this condition indeed the females ultimately became most aggressive, and finally used electric shocks averaging more than twice their initial intensity against their male antagonists. These results suggest that even within a fairly narrow type of aggression, such as the use of physical punishment, sex differences are moderated by numerous conditions—in this instance depending as much on the sex of the victim as on the sex of the aggressor. The findings also showed that sex-typed behaviors in different modes, such as verbal aggression and physical aggression, are not necessarily correlated. Recall that while males became increasingly abusive verbally to their sadistic female opponents they did not increase the shock levels they used against them.

In the socialization of sex-typed behaviors discrimination training plays a major and continuous role. Social agents do not usually reinforce situation-free versions of all forms of behavior. Parents do not, for example, condone all types of aggression for boys regardless of circumstances and setting. This fact is illustrated in the finding that boys who were aggressive at school had parents who encouraged aggression toward peers; these boys, however, were nonaggressive at home and their parents indeed punished aggression at home (Bandura, 1960). Similarly, Trinidadian lower-class Negroes rarely chose to wait for promised delayed rewards and instead usually preferred immediately available albeit smaller gratifications (Mischel, 1958b, 1961a). In the past experiences of these people, promises of future rewards had been broken frequently by promise-makers, and they had participated in a culture in which immediate gratification was modeled and rewarded extensively (Mischel, 1961b, 1961c). Nevertheless, the same people saved money, planned elaborately, and gave up competing immediate gratifications to make long-term preparations for annual feasts, religious events, and carnival celebrations (Mischel and Mischel, 1958).

As another illustration, consider the finding that women tend to be more "persuasible" than men (Hovland and Janis, 1959). A closer examination of social influence phenomena indicates that this sex difference is not so simple. One study investigated sex differences in attitude and behavior change under various conditions of fear arousal and instructions (Leventhal, Jones, and Trembly, 1966). College students were exposed to communications designed to alter their attitudes toward taking tetanus shots and their actual taking of these protective innoculations. The stronger the threat stimulus, the more anxious the women became in their self-reported fears. In comparison to men, the women reported that they felt more vulnerable to tetanus and more favorable to the shots, and they said the threat was more serious. The behavioral data, however, showed that the women were no more likely than the men to take the shots. The sex differences in self-reports of persuasability thus were not accompanied by sex differences in the influencability of relevant actions. As these results show, studies that compare behavior change in the two sexes in response to influence attempts must take into account sex differences in self-reports of persuasability and sex differences in alterations of the target behavior itself.

From the viewpoint of social learning theory modest associations across response modes are not surprising because the mode in which behavior occurs usually influences markedly the consequences to which the behavior leads. An individual's verbalizations, thoughts, stories, self-reports, daydreams, and overt enactments all dealing with the theme of aggression, or of sexual acts, rarely lead to the same consequences or even to highly correlated consequences. To the degree that the outcomes for behavior in different response modes and eliciting conditions are uncorrelated, and the stimulus conditions are unrelated, consistencies across these response modes should not be anticipated. The consequences for similar content expressed in different response modes usually are drastically different. A person whose stories on a projective test abounded with aggressive themes might be judged to have a healthy, active fantasy life, but the same individual probably would be institutionalized if he enacted similar content in his interpersonal relations. In light of these considerations it should not be unexpected that even seemingly slight differences in the response medium and setting used to sample behavior have provided relatively unrelated results, and that trait scores from one medium (e.g., questionnaires) show limited relations to scores for the same disposition elicited in any other different medium (e.g., Campbell and Fiske, 1959; Skolnick, 1966a, 1966b).

Changes in statements about expectancies for academic success following manipulated success and failure experiences provide a further example. The specific academic performance area involved may have different value for the sexes (e.g., mechanical engineering versus home economics). In addition, the act of changing such verbal expectancy statements may have different reward values for the sexes. Female college students were more likely than males to lower their expectancy statements following failure, particularly in public situations, although there were no sex differences following success (Mischel, 1958a). These results suggest that the public acknowledgement of generalized or pervasive failure was probably more negative for males than for females. Sex differences in self-reported expectancy changes, however, are not necessarily accompanied by other differences in the relevant behavior (e.g., Mischel, 1962).

In another study, achievement needs inferred from TAT themes were found to be positively related to choice preferences for delayed, larger, as opposed to immediate, smaller rewards for adolescent boys tested by male experimenters, but they were *negatively* related for adolescent girls tested by female experimenters (Metzner and Mischel, 1962). With cross-sex pairs of subjects and experimenters the relationships between the two variables were negligible. These re-

lationships (which have been replicated) may reflect that adolescent girls who have learned to delay rewards and to anticipate the consequences of their own behavior are less likely to expect positive consequences for telling achievement-oriented stories to women. Young men who delay immediate gratification, on the other hand, may have learned that achievement-oriented stories are appropriate and expected when the stories are elicited by male experimenters. Sex differences in correlational patterns often may reflect mediation by such situational variables.

The manner in which sex differences in the value of rewards may produce sex differences in the amount of behavior change was illustrated by the work of McClelland and his colleagues (1953). Achievement motivation was increased for males but not for females following a test reported to measure intelligence under conditions designed to stimulate achievement needs. When the intervening experience involved a challenge to social rather than to intellectual acceptability, however, achievement scores increased significantly in females but not in males.

The behaviors in particular contexts that are appropriate for males as opposed to females also change as a function of the individual's age. Different forms of dependency, for example, may be labeled as broadly acceptable and may lead to positive outcomes across many situations for both sexes at early ages but not in later phases of development. When dependency is manifested by older boys it may be unacceptable, whereas similar dependent behaviors may be condoned for girls. As previously noted, longitudinal studies of the temporal stability of personality dimensions also have found sex differences in the durability of various sex-typed behavior patterns. In the Fels Longitudinal Study, Kagan and Moss (1962) found some significant consistency between childhood and early adulthood ratings of achievement behavior, sex-typed activity, and spontaneity for both sexes. Stability was found for certain other variables, like dependency and aggression, for one sex but not for the other. In particular, Kagan and Moss found that childhood dependency and passivity were related to adult dependency and passivity for women, but not for men and, conversely, "the developmental consistency for aggression was noticeably greater for males" (p. 95). It has been suggested that these sex-linked differences in the continuity of behaviors may reflect differences in their "congruence with traditional standards for sex-role characteristics" (Kagan and Moss, 1962, p. 268). Kagan and Moss argued that "Passive and dependent behavior are subjected to consistent cultural disapproval for men but not for women" (p. 268), whereas the reverse characterizes men. This seems plausible, but it is more difficult to understand just how these sex-typed differences in sanctions would prevent continuity in the sex-inappropriate behavior. "Cultural disapproval" might be expected to decrease uniformly the overall frequency of sex-inappropriate behaviors by inhibiting them. It is less clear, however, why such disapproval of sex-inappropriate behaviors would eliminate intra-individual stability in them. Assume for example, that girls tend to be consistently unrewarded or punished for aggressiveness in the course of development. As a result, their aggressive tendencies would be expected to decrease in their total frequency over time. But it is unclear why such a mean decrease would change any individual girl's position relative to other girls. While all girls might show a decrease, each girl could still retain her relative position or rank order within the distribution. To illustrate, the girl who showed most aggression at the early age could still be the most aggressive one in the sample years later, although her overall aggressiveness was greatly reduced as a result of sex-linked cultural sanctions. To account for reduced intra-individual consistency one would have to hypothesize inconsistent or random training over time rather than "consistent cultural disapproval." One would have to hypothesize that sex-inappropriate behaviors are inconsistently reinforced over the course of development so that the reinforcement a child receives for sex-inappropriate behaviors at any one time are unrelated to those obtained at other times.

On the other hand, sex-appropriate behaviors (e.g., dependency in females and physical aggressiveness in males) may be more consistent than sex-inappropriate behavior even at the relatively early stages in development when the first measurements were made in the reported longitudinal studies. The pre-viously discussed data of Sears and others (e.g., Lansky et al., 1961; Sears, Rau, and Alpert, 1965) have indicated that, already at preschool age, boys show virtually no consistency in their dependent behaviors but do manifest some consistency in aggressiveness across situations, whereas the reverse patterns characterize girls. If that is generally true, then the greater temporal instability of sex-inappropriate behaviors may reflect that they were never very consistent dispositions in the first place and therefore cannot be expected to remain stable.

Just as the probable consequences of any behavior pattern depend on numerous specific situational considerations, so does the affective value or valence of any stimulus hinge on the exact conditions in which it occurs. The subject's sex and the social agent's sex often interact in influencing the valence and the behavioral effects of a host of independent variables (e.g., Sarason, 1966). It has been found repeatedly that responsiveness to such social reinforcers as verbal approval depends, in part, on interactions between the sex of the child and the sex of the reinforcing adult (Epstein and Liverant, 1963; Gewirtz, 1954; Gewirtz et al., 1958; Hartup, 1961; Stevenson, 1965; etc.). The differential effectiveness of social reinforcement, depending upon the relationship between the child's sex and the experimenter's, has been studied thoroughly. Although the relationships are not always consistent, in general the main trend seems to be for greater effectiveness in social reinforcers when they come from a cross-sex social agent (Stevenson, 1965). To illustrate, one of the first studies on this topic (Gewirtz, 1954) examined attention-seeking by preschool children. Each child was engaged in easel painting in front of an adult whose availability to the child was either high or low. The highest attention-seeking was by boys interacting with a female adult. A second study (Gewirtz et al., 1958) also revealed that after a brief social deprivation (20 minutes in a room alone) or approval (20 minutes with a friendly adult) susceptibility to social reinforcement tended to be greatest in cross-sex relationships, again most notably for boys paired with female experimenters, especially after social deprivation.

Later studies also have indicated that social approval from a cross-sex adult tends to be more potent than social reinforcement from a same-sex adult. These studies were conducted with a variety of subject samples of varying ages. The main finding in general tends to be an enhancement in the efficacy of verbal social reinforcement when it is dispensed by a cross-sex experimenter (e.g., Stevenson, 1961; Stevenson and Allen, 1964; Stevenson and Knights, 1962). These results might be taken as evidence for the greater attractiveness or salience to children (and to adults) of cross-sex persons. On the other hand, there is a strong and pervasive tendency for boys and girls to prefer (at least in ratings) adults of their own sex (e.g., Kagan and Lemkin, 1960; Minuchin, 1965; Stevenson et al., 1967). The greater efficacy of cross-sex adults in the experiments on social reinforcement also seems to conflict with the previously discussed tendency for people to attend more closely to same-sex models. Stevenson (1965) has suggested that social reinforcement from cross-sex adults may be relatively less available and that this greater deprivation enhances (perhaps by contrast) the potency of cross-sex social reinforcement when it does occur. However, it would seem that greater attentiveness to cross-sex adults (and hence greater susceptibility to their influence attempts) is consistent with the finding that parents may be more permissive and nurturant to their cross-sex children (Rothbart and Maccoby, 1966). Stevenson also noted that the cross-sex effect in conditioning may be due not to the children's evaluations of the adults but perhaps to more affectionate social reinforcement inadvertently emitted by adult experimenters to opposite-sex children.

Epstein and Liverant (1963) studied the relationships between sex-role preferences expressed by boys on the IT Scale and the youngsters' susceptibility to verbal conditioning conducted by a male or female adult. More specifically, boys between the ages of 5 and 7 were divided into those who were either very high or very low in masculinity as judged by their IT Scale preferences. They then were exposed to a male or female adult experimenter. The experimenter verbally approved their saying "mother" or "father" (depending on the condition) repeatedly in answer to many questions. The results indicated the masculine boys were more readily conditioned by a male than by a female, suggesting that adult men had acquired greater reinforcement value for these youngsters. Regardless of masculinity scores, all the boys tended to condition more readily when the response was "father" than when it was "mother."

Sex of child may also interact with sex of adult in determining the extent to which observational learning influences subsequent performance (Bandura, Ross, and Ross, 1961, 1963a, 1963b; Bandura and Walters, 1963; Rosenblith, 1959, 1961; etc.). In addition, the sex of the child and the sex of the social agent may affect the potency of more direct types of social influence. One study examined how the sex of experimenter, sex of child, and withdrawal of attention affect resistance to temptation in 4-year-old boys and girls (Burton, Allinsmith, and Maccoby, 1966). There were no significant main effects, nor were there any sex differences in the children's resistance to temptation. An interaction, however, was found between sex of child and sex of experimenter. The interaction indicated somewhat greater resistance to temptation in cross-sex groups. This tendency to resist temptation more for a cross-sex experimenter seems consistent with the previously cited findings that children may be more influenced by social approval from cross-sex experimenters (e.g., Stevenson, 1965).

Borstelmann (1961) found that the sex of child and sex of experimenter did not interact significantly to influence preschool children's sex-typed preferences. He also found that the relations among different sex-typing measures were small. A later study (DeLucia, 1963) investigated sex-typed toy preferences in children ranging in age from kindergarten to the fourth grade. Consistent with findings from numerous other studies, appropriate sex-typing tended to increase with age, and boys made more sex-appropriate choices than did girls. The data on the test-retest reliability of the children's preferences reassessed after intervals ranging from 1 to 4 weeks were most interesting. In all grades, when both tests were administered by a cross-sex experimenter the children's sex-typed preferences remained fairly consistent and stable, the coefficients being .64, .67, .70, and .72. But when the two tests were administered by same-sex experimenters the coefficients were very low: .21, .13, .37, and −.13. Thus even the relatively short-term temporal stability of sex-typed preferences may be appreciably influenced by the sex of the person who *elicits* them. It might be speculated that the child's expectations about the preferences that he *ought* to display are influenced by the sex of the experimenter, with greater pressure for maintaining consistent and stable sex-appropriate choices when they are elicited by a cross-sex experimenter.

The findings reviewed in this section indicate that sex-typed responses often are affected by the situation in which they are made and by such variables as the sex of the person eliciting the response, with interaction effects between the experimenter's sex and the sex of the subject. Although the value and consequences of many social behaviors often depend on the person's sex, the outcomes even for highly sex-typed behaviors usually hinge on many variables in addition to the performer's sex. As the examples in this section point out, the reinforcing consequences produced by behavior in naturalistic life contexts depend not only on the performer's sex and on the content of the behavior, but also on the particular circumstances in which it occurs and on the social agent who controls outcomes. Individuals discriminate between contingencies to a great degree even in behaviors often used as referents for supposedly stable generalized traits like dependency, aggressiveness, self-control, and "ego strength." Since the bulk of social behaviors yield positive outcomes in some contexts but negative consequences in other situations, the behaviors may tend to become remarkably specific, as the modest consistency coefficients for sex-typed behaviors have indicated.

If one assumes, in accord with broad trait theories, that people have highly generalized dispositions, then seemingly discrepant behaviors from the same individual need special interpretations to explain his inconsistency. Having judged a woman to be "basically aggressive and masculine," for example, new evidence that she is passive and dependent in some situations, and nurturant in others, might be construed as signs of her conflicted efforts to defend against her fundamental aggressiveness and her masculine identification. If, on the other hand, one emphasizes subtle discrimination training throughout socialization, as do social learning

theories, then it is not necessary to call upon special defensive mechanisms to mediate between hypothesized unitary dispositions and supposedly discrepant surface behaviors. The diverse behaviors themselves are seen as the predictable, expected results of socialization processes in which discrimination training has a central role. If in the course of an individual's development masculine striving and assertiveness is modeled, expected, and rewarded in some situations but passivity is learned and encouraged in other settings, then she will display both kinds of behavior, depending on just where she is. Special defense mechanisms, conflicts, displacement, or other underlying processes need not be invoked to account for these "inconsistencies," since the hypothesis of broad trait generality across diverse situations was not made at the start.

CONCLUSIONS

This chapter has illustrated some of the main psychological differences found between the sexes and has explored some of the causes, correlates, and ramifications of these differences. Although the focus has been on sex-typed behaviors, the intent has been to show that the problems found and the theorizing required in this domain are basically similar to those in other areas of socialization.

Guided by the trait or dispositional approach to personality, one of the most popular strategies of personality study has sought to identify broad trait dimensions. Perhaps the most prototypic of these dimensions has been "masculinity-femininity," or the degree of appropriate sex-typing. The personality correlates and the child-rearing practices associated with the individual's standing on this dimension have been pursued vigorously.

Traditional conceptions of the socialization process in general, and of sex-typing in particular, have been most influenced by Freud's theorizing about identification as a unitary process. This approach rests on the belief that a host of broad personality variables—such as sex-typing, conscience, and adult-role taking in the child—are the closely intercorrelated products of his identification with his parents, particularly the same-sex parent. Although some consistency has been found in the hypothesized products of identification, the empirical results do not support identification as a distinctly unitary process that leads to closely integrated behavioral products. The relationships obtained by correlational research on personality dispositions are large enough to demonstrate that behavior is not haphazard. However, while people may construe themselves and each other as characterized by consistent dispositions, their behavior across settings is far from homogenous. This relative specificity is seen in the modest consistency coefficients obtained among seemingly close indices of such sex-typed behaviors as dependency and of sex-typing itself. The results reviewed suggest that personality organization is much more subtly differentiated than broad unitary dispositional theories of personality would suggest. The persistent finding that complex behavior is regulated by interactions that depend intimately on situational conditions or stimulus variables suggests that global traits are excessively gross units for personality study. Such global units do not properly encompass the richness and complexity of human social behavior. A more adequate conceptualization of personality must deal with man's extraordinary adaptiveness and capacities for discrimination, for self-regulation, and for constructive change as he copes with a changing environment.

Recognizing the diversity existing within the behavior of every person, cognitive consistency theorists have given an important role to man's strivings to create consistency, balance, and dissonance reduction. Drawing on this conceptualization, cognitive-developmental theory (particularly Kohlberg, 1966) has emphasized the importance of cognitive processes in socialization, and of self-categorizations of one's gender in the development of sex-typing. A considerable amount of evidence does suggest that people strive for cognitive consistency and reduce discrepancies among cognitions. Much less clear, however, is the causal role of such cognitive processes in directing behavior and in generating changes in what the person actually does.

There is little doubt, for example, that children soon do categorize themselves as males or females invariantly, and that their sex in turn influences the value and meaning of a multitude of events for them. More controversial are the causal mechanisms through which the individual's self-categorization as male or female would determine his subsequent sex-role behaviors. From the viewpoint of cognitive-developmental theory the person's gender self-categorization is the basic organizer of sex-role attitudes; in that view basic self-categorizations determine basic attitudes and values. Empirically, the relations between the individual's attitudes and values and other indices of his behavior, however, are far from strong. Moreover, the causal effects of attitudes and cognitions on other aspects of behavior are not clear, and it may be hazardous to assume a unidirectional causal chain in which attitudes and cognitions are taken as the invariable causes of other forms of behavior.

Formulations of the identification process that were influenced heavily by Freud's theorizing have viewed it as a special phenomenon through which children come to identify with the same-sex parent early in the course of socialization. More recent formulations, focusing on social learning variables, have construed identification as similar to any interpersonal modeling phenomena through which observers learn and adopt the attributes and actions of other people. Viewed in this perspective, the study of identification becomes part of the investigation of observational learning. Extensive research on that topic has explored in detail many of the conditions than enhance observational learning. Consistent with the expectations of several identification theories, it has been found that such attributes as the model's noncontingent rewardingness and nurturance, his power and control over resources, and his similarity to the observer may facilitate the observer's tendency to emulate him. Although these model attributes often increase imitation, they are not an essential prerequisite for observational learning, at least in the older children usually studied. Moreover, the characteristics of the model that exert the most potent influences depend, in part, on the type of behavior that is modeled and on the conditions in which the observer must later rehearse or transmit it. Components from the behaviors of many models are adopted and synthesized into unique new patterns. Careful analyses of identificatory processes also show that they are not confined to the child's imitation of his parents but involve observational learning from numerous sources and models throughout his life.

The emphasis on observational and cognitive-symbolic processes in modern social learning theories of identification reveals that these positions do not rely simply on reinforcement principles. On the contrary, the acquisition or learning of social behaviors (such as appropriate sex-typing patterns) is seen to depend on observational, attentional, and rehearsal processes that are relatively independent of immediate external reinforcement. The probable reinforcing consequences to which behavior leads are viewed as important, however, in social learning conceptualizations of the individual's choice among the numerous behaviors potentially available to him in a particular situation. Even here cognitive processes are important since the reinforcing consequences that are associated with alternative behaviors presumably are learned through vicarious and symbolic reinforcement, as well as by directly administered rewards and punishments.

The chief difference between current social learning views and those of cognitive-developmental theory thus is not that the former depend exclusively (or even primarily) on the concept of reinforcement while ignoring cognitive-perceptual processes. The difference hinges rather on the heavy emphasis that cognitive-development formulations place on the *causal role* of cognitions and self-concepts about sex-role identity as pervasive determinants of personality. The question is not the existence of such cognitions and self-concepts, but rather how adequately they in themselves account for complex sex-typing and socialization phenomena. From the viewpoint of social learning theory, the individual's constructions and self-categorizations do not necessarily parallel his other behaviors, nor do they necessarily cause them.

While attributing less of a causal role to self-categorizations of gender, social learning theories do view the child's sex itself as one critical determinant of his social development. As a result of their different socialization histories the sexes come to differ in the meaning and value that stimuli have for them and therefore also in their subsequent preferences and choices. As we have seen, the reinforcing outcomes obtained directly and vicariously for many forms of behavior are sex-typed

and hinge in part on the sex of the performer. The individual's sex influences the consequences he gets for many of his behaviors, but these consequences also depend on numerous other moderating considerations. The type of behavior, the setting in which it occurs, the individual's age, status, and other attributes, the characteristics of the social agents who evaluate him—these are some of the many variables that interact with sex to determine the probable direct and vicarious consequences to which behavior is likely to lead in particular situations. Considering the multiplicity of these determinants of response consequences, both to oneself and to relevant models, it becomes understandable that individuals learn to discriminate sharply and show only modest consistency even across seemingly similar situations.

The external control of sex-contingent reinforcement may have an especially important part in early socialization. In later phases of development, however, the person's own self-reactions and self-evaluations play an increasingly important role. Therefore an adequate approach to socialization must also deal with the manner in which persons acquire standards and rules for regulating their own behavior. The individual judges his own actions, feelings, and accomplishments, and the stream of behavior involves a constant reaction to one's own behavior, as well as to environmental events. In his own self-reactions the person also compares himself to other people, and he transmits his standards to others. These interactions between the person and the environment as they change each other are importantly influenced by the individual's sex. Sex-role stereotypes and standards probably serve as important guides in the self-evaluative process. However, considering the extensive discriminations found within any domain of sex-typed behaviors, it seems likely that self-evaluations would generally depend not only on one's broad stereotypes about sex-appropriate behavior in general but also on a multitude of more specific moderating conditions.

All social behavior, regardless of the particular dependent measure selected as the unit of study, can hopefully be understood by fundamentally similar causal principles—such as cognitive consistency strivings, observational learning, and reinforcement. The particular principles preferred as the best available explanations for personality phenomena are controversial and sure to change. But it would be surprising if different basic laws were needed ultimately to understand sex-typed behaviors and nonsex-typed behaviors, or if a different set of theoretical rules were required for every possible dimension of personality, such as dependency, aggression, self-control. If observational learning processes, for example, are important determinants of behavior, one would expect them to function in fundamentally similar ways regardless of the substantive content that is being displayed by models. Obviously the specific behaviors displayed by a "masculine" father would differ from those shown by a more "feminine" parent, but the variables that regulate a child's adoption of the modeled behavior should be similar. Likewise, if reinforcement is an important determinant of performance, one would expect the same reinforcement principles to apply, regardless of whether the performance of interest occurs in school, in the home, in children, in adults, with peers, with teachers, and so on. Although the specific events that constitute reinforcers would differ, the principles of learning needed would be the same. Thus sex-typing, in the present view, should be governed by the same fundamental principles that regulate the development and occurrence of other complex forms of social behavior. As these mechanisms become increasingly clear, they should permit us to go beyond the traditional categorization of personality as a set of discrete, unitary dimensions and to elucidate, instead, the causes of socialized behavior regardless of its particular content.

References

Abelson, R. P., and Rosenberg, M. J. Symbolic psycho-logic: a model of attitudinal cognition. *Behav. Sci.*, 1958, **3**, 1–13.

Allen, E. K., Hart, B. M., Buell, J. S., Harris, F. R., and Wolf, M. M. Effects of social reinforcement on isolate behavior of a nursery school child. *Child Dev.*, 1964, **35**, 511–518.

Allinsmith, W. The learning of moral standards. In D. R. Miller and G. E. Swanson (Eds.), *Inner conflict and defense*. New York: Holt, 1960. Pp. 141-176.

Allport, G. W. *Personality: a psychological interpretation*. New York: Holt, 1937.

Allport, G. W. Traits revisited. *Am. Psychol.*, 1966, **21**, 1–10.

Allport, G. W., and Odbert, H. S. Trait-names: a psycho-lexical study. *Psychol. Monogr.*, 1936, **47** (Whole No. 211).

Anastasiow, N. J. Success in school and boys' sex-role patterns. *Child Dev.*, 1965, **36**, 1053–1066.

Anderson, N. H. Primacy effects in personality impression formation using a generalized order effect paradigm. *J. pers. soc. Psychol.*, 1965, **2**, 1–9.

Aronfreed, J. The nature, variety, and social patterning of moral responses to transgression. *J. abnorm. soc. Psychol.*, 1961, **63**, 223–240.

Aronfreed, J. The origin of self-criticism. *Psychol. Rev.* 1964, **71**, 193–218.

Aronfreed, J. The concept of internalization. D. A. Goslin (Ed.), *Handbook on socialization theory*. Chicago: Rand McNally, 1969. Pp. 263–324.

Aronfreed, J., and Reber, A. Internalized behavioral suppression and the timing of social punishment. *J. pers. soc. Psychol.*, 1965, **1**, 3–16.

Asch, S. E. Forming impressions of personality. *J. abnorm. soc. Psychol.*, 1946, **41**, 258-290.

Ayllon, T., and Azrin, N. H. The measurement and reinforcement of behavior of psychotics. *J. exp. Analysis Behav.*, 1965, **8**, 357–383.

Bach, G. R. Young children's play fantasies. *Psychol. Monogr.*, 1945, **59**(2).

Bach, G. R. Father-fantasies and father-typing in father-separated children. *Child Dev.*, 1946, **17**, 63–80.

Baldwin, A. L. The effect of home environment on nursery school behavior. *Child Dev.*, 1949, **20**, 49–61.

Bandura, A. Relationship of family patterns to child behavior disorders. Progress Report, U.S.P.H. Research Grant M-1734, Stanford University, 1960.

Bandura, A. Behavioral modification through modeling procedures. In L. Krasner and L. P. Ullmann (Eds.), *Research in behavior modification*. New York: Holt, Rinehart & Winston, 1965. Pp. 310–340.

Bandura, A. Social learning theory of identificatory processes. In D. A. Goslin (Ed.), *Handbook of socialization theory and research*. Chicago: Rand McNally, 1969. Pp. 213–262.

Bandura, A., Grusec, J. E., and Menlove, F. L. Observational learning as a function of symbolization and incentive set. *Child Dev.*, 1966, **37**, 499–506.

Bandura, A., Grusec, J. E., and Menlove, F. L. Vicarious extinction of avoidance behavior. *J. pers. soc. Psychol.*, 1967, **5**, 16–23.

Bandura, A., and Harris, M. B. Modification of syntactic style. *J. exp. child Psychol.*, 1966, **4**, 341–352.

Bandura, A., and Huston, A. C. Identification as a process of incidental learning. *J. abnorm. soc. Psychol.*, 1961, **63**, 311–318.

Bandura, A., and Kupers, C. J. Transmission of patterns of self-reinforcement through modeling. *J. abnorm. soc. Psychol.*, 1964, **69**, 1–9.

Bandura, A., and McDonald, F. J. Influence of social reinforcement and the behavior of models in shaping children's moral judgments. *J. abnorm. soc. Psychol.*, 1963, **67**, 274–281.

Bandura, A., and Mischel, W. Modification of self-imposed delay of reward through exposure to live and symbolic models. *J. pers. soc. Psychol.*, 1965, **2**, 698–705.

Bandura, A., Ross, D., and Ross, S. A. Transmission of aggression through imitation of aggressive models. *J. abnorm. soc. Psychol.*, 1961, **63**, 575–582.

Bandura, A., Ross, D., and Ross, S. A. Imitation of film-mediated aggressive models. *J. abnorm. soc. Psychol.*, 1963, **66**, 3–11. (a)

Bandura, A., Ross, D., and Ross, S. A. Vicarious reinforcement and imitative learning. *J. abnorm. soc. Psychol.*, 1963, **67**, 601–667. (b)

Bandura, A., and Walters, R. *Social learning and personality development*. New York: Holt, Rinehart & Winston, 1963.

Bandura, A., and Whalen, C. K. The influence of antecedent reinforcement and divergent modeling cues on patterns of self-reward. *J. pers. soc. Psychol.*, 1966, **3**, 373–382.

Becker, W. C. The matching of behavior rating and questionnaire personality factors. *Psychol. Bull.*, 1960, **57**, 201–212.

Becker, W. C. Consequences of different kinds of parental discipline. In M. L. Hoffman and L. W. Hoffman (Eds.), *Review of child development research*. Vol. 1. New York: Russell Sage Foundation, 1964. Pp. 169–208.

Bell, R., and Darling, J. The prone head reaction in the human newborn: relationship with sex and tactile sensitivity. *Child Dev.*, 1965, **36**, 943–949.

Beller, E. K. Dependency and independence in young children. *J. Genet. Psychol.* 1955, **87**, 25–35.

Beller, E. K. Personality correlates of perceptual discrimination in children. Unpublished Progress Report, 1962.

Beller, E. K., and Neubauer, P. B. Sex differences and symptom patterns in early childhood. *J. Child Psychiat.*, 1963, **2**, 414–433.

Beller, E. K., and Turner, J. L. A study of dependency and aggression in early childhood. From progress report on NIMH project M-849, 1962.

Bennett, E. M., and Cohen, L. R. Men and women: personality patterns and contrasts. *Genet. Psychol. Monogr.*, 1959, **59**, 101–155.

Bettelheim, B. Individual and mass behavior in extreme situations. *J. abnorm. soc. Psychol.*, 1943, **38**, 417–452.

Bijou, S. W. Experimental studies of child behavior, normal and deviant. In L. Krasner and L. P. Ullmann (Eds.), *Research in behavior modification.* New York: Holt, 1965. Pp. 59–81.

Blake, R. R., and Vanderplas, J. M. The effect of pre-recognition hypotheses on veridical recognition thresholds in auditory perception. *J. Pers.*, 1950, **19**, 95–115.

Block, J. *The challenge of response sets.* New York: Appleton-Century-Crofts, 1965.

Bonarius, J. C. J. Research in the personal construct theory of George A. Kelly: Role Construct Repertory Test and Basic Theory. In B. A. Maher (Ed.), *Progress in experimental personality research.* Vol. 2. New York: Academic Press, 1965. Pp. 1–46.

Borstelmann, L. J. Sex of experimenter and sex-typed behavior of young children. *Child Dev.*, 1961, **32**, 519–524.

Brehm, J. W., and Cohen, A. R. *Explorations in cognitive dissonance.* New York: Wiley, 1962.

Brim, O. G., Jr. Family structure and sex role learning by children: a further analysis of Helen Koch's data. *Sociometry*, 1958, **21**, 1–16.

Brim, O. G., Jr. Personality development as role-learning. In I. Iscoe and H. W. Stevenson (Eds.), *Personality development in children.* Austin: University of Texas Press, 1960. Pp. 127–159.

Brim, O. G., Jr., and Wheeler, S. *Socialization after childhood: two essays.* New York: Wiley, 1966.

Brody, Grace F. Relationship between maternal attitudes and behavior. *J. pers. soc. Psychol.*, 1965, **2**, 317–323.

Bronfenbrenner, U. The study of identification through interpersonal perception. In R. Tagiuri and L. Petrullo (Eds.), *Person perception and interpersonal behavior.* Stanford, Cal.: Stanford University Press, 1958. Pp. 110–130.

Bronfenbrenner, U. Freudian theories of identification and their derivatives. *Child Dev.*, 1960, **31**, 15–40. (a)

Bronfenbrenner, U. Some familial antecedents of responsibility and leadership in adolescents. In L. Petrullo and B. M. Bass (Eds.), *Studies in leadership.* New York: Holt, 1960. (b)

Broverman, D. M., Klaiber, E. L., Kobayashi, Y., and Vogel, W. Roles of activation and inhibition in sex differences in cognitive abilities. *Psychol. Rev.*, 1968, **75**, 23–50.

Brown, D. G. Masculinity-feminity development in chldiren. *J. consult. Psychol.*, 1957, **21**, 197–202.

Brown, R. *Social psychology.* New York: Free Press, 1965.

Bruner, J. S. Social psychology and perception. In E. E. Maccoby, T.M. Newcomb, and E. L. Hartley (Eds.), *Readings in social psychology.* (3rd ed.) New York: Holt, 1958. Pp. 85–94.

Bruner, J. S., Olver, R. R., and Greenfield, P. M. *Studies in cognitive growth.* New York: Wiley, 1966.

Burnstein, E., Stotland, E., and Zander, A. Similarity to a model and self-evaluation. *J. abnorm. soc. Psychol.*, 1961, **62**, 257–264.

Burton, R. V. Generality of honesty reconsidered. *Psychol. Rev.*, 1963, **70**, 481–499.

Burton, R. V., Allinsmith, W., and Maccoby, E. E. Resistance to temptation in relation to sex of child, sex of experimenter, and withdrawal of attention. *J. pers. soc. Psychol.*, 1966, **3**, 253–258.

Burwen, L. S., and Campbell, D. T. The generality of attitudes toward authority and nonauthority figures. *J. abnorm. soc. Psychol.*, 1957, **54**, 24–31.

Buss, A. H. Physical aggression in relation to different frustrations. *J. abnorm. soc. Psychol.*, 1963, **67**, 1-7.

Byrne, D. *An introduction to personality.* Englewood Cliffs, N.J.: Prentice-Hall, 1966.

Campbell, D. T. Recommendations for APA test standards regarding construct, trait, or discriminant validity. *Am. Psychol.*, 1960, **15**, 546–553.

Campbell, D. T. Conformity in psychology's theories of acquired behavioral dispositions. In I. A. Berg and B. M. Bass (Eds.), *Conformity and deviation.* New York: Harper, 1961. Pp. 101–142.

Campbell, D., and Fiske, D. Convergent and discriminant validation by the multi-trait-multimethod matrix. *Psychol. Bull.*, 1959, **56**, 81–105.

Carlin, M. T. The effects of modeled behavior during imposed delay on the observer's subsequent willingness to delay rewards. Unpublished doctoral dissertation, Stanford University, 1965.

Carlson, R. Identification and personality structure in preadolescents. *J. abnorm. soc. Psychol.*, 1963, **67**, 566–573.

Cattell, R. B. Confirmation and clarification of primary personality factors. *Psychometrika*, 1947, **12**, 197–220.

Cattell, R. B. *Personality: a systematic theoretical and factual study.* New York: McGraw-Hill, 1950.

Cattell, R. B. *Personality and motivation: structure and measurement.* Yonkers-on-Hudson, N.Y.: World, 1957.

Cava, E. L., and Rausch, H. L. Identification and the adolescent boy's perception of his father. *J. abnorm. soc. Psychol.*, 1952, **47**, 855–856.

Chittenden, G. E. An experimental study in measuring and modifying assertive behavior in young children. *Monogr. Soc. Res. Child Dev.*, 1942, **7**, No. 1 (Serial No. 31).

Christie, R. Authoritarianism re-examined. In R. Christie and M. Jahoda (Eds.), *Studies in the scope and method of "The Authoritarian Personality."* Glencoe, Ill.: Free Press, 1954. Pp. 123–196.

Couch, A. S., and Keniston, K. Yea-sayers and nay-sayers: agreeing response set as personality variable. *J. abnorm. soc. Psychol.*, 1960, **60**, 151–174.

Crandall, V. J., Katkowsky, W., and Preston, A. Motivational and ability determinants of young children's intellectual achievement behaviors. *Child Dev.*, 1962, **33**, 643–661.

Cronbach, L. J. Processes affecting scores on "understanding of others" and "assumed similarity." *Psychol. Bull.*, 1955, **52**, 177–193.

Cronbach, L. J. *Essentials of psychological testing.* (2nd ed.) New York: Harper, 1960.

D'Andrade, R. G. Trait psychology and componential analysis. *Am. Anthrop.*, 1965, **67**, 215–228.

D'Andrade, R. G. Sex differences and cultural institutions. In E. E. Maccoby (Ed.), *The development of sex differences.* Stanford, Cal.: Stanford University Press, 1966. Pp. 174–204.

Davison, G. C. The negative effects of early exposure to suboptimal visual stimuli. *J. Pers.*, 1964, **32**, 278–295.

Davison, G. C. Systematic desensitization as a counterconditioning process. *J. abnorm. Psychol.*, 1968, **73**, 91–99.

Davitz, J. R. The effects of previous training on postfrustrative behavior. *J. abnorm. soc. Psychol.*, 1952, **47**, 309–315.

Dawe, H. C. An analysis of 200 quarrels of preschool children. *Child Dev.*, 1934, **5**, 139–157.

DeLucia, L. A. The toy preference test: a measure of sex-role identification. *Child Dev.*, 1963, **34**, 107–117.

Deutsch, J. A., and Deutsch, D. *Physiological psychology*. Homewood, Ill.: Dorsey Press, 1966.

Digman, J. M. Principal dimensions of child personality as inferred from teacher's judgments. *Child Dev.*, 1963, **34**, 43–60.

Distler, L. S., May, P. R., and Tuma, A. H. Anxiety and ego-strength as predictors of response to treatment in schizophrenic patents. *J. consult. Psychol.*, 1964, **28**, 170–177.

Dornbusch, S. M., Hastorf, A. H., Richardson, S. A., Muzzy, R. E., and Vreeland, R. S. The perceiver and the perceived: their relative influence on the categories of interpersonal cognition. *J. pers. soc. Psychol.*, 1965, **1**, 434–440.

Douvan, E., and Kaye, C. *Adolescent girls*. Ann Arbor: Survey Research Center, University of Michigan, 1957.

Droppleman, L. F., and Schaefer, E. S. Boys' and girls' reports of maternal and paternal behavior. Paper read at American Psychological Association, New York City, August 31, 1961.

Duncker, K. Experimental modification of children's food preferences through social suggestion. *J. abnorm. Psychol.*, 1938, **33**, 489–507.

Durrett, M. E. The relationship of early infant regulation and later behavior in play interviews. *Child Dev.*, 1959, **30**, 211–216.

Edwards, A. L. *The social desirability variable in personality assessment and research*. New York: Dryden, 1957.

Edwards, A. L. Social desirability and the description of others. *J. abnorm. soc. Psychol.*, 1959, **59**, 434–436.

Edwards, A. L. Social desirability or acquiescence in the MMPI? A case study with the SD scale. *J. abnorm. soc. Psychol.*, 1961, **63**, 351–359.

Emmerich, W. Parental identification in young children. *Genet. Psychol. Monogr.*, 1959, **60**, 257–308.

Epstein, R., and Liverant, S. Verbal conditioning and sex-role identification in children. *Child Dev.*, 1963, **34**, 99–106.

Farina, A. Patterns of role dominance and conflict in parents of schizophrenic patients. *J. abnorm. soc. Psychol.*, 1960, **61**, 31–38.

Fauls, L. B., and Smith, W. D. Sex-role learning of five-year-olds. *J. genet. Psychol.*, 1956, **89**, 105–117.

Fenichel, O. *The psychoanalytic theory of neurosis*. New York: Norton, 1945.

Feshbach, S. The catharsis hypothesis and some consequences of interaction with aggressive and neutral play objects. *J. Pers.* 1956, **24**, 449–462.

Festinger, L. *A theory of cognitive dissonance*. Stanford, Cal.: Stanford University Press, 1957.

Festinger, L. Behavioral support for opinion change. *Publ. Opin. Q.*, 1964, **28**, 404–417.

Finch, H. M. Young children's concepts of parent roles. *J. Home Econ.*, 1955, **47**, 99–103.

Freud, A. *The ego and the mechanisms of defense*. New York: International Universities Press, 1946.

Freud, S. *An outline of psychoanalysis*. (1st ed., 1940.) New York: Norton, 1949.

Gewirtz, J. L. Three determinants of attention-seeking in young children. *Monogr. Soc. Res. Child Dev.*, 1954, **19**, No. 2, (Series No. 59).

Gewirtz, J. L. A factor analysis of some attention-seeking behaviors of young children. *Child. Dev.*, 1956, **27**, 17–36.

Gewirtz, J. L., and Baer, D. M. The effect of brief social deprivation on behaviors for a social reinforcer. *J. abnorm. soc. Psychol.*, 1958, **56**, 49–56.

Gewirtz, J. L., Baer, D. M., and Roth, C. H. A note on the similar effects of low social availability of an adult and brief social deprivation on young children's behavior. *Child Dev.*, 1958, **29**, 149–152.

Gewirtz, J. L., and Stingle, K. G. The learning of generalized-imitation as the basis for identification. *Psychol. Rev.*, 1968, **75**, 374–397.

Gill, L. J., and Spilka, B. Some nonintellectual correlates of academic achievement among Mexican-American secondary school students. *J. educ. Psychol.*, 1962, **53**, 144–149.

Glass, D. C. Theories of consistency and the study of personality. In E. F. Borgatta and W. W. Lambert (Eds.), *Handbook of personality theory and research*. Chicago: Rand McNally, 1968. Pp. 788–854.

Goldberg, S., and Lewis, M. Play behavior in the year-old infant: Early sex differences. *Child Dev.*, 1969, **40**, 21–31.

Goldberg, L. R., and Werts, C. E. The reliability of clinicians' judgments: a multitrait-multimethod approach. *J. consult. Psychol.*, 1966, **30**, 199–206.

Goodenough, E. W. Interest in persons as an aspect of sex differences in the early years. *Genet. Psychol. Monogr.*, 1957, **55**, 287–323.

Gordon, J. E., and Smith, E. Children's aggression, parental attitudes, and the effects of an affiliation-arousing story. *J. pers. soc. Psychol.*, 1965, **1**, 654–659.

Gough, H. G. Identifying psychological femininity. *Educ. psychol. Measur.*, 1952, **12**, 427–439.

Gough, H. G. *Manual for the California Psychological Inventory*. Palo Alto, Cal.: Consulting Psychologists Press, 1957.

Gray, S. W. Perceived similarity to parents and adjustment. *Child Dev.*, 1959, **30**, 91–107.

Greenstein, J. M. Father characteristics and sex typing. *J. pers. soc. Psychol.*, 1966, **3**, 271–277.

Grinder, R. E. Parental childrearing practices, conscience, and resistance to temptation of sixth-grade children. *Child Dev.*, 1962, **33**, 803–820.

Grinder, R. E. Relations between behavioral and cognitive dimensions of conscience in middle childhood. *Child Dev.*, 1964, **35**, 881–891.

Grusec, J. Some antecedents of self-criticism. *J. pers. soc. Psychol.*, 1966, **4**, 244–252.

Grusec, J., and Mischel, W. Model's characteristics as determinants of social learning. *J. pers. soc. Psychol.*, 1966, **4**, 211–215.

Guilford, J. P. *Personality*. New York: McGraw-Hill, 1959.

Hamburg, D. A., and Lunde, D. T. Sex hormones in the development of sex differences in human behavior. In E. E. Maccoby (Ed.), *The development of sex differences*. Stanford, Cal.: Stanford University Press, 1966. Pp. 1–24.

Hampson, J. L. Determinants of psycho-sexual orientation. In F. A. Beach (Ed.), *Sex and behavior*. New York: Wiley, 1965. Pp. 108–132.

Harding, J., Kutner, B., Proshansky, H., and Chein, I. Prejudice and ethnic relations. In G. Lindzey (Ed.), *Handbook of social psychology*. Reading, Mass.: Addison-Wesley, 1954. Pp. 1021–1061.

Harris, D. B. Sex differences in the life problems and interests of adolescents, 1935 and 1957. *Child Dev.*, 1959, **30**, 453–459.

Hartley, R. E. Children's concepts of male and female roles. *Merrill-Palmer Q.*, 1960, **6**, 84–91.

Hartley, R. E., and Hardesty, F. P. Children's perceptions of sex roles in childhood. *J. genet. Psychol.*, 1964, **105**, 43-51.

Hartshorne, H., and May, M. A. *Studies in the nature of character*. Vol. 1. *Studies in deceit*. New York: Macmillan, 1928.

Hartup, W. W. Nurturance and nurturance-withdrawal in relation to dependency behavior of preschool children. *Child Dev.*, 1958, **29**, 191–201.

Hartup, W. W. Sex and social reinforcement effects with children. Paper read at the American Psychological Association, New York City, 1961.

Hartup, W. W. Dependence and independence. In H. W. Stevenson et al. (Eds.), *Child psychology.* 62nd Yearbook of the National Society for the Study of Education. Part 1. Chicago: University of Chicago Press, 1963. Pp. 333–363.

Hartup, W. W., and Himeno, Y. Social isolation vs. interaction with adults in relation to aggression in preschool children. *J. abnorm. soc. Psychol.,* 1959, **59,** 17–22.

Hartup, W. W., and Zook, E. A. Sex role preferences in three- and four-year-old children. *J. consult. Psychol.,* 1960, **24,** 420–426.

Hathaway, S. R., and Briggs, P. F. Some normative data on new MMPI scales. *J. clin. Psychol.,* 1957, **13,** 364–368.

Hattwick, L. A. Sex differences in behavior of nursery school children. *Child Dev.,* 1937, **8,** 343–355.

Heathers, G. Emotional dependence and independence in a physical threat situation. *Child Dev.,* 1953, **24,** 169–179.

Hebb, D. O. *Psychology.* Philadelphia, Pa.: Saunders, 1966.

Heider, F. *The psychology of interpersonal relations.* New York: Wiley, 1958.

Heilbrun, A. B., Jr. The measurement of identification. *Child Dev.,* 1965, **36,** 111–127.

Helper, M. M. Learning theory and the self-concept. *J. abnorm. soc. Psychol.,* 1955, **51,** 184–189.

Hetherington, E. M. A developmental study of the effects of sex of the dominant parent on sex-role preference, identification, and imitation in children. *J. pers. soc. Psychol.,* 1965, **2,** 188–194.

Hetherington, E. M., and Frankie, G. Effect of parental dominance, warmth, and conflict on imitation in children. *J. pers. soc. Psychol.,* 1967, **6,** 119–125.

Hicks, D. J. Imitation and retention of film-mediated aggressive peer and adult models. *J. pers. soc. Psychol.,* 1965, **2,** 97–100.

Hill, W. F. Learning theory and the acquisition of values. *Psychol. Rev.,* 1960, **67,** 317–331.

Hoffman, M. L. Child-rearing practices and moral development: generalizations from empirical research. *Child Dev.,* 1963, **34,** 295–318.

Holmes, D. S. Male-female differences in MMPI ego strength: an artifact. *J. consult. Psychol.,* 1967, **31,** 408–410.

Honzik, M. P. Sex differences in the occurrence of materials in the play constructions of preadolescents. *Child Dev.,* 1951, **22,** 15–35.

Horowitz, R. A pictorial method for study of self-identification in preschool children. *J. genet. Psychol.,* 1943, **62,** 135–148.

Houwink, R. H. The attitude-interest analysis test of Terman and Miles and a specimen revision for the Netherlands. (In Dutch.) *Ned. Tijdschr. Psychol.,* 1950, **5,** 242–262.

Hovland, C. I., and Janis, I. L. (Eds.) *Personality and persuasability.* New Haven, Conn.: Yale University Press, 1959.

Hovland, C. I., Janis, I. L., and Kelley, H. H. *Communication and persuasion.* New Haven, Conn.: Yale University Press, 1953.

Insko, C. A., and Schopler, J. Triadic consistency: a statement of affective-cognitive-conative consistency. *Psychol. Rev.,* 1967, **74,** 361–376.

Jackson, D. N., and Messick, S. Content and style in personality assessment. *Psychol. Bull.,* 1958, **55,** 243–252.

Jakubszak, L. F., and Walters, R. H. Suggestibility as dependency behavior. *J. abnorm. soc. Psychol.,* 1959, **59,** 102–107.

Jegard, S. F., and Walters, R. H. A study of some determinants of aggression in young children. *Child Dev.,* 1960, **31,** 739–747.

Jersild, A. T., and Markey, F. V. Conflicts between preschool children. *Child Dev. Monogr.*, No. 21, 1935.

Jones, A. Information deprivation in humans. In B. A. Maher (Ed.), *Progress in experimental personality research.* Vol. 3. New York: Academic Press, 1966. Pp. 241–307.

Kagan, J. The child's perception of the parent. *J. abnorm. soc. Psychol.*, 1956, **53,** 257–258.

Kagan, J. The concept of identification. *Psychol. Rev.*, 1958, **65,** 296–305.

Kagan, J. Acquisition and significance of sex typing and sex role identity. In M. Hoffman and L. Hoffman (Eds.), *Review of child development research.* Vol. 1. New York: Russell Sage, 1964. Pp. 137–167.

Kagan, J., Hosken, B., and Watson, S. The child's symbolic conceptualization of the parents. *Child Dev.*, 1961, **32,** 625–636.

Kagan, J., and Lemkin, J. The child's differential perception of parental attributes. *J. abnorm. soc. Psychol.*, 1960, **61,** 440–447.

Kagan, J., and Moss, H. A. *Birth to maturity: a study in psychological development.* New York: Wiley, 1962.

Kanfer, F. H., and Marston, A. R. Determinants of self-reinforcement in human learning. *J. exp. Psychol.*, 1963, **66,** 245–254.

Kelly, E. L. Consistency of the adult personality. *Am. Psychol.*, 1955, **10,** 659–681.

Kelly, G. A. *The psychology of personal constructs.* Vols. 1 and 2. New York: Norton, 1955.

Kogan, N., and Wallach, M. A. *Risk taking: a study in cognition and personality.* New York: Holt, Rinehart & Winston, 1964.

Kohlberg, L. The development of moral character and ideology. In M. Hoffman and L. Hoffman (Eds.), *Review of child development research.* Vol. I. New York: Russell Sage, 1964. Pp. 383–431.

Kohlberg, L. A cognitive-developmental analysis of children's sex-role concepts and attitudes. In E. E. Maccoby (Ed.), *The development of sex differences.* Stanford, Cal.: Stanford University Press, 1966. Pp. 82–173.

Kohlberg, L., and Zigler, E. The impact of cognitive maturity on the development of sex-role attitudes in the years 4 to 8. *Genet. Psychol. Monogr.*, 1967, **75,** 84–165.

Korchin, S. J., and Heath, H. A. Somatic experience in the anxiety state: some sex and personality correlates of "autonomic feedback." *J. consult. Psychol.*, 1961, **25,** 398–404.

Lambert, W. E., Amon, S. and Goyeche, J. R. The effects on pain tolerance of increasing the salience of sex-group membership. Montreal: McGill University. (mimeo) 1967.

Landfield, A. W., Stern, M., and Fjeld, S. Social conceptual processes and change in students undergoing psychotherapy. *Psychol. Rep.*, 1961, **8,** 63–68.

Lansky, L. M., Crandall, V. J., Kagan, J., and Baker, C. T. Sex differences in aggression and its correlates in middle-class adolescents. *Child Dev.*, 1961, **32,** 45–68.

Lazowick, L. On the nature of identification. *J. abnorm. soc. Psychol.*, 1955, **51,** 175–183.

Lefkowitz, M. M., Blake, R. R., and Mouton, J. S. Status factors in pedestrian violation of traffic signals. *J. abnorm. soc. Psychol.*, 1955, **51,** 704–706.

Leventhal, H., Jones, S. and Trembly, G. Sex differences in attitude and behavior change under conditions of fear and specific instructions. *J. exp. soc. Psychol.*, 1966, **2,** 387–399.

Levy, D. M. *Maternal overprotection.* New York: Columbia University Press, 1943.

Liebert, R. M., and Ora, J. P., Jr. Children's adoption of self-reward patterns: incentive level and method of transmission. *Child Dev.*, 1968, **39,** 537–544.

Lindzey, G., and Goldberg, M. Motivational differences between males and females as measured by the TAT. *J. Pers.*, 1953, **22**, 101–117.

Livson, N., and Peskin, H. Prediction of adult psychological health in a longitudinal study. *J. abnorm. Psychol.*, 1967, **72**, 509–518.

Loevinger, J. Objective tests as instruments of psychological theory. *Psychol. Rep. Monogr.*, 1957, No. 9.

Lovaas, O. I., Berberich, J. P., Perloff, B. F., and Schaeffer, B. Acquisition of imitative speech by schizophrenic children. *Science*, 1966, **151**, 705–707.

Lynn, D. B., and Sawrey, W. L. The effects of father-absence on Norwegian boys and girls. *J. abnorm. soc. Psychol.*, 1959, **59**, 258–262.

Maccoby, E. E. Role-taking in childhood and its consequences for social learning. *Child Dev.*, 1959, **30**, 239–252.

Maccoby, E. E. Sex differences in intellectual functioning. In E. E. Maccoby (Ed.), *The development of sex differences.* Stanford, Cal.: Stanford University Press, 1966. Pp. 25–55.

Maccoby, E. E., and Wilson, W. C. Identification and observational learning from films. *J. abnorm. soc. Psychol.*, 1957, **55**, 76–87.

Maccoby, E. E., Wilson, W. C., and Burton, R. V. Differential movie-viewing behavior of male and female viewers. *J. Pers.*, 1958, **26**, 259–267.

MacKinnon, D. W. Violation of prohibition. In H. A. Murray et al., *Explorations in personality.* New York: Oxford University Press, 1938. Pp. 491–501.

Mann, R. D. A review of the relationships between personality and performance in small groups. *Psychol. Bull.*, 1959, **56**, 241–270.

McCandless, B. R., Bilous, B., and Bennett, H. L. Peer popularity and dependence on adults in preschool age socialization. *Child Dev.*, 1961, **32**, 511–518.

McClelland, D. C. Longitudinal trends in the relation of thought to action. *J. consult. Psychol.*, 1966, **30**, 479–483.

McClelland, D. C., Atkinson, J. W., Clark, R. A., and Lowell, E. L. *The achievement motive.* New York: Appleton-Century-Crofts, 1953.

McMains, M. J., and Liebert, R. M. Influence of discrepancies between successively modeled self-reward criteria on the adoption of a self-imposed standard. *J. pers. soc. Psychol.*, 1968, **8**, 166–171.

Meehl, P. E. The cognitive activity of the clinician. *Am. Psychol.*, 1960, **15**, 19–27.

Messick, S., and Jackson, D. N. Acquiescence and the factorial interpretation of the MMPI. *Psychol. Bull.*, 1961, **58**, 299–304.

Metzner, R., and Mischel, W. Achievement motivation, sex of subject, and delay behavior. Unpublished manuscript, Stanford University, 1962.

Miller, G. A. The magical number seven, plus or minus two: some limits on our capacity for processing information. *Psychol. Rev.*, 1956, **63**, 81–97.

Miller, N. E., and Dollard, J. *Social learning and imitation.* New Haven, Conn.: Yale University Press, 1941.

Minuchin, P. Sex-role concepts and sex typing in childhood as a function of school and home environments. *Child Dev.*, 1965, **36**, 1033–1048.

Mischel, W. The effect of the commitment situation on the generalization of expectancies. *J. Pers.*, 1958, **26**, 508–516. (a)

Mischel, W. Preference for delayed reinforcement: an experimental study of a cultural observation. *J. abnorm. soc. Psychol.*, 1958, **56**, 57–61. (b)

Mischel, W. Preference for delayed reinforcement and social responsibility. *J. abnorm. soc. Psychol.*, 1961, **62**, 1–7. (a)

Mischel, W. Delay of gratification, need for achievement, and acquiescence in another culture. *J. abnorm. soc. Psychol.*, 1961, **62**, 543–552. (b)

Mischel, W. Father absence and delay of gratification: cross-cultural comparison. *J. abnorm. soc. Psychol.*, 1961, **63**, 116–124. (c)

Mischel, W. Delay of gratification in choice situations. NIMH Progress Report, Stanford University, 1962.

Mischel, W. Predicting the success of Peace Corps Volunteers in Nigeria. *J. pers. soc. Psychol.*, 1965, **1**, 510–517.

Mischel, W. A social learning view of sex differences in behavior. In E. E. Maccoby (Ed.), *The development of sex differences*. Stanford, Cal.: Stanford University Press, 1966. Pp. 56–81. (a)

Mischel, W. Theory and research on the antecedents of self-imposed delay of reward. In B. A. Maher (Ed.), *Progress in experimental personality research*. Vol. 3. New York: Academic Press, 1966. Pp. 85–132. (b)

Mischel, W. *Personality and assessment*. New York: Wiley, 1968.

Mischel, W., Coates, B., and Raskoff, A. Effects of success and failure on self-gratification. *J. pers. soc. Psychol.*, 1968, **10**, 381–390.

Mischel, W., and Gilligan, C. Delay of gratification, motivation for the prohibited gratification, and responses to temptation. *J. abnorm. soc. Psychol.*, 1964, **69**, 411–417.

Mischel, W., and Grusec, J. Determinants of the rehearsal and transmission of neutral and aversive behaviors. *J. pers. soc. Psychol.*, 1966, **3**, 197–205.

Mischel, W., and Liebert, R. M. Effects of discrepancies between observed and imposed reward criteria on their acquisition and transmission. *J. pers. soc. Psychol.*, 1966, **3**, 45–53.

Mischel, W., and Liebert, R. M. The role of power in the adoption of self-reward patterns. *Child Dev.*, 1967, **38**, 673–683.

Mischel, W., and Mischel, F. Psychological aspects of spirit possession. *Am. Anthrop.*, 1958, **60**, 249–260.

Money, J. Influence of hormones on sexual behavior. *Ann. Rev. Med.*, 1965, **16**, 67–82. (a)

Money, J. Psychosexual differentiation. In J. Money (Ed.), *Sex research, new developments*. New York: Holt, Rinehart & Winston, 1965. Pp. 3–23. (b)

Money, J., Hampson, J. G., and Hampson, J. L. Imprinting and the establishment of gender role. *A. M. A., Arch. Neurol. Psychiat.*, 1957, **77**, 333–336.

Moore, S. and Updegraff, R. Sociometric status of preschool children related to age, sex, nurturance-giving and dependency. *Child Dev.*, 1964, **35**, 519–524.

Mowrer, O. H. *Learning theory and behavior*. New York: Wiley, 1960.

Mulaik, S. A. Are personality factors raters' conceptual factors? *J. consult. Psychol.*, 1964, **28**, 506–511.

Mussen, P. H. Some antecedents and consequents of masculine sex-typing in adolescent boys. *Psychol. Monogr.*, 1961, **75**, No. 2 (Whole No. 506).

Mussen, P. H. Long-term consequents of masculinity of interests in adolescence. *J. consult. Psychol.*, 1962, **26**, 435–440.

Mussen, P. H. and Distler, L. Masculinity, identification and father-son relationship. *J. abnorm. soc. Psychol.*, 1959, **59**, 350–356.

Mussen, P. H., and Distler, L. Child rearing antecedents of masculine identification in kindergarten boys. *Child Dev.*, 1960, **31**, 89–100.

Mussen, P. H. and Jones, M. C. Self-conceptions, motivations, and interpersonal attitudes of late- and early-maturing boys. *Child Dev.* 1957, **28**, 243–256.

Mussen, P. H. and Jones, M. C. The behavior-inferred motivations of late- and early-maturing boys. *Child. Dev.*, 1958, **29**, 61–67.

Mussen, P. H., and Jones, M. C. Self-conceptions, motivations, and interpersonal attitudes of late- and early-maturing boys. *Child Dev.*, 1959, **28**, 243–256.

Mussen, P. H., and Rutherford, E. Parent-child relations and parental personality in relation to young children's sex-role preferences. *Child Dev.*, 1963, **34**, 589–607.

Norman, W. T. Toward an adequate taxonomy of personality attributes: replicated factor structures in peer nomination personality ratings. *J. abnorm. soc. Psychol.*, 1963, **66**, 574–583.

Odom, R. D., Liebert, R. M., and Hill, J. H. The effects of modeling cues, reward, and attentional set on the production of grammatical and ungrammatical syntactic constructions. *J. exp. child Psychol.*, 1968, **6**, 131–140.

Oetzel, R. M. Selected bibliography on sex differences. In E. E. Maccoby (Ed.), *The development of sex differences in behavior*. Stanford, Cal.: Stanford University Press, 1966. Pp. 223–351.

Osgood, C. E., Suci, G. J., and Tannenbaum, P. H. *The measurement of meaning*. Urbana: University of Illinois Press, 1957.

Parsons, T. Family structure and the socialization of the child. In T. Parsons and R. F. Bales (Eds.), *Family socialization and interaction process*. Glencoe, Ill.: Free Press, 1955. Pp. 35–131.

Passini, F. T., and Norman, W. T. A universal conception of personality structure? *J. pers. soc. Psychol.*, 1966, **4**, 44–49.

Patterson, G. R., and Anderson, D. Peers as social reinforcers. *Child Dev.*, 1964, **35**, 951–960.

Payne, D. E., and Mussen, P. H. Parent-child relations and father identification among adolescent boys. *J. abnorm. soc. Psychol.*, 1956, **52**, 358–362.

Pedersen, F. A. Consistency data on the role construct repertory test. Unpublished manuscript, Ohio State University, 1958.

Piaget, J. *Play, dreams, and imitation in childhood*. New York: Norton, 1951.

Pittel, S. M., and Mendelsohn, G. A. Measurement of moral values: a review and critique. *Psychol. Bull.*, 1966, **66**, 22–35.

Rorer, L. G. The great response-style myth. *Psychol. Bull.*, 1965, **63**, 129–156.

Rosekrans, M. A. Imitation in children as a function of perceived similarity to a social model and vicarious reinforcement. *J. pers. soc. Psychol.*, 1967, **7**, 307–315.

Rosenberg, B. G., and Sutton-Smith, B. Family interaction effects on masculinity-femininity. *J. pers. soc. Psychol.*, 1968, **8**, 117–120.

Rosenblith, J. F. Learning by imitation in kindergarten children. *Child Dev.*, 1959, **30**, 69–80.

Rosenblith, J. F. The modified Graham Behavior Test for Neonates: test-retest reliability, normative data, and hypotheses for future work. *Biologia Neonat.*, 1961, **3**, 174–192.

Rothaus, P., and Worchel, P. Ego-support, communication, catharsis, and hostility. *J. Pers.*, 1964, **32**, 296–312.

Rothbart, M. K., and Maccoby, E. E. Parents' differential reactions to sons and daughters. *J. pers. soc. Psychol.*, 1966, **4**, 237–243.

Rotter, J. B. *Social learning and clinical psychology*. Englewood Cliffs, N.J.: Prentice-Hall, 1954.

Rubin, M., and Shontz, F. C. Diagnostic prototypes and diagnostic processes of clinical psychologists. *J. consult. Psychol.*, 1960, **24**, 234–239.

Sanford, N. The dynamics of identification. *Psychol. Rev.*, 1955, **62**, 106–118.

Sanford, R. N., Adkins, M., Miller, R. B., and Cobb, E. A. Physique, personality, and scholarship. *Monogr. Soc. Res. Child Dev.*, 1943, **8**(1).

Sarason, I. G. *Personality: an objective approach*. New York: Wiley, 1966.

Sarason, I. G., Ganzer, V. J., and Granger, J. W. Self-description of hostility and its correlates. *J. pers. soc. Psychol.*, 1965, **1**, 361–365.

Sarason, S. B., Davidson, K. S., Lighthall, F. F., Waite, R. R., and Ruebush, B. K. *Anxiety in elementary school children*. New York: Wiley, 1960.

Schachter, S. *The psychology of affiliation*. Stanford, Cal.: Stanford University Press, 1959.

Sears, P. S. Doll play aggression in normal young children: influence of sex, age, sibling status, father's absence. *Psychol. Monogr.*, 1951, **65**, (6).

Sears, P. S. Child-rearing factors related to playing of sex-typed roles. *Am. Psychol.*, 1953, **8**, 431. (Abstract)

Sears, R. R. Identification as a form of behavior development. In P. B. Harris (Ed.), *The concept of development*. Minneapolis: University of Minnesota Press, 1957. Pp. 149–161.

Sears, R. R. Relation of early socialization experiences to aggression in middle childhood. *J. abnorm. soc. Psychol.*, 1961, **63**, 466–492.

Sears, R. R. Dependency motivation. In M. R. Jones (Ed.), *Nebraska symposium on motivation*. Lincoln: University of Nebraska Press, 1963. Pp. 25–64.

Sears, R. R. Development of gender role. In F. A. Beach (Ed.), *Sex and behavior*. New York: Wiley, 1965. Pp. 133–163.

Sears, R. R., Maccoby, E. E., and Levin, H. *Patterns of child rearing*. Evanston, Ill.: Row, Peterson, 1957.

Sears, R. R., Pintler, M. H., and Sears, P. S. Effect of father separation on preschool children's doll play aggression. *Child Dev.*, 1946, **17**, 219–243.

Sears, R. R., Rau, L., and Alpert, R. *Identification and child rearing*. Stanford, Cal.: Stanford University Press, 1965.

Sears, R. R., Whiting, J., Nowlis, V., and Sears, P. Some child rearing antecedents of aggression and dependency in young children. *Genet. Psychol. Monogr.*, 1953, **47**, 135–234.

Shure, G. H., and Rogers, M. S. Note of caution on the factor analysis of the MMPI. *Psychol. Bull.*, 1965, **63**, 14–18.

Siegel, A. E., Stolz, L. M., Hitchcock, E. A., and Adamson, J. Children of working mothers and their controls. *Child Dev.*, 1959, **30**, 533–546.

Sines, L. K. The relative contribution of four kinds of data to accuracy in personality assessment. *J. consult. Psychol.*, 1959, **23**, 483–492.

Skolnick, A. Motivational imagery and behavior over twenty years. *J. consult. Psychol.*, 1966, **30**, 463–478. (a)

Skolnick, A. Stability and interrelations of thematic test imagery over 20 years. *Child Dev.*, 1966, **37**, 389–396. (b)

Sopchak, A. Parental "identification" and "tendency toward disorders" as measured by the MMPI. *J. abnorm. soc. Psychol.*, 1952, **47**, 159–165.

Staub, E. The effects of persuasion, modeling, and related influence procedures on delay of reward choices and attitudes. Unpublished doctoral dissertation, Stanford University, 1965.

Stevenson, H. W. Social reinforcement with children as a function of CA, sex of E, and sex of S. *J. abnorm. soc. Psychol.*, 1961, **63**, 147–154.

Stevenson, H. W. Social reinforcement of children's behavior. In L. P. Lipsitt and C. C. Spiker (Eds.), *Advances in child development*. Vol. 2, New York: Academic Press, 1965. Pp. 97–126.

Stevenson, H. W., and Allen, S. Adult performance as a function of sex of experimenter and sex of subject. *J. abnorm. soc. Psychol.*, 1964, **68**, 214–216.

Stevenson, H. W., Hale, G. A., Hill, K. T., and Moely, B. E. Determinants of children's preferences for adults. *Child Dev.*, 1967, **38**, 1–14.

Stevenson, H. W., and Knights, R. M. Social reinforcement with normal and retarded children as a function of pretraining, sex of E and sex of S. *Am. J. Ment. Defic.*, 1962, **66**, 866–871.

Stotland, E., Zander, A., and Natsoulas, T. The generalization of interpersonal similarity. *J. abnorm. soc. Psychol.*, 1961, **62**, 250–256.

Tannenbaum, P. H., and Gaer, E. P. Mood change as a function of stress of protagonist and degree of identification in a film-viewing situation. *J. pers. soc. Psychol.*, 1965, **2**, 612–616.

Taylor, S. P., and Epstein, S. Aggression as a function of the interaction of the sex of the aggressor and the sex of the victim. *J. Pers.*, 1967, **35**, 474–486.

Terman, L. M., and Miles, C. C. *Sex and personality: studies in masculinity and femininity.* New York: McGraw-Hill, 1936.

Toigo, R., Walder, L. O., Eron, L. D., and Lefkowitz, M. M. Examiner effect in the use of a near-sociometric procedure in the third grade classroom. *Psychol. Rep.*, 1962, **11**, 785–790.

Tuddenham, R. D. Studies in reputation: I. Sex and grade differences in school children's evaluations of their peers. *Psychol. Monogr.*, 1952, No. 333, 1–39.

Tupes, E. C., and Christal, R. E. Recurrent personality factors based on trait ratings. *USAF ASD Technical Reports*, 1961, No. 61–97.

Vernon, P. E. *Personality assessment: a critical survey.* New York: Wiley, 1964.

Wagman, M. Sex differences in types of daydreams. *J. pers. soc. Psychol.*, 1967, **7**, 329–332.

Wallace, J. An abilities conception of personality: some implications for personality measurement. *Am. Psychol.*, 1966, **21**, 132–138.

Wallach, M. A. Commentary: active-analytical vs. passive-global cognitive functioning. In S. Messick and J. Ross (Eds.), *Measurement in personality and cognition.* New York: Wiley, 1962. Pp. 199–218.

Walters, R. H., Parke, R. D., and Cane, V. A. Timing of punishment and the observation of consequences to others as determinants of response inhibition. *J. exp. Child Psychol.*, 1965, **2**, 10–30.

Walters, J., Pearce, D., and Dahms, L. Affectional and aggressive behavior of preschool children. *Child Dev.*, 1957, **28**, 15–26.

Watson, G. Some personality differences in children related to strict or permissive parental discipline. *J. Psychol.*, 1957, **44**, 227–249.

Weller, G. M., and Bell, R. Q. Basal skin conductance and neonatal state. *Child Dev.*, 1965, **36**, 647–657.

Wells, W. D., Goi, F. J., and Seader, S. A change in a product image. *J. appl. Psychol.*, 1958, **42**, 120–121.

Whitehouse, E. Norms for certain aspects of the thematic apperception test on a group of nine-and ten-year-old children. *Personality*, 1949, **1**, 12–15.

Whiting, J. W. M. Sorcery, sin, and the superego. A cross-cultural study of some mechanisms of social control. In M. R. Jones (Ed.), *Nebraska symposium on motivation.* Lincoln: University of Nebraska Press, 1959. Pp. 174–195.

Whiting, J. W. M. Resource mediation and learning by identification. In I. Iscoe and H. W. Stevenson (Eds.), *Personalty development in children.* Austin: University of Texas Press, 1960. Pp. 112–126.

Whiting, J. W. M., and Child, I. L. *Child training and personality.* New Haven, Conn.: Yale University Press, 1953.

Whiting, J. W. M., and Whiting, B. Personal communication on a current research project, 1962. Reported in R. Oetzel, Annoted Bibliography, In E. E. Maccoby (Ed.), *The development of sex differences.* Stanford, Cal.: Stanford University Press, 1966. P. 316.

Wiggins, J. S. Strategic, method, and stylistic variance in the MMPI. *Psychol. Bull.*, 1962, **59**, 224–242.

Wishner, J. Reanalysis of "impressions of personality." *Psychol. Rev.*, 1960, **67**, 96–112.

Wyatt, D. F., and Campbell, D. T. On the liability of stereotype or hypothesis. *J. abnorm. soc. Psychol.*, 1951, **46**, 496–500.

Wyer, R. S., Weatherley, D. A., and Terrell, G. Social role, aggression, and academic achievement. *J. pers. soc. Psychol.*, 1965, **1**, 645–649.

21. Attachment and Dependency

ELEANOR E. MACCOBY AND JOHN C. MASTERS[1]

The behavior which has been labeled attachment or dependency is a conspicuous feature of early childhood. Young children seek physical contact with or at least seek to be near certain other people. Their attachment tends to be directed toward specific individuals, not to all social objects that are available. Children resist separation from these individuals and behave in such a way as to get their attention and approval.

These behaviors may be observed nearly universally in young children, and sometimes they are remarkably intense. The fact that the behavior occurs is not in doubt. The extensive literature on the subject has sought to deal with the following issues: What is the developmental progression in the nature of the behavior, the conditions under which it occurs, and the identity of the individuals toward whom it is directed? What is the origin of the behavior? Are there consistent individual differences in the frequency or intensity of the behavior and, if so, what factors underlie such differences? Is there any relationship to be found between attachment behavior in the human child and similar behavior in other mammalian species? What generalizations can be made concerning the motivating or eliciting conditions?

In this chapter these issues are discussed in the light of available evidence. After a brief discussion of terminology, we present the major theoretical formulations concerning the origins of attachment and dependency. Later in the chapter, as research findings are reviewed under topical headings, the relevance of the findings to the theories will be discussed. The review will be concerned primarily with attachment and dependency behavior as they occur in childhood and relatively little with analogous behavior in adulthood.

DEFINITIONS AND TERMINOLOGY

Hartup (1963) has said: "Whenever the individual gives evidence that people, as people, are satisfying and rewarding, it may be said that the individual is behaving dependently." In using this definition, Hartup is consistent with the dominant usage in American writings, where the emphasis is placed upon the child's seeking the nearness, attention, and approval of adults for their own sake rather than as a means for satisfying other needs. Some writers have explicitly distinguished between "instrumental" and "emotional" or "affectional" dependency (Heathers, 1955; Kagan and Moss, 1962), and Sears et al. (1967) note that the two categories of dependency have different developmental histories. The large majority of American research and theoretical writing has attempted to deal with "emotional" rather than "instrumental" dependency, although in research operations, the two are often difficult to distinguish.

Many research workers agree in including

[1] The authors wish to thank the following people for reviewing and commenting on portions of this manuscript in early draft: Justin Aronfreed, John Bowlby, Robert Cairns, Jacob Gewirtz, Hilde Himmelweit, Michael Maccoby, Lois Murphy, and Robert Sears.

the following as part of the cluster of behaviors to be considered "dependent":

> Seeking physical contact
> Seeking to be near
> Seeking attention
> Seeking praise and approval
> Resisting separation

Researchers have differed in whether they include "seeking help" or "asking questions" in the list. The difficulty of interpreting the motivational base of these items of behavior will be discussed later; for the present, it is sufficient to note that some researchers have attempted to include as "dependent" only those instances of help-seeking and question-asking in which the child did not appear to need the information or help per se but was using bids for information or help as a means of getting and keeping contact with an adult.

Bandura and Walters (1963) abandon the attempt to distinguish between instrumental and emotional dependency, defining dependency simply as "a class of responses that are capable of eliciting positive attending and ministering responses from others."

There are a number of other terms which have been employed to distinguish between different classes of dependent behavior. These include "passive" versus "active" dependency (see Kagan and Moss, 1962; Gewirtz, 1966); "oral" dependency (a term originating in psychoanalytic theory); and "secure" versus "insecure" or "anxious" attachment (Ainsworth, 1963).

Bowlby prefers the term "attachment." He uses this term to refer to behavior that maintains proximity to another individual or restores that proximity when it has been impaired. For Bowlby there is a further requirement for behavior that is to be called attachment: it must have one or more specific objects, and behavior toward these objects must be different from behavior toward other individuals in the same setting. A number of recent writers have adopted Bowlby's terminology (Walters and Parke, 1964b, 1965; Schaffer and Emerson, 1964a; Ainsworth, 1963). Bowlby criticizes the term "dependency" as follows:

"To be dependent on a mother-figure and to be attached to her are very different things. Thus in the early weeks of life an infant is undoubtedly dependent on his mother's ministrations, but he is not yet attached to her.[2]"

Bowlby holds that the term "dependency" refers to the extent to which one individual relies on another for his physical needs. He thus uses the term to refer to a state of helplessness and not to any activity on the part of the dependent organism that might be designed to obtain or maintain contact or help. However, it is evident from the list of behaviors previously given, which are usually measured as indicators of dependency by researchers in the social-learning tradition, that the term dependency has come to have a technical meaning different from the one Bowlby attributes to it. In most respects it includes the same classes of behavior that Bowlby would call attachment. The primary difference appears to be that a child may be referred to as having a given degree of dependency, without reference to the identity of the target figure toward whom the behavior is directed. In some research "dependency toward adults" has been distinguished from "dependency toward children," but the term does not usually imply the requirement that a child's dependency shall be directed toward one or more specific attachment figures, whereas Bowlby's use of "attachment" does carry this implication. It might be noted that Freud's term "object cathexis" is thus closer to the term "attachment" than to the term "dependency."

Bowlby has a further objection to the use of the term "dependency": he believes that it has negative connotations, carrying the implication that the behavior referred to is undesirable and must be subject to socialization pressure for its change or elimination. As will be seen, he views attachment behavior as natural, inevitable, and functional and holds that its continuance in some form into adult life does not imply any sort of pathology, regression, or fixation. Therefore he would like to rid the literature of the surplus meanings which he believes the term dependency entails.

In the present review, the terms depen-

[2] From Volume I of *Attachment and Loss* (forthcoming). At the time of this writing, the book is nearing completion. The writers are grateful to Dr. Bowlby for the opportunity to read portions of manuscript in draft.

dency and attachment are both used to refer to a class of behavior of the child, not to his state of helplessness. They refer to the behavior that maintains contact of varying degrees of closeness between a child and one or more other individuals and elicits reciprocal attentive and nurturant behavior from these individuals. The behavior may or may not occur instrumentally in the service of another drive or motive. In discussing the work of an author, his own choice of terminology will be followed whenever clarity permits. The matter of the specificity of attachment or dependency targets will be left open as a topic for debate between different theoretical viewpoints and for empirical study.

The term "dependency anxiety" will be used to refer to anxiety responses which are attached to either (1) external cues which elicit incipient or overt dependency behavior, or (2) dependency responses themselves. The term will *not* be used to mean anxiety states for whose reduction dependent behavior has become an instrumental response.

THEORIES

Ethological Theory

The most complete statement of ethological instinct theory as it applies to the development of attachment in human children is made by John Bowlby in his book *Attachment and Loss*. Earlier, partial statements of the theory appeared in two articles by Bowlby (1958, 1960) and the theory has been influential in the work of Ainsworth (1963) and Schaffer (Schaffer and Emerson, 1964; Schaffer, 1963).

The theory draws upon the theory and findings of modern ethology (e.g., Hinde, 1966) and also upon control systems theory. It rejects the antithesis "innate" versus "acquired." Using as an example imprinting in birds, Bowlby points out that although the fact of becoming attached to some object (following it and not others) is "environmentally stable" in certain species of birds—i.e. it is found in all members of the species not reared in isolation and is relatively little influenced by variations in environment—the identity of the object followed is "environmentally labile," depending upon which moving object the newly hatched chick happens to be exposed to first. Similarly, while nest-building behavior, taken

as a large behavioral unit or "system" is instinctive, the bird's behavior at any particular moment will be determined by how nearly completed the nest is, how far away the materials for the nest are to be found, and other inputs from the environment. When Bowlby says that attachment behavior is instinctive, he means that it is environmentally stable within the environment of adaptation in which it evolved. With the human being, there is no requirement that behavior be adapted to man's current environment. Bowlby assumes that human attachment behavior evolved during the long period of man's history when he lived in small nomadic groups, engaged in hunting and gathering. He assumes further that there is a continuity between attachment behavior in man and in other mammals, particularly in the primates, so that observation of these species will provide information relevant to our understanding of the human mother-child pair.

Instinctive behavior can involve control systems of varying degrees of complexity. It can involve fixed action patterns, which are reflexlike and sterotyped. Such action patterns may not properly be called goal-directed, even though they have a function in the survival of the species. Social display in fish and egg-retrieving in the goose are examples of such simple systems. Some instinctive behavior, however, is governed by a control system which makes use of feedback; this may be a simple on-off system in which a piece of behavior is set in motion when a given deviation from a set-goal occurs, and continues until the deviation disappears (e.g., the furnace under the control of the thermostat); or it may be more sophisticated, so that the intensity of the response is a function of the amount of discrepancy from the set-goal, or so that the response is geared to movement (changes) in the set-goal, as in the case of the pursuit movements of a predatory bird whose prey is in flight, or the tracking of an aircraft by an anti-aircraft gun. Such control systems may be properly called goal-directed or, perhaps better, goal-*corrected*: they make use of feedback concerning the location of the goal-object and behavior changes on the basis of this feedback. Applying concepts of this kind to attachment behavior, Bowlby holds that there is a developmental progression from fixed action patterns in early infancy to more sophisticated goal-corrected systems in later infancy and early childhood. Much, though not all, attachment behavior is thought to be mediated by homeostatic control systems, tending to keep the organism within a particular range of relations to a goal-object.

Drawing on experimental and observational work with animals, Bowlby describes attachment behavior (and the reciprocal maternal behavior) as follows: both mother and infant behave so that they maintain proximity to one another. The attachment is specific, in that infant and mother recognize one another and show reciprocal attachment and caretaking behavior almost exclusively toward one another. Among primates, the newborn is constantly in contact with its mother's body. In the less advanced primates, this proximity is achieved primarily by the infant's clinging (with its hands to the mother's fur, with its mouth to a nipple). Chimpanzee and gorilla infants are too immature at birth to cling effectively, and the mother must support them, but the balance soon shifts to the infant's doing most of the work in maintaining contact. As the infant grows older, it begins to spend more time away from the mother, at first only a few feet away, moving in a circle of ever-increasing radius. At any alarm the infant moves to rejoin the mother and she moves to retrieve him. The infant also runs to her if she begins to move away, or if she signals that she is about to do so. The intensity and frequency of attachment behavior gradually wanes, till the young animal spends most of its time with age-mates; for some species of primates, however, some degree of attachment to the mother continues into adulthood. There is some evidence that attachment behavior lasts longer in females than in males, and in some primates there are social groupings made up of a grandmother, her daughters, and the daughters' female offspring.

Bowlby sees attachment behavior as having the function of protecting the young from predators. He argues that only organisms equipped with a behavior system to perform this function could survive. However, the function of a behavior is not the same thing as its goal. The set-goal of attachment behavior is a given degree of proximity to a specific other individual. Two conditions will activate this behavior: separation and threat. The behavior is terminated by sound, sight,

and/or touch of the mother. The intensity of activation can vary, and the terminating conditions vary according to the intensity of the activation. When the attachment system is intensely active, nothing but physical contact with the mother will serve to terminate the behavior. With lesser degree of activation, distance-contact with the mother (seeing her, hearing her) may serve, or proximity to a surrogate figure may constitute a terminating condition. The degree of separation that will be tolerated before the system is activated increases with age; one reason for this is the increasing strength of competing systems, especially curiosity (exploration). The fact that attachment behavior depends upon the recognition of a particular mother means that perceptual factors loom large in eliciting it. The infant must attend to the mother's appearance, smell, or any other cues that will permit him to distinguish her from other animals. Perceptual factors are also important in determining what will be reacted to as "threat." The infant tends to be alarmed by strange situations, but perceptual experience is required before anything is "familiar," and before the "familiar" can be discriminated from the "strange."

The behavior of a mother-infant pair at any moment will depend on fluctuations in the eliciting conditions for (1) attachment behavior in the child; (2) child behavior antithetical to attachment behavior, (3) caretaking behavior in the mother, and (4) antithetical behavior in the mother.

The attachment behavior of the infant has two components: the items in the infant's behavior repertoire that serve a *signal* function (crying, smiling, babbling, and later calling) and those that serve an *executive* function (clinging, and later approach and following). The signaling aspects of the infant's attachment behavior serve as elicitors of the mother's caretaking; certain aspects of the mother (her face, her voice) serve as elicitors of the child's attachment behavior. Although Bowlby fully agrees that perceptual experience plays a large part in establishing particular stimuli as elicitors of the mother's and infant's reciprocal behavior, he holds that all stimuli are not initially equipotential for playing this role. With respect to the infant, Bowlby says:

"When he is born, an infant is far from being a *tabula rasa*. On the contrary, not only is he equipped with a number of behavioral systems ready to be activated, but each system is already biased so that it is activated by stimuli falling within one (or more) broad ranges, is terminated by stimuli falling within other broad ranges, and is strengthened or weakened by stimuli of yet other kinds. . . . Some of the motor patterns themselves are organized on lines little more elaborate than those of a fixed action pattern, whilst the stimuli that activate and terminate them are discriminated in only the roughest and readiest of ways. Even so, some discrimination is present from the start; and also from the start there is a marked bias to respond in special ways to several kinds of stimuli that commonly emanate from a human being—the auditory stimuli arising from a human voice, the visual stimuli arising from a human face, and the tactile and kinaesthetic stimuli arising from human arms and body (Chap. 11, p. 1)."

The influence of ethology is clear in this formulation. The term "elicitors" is used here analogously to the term "releasers" in ethology. Bowlby cites the work of Hetzer and Tudor-Hart (1927), who found that the newborn infant reacts differently to soft sounds than to loud ones and by the third week responds quite specifically to the human voice with sucking and gurgling and "expressions suggestive of pleasure." Bowlby points out that noises arising from the preparation of a feeding bottle did *not* come to produce these reactions during the same 3-week period, so that although perceptual experience undoubtedly sharpened the infant's discrimination of a voice from other sounds, there was an innate bias in favor of the infant's attachment behavior becoming aroused by this stimulus and not others that were also available and also associated with feeding.

Bowlby explicitly eschews the concept of *drive*, or attachment *motive*, in his formulation. The attachment behavior system is *activated* by certain eliciting stimuli, the activity of the system is terminated by other stimuli, not by "drive reduction." An infant does not have a "need" for a certain quantum of "mothering." Nevertheless, he may be counted on to behave so as to elicit mothering behavior from his caretaker, and efforts to discourage him from this behavior usually will not succeed. Bowlby holds that the punishment of attachment behavior only intensifies it, for such punishment is a threat, and threat is a natural elicitor of an infant's attachment behavior. It may be noted that in using the concept "threat" or "fear-producing stimulus," Bowlby appears to have allowed a drive construct to enter his system by the back door, since such a class of stimuli is defined by the emotional state aroused in the organism.

What brings about the decline in the intensity and frequency of attachment behavior after age 3? Bowlby refers to observations of nonhuman primates, noting that while in some species the mother actively discourages her growing infant from clinging to her or riding on her back, among chimpanzees and gorillas this has not been observed. The "dependency weaning" seems to occur at the initiative of the young animal rather than that of the mother. He therefore does not think that negative socialization pressures emanating from parents play a very significant role in the decline of attachment behavior; at least, the behavior will wane without such pressure. With reference to other instinctive behavior, Bowlby notes that such behavior (nesting, mating) will occur only if *two* conditions are fulfilled: the relevant eliciting stimuli are present, and the animal is in an appropriate hormonal state. With reference to attachment behavior, he does not discuss the possibility of any internal "state" whose waning could bring about the decline of attachment behavior in the young child. Studies of hormonal factors in maternal behavior may offer some bases for explaining the decline in material care taking behavior in these terms. Furthermore, there appear to be specific elicitors for maternal behavior which disappear as the infant matures. Jay (1963) and DeVore (1963) suggest that in baboons and langurs maternal behavior is elicited by the sight of an infant which is quite dark in color, as the newborn infants of these species are. The infant changes color at a certain point in its growth cycle, after which maternal behavior declines sharply. Perhaps, with humans, the child's outgrowing his "babyish" appearance has the same effect.

From the standpoint of the activation of the child's attachment behavior, Bowlby does say, as noted previously, that the increase in exploratory behavior operates to counteract attachment behavior and hence could be partly responsible for the age-related decline. Something Bowlby does not say, which would be a reasonable deduction from his theory, is that the decline is also partly due to a decline in the frequency of occurrence of the eliciting conditions. With increasing experience, fewer situations that the young organism encounters are strange and hence feared, so that the occasions on which flight-to-mother occurs should become infrequent.

In human children, there occurs not only a decline in the total frequency and strength of attachment behavior but an increase in the number of attachment figures. This fact appears to pose something of a problem for instinct theory. In other instinctive behavior, as Bowlby documents, the tendency is for the behavior to be elicited initially by a fairly wide range of stimuli, and for the range to narrow with experience. Why is the reverse true with attachment, if it is truly an instance of an instinctive system? A related question is: why do we often see a shift in attachment figures, during childhood, from the mother to the father or to some other nonmaternal figure?

Another issue concerns the consequence to the individual when attachment behavior has no opportunity to occur, as for example when the infant is reared in isolation. In Bowlby's system, the infant would not be described as frustrated; that is, he would not be thought of as having an unsatisfied "need" for contact with an attachment figure. However, maternal deprivation would have the important consequence that the normal means of quieting fear in strange situations would not be available; hence exploration and other normal activities would be interfered with through abnormal intensity and perseveration of fear responses.

There remains an interesting question in relation to ethological theory: What kind or degree of attenuation of the "natural" mother-child attachment relationship is possible without disturbance? Bowlby sees the "natural" human situation as one in which the infant is in fairly constant contact with its mother's body (or that of a constant surrogate) for an extended period during infancy, and then is within sight and sound of her constantly for another extended period. In modern Western societies, the infant sleeps apart from the mother, is carried relatively infrequently, and

is quite often out of sight and hearing of his mother. The degree of attenuation varies, indeed, up to the communal child-rearing situations in the Russian residential nursery where the child cannot be said to have continued access to a single, fixed attachment figure at all. If children can be shown to develop normally in these situations, then the "instinctive" attachment system Bowlby describes must be one that is easily replaced, whose functions may be easily fulfilled in other ways.

Instinct theory attempts to explain species-wide developmental sequences. It is not primarily a theory of what underlies individual differences. Bowlby refers to Ainsworth and to Schaffer and Emerson in documenting the existence of striking differences among infants in the degree to which attachment behavior occurs; indeed, there appear to be some human infants who do not display the behavior at all during the first year of life. In seeking an explanation for this fact, Bowlby has emphasized the importance of the mother's responsiveness to the infant in maintaining his attachment behavior. The infant is equipped with easily elicited bits of behavior (smiling, vocalizing) which under normal circumstances will get a maternal response; if they do so, they will be strengthened, but if there is no maternal response, the infant's attachment behavior will become progressively weaker. The fact that attachment behavior is thus dependent upon environmental support does not in any way weaken the case for its being instinctive, Bowlby holds. There is a considerable body of evidence on the instinctive behavior of lower animals, showing that such behavior will die out when there has been no opportunity to exercise it, even though it was initially present and unlearned. However, in the case of attachment behavior, the behavior is *not* initially present; it appears and grows stronger as the infant develops. If Bowlby attributes individual variations in the rate of this development to differences in the amount and kind of environmental support, his theory, at least with respect to this particular issue, becomes scarcely distinguishable from social learning theory.

Psychoanalytic Theory

The Freudian theory of attachment may also be regarded as an instinct theory, in that it postulates biological predispositions in the infant not only to satisfy basic needs, but also to relate to the human objects in its environment. These two types of instinct are seen as interrelated not only in early infancy but throughout the developmental cycle as postulated in the theory of psychosexual stages.

In early Freudian theory, there were two classes of instincts: the self-preservation or ego instincts (including breathing, hunger, and thirst) and the sexual instincts. The activities of infants and children that are interpreted as sexual are quite varied, and in the course of normal development these are thought to be replaced by, or transformed into, new activities which are thought to satisfy the same aim and stem from the same source. Attachment was seen as pertaining primarily to the sexual rather than the self-preservative instincts.

The existence of an attachment is termed an object choice. The object is "cathected with libidinal energies"—that is, the chosen object becomes an object of the instinct, and the attainment or manipulation of such objects is the instinctual aim. The object itself may be another person (or, occasionally, an animal or inanimate object), or the individual may take *himself* as an object. At a later point, Freud introduced the concept of narcissism and viewed self-attachment as a universal primary stage:

Originally, at the very beginning of mental life, the ego's instincts are directed to itself and it is to some extent capable of deriving satisfaction for them on itself. This condition is known as narcissism and this potentiality for satisfaction is termed auto-erotic. The outside world is at this time, generally speaking, not cathected with any interest and is indifferent for purposes of satisfaction (S. Freud, 1959, Vol. IV, pp. 77–78).

The first external object choice, termed "anaclitic" (or, translated more literally, "leaning-up-against-type"), emerges initially from both the ego and sexual instincts:

The sexual instincts are at the outset supported upon the ego-instincts; only later do they become independent of these, and even then we have an indication of that original dependency in the fact that those persons who have to do with the feeding, care, and pro-

tection of the child become his earliest sexual objects: that is to say, in the first instance the mother or her substitute (S. Freud, 1959, Vol. IV, pp. 44–45).

The anaclitic object choice is the first example of a real attachment or love the child may have for something outside his own body, and Freud uses the oral analogy of "incorporation" in describing it:

When the object becomes a source of pleasurable feelings, a motor tendency is set up which strives to bring the object near to and incorporate it into the ego. We then speak of the "attraction" exercised by the pleasure-giving object, and say that we "love" that object (S. Freud, 1959, Vol. IV, p. 79).

Erikson is even more explicit about the oral character of the infant's early attachment:

As the newborn infant is separated from his symbiosis with the mother's body, his inborn and more or less coordinated ability to take in by mouth meets the mother's more or less coordinated ability and intention to feed him and to welcome him. At this point he lives through, and loves with, his mouth . . . (Erikson, 1954, pp. 56–57).

Psychoanalytic theory assumes a relationship between the nature of infantile attachments and the level of perceptual organization of which the infant is capable. In the beginning, the infant's perception is thought to be of a global, diffuse nature, and at this time there are no images of objects. Gradually, through experience with pleasure and pain, the self and the external world come to be differentiated. Fenichel says:

The idea of mother is certainly not present at the beginning. Though it is very difficult to describe, we must assume that the first ideas concerning things which may bring satisfaction but which are momentarily absent include simultaneously the mother's breasts (or the bottle), the person of the mother, and parts of the child's own body (Fenichel, 1945, p. 87).

Toward the last third of the first year, the infant begins to "experiment" concerning the separateness of himself and mother (see Mahler, Furer, and Settlage, 1959). It could be at this point that the mother, perceived as an external object, may become a true anaclitic object choice and no longer be merely a part of narcissistic libidinal cathexes.

The first anaclitic love object was so-called because the erotic attachment was formed with the caretaker, who was important for self-preservation. Freud's later usage of the term is less limited, however. In later childhood and adulthood, two types of object choice still prevail. In this case the anaclitic type covers all those objects which are cathected because they resemble a nurturant person in the individual's past (usually a parent, sometimes a sibling). Narcissistic object-choices resemble the person himself.

The course of the psychosexual stages, parallelled as they are by stages in the development of object choice, are of central importance in determining the character and "mental health" of the grown individual. At any particular stage of development "fixation" may occur.

Fixation at the "oral" stage would imply a continuing importance of oral activities and the associated "clinging" sort of attachment behavior, as well as a continuation of the feelings characteristic of the stage and a tendency, under stress, to resort to increased oral and dependent behaviors (regression). All stages of development are slightly fixated, but fixation varies in degree, and when it is in-

tense, it impairs the adequacy of subsequent development.

Table 1, taken from Fenichel, illustrates stages of psychosexual and object-choice development, and some of the postulated aberrations which may result from fixations. All the stages except 3 and 5 are commonly construed in terms of attachment.

Factors postulated to evoke fixations include certain caretaking activities. Fixations may be produced either by oversatisfaction or frustration of the desires characteristic of a given stage (Fenichel, 1945, pp. 65–66). It is also postulated that abrupt changes from satisfactions to frustrations may have fixating effects. It would appear, then, that the behavior of the caretaker or the experiences of the individual have a determining effect not only on the type of attachment objects chosen, but also on the nature of the attachment behavior toward those objects in later life. Fixations of varying strength in the oral stage, which thereby affect the course of later development, may be major (resulting in schizophrenia and self-absorption—see Table 1), or they may be of lesser degree, in which case relations with the object-choice would be dependent and reflect the self-preservative nature of the early interaction.

The primary outcome of fixation at the oral stage is thought to be the development of "oral character." Descriptions of this type of character usually emphasize as the central core a passive-dependent, receptive orienta-

Table 1.   Steps of psychosexual and object choice development. From Fenichel, 1945, p. 101.

Stages of Libidinal Organization	Stages in Development of Object Love	Dominant Point of Fixation in:
1. Early oral (sucking stage)	Autoeroticism (no object, pre-ambivalent)	Certain types of schizophrenia (stupor)
2. Late oral-sadistic (cannibalistic)	Narcissism: total incorporation of the object	Manic-depressive disorders (addiction, morbid impulses)
3. Early anal-sadistic stage	Partial love with incorporation	Paranoia, certain pregenital conversion neuroses
4. Late anal-sadistic stage	Partial love	Compulsion neuroses, other pregenital conversion neuroses
5. Early genital (phallic) stage	Object love, limited by the predominant castration complex	Hysteria
6. Final genital stage	Love (postambivalent)	Normality

tion toward life. Either positive or negative emphasis upon taking and receiving may be interpreted as residues of early oral experience. Some theorists link oral overindulgence in infancy to later feelings of optimism and self-assurance, whereas early oral deprivation or frustration may determine a pessimistic or even sadistic attitude. Descriptions of the behavioral tendencies defining oral character lean heavily upon analogy; for example, Blum says: "Persons in whom the oral-sadistic component is marked are aggressive and biting in their relationships. They continually demand supplies in a vampire-like fashion, and affix themselves by 'suction'" (Blum, 1953, p. 160). Thurston and Mussen (1951) summarize some of the adult traits which have been alleged to be part of oral character, including needing to be ministered to, attempting to recapture the blissful state of passive dependency and assimilation, talking, singing, drinking, chewing, craving to receive, needing protection, being a "yes man." Oral traits thought to be specifically the outcomes of negative fixation include pessimism, depressive tendencies, being aggressively demanding, being constantly dissatisfied, frequently feeling cheated. One consequence of the infantile feeding situation is the association of food or feeding with love. It is this association which presumably leads some persons suffering from oral fixation to eat in self-prescribed therapy when they feel depressed (unloved), and hence an association is expected between obesity and either dependency or conflict over dependency.

Much of the research growing out of psychoanalytic theory has involved efforts to operationalize "oral indulgence" and "oral frustration" in infancy, and to measure not only specifically oral behaviors in childhood and adulthood, but the precipitates and transformations of oral fixation in the other aspects of "oral character" described above. Whiting and Child (1953) have extended the theory to the prediction of culture-wide belief systems, which are seen as "projective" systems, having their motivational origins in early childhood experiences.

Erikson reinterprets the psychosexual stages in terms of the social interactions that characterize them. His discussions of the oral or incorporative mode of interaction, characterized by the feeding situation, presents a synthesis of narcissistic and anaclitic development. Erikson postulates that the loving interaction between mother and child creates within the child a sense of "basic trust." The concept of basic trust includes not only "that one has learned to rely upon the sameness and continuity of the outer providers" (p. 61) but also an element of mastery—"that one may trust oneself and the capacity of one's own organs to cope with urges; that one is able to consider oneself trustworthy enough so that the providers will not need to be on guard or to leave" (p. 61).

Fromm, like Erikson, de-emphasizes the sexual component in the child's ties to its mother. Rather, the childhood tie and its adult transformations are seen as growing out of the child's need to be fed and cared for, and he sees the child and adult as being in conflict between the wish to continue the pleasures and safety of dependency and the equally powerful desire for independence and freedom. Fromm says:

This pre-Oedipal attachment of boys and girls to their mother which is qualitatively different from Oedipal attachment of boys to their mother, is in my experience by far the more important phenomenon, in comparison with which the genital incestuous desires of the little boy are quite secondary. I find that the boy's or girl's pre-Oedipus attachment to mother is one of the central phenomena in the evolutionary process and one of the main causes of neurosis and psychosis. Rather than call it a manifestation of the libido, I would prefer to describe its quality which, whether we use the term libido or not, is something entirely different from the boy's genital desires. This "incestuous" striving, in the pregenital sense, is one of the most fundamental passions in men or women, comprising the human being's desire for protection, the satisfaction of his narcissism; his craving to be freed from the risks of responsibility, of freedom, of awareness; his longing for unconditional love, which is offered without any expectation of his loving response. It is true these needs exist normally in the infant, and the mother is the person who fulfills them. The infant could not live if this were not so; it is helpless, cannot depend on its own resources, needs love and care which do not depend on any merits of its own. . . .

But the more obvious fact—that the infant needs a mothering person—has obscured the fact that not only the infant is helpless and craves certainty; the adult is in many ways not less helpless. Indeed, he can work and fulfill the tasks ascribed to him by society; but he is also more aware than the infant of the dangers and risks of life; he knows of the natural and social forces he cannot control, the accidents he cannot foresee, the sickness and death he cannot elude. What could be more natural, under the circumstances, than man's frantic longing for a power which gives him certainty, protection and love? This desire is not only a "repetition" of his longing for mother; it is generated because the very same conditions which make the infant long for mother's love continue to exist, although on a different level (Fromm, 1964, pp. 97–98).

Like other psychoanalytic writers, Fromm looks upon the infant's tie to his mother as a primary basis for the development of healthy, mature attachments (to spouse and children) in adult life. But unlike these others, he emphasizes the view that the continuance of symbiotic dependency into adulthood is a destructive force, antagonistic to the development of autonomy and the ability to give love.

Henry Murray (1938), in developing his "personalogy," has been concerned primarily with the later ramifications of early experience, not so much in the global adjustment sense (as were the major psychoanalytic theorists) but rather along the lines of more subtle individual differences. Murray's concern is less with the infant or parent-child interaction than with the description of adult personality. The remnants of the child's attachment experience in the adult's need configurations will be found in his needs for succorance, for affiliation, and in the interaction or fusing of these needs. Murray (1938) defines these needs as follows:

n Affiliation. Under this heading are classed all manifestations of friendliness and good will, of the desire to do things in company with others.

n Succorance. This describes the need for or dependence upon a nurturing object that must be always at hand or within call in case the S wants anything: food, protection, assistance, care, sympathy, undivided devotion (p. 325).

And these two needs may fuse, creating what Murray terms:

Dependency. n Affiliation fused with *n* Succorance: here we would include instances of enduring love and friendship for stronger sympathizing or protecting objects, usually both parents . . . (p. 320). . . . The manifestations of anaclitic love (childish dependence on an adult) are classed here. Affectionate adherence, seeking protection, cuddling, and homesickness are among the common signs (p. 325).

Other needs that may fuse with affiliation are *n* Deference and *n* Nurturance, which result in respect and kindness, respectively, toward others.

Harry Stack Sullivan (1953) has presented an interpersonal theory of personality development in which he describes the growth of the personality in terms of the kinds of attachment figures that are most important at successive stages of development. Sullivan postulates a constellation of needs in the infant, which may be called the need for "tenderness." Under this rubric are included all the physical needs of the infant that have to do with the "necessary communal existence of the infant and the physio-chemical universe" (Sullivan, 1953, p. 40). There is also a complementary need in the mothering individual to respond appropriately to the evocative behavior of the infant. Sullivan does not specify whether the interaction between infant and caretaker is due entirely to the infant's helplessness, or whether there is social interaction engendered by something other than physical necessity (cf. Bowlby's concept of attachment). Infancy, as a period of development, is superseded by childhood, which Sullivan defines as the age that extends "from the appearance of the ability to utter articulate sounds of or pertaining to speech, to the appearance of the need for playmates—that is, companions, cooperative beings of approximately one's own status in all sorts of respects" (p. 33). Succeeding stages are marked by the need for an intimate relation with an individual of one's own sex, then by the shift to an attachment object of the opposite sex. There is a parallel between this formulation and the description by Harlow (1966) of the successive development of several "affectional systems."

An important outgrowth of psychoanalytic theory is the position presented by Bowlby (1952) in his monograph on maternal deprivation. It should be noted that Bolwby's writing on this subject preceded his theoretical statements concerning the ethological foundations of attachment summarized earlier in this chapter. Bowlby's 1952 statement differs from that of Freud and a number of his followers in that it places less emphasis on the problems of object choice and fixation, and more on the *function* of attachment for the development of ego and superego. Bowlby says:

It is evident that both ego and super-ego are absolutely dependent for their functioning on our ability to maintain the abstract attitude, and it is not surprising that during infancy and early childhood these functions are either not operating at all or are doing so most imperfectly. During this phase of life, the child is therefore dependent on his mother performing them for him. She orients him in space and time, provides his environment, permits the satisfaction of some impulses, restricts others. She is his ego and his super-ego. Gradually he learns these arts himself and, as he does so, the skilled parent transfers the roles to him. . . . If mental development is to proceed smoothly, it would appear to be necessary for the undifferentiated psyche to be exposed during certain critical periods to the influence of the psychic organizer—the mother" (Bowlby, 1952, p. 53).

In Bowlby's view, the early social relationship between the mother and child must be both continuing and satisfactory for the child's intrapsychic structures to develop adequately. This is true, he believes, partly because the child's motivation to take over the controlling and planning functions depend upon a positive relationship with those who are attempting to teach him to do this:

An individual cannot learn a skill unless he has a friendly feeling towards his teacher, and is ready to identify himself with her and to

incorporate her (or some part of her) into himself. Now this positive attitude towards his mother is either lacking in the deprived child or, if present, is mixed with keen resentment. How early in a child's life deprivation causes a specifically hostile attitude is debatable, but it is certainly evident for all to see in the second year.

Bowlby describes a series of stages in the nature of attachment and the functions served by it, and he indicates that the effects of separation or deprivation should depend upon the stage at which the child has arrived at the time these conditions prevail. He does argue for the great importance of the first two years of life. Bowlby's statement has been influential in the subsequent research and writing on maternal deprivation and separation, where an emphasis may be seen on impairments of ego development or regression in ego functioning, as well as upon disturbances in object relationships.

Social Learning Theory

Social learning theories of dependency and attachments have been formulated by Sears (Sears et al., 1953, 1957, 1965; Sears 1963), Whiting (1944), Dollard and Miller (1950), Bandura and Walters (1963), Gewirtz (1961), and Bijou and Baer (1965). A review of several theories and a statement of two operant conditioning positions are offered by Gavalas and Briggs (1966). The formulations of the preceding theorists are by no means identical, but they have certain elements in common. The common elements will be discussed first; a discussion of the variants follows.

In social learning theory, the child's attachment to the mother (or other caretaker) is held to be based upon her nurturance of him —on the fact that she satisfies his needs. Sears states this basic proposition as follows:

Dependency appears to result from the pervasive presence of others' performances of this nurturant role. From birth the child is fed, warmed, dried, snuggled, has his thirst quenched, and his pains and discomforts reduced, by others. In American society, this "other" is usually the mother. As a consequence, the child early learns to manipulate his mother, to secure her help whenever his primary drives require some change in his environment in order that they may be reduced (Sears et al., 1953, p. 178).

In the terminology of Bijou and Baer (derived from Skinner),

The mother herself will, as a stimulus object, become discriminated as a "time" and a "place" for either the addition of positive reinforcers to the baby's environment or the subtraction of negative reinforcers from it. Thus she is discriminative, as a stimulus, for the two reinforcement procedures which strengthen operant behavior. Thereby, she acquires positive reinforcing function, and lays the foundation for the further social development of her infant (Bijou and Baer, 1965, p. 123).

These writers list the ways in which a mother initially (without learning) provides positive reinforcement. They include giving food and water, regulating temperature, providing tactile stimulation, sometimes assisting breathing, and providing stimulus change. These and other writers have used the terms "secondary reinforcers," "conditioned reinforcers," or "acquired reinforcers" for maternal stimuli (sight, sound, etc., of mother) which have acquired reinforcing power through their contiguity with primary reinforcement.

It should be noted that the particular social stimuli which become reinforcing for the child will vary from family to family, depending upon the nature of the mother's responses. This point has been emphasized by Gewirtz (1961). If a mother characteristically does not smile much, but holds and pats the infant frequently, body-contact stimuli will come to be the ones this particular infant seeks, and he will not be particularly responsive to "distance cues" of maternal affection and approval; with a mother who responds in a more distant manner—who looks at the child or smiles at him when he vocalizes or smiles, but does not usually touch him—the child will seek, and be responsive to, the more distant aspects of maternal warmth. He will like to be near his mother, but he will not try to climb onto her lap as frequently as the child

whose mother has done more kissing and cuddling with her ministrations.

Any behavior of the child that is consistently followed by either primary or conditioned reinforcers will be strengthened; that is, the probability of its occurrence in the presence of the discriminative stimuli will be increased. The reader will note that in Skinnerian learning theory this statement does not add anything to the theory, beyond what was already implied in the definition of primary and secondary reinforcers, for these reinforcers are defined as any stimuli which, occurring just after a response, strengthen that response. The point of interest is that dependent or affiliative responses are more likely to be reinforced, and hence strengthened, than are other classes of responses. If the infant kicks his foot, this does not ordinarily bring about the occurrence of a reinforcer. If the infant cries, however, or clutches at his mother, he is likely to get either a primary reinforcement (such as tactual stimulation, feeding, and substantial stimulus change), or the conditioned reinforcement of his mother's looking at him and coming closer.

The strength of the child's dependency responses will depend first upon the frequency with which they have been reinforced. But the scheduling as well as the frequency of reinforcement is important in controlling behavior. It has been shown that both the rate at which a response is emitted and its resistance to extinction are a function of the proportion of responses that are reinforced, and whether reinforcement is time-bound or response-bound (e.g., whether reinforcement comes for the first response after the lapse of a given period of time, or for every N response). Perhaps the best known fact concerning scheduling is that response-correlated intermittent schedules yield responses that are both more frequent and more resistant to extinction than responses under 100% reinforcement. Applying this principal of learning to the acquisition of dependent responses, it would follow that the child who must call or cry several times before his mother responds to him ought to develop a stronger calling or crying response than a child whose mother responds to the first signal.

Social learning theory's emphasis on the importance of the contingency between the child's response and some form of reinforcement constitutes an important difference between this theory and instinct theory. Gewirtz underlines this point:

Our analysis focuses on whether the particular stimuli available to the infant are functional, and with his behaviors enter into effective contingencies for learning. . . . Most parents, like most theorists in this area, seem to emphasize the importance alone of the simple fact of giving a commodity, like food or love (assumed to be indispensible for every child) and do not emphasize . . . how, as potential discriminative and reinforcing stimuli, these events could relate to the child's behaviors (Gewirtz, 1961, pp. 227; 229).

Do social learning theorists consider any particular aspect of maternal ministrations to the infant as being of special importance in the development of the infant's dependency? In the selection from Sears et al. quoted above, a list of things the mother can do to provide primary (unlearned) reinforcement is given, and any of these is presumably an adequate basis for the establishment of conditioned reinforcers. Gewirtz, and Bijou and Baer, give similar lists of primary reinforcers and do not distinguish among them in terms of saliency. Whiting and Child (1953), influenced by psychoanalytic theory, consider feeding to be more important than other forms of reinforcement for the establishment of dependency. Sears and his colleagues, who advance no reason derived from learning theory to suggest that feeding should have any greater role than other primary reinforcement situations, do concentrate upon the infant feeding situation in the research operations they use to uncover the origins of different degrees of dependency among young children. Here, again, the choice appears to be dictated by psychoanalytic theory.

Social learning theorists appear not to have been very clear concerning the role of physical contact-giving as a reinforcer. The ambiguity is illustrated in the following passage from Sears:

One apparent result of this mutually satisfying relationship is the creation of secondary rewards or reinforcers for both members of the pair. That is, the mother's talking, patting, smiling, her gestures of affection or concern, are constantly being presented to the baby in context with primary reinforcing stimulations, such as those involved in eating, fondling and caressing (Sears, 1963, p. 30).

Here patting is listed as a secondary reinforcer, while fondling and caressing are listed as primary. Bijou and Baer list tactual stimulation as probably primary, as does Gewirtz, although they do not give it any greater role than other primary reinforcers. J. B. Watson (1928), in his diatribe concerning the pernicious effects of fondling infants, looked upon the development of infant affection toward caretakers as an instance of classical conditioning, and he did single out contact-giving as the single important basis for the establishment of the infant's "love" for its parents:

Our laboratory studies show that we can bring out a love response in a newborn child by one stimulus—by stroking its skin. The more sensitive the skin area, the more marked the response. . . . Loves grow up in children just like fears. Loves are home made, built in. In other works, loves are conditioned. You have everything at hand all day long for setting up conditioned love responses. The touch of the skin takes the place of the steel bar, the sight of the mother's face takes the place of the rabbit in the experiments with fear. The child sees the mother's face when she pets it. Soon the mere sight of the mother's face calls out the love response. The touch of the skin is no longer necessary to call it out. A conditioned love reaction has been formed. Even if she pats the child in the dark, the sound of her voice as she croons soon comes to call out a love response (Watson, 1928, cited in Kessen, 1965, p. 241).

For operant conditioning theorists, it does not make much difference whether skin contact is a primary or secondary reinforcer. It is enough for their purposes to know that it does function as a reinforcer, and that it will strengthen whatever infant behavior it is regularly contingent upon. Gewirtz' emphasis on stimulation per se as an unlearned reinforcer presents an important recent modification of social learning theory.

A point of difference among social learning theorists has been whether they look upon dependency as a *drive*. The concept of secondary drive as well as secondary reinforcer has been widely employed.

Numerous authors have noted that the mere establishment of a secondary reinforcer need not imply a secondary drive. (For a full discussion of the drive concept as it applies to social attachments, see Walters and Parke, 1964.) That is, although an infant may come to seek the mother's attention and approval after these have become secondary reinforcers through association with primary gratification, this fact alone would not justify postulating a "drive for attention" or, more generally, a "dependency drive." The concept of drive would be redundant here, unless something more is implied beyond the fact that formerly neutral cues are now sought out.

Why have theorists attempted to describe dependency as a drive or "motive system" rather than simply as a class of behaviors having maternal stimuli as their goal? There are the common-sense reasons having to do with the fact that dependent behavior is persistent, energetic, and maintained or even increased in intensity in the presence of obstacles to goal attainment. Beyond this, there is the possibility that dependent behavior becomes to some degree autonomous from the original motivating conditions under which it was established. Many of the primary reinforcements administered by a mother have reinforcing power only when the relevant motivating conditions exist; food is not reinforcing to a child who has just been fed, nor is warmth to a child who is not cold, and previously neutral stimuli will not become secondary reinforcers through contiguity with the giving of food and warmth under these conditions. Furthermore, there is some evidence from animal experimentation that a secondary reinforcer, once established, will be effective only when the original motivating condition is present (e.g., the click of the food mechanism is not reinforcing except when the animal is hungry). If it could be shown that a child displays dependent behavior only when he is tired, hungry, cold, afraid, etc., then it would be reasonable to look upon dependency as a learned set of responses, motivated by these other drives and having social stimuli as the goal. There are two difficulties with this position, however. First, it is very difficult to test whether dependent behavior occurs independently of other motive states, since it is difficult to be sure that all of these drives are satiated at a given moment. Second, some of the "primary" reinforcers that establish social stimuli as secondary reinforcers (e.g., stroking of the skin, stimulus change) seem to be effective in the absence of any specific drive state. Here we face the familiar problem in motivation theory of whether we should postulate a drive for every class of unlearned reinforcers. If this is not done for unlearned reinforcers, there seems little reason to do so for learned reinforcers. Thus even if it could be shown that children do seek social stimulation (conditioned reinforcers) in the absence of other drives, there would be no more reason to describe this fact in terms of a dependency *drive* than to postulate a "stimulus change drive" or a "tactual stimulation drive" to account for the pursuit of these classes of unlearned reinforcers in the absence of specific drive states.

In attempting to account for the seeming autonomy of social stimuli as reinforcers, Gewirtz has made use of Skinner's concept of *generalized reinforcers*:

There exists further the possiblity of pairing regularly a cue stimulus with more than one reinforcing stimulus. . . . These events may be said to function as conditioned reinforcing stimuli because they represent occasions on which the probability is high that behaviors can be reinforced by many other reinforcing stimuli important to the organism, some of which would depend on particular deprivation conditions. Conditioned reinforcers so established would be powerful and effective under a wide range of conditions, and have been labeled *generalized* reinforcers by Skinner (1953). It is assumed that the effectiveness of such reinforcers would not be limited, for example to the circumstances under which there are present the deprivation states that control the efficacy of some of the functioning reinforcing stimuli on which their acquisition of reinforcer value is based (Gewirtz, 1961, p. 221).

The concept "generalized reinforcer" is currently under both theoretical and empirical attack (see Myers and Trapold, 1966). Even if clear evidence could be produced for the existence of such reinforcers, the important question remains as to the reason for the variations from time to time in the vigor with which such a reinforcer is sought. When the mother is present, the young child does not constantly demand her attention and does not insist on remaining in physical contact with her at all times. One reason that the "drive" concept has been attractive to people attempting to understand dependency is that the occurrence of the behavior in a given child varies from time to time, and that this variation is not entirely a function of whether the "goal object" of the dependent behavior is available. If a child sometimes eats when food is present and sometimes does not, we explain this variation in terms of changes in an internal drive state—hunger. Can the variations in dependent behavior under constant "external" conditions (i.e., mother present at a constant distance) be explained as due to variations in the intensity, or degree of arousal, of an internal motivating state?

In an early paper, Gewirtz and Baer argued that one is only justified in postulating such a drive state if one can point to a deprivation operation following which the behavior occurs and a satiation operation that reduces the probability of its occurring. If such operations can be shown to control the behavior, then the situation is analogous to that which prevails for the primary drives such as hunger, thirst, and fatigue. Gewirtz and Baer (1958) did show that dependency responses (specifically, responsiveness to social reinforcement) increased after social deprivation and decreased after "satiation" of social stimuli. Hence they felt that it *was* legitimate to infer a dependency drive or motive which was activated by social deprivation, and which motivated the learning of instrumental behavior that would increase the supply of social stimulation. This formulation led to a body of research designed to discover whether the effects of social deprivation could be best understood in terms of the arousal of a specific dependency drive, or whether instead social deprivation aroused *another* specific drive (fear or anxiety) or simply served as a generalized arouser.[3] This research and the implications of the findings will be discussed below. In his later work, Gewirtz abandoned the drive formulation and instead formulated his work in terms of the discriminative stimuli which determine whether learned dependency behavior will or will not occur in a given situation.

Sears et al. (1953) also postulate a "dependency drive," but they formulate the matter in a different way. They say that dependency is first established as a response to maternal stimuli that have become conditioned as secondary reinforcers. But dependent behavior then "acquires drive properties":

Whiting has reasoned that there must be some differential factor, beyond simple reinforcement, to account for the fact that only some, not all, instrumental acts develop the properties of goal responses, and only some, not all, persons and objects that are necessary for gratification in a behavior sequence become goal objects.

Whiting has suggested that only those actions which are followed by both reward and punishment become part of a secondary motivational system. Simple reinforcement by reward establishes a given action as a response to some particular set of instigators. Reinforcement also establishes an anticipatory goal response, or expectancy of reward. Neither the action nor the expectancy has drive strength in its own right. But if the action sometimes meets with punishment or non-reward, an additional expectancy is established, an expectancy of failure to secure the reward. The conflict between two incompatible expectancies provides the drive strength for instigating the originally reinforced action. With conflict-induced drive as the moving force, then, such groups of actions as those described in the preceding section become secondary drive systems (Sears et al., 1953, p. 180).

There is no statement here that dependent behavior would fail to occur in the absence of conflict, only that conflict "provides the drive strength" or serves as the "moving force." Perhaps what is implied is that conflict energizes the response—makes it more intense

[3] E. K. Beller (1959) argues that "a fear or anxiety mechanism" becomes an integral part of dependency, in that the "threat of losing the attention and presence of a parental figure becomes synonymous with being in danger of not getting relief from pain."

or more vigorous. A first question would be whether conflict does indeed always increase the vigor of a response. In the case of a child's approach to a partly attractive, partly threatening object, the approach is likely to be more slow and tentative than it would be in the absence of threat, rather than more vigorous. But given that some energizing function of conflict can be documented, it would seem equally plausible to look upon conflict as a generalized arouser rather than as a producer of a specific "dependency drive."

In formulating hypotheses for research, it has been difficult to distinguish the predictions based on "conflict-drive" theory from those based on the effects of various eliciting conditions. For example, Sears has argued plausibly that since maternal actions play a large role in removing many sources of frustration for the child, the state of frustration itself will become an occasion (an elicitor) for dependency responses. A state of conflict could be looked upon in the same way—as an aversive condition which the child will have learned to try to remove by securing the mother's help and attention. In his recent writing about dependency, Sears (1963) says: "If we acknowledge, as we must, that there is no critical evidence to support the drive conception, then we must ask what alternative explanations can be used to account for the phenomena." He refers to Skinnerian principles of operant conditioning as a viable alternative, but does not consider the evidence sufficient for making a definitive choice at the time of writing.

An important difference in emphasis between social learning theory and instinct theory is that instinct theory tends to describe attachment in terms of species-wide regularities in the topography of the behavior, in eliciting conditions, and in the developmental changes that occur in these during the life-history of the organism. Social learning theory, while encompassing the similarities among children that presumably arise from uniformities in their learning experiences, has focused extensively upon individual differences. Earlier we referred to the conditions that could bring about differences among children in the nature of the maternal stimuli that became particularly reinforcing for them. Similarly, different dependent responses will be strengthened in particular children, depending on which of their behaviors their parents are most responsive to. Some children will become "whiners," others "clingers," others "show-offs," and others "mother's helpers," depending on which of these behaviors have been most effective in eliciting parental attention and ministration.

The learning theorist concerns himself with explaining why one child is more upset over separation from a parent than others, or why some demand more of the teacher's attention than others, and he searches for the explanation in the history of each child's interaction with his primary caretakers, inquiring, for example, about the frequency and scheduling of maternal reinforcements, and the contingencies these entered into with the child's behavior. Although these individual differences are of some intrinsic interest, social learning theorists have used them primarily as a means of searching for general formulations about the origins of dependency.

Of special interest is the problem of punishment and its effects. In learning theory, the effect of punishment upon dependency will vary with the frequency, intensity, and form of the punishment and the amount of reward that has been contingent on the same behavior. Since some dependency responses are inevitably rewarded during necessary caretaking, punishment for dependency will produce conflict; in the conflict-drive formulation previously described, this means that punishment for dependency will strengthen the dependency "drive." Sears et al. (1953) say that while the strength of dependency will be increased with punishment, the manifestations of the drive in overt behavior may not be more pronounced, and the mode of expression may be changed. Specifically, punishment may lead to displacement of dependency behavior from mother to other objects—the object being more unlike the mother with increasingly severe punishment.

Bandura and Walters (1963) emphasize the importance of the balance between punishment and reward. In severe rejection, where there is more punishment than reward, dependency may be expected to be infrequent. With mild rejection, where reward outweighs punishment in terms of frequency, or where punishment is mild, one may even get an intensification of dependency. This last effect is especially likely, they hold, when the parent's negative responses to dependency have the form of withholding positive reinforcement rather than the presentation of aversive stimulation. Withholding positive reinforcement for behavior that is quite often reinforced produces, in effect, an intermittent schedule, which should strengthen the behavior.

If dependent behavior is punished, anxiety responses will be attached to the behavior itself (including the incipient, pre-overt elements of a dependent sequence) and to the external cues which have been associated with arousal of dependency. This anxiety can then motivate a number of behaviors, including avoidance of the punitive agent, avoidance of the stimuli that arouse dependent impulses, and acquisition of acceptable behavior which will terminate the punishment or the anxiety-arousing cues.

In recent years, social learning theorists have been emphasizing the importance of "modeling," or observational learning, in the acquisition of social behavior (see Bandura and Walters, 1963). This theme has been conspicuously missing from the theoretical writing on dependency, probably because in behaving dependently, a child is usually not matching his behavior to that of another person, but is acquiring behavior that is *reciprocal* to that of another person. It remains an open question whether any aspects of dependent behavior are normally acquired through modeling.

Learning theorists have given little attention to the changes in dependent behavior occurring in a systematic way with the age of the child. They do take note, of course, of the fact that certain forms of dependency do not occur until physiological maturation has made them possible, for example, the child does not follow his mother until he can crawl or walk. In the early Sears formulation (Sears et al., 1953) these changes in forms of the behavior are not seen to imply changes in strength of the underlying motive:

Dependency behavior is discernible by the second month. . . . It may be suggested that the child begins to develop dependency actions and drive from birth. The actions change continuously as new understanding of how to get help occurs, but the dependency drive reaches an asymptote early in infancy (p. 187).

In a later formulation Sears et al. (1957) seem to put the asymptotic level of drive strength later in the first year. The changes in kind and amount of dependency as the child grows older are seen, in learning theory, to be a function of changes in the reactions of socialization agents to them. Clinging and demanding behavior which is appropriate for very young infants is seen as "changeworthy" by adults as the child grows older. These adults now punish, or refuse to reward, behavior which was previously supported. Thus the decline in infantile forms of dependency and the shift to more mature forms are seen as an outcome of what has sometimes been called "dependency weaning," and the role played by socialization agents in this process is held to be a crucial one. This is a clear point of difference between instinct theory and social learning theory.

Concerning the extent of focusing upon a single attachment figure, the two theories also differ, although learning theorists have not dealt extensively with this point. The primary caretaker is seen as the person whose characteristics will be associated with gratification and hence sought by the child. But similar stimuli emitted by others should presumably be effective as well (as elicitors of dependent responses, as discriminative cues, and as secondary reinforcers) along a generalization gradient. Thus people similar to the primary caretaker should be the next most likely targets for attachment, dissimilar people and objects least likely. Learning theorists encounter a problem in attempting to define the similarity dimension. Will generalization of dependency occur primarily to other adults? To others of the same sex as the primary caretaker? To people who are perceptually similar (e.g., do or not wear glasses)? Experimental exploration of the dimensions has not been carried out; presumably the nature of the dimensions would change with age, as verbal mediation becomes available and the child can manage more sophisticated categorizing. But social learning theory does not predict the degree of focusing of attachment behavior on a single object (or limited number of objects) that is implied in theory based on ethology, and attachments to other children, nursery school teachers, etc., are seen as extensions of the primary attachment to the mother.

Another point of difference lies in the treatment of elicitors. Instinct theory treats fear-producing stimuli as specific elicitors. While there appears to be nothing in social learning theory which would preclude including fear as an elicitor, in fact it has not usually been included; the eliciting conditions emphasized in social learning theory are, as noted earlier: (1) frustration of all kinds, including as a subclass of frustration the "social frustration" involved in non-nurturance or withdrawal of love; and (2) social deprivation.

A modification of social learning theory has been offered by Walters and Parke (1964a, 1965). They argue that the common component in the varied behaviors that have been labeled "dependent" or "attached" is the development of attentive (orienting) responses toward other individuals. These orienting responses are learned. They are affected by changes in the general arousal level in several ways:

1. A given arousal level has cue properties, and these cues can be linked through learning to increases or decreases in orienting toward others.

2. Arousal affects perceptual behavior (by narrowing or broadening the range of information taken in).

3. Arousal intensifies behavior.

It should be noted that in this formulation "arousal" does *not* refer to a specific social motive (e.g., dependency or aggression) but to a general physiological state, whose nature is independent of the nature of the external conditions which produced the arousal.

Walters and Parke, with their emphasis on orienting toward others as the core "meaning" of dependency and attachment, follow Rheingold (1961) in stressing the importance of vision and hearing in the child's maintenance of contact with the mother, and they hold that the role of physical contact has been overstressed. Rheingold states the case as follows:

The earliest and most common response of the infant rhesus to its mother is to cling. Not so the human infant. At three months of age he is already fully responsive to people, yet he will not *cling* to them for months to

come. I suggest, therefore, that not physical, but visual contact is at the basis of human sociability (p. 169).

An interesting question in this connection is whether, in Bowlby's terms, distance perception is equally effective in terminating as in eliciting attachment behavior. In instinct theory, the sight and sound of the mother coming and going are the effective cues in eliciting smiles, cries, or following from the infant, so this theory, too, emphasizes distance receptors. In early infancy, however, it is thought to be physical contact with the mother that will terminate the sequence of attachment behavior. (Harlow takes this position as well in relation to infant monkeys.) In later infancy, the childs efforts will be terminated upon achieving a given degree of proximity to the mother—and this must presumably be judged on the basis of distance cues. Hence Bowlby's theory would appear to postulate a shift, during the early life of the child, from contact cues to distance cues as effective terminators of an attachment sequence. Neither Rheingold nor Walters and Parke distinguish between the eliciting and terminating functions of stimuli.

Cairns (1966) has offered a theory of attachment growing out of comparative work with several species of mammals, based upon a Guthrie-Estes contiguity and stimulus-sampling model, omitting reinforcement from the formulation. His position, briefly, is that any object which is constantly present in the organism's immediate environment has a certain probability of becoming a conditioned stimulus for all the behavior the organism regularly performs. Stimuli differ with respect to the probability that responses will become conditioned to them—they differ with respect to "weight," "importance," or "salience." The salience of a stimulus will be a function of the size of the stimulus subset, and also (among other attributes) of the intensity of the stimulus, its vividness, and whether it is in motion. In addition, a stimulus is more salient if it is involved in an interactive way with the S's responses. An adult animal (it may or may not be a member of the same species) that is continuously present in the young animal's environment is likely to be a salient stimulus because it is relatively large, vivid, and mobile, and moreover it responds to the activities of the infant so that the responses of each member of the pair become cues for the behavior of the other in a dyadic chain (see Sears, 1951). The other animal (or other salient object) acquires an essential cue function for the maintenance of the young animal's behavior, and if it is removed, the young animal's behavior will be disrupted, and he is likely to learn to perform behavior that will restore the object. He would therefore be described as "attached" to the object. However, if separation continues, extinction will occur as the young animal's behavior becomes conditioned to the new stimuli that have replaced the old. The prediction from this theory therefore is that separation reactions will be most intense immediately following the separation and will decline with time. This prediction is different from that based on drive theory, which would hold that the intensity of the motivation should increase with the number of hours "deprivation." The Cairns prediction has been confirmed in a study of social attachment in lambs (Cairns, 1966). Although behavior disruption following water deprivation increased with the number of hours of deprivation, disruption following separation from the primary attachment figure was greatest immediately following the separation and declined sharply thereafter. A study by Lewis (1965) with children confirms that the effect of social isolation does not increase monotonically with the duration of the isolation.

Cairns' work is an instance of a substantial body of comparative work which helps to bridge the gap between ethological and social learning theory. In this category is the work on the nature of the environmental and organismic conditions which affect the occurrence, intensity, and timing of imprinting (Hess, 1959; Sluckin, 1962; Moltz, 1963). The work of Harlow and his colleagues (reviewed later in this chapter) identified certain specific aspects of maternal response which serve to maintain an infant's attachment behavior. Rheingold (1963) and Hinde (1966) have focused upon the interaction between physicochemical determinants of behavior and the modification of behavior through experience with the environment. Consistently typical courses of social development are described for mother-infant pairs of given species, and the importance of learning in the development of these response chains is shown in studies utilizing infant isolation techniques (Schneirla and Rosenblatt, 1963; Rosenblatt et al., 1961). These studies have concentrated more upon maternal behavior and the nature of the inputs from the infant that maintain it than upon infant attachment behavior as such. Nevertheless, they serve to underline the current emphasis upon the interactions between "instinctual" and experiential components in the control of behavior.

We now turn to a brief presentation of three "subtheories." These theories have been less extensively elaborated, at least with respect to their developmental implications, than the three already discussed and do not purport to encompass as wide a range of ages or behaviors.

Cognitive-Developmental Theory

Schaffer and Emerson (1964a) have used cognitive-developmental theory extensively to interpret their findings on attachment during infancy. The basic tenet is that any behavior of a child is a function of the level of cognitive development he has achieved. An illustrative derivation of this principal applied to attachment is that: a child cannot develop a specific attachment until he can both discriminate and recognize an individual person. Even after an infant can do these things, however, he still may not know that the person continues to exist when out of sight. The development of object constancy should introduce a new phase of attachment behavior, for example, signaling when the attachment figure is not in view. When time concepts begins to be mastered, this should mean both that the child will begin to respond to signs of the mother's impending departure (showing anticipatory protest), and that he will be able to anticipate her return during an absence and derive some comfort thereby. Reactions to death of an attachment figure should vary greatly with the age of the child, depending on the level of understanding of the permanence of death.

Leading cognitive developmental theorists (e.g., Piaget, Kohlberg) have not explicitly formulated a theory of attachment or dependency. Kohlberg (1966) has done so tangentially, in his analysis of sex-typing and the development of differential attachment to the same-sex parent. Since the theory has not been fully developed, it will be given only very brief treatment here, with a view to indicating its potential.

Kohlberg, in his theory of sex-typing, postulates (and presents some evidence for) the following developmental sequence:

1. The child can label itself correctly as a boy or girl.
2. The child then differentiates cognitively the objects and activities that are considered masculine or feminine.
3. Self-categorization determines valuings: there is a need to value things that are consistent with or like the self; thus when the child understands what things or activities are masculine or feminine, he will value (choose) those which are consistent with his self-label.
4. When sex-appropriate values have been acquired, the child tends to identify with like-sex figures (particularly the same-sex parent). The child begins to imitate the same-sex parent more, and this leads to a differential attachment to that parent.

Stage 4 of this sequence is delayed until the age of 6 to 8, because up until this time the child does not understand that an individual's sex is a constant property (the achievement of sex-constancy is thought to be related to the achievement of other constancies, such as distance and quantity), and he cannot reliably group other individuals into same-sex categories. Until he can do this, the "we-men" or "we-girls" basis for differential attachment is missing.

Kohlberg's theory is a cognitive balance theory. The choice of an attachment object depends upon a perception of similarity in the characteristics of self and others. The theory can, of course, be generalized to include other dimensions of similarity than sex as a basis for selective attachment. A fairly high degree of cognitive maturity is needed, as Kohlberg has shown in connection with sex-typing, for a child to perceive similarities between himself and others. This aspect of cognitive-developmental theory therefore does not account for attachment in the early years of life.

From the cognitive developmental point of view, individual differences would be studied in relation to variations in level of cognitive development among children of a given age.

Assuming that frequency and kind of dependency behavior change regularly with age, then the brighter the child, the sooner will he achieve more mature dependency behavior, since he will have more rapidly achieved the cognitive structures that underlie the age changes in dependency behavior. Negative correlations would therefore be expected between IQ and the frequency or intensity of the more infantile forms of dependency. The cognitive theorist does not say that variations in socialization practices are unimportant in accounting for individual differences, only that socialization practices, like any other environmental input, must themselves be mediated through the cognitive capabilities of the child.

Social Comparison Theory

Schachter (1959) argues that affiliative behavior serves two functions: (1) anxiety reduction (at least for some individual), and (2) social comparison. Drawing on the statement of the theory by Festinger (1954), Schachter states the social comparison hypothesis as follows:

A drive exists in man to evaluate his opinions and abilities. . . . When an objective, non-social means . . . of evaluation is not available, evaluation will be made by comparison with the opinions and abilities of other people. . . . Stable and precise evaluation by social comparison is possible only when the opinions and abilities available for comparison are not too divergent from one's own; the tendency to compare oneself with others decreases as the discrepancy in opinion or ability increases (1959, p. 113).

Individuals, then, are drawn to seek the company of others when they are unsure of the evaluation of some aspect of their own attitudes, performance, or feelings. Schachter emphasizes emotional states as especially likely to produce the need for comparison:

Since emotion-producing situations are often novel and outside the realm of our past experience, it could be expected that the emotions would be particularly vulnerable to social influence (p. 128).

Schachter has applied his theory to affiliative behavior among young adults. He has identified stable individual differences, and he assumes that these differences are related to differential early childhood histories. Specifically, he suggests that individuals who show high affiliative tendencies under stress conditions are those whose mothers have been more effective in reducing anxiety by being more immediately attentive when the young child was upset. Furthermore, the affiliative adult should be one who did not have a threatening person close at hand in childhood. Schachter assumes that an older sibling is more likely to arouse anxiety than to reduce it; hence affiliative tendencies should be weaker among adults who have grown up as younger children in a family,

What are the implications of this theory for affiliative behavior in childhood? On the basis of its anxiety-reducing value, affiliative behavior toward nurturant adults should develop quite early in childhood, assuming that young children do experience anxiety fairly frequently.

The social comparison motive is more problematical. One may assume that children are even less able than adults to identify their own emotional or drive states. When a child is emotionally aroused, he ought to be more likely than an adult to wonder whether he is afraid, exhilarated, or in need of going to the bathroom. Mothers do provide definition for these states. For example, one of the writers observed the following scene on a transoceanic flight. The plane had encountered severe turbulence; passengers were alarmed and many were sick; when the plane hit a pocket and plunged downward, the mother of an 18 month-old child would lift the child gaily, smile at him, and exclaim, "Whee! Isn't this *fun!*" The child was excited, but he seemed to be enjoying the trip. It is not unlikely that when unsure of the nature of his arousal state, a child might come to seek definition from his mother.

However, Schachter's formulation of social comparison as it applies to affiliative behavior involves an individual's defining his own motive by *observing* the reactions of others in a similar situation, and inferring the emotional state implied thereby. We have little evidence concerning the ability of young children to interpret the emotional states of others; they can probably make rudimentary distinctions

between "happy" and "sad," but perhaps little beyond this. Furthermore, the work on egocentrism would suggest that they do not make good use of inferences concerning the stimulating situations impinging upon others. They would thus not be sure of the identity of the people who are "in the same boat," and therefore appropriate for social comparison. For these reasons, it appears likely that the social comparison motive for affiliation develops slowly, but the necessary tests of the theory at different age levels have not been done.

Dependency as Immaturity

Modern clinical psychologists who stress the importance of the development of "ego controls" regard a child's flight to the mother for nearness or physical contact as a manifestation of the insufficient development of other "coping" devices. Lois Murphy's work (1962) embodies this point of view. Like the ethologists, she emphasizes the importance of strange situations as producers of fear or tension in young children, and the positive function of the child's contact with his mother in reducing this tension and permitting exploration and other coping behavior to occur. From this standpoint, the decline with age in frequency and intensity of mother-contacting or upset over separation from mother would be a function of (1) cognitive growth, which allows the child to understand new situations better and to bridge the time gap involved in separations from mother, (2) the learning of a wide variety of skills, which gives the child confidence that he can function effectively in a new situation, and (3) learning to select or reject segments of a total stimulus situation, so that the total stimulation involved in certain new situations will not be overwhelming.

The passive child as distinct from the active child (and this temperamental factor is seen as being at least in part constitutional) is likely to be slower in acquiring behavior that will replace mother-contacting and hence is likely to show mother-contacting with more intensity and frequency (or at a later age) than the active child. But passivity and dependency are by no means synonymous. The active child, when faced with a situation beyond his level of coping ability, will be especially demanding of his mother's support. The seeking of help can sometimes be a manifestation of insecurity, but on the other occasions it can be part of an autonomous sequence of behavior—a sequence initiated by the child and under his control. Murphy illustrates this point from observations of preschool, task-oriented behavior: one child said to the adult experimenter: "I wanna put the big one in; *you* put the little one in." Another child asked, "Will you hold the paper while I cut?" In these instances, help-seeking is a response in which the child dominates or controls others; in other instances, it is submissive. Summarizing the observations of a group of "autonomous" children, Murphy says:

It is not surprising that all the children who showed strong autonomy drives and intiative expressed their own self-sufficiency and refused help insofar as they could manage by themselves. However, we might not have taken it for granted that these autonomous self-sufficient children would be flexibly able to accept help when they got beyond their depth or confronted situations which they could not manage alone; yet many of the children mentioned over and over again as sturdily independent were equally able to reject help if they did not need it and to accept it when they did. They could be autonomous but were not compulsively so, and for them there was no conflict between autonomy and dependence (1962, p. 224).

In Murphy's terms, help-seeking is sometimes part of competent coping behavior, sometimes not. This statement points to the problems of defining "independent" versus "dependent" behavior, and identifying the behaviors which may be expected to cluster as traits of a given child.

For Murphy, then, help-seeking per se would not form part of the passive (nonindependent) cluster. Attributes considered more likely to form part of this cluster include: frequent mother-contacting, timidity in new situations and a tendency to take a long time to become relaxed in such situations, and waiting for others to take the initiative in starting a new behavior sequence. What "antecedent" conditions would one look for in studying the development of individual differences in this cluster? Murphy has not explicitly delineated these, other than to say

that constitutional factors would contribute. One may infer, however, that the factors which govern the acquisition of "coping" responses would be considered more important than the factors which affect passive behavior directly. This would constitute a major difference between the Murphy approach and that of social learning theory. That is, while social learning theorists tend to study the development of dependency responses in terms of the history of reinforcement contingencies for these responses, or the opportunities to learn dependency behavior through modeling, or the frequency of arousal of motivating conditions which govern the output of these responses, Murphy would look upon passive-dependent behavior as a kind of residual whose frequency depends upon the extent to which *alternative* behaviors have been acquired.

If one wanted to study learning histories, then, as a means of predicting the frequency of passive-dependent behavior in individual children, one would study the frequency of opportunities to learn active "coping" behavior, including such attributes as the ability to plan and organize a sequence of behavior, good motor control, and "using the environment selectively."

The preceding review of theories will serve as a background to the topically organized presentation of research findings which follows. In part, the power of each of the theories can be evaluated in terms of the research that has been stimulated and influenced by it. The first topic, developmental changes, reports findings which have greatest relevance to ethological and cognitive-developmental theory. Later topics, such as social deprivation and socialization effects, have their primary base in social learning theory and psychoanalytic theory.

DEVELOPMENTAL CHANGES

In this section, we chart the changes occurring with age in normal attachment and dependency behavior that have thus far been identified. During infancy there are developmental changes in the responsiveness to social stimuli (human voice, facelike configurations) and in the social responses elicited by the infant (e.g., smiling). The relevant literature is reviewed in detail in Chapter 5 by Kessen.

Although these developments are of course relevant to attachment, we focus here upon attachment behavior at a somewhat more molar level.

Schaffer and Emerson (1964a) followed a group of 60 Scottish infants from fairly early infancy (the age at initial contact ranged from 5 to 23 weeks) to 18 months of age. They conducted monthly mother interviews, focused upon the child's reactions to a specified set of separation situations (e.g., being put down after being held; being left alone in a room), and they also carried out monthly observations of the infant's response to various degrees of approach by the interviewer. Figure 1 shows the age trends in attachment that were identified in this study. In an early phase, called "indiscriminate attachment," the infants protested over separation, but the incidence of protest was not related to the identity of the person from whom they were being separated. At about the age of 7 months, specific attachments emerged, and they became more intense during the next 3- or 4-month period.

There were pronounced individual differences in the age of onset of specific attachment. The youngest child to show this behavior was 22 weeks old, and there were two infants in the sample who did not show the behavior until after their first birthday.

There were changes over time in the nature of the situations that elicited protest from the infants. The youngest infants protested over being put down after being held, but this became less frequent as the infants grew older. On the other hand, protest over being left alone in a room, being left with someone other than the attachment figure, or being left in a pram outside the house or outside a shop all increased in effectiveness as elicitors of protest up to 18 months of age.

Schaffer and Emerson (1964a) found that fear of strangers emerged, on the average, about 1 month after the appearance of specific attachments, although there was a group (about one-fourth of the total sample) in which stranger fears preceded the onset of specific attachments.

Most commonly, the mother was the first object of specific attachment, although there were a few instances in which the father or a grandparent was the sole initial object of attachment, or in which attachments were formed initially to the mother and another figure simultaneously. Following the onset of specific attachment, there was an increase in the number of attachment figures. Although most infants initially formed an attachment to a single figure and then broadened their attachments to other objects, some infants (29% of the sample) formed multiple attachments from the time that any specific attachments were noted. The formation of additional attachments usually proceeds rapidly:

This is not a slow and gradual process: by the third lunar month following onset, over half the subjects were showing attachment toward more than one person, and by the sixth month, this proportion had risen to three quarters of the group. By 18 months, finally, only 13 percent were showing attachments to just one person, while almost a third of all cases now had five or more attachment objects (Schaffer and Emerson, 1964a, p. 31).

Mary Ainsworth (1963, 1967) spent a period of 9 months observing a group of 28 infants and their mothers in Ganda, Africa.

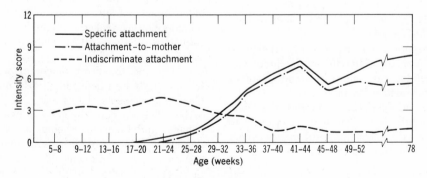

Fig. 1. Developmental course of attachments.

The age range spanned by the period of observation was 2 to 14 months. Attachment to mother was judged to have occurred when the infant "discriminated her from other people and responded to her differentially." Differential smiling, crying, and vocalization were used as criteria of attachment, as well as separation reactions, visual-motor orientation toward the mother, following, making physical contact with her, gestures of greeting, and using her as a base for exploration. On these bases, 23 of the infants developed a clear-cut attachment to the mother during the 9-month period of observation, whereas 5 did not. While there were a few signs of specific attachment during the first few months of life, it was not until the second quarter of the first year that unequivocal signs of differential attachment to the mother appeared. At this time, the infants would accept attention from other people. During the third quarter, attachment became intensified and was shown by crawling after the mother and greeting her after separation. At this age, and also during the fourth quarter of the first year, following the mother tended to replace crying when she left the room. Fear of strangers tended to emerge during the fourth quarter, although there were two infants who "showed a sudden aversion to strangers, even though they had previously accepted them" at about 8 months.

Ainsworth differentiated three groups of infants: the "secure attached" $(N = 16)$, the "insecure attached" $(N = 7)$, and the non attached $(N = 5)$. The insecure group were described as children who "were said to cry a great deal, and were observed to do so during our visits, even while held by their mothers. They demanded much attention from the mother, fussing while doing so, and they stayed close to her rather than using her as a secure base from which they could explore the world" (p. 84).

The secure group, in contrast, cried little and showed their attachment by following, and greeting, and seeming especially content when with their mothers.

While the development pattern described by Ainsworth is similar in most respects to that outlined by Schaffer and Emerson, there are some points of difference:

1. Specific attachments appeared somewhat earlier among the Ganda infants.

2. Intense stranger fears appeared later among the Ganda, with a greater lapse of time between the onset of specific attachment and a "panicky" reaction to strangers.

3. The initial attachment was always to the mother, though this was quickly followed by the formation of attachments to additional figures.

The difference in age of onset of specific attachments may be due to one of several factors. First, Schaffer and Emerson visited the families in their study once a month, Ainsworth every two weeks, and the more frequent visits may have permitted identifying a developmental change sooner for the Ganda children. Second, there is some evidence of a faster rate of locomotor development among Ganda infants than among American and European infants, and the development of attachments could be geared to this accelerated timetable. Finally, Schaffer and Emerson measured attachment primarily through separation reactions; Ainsworth used a wider range of behaviors. Ainsworth has pointed out elsewhere (1967) that infants who show strong attachment in other respects may not show reactions to mild degrees of separation unless there are other elements of stress in the situation.

Discussing the concept of a "critical period" in the formation of attachments, Caldwell (1962b) cites some unpublished data from a study by Yarrow on adopted children. Infants placed in adoptive homes at 3 months of age showed few signs of upset during the postplacement period, whereas 86% of the cases placed at 6 months did so, and progressively more severe disturbances were found at each 1-month interval from 3 to 12 months. These disturbances may be interpreted as reflecting the greater frequency and intensity among older infants of attachments formed to the pre-adoption caretakers, although direct information on these attachments is not provided.

Concerning the development of stranger-fears, a study by Rheingold (1961) indicates that some elements of this fear may develop earlier than was noted by either Ainsworth or Schaffer and Emerson. Rheingold contrasted a group of home-reared infants approximately 3½ months old with some like-aged institutional babies who had had a variety of caretakers and a lower level of total social stimulation. The institutional babies were more responsive to a stranger, and the home-reared babies showed more "negative" reactions—sobering or protesting when approached by the examiner. This could mean either that the home-reared babies were showing stranger-fear or that the institutional babies were showing the effects of social deprivation. Other data in the literature would indicate that 3½ months is very early for babies to recognize familiar caretakers and distinguish them from strangers, but further evidence is needed. Ainsworth (1967) has noted several stages in the early development of stranger fears, with "sobering" and "staring" and other mild differential reactions preceding full-blown anxiety reactions.

The published literature contains very little data on age changes in attachment or dependency behavior after infancy. We have been able to locate only one clearly longitudinal study, a short-term one covering a 2-year period at a nursery school (Martin, 1964). There were four groups of children, starting nursery school in successive years. During the 2-year span studied for each group, there was a significant increase in the absolute frequency of dependent responses for one group, no change for the other three. Analysis of the component subscores on dependency[4] reveals that the increase was confined to the "seeks positive attention" category; there was a small decline in the frequency of touching and holding. It should be noted that the *relative* frequency of dependent responses (all subscores summed) to other classes of responses declined significantly over the 2-year period for all groups, while the relative frequency of autonomous achievement and friendship-affiliation responses increased.

An early study of age trends in responses to separation (Shirley and Poyntz, 1941) included children ranging in age from 2 to 7. Children were rated on the amount of upset they showed upon parting from their mothers to go to a day care center. In some instances the children were picked up at home, so that the parting occurred there. In other instances the mothers brought the children to the center and parted from them there. A total of 199

[4] The original publication did not present time-trends for the component scores. The authors are grateful to William Martin and Walter Emmerich for making the data available for this analysis.

children were included in the study, and many of the children were observed several times, on the occasions of successive visits to the center every 6 months. Thus the study is semilongitudinal. Data are reported separately for observations taken at 11 different ages (grouped into 6 month intervals). There is a decline with age in the proportion of children who show upset over parting from their mothers either at home or at the day center, and also a decline in the proportion who ask for their mothers during her absence while they are at the center. Children aged 2 to 4 seem to be fairly similar in their amount of upset, with the greatest decline in separation reactions occurring between age 4 and 4½.

Heinicke and Westheimer (1965, pp. 307–311) have studied reactions to more extended separations. They observed a group of 10 children ranging in age from 1 year, 1 month to 2 years, 8 months. The intensity of separation reactions within this sample was not related to the age of the child when the separation occurred. In contrasting their findings with those of other investigators who have studied younger or older children, Heinicke and Westheimer suggest that (1) younger children react with loss of appetite, whereas children of approximately 2 years of age are more likely to overeat, at least during certain phases of the separation; (2) that younger children have not been observed to show as much ambivalence toward their attachment figure upon reunion; and (3) that older children (aged 4 to 6), while showing very similar initial separation reactions to those of younger children, regain their equilibrium more quickly.

Cox and Campbell (1968) studied the effects of brief mother absence on two groups of subjects: 20 children between 13 and 15 months of age, and 20 children of age 23 to 37 months. Half of each group was the experimental group in which the mother left the child alone for the central 4 minutes of a 12-minute session in an experimental room. The control-group mothers remained with the children throughout the session. Observers measured the decline in play, speech, and movement during the mother's absence. The decline was significant in all three categories of behavior for both groups, but the effects of mother-absence were greater for the younger children.

Heathers (1955) selected two samples of differing ages to permit age comparisons. He used time-sampled behavior observations with 20 2-year-olds and 20 4-year-olds and found the changes from the first to the second age level, as given in Table 2.

During the 2½ year age span covered by this study, then, there is a decline in teacher-oriented dependency and an increase in social interaction with other children. This increased sociability with peers involves some components traditionally labeled "dependent"— that is, attention-seeking and approval-seeking —but also some components involving dominance (structuring other children's play) and independence (resisting interference from other children). A growth in social skills is suggested by the fact that increased interaction and increased structuring of other children's play are *not* accompanied by increased interference with other children's ongoing activities.

Sears et al. (1965) obtained time-sampled observational data on several aspects of dependency for nursery-school aged children. The age range for the boys in the sample was 20 months, for the girls, 18 months. Within this age range, the correlations between chronological age and dependency scores are given in Table 3.

Although the age range is narrow, and hence no substantial developmental changes may be expected, there is some indication here of a decline with age, especially among

the girls, in the more passive forms of dependency *directed toward adults.* No such decline is apparent in proximity-seeking directed toward other children. Over the whole sample, attention-seeking does not decline with age, regardless of target, although there is some evidence that there are counteracting tendencies in the two sexes. Girls seem to improve their discrimination of the cues that indicate whether their mothers are free to respond to bids for attention.

Stith and Connor (1962), working with an age range of 38 to 75 months, report a substantial decline with age in frequency of the children's dependent contacts with adults. Within this same age range, they found a slight increase (not significant) in total dependent contacts with other children, accompanied by a significant increase in "helpful" contacts. It would seem, then, that there is an increase in reciprocity in the child's relationships with his age-mates, in which there is a simultaneous increase in both asking and offering help and support.

Emmerich (1964) similarly emphasizes the interrelatedness of dependent behavior with the development of other social behavior. Working with the same 2-year longitudinal data initially reported by Martin (1964), he factor analyzed a variety of social behaviors and found a dimension that remained relatively stable through the 2-year period: interpersonal versus impersonal orientation. Interpersonal orientation had positive loadings

Table 2.   Change with age in Dependence and Independence behavior, and in type of play activities. From Heathers, 1955.

	Direction of change from age 2 to 4-5	Significance Level
Clings to or seeks affection from teacher	Decrease	.01
Clings to or seeks affection from child	Decrease	N.S.
Seeks attention or approval from teacher	Decrease	.05
Seeks attention or approval from child	Increase	.01
Ignores stimuli from teacher	Increase	.01
Ignores stimuli from child	Increase	N.S.
Plays alone intently	Increase	N.S.
Structures child's play	Increase	.01
Interferes with child's play	Decrease	N.S.
Resists child's interference or aggression	Increase	N.S.
Not playing	Decrease	.02
Alone play	Decrease	.01
Social play	Increase	.01
Social interaction with children	Increase	.01

Table 3.   Correlations between dependency components and chronological age. (Sears et al., 1965)

	All Sample	Boys	Girls
Behavior unit observation			
Proximity seeking toward children (touching, being near)	.21	.12	.35
Proximity seeking toward adults	−.25	−.09	−.40
Positive attention seeking from children	−.04	−.42[a]	.22
Seeking positive attention from adults	.03	−.10	.12
Mother-child interaction			
Bids for attention when mother busy	—	−.26	−.50[a]
Bids for attention: mother attentive	—	.06	−.11
N	40	21	19

[a] In the original publication, correlations were not reported separately according to whether the target of the behavior was an adult or child. We are grateful to R. R. Sears for making the data available to permit computation of the present table. For this analysis, we have excluded dependency toward the mother on those occasions when she was present, since she was not present for most of the children most of the time, and on the same ground we have excluded the few instances of dependency toward siblings.

on some components of dependent behavior and some components of social-affiliative behavior. Children who were highly "interpersonal" in their orientation at the time they entered nursery school were also characterized by "negative attitude." Emmerich discussed this finding in the following terms:

A straightforward interpretation is that the outgoing child's greater frequency of direct contacts with others results in more interpersonal conflicts and consequent expressions of hostility (p. 329).

At the end of the 2-year period, however, the child with a strong interpersonal orientation was no longer typically negative. Emmerich interprets the temporal changes in correlation patterns as reflecting "a developmental transformation during the fourth semester, when the previously interpersonal-negative child becomes poised, while his previously impersonal-positive counterpart manifests social insecurity." Emmerich (1964) adds:

Perhaps in anticipation of the child's entry into the more formal kindergarten setting, socializing agents at this time are putting pressure upon the outgoing child to modulate his aggressiveness, while a simultaneous attempt is being made to influence the self-contained child to become more outgoing. It is also likely that certain changes in the child's social orientation complement the more deliberate socializing efforts of adults. The outgoing child is probably discovering through the reactions of others that assertiveness is more effective than aggression in satisfying his social needs. And the impersonal child may be discerning the value in relating more directly to others, but, since he will not have developed the requisite interpersonal skills, and/or because of aggression conflict, his initial efforts result in increased social tension and insecurity" (pp. 330–331).

Susceptibility to social reinforcement has been used as an indicator of dependency motivation. There is some evidence that this susceptibility declines with age (McCuller and Stevenson, 1960; Lewis, Wall, and Aronfreed 1963; Rosenhan and Greenwald, 1965; Allen, 1966). In other studies social deprivation has been used as an antecedent condition, with social reinforcement used to measure the effects of this manipulation. Walters and Parke (1964b, pp. 248–251) have summarized the age trends in effectiveness of social isolation, citing a number of studies in which social isolation clearly affected preschool or early grade-school aged children, and two studies among adolescents in which social isolation by itself did not increase responsiveness to social reinforcement. They explain these age changes as follows:

Whereas for a child, even brief isolation may be a conditioned stimulus for emotional arousal, older subjects are more habituated to spending time alone and are unlikely to react to isolation in an emotional manner. Age changes in response to isolation are undoubtedly a function of a number of physiological and psychological changes that ordinarily occur as an individual matures. Being alone is not usually a threatening state of affairs for an older child, adolescent, or adult who can take care of his everyday physical needs and who, even if deprived of occupational or recreational activities, can spend his time in thought" (pp. 248–249).

It may be noted that almost all the studies of social reinforcement effectiveness have involved *adults* as the dispensers of this reinforcement. The previously noted developmental shifts in orientation from adults to age-mates may mean that the decline in susceptibility to social reinforcement would be found only in relation to adult experimenters; there might even be an increase in susceptibility to social reinforcement dispensed by peers, but this possibility remains to be tested empirically.

An interesting hint as to one aspect of developmental change may be found in data obtained by Rosenthal (1965).[5] In Table 4 are presented the correlations between chronological age, which in this study ranges from 3.1 years to 5.0 years, and the frequency of two kinds of dependent acts directed toward (1) mother, and (2) a female stranger (when mother is not present), under conditions of either high or low anxiety.

Attention-seeking does not show significant age effects. For proximity-seeking, however, under conditions of low anxiety, there is a tendency for older children to show less of the behavior, both toward the mother and toward a stranger. When anxiety-producing cues are introduced, however, the older chil-

[5] An analysis by age was not included in the original report of this study; the author has made the data available to us to permit the computation of the correlations seen in Table 4.

Table 4. Correlations between chronological age and amount of attention-seeking and proximity-seeking by target of dependency and level of anxiety (from Rosenthal, 1965).

	High Anxiety	Low Anxiety
Attention-seeking directed toward		
Mother	−.17	−.04
Stranger	.27	−.13
Proximity-seeking directed toward		
Mother	.08	−.44
Stranger	.25	−.31
$N =$	32	32

dren are somewhat more likely to generalize their dependent responses to a stranger. The difference between the age correlations .25 and −.31 (proximity-seeking toward strangers under high-versus low-anxiety conditions) is significant at the .002 level. This suggests that older children are more able to make use of strangers as a source of security for dealing with anxiety than are younger children. Inspection of the means indicates that anxiety arousal increases proximity-seeking among the older children in the sample, among whom it is otherwise low, whereas for the younger children, whose normal rate is higher, anxiety does not clearly increase the incidence of proximity-seeking.

Kohlberg (1966) argues that in charting developmental trends it is necessary to take account not only of age but also of the different levels of cognitive development achieved by children of similar age. Kohlberg and Zigler (1966) have charted the frequency of verbal dependency responses directed toward male and female experimenters. They find that boys of average intelligence shift toward greater dependency upon male (as compared with female) experimenters during the age period 4 to 7 years. Brighter boys, on the other hand, are already more dependent upon males at the age of 4 and shift back toward neutrality in sex of dependency target. These age shifts are associated with the growth of sex-role concepts, with the brighter boys having achieved a stereotyped concept of masculinity and an understanding of the constancy of sex identity at the time of their greatest preference for males, followed by a more differentiated set of sex role concepts at the time of their shift toward impartiality with respect to sex of experimenter. Kohlberg reports similar differential trends for bright and average children with respect to choices of father versus mother dolls in doll play. He interprets his findings as supporting the view that the choice of dependency targets is not simply a function of the child's experience with certain individuals, and generalization from these experiences to new encounters, but that orientation toward other individuals is in some degree determined by perception of similarity between the self and the other, and that such perceptions undergo systematic changes with cognitive development.

Consistent with Kohlberg's view of developmental change is the fact that bright children tend to be less dependent (Emmerich, 1966a) and less susceptible to social influence in a perceptual judgment situation (Hottel, 1960) than do children of the same age but lower IQ.

SITUATIONS WHICH AROUSE, INTENSIFY, OR REDUCE ATTACHMENT OR DEPENDENT BEHAVIOR

The frequency and intensity of the attachment or dependent behavior shown by a given child varies considerably from time to time and from one situation to another. This fact has been emphasized by Schaffer and Emerson (1964a), who report the observations of mothers concerning their infant's behavior as follows:

There are certain conditions which prevent, suppress or minimize the infant's protests at the removal of his attachment object, and amongst these the influence of newly developed motor skills and the infant's often intense curiosity and exploratory tendency may be enumerated. . . . In general, amongst the factors that minimize intensity the distracting influence of environmental stimulation is perhaps the most powerful, so that an infant's reactions to the withdrawal of his attachment object may be frequently influenced by the presence or absence of other sources of stimulation. . . . There are, on the other hand, certain other conditions which are frequently found to evoke or intensify proximity seeking.

Pain, illness, fatigue and fear are amongst the most potent of these: the infant, for instance, who shows no objection to his mother's departure during most of the day may require her continuous presence in the last hour or so before bedtime. A period of absence on the part of the attachment object was also commonly reported as producing an intensification of proximity seeking (pp. 26–27).

The authors note that a sudden increase in the amount of social stimulation—such as would occur during the visit of a doting relative—would also increase the level of the infant's demands for attention. Ainsworth (1963), from her study of the Ganda, adds weaning as a time when attachment behavior is intensified.

This section is concerned with systematic studies dealing with the eliciting or arousal conditions that have been shown to affect the level of attachment or dependent behavior that normal children (or young, subhuman primates) display and will also discuss any evidence that the attachment behavior serves to alleviate or reduce these arousal states.

Fear, Anxiety, and Stress

The arousal of fear or anxiety in a young child or animal is usually inferred either from the stimulus situation or from emotional responses such as crying, shrieking, crouching, or rocking. Few investigators have taken direct physiological measures of arousal. In the following report, the nature of the evidence from which the arousal of fear or anxiety is inferred will be described.

Students of the relationships between fear and attachment behavior have focused upon two issues: (1) the role of fear in arousing or intensifying attachment behavior, and (2) the role of attachment behavior in reducing fear or permitting the child to cope with emotional tension. The work of Harlow and his colleagues illustrates this dual emphasis. They have found that when a young monkey that has been raised with a cloth surrogate mother is placed in a strange open-field situation or presented with a toy bear beating a drum, he immediately makes contact with the mother surrogate, clinging intensely. After a brief period of clinging, the signs of distress diminish, and the infant begins first to look at the frightening stimuli, and then to approach and explore them. In the absence of the mother surrogate, distress (e.g., wailing, crouching) does not diminish and exploration and play are radically diminished (see Harlow and Zimmerman, 1958; Harlow, 1959, 1961). It is notable that monkeys raised either in total isolation or with a wire surrogate mother do not use a surrogate for initial clinging and then as a base for exploration when a surrogate is made available in a fear-producing situation; rather, they behave like animals placed in the situation alone.

The function of the human mother's presence in moderating the effects of a strange environment and freeing the child to explore is described and discussed by Murphy (1962, pp. 204-205) and has been studied by Arsenian (1943) and Ainsworth and Wittig (1967). Arsenian worked with 24 children from the nursery of a state reformatory for women. The children ranged in age from 11 to 30 months. During the study they were taken to a strange room which was attractively decorated and equipped with toys. One group entered the room alone and remained alone; another group entered and remained in the room with their mothers or another familiar adult. The reactions of the subjects to the strange room were rated on a scale of security-insecurity on the basis of observation of such behaviors as crying, nonmotile withdrawal, approach to toys. The security ratings of the alone group were considerably lower than those of the group with a familiar adult present, and this remained true through a series of 11 trials. In the cases of the children who were with their own mothers, Arsenian reports:

The children were maximally secure and the mothers were focal attractions in the situation. These children seemed to be unable to sustain any activity without referring it to the adult: they talked to her, showed her the new toys, and played in proximity to her (p. 241).

This report presents no evidence as to whether the amount of attachment behavior shown by these children toward their mothers was greater in the strange room than would be usual in a familiar environment. Several of the children who had been in the mother-present group were left alone after the fifth

trial. The security of their behavior diminished sharply after the adult left. The reverse procedure, however—introducing a familiar adult on the fifth trial for children who had been alone—did not appreciably increase security ratings.

Ainsworth and Wittig (1967) worked with a group of 14 normal 1-year-olds (median age 51 weeks) and observed their behavior in a strange room through a series of 3-minute episodes in which the child was either alone, with his mother, with a stranger, or with both the mother and the stranger. The amount of exploratory and play behavior was greatest when the mother and child were alone together. When a stranger entered the room, with the mother still present, the child was not greatly disturbed, but the amount of exploration declined significantly. During this episode, the child tended to look more at the stranger than at the mother. While the published report does not include data on the amount of the mother-contacting, it may be inferred from the descriptive material that after the entrance of the stranger the child tended to stay nearer the mother than he had done before, although there were instances of approach to the stranger and most of the children tolerated approaches by the stranger without resistence. Clear evidence of the security-giving function of the mother is seen in the fact that the amount of exploratory and play behavior were considerably greater, and the amount of crying considerably less, when the mother was present than when the child was either alone or with only the stranger.

Studies of the effects of fear-arousal on the dependent behavior of children beyond infancy are rare. There is one study of 64 English preschool girls (Rosenthal, 1965, 1967, 1968). Rosenthal measured dependency responses toward the child's mother in one session and toward a strange female in another session. Half the subjects were tested under low-anxiety, half under high-anxiety conditions. The anxiety manipulation is described by Rosenthal as follows:

In the low anxiety condition, the child played in the observation room with the various toys available; a picture of smiling faces was hanging near the toys. The only stimulation from outside the room was the sound of a gramophone in an adjacent room, which played first lines of various children's songs at regular intervals of three minutes. In the high anxiety condition the child, on entering the room, faced a slow burning alcohol lamp standing on a stainless steel tray. Next to it was a pair of scissors, a white paper tissue, and a pencil. The pictures of the smiling faces were replaced with a group of sad faces. The sound track heard from the adjacent room was made up of the following sounds: a loud banging on a metal object, a child crying and a high-pitched shriek. Each sound was on for about 20 seconds. The sounds came on at regular three minute intervals. The tray with the burning lamp stood on a chair next to the red door leading to the room from which the sounds came. After about 12 minutes, and following a loud continuous shriek, the red door opened very slowly (provided the child looked in that direction) and a hand in an arm-length black glove reaching in slowly, put out the lamp and withdrew, closing the door once more. Within two or three minutes, a crying sound was heard (1967, pp. 122-123).

The effect of this manipulation on dependency may be seen in Table 5. Attention-seeking (a combined score summing asking for attention, approval, and help) was not appreciably affected. Proximity-seeking (being near, clinging) was significantly greater under high-anxiety conditions. ($p < .025$, one-tailed test).

This study, then, provides evidence of the fact that stress will increase proximity-seeking in children. That this behavior is functional as instrumental behavior to reduce stress is suggested by the findings of Kiesler. Kiesler (1966) studied children's performance on simple as compared with complex tasks, and found that under conditions of stress (medical instruments in room) the presence of others hindered performance on simple

tasks and helped performance on conplex tasks; with low arousal this was not the case. Using the Taylor-Spence formulation of the relationships between drive level and task performance, Kiesler inferred that the presence of others had reduced stress.

At the adult level, Schachter (1959) has shown that the threat of strong shock increases affiliative tendencies among college women. Subjects were told there would be a delay before the shock-administering sessions could begin, and they were asked whether they would like to wait alone or with other students (in most instances people with whom they were not acquainted). The subjects who expected strong painful shocks more often chose to wait with others than did subjects under threat of mild shock.

Helmreich and Collins (1967), working with high school boys, found that subjects under the threat of shock preferred to be in a leader-dominated group, rather than simply being with an unstructured group of peers, a finding which strengthens the view that affiliative responses under stress, as they are seen in young adults, are related to the dependency responses seen in younger children under similar conditions. Sarnoff and Zimbardo (1961) replicated Schachter's results on the effects of the threat of shock, using male undergraduates as subjects, but found that arousing anxiety through telling subjects they would have to suck baby bottles during a forthcoming experimental session did not increase affiliative choices but, on the contrary, decreased them. It would appear, then, that not all threats of forthcoming discomfort arouse affiliative tendencies among adults, and one may speculate as to whether fear of ridicule or "loss of face" would cause adults to avoid rather than seek contact with others.

Walters and Parke (1964b, p. 246) point out that the patterns of reward and punishment for emotional behavior differ according to the nature of the stimulus situation. Ridicule and other forms of social punishment are delivered to persons who display "irrational fears," but not—at least not to the same extent—to those who seek to avoid objectively dangerous situations. Hence subjects might want to conceal their emotional arousal when they believe it would be judged irrational by others, and this might lead them to avoid company rather than seek it in the

Table 5. Mean Frequency of Attention- and Proximity-seeking under Two Anxiety Conditions

	Attention-Seeking	Proximity-Seeking
High anxiety	22.30	21.22
Low anxiety	21.08	13.14

bottle-sucking condition used by Sarnoff and Zimbardo.

Wrightsman (reported in Schachter, 1959) has shown that there is a reduction in self-rated anxiety among firstborn college students who wait for shock in the presence of others (by comparison with waiting alone), whereas there is no such reduction for later-borns. This is consistent with other work on ordinal position; the point of importance here is that the anxiety-reducing effect of affiliative behavior was shown at least for one subgroup of the experimental population.

We see, then, that work with adults is consistent with the main points emerging from the work with young children and animals: (1) at least some stressful situations increase affiliative tendencies, and (2) the presence of certain other people, at least for certain adults, will reduce stress. We do not know, however, whether the adult phenomena are truly continuous with those observed in early childhood. The adult studies have been concerned with affiliative tendencies toward peers, while the early childhood work has usually dealt with attachment behavior directed toward a primary attachment object. It is not clear that affiliative behavior directed toward peers represents a generalizations or extension of attachment toward significant adults. Schachter and others working since his original publication have conducted a series of experiments designed to explain the increase in affiliative behavior under stress. We shall not review these experiments in detail here, since they deal only tangentially with developmental issues. It is important to note, however, that these experiments have pointed to the social comparison motive as the important factor in adults. As we noted earlier, it is unlikely that the social comparison motive can underlie fear-produced attachment behavior in very young children, but the relevant experiments have not been done over a sufficient span of ages to permit determination of the age at which it does become operative.

In the work on social isolation, and its effect on enhancing the effectiveness of social reinforcement, there have been several experiments which have involved an experimental manipulation of anxiety level. These experiments will be discussed with the work on social isolation.

Separation from Attachment Object

It is fairly well established that separation of an infant from its attachment object not only produces distress at the time of separation but also results in an increase in the amount and/or intensity of attachment behavior shown by the infant when the pair are reunited. Seay, et al. (1962) report the post-separation behavior of four young monkeys that had been physically separated from their mothers for 3 weeks (although they could see them through a glass barrier). During the reunion period, in comparison with the pre-separation period, there was a significant increase in infant-mother clinging and mother-infant cradling. Kauffman and Rosenblum (1967) have also demonstrated an increase in mother-infant ventral contacting during the reunion period. The duration of this period of increased clinging varies, and the behavior is gradually supplanted by a resurgence of social play and exploration.

In the study by Anisworth and Wittig (1967) described above, there were two brief episodes in which the mother went out of the room, leaving her 1-year-old baby. In the first episode, the baby was left in the presence of a stranger; in the second episode the baby was left alone, and then a stranger entered and attempted to comfort the infant if it was distressed, after which the mother reappeared. There appeared to be a cumulative effect of the successive separations, although this was not shown conclusively since the order of episodes was not counterbalanced. The infants were more upset the second time the mother left the room than they were the first time (although this may of course have been due to the fact that another adult was present on the first occasion and not the second). On the occasion of the mother's first return, the infants usually simply approached her. On the second occasion, they clung strongly and resisted being put down by their mothers after the reunion.

Schaffer and Callender (1959) describe reactions of a group of infants to separations from their families for short-term hospitalization. The children who were 7 months old or older were more upset than younger infants, and their behavior after reunion with their mothers is described as follows:

These infants cried whenever left alone by the mother, physically clung to her and refused to be put down, showed fear when approached by strangers, and when sometimes even apprehensive of such familiar figures as fathers or siblings. (Schaffer and Callender, 1959, p. 536)

These postseparation reactions could be described as intense attachment behavior.

An interesting documentation of certain postseparation reactions may be found in the book *Brief Separations* by Heinicke and Westheimer (1965). They studied 10 children in their second and third years of life (median age 22 months) who were brought to a residential nursery and separated from their families for periods ranging from 2 weeks to 3 months. A matched control group of 10 nonseparated children was also studied. Unlike the younger children described by Schaffer and Callender, these children did not show an immediate increase in most aspects of attachment behavior upon being reunited with their mothers. There was an initial period when the child turned away and avoided affectionate interaction with its mother. The authors believe that this was not simply lack of recognition of the mother, since the children generally showed more positive reactions to their fathers and resumed affectionate interaction fairly quickly with them, indicating that fathers were recognized. However, the fathers visited the children during their stay at the residential nursery, whereas the mothers for the most part did not, so there might easily be a difference in the degree to which the two parents were forgotten during the separation. When the children did begin to accept interaction with their mothers following reunion, there was a period of ambivalence, during which they showed both affection and hostility before a normal level of interaction was restored. The authors do not report the amount of mother-contacting that occurred during the period of ambivalence, so we cannot be sure whether there was an intensification during this time of dependency or attachment as usually defined, although the authors do mention manifestations of apprehension among the children concerning possible further separations.

On the whole, then, brief separations are generally followed by an intensification of at least some aspects of attachment behavior, particularly for very young children.

Social Deprivation and Satiation

Extensive research effort has been devoted to studies of the effects of "social deprivation," involving either (1) isolation from social contacts of all kinds, or (2) reduction in the normal level of social interaction. Some studies have also dealt with the effects of "satiation"—the provision of a higher-than-normal level of social interaction. Deprivation and satiation have been studied primarily in relation to their impact upon the effectiveness of social reinforcement. That is, the extent of change in an individual's base-rate performance on a task that results from contingent reinforcement of a social nature (e.g., the experimenter's nodding, giving praise or approval, or simply saying "um-humm") is usually taken as the dependent variable in studies of the effects of social deprivation or satiation, although there are instances of other aspects of affiliative behavior being studied as outcomes as well. Work on the conditions that govern the effectiveness of social reinforcement is included in this review because we assume that susceptibility to social influence may be regarded as either an indicator of the arousal of an affiliative need or, perhaps more parsimoniously, as an indicator of orientation toward social cues. The evidence that susceptibility to social reinforcement is related to other aspects of "dependency" will be reviewed in a later section.

We have noted earlier the relevance of the work on social deprivation and social reinforcement for theories of social motivation. There is an excellent formulation of the theories and the issues they face, as well as a review of the experiments relevant to them, in Walters and Parke (1964b). Another excellent review, dealing primarily with the conditions that influence the effectiveness of social reinforcement, may be found in Stevenson (1964).

One of the earliest studies of social deprivation is that of Gerwirtz (1948). In one experimental condition, preschool children were placed in a situation where an adult experimenter sat nearby and was consistently attentive to the child. In another condition the experimenter pretended to be busy with his own work and sat away from the child. The children in the "low availabil-ity" condition more often sought the adult's attention than did the children in the high availability condition. These results were rep-licated in a later study (Gewirtz, 1956) in an easel-painting session in which the adult was either "busy" or fully attentive. Erikson (1962), using a similar manipulation of adult availability, found that sixth-grade children were more responsive to social reinforcement following the low-availability treatment. Sears et al. (1965, pp. 49–50) found that nursery-school aged children made more bids for maternal attention during a mother-child interaction observation session when the mother was busy than when she was attentive. Beller (1959) reports that perceptual orienta-tion toward an adult increases in a free-play situation where the adult is relatively unavail-able, in comparison to an organized play situ-ation where the adult is readily and constantly available. Increased attentiveness to social cues was also demonstrated by Canon (1967), who found that following social isolation, children were more distracted from a con-ceptual task by a social distractor (woman's voice telling a nurturant story) than by non-human noises, whereas the reverse was true for children who had not undergone social isolation.

The one possibly negative item in the lit-erature is a study by Cairns (1962) in which, for one condition, the adult was available dur-ing a 15-minute session in which the child was allowed periodically to choose an attractive toy from a cupboard. In the contrasting situation, the adult was nonavailable (busy) and would not allow the child to touch the attractive toys. Under these conditions, low-availability did not result in enhanced effectiveness of subsequent social reinforcement from a sec-ond experimenter, but of course this outcome may be a function of the adult's being frus-trating rather than nonavailable.

The experimental use of "nurturance with-drawal" has been one method of producing a temporary state of social deprivation. These studies create a climate of social satiation or of positive social interaction and then remove the conditions creating this climate. The initial study employing this technique was that of Hartup (1958). His work grew out of cor-relational studies by Sears et al. (1953) and Whiting and Child (1953) in which it was hypothesized that parental use of "withdrawal of love" as a technique of discipline should be positively related to the frequency of de-pendency behavior among young children. Hartup defined nurturance as "adult behavior which rewarded, encouraged, supported or showed affection to the child." One group of children in the study were given 10 minutes of continuous "nurturance," while another group were nurtured for 5 minutes, after which the adult withdrew from the child and refused to interact with him for 5 minutes. In a con-cept formation task in which verbal approval was the reinforcer, children from whom the nurturance had been withdrawn learned faster. The effect was significant only for girls. A within-sample analysis revealed that boys who were observed to be highly dependent in their behavior at nursery school did show greater learning following nurturance withdrawal, whereas for low-dependent boys the reverse was true.

Gewirtz and Baer (1958) produced social deprivation by isolating preschool subjects for 20 minutes before their participation in a simple two-response marble-dropping task. In this task subjects were rewarded by social approval for the correct response. The first study compared the performance of an iso-lated and a nonisolated group. The frequency of correct responses was greater following iso-lation than in the control condition. In the second study, a "satiation" condition was added in which, prior to the marble-dropping session, the subjects were given 20 minutes of frequent attention and approval. The fre-quency of correct responses—hence, by im-plication, the effectiveness of social reinforce-ment—was greatest after isolation and least after satiation.

In the research that has followed the initial Gewirtz and Baer publications, there have been many replications of the finding that social isolation enhances the effectiveness of social reinforcement. Significant isolation ef-fects have been found, either for all groups of subjects or for certain subgroups of sub-jects, in the following studies: Walters and Ray, 1960; Walters and Quinn, 1960; Steven-son and Odom, 1962; Hill and Stevenson, 1964; Lewis and Richman, 1964; Lewis, 1965; Rosenhan, 1967. Significant isolation effects were *not* found in the following studies: Walters and Parke, 1964a; Walters and Henning, 1962; Walters, Marshall, and Shooter, 1960; Walters and Karal, 1960. As noted earlier, differences in age of the subjects may be a partial explanation for the negative findings: three out of the four negative studies were done with college students, the fourth with fourth-graders. The studies with positive findings were all done with preschool children or children of early grade-school age, with the exception of the Walters and Quinn study (college students) and one of two age groups studied by Rosenhan (sixth graders). The generalization seems warranted that social isolation does have the stated effect with young children. Most recent research has been devoted not so much to the question of *whether* social deprivation has an effect, but to a more precise determination of what the effect is and a better understanding of exactly what it is about social deprivation (or more specifically, social isolation) that produces the effects.

A first question has been whether social deprivation enhances only the value of *social* reinforcers or of other reinforcers as well. If subjects who have undergone social deprivation perform better in all kinds of learning situations, regardless of the nature of the reinforcement, this might indicate that the effect of deprivation had been to raise the general level of motivation or responsiveness rather than to produce a specifically social motivation. Erikson approached this issue by comparing the value of verbal approval as a reinforcer with that of marbles from an automatic dispenser, following a 15-minute period of either deprivation of adult attention or continuous communication with an adult. She found that social deprivation increased the value of verbal reinforcement only, not that of the material reward. Dorwart et al. (1965) used a very mild manipulation of "social deprivation"—the experimenter was either not introduced to the child and silent during the 3-minute walk to the experimental room, or introduced and warmly chatty. They found that their "deprived" subjects were more likely to match input or maximize in a probability learning situation if the reinforcement was social, but that the manipulation had no effect upon the value of a red light as a reinforcer. Rosenhan (1967) studied the interaction between deprivation and satiation of social interaction and the effectiveness of social and nonsocial (light turned on for cor-

rect response) reinforcers. First-and sixth-grade children served as subjects, and the deprivation situation involved the experimenter's leaving the room for 15 minutes, while "satiation" involved engaging the child in conversation and play and giving social reinforcement for actions or statements. The findings were that satiated children were more responsive to nonsocial reinforcement or pure information feedback than they were to social reinforcement, whereas the reverse was true for the deprived children, who showed little learning with the light and whose rate of learning under social reinforcement was nearly identical to the rate observed for satiated children with nonsocial reinforcers. Walters and Parke (1964a) studied the effects of (1) arousal, and (2) isolation on responsiveness to verbal versus material reinforcement. Girls in the sample were more responsive to verbal reinforcement and less responsive to material reinforcement following isolation, but this interaction was not significant, and the relationship did not occur for boys.

Taking these studies as a whole, there is fairly good evidence that the effect of varying degrees of social deprivation is to enhance the effectiveness of specifically social reinforcers, not to improve learning under all reinforcement conditions. These results would be compatible with the position that social deprivation produces or enhances an affiliative or "dependent" motivational state.

A second set of experiments has investigated the question of whether social deprivation is effective in enhancing socially oriented behavior because it usually involves stimulus deprivation. It has been shown that isolation in stimulus-impoverished environments will increase stimulus-seeking (Butler, 1953; Stevenson and Odom, 1962). Perhaps children have learned that other human beings are good providers of a variety of stimulation, so that when stimulus-deprived they seek social interaction and are more attentive to social cues. Stevenson and Odom attacked this issue by comparing the following conditions: social isolation in a room containing attractive toys; social isolation without the toys; and a non-isolated control group. Both of the isolated groups showed greater responsiveness to social reinforcement than did the no-isolation control, and the two isolated groups did not differ significantly from each other, indicating that the presence of attractive and engaging stimuli during social isolation does not mitigate the effects of such isolation upon responsiveness to social reinforcement, and that the primary factor in such effects is social isolation per se. Walters and Quinn (1960) ran one group of college students who performed a tactual sorting task under conditions of sensory deprivation, in which their eyes were covered, their ears shielded from sound, and their nonused hand gloved. The experimenter was present and handed them the materials for sorting, with manual contact providing at least a minimum of social interaction. Another group performed the task with the experimenter absent from the room (social isolation), another group underwent both stimulus and social isolation, and a control group had neither. Following these initial manipulations, the subjects were run in an autokinetic judgment task, with a new experimenter telling the subject, after the first few trials, that he had severely underestimated the movement of the light. Other trials followed and the experimenter reinforced the subjects' more extreme judgments by "yes" and other responses by "no." Subjects who had experienced *both* sensory and social isolation showed the shortest latencies of response and the greatest amount of change in distance estimates (in the direction suggested by experimenter) from the first to the second series to trials. The influence for experimenter, as reflected in the changes in judgments, was equally great for social deprivation alone and sensory deprivation alone, and from inspection of the tables appears to be greater under both of these conditions than for the no-deprivation control group, although statistical tests for comparisons of individual groups are not provided. Tentatively, this experiment supports the view that both stimulus deprivation and social deprivation contribute to the enhancement of social reinforcer effectiveness.

A third experiment comparing stimulus deprivation with social deprivation does not show an independent effect of social deprivation. Hill and Stevenson (1964) compared the following isolation conditions: (1) subjects waited alone in an empty room, (2) subjects waited alone while watching an abstract movie, and (3) subjects watched the movie in the company of the experimenter. The subsequent rate of marble-dropping for social reinforcement was greatest for the alone, no-movie group; the other two groups did not differ, and both actually showed a decline in performance under social reinforcement in comparison to their no-reinforcement base rate. It should be noted in this experiment, as well as that of Walters and Quinn, the social-only deprivation condition involved an isolation period which was filled with interest-absorbing activity for the subject—more absorbing, perhaps, than the mere provision of toys in the Stevenson-Odom study. There is the possibility that sensory satiation is occurring, and, if so, it might conceivably counteract the effects of social isolation.

A vigorously pursued line of research has focused on the possibility that social isolation has its effects because it arouses anxiety. This is the position taken by Walters and his co-workers,[6] who point out that social contact is anxiety-reducing, so that the seeking of social interaction and increased attentiveness to social cues would be predictable instrumental responses following anxiety arousal. Walters and Ray (1960) manipulated both isolation and anxiety. First and second-grade subjects either were isolated for 20 minutes or proceeded directly to the experimental room. Half were called for initially by the school secretary, with whom they were familiar, and half by a brusque stranger. Responsiveness to subsequent social reinforcement was clearly enhanced under the anxiety conditions; there was a weaker but significant ($p < .05$) main effect of social isolation. Although the interaction is not reported as significant, inspection of the tables indicates that the social isolation effect occurred for the anxious subjects only. In a later study using fourth-grade children as subjects, Walters and Parke (1964a) found a significant effect for "arousal" only. In this study arousal was induced by having a stranger as the experimenter and giving the subject no information concerning the nature of the experiment. The fact that this manipulation actually did produce physiological changes that are part of the arousal pattern was documented through the recording of finger temperatures, which showed a significant difference in degree of change between the arousal and no-arousal conditions. While

---

[6] In their later work, Walters and his colleagues prefer the term "arousal" to the term "anxiety."

interactions were not significant, Walters and Parke (1964b) note, in discussing the experiment in their review paper:

Subjects placed under the threat condition and subsequently isolated both exhibited greater emotionality—assessed from finger-temperature records—and learned faster than any other group of subjects. Possibly isolation has a catalytic effect. A person in whom a state of anxiety or uncertainty has already been created may become increasingly apprehensive in the absence of stimuli capable of eliciting responses incompatible with the anxiety or uncertainty (p. 246).

There is some evidence, then, that social isolation per se does contribute, in interaction with anxiety, to social reinforcer effectiveness, but the evidence is weak. In a third study with older subjects, even this small contribution is not apparent. Walters and Henning (1962), working with adolescent boys, again compared the effects of social isolation with those of an anxiety arousing situation. Subjects were isolated for either 3 or 6 hours; the manipulation of anxiety involved the subjects either being told or not told that their performance in a speech-making task would be an indicator of intelligence and emotional stability. The anxiety condition clearly affected the subjects' susceptibility to social reinforcement; even the unusually long periods of social isolation employed in this study did not.[7] In the series of arousal experiments, there is only one (Walters and Foote, 1962), done with first- and second-grade girls, that did not show a significant effect of an anxiety manipulation.

Walters and his colleagues have demonstrated that arousing the subject through some sort of stress manipulation will increase his susceptibility to social reinforcement. Other investigators have obtained consistent results; for example, Hartup (1964) found that the rate of marble dropping by nursery school children is better maintained if the children are rewarded with the attention and verbal

approval of disliked rather than liked peers. Patterson and Anderson (1964), however, obtained an opposite result with children in the 7 to 10 age range, whose preference behavior was more influenced by reinforcement from liked peers than from disliked peers. Lewis and Richman (1964) found that children who had previously encountered a hostile adult were more responsive to social reinforcement than children whose pre-experimental encounter had been with a friendly adult. Berkowitz and Zigler (1965) found that prior contact with an adult who made critical and disapproving statements concerning a child's performance would result in subsequently greater effectiveness for social reinforcement than did prior contact with an approving adult. This occurred, however, only when the child was tested immediately after such contact. When the testing was delayed for a week the opposite effect was found. Consistent with this is the finding of McCoy and Zigler (1965), who varied the amount and nature of subjects' prior contact with the experimenter and tested them after a week's time, measuring the length of time they were willing to continue playing a game with the experimenter. The children stayed longest with the experimenter with whom they had previously had positive interaction, and least long with a strange experimenter, with scores for children who had had a "neutral" previous interaction with the experimenter being intermediate. These results suggest the hypothesis that a hostile person arouses fear in the child, and as long as the fear lasts it motivates the child to conform to the demands of the feared person. With the passage of time, however, the fear dies out and the child simply avoids or ignores the hostile person.

In an unpublished study, Mark Lepper tested this hypothesis by reinstating fear after the passage of time (by showing the children a mildly frightening movie). Under these conditions, the children again became more responsive to an experimenter with whom their previous contact had been negative; without the arousal condition, they were more responsive to a previously friendly experimenter. These experiments are consistent with the view that "arousal" does increase susceptibility to social reinforcement. There are a few entries in the literature, however, which are not consistent with an arousal hypothesis.

[7] In view of Cairns' (1966) finding that separation from an attachment object has its greatest effect immediately, with the effect diminishing rather quickly with time, it may be that the social isolation period in this study was too long!

Ruebush and Stevenson (1963) found that children who exhibited *low* anxiety levels on an anxiety questionnaire were more responsive to social reinforcement. However, self-rated "anxiety" may not reflect the same internal state as that produced by arousal operations. Stevenson and Hill (1965) compared the effects of previous success or failure upon responsiveness to social reinforcement. Following success, children's performance was at a higher level when social reinforcement was employed; following failure, however, performance was better when followed by nonreinforcement. Walters and Parke (1964b) point out that an experimenter who himself is the vehicle of a failure experience may acquire aversive properties and his subsequent "social reinforcement" behavior may itself be negative, but this explanation would not be consistent with the previously noted finding that responsiveness is greater to a hostile than neutral or friendly person, at least during the period immediately following the encounter.

The bulk of the evidence seems to indicate that social deprivation is not a necessary condition for the enhancement of social reinforcer effectiveness—a variety of stress manipulations have the same effect. This fact is consistent with the literature reviewed earlier that points to a functional relationship between fear or anxiety and a variety of manifestations of attachment or dependent behavior. The problem is to determine whether social deprivation is effective *only* if the subjects are anxious, or whether social deprivation is also, in itself, a sufficient condition. The fact that the isolated and nonisolated children in Walters and Ray's low-anxious group did not differ in their responsiveness to social reinforcement would suggest that social isolation by itself is not sufficient to produce this affiliative behavior. In the experiment of Stevenson and Odom, however, we find that social isolation *did* produce the effect, even for the children who were given toys to play with and were presumably made comfortable before the experimenter left them alone. But there may have been some residual anxiety attendant upon the isolation. With the two-by-two design in which isolation and an anxiety-arousing manipulation are covaried, one can never be sure that the isolated low-anxiety condition has actually been produced.

Because of this dilemma, Gewirtz (1967)

argues that the satiation operation is more satisfactory than the deprivation operation in testing the effects of previous level of social interaction on subsequent social behavior. In three recent experiments (Landau and Gewirtz, 1967; Gewirtz, 1967, experiments I and II), satiation for social reinforcers has been employed *without* isolation. In the Landau and Gewirtz study, contingent social reinforcement was given in a treatment period immediately preceding a test for social-reinforcer effectiveness, and the study showed that reinforcer effectiveness was an inverse function of the number of times that the reinforcer stimulus had been received in the pretraining period. An earlier study by Stevenson and Knights (1962) also showed that pretraining with positive contingent reinforcement by a given experimenter reduced the later effectiveness of this experimenter as a social reinforcement agent. In the second study in the recent Gewirtz series, the social reinforcer ("good") was administered *non*-contingently during the pretraining period (while the subject was looking at books), and again an inverse relationship was found between the number of reinforcers administered during pretraining and the responsiveness to reinforcement in the test. In the third experiment, intervals for "recovery from satiation" were interpolated between pretraining and test, and it was found that when more time had been allowed for recovery, social reinforcement was subsequently more effective.

Gewirtz points out that the satiation operations used in these experiments do not interfere with the provision of other stimuli, so the results cannot be interpreted in terms of "stimulus deprivation or satiation" of a more general kind. Furthermore, the adult is always with the child, and it appears unlikely that there would be an inverse relationship between the number of times the adult says "good" and the amount of anxiety or arousal produced in the situation; hence the anxiety hypothesis also does not account for the regular relationships obtained. Gewirtz argues, then, that these findings support the position that there is a functional relationship between deprivation or satiation of social stimuli and the enhancement or reduction of social reinforcer effectiveness of just the sort that obtains between such appetitive stimuli as food and water and the deprivation or satiation conditions that govern their reinforcement value. Concerning whether this implies that social deprivation arouses a "social drive," Gewirtz says:

Gewirtz and Baer viewed the functional relationship as comparable to those involving deprivation and satiation of appetitive stimuli to which the term "drive" has traditionally been applied. For heuristic reasons, they suggested that the term "social drive" could be applied to describe this functional relationship, although they recognized that the drive label was gratuitous, adding only historical context to the analysis (1967, p. 2).

It should be noted that Gewirtz' zero satiation condition bears some resemblance to what has been called "withdrawal of nurturance" in other experiments. In his procedure, the experimenter interacts with the child in a friendly way on the walk to the experimental room. Then the experimenter administers a demographic questionnaire to the child and says: "I have a game here I want to play with you and then there are some things for us to talk about, but first I have some paper work to finish. If you don't mind waiting for a few minutes, I brought along some books you can look at while I work. Okay?" The experimenter then sits opposite the child and busies himself with note-taking, during which time he is either silent or says "good" the required number of times. While this sequence can hardly be regarded as one that threatens the child, it does involve changing the level of interaction in a downward direction, so that it is still unclear whether the experimental manipulation is best described as deprivation, satiation, or a combination of the two.

It is worth noting that satiation effects are not obtained if the prior reinforcement is contingent upon dependency responses. Cairns (1962) compared two groups, both run under high adult-availability conditions, in one of which the child could not get some attractive toys until the adult handed them to him. In this condition, the adult complied with the child's requests for help, and during the session thus provided a number of reinforcements for help-seeking behavior. In the other condition the children had direct access to the toys, and while the adult was generally rewarding, the reinforcements dispensed were not contingent on help-seeking. The group rewarded for help-seeking showed greater susceptibility to social reinforcement in a subsequent session.

We have already seen that an increased level of social reinforcement is associated with decreased responsiveness to social reinforcement in a subsequent period. That this phenomenon may span a longer time than the time periods usually used in experimental studies is suggested by Cairns' (1963) finding that the children who are most responsive to social reinforcement in laboratory studies are the ones who receive the *least* praise at home. We may speculate that one factor underlying this relationship—apart from any arousal properties the parents' sparse use of praise may have—is that praise, like any other stimulus, may be more attention-getting, and more valued, when it is rare. In other words, the child may establish an adaptation level to the normal rate of input of a reinforcer and respond primarily to deviations from this level. Support for this hypothesis may be found in the Cairns (1962) findings that (1) children prefer a class of tokens which they have not had a previous opportunity to play with, and (2) the rating adults give to the verbal reinforcer "um-humm" on the Semantic Differential varies inversely with the number of times this reinforcer has been used in a preceding experimental session.

The studies involving pretraining operations varying the availability of social stimuli would appear to have shown that such operations are *sufficient* condition (though not, as we noted above, necessary) for changes in the effectiveness of social reinforcers. Arousal (or anxiety) stands as a second sufficient condition.

Closely allied to the arousal hypothesis is the view that frustration acts as a mediator of dependency behavior. Whiting (1944) argued that a number of different responses may be activated under frustration, depending upon previous learning conditions and the social context in which the frustration occurs, and that dependency is one of the responses (along with aggression, avoidance, and submission) likely to be acquired. Whiting held that a variety of frustrations (including weaning and toilet training) should lead to increases in dependent behavior, and indeed he observed that this was the case in the preliterate society where he worked. Hartup and Himeno (1959) suggested that social isolation is a form of frustration and as such should produce increases in aggression as well as the increases in dependent behavior documented in the studies previously reviewed. These investigators did find an increase in aggressive responses in doll play sessions which followed social isolation. Walters and Parke (1964b) hold that this finding "provides strong evidence against the social drive hypothesis," on the grounds that aggression "can hardly be regarded as behavior aimed at eliciting positive social reinforcement." Apart from the work on *negative-attention-getting* (Sears et al., 1953, 1965), which indicates that there is a class of aggressive behavior having just this aim, there is the question of whether the social drive hypothesis claims that the *only* effect of social deprivation is to enhance the value of social reinforcers. There seems to be no necessary reason to place this restriction on the theory, and we do not find that Gewirtz and Baer did so.

The view that social deprivation has its effect because it serves as a source of frustration is called into question by the findings of Cairns (1962) cited above. When an adult is not only unavailable but also actively frustrating (by blocking the child's access to toys), the usual findings for low-availability are reversed, and the child becomes *less* susceptible to social reinforcement than he is following a high-availability, nonfrustrating sequence.

Beller and Haeberle (1961) present evidence that the effects of social deprivation on dependency behavior may depend upon the initial level of dependency shown by the child. These authors classified children as high or low dependent, and they found that only the high dependent children became more dependent under the withdrawal of positive reinforcers. Other evidence (Baer, 1962) also indicates that withholding positive reinforcers produces increases in dependency behavior only in children whose past social learning experiences have made them relatively high in dependency. Hartup (1958) obtained similar results with his male subjects.

Several studies have explored social reinforcement effects among retarded, institu-

tionalized children. These studies may be considered "naturalistic" studies, combining elements of social deprivation and stimulus deprivation that are common in the history of these children and in institutional settings.

In one study (Zigler, 1961) two psychologists examined the case histories of 60 institutionalized retarded children and rated the children according to the degree of social deprivation they had experienced. Children were categorized as having had low or high deprivation. Children rated as more socially deprived spent a significantly longer time at a marble-sorting task that utilized social reinforcement than did the less socially deprived children. In addition, twice as many of the more socially deprived children made the maximum number of responses (400) compared to the less socially deprived subjects.

In a follow-up study, Zigler and Williams (1963) found that during a 3-year period following the original study the children with *less* social deprivation in their history showed a significantly greater increase in the effectiveness of social reinforcement than did children rated as highly deprived. Residence in an institution apparently had little effect upon the more socially deprived children but appeared to act as a deprivation condition upon the children rated as less socially deprived before admission to the institution.

Stevenson and Fahel (1961) studied both institutionalized and noninstitutionalized normal and retarded children. For half of the children, a marble-dropping game was played during which the experimenter was attentive but unresponsive to the children's behavior; for the rest of the children, the experimenter delivered two supportive comments for each minute for 5 minutes following a 1-minute base-line period. Upon the introduction of social reinforcement, institutionalized subjects increased their rate of marble-dropping significantly more than did noninstitutionalized children.

In a study by Stevenson and Knights (1962a), normal and retarded children of the same mental age played a marble game in which responses were reinforced by supportive comments by the experimenter. The performance of both normal and retarded children was reduced if the criterion game had been preceded by a pretraining period of positive interaction with the experimenter. The performance difference between a group who had had no pretraining and the pretrained subjects was greater for the normal children. This finding, indicating that retarded children are less likely than normals to satiate given the same amount of social interaction, also implies that retarded children may already be in a state of social deprivation. In addition to the fact that institutional retardates are more responsive to social reinforcement and less susceptible to social satiation than normal children, there are other indications of a higher level of "dependency" among these children. For example, Turnure and Zigler (1964) found that a group of retardates (1) were more imitative, (2) glanced more often toward the experimenter, and (3) were more disrupted in their task performance by incompatible social cues than were a group of normal children of similar mental age.

There is no consistent evidence that the length of institutionalization is associated with the effectiveness of social reinforcement. The Zigler and Williams (1963) study indicates that change in reinforcer effectiveness during institutionalization depends largely upon children's deprivation states before institutionalization. In another study, Stevenson and Knights (1962b) found that girls who had returned to an institution after a summer vacation with their families were more responsive to social reinforcers immediately after their return than following 12 weeks in the institution. This finding is contrary to the social and stimulus deprivation hypotheses. However, as we have seen earlier, separation from attachment objects augments dependent behavior under some conditions, and the girls' leaving their families to return to an institution may have been the significant factor in these cases.

INDIVIDUAL DIFFERENCES

Thus far in our review we have been concerned with the modal developmental sequence in attachment and dependent behavior, and with the environmental conditions that will bring about changes in this behavior on the part of all or most children. We have noted, however, that children of a given age may differ considerably in the intensity and frequency with which they exhibit various types of dependent behavior, and a great deal of research effort has been devoted to uncovering the factors that underlie these individual differences. The study of the reasons why some children are more dependent or attached than others is not, of course, independent of the studies of situational determinants reviewed previously. For example, we have seen that fear or anxiety-producing situations will usually intensify attachment behavior. It follows that a child who is growing up in an unusually fear-producing environment should show more dependent behavior than one whose life situation is more secure. Similarly, we have seen that children who have just been rewarded for help-seeking are more responsive to social reinforcement in a subsequent experimental session. Children who are frequently rewarded for help-seeking in the course of their daily lives, then, ought to have high susceptibility to social reinforcement as a personality trait, and perhaps other aspects of dependency as well.

It has been the assumption of students of personality development that if one can uncover some of the conditions associated with the acquisition of certain stable individual response-tendencies, one will have identified conditions that could be experimentally manipulated to produce "situationally controlled" behavior change in most children. The basic strategy in studies of personality has been to identify individual differences along one or more dimensions of concern, and then to search for "antecedent" conditions (e.g., parental socialization practices) which are correlated with or predictive of these differences.

As we begin to examine and describe the empirical work on individual differences, we note that there has been great variety in the operations defining the dimensions along which measurements are taken, and along which individuals are compared. Although a few researchers have taken the position (derived from ethological theory) that attachment is an all-or-none phenomenon—a child is either attached to a given individual or he is not—most have considered attachment or dependency to be a matter of degree and have attempted to obtain measures that will reflect the level of strength of the behavior.

Possible measures of behavior strength include:

1. The distance from an attachment figure that a child can go (or be taken) before his attachment behavior is activated.
2. The degree of strangeness in the environment that is tolerated without the activation of attachment behavior.
3. The length of time a child can be separated from his attachment figure before protest or efforts to regain begin.
4. The vigor of the behavior (e.g., intensity of crying, strength of clinging).
5. The number of persons toward whom the behavior is shown.
6. The number of situations in which the behavior is shown.
7. The number of different types of the behavior shown.
8. The frequency of the behavior.
9. The degree of maturity the attachment behavior shows (whether it is primarily like that shown characteristically by older or younger children).
10. The salience of dependency as a dimension for organizing the individual's behavior (i.e., the extent to which it is correlated with his other behavior, so that it would emerge as a central dimension in factor analysis).

All these attributes may be considered measures of behavior strength, yet only a limited subset has actually been used in research.

The age of onset of certain forms of attachment behavior—particularly of specific attachments and stranger fears—has been studied as a dimension of individual differences; this dimension would be thought of as related to the "strength" measures listed above only if one assumes that the conditions producing high intensity or frequency of the behavior would also contribute to its early appearance. This is an empirical question that will be considered shortly.

The most commonly used measure is *frequency,* although this is often used in conjuction with some other strength measure. For example, a "total dependency" or "total attachment" score may be derived by adding frequency subscores based upon several different situations or several different "kinds" of dependent behavior. Ratings of dependent behavior commonly direct the rater's attention primarily to frequency, although other indicators of strength may be involved. For example, Beller's rating scale: "How often does the child seek help?" runs from "Very often and very persistently" to "Very rarely and without persistence."

The Stability and Consistency of Individual Differences

As noted previously, when a population of like-aged children is measured with respect to the frequency or intensity of the children's attachment or dependent behavior, marked individual differences may be observed. The etiology of these differences is a matter of considerable interest, but before this problem can be studied, it is necessary to determine to what degree it is possible to characterize a given child as being consistently highly attached, or highly dependent, by comparison with other children.

The first requisite for identifying such stable individual differences is, of course, that there shall be a reliable scoring system for the behavior under study. Many researchers report figures on interobserver reliability where both observers are observing the same sample of behavior, or on interscorer or interrater reliability where two scorers or raters are scoring the same set of behavior protocols.

High scoring reliability is a necessary prerequisite for detecting trait consistency, but of course it does not imply that such consistency exists. Assuming that adequate scoring reliability has been obtained, the further questions are: (1) Does a child who frequently displays one kind of dependent behavior (e.g., seeking physical contact with an adult) also frequently display other kinds of dependent behavior (e.g., seeking attention, or being upset over separation)? (2) Is a child who frequently displays a given kind of dependency behavior in one situation likely to show this same kind of behavior in a variety of other situations and toward a variety of other targets? (3) And to what degree is the rank-ordering of a group of children with respect to dependent behavior maintained over time? This last question can refer to a brief test-retest interval of a few weeks, or to a longer-range stability over a range of many years.

We begin our review of intrapersonal consistency in dependency with question 1. This question may be put in a slightly different way: How wide a range of behavior may be legitimately regarded as part of the "trait" *dependency*?

Correlations among Different Dependent Behaviors. We noted earlier that responsiveness to social reinforcement and susceptibility to social influence, in general, are thought to form part of a larger cluster of dependent behavior tendencies. We have already seen that in some studies it was only the children known to be dependent on the basis of some other measure who were affected by social deprivation. We may now summarize the evidence that, even in the absence of any social deprivation manipulation, there is a relationship between dependency in the more general sense and susceptibility to social influence.

Kagan and Mussen (1956), measuring dependency themes in TAT stories, showed that the more dependent adults are especially likely to conform to the judgments of others in a group perceptual judgment situation. Jakubczak and Walters (1959) assessed dependency in 9-year-old boys by means of a semiprojective technique. They then tested high- and low-dependent boys in the autokinetic judgment situation. In the early stages of the testing they found that the high-dependent boys matched the judgments of the confederates of the experimenter to a greater degree than did the low-dependent boys.

Endsley (1960) demonstrated that children who are dependent in the sense of seeking praise from teachers perform better on a learning task in which social reinforcement is used than do children who seek praise relatively seldom. By using other measures of dependency, the relationship of dependency to susceptibility to social reinforcement has been verified by Adler (1961), Ferguson (1961), Epstein (1964), and Cairns and Kaufman (1962).

Cairns has worked with the hypothesis that not only does high dependency increase susceptibility to social reinforcement, but inhibition of dependency (dependency anxiety) decreases it. Cairns and Lewis (1962) assessed dependency in adults by the Edwards Personal Preference Scale, the Leary Interpersonal Checklist, and a behavioral measure. They found that subjects with low scores on these measures judged verbal reinforcing stimuli to be neutral or *negative*, and the low

group showed a significant decrement when they were verbally reinforced for producing aggressive sentences. Cairns also found (1961) that adolescents who are reluctant to accept help from others respond relatively little to social reinforcement.

Most of the previously cited studies involve comparing groups of highly dependent subjects with groups of low-dependent subjects with respect to their performance on a conformity task or a task that involves social reinforcement. The differences between the groups are tested for significance, but we do not have a measure of the magnitude of the effect. Thus it appears to have been demonstrated that susceptibility to social influence is related to measures of a more general "trait" of dependency, but we do not know the degree of the relationship.

We turn now to studies dealing with the interrelationships among other aspects of dependency. In most of these, correlation coefficients are reported, so that it is possible to determine not only whether a relationship is statistically significant, but something about its magnitude as well.

Working with a sample of 64 girls aged 3 to 5, Rosenthal (1965) conducted three observational sessions with each child; for two of these, the child was in the mother's presence; for the third, in the presence of a strange female adult. Behavior was scored into the following categories: negative attention-seeking, positive attention-seeking, approval-seeking, help-seeking, proximity-seeking, and physical contact-seeking. Indices of relationship were obtained among all these categories except negative attention-seeking, which was too infrequent to permit analysis. Within a single observational session, positive attention-seeking, approval-seeking, and help-seeking were significantly interrelated (coefficients of contingency averaging .41), and proximity-seeking and physical contact-seeking were related (c ± .50), but scales were not related from one of these clusters to the other.

Gewirtz (1956) observed the behavior of 66 4- and 5-year-old children during a structured easel-painting situation in the presence of an adult, scoring the following categories: attention-seeking, questions, comments, glances, praise-seeking, help-seeking, permission-seeking, number of paintings completed, and the length of time the child chose to remain at the task. The matrix of intercorrelations among these variables was factor analyzed and two major factors emerged. The first, accounting for 28% of the total item variance, was one which appeared to involve active, overt attempts to gain or maintain the adult's attention; items having high loadings on this factor were question-asking, attention-seeking, comments, help-seeking and praise-seeking. The second factor, accounting for 22% of the total variance, appeared to reflect a more passive compliance with what the child perceived to be the adult-imposed requirements of the situation. High loadings on this factor were found for the number of glances the child directed to the adults and for task persistence—the amount of time the child remained at the task and the number of paintings completed.

As part of a study of 19 girls and 21 boys done at Iowa (Sears et al., 1953), standardized behavior observations were made by Gewirtz on five aspects of dependency: touching and holding, being near, positive attention-seeking, negative attention-seeking, and reassurance-seeking. The intercorrelations among these measures were slightly positive for boys (mean $r = .16$), essentially zero for girls, and were not significant.[8]

In a later study, Sears and his colleagues (Sears, Rau, and Alpert, 1965) used a time-sampling method of behavior-unit observation, and scored the same categories of dependency as those used in the Iowa study. For boys the intercorrelations among these variables were approximately zero. For girls there was a strong positive relation between "touching and holding" and "being near" ($r = .71$)— the cluster which Rosenthal also found to be a coherent one among girls, and which she labeled proximity-seeking. The correlations among the remaining girls' measures were low positive (mean correlation: .16) and insignificant, and for boys the correlations clustered around zero. One might ask whether there is a "forced" correlation between "touching and holding" and "being near" in these observational studies, since a child must approach another individual in order to touch him, so that whether he is scored as "touching"

[8] These correlations were not included in the original publication and have been computed for the present report.

or "being near" would depend on the point in time when the observation was made. Actually, however, "being near" is defined as sitting near or playing near another person, without any continued approach being implied. And, in fact, the two measures are uncorrelated for boys (.13) in the 1965 Sears study, and uncorrelated for both sexes in the Iowa study.

A reanalysis of the Sears (1965) data, separating the scores according to whether the target of the dependent behavior is an adult or another child, reveals the following relationships ($N = 40$):

	2	3—	4
1. Positive attention-seeking toward children	.49	.13	−.19
2. Positive attention-seeking toward adults		−.23	.12
3. Proximity-seeking toward children			−.20
4. Proximity-seeking toward adults			

Even though the correlations are small, it is interesting that the relationship between proximity-seeking toward adults and either type of dependent behavior directed toward children is negative.

A very similar pattern of intercorrelations was obtained by Heathers (1955), who observed behavior during free nursery school play and scored two categories of dependency: clinging (including seeking affection), and seeking attention or approval. Total scores for these two categories were uncorrelated. When scores were distinguished according to whether dependent behavior was being directed toward adults or children, the following pattern of intercorrelations emerged:

	2	3	4
1. Seeks attention or approval, child	.64	.16	−.27
	.57	−.05	−.29
2. Seeks attention or approval, teacher		.33	.07
		−.50	.23
3. Clings, seeks affection, child			.08
			.06
4. Clings, seeks affection, teacher			

(From Heathers, 1955. The upper number in each pair of correlations is for 2-year-olds, the lower number for children aged 4 to 5. $N =$ 20 for each age group.)

In both the Sears and the Heathers studies, then, there is evidence that attention-seeking "generalizes" from adults to children, but no evidence that proximity-seeking does so.

There is very little work dealing with the generalization of dependency responses from one target to another. An exception is the previously mentioned study by Rosenthal (1965) in which children were observed once in the presence of their mothers and once in the presence of a stranger. Rosenthal found a generalization gradient, with fewer dependency responses being directed to the stranger than to the mother. When anxiety-producing cues were introduced into the experimental situation, the total frequency of dependent responses to both targets was increased, but the slope of the generalization gradient remained unchanged. When the sample was subdivided according to an independent assessment of the child's normal level of dependency, it was found that high-dependent children showed more dependent responses toward both the mother and the stranger than normally low-dependent children, with the slope of the gradient being the same for the two groups. Thus having a higher-than-average level of pre-existing dependency operated in the same way as an experimental induction of anxiety, that is, it increased the amount of the child's dependency toward both mother and stranger to the same degree.

In the longitudinal study conducted at the Fels Institute, ratings of several aspects of dependency were made, based upon repeated behavior observations (at home and at school), interviews with the child, the interviews with the mother. Kagan and Moss (1962) have reported data concerning the long-range stability of the behaviors they studied, and these findings will be discussed later. The intercorrelations among the different dependency scores are reported separately for four different age levels (Kagan and Moss, 1962, Appendix Table 32C, p. 365 then ff). Ratings of passivity are correlated, significantly at most age levels, with ratings of general dependency, affectional dependency, and instrumental dependency, the mean intercorrelation being .42 for boys and .62 for girls. After the age of 6, ratings of passivity and dependency are negatively related to ratings of independ-

dence, the mean figures (across all age levels) being −.57 for boys, −.71 for girls. The ratings at any given age level were made by the same rater at the same time; hence these figures may reflect to some degree the implicit assumptions of the rater concerning relationships among the behaviors indexed by the subscales.

In another study based on a sample of Fels children, Crandall et al. (1960) made ratings on the basis of time-sampled observation. They rated (1) approval-seeking, (2) emotional support-seeking, and (3) help-seeking, all from adults. The intercorrelations of these ratings were: 1 and 2, .41; 1 and 3, .16; and 2 and 3, .72.

As part of the Iowa study referred to earlier (Sears et al., 1953), Beller obtained a set of ratings by nursery school teachers on the following aspects of dependency: seeking help, seeking praise and approval, seeking physical contact, seeking attention, and being near. These ratings were made separately for behavior directed toward the teacher and behavior directed toward other children. The ratings showed substantial intercorrelations, the mean value for the intercorrelations among measures of dependency toward the teacher being .67; toward other children, .71. In a later study, Beller (1959) reports a set of ratings made by nursery school teachers who had had extensive opportunities to observe a group of 74 children, and who were trained to take note of dependency-relevant behavior. They rated the children on: seeking help, seeking recognition, seeking physical contact, seeking attention, and seeking physical nearness. The ratings of adult-directed dependency were significantly intercorrelated, with the mean correlation being .63 for the five measures of dependency on adults; a similar level of intercorrelation was obtained for the five measures of dependency directed toward other children. There was no indication of separate "clusters" or subgroups of measures in either of these studies.

In these studies, as well as the Fels study, ratings were not independent—that is, the rater, while rating one subscale, knew what ratings were being given on the other subscales, and hence there is an opportunity for "halo" effect to operate to an unknown degree. Another possible problem in the interpretation of the 1959 Beller data lies in the wide age range used. The ages in this sample range from 2½ to 6—a wider range than that included in the other studies cited. If there were a general decline, throughout the preschool years, in the frequency of all the varieties of dependent behavior measured, then a wide age range would inflate the intercorrelations among these measures. In his publications Beller does not report the correlations of his subscales with chronological age, but a subsequent analysis[9] reveals no relationship with age for any of the subscales, and no changes with age in mean ratings on "total dependency." This age stability may simply reflect the fact that teachers tend to rate children with reference to their own age group, so that age in a sense is already partialled out of such ratings. In any case, it would appear that the intercorrelations among the Beller subscales are not inflated by common age trends.

The work summarized thus far points to a fairly high degree of "trait consistency" when ratings are used, and a much more differentiated picture with behavior-observation scores. It is possible that an important reason for the lack of intercomponent correlations in data derived from behavioral observations is the lack of standardization of eliciting conditions. Here the contrast between measures of intellectual performance and measures of "personality" attributes, with respect to intrapersonal stability, is an instructive one. Intelligence tests, which yield stable individual profiles, have employed standardized eliciting conditions; observational measures of attributes have done so to a considerably lesser degree. In the usual time-sampling procedures, for example, the behavior of the child is recorded wherever he happens to be in the nursery school. Sometimes there is an adult nearby, sometimes there is not. Sometimes the child has been put in a structured situation where a given activity is highly probable (e.g., he has been given a painting smock and some paints and placed in front of an easel), sometimes he has not. Sometimes the nearest adult is one to whom the child has formed a fairly close attachment, on other occasions the child's favorite target may be out of sight and another, less favored person may be nearby. All these variations should

affect the chances of a dependent response being made and reduce the chances of identifying any trait consistency that may exist. When the eliciting conditions are more standardized, a certain amount of trait consistency does emerge, even when behavior unit observations are being used (e.g., Gewirtz, 1956; Rosenthal, 1965), although the trait consistency is narrower than that found in rating studies.

Relation of Dependency to Other Social Behavior. So far we have been discussing "trait consistency" in terms of the interrelationships among different manifestations of dependency. Factor analysis involving measures of a large variety of behaviors provides a somewhat different approach. In such analyses, it is possible to see whether the different aspects of dependent behavior correlate more strongly with one another than they do with other, presumably nondependent behaviors. In other words, it is possible to determine whether they have high loadings on the same factors. Cluster analysis provides a similar approach to the same question.

In several studies, the two primary factors accounting for the largest portion of the covariance among a variety of measures have been chosen for circumplex analysis (Schaefer, 1961). In such an analysis, a variable can be plotted graphically in terms of its position on the two main factors, and it can be determined which variables occupy neighboring spaces in the sense of having similar loadings on these two factors. Becker and Krug (1964), starting with 72 bipolar seven-point rating scales (rated independently by two teachers and each parent for a given child), and a sample of 71 kindergarten-aged children, present a circumplex plot, organized around the two primary dimensions "emotional stability-instability" and "extroversion-introversion" (see Fig. 2). The "dependent" end of the "dependent-independent" scale falls in the area of the circumplex labeled "submissiveness," fairly close to introversion, and somewhat more in the emotionally stable than the unstable region. However, it should be noted that other attributes commonly thought of as part of the dependency cluster occupy quite different space. For example, "attention-seeking" is related to behaviors in the "emotional-demanding" and "unstable" region, and "sociability" is highly loaded on

---

[9] We are grateful to E. K. Beller for making his data available for this analysis.

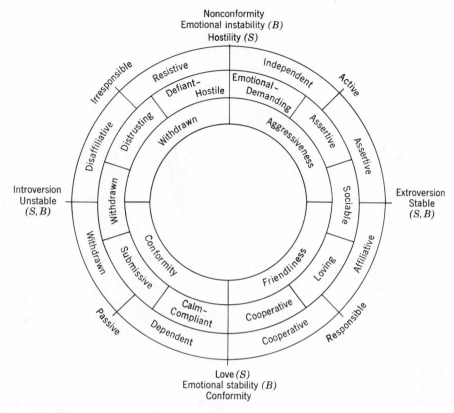

Fig. 2. A comparison of two-factor child behavior models. Outer ring: four-cluster solution from Baumrind and Black. Middle ring: Becker and Krug's (1964) model. Inner ring: Schaefer's (1961) model. Becker and Krug's major axes are indicated by B and Schaefer's by S. (From Baumrind and Black, 1967.)

extroversion but orthogonal to emotional stability. In short, these three aspects of dependency proved to be part of quite different behavioral clusters. Becker and Krug present a circumplex ordering based on the rating intercorrelations from five other studies and obtain a high degree of concordance for their ordering.

Baumrind and Black (1967) present a circumplex analysis which begins with a somewhat different set of measures—a Q sort of 95 behavior-descriptive items including a fairly large set dealing with aspects of competence and degree of planning of behavior. They compare their ordering with that of Becker and Krug, and with that of Schaefer (1961). It may be seen in Fig. 2 that "dependent" behavior is associated with passivity and conformity, whereas affiliative behavior is on a dimension almost completely orthog-

onal to the dependent-independent dimension.

The different factorial loadings for the different components of dependency provide some insight into the findings that have been obtained in studies which select other personality attributes for correlation with various measures of dependency, and we digress briefly to consider some of these studies. Hartup and Keller (1960) found that nurturance-giving was positively related to "seeking help," but negatively related to "being near." On the circumplex, both seeking help and nurturance-giving would probably be located in the region described as active and sociable, while being near would be located with passive dependency. Marshall and McCandless (1957) report that dependence on adults is negatively associated with the amount of interaction with peers and the number of dependent bids directed toward peers. This study and a later one by McCandless et al. (1961) also show that popularity with peers and acceptance by them are negatively associated with the level of a child's adult-oriented dependency, a relationship also found by Moore and Updegraff (1964). These findings are consistent with the data reported earlier reflecting a developmental shift from orientation toward adults to orientation toward age-mates; in addition, they may reflect a tendency for adult-oriented dependency to be more passive.

Studies reporting the relationship between dependency and aggression have yielded conflicting results, some of which may be understood by reference to the circumplex model. Theoretically there are two possible viewpoints about what the relation between dependency and aggression ought to be. On the one hand, if both are viewed as responses to frustration (and as *immature* responses that occur primarily when the child has not yet acquired other modes of coping with frustration), then the frequency of dependent and aggressive responses might prove to be positively correlated. On the other hand, one might view the two classes of responses as conflicting, in that affiliative tendencies involve the need to be liked and approved and aggression generally elicits hostile rather than supportive responses from others. Empirically, one does observe responses which are difficult to classify as either dependent or aggressive (e.g., "negative attention seeking"; whining). In a number of studies high positive correlations have been obtained between measures of dependency and measures of aggression. Winder and Rau (1962) report a correlation of .73 between the two classes of behavior, as reflected in scores on a Peer Nominations Inventory, and Maccoby and Rau (1962) also obtained a strong positive correlation with a more representative sample of children using the same measurement technique. These correlations were not simply a product of negative halo, since dependency and aggression were considerably more strongly correlated with one another than either was with a Likeability scale.

Sears et al. (1953) also found positive correlations between dependency and aggression on both ratings and observational measures. Much (not all) of the interrelationship was accounted for by the association of each attribute with activity level. These results are consistent with the early finding by Murphy (1937) that the amount of "sympathy" shown by children was positively associated with their level of aggression, and with the work of Emmerich (reported above), who found that the most socially interactive children were also most given to "negative attitude," at least during the initial period of their stay in nursery school. Bandura and Walters (1959) report considerable *inhibition* of overt dependency in a group of adolescent aggressive boys, accompanied by signs of anxiety concerning dependency; a study of a group of pre-adolescent aggressive boys, however (Bandura, 1960), revealed high levels of overt dependency toward parents among these boys.

That dependency and aggression are functionally positively related is suggested by the fact that the same experimental manipulations change at least some manifestations of both in the same direction. Keister and Updegraff (1937) have shown a simultaneous decline in the two classes of behavior following a training session in which children are taught task persistence and constructive solution strategies in the face of a frustrating task. Also, as previously noted, social isolation tends to augment a variety of dependent responses, while one study (Hartup and Himeno, 1959) reports an increase in doll-play aggression following social isolation.

There is some evidence of a negative association between the two classes of behavior, however. An experimental arousal of affiliative tendencies, accomplished through reading a story about a child searching for friends, resulted in a decrease of aggressive responses in a subsequent doll-play session in which the child's thematic interactions between two child dolls were scored (Gordon and Cohn, 1963). Faigin (1958), in an observational study of children aged 19 to 38 months living in two Israeli kibbutzim, found a strong negative correlation (−.73) between dependency and aggression. This correlation was confined to the children's relationships with adults. In their interactions with age-mates, the two classes of behavior correlated slightly positively. In Faigin's study, dependency toward adults was heavily weighted with the more passive forms of behavior such as crying and "seeking affection" (touching, holding, being near), and perhaps it is for this reason that correlations with aggression are negative. In the studies which yield positive correlations, dependency usually includes a larger component of attention- and approval-seeking, and usually involves dependency directed toward age-mates as well as that directed toward adults. In this connection, the findings of Sears et al. (1965) are instructive: observational measures of aggression, in their study, tended to correlate positively with attention-seeking, and negatively with touching, holding, and being near (see their Appendix Table K-5). In a study by Beller (1962) ratings of aggression had correlations with rated attention-seeking ranging from .37 to .57, while the correlations with ratings of seeking physical nearness were lower (.12 to .29).

We return now to our consideration of the factor-analytic studies of children's behavior and the nature of the clusters of which various dependent behaviors form a part. Emmerich (1964, 1966a) has carried out two different factor analyses, with two sets of data taken from the same group of children and covering the same period of time. In one case, the data were teacher ratings; in the other, time-sampled behavior observations. For the behavior observations, 34 categories of behavior were recorded, including six that would form part of the usual definition of dependency: touching or holding, being near, seeking positive attention, securing aid for self, securing reassurance, securing negative attention, and seeking affiliation. The factor analysis yielded three major dimensions, which Emmerich designated as follows: (1) interpersonal versus impersonal orientation; (2) positive-negative attitude; and (3) active-passive mode. The presumably dependency-related behaviors did not clearly cluster together, nor did they load on the same factors. The situation is quite different when the analysis is based on teacher ratings of 34 subscales taken from Beller; the 34 attributes rated by the teachers are not the same as those scored in the behavior observation, although there is considerable overlap in the dependency area, where seeking help, attention, physical contact, proximity, and recognition are rated. From the factor analysis of the 34 rating scales three clear factors

emerge: (1) aggression-dominance, (2) dependency, and (3) autonomy. A very similar set of three factors emerge from the factor analysis carried out by Beller and Turner (1964) on a subset of these same rating scales. A factor analysis of a set of 72 ratings that did not include the Beller scales, however, and focused on somewhat different attributes, did not reveal a coherent dependency factor (Becker, 1960).

It would appear, then, that when one uses behavior observation of a restricted set of behaviors all theoretically related to dependency, dependency does not emerge as a coherent dimension (as in the work of Gewirtz, Heathers, and Sears). When behavior observations include a wider range of behavior, dependency breaks down into two or sometimes three components, each part of different but stable clusters (Emmerich, Becker and Krug, Baumrind and Black, and Schaefer). When ratings are used, dependency does emerge as a coherent dimension for ordering individual differences in children's behavior (Kagan and Moss, 1962; Beller, 1959; Emmerich, 1966a), provided dependent behavior was the focus of a number of the original rating scales. Does this mean that dependency exists primarily "in the eye of the beholder"—that it is a salient dimension among adult judges, and that they tend to superimpose it where the more objective measures provided by behavior observation do not detect it? Mischel (1968) argues that "trait generality" for a wide variety of personality attributes is produced in just this artifactual way.

The situation is not entirely simple, however. As we have seen from a review of the circumplex studies, not all rating studies do yield a dependency dimension; therefore this trait must not be "salient" for all raters, or the set to perceive it must not be induced by all rating procedures. Beyond this, there is the question of whether independent ratings of the "same" attribute correlate positively and significantly with one another. If they do, then the ratings must reflect something "real" about the individual differences among the group being rated. Emmerich (1966b) discusses this issue from a transactional approach, arguing that the rating process is one of person-perception, in which the characteristics of the rater, as well as those of the ratee, are involved. "Traits" are organizing concepts in the minds of raters, by means of which they make a selection from among the available behavioral cues emitted by the ratee. There exists a variety of possible organizing dimensions a rater might use, but the value arrived at along a dimension for a given rater-ratee pair is not independent of the "real" behavior of the child. In other words, the rating dimension, though superimposed during the rating process, can yield valid and reliable data for ordering subjects. It is an empirical question as to whether it does so.

Correlations among Independent Assessments of Dependency. We turn now to a different aspect of the problem of consistency: To what extent is the rank-ordering of a group of individuals (either on a total dependency score or a subscore representing a component) maintained when different behavior samples, taken from the same group of children, are compared?

In the Rosenthal (1965) study described earlier, mother-daughter pairs were observed on two different occasions. Total proximity-seeking (a summary score of proximity-seeking and physical-contact-seeking) was moderately stable from one session to another. The stability was greater when the second session occurred under high anxiety conditions than when anxiety-producing stimuli were not introduced. Total attention-seeking behavior (a summary of seeking positive attention, negative attention, approval, and help), however, did not show inter-session stability. The relevant correlations are given in Table 6.

Hatfield et al. (1967) computed total dependency scores for two sessions of mother-child interaction. The intersession correlation was .39. Coz and Campbell (1968) observed a group of young children (aged 13 to 15 months) with their mothers on two occasions

Table 6. Inter-session correlations. (From Rosenthal, 1965).

	High Anxiety	Low Anxiety
Total attention seeking	.06	.05
Total proximity-seeking	.68[a]	.38[b]
N	32	32

[a] $p = <.01$.
[b] $p = <.05$.

three weeks apart. The correlation was .48 between Session I and Session II scores on the frequency of "touching and holding mother."

Sears et al. (1965) computed total dependency scores for a group of 40 children for three different time periods. The scores were based on time-sampled behavior observations, and the time periods covered were weeks 2 to 3, 4 to 6, and 7 to 8 of an 8-week summer nursery school session. The average of the three correlations among time periods was .36.

By computing a measure of "trait-consistency" in a different way, the Sears study reports the correlations between scores obtained by four different observers, each observer having observed a different time sample of the child's behavior over the entire summer session period. The average intercorrelation among observers was .42 for total dependency scores. This analysis was not done separately for dependency subscores.

A similar measure of consistency is reported by Heathers (1955). The correlations of scores based on two independent observational samples are given in Table 7. It is possible that the high level of interobserver agreement in this study is a function of the fact that the subscores distinguish both target of dependency and type of dependency—

Table 7. Inter-observer correlations. (From Heathers, 1955).

	Two-Year-Old Group	Four- and Five-Year Old Group
Clings to or seeks affection from teacher	.51[a]	.62[b]
Clings to or seeks affection from child	.10	.80[b]
Seeks attention or approval from teacher	.90[b]	.76[b]
Seeks attention or approval from child	.82[b]	.50[a]
N =	20	20

[a] $p < .05$
[b] $p < .01$

Table 8. Inter-rater correlations. (From Emmerich, 1955).

| | Semester Reliabilities | |
	Median	Highest
Seeks recognition from teacher	.29	.45
Seeks to be near teacher	.67	.82
Seeks physical contact with teacher	.62	.75
Seeks recognition from teacher	.37	.42
Seeks attention from teacher	.53	.71
Seeks help from teacher	.43	.53

distinctions which, as we have seen, are important to make since these classes of subscores tend to be uncorrelated.

Several studies have compared the ratings made by different raters of the same group of children. Table 8 reports the intercorrelations Emmerich found among ratings made by the head teacher and the assistant teacher. These ratings were independent in the sense that the teachers did not consult one another in making their ratings. However, they had opportunities to talk together during the semester about individual children, and hence could influence one another's appraisal of individual children prior to the time that the ratings were made. Also, of course, they may have been basing their ratings, in part, on certain salient episodes that both had observed, so the samples of behavior being rated partially overlap.

Becker (1960) obtained four sets of ratings on a group of 64 children—each child being rated by two teachers, his mother, and his father. Factor analysis of the ratings did not reveal a factor which could be reasonably labeled dependency (unless "submission" be so interpreted), so the findings are only tangentially relevant to our summary. It is of interest, however, that the factor scores based on ratings by the two teachers correlated with one another .76; the pooled teacher-rating factor scores correlated .31 with mothers' ratings, and .28 with fathers' ratings, while the ratings of the two parents correlated .52 with each other. Thus we see that there is some small degree of stability in the rated rank-ordering of children from a home to a nursery school setting, with raters who are observing different samples of behavior and who have relatively little opportunity to talk about the child (teachers and parents). When two raters are rating behavior that occurs in the same setting, and have more opportunity to discuss the child, correlations go up.

Let us summarize the differences between rating studies and behavior-observation studies with respect to the picture they yield of the degree and nature of intrapersonal consistency in dependency. First, ratings of different kinds of dependency tend to correlate with each other fairly substantially (in the .60s). Behavior-observation subscores generally do not, although in some studies "touching and holding" correlates with "being near," and these two subscores form a different cluster from the attention- and approval-seeking group. To date, rating studies have not found these subclusters, and in general it is accurate to say that ratings find (or produce!) a considerably greater degree of "trait generality" than do observational scores. Consistency can be measured in a different way, by comparing different samples of the same group of children's behavior. There are few studies that provide relevant data, but the available information indicates that the scores of different observers working with different time-samples in the same setting correlate positively, with the magnitude of the relationship possibly depending on how global the scores are. Among preschool children, the obtained correlations range from .42 (for total dependency) to .80 (clinging or seeking affection from other children). Correlations in a similar range are obtained between the scores of two raters rating the same group of children in the nursery school setting; in the case of ratings, however, it is difficult to make sure that the judgments of the two raters are truly independent. Tentatively, the data suggest that both ratings and observational scores are measuring "real" individual differences, in that scores produced by different raters or different observers yield similar rank-orderings of a group of children. We have very

Table 9. Correlations between ratings and behavior observation scores. (From Sears, 1953).

| | Behavior Observation Scores | | | | | |
| | Touching and Holding | | Being Near | | Seeking Positive Attention | |
Teacher Ratings for Seeking:	Boys	Girls	Boys	Girls	Boys	Girls
Help from teacher	.34	.11	.15	.20	−.08	−.01
Help from child	.01	.20	.07	.13	.31	.09
Praise and approval from teacher	.18	.31	−.24	.28	.17	−.05
Praise and approval from child	.19	.20	.13	−.08	.40	.28
Physical contact from teacher	.24	.36	.25	.49	.03	−.38
Physical contact from child	.17	.22	.01	.01	.26	.32
Attention from teacher	.15	.23	.13	.36	.46	−.08
Attention from child	.07	.12	−.09	−.03	.38	.30
To be near teacher	.19	.28	.32	.51	.22	−.25
To be near child	.19	−.06	.04	−.02	.34	.33

little information concerning how stable these rank-orderings would be from one setting to another, although the Becker study would indicate that such stability, at least when ratings are used, is small ($r =$ approximately .30).

To what extent are ratings and observations measuring the same thing? Sears et al. (1953) report scores for total dependency for both observational measures and ratings; the two kinds of measure correlate .44 for boys, .06 for girls. When the two sets of scores are broken down into their components,[10] the following patterns shown in Table 9 emerge. The behavior observation scores were not differentiated as to target, and hence it is not possible to make as fine-grained a comparison as would be desirable. For boys, the consistency between the two sets of measures is no greater when one uses component scores than it was with the use of a total dependency score. For girls, the consistency is considerably greater, and the improvement appears to be due to the fact that girls' proximity-seeking is directed primarily toward adults (the teacher), whereas their attention-seeking tends to be directed toward age-mates. In fact, their attention-seeking is *negatively* related to proximity-seeking directed toward adults. Thus there are counteracting trends

which reduce correlations greatly when they are based on "total dependency" scores.

Emmerich (1964, 1966a) has reported both observational scores and teacher ratings on a group of 38 preschool children. The rated subscores on dependency (the Beller scales) were highly intercorrelated; a factor score combining these subscales correlates as follows with the component behavior observation scores:[11]

Touching and holding	.33
Being near	.02
Securing positive attention	.23
Securing reassurance	.22
Securing negative attention	.30

In this study, neither the ratings nor the observational scores were differentiated as to target, and this may be one reason the correlations are so low.

We suggest the following interpretation of the relationships between ratings and behavior observations: ratings tend to be more global. The components that will be weighted most heavily in them will probably depend on the relationship of the rater to the child. If the teacher does the rating, she will weight the elements that attract her attention when she is busy—the more active forms of dependency, and those that are directed toward herself rather than toward children. There is a small amount of variance in common be-

---

[10] These figures were not included in the original publication and have been computed for the present report. The underlined figures are the ones most nearly approximating measures of the same component.

[11] The authors wish to thank Walter Emmerich for making these figures available for the present report. They were not included in the original publications.

tween the global rating scores and the more differentiated observational scores: even though the latter do not correlate consistently with one another, each may have a small independent correlation with rated dependency, arising from the fact that raters draw from a variety of component behaviors in making their global ratings. Ratings of components, however, are heavily influenced by one another and by the rater's concept of the total score.

Stability over Time. In their longitudinal study of 60 Scottish infants, Schaffer and Emerson (1964a) inquired whether those infants that showed the most intense attachments at one age remained more intensely attached than other infants as they grew older. They demonstrate a moderate level of short-term consistency, but relatively little over long time periods (See Table 10). From the standpoint of method, it is interesting to note that Schaffer and Emerson initially correlated intensity scores for successive chronological ages; that is, scores for all children at 6 months of age were correlated with the scores of the same children when they were 7 months old. Low correlations were found (Personal communication, Rudolph Schaffer). When the children were grouped by *developmental level*, however (i.e., how many months had passed for each child since the onset of specific attachments), the pattern of intercorrelations seen in Table 10 emerged. The month-to-month consistency in the intensity of nonspecific attachments was somewhat higher than that for specific attachments (see Schaffer and Emerson, 1964a, Table 5), but again, only when children are grouped by age at onset of specific attachments. The correlations in attachment intensity for successive months are lowest just at the time of

onset of specific attachments, indicating (as Schaffer and Emerson note) a period of upset and instability at this time.

In the previously mentioned short-term longitudinal study conducted by Martin and Emmerich, children were studied through a 2-year period. The behavior observation scores revealed a considerable degree of stability of individual differences over time, but the nature of the stability is complex. The published report does not include a full matrix of intercorrelations among the factor scores at successive ages. We do find that the factor named "interpersonal-impersonal orientation" is correlated .62 between semester 2 and semester 3, and .74 between semester 3 and semester 4, but the factor scores are not made up of the same components at these successive ages. For example, during semester 2, this factor has high loadings on "authoritarian control" of other children and on being dependent on the approval of others; in semester 4, a child who receives a high score on "interpersonal orientation" is one who frequently *offers* physical contact and positive attention to other children and carries out tasks in groups rather than alone. But it is the same children who tend to behave in these ways at the two time periods. Thus Emmerich demonstrates the existence of stable individual differences in the sense that what a child will do at age 5 is predictable from his behavior at age 3, but not in the sense of continuity in the "same" behavior. In some instances, the predictions from a set of factors (via multiple correlations) were as high as the .80s from one semester to the next, and predictions over the 2-year span were substantial.

As noted earlier, teacher ratings were collected for this same group of children over the same 2-year period, and a factor analysis

Table 10. Rank Order Correlations of Scores for Specific Attachment Intensity as Obtained for (A) Successive Lunar Months and (B) Longer Time Intervals

Age Periods		N	Rho	P
Lunar months following onset				
A.	1st and 2nd	51	.488	<.001
	2nd and 3rd	45	.608	<.001
	3rd and 4th	42	.578	<.001
	4th and 5th	33	.317	<.10
	5th and 6th	20	.403	<.05
B.	1st and 6th	20	.309	n.s.
	6th and 18th (CA)	19	.099	n.s.

From Schaffer and Emerson, 1964a, p. 27.

Table 11. Dependency Factor-Stability
        Coefficients.

	Semester			
	1	2	3	4
1				
2	.83			
3	.61	.56		
4	.48	.45	.69	

From Emmerich, 1966a, p. 20.

of the ratings revealed a clear dependency factor at each of the four semesters. The dependency factor scores correlated with one another at successive time periods as given in Table 11.

The ratings made of an individual child at successive time periods were partially independent of one another. The children were rated by a head teacher and an assistant teacher; they had different head teachers in successive years, and most children also had different assistant teachers, sometimes in successive semesters as well as successive years. The amount of communication that occurred among teachers about individual children is unknown. It should be noted that there was a decline during the age range studied in the amount of individual difference variance accounted for by the dependency factor. That is, although it was stable to the degree revealed by Table 11, it became progressively less salient as a variable accounting for a major portion of an individual's rated behavior. Furthermore, there are changes with time in the nature of the specific behaviors that have high loadings on the dependency factor. Emmerich notes:

The two scales reflecting *instrumental dependency* loaded more heavily on Dependency than on Autonomy during the first year, whereas the converse was more frequent during the second year. This structural change bears on the questions of the relations among instrumental dependency, emotional dependency, and independence. It indicates that instrumental dependency was initially associated with emotional dependency but then increasingly came to signify an *alternative* to autonomy (1966a, p. 22).

Emmerich's work highlights the problem that is, of course, the most difficult one in studies of stability over time in a personality trait: What behavior at age 6 or age 9 is to be regarded as sufficiently similar to behavior seen at age 2 or 4 so that we can say that if a child displays each of them frequently at successive ages he has demonstrated "stability" in a trait? Like Emmerich, Schaffer and Bayley (1963) have followed the strategy of carrying out separate factor analyses of the scores obtained at each successive age in a longitudinal study. They report data on 27 boys and 27 girls studied from infancy through adolescence. Behavior ratings were made at the time the children were seen for the administration of tests of mental and physical development. Ratings at successive ages were made by the same rater. Separate factor analyses were carried out for each of the following age periods: 10 to 36 months, 27 to 96 months, 9 to 10 years, and adolescence (after 12 years). The factorial structure was not the same at successive ages, and at no age did a factor emerge which corresponded to what is usually defined as dependency; hence we summarize these extensive findings in only the briefest way. Friendliness, sociability (responsiveness to persons), and the absence of shyness did form a reasonably coherent cluster that served to order individual differences at each age level. In general, the correlations at successive age levels were sizable and significant between closely adjacent ages and grew smaller as the time gap increased. Holding time gap constant, the older the child, the higher the correlations between successive time periods. Thus the picture for this aspect of social behavior is similar to that obtained in studies of constancy of the IQ. The predictive picture over long time periods is complex and differs for the two sexes, but in general it can be said that friendliness and absence of shyness during the preschool years do predict friendly and cooperative behavior in a testing situation in middle childhood and, to a lesser extent, in adolescence.

The most comprehensive effort to trace stability over time in behavior that is more specifically "dependent" has been carried out by the staff of the Fels Institute, the data being analyzed and reported by Kagan and Moss in their book *Birth to Maturity* (1962). Information was collected on a group of 44 boys and 45 girls from infancy into adulthood. During childhood regular visits were made by a home visitor, who observed the behavior of the child and the parents in the home setting; in addition, there were systematic observations of the child at nursery school, at elementary school, and at summer camp, plus interviews with the child, the mother, and the child's teachers. All the information concerning a given child was assembled in his folder and divided by age levels; on the basis of the total material available for an age period (e.g., 0 to 3 years), ratings were made on the dimensions of interest in the study, and these included ratings of several aspects of dependency. Up to age 6, there was a global rating for dependency on adults. In the next two age periods separate ratings were made for instrumental and affectional dependency. The age levels for which separate ratings were made (I) 0 to 3 years, (II) 3 to 6 years, (III) 6 to 10 years, (IV) 10 to 14 years. In addition to the childhood data, there was information concerning the personality structure of each individual at adulthood. A systematic assessment was carried out, including an intensive interview and a battery of tests. The childhood ratings of successive ages were made by the same rater, but not at the same time—the rater allowed a period of 6 to 8 months to intervene between his ratings of each age level, in order to minimize "halo" in the ratings due to memory of how individual cases had been rated at earlier age levels. The adult assessment was completely independent of the childhood ratings, being done by different personnal who had no knowlelge of the childhood data.

Table 12 shows the correlations between different age levels for the aspects of dependency that were rated. In one respect the pattern is the same as that seen in the Schaefer and Bayley study: correlations between adjacent age levels are higher than those for more widely separated ages. However, it is not true that there is uniformly greater stability as the child grows older. For passivity, for example, the period of greatest stability is between age periods II and III.

We have seen earlier that the passivity, affectional dependency, and instrumental dependency subscales all were substantially intercorrelated. And these scales had substantial negative correlations with independence. Hence we may expect to find fairly comparable patterns of stability and instability for

these scales. Table 12 does suggest, however, that passivity may be somewhat more stable than dependency upon adults.

There is somewhat greater stability for girls than for boys. If one takes a difference of .15 as indicating a directional trend, there are 11 instances in which the stability coefficient is greater for girls than boys, two in which the boys' figure is greater than girls', and 10 instances in which the coefficients do not differ.

The correlations between childhood dependency and adult measures reflect many of the trends already noted. With a few exceptions the prediction of adult characteristics is best from the adolescent ratings, and quite poor from the measures taken at age 0 to 3. Moreover, the prediction is much better for women than men. Specifically, girls who were relatively passive, dependent on adults, and lacking in independence in middle and late childhood display the following characteristics in young adulthood: they maintain a dependent relationship with their parents, they withdraw from stress situations, they choose secure jobs and avoid risks in the choice of a vocation, and they show little conflict over dependency. The corelations fell largely in the range .30 to .60. It is interesting that the girls who were *independent* during childhood and adolescence tend to form dependent ties with women friends in adulthood. Perhaps we see here a reflection of a tendency which we noted earlier at the preschool years for the shift away from adult-oriented dependency to be accompanied by a high level of social interaction with peers. In general, the childhood variables "passivity" and "independency" predict girls' adult characteristics better than do childhood emotional or instrumental dependency. For men, the predictions to adulthood are strikingly poor. For them there is considerably more stability through childhood and adolescence than there is between adolescence and adulthood, where a marked transition seems to occur. This is not to say that the total level of dependent behavior declines at this point—though it may—but that the rank order of individuals is rearranged. We do see some tendency for boys who were passive to become men who withdraw from stress, but the correlation is relatively small (.36). Furthermore, boys who were independent in adolescence show conflict over dependency

Table 12. Stability of Passivity and Dependency Over Childhood Periods I to IV.

Variable	I to II	I to III	I to IV	II to III	II to IV	III to IV
13. Passivity						
Boy	.67[a]	.50[b]	.00	.75[a]	.24	.60[a]
Girl	.58[a]	.66[a]	.44[c]	.79[a]	.51[d]	.76[a]
Total	.59[a]	.59[a]	.36[b]	.73[a]	.39[d]	.69[a]
14. Dependency (on adults)						
Boy	.58[a]					
Girl	.64[a]					
Total	.60[a]					
14–91. Dependency—affectional (on adults)						
Boy		.36[c]	.66[b]	.33[c]	−.03	
Girl		.33[c]	.17	.29[c]	.26	
Total		.33[b]	.33[c]	.29[b]	.07	
14–92. Dependency—instrumental (on adults)						
Boy		.45[b]	.04	.24	−.13	
Girl		.36[b]	.23	.54[a]	.24	
Total		.38[d]	.26	.39[a]	.14	
91. Affectional dependency (on adults)						
Boy						.41[c]
Girl						.34[c]
Total						.35[b]
92. Instrumental dependency						
Boy						.56[d]
Girl						.34[c]
Total						.45[d]
77. Independence						
Boy				.28	−.33	.52[b]
Girl				.55[a]	.64[a]	.65[a]
Total				.43[a]	.21	.63[a]
16. Anxiety loss of nurturance						
Boy	.25	.24		.08		
Girl	.30	.29		.36[c]		
Total	.28[c]	.33[c]		.30[c]		

[a] $p < .01$; two tails.
[b] $p < .05$; two tails.
[c] $p < .10$; two tails.
[d] $p < .01$; two tails.

in adulthood ($r = .49$)—an indication that what we see as independence in boys may not reflect a lack of dependent tendencies so much as a strong acquisition of counteracting tendencies.

There is one instance in the Kagan and Moss study which points to a continuity over the whole span of childhood into adulthood: passivity in the earliest period (age 0 to 3) is moderately correlated with dependency on love object in adulthood. For boys, in fact, there is better prediction from this earliest period than from later periods. In general, however, the overall picture is one of stability over 3- or 4-year periods or sometimes longer, but with changes occurring through the whole span of childhood that result in little similarity between what a child is like in early childhood and what he is like as an adult. We hasten to add that this does not mean that the characteristics seen in early childhood are unrelated to mature personality organization. It is quite possible that antecedents or predictors exist, but that they do not take the form of similarities in any easily detected phenotypical aspects of the behavior. The work of Schaefer and Bayley alerts us to this possibility. They point out, for example, that activity level in infancy and the rapidity with which the child carries out motor activity are related (negatively) to the child's later attentiveness in a test and his skill in carrying out intellectual tasks. It is possible that "independence" in adolescence might be more closely related to early problem-solving skill than to early dependence or independence, but we lack longitudinal data that permit us to study the transformations that may occur from age to age in the "meaning" of dependent behavior or to identify the best predictors from early to later behavior. Emmerich has approached the problem of stability over time with this question in mind, and it is to be hoped that this strategy will be employed over longer spans of time than have so far been studied.

Dependency, Conflict, and Anxiety

So far we have been discussing the intra-personal stability of the tendency to behave in a variety of dependent ways. It is also of interest to know whether certain individuals, more than others, are characterized by the tendency to be in conflict over dependency and to become anxious when dependency-arousing situations occur. Despite the fact that dependency conflict has been an important concept in a number of theoretical discussions, there have been surprisingly few efforts to measure it and use it in research. An exception is the work of Beller and his colleagues, who have conducted an extensive series of studies on dependency conflict (Beller, 1957, 1962; Beller and Haeberle, 1961). They assess conflict through two classes of raters' assessments. Dependency is defined by observer ratings based upon "how frequently and how persistently a child seeks help, physical contact, and attention from adults" (Beller and Haeberle, 1959, p. 3). A measure of independent striving is based on five components: "trying to initiate activities, overcome obstacles, and complete activities unaided, to try to do things by oneself, and to

derive satisfaction from work as measured by overt indications of tension reduction" (*ibid.*, pp. 3–4). Conflict is assessed through a comparison of the scores on dependency and independence-striving: when the two scores are similar (either both high or both low) the child is said to be in conflict; if the scores differ, the child may be designated as free from conflict and either dependent or independent. Beller reports that in a normal population scores on dependency are negatively correlated with scores on independence-striving; among a group of children who are being seen in a clinic, the two scores are uncorrelated, indicating that there is a higher proportion of dependency-conflicted children in the clinic population.

Beller and Haeberle (1961) studied the relationship between dependency conflict and fantasy. Simple scores on dependency (without regard to the subjects' scores on independence-striving) were positively related to fantasies of seeking and obtaining help in doll play. After an experimental induction of dependency frustration, the highly dependent children introduced more family figures and help-seeking themes in their fantasies to a CAT separation-anxiety card than did low-dependent children. Beller's measure of dependency conflict did not relate to help-seeking fantasies in doll play nor to the introduction of parental or family figures in responses to the separation card. Children with high dependency conflict did, however, introduce more threatening figures in the responses they gave to all dependency cards from the CAT. The high-conflict children also produced more fantasies of an aggressive or punitive nature in their responses to the card intended to elicit feeding themes, and to a lesser extent this was also true for the card intended to elicit toilet themes. In discussing this finding Beller mentions another study in which he found high conflict to be related to a higher incidence of behavior problems in the areas of feeding and toileting. These findings suggest a history of punishment in connection with feeding, toileting, and dependency for the high-conflict children.

In a further effort to test for the generality of the dependency-conflict trait, Beller (1957) placed children in a situation where a desirable toy was out of reach and determined how soon they would ask for help. The children who were classified as having high conflict (on the basis of observers' ratings of their normal levels of dependent and independent behaviors) were slow to ask for help, by comparison with the children who were unconflicted with respect to dependency. The children who were inhibited in asking for help also differed from other children with respect to certain aspects of aggressive behavior. In previous work, Beller and Haeberle (1961) had found that frustration, whether frustration of dependent or nondependent responses, inhibited constructive aggression and enhanced the expression of destructive, noninstrumental aggression. In the study of help-seeking, however, Beller found that the children who were inhibited in asking for help showed a positive relationship between their more destructive aggression in the nursery school and their "constructive aggression" during an experimental session in which knocking down a pile of pans would gain them a toy. No such relationship was found among children who were uninhibited in instrumental dependency in the experimental situation, or unconflicted in their normal observed dependency.

The relationship between dependency and perceptual orientation is attenuated for the high-conflict children. Beller (1962) had observers record, in 30 2-minute samples, how often children looked at adults, at interactions between adults and other children, and at physical objects. As may be seen in Table 13, the dependency striving of children is positively correlated with the frequency with which they look at people and interactions, and negatively correlated with their tendencies to look at the physical environment. However, if the children are grouped according to the measure of dependency conflict, it is apparent that low-conflict children evidence highly significant relationships between dependency and perceptual orientations, whereas highly conflicted children show relationships in the anticipated direction but insignificant. High conflict may thus be seen to have an attenuating effect upon the expression of behavior correlated with or attributable to dependency motivation.

As previously noted, Kagan and Moss, in their adult assessments of the subjects in the Fels longitudinal sample, included measures of dependency conflict. They inferred the existence of conflict from slow recognition times for tachistoscopically presented dependency scenes, and also made a rating of dependency conflict from intensive interviews. These two measures of "conflict" were not significantly correlated. Kagan and Moss found that adult conflict, assessed by interview ratings, was related negatively to passivity at ages 6 to 10 and 10 to 14. It was also negatively related to instrumental dependency at ages 10 to 14, and positively to independence at ages 10 to 14, primarily for males. It seems that passivity in later childhood as well as an active instrumental dependency at that time is indicative of an acceptance of dependency behavior with no particular conflict.

In the tachistoscopic portion of the study, no relationships for women were significant. For men, the interview ratings of the adult subjects' fear of failure, dependency on love object, and dependency on friends were associated with a lack of conflict as inferred from the early recognition of dependency scenes. The men who were instrumentally dependent at 10 to 14 recognized the dependent pictures earlier as adults.

Just as Beller found more incidence of dependence conflict in young boys, Kagan and Moss found that men had generally higher recognition thresholds, as well as lower correlations between self-rated dependency and interview ratings of dependency, than did the women. They also found that delayed recognition of the dependency scenes was more closely associated with inhibition of dependency behavior for men than for women.

Working with groups of delinquent boys, Cairns (1961) studied the relationship between dependency anxiety and the effective-

Table 13. Correlations between Perceptual Orientation and Ratings of Dependency Striving

	Dependency Striving		
Child Orients toward:	Total Group (N = 29)	Low Conflict (N = 8)	High Conflict (N = 11)
Adults	.50[a]	.83[a]	.24
Adult-child interactions	.27	.74[b]	.05
Physical environment	−.43[b]	−.83[a]	−.20

From Beller, 1962.
[a] p = <.01.
[b] p = <.05.

ness of social reinforcement. Dependency anxiety was measured in two ways: a rating by counselors of the extent to which a boy actively avoided help-seeking even when needed, and resisted placing himself in a dependent role; and story completions, which were scored in terms of whether the boys expected a dependent bid to be punished or rewarded. For the boys who were low in dependency anxiety, verbal reinforcement resulted in improvement in two types of task: a conditioning procedure in which confiding responses were reinforced, and a paired-associates learning task. For the boys who were anxious about dependency, however, the frequency with which confiding responses were given *declined* following verbal reinforcement, and their performance on the paired-associates task also declined after an initial improvement. Thus it is found that high dependency anxiety is associated with poor responsiveness to social reinforcement in comparison with the responsiveness of subjects who have lesser dependency anxiety.

The work we have cited would appear to have demonstrated that "dependency conflict" or "dependency anxiety" is a valid dimension of individual differences. It has predictive value for a range of related behaviors, and also has proved useful as a cross-cutting variable for isolating subpopulations in which relationships between other variables are particularly strong.

Genetic Factors in Individual Differences

The research which has attempted to explore the etiology of individual differences in attachment and dependency behavior has focused almost entirely on variations in environmental conditions—particularly in socialization and parent-child interaction patterns —which might produce variations in development of such behavior. Recently more consideration is being given to the possible role of genetic factors. Schaffer and Emerson (1964b) point out that among the infants they studied, some could be identified as "cuddlers" and others as "noncuddlers." They found that this characteristic of an infant could be identified early in infancy and tended to be maintained at least through the first year of life. They noted further that the noncuddling infants in their study tended to have noncuddling siblings, and that the "cuddli-

ness" of an infant did not appear to be related to the mother's customary mode of handling the child. They say:

Thus the avoidance of close physical contact may be interpreted as stemming from a pervasive innate response tendency which will affect the initial development of social behavior and which may, in some cases, even be responsible for imposing a considerable strain on the mother-child relationship (1964b, p. 13).

A twin study has likewise pointed to a genetic contribution to early attachment behavior. Freedman (1965) reports a greater concordance between identical than between fraternal twins in social orientation during the first 5 months of life, and in the occurrence of stranger fears between ages 5 and 12 months. Not only the frequency and intensity of such behavior but also the age at which it appears is highly similar for identical twins.

Other investigators have done twin studies of "sociability" or "extroversion," computing a heritability index on the basis of comparative concordance scores for identical versus fraternal twins. Scarr (1965), working with children between 6 and 10 years old, found higher concordance for identical than for fraternal twins on measures of N Affiliation (based on mothers' reports) and on the Fels behavior scales *Friendliness* and *Social Apprehension* (rated by an observer). It is interesting that in the instances when parents were wrong about whether their twins were identical or fraternal, the degree of similarity between the twins was more a function of their actual zygocity than of whether their parents believed them to be identical—a fact which strengthens the genetic interpretation of the data. A substantial heritability factor among adolescent or adult twins has been found by Eysenk (1956) for *Extroversion*, by Gottesman (1966), for *Person Orientation*, and by Vandenberg (1962) for *Sociable*.

Although sociability and extroversion are of course not the same as attachment and dependency as we have defined them, these findings do alert us to the probable existence of genetic factors that may affect the social behavior we are interested in. Further indications of the possible importance of such factors may be seen in the findings of Schaefer and Bayley (1963) and Kagan and Moss (1962) that early temperamental characteristics (particularly activity or passivity) were related to later social behavior. As we go on to discuss the effects of socialization practices, we should keep two points in mind: (1) when we find effects of environmental inputs, this does not imply that genetic factors are unimportant; and (2) it is possible that a given socialization input will have a different effect on genetically different children. The research literature has dealt only very minimally with this difficult issue, introducing it primarily in discussions of sex differences.

SOCIALIZATION ANTECEDENTS

Some Methodological Considerations

We now turn to a review of the research dealing with the socialization conditions that are associated with the development of high or low levels of dependent behavior in individual children. We are here using the term "socialization" broadly, to include all aspects of the child-directed behavior of parents or other agents who are charged with teaching the child and caring for it. In some instances, the term socialization has been used more narrowly. Schaffer and Emerson (1964a), for example, distinguish "socializing variables" (including weaning and toilet training) from "relationship variables" (including responsiveness to crying and frequency of maternal interaction). We recognize that some maternal behavior is part of the mother's conscious effort to train the child toward the social behavior she considers desirable, while part is not, but in practice it is difficult to distinguish the two. Thus some mothers refuse to pick up a crying baby because they do not wish to "spoil" it; they regard this early interaction as the first episode in a long series of efforts to teach the child to adjust himself to the authority of his parents and the needs and wishes of the other people he lives with. For other mothers the infant's crying is differently perceived and responding to it is not seen as related to character-building. For present purposes, we are using the term "socialization" to refer to child-directed maternal behavior (and the behavior of other agents) whether it is intended to train the child toward social norms or not.

It will be evident from the preceding section that the success of efforts to predict individual differences in dependency from child-training practices will depend heavily on the choice of the aspect or aspects of dependency to be predicted and how they are measured. Since, for example, observational measures of proximity- and attention-seeking tend to be unrelated, it will be difficult to generate correlations between antecedent variables and a summary score in which measures of these two attributes are combined. Furthermore, summary scores in which dependent bids directed toward adults are summed with similar bids toward children will be even more difficult to predict, considering that the proximity-seeking portion of these two component scores tends to be *negatively* related to one another. It should be noted that predictions of childhood dependency are based upon theories that are concerned with the development of dependency toward the mother. If dependency toward other persons (children, or strange adults) is measured observationally and included in the childhood dependency score, this is done on the basis of the assumption that mother-directed dependency generalizes to other targets. As we have seen, this assumption is not justified with respect to all classes of dependent behavior or all classes of targets. Prediction of ratings may be more promising than prediction of observational scores, since there is greater "trait consistency" with the use of this kind of measure, but it is difficult to be sure how much of this consistency is produced by rater halo effects and how much by the rater's success in selecting and responding to behavioral cues that reflect a stable response disposition in the child. To the extent that the latter occurs, ratings should be predictable from independently measured antecedents.

Other formidable problems of method reside in the measurement of socialization practices. Especially during the pioneering phases of research on the antecedents of dependence, there was almost exclusive reliance on the mother interview. Since that time, evidence has been accumulating that while reliable and valid interview data can be obtained concerning concurrent events (e.g., Shaffer and Emerson, 1964a, p. 17), mothers' retrospective reports concerning their own child-rearing practices or their children's responses occurring some years prior to the interview are of questionable value (see Brekstad, 1966; Haggard et al., 1960; McGraw and Molloy, 1941; Mednick and Schaffer, 1963; Robbins, 1963; Wenar, 1961; Wenar and Coulter, 1962; Yarrow et al., 1964). Several of the major socialization studies have been done with children of preschool age, and the data on infancy socialization experiences are retrospective. We should therefore be prepared for the likelihood that it will be difficult, in this review, to locate strong evidence concerning the relationships between infancy socialization practices and later levels of dependency.

An additional methodological problem has to do with the interrelationships of various socialization practices with one another. In naturalistic studies, where parental behavior is studied as it occurs in daily life rather than being experimentally varied, a given parental practice covaries systematically with other characteristics of the parents' behavior and the child's environment. For example, as Becker (1964) has noted, parents rated as "cold" or "hostile" toward their children also tended to employ physical punishment relatively frequently. Thus it is difficult to study the effects of either of these aspects of socialization in isolation from the other. One research strategy for dealing with this problem has been to factor-analyze the scores given to a group of parents on a number of variables, in order to discover the dimensions which are orthogonal to one another and account for as much as possible of the variance between individual parents. Of course, the dimensions that emerge are a function of the choice of variables included in the initial set of measures. Following is a list of some of the dimensions of parental behavior which have been identified by factor analysis:

Warmth (versus hostility or rejection)
Permissiveness (versus restrictiveness)
Child-rearing anxiety
Sex anxiety
Inhibitory demands and discipline
Responsible child-rearing orientation
Physical punishment
Dependency encouragement
Democratic attitudes
Authoritarian control
Punishment (versus non-punishment); punitiveness; punishment orientation
General family adjustment

Marital conflict
Firm discipline
Independence-achievement orientation
Seclusiveness
Involvement versus laissez-faire

(Lorr and Jenkins, 1953; Sears et al., 1957; Slater, 1962; Becker et al., 1962; Nichols, 1962; Cline et al., 1963; Baumrind and Black, 1967; Hatfield et al., 1967).

Schaefer (1959) has attempted to order a variety of child-rearing variables with respect to two basic dimensions: warmth-hostility and control-autonomy. He has shown that these dimensions fit the data from several studies of socialization practices, although some studies have identified additional dimensions orthogonal to these. Becker (1964) has subdivided the control-autonomy dimension into a restrictiveness-permissiveness dimension and one of calm detachment versus anxious emotional involvement, while maintaining the warmth-hostility dimension as separate and unitary. The number and kind of dimensions that can be distinguished in a study of child-rearing practices will probably be a function of the way these practices are measured. If ratings or attitude scales are used (either self-ratings made by observers or interviewers), there will probably be only a limited number of dimensions which raters can keep distinct; they will tend to assimilate a variety of behaviors to these dimensions (see the earlier discussion of halo effects in the rating of child behavior). The method of behavior unit observation has been rarely used for measurement of parent behavior. As may be seen in Baumrind and Black (1967), the use of this method may yield a very different set of dimensions than that ordinarily emerging from a parent interview. In this study, the analysis of observational data (called Home Visit Sequence Analysis) produced information concerning interactions in which either the parent or the child tried to influence the other, and the coders scored whether it was the parent or child who usually took the initiative in such attempts, whether the attempt succeeded (whether the other person complied), whether or not coercive power was employed to obtain compliance, and the amount and kind of verbal give-and-take that occurred in connection with such demands. Such scores were useful in Baumrind and

Black's study in predicting children's level of dependent behavior, but they will not figure centrally in the review which follows, since until very recently the usual methods of measuring parent behavior (by interview of attitude scales) have not been such as to produce measures of these kinds of characteristics.

Socialization and Attachment in Infancy

We begin by considering studies of attachment in infancy and the aspects of mother-child interaction that appear to affect it. As we noted earlier, Schaffer and Emerson (1964a) report wide individual differences among infants with respect to the age at which specific attachments begin, the number of persons to whom attachments are formed, and the intensity of the attachment. In this study, the intensity of attachment did not prove to have any relationship to the following infancy socialization variables: scheduling of feeding, age of weaning, duration of weaning, age of toilet training, or severity of toilet training. Furthermore, the sheer availability of the mother (measured in terms of the frequency and duration of her absences) was not a factor in the intensity of the infant's attachment. There was a tendency for infants cared for exclusively by the mother to be more intensely attached than infants who were cared for and played with by a number of people, although this finding did not reach the .05 level of significance. The trend is consistent with a finding by Caldwell (1962) that more attachment behavior is seen in infants for whom maternal care has been provided by the mother alone than among infants whose caretaking has been shared among a number of individuals.

In the Schaffer and Emerson study, however, the variables that are more strongly related to the intensity of the infant's attachment are (1) maternal responsiveness and (2) amount of interaction. The mothers who responded immediately when their babies cried—going to the child to pick him up or minister to him in some other way—had infants who were more intensely attached than the mothers who allowed the child to cry for some time before responding. Similarly, the mothers who give the child a great deal of time and attention have more strongly attached infants than the mothers who interact

with the child only when giving routine care. The function of this attachment for exploratory behavior is suggested by the work of Rubenstein, (1967) who time-sampled maternal attentiveness toward infants 4 and 5 months old and found that the infants of the more attentive mothers showed greater visual attention to and manual manipulation of test objects during a later (6-month) test.

It is interesting that, in the Schaffer and Emerson study, the *kind* of interaction did not appear to make much difference: some mothers interacted primarily by giving physical contact, others by talking, smiling, and looking, still others by directing the child's attention to other things than herself (to toys, food, etc.), and these various forms of interaction appeared to be about equally effective in building attachment intensity. Schaffer and Emerson also point out that when attachments are formed to others than the mother, the attachment figures tend to be people who provide large amounts of stimulation to the infant, but that this need not be of a caretaking kind.

While the type of maternal interaction may not be especially important in the development of attachments, Korner and Grobstein (1966) show that, in neonates, picking up the crying infant and putting it to the shoulder is a procedure that facilitates the infant's alerting and scanning responses, whereas other forms of handling do not have this effect. It should be noted that the attentiveness of the mother is more effective than that of a stranger in building the infant's social behavior (Walker, 1967).

The number of figures to whom the child forms attachments is a function of the number of different people who interact with him, either in caretaking or playful ways. Schaffer and Emerson say: "Breadth, we may conclude, is essentially a function of the opportunities which a child has of meeting other people who will offer relevant stimuli" (p. 59). With infant animals, Collard (1967) has shown that there is less stranger fear among kittens that have been played with by several people than among kittens played with by a single person.

The age of onset of specific attachments was not related to the maternal behavior variables measured in the Schaffer and Emerson study. Rather, age of onset was related to

Developmental Quotient, suggesting that the rate of maturation is more important than environmental variables in determining the point in time when attachment will develop. Schaffer and Emerson point out, however, that although in the sample of families studied environmental conditions were probably adequate for the appearance of attachment behavior on schedule, there may very likely be more extreme environments (e.g., stimulus-poor environments) in which the onset of the behavior would be delayed.

Turning to another study of attachment in infancy in which assessments were made of a number of aspects of maternal behavior, we find that among Ganda infants (Ainsworth, 1963) the strength and security of the child's attachment to the mother is not related to her "warmth" (the amount of affection she expresses toward the child), or to scheduling of feeding, or to whether she is the exclusive caretaker. However, the greater the total amount of time the mother spends in caretaking and other interaction with the child, the more securely attached he is. Furthermore, Ainsworth found that the mothers of securely attached infants were better informants than other mothers—they seemed more interested in their children and better informed about them, as though they had paid close attention to details of their behavior. Finally, one aspect of the feeding situation was associated with the strength of the child's attachment, namely, whether the mother enjoyed breast feeding. We can only wonder why this aspect of feeding, rather than the scheduling of feeding or the quality of the mother's milk supply or the age of weaning should be related to attachment. Perhaps the mother's enjoyment of breast feeding serves as another index of her responsiveness to the infant.

With respect to the role played by feeding in the development of attachment, the work and conclusions of Harlow and his associates are well known. They find that infant monkeys strongly prefer a cloth mother surrogate who has not fed them to a wire one who has (Harlow and Zimmerman, 1958), although there is some small effect of feeding, in that when an infant has the opportunity to choose between a lactating cloth mother and a non-lactating one, he tends to choose the cloth mother, at least initially. Harlow (1961, p. 81) reports that this preference disappears

after about 100 days of age. Ingel and Calvin (1960) found that puppies prefer a lactating "comfortable" surrogate to one that is equally comfortable but on which they are not fed, but they did not continue the experiment long enough to permit a check on whether this preference disappears with time.

In the work with human infants it is difficult to assess the importance of the feeding factor. In most instances, the person to whom the infant becomes attached (at least, for the initial attachment) is the person who feeds him and provides other comfort and stimulation as well. For the most part, the individual differences that must be explained have to do with variations among infants in the intensity of attachment to mothers all of whom feed the infants, so that we are comparing, for example, attachment to a mother who feeds and is highly responsive to crying with attachment to a mother who feeds and who is unresponsive to crying. If responsiveness emerges as an important factor in such a comparison, this of course does not mean that feeding was unimportant, or less important—only that its importance was not tested. It does appear to be true that the way feeding is done (e.g., scheduled or self-demand) does not make much difference in attachment intensity, nor does the age of weaning, but of course variations in these dimensions do not alter the fact that the mother continues to provide food to the child and that attachment to her may be formed at least partly on this basis. Perhaps more crucial to the argument is the fact that attachments are sometimes formed to individuals who play with the child but do not participate in feeding or other caretaking (see Schaffer and Emerson, 1964a). This does not demonstrate that feeding per se cannot produce attachment, but only that other factors can also be sufficient. In the Schaffer and Emerson study, attachment to a non-nurturant figure is never the infant's only attachment—he is also attached to mother, father, or grandparent, and the attachments to nurturant figures develop first. It would be interesting to know whether the attachment to nurturant and non-nurturant figures is qualitatively different. Schaffer and Emerson test for the existence of attachment by measuring separation reactions. It is possible that a child might resist separation from, for example, a somewhat older sibling who provides only interesting stimulation, but that the same child would not run to this sibling if hurt or afraid, but would seek instead the attachment figure who has provided nurturance. Whether the crucial element in such previous nurturance would be provisions of body-contact comfort (as Harlow suggests), or whether feeding would contribute independently to the attractiveness of the attachment figure as a comfort-giver, we simply cannot tell on the basis of existing evidence with human children.

The importance of the amount and kind of interaction a mother-figure provides in the development of social attachment behavior is clearly demonstrated in an experiment by Rheingold (1956). The experimenter "mothered" eight 6-month-old institutional babies, in groups of four at a time. During an 8-week period, the experimenter alone took care of the group of four babies for 7½ hours a day 5 days a week, doing all the routine caretaking and a good deal of additional social stimulation as well. At the end of the experimental period this group was contrasted with a group of control babies who had been cared for under the normal institutional routine, with multiple caretakers and a lower total level of social interaction. The experimental babies were more socially responsive to the experimenter, in that they quickly fixed their attention on her and brightened or smiled at her approach. They were also more responsive than were the control babies to the examiner, who saw the babies only during the administration of tests and did not know which babies were in the experimental group. There is evidence here, then, of the greater development of what Schaffer and Emerson would call indiscriminate attachment among babies who have had more social interaction and whose interaction has been concentrated more with a single individual. We do not know which of these factors is the more important or whether feeding per se plays a role, but the role of the interpersonal environment in enhancing certain aspects of attachment behavior is clear. The babies in this study were followed up later, when they were between 18 and 22 months old (Rheingold and Bayley, 1959). They had been placed in adoptive homes, or returned to their own homes, after spending, on the average, 9 to 10 months in the institution. Both experimental and control

babies appeared to be normal in social responsiveness and in other aspects of their development, and they no longer differed in their responsiveness to either the experimenter or the examiner. Thus the increases in social responsiveness produced by the earlier experimental treatment did not last through the subsequent year when the children were shifted to a normal home environment.

Casler (1965) has obtained tentative findings suggesting that tactile stimulation may be an important element in stimulating social development (or preventing its deterioration) in institutionalized babies. After a 10-week period during which eight babies received two 10-minute sessions a day of stroking (by an experimenter who neither held them nor looked them in the face, but did occasionally say "hello baby") they showed somewhat less loss in personal-social scores on a Gessell DQ test than did a control group, although the difference was not statistically significant.

A further indication of the importance of the amount and kind of stimulation offered by the environment in the development of social responsiveness is seen in the work by Gewirtz (1965). Gewirtz studied the amount of smiling to the stimulus of an unresponsive human face[12] during the first 18 months of life among children growing up in four different environments: town families, kibbutz, residential institution, and day nursery. From the age of about 10 months on, the amount of smiling is greater for the children growing up in families than in the other three environments.

It has been widely reported that institutional babies tend to be socially unresponsive, by comparison with home-reared babies (see Spitz, 1945; Goldfarb, 1945; Bowlby, 1953), and this deficit is often assumed to be a function of the low level of interaction these infants have with adult caretakers. These and other studies have been reviewed by Casler (1963) and Yarrow (1964). In animal studies it has been possible to study the effects of various kinds and degrees of social deprivation in infancy. Cairns (1967) has reviewed some of this work, showing that animals reared in isolation show a diminished tendency to ap-

12 The face was that of a relative stranger, but before testing the observer played with the child briefly so that the response to the test would not reflect "stranger fear."

proach other members of their own species. Harlow and his colleagues (Mitchell et al., 1966; Harlow et al., 1965; Griffin and Harlow, 1966) have shown that the effects of isolation depend in part upon its duration, and that while the effects of the 3 months of isolation appear to be reversible, animals isolated for the first 6 months or year of their lives will continue to show serious deficiencies in their social behavior as adults. It is not clear, so far, exactly what aspects of maternal-infant interaction during the early period of life are essential for later social development. An infant reared with a cloth surrogate becomes attached to it, is able to use this surrogate for contact comfort, and can explore fearful stimuli normally using this surrogate as a base, yet does not become a socially adequate adult (e.g., does not display normal sexual or maternal behavior).

What does the live mother do that the cloth mother does not do that enables the young monkey to approach other members of the species and interact with them normally? Cairns (1967) has suggested that the degree of attachment to a stimulus object will depend on how salient that stimulus is, and that both movement of a stimulus and physical involvement of the stimulus in the subject's ongoing responses make it salient. A live mother moves and is involved in an interactive way with her infant, and hence he may become more fully attached to her than to the cloth surrogate. However, the importance of mother-infant interaction is called into question by the findings that young monkeys that are reared so that they can *see* other members of their species are more socially adequate as adults than fully isolated animals, even though they do not have an opportunity for physical contact or interaction (see Rowland, 1964). Furthermore, Cairns has found that lambs can form attachments to television sets, or to dogs that are always in sight but separated by a glass panel. Cairns (1966, p. 418) says that these findings "support the assumption that environmental events do not have to serve as manipulanda in order to become significant components of the stimulus patterns that support subjects' behavior." The extent of the role played by visual contact in comparison with physical interaction has not been fully explored. The primary point to be derived from the animal studies is that con-

tinuing contact over a period of time with living members of a species is necessary for the development of general social responsiveness to numbers of that species. There is some evidence that there is a critical period for social exposure during infancy, at least among primates, although Cairns (Cairns, 1966; Cairns and Johnson, 1965) has shown that it is possible to shift attachments from one species to another after infancy. From work with human infants we derive the further point that, beyond the baseline amount of interaction necessary to establish attachment, variations in the amount of interaction will produce variations in the degree of social responsiveness and the intensity of attachment behavior a young child displays.

Infant Socialization and Later Dependency

We have seen that the more responsive a mother is to an infant, and the greater the total amount of social stimulation she provides, the more strongly attached her infant will be. Will the effects of these attachment-building experiences in infancy carry over into preschool years? The follow-up study by Rheingold and Bayley suggests that they will not, unless the conditions that prevailed during infancy are maintained for a considerable time—perhaps beyond infancy into the preschool years themselves. Efforts have been made to relate infancy experiences to later dependency, but in most instances it is not clear whether the infancy experiences represent socialization practices initiated in infancy and maintained into childhood, or whether they are discontinuous. In some instances (e.g., age at weaning), the socialization variable measured in infancy has no counterpart for the next age period. In other instances, such as "responsiveness to crying," the variable would be relevant for successive age periods but has been directly measured only for infancy.

In general, infancy socialization practices do not consistently predict dependency at preschool age. Studies done at this age have tended to be concerned with testing psychoanalytic theory, and therefore have usually inquired about such infant practices as feeding and toilet training, rather than about the variables which have more recently proved to be important in the studies of infant attachment. A summary of some of the findings follows.

Rigid feeding schedule in infancy is associated with:

1. High dependency toward teacher, girls only (Sears et al., 1953) when dependency is measured with ratings not observation.

2. Low dependency, in boys only (Sears et al., 1957), child's dependency measured by mother interview; *r* for boys is significant but small.

3. No measure of dependency in either sex (Sears et al., 1965), observational measures.

4. High dependency in girls only (Smith, 1958).

Severe weaning is associated with:

1. High dependency on teacher (Sears et al., 1953) when rating measure of dependency is used; no relationship with observational measure.

2. No aspect of dependency (Sears et al., 1957), dependency measured through mother's report.

3. Low touching and holding and being near, girls only (Sears et al., 1965), observational measures.

4. High total dependency, particularly negative-attention-seeking, boys only (Sears et al., 1965), observational measures.

There are numerous possible reasons for the lack of replication across studies—variations in method being a major candidate. In general, it must be said that a relationship between these infant socialization practices and later dependency has not been demonstrated. Similarly, over a series of studies, severity of toilet training has not been found to bear a consistent relationship to later dependency.

The absence of replicable relationships is consistent with the work of Schaffer and Emerson in indicating that normal variations in infant feeding and toilet training do not have much bearing upon the concurrent development of attachment. In one of the Sears studies (1957) an effort was made to determine whether the mother's responsiveness to the infant's crying had any enduring effect. This variable, as measured retrospectively from mother interview when the child was 5 years old, revealed no relationship to current dependency. Whether this was true because

of poor retrospective report, or whether the initial effects of unresponsiveness were counteracted by changes in maternal responsiveness as the child grew older, we do not know. Similarly, in two studies (Sears et al., 1957, 1964) no effects were detected of separations from the mother during infancy upon preschool dependency. In the samples used, separations were rare and brief, so there is no adequate assessment here of the effects of extensive mother-child separation in early childhood upon later manifestations of attachment and dependency, nor are there enough cases of separation at specific early ages to test for the existence of a "critical period." In the Sears et al. (1965) study severity of current separation was positively associated with attention-seeking in girls (.53) and with touching and holding in boys ($r = .51$).

There is some evidence from the Fels longitudinal work (Kagan and Moss, 1962) that maternal behavior during the child's earliest years (0 to 3) does have a lasting effect. In this study maternal behavior was rated on four global characteristics: protection, restriction, hostility, and acceleration. At each level, the maternal characteristics and child characteristics were rated by the same rater at the same time, so that the two sets of measures are not independent. Furthermore, there was a substantial degree of stability in maternal behavior over the age span studied, so that if early maternal behavior predicts later child behavior, this may not be due to the effects of early experience but rather to the fact that the mother who is restrictive or protective while the child is very young continues to be so, so that relationships that appear to be predictive are actually concurrent.

Despite these problems, it is interesting that there are some instances in which maternal practices during the first 3 years of life predict the child's later characteristics *better* than do the concurrent measures or measures during the intermediate years. For example, girls who had been highly protected during their first 3 years of life tended to withdraw from stressful or challenging situations as adults ($r = .52$), whereas maternal protection from age 3 to 10 was not related to this aspect of adult behavior. Similarly, maternal hostility toward girls during the earliest age period predicted adult independence, while maternal hostility during the intermediate years did not. Among boys, maternal restrictiveness at age 0 to 3 was associated with low adult dependency on love objects and friends while maternal restrictiveness occurring during the preschool and early school-age years was positively associated with these characteristics. Furthermore, early maternal restriction was not associated with manifestations of dependency during childhood years among these boys. Thus there is evidence of delayed (or "sleeper") effects of early socialization experiences. In general, however, the Fels study reveals a few continuous relationships that prevail throughout childhood: *protection* of boys is associated with passive and dependent behavior, while *restriction* of girls has a like effect.

Childhood Socialization and Dependency

Efforts to understand the effects of concurrent socialization practices on dependency have focused on certain global dimensions of parental behavior, particularly the warmth-hostility dimension and the permissiveness-restrictiveness (or controlling versus autonomy-giving) dimension. This has been true partly because, as we have noted, factor analysis of measures of parent characteristics have shown that these two dimensions are fairly pervasive and account for variance in other measures (e.g., in the frequency of use of physical punishment or reasoning as techniques of discipline). In addition, "warmth" has figured centrally as a predictive dimension because it is presumed to represent a cluster of parent behaviors that have theoretical importance in the development of dependency. A warm parent is one who is interested in the child, oriented toward him, responsive to him, and whose responses tend to be rewarding and supportive. The warm parent provides a relatively large amount of contact comfort, and praises the child for desired behavior. All these parent behaviors should presumably be conditions for the establishment of a strong attachment to the parent on the part of the child. It is therefore surprising, at least on first consideration that this global variable has proved to be a poor predictor of dependency. We have seen that in the work on infant attachment, warmth per se was not associated with either the intensity or breadth

of attachment. The research on the effect of warmth on the dependency of children of preschool and early school age may be summarized as follows:

Finney (1961). Maternal nurturance (defined as equivalent to warmth unrelated to child's dependency ($r = -.09$). $N = 31$ boys who were patients at a mental health clinic; age range 5 to 16.

Cairns (1962). Maternal and paternal warmth (as determined from mother interview) unrelated to child's responsiveness to social reinforcement. $N = 60$ second- and third-grade children.

Baumrind and Black (1967). No relationship between maternal or paternal warmth and childhood dependency. Nonsignificant trend: parental warmth associated with *autonomy* in boys. (Mother and father interviews; $N = 95$, preschool age).

Sears et al. (1953). Nonsignificant trend: rated dependency positively associated with parental "nurturance" (mother interview). Observed dependency positively related to nurturance in girls, negatively in boys. $N = 40$, preschool age.

Sears et al. (1957). Maternal warmth unrelated to child's current dependency (both measured by mother interview). $N = 379$, kindergarten age.

Sears et al. (1965). Maternal and paternal warmth unrelated to any measure of dependency. (Mother and father interview, $N = 40$, preschool age.) Mothers who were not as warm in the mother-child interaction had sons who were low in dependency ($r = -.56$).

Siegelman (1966). Small but significant negative relationship between mother love and child's dependency in school setting. Subjects fourth-, fifth-, and sixth-grade boys. Parents' characteristics measured with Bronfenbrenner Parent Behavior Questionnaire; child characteristics assessed with Winder-Wiggins peer-nominations inventory.

Hatfield et al. (1967). Maternal warmth positively correlated with the child's *independence* during a mother-child interaction session ($N = 40$, boys and girls of nursery-school age).

Bandura (1960). Parental warmth associated with high dependency in pre-adolescent boys.

Bandura and Walters (1959). Parental warmth associated with dependency and nonaggressiveness in adolescence.

There is evidence that dependency is associated not with warmth but with its polar opposite, *rejection or hostility*. This relationship has been found in the following studies:

Winder and Rau (1962). Maternal rejection associated with dependency but not with aggression. Paternal rejection associated with both dependency and aggression. Sixth-grade boys. Child characteristics measured by peer nominations; parents' by attitude questionnaire.

Sears et al. (1957). Slight but significant positive correlation between rejection and dependency.

Marshall (1961). Parental "interpersonal distance" from child (parent attitude inventory) related to high frequency of teacher-contacting among nursery school-aged girls.

McCord et al. (1962). More dependency if either father or mother rejecting. Boys studies through period of pre-aolescence and adolescence. Case records.

Wittenborn (1956). Rejection of child related to dependency on adults ($r = .30$). Dependency assessed through child questionnaire; adopted children.

Smith (1958). Rejection (measured by mother interview) positively related to observed dependency in preschool aged children.

An exception is found in Bandura and Walters (1959), where rejecting parents had adolescent sons who were aggressive and *low* in dependency. However, in this study a group of boys were selected who were known to be "acting-out" aggressive delinquents or predelinquents, in whom overt dependency manifestations would be minimal.

Another exception is the finding by Sears et al. (1965) that for girls, maternal hostility was associated negatively with the child's observed dependency ($r = -.52$).

Why should dependency so often be associated with rejection rather than warmth? Sears et al. (1957) and Sears (1963) have analyzed the problem in terms of conditions that lead to the acquisition of dependent behavior and the conditions that lead to its performance once learned. High maternal nurturance in infancy should be associated with strong acquisition of the behavior. At a later point, frustration of this already-learned behavior sequence should intensify the behavior for two reasons. First, if the mother does not give the nurturance the child wants, the child performs the actions he has learned to get such nurturance, that is, he performs further dependent responses. Furthermore, nonreward or punishment of the dependent behavior which has been so frequently rewarded in the child's earlier experience generates conflict, and conflict, according to the hypotheses, energizes whatever responses occur.

How much nurturance in infancy is necessary for the strong establishment of attachment? Harlow has pointed out that although a group of "motherless mothers" he studied were abusive and rejecting toward their infants, the infants nevertheless became attached to them and continued to attempt to cling despite vigorous rebuffs. It is likely that within the normal sample of families included in the studies listed above, almost all mother-child interaction would be of sufficient quality to establish attachment as approximately asymptotic strength. If this were true, then the variance in the frequency and intensity of children's dependency responses at a later age would be primarily a function not of acquisition conditions but of eliciting conditions. We have seen in our review of the experimental work on social deprivation that such deprivation is an effective eliciting condition for a variety of dependent behaviors. A rejecting parent may be seen as one who frequently withdraws himself from interaction with the child—who is unavailable—and who thus frequently provides the eliciting conditions for dependent behavior.

He probably also frequently arouses anxiety in the child over whether he is loved, and, as we have seen earlier, a firmly established response to anxiety is the seeking of comfort from attachment figures or their surrogates.

We must not overlook the possibility that dependent children tend to have rejecting parents because they are dependent—that dependent behavior, beyond a tolerable level of intensity and frequency that is graded according to age, alienates parents. In correlational studies it is not possible to determine how important a factor this is. However, the studies in which social deprivation has been manipulated experimentally have indicated that social deprivation does exert some degree of direct control over dependent behavior regardless of the pre-existing characteristics of the child, and it may be assumed that this is true in family interaction settings as well.

There may be another reason for the association between rejection and dependency. As shown previously, dependency is an immature response system, in the sense that the frequency of this behavior declines with age, as the child acquires a more adaptive repertoire of alternative techniques for getting what he wants. Among children of a given age, then, the more dependent children are the ones who have proceeded slowly in the process of acquiring these alternative repertoires. The rejecting parent probably does a poor job of helping the child to acquire more mature behavior. He is probably not sufficiently interested or patient or perceptive about what the child can and cannot be expected to do for himself to support the child's first fumbling efforts at independence. There is little research, however, on what the rejecting parent actually does or fails to do as a teacher, and we can only suggest this as a promising line of inquiry for the future.

Although warmth per se does not appear to be directly related to dependency (and may be inversely related), there are indications in the literature that it may be a positive factor in interaction with other socialization conditions. Becker (1964) has summarized some of the interactions with the permissiveness-restrictiveness dimension, suggesting that high levels of dependency are found primarily among children growing up in homes that are both warm and restrictive. However, he does not report any studies of dependency in which different levels of warmth were compared at two or more levels of restrictiveness within a given study, so the inference must rest on a comparison of studies that differed in the nature of their samples and their methods.

In socialization in the home setting, the theme of social deprivation is embodied in the use of "withdrawal of love" as a technique for controlling the child. Love, affection, and approval are given contingently upon the child's behaving as the parent wishes. When the child deviates from this pattern, the parent witholds affection. Isolating the child from the family for undesired behavior (e.g., sending him to his room) is another form of social deprivation used in day-to-day discipline and control. The effects of these socialization practices have been most widely studied in connection with the development of internalized controls over deviant behavior. But following the line of reasoning presented above in connection with the effects of rejection, the use of withdrawal of love or isolation should increase children's dependency toward their parents. This hypothesis was tested in the Sears et al. (1957) study, where it was found that the use of withdrawal of love as a disciplinary technique was somewhat related to the frequency and intensity of the dependent behavior shown by the child at home (as measured by mother's report).

The effects of direct reinforcement for dependency have been investigated in a number of studies. As mentioned earlier, Cairns (1962) found that children were more responsive to social reinforcement if they had been rewarded for help-seeking immediately before the testing session. In another experimental study, Nelson (1960) gave one group of children approval for behaving in a dependent manner, while another group received mild verbal rebukes for such behavior. Pretest to posttest changes revealed that reward resulted in an increase in dependency responses toward the rewarding agent, whereas mild punishment for dependency resulted in a decrease of such responses.

In nonlaboratory studies it has sometimes been difficult to distinguish reward for dependency from parental interference with, or prevention of, the acquisition of independent behavior. Levy's (1943) classic study of overprotected boys was one of the earliest naturalistic reports. Overprotection, in this group of families, involved not only continuing provision of help and contact comfort to a degree unusual for the child's age; it also involved restricting the child's opportunities to develop independence. The boys treated in this way were either passively dependent (if their mothers were dominant) or demandingly dependent (if their mothers were submissive). In a later study by Heathers (1953), children had to walk along a raised board mounted on springs, and were offered the opportunity to take the experimenter's hand. The children who accepted this help were found to have parents who "encourage their children to lean on others," and Heathers pointed out that these parents also tended to hold their children back from developing age-appropriate behavior.

Finney (1961), working with a group of boys who were patients in a mental health clinic, found only a small and insignificant relationship between the mother's selective reinforcement of dependency responses and the child's rated dependency ($r = .18$), but this correlation rose to .40 when the level of maternal nurturance was partialled out. Finally, Bandura (1960), working with a group of aggressive pre-adolescent boys and a control group, found that the more dependent boys had parents who rewarded dependent behavior. In sum, the research on direct reward of dependent behavior is consistent in pointing to a positive relation between such reward and the frequency of dependent behavior displayed by the child.

The findings are not so clear with respect to the effects of punishment. As mentioned earlier, Harlow found that infant monkeys became attached to abusive mothers. Consistent with this is Cairns' (1966) finding that lambs reared with adult dogs became attached to the dogs even if the dogs mauled them. With human children, Nelson (1960) found, as noted above, that mild verbal rebuke for dependent responses reduced the frequency with which such responses were shown toward the person who administered the rebuke. Sears et al. (1965) found that punishment for dependency is negatively associated with total observed dependency in girls. Bandura and Walters (1959) reported that aggressive adolescent boys who had experienced a good deal of parental rejection showed less dependent behavior than more accepted, nonaggressive boys, and reported further that parents who expressed rejection of their children also directly punished de-

pendency to a greater extent than those who were more accepting. In a later study with somewhat younger boys, however, Bandura (1960) reported that punishment for dependency decreased the frequency of its occurrence directly toward the punishing agent, but not its total frequency toward all targets and in all situations. There were, in fact, a group of highly aggressive boys among whom maternal punishment for dependency seemed to have the effect of *increasing* dependency responses toward adults. McCord et al. (1962) also found a positive relation between punishment for dependency and a dependent orientation toward either adults or peers, or both. In a cross-cultural study, Whiting and Child (1953) reported that high punishment for dependency in childhood was not associated with fear of others in adulthood and thus, by implication, was not associated with low adult dependency.

There are several indications that the effect of punishment for dependency depends upon whether the punishment is intermittent and mixed with reward for the same behavior. Fisher (1955) compared the social responses of two groups of puppies. One group was consistently petted and fondled by the experimenter for approach responses, while the second group was given the same kind of reward treatment on many occasions, with the addition of training sessions in which the puppies were handled roughly and on occasion electrically shocked for approach responses. Tests of dependency behavior conducted toward the end of, and following, 13 weeks of training showed that the puppies which had received both reward and punishment exhibited greater dependency behavior in the form of remaining close to a human than did the puppies in the reward-only group.

In a correlational study of kindergarten-aged children, a similar pattern of results was obtained. Sears et al. (1957) found that the amount of punishment[13] for dependency was positively related ($r = .39$) to the amount of dependency the child showed at home only when the parents also rather frequently rewarded such behavior (see Table 14). In

---

[13] There were very few instances in which the mothers administered physical punishment for dependent behavior. "Punishment" in this table refers primarily to maternal irritation and verbal scolding.

Table 14. *Relationship of Child's Current Dependency to Combined Reward and Punishment for Dependency*

	Percentage Showing Considerable Dependency at Kindergarten Age	Number of Cases
High reward for dependency		
Low punishment	9%	68
Medium punishment	25	59
High punishment	42	31
Low reward for dependency		
Low punishment	21	28
Medium punishment	38	45
High punishment	33	85

From Sears et al., 1957, p. 526.

this study the same pattern of results appears if the cases are divided according to the level of infant nurturance rather than according to the amount of current reward for dependency.[14] That is, it is only for the children who received a relatively high level of infant nurturance (whose mothers were quite responsive to their crying and who were fed on demand) that the effect of current punishment for dependency is to increase it. These results may be interpreted either as a reflection of the well-known principle from animal learning studies that intermittent reinforcement makes responses more resistant to extinction, or they may be interpreted in terms of the energizing effects of conflict.

The effect of general punitiveness—frequent punishment for a wide range of responses, not specifically for dependency—may depend upon the sex of the child. In the 1953 Sears study, parental punitiveness was positively related to dependency for boys, negatively for girls. Winder and Rau (1962) found high punitiveness to be associated with high dependency in their sample of boys (girls were not included in the study), and Baumrind and Black (1967) found punitiveness to be associated with autonomy (indipendence) in girls but not among boys. Consistent with these findings on sex differences in the effects of punitiveness are some of the earlier-mentioned sex differences in the cor-

[14] This tabulation was not included in the published report of the study.

relates of rejection or hostility: Sears et al. (1965) showed that maternal hostility was negatively associated with dependency in girls but not in boys, and Kagan and Moss (1962) report that maternal hostility during the first 3 years of life is associated with independence in adulthood among women, but not among men.

In our earlier discussion of rejection, we offered some reasons why the production of anxiety ought to facilitate dependency. The effects of punitiveness and rejection on boys is not difficult to understand in terms of that reasoning. The fact that the situation is different for girls is puzzling. Sears (1953) argued that a given amount of punishment is more severe for girls than it is for boys because girls are more fully identified with the punisher. Another possibility is that the social roles (and perhaps certain inborn tendencies) of girls are such that they will remain dependent unless driven into independence by aversive treatment from their attachment object. This is speculation, however, and for the present we must simply note that some intriguing sex differences do exist in this region of parental child influences.

As pointed out earlier, a major dimension of child-rearing is the permissiveness-restrictiveness (or control versus autonomy-giving) dimension. The simplest hypothesis concerning the relation of this dimension to dependency is that restrictiveness will prevent the child from acquiring autonomous skills for coping with his needs, and will therefore be associated with continued high dependence upon parents and other adults. The development of social skills with age-mates should be one of the things interfered with by parental restrictiveness, and therefore such restrictiveness ought to be reflected in low "dependency" behavior directed toward peers. There are a number of studies which support this hypothesis:

Watson (1957). Children raised in warm and permissive homes (as measured by parent-self ratings) are more independent than children raised in warm but restrictive homes. The children's characteristics were assessed through behavior observation and projective tests. $N = 328$, grades kindergarten through six.

Faigin (1958). Children being raised in a kibbutz with a structured (relatively restrictive) program were compared with those raised in a kibbutz with a more permissive philosophy. In the structured kibbutz there was more seeking of attention and help from adults; in the permissive kibbutz there was more crying and thumbsucking among children under 2, dependency directed toward peers among children over 2.

Winder and Rau (1962). High restrictiveness on the part of either father or mother associated with dependency and aggression in boys.

McCord et al. (1962). Dependency upon adults during middle childhood and adolescence among boys was associated with high parental demands, strict parental supervision, and high restrictions imposed by parents. Dependency upon age-mates, on the contrary, was associated with a total lack of parental restrictions and supervision.

Levy (1943). Boys who were restricted by "overprotective" mothers were either passively dependent or demandingly dependent upon their mothers.

Kagan and Moss (1962). Maternal restrictiveness is consistently associated with dependency in girls throughout childhood and into adulthood. For boys, there is a reversal: maternal restriction during the 0 to 3 age period is associated with *independence* in adulthood, while restrictiveness during the ages 3 to 6 predicts *dependence* in adulthood.

Finney (1963). Maternal "overprotectiveness" is positively correlated with children's "submissiveness."

Murphy (1962). Maternal permissiveness for autonomy in the infant feeding situation correlated with autonomy at preschool age. Correlations reported for boys only.

Smith (1958). Dependency toward the mother positively related to maternal overprotectiveness ($r = .49$, subjects of preschool age).

Before concluding that there is a simple direct relationship between "permissiveness" and low dependency toward adults, we should specify in greater detail what is meant by permissiveness and what is the alternative behavior that develops in place of adult-directed dependency. Allowing the child freedom to explore, to express his emotions and opinions, and to make decisions concerning his own course of action may or may not be accompanied by efforts to teach him how to be successfully independent and by demands for mature and responsible behavior. The distinction has often been made between permissiveness that stems from parental indifference (and is akin to neglect) and permissiveness that stems from trust, is accompanied by guidance, and is paced appropriately to the child's level of competence. It is likewise useful to distinguish the child who is nondependent toward adults but dependent toward peers in the sense of being clinging and conforming, from the child who is nondependent toward adults but autonomously interactive with peers. It was shown earlier that among children who frequently initiate contact with other children and seek their attention, some also frequently *give* contact and attention and may also characteristically resist interference from other children in their ongoing behavior sequence. In other words, children who are nondependent toward adults and socially interactive with peers may or may not be autonomous. Some of the studies mentioned have not made these distinctions and it is difficult to know what kind of parental behavior is being contrasted with restrictiveness, and what kind of child behavior is contrasted to adult-directed dependency. Baumrind and Black (1967) have studied some of the child-rearing correlates of autonomy in preschool aged children, reporting that autonomy (and independence) are associated with the following aspects of parental behavior:

Boys:
  Consistent dicipline
  High maturity demands
  Encouragement of the child's making independent contacts
  Use of reasoning to obtain compliance
  Low restrictiveness
  Low use of coercive power

Girls:
  High socialization demands
  Low use of coercive power
  Punitiveness

Parent initiation (rather than child initiation) of control sequences

In the case of boys, at least, we see that the low restrictiveness that is associated with children's independent behavior is not of the neglecting sort—it is embedded in a context of parental guidance and standard-setting. Similarly, in the study by Sears et al. (1965), it was found that independence among boys was associated with maternal pressure for the child to be independent, but also with high maternal expectancy for the child to take responsibility.

SUMMARY

There are a number of serious gaps in our knowledge about the behavioral realm we have been discussing. One of these concerns the normal course of developmental change and transformation that occurs after infancy. The scraps of information we do have point to a decline in proximity-seeking, with attention-seeking and approval-seeking either maintaining a constant level or increasing. There appears to be a shift in target from the mother and other adults to age-mates. With respect to these changes, one is struck by the parallels with subhuman primates, in whom infant-infant play and other social contact with age-mates take more and more of the infant's time, while the occasions upon which the infant flees to the mother for comfort or protection decline in frequency, and the amount of time spent simply staying near the mother becomes progressively less.

Harlow has discussed these shifts in terms of the development of distinct "systems":

We have broadly defined the socialization motives as the affectional systems and have presented the position that within, and probably even without, the primate order there are at least five affectional systems. These are: the mother-infant or maternal affectional system, the closely related and complementary infant-mother affectional system, the age-mate or peer affectional system, the heterosexual affectional system, and the paternal affectional system (Harlow, 1966, p. 224).

We confess that upon first reading this formulation, we were skeptical about the utility of conceptualizing affectional behavior as separate systems. The primary phenomenon being observed is that the animal is able to form attachments to a variety of different other individuals at different points in his life cycle. This could be thought of as simple generalization of a behavior pattern from one object to another. Harlow's own finding that deprivation in one "system" (the infant-mother-system) results in abnormal development of other "systems" (the adult heterosexual and the maternal affectional systems) would indicate that these are not separate systems, but that one is the direct outgrowth of the other.

What evidence would justify postulating separate systems? One would have to look for differences in the topography of the behavior itself, and in the nature of the conditions that elicit or control it. If one followed the lead of the ethologists, one would have to ask in addition whether the behavior served different functions. In the infant monkey, it would appear to be reasonably clear that the infant's behavior toward his age-mates is not a simple generalization of the "same" behavior that he has been displaying toward his mother. For example, a primary element in the infant-mother behavior pattern is ventral contacting and clinging. This pattern is almost completely absent in the infant-infant response sequences. The infant-infant interactions are largely rough-and-tumble play. Furthermore, a primary elicitor of the infant's mother-contacting is the introduction of fear-producing stimuli. We cannot find a report in the literature of an experiment in which an infant monkey, raised with a normal live mother and also with opportunities to play with age-mates, is subjected to a stress situation when both his mother and an age-mate are present; we suspect the infant would run to the mother and not the age-mate, even though he might spend far more of his time normally with the latter. Furthermore, he would probably use the mother and not the age-mate as a "safe base for exploration." If this were the case, we would begin to have evidence that the two kinds of relationships did indeed constitute different systems. Of course, an infant may be able to use an age-mate as though it were a mother if a normal mother is not available. Harlow's descriptions of the motherless infants raised in each other's company reveals that in these circumstances ventral clinging of one infant to another does occur, and it is likely that if these monkeys were in each other's presence in a strange situation or when a potentially dangerous stimulus appeared, they would seek and obtain contact comfort from one another.

In the case of the human child, can we see similar distinctions in the nature of the "dependent" behavior toward the mother compared to that directed toward age-mates? And are there comparable differences in the nature of the occasions when the behavior is likely to occur? The young human infant does not cling, although clinging does develop by the end of the first year and can be very vigorous when the child is emotionally upset. The earliest attachment behavior would appear to be crying and smiling, followed by the development of lifting the arms to be picked up; finally, when the child can walk, he follows his attachment object and stays within a given range, making closer contact and hiding behind his mother or climbing into her arms at moments of stress. He also develops a variety of behaviors that will attract the mother's attention, including calling to her. Throughout this developmental sequence the distance receptors play an important role: the child looks at his mother a great deal, and listens for her. Nevertheless, we do not feel it is satisfactory to regard the development of this receptor orientation as the primary element in attachment, or a sufficient criterion of its occurrence, because it is too general and forms part of too many other behavior patterns. Ainsworth's observations of 1-year-olds are instructive in this connection. When the child was playing in the mother's presence and a stranger entered the room, the child retreated to the mother and *looked at the stranger*. Furthermore, the children who were securely attached (to use Ainsworth's term) would spend most of their time looking at the things they were playing with when the mother was present. It was only when she was not present that the child would stop attending to his toys and restlessly look for his mother. Thus it is difficult to identify the object of attachment (or to estimate the intensity of the attachment) simply by noting the orientation of the child's distance receptors, and the topography of child-mother attachment behavior is more adequately de-scribed in terms of the approach and contacting responses described previously.

Is child-child dependent behavior made up of the same responses? We do not have good observations of the topography of the child-child behavior. We can only speculate that children rarely hold out their arms to another child, or run to another child for contact comfort under stress, or cling to another child. [Exceptions would occur in the case of children who had learned to use one another as mother surrogates, as in the case of the children described by Freud and Dann (1951) or perhaps in some instances among kibbutz children.] In making social approaches to other children, do they smile as they would at their mothers? Do they cry when the help they want from other children is not quickly forthcoming? We cannot be sure of these items, but certain common elements are easily observed: a child will follow another child around, try to get his attention, and some-times ask for help. Beyond this, there are a number of aspects of the child-child interaction system that are farily unique to this system and do not appear to be transferred as previously learned items from infant-mother interactions. This category includes much of what we call play.

Thus we see that with respect to some behaviors—certain aspects of proximity-seeking versus play—there is justification for looking upon child-mother interactions and child-child interactions as different behavioral systems. With respect to attention-seeking there is not. Let us underline some of the differences between these classes of behavior: (1) proximity-seeking declines with age, attention-seeking does not; (2) proximity-seeking is increased under fear arousal, attention seeking is not; (3) attention-seeking generalizes from adult targets to child targets, proximity-seeking does not (i.e., there is a positive correlation between frequency scores for attention-seeking directed toward the two kinds of targets, whereas for proximity-seeking this correlation is zero or negative); and (4) by preschool age attention-seeking is a part of a behavioral cluster that involves not only asking for help, attention, and nurturance, but *giving* help, attention, and nurturance to others—it is part of a reciprocal interaction system and is positively related to aggression and sociability as well; proximity-seeking tends to be negatively related to all these things, and is part of a different, more passive behavioral cluster.

How did these differences come about? Were attention-seeking and proximity-seeking separate behaviors from the start, with different elicitors and maintaining conditions, or did they start out as part of the same behavioral system in the early life of the child and become separate through a process of differentiation? There is very little evidence that will help to answer these questions. Heathers (1955) did find a small positive relationship between attention-seeking and proximity-seeking directed toward adults at age 2 and a negative correlation between these two variables at age 4 to 5—a finding which would support the differentiation position. It appears likely that the primary maternal behaviors which furnish the maintaining stimuli for proximity-seeking are picking up the child, holding it, cuddling it—in short, the provision of contact comfort. As the child grows larger and heavier the mother cannot so easily provide these maintaining stimuli, while she can easily continue to provide attention, help, and approval, thus maintaining the behaviors of the child that we see as seeking for these things. Similarly, the lack of generalization of proximity-seeking from adult to child targets may be viewed as an outcome of the fact that age-mates are not large and strong enough to pick the child up, nor do they have the giving of other forms of contact-comfort as a strongly established part of their behavior repertoires, at least not in early childhood. They *can* give attention, however, and are likely to do so toward a child who is active, sociable, and/or aggressive—hence the development of a relationship between these qualities and attention-seeking.

There is one fact that argues against the differentiation hypothesis, and this is the different effect of fear-arousal on the two classes of behavior. It is difficult to see why or how fear should affect both classes of behavior early in life, and only proximity seeking later on. Is there any age at which fear seems to offer attention seeking as well? In the work with primates, we have not encountered any description of young animals "showing off" when afraid. Instead, they run to the mother and cling. With human children, the only piece of direct evidence is the Rosenthal study, in which an arousal produced by the sound of a child crying (and other mildly threatening elements) led to increased proximity-seeking but not to increased attention-seeking. On the other hand, it is true that in the research on social reinforcement, certain "arousal" conditions have been associated with increased responsiveness to social reinforcement, and such responsiveness seems to have more in common with attention-seeking than with proximity-seeking. But the arousal in these studies has been produced by a social threat. That is, an experimenter has shown (or threatened to show) social distance, inattentiveness, and/or disapproval. The child's response is to try to get a restoration of attention and approval. These studies have not demonstrated that increased responsiveness to social reinforcement, or other forms of seeking for attention and approval, would occur with the arousal of nonsocial fears. We suspect that the introduction of, say, a feared animal into the experimental situation would increase proximity-seeking and not attention-seeking, unless the situation were arranged in such a way that the only way a child could stay in contact with the experimenter was by dropping marbles into a slot and hearing the experimenter say "good." But the issue must remain open, since evidence is not available which would tell whether, and how early in life, the two kinds of behavior are functionally distinct and, if so, how early in life the distinction emerges.

In infancy, "crying for attention" and other actions that draw the mother's attention to the child are certainly part of the primary attachment system. When the infant is too young to crawl, or when he can crawl but is confined in a playpen or crib, he can only achieve proximity by bringing the mother to him, and attention-seeking is a necessary part of this process. Crying and calling to the mother undoubtedly continue to serve this function after the child can crawl and walk. But with the acquisition of a range of social skills, attention-seeking comes to have a more general function. In any social interaction, each participant must get and maintain the attention of the other participants. In a conversation between two people, if the attention of one person wanders, the other person must raise his voice, make a sudden movement, say or do something startling, or otherwise seek to recapture the other's attention, or the conversation will break off. It is understandable, then, that by preschool age, when children have begun to participate in interactions with others that continue for progressively increasing periods of time, they have learned how to maintain the attention of the other participants, and attention-seeking has become part of a cluster of socially interactive behaviors (including attention-*giving*), and no longer merely serves to bring about proximity with a comfort-giving figure.

Approval-seeking comes to play a central role in a cluster of behaviors that contains "dependent" and "nondependent" elements—namely, the maintainance of self-esteem and the validation of judgments about the rightness or fitness of the individual's actions. Presumably, the frequency of approval-seeking and the conditions under which it occurs would be related to the development of the self-concept and would become more differentiated from other aspects of attention-seeking as this development progresses.

The preceding comments all relate to the basic point that "dependency" is too global a concept to be useful in the analysis of behavior beyond the first year or two of life. There seems good reason to speak of a unitary, primary "affectional system" in infancy and early childhood. The term *attachment* seems a good choice to designate the behavior involved at this age, and the parallels between the development of this behavior in the human infant and in subhuman primates suggests the possible importance of an instinctual component in this behavior. At the very least, we can say that some species show attachment in infancy, whereas others (e.g., lizards) do not, and mankind is one of the species in which the probabilities are great that the behavior will develop in any given

individual. However, from the outset, inputs from the environment (particularly the interpersonal environment) affect the course of development of the behavior. By the age of 3 or 4 years, specific learning and general cognitive growth have brought about a considerable differentiation of attachment and dependent behavior with respect to its topography, its targets, and its eliciting conditions, and new clusters of behavioral dispositions have become organized which incorporate elements of the formerly unitary system. Different cultural settings differ, of course, in the nature of the learning experiences they provide, and they differentially affect the rate and course of this development.

By preschool age, then, it is no longer useful to attempt to rank-order children along a single dimension of "dependency." This is not to say that there is no individual consistency across time and varied settings with respect to dependency-related behavior. There is evidence for relatively enduring intra-individual dispositions—the behavior of the individual is predictable, to a significant degree, from his past behavior. It is only that these dispositions appear to be narrower, and clustered in different ways, than much of the research and theorizing on dependency has assumed.

We have seen that the research on socialization has produced a number of inconsistent findings, and that the correlations which have been found tend to be low. It is reasonable to expect that better predictions could be made from socialization variables if the aspects of dependency being predicted were chosen and defined in relation to the developmental level of the children being studied, with separate predictions being made for aspects of dependency which normally vary independently at a given point in the developmental sequence.

References

Adler, P. T. The relationship of two types of dependency to the effectiveness of approval as a reinforcer among a group of emotionally disturbed children. Doctoral dissertation, New York University, 1961.

Ainsworth, M. D. S., The development of infant-mother interaction among the Ganda. In B. M. Foss (Ed.), *Determinants of infant behavior*. Vol. II. New York: Wiley, 1963.

Ainsworth, M. D. S., and Wittig, B. A. Attachment and exploratory behavior of one-year-olds in a strange situation. In B. M. Foss (Ed.), *Determinants of infant behavior*. Vol. IV. London: Methuen and New York: Wiley, 1967.

Allen, S. Effects of verbal reinforcement on children's performance as a function of type of task. *J. exp. Child Psychol.*, 1966, **3**, 57–73.

Anderson, J. E. *The young child in the home: a survey of three thousand American families*. New York: Appleton-Century, 1936.

Arieti, S. *American handbook of psychiatry*. New York: Basic Books, 1959. 2 vols.

Arsenian, J. M. Young children in an insecure situation. *J. abnorm. soc. Psychol.*, 1943, **38**, 225–249.

Baer, D. M. A technique of social reinforcement for the study of child behavior: behavior avoiding reinforcement withdrawal. *Child Dev.*, 1962, **33**, 847–858.

Bandura, A., and Walters, R. H. *Adolescent aggression*. New York: Ronald Press, 1959.

Bandura, A., and Walters, R. H. Aggression. In H. W. Stevenson (Ed.), *Child psychology*. National Society for the Study of Education Yearbook, Part 1. Chicago: University of Chicago Press, 1963. Pp. 364–415.

Baumrind, D., and Black, A. E. Socialization practices associated with dimensions of competence in preschool boys and girls. *Child Dev.*, 1967, **38**, 291–328.

Becker, W. C. The relationship of factors in parental ratings of self and each other to the behavior of kindergarten children as rated by mothers, fathers and teachers. *J. consult. Psychol.*, 1960, **24**, 507–527.

Becker, W. C. Consequences of different kinds of parental discipline. In M. L. Hoffman and L. W. Hoffman (Eds.), *Review of child development research*. New York: Russell Sage, 1964.

Becker, W. C., and Krug, R. S. A circumplex model for social behavior in children. *Child Dev.*, 1964, **35**, 371–396.

Becker, W. C., Peterson, D. R., Luria, Z., Shoemaker, D. J., and Hellmer, L. A. Relations of factors derived from parent-interview ratings to behavior problems of five-year-olds. *Child Dev.*, 1962, **33**, 509–535.

Beller, E. K. Dependency and autonomous achievement striving related to orality and anality in early childhood. *Child Dev.*, 1957, **28**, 287–315.

Beller, E. K. Exploratory studies of dependency. *Trans. N. Y. Acad. Sci.*, 1959, **21**, 414–426.

Beller, E. K. A study of dependency and aggression in early childhood. Unpublished progress report, 1962, Project M-849. Child Development Center, New York City.

Beller, E. K., and Haeberle, A. W. Motivation and conflict in relation to phantasy response of young children. Paper read at the 25th anniversary meeting of the Society for Research in Child Development, Bethesda, Md., 1959.

Beller, E. K., and Haeberle, A. W. Dependency and the frustration-aggression hypothesis. Unpublished paper, Child Development Center, New York City, 1961.

Beller, E. K., and Turner, J. L. Sex differences: the factorial structure of personality variables in "normal" and "emotionally disturbed" preschool children. Paper presented at the meetings of the Eastern Psychological Assn., Philadelphia, 1964.

Berkowitz, H., and Zigler, E. Effects of preliminary positive and negative interactions and delay conditions on children's responsiveness to social reinforcement. *J. Pers. Soc. Psychol.*, 1965, **2**, 500–505.

Bijou, S. W., and Baer, D. M. *Child development*. Vol. II. New York: Appleton-Century-Crofts, 1965.

Blum, G. S. *Psychoanalytic theories of personality*. New York: McGraw-Hill, 1953.

Bowlby, J. *Maternal care and mental health.* (2nd ed.) Geneva (World Health Organization: Monograph Series, N. 2), 1952.

Bowlby, J. The nature of the child's tie to his mother. *Int. J. Psychoanal.,* 1958, **39,** 350.

Bowlby, J. Symposium on "psychoanalysis and ethology." II. Ethology and the development of object relations. *Int. J. Psychoanal.,* 1960, **41,** 313.

Brekstad, A. Factors influencing the reliability of anamnestic recall. *Child Dev.,* 1966, **37,** 603–612.

Butler, R. A. Discrimination learning by rhesus monkeys to visual exploration motivation. *J. comp. physiol. Psychol.,* 1953, **46,** 96–98.

Cairns, R. B. The influence of dependency inhibition on the effectiveness of social reinforcement. *J. Personality,* 1961, **29,** 466–488.

Cairns, R. B. Antecedents of social reinforcer effectiveness. Progress Report, USPHS research grant M-4373, 1962.

Cairns, R. B. Antecedents of social reinforcer effectiveness. Paper presented at the Society for Research in Child Development biennial meetings, 1963.

Cairns, R. B. The development, maintenance, and extinction of social attachment behavior in sheep. *J. comp. physiol. Psychol.,* 1966, **62.**

Cairns, R. B. The attachment behavior of mammals. *Psychol. Rev.* 1967, **73,** 409–426.

Cairns, R. B., and Johnson, D. L. The development of interspecies social preferences. *Psychonom. Sci.,* 1965, **2,** 337–338.

Cairns, R. B., and Kaufman, H. Prestige suggestibility and dependency inhibition. Unpublished manuscript, University of Indiana, 1962.

Cairns, R. B., and Lewis, M. Dependency and the reinforcement value of a verbal stimulus. *J. consult. Psychol.,* 1962, **26,** 1–8.

Caldwell, B. M. Mother-infant interaction in monomatric and polymatric families. *Am. J. Orthopsychiat.,* 1962a, **32,** 340–341. (a)

Caldwell, B. M. The usefulness of the critical period hypothesis in the study of filiative behavior. *Merrill-Palmer Quart.,* 1962b, **8,** 219–242. (b)

Canon, L. K. Motivational state, stimulus selection, and distractibility. *Child Dev.,* 1967, **38,** 589–596.

Casler, L. Maternal deprivation: a critical review of the literature. *Monogr. Soc. Res. Child Dev.,* 1961, **26,** No. 2.

Casler, L. The effects of extratactile stimulation on a group of institutionalized infants. *Genet. Psychol. Monogr.,* 1965, **71,** 137–175.

Cline, V. B., Richards, J. M., Jr., and Needham, W. E. A factor analytic study of the father form of the parental attitude research instrument. *Psychol.,* 1963, **13,** 65–72.

Collard, R. R. Fear of strangers and play behavior in kittens, with varied social experience. *Child Dev.,* 1967, **38,** 877–892.

Cox, F. N. Some effects of text anxiety and presence or absence of other persons in boys' performance on a repetitive motor task. *J. Exp. Child Psychol.,* 1966, **3,** 100–112.

Cox, F. N., and Campbell, D. Young children in a new situation with and without their mothers. *Child Dev.,* 1968, **39,** 123–131.

Crandall, V. J., Preston, A., and Rabson, A. Maternal reactions and the development of independence and achievement behavior in young children. *Child Dev.,* 1960, **31,** 243–251.

Denenberg, V. H., and Grota, L. J. Social-seeking and novelty-seeking behavior as a function of differential rearing histories. *J. abnorm. soc. Psychol.,* 1964, **69,** 453–456.

DeVore, I. Mother-infant relations in free-ranging baboons. In H. Rheingold (Ed.), *Maternal behavior in mammals.* New York: Wiley, 1963.

Dollard, J., and Miller, N. E. *Personality and psychotherapy: an analysis in terms of learning, thinking and culture.* New York: McGraw-Hill, 1950.

Dorwart, W., Ezerman, R., Lewis, M., and Rosenhan, D. The effect of brief social and nonsocial reinforcement. *J. Pers. soc. Psychol.*, 1965, **2**, 111–115.

Emmerich, W. Continuity and stability in early social development. *Child Dev.*, 1964, **35**, 311–332.

Emmerich, W. Continuity and stability in early social development: II. Teacher's ratings. *Child Dev.*, 1966, **37**, 17–27. (a)

Emmerich, W. Personality assessments conceptualized as perspectives. *J. Project. Tech. pers. Assess.*, 1966, **30**, 317–318. (b)

Endsley, R. C. Dependency and performance by preschool children on a socially reinforced task. Unpublished Masters thesis, State University of Iowa, 1960.

Epstein, R. Need for approval and the conditioning of verbal hostility in asthmatic children. *J. abnorm. soc. Psychol.*, 1964, **69**, 105–109.

Erickson, M. T. Effects of social deprivation and satiation on verbal conditioning in children. *J. comp. physiol. Psychol.*, 1962, **55**, 953–957.

Erikson, E. H. Identity and the life cycle, selected papers. *Psychol. Iss.*, (I, Whole No. 1). New York: International Universities Press, 1959.

Eysenck, H. J. The inheritance of extraversion-introversion. *Acta psychol.*, 1956, **12**, 95–110.

Faigin, H. Social behavior of young children in the kibbutz. *J. abnorm. soc. Psychol.*, 1958, **56**, 117–129.

Fenichel, O. *The psychoanalytic theory of neurosis.* New York: Norton, 1945.

Ferguson, P. E. The influence of isolation, anxiety and dependency on reinforcer effectiveness. Unpublished Masters thesis, University of Toronto, 1961.

Festinger, L. A theory of social comparison processes. *Hum. Relat.*, 1954, **7**, 117–140.

Finney, J. C. Some maternal influences on children's personality and character. *Genet. Psychol. Monogr.*, 1961, **63**, 199–278.

Finney, J. C. Maternal influences on anal or compulsive character in children. *J. genet. Psychol.*, 1963, **103**, 351–367.

Fisher, A. E. The effects of differential early treatment on the social and exploratory behavior of puppies. Unpublished doctoral dissertation, Pennsylvania State University, 1955.

Freedman, D. G. Heredity control of early social behavior. In B. M. Foss (Ed.), *Determinants of infant behavior.* Vol. III. New York: Wiley, 1965. Pp. 149–159.

Freud, A., and Dann, S. An experiment in group upbringing. In *The psychoanalytic study of the child.* Vol. VI. New York: International Universities Press, 1951.

Freud, S. *Collected papers.* Vols. I, II, III, IV. New York: Basic Books, 1959.

Fromm, E. *The heart of man.* New York: Harper and Row, 1964.

Gavalas, R. J., and Briggs, P. J. Concurrent schedules of reinforcement: a new concept of dependency. *Merrill-Palmer Quart.*, 1966, **12**, 97–122.

Gewirtz, J. L. Succorance in young children. Unpublished doctoral dissertation, State University of Iowa, 1948.

Gewirtz, J. L. A factor analysis of some attention-seeking behaviors of young children. *Child Dev.*, 1956, **27**, 17–36.

Gewirtz, J. L. A learning analysis of the effects of normal stimulation, privation and deprivation on the acquisition of social motivation and attachment. In B. M. Foss (Ed.), *Determinants of infant behavior.* London: Methuen and New York: Wiley, 1961. Pp. 213–299.

Gewirtz, J. L. The course of infant smiling in four child-rearing environments in

Israel. In B. M. Foss (Ed.), *Determinants of infant behavior*, Vol. III. London: Methuen, 1965.

Gewirtz, J. L. Deprivation and satiation of social stimuli as determinants of their reinforcing efficacy. In J. P. Hill (Ed.), *Minnesota Symposia on Child Psychology*. Vol. 1. Minneapolis: University of Minnesota Press, 1967. Pp. 3–56.

Gewirtz, J. L., and Baer, D. M. Deprivation and satiation of social reinforcers as drive conditions. *J. abnorm. soc. Psychol.*, 1958, **56**, 49–56.

Goldfarb, W. Psychological deprivation in infancy and subsequent adjustment. *Am. J. Orthopsychiat.*, 1945, **15**, 49–56.

Gordon, J. E., and Cohn, F. Effect of fantasy arousal of affiliation drive on doll play aggression. *J. abnorm. soc. Psychol.*, 1963, **66**, 301–307.

Gottesman, I. I. Genetic variance in adaptive personality traits. *J. Child Psychol. Psychiat.*, 1966, **7**, 199–209.

Griffin, G. A., and Harlow, H. F. Effects of three months of total social deprivation on social adjustment and learning in the rhesus monkey. *Child Dev.*, 1966, **37**, 533–547.

Haggard, E. A., Brekstad, A., and Skard, A. G. On the reliability of the anamnestic interview. *J. abnorm. soc. Psychol.*, 1960, **61**, 311–318.

Harlow, H. F. Love in infant monkeys. *Scient. Am.*, 1959, **200**, 68–74.

Harlow, H. F. The development of affectional patterns in infant monkeys. In B. M. Foss (Ed.), *Determinants of infant behavior*. New York: Wiley, 1961. Pp. 75–100.

Harlow, H. F. The primate socialization motives. *Trans. Stud. Coll. Phys. Philad.*, 1966, **33**, 224–237.

Harlow, H. F., Dodsworth, R. O., and Harlow, M. K. Total social isolation in monkeys. *Proc. Nat. Acad. Sci.*, 1965, **54**, 90–97.

Harlow, H. F., Rowland, G. L., and Griffin, G. A. The effect of total social deprivation on the development of monkey behavior. *Psychiatric Research Report* 19, American Psychiatric Association, December, 1964.

Harlow, H. F., and Zimmerman, R. R. The development of affectional responses in infant monkeys. *Proc. Am. phil. Soc.*, 1958, **102**, 501–509.

Hartup, W. W. Nurturance and nurturance-withdrawal in relation to the dependency behavior of young children. *Child Dev.*, 1958, **29**, 191–201.

Hartup, W. W. Dependence and independence. In Stevenson, H. W. (Ed.), *Child psychology*. National Society for the Study of Education Yearbook, Part 1. Chicago: University of Chicago Press, 1963. Pp. 333–363.

Hartup, W. W. Friendship status and the effectiveness of peers as reinforcing agents. *J. exp. Child Psychol.*, 1964, **1**, 154–162.

Hartup, W. W., and Himeno, Y. Social isolation versus interaction with adults in relation to aggression in preschool children. *J. abnorm. soc. Psychol.*, 1959, **59**, 17–22.

Hartup, W. W., and Keller, E. D. Nurturance in preschool children and its relation to dependency. *Child Dev.*, 1960, **31**, 681–689.

Hatfield, J. S., Ferguson, P. E., Rau, L., and Alpert, R. Mother-child interaction and the socialization process. *Child Dev.*, 1967, **38**, 365–414.

Havighurst, R., and Neugarten, B. *American Indian and white children*. Chicago: University of Chicago Press, 1955.

Heathers, G. Emotional dependence and independence in a physical threat situation. *Child Dev.*, 1953, **24**, 169–179.

Heathers, G. Emotional dependence and independence in nursery school play. *J. genet. Psychol.*, 1955, **87**, 37–57.

Heinicke, C. M., and Westheimer, I. *Brief separations*. New York: International Universities Press, 1965.

Helmreich, R. L., and Collins, B. E. Situational determinants of affiliative preference under stress. *J. pers. soc. Psychol.*, 1967, **6**, 79–85.

Hess, E. H. Two conditions limiting critical age for imprinting. *J. comp. physiol. Psychol.*, 1959, **52**, 515–518.

Hetzer, H., and Tudor-Hart, B. H. Die Fruheston Reaktionen auf die monschliche Stimme. *Quellen und Studien zur Jugenkind,* 1927.

Hill, K. T., and Stevenson, H. W. Effectiveness of social reinforcement following social and sensory deprivation. *J. abnorm. soc. Psychol.*, 1964, **68**, 579–584.

Hinde, R. *Animal behavior.* New York: McGraw-Hill, 1966.

Hottel, J. V. The influence of age and intelligence on independence-conformity behavior of children. Unpublished doctoral dissertation, George Peabody College for Teachers, 1960.

Ingel, G. J., and Calvin, A. D. The development of affectional responses in infant dogs. *J. comp. physiol. Psychol.*, 1960, **53**, 302–305.

Jakubczak, L. F., and Walters, R. H. Suggestibility as dependency behavior. *J. abnorm. soc. Psychol.*, 1959, **59**, 102–107.

Jay, P. Mother-infant relations in langurs. In H. Rheingold (Ed.), *Maternal behavior in mammals.* New York: Wiley, 1963.

Kagan, J., and Moss, H. A. *Birth to maturity,* New York: Wiley, 1962.

Kagan, J., and Mussen, P. H. Dependency themes on the TAT and group conformity, *J. consult. Psychol.*, 1956, **20**, 29–32.

Kaufman, I. C., and Rosenblum, L. A. The reaction to separation in infant monkeys: anaclitic depression and conservation-withdrawal. *Psychosom. Med.*, 1967, **29**, 648–675.

Kessen, W. *The Child.* New York: Wiley, 1965.

Keister, M. E., and Updegraff, R. A study of children's reactions to failure and an experimental attempt to modify them. *Child Dev.*, 1937, **8**, 241–248.

Kiesler, S. B. Stress, affiliation and performance. *J. exp. res. Pers.*, 1966, **1**, 227–235.

Kohlberg, L. A cognitive-developmental analysis of children's sex-role concepts and attitudes. In E. Maccoby (Ed.), *The development of sex differences.* Stanford, Cal.: Stanford University Press, 1966.

Kohlberg, L., and Zigler, E. The impact of cognitive maturity on the development of sex-role attitudes in the years 4–8. *Genet. Psychol. Monogr.*, 1967, **75**, 89–165.

Korner, A. F., and Grobstein, R. Visual alertness as related to soothing in neonates: implications for maternal stimulation and early deprivation. *Child Dev.*, 1966, **37**, 867–876.

Landau, R., and Gewirtz, J. L. Differential satiation for a social reinforcing stimulus as a determinant of its efficacy in conditioning. *J. exp. Child Psychol.*, 1967, **5**, 391–405.

Levy, D. M. *Maternal overprotection.* New York: Columbia University Press, 1943.

Lewis, M. Social isolation: a parametric study of its effect on social reinforcement. *J. exp. Child Psychol.*, 1965, **2**, 205–218.

Lewis, M., and Richman, S. Social encounters and their effect on subsequent social reinforcement. *J. abnorm. soc. Psychol.*, 1964, **69**, 253–257.

Lewis, M., Wall, A. M., and Aronfreed, J. Developmental change in the relative value of social and non-social reinforcement. *J. exp. Psychol.*, 1963, **66**, 133–138.

Lorr, M., and Jenkins, R. L. Three factors in parent behavior. *J. consult. Psychol.*, 1953, **17**, 306–308.

Maccoby, E. E. The taking of adult roles in middle childhood. *J. abnorm. soc. Psychol.*, 1961, **63**, 493–503.

Maccoby, E. E., and Rau, L. *Differential cognitive abilities.* Final report cooperative research project No. 1040, Stanford University, 1962.

Mahler, M. S., Furer, M., and Settlage, C. F. Severe emotional disturbances in childhood; psychosis. In S. Arieti (Ed.), *American handbook of psychiatry*. Vol. 1. New York: Basic Books, 1959. Pp. 816–839.

Marshall, H. R. Relations between home experiences and children's use of language in play interactions with peers. *Psychol. Monogr.*, 1961, **LXXV** (Whole No. 509).

Marshall, H. R., and McCandless, B. R. Relationships between dependence on adults and social acceptance. *Child Dev.*, 1957, **28**, 413.

Martin, W. Singularity and stability of social behavior. In C. B. Stendler (Ed.), *Readings in child behavior and development*. New York: Harcourt, Brace, 1964.

McCandless, B. R., Belous, C. B., and Bennett, H. L. Peer popularity and dependence on adults in preschool age socialization. *Child Dev.*, 1961, **32**, 511–518.

McCord, W., McCord, J., and Verden, P. Familial and behavioral correlates of dependency in male children. *Child Dev.*, 1962, **33**, 313–326.

McCoy, N., and Zigler, E. Social reinforcer effectiveness as a function of the relationship between child and adult. *J. Pers. Soc. Psychol.*, 1965, **1**, 604–612.

McCullers, J. C., and Stevenson, H. W. Effects of verbal reinforcement in a probability learning situation. *Psychol. Rep.*, 1960, **7**, 439–445.

McGraw, M. B., and Molloy, L. B. The pediatric anamnesis: inaccuracies in eliciting developmental data. *Child Dev.*, 1941, **12**, 255–265.

Mednick, S. A., and Shaffer, B. P. Mothers' retrospective reports in child-rearing research. *Am. J. Orthopsychiat.*, 1963, **33**, 457–461.

Mischel, W. *Personality and assessment*. New York: Wiley, 1968.

Mitchell, G. D., Raymond, E. J., Ruppenthal, G. C., and Harlow, H. F. Longterm effects of total social isolation upon behavior of rhesus monkeys. *Psychol. Rep.*, 1966, **18**, 567–580.

Moltz, H. Imprinting: an epigenetic approach. *Psychol. Rev.*, 1963, **70**, 123–138.

Moore, S., and Updegraff, R. Sociometric status of preschool children related to age, sex, nurturance-giving, and dependency. *Child Dev.*, 1964, **35**, 519–524.

Murphy, L. *Social behavior and child personality*. New York: Columbia University Press, 1937.

Murphy, L. B. *The widening world of childhood*. New York: Basic Books, 1962.

Murray, H. A. *Explorations in personality*. New York: Oxford University Press, 1938.

Mussen, P., and Kagan, J. Measures of group conformity related to personality measure of dependency. *J. consult. Psychol.*, 1956, **20**, 29–32.

Myers, W. A., and Trapold, M. A. Two failures to demonstrate superiority of a generalized secondary reinforcer. *Psychon. Sci.*, 1966, **5**, 321–322.

Nelson, E. A. The effects of reward and punishment of dependency on subsequent dependency. Unpublished manuscript, Stanford University, 1960.

Nichols, R. C. A factor analysis of parental attitudes of fathers. *Child Dev.*, 1962, **33**, 791–802.

Patterson, G. R., and Anderson, D. Peers as social reinforcers. *Child Dev.*, 1964, **35**, 951–960.

Rheingold, N. L. The modification of social responsiveness in institutional babies. *Soc. Res. Child Dev. Monogr.*, 1956, **23**.

Rheingold, H. L. The effect of environmental stimulation upon social and exploratory behavior in the human infant. In B. M. Foss (Ed.), *Determinants of infant behavior*. Vol. I. New York: Wiley, 1961.

Rheingold, H. L. (Ed.) *Maternal behavior in animals*. New York: Wiley, 1963.

Rheingold, H. L., and Bayley, N. The later effects of an experimental modification of mothering. *Child Dev.*, 1959, **30**, 363–372.

Robbins, L. C. The accuracy of parental recall of aspects of child development and of child rearing practices. *J. abnorm. soc. Psychol.*, 1963, **66**, 261–270.

Rosenblatt, J. S., Turkewitz, G., and Schneirla, T. C. Early socialization in the domestic cat as based on feeding and other relationships between female and young. In B. Foss (Ed.), *Determinants of infant behavior.* London: Methuen, 1961.

Rosenhan, D., and Greenwald, J. A. The effects of age, sex, and socioeconomic class on responsiveness to two classes of verbal reinforcement. *J. Personality,* 1965, **33**, 108–121.

Rosenhan, D. Aloneness and togetherness as drive conditions in children. *J. exp. res. Pers.*, 1967, **2**, 32–41.

Rosenthal, M. K. The generalization of dependency behaviors from mother to stranger. Unpublished doctoral dissertation, Stanford University, 1965.

Rosenthal, M. K. The generalization of dependency behavior from mother to stranger. *J. Child Psychol. Psychiat.*, 1967, **8**, 117–133.

Rosenthal, M. K. The effect of a novel situation and anxiety on two groups of dependency behavior. *Br. J. Psychol.*, 1967, **58**, 357–364.

Rowland, G. L. The effects of total social isolation upon learning and social behavior in rhesus monkeys. Unpublished doctoral dissertation, University of Wisconsin, 1964.

Rubenstein, J. Maternal attentiveness and subsequent exploratory behavior in the infant. *Child Dev.*, 1967, **38**, 1089–1100.

Ruebush, B. K., and Stevenson, H. W. The effects of mothers and strangers on the performance of anxious and defensive children. *J. Personality*, 1964, **32**, 587–600.

Sarnoff, I., and Zimbardo, P. Anxiety, fear and social isolation. *J. abnorm. soc. Psychol.*, 1961, **62**, 356–363.

Scarr, S. The inheritance of sociability. *Am. Psychol.*, 1965, **20**, 524. (Abstract)

Schachter, S. *The psychology of affiliation.* Stanford, Calif.: Stanford University Press, 1959.

Schaefer, E. S. A circumplex model for maternal behavior. *J. abnorm. soc. Psychol.*, 1959, **59**, 226–235.

Schaefer, E. S. Converging conceptual models for material behavior and for child behavior. In J. C. Glidewell (Ed.), *Parental attitudes and child behavior.* Evanston, Ill.: Thomas, 1961.

Schaefer, E. S., and Bayley, N. Maternal behavior, child behavior, and their intercorrelations from infancy through adolescence. *Monogr. Soc. Child Dev.*, 1963, **28** (3).

Schaffer, H. R. Some issues for research in the study of attachment behavior. In B. Foss (Ed.), *Determinants of infant behavior.* Vol. II. London: Methuen, 1963.

Schaffer, H. R., and Callender, W. M. Psychologic effects of hospitalization in infancy. *Pediat.*, 1959, **24**, 528–539.

Schaffer, H. R., and Emerson, P. E. The development of social attachments in infancy. *Monogr. Soc. Res. Child. Dev.*, 1964, **29** (3). (a)

Schaffer, H. R., and Emerson, P. E. Patterns of response to physical contact in early human development. *J. Child Psychol. Psychiat.*, 1964, **5**, 1–13. (b)

Scott, J. P. "Critical periods" in the development of behavior. *Science*, 1963, **139**, 673–674; 1110–1115.

Sears, R. R. A theoretical framework for personality and social behavior. *Am. Psychol.*, 1951, **6**, 476–483.

Sears, R. R. Dependency motivation. In M. Jones (Ed.), *Nebraska symposium on motivation.* Lincoln: University of Nebraska Press. 1963. Pp. 25–64.

Sears, R. R., Maccoby, E. E., and Levin, H. *Patterns of child rearing*, Evanston, Ill.: Row, Peterson, 1957.

Sears, R. R., Rau, L., and Alpert, R. *Identification and child rearing*. Stanford, Calif.: Stanford University Press, 1965.

Sears, R. R., Whiting, J. W. M., Nowlis, V., and Sears, P. S. Some child rearing antecedents of dependency and aggression in young children. *Genet. Psychol. Monogr.*, 1953, **XLVII**, 135–234.

Seay, B., Hansen, E., and Harlow, H. F. Mother-infant separation in monkeys. *J. Child Psychol. Psychiat.*, 1962, **3**, 123–132.

Shirley, M. Children's adjustments to a strange situation. *J. abnorm. soc. Psychol.*, 1942, **37**, 201–217.

Shirley, M., and Poyntz, L. The influence of separation from the mother on children's emotional responses. *J. Psychol.*, 1941, **12**, 251–282.

Siegelman, M. Loving and punishing parental behavior and introversion tendencies in sons. *Child Dev.*, 1966, **37**, 985–992.

Skinner, B. F. *Science and human behavior*. New York: Macmillan, 1953.

Slater, P. E. Parental behavior and the personality of the child. *J. genet. Psychol.*, 1962, **101**, 53–68.

Sluckin, W. Perceptual and associative learning. *Symp. zool. Soc. Lon.*, 1962, **8**, 193–198.

Smith, H. T. A comparison of interview and observation measures of mother behavior. *J. abnorm. soc. Psychol.*, 1958, **57**, 278–282.

Spitz, R. A. Hospitalization: an inquiry into the genesis of psychiatric conditions in early childhood. *Psychoanal. Study Child*, 1945, **1**, 53–74.

Stevenson, H. W. Social reinforcement of children's behavior. In L. P. Lipsitt and C. C. Spiker (Eds.), *Advances in child development and behavior*. Vol. 2. New York: Academic Press, 1965. Pp. 97–126.

Stevenson, H. W., and Fahel, L. S. The effects of social reinforcement on the performance of institutionalized and noninstitutionalized normal and feebleminded children. *J. Personality*, 1961, **29**, 136–147.

Stevenson, H. W., and Hill, K. T. The effects of reinforcement and non-reinforcement following success and failure. *J. Personality*, 1965, **33**, 418–427.

Stevenson, H. W., and Knights, R. M. Social reinforcement with normal and retarded children as a function of pretraining, sex of E, and sex of S. *Am. J. mental Defic.*, 1962a, **66**, 866–871.

Stevenson, H. W. The effectiveness of social reinforcement after brief and extended institutionalization. *Am. J. ment. Defic.*, 1962b, **66**, 589–594.

Stevenson, H. W., and Odom, R. D. The effectiveness of social reinforcement following two conditions of social deprivation. *J. abnorm. soc. Psychol.*, 1962, **65**, 429–431.

Stith, M., and Connor, R. Dependency and helpfulness in young children. *Child Dev.*, 1962, **33**, 15–20.

Sullivan, H. S. *The interpersonal theory of psychiatry*. New York: Norton, 1953.

Thurston, J. R., and Mussen, P. H. Infant feeding gratification and adult personality. *J. Personality*, 1951, **19**, 449–458.

Turnure, J., and Zigler, E. Outer-directedness in the problem solving of normal and retarded children. *J. abnorm. soc. Psychol.*, 1964, **69**, 427–436.

Vandenberg, S. G. The hereditary abilities study: hereditary components in a psychological test battery. *Am. J. hum. Genet.*, 1962, **14**, 220–237.

Wahler, R. G. Infant social attachments: a reinforcement theory interpretation and investigation. *Child Dev.*, 1967, **38**, 1079–1088.

Walters, R. H., and Foote, A. A study of reinforcer effectiveness with children. *Merrill-Palmer Quart.*, 1962, **8**, 149–157.

Walters, R. H., and Henning, G. B. Social isolation, effect of instructions and verbal behavior. *Can. J. Psychol.*, 1962, **16**, 202–210.

Walters, R. H., and Karal, P. Social deprivation and verbal behavior. *J. Personality*, 1960, **28**, 89–107.

Walters, R. H., Marshall, W. E., and Shooter, J. R. Anxiety, isolation and suspectibility to social influence. *J. Personality*, 1960, **28**, 518–529.

Walters, R. H., and Parke, R. D. Emotional arousal, isolation and discrimination learning in children. *J. exp. Child Psychol.*, 1964a, **1**, 163–173.

Walters, R. H., and Parke, R. D. Social motivation, dependency and susceptibility to social influence. In L. Berkowitz (Ed.), *Advances in experimental social psychology*. Vol. 1. New York: Academic Press, 1964b.

Walters, R. H., and Parke, R. D. The role of the distance receptors in the development of social responsiveness. In L. P. Lipsitt and C. C. Spiker (Eds.), *Advances in child development and behavior*. Vol. 2. New York: Academic Press, 1965.

Walters, R. H., and Quinn, M. J. The effects of social and sensory deprivation on autokinetic judgments. *J. Personality*, 1960, **28**, 210–219.

Walters, R. H., and Ray, E. Anxiety, social isolation and reinforcer effectiveness. *J. Personality*, 1960, **28**, 358–367.

Watson, G. Some personality differences in children related to strict or permissive parental discipline. *J. Psychology*, 1957, **44**, 227–249.

Watson, J. B. *Psychological care of infant and child*. New York: Norton, 1928. (Reprinted in W. Kessen, *The child*. New York: Wiley, 1965.)

Wenar, C. The reliability of mothers' histories. *Child Dev.*, 1961, **32**, 491–500.

Wenar, C., and Coulter, J. B. A reliability study of developmental histories. *Child Dev.*, 1962, **33**, 453–462.

Whiting, J. W. M. The frustration complex in Kwoma society. *Man*, 1944, **44**, 140–144.

Whiting, H. W. M., and Child, I. *Child training and personality*. New Haven, Conn.: Yale University Press, 1953.

Winder, C. L., and Rau, L. Parental attitudes associated with social deviance in preadolescent boys. *J. abnorm. soc. Psychol.*, 1962, **64**, 418–424.

Wittenborn, J. R. A study of adoptive children: III, Relationship between some aspects of development and some aspects of environment for adoptive children. *Psychol. Monogr.*, 1956, **LXX** (410).

Yarrow, L. J. Separation from parents during early childhood. In M. L. Hoffman and L. W. Hoffman (Eds.), *Review of child development research*. Vol. 1. New York: Russell Sage, 1964.

Yarrow, M. R., Campbell, J. D., and Burton, R. V. Reliability of maternal retrospection: a preliminary report. *Family Process*, 1964, **3**, 207–218.

Zigler, E. F. Social deprivation and rigidity in the performance of feebleminded children. *J. abnorm. soc. Psychol.*, 1961, **62**, 413–421.

Zigler, E., and Williams, J. Institutionalization and the effectiveness of social reinforcement: a three-year follow-up study. *J. abnorm. soc. Psychol.*, 1963, **66**, 197–205.

22. Aggression

SEYMOUR FESHBACH[*]

THEORIES OF AGGRESSION

Overview of Major Issues. The record of man's aggressions runs the gamut of human history—from the Biblical era and the pre-Homeric sagas to the series of conflicts and upheavals that have marked the twentieth century. War, murders, fighting, and the destruction of property are the obvious manifestations of aggression. More subtle forms can be observed in the complex fabric of interpersonal relationships—in barbed exchanges between husband and wife, in the merciless teasing in which children sometimes engage, in the sundry and devious manners by which siblings can be cruel to each other. Very cogent arguments have also been made suggesting that aggression is an important component of such self-defeating behaviors as academic failure (Kornrich, 1965; Spache, 1954), alcoholism (Schilder, 1941), social withdrawal, and suicide (Menninger, 1938). The range and persistence of human aggression present a major problem to clinicians who deal with individual psychopathology and are

* The writing of this review was facilitated by the support of U.S.P.H. Grant No. MH-10973, concerned with the "Organization and Regulation of Anger and Aggression." The chapter was read at various stages of completion by Norma Feshbach, who made many helpful theoretical and editorial suggestions. Her contribution is gratefully acknowledged. Appreciation is also expressed to the editorial advisory committee of this book, whose critical appraisal resulted in a number of improvements in the manuscript. The final responsibility for the literature reviewed and the cogency of the theoretical arguments rest, of course, with the author.

a central concern, if not *the* central concern, of social reformers. Concerns for the regulation and modification of aggression—whether intragroup, interpersonal and intrapersonal—have stimulated interest in the origins and development of aggressive behavior. Most social and political philosophies rest, in part, on assumptions and speculations regarding the instinctive or learned nature of aggression and the procedures required for its control and socially approved expression. These same issues influence the often conflicting child-rearing recommendations made to parents by experts.

The justification for the study of aggression in children need not rest on its manifestations in adults. Aggressive behaviors can be readily observed in children's social interactions with peers, with parents, and with authority. The control of aggressive behavior poses a fundamental developmental problem for the child, who must learn to inhibit his rage, to discriminate between those situations in which it is appropriate or inappropriate to behave aggressively, and to modulate his aggressive response to match the degree of frustration or provocation to which he may be subjected. And, if aggression is an instinctual human drive rooted in the child's biological inheritance, as some theorists believe, the problem of its control, mode of expression, and means of satisfaction is no less challenging. Although its instinctual basis may be in dispute, aggression appears to be intimately linked to biological states and structures. At the same time, aggression is a social act and, as such, is strongly influenced by familial and broader cultural factors. The interaction between biological and social processes in determining the development and manifestation of aggressive behavior in children might well serve as one major focus for this chapter. Unfortunately, data on the physiological and instinctive mechanisms governing aggression are primarily based on animal subjects. And, although studies of aggression in animals are certainly relevant to an understanding of the development of aggression in children, generalizations from animal studies to children's aggressions can be offered only as tentative hypotheses since the range of aggressive responses in humans is much greater and the behavioral options much more diverse and complexly determined. For this reason, we shall consider only briefly some of the possible implications of the animal literature for a theory of human aggression.

Primary emphasis will be placed on the literature that deals directly with children's aggression. Alternate theoretical approaches to the analysis of aggressive behavior will be presented, followed by a review of the various manifestations of aggression in different subgroups of children. Problems of measurement will also be considered, the major question here being the structure of patterns of aggression and the consistency of different aggressive behaviors. The issue of consistency comprises two related but distinct problems—stimulus generalization and response equivalence. Stimulus generalization refers to the correlation between similar aggressive responses in different situations (e.g., home, school, and classroom), while response equivalence pertains to the relationship among different aggressive responses to similar situations (e.g., physical aggression, verbal aggression, self-punitive behavior, displacement). The complexity of social behavior does not readily permit the independent variation of situation and responses, and, as a consequence, studies of consistency of aggression usually entail comparisons of different responses to varied situations.

Issues generated by comparisons of age, social class, and other relevant demographic groupings and by personality correlates of aggression will be covered in a third section. Particular attention will be given to developmental changes in patterns of aggression and to variations with age in the relationships of demographic and personality variables to aggressive behaviors. The study of the pattern-

ing and structure of aggressive behaviors, although largely descriptive, inevitably raises questions related to the antecedents of aggression, which is a central concern of this chapter. With regard to the immediate antecedents of an aggressive response, it might be parenthetically noted that most dynamic relationships between specific stimulus events and children's aggressive responses are influenced by the history of the child. For example, the response to frustration is markedly affected by the models to whom the child has been exposed and by selective reinforcement of the child's reactions. Also to be reviewed in this section are the effects of early deprivations and of parental response to aggressive acts by the child upon his subsequent aggressive behavior. The central question here is the effects of various child-rearing practices upon the acquisition, manifestation, and control of aggression.

The final section is concerned with the regulation of aggression, particularly with the role of inhibitory and drive-reducing mechanisms. An intriguing issue to which inhibitory effects give rise is the strength and fate of the aggressive tendency pursuant to inhibition. Displacement and fantasy aggression are of special interest in this regard. These indirect modes of aggressive expression presumably serve to reduce the instigation to aggression. Particular attention will be given to the possible cathartic role of aggressive fantasy and to the effects of the mass media upon aggressive behavior.

Problems of Definition. Punching and kicking another child, flailing of the hands and feet, a derogatory comment, bursting of a balloon, tearing the wing off a butterfly, running away from home—these are all behaviors which have been labeled aggressive by various investigators. Such responses are only a sample of the vast repertoire of behaviors that are considered to be manifestations of aggression. It is attractive to utilize concepts that embrace a broad range of behaviors and thereby give coherence to otherwise disparate and scattered observations. At the same time, one may be placing under the same rubric behaviors which are functionally different with respect to their antecedents, correlates, and effects. The conflicting results, which are frequently yielded by studies of aggression, are partly due to the ambiguity of the referent of aggression and the use of behaviors that are only superficially related to each other.

A related source of ambiguity in the literature is the frequent assumption that a behavior manifested by one individual under varying circumstances or elicited in different individuals in the same circumstance maintains the same meaning or significance. Child A may strike child B because he enjoys striking B, because he wants the bicycle child B has monopolized, or because in his anger he has flailed out at the most available target. These behaviors are all aggressive in an implicit sense of that term, but the mediating processes appear to be dissimilar. In the first case the reinforcement for the behavior is the pain inflicted on B, in the second case the reinforcement might be gaining possession of the bicycle, while in the third instance the reinforcement may be more clearly linked to the expressive components of the act itself than to its social consequences. These distinctions are extensively discussed elsewhere by the author (Feshbach, 1964).

The major focus of this analysis is on the distinction between aggressive drive and other mechanisms mediating aggressive behavior. At a descriptive level, the term aggression may be applied to any behavioral sequence or subset thereof, which results in injury to or destruction of an animal, human, or inanimate object. At the level of construct, or mediating process, this definition is much too broad. One obvious distinction that needs to be made is between acts that accidentally lead to injury and acts that are "intentional" or "motivated." By unintentional aggression, we refer to acts which, although resulting in injury, were not contingent upon their injurious consequence. The behavior of a hyperactive or clumsy child may result in physical pain to others and in the destruction of valued property. However, these injurious effects are incidental consequences of the child's behavior and are irrelevant to the child's response and, in fact, may result in subsequent inhibition of hyperactive tendencies. It is, of course, possible that in some children clumsiness and "excessive activity" may have unconscious aggressive components. However, it would be farfetched to argue that every act that results in damage is aggressive.

"Intentional" or "motivated" aggression does not imply that the child is aware of or

is consciously directing his aggressive behavior; it means only that the aggressive component of this behavior is an essential part of its function. The class of motivated aggressive acts can be further subdivided into *instrumental* aggression, which is directed toward the achievement of nonaggressive goals, and *hostile* aggression, or aggressive *drive,* for which the goal response is injury to some object (Sears, Maccoby, and Lewin, 1957). As an instrumental act, aggressive behavior is viewed as one among a number of possible alternative routes for satisfying the organism's needs and desires. A 4-year-old may want to play with an attractive toy which a peer refuses to relinquish. He can negotiate and offer the other child a positive exchange (e.g., candy, another toy), he can resort to help from authority by asking the nursery school teacher to intervene, he can also urge, cry, and engage in a number of other responses including hitting the peer. The goal in this situation is the toy rather than hurting the other child. If hitting the child is reinforced by obtaining the toy, then this aggressive behavior is strengthened and presumably will be more likely to occur the next time a similar situation arises. Even though aggressive behavior may become prepotent in this manner, the reinforcement is still the attainment of the desired object. If the other child relinquishes the object, the aggressive interaction will be avoided or aborted. In situations where the aggressor persists in hitting his peer, regardless of the fate of the toy, or strikes another child simply because he "wants to," the behavior is indicative of the expression of aggressive drive as compared to instrumental aggression. There are many situations, of course, in which both instrumental and drive aggression are present, and it becomes difficult to disentangle the functions of each.

The research literature bearing on children's aggression has, for the most part, concerned itself with observations of aggressive behaviors, without attempting to distinguish between instrumental aggressive acts and aggressive drive instigated behavior. Empirical operations for discriminating among different classes of aggressive behaviors are not readily available, and their implementation poses serious methodological problems. Theories of aggression in children employ both aggressive drive and instrumental aggression concepts, and theoretical differences and controversies arise from the differential emphasis placed upon these possible functions of aggressive activity. These theoretical differences may occasionally prove to be more illusory than real upon analysis of the aggressive behaviors which the respective theories attempt to explain. Thus the assertion that aggression is innate may be intended to imply that children are born with an innate drive to inflict injury upon others or may imply only that aggression is a prepotent response to certain classes of stimulus situations. In the latter instance, the aggressive response is conceived of as being in the response hierarchy of behaviors elicited by a stimulus configuration. Drive properties may or may not be attributed to the aggressive response, depending upon the particular theoretical model.

The necessity for discriminating other classes of aggressive behaviors, in addition to instrumental aggression and aggressive drive, will become evident as various theoretical approaches to the problem of aggression are reviewed. For example, the affective response of anger or rage is closely associated with aggressive drive but need not entail the motivated infliction of injury. It is apparent that the affective display indicative of anger has adaptive functions, communicating the organism's frustration and threat to potential adversaries. However, these adaptive consequences, which result from the evolutionary history of the organism, should not be interpreted as the cause or antecedent of the infliction of injury. Although the destructive consequences of anger and rage may be incidental to the expression of these affects, these responses can be considered a form of "motivated" aggression because of the "built-in" relationship between the anger response and its injurious potential. The mechanism by which anger acquires aggressive drive properties, in the sense of performance of the act in order to bring about injurious consequences, is an intriguing developmental problem about which we have few empirical data.

The relationship between anger and aggressive drive is partly a definitional issue, depending upon the theoretical functions ascribed to aggressive drive. The anger response may be considered to have drive properties in the sense of an energizer of ongoing behavior. Anger may also have noxious qualities, resulting in the activation of diffuse behavior, which ceases when the organism makes a response that removes the antecedents of the anger reaction. In the theoretical position to be subsequently amplified, anger is treated primarily as an energizer and as an expressive response rather than as a noxious state. Even if the affective reaction of anger was assumed to have a noxious stimulus function, a distinction should still be maintained between this aspect of anger related drive, including the associated instrumental responses, and the motivated infliction of injury. The proposition is suggested that an organism can learn to reduce anger through methods other than the infliction of injury. Thus, while the affective reaction of anger may have drive properties and may be closely related to "aggressive drive," as that construct is employed in this paper, the aggressive drive may be rooted in other antecedents than those fostering anger and, in addition, may be implicated in other behaviors.

A further distinction between assertiveness and hostility is necessary in clarifying the current discussion of aggressive phenomena. Common usage of the term "aggressive" carries connotations of assertiveness as well as hostility. Assertiveness or the legitimate expression of one's own interests may result in pain to some other party, for example, a competitor. Social conventions attest to the difference between competition-produced and aggression-instigated injury and loss. However, this discrimination is not easily made, and the inhibition of aggression can be seen to generalize in many instances to the inhibition of assertions of self-interest. There are psychoanalytic theorists who assume that the energy of the self-assertive motive is derived from aggressive drive energy (Hartmann, Kris, and Lowenstein, 1949). Hence one may find the term aggressiveness applied to behaviors that seem quite remote from hostile, injurious actions. The empirical problem is to demonstrate that these diverse behaviors are functionally related.

Psychoanalytic Theories

Freud's Instinct Theory of Aggression. The concept of aggression had a subordinate, basically minor role in psychoanalytic theory until Freud's reformulations of his instinct theory, which he proposed in *Beyond the*

Pleasure Principle (Freud, 1927), written shortly after World War I. Freud had initially postulated two groups of instincts, the sexual instincts and the ego instincts, the latter being a mixture of self-preservative tendencies, cognitive functions, and moral restrictions. Freud himself wryly selected Schiller's aphorism, "hunger and love make the world go round," (Freud, 1930, p. 95) as the starting point for his model of instinctual drives. He subsequently found, however, that this categorization failed to provide a satisfactory account of sadistic and masochistic behaviors, of the tendency to repeat essentially unpleasant and often self-destructive acts (repetition-compulsion), and of the frequent opposition of love and hatred. Sadistic tendencies which had been grouped with the love or object instincts clearly stood out from other libidinal manifestations in that its aim "was so very unloving" (Freud, 1930, p. 95). He subsequently proposed a new dichotomy in which the libidinal instinct, Eros, was enlarged to embrace all of the life enhancing and constructive drives in contrast with the death instinct, Thanatos, which encompassed the organism's tendencies toward aggression, self-destruction and ultimately death (Freud, 1927).

The aim of the death instinct, which Freud linked to biological, catabolic processes, is Nirvana, or the cessation of stimulation. The death instinct, like the libido, also has its vicissitudes. The major variation is in the external versus internal direction of the instinct. When directed toward an external object, it takes the form of destruction of others. It is the libidinal, self-preservative, and enhancing tendencies which block the primary self-direction of these destructive urges, and cause them to be manifested outwardly. In this formulation, aggressive drive, although derived from the death instinct, is still an innate urge, arising from the conflict of two fundamental biological processes. Freud had earlier viewed aggressive striving as primarily reactive to frustration and pain—"the ego hates, abhors and pursues with intent to destroy all objects which are for it a source of painful feelings" (Freud, 1925, p. 81). This conception of aggression as a reaction to particular experiences was supplanted by a biological emphasis on the origins of aggression. Aggressive urges, like sexual impulses, became psychic manifestations of innate somatic sources of excitation. With the publication of *Civilization and Its Discontents* (Freud, 1930), aggression assumes an even greater importance in Freud's thinking and parallels, if not supersedes, libido as the factor responsible for the emergence of social codes and restrictions. He writes:

Civilized society is perpetually menaced with disintegration through this primary hostility of men toward one another. . . .Culture has to call up every possible reinforcement in order to erect barriers against the aggressive instincts of men and hold their manifestations in check by reaction-formation in men's minds. Hence, its system of methods by which mankind is to be driven to identification and aim-inhibited love-relationships; hence, the restrictions on sexual life, and love too, its ideal command to love one's neighbor as oneself (Freud, 1930, p. 86).

Freud was not very sanguine about the success of these techniques for controlling natural aggressive impulses, and his pessimism was reinforced by the incredible display of violence and brutality he witnessed during the Nazi hegemony in Europe.

Modified Psychoanalytic Instinct Theories. The death instinct is one of Freud's more speculative constructs, which has an ambiguous status within psychoanalytic orthodoxy and is largely rejected by other schools of psychoanalysis. The notion is patently teleological and its presence in the young child is not amenable to direct observation. Whereas the concept of a death instinct has gained little acceptance, the assumption of an instinctual aggressive urge is still held by many psychoanalysts (Munroe, 1955). The range of views among psychoanalysts concerning the nature and function of aggression is almost as broad as the heterodoxy among psychoanalytic theorists.

The reactive character of human aggression is accepted by most psychoanalysts. The principal areas of difference arise from the following sources: (1) the particular frustrations or blocked impulses that are assumed to be the primary antecedents of aggression, (2) acceptance of the death instinct and the extent to which aggression is believed to be a reflection of a biological "need," (3) the patterns of behavior believed to be indicative of aggression, and (4) the mechanisms postulated for controlling and expressing aggressive impulses. One finds varied, almost antithetical theoretical conceptions of aggression even among psychoanalysts operating within the Freudian tradition. Nunberg (1955) and Saul (1956) represent two ends of a continuum, the former finding evidence of the death instinct in the mouthing by an infant of its body extremities, the latter arguing that the roots of aggression are in the child's experiences during his early formulative years. In Saul's view, hostility is basically a reflection of developmental disturbances arising from diverse sources such as overindulgence of the child, inadequate handling of sibling and other familial relationships, parental rejection, and identification with punitive parental images. While aggression is reactive rather than instinctive for Saul, it nevertheless assumes a paramount place in his description of normal and neurotic personality functioning. A more typical position among Freudian analysts, perhaps best represented by Waelder (1956), is one that accepts the validity of both reactive and instinctive sources of aggression. Waelder sees reactive aggression as derived from three sources. Like Saul, Waelder notes that aggression may arise from the frustration of ego drives and libidinal impulses. It may be an aspect of libidinal strivings, penetration fantasies, or it may come about as a by-product of the child's attempts at self-mastery and control of the environment. The assertive and problem centered aspect of aggressive behavior is further developed by the neo-Freudian psychoanalytic ego psychology theorists (Hartmann, Kris, and Lowenstein, 1949). There are some forms of aggression, however, which Waelder feels are so deep-rooted and disproportionate to the frustrating stimulus, that they must be attributed to an instinctive destructive drive. A sudden psychotic outbreak of mass murder, an inexplicable act of suicide, and the harboring and activation of vengeful feelings over decades are examples of essential destructiveness which is instinctive in origin.

The neo-Freudian position, elaborated in various individual and joint publications of Lowenstein, Hartmann, and Kris (Lowenstein, 1948; Hartmann, Kris, and Lowenstein, 1949) concur with Freud's assumptions regarding the instinctual origins of aggression. However, whereas Freud interpreted outward aggression as a manifestation of the death instinct, these theorists view self-destructive behavior as a deflection of aggressive impulses. In addition, although these writers consider the aims of aggression to be more rigid and narrow than libidinal aims, they suggest that the destructive function of aggressive energy can become modified through the process of neutralization and sublimation. This neutralized energy is necessary for the normal development of the child, constituting part of the ego and superego resources available to the child in his problem-solving activity and in the control and inhibition of socially unacceptable impulses. As in the case of libidinal transformation, neutralized and instinctual aggressive energies may, in some areas, prove to be in conflict. Aggressive impulses may conflict with introjected superego standards, with reality considerations, with libidinal impulses directed toward an external object, or with narcissistic investment in an object person with whom the child has identified. The grouping of neutralized aggressive energy and instinctual destructive urges under the rubric of aggression is theoretically troublesome and is difficult, if not impossible, to test empirically. Munroe (1955), in her review of psychoanalytic models of aggression, suggests that the phenomena involved are conceptually distinct as well as phenotypically different. She states that it is "a mistake to lump all of the phenomena commonly called aggression (mainly by Freudians) under the single heading of a single instinctual drive. Many of these same phenomena result from the operation of what I have called the nonsexual drive system, with special emphasis on motility" (p. 635).

It is evident that the treatment of aggression among the major Freudian psychoanalytic theorists is both variable and in certain respects inconsistent. For the non-Freudian psychoanalysts, the status of aggression is equally variable, though they all give more consideration to the functions of cultural mores and of the child's socialization experiences. Both Fromm (1941) and Horney (1937, 1945) incorporate aggressive behaviors in their characterological schemes. The sadomasochistic personality pattern, as described by Fromm, represents a means of

reducing feelings of powerlessness and alienation from the social structure. For Horney,
aggression is one fundamental mode of response used by the child to cope with feelings
of helplessness or "basic anxiety." It also
embraces the neurotic need for power and for
exploitation of others. Horney distinguishes
between reactive aggression which has an
injurious intent and reactive aggression which
is largely instrumental. She states: "Hostility
toward others may also be merely reactive.
. . . [W]e could say that although the kinds
of action we refer to here are aggressive and
even hostile they are not perpetrated in a
mean spirit. There is no conscious or unconscious satisfaction derived from the fact of
hurting" (1945, p. 193). It should be noted
that reactive hostility or aggression is an omni-
present response for Horney and consequently, on an empirical and clinical level, it
becomes difficult to distinguish from Freud's
concept of instinctual aggressive drive.

Aggression, of course, appears in the writing of representatives of psychoanalytic
schools other than those previously reviewed.
These treatments of aggression tend to be
fairly similar to those we have discussed, with
the possible exception of Rank. For Rank,
hostility may sometimes reflect constructive
personality forces (Munroe, 1955). It can
represent an attempt to cope with the pain
of separation and to maintain rather than
sacrifice one's identity. Thus the child's efforts
at individualization may take the form of resistance and aggression.

Manifestations of Aggression in Psychological Development

Aggressive Orality and Sadism. The theoretical conceptions of Freud and other psychoanalysts concerning the nature of aggression are based partly upon observations of
adult behavior and also upon certain aspects
of children's behavior. Some insight into the
psychoanalytic model can be gained by considering the kinds of behavior occurring during the course of the child's development
which are believed to be manifestations of
aggression, and the major stimulus situations
which appear to evoke these behaviors. For
psychoanalytic theorists who view aggression
as an innate, biologically rooted drive, seeking
constant expression, it is more accurate to
consider these stimuli as providing oppor-

tunities for the discharge or neutralization of
aggressive energy rather than as evoking
aggressive behaviors.

There are two primary ways in which the
young infant is seen to display aggressive
tendencies. One is the rage reaction, an af-
fectomotor pattern consisting of agitated
movements of the limbs, vocal cries, and
changes in various indices of autonomic
arousal—particularly, increased heart rate and
blood pressure and reddening of the skin.
The rage response for Munroe (1955) is an
example of reactive aggression and, as in
other species, reflects the evolutionary function of mobilizing the organism for active
combat when subjected to danger. For
Hartmann, Kris, and Lowenstein (1949),
the aggressive energy initially discharged
through the rage response to danger, through
subsequent neutralization becomes part of the
ego apparatus and is also discharged through
active, coping motoric behaviors of the infant.
The rage reaction differs quite strikingly from
the second principal mode of aggressive discharge, oral activity. The oral incorporative
behavior of the infant is seen as the prototype
of aggressive greed (Freud, 1949; Klein,
1937). The infant is said to "destroy what he
appropriates—sucks the object dry, tries to
take everything into himself" (Freud, 1949,
p. 40). An aggressive response to food deprivation may then be a function of the
frustration of hunger drive and also of aggressive drive; for example, Hartmann, Kris, and
Lowenstein state that "the absence of food
deprives the child of the opportunity to discharge aggressive tension in its incorporation."
Since the topography of the neonate's oral
behavior bears little resemblance to responses
ordinarily classified as aggressive, the rationale for considering such behaviors to be aggressive is the assumption that one aim of
oral activity is the destruction of objects that
are incorporated by the infant. The value of
this assumption is questionable since, operationally, it would be very difficult to separate
the aggressive aim of an oral act from its
other functions of satisfying hunger needs and
sucking tendencies.

The later stage of oral development, in
which teething and biting appear, can be
more obviously related to aggression, although
here too the consequence of biting is not
necessarily its aim. Biting, however, is a be-

havior that can produce pain and injury to the self and others, and appears to be a pleasurable act for the infant (Erikson, 1950; Munroe, 1955). As such, biting can be viewed as a stimulus-specific aggressive response. The child may learn to use biting behavior as a means of satisfying aggressive impulses, but this possibility is to be distinguished from the proposition that occurrence of biting is ipso facto evidence for the discharge of aggressive drive. Erikson suggests a process by which the pain produced by biting can become a source of satisfaction to the infant. If teething is very painful to the child and the act of biting hard provides some relief for that pain, then the child, in the absence of other objects, may derive some gratification from biting himself. This process may be one antecedent of masochistic behavior (Erikson, 1950). While the infant is likely to encounter frustration in biting other people, in some instances he may learn to associate biting of others and the expressive response to being bitten with the reduction of his own discomfort, thereby establishing a basis for sadistic trends.

Melanie Klein proposes that the incidental sadism of biting acquires a hostile purpose when the child is frustrated in weaning or by delay in feeding. The infant's oral-sadistic tendencies then become integrated with fantasies or observations of coitus which is fantasied as an act of biting, by which the mother incorporates the penis. At the same time, the sexual organs are believed to acquire hostile instrumental properties—the vagina being equated with the biting mouth and the penis with the frustrating breast. According to Klein, under persistent frustration, the infant may project his hostility onto the mother, thereby exacerbating his anxiety and also his aggressive feelings. In a well-known statement concerning the paranoid position of some infants, Klein writes, "The idea of an infant from six to twelve months trying to destroy its mother by every method at the disposal of its sadistic tendencies—with its teeth, nails and excreta and with the whole of its body, transformed in imagination into all kinds of dangerous weapons—presents a horrifying, not to say an unbelievable picture to our minds" (Klein, 1937, p. 187). In considering this portrayal of infant hostility, it should be noted that these observations are based on and apply primarily to clinical cases, and that

the views of Klein are not shared by most psychoanalysts.

Anal Expression and Negativism. In many ways, the aggressive development of the child is seen as paralleling his psychosexual development. The anal mode can serve to discharge aggressive impulses, just as the oral mode of libidinal expression does. Thus Fenichel (1945) refers to the anal period as the "anal sadistic" stage. There are at least two aspects of anal activity which, according to psychoanalytic theory, may be considered as having aggressive aims. The expulsion of the feces itself has an aggressive component, "their 'pinching off' being perceived as a kind of sadistic act" (Fenichel, 1945, p. 66). Fenichel comments that this eliminative treatment of feces may become the prototype for subsequent treatment of people. Second, the process of toilet training provides the child with a weapon he may use against adults. The mastery he attains over his sphincter muscles permits him, through his ability to determine whether and where he will defecate, to express opposition toward the socializing agents. The child readily discerns that the feces, which are for him primarily an object of libidinal investment, have noxious properties for many adults. He may then learn to use anally related behaviors such as smearing feces and expelling flatus as a means of discharging hostile feelings.

Psychoanalytic theory attributes to oral and anal behaviors intrinsic and acquired instrumental aggressive functions. It is the intrinsic aggressive component—the destruction of objects through incorporation, the "pinching off" of the feces—which appear to adherents of other theoretical persuasions as speculative and improbable. The possible use of the noxious consequences of oral and anally related behaviors to bring about various desired outcomes is certainly more compatible with contemporary learning theory views.

The relationship between the acquisition of anal control and the appearance of stubborn, negative behaviors has particular relevance to the matter of ego development. While the child is acquiring many skills in his second and third year which contribute to his feelings of autonomy, the sequelae of toilet training may be of significance because of their libidinal aspects and because of the pressures surrounding toilet training in Western cultures (Ericson, 1950). For this reason, the resolution of the anal conflict situation may have profound effects upon the child's subsequent personality development. It may influence such traits as independence (Ericson, 1950) as well as the well-known triad of obstinacy, parsimony, and pedantry, and it may also be one source of the negativism which children typically display during their third year (Gesell and Ilg, 1943; Ausubel, 1950). Ausubel's (1950) analysis of this behavior suggests that the temper tantrums of the child and the pain inflicted upon his parents by his obstinacy are secondary products of his newly achieved degree of skill and initiative and accompanying feeling of omnipotence. The parent may perceive the child as acting "mean," but the child's negativistic behavior may or may not have aggressive aims, depending upon the individual situation.

Intrafamilial Rivalry. One of Freud's most significant contributions to the understanding of personality development is his description of the complex pattern of interrelationships that exist between the members of the family unit. The attachments that the child acquires toward people and objects in his environment and the real and fantasied anxieties and threats that he perceives toward these attachments create deep ambivalences in his feelings toward sibling and parents and may, indeed, provide the foundation for subsequent interpersonal feelings throughout his development. Although many diverse interpretations may be made of these conflicts and specific age periods during which they become salient, the presence of positive and aggressive feelings toward significant family members appears to be inevitable for children raised in Western and other cultures.

During the course of socialization, normal children develop a strong attachment to their primary caretaker, who is usually the mother. The child typically finds that he must share the attention and affection of the mother with his father and his siblings. Psychoanalytic theory hypothesizes that the frustration entailed in this competition for a parent will elicit hostile, envious feelings in the child toward his rivals. Rivalry and aggression between siblings is so commonly observed in Western cultures that quantitative documen-tation of sibling aggression would appear to be superfluous.

A rich source of information concerning the conditions and patterns of sibling rivalry has been provided by observations of children's doll play behavior (Levy, 1933, 1936). Doll play is widely used by child psychoanalysts as a therapeutic technique (Levy, 1936; Klein, 1937; Freud, 1948) and analysts have used the child's aggressive behavior in the family doll play situation to buttress and modify inferences concerning family rivalry based on retrospective accounts of the adult analysand. Studies of factors determining degree of sibling rivalry and the manner of its resolution would be of considerable value. Since a great many conflicts between siblings are over the same kinds of situations that occur in peer interactions, observations of sibling rivalry are confounded with typical struggles that occur between peers. Peer interaction effects should be empirically separated from those produced by rivalry for the parent in order to ascertain the special significance of the latter.

The core family conflict, for psychoanalytic theory, is the rivalry of the child with his same-sex parent. The motivational basis for this rivalry and significance for the child's subsequent personality development is a matter of controversy (Mullahy, 1952), but psychoanalysts of all schools agree to its reality. An example of contrasting views is Fromm's revision of Freud's libidinal interpretation of the Oedipal conflict. Whereas Freud postulated that the son's aggression toward his father is a consequence of incestuous feelings toward his mother, Fromm interprets the conflict between father and son as a product of a patriarchal society in which the father is the authority figure in the family and the son attempts to achieve independence and freedom through rebellion against the arbitrary authority of the father (Mullahy, 1952). In addition to reinterpreting the Oedipal conflict, reservations are raised concerning its universality since Fromm makes the boy's struggle with his father contingent upon a particular family constellation and social structure.

There is an obvious sense in which Fromm's position is probably valid. The degree to which a father exerts arbitrary authority and the extent to which this behavior is consonant with the norms of the culture will undoubtedly influence the son's relationship to his father. The absence of a father or the presence of a father surrogate, as in the Trobriand Islanders (Malinowski, 1929), will affect the degree and object of aggressive expression. However, also germane to the Oedipal situation are the child's dependency upon his mother, his envy of his parents' prerogatives, conflicts over discipline, frustration experienced in attempting to meet parental goals, and related problems which are likely to contribute to aggressive feelings toward a father by his son. Fromm, like many culturally oriented psychoanalysts, tends to minimize the developmental problems that all children share. A rapprochement between recognition of the powerful shaping effects of culture and sensitivity to the developmental tasks of socialization is found in the work of Erikson (1950). Erikson represents the Oedipal situation as a complex mixture of libidinal interests, striving for autonomy, and locomotor and cognitive changes as well as cultural patterning and unique familial demands.

According to classic psychoanalytic theory, the legacy of the Oedipal conflict is the perpetuation of its aggressive component in a fundamentally different form—guilt. The hostility of the son toward his father is resolved as a consequence of the child's identification with his father and subsequently is manifested in the guise of guilt and self-criticism. The motivational energy available to the child's superego is derived from the child's aggression toward a parent, a touch of irony and paradox. It is Freud's contention that the internal forces which compel the child to conform to social prohibition are the same forces which fostered social destruction and personal aggrandizement. Under certain circumstances, the child's identification with the parent may facilitate the acquisition rather than inhibition of aggressive behaviors. This can occur if a powerful parent is a destructive, punitive individual and the child defensively identifies with this parent and adopts his behaviors as a means of reducing his conflict and fear. This process of "identification with the aggressor" (A. Freud, 1946a) is to be contrasted with identification mediated by positive feelings toward the parent.

The internalized system of norms and values which constitute the superego is one of two major control mechanisms postulated by psychoanalytic theory to account for the inhibition of libidinal and aggressive impulses. The second major source of control are the so-called ego functions. Perhaps the most significant change that has occurred in psychoanalytic theory since Freud has been the increasingly important role in personality functioning that is ascribed to such ego capacities as reality testing, information processing, frustration tolerance, and ability to delay gratification. Whereas Freud had viewed the ego system as essentially a passive arbitrator of the conflicts between id, superego, and reality demands, psychoanalytic ego psychology proposes a more autonomous and positive role for these ego functions. With respect to the problem of aggression, reference has been previously made to the position of some psychoanalysts that the active, coping responses of the child in his attempt at environmental mastery are a form of aggression (Hartmann, Kris, and Lowenstein, 1949; Ericson, 1950). This equation of certain ego functions with aggression has been judged by the present author to be of dubious theoretical value. The relationship between ego capacities and control of aggressive and other impulses is a quite different matter.

Clinical studies indicate that hyperaggressiveness in children and adolescents is a consequence of ego deficiencies as well as heightened aggressive drive and an inadequate superego (Lowry et al., 1943; Dittman and Goodrich, 1961; Redl and Wineman, 1957). In their description of an intensive treatment program for disturbed, hostile pre-adolescent youngsters, Redl and Wineman (1957) enumerate 22 patterns of behavior reflecting deficiencies in ego function. These include such characteristics as diffuse flight and destructive attack when threatened, inability to resist temptation, susceptibility to behavioral contagion, and failure to discriminate between a past trauma and the present reality and between their own and other's experiences. Redl and Wineman, in describing the intimate relationship between these ego deficiencies and the extreme hostility manifested by these children, state:

For example, such children are not able to face up to fear, anxiety or insecurity of any kind without breakdown into disorganized aggression. . . . Should the adult have succeeded, by dint of great effort and detailed planning, in pulling them through a pleasurable activity, they just can't seem to store up enough of a memory of it to remember how much fun it was. So, in moments of boredom, instead of having saved up something to fall back upon and use, they again break out into wild, disruptive, and impulsive behavior. Then too, they can't wait for anything: whatever they want has to be granted *right now*. . . . If the adult does not come through —the inevitable explosion of hate (p. 259).

Ego deficiencies are only part of the clinical problem posed by these children. Redl and Wineman also describe capacities for ingenuity and vigilance, which are used to defend "impulse gratification at any cost" (p. 143). The children display a variety of rationalizations and seek environmental supports from delinquency-prone peer groups which enable them to evade their conscience and defend against change. Their behaviors constitute ego defenses which, although creating immeasurable difficulties for the clinician and other social agents who attempt to modify the children's hostility, also represent skills which a therapeutic program will make use of and hope to turn to better advantage.

The aggression of the children observed by Redl and Wineman is atypical and, fortunately, most pre-adolescent youngsters display greater controls and more responsiveness to social influence. Their pathology, however, by exaggerating the effects of mediating processes, may provide suggestive insights into the mechanisms regulating aggressive behavior. The earlier psychoanalytic formulation of aggression had placed primary emphasis on instinctual aggressive impulses and upon the frustration of libidinal strivings as antecedents of hostility. Subsequent psychoanalytically oriented studies of delinquency and of extreme aggressive response patterns (Bettelheim, 1952; Eichorn, 1935; Redl and Wineman, 1957) have resulted in an important modification of this view, greater recognition being given to the role of ego functions. The child's level of ego development is seen to have a twofold influence upon aggression. The adequacy of the child's ego capacities is a determinant of the degree of frustration he will experience and, in addition, determines the degree of control he manifests in expressing aggression.

Learning Theory Models

The Frustration-Aggression Hypothesis. *Frustration and Aggression* by Dollard, Doob, Miller, Mowrer, and Sears (1939) marked the first systematic treatment by experimental psychologists of aggressive phenomena. In formulating their theoretical analysis, the authors acknowledge a strong debt to Freud. Their treatment, particularly in relation to the types of phenomena subsumed under aggression and the mechanisms mediating the displacement and reduction of aggression, is quite similar to that of Freud. However, with regard to the antecedents of aggression, they reject the notion of a death instinct and of an aggressive instinct. Rather, they hold to a reactive theory of aggression and assume that aggression is a consequence of the organism's exposure to frustrating experiences.

The frustration-aggression hypothesis asserts that frustration of an ongoing activity produces an instigation whose goal response is injury to some person or object. While the concept of instigation is used in a broad, general sense to refer to the antecedent conditions correlated with an aggressive response, the functions associated with instigation are similar to those attributed to a drive construct. This conceptualization retains most of the dynamic properties of the psychoanalytic theory of aggression without the limiting assumption of an instinctive drive. Aggressive drive is not innate but its strength is directly linked to the frequency and intensity of frustrating experiences. Miller (1941) and Sears (1941) acknowledge that frustration reactions can be altered through learning. They state that aggression may be one of a number of behaviors innately elicited by frustration but that a strong connection between the two becomes established very early. The instigation to aggression might be viewed as the dominant response in a hierarchy of responses innately elicited by frustration. The relative positions of the responses in the hierarchy are subject to modification through the reinforcement contingencies provided by the environment for each of these responses.

The initial statement of the frustration-aggression hypothesis was a strong one: "aggression is always a consequence of frustration"

(p. 1). There are two implications contained in this proposition: (1) all aggressive behavior is due to frustration; and 2) frustration always leads to aggression. The logical equivalents of these implications are $A>F$ and $F>A$. Although the two statements are often treated equivalently, logically, and theoretically, one may be false while the other is true. Berkowitz (1962) provides an excellent discussion of the issues bearing on each of these implications. Conclusions regarding their validity depend, in large degree, upon the range of situations considered to be frustrating and upon delimiting the propositions to behavior mediated by aggressive drive and excluding instrumental aggression. For example, Durbin and Bowlby (1939), in their classification of the causes of fighting in children and apes, distinguish between disputes over the possession of external objects, the intrusion of a stranger into a group, and "frustration." The presence of a strange animal as the occasion for an aggressive response is also noted by Scott and Fredericson (1951), Seward (1945), and Lorenz (1966). Menninger (1942) cites the example of an aggressive reaction to having one's toe stepped on (which he states is not a frustration) as an obvious exception to the hypothesis.

Several critics have argued that there are qualitative differences among frustrations which must be taken into account in predicting aggressive reactions. Both Rosenzweig (1944) and Maslow (1941, 1943) believe that hostility is primarily elicited by one class of frustration, ego threats, and that the thwarting implicit in an unsatisfied primary drive does not necessarily evoke aggressive behavior. Berkowitz (1962) has pointed out that these presumed exceptions can be viewed as compatible with the frustration-aggression hypothesis providing one uses a broad definition of frustration. He suggests that frustrations which appear qualitatively different may vary quantitatively and consequently elicit different degrees of hostility.

In elaborating the frustration-aggression hypothesis, Dollard and his collaborators (1939) formulated a number of specific hypotheses that were amenable to empirical test. These pertain to the factors governing the strength of instigation to aggression, the inhibition of aggression, the displacement of aggression, and the reduction of aggression. With regard to the first of these parameters, they propose that the strength of instigation to aggression should vary directly with "(1) the strength of instigation to the frustrated response, (2) the degree of interference with the frustrated response, and (3) the number of frustrated response-sequences" (p. 28). As an example of the first proposition, a child should be more annoyed if an attractive rather than a dull toy is taken away from him or his feeding is delayed when he is very hungry as compared to when he is almost satiated. The second hypothesis implies that a toddler digging in a sand box with two shovels will be less angry if one rather than both shovels is taken away from him. The third proposition states that frustrations exercise a cumulative effect, so that a child who has a bad day in school, for example, will take less kindly to a restriction at home on his TV viewing than when he has had a pleasant day.

In addition to being influenced by variables affecting the degree of frustration, aggression is also influenced by inhibitory factors. In general, it is proposed that "the strength of inhibition of any act of aggression varies positively with the amount of punishment anticipated to be a consequence of that act" (p. 33). The anticipation of punishment may be restricted to overt behaviors discernible by parental and authority figures but can extend to covert thoughts and feelings. The concept of punishment is used broadly to include failure and injury to a loved object as well as infliction of sanctions. It would appear to follow from this hypothesis that children who have been punished for aggression will tend to express less aggression than children who have not been punished. This is a rather obvious, almost commonsense prediction. However, as Dollard and his colleagues (1939) recognize, the effects of punishment may tend to facilitate aggressive behavior. Anticipation of punishment as well as the experience of punishment may be frustrating and therefore increase the instigation to aggression while, at the same time, inhibiting the overt expression of a particular aggressive act. It has also been noted (Bandura and Walters, 1963) that the punishing agent can serve as a model for the child, who may incorporate or imitate these punitive behaviors. The father who spanks his child for an aggressive act may be simultaneously "teaching" the child to be physically aggressive. The possibility that punitive behavior may be imitated and that it can further frustrate the child greatly complicates predictions of the effects of punishment on subsequent aggressive behavior.

These factors, relating to the degree of inhibition and frustration, govern the strength of the aggressive response. In order to account for directionality and variations in the mode of the aggressive responses as well as in the stimulus object, Dollard and his associates made the following additional assumption: "The strongest instigation, aroused by a frustration, is to acts of aggression directed against the agent perceived to be the source of the frustration and progressively weaker instigations are aroused to progressively less direct acts of aggression" (p. 39). No explicit definition is provided for the degree of directness but operationally it is usually defined in terms of similarity. The dimension of directness pertains to both the stimulus object and to the form of the aggressive responses. With respect to the stimulus dimension, the proposition implies that if a child has been frustrated by a male peer, then, other things being equal, the instigation to aggress against a female peer will be weaker than the instigation to aggress against some other male peer. The stimulus dimension is more readily specified than the response dimension, which presumably varies according to the degree to which a response accomplishes the aggressive goal as well as its similarity to a prepotent

aggressive response. Thus it is not apparent whether a fantasy about hitting the frustrating peer is less or more direct than making some critical remarks about him to a friend.

The effects of inhibition of a direct act of aggression upon less direct aggressive acts is of particular relevance to phenomena of displacement and other substitute behaviors. In their original statement, Dollard et al. assume that inhibition of direct aggression constitutes, in itself, an additional frustration, which instigates aggressive acts toward the source of inhibition and indirectly heightens the instigation to other forms of aggression. Inhibitions, then, may operate to increase the strength of indirect aggressive responses, particularly when the inhibition is specific to more direct acts. The interaction between inhibition of and instigation to aggression may be viewed as an approach-avoidance conflict situation. In a number of papers subsequent to the frustration-aggression volume, Miller (1944) has proposed and tested a formal model of approach-avoidance conflicts, where one arm of the conflict is an avoidance tendency and the other arm is an approach motivation. The model has been applied to a wide range of conflict situations, including conflict over aggressive tendencies. It is to be noted that this formulation by Miller does not include the assumption that inhibition of aggression provides a further instigation to aggression. The model only assumes that avoidance tendencies decelerate more rapidly than approach tendencies with increasing distance (or indirectness) from the goal, and that the net strength of an indirect response will be a function of

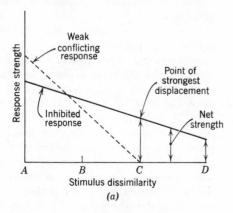

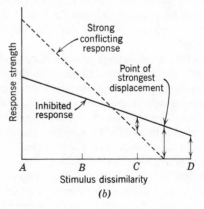

Fig. 1.   Model of displacement of aggression.   (From Miller, 1948, p. 169.)

its own strength minus that of the conflicting tendency.

This model is illustrated in Fig. 1, taken from Miller's paper (1948) on the displacement of aggression. To relate this model to a concrete example, we might imagine the conflict experienced by a 5-year-old boy whose younger brother has just destroyed a carefully constructed tower of blocks. The older sibling has been previously punished for aggression toward his brother and his impulse to hit his brother, located at point A in Fig. 1a, is inhibited by anticipation of subsequent punishment. Point B might represent another child who resembles his brother, point C a third child unlike his brother, and point D, a dog. According to the conditions specified in Fig. 1a, one would predict that hitting the third child is the response most likely to occur.

Figure 1b postulates an increment in the strength of the avoidance tendency. The effect of this increment is to increase the relative probability of more indirect aggressive responses; now the boy is more likely to strike the dog than hit the third child. The *absolute strength* of the displaced responses remains unaffected by the presence of inhibition. If there were no avoidance operating, and stimuli A, B, and C were absent from the situation, the boy would direct his aggression toward the dog, stimulus D, with an intensity equal to that when inhibition is present. In contrast to the original formulation, in the Miller model inhibition can only reduce the absolute strength of an indirect response, although it may increase its relative probability. More recently, Miller (1959) has considered the implication of conflict-produced tension for the model. We shall have occasion to review applications of the conflict model to experimental studies of displaced aggression in children.

We might at this point simply note that additional variables have to be considered when applying the model to most conflict situations in which children or adults find themselves. The response to stimulus objects B, C, and D is influenced by specific attitudes and habits associated with these stimuli as well as by the generalized avoidance and approach tendencies. Also, depending upon the cultural norms, inhibitory tendencies may embrace categories of stimulus persons—younger children, girls, helpless animals, etc. The in-

hibition might well apply to the mediating aggressive drive stimulus (Feshbach, 1956) rather than to the aggressive response and operate as a blanket rather than a gradient. Nevertheless, even with these limitations, the model has proved to be a useful and productive analytic tool.

Perhaps even more complicated than the effects of inhibition on aggressive behavior is the relationship between the expression of aggression and subsequent aggressive activity. In the book *Frustration and Aggression* it was assumed that acts of aggression were functionally equivalent, so that direct and indirect aggressive behaviors would serve to reduce in varying degrees the intensity of the aggressive impulse. Specifically, it was asserted that "the occurrence of any act of aggression is assumed to reduce the instigation to aggression. In psychoanalytic terminology, such a release is called catharsis" (Dollard et al., 1939, p. 50). This assumption, which corresponds to the psychoanalytic view of motivational dynamics, has important social as well as theoretical implications. It suggests that if children are provided socially approved aggressive "outlets," as in play activities or through such vicarious experiences as exposure to aggressive content in films and television, they will display less aggression in other situations. Presumably a child who is permitted to express his aggression freely toward sources of frustration in the home will be less aggressive at school and in the play yard. Thus it follows from the principles of displacement and catharsis that "with the level of original frustrations held roughly constant, there should be an inverse relationship between the occurrence of different forms of aggression" (p. 51).

As will become evident when other learning models are discussed, the effects of an aggressive response upon subsequent aggressive behaviors are not only mediated by changes in the strength of aggressive instigation or drive but also by changes at the response level. If, following frustration, an aggressive response is successfully directed toward the source of frustration, any reduction in instigation that may ensue occurs in conjunction with reinforcement of the aggressive response. Furthermore, anxieties that may be associated with the aggressive act would be reduced by the occurrence of aggression without punishment. Both the reduction in inhibition and the increase in aggressive response strength function to increase the probability of aggressive behavior and to exert an effect opposite to that of the reduction in aggressive instigation. Whether an aggressive act will result in an increment or in a decrement on some other measure of aggression will then depend upon the relative strengths of these opposing factors.

Although the S-R theoretical framework of the authors as reflected in other writings (Miller and Dollard, 1941; Dollard and Miller, 1950; Sears, 1941) certainly takes cognizance of these response variables, the frustration-aggression volume emphasized the role of motivational antecedents of aggressive behavior. This focus served as an excellent bridge between psychoanalytic theory and the more formal learning theory models then extant. However, subsequent analysis and research has made it evident that one cannot test the consequences of the frustration-aggression hypothesis without taking into account learning parameters.

Reinforcement and Modeling. All theoretical models of aggression assume that aggressive behavior is, to some degree, acquired. The disagreements among theorists lie in the importance ascribed to learning as a determinant of aggression and in the kinds of aggressive behavior that are assumed to be influenced by past learning. The role of learning can be restricted largely to determining the form of the aggressive response while the impetus for the aggressive act is attributed to instinctual drives or to frustrating experiences. This is essentially the psychoanalytic position. In shifting the source of aggression from an instinctive to a frustration-produced drive, the importance of the organism's experiences is recognized but the role of learning is still relatively minor.

Psychoanalytic theorists who stress the importance of frustration still assume that aggressive impulses are innately elicited by frustrating events. The conditions that produce frustration may, of course, be influenced strongly by learning. However, given a frustrating event, it is posited that aggressive impulses will inevitably be aroused. In *Frustration and Aggression* the authors leave open the question of the origin of the connection between frustration and aggression but proceed on the assumption that the connection, if not innate, has a high probability of being acquired in the course of socialization. Possible mechanisms by which aggressive drive is acquired have been suggested by Sears (1958) and by Feshbach (1964). Sears proposes that the motive to injure others becomes acquired through a process of secondary reinforcement. A successful instrumental aggressive act eliminates frustration and also evokes pain responses from the frustrator. The consistent association of the perception of pain in others with the removal of frustration results in the former acquiring secondary reinforcement properties. Feshbach, questioning the secondary reinforcement hypothesis, postulates that the motivation to inflict pain is rooted in the child's exposure to behaviors and cultural norms which indicate that the infliction of pain upon others is the appropriate response made to the experience of pain. Both the secondary reinforcement and the internalized cultural standard hypotheses are largely speculative, there being little in the way of empirical evidence that directly bears on the issue of the acquisition of aggressive drive.

Research on the influence of learning upon aggression has largely stressed the acquisition of aggressive responses without attempting to distinguish between aggressive behavior that is instrumental to nonaggressive goals and aggressive behavior that is mediated by aggressive drive. Operationally, the distinction is very difficult to make. Moreover, it can be argued that much of human aggression is instrumental in character, and research effort should therefore be directed to the study of the reinforcement contingencies which maintain and inhibit aggressive responding and the discriminative stimuli eliciting an aggressive response. Scott (1958) has shown that this mode of analysis can provide a satisfactory account of many forms of aggressive interaction in infrahuman species while other investigators have demonstrated that it can be applied with considerable success to particular aggressive behaviors manifested by young children and adolescents (Bandura and Walters, 1959; Bandura, Ross, and Ross, 1961, 1963; Buss, 1961; Walters and Brown, 1964). These studies can be separated into two broad classes. In one, emphasis is placed upon the acquisition of aggressive responses through reinforcement of the response after it has occurred (Davitz, 1952; Lovaas, 1961; Buss, 1958; Cowan and Walters, 1963), whereas the other examines the role of such processes as modeling and identification in the acquisition of the response (Bandura, 1962). These two emphases are by no means incompatible but rather deal with different stages of the aggressive behavior.

In analyzing the behavior of a child, an aggressive response can be treated essentially as a conditioned operant, the problem then being to determine the stimulus contingencies that reinforce the behavior. In some cases the reinforcement may be obvious. The mother who yields to her child whenever he displays a temper tantrum is clearly reinforcing the tantrum. The behavior of the bully who terrorizes his peers is rewarded whenever they conform to his wishes. The reinforcement for aggressive behavior also takes a more subtle form. A teacher rebuking a child who repeatedly aggresses against classmates may be inadvertently rewarding the aggressive response if the function of the behavior is to seek the teacher's attention. Aggressive behavior in this context and in the preceding examples is functionally similar to crying, ingratiation, cajoling, or any other mode of response that brings about these particular reinforcing contingencies. The parameters governing the maintenance of aggressive behavior, its generalization, inhibition, and extinction are the same as those that apply to instrumental behaviors in general. In terms of this theoretical framework, there is no unique class of goal responses consequent to the aggressive act. The infliction of pain may still be one among a number of reinforcers that may maintain an aggressive act. However, there is no intrinsic reason to emphasize this possible reinforcer of aggression over others. The question of the reinforcements for aggression in any particular situation has to be resolved empirically.

There still remains the problem of accounting for the initial occurrence of an aggressive act. Learning models have suggested a number of possible mechanisms. The simplest would be to assume that the aggressive response occurs during trial and error behavior, and that once it occurs, its subsequent probability depends upon whether or not it is reinforced. A modified view is the assumption that aggression is a dominant or prepotent response in a hierarchy of responses elicited by such stimulus situations as frustration. Reinforcement contingencies can then operate to enhance the aggressive response or to lower its position in the hierarchy. These explanations can account for some aggressive responses that may innately occur, but more complex, aggressive behaviors are clearly acquired in another manner. One possibility is that these complex behaviors are gradually shaped through selective reinforcement of successive approximations of the behavior. Bandura (1962) has cogently argued that the mechanism of gradual shaping is highly inefficient and does not fit developmental observations. He has proposed instead that most social behaviors are acquired through the process of imitation or modeling. In a series of experiments, Bandura has shown that children do indeed imitate aggressive behaviors of models, and he has also investigated some of the variables influencing the degree of imitative behavior manifested by the child.

The mechanism of imitation, particularly as elaborated by Bandura and Walters (1963), has interesting implications for the acquisition of aggressive behaviors. In their view, a major determinant of children's aggressive behavior is the aggression displayed by parental figures and other significant persons in the child's environment who function as models for the child. Aggressive acts may or may not be attached to frustrating stimuli, depending upon the conditions under which the models displayed the aggression. As Bandura (1962) has demonstrated, acquisition of the response by the child does not depend upon direct reinforcement of the behavior and can occur without the child actually reproducing the model's response during acquisition. Bandura and Walters suggest that the role of reward, whether administered to the model or to the child, is to influence the observer's performance of the imitative response, but the acquisition of these responses depends primarily upon sensory contiguity.

The mechanism of modeling, like the mechanism of selective reinforcement of aggressive behavior, greatly increases the variety of stimulus conditions that may elicit aggressive behavior. Both tend to deemphasize the importance of frustration as an antecedent of aggressive behavior and reduce the necessity for positing an aggressive drive construct to account for aggressive behaviors.

Modified Instinct-Learning Approach

Ethology. The study of animal aggression has become sufficiently extensive to warrant a chapter or a book devoted to that topic alone. Among the animals whose aggressive behavior has been intensively studied are fish (Tinbergen, 1953a; Zumpe, 1965), lizards (Noble, 1933, 1934), birds (Tinbergen, 1951a, 1951b, 1951c, 1961), mice (Scott, 1946, 1947; Frederickson, Story, Gurney, and Butterworth, 1955; Beeman, 1947), rats (Seward, 1945; Scott and Frederickson, 1951; Richter, 1954), dogs (James, 1951; Fuller, 1953), wolves (Young and Goldman, 1944), and apes (Carpenter, 1934; Zuckerman, 1932). Although the study of aggression in animals is of considerable importance in its own right, we are concerned here primarily with those aspects of animal aggression that bear upon human aggressive behavior.

The relevance of animal aggression to human aggression is itself a matter of some controversy because of the danger of drawing loose analogies from animal to human behavior on the basis of superficial similarities. The fact that many animals display strong territorial attachments and will fight when the territory is violated by an intruder (Ardrey, 1966) affords some resemblance to the human phenomenon of nationalism. However, to argue on the basis of these animal observations that humans have an instinctive territorial impulse and an instinctive tendency to fight to defend their "territory" tends to obscure important, perhaps fundamental, differences in the behaviors manifested and in the processes regulating these behaviors. In addition to the problem of making inferences from animal data to human activities, there is by no means agreement among students of animal behavior on the mechanisms accounting for aggression and, in some instances, on the basic data (Barnett, 1967). Nevertheless, there are continuities in species development, and the hypotheses and perspective provided by ethologists may be useful in the analysis of human aggressive phenomena.

Animal aggression, although less varied than the behavior encompassed in human aggression, also embraces a rather diverse set of behaviors, ranging from "threatening" gestures to physical attack. Moyer (1967) has proposed a useful classification of these aggressive behaviors, based on the topography of the aggressive response and on the class of stimulus situations that will evoke the destructive tendencies. He distinguishes the following types of aggression:

1. Predatory aggression. Here the eliciting stimulus is the presence of a natural object of prey.

2. Intermale, spontaneous aggression. The releaser of this aggressive pattern is typically the presence of a male of the same species, and a male to which the attacker has not become habituated.

3. Terror-induced aggression. This type of aggression is always preceded by escape attempts and usually occurs under conditions of confinement in which the animal is cornered by some threatening agent.

4. Irritable aggression. This response is elicited by a wide range of stimuli and is characterized by an affective display. It is not preceded by attempts to escape.

5. Territorial defense. The stimulus situation eliciting this behavior entails an area which the animal has established as its "territory" and an intruder, typically but not necessarily an animal of the same species.

6. Defense of the young. This form of aggression among mammals is usually displayed by the female. The stimulus complex evoking the aggression consists of the presence of the young and the proximity of a threatening agent to the young of the animal.

7. Instrumental aggression. Any of the preceding classes of aggression may produce a stimulus change resulting in reinforcement of the behavior. Instrumental aggression is characterized by the increase in the probability of an aggressive response to a particular stimulus situation as a result of prior reinforcement.

This categorization is not exhaustive. There are certain patterns of aggressive behavior, for example, the aggressive components of the triumphal ceremony in Greylag geese (Lorenz, 1966), which do not readily fit any of these categories. In addition there are species differences and differences within species in the occurrence of each of these types of aggression. However, the categories do encompass most types of aggressive behavior, particularly those observed in mammalian species. One important value of the distinctions made in this categorization is the delineation of classes of aggressive behavior which may be genotypically as well as phenotypically different. In discussions of human aggression, the distinction has been made between instrumental aggression and aggressive drive mediated behavior, the latter being ascribed to an innate instinct (Freud, 1930), to frustration (Dollard et al., 1939), or to social learning (Feshbach, 1964).

Moyer's analysis is of particular interest because of its focus on stimulus antecedents and the suggestion that these antecedents may innately elicit aggressive behaviors which are functionally different. Predatory aggression, for example, a severe form of aggressive behavior resulting in destruction of the prey, is sometimes used as the prototype of bestial impulses; humans are described as having a "killer instinct"; the destructive fantasies and behavior of a child are seen as analogous to the ferocity displaced by our mammalian forebearers in their pursuit of jungle enemies. Yet there is both physiological and behavioral evidence that predatory aggression is fundamentally different from the various forms of intraspecies aggression. Predatory aggression appears to be very closely related to food seeking and consummatory behavior (Hutchinson and Renfrew, 1966) and is mediated by a different area of the hypothalamus than is implicated in the control of irritable aggression (Wasman and Flynn, 1962). Not only is the topography of the predatory response strikingly different from the behaviors characterized as irritable aggression, but the neural correlates and stimulus antecedents differ. Intermale spontaneous aggression, like predatory aggression, is intimately related to changes in another drive system of the organism, in this case the hormonal and stimulus factors regulating sexual behavior. There is evidence that in some species the form of the aggressive response is specific to this eliciting stimulus situation; for example, certain deer use their antlers when engaged in intermale fighting but use their front horns against predators (Tinbergen, 1953) and, in the rat, this response appears to be highly stereotyped (Eibl-Eibesfeldt, 1961; Barnett, 1963).

These observations in animals suggest the possibility that there may also exist for hu-

mans stimulus situations other than frustration, which innately elicit behavior with destructive consequences but which are governed, at least initially, by different mechanisms. The late oral biting stage, which many psychoanalysts view as having significant aggressive as well as libidinal components (Ericson, 1951; Munroe, 1955), is a case in point. The biting response may help relieve the pain associated with teething; it may also be part of the set of consummatory reflexes involved in eating. In either instance, the response pattern is very different from the anger or rage elicited in the infant by frustration. The infant may then learn to use the biting response, as he may learn to use aggressive behaviors acquired through modeling in an instrumental manner where the *pain* inflicted by the behavior produces a stimulus change which is reinforcing. The hitting, biting, scratching, kicking behaviors infants display may be elicited by functionally dissimilar mechanisms; the injurious consequences, which are the basis for classifying them as aggressive, being incidental to the behavior.

It is confusing and misleading to cite these behaviors as evidence for an aggressive instinct in the sense of an innate cyclic or constant driving force. The animal literature (Scott, 1958; Lorenz, 1966) indicates that these seemingly aggressive behaviors are highly controlled by external stimulus factors and the data fail to support the notion of an innate, internally governed drive that seeks out such aggressive interactions to reduce its intensity. While Konrad Lorenz views aggressive drive as a "true, primarily species-preserving instinct" (1966, p. 50) in humans as well as animals, his conception and analysis of the aggressive "instinct" is very different from the instinctual aggressive drive postulated by Freud. Aggression is reactive in almost all of the evidence that Lorenz cites, with the exception of occasional observations of apparently spontaneous aggressive discharge. For Lorenz, the concept of instinct primarily implies that aggressive tendencies are innately elicited by particular stimulus configurations. Moreover, the destructive consequences of the behaviors are species-preserving from an evolutionary point of view, but it is not assumed that these destructive consequences determine the behavior.

Similar restrictions are found in the views

of Ardrey (1967), who, perhaps more than Lorenz, stresses the continuity between "instinctive" aggression in humans and instinctive aggression in animals. On the basis of speculations concerning the behavior of a possible prehistoric ancestor of man, Australopithecus africanus, Ardrey argues that "man is a predator whose natural instinct is to kill with a weapon" (Ardrey, 1967, p. 322). However, this predatory, killer-instinctive behavior is elicited in the pursuit of more fundamental drives to protect and maintain territory and to achieve dominance (Ardrey, 1966, 1967). Whether these drives, which appear to be so powerful in many animal species, are equally significant for humans and whether the blocking of these drives will innately elicit strong aggressive behaviors are interesting empirical questions. The animal data summarized by Lorenz and Ardrey can best be seen as offering hypotheses as to the stimulus conditions that may be potent elicitors of aggression in humans.

Ardrey and to a lesser extent Lorenz neglect the role of learning as a determinant of aggressive behavior in animals. Scott's (1958) review of the animal literature points to the significant extent to which aggressive behavior in animals is dependent upon the reinforcement of that behavior. Mice and dogs can be readily trained to be fighters or to adopt more passive behavior. If training begins before the animal develops strong aggressive habits, it is possible to develop nonaggressive behaviors that successfully compete with or inhibit aggressive reactions. Scott suggests that "If it can be established that aggression is produced by training in all species of animals, including human beings, there is a hopeful outlook for the control of human aggression" (p. 20). The first half of this statement reflects a conception of aggression sharply differing from that of Lorenz.

The views of Scott and Lorenz are in part based upon different sets of observations; Scott used experimental laboratory studies in which the behavior of the animal is systematically manipulated, whereas Lorenz made controlled observations of animal behavior in natural settings. These differences in methodology and in theoretical outlook notwithstanding, there are nevertheless important areas of agreement. Scott's own research indicates a sensitivity to genetic differences between

species in aggressive thresholds (Scott, 1942) and in the modifiability of aggressive behaviors (Scott, 1954). Also, Scott acknowledges the role of both endogenous and exogenous factors in controlling aggressive behavior. The major difference lies in the importance ascribed to learning. Where Lorenz emphasizes innate mechanisms, Scott emphasizes the degree to which the organism's innate hierarchy of behaviors can be altered through experience. The role of innate, structured variables is evident in such observations as those of Richter (1954), contrasting the consistent aggressiveness and suspiciousness of the wild Norway rat with the gentleness and docility of the domesticated species, and in Eibl-Eibesfeldt's (1961) demonstration that wild Norway rats, reared in isolation before manifesting any aggressive behavior, will "spontaneously" fight when two males are put together. At the same time, as Seward's studies with rats and Scott's experiments with mice (1946, 1947, 1953) and goats (1948) indicate, fighting behavior is radically influenced by experience. Seward found that rats trained to fight each other under low hunger drive conditions actually fought less than usual when they were subsequently food deprived and placed in a situation in which they had to compete for food. Scott showed that the effects of food deprivation upon a flock of goats which had a well established dominance order in competing for grain were dependent upon the animal's position in the dominance hierarchy. The amount of aggression increased in the dominant goats, the subordinate member behaving aggressively only if paired with an even more subordinate animal. These studies lead Scott to suggest that "frustration leads to aggression only in situations where the individual has a habit of being aggressive" (1958, p. 35).

It is evident from the animal data that aggression is both species specific and subject to general behavioral influences. Generalizations from an animal species to the human species are therefore highly questionable. The animal data may suggest the kinds of physiological mechanisms and situational variables that should be investigated in humans but cannot substitute for direct empirical studies of human aggression. It is also apparent that there are major differences between animal aggression and human aggression. Animal aggression is, on the whole, regulated by immediate stimulus changes. Human aggression can be maintained by mediating cognitive structures and is, to a much smaller degree, stimulus bound. As Tinbergen (1953) and Lorenz (1966) have so amply documented, intraspecies aggression in most animals is regulated by inhibiting stimuli which can divert or modify an opponent's aggressive behavior before serious injury occurs. A deer in the midst of an antler fight will stop the forward movement of his antlers when aimed at the unprotected flank of his rival; a cock, beaten in a fight, puts his head in a corner and thereby removes from his opponent the fight-eliciting stimuli; a dog who is the loser of a fight may present his unprotected neck to the mouth of the victor (Lorenz, 1966). Tinbergen (1953), who has extensively studied fighting behavior in fish, describes an intricate set of "signals" that elicit and inhibit aggression in different species, regulating the intensity of the aggressive interaction so that it amounts to little more than a ritualized "threat" ceremony, with few, if any, actual blows being exchanged. Intraspecies killing in animals is much rarer than in humans, and the pursuit of a rival over space and time in order to inflict injury upon him is a peculiarly human phenomenon.

If innate inhibitory signals—gestures, facial expressions, cries—are present in humans, they are less effective than in animals and require the additional support of social learning. An interesting and neglected research problem are the factors involved in the development of expressive behaviors in humans which have the capacity to inhibit an opponent's aggression. Lorenz has noted that many aggressive interactions among humans, especially modern warfare, are carried out at such a distance that a "killer" is screened against the stimulus situation which might otherwise activate inhibitions of his aggression (1966). Lorenz feels that one method of compensating for the weaker inhibition of aggression in man is to provide adequate substitution outlets for the discharge of his aggressive drive. Scott, on the basis of observations of displacement of aggression following the interruption or blocking of an activated aggressive behavioral sequence, makes a similar recommendation for socially approved aggressive substitutes. However, the animal data would appear to suggest more strongly the strengthening of inhibitory signals and the reinforcement of social interactions incompatible with destructive behavior as methods for controlling aggression.

THE MEASUREMENT OF AGGRESSION

Process and Structure of Aggressive Behavior

A basic and persistent problem in the investigation of aggression is its measurement. Kaufmann (1965), in his detailed review of methodological problems in the study of aggression, emphasizes the importance of the operational definition of aggression in clarifying theoretical issues and in integrating research findings. Difficulties of measurement derive from the complexity of the construct and from a lack of consensus concerning operational definitions and theoretical premises. The following statement, made almost a decade ago by Bronfenbrenner and Ricciuti in their review of assessment methods appropriate for use with children still applies:

[A]lthough many promising techniques for the appraisal of aggression in children have been developed, the research worker will find few refined psychometric instruments available. To some extent, this state of affairs reflects the overall status of psychological measurement in the field of personality study. However, the paucity of standardized techniques is partly due to the complex nature of aggression as a psychological variable (1960, p. 790).

The availability of standardized procedures is a less serious difficulty than the ambiguity of the referent which is being assessed. Although considerable ingenuity and effort have been invested in designing procedures for measuring aggressive behavior, the validity and often the objectives of these measures are unclear. The measure may be intended to be specific to the situation in which aggression is assessed—for example, observation of aggressive behaviors in school—or the same measure may be used as an indicator of free-floating aggressive drive or generalized aggressive tendencies. The requirements for assessing aggressive tendencies will depend in large degree upon the theoretical model of the investigators. Figure 2 illustrates some

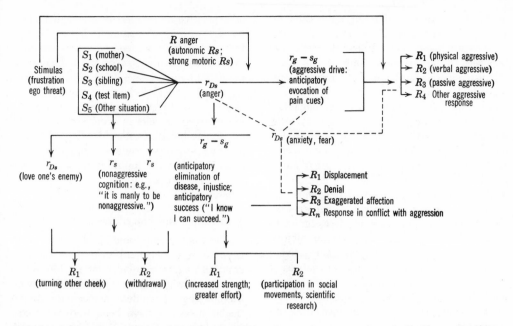

Fig. 2. Schematic representation of response patterns to aggression instigation situations. (Modification of diagram in Feshbach, 1964, p. 267.)

of the measurement questions that may be generated by a particular theory, by a schematic representation of a mediating drive stimulus model of aggression. The diagram is based on a modification of a similar scheme outlined elsewhere by the author (Feshbach, 1964). The top row of the diagram depicts a possible chain of events, beginning with an instigating stimulus and culminating in an overt aggressive response. Alternative responses initiated by nonaggressive reactions and by anxiety are outlined by the bottom rows. The model distinguishes between anger and the motivation to inflict pain, but this distinction is not essential to the present discussion. It it included to suggest the possible separation of anger and aggressive drive, although under most circumstances they can be considered equivalents. The line from the stimulus past the mediating response drive stimulus (rDs) of anger indicates that a stimulus elicits aggressive drive without anger or a component of the affective reaction. The longer line from the stimulus, bypassing aggressive drive, encompass those circumstances in which aggressive drive is short-circuited and the overt aggressive response is directly connected to the stimulus.

The elements described in the diagram and their interconnections suggest the kinds of measurement issues that are encountered in the assessment of aggression. Individuals may differ in the range of stimulus situations that may elicit an aggressive response, in the intensity of aggressive affect and aggressive drive, in the range of aggressive behaviors influenced by aggressive drive, and in the degrees and mode of inhibition of covert aggressive attitudes and overt aggressive reactions. These dimensions are not completely independent. Under heightened drive conditions, one would expect a lowered threshold for aggression so that a greater number of stimuli evoke an aggressive response. An increase in drive should also facilitate response generalization and thereby increase the range of behaviors reflecting aggressive motivation. However, the arousal of inhibitory factors could sharply modify these relationships, which are further complicated by the stimulus and response specificities resulting from the individual's reinforcement history. In an effort to disentangle these potential effects, a number of measuring procedures have been developed which are presumably differentially sensitive to aggressive drive, instrumental response, and inhibitory factors.

A related measurement effort is the investigation of the degree of generality of aggressive behavior. The interpretation of the relationships among different aggressive responses depends to a considerable extent upon one's theoretical framework. Behaviors believed to be manifestations of the same construct are expected to be positively correlated. However, there are other possible relationships. To demonstrate that behaviors are related to the same construct, they must be linked in some manner. At issue is the nature of the linkage. If aggression is conceived of as a response trait, then the research problem becomes one of determining the intercorrelations among a set of behaviors. An aggressive label, based upon a marker variable or upon similar content, is assigned to those behaviors that share common factors. Behaviors that are uncorrelated or negatively correlated would be given different labels. It is also possible within this framework to take into account the effects of inhibitory factors by the appropriate choice of measuring instruments.

If aggression is conceptualized as a motive, the task of establishing the functional equivalence of behaviors assumed to be aggressive is twofold. First, the behaviors must be related to antecedent events which elicit the motive. Since individuals may differ in the preferred mode of aggressive responses, the aggressive behaviors may be indifferently or negatively related to each other while positively correlated with the antecedent condition. Thus, under conditions of frustration, some children may respond with physical aggression, whereas others may resort to hostile verbalizations. A systematic relationship with the antecedent event is clearly not a sufficient condition since the same event may produce increments in nonaggressive behaviors in some children. Thus frustration may result in nonaggressive responses ranging from withdrawal to increased striving for the blocked goal object. In order to establish the relationship of a behavior to the aggressive drive construct, a second step, in which the behavior is linked to the theoretical consequences of aggression, must be carried out. This is frequently done at a more or less intuitive level through consensual agreement on the injurious implications of a response. The task of empirically demonstrating that the goal of or reinforcement for the behavior is its injurious effects is a very difficult one, and relatively few studies have attempted to do this. A finding of a positive correlation between diverse behaviors whose one common element appears to be their injurious consequences would be presumptive evidence that the behaviors are mediated by aggressive drive. Direct evidence would be provided by procedures enabling one to show that the expression of one form of aggression results in a decrement in other aggressive behaviors, the blocking of one aggressive response produces an increment in others, or that the injurious consequences of a response serves to reinforce other correlated behaviors.

Instruments and Procedures

The instruments and procedures which have been used to assess various facets of children's aggressive behavior are too numerous to consider in detail in this review. Methodological problems associated with particular measures have been frequently commented upon in connection with a specific empirical question. An enumeration of the variety of procedures is instructive. These include:

1. Direct observation and behavior sampling (Feshbach, 1967; Murphy, 1937; Patterson et al., 1967; Sears et al., 1965).

2. Interviews of the child (Bandura and Walters, 1959; Kagan and Moss, 1962; Nakamura, 1959) and interviews of the parents (Sears et al., 1957) and schoolteachers (Kagan, 1956), including the administration of questionnaires, rating scales, and autobiographical workbooks.

3. Peer nominations and related sociometric devices (Lesser, 1959; Walder et al., 1961; Wiggins and Winder, 1961).

4. Personality inventories (Feshbach, 1967; Sears, 1961; Zaks and Walters, 1959).

5. Situational tests of aggression toward other children (Mallick and McCandless, 1966) and of aggression to play objects (Bandura, Ross, and Ross, 1961; Stone, 1956; Walters and Brown, 1963); doll play (Bach, 1945; Chasdi and Lawrence, 1955; Phillips, 1945; Pintler, 1945; Robinson, 1946; P. Sears, 1951).

6. Projective tests, among which have been the Thematic Apperception Test and its variants (Feshbach, 1955; Jensen, 1957; Kagan, 1956, 1959; Lesser, 1958b; Mussen and Naylor, 1954; Smith and Coleman, 1956); the

Rorschach (Garlow, Zimet, and Fine, 1952; Long and Miezitis, 1966; Smith and Coleman, 1956); the Human Figure Drawing Test (Koppitz, 1966); the Rosenzweig Picture Frustration Test (Chorost, 1962; Rosenzweig, 1960); a nonverbal cartoon test (Patterson, 1960) and the sentence completion method (Beech and Graham, 1967).

This list, although not exhaustive, reflects the diversity of methods employed in assessing aggression and, by implication, some of the problems entailed in comparing and integrating findings based on these varied procedures. For a review of methodological issues bearing on the assessment of children's behavior, the reader is referred to Bronfenbrenner and Ricciuti (1960). Several reviews of projective techniques bear upon their validity in the assessment of children's aggression (Murstein, 1965; Zubin, Eron, and Schumer, 1965) while Buss' (1961) book on aggression includes chapters on projective and inventory measures. Cohn (1962) has provided a summary of the extensive literature on doll play, the technique most widely used in the study of aggression in preschool children.

It is apparent from these reviews that the measures of aggression currently available have limited utility and are appropriate for different kinds of problems. Projective measures, including doll play, have proved to be sensitive to experimental manipulation of aggression-related variables and to antecedents of aggression associated with socialization practices. They have been much less successful as predictors of aggression in other situations. The inventory measures developed by Sears (1961) to assess antisocial aggression, prosocial aggression, self-aggression, aggression-anxiety, and projected aggression offer promise for the differentiation of the response modes children use to cope with their aggressive impulses. These measures have, as yet, been employed in too few studies to establish their validity in making these theoretically significant distinctions. A factor analytic study by Sanner (1964) suggests that the behavior dimensions assessed by the Sears Aggression Scales bear little relationship to the dimensions assessed by sociometric rating procedures. Sociometric rating procedures, including both the Peer Nomination Inventory (Wiggins and Winder, 1961) and the Rip Van Winkle peer rating aggression index (Walder et al., 1961), have been shown to be reliable, and initial reports concerning their validity as measures of overt aggressive tendencies have been encouraging (Eron et al., 1963; Winder and Wiggins, 1964). However, the predictive utility of sociometric, projective, and inventory measures is limited by the substantial methods variance yielded by each procedure (Magee, 1964; Sanner, 1964), and it is evident that the more dissimilar the test of aggression is to the aggression criterion, the weaker are the relationships obtained.

Fantasy and Overt Aggression

The extensive literature on the assessment of children's aggression by means of thematic apperception fantasy type procedures provides a useful illustration of general problems encountered in the measurement of aggression and of the more specific advantages and limitations of projective devices. The central issue to which the majority of these studies have been addressed is the relationship between aggression expressed in fantasy and aggression expressed in an overt, interpersonal form. The correlation between fantasy aggression and overt aggression has been of interest because of its theoretical implications as well as its relevance to the problem of the prediction of aggression by means of psychological tests.

The stories which the child constructs in response to TAT type stimuli can be viewed as a sample of cognitive activity which represents the same response dispositions that are reflected in the child's social behaviors. Thus a child who has strong aggressive tendencies can be expected to manifest these tendencies over a broad range of stimulus situations and behaviors, including his overt reactions to other people and his verbal responses elicited by an ambiguous pictorial stimulus. Other factors being equal, fantasy and overt aggression should be positively correlated. However, because of the anticipation of punishment for many forms of overt aggressive expression, there is likely to be differential inhibitions of overt and covert aggression, thereby attenuating or eliminating the relationship.

According to Miller's (1944) conflict and displacement model, there should be less generalization of avoidance than of aggressive responses from the goal situation to the test situation. Because of its projective nature, the TAT has also been assumed to be more sensitive to generalized aggressive drive and less sensitive to situational influences than overt, interpersonal aggressive reactions. For these reasons, the presence of aggressive themes on the TAT has been viewed as a more valid indicator of the strength of aggressive disposition than the individual's nontest behaviors. The absence of aggressive TAT themes is, of course, subject to many more interpretations than their presence. A low aggression score on the TAT may reflect low aggressive drive, high aggression anxiety, limited linguistic skills, or the inappropriateness of the test stimuli. A high score, while more diagnostic, also has its theoretical limitations; thus a high score may be indicative of a rich fantasy life as well as of strong aggressive drive. Moreover, if fantasy is conceived of as a substitute for the expression of unacceptable impulses in everyday life, then the strength of aggressive fantasy should be a direct function of the degree of inhibition of overt aggressive behaviors.

As previously indicated, Miller's (1944) conflict model predicts that the fantasy response resulting from overt inhibition can be either weaker or equal to, but never stronger than a fantasy response which would occur if no inhibition was operating. The possibility that conflict between approach and inhibitory responses may increase the strength of indirect, displaced responses such as fantasy has been suggested by Whiting and Child (1953) and also by Miller (1959). The conception of fantasy as a compensatory response, resulting from the inability to express overtly a socially unacceptable impulse, is consistent with psychoanalytic theory. Psychoanalytic ego psychology has also emphasized the control function of fantasy, which, by binding energy associated with a drive, can serve to regulate its expression (Rapaport, 1959). According to the psychoanalytic model, then, fantasy aggression should be negatively correlated with the overt acting out of aggression.

The research data, although not conclusive with respect to these theoretical issues, have nevertheless yielded interesting and fairly consistent relationships between certain aspects of TAT fantasy and overt aggressive responses. Murray (1943), on the basis of his initial studies of the TAT, concluded that culturally discouraged motives such as sex and aggression are likely to show little or no relationship between strength of fantasy and overt expression. Subsequent studies of both children and adults, in which the amount of aggression in fantasy has been correlated with a measure of overt aggression, tended to confirm this conclusion. While there have been reports of significant positive correlations (Kagan, 1956; Lesser, 1958a; Mussen and Naylor, 1954) and negative correlations (Horrocks and Gottfried, 1966) for samples of children and adolescents, the modal finding has been inconclusive (Gluck, 1955; Hymann, 1956; Jensen, 1957; McCasland, 1961; Symonds, 1949). This discouraging picture changes when more refined analyses of fantasy responses have been undertaken. Mussen and Naylor (1954) compared the TAT response of lower-class 9- to 15-year-old Negro and white delinquent boys, residing in cottages, with incidents of aggressive behavior observed over a 2-week period. The TAT protocols were scored for the number of times the heroes were subjected to punishment and also for the number of aggressive acts appearing in the stories. The positive association obtained for this population between fantasy and overt aggression was improved when the punishment scores were taken into account.

Enhancement of the predictive value of fantasy aggression, when allowance is made for the negative relationship between overt aggression and fantasy expressions of punishment, guilt, and aggression anxiety, has been obtained with impressive consistency (Bandura and Walters, 1959; Jensen, 1957; Lesser, 1958a; McCasland, 1961). Lesser (1958a) used a modified sociometric peer rating procedure to assess overt aggression in 10- to 13-year-old white upper-lower-class boys and a specially designed set of stimulus cards to elicit fantasy aggression. Several measures of aggression anxiety were derived according to the point at which the anxiety intervened in an instigation to aggression-expression of aggression sequence. The fantasy aggression measure was similar to that employed by Mussen and Naylor (1954) and a comparable small, positive relationship between fantasy and overt aggression was found. This finding is consistent with Mussen and Naylor's contention that lower-class children who have heightened fantasy aggression needs are likely to express these needs in their overt behavior because of the greater permissiveness of peer aggression in the lower-class culture. Of particular interest is the role of individual variations in the inhibition of fantasy aggression. The most striking result in Lesser's study (1958a) is the strong negative correlation between overt aggression and the degree to which inhibitory controls appeared early in the fantasy aggression sequence. Also noteworthy were the differences obtained when the agent of punishment in fantasy was analyzed. Punishment by peers was found to be negatively related to overt aggression, whereas punishment by parents, teacher, or police was found to be associated with a high degree of overt expression of aggression. It is possible that a different pattern of correlates of peer and adult punishment may have been obtained if the measure of overt aggression had been based on aggression toward authority figures.

An encouraging outcome of TAT fantasy research has been the extent to which theoretically relevant distinctions in fantasy measures of aggression inhibition have proved to be useful in differentiating children who vary in overt aggressive behavior. Bandura and Walters (1959), in their investigation of the factors associated with antisocial aggressive behavior in male adolescents, developed a series of pictures depicting boys in socially deviant acts. They found evidence of greater guilt in the controls as compared to the aggressive acting out adolescents but little difference between the two groups in fear and external punishment scores. These data suggest that the aggressive acting out adolescents have weak internalized controls and that the restraint of aggression is dependent upon the likelihood of external punishment. MacCasland (1961) distinguished between manifestations of external and internal inhibition of fantasy aggression and also found external aggression inhibition scores to be unrelated to overt aggression while the measure of internal inhibition was inversely related to aggressive acting out behavior. The TAT stories of disturbed boys who obtained high aggression scores on a rating scale and on a behavior checklist contained fewer instances- of restraints, guilt, or remorse than the stories of low aggression scorers. MacCasland's method

for categorizing internal and external inhibition is similar to that employed by Purcell (1956), who obtained an inverse relationship between the extent of social behavior in a group of young adult males and the ratio of internal punishment to aggression in fantasy. The relationships found between measures of external controls and overt behavior were less striking than the correlations obtained for the internal inhibition measure.

Jensen's (1957) monograph comparing the TAT fantasies of overtly aggressive, passive, and assertive adolescent boys should also be added to the group of studies reporting an inverse relation between inhibition of fantasy aggression and overt aggressive behavior. Jensen's method of scoring inhibition included instances of both internal and external controls and consequently his findings are not directly comparable to those previously cited. An additional feature of Jensen's scoring procedure was the inclusion of a measure of the frequency of socially tabooed content and language, which proved to be the most discriminating of the TAT scores. The overtly aggressive boys were much more likely than either of the other groups to express socially taboo sexual content and other disapproved thoughts in their fantasies, and to make use of socially disapproved language in so doing. Although there may be a dynamic relationship between preoccupation with tabooed sexual themes and overt hostility, the most ready interpretation of this finding is in terms of the lack of control and defiance of propriety manifested in the testing situation and in the criterion situation.

It is a well known dictum in test construction that the predictive value of a test increases as a function of its similarity to the criterion. Greater similarity can be brought about by examining selected response dimensions, as Jensen did (1957), or by systematically modifying the stimulus properties of the standard TAT stimuli. Lesser, in the studies already reported, has utilized a set of 10 pictures of boys interacting which are particularly appropriate for the predictions of peer aggression. These pictures differ in ambiguity and aggressive "pull" and the responses to them have been shown to have the properties of an unidimensional Guttman Scale (Lesser, 1958b). The advantages of this instrument are reflected in the systematic relationships which Lesser (1957, 1958a) has reported between overt aggression and fantasy aggression and inhibition. The importance of TAT stimulus content for prediction is more directly illustrated in a study by Kagan (1956) in which he administered specially devised pictures to 6- and 10-year-old boys and used as a measure of overt aggression, teachers' ratings of the tendency of the boys to imitate fights. The stimuli were of varying ambiguity and depicted a boy interacting with another boy or with an adult. The results indicated that fighting themes were predominantly elicited by the boy-boy scenes and that the frequency of fighting themes was significantly higher in the aggressive than in the nonaggressive boys. Other categories of aggressive fantasy did not reliably relate to the criterion. It was also found that the stimulus picture most suggestive of fighting differentiated overtly aggressive and nonaggressive boys more successfully than the least suggestive picture. The failure to give aggressive themes to pictures suggestive of aggressive content is probably indicative of strong inhibition rather than weak aggressive tendencies. Thus, increasing the structure of the test provides greater predictive accuracy, although some of the advantages of projective tests in circumventing inhibition are lost.

In addition to stimulus properties of the TAT pictures and the response dimensions assessed, the relationships between fantasy and overt aggression have been shown to vary with characteristics of the population. Lesser (1957, 1959) obtained a significant positive correlation between fantasy aggression and peer ratings of aggression in boys whose mothers were relatively encouraging of aggressive behavior and a negative correlation, just short of statistical significance, for boys, considered likely to be high in anxiety, whose mothers tended to discourage aggression. Correlations obtained for the latter group of boys with other measures, such as the Rosenzweig Picture-Frustration study, were generally lower than comparable relationships obtained for the less anxious children. Studies of seriously emotionally disturbed children who tend to be anxious and also highly aggressive have generally yielded a pattern of relationships different from the results obtained with more normal children. McNeil (1962) found negligible relationships between anger in fantasy and daily recording of aggressive behavior in a sample of aggressive, antisocial boys attending a therapeutic summer camp. Significant relations were obtained only between fantasy in which the hero suffers and friendly, nonaggressive behavior. One would expect that a more overtly and uniformly aggressive population of children would, because of the restricted range, result in lowered correlations. However, inasmuch as Marquis (1961) found in a group of similarly disturbed children that aggression in fantasy relates positively to constructive behaviors and negatively to overt aggression, methodological explanations of the findings obtained for this population are not sufficient. If one assumes that many of these disturbed youngsters are in conflict and highly fearful, Marquis' findings and the negative relationship between fantasy and overt aggression reported by Lesser for his high anxious group suggest that fantasy may serve to control aggression in children who have strong aggressive impulses coupled with high anxiety.

The sex of the child is undoubtedly a relevant population parameter. However, the absence of information concerning the relationship between fantasy aggression and overt aggression in girls is noteworthy. The hypothesis concerning the role of aggression anxiety suggests that girls should tend to show inverse relationships between aggression in fantasy and overt aggression. There is little question concerning the importance of obtaining information concerning this issue and other aspects of female aggression. Investigations of the utility of fantasy and other techniques in predicting aggressive behaviors in girls would be of considerable empirical interest as well as having theoretical relevance to problems of sex differences in the control of aggression.

PATTERNS OF AGGRESSION

Age Changes

A comparative study of aggression at different age levels requires the use of standard situations or environmental settings in which the aggressive behaviors of children of varying ages can be observed. This ideal has rarely been approximated. Children at various age periods, toddlers, preschool and elementary school age children, have been studied under very different conditions and with different measures of aggression. Because of the variation in method of observation, one cannot readily determine whether a 6-year-old child, for example, is more aggressive than a 2-year-old. One can, however, make comparisons among different age groups with regard to the repertoire of behavior modes by which aggression is manifested. Generalizations concerning age changes are further restricted by sampling considerations, since most of the quantitative studies have been derived from observations of American children. Since even the most confirmed instinct theorist would agree that the intensity and forms of aggressive behavior are profoundly influenced by the child's experiences, the lack of cultural breadth places serious limitations upon any normative statement that can be made concerning children's aggression at different age periods. There is little doubt, however, that children in all cultures manifest aggressive behaviors with which each society deals in terms of its own values and socialization practices (Whiting and Child, 1953; Whiting, 1963).

Normative assertions concerning children's aggression are also restricted by the particular environmental setting in which the behavior was elicited. The degree and type of aggression observed in nursery school or in doll play are only weakly, if at all, related to the child's aggressive displays in the home (Korner, 1937). Thus a tabulation of the frequency of temper tantrums or of fighting at school may yield a statistic very different from a tabulation of the same behaviors in the child's home, and the age trends of these two samples of behavior may also differ. Studies of aggressive behavior in different contexts have, in fact, yielded conflicting age trends, in part due to the aggressive response and populations assessed as well as the varied setting. Moreover, within a particular setting such as nursery school, changes in aggression during the preschool period may be obscured by the substantial influence of the nursery school structure and atmosphere upon the frequency of aggressive behaviors occurring in that school (Body, 1955; Jersild and Markey, 1935; Muste and Sharpe, 1947; Roff and Roff, 1940).

Developmental changes in aggression in the preschool age range of 2 to 5 have been more thoroughly investigated than those in any other age period. Jersild and Markey (1935), observing children in nursery school, found an irregular decline in frequency of social conflicts with age, two of the three groups studied showing a negligible correlation. Concomitantly, crying and physical aggression decreased while the frequency of verbal aggression increased. Similar findings have been reported by Green (1933) and Bridges (1931), the latter study based on British schoolchildren. Decreased aggression with age is suggested by Dawe (1934), who obtained a decline in children's quarrels over the 2 to 5 age range. Several studies have failed to find any significant age differences in the aggression of preschoolers (McKee and Leader, 1955; Roff and Roff, 1940) while a number have reported more aggressiveness in the older nursery school children (Murphy, 1937; Muste and Sharpe, 1947; Walters, Pearce, and Dahms, 1957). Walters et al. (1957), in a study of 124 children, found little difference in the frequency of physical and verbal aggression, both increasing from ages 2 to 4 and leveling off at age 5.

The method used by Muste and Sharpe (1947) combines certain characteristics of free play interaction with the standardized doll play situation. In this situation, two children at a time were observed for 15 minutes after being exposed to a set of play materials. Each child was paired with every other child of the same sex in his nursery school. The experimenters report a correlation of +.54 between aggression and age (ranging from 2 years, 10 months to 5 years, 4 months). The type of aggression varied with the age of the subject and with the age of the playmate. Older children made relatively many more verbal demands on younger children, whereas the younger children were more prone to seize materials, especially from a child of similar age. These breakdowns in types of aggression are presented as percentages of total aggression rather than absolute frequencies and can best be interpreted as modal responses. Muste and Sharpe (1947) also obtained correlations between frequency of aggression and amount of time spent in social interchange and other positive social behaviors which increase with age. Thus they obtained a correlation of +.39 between sharing and aggression, a finding reminiscent of Murphy's (1937) earlier report of a positive relationship between sympathy and aggression.

The shift from parallel play to cooperative play during the preschool years provides greater opportunity for interpersonal conflicts as well as for more socially desirable interactions. From this vantage point, the doll play method in which the child plays alone with a set of designated objects should provide a clearer indication of aggressive trends, although, in other respects, the fantasy and self-centered nature of doll play may be considered a disadvantage. The results of the few studies that have related the age of the preschool child to aggression in doll play are no less ambiguous than those based on observations of nursery school behavior. In an investigation by P. Sears (1951), 150 children—25 boys and 25 girls at the ages of 3, 4, and 5—participated in two 20-minute doll play sessions. The correlation between overall aggression score and age was insignificant for girls and approached statistical significance for boys, the 3-year-olds tending to display less aggression than the 4- and 5-year-olds. A breakdown of the aggression scores revealed significant increases between the age of 3 and 4 in about one-fifth of the subcategories for both boys and girls. As in the Walters et al. (1957) study, the 4- and 5-year-old child displayed similar patterns of aggressive behavior.

In contrast with these findings, Ammons and Ammons (1953), using a doll play interview procedure, found a tendency for physical counteraggression to peak at age 3, while the variety of aggressive behaviors was greatest at ages 4 and 5. None of these differences, however, were significant. The Ammons and Ammons (1953) method, unlike the ordinary doll play procedure, presents the subject with a series of frustrating social interactions between two doll figures. The child is then asked to state what one of the dolls would do in the indicated circumstances. The method is similar to the Rozensweig Picture Frustration Test, but is adapted for preschool use.

The most consistent finding that emerges from these doll play and nursery school data is the indication of an increase in verbal aggression between 2 and 4 years of age. The development of aggressive verbal responses probably facilitates the maintenance of aggressive attitudes and behaviors through verbal mediation and may account for the regular increment Goodenough (1931) found between ages 1 and 8 in the duration of sulking and resentment following outbursts of anger. Goodenough's study was based upon daily parental records of aggressive outbursts of their children. Although this study is more than 35 years old, it still constitutes the most extensive, descriptive study of age changes in aggressive behaviors. The major limitation of the study is the small sample size of 26 boys and 19 girls ranging in age from 7 months to 8 years. Moreover, the sample was largely composed of children of professional parents, and generalizations from this study are further limited by the reliance on diaries kept by the mother. The data are, nevertheless, of considerable interest.

The increase in the duration of the aftereffects of aggression occurred after the age of 4, there being little difference between children under 2 and those in the 2- to 4-year age range. The frequency of aggressive outbursts, however, reached a peak for both sexes at the age of 2, gradually declining until about age 5. The mode of aggressive behaviors differs markedly over this age period. The proportion of undirected, temper-tantrum type aggressive acts decreases gradually during the first 3 years, and then shows a sharp decline after the age of 4. In contrast, the relative frequency of retaliatory responses increases with age, the greatest increment occurring after the child attains his third year. A response was classified as retaliative whenever there was "clear motor or verbal evidence of an attempt on the part of the child to secure revenge for an immediate injury" (p. 56). The increase in retaliatory responses can be taken as evidence for the development of aggressive drive as distinguished from the affective, undirected expression of anger.

The immediate antecedents of aggressive outbursts also vary with age. Desire for attention and minor physical discomforts constituted the primary occasions for anger display in the two infants who were under 1 year of age. Restriction of movements, which Watson had theorized to be the primary stimulus to anger in the infant, occurred as precursors to aggression relatively often in this age group in comparison to the older groups but accounted for only a small percentage of their total aggressive outbursts. During the second and third years, establishment of routine physical habits and authority conflicts proved to be major irritants. Social difficulties with playmates began to assume importance during the third year and became more significant as sources of aggression in subsequent years.

The age changes in the frequency and mode of aggression expression were accompanied by differences in the methods the parents report using in controlling aggression. Physical force, persuasion, diverting the child's attention, and ignoring of outburst were less frequently used with the older children, who, more often than their younger peers, were subjected to scolding, threatening, and isolation. Yielding to the child also decreased with advancing age, as the proportion of compromise solutions showed a steady increase. These data suggest that the parent is more authoritarian with the younger child and makes greater use of verbal controls as the child increases in age. An interesting methodological note was the lack of agreement obtained between statements made by the parent at the beginning of the study concerning methods used for the control of aggression and the actual records of their own behaviors during the ensuing period of observation. The parents tended to exaggerate, in their questionnaire response, the frequency of such methods as reasoning, appeal to self-esteem, and humor, while minimizing the use of negative sanctions. The diary procedure proved to be a useful compromise between direct observation and parental recollection, suggesting developmental trends in aggressive patterns which warrant additional investigation, employing larger and more representative populations.

Comparative age studies of aggressive behaviors after the preschool period are few in number and tend to deal with isolated observations. Feshbach (1956), in an investigation in which groups of children played for 50-minute sessions with either aggressive or nonaggressive toys, found that 7- and 8-year-olds engaged in reliably more fantasy aggression than did 5- and 6-year-olds when interacting with the aggressive toys, whereas the amount of aggression directed toward peers was similar for both age groups. This difference in fantasy behavior may be a function of greater aggressiveness in the older

group, which is displaced onto fantasy or may reflect a cognitive difference between the two age groups. Additional data are needed to verify and clarify this observation. A report by Bender and Schilder (1936), based on a study of 3- to 15-year-old patients in a children's ward, suggests that the propensity for the use of fantasy aggression does not extend to early adolescence. Their pre-adolescents and young adolescents were less free in expressing aggression in play and fantasy than the younger children. Rosenzweig and Rosenzweig (1952), using the Picture Frustration Test, also found the projective expression of direct aggression to decrease with age, extrapunitive responses declining from age 4 to age 13, while intrapunitive responses increased in frequency over this period.

The longitudinal study of the stability of aggressive behaviors constitutes still another approach to the problem of age trends. Tuddenham (1959), reporting on a follow-up of the Berkeley adolescent growth study, found a strikingly high correlation for male subjects between ratings of aggressive motivation obtained during adolescence and ratings based on interviews conducted when the subjects were approximately 33 years old. Greater stability of aggressive behavior for males than for females was also found by Kagan and Moss (1962) in their extension and analysis of the Fels longitudinal data. Ratings were made of personality attributes, including several dimensions of aggression, for each of four age periods—0 to 3, 3 to 6, 6 to 10, and 10 to 14. In addition, 71 of the 89 subjects for whom longitudinal ratings had been made participated in an assessment program as young adults. The correlations between age periods reflect a moderate degree of stability for several aggression-related variables. Physical aggression to peers was highly stable over the first 10 years. It was not rated for the 10 to 14 age range because of its low incidence during that period, an interesting finding in itself. Dominance and competitiveness, which were not rated for the earliest age period, and indirect aggression to peers also showed considerable stability. Aggression toward the mother during the first 3 years of life failed to predict subsequent aggression, and, overall, the stability coefficients for this dimension were variable, only adjacent age periods showing substantial correlations.

One might expect the mother to be less tolerant of hostile expressions directed toward her than she is to aggression toward peers, and the fluctuation in aggression toward the mother may reflect the influence of inhibition and changes in maternal attitudes toward aggression as well as changing feelings about her. The pattern of stability coefficients obtained for conformity to adult authority was similar in most respects to that found for the expression of aggression toward the mother. These two variables were highly negatively correlated in each age period and are probably assessing the same dimension. The variable of behavioral disorganization, a measure of diffuse anger reactions such as temper tantrums, violent crying, and rage, was consistently related to the ratings of aggression directed toward the mother. The occurrence of these diffuse anger reactions during the first three years was unrelated to subsequent manifestations of similar behaviors while, after this early period, behavioral disorganization displayed moderately high stability.

The Kagan and Moss data reflect a surprising degree of continuity in a number of aggressive behaviors. Aggressive predispositions manifested early in life, especially during the 3- to 6-year age period, persist into adolescence. Several of the adult measures indicate that these childhood behaviors are also correlated with aggression in adulthood. Aggression to the mother and behavioral disorganization during ages 6 to 14 were positively related to the ratings of adult aggressive retaliation, anger arousal, and competitiveness for males and negatively related to ratings of aggression anxiety and repression of aggression. Physical aggression and indirect aggression to peers were related to adult competitiveness for the males but not to the more direct aggressive measures. These findings suggest that peer aggression in males is a reflection of instrumental aggression rather than hostility or aggressive drive.

The relationship between ratings of childhood aggression and adult aggression was weaker and also more complex for the girls than for the boys. Physical aggression to peers by girls younger than age 6 was negatively correlated with adult competitiveness and, after age 6, with aggression anxiety. The mixed pattern for the girls suggests that early aggression is subsequently inhibited in

girls and is a source of conflict, at least in the middle-class sample studied by Kagan and Moss (1962), whereas in boys early aggression is a sex-appropriate response which is continuous with aggressive and competitive behaviors as an adult. One can, of course, also account for sex differences in the stability of aggression by emphasizing the role of constitutional determinants as well as by placing the explanatory burden upon cultural influences.

Sex Differences

Since the area of sex differences has been reviewed elsewhere in this book, we shall restrict our discussion to special issues concerning aggression and the sex of the child. A major factor distinguishing the two sexes at the behavioral level is the extent of participation in aggressive activities, particularly physical aggression. For many cultures, aggression, as epitomized in the young warrior, is the hallmark of masculinity. Boys are expected to be aggressive and even where parents discourage fighting, the activity may be perceived as a "natural" male activity which requires modulation only. Inhibition of aggression in boys may elicit labels of "sissy," "fairy," and similar epithets connoting feminine behavior. Conversely, the young girl who engages in fighting may be labeled a "tomboy" and her behavior considered "unladylike." Sears, Maccoby, and Levin (1957), in their study of child-rearing practices, found that the greatest distinction parents made in the rearing of boys and girls was in the area of aggression.

It is clear that the role demands placed by the culture upon boys and upon girls are a major source of sex differences in behavior. It is also evident that the pattern of aggression for each sex is not universal but is subject to considerable cultural variation (Mead, 1935; B. Whiting, 1963). More ambiguous and more difficult to establish are the effects exerted by constitutional determinants upon aggressive behavior. To state the issue in the form of biological antecedents versus cultural reinforcements is a gross oversimplification which precludes the examination of subtle developmental interactions. Constitutional differences may not lie in aggressive dispositions as such but rather in physical strength and in motoric impulses, which may lead to a different constellation of experiences and reinforcements for males and for females. The indications that newborn females have greater skin sensitivity (Bell and Costello, 1964; Weller and Bell, 1965) and pain sensitivity (Lipsitt and Levy, 1959) than newborn males provide examples of constitutional factors which, though not directly implicated in aggression, could exert a profound influence upon its development. For example, greater skin sensitivity might predispose the child to prefer more passive forms of bodily contact and to reduce its participation in subsequent rough-and-tumble activities which are prototypic of physical aggressive responses.

From a biosocial view, it is also reasonable to ask whether it is "easier" to facilitate aggressive behaviors in boys than in girls and what the implications of this training might be for other behaviors of the child. Operationally, the problem of the modifiability of an aggressive response pertains to the incentives, amount of practice, and reinforcement scheduling required to bring about a particular level of aggressive or nonaggressive performance. Thus it may require less effort for parents to inhibit physical aggression in girls than in boys. Conversely, it may take more effort to promote fighting behaviors in girls than in boys. Although exhibitions featuring female boxers might even be more profitable than the occasional spectacles of female wrestlers, female boxers are a rare phenomenon. It is in this sense of a predisposition to motoric aggressive responses that aggression may be a more natural response for males than for females. Evidence from several primate studies suggests that males are more highly disposed to such aggression than females. Harlow (1962) has reported that infant male Macaques manifest more aggressive behaviors when attacked than do infant female Macaques. Field studies of ground-dwelling old world monkeys have indicated that there is much more rough-and-tumble play among males than females and that their "play" behavior provides an opportunity to rehearse the aggressive behaviors the adult male will need to defend his group (DeVore, 1965). At the biochemical level, the administration of the male hormone, testosterone, to newborn female rats has been shown to enhance aggressive behaviors (Harris and Levine, 1967) and a similar observation has been made on female Macaques who were structurally and behaviorally influenced in a masculine direction by the prenatal administration of testosterone (Young, Goy, and Phoenix, 1964). Hamburg and Lunde (1966), in their review of the role of sex hormones in the development of sex differences, suggest that the primary effect of early exposure of the central nervous system to the male hormone may be to subtly predispose the organism to the subsequent acquisition of aggressive behaviors rather than to establish a fixed, enduring, aggressive response structure.

Evidence of biological determinants of sex differences in human aggression would not minimize the significance of cultural and individual experiential factors. Such factors may reinforce or exaggerate constitutionally rooted differences or completely overwhelm them. Whatever the relative potency of these determinants, an appropriate subject of inquiry is the interaction over time between constitutional dispositions and the cultural milieu. Moreover, confirmation of biological determinants does not, in itself, resolve the question of the optimal level of aggression for each sex. The problem of how aggressive a girl and boy ought to be entails considerations of values, role demands, and interrelationships between aggression and other areas of behavior. The dimensions of aggression also need clarification. The readiness to inflict injury should be distinguished from the readiness to engage in physical aggression. The animal findings pertain only to the physical aggression and a similar restriction may hold for sex differences in human aggression. The concept of aggression when applied to sex differences in behavior also carries connotations of dominance-submissiveness hierarchies which are governed by differences in physical strength and aggressive prowess (Scott, 1958). The position in the dominance hierarchy will influence the animal's activity in competition for food and sex partners. In addition, physical aggression typically is a vigorous behavioral act carried out when the organism is excited, and its reinforcement may foster more active behavior patterns. At the human level, physical aggression is only one of a number of instrumental behaviors which can be employed to overcome a competitor or some other form of frustration. Consequently, we would expect that the relationships among dominance, activity, aggression, and sex in humans would be greatly attenuated except in very primitive social structures.

Studies of sex differences in children's aggression have shown boys to be more aggressive than girls when direct physical aggressive responses are assessed. Where other forms of aggression are measured, the findings are much less consistent. An excellent summary of this literature has been provided by Oetzel (1966) and is duplicated in Table 1. The studies are categorized by the method of observation and the age of the sample; the nature of the differences obtained is also specified. It can be seen that sex differences

Table 1. Sex Differences in Aggression: Summary of Studies

Study	Age	Sex Group with Higher Scores	Comments
		Observational Studies	
Dawe, 1934	Nursery school	Boys	Boys participated in more quarrels
Green, 1933	Nursery school	Boys	Boys had more quarrels
Sears et al., 1953	Nursery school	No diff.	Total aggressive responses—boys slightly higher, but not significantly so
Sears et al., 1965	Nursery school	Boys— No diff.	In 7 out of 10 types of aggression Verbal disapproval, tattling, and prosocial aggression
Jersild and Markey, 1935	2-5	Boys No diff.	More physical quarrels Verbal quarreling
Muste and Sharpe, 1947	2-5	No diff.	Boys slightly more physical and girls slightly more verbal aggression
McKee and Leader, 1955	3-4	No diff.	Pairs of children playing
Siegel, 1956	3-5	Boys	Like-sex pairs playing
McCandless et al., 1961	3½-5	Boys	Initiated more conflicts and resisted attack more frequently
Siegel et al., 1959	5	Boys	In type of interaction, aggression was rank order 3 for boys, and 7 for girls, out of 9 possible categories
Walters et al., 1957	2-5	Boys	Aggressive contacts with peers
Whiting and Whiting, 1962	3-6	Boys	Physical aggression in six cultures
		Rating Studies	
Hattwick, 1937	2-4½	Boys	Negativistic behavior
Beller and Neubauer, 1963	2-5	Boys	Mothers' reports of hyperaggression and hyperactivities in clinic children
Beller and Turner, 1962	Preschool	Boys	Several subscales of aggression
Sears et al., 1957	5	No diff.	Mothers' reports
Beller, 1962	5½-6	Boys	General aggression
Digman, 1963	6-7	Boys	Teachers' ratings—more negativistic, aggressive, noisy

Table 1 (Continued)

Study	Age	Sex Group with Higher Scores	Comments
Feshbach, 1956	5-8	Boys	Teachers' ratings
Toigo et al., 1962	8	Boys	Nominated by peers as more aggressive
Tuddenham, 1952	8 and 10	Boys	Considered more quarrelsome by peers
Sanford et al., 1943	5-14	Boys	Teachers attributed aggression more to boys

Experimental Studies

Study	Age	Sex Group with Higher Scores	Comments
Bandura et al., 1961	Nursery school	Boys No diff.	Imitative physical aggression Imitative verbal aggression
Bandura et al., 1963	Nursery school	Boys	Total aggression and nonimitative aggression
Bandura et al., 1963	Nursery school	Boys	Imitative and nonimitative aggression
Bandura, 1965	Nursery school	Boys	Aggressive acts
Hartup and Himeno, 1959	Nursery school	Boys	More doll-play aggression with isolation as a precondition
Hicks, 1965	Nursery school	Boys	Imitative aggression
Moore, 1964	4-6	Boys	Directed aggression with less displacement after frustration
Jegard and Walters, 1960	4-6	Boys	Hitting a punch toy after frustration
Buss, 1963	College	Men	Aggressive to a frustrating "victim"

Projective Tests

Study	Age	Sex Group with Higher Scores	Comments
Sanford et al., 1943	5-14	Boys	TAT aggression
Spache, 1951	6-13	Boys	Outward aggression toward peers on the Rosenzweig P-F Test
		Girls	Outward aggression toward adults on the P-F Test
Sarason et al., 1965	College	Men	Formed hostile rather than neutral sentences in sentence completion
Lindzey and Goldberg, 1953	College	No diff.	TAT protocols
Kagan and Moss, 1962	20-29	Men	Recognized more tachistoscopic pictures of aggression

Self-Report

Study	Age	Sex Group with Higher Scores	Comments
Sears, 1961	12	Boys Girls	Antisocial aggression Prosocial aggression
Gill and Spilka, 1962	12-18	Boys	Manifest hostility (Ss were Mexican-Americans)
Lansky et al., 1961	13-18	Boys	Aggression toward father, self-rating on aggression
Rothaus and Worchel, 1964	College	Men	Hostile to an E before and after hostility arousal

Table 1 (Continued)

Study	Age	Sex Group with Higher Scores	Comments
Wyer et al., 1965	College	Men	Direct expression of aggression
Bennett and Cohen, 1959	15-64	Men	Overt aggressiveness
		Women	Covert hostility
Fantasy Aggression in Doll Play			
Bach, 1945	Preschool	Boys	Hostile, aggressive acts
Sears, 1951	Preschool	Boys	Direct physical aggression
		No diff.	Verbal and indirect aggression
Sears et al., 1965	Nursery school	Boys	Antisocial and total thematic aggression
Pintler et al., 1946	3-6	Boys	Aggressive themes
Moore and Ucko, 1961	4-6	Boys	Aggressive responses to home problems
Durrett, 1959	4-6	Boys	Total and physical aggression
		Girls	Verbal aggression
Gordon and Smith, 1965	Nursery school and 6 years	Boys	Overall aggression
Anxiety and Guilt about Aggression			
Sears, 1961	12	Girls	Self-report, aggression anxiety
Buss and Brock, 1963	College	Women	Guilty about having been aggressive to a "victim"
Rothaus and Worchel, 1964	College	Women	TAT aggression anxiety
Wyer et al., 1965	College	Women	Guilt over aggression

(Complete references for all studies cited may be found there.)

in aggression are present at the age of 2 and persist into adulthood. The number of studies in which males are reported to be more aggressive than females far exceeds the reports of no differences plus the few instances of greater aggression in females. The exceptions to the overall trend are instructive. Reversals and the absence of differences tend to occur when verbal and indirect forms of aggression are assessed. One cannot determine from these data whether the verbal and covert forms of aggression are a substitute for more direct aggressive expression or represent response modes that are differentially reinforced and inhibited.

Additional evidence suggesting that girls make greater use than boys of indirect forms of aggression has been reported by N. Feshbach (1965) and in a masters dissertation by one of her students (Sones, 1968). In the first of these studies, two-person, same-sex groups of 6- to 7-year-old children were established and a same- or opposite-sex peer was subsequently introduced to the group. Observations of the children's response to the newcomer showed the girls to be more unfriendly and rejecting than the boys. A similar finding was obtained with junior high school adolescents where pairs of boys and pairs of girls were given the opportunity to interact with a same-sex newcomer. In addition to sex differences in attitudes toward the newcomer as measured by a questionnaire administered after the experimental session, the girls engaged in less participation with the newcomer than the boys, more often rejected the newcomer's suggestions, and were also more critical of the newcomer. It would be premature to infer from these findings that girls are more hostile than boys. However, these data along with evidence that girls are higher in prosocial forms of aggression (Sears, 1961) and also have more conflict over aggression (Kagan and Moss, 1962) and greater aggression anxiety than males (Feshbach, 1967; Sears, 1961) suggest that the difference between boys and girls in aggression does not lie in the strength of aggressive drive but in the mode of behavior by which aggression is manifested. The evidence is compelling that boys are more physically aggressive than girls, yet a different pattern of results is obtained when more indirect, nonphysical forms of aggression are evaluated.

An apparent exception to the generalization concerning sex differences in physical and verbal aggression has been reported by Mallick and McCandless (1966). Girls of 8 and 9 years, in comparison to same-age boys, expressed less dislike on a rating scale toward a sixth-grade child who had been a source of frustration. However, there were no sex differences in the extent to which they pushed a button which in one experiment presumably resulted in the delivery of electric shock and in a second experiment could interfere or facilitate the older child's success on a task. The authors note that the children were assured they could not be detected and that in a permissive situation, girls may behave just as aggressively as boys. To explain the like-dislike difference obtained in the study quoted above, it might be argued that the expression of aggressive feelings in this form is more overt and direct and subject to greater aggression anxiety than the button-pressing response. Although the delivery of shock is generally considered to be a direct form of physical aggression and has been shown to differentiate adult males and females (Buss, 1963), it differs from more usual forms of physical aggression that have been studied in that it entails minimum bodily involvement. Fighting and the delivery of punishment through pressing a particular button are very different modes of response, although both may produce physical pain. The hypothesis is proposed here that sex differences in aggression are direct functions of the amount of large muscle involvement in the performance of an aggressive act.

Variations in mean aggression scores as a function of the sex of the child provide one source of information concerning the development of aggression in males and females. Also relevant are differences between the sexes in the relationships of aggression with child-rearing and personality variables. In view of the fact that, in general, aggression is more tolerated in boys than in girls and that there may also be constitutional factors contributing to sex differences, the implications of a high aggression score for a girl should be different from the meaning of the same score for a boy. In one case aggression is deviant from and in the other consistent with the social role ascribed to that sex. The route to deviance is likely to be different from the route to social conformity. The Kagan and Moss (1962) finding of greater stability of aggressive behaviors in males than in females is consistent with what would be predicted on the basis of the sex-typing of aggression. Lansky et al. (1961) have reported greater consistency among measures of aggression in male than in female adolescents. However, there were more significant associations between aggression and other behaviors for girls than for boys. For boys the focal measure of aggression was aggressive imagery on the Rorschach, which was negatively related to interviewer ratings of conformity but, surprisingly, was positively related to a measure of femininity. In addition, aggression in boys was positively correlated with the free expression of dependency strivings. For girls, high aggression was associated with achievement preoccupation, low affiliation, anxiety about sexuality, and other measures suggesting a "masculine" orientation. Because of the large number of correlation coefficients calculated, the specific patterns obtained must be considered tentative until cross-validated. Regarding dependency, there have been several studies indicating low positive correlations in boys between aggression and dependency (French, 1964); Sanner, 1964) while evidence of strong dependency conflicts in aggressive, acting out adolescent boys has also been reported (Bandura and Walters, 1958).

Differences in child-rearing antecedents of aggression in boys and in girls have been found in a number of studies, although, as a review later in this chapter will indicate, there are many instances of common relationships. A number of these differences reflect the differential impact of the parental model and socializing agent upon same-sex and opposite-sex children (Gordon and Smith, 1965; Levin and Sears, 1956; Sears, 1961). The presence or absence of the father in the home has been related to sex differences in the development of aggression. Bach (1946) found that 6- to

10-year-old boys whose fathers were absent from the home due to military service engaged in fewer aggressive doll play fantasies involving the father than boys whose fathers were present in the home. While girls displayed less aggression than boys, a similar relationship between aggression in girls and the presence or absence of the father was obtained. Sears (1951; Sears, Pintler, and Sears, 1946) also reported less doll play aggression in preschool boys as a result of the father's absence from the home but found no difference in aggression between father-absent and father-present girls. In addition, by the age of 5, the effects of the father's absence upon boys' aggression were barely discernible, the principal difference occurring at ages 3 and 4. At these younger ages, the level of aggression of the father-absent boys is about equal to that for the girls. It is not clear why the father-absent boys "catch up" in the Sears study, whereas in the Bach study they maintain lower aggression scores.

Correlates of a self-administered aggression-anxiety scale were obtained by Sears (1961) in a study of 12-year-olds whose mothers had been interviewed when the children were 5. The data suggested that aggression anxiety in boys is part of a conformity syndrome, related to nonpermissiveness of impulse expression in a love-oriented home. In girls, high aggression anxiety was associated positively with measures reflecting instigation to aggression at age 5 and, more generally, with conditions that appear to be antithetical to appropriate sex-typing. This pattern of correlates of aggression anxiety in girls was only partly confirmed in a study by Oetzel (1964) in which she compared the following groups: girls with high feminine interests at ages 5 and 10; girls whose mothers indicated they were tomboys at both ages; girls who changed from a tomboy at age 5 to feminine interest at age 10; and "average" girls who scored at the mean of the total sample at both ages. The feminine girls were higher in aggression anxiety than the tomboys and were somewhat less aroused by an aggressive role playing situation. However, the prediction that the girls who became more feminine between ages 5 and 10 would show high aggression anxiety because of a need to inhibit their earlier masculine-aggressive tendencies was not substantiated by the data. The re-

sults, contrary to the hypothesis, indicated that high anxiety was associated with an increase in masculinity from 5 to 10. This particular outcome may have been due, in part, to the tolerance of early tomboy behavior in the highly educated, middle-class sample of parents who were the participants in the study.

The Sears (1961) and Oetzel (1964) data and the results of the studies of the effects of father's absence upon aggression in boys and in girls are consistent with the view that sex differences in the correlates of aggression are a consequence of the masculine typing of aggressive behavior. Again, explanations relying either on social role variables or on constitutional determinants can account for much of these data. There is little question that social role and child training variables exert a major influence upon the differential development of aggression in boys and in girls. Nevertheless, the possible importance of constitutional factors cannot be dismissed. However, much less is known regarding the mechanisms by which constitutional as compared to social reinforcement variables might affect aggressive interactions in humans.

If constitutional factors relevant to differences in aggression are largely matters of muscularity, one should expect to find within-sex variations in aggression associated with differences in physique. Demonstrations of significant relationships between physique and aggression are, of course, subject to the same alternative interpretations that have been offered for sex differences. Both physique and degree of aggressiveness could be manifestations of the same underlying biological structure. This is essentially Sheldon's position (1944). Differences in physique might also influence the success of instrumental aggressive responses. A strong, muscular child should experience greater reinforcement for physical aggressive acts than a weaker child. Finally, because of cultural stereotypes regarding temperament and physique, there might be differences in the reactions of socializing agents to children of varying physiques. A parent might *overprotect* a thin, asthenic child but accept and even encourage aggressive responses from his muscular sibling. The theoretical ambiguity of the findings notwithstanding, the empirical relationships are of interest for predictive purposes and because they still have some bearing upon the utility of explanations of differences in aggression based on constitutional factors.

Studies of physique and behavior have generally used Sheldon's (1944) typology of ectomorphy, mesomorphy, and endomorphy for classifying the physique of the child: ectomorphy denotes a slender, linear body; mesomorphy refers to the predominance of muscle, bone, and connective tissue; endomorphy is primarily defined by roundness of physique and highly developed viscera. Of particular interest is the mesomorphic body type, which Sheldon hypothesized to be related to the trait dimension of somatonia, which has a strong aggressive component. Sheldon's (1944) initial findings of very strong correlations between physique and temperament have been criticized because of possible rater bias and because of the overlap of physique items with the temperament rating scale. Nevertheless, there have been several studies in which a positive relationship has been found in children between mesomorphy and an index of aggressive disposition. Davidson et al. (1957), in an investigation of physique, temperament, and intellectual functioning in 7-year-old children, found that mesomorphs, as seen by their mothers, were more dominant and assertive than ectomorphs or endomorphs. Walker (1962) obtained a similar positive relationship between aggressiveness as determined by teacher ratings and mesomorphy for a younger age group of preschool boys. Evidence of a predominance of mesomorphy in delinquent boys has been reported by Sheldon (1949) and by Glueck and Glueck (1950). The Gluecks matched 500 delinquent with 500 nondelinquent boys for IQ, age, ethnic origin, and residential area. Impressive differences between the two groups in physique were found, the ectomorphs being grossly underrepresented and the mesomorphs generally overrepresented among the delinquents when compared with their matched controls. Although delinquency is a complex, socially defined act rather than a personality attribute, there is ample evidence that delinquents are more hostile, impulsive, and overactive than nondelinquents (Capwell, 1945; Hathaway and Monachesi, 1953; Glueck and Glueck, 1950).

Although additional research relating variations in physique to particular modes of aggressive expression is needed, there appears to be a relationship between muscularity and aggressive acting out behavior. The clarification of the source of this relationship will ultimately depend upon detailed studies tracing the development of aggression in children of varying sex and body types.

Another factor which has been shown to vary in importance, depending upon the sex of the child, is birth order. Studies of birth order effects on samples ranging from preschoolers to adults have, with a few exceptions, indicated that first born children are less aggressive than their later-born siblings, who generally tend to show weaker impulse controls (Goodenough and Leahy, 1927; Patterson and Ziegler, 1941; P. Sears, 1951). These effects have been especially evident in male children (Koch, 1955; MacFarlane, Allen, and Honzik, 1954), although Pauline Sears (1951) found significantly greater doll play aggression in later-born females as compared to first-born females, the trend for the males failing to attain statistical significance. Conflicting evidence has been obtained for females, several studies reporting the first-born to be more aggressive than later-born female children (Koch, 1955; MacFarlane et al., 1954). A number of possible explanations might account for the apparent interaction between birth order and sex of the child and there is little empirical basis for deciding among them. Evidence that only children tend to be high in aggression (Goodenough and Leahy, 1927; Sears, 1951; Wile and Davis, 1941) suggests that the lesser aggressiveness of the first-born male child is due not only to his greater dependency upon and identification with adults, but also to the presence of younger siblings in the family. Since boys tend to be more overtly aggressive than girls, parents may have to exercise more restraint in preventing older boys from manifesting aggression toward siblings. The possibility that the subtle influence of birth order may significantly modify sex differences in aggressive behavior is intriguing and well worth additional exploration.

Social Class and Cultural Factors

The concept of social class is a sociological dimension denoting, among other implications, a patterned set of experiences of importance for various areas of psychological development. One of these areas is anger and aggression. Earlier studies of social class differences in aggression have consistently indicated that middle-class families suppress impulse expression, including the inhibition of aggressive behaviors, whereas lower-class families exercise fewer controls over their children's display of anger and aggression (Aberle and Naegele, 1952; Bettelheim, 1952; Davis, 1943, 1947, 1948; Havighurst and Taba, 1949). Davis, in describing the impulse-free quality of the lower-class subculture, makes the following comments:

To express violent anger is a tremendously gratifying and cathartic experience. In its end forms of hitting, aggressive behavior is a basic goal response and one which middle class and upper class people learn to inhibit only at the expense of great strain and anxiety. The necessity of continually repressing the aggressive impulse is a conflict which lower class children escape. . . . For this reason, the lower class person, unlike the lower middle class individual, does not have to endure in his class world the feelings of incoherent rage and helplessness which result from the chronic suppression of aggressive impulses (1943, p. 614).

There are two assertions made in this statement, the validity of each being independent of the other. One is the generalization that aggression is suppressed in middle-class families and permitted, if not encouraged, in the lower class. Second is the assumption that the inhibition of aggressive impulses is psychologically maladaptive. We shall return to this issue at the end of the chapter, noting only that this assumption can be controverted. The relatively simpler matter of class differences in aggression is also subject to question, more recent studies yielding conflicting findings.

The view that punishment for aggression tends to be more severe in middle- than in lower-class families was initially questioned by Maccoby and Gibbs (1954). The lower-class mothers of their preschool sample reported using more severe forms of punishment in disciplining aggression than did the middle-class mothers. Subsequent research has generally confirmed the Maccoby and Gibbs findings, and has indicated that middle-class

parents tend to be warmer, less restrictive, tend to make greater use of psychological punishment, and are less likely to employ physical punishment than lower-class parents (Bronfenbrenner, 1958; Kohn, 1963; Miller and Swanson, 1960). An exception to this pattern has been reported by Lefkowitz, Walder, and Eron (1963), who found negligible relationships between social status and their inventory of punishment for aggression. Absence of a relationship between the use of physical punishment and social class has also been reported by Kohn (1959). Of interest is Kohn's finding that lower-class parents tend to be more concerned with the potential damage a child's behavior might inflict while the middle-class parents were more oriented toward determining the aggressive intent of the child, although they employed a similar degree of physical punishment. The Lefkowitz et al. (1963) finding of class similarity in punishment for aggression may have been influenced by the sample of parents interviewed who were selected from a semirural area rather than urban centers. It is likely that social class differences in the socialization of aggression will vary with social structure within class levels and also with ethnicity, although Davis and Havighurst (1946) did find social class effects overriding the influence of the ethnic variable of race. Nor can it be assumed that social class patterns will remain invariant over time. Some of the discrepancy between the earlier and late data may reflect a change in the middle-class tolerance of impulse expression (Bronfenbrenner, 1958). Part of the discrepancy may also result from procedural differences and from the inferences that were drawn from the data since both Davis (1943) and Havighurst and Taba (1949) comment on the violence and use of physical punishment in the lower-class home.

A correlate to the initial conception of the lower classes as more indulgent of aggression than the middle classes was the implication that lower-class children express aggression more freely than middle-class children. Evidence that children from lower-class backgrounds tend to be more aggressive than middle-class children has been reported in studies by Goldstein (1955), McKee and Leader (1955), and Stoltz and Smith (1959). Sears et al. (1957), however, found that social class was unrelated to the aggression reported by mothers of preschool children. Similarly, no difference was obtained by Bene (1958) between English middle- and working-class adolescent boys in the degree to which they suppressed aggressive responses on a self-report inventory. A further complication is introduced by the Eron et al. (1963) study in which sociometrically derived aggression scores of high-status boys proved to be significantly higher than the scores for the middle- and low-status boys. A similar but nonsignificant trend was obtained for the girls. In a more refined analysis of these same data, breaking down occupational level into nine categories, Toigo (1965) found a small, significant curvilinear relationship between occupational status and aggression for the combined sample of boys and girls. Children whose parents were at the extremes of the occupational status hierarchy tended to be more aggressive than children from the middle status ranks. The data showed children of rural, farm background to have the highest level of aggression of any of the groups in the sample. These results held with classroom context controlled, although the latter also contributed to the variance in aggression scores.

The data bearing on the relationship between the social class background of the child and his aggressiveness are contradictory and not easily reconcilable. In order to attain clearer empirical generalizations, the psychological factors theoretically linking social class and aggression need to be more systematically investigated. Such factors include the socialization techniques employed and also the degree of frustration and other instigations to aggression experienced by children from different social strata. Miller and Swanson (1960) have demonstrated that within the middle-class there are important differences in the psychological environment of children raised in entrepreneurial versus bureaucratic social settings. The lower-class is no less heterogeneous and distinctions among lower-class subgroups might reveal social substructures which are more homogeneous in behavior and in impact upon the child.

The social organization and pattern of living in rural as compared to urban areas provide a variable that might sharply modify class-linked practices related to the develop-

ment and expression of aggression. Madsen's (1966) comparative study of urban and rural Mexican and American (U.S.) 8- to 10-year-old children revealingly illustrates rural-urban differences. A sentence completion test, in which the stem described a frustrating situation, was used to assess the expression of manifest aggressive tendencies. A second measure of manifest aggression, teachers' rankings, was applicable only to within-group analyses. The Rorschach Test was administered as a measure of covert aggression. The results showed the urban Mexican children to be the most aggressive on the sentence completion measure while the rural Mexicans obtained the lowest scores of the four groups. The means of the rural and urban North American children were similar on this measure. In contrast to these findings for verbalized aggressive tendencies, the rural children in both Mexico and the United States obtained significantly higher covert aggression scores on the Rorschach than did their urban counterparts. In all four settings, the boys' mean Rorschach aggression scores were higher than those of the girls. This finding is rather surprising in view of the negative correlations found between Rorschach aggression and teachers' rankings of aggression, particularly in the rural Mexican sample, which also showed an inverse relationship between the Rorschach and the sentence completion measure. The rural Mexican children lived in a closely knit cooperative society which exercised marked restraint over the direct expression of aggression. The data are consistent with the hypothesis that the blocking of overt aggressive reactions in these children facilitated the displacement of aggression to indirect response modes that are not punished by the society. The hypothesis is further supported by a separate phase of the study, which indicated that sixth-grade children from this same rural Mexican community were much more rejecting of social deviancy than sixth graders from the other three groups.

In contrast with Toigo's (1963) findings, the Madsen (1966) study indicates that rural children tend to express aggression in a covert, as compared to urban children, who use a more overt manner. It is possible that the data reflected a class difference since the rural children came from less economically advantaged backgrounds than did the urban samples. However, it is also evident that social class and rural-urban distinctions inadequately describe the striking differences in life style that exist in a rural Mexican village and in an urban Mexican community, nor do they capture the more subtle differences between the particular North American rural and urban communities from the Pacific Northwest that had been sampled.

Personality Correlates

It is evident from the investigation of group differences in aggression that there are different routes to the development of aggressive behaviors and that personality studies are not likely to yield a general personality composite, descriptive of *the* aggressive child. The significance of aggressive behaviors varies with the sex and age of the child and also with the nature and context of the aggressive act. The child whose aggressive responses require his incarceration or institutionalization is probably qualitatively as well as quantitatively different from the child who is quick to react with overt aggression and also quick to forget. In addition, from a theoretical standpoint, it is possible to make directly opposite predictions regarding the relationship of aggression with such personality dimensions as need for nurturance, achievement strivings, and anxiety, depending upon the relative strengths of motivational and response parameters that influence the manifestations of these traits.

Since the aggressive child is, in most cultures, a deviant child whose behavior is socially disruptive, it can be anticipated that, at a gross level, he will display other maladaptive attributes. Butcher (1965) administered the M.M.P.I. to eighth-grade boys who had been categorized as high, middle, or low in aggression on the basis of teacher ratings and peer nominations. Both the high and low aggressive boys proved to be more disturbed than the boys whose aggression scores fell in the middle range. The low aggression boys were more neurotic, withdrawn, and socially inhibited while the high aggression boys were more rebellious, excitable, and schizoid. However, in a study by Magee (1964), high and average aggressive boys in grades 3 to 6 did not differ on a measure of impulsiveness or on subsets of items selected from the psychopathic deviate

scale of the M.M.P.I. and the Gough delinquency scale. Magee did find that the self-perceptions of the high aggressive boys were more negative than those of the average aggressive boys.

In contrast to Magee's findings, a negligible relationship between self-esteem and aggression for tenth-grade boys has been reported by Toews (1966); in this same study a significant inverse relationship was obtained for girls. Since aggression is a more acceptable behavior pattern for boys than for girls, one might expect to find the correlation between indices of adjustment and aggression to be more greatly attenuated in boys than in girls. Silverman (1963), on the basis of an analogous argument, hypothesized that self-esteem and aggression should be negatively related in middle-class children but indifferently related in lower-class children for whom aggression was assumed to be a more normative behavior. His results, based on measures of fifth to eighth graders, were consistent with these hypotheses. Also suggestive of low self-esteem in aggressive children are findings indicating that these children are more likely to feel rejected by their parents than are less aggressive children (Bandura and Walters, 1959; French, 1964).

In considering the relationship between self-esteem and aggression, a distinction should be made between persistent aggressive behaviors and an aggressive response to a provocation. Although an individual with high self-esteem may be low in aggressive motivation and may typically behave in a nonaggressive manner, he may be freer to respond aggressively to provocation (Licht, 1967). Similar considerations apply to the relationship between anxiety and aggression and between dependency and aggression. Children who are low in anxiety and dependency may be less inhibited in expressing aggression when unfairly treated than are children who are easily threatened and concerned with affection and support from others, who may be more hostile. The relationships obtained between aggression and such response systems as anxiety and dependency will be influenced by the degree to which these response patterns are specific to aggression-instigation situations or represent more general behavior tendencies. Thus generalized anxiety, assessed by the children's manifest anxiety scale, has been shown to be positively correlated with aggression as determined by peer nomination in a study of 9-year-old boys (Ross, 1963), while aggression-anxiety has been shown to be negatively correlated with peer nominations of aggression and a self-report measure of antisocial aggression in 11- and 12-year-olds (Sanner, 1964; Sears, 1961). Aggression-anxiety, though inversely related to direct aggressive expressions, appears to be positively correlated with socially acceptable, morally justified aggressive attitudes (Sanner, 1964; Sears, 1961).

Studies relating dependency and aggression have yielded conflicting results. Sears et al. (1953) obtained a positive correlation between dependency and aggression in preschool age children, attributing this relationship to the correlation of both variables with the activity level of the child. Sears, Maccoby, and Levin (1957) found a small positive relationship between aggression toward parents and dependency for girls but not for the boys. Winder and Rau (1962) obtained a strong positive correlation between aggression and dependency in a sample of preadolescent boys, using a sociometric device, the Peer Nomination Inventory, to assess both variables. However, the peer rating measure is affected by the general "likeability" and social deviance of the subjects nominated, a factor which would tend to inflate the correlation between subcategories of the instrument. An interesting study by Beller (1959) of aggression and dependency in a group of emotionally disturbed nursery school children demonstrates the importance of employing more refined analyses of aggression. He found that dependency was positively correlated with destructive aggressive behaviors but was negatively correlated with assertive, instrumental aggressive acts. The Kagan and Moss data (1962) reflect the utility of distinguishing between different types of dependency, as well as aggression. Before age 6, generalized dependency is weakly, although negatively related to aggression toward the mother and aggression toward peers. For boys, the inverse relationships tend to become stronger after age 6, a highly significant negative correlation being obtained between aggression toward the mother and affectionate dependency in the 10- to 14-year-age period. For girls in this age period, the correlations tend to

be positive, particularly the relationship between aggression toward the mother and instrumental dependence. In view of the large number of correlations reported in the Kagan and Moss study, these data must be interpreted with caution. Nevertheless, the pattern of correlations reflect the utility of the empirical distinctions made in assessing several types of dependency and aggression.

These distinctions can account for part but not all of the inconsistency in the relationships reported between aggression and dependency. Bandura and Walters' (1959) comparison of highly aggressive adolescent boys with a normal control population indicated that the aggressive boys were significantly less dependent upon their parents than the controls. However, in a subsequent study of 6- to 10-year-olds, aggressive boys proved to be more dependent than an inhibited group of boys (Bandura, 1960). It is unlikely that the age difference is the critical factor responsible for the discrepancy. The Lansky et al. (1961) study suggested that aggression is positively correlated with dependency in adolescent boys, whereas Kagan (1958) reported a nonsignificant tendency in 6- to 10-year-old boys, who are high in aggression, to respond with fewer dependency themes on a thematic apperception measure than a comparable group of boys low in aggression. French (1964) observed 8- to 10-year-old boys who were attending a summer camp and found a negligible relationship between a sociometric measure of aggression and an overall measure of overt dependency behaviors. However, aggression was positively correlated with attention-seeking responses. The association between aggression and attention seeking is confirmed by Sanner (1964), who found that a positive correlation between aggression and dependency was largely due to the attention-seeking component. Moreover, in factor analyzing the data, attention seeking emerged as a marker of general aggressiveness.

There are a number of other personality attributes of theoretical interest which have been related in scattered studies to some aspect of children's aggression. Recent psychoanalytic models of children's behavior have placed increasing emphasis on the development of ego controls and their role in the regulation of impulse expression. Evidence of a link between these control factors and aggressive behavior in preschool children is provided by two studies in which negative correlations were obtained between measures of ego control and aggressive behaviors (Block and Martin, 1955; Livson and Mussen, 1957). The inverse relationship of ego control and aggression did not appear to be a function of the child's general maturity since age variations were controlled and, in addition, dependency was unrelated to ego control (Livson and Mussen, 1957). Shifting to an older age group, studies of late-maturing adolescent boys as compared to early maturers (Mussen and Jones, 1957, 1958) indicate that the physical status of the child may exert a significant influence upon core personality dimensions, physical retardation apparently resulting in adverse effects. The later maturer feels more inadequate, rejected, and dependent and is also rated by observers as more aggressive and rebellious than the early maturer. Although more overtly aggressive, the later maturer expressed less hostility in fantasy (TAT) than the early maturer.

In confirmation of the hypothesis that the rebelliousness of the aggressive child should make him more resistant to social influence, Lesser and Abelson (1959) obtained negative correlations between aggression and persuasibility. Roland's (1962) data indicate this relationship is curvilinear, both high and low persuasibility boys being more aggressive than medium persuasibility boys. The high persuasibility subjects displayed more aggression anxiety and initial inhibition of aggressive responses than did those of low persuasibility. If we assume that a moderate degree of responsiveness to social influence is more adaptive than either high conformity or nonconformity, these results provide still further evidence of the association between aggressiveness in children and behaviors indicative of maladjustment. To this list should be added the positive correlations of aggression with reading disability (Norman and Daley, 1959; Spache, 1954) and underachievement in school (Shaw and Grubb, 1958).

An interesting problem area, and one which has been only barely investigated, is the relationship between aggressive behavior and the development of empathy and other positive social feelings. Observation by an empathic child of the consequences of an aggressive act directed toward another child should tend to elicit distress responses in the observer even if he himself is the instigator of the aggressive act. These vicarious, painful responses provide feedback to the child, which can be expected to function as inhibitors of the child's own aggressive responses; thus children high in empathy should manifest less overt aggression than children low in empathy (Feshbach, 1964). In apparent contradiction to this hypothesis, Lois Murphy (1937) obtained a positive correlation between teachers' ratings of aggressive behavior in nursery school children and ratings of sympathetic behaviors which in a number of instances were similar to empathic responses. She notes, however, that both aggressive and sympathetic responses are instances of socially oriented behavior, and the correlation can be attributed to their common relationship with the social maturity of the child during the pre-school period.

Feshbach and Feshbach (1968) investigated the relationship between empathy and aggression in preschoolers and in a 6- to 7-year-old sample. The measure of aggression was based on teacher ratings while empathy was elicited by presenting the subject with a series of pictorial sequences, each conveying an affective experience of a child. The degree to which the subject's self-reports of his affective reactions matched the affect depicted by the stimuli constituted the measure of empathy. A positive relationship, similar to that reported by Murphy, was found between empathy and aggression for the younger age group. Consistent with the prediction, the relationship was reversed for the older children. Experimental support consistent with this proposed inhibitory effect of empathy upon aggressive behavior is provided by Aronfreed and Paskal's (1968) demonstration of the conditioning of an empathic response and subsequent reduction in the administration of a painful stimulus. An intriguing aspect of the possible role of empathy in regulating aggression is the analogy to aggression-inhibitory mechanisms in animal species. Empathy unfortunately appears to be much more vulnerable to disruption than animal inhibitory processes and more information is needed concerning its development and the circumstances that affect its stability and influence.

ANTECEDENTS OF AGGRESSION

Studies of age, sex, social class and other group differences in aggression provide useful descriptive data and also offer insight into the factors influencing the development of aggressive behaviors. Their inclusion in the previous section on group differences was based upon methodological and content criteria rather than upon conceptual issues to which they may have been addressed. These studies are clearly relevant to questions pertaining to the antecedents of aggression. The antecedents will be reviewed more fully in the present section, which is subdivided into two principal areas. The first is concerned with the experimental analysis of motivational and learning mechanisms mediating the acquisition and performance of aggressive behaviors. The second is concerned with similar issues, as reflected in the context of child-rearing antecedents of aggression. Although two studies may be concerned with the same problem—for example, the effects of frustration as determined through experimental goal blocking or through assessing variations in the age of weaning—the methodologies employed are so very different with respect to the procedures and measures used that it is useful, in considering the antecedents of aggression, to group the studies according to the methods employed as well as the experimental questions investigated.

Experimental Manipulation of Antecedents

Frustration. Very shortly after the publication of *Frustration and Aggression* (Dollard et al., 1939), Miller (1941) and Sears (1941) amplified the role of learning in altering the response to frustration. The instigation to aggression, rather than an inevitable reaction to frustration, was viewed as a prepotent response in a family of responses whose respective probabilities could be sharply modified by their reinforcement history. Serious questions have nevertheless been raised and still persist regarding the viability of the frustration-aggression hypothesis (Bandura and Walters, 1963; Buss, 1961; Sargent, 1948). These questions have been concerned with (1) distinctions among the kinds of frustrating situations that elicit aggression, (2) the specificity or generalized nature of

the affective response to frustration, (3) the utility of singling out aggression as a unique reaction to frustration (rather than, for example, withdrawal), and (4) the role of stimuli other than frustration which appear to be powerful instigators of aggression.

Agreement as to what constitutes a frustrating event has proved to be troublesome. Varying degrees of emphasis have been placed upon external interferences as a defining criterion (Buss, 1961; Dollard et al., 1939) and upon the internal affective reaction to goal blocking (Amsel, 1958; Brown and Farber, 1951). Buss has noted that frustration can occur through the blocking of instrumental behaviors by externally imposed barriers such as delay and by internal conflict between incompatible responses. He also lists, as sources of frustration, omission of rewards through failure to achieve a goal and through preventing the individual from making the appropriate consummatory or goal response (Buss, 1961, pp. 17-20). He further raises the relevant question as to whether the diverse operations subsumed under frustrations are functionally similar. It is certainly evident that having empirically demonstrated a relationship between one mode of frustration and aggressive reactions one cannot readily generalize this relationship to other forms of frustration. Without a clear conception of the operations that define the set of frustrating events that are theoretically linked to aggression instigation, the construct power of frustration as an antecedent of aggression is seriously limited.

It has been pointed out by Maslow (1941) that frustrations which threaten the organism's basic ego and security needs are much more likely to evoke hostile reactions than frustrations which entail physiological drive deprivation. Rosenzweig's (1944) categorization of aggressive responses to frustration is based upon a similar emphasis upon the ego-threatening properties of the frustration. He distinguishes between need-persistive and ego-defensive reactions to frustration. Ego-defensive behaviors are categorized into extrapunitive responses in which aggression and the attribution of blame is directed toward external persons and things, intrapunitive responses in which the aggression and blame are self-directed, and impunitive responses in which aggression is denied or absent. The particular significance of ego threat as an antecedent of hostility may also be reflected in the distinction made between frustration and attack (Buss, 1961; Levy, 1941), although Buss has emphasized the role of the noxious stimuli inflicted by physical attack rather than its ego threat implications.

Whatever the mediating mechanisms may be, both observation and experimental data indicate that physical attack is a potent elicitor of aggression. Graham, Charwat, Honig, and Welty (1951) found that junior high school students responded with much stronger aggressive reactions to hypothetical situations in which a protagonist was physically attacked than situations in which he was subjected to criticism and less direct forms of attack. Buss (1963), using college students and a situational measure of aggression as the dependent variable, reports that the infliction of physical pain is a much stronger instigator of aggression than response interference.

It is evident that the differences in aggression produced by supposedly qualitatively different types of frustration can be attributed to quantitative variations in the degree of goal blocking each category of frustration entails. Berkowitz (1962), who is sympathetic to a modified frustration-aggression hypothesis, argues that the distinctions made by Maslow, Rosenzweig, and other critics of the frustration-aggression hypothesis do not represent exceptions to the proposition but rather describe situations that vary in the degree of frustration they impose. He makes a similar observation regarding the demonstration that arbitrary frustrations will elicit aggressive reactions while the same frustrations imposed in a nonarbitrary or accidental manner are much less likely to elicit hostility (Cohen, 1955; Pastore, 1952). Arbitrary frustrations, such as deliberate as compared to accidental tripping or the failure to obtain a job because the employer was capricious rather than the position's having been filled previously, entail the violation of expectancies and often ego injury as well. Reference group theory tells us that the frustrating properties of a deprivation depend on the extent of deprivation relative to cultural norms of expectation rather than on the absolute degree of deprivation. A low income in a fixed social structure with little opportunity for economic mobility, or a society in which the same economic level characterizes all members, is much less frustrating than the same income in a fluid society where there is not only evidence of disparities in income but also expectancies for economic improvement. A similar analysis holds for other patterns of behavior. We expect some degree of discomfort in a crowded subway car and when our feet are stepped on in this context, we react with less anger than when they are unnecessarily and deliberately stepped upon. The implicit expectancies present in all social situations can be conceptualized as subgoals or goal related, and negative discrepancies from these expected behaviors and their consequences then correspond to goal interferences or sources of frustration.

In the writer's judgment, it is more important to determine the kinds of interfering events that are most likely to evoke hostility and aggression than to salvage the universality of the frustration-aggression hypothesis through extensions of these concepts. The observation that ego injuries are particularly potent elicitors of hostility, if substantiated by further research, provides insights into the development of aggression which are not present in any obvious manner in the frustration-aggression hypothesis. It suggests, for example, that parental rejection of the child should produce more aggressive children than severe weaning or toilet training. The proposition that arbitrary or intentional frustrations are more likely to elicit aggression than unintentionally or accidentally posed frustrations also raises important developmental questions which are not implied by the concept of frustration as such. Arbitrary frustrations may entail more goal blocking than unintentional frustrations and therefore, as Berkowitz suggests, evoke more aggression. However, social learning may also exert a significant role in determining the response to different types of frustration. Certainly it would appear that socializing agents exert a great deal of effort in teaching children to discriminate between intentional and accidental infliction of injury.

Our expectations that children make a cognitive distinction between these two antecedent factors is reflected in one of the comprehension items on the Stanford-Binet (Terman, 1916, 1960): "What's the thing for you to do if a playmate hits you without meaning to do it." In order to be given credit for the item, the child is required to offer a nonaggressive response. Responses such as "I would excuse him," "I would not fight or run and tell on him" are also considered satisfactory, whereas the manual (Terman, 1916; p. 217) lists such responses as "I would hit them back," "Would not play with him," and "He is supposed to say 'excuse me,'" as unsatisfactory. The item is included at the 8-year-old level, fewer than 50% of children under 8 giving the socially correct response, which requires the child to have a concept of intentionality and apply it to social sources of frustration. This discrimination is probably acquired by the child through the same kinds of processes of instruction, modeling, and differential reinforcement as other learned discriminations. Parents respond very differently to a child's destructive act if they believe it is to be "deliberate" than if they view it as an "accident." Within the accident category even finer distinctions are made as to the degree of carelessness entailed in this unintended event. The punishment which the child may receive is gauged to the parents' appraisal of his responsibility for the act; severer forms of punishment are usually reserved for deliberate destruction, with acts of carelessness also receiving some form of negative sanction. If the child is not judged in any way responsible for the destruction, the probability of no punishment is increased. This differential treatment of destructive behavior according to its motivation is formally recognized in our legal codes.

The child, then, is exposed to a number of socializing influences which foster discrimination among types of frustrations and determine the matching of aggressive and nonaggressive responses to these discriminations. Implicit in this analysis is the assumption that aggression is readily elicited by strong frustration, whether innately or through very early social conditioning. The problem of socialization is the training of nonaggressive reactions to provocations which inevitably occur in the course of social living. The assumption implies that the child does not have to be taught to be angry when he is subjected to frustration, although, of course, the strength and mode of instrumental aggres-

sive behaviors are highly dependent upon learning, and the linkage between frustration and anger can also be enhanced through direct reinforcement or modeling. It seems unlikely that in the course of the discrimination process we have outlined, the affective response to frustration is eliminated through extinction. Rather, it is probably inhibited by negative sanctions or replaced by the strengthening of other reactions.

A question may be raised as to the "fate" of the aggressive impulse under these circumstances. The response to this question depends upon one's theoretical orientation. From a learning theory point of view, the aggressive tendency may never be activated and expressed, in direct or disguised form, if the nonaggressive response tendencies have been adequately learned and strengthened. However, when the competing response tendencies are similar in strength, one can expect to find evidence of conflict and indirect aggressive expression. Moreover, should nonaggressive responses be weakened through nonreward or through disruptions in mediating cognitive controls, for example, under conditions of excitement, there may be a loss in discrimination of the intentionality of a frustrating action. Aggressive reactions which are not characteristic of past behaviors may be evoked. One can then expect to find that the response to frustration will vary between individuals and also within the same person, depending upon past learning experiences, constitutional factors, and the stimulus context in which the frustration occurs.

Evidence for the unlearned basis of the frustration-aggression relationship is most readily obtained in animal studies. Seay and Harlow (1965) frustrated 6-month-old rhesus monkeys by separating them from their mothers and observed their subsequent interactions with peers. They found the monkeys exhibiting aggressive behavior toward peers despite the fact that aggression in rhesus monkeys is quite rare at this age. If one views pain as a form of frustration, then the Hutchinson, Ulrich, and Azrin (1965) study, in which electric shocks were found to produce fighting in pairs of rats raised in isolation from the time of weaning, can be taken as support for the aggression instigating properties of frustration. Rather striking evidence of aggression following frustration, although not in organisms reared in isolation, is provided by Azrin, Hutchinson, and Hake (1966). These investigators trained pigeons to peck at a keg for food, using a 100% reinforcement schedule. When food was suddenly withheld, the bird would vigorously attack another pigeon who had been placed in the cage. They report additional observations indicating that the attack behavior was not simply a displacement of the bar-pressing response.

Animal studies further indicate that the absence of a reinforcement in situations where the organism has been typically rewarded has aversive stimulus properties with functions similar to those of punishment (Amsel, 1962; Azrin et al., 1966; Ferster, 1957; Ulrich, 1966). There is also evidence that frustrative nonreward has energizing effects on behavior (Miller and Stevenson, 1936; Amsel and Roussel, 1952; Wagner, 1959). It appears, then, that certain frustrations, having energizing and noxious properties, will foster aggressive behaviors when appropriate stimulus targets are present. While acknowledging the gap between observations of animals and inference about humans, it seems reasonable to assume as a working hypothesis that frustration can have similar noxious, energizing, and aggression-eliciting functions for children.

One of the earliest studies of the effects of frustration on children is that of Sears and Sears reported in the book *Frustration and Aggression* (Dollard et al., 1939, pp. 28–29). The feeding of a 5-month-old baby was systematically interrupted by removing the bottle after he had ingested differing amounts of milk. The latency of crying was the criterion measure. Their data indicated that the time between the removal of the bottle and a crying response increased with the amount of milk ingested before interruption. Crying is an undifferentiated emotional response, and whether it reflects aggression is equivocal. Although it would be tenuous to consider the crying reaction an index of aggressive drive (i.e., the motivation to inflict injury), it seems reasonable to view it as a possible manifestation of rage or anger. Using the amount of milk drunk as an inverse measure of drive strength, the findings are consistent with the hypothesis that the effects

of frustration vary with the intensity of the drive instigated behavior that is thwarted.

With increasing age, the anger reaction becomes associated with instrumental aggressive behaviors while grosser affective expressions such as crying may be inhibited or modified. Nevertheless, as temper tantrums demonstrate, the constellation of crying, anger, and frustration in children persists well beyond infancy. There have been few experimental data that bear on the relationship between frustration and these rather dramatic affective reactions since investigators, of necessity, have studied relatively mild forms of instrumental aggression and anger. For ethical reasons alone, children can be subjected to only limited amounts of experimentally manipulated degrees of frustration. Experimenters have experienced difficulty in implementing even relatively weak frustrating procedures because of the restraints which humane adults have against arbitrarily exposing children to possible pain (Frederickson, 1942). In view of these necessary and laudable restrictions, it is not surprising that there is conflicting evidence concerning the aggression-instigating effects of frustration. Burton (1942), in a study of factors influencing satiation on a pegboard task in preschool children, incidentally observed aggressive reactions in a number of the children as they experienced satiation. Negative evidence is reported by Yarrow (1948), who compared changes in doll play in preschoolers resulting from the introduction of satiation, failure, or success (control) prior to a second doll play session. The failure procedure consisted of giving the child a difficult tinker toy to assemble, while the method of inducing satiation was similar to, but not as prolonged as that employed by Burton. All groups, including the success group, increased in aggression during the second session. Neither of the frustration groups showed greater increase than the controls.

Jegard and Walters (1960) similarly failed to find an increase in aggression following frustration in nursery school children, although in the description of the frustration procedure it is reported that several of the children manifested signs of anger. As Jegard and Walters note, the striking of an inflated toy punch-bag, which constituted the primary measure of aggression, may have a playful rather than hostile significance. Perhaps a similar statement can be made about the popping of balloons. Mussen and Rutherford (1961) frustrated a group of first-grade pupils by having them perform a repetitive task of copying numbers while their teacher criticized their performance. The children were then shown either an aggressive cartoon, a nonaggressive cartoon, or no cartoon, following which they were asked a series of eight questions concerning their desire to pop a balloon. The same procedure was carried out with a nonfrustrated group of children. There was little difference between the frustrated and nonfrustrated children in the number of aggressive responses on the balloon test, although the measure was sensitive to the cartoon variation.

Evidence of increased aggression following mild, repeated frustration of nursery school children is reported by Otis and McCandless (1955). Experimenter and child played a game in which each pushed a toy car starting from opposite ends of a road. For eight such trials, the experimenter's car would meet the child's car at the middle of the road, thereby presenting an obstacle to the child's movement. The child's response to this frustration was scored as dominant-aggressive or submissive-complaisant, depending upon his insistence upon his own car passing or his yielding to the experimenter. Children previously rated by their teachers as high in power-dominance gave more dominant aggressive responses and showed a greater increase over the eight trials than children lower in power-dominance. A similar finding was obtained for children rated low in love-affection as compared to those rated high in love-affection. There is some question whether the dependent measure is more closely related to assertiveness than it is to aggression. The increase in dominant-aggressive responses over the last four trials suggests an aggressive component, paralleling the increase in aggression observed in successive doll play periods.

A number of other studies employing diverse operations for assessing aggression have found increments in aggressive tendencies resulting from frustration (Miller and Bugelski, 1948; Moore, 1964; Mallick and McCandless, 1966). In the frequently quoted experiment by Miller and Bugelski (1948), boys attending a work camp were required to take a long series of boring and difficult tests instead of attending "bank night" at a local movie, an event which they had been eagerly anticipating. Attitude questionnaires toward Mexicans and Japanese administered before and after this frustration reflected a reliable decrease in the number of favorable traits ascribed to these groups. Using a more direct measure of displaced aggression, Moore (1964) found that highly frustrated boys ranging in age from 4 to 6, who had lost chips that could be exchanged for a toy, fired a pop gun significantly more often at figure cards associated with the loss of these chips than boys in low frustration and control groups. No experimental effects were reported for girls, who, under all conditions, fired the pop gun less often than did the boys.

Increases in doll play aggression in both boys and girls were found by Hartup and Himeno (1959) in preschool children following social isolation. Children in the isolation condition were left alone for a 10-minute period while a control group participated in social interaction with an adult. Measures of doll play aggression taken before and after the experimental intervention showed a significant increase in the isolation group while the controls failed to manifest the increment in aggression usually observed from the first to the second doll play session. Therefore, one cannot ascertain whether the observed difference is due to the evocation of competing nonaggressive responses by the control condition or the arousal of aggression by the dependency deprivation and the activity frustration fostered by the isolation condition. Significant differences in aggression in both boys and girls following frustration were also obtained by Mallick and McCandless (1964) in a series of three experiments on catharsis in which a sixth-grade "confederate" interfered with completion of a task for which third graders were to receive a reward. The measures of aggression in these studies included the administration of shock, interference with the sixth grader's performance, and assessment of dislike of the frustrator. The condition combined the use of sarcastic remarks along with task interference, and the consistent increments in aggression in both sexes may well have been due to the ego injury inflicted by the sarcasm.

It is a maxim of personality research that there are systematic individual differences in the response to changes in the social environment, and the frustration-aggression relationship is no exception to this rule (Block and Martin, 1955; Waterhouse and Child, 1953; Otis and McCandless, 1955). The classic study of Barker, Dembo, and Lewin (1941) demonstrated that children display varied reactions when frustrated, including aggressive behavior toward experimenters and toward a barrier interposed between the child and a highly attractive set of toys. Replicating the principal features of this study, Block and Martin (1955) were able to identify a personality dimension that predicted the child's response to the interposition of the barrier. Whereas the Otis and McCandless study had assessed individual differences in motivational dispositions, Block and Martin obtained measures of self-control abilities, including ratings of the child's degree of ego control as displayed in the nursery school and situational tests determining the child's persistence in a monotonous task and the degree to which he could delay gratification. The children whose scores on these measures reflected weak ego controls gave predominantly aggressive responses when prevented access to the attractive toys, whereas the "overcontrollers" played constructively with less attractive toys which were still available to them.

In addition to studies of individual predispositional sources of variations, there have been investigations demonstrating situational and learning effects upon the child's response to frustration. Wright (1942, 1943) introduced pairs of close friends and casual friends of preschool age into the attractive toy-barrier situation. The close-friend pairs showed less of a decrement in constructiveness of play than the casual pairs, were more cooperative and *less* hostile toward each other, and reacted with more joint aggression toward the experimenter, who was the source of their frustration. These data suggest that direct aggressive responses to frustration were inhibited and this inhibition was reduced by the support provided by the presence of a good friend. Part of the aggressive influence upon children of exposure to aggressive adult models (Bandura and Huston, 1961; Bandura, Ross, and Ross, 1961, 1963)

and of aggression training (Davitz, 1952; Walters and Brown, 1963) may be due to a similar mechanism of reduced inhibition as well as to a strengthening of aggressive response tendencies. Impressive differences in aggressive free play following frustration were demonstrated by Davitz (1952) in 7- to 9-year-old children who had been differentially reinforced for aggressive and constructive behavior. After seven 10-minute training sessions in which half the groups were praised and given recognition for aggressive behaviors and half for cooperative, task-oriented responses, the children were led to believe they would be shown several movies. During the second reel, the movie was interrupted as it approached its climax and a candy bar was taken away from the children. A free play session, in which the children were filmed, followed these frustrations. The children who had been trained to respond aggressively in competitive game situations displayed more aggression in free play than the group trained in constructive activities, who responded more constructively.

This study has been interpreted as demonstrating "both the inadequacy of the frustration-aggression hypothesis and the importance of direct training in the development of aggressive modes of response" (Bandura and Walters, 1963a, p. 382). The second part of this conclusion appears to be justified by the data but the first part is questionable. Perhaps if one had assessed the children's responses to the source of frustration, evidence might have been obtained of aggressive behavior in both experimental groups. Also, Walters and Brown's (1963) finding that a similar frustration has a negligible effect on the play behavior of this age group suggests that children aged 7 to 9 may be better able to tolerate minor frustrations than those of preschool age. The pain or tension induced by the frustration may be weaker in the older children who, at the same time, have a larger repertoire of coping responses. These developmental trends in reactions to frustration should be considered along with the demonstrations by Updegraff and Keister (1937), Davitz (1952), and Walters and Brown (1963) that the response to frustration can be modified by training. The initial statements of the frustration-aggression hypothesis specifically eschewed but did not deny the role of instrumental training. The significant finding that frustration reactions can be modified does not negate the hypothesis that the instigation to aggression is a potent reaction in the hierarchy of responses to frustration.

There is more general agreement that frustration increases drive, the issue being whether the drive is aggressive or nonspecific. A number of studies with children have found, consistent with the previously cited animal experiments, an increase in the strength of responses concomitant with or immediately succeeding a frustrating event. Haner and Brown (1955) assigned grade school children the task of placing a designated number of marbles into holes, promising the child a reward if he had four successful trials. The subjects were failed at varying distances from the goal in terms of the number of holes filled, a loud buzzer signaling the end of each trial. The subject terminated the buzzer by pushing a plunger and the amount of pressure exerted on the plunger was recorded. A positive relationship was obtained between the intensity of frustration, defined by proximity to the goal, and the pressure placed on the plunger. Haner and Brown considered the degree of pressure exerted as a measure of aggression, a questionable equivalence (Buss, 1961, p. 21). The study, however, does support the hypothesis that frustration has drive properties and will lead to more vigorous responding. Similar findings were obtained by Holton (1961), who varied response strength as well as distance from the goal. Preschool children pressed one of two identical stimulus panels for marble rewards which were exchangeable for toys. Two groups of subjects received the same number of reinforcements but differed in nearness to completion of the task when nonreward was introduced. A third group received half the number of reinforcements but was near completion when the reward was omitted. All groups of subjects showed an increase in response vigor on the first four nonreinforced trials, subjects who received the larger number of reinforced and who were blocked nearer to the goal showing the greatest increase. Both the Holton and the Haner and Brown studies indicate that the intensity of response to frustrative nonreward is a function of the strength of the frustrated response. Supporting evidence for this relationship has been provided in studies employing speed as a response measure (Penny, 1960) and experimental extinction for reward omission (Longstreth, 1960; Screven, 1954).

Frustration produced by delay rather than omission of reward has also been shown to increase response strength. In a study by Olds (1953), preschoolers were trained to crank a token machine a specified number of turns of the crank for each chip received. These chips subsequently could be traded in for penny goods. Measures of the amount of effort the child expended in cranking the machine were taken. During the testing situation, delay of reward was introduced by varying the number of turns required to turn the crank for each chip. It was found that the amount of force exerted on the crank increased from the training to the test situation in those groups who were subject to a delay in testing relative to the number of turns required in training.

These studies are consistent with the Brown and Farber (1951) formulation of frustration as an internal affective state which can energize behavior. The behavior may be aggression, withdrawal, button pressing, or any other response pattern that is dominant in the frustrating situation. Bandura and Walters (1963a) further suggest that mild responses which are initially not classified as aggressive are considered aggressive when the response is intensified. They pose the interesting possibility that the evocation of so-called "aggressive" responses under conditions of frustration may represent a quantitative change in response magnitude rather than a qualitative change in the content of the behavior. The Bandura and Walters (1963a) reinterpretation of the frustration-aggression hypothesis poses a tenable alternative to the proposition that frustration tends to elicit a motive or tendency to inflict injury. However, it does not provide a satisfactory account of those experimental studies in which the change of behavior resulting from frustration is a choice of an aggressive option rather than an intensification of a response (Mallick and McCandless, 1966; Miller and Bugelski, 1948). Here one has to appeal to prior learning to account for the preference for aggressive alternatives in certain frustrating situations.

Experiments demonstrating that frustration

energizes behavior do not negate the possibility that frustration may also elicit aggressive response tendencies. These studies were not designed to detect aggressive behaviors. The child was given only one option—that of pressing a plunger, turning a crank, or pushing a panel. Under these same stimulus conditions, if provided by the response opportunity, he might have expressed dislike of the frustrator and even chosen to punish him. The situation must provide adequate response alternatives and, as Berkowitz has shown in a series of studies of college students (Berkowitz, 1964; Berkowitz and Buck, 1967; Berkowitz and Green, 1962), the presence of appropriate aggression-eliciting stimuli facilitates the evocation of aggressive tendencies which may otherwise have not been expressed. Buss (1961, p. 61) makes a similar observation in suggesting that displacement of aggression requires a provoking target as well as an angry individual.

These situational requirements coupled with the influence of previous learning place important restrictions upon the utility of the frustration-aggression hypothesis. The relationship between these two variables is clearly more complex than indicated in the original formulation. The terms "frustration" and "aggression" and the conditions under which frustration will elicit aggressive tendencies require additional specification. In addition, a detailed developmental study of the child's response to various frustrating stimuli is very much needed. One might posit that initially strong frustrations tend to elicit rage or anger responses (Feshbach, 1964). Rage can be defined as a noxious affective state, characterized by agitated motoric behavior and differentiated from fear in that the organism approaches rather than withdraws from the provoking stimulus. It is also likely that there are physiological differences between fear and rage, although this question is still very much at issue. The diffuse movements of the child—hitting, kicking, biting— may become more focused and directed toward the frustrating stimulus if they succeed in removing the frustration, thereby strengthening the relationship among frustration, anger, and instrumental aggressive responses. To rephrase the frustration-aggression hypothesis, "in this early stage of development (from infancy through approx-imately the second year), frustration produces an instigation to hit rather than to hurt" (Feshbach, 1964, p. 262). The acquisition of the motivation to inflict injury, as distinguished from discharge of affect and elimination of a disturbing stimulus, poses a second developmental issue. It has been suggested that aggresive drive is learned as a consequence of secondary reinforcement (Sears, 1958) or internalization of social norms (Feshbach, 1964) and is closely related to efforts at the restoration of self-esteem (Feshbach, 1964; White and Lippett, 1960; Worchel, 1960). To the extent that this theoretical distinction has merit, the evocation of the instigation to inflict injury (aggressive drive) by frustration is dependent upon the age of the child and his learning history.

Reinforcement. The review of group differences in aggressive behavior has indicated the importance of cultural values concerning aggression and the reinforcements, or lack thereof, provided for different modes of aggressive responding. Aggressive behavior may be elicited by nonfrustrating stimuli that have been associated with past reinforcement of the aggressive response in the absence of frustrating, painful, or other stress conditions. When viewed in this manner, aggressive behaviors are conceptually no different from other instrumental acts and should be subject to the same laws of reinforcement, extinction, discrimination, and generalization. The reinforcers for the aggressive act may be such noninjurious events as approval, toys, candy, or other material and social rewards that have been shown to influence children's learning.

The analysis of aggression as an instrumental response is largely an outgrowth of the theoretical and technical advances in the investigation of operant behavior. Earlier indices were primarily concerned with the modification of aggressive behaviors, whereas more recent interest has been in the reinforcing contingencies governing the acquisition and generalization of the aggressive response. Chittenden (1942) demonstrated that aggressive preschoolers can be trained to make less competitive, socially approved responses, while Updegraff and Keister (1937) taught nursery school children to respond in a constructive manner to frustration. Their report is of particular interest inasmuch as their subjects showed a striking decrement in aggressive responses to frustration and an equally striking increment in the time spent in task oriented behaviors after a 6-week training session in which they were taught to make constructive responses to a series of tasks of gradually increasing difficulty. Reference has already been made to the study by Davitz (1952), who, through the encouragement of aggression in one group of children and constructive behavior in another, demonstrated the generalization of these behaviors to a free play situation.

Successful manipulation of aggressive behavior in 3- to 4-year-old boys through the use of operant procedures has been demonstrated by Brown and Elliot (1965). After 1 week of observation to establish base rates, the nursery school teachers directed their attention, as far as possible, to cooperative or nonaggressive behaviors while ignoring aggressive acts. A 2-week treatment period was followed by an interval of 3 weeks, after which a second 2-week treatment period was initiated. The results reflected a striking decline in physical and in verbal aggression during the second week of the experimental periods. Verbal aggression did not recur after the first treatment, whereas physical aggression did, possibly because the teachers found it more difficult to ignore fighting than to ignore verbal threats.

Lovaas (1961) has reported on the interaction between two aggressive response modalities. The effects of reinforcement of aggressive verbal responses upon nonverbal behaviors were investigated in a sample of 14 nursery school children. Half of the children were reinforced with trinkets for verbally aggressive responses to a doll figure such as "bad doll," "doll should be spanked," while half were reinforced for emitting nonaggressive verbal responses. For the latter group an effort was made to avoid reinforcing friendly, affectionate verbal responses in order to minimize the possibility that any subsequent difference in aggressive responding between the two experimental groups might be due to the reinforcement of behaviors incompatible with aggression. Following the training period, children were given an opportunity to play for a 4-minute period with two pieces of equipment, a "striking doll apparatus," which was arranged so that by depressing a lever the child could make one doll strike another on the head with a stick, and a ball-toy consisting of a ball which could be flipped up and down inside a cagelike structure by depression of a lever. The child had been familiarized with both pieces of apparatus before the verbal reinforcement training session. During the training session, a marked increase in verbal aggression was obtained in the subjects rewarded for verbally aggressive responses. An analysis of the subject's behavior during the subsequent play period indicated a significantly higher mean proportion of doll striking than ball tossing responses in the group reinforced for verbal aggression as compared to the group reinforced for nonaggressive verbal behaviors. There are several possible explanations of these findings: the aggressive verbal response acting as a discriminative stimulus for the aggressive nonverbal behavior, or as a verbal mediator, reduction in aggression anxiety, the sharing of common reinforcing stimuli by the two verbal and nonverbal aggressive behaviors, etc. Central to all these alternatives is the functional relationship between verbal and motoric aggressive response systems and the finding that alterations in one can produce alterations in the other.

Walters has carried out a series of studies in which parameters influencing the acquisition and generaliation of aggressive responses have been examined (Cowan and Walters, 1963; Hops and Walters, 1963; Walters and Brown, 1963). In each of these studies, the striking of an inflated, automated Bobo doll was reinforced by the delivery of a marble. In the first experiment (Cowan and Walters, 1963), 29 boys between the ages of 8 and 13 institutionalized for emotional problems and a noninstitutionalized public school sample matched for age, were assigned to one of three reinforcement schedules—100% reinforcement, fixed ratio on a three-trial interval, and a fixed ratio on a six-trial interval. No differences were found during an operant period or while reinforcers were being dispensed. However, differences appeared during extinction. The institutionalized children took longer to extinguish than the normals and the FR_6 partial reinforcement schedule resulted, as anticipated, in the largest number of trials to extinction for both samples. The authors suggest that the greater resistance of the institutionalized children to extinction is a function of their higher emotional arousal and drive level. An alternative interpretation can be offered in terms of the added strengthening of the aggressive operant through fear reduction in the emotionally disturbed children. In either case, the implication that it may be more difficult to modify the aggressive behavior of disturbed than emotional children, although the behavior was acquired under similar circumstances, is an interesting one to pursue.

In a subsequent study Hops and Walters (1963) investigated the effects of emotional arousal by experimentally manipulating isolation and anxiety in first- and second-grade public school children before placing them in the aggression reinforcement situation. A 2 × 2 factorial design was utilized in which isolation was manipulated by having children wait alone or on the playground for a 20-minute period before the experiment, and anxiety was varied by the experimenter acting in either a cold and brusque or friendly manner. Neither of these variables produced any effects in the second-grade children, possibly because the experimental manipulations were less threatening for them as compared to the first graders. For the first graders, the anxiety condition resulted in a higher response rate during reinforcement and both anxiety and isolation produced greater resistance to extinction.

A reservation which inevitably occurs in connection with these experiments is the relevance of the Bobo doll situation to more realistic aggressive phenomena. The previously cited study by Walters and Brown (1963) was addressed to this issue. Seven-year-old boys were assigned to one of two reinforcement or control conditions, and following a frustrating or nonfrustrating experience, each participated with another child in competitive games similar to those used by Davitz (1952). They were also observed in a brief free play session. The children who had been reinforced on a fixed ratio 1:6 schedule manifested significantly more aggressive responses, other than the pushing and shoving demanded by the games, than did groups who had been either continuously reinforced, who had not been reinforced, or who had not been previously exposed to the Bobo doll, there being no significant differences among the three latter groups. These results indicate that intermittent reinforcement for aggressive behavior toward a doll object increases the probability of aggressive behavior toward another child.

This demonstration of generalization of aggression from a fantasy object to an interpersonal situation is a significant finding. Its full implication cannot be ascertained, however, without a better understanding of the factors mediating the experimental effect. The gamelike quality of the test situation, even though involving some free play, could be a critical variable mediating the generalization. Moreover, if one adopts a cognitive framework, it becomes relevant to ascertain the meaning of the experimental situation for the child and determine precisely what was reinforced. Thus instead of simply the hitting response being strengthened, the child, under the partial reinforcement schedule, may have learned that in order to gain the approval of the experimenter (signified by a marble) he must emit a substantial number of aggressive responses. It would have been interesting to determine whether the aggression training would have generalized if the child had been taken out of the experimental situation and had been observed interacting with peers on the playground.

A detailed analysis of the acquisition of aggressive behaviors in a naturalistic setting has been reported by Patterson, Littman, and Bricker (1967). Aggressive events occurring among 3- to 4-year-old children were recorded for approximately 60 sessions in two middle-class nursery schools over a period of 26 weeks. For each aggressive event, the act, the consequence provided by the victim, and the teacher's behavior were noted. Ratings were also made of activity level and intensity of verbal and motor behavior. It was postulated that the consequences of an aggressive response would be a critical determinant of subsequent aggressive behavior; specifically, positive reinforcement by the victim would increase the probability of the aggressor emitting a subsequent aggressive response toward that victim and counterattack by the victim or intervention by the teacher would temporarily suppress and redirect the response to another victim. In addition, it was hypothesized that the frequency of both aggressive interaction and being victimized was a function of the child's activity level and the degree to which he engaged in social interaction. The data revealed that in both nursery schools, a large majority of aggressive responses culminated in a positive reinforcement for the aggressor suggesting that the nursery school setting should function to maintain aggressive behavior in children initially high in aggressive output and enhance aggressive behaviors in children who are initially low in aggression. The results of sequential analyses of individual aggressive behavior protocols were generally consistent with the experimental hypotheses. The data for the children who enter nursery school with weak aggressive tendencies are particularly striking. These children show an increment in aggressive responses provided that they are also socially active. Their protocols suggest a sequence of victimization, successful counterattack, and initiation of aggressive episodes. In contrast, the aggressive behavior of the children who were noninteractors remained at a low rate.

The Patterson et al. (1967) findings are based on correlational methods and, as such, the possible influence of correlated factors, other than the reinforcement contingencies that were observed, cannot be excluded. Nevertheless, these data provide an important insight into the influence of the peer group upon the acquisition and maintenance of instrumental aggressive behaviors. These field observations are consistent with and are significant extensions of the studies reporting experimental manipulations of aggressive and nonaggressive responses through reinforcement procedures. They leave little doubt concerning the role of reinforcement in the development of instrumental aggression. However, their implications are also limited to the dimensions of aggression upon which these studies have focused. The influence of such variables as dislike, jealousy, and ego-injury and of consequences which entail preference for the infliction of noxious stimuli need also to be considered and investigated in similar detail.

Modeling. Parents, teachers, peers, and other socializing agents influence the development of aggressive and nonaggressive behaviors through the rewards they dispense and, more indirectly, through behavior patterns which serve as a model to the child. The effect upon the child of exposure to the behavior of others, although often incidental and unintended, may nevertheless be very potent. The acquisition of language vocabulary is the most obvious example of this process. Children acquire a substantial part of their behavioral repertoire by imitation of other people as well as through direct instruction, shaping, and reinforcement. Although the application of concepts of imitation and identification to social behavior is very old to psychology, experimental studies and theoretical analysis of imitative phenomena are relatively recent.

Interest in the role of imitation in the development of aggression has been greatly stimulated by the research of Bandura and his associates (Bandura and Huston, 1961; Bandura, Ross, and Ross, 1961, 1963a, 1963b). The first of these studies (Bandura and Huston, 1961) examined the influence upon preschool children of nurturant versus non-nurturant interaction with an adult model upon imitation of the incidental responses of the model made while performing a discrimination task. Subjects assigned to the experimental modeling condition observed the model aggressively knock down a small rubber doll located on the lid of a discrimination box as well as exhibiting other discrete behaviors irrelevant to the task. The children in the control condition observed a different set of acts, none of them aggressive. On trials in which the subjects were given the discrimination task, a high degree of duplication of the model's behavior was reported, 90% of the experimental subjects and only 13% of the controls exhibiting the model's aggressive response toward the doll. The children who had previously had a nurturant, rewarding interaction with the model showed greater imitation of the model's non-aggressive incidental behaviors than did the children who had had minimal interaction with her. Bandura and Huston (1961), on the basis of the ready imitation by the subjects of the model's aggressive acts, regardless of the variation in their earlier contact with her, suggest that "mere observation of aggressive models, regardless of the quality of the model-child relationship, is a sufficient condition for producing imitative aggression in children" (Bandura and Huston, 1961, p. 317). This inference seems overstated in view of the novelty of the aggressive behavior, its essential innocuousness, and other special properties which may have facilitated its imitation.

In a subsequent study, the imitative effects of exposure to a model were extended to settings in which the model is absent (Bandura, Ross, and Ross, 1961), and influence of similarity between the sex of the model and the sex of the child was examined. Nursery school children of both sexes observed a same-sex or opposite-sex model behaving in an aggressive or nonaggressive manner. A group of children who were not exposed to any model constituted an additional control. In the aggressive condition, the model exhibited distinctive verbal and physical aggressive acts toward a Bobo doll, whereas in the nonaggressive treatment, the model ignored the Bobo doll. Following exposure to the model, the children were subjected to a mild frustration before being given the opportunity to play with a set of toys, including the Bobo doll. The behavior of the children in the test situation reflected the behavior of the model they had previously observed. In addition to imitating the aggressive model, children in the aggressive condition expressed more nonimitative aggression than the controls. The sex of the child and of the model exerted significant effects upon the degree and type of imitation obtained. Boys reproduced more imitative physical aggression than girls regardless of the sex of the model. Boys also showed greater imitation of verbal aggression than girls when the model was a male; the difference was reversed for the female model. Overall, the sex of the model made a greater difference for boys than for girls, the boys showing much more imitative aggression of the male model than of the female model.

The findings of the first of these studies by Bandura, Ross, and Ross are consistent with other data relating to the sex-typing of aggression and also suggest that the imitation of aggression by the child is influenced by his similarity to the model. A later experiment (Bandura, Ross, and Ross, 1963a) explored the effects on the aggressive behaviors of preschool children of real-life aggressive

models, films depicting an aggressive human model, and films depicting an aggressive cartoon model. The results indicated that although all three conditions produced imitative aggression, exposure to the human models, especially human on films, exerted the greatest influence on the child's aggressive behavior. The differential effectiveness of the human model on film was most evident for aggressive gun play, a nonimitative aggressive act. Sex differences consistent with those reported in the earlier study were again obtained. The finding that children imitate the aggressive behavior of characters in films has an obvious bearing on the important social issue of the effects of violence in movies and television upon the aggressive behavior of young viewers. This issue shall be considered in greater detail at a subsequent point in this chapter. For the present, we wish only to note the disparity between the laboratory and the living room setting, and between the aggressive play behaviors imitated or stimulated and the antisocial aggressive acts that are a matter of social concern.

Although caution is necessary in extrapolating from the modeling experiments to more complex social phenomena, the ingenious method developed by Bandura and his co-workers provides an opportunity to investigate variables governing the imitation of aggression and to test theoretically relevant hypotheses. In a further investigation of the factors governing the degree of imitation of film models, Bandura, Ross, and Ross (1963b) manipulated the consequences of the model's aggressive acts. A series of films were prepared in which two male adults engaged in aggressive or in vigorous nonaggressive play. In one of the aggressive versions the aggressor is punished for his actions; in the other version his aggressive behavior is rewarded. Nursery school age children were randomly assigned to one of these film conditions or to a control treatment in which they were not exposed to a model. Consistent with prediction, witnessing of the reinforced model produced significantly greater imitative aggression than the other treatments. The degree of imitative aggression in the children who observed the punished model was comparable to the behaviors of the control groups. The effects of the experimental treatments on nonimitative aggressive behavior were more complex, there being little difference on this measure for the girls. The boys, however, showed more nonimitative aggression in the nonaggressive model and aggressive-reinforced model treatments as compared to the means for the no-model control and aggression-punished-model groups. The stimulating or disinhibiting efects of the nonaggressive but vigorous model on boys suggests that an exciting stimulus, regardless of its aggressive content, may facilitate aggressive behavior in boys.

Another observation of interest yielded by the study was the children's negative labeling of the attributes of the successful aggressive model; that is, they imitated the model despite their negative evaluation of his behavior. The weakness of the children's value structure relative to the strength of instrumental success influencing imitation may be exaggerated in this young age group but is not peculiar to it. Historical examples of success assuming precedence over morality in older individuals are not infrequent. In a somewhat older group of kindergarten boys, Walters, Leat, and Mezei (1963) found a similar effect of vicarious reinforcement upon imitation of the deviant behavior of a film model who played with some attractive toys the children had been forbidden to touch.

The laboratory studies of modeling that have been reviewed have demonstrated that observation of models displaying aggressive and other socially deviant responses produces strong, immediate effects on the observer's behavior. Persistence of modeling influences on imitative aggression after a 6-month interval has been reported by Hicks (1965). Three- to six-year-old children observed the aggressive behaviors of a male or female adult or peer model. The experimental procedure was similar to that employed by Bandura, Ross and Ross (1962). A test for imitative aggression was made directly following exposure to the film and also after a lapse of 6 months. On the initial test, all the model conditions were found to be highly effective in shaping the children's aggressive responses, although exposure to the peer male model produced the greatest amount of imitative aggression. Modeling effects were still present but much weaker on retest, only the difference between the adult male and the no-

model control condition attaining statistical significance. Nevertheless, the evidence of retention and performance of the imitative response after a very substantial lapse of time is an impressive demonstration of the effects of brief exposure to a model. It seems reasonable to infer that the repeated exposure to adult and peer models which the child experiences during the normal course of his development exerts a profound influence upon the acquisition of aggressive behaviors.

However, it is unlikely that imitative influences independent of other antecedents can adequately account for the acquisition of aggressive behaviors. The child, as he increases in age, is exposed to many models who may display competing response tendencies. He clearly does not imitate everyone in his environment nor does he imitate all of the behavior of those models which have the strongest influence upon him. Thus, despite the power of parental models, children are not little adults. Certain behaviors are more readily imitated than others (especially, as many parents of young children have wryly noted, if they are the socially deviant behaviors of their peers). In addition, we can assume that there are individual differences among children in the attractiveness of various behaviors so that, for example, children predisposed to aggression are probably more likely to imitate aggressive models than children who have weak aggressive tendencies. It can be argued that both the aggressive and the nonaggressive child acquire cognitive representations of the observed behavior, whereas its overt expression depends upon its motivational consequences for the child. Thus Bandura (1962) has shown that the relatively few imitative aggressive responses produced by a film-mediated model who is punished for his behavior can be significantly enhanced by offering the children who had been exposed to the model an attractive incentive contingent upon their reproducing the model's behavior. In this sense, any information acquired by the child as a result of instruction or reading becomes part of his behavioral repertoire. However, the amount of information a child has about aggressive acts and implements does not determine his aggressiveness. Rather, individual differences in aggression lie in the tendency to use this information and in the extent to which it becomes integrated in behavior.

Parental Influences

The analysis of parental influences upon children's personality development poses an array of methodological and theoretical difficulties which are perhaps even more exaggerated when one considers the development of aggrssion. Children's aggressive actions are salient behaviors which often directly impinge upon the parent and which also relate to core cultural and personal values concerning the desirability and appropriateness of these actions. A temper tantrum, destruction of household objects, hostile reactions toward parental restrictions, conflicts with siblings—all present decision situations for the parent. He or she may choose to ignore or encourage the behaviors, restrain and/or punish the child, distract him, reason with him, or respond with involuntary anger and abuse. The parents' responses may vary, depending upon the object of aggression, the mode of aggression, the degree of provocation, and the parents' own mood at the time the aggressive act occurs. Some parents may react in terms of a well articulated value system; the response of others may be rooted in vaguely defined attitudes and be highly susceptible to situational factors. This complex patterning of parental responses and values relating to children's aggressive behaviors constitutes the parent's efforts at the socialization of aggression.

The socialization practices directly relating to aggressive responses of children represent only part of the parental influence upon the child's aggressive behavior. Many family interactions occur which, although not directly connected with the specific training of aggression, may have a profound effect upon the development of aggression. Parental affection or rejection and the degree of emotional stability and strife in the household (McCord, McCord, and Howard, 1961) are two examples of more indirect influences. In addition, the effects of parental practices concerning areas of behavior other than aggression must be considered. According to some psychoanalytic and learning theories, the frustrations imposed upon the child in the course of weaning, toilet training, and the more general imposition of restraints upon

impulse expression are factors that increase instigation to aggression. Many parents, guided by these assumptions, have indulged their children in order to avoid the presumed aggressive and other undesirable consequences of frustration. In this connection, mention should also be made of the set of training procedures relating to the acquisition of ego control functions which serve to inhibit aggressive acting-out behaviors.

The behavioral model which the parent presents (Bandura and Walters, 1963b) is another significant influence upon the child's development of aggression. The parent, directly or inadvertly, sets an example for the child, who will often approximate in his own behavior the reactions he observes in significant others. To the extent that children imitate and identify with a same-sex parental model, aggressive mothers should raise aggressive daughters and aggressive fathers should produce aggressive sons. Unfortunately, the testing of this straightforward proposition is complicated by other consequences of the parents' behavior. Thus aggression in parents may be associated with a lesser degree of nurturance and related dispositions which are believed to facilitate identification. The child may therefore be less disposed to identify with an aggressive parent. Also, the aggressive parent may inhibit and discourage in the child those very behaviors which the parent himself exemplifies. One can enumerate other correlated variables that could attenuate and exaggerate the predicted relationship between parental and children's aggression. Aggressive parents may reward aggressive behavior in their children, may provoke aggressive reactions, or may even be responding with aggression to provocation from the child. Further, there is the possibility that genetic factors may exert an indirect influence on aggression through physiological and temperamental variables which may affect aggressive reactivity.

This example of the complexities contributing to the testing of one proposition can be extended to the general problem of determining the effects of parental influences upon the child. There is an intricate matrix of interdependent variables operating in the home which are correlated over time and with influences stemming from outside the immediate family. The practicalities of research are such that one is ordinarily unable to control for more than two or three correlated factors when attempting to isolate the effects of a particular parental influence. It is clear that one cannot hope to establish etiological relationships studying the correlations of parental influences with the child's aggressive behaviors. However, as a number of studies have demonstrated (Sears, Maccoby, and Levin, 1957; Bandura and Walters, 1959), these correlations can be fruitfully used as one source of evidence bearing upon a clearly formulated hypothesis or theoretical model.

The welter of variables on the antecedent side of the parental influence—children's aggression equation is almost matched by the parameters on the dependent side. A child's aggression is not a unidimensional trait. As previously noted, aggressive behaviors vary with the stimulus object, and different aggressive response modes tend to be weakly correlated. Related to these stimulus and response variations affecting the assessment of the child's aggression are a number of attributes mediating his aggressive behaviors. These include the degree of instigation to aggression or aggressive drive, the strength and repertoire of aggressive responses available to the child, the degree of inhibition of

aggression, and the effectiveness of such ego control mechanisms as the child's level of reality testing and his ability to delay gratification. In reviewing the pertinent literature, wherever possible, attempts will be made to link a particular source of parental influence to a particular factor or factors mediating aggressive expression. A schematic ordering of parental influences that have been theoretically linked to one or more of these variables mediating aggression is presented in Table 2.

Generalized Parental Attitudes and Behaviors. There is a considerable amount of clinical evidence indicating that children who are unwanted, who are afforded little warmth and affection by their parents, and who are in other ways subjected to serious emotional deprivation and to frustration of their dependency needs are likely to develop hostile behavior patterns (Banister and Ravden, 1944; Bender, 1947; Lowrey, 1940; Lowrey et al., 1943). Comparisons of delinquent boys with their nondelinquent siblings (Healy and Bronner, 1936) and with nondelinquent peers matched for socioeconomic backgrounds (Glueck and Glueck, 1950) have revealed a history of rejection and affectional deprivation in the backgrounds of the delinquent children. Goldfarb (1945) and Lowrey (1940) report a high frequency of aggressive

Table 2. Linkages between Parental Influences and Variables Mediating the Child's Aggressive Behavior

Parental Influences	Attributes of the Child Mediating His Aggressive Behavior

Generalized parental attitude and behaviors:
  Acceptance, warmth-rejection,
    hostility
Permissiveness-restrictiveness
Emotional stability-instability
	Instigation to aggression
	  (aggressive drive)
	Ego controls

Socialization of specific
  behavior systems:
  Weaning, toilet training,
    independence training
	Instigation to aggression
	Ego controls

Permissiveness and reinforcement
  of aggression
	Strength and repertoire
	  of aggressive behaviors

Punishment of aggression	Inhibition of aggressive behaviors, Instigation to aggression

Aggressive versus nonaggressive
  parental models
	Strength and repertoire of
	  aggressive behaviors

disturbances in institutionally reared children who had experienced early emotional deprivation while Menlove (1965) found a significantly greater incidence of hostility and negativism in a group of adopted children than in a matched sample. To the extent that degree of emotional deprivation is associated with age of adoption, early adoption should result in less aggression. However, possibly because of the restricted nature of her clinical sample, Menlove did not find a difference in aggressive symptomatology in children adopted before the age of 6 months when compared to those adopted after they were 6 months old.

Studies of clinical populations suggest that a background of early separation and emotional deprivation is found more often in behavior disorders in which aggressive symptoms are salient than in other forms of behavior pathology. Bowlby (1946) and Friedlander (1949) report similar findings indicating a higher proportion of delinquent than disturbed, nondelinquent children having experienced prolonged separation from their mothers during early childhood. Comparisons of family backgrounds of overinhibited and aggressive children (Hewitt and Jenkins, 1946; Lewis, 1954) reveal a history of severe maternal rejection in the aggressive children. Goldfarb (1943) found a predominance of aggressive disorders in adolescents reared during their first three years in an institution and a pattern of inhibition and timidity in adolescents raised in foster homes. These data provide further support for the proposition that early experiences of separation and associated emotional deprivation and frustration of dependency needs facilitate the development of aggressive personality problems in children. An exception to this generalization is reported by Bandura (1960), who compared a group of nondelinquent, aggressive male schoolchildren with a demographically matched group of boys judged to be inhibited and withdrawn. There was little difference between the two groups in the extent to which they had been deprived of parental affection. Both the aggressive and inhibited samples were less emotionally disturbed and their behaviors less extreme than the clinical populations compared in the other studies, a factor which could account in part for the discrepancy in findings.

In interpreting the comparisons between aggressive and nonaggressive behavior disorders, or between delinquents and nondelinquents, it must be recognized that there are many differences in the histories of these children in addition to the observed differences in early separation and emotional deprivation. Separation, for example, denotes a critical event in the child's life. It does not describe, however, the factors that led to this event or the particular experiences of the child subsequent to the event. Variables of the order of separation, institutionalization, and severe rejection of the child denote syndromes of experiences, much as do demographic variables such as age, sex, and social class. Nevertheless, these studies are of theoretical importance as well as having practical, social significance. If no associations were found between aggressive behavior and maternal rejection and separation, given the profound frustration that these early experiences imply, the utility of the frustration-aggression hypothesis would be seriously diminished.

The relationship of parental warmth and hostility to aggressiveness in children is by no means restricted to seriously disrupted family structures. Bandura and Walters (1957), in an effort to minimize the role of social disorganization and also to isolate aggressive, antisocial acts from other forms of delinquency, compared adolescents who had been involved in such acts with a control group of normal adolescents. Their design differed in several important respects from the approach used by the Gluecks: they selected delinquent boys who had been involved in aggressive, antisocial behaviors, who were of at least average intelligence, who came from intact homes, whose parents were steadily employed, and who did not live in high-delinquency neighborhoods. The matched control boys were identified by high school counselors as neither markedly aggressive, withdrawn, or disruptive. The results provide evidence of less warmth and greater rejection by the parents of the aggressive adolescents. The pattern of response to the child's dependency needs differed, however, for the father and mother of the aggressive children. The mothers of the aggressive boys apparently engaged in adequate affectionate interaction with the child during infancy and early childhood. Their more critical attitude toward the boys, as compared to attitudes of the control mothers, appeared to be a reaction to their sons' aggressive behaviors. They also tended to discourage and punish the boys' help-seeking behavior, a lack of support which may have been particularly frustrating for the children in view of their early affectionate attitudes. The differences between the fathers of the aggressive and control boys were more pronounced. The fathers of the aggressive boys were colder, more intolerant, and less interested in their sons apparently long before the boys' aggression had become serious problems.

Significant correlations between lack of parental affection and aggression in their offspring have also been found for children who are not delinquent or manifesting other clinical problems. McCord, McCord, and Howard (1961) categorized a sample of relatively nondelinquent, predominantly lower-class boys who had been observed over a 5-year period, beginning at the age of 9, into aggressive, normally assertive, and nonaggressive groups. Their data indicate that 95% of the aggressive boys were raised in homes where one or both of the parents was rejecting, whereas the majority of the assertive and nonaggressive children were raised by affectionate parents. Less strong but significant relationships have been obtained with measures reflecting a continuum of aggression rather than distinct categories.

Sears, Maccoby, and Levin (1957), in their retrospective study of the child-rearing antecedents of social behaviors in 5-year-olds, found a small negative correlation between warmth of the mother and the extent to which the mother described her child as aggressive. A similar finding was obtained by Wittenborn (1954), but the correlation disappeared when his measure of aggression was based on an interview with the child rather than a report from the mother. Lesser (1952), however, found a marked positive relationship between parental rejection and a measure of aggression in pre-adolescent boys based on peer ratings while Bayley and Shaefer (1963) reported a positive relationship between maternal love and contented, happy behavior of boys and of girls from 1 to 3 years of age. Working with a much older sample, Bornston and Coleman (1956) ob-

tained higher aggression scores on the Rosenzweig Picture-Frustration for the college student offspring of relatively cold mothers. A cross-cultural study indirectly bearing upon the relationship between early nurturance and subsequent aggressive attitudes has been reported by Lambert, Triandis, and Wolf (1959). Societies with predominantly benevolent deities were more often characterized, although not significantly so, by a high display of affection and overall nurturance toward the infant, than were societies with predominantly aggressive deities. A statistically reliable association was found between the belief in aggressive deities and a relatively high degree of pain inflicted on the infant by nurturing agents.

There are occasional exceptions to the proposition that cold, rejecting parents produce hostile offspring, some studies yielding complex interactions with sex of the child and with the age period during which parental nurturance was assessed (Kagan and Moss, 1962; Sears et al., 1953). However, a preponderance of evidence indicates that the absence of warmth and nurturance in the household is associated with aggressiveness in the child. This association is not necessarily unidirectional. The child's aggressiveness may elicit rejecting responses from the parent, which in turn fosters further aggression, thereby establishing an unhappy cycle of rejection-aggression. Insofar as rejection may be regarded as a form of frustration—and this issue will be discussed later—the relationship between rejection and aggression is not surprising, although as Child (1954) has pointed out, there is no sound theoretical reason from a learning point of view to expect a simple, direct relationship between frustrating experiences in socialization and the strength of aggressive tendencies. Experimental data indicate that aggression is only one of a number of response tendencies which are heightened by frustration. The long-term effects of frustration depend upon reactions of the socializing agents to the child's response to frustration, upon whether aggressive responses or behaviors incompatible with aggression are systematically reinforced, ignored, or punished.

Parental coldness to the child, however, has rather unique characteristics as a source of frustration, and because of these properties may be more likely than other types of frustration to lead to the development of hostility in the child. The parent who has little warmth for and interest in the child is likely to expose the child to constant frustration. Since the infant's expressions of discomfort may be ignored or attended to only after prolonged delay, he may receive less of the stimulation and support needed to develop skills facilitating effective responses to developmental problems; and his needs for affection and nurturance, to the extent that they have been acquired, will be repeatedly thwarted. Rejecting parents are difficult to please, and nonaggressive no less than aggressive reactions may be responded to with minimal rewards.

In addition to increasing the probability of frustrations and reducing the likelihood that nonaggressive reactions to goal-blocking will be adequately reinforced, the lack of parental affection has other implications for the acquisition of aggression. Affection from the parent plays an important role in the development of affectionate behavior tendencies in the child. The cold parent not only frustrates the child but he fails to elicit loving reactions, which would be incompatible with and inhibit aggressive expression. Also, the warmth and nurturance provided by the parent is linked to the development of ego controls, which, through the process of identification, facilitates the acquisition of internalized prohibitions that serve to inhibit and prevent the expression of aggression and other socially unacceptable behaviors. Thus the child who has been given little affection and attention is likely both to experience persistent frustration and develop deficiencies in capacities which would help him cope with the frustrations. These are the ingredients that lead to hyperaggressive, impulse-ridden youngsters.

Weaning and Toilet Training. The frustrations associated with specific child-training areas seem less pervasive and persistent than those stemming from parental coldness toward the child. At the same time, frustration of early modes of psychosexual expression, according to psychoanalytic theory, could have profound effects upon personality development, including the fostering of basic hostile attitudes in the child. Studies bearing upon the relationship between aggression and the severity of oral training have yielded weak or indifferent findings (Sears et al., 1953; Sears, Maccoby, and Levin, 1957; Sears, 1961; Sewell, 1952; Sewell and Mussen, 1952). The results obtained for anal training are mixed. Sewell (1952) and Sears et al. (1953) related measures of aggression to toilet training variables and obtained inconsistent findings, there being some evidence in the Sears study of a relationship for boys between severe toilet training and aggression. Wittenborn (1954), however, in separate studies of 5-year-olds and 8-year-olds, obtained consistent, significant correlations between rating of the severity of toilet training and the child's aggression. Since the toilet training data were obtained through retrospective interviews, these results may have reflected in part the mothers' current attitudes rather than the children's past behavior. Additional data on this issue are provided by the Sears, Maccoby, and Levin (1957) analysis of child-rearing practices. Although no significant relationships were reported between toilet training practices and aggression, there were strong indications that severe toilet training was frustrating and emotionally upsetting to the child. Especially revealing is the dependence of these effects upon the degree of the mother's warmth toward the child. The extent of emotional upset with mild training is similar to that with severe toilet training practices when the mother, in both instances, is rated as high on warmth. However, a very marked difference in emotional upset as a function of severity of toilet training was obtained for mothers who had been rated as relatively cold.

These data underline the methodological limitations of considering child-rearing variables in isolation. Just as a significant relationship between a practice and some aspect of the child's behavior may depend upon the presence of other conditions, the absence of a relationship may be due to the influence of unmeasured moderator variables. Judgments on the importance of a child-rearing technique should be made only in the context of other dimensions of the parent-child relationship.

Permissiveness-Restrictiveness. Cognizance of the interactive nature of the variables influencing aggressive behavior is also required in studies of the effects of more global dimensions of parental behavior such as the extent of permissiveness exercised in regulating the child's behavior. Parents who are restrictive in one area of child rearing also tend to be restrictive in other areas (Sears et al., 1957; Becker et al., 1962; Becker, 1964; McCord, 1964). The degree of restriction or strictness employed by the parents bears a complex theoretical relationship to the development of aggression. Restrictive discipline should increase the amount of frustration the child experiences, but at the same time should tend to inhibit behavior that deviates from parental standards. The increased frustration would lead to a prediction of increased aggression, whereas the inhibitory effect leads to an opposite prediction.

A closer examination of the role of restrictive discipline suggests that the assumption that strictness promotes frustration may be an oversimplification. As Berkowitz (1962) has noted, frustration is a function of expectancy or the strength of the approach tendency that is blocked. If nonconforming behaviors are treated permissively by the parents, the strength of these behavioral tendencies will be increased. Interference with these behaviors will then be more frustrating as compared to the situation for the child who, because of exposure to restictive discipline, has received less reinforcement for such behaviors; that is, if restrictive practices decrease the expectancy that careless, disobedient, aggressive, untidy, and other deviant behaviors will be reinforced and strengthened, the frustration produced by the restrictions will be lessened.

In terms of this analysis, the overall effects of restrictive discipline should be the lowering of aggressive tendencies in the child. In arriving at this hypothesis, we have not taken into consideration the type and consistency of punishments employed and the warmth-coldness of the parent, both relevant parameters. Other relevant dimensions are the consistency of discipline, the principal disciplining agent, and the specific control techniques used by the parents in responding to acts of aggression. With respect to the last consideration, although a general factor of permissiveness-restrictiveness has been demonstrated, there still remains substantial variance in the disciplinary measures used for specific behavior areas. Because the parent's handling of aggression should have a particularly close relationship to subsequent manifestations of aggression, investigations bearing on parental control of aggression will be separated, where possible, from those dealing with the effects of more general parental control practices.

In view of the multiplicity of factors influencing the outcome of permissive versus restrictive practices, it is not surprising to find some inconsistencies in the research findings. In an early study of a parental pattern related to but more embracing than the permissive dimension, Symonds (1939) found that children of submissive parents were disobedient, assertive, and irresponsible as compared to children of dominant parents, who were more courteous, obedient, and generally more socialized. Symond's submissive category included parents who were indifferent to the child as well as indulgent, whereas the dominant parents were often overprotective and also punitive. Perhaps an indirect measure of aggression may have reflected greater hostility in the children of the dominant parents. Subsequent investigations, assessing the effects of parental restrictiveness, have revealed rather striking sex differences, particularly with regard to effects on aggressive behaviors.

Delaney (1965) administered separate measures of restrictiveness to mothers and fathers, derived from McCord's (1964) factor analysis of parent interview rating scales. These factor scores were then compared with ratings of their child's aggression, based on two semesters of nursery school attendance. The overall trend of her findings suggested that parental restrictiveness, rather than permissiveness, was positively related to the child's aggressive behavior. The correlation between father restrictiveness and aggression in boys was highly significant, whereas correlations between paternal restrictiveness and aggression in girls, and maternal restrictiveness and aggression in boys or girls, were not significant. It may be that boys, receiving less dependency gratification from the father than the mother, particularly resent the father's controls. However, since restrictiveness by the father is likely to be associated with the use of punitive techniques, the greater aggressiveness observed in the sons of restrictive fathers could also be a consequence of sex-typed modeling. These factors are evident in the Gordon and Smith (1965) study, in which the general strictness of mothers was separated from the degree to which they punished aggression. For girls, the stricter the mother, the more aggressive was the daughter, but only if the mother used physical punishment. In contrast, a negative association was obtained between mothers' strictness and aggression in boys, especially when physical punishment was not employed by the mother.

The subtle interaction between maternal restrictions and the sex of the child at different age periods is examined by Kagan and Moss (1962) in their report of the Fels Longitudinal study. Restrictiveness exercised during the first three years was unrelated to the child's aggression during that time period. There was some evidence of negative correlations with indirect expressions of aggression during the ages of 3 to 10, but the most striking finding was the lesser amount of aggression expressed toward restrictive mothers by their sons during pre-adolescence. This effect did not extend to aggression in adulthood despite the consistency in aggression between these two age periods. Restrictiveness assessed during the ages of 3 to 6 bore little relationship to the child's behavior until he entered adolescence. Children of restrictive mothers show a moderate tendency, as young adults, to be less critical of their mothers and, in the case of the males, of their fathers as well. Further, these same males evidenced greater retaliatory tendencies, and the females showed greater ease of arousal in comparison to the children of permissive mothers. When mother's permissiveness is considered during the 6- to 10-year period, further support is provided for the presence of anger and counteraggression in adult sons of restrictive mothers.

The Kagan and Moss (1962) findings suggest that early and later restrictiveness have different effects upon the development of aggression in boys. For boys, early restrictiveness tends to be associated with reduced aggression while restrictiveness at later ages is related to hostile trends in adulthood, although the hostility is not expressed toward the parents. For girls, there was less consistency in the correlations and there appears to be little overall relationship between the mother's restrictiveness and her daughter's aggressive behavior. The prediction of ag-

gression in girls from child-rearing parameters is greatly complicated, as Kagan and Moss have suggested, by the sex-typed sanctions against female aggression. The varying effects of restrictiveness upon boys can be accounted for partly by the low degree of consistency between the mother's demands on her son before the age of 3 and her subsequent restrictiveness. The older child is more cognizant of restrictive practices and may experience more resentment, particularly if his mother had previously been permissive and had made relatively few demands of the child.

Permissiveness-Restrictiveness in a Hostile Context. The results reviewed thus far indicate that the effects of parental permissiveness versus restrictiveness vary with the sex of the parent, the sex of the child, and the age during which these practices and their consequences are assessed. They also vary, as one might anticipate, with the parental feeling toward the child. Permissiveness in the context of parental rejection and hostility implies a failure to provide adequate controls either through restraint or identification with the parents. Given this combination plus a sprinkling of severe punishments, one has an ideal formula for maximizing aggression in the child. Studies of delinquents have consistently reported a high incidence of lax controls (Healy and Bronner, 1936; Burt, 1929; Glueck and Glueck, 1950) as well as parental rejection. The image, however, of the households of delinquent children as characterized by a laissez-faire attitude toward the child's behavior is oversimplified.

The Bandura and Walters (1959) study indicates that the fathers of the aggressive, antisocial adolescent group resembled the control parents in the restrictions they imposed on their children. The mothers of the aggressive boys, however, tended to place fewer curbs on the child's behavior in the home and were much less demanding of obedience and less consistent in enforcing demands than the control mothers. The extent to which the greater permissiveness of these mothers may have been a response to their sons' resistance to demands and, possibly, an overcompensation for the fathers' lack of involvement with the boys is not clear. The McCords' study (McCord, McCord, and Howard, 1961) of a nondelinquent sample of aggressive boys provides further evidence that the aggressive child is likely to come from a family that makes few demands for polite, conforming behavior and also fails to supervise behavior adequately. The degree of maternal control, in the sense of parental domination of the child's choices, was distinguished from the measures of parental demands and supervision. The aggressive boys tended to be raised by mothers who either "overcontrolled" or "minimally controlled" their behavior while the mothers of the nonaggressive boys predominantly fell in the "overcontrol" and "normal control" categories. The mothers of the assertive boys were distributed in all three categories, with the highest proportion displaying "normal controls."

Both the McCord and the Bandura and Walters data suggest that the parents of aggressive and nonaggressive boys differ more markedly in the demands they place on the child for conformity to social convention than in the restraints they exercise on impulse expression. The parent of the aggressive boy may restrict the child's freedom to behave in a deviant manner but appears to be lax in fostering socially desirable behaviors. The child is thus aware of unacceptable behaviors but has an inadequate conception of the approved behaviors that are required of him.

The fact that the aggressive boys studied by the McCords and by Bandura and Walters have experienced fewer parental demands, especially maternal demands, is suggestive of the specific role of permissive practices only in the context of rejecting and punitive parental behaviors. It would be informative to determine the extent of aggression in children who are exposed to restrictive practices in otherwise similar types of families. The family characteristics are highly patterned and do not conveniently array themselves for the investigator, so that one significant dimension of parental practices fluctuates while all others remain constant. However, there are a few studies of children raised by restrictive parents who are also ambivalent or hostile to the child, which provide a contrast to the studies of families employing lax disciplines coupled with similar negative attitudes. The combination of parental punitiveness plus the exercise of strict controls should induce in the child a strong conflict between anger toward the parents and anxiety over the expression of aggressive feelings. The constraint of the parents reduces realistic alternatives available to the child for resolution of the conflict. The probable outcome is internalization of the conflict manifesting itself in persistent tension, anxiety, self-devaluation, and displacement of hostility. Clinical studies of inhibited, neurotic children as compared to aggressive, acting-out youngsters indicate more severe parental control by the parents of the former group (Lewis, 1954; Rosenthal et al., 1962). Some of the case studies of homicides reviewed by Bromberg (1961) reflect a family background of puritanical restraints, often with a religious overlay, in adolescents who have committed "senseless" murders inexplicable in terms of past deportment or immediate provocation.

Less extreme manifestations of this pattern are provided in an early study by Watson (1934) employing student self-descriptions and reports of parental discipline. While parents were primarily categorized according to degree of strictness, Watson (1957) has subsequently noted that the criteria also included behaviors indicative of rejection and hostility. The students who described their parents as most punitive and restrictive reported more feelings of unhappiness, anxiety, and guilt, more resentment of parents, and more difficulty with classmates. Sears (1961), in a follow-up study of 12-year-olds whose mothers had been interviewed 7 years earlier (Sears, Maccoby, and Levin, 1957), found the maximum degree of self-aggression in boys whose mothers were in the lower half of the distribution on permissiveness and in the upper half in punitiveness. The self-aggression measure consisted of a set of items dealing with self-punishment, suicidal tendencies, and accident proneness, which, though statistically unrelated, tap some form of self-injury. Parental coldness, although associated with severity of punishment, especially withdrawal of love, was negligibly related to self-aggression. Baumrind (1967), using a younger population and comprehensive observation procedures for assessing both child and parental behavior, obtained a strong relationship between social inhibition in the child and parental restraint coupled with parental coldness. She found that nursery school children who displayed a behavior pattern reflecting discontent, insecurity, low affiliation toward peers, and a tendency to become hostile or regressive under stress had parents who were low in involvement with their children and who exerted firm control but offered little affection. The Baumrind study, while not directly concerned with aggressiveness in the child, lends addtional support to the consistent indications that parental strictness combined with punitive and rejecting attitudes fosters overconformity, dissatisfaction, and displaced aggressive tendencies in the child.

Permissive-Restrictiveness in a Nurturant Context. Much of the debate during the past three decades between different "schools" of child-rearing has centered on the role of permissive versus restrictive practices in an intact household where the child is accepted by parents who provide a reasonable degree of warmth and nurturance. From a theoretical standpoint, it is difficult to make any predictions concerning the probable effects of variations in permissive practices by these parents upon the development of aggressive behavior in their children. Generalized permissiveness is likely to facilitate the reinforcement of aggressive as well as deviant behaviors. However, restrictive practices should increase the child's experiences of frustration, although, as previously noted, such practices may eventually lead to more modest expectancies and perhaps less frustration relative to these expectancies. The balance between these opposing effects will depend to a great extent upon situational variables affecting the generalization of frustration-instigated aggressive drive and the generalization of aggressive response tendencies.

The few empirical studies that relate to this issue have yielded conflicting outcomes. Watson (1957) categorized intact families as consistently strict or consistently permissive on the basis of nominations from parents, teachers, and social workers and a home interview. The parents in both groups, while characterized as adequately warm, were not matched for degree of warmth, or acceptance of the child. Differences in the range of these parental attitudes may have contributed to the differences in aggressive behavior reported between the children of the strict versus those of permissive families. The behavior of the children was assessed through direct observation and through the adminis-

tration of projective measures. The results indicated that the children reared in permissive homes were friendlier and showed less hostility on the projective measures than the children from the restrictive families.

Baumrind's previously cited study (1967), which was not directly concerned with aggression, nevertheless provides a different image of the effects of variation in parental control exercised in a nurturant setting. The results for two of the behavior patterns she investigated are pertinent here. The parents of preschool children reliably rated as self-reliant, self-controlled, buoyant, and affiliative were similar in nurturance and warmth to parents of children who were observed to be low in self-control and self-reliance and who avoided novel experiences. The two groups of parents differed markedly in the control which they exercised over their children and in independence training, the former group obtaining significantly higher scores on each of these dimensions. The parents of the self-reliant and explorative children made greater demands upon their children and were less permissive of infantile behaviors.

In considering the apparent discrepancy between Baumrind's and Watson's findings, one should note the important differences in methodology and samples in the two studies. It is our impression that Watson's restrictive parents were less permissive than the authoritative, nurturant parents of Baumrind's high-ego strength children. Baumrind's samples were drawn from a middle-class, highly educated population, whose disciplinary practices are more likely to be skewed in the permissive than in the restrictive direction. The combination of warmth and firm control in these parents was also accompanied by the use of reasoning and consistency in enforcing rules, and by consideration for the child's independent decisions. In this last regard, authoritative, nurturant families resemble Baldwin's (1949) democratic households, which, although more permissive, were also characterized by warmth and rationality. The children reared in democratic households were outgoing, assertive, and aggressive in the domineering rather than hostile sense of that term.

The Watson and Baldwin studies suggest that permissive practices in a nurturant context foster outgoing, friendly, nonhostile attitudes, and instrumentally appropriate aggressive behaviors. It is possible to reconcile the Baumrind findings with this generalization, yet it is clear that the issue must remain in doubt until other parameters are controlled and comparable operational definitions of the key variables of permissiveness-strictness, warmth, and aggressiveness are employed. One important parameter is the sex of the child. Maccoby (1961), studying rule enforcement in the same children followed up by Sears (1961), found maximum rule enforcement in 12-year-old boys whose mothers had been rated as restrictive and warm when the children were 5-year-olds and minimum enforcement in the pre-adolescent boys whose mothers were warm but permissive during the earlier period. Rule enforcement in boys was associated with less overt aggression and less misbehavior when the teacher was out of the room. For girls, however, rule enforcement was associated with more misbehavior when the teacher was absent and appeared to be an expression of socially approved aggression as well as conformity. Thus punitiveness by the mother rather than restrictiveness was correlated with rule-enforcement for the girls.

As noted previously, Sears' (1961) analysis of self-inventory measures, based on these same children, indicated that the antecedents of aggression anxiety and self-aggression differ for the two sexes. Particularly germane to the present issue concerning the interaction of parental warmth and degree of permissiveness is Sears' finding that strictness is associated with greater self-aggression in boys, when the father is both warm and the chief disciplinarian. Bronfenbrenner's evidence (1961) that a similar level of parental discipline appears to foster responsibility and controls in boys but is disruptive in girls accentuates the importance of taking into account the sex of the child in assessing the influence of parental discipline. The need for obtaining measures of covert and displaced aggression as well as overt, direct aggression is also evident. Levy's study (1943) of overprotective mothers underlines the importance of assessing aggression in different situations. He reports that where the overprotective mother was also dominating, the child was submissive at home and obedient in school. Children with indulgent mothers were also conforming at school but more rebellious and aggressive at home. One wonders how these children will behave as adults. The permissive parent may take some reassurance from the Kagan and Moss longitudinal data, which suggest that maternal restrictiveness rather than maternal permissiveness is more likely to foster the development of hostile, inappropriate aggressive behavior.

Permissiveness and Punishment of Aggression. The parent's aggressive values and his response to the child's aggressive behaviors can be expected to have a stronger, as well as a more direct impact upon the child's aggressive behaviors than the more generalized influence of restrictive practices. Since the parent's handling of aggression is related to broad parental attitudes and to the techniques utilized in training other behaviors (Becker et al., 1962; McCord, 1964; Sears et al., 1957), the data bearing on the effects of permissiveness and punishment for aggression may reflect the influence of these correlated variables. Nevertheless, the investigation of the specific responses made to the child's aggression provides a clearer demonstration of the effects of specific parental behaviors upon the subsequent development of aggression. The effects of different classes of punishment, with particular interest in physical punishment, will be reviewed here.

The mode of punishment used by a parent is related to its severity: spanking, thrashing, and other physical means generally are considered more severe forms of punishment. The severity of punishment appears to be judged in terms of some implicit evaluation of the extent to which the punitive act possesses an aggressive component, that is, inflicts physical injury on the punished object. The aggressive features of different modes of punishment may play a special role in the acquisition of aggression through the mechanism of imitation. It is of importance then to consider the mode of punishment used by the parent, including punishment for non-aggressive infractions.

The complex effects of punishment upon aggression renders uncertain predictions of its consequences. A major, and intended effect of punishment is the inhibition of a disapproved response. However, punishment is also a source of frustration and pain and may therefore increase the instigation to aggression. In addition, the parent who uses an aggressive form of punishment may be indirectly fostering the acquisition of aggression if the child uses or models his behavior. It is for these reasons that investigators have been attracted to projective procedures for the assessment of aggressive motivation. According to the Miller conflict model, the strength of avoidance responses relative to the strength of approach (aggressive) responses decreases with increasing stimulus and response dissimilarity from the goal-stimulus and goal response. Thus the child may display little or no aggression in situations in which he has been punished by his parents for aggression but may reveal his aggressive response tendencies in fantasy.

Fantasy measures of aggression, despite their methodological limitations, have yielded, on the whole, consistent positive relationships with severity of punishment by socializing agents. Hollenberg and Sperry (1951) found that high punishment for aggression at home was associated with a greater amount of aggression in doll play. This tendency achieved statistical significance when the joint effects of both severity of punishment and of frustration were taken into account. Sears et al. (1953) reported significant positive correlations for boys and for girls between maternal reports of punishment for the expression of aggression and doll play aggression. Levin and Sears (1956), in a study primarily aimed at determining the influence of identification upon the relationship between parental punishment and aggression, failed to replicate these findings with a somewhat older group of nursery school children. The results did, however, confirm their hypothesis that the primary agent of discipline in the family and the level of the child's identification as assessed by internalization of parental standards exert an important influence upon the punishment-aggression relationship. Boys who were high in identification were more aggressive than boys low in identification when the father was the chief disciplinary agent. For girls, high aggression in doll play was associated with a punitive mother who was the chief disciplinary agent. These data suggest that modeling is a significant mechanism mediating the effects of parental punishment upon the child's aggression.

Indirect support for the aggression-instigating effects of punishment is provided by Whiting and Child's (1953) cross-cultural investigation of the relationship between socialization practices in preliterate cultures and normative beliefs concerning the sources of and remedies for illness. They obtained a highly significant positive correlation between the severity of socialization in a society and the degree of fantasy concerning malignant spirits and sorcerers. An incidental but theoretically interesting result was the finding that the strength of these aggressive fantasies increased with their indirectness as a function of severity of socialization. Similar results were obtained by Wright (1954) in a cross-cultural study relating projection and displacement of aggression in folk tales to punishment of children's aggression. It may be recalled that Miller's conflict model assumes that at any point on a generalization continuum, the response tendency elicited is a function of the net strength of the approach and avoidance tendencies of that point. This model does not predict that displaced aggressive tendencies will become stronger with increased dissimilarity; only that with strong inhibition, the likelihood of finding evidence of aggressive tendencies becomes greater with distance from the goal situation, because of the differential rates of decline of the approach and the avoidance gradients. The cross-cultural data suggest an additional assumption: conflict increases drive and can lead to an increment in the absolute strength of displaced responses.

Two studies using the responses to thematic apperception type stimuli as the measure of aggression have reported more complex but theoretically consistent relationships with parental treatment of aggression (Lesser, 1952, 1957; Weatherly, 1962). Lesser (1957) administered a structured questionnaire to mothers of 10- to 13-year-old males and assessed the boys' overt aggression by means of a peer nomination procedure and their covert aggression by means of a set of stimulus cards specifically prepared for that age group. The extent to which the mother permitted aggression was related to the overt aggression measure. In addition, for boys of permissive mothers, overt and fantasy aggression were correlated positively, whereas for boys whose mothers discouraged aggression, a significant negative correlation was obtained between overt and fantasy aggression. The absence of a positive correlation between fantasy aggression and maternal inhibition of aggression in Lesser's study cannot be taken as an exception to the overall findings for punishment and aggressive fantasy since Lesser's questionnaire focused on the degree to which aggression was encouraged or discouraged. This dimension, as Sears, Maccoby, and Levin (1957) have demonstrated, can be distinguished from the severity with which the parents punish aggression.

A similar reservation holds for Weatherly's (1962) study in which the mothers of female undergraduates responded to a brief questionnaire concerning their early handling of their daughters' aggressive behaviors. Weatherly experimentally varied the stimulus pull of the thematic apperception cards and also the level of aggressive arousal of his subjects. The results revealed a significant triple interaction, which, unlike most higher-order interactions, was theoretically interpretable. Daughters of permissive mothers, under arousal, showed a significant increase in aggressive themes to high aggressive cue cards only while the low permissive subjects showed no change. Weatherly sees the permissively reared girls as responding in an appropriate manner to the experimental provocation while the daughters of the restrictive mothers tended to inhibit aggression under arousal conditions. Evidence that the latter group did not simply have weaker aggressive tendencies is provided by self-report descriptions obtained during the course of the experiment. Regardless of the arousal condition, the daughters whose mothers had been nonpermissive of aggression rated themselves as less happy, more tense, and more angry than the daughters of the permissive mothers.

Allinsmith (1954), in a doctoral dissertation reprinted in part in Miller and Swanson's (1960) study of the socialization antecedents of psychodynamic mechanisms, used story completions as her measure of fantasy aggression. Her measure of punishment included parental responses to nonaggression as well as aggressive deviations by the child, and she differentiated the parents according to their relative use of physical versus psychological punishments such as shaming and withdrawal of love. This qualitative distinction is undoubtedly correlated with the severity of punishment employed, at least insofar as punishment severity is typically assessed. The data, based on a sample of junior high school boys and their mothers, reflected a strong positive relationship between exposure to a predominance of physical punishment and the child's projective expressions of aggression. Although lower-class families made greater use of physical punishment and middle-class families more often employed psychological punishment, the fantasy aggression scores were shown to be a function of mode of punishment rather than social class membership. The boys' reports of parental punishment were consistent with those provided by the mothers' interviews. There was also an indication of internalization of parental punitive standards, the boys tending to find more acceptable the predominant mode of punishment to which they had been subjected. The positive correlation between the child's experience of punishment and his attitudes toward the appropriateness of the punishment is somewhat surprising since the physical punishments were administered with greater anger and less emotional control than psychological punishments. Buss (1961, p. 290) has suggested that lack of control by the parent may be a more crucial variable than severity of punishment, the inhibitory effects of the punishment being counteracted by the angry display of the parent and its subsequent imitation by the child.

A more detailed analysis of the story completions indicates that physical punishment facilitates attack and escape responses to the frustration depicted in the stories, whereas psychological punishment is associated with greater manifestations of self-directed aggression. Beardslee (1960), however, using the same instrument and population as Allinsmith, failed to find any relationship between mode of punishment and changes in the child's story completion following experimental arousal of anger. Since mode of punishment was correlated with initial story completion, ceiling effects may have obscured relationships with the change scores. Beardslee did find a significant positive relationship in a middle-class group between strictness of parental demands for obedience and an increase in defenses against expressing aggression in the story completion task. These results are reminiscent of Weatherly's (1962) finding of an increase in TAT aggression following anger arousal in girls whose mothers had been permissive of aggressive expression.

There is other evidence in addition to the fantasy literature which indicates that parental punishment of aggression fails to inhibit and may, indeed, even foster aggressive behaviors. Greater use of physical punishment, though not necessarily specific to aggressive behaviors, by parents of delinquents is reported by the Gluecks (1950) and by Bandura and Walters (1959). The McCords (McCord, McCord, and Howard, 1961) found that parents of the aggressive boys made more frequent use of threats than the parents of the assertive and nonaggressive boys. Fewer mothers of the nonaggressive boys used physical punishment while the father's use of physical punishment was unrelated to the child's aggression. Contrary to a modeling hypothesis, ratings of the father's aggressiveness were unrelated to the son's aggression. Many more of the fathers of the aggressive boys, however, were socially deviant, for example, psychotic, alcoholic, or criminal. Although in these studies the mode of punishment cannot be separated readily from the influence of other factors, it appears that parents of aggressive boys make little use of reasoning, are irrationally and inconsistently punitive, and are prone to use severe punitive measures.

Studies of intact families yield equally consistent evidence of a positive correlation between parental punishment for aggression and overt aggressiveness in the child. Sears et al. (1953) observed the children's preschool behavior and found a strong, positive correlation between severity of punishment and overt aggression for the boys and a curvilinear relationship for the girls, both high and low punishment being associated with low aggression. In the previously cited study by Sears, Maccoby, and Levin (1957), separate measures of permissiveness and punitiveness for aggression were obtained. Permissiveness and punitiveness, although negatively correlated with each other, were both positively related to the mother's reports of the child's aggression. The positive relationships held for both boys and girls. The most aggressive children were those whose mothers were relatively high on permissiveness but would, on occasion, severely punish aggression. The Levin and Sears (1956) study of

aggression in doll play was based on this same sample of children and points to the importance of the sex-typing of aggression and of role identification in mediating the effects of parental punitiveness upon aggression. Aspects of the Sears (1961) follow-up study of these children have previously been reviewed. With respect to the effects of permissiveness and punitiveness for aggression, these variables, assessed at age 5, bear little relationship to the children's self-reports of antisocial aggressive tendencies some 7 years later. There was a nonsignificant tendency for parental punitiveness to be negatively correlated with the antisocial aggression scores, which, when considered in conjunction with the positive relationship obtained for girls between punishment for aggression and aggression anxiety, suggests the inhibition of direct aggressive expression as a result of aggression anxiety. The positive correlation between punishment and prosocial aggression in girls further suggests that while direct aggressive behaviors may be inhibited, punishment facilitates socially approved forms of aggressive expression in girls.

Although Sears failed to find a relationship between early punishment and subsequent aggression in boys and obtained only a weak relationship between punishment and aggression in girls, he did not assess parental disciplinary practices at the time at which the aggression questionnaires were administered. Eron, Walder, Toigo, and Lefkowitz (1963) used a peer nomination technique to obtain aggressive behavior scores for a large sample of third graders. They also assessed, on the basis of parental interviews, the degree of maternal and paternal punishment for aggressive behaviors. The results provide striking evidence of a positive relationship between the severity of punishment as reported by the parents and the extent to which aggressive behaviors were attributed to their child by his classroom peers. The mean aggression scores of boys and girls of high punitive fathers or mothers were consistently greater than the scores obtained by the children of low punitive parents. Even though the means for the children of parents in the moderate punishment range, with only one exception, fell in between those of the other two groups, it is evident from their analysis and from a subsequent report (Lefkowitz,

Walder, and Eron, 1963) that aggression is not linearly related to punishment.

Enhanced aggressiveness is primarily a function of severe punishment, especially of physical punishment. The effects of maternal punishment proved to be uniform over variations in the social status of the parents as determined by father's occupation. The effects of father's punishment, however, depended dramatically on his occupational level, the positive relationship between punishment and aggression in boys holding only for the high-status fathers. The sons of high-status fathers who used severe punishment were, by a considerable margin, the most aggressive of all of the subgroups. A similar trend was noted in the daughters of these high-status, punitive fathers. These findings are puzzling and the data do not provide any ready explanation for them. Thus there were no social class differences in the severity of punishment favored for different types of offenses. Perhaps, in terms of actual behavior, the middle-class father reserves physical punishment for more serious infractions by the child, thereby accounting for the association between high aggressiveness and paternal severity of punishment. It is also possible that the use of severe punishment by lower-class fathers is more in accord with social expectation and is therefore less resented by the child. For the middle-class family, severe punitive action by the father is more likely to be indicative of hostility and emotional disturbance.

There are, in addition, sampling variations in social class behaviors in different geographic areas as well as variations due to procedural differences whose effects are difficult to evaluate (Allinsmith, 1954; Sears, Maccoby, and Levin, 1957). Langston (1960), in a doctoral dissertation based on fifth and sixth graders in a southern urban community, failed to find any consistent relationship between peer ratings of aggression and reports provided by the subjects of punishment practices by the father or the mother. For boys, moderate punishment by the father was associated with greater aggression than low or high punishment. These findings are consistent with the curvilinear relationship obtained by Sears et al. (1953) between maternal punishment and girls' aggressive behaviors in nursery school. Langston predicted

that severe punishment, administered by the same-sex parent, would facilitate, through identification, the internalization of aggression-anxiety by the child. However, it is equally logical to predict greater aggressiveness on the basis of identification (Levin and Sears, 1956). Whereas a positive linear relationship was found between maternal punishment and aggressiveness in lower-class boys, this relationship was curvilinear for middle-class boys, rendering the possible role of identification even more ambiguous.

The conflict between the Eron et al. (1963) findings and those reported by Langston may be due to the method by which the parental punishment data were obtained. Langston based the measure of parental punishment on the children's reports. More important, his scale did not allow for the severity of physical punishments which were provided in the set of alternatives used by Eron and his associates in their structured interview of the parents. This omission may be a critical factor since one generalization that emerges with great consistency is the association of children's aggression with parental use of severe physical punishment.

Studies of parental punishment have provided surprisingly little evidence of inhibitory effects. There is some indication that the use of love-oriented psychological punishment may lead to the inhibition or self-direction of aggression (Allinsmith, 1954; Sears, 1961). However, the data linking physical punishment to the exacerbation of aggression are much more extensive. Belief in the homily "spare the rod and spoil the child" is little justified by these empirical findings. Parents who believe that by being nonpunitive of aggression they will raise children who bear a minimum of hostility can derive some amount of support from these data, providing they do not encourage aggressiveness in the child. Scientists who are interested in the mechanisms mediating the relationship between parental response to aggression and the child's manifestation of aggression can derive little comfort from the results thus far. It is evident that a number of variables must be disentangled: the degree to which aggression is valued, ignored, or discouraged; the method by which aggression is assessed; the severity of punishment used; the frequency of punishment; the mode of punishment; the child's relationship to the punishing agent; the parental affection for the child; the sex of the child; the principal punitive agent and the consistency and pattern of punishment procedures employed by the parents; the range and type of aggressive behaviors for which particular punishments are administered; the normative punishments used in the subculture; and, to conclude without exhausting the list of relevant variables, the age at which punishment is administered.

In analyzing the effects of any of these factors, it is assumed that the behavior of the child is a constant. Parents, however, are not immune to their children's behavior and their response to a particular act may be influenced by the history of their interaction with a child. A parent who uses severe punishment may have begun with soft words, which failed to achieve their objective of aggressive control. Children differ in their predisposition to aggression and in their docility. These variations in aggressiveness may evoke from the parents some portion of those very punitive behaviors which are assumed to be their antecedents. Although one can exaggerate the influence of the child's aggression upon the parents' disciplinary practices, the possible contribution of the child's behavior to the parent-child interaction has been largely ignored and some attention to this dimension is required.

THE REGULATION OF AGGRESSION

Inhibition and Facilitation

The acquisition of a repertoire of aggressive behaviors and the motivation to use these behaviors are necessary antecedents to the performance of an aggressive response. For aggression to attain overt expression, these antecedents must overcome the internal and external restraints that contribute to the regulation of aggressive behaviors. Indeed, for the Freudian psychoanalytic theorist, aggressive impulses are treated more or less as given, the psychologically interesting question being the source, strength, and consequences of inhibitions against aggression.

Issues pertinent to the role of inhibition have previously been considered in the context of personality correlates of aggression, the measurement of aggression, and the use

of punishment in the socialization of aggression. These data are, on the whole, consistent with the assumption that anxiety over aggression acts to inhibit the direct expression of aggressive tendencies (Lesser, 1958; MacCasland, 1961; Sears, 1961); however, the effects of inhibiting factors upon the persistence and displacement of aggressive impulses are much more ambiguous. It is very difficult to establish with correlational methods the functional relationship between inhibition and indirect aggressive behaviors. Consider, for example, Sears' (1961) findings that aggression anxiety is negatively correlated with antisocial aggression but is positively correlated with prosocial aggression and that girls display less antisocial and more prosocial aggression than boys. One can interpret these findings as indicating that the inhibition of antisocial aggression impulses increases the amount of aggression expressed in a prosocial form. However, it is also tenable to view these relationships in terms of sex-typing and the differential reinforcement of aggressive behaviors in boys and girls. In view of these alternative explanations and in view of the positive and indifferent as well as negative empirical relationships that have been reported between direct and indirect forms of aggression, these data offer little support to the notion of a fixed aggressive drive and a vicarious relationship between direct and indirect modes of aggression such that the latter is enhanced when the former is inhibited.

The antecedents of inhibition are equally murky. The relationship between parental use of punishment for aggression and the child's subsequent aggressive behavior is complicated by the drive-arousing and behavior-modeling effects of exposure to punishment. The evidence that parental punishment increases the probability of the aggressive behavior in the child is far more impressive than the evidence for inhibitory effects (Bandura and Walters, 1959; Eron et al., 1963; Glueck and Glueck, 1950; McCord, McCord, and Howard, 1961; Sears et al., 1953, 1957). In contrast to the results obtained for punishment, the use of reasoning as a method of discipline, parental warmth, and other factors related to conscience development are associated with the inhibition of aggression (Bandura and Walters, 1959; Baumrind, 1967;

Lesser, 1952; Sears, 1961; Sears et al., 1957).

The effects of punishment for aggression are most readily revealed through experimental manipulation and control of the type and agent of punishment, its timing, consistency, and other parameters. Nevertheless, controlled studies of children in which punishment for aggression has been systematically varied are rare for obvious ethical reasons. An experiment by Hollenberg and Sperry (1951), which was first published in 1951 and reprinted four years later (Chasdi and Lawrence, 1955), remains a basic study in this area, although knowledge of the more general effects of punishment has been considerably augmented in the ensuing years (Bandura, 1962; Mowrer, 1960; Solomon, 1964; Walters and Demkow, 1962). Hollenberg and Sperry (1951) observed the aggressive behavior of nursery school children over four doll play sessions. In the first session, experimental and control children were treated in a customary permissive manner by the experimenter. During the second session, children in the experimental group were administered mild verbal reproofs for aggressive behavior. In all other sessions with both the experimental and control subjects, the experimenter maintained a permissive attitude. The results showed the verbal punishment to have a temporary suppressing effect upon aggressive responses. While the control children increased in doll play aggression from one session to the next, the experimental group showed no increase between the first two sessions and, in addition, their aggressive behavior sharply declined in the third session. By the fourth session, however, the aggressive response level of the experimental group had recovered and was comparable to that of the control children.

Generalizations from this experiment to the social application of punishment are limited by the relatively mild rebukes employed. In addition, there was no attempt in this study to determine the effects of sustained punishment upon the strength of direct and indirect aggressive response tendencies. In view of the necessary restraints upon experimental manipulations of punishment for children's aggression, investigators will have to look to naturally occurring punishment situations, despite their greater complexity. In this regard, although there have

been extensive studies of the effects of parental punishment, insufficient attention has been given to the use of punishment for aggression by other socializing agents such as teachers. The numerous reports of marked variations in preschool children's aggression as a function of the particular nursery school attended (Muste and Sharpe, 1947; Jersild and Marky, 1955; Patterson et al., 1967; Roff and Roff, 1940) suggest that it would be fruitful to examine the influence of the teacher's attitude and response to aggression, controlling insofar as possible for concomitant variations in the structure and contents of the nursery school program.

Levin's (1955) study of classroom control and doll play aggression in kindergarten groups is illustrative of the potential usefulness of this approach. Judgments were made of the degree of control exercised in eight kindergarten classrooms, five characterized as high and three as low in dominance control. Children from these classrooms individually participated in two 20-minute doll play sessions separated by a 1-week interval. A reliable increase in aggression from the first to the second session was observed in both boys and girls from high-dominance classrooms while no significant change occurred in the low-dominance groups. Also, the children from high-dominance classrooms manifested less initial doll play aggression than the children from low-dominance classrooms, this tendency approaching statistical significance for the boys. The Levin (1955) study suggests that the exercise of strong control by teachers promotes the inhibition of aggressive responses but that this inhibition is dissipated in a permissive context such as is typical of doll play. These findings are reminiscent of the results reported by Lewin, Lippett, and White (1939) in their classic study comparing the effects of "democratic," "authoritarian," and "laissez-faire" atmospheres upon the pattern of aggressive behaviors manifested in boys' groups.

The increment in aggression with repeated doll play sessions observed by Levin (1955) in youngsters from high-dominance classrooms and by Hollenberg and Sperry (1951) in their control children appears to be a reliable phenomenon. It has been obtained in a majority of the studies in which children have been administered more than one doll play session (Bach, 1945; Sears, 1951; Yarrow, 1948). This result is generally believed to reflect a reduction in inhibition of aggression, although Buss (1961) has argued that the presence of a permissive adult during doll play may serve as a positive reinforcer for aggression. There are a number of studies indicating that the presence or absence of an adult and his relationships to the child exert a critical influence upon changes in doll play aggression (Levin and Turgeon, 1957; Siegel, 1957; Siegel and Kohn, 1959), although the mechanism mediating this influence is still unresolved. Levin and Turgeon (1957), for one group of preschool children, had both the child's mother and the experimenter present in the second doll session while for another group a stranger accompanied the experimenter. It was hypothesized that less aggression would be manifested in the "mother present" than in the "stranger present" situation. This hypothesis was based on the assumption that the strongest aggressive response tendencies and aggressive inhibitory tendencies are evoked in the home and, according to Miller's (1948) displacement model, generalization of aggression should be greater than the generalization of inhibition to the more dissimilar, "stranger present" situation. Results directly opposite to predictions were obtained, the "mother present" children showing an increase from the first to the second session while, with the stranger present, a nonsignificant decrement in aggression was observed.

Levin and Turgeon, as an explanation of their findings, proposed that the child abdicated to his mother the responsibility for aggressive behavior and assumed that she would inhibit disapproved actions. Bandura and Walters (1963a) have questioned this interpretation, noting that the increment in doll play aggression characteristically occurs with only the experimenter present and that the stranger may have had an inhibitory effect upon the children's play behavior. Siegel (1957), in an effort to isolate the effects of the presence of one adult, observed changes in aggression over two play sessions in which no adults were present in either session. Preschool children were assigned to like-sex pairs and were given the opportunity to play with a varied set of materials which lent themselves to both aggressive and nonaggressive activities. A significant *decrement* in aggression was found from the first to the second experimental session. This result was subsequently replicated in a study directly comparing the effects on the aggressive play activities of boys of an adult present in both play sessions with an adult absent (Siegel and Kohn, 1959). All of the subjects in the adult-absent condition decreased in aggression while two thirds of the subjects in the adult-present condition increased in aggression. These findings are consistent with the hypothesis that a child taught to inhibit aggression will assume responsibility for his behavior when alone and will "abdicate" that responsibility to an adult when one is present. They are also consistent with an explanation based on the reinforcing function of the adult (Bandura and Walters, 1963; Buss, 1961).

An inhibition interpretation of these data can be made which does not depend upon the rather abstruse assumption of the child temporarily relegating his superego to an adult. One need only assume that aggression anxiety is evoked by the stimulus cues of an adult in conjunction with the performance of an aggressive act. In order for anxiety reduction to occur, the child should aggress in the presence of a nonpunitive adult so that the permissive response of the adult to the child's aggressive acts would then facilitate extinction of the child's anxiety over aggression. This explanation also accounts for the finding that a high degree of experimenter-child interaction results in more doll play aggression than a low degree of experimenter-child interaction (Pintler, 1945), for the gradual increase in aggressive responses within a 10-minute doll play session (Hartup and Himeno, 1959) and for the eventual leveling off and variability of aggressive doll play beyond half-hour periods (Phillips, 1945). It is aso possible to account for these same observations by assuming that the experimenter reinforces aggressive play responses to the doll play stimuli. Operationally, the difference between a reduction in inhibition and the strengthening of a response tendency is difficult to discriminate, particularly when "no response" by an experimenter has been shown to function under some circumstances as a positive reinforcer (Adelman, 1967; Crandall, Good, and Crandall, 1964).

The fear that children may have of being punished for aggressive behaviors is only one source of inhibition of aggression. From the point of view of social control, fear of external punishment may be less important than the child's internalization of standards which motivate him, through self-administered disapproval or other means, to conform to social prohibitions (Aronfreed, 1961). In investigating the antecedents of conscience-produced inhibition, one looks to such variables as parental affection, nurturance, and the use of cognitive labeling in enforcing discipline rather than severity of punishment (Kohlberg, 1964). Clearly, additional attention needs to be given to aggression inhibitory mechanisms other than fear of punishment. The negative correlations that have been reported between empathy and aggression (Feshbach and Feshbach, 1968), between ego control and aggression (Livson and Mussen, 1957), and between affiliation arousal and aggression (Gordon and Smith, 1965) suggest that these may also be fruitful areas for the investigation of inhibitory processes.

Displacement

The concept of displacement is a powerful but loosely defined process that has been employed to account for aggressive behavior in stimulus situations to which an aggressive response appears unwarranted. It is assumed that the inhibition of aggression toward an instigating stimulus results in the expression of this aggressive disposition toward less threatening targets, which may be innocent of any provocation. Usually, it is also assumed that the displaced target is at some point along a similarity continuum with the instigating stimulus (A. Freud, 1946a; Miller, 1948). Miller's (1944, 1948) conflict model represents an explicit formulation of this conception of displacement, with the important additional assumption that the avoidance gradient is steeper than the approach (or aggression) generalization gradient. As previously indicated, for Miller's model conflict as such is incidental to displacement, which essentially is conceptualized as the resultant

of two generalization gradients. Although data have been cited suggesting that conflict may increase the strength of a displaced aggressive response (Whiting and Child, 1953; Wright, 1954), the evidence is not sufficiently compelling to require modification of the Miller model on this account.

The primary difficulty with the Miller model and, more broadly, with the concept of displacement lies elsewhere. In view of the many dimensions on which stimuli can vary, one is often at a loss to determine, a priori, along which of these dimensions aggression will generalize. For example, the inverse correlation reported between cotton yields in the Southern United States and lynching of Negroes (Hovland and Sears, 1940) suggests that the aggression induced by economic frustration is displaced to Negroes, but the similarity dimension along which the generalization of aggression to Negroes presumably took place is by no means obvious. In another context, Sears et al. (1953) have used the Miller model to account for the finding that children of highly punitive mothers showed little aggression in school and a great deal of aggression in doll play. As Bandura and Walters have noted, "the assumption that a doll play kit containing parent and child dolls and a house with furniture has *fewer* elements in common with the child's home than has the regular school setting is open to question" (1963a, p. 399). The analysis of displacement effects is further complicated by the specific aggressive and avoidance tendencies that have been acquired to each of the stimuli that make up the generalization continuum. Whether hostility generated at home is expressed in school activities depends upon the reinforcements, punishments, and instigation to aggression that characterize the school setting as well as its similarity to the home situation.

Although our ability to predict the displacement of aggression and our knowledge of the mediating processes are very limited, there have been a number of studies with children and adults which demonstrate that displacement is indeed a genuine phenomenon (Berkowitz and Holmes, 1959, 1950; Berkowitz and Green, 1962; Ferson, 1958; Kaufman and Feshbach, 1963; Miller and Bugelski, 1948; Weiss and Fine, 1956). The previously cited experiment of Miller and Bugelski (1948) can also be considered as evidence for the displacement of aggression. The decrease in positive evaluations of Mexican and Japanese on checklists given before and after the frustrating experience indicates that the hostility aroused by the frustration was displaced toward these minority groups. Inasmuch as no control was included to determine the effect of retaking the dependent measures after a nonfrustrating experience, these findings must be considered as providing only tentative support for the displacement hypothesis.

Indirect evidence of displacement is provided by Mussen's (1950) study of racial attitudes in Caucasian boys before and after an interracial summer camp experience with Negro children. While many of the white youngsters became more favorable toward Negroes as a result of the experience, some increased in prejudice. The latter displayed strong aggressive dispositions and needs to defy authority on projective tests. Mussen hypothesized that these boys were dissatisfied with many aspects of the camp experience and vented their negative feelings on to the Negro children. Berkowitz (1962) has suggested that the boys who increased in prejudice may have been initially hostile toward the Negro boys (suggesting an initial displacement reaction) and misinterpreted their actions, thereby actually feeling more frustrated by the Negro boys.

The irrationality of social prejudice lends itself to a displacement interpretation (Adorno et al., 1950), although there are serious reservations as to the adequacy of this interpretation (Asch, 1952; Christie and Jahoda, 1954). The fact that minority group members are often convenient scapegoats for the inadequacies and frustrations of the prejudiced is an example of displaced aggression but does not explain prejudice, which may well precede scapegoat behavior. However, the study of scapegoating, which is intimately related to the mechanism of displacement, could provide essential insights into the condition facilitating displacement. Nevertheless, although scapegoat behavior is not restricted to intergroup relations and appears to occur frequently in schoolchildren, there are surprisingly few systematic investigations of this phenomenon in children. The early group

atmosphere experiments (Lewin, Lippitt, and White, 1939; White and Lippitt, 1960), actually concerned with a broader range of behaviors, may be viewed partly as an investigation of scapegoat behavior in children. In these studies, clubs, consisting of five 11-year-old boys, were subject to three different types of adult leadership and group atmosphere: democratic, authoritarian, and laissez-faire. Under democratic leadership, group activities and goals were arrived at through group discussions and decisions, the leader primarily offering guidance, evaluation, and support. Under authoritarian conditions, the adult leader remained distant from the group, determined policies and assignments, and arbitrarily dispensed praise and criticism. In the laissez-faire atmosphere, the leader remained passive and provided information only when solicited; this group was essentially free to make its own decisions about goals and procedures.

The authoritarian atmosphere elicited both greater aggression and greater passivity than either of the other conditions. The least aggression, the most constructive responses, and the highest morale were evidenced under democratic leadership. The children in the authoritarian groups not only displayed more aggression toward their leader but also engaged in more bickering and internal strife. There were several indications of displaced aggression produced by the autocratic atmosphere, including instances of scapegoat behavior in which authoritarian club members focused their hostility on one of their own group members. In two cases, the "scapegoats" were treated so badly that they left the club. In addition to the spontaneous emergence of scapegoat behavior in the authoritarian groups, aggressive displacement reactions toward an out-group were manifested by these children when they were subjected to hostile criticism by a stranger (actually a confederate of the experimenter).

Any generalizations of the superior effects of the democratic atmosphere and the hostility created by the authoritarian atmosphere must be restricted to populations similar to those employed in the experimental studies. These children had been raised under child-rearing conditions more comparable to the democratic than the autocratic structure. However, children raised in an authoritarian society and family setting may find the autocratic leadership satisfying and the democratic atmosphere frustrating.

With regard to the problem of displacement, the antecedents of aggression in these experiments—that is, the autocratic versus democratic group atmosphere—are less relevant than the factors which appeared to direct scapegoat behavior. White and Lippitt (1960) observed that the displaced aggression manifested toward club members was directed toward the restoration of self-esteem. They noted that the scapegoats were never the weakest or safest targets. Rather they were boys who were quite capable of self-defense in an individual struggle. It was because of the relative physical strength of the scapegoat that the authors derived the hypothesis that the function of the displaced aggression was the recovery of status or self-esteem. It is also conceivable that the choice of the displaced object was influenced by his similarity to the powerful autocratic leader. It is not possible to decide between these alternatives on the basis of the available data.

White and Lippitt (1960, p. 158), on the basis of qualitative observations, offered several hypotheses concerning the conditions that prevent the dissatisfaction created by an autocracy from being translated into direct or displaced aggression. Aggression is purportedly not evoked when (1) the followers develop an attitude of hero worship toward the leader, (2) the boys are preoccupied with continual activities incompatible with rebellious behavior, (3) aggression appears completely nonfunctional and futile, (4) aggressive behavior does not occur as a possibility, either because no one sets an aggressive example or because nonaggressive attitudes have been reinforced in comparable situations.

Each of these hypotheses would be well worth additional investigation. In essence they imply that while the potential for aggression may be created by a frustrating state of affairs, aggressive impulses are not evoked, even in disguised form, when the individual is engaged in behaviors incompatible with aggression and when aggression has a low probability of success. The latter stricture may hold for the instrumental components of aggression but seems less applicable to the expressive components.

The proposition that the displacement of aggression reduces feelings of powerlessness in the aggressor and acts to restore his self-esteem has important implications for the management of aggression but is difficult to test directly. One would have to show an increase in self-esteem following the performance of an aggressive act and demonstrate that this restoration of self-esteem reinforces or motivates the aggressive behavior. There is evidence for adults that threats to self-esteem as compared to more impersonal and "shared" threats facilitate the displacement of aggression (Feshbach and Singer, 1956). The more general problem of the conditions under which a threat promotes cohesion in a group or creates disruption and internal strife has been a matter of considerable interest to social psychologists (Burnstein and MacRae, 1962; Hamblyn, 1958; Mulder and Stemerding, 1963). The previously cited study by Wright (1943), who found that strong friends increased cooperativeness and weak friends decreased cooperativeness following frustration, suggests that the structure of a group or the relationship existing among the members is a critical variable determining when a displaced aggressive response to threat will occur.

The most extensive study of this problem with children's groups is that of Sherif et al. (1961). These investigators carried out a number of field experiments that were designed to elicit and reduce intergroup hostility. Boys, shortly after they arrived at a summer camp, were assigned to one of two groups—the Bull Dogs or the Red Devils. A period of cooperative activity was implemented within each group to foster cohesiveness and the development of an internal group structure. A series of competitive games and contests was then introduced between the two groups. An initially friendly competition was gradually replaced by intergroup hostility. Within-group solidarity was also fostered during the early part of the competition. However, when members of one group realized they were losing in the cumulative competition, internal bickering and strife developed. The experimenter, after deliberately exaggerating the hostility between the two groups, then tried out several techniques for reducing the hostility between the two groups. The only strategy found effective in this first experiment required the group as a whole to compete against an outside camp in an athletic game, a technique which involves the focusing of hostility onto another group or scapegoat. In order to further investigate alternative strategies, intergroup hostility was generated in a subsequent experiment, where one of the most effective hostility reducing techniques actually entailed subjecting the boys to a frustrating event. The groups were on an overnight camping trip and an old truck, which was to deliver their midday meal, ostensibly broke down. A large rope, used in intergroup tug-of-war contests, was employed by both groups in a joint effort to pull the truck. When the truck returned with the food, the two groups again spontaneously engaged in cooperative behavior by preparing the food together.

The Sherif et al. (1961) study rather dramatically demonstrates that a frustrating event need not result in the displacement of aggression toward another target, even when a negative attitude toward that target already exists. The positive response to the frustration appeared to be due to the perception that the frustration was jointly shared by the antagonists and to the cooperative, task-oriented responses which were required to overcome the frustration.

The study of frustration and displacement in group settings requires the consideration of parameters that are completely absent in the individual displacement paradigm. For this reason, the Miller (1945) model is of limited utility in understanding and predicting the patterns of aggression displayed in the Sherif et al. (1961) studies. The model is more appropriate to simpler situations in which aggression is evoked by a provoking stimulus and aggressive behaviors are observed toward new stimuli with which the subject has no prior experience except that mediated by its similarity to the goal object. One of the difficulties in applying the model to even this restricted situation is the need for prior assessment of the slopes and elevation of the approach and avoidance gradients in order to predict the displacement response. This difficulty is illustrated in the previously cited study by Moore (1964), involving a shooting game in which targets varying in similarity to a frustrating stimulus were selected by the subject. The hypothesis that the children would prefer, as targets, objects sim-

ilar to the frustrating stimulus was partially supported by the choices of the boys, whereas the girls tended to choose dissimilar targets. The Miller model nicely accounts for this difference if one makes the reasonable assumption that the girls were higher in aggression anxiety than the boys. However, depending upon the respective strengths of the aggression and avoidance gradients, a finding that both boys and girls chose dissimilar targets or similar targets would also be compatible with the model.

In summarizing the empirical data bearing upon the displacement of aggression by children, it appears that much greater attention has been given to stimulus displacement than to response displacement, although changes in the form of the aggressive response usually accompany changes in the stimulus object. It is also evident that displacement of aggression is an important and real phenomena. Investigations of displacement have pointed to the complexity of this behavior but have also yielded some interesting and plausible suggestions as to the conditions that govern displacement responses. However, these hypotheses have yet to be supported by "hard" data and must still be considered as largely conjectural.

Catharsis

The concept of catharsis has been used to describe the process through which emotion, particularly anger, is discharged. It has its origins in the Greek drama, referring to "the state of feeling produced by the dramatic tragedy. It meant the stillness at the center of one's being which came after pity or fear had been burned out. The soul is purified and calmed, freed from the violent passions" (Schaar, 1961, p. 520). When first introduced into contemporary psychological theory by Freud and Breuer in their papers on the treatment of hysteria, it referred to the tension-reducing consequences of emotional expression. It was assumed that giving vent to one's hostile feelings, even without inflicting damage, would reduce the intensity of the hostility. The emphasis in this formulation was upon the affective-expressive aspects of aggression. The meaning of the concept was subsequently modified in the frustration-aggression volume (Dollard et al., 1939) to denote a reduction in aggressive drive consequent to the infliction of injury. Thus the catharsis hypothesis, as formulated by Dollard and his colleagues, asserts that any act of aggression, including a displaced aggressive response, reduces the instigation to aggression.

This ostensibly straightforward proposition has proved exceedingly difficult to test. The principal source of the difficulty lies in the competing effect of a rewarding aggressive action. A successful aggressive act, although reducing aggressive drive, may actually increase the probability of subsequent aggression through reinforcement of the aggressive response, a reduction in aggression-anxiety, or through the aggressive response-eliciting properties of aggressive stimuli. The recommendation to discharge hostile feelings by practicing on a punching bag may have the unintended effect of increasing boxing skills and decreasing anxiety over fighting. In order to predict the theoretical effects of an aggressive act upon subsequent aggressive behavior, the relative strengths of the drive decrement and response increment effects must be assessed or inferred. These will vary with the conditions antecedent to the intervening aggressive act, with the dependent measures used to assess subsequent aggressive tendencies and with the time interval between the two aggressive actions. It is not surprising, then, that the research literature on catharsis has yielded mixed results.

While the catharsis hypothesis, as formulated by Dollard et al. (1937), pertains to the functional value of any act of aggression, the principal focus of experimental interest has been in the cathartic effects of substitute, especially fantasy modes of aggressive expression. Experimenters have determined the impact upon the child's aggressive behavior of participation in aggressive play (Feshbach, 1956; Kenny, 1953; Mallick and McCandless, 1966), the evocation of aggressive fantasies in response to TAT type stimuli (L. Lesser, 1962), and of vicarious aggressive fantasy through exposure to filmed aggressive content (Bandura, Ross, and Ross, 1963a; Lovaas, 1961; Mussen and Rutherford, 1961; Siegal, 1956; Walters and Thomas, 1963). The predominant finding, with certain important exceptions, has been a relative or absolute increase in children's aggressive behavior following aggressive play or witnessing aggressive interactions on film.

Findings contrary to the catharsis hypothesis were first reported by Kenny (1953) in a study comparing the aggressive story completions of an experimental group of grade school children who participated in two release-therapy type doll play sessions with those of a control who were given two sessions of nonaggressive play with jigsaws and swings. It was anticipated that the opportunity for physical and verbal aggression provided in the experimental doll play sessions would facilitate the catharsis of aggression. A before-after comparison of the responses to the Korner Incomplete Stories Test (1949) showed, however, a significantly greater *decrease* in aggression in the control than in the experimental subjects.

Feshbach (1956) investigated the effects of aggressive play on children's social interactions. The initial level of aggressiveness of children, varying in age for 5 to 8 years, was determined by teacher ratings. High- and low-aggressive children were then randomly assigned to an aggressive toy group, to a neutral toy group, or to a control group who followed their regular classroom activities. Each of the two experimental groups was subdivided into four play groups of five children, which met for one 50-minute session a week for a period of 4 weeks. Children in the aggressive toy group listened to a record and story with aggressive themes and were then provided with objects such as soldiers, pirates, guns, which lent themselves to aggressive play. The neutral toy groups were told nonaggressive stories and were given nonaggressive toys such as farm implements and trains with which to play. Thematic aggression expressed in the context of ongoing play and appropriate to that play was distinguished from nonthematic aggressive responses, which were not part of the play activity. Examples of nonthematic responses were taunting or striking another child independently of the content of a play theme. These responses occurred with much greater frequency in the aggressive toy group than in the control group. The two groups did not differ in before and after changes in teacher ratings of aggression and were consequently combined for comparison with the controls. Boys initially low in aggression who participated in the play sessions showed significantly greater increments in aggression ratings than did low-aggressive boys in the control group. High-aggressive boys tended to decrease in aggression, but this effect, probably due to statistical regression, was no greater in the experimental groups than in the control group. No significant changes on teachers' ratings were reported for the girls.

These findings appeared to be inconsistent with the results of a previous investigation by Feshbach (1955) with college students in which a reduction in aggression was reported in angered subjects who had been given the opportunity to express hostility in TAT type fantasy. The apparent inconsistency can be resolved if it is assumed that aggressive drive must be elicited at the time of vicarious or direct aggressive behavior if the aggressive act is to have a drive-reducing effect. Evidence in support of this hypothesis was obtained by Feshbach (1961) in an experiment in which groups of angered and neutral college students witnessed either a fight film or a control film. A reduction in aggression subsequent to the fight film as compared to the control film was found for the angered subjects only.

The assumption that aggressive drive must be evoked in order for an aggressive act to have a cathartic effect accounts for most, although not all of the discrepant findings in this area. The studies by Bandura and his associates on modeling effects (Bandura, 1961; Bandura, Ross, and Ross, 1961, 1963a) bear upon the catharsis issue. In these studies, children were mildly frustrated before the measurement of modeling effects but not before exposure to the model. One might expect, under these circumstances, that watching a model perform an aggressive act would have a stimulating or disinhibiting effect on the observer. Thus Lovaas (1961) found that preschool children shown an aggressive cartoon film depressed a lever operating a hitting doll more frequently than children who had been shown a nonaggressive cartoon film. Although this effect was not observed in two initial experiments, it attained statistical significance in a third experiment in which the dependent measure was modified so that the child was given a choice between pressing the lever operating the hitting doll or a lever operating a ball toy. Larder (1962) observed

a similar increment in the frequency of operating a hitting doll toy in preschool children who had been read an aggressive story in comparison to a control group which heard a neutral story.

Siegal (1956) employed a social interaction play situation to determine the effects of a film-mediated fantasy aggression experience. Same-sex pairs of nursery school children witnessed a highly aggressive cartoon film and a nonaggressive cartoon film of equal interest, the showing of each film being separated by a 1-week interval. Following each film showing, the two children were left alone in a playroom while their behavior was scored for aggression and for anxiety and guilt by an observer. Difference scores between the nonaggressive and aggressive condition failed to yield any significant effects, although a trend toward increased aggression in the aggressive film group was obtained. Walters and his collaborators (1962, 1963), however, have effectively demonstrated that exposure to aggressive film content can affect social interaction as well as individual play activities. In a series of experiments using hospital attendants, high school boys, and young women from a hostel for working girls, experimental subjects witnessed an aggressive scene from the motion picture "Rebel Without a Cause" while control subjects watched a film of adolescents cooperating in constructive activities. The dependent measure, administered before and after the film exposure, consisted of the subject administering electric shock in a fictitious learning experiment to a confederate of the experimenter. All three experimental groups showed a significant increase in the shock levels used in comparison to the changes obtained in their respective controls. In addition, the experimental males scored higher than the control males on the Buss-Durkee inventory of aggression, the difference for girls being insignificant.

The results obtained are particularly impressive in the view of the replication and of the direct, interpersonal character of the dependent measure of aggression. It is possible that the control film as well as the aggression film contributed to this consistency in that the control film may have encouraged cooperative behaviors that were incompatible with infliction of electric shock. In a sense, any "control" condition is an experimental treatment which serves as a reference for the evaluation of the effects of some other treatment. No matter what control film was used, the difference obtained would be relative to the two conditions and could be attributed to either one independently. If one employed a wide array of nonaggressive "control" films, all of which resulted in less aggression than the aggressive film, it would still be logically tenable, even if not theoretically probable to attribute the differences to the competing responses produced by the control film as well as to the facilitation of aggression by the experimental film. In any case, these experiments indicate that there is greater rather than less aggression following a vicarious aggressive experience as compared to a nonaggressive experience, when aggressive drive has not been experimentally aroused before the experimental treatment.

There have been several experiments with children in which the initial level of aggression has been manipulated immediately before the subject participates in an aggressive or nonaggressive treatment. In the Mussen and Rutherford (1961) study cited earlier, groups of frustrated and nonfrustrated first-grade children were shown an aggressive animated cartoon, a nonaggressive cartoon, or no cartoon. Subjects who saw the aggressive cartoon obtained significantly higher aggression scores than either of the other two groups on the balloon test administered after the experimental treatment. Since there was no difference between frustrated and nonfrustrated children on this test, it is possible that the frustration condition was not very effective and that aggressive drive was only minimally evoked. The study, while demonstrating the stimulating effects of exposure to an aggressive cartoon, does not permit an adequate evaluation of the influence of initial level of aggression arousal.

The same restriction does not hold for the previously cited Mallick and McCandless study (1966), in which a strong aggressive effect of frustration was obtained. In their last two experiments, third graders, following frustration or nonfrustration, were assigned to an aggressive play, social talk, or "interpretation" of frustration treatment before the dependent measures of aggression were administered. The aggressive intervening experience consisted of shooting guns at a target on

which was placed a picture of a child of the same age and sex of the frustrating or nonfrustrating agent. The social talk treatment consisted of an 8-minute conversation with the experimenter while in the "interpretation" condition, the behavior of the frustrator was attributed to his being upset and was otherwise rationalized. The results indicated that under nonfrustration conditions, there was a consistent tendency for the aggressive play group to respond more aggressively than the social talk group on the criterion measure. The criterion measure consisted of the number of responses interfering with or facilitating the performance of the older child who had initially participated in the frustrating or nonfrustrating task with the subject. Under frustrating conditions, there was little difference between the aggressive play and social talk groups. The "interpretation" group, however, displayed significantly less aggression than the other two groups. Comparable results were obtained with a verbal "like-dislike" aggression rating.

An incidental finding of interest was obtained in the third experiment in which the like-dislike rating was omitted for half the children. The subjects who had been administered the like-dislike ratings obtained higher aggression scores on the task interference measure than the subjects who had not made the rating. On the basis of this finding, Mallick and McCandless (1966) suggest that verbal expression of hostility, say, in therapy, could actually increase aggressive behavior rather than exert a cathartic effect. The gap between a rating and verbal behaviors in therapy is too large to permit any generalization, but the possibility merits investigation. More directly relevant to the catharsis hypothesis are the effects of the experiences intervening between frustration and the criterion measure. While the reduction in aggression following the "interpretation" condition was very clearly demonstrated, the explanation is more ambiguous. The effect may have been mediated by a cognitive reevaluation of the frustrator's behavior so that it no longer appeared to be mean or arbitrarily threatening. It is also quite possible that the subjects felt inhibited because of the experimenter's positive attitude toward the frustrator or conformed to an implicit "message" that the frustrator was a good fellow and should not be aggressed against. The failure of the aggression play condition to lower aggression in the frustrated subjects cannot be taken as strong negative evidence since there is no a priori theoretical reason for one to expect the subjects to have identified the target with the frustrator or the shooting of a gun at this target to have high substitute value. Nevertheless, this experiment, coupled with the evidence of aggressive stimulating effects reported in other studies, places the burden for the positive demonstration of catharsis upon those investigators, such as this writer, who would argue that substitute aggressive activities can serve to control and reduce aggressive tendencies.

Moderate support for the cathartic effects of aggressive fantasy in children is reported by N. Lesser (1962). Seven- to nine-year-old boys were initially administered part of the Michigan Picture Test and then categorized as High and Low Fantasy on the basis of their scores on the Weisskopf Transcendence Index (1950). Following the induction of frustration through administration of an unsolvable puzzle and the loss of an attractive toy, the boys engaged in immediate free play or were given a fantasy task or a neutral task before free play. For the fantasy task, they were administered three cards from the Michigan Picture Test while the subject in the neutral task condition played with a "Bird Bingo" game. Contrary to the expected outcome, the High Fantasy subjects showed more overt aggression in free play than the Low Fantasy subjects. The positive relationship between TAT type fantasy and individual free play aggression is not surprising if one considers that both tasks tap the child's expressiveness and lack of inhibition. Of greater relevance to the cartharsis issue were the significantly higher aggression scores obtained by the boys who particpated in the neutral task as compared to the boys who had the opportunity to express aggression in fantasy. The aggression means for the immediate free play group and the fantasy group were comparable, suggesting that the neutral task increased aggression rather than the fantasy task reducing it. However, the immediate free play task does not control for the lapse of time, possible incubation effects, the interaction between the frustration and an intervening task and other factors which

may contribute to an increase in aggression. A finding that most neutral tasks under these conditions resulted in higher aggression than a fantasy task would imply that fantasy does serve to control aggressive impulses and "reduces" aggression relative to the amont that would be displayed under nonfantasy conditions.

The investigations of catharsis that have been reviewed here suggest that the prior or simultaneous evocation of aggressive drive may possibly be necessary but is not a sufficient condition for an aggressive act to have a cathartic effect. There also needs to be a functional relationship between the goal behavior and the substitute act. From the Lewinian studies on substitute value, it appears that the degree of similarity between the substitute act and the goal response is a significant determinant of the tension-reducing properties of the substitute behavior (Escalona, 1954). Although similarity is not a well defined theoretical dimension, it does point to characteristics of indirect aggressive acts, which may partly determine their cathartic effects. In evaluating the cathartic effect, it may be necessary to distinguish between a reduction in expressive aggression and hostile aggressive drive. Both of these effects may be obscured by an increment in instrumental aggression. In order to evaluate hypotheses regarding the consequences of an aggressive act, a number of measures which are differentially responsive to these diverse effects should be utilized. Assuming that these measures are about equally responsive to changes in drive strength, then the more similar the response assessed in the dependent measure is to the rewarding, drive-reducing aggressive act, the more likely one is to find evidence of an increment in aggression. In comparison, dissimilar measures will be more likely to reflect decrements in aggression. Consequently, in evaluating the effects of an aggressive activity upon subsequent aggression, opposite inferences can be drawn, depending upon the measures of aggression used.

Effects of Mass Media

The studies of modeling and catharsis through vicarious aggression pertain directly to the issue of the influence of the mass media upon children's aggression. The experiments on the effects of witnessing aggression depicted on film have, with few exceptions, reported a stimulating effect on aggressive behavior (Bandura, Ross, and Ross, 1963a; Lovaas, 1961; Mussen and Rutherford, 1961; Siegal, 1956; Walters et al., 1962, 1963). There is a wide gap, however, between the isolated influence of a brief exposure of an aggressive film and the impact of prolonged exposure to aggressive content in television and films. The laboratory measures of aggression and the context in which they have been assessed often differ markedly from the aggressive behavior and social setting in which the influence of the mass media is presumably manifested. There have been a number of investigations which have manipulated conditions closer to the actual functioning of the media (Albert, 1957; Bailyn, 1959; Emery, 1959; Feshbach, 1967a, 1967b; Maccoby and Wilson, 1957) and these help to bridge the gap between the laboratory experiments and field surveys of reactions to the mass media.

There is no doubt that acts of crime and violence are depicted in the mass media (Head, 1954; Wertham, 1954) and that children are exposed to these aggressive stimuli (Himmelweit, Oppenheim, and Vince, 1958). Survey studies indicate that violence on television is believed to be responsible for delinquent behaviors and that parents and professionals are very concerned about the effects upon children of continual exposure to aggressive content in television (Klapper, 1954; Smythe, 1955). This concern is reflected in the research issues which are raised regarding the specific impact of television upon human behavior (Arons and May, 1963). The recognition of the need for additional research is matched by the confidence with which some authorities assert that violence in the mass media is responsible for delinquent behavior and sundry forms of psychopathology (Banay, 1955; Wertham, 1954). It has been surprisingly difficult to demonstrate this proposition empirically. If the mass media do stimulate and reinforce aggressive behaviors, the effects are subtle and restricted to a small and probably disturbed segment of the population.

In an extensive study performed in England by Himmelweit, Oppenheim, and Vince (1958), 1854 children, aged 10 to 11 and 13 to 14, were divided into "viewers," who had television available at home, and "con-trols," who did not have television sets at home and did not regularly watch television elsewhere. Members of the two groups were individually matched on a number of demographic variables and, insofar as possible, were selected from the same classrooms. In addition, the subsequent introduction of television in one geographic area permitted the comparison of a subsample who had acquired a television set with a matched group of those who had not. A substantial minority of the viewers reported having been frightened occasionally by TV fare. Nevertheless, there were no significant differences between viewers and nonviewers on measures of aggression, delinquency, and maladjustment. Comparable negative findings have been obtained for exposure to violence in radio (Riccutti, 1951), with conflicting data reported for exposure to violence in comic books (Hoult, 1949; Lewin, 1953).

There are several studies demonstrating a relationship between aggressive personality predispositions and a preference for aggressive content in pictorial media (Bailyn, 1959; Eron, 1963; Schramm, Lyle, and Parker, 1961), although the functional value for the aggressive child of this selective exposure is uncertain. Bailyn (1959), in an elaborate study of children's habits pertaining to various media, found that boys who particularly liked aggressive hero material tended to be emotionally disturbed, to come from problem families, and also to show a disposition to project blame onto others. Eron (1963) obtained a significant positive relationship between degree of aggression of third-grade boys, as determined by peer judgments, and the violence ratings of their favorite programs, as reported by both fathers and mothers. The amount of television observed, however, was related negatively to the sociometric aggression scores. Both Bailyn (1961) and Eron (1963) found inconsistent or negligible relationships between the personality measures of girls and their reactions to the mass media.

Schramm et al. (1961) have reported stronger relationships between personality dispositions and media behavior in middle than in low socioeconomic groups and in adolescents than in pre-adolescents. They divided sixth- and tenth-grade children into four groups based on the joint use of television and printed material and, in addition, administered the Sears (1961) aggression scales to the entire sample. For the tenth-grade children, the fantasy-oriented groups ("high TV, low print") was significantly higher than the other groups in antisocial aggression, whereas the reality-oriented group ("low TV, high print") was lowest in anti-social aggression and highest in aggression anxiety. These relationships were not sig-nificant for the lower socioeconomic group, partly because of their generally high anti-social aggression scores. The fantasy-oriented children appeared to have experienced greater frustrations than the other groups, as re-flected in the high frequency of parental and peer conflicts reported for these children. Comparable relationships between apparent level of frustration and preference for violent and action programs were obtained by Riley and Riley (1951) and by Bailyn in the pre-viously cited study (1961). It is tempting to infer that the frustrated, conflict-ridden chil-dren seek out television to obtain satisfactions they cannot achieve in everyday life. How-ever, an equally cogent argument can be made that television serves to support and reinforce their aggressive attitudes.

Experimental manipulation of relatively standard motion picture or television fare has provided more direct information concerning the behavior consequences of exposure to the film media and has helped define some of the mediating processes through which the stim-uli portrayed in the films influence the child. Thus Siegal (1958) has shown that children acquire role expectancies from the manner in which a particular occupation was depicted in a series of radio dramas. Maccoby, Levin, and Selya (1955) and Maccoby and Wilson (1957) have reported results indicating that what children learn from the media is also dependent upon predispositional variables and their interaction with the stimulus con-tent presented. Fifth- and sixth-grade chil-dren, after a frustrating or neutral experience, were exposed to a film depicting aggressive and nonaggressive interactions (Maccoby, Levin, and Selya, 1955). Consistent with ex-pectation, the frustrated children remem-bered more of the aggressive and less of the neutral material than the control group. These results were not confirmed, however, in a subsequent replication (Maccoby, Levin, and Selya, 1956). In a later study, Maccoby and

Wilson (1957) showed complete motion pic-tures to seventh-grade students and found that the subjects remembered more of the events and behaviors relating to the film character with whom they identified. Thus boys recalled more aggressive content than girls when the agent of aggression in a film was a boy. The results suggested that the child's self-perceptions and self-ideal influ-enced his choice of identification figure, which in turn affected his recall of the film content.

Albert (1957) and Emery (1959) have examined the influence of exposure to films upon aggressive tendencies. Albert (1957) divided 8- to 10-year-old children into high-, medium-, and low-aggression groups on the basis of their scores on the Rosenzweig Picture Frustration Test. Children from each aggression group witnessed a western film with one of three endings. For one group, the conclusion of a western was doctored so that the villain was successful, for a second variation the film was left incom-plete in that there was no resolution of the conflict, while a third group was adminis-tered the conventional western version. After seeing the films, the children were readmin-istered the Picture Frustration Test. The changes in aggression that were observed were unsystematic and were not statistically stable. There was some tendency for the in-complete version of the film to produce a greater decrement in aggression in the high- and medium-aggression groups, relative to the changes produced by the standard and the doctored versions. Of interest was the greater dislike manifested for the villian when he was successful. This result is in conflict with Bandura's findings with preschool sub-jects and may reflect a developmental differ-ence in attitudes toward villainy.

Emery (1959) showed a complete motion picture to 10- and 13-year-old children and assessed changes in aggression with the Pic-ture Frustration Test and the Thematic Ap-perception Test. He found indications of an increase in threatening percepts and in the tendency to defend one's current situation. Such defense was distinguished from hostile aggression, which was not significantly modi-fied by exposure to the film. These findings, in conjunction with Albert's results, provide little support for either the aggression-en-hancing or aggression-reducing hypothesized effects of exposure to aggressive interactions on film. Conclusions from these studies are limited, however, by the reliance on projective procedures to evaluate changes in aggressive tendencies and by the restricted stimulus content sampled.

Feshbach (1967a, 1967b) has recently reported on a field study, conducted in collaboration with R. D. Singer, in which television content was experimentally varied over a 6-week period in order to assess the influence of differential exposure to aggressive stimuli upon aggressive attitudes and behavior. The subjects were 665 boys in seven different institutional settings, five in Southern California and two in New York City. The boys were randomly assigned within each institution to a television schedule containing predominantly aggressive programs or to a control treatment of predominantly nonaggressive programs. The institutional setting included three private schools (one a military school) and four boys' homes. The homes were residential settings for boys from a predominantly low socioeconomic background whose families are unable or unfit to take care of them. The students at the private schools were from predominantly upper middle- to lower upper-class backgrounds. The boys ranged in age from 10 to 17 years old and, with the exception of two institutions, volunteered for the project. The subjects and the cottage supervisors who were to record and rate their behavior were informed that the study was concerned with the relationship between the evaluation of different types of TV programs and the personality and attitudes of the viewer. A rationale for viewing the same program series and similar types of programs was also provided. Questionnaire measures of Overt and Covert Hostility, Aggression-Anxiety, Impulsiveness, Aggressive values, and peer ratings of aggression and a TAT measure of fantasy aggression were administered before and after the 6-week experimental period. In addition, daily behavior ratings were submitted for each boy by his immediate supervisor. The boys also rated each TV program they observed, in part as a check on the effectiveness of the experimental manipulation. All subjects were required to watch a minimum of 6 hours of television a week and were permitted to view as much television as they wanted, provided they observed programs from the designated list or "diet."

The most impressive differences were yielded by the behavior ratings, which essentially consisted of the recording of aggressive incidents. The frequency of verbal aggression and physical aggression, whether directed toward peers or authority figures, was consistently higher in the control group exposed to the nonaggressive programs as compared to the experimental group who had been placed on the aggressive "diet." This effect was significant for the subjects in the boys' homes, but not for the private school samples. Similar trends were observed for the elementary, junior high, and high school samples. The difference between the control and experimental groups in aggressive behavior directed toward peers was greatest in boys who were initially aggressive, especially boys above the mean on the questionnaire measures of hostility. Significant effects on two measures of aggressive values and on the sociometric rating scale were obtained for subsamples initially predisposed to aggression. The TAT fantasy measure was the only one on which the aggressive TV group increased relative to the change in the control group. This difference is readily attributable to generalization of the TV content to the TAT stories they were asked to construct.

These data offer little support for the hypothesis that exposure to aggressive content in television leads to an increase in aggressive behavior. On the contrary, the experimental findings provide some evidence suggesting that exposure to aggressive content in television serves to reduce or control the expression of aggression, although in a select sample of children. The provision of a reward for all participants and the use of volunteers were designed to foster a positive attitude toward participation in the study, regardless of the experimental assignment. The favorable attitudes of the boys toward both the aggressive and nonaggressive programs indicated that this goal was accomplished and that it is unlikely that the experimental difference was a function of differential preference for one or the other diet.

One possible interpretation of the main experimental effect is in terms of the cognitive support which aggressive television content provides in "binding" and regulating the aggressive impulse of boys with strong aggressive tendencies. Removal of this support may have produced the increment in aggression observed in the control group. This explanation is predicated on the assumption of a population that has been socialized in a cultural setting which has enabled the children to become accustomed to witnessing aggression on television. The group for whom there was no significant effect—the higher IQ, private school samples—had had relatively little access to television before the implementation of the experiment. These boys are reminiscent of the "reality" group of Schramm et al. (1961), who had little need for fantasy experience and control.

Since single experiments are rarely definitive, and since alternative interpretations of these data are possible, it would be inappropriate to advocate, on the basis of the preceding findings, that aggressive boys be encouraged to watch aggressive television programs. In addition, the studies of Siegal (1958), Bandura, Ross, and Ross, (1963a), Maccoby and Wilson (1957), and Walters and Thomas (1963) indicate that children learn aspects of the aggressive content depicted on films and that, under some circumstances, their level of aggression is increased by exposure to this content. Nevertheless, the Feshbach (1967a, 1967b) findings suggest that the playlike behavior frequently used in laboratory studies to assess aggression may not be on the same continuum as the aggressive social interaction, which is the object of parental and professional concern. It may be that the "message" of fantasy conveyed by fictional presentation in the mass media is perceived as such by children and is much less influential in shaping their aggressive attitudes than the "message" of reality.

CONCLUDING OBSERVATIONS

The methodological problems that limit the inferences that can be drawn from research on aggression have been alluded to throughout the chapter and will not be further elaborated in this concluding statement. Also, rather than summarizing areas of conflict or agreement, we shall consider research issues that are believed to be central to an understanding of aggression, and, either through

neglect or procedural difficulty, have been only barely investigated, if at all.

The most obvious hiatus and, in many respects, the most important, is the absence of descriptive, normative data bearing on the development of aggression. Of particular interest are the patterns of aggression and the transformation in these patterns that occur during the period from birth to the child's fifth year. During this period the rudiments of instrumental aggressive behaviors and of the affective drive structure of aggression motivation are established. Reinforcement theory provides us with a ready framework for the analysis of the development of instrumental aggression but the origins of drive-related aggressive behaviors such as those reflected in acts of meanness and sadism have been inadequately described and are poorly understood. A detailed longitudinal analysis focusing on the emergence of these different facets of aggression, coupled with cross-sectional sampling of aggressive behaviors during this age period, would provide the normative data necessary for the formulation of an adequate theoretical description of this development.

Information is needed on the antecedent as well as on the response side of the developmental sequence. Our knowledge of the stimuli that evoke aggressive behavior in the young child, particularly at different age levels, is surprisingly limited; the Goodenough (1931) monograph, which is more than three decades old, remains the best source of information on this question despite the small size and middle-class bias of the sample. A systematic appraisal of changes in the events that provoke aggression would facilitate the integration of the developmental data on aggression with more general developmental theories. For example, it is very possible that the stimulus antecedents of aggression follow the developmental sequence of cognitive structures. Thus for a frustrating stimulus to have ego-threatening properties or to be perceived as unintentional, the child may have to be beyond the pre-operational stage of development. The determination of the stimuli which typically provoke aggression in young children should relate and contribute to more general conceptualizations of development as well as provide insight into the conditions that govern the evocation of aggressive impulses. The developmental tracing of the antecedents and the patterning of aggressive behavior would also facilitate comparisons between human aggression and animal aggression. The relevance of the research and theory of the ethologists to human aggression remains largely speculative despite the recognition that from an evolutionary and also an ontogenetic point of view, it would be useful to make a comparative study of those aggressive reactions in young children that have analogues in animal behavior.

The study of the early development of aggressive behavior directly bears on another issue of central importance to an understanding of the roots of aggression—namely, the functional relationship between aggression and assertiveness. The psychoanalytic ego psychologists (Hartmann, Kris, and Lowenstein, 1949) have hypothesized that both of these behavior tendencies emerge from the same developmental structure; indeed, at an empirical level, they are often treated synonymously during the preschool years (Otis and McCandless, 1955; Patterson et al., 1967). By adolescence, however, assertiveness and aggression are usually considered theoretically and empirically distinct (Kagan and Moss, 1962). Assertiveness describes a behavioral pattern of active coping with the environment and persistence in the pursuit of one's own needs when confronted with counterpressure. Although aggression, as an instrumental response, may share some of these properties, the distinguishing characteristic of aggressive behavior is its painful and destructive consequences. Whereas assertive behaviors are likely to be seen as positive adaptive efforts by the child, aggression is more negatively viewed and is more likely to be discouraged and subject to punishment. In terms of child-rearing practices, it would be important to establish how closely related these two behavior patterns are and therefore how difficult a discrimination the child is required to make in being differentially reinforced for assertiveness and aggression. We have no information as to the effects of inhibition of instrumental aggression upon the young child's assertive, coping responses. Presumably, it should be possible to modify instrumental aggression through extinction and

punishment procedures without fostering passivity. However, this needs to be empirically established.

At a more general level, an encouraging development is the recent interest in alternatives to aggression controls other than punishment and substitute outlets. If aggressive affect or aggressive drive is conceptualized as a mediating response to an instigating stimulus, then it should be possible to reduce aggression by modifying the stimulus or by fostering responses which are incompatible with aggression. More precise data on the factors influencing aggressive affect and aggressive drive would be relevant to this issue also. To the extent that aggressive drive-mediated behavior reflects retaliatory attempts at the restoration of self-esteem, it should be possible to reduce the drive, or interfere with its evocation, by the culture's encouraging nonaggressive means for restoring self-esteem. The issues here are similar to those involved in the modification of instrumental aggression, but there are differences as well. In the case of instrumental aggression, it is by definition a learned behavior pattern which can be modified through appropriate reinforcement and extinction procedures. However, with regard to anger, there may well be strong, unlearned affective reactions to particular stimulus constellations and it may be very difficult to modify these reactions or provide effective alternatives without producing undesired consequences. For example, in reinforcing nonangry behaviors, one may also be modifying the responsiveness to other affective stimuli. The child who has difficulty in experiencing anger may have difficulty in experiencing pleasure. The principal import of these comments is that in examining the consequences of socialization practices, it is essential to consider effects on behaviors beyond those specifically being trained.

A final comment may be made concerning the role of social variables in determining violence and other forms of aggression. Social variables have indeed been emphasized but primarily as reinforcers of individual aggressive behaviors. Thus cultural and class differences in aggression are attributed to differences in social norms and to the selective reinforcement of particular behavior patterns. The social context, however, also contributes to the determination of aggressive behavior as a group influence. Although much of human aggression—both child and adult—occurs in the context of a group activity, there are few empirical data that bear on differences in aggression when a child is part of a group compared to when he is acting as an individual aggressor. The extreme aggressive behaviors in which a group may sometimes participate are hardly touched upon by the studies considered in this review. Somewhere in between the sociology of aggression and the psychology of aggression lies a significant research area which is in need of systematic study.

References

Aberle, D. F., and Naegele, K. D. Middle-class fathers' occupational role and attitudes toward children. *Am. J. Orthopsychiat.*, 1952, **22**, 366–378.

Adelman, H. Reinforcing effects of adult nonreaction on achievement expectancy in underachieving boys. *Child Dev.*, 1969.

Adorno, T., Frenkel-Brunswik, E., Levinson, D., and Sanford, R. *The authoritarian personality*. New York: Harper, 1950.

Aichhorn, A. *Wayward youth*. New York: Viking Press, 1935.

Albert, R. The role of mass media and the effect of aggressive film content upon children's aggressive responses and identification choices. *Genet. Psychol. Monogr.*, 1957, **55**, 221–285.

Allinsmith, B. B. Parental discipline and children's aggression in two social classes. *Diss. Abstr.*, 1954, **14**, 708.

Allinsmith, B. B. Expressive styles: II. Directness with which anger is expressed. In D. R. Miller and G. E. Swanson (Eds.), *Inner conflict and defense*. New York: Holt, 1960.

Ammons, C., and Ammons, R. Aggression in doll-play; interviews of two- to six-year-old white males. *J. genet. Psychol.*, 1953, **82**, 205–213.

Amsel, A. The role of frustrative-nonreward in noncontinuous reward situations. *Psychol. Bull.*, 1958, **55**, 102–119.

Amsel, A. Frustrative nonreward in partial reinforcement and discrimination learning: some recent history and a theoretical extension. *Psychol. Rev.*, 1962, **69**, 306–328.

Amsel, A., and Roussel, J. Motivational properties of frustration: I effect on a running response of the addition of frustration to the motivational complex. *J. exp. Psychol.*, 1952, **43**, 363–368.

Ardrey, R. *The territorial imperative*. New York: Atheneum, 1966.

Ardrey, R. *African genesis*. New York: Dell, 1967.

Aronfreed, J. The nature, variety, and social patterning of moral responses to transgression. *J. abnorm. soc. Psychol.*, 1961, **63**, 223–240.

Aronfreed, J. The concept of internalization. In D. A. Goslin and D. C. Glass (Eds.), *The handbook on socialization theory*. Chicago: Rand McNally, 1967.

Aronfreed, J., and Paskal, V. The development of sympathetic behavior in children: an experimental test of a two-phase hypothesis. Unpublished manuscript, University of Pennsylvania, 1966.

Arons, L., and May, M. A. *Television and human behavior*. New York: Appleton-Century-Crofts, 1963.

Asch, S. *Social psychology*. New York: Prentice-Hall, 1952.

Ausubel, D. Negativism as a phase of ego development. *Am. J. Orthopsychiat.*, 1950, **20**, 796–805.

Azrin, N. H., Hutchinson, R. R., and Hake, D. F. Extinction-induced aggression. *J. exp. Analysis Behav.*, 1966, **9**, 191–204.

Bach, G. R. Young children's play fantasies. *Psychol. Monogr.*, 1945, **59** (2).

Bach, G. R. Father-fantasies and father-typing in father-separated children. *Child Dev.*, 1946, **17**, 63–80.

Bailyn, L. Mass media and children: a study of exposure habits and cognitive effects. *Psychol. Monogr.*, 1959, **73** (471).

Baldwin, A. L. The effect of home environment on nursery school behavior. *Child Dev.*, 1949, **20**, 49–62.

Banay, R. S. Testimony before the subcommittee to investigate juvenile delinquency, of the Committee on the Judiciary, United States Senate, Eighty-fourth Congress, S. Res. 62, April, 1955. Washington, D.C.: United States Government Printing Office, 1955.

Bandura, A. Relationship of family patterns to child behavior disorders. U.S.P.H. Research Grant Reference No. M-1734. Progress Report, June 15, 1960.

Bandura, A. Punishment revisited. *J. consult. Psychol.*, 1962, **26**, 298–301.

Bandura, A., and Walters, R. H. Aggression. In H. Stevenson (Ed.), *Child psychology*. Chicago: University Chicago Press, 1963, 364–415.

Bandura, A., and Huston, A. Identification as a process of incidental learning. *J. abnorm. soc. Psychol.*, 1961, **63**, 311–318.

Bandura, A., Ross, D., and Ross, S. Transmission of aggression through imitation of aggressive models. *J. abnorm. soc. Psychol.*, 1961, **63**, 575–582.

Bandura, A., Ross, D., and Ross, S. Imitation of film-mediated aggressive models. *J. abnorm. soc. Psychol.*, 1963, **66**, 3–11 (a).

Bandura, A., Ross, D., and Ross, S. Vicarious reinforcement and imitative learning. *J. abnorm. soc. Psychol.*, 1963. **67**, 601–607 (b).

Bandura, A. ,and Walters, R. H. *Adolescent aggression*. New York: Ronald Press, 1959.

Bandura, A., and Walters, R. H. Aggression in child psychology; sixty-second yearbook of the National Society for the Study of Education, Part 1, 1963, 364–415 (a).

Bandura, A., and Walters, R. H. Social learning and personality development. New York: Holt, Rinehart, and Winston, 1963 (b).

Banister, H., and Ravden, M. The problem child and his environment. *Br. J. Psychol.*, 1944, **34**, 60–65.

Barker, R. G., Dembo, T., and Lewin, K. Frustration and regression: an experiment with young children. *Univ. Iowa Stud. Child Welfare*, 1941, XVIII, 1–314.

Barnett, S. A. *A study in behavior*. London: Methuen, 1963.

Baumrind, D. Child care practices anteceding three patterns of preschool behavior. *Genet. Psychol. Monogr.*, 1967, **75**, 43–88.

Bayley, N., and Schaefer, E. S. Correlations of maternal and child behaviors with the development of mental abilities. *Monogr. soc. res. Child Dev.*, 1964, **29** (6), 97.

Beardslee, B. A. The learning of two mechanisms of defense. In D. R. Miller and G. E. Swanson (Eds.), *Inner conflict and defense*. New York: Holt, 1960.

Becker, W. C. Consequences of parental discipline. In M. L. Hoffman and L. W. Hoffman (Eds.), *Review of child development research*. Vol. 1. New York: Russell Sage, 1964.

Becker, W. C., Peterson, D. R., Luria, Z., Shoemaker, D. J., and Hellmer, L. A. Relations of factors derived from parent-interview ratings to behavior problems of five-year-olds. *Child Dev.*, 1962, **33**, 509–535.

Beech, H. R., and Graham, M. Note on use of sentence completion in assessing overt aggression in normal school children. *Psychol. Rep.*, 1967, **20**, 9–10.

Beeman, E. A. The effect of male hormone on aggressive behavior in mice, *Physiol. Zool.*, 1947, **20**, 373–405.

Bell, R., and Costello, N. Three tests for sex differences in tactile sensitivity in the newborn. *Biologia Neonat.*, 1964, **7**, 335–347.

Beller, E. K. Exploratory studies of dependency. *Trans. N. Y. Acad. Sci.*, 1959, Ser. II, **21** (5), 414–426.

Bender, L. Psychopathic behavior disorders in children. In R. M. Lindner and R. V. Seliger (Eds.), *Handbook of correctional psychology.* New York: Rinehart, 1947.

Bender, L., and Schilder, P. Aggressiveness in children. *Genet. Psychol. Monogr.*, 1936, **18**, 410–425.

Bene, E. Suppression of heterosexual interest and of aggression by middle class and working class grammar school boys. *Br. J. educ. Psychol.*, 1958, **28**, 226–231.

Berkowitz, L. *Aggression: a social psychological analysis.* New York: McGraw-Hill, 1962.

Berkowitz, L. Aggressive cues in aggressive behavior and hostility catharsis. *Psychol. Rev.*, 1964, **71**, 104–122.

Berkowitz, L., and Buck, R. W. Impulsive aggression: reactivity to aggressive cues under emotional arousal. *J. Personality*, 1967, **35**, 415–424.

Berkowitz, L., and Green, J. A. The stimulus qualities of the scapegoat. *J. abnorm. soc. Psychol.*, 1962, **64**, 293–301.

Berkowitz, L., and Holmes, D. S. The generalization of hostility to disliked objects. *J. Personality*, 1959, **27**, 565–577.

Berkowitz, L., and Holmes, D. S. A further investigation of hostility generalization to disliked objects. *J. Personality*, 1960, **28**, 427–442.

Bettelheim, B. *Love is not enough; the treatment of emotionally disturbed children.* Glencoe, Ill.: Free Press, 1952 (a).

Bettelheim, B. Mental health and current mores. *Am. J. Orthopsychiat.*, 1952, **22**, 76–88 (b).

Block, J., and Martin, B. Predicting the behavior of children under frustration. *J. abnorm. soc. Psychol.*, 1955, **51**, 281–285.

Body, M. Patterns of aggression in the nursery school. *Child Dev.*, 1955, **26**, 5–11.

Bornston, F. L., and Coleman, J. C. The relationship between certain parents' attitudes toward child-rearing and the direction of aggression of their young adult offspring. *J. clin. Psychol.*, 1956, **12**, 41–44.

Bowlby, J. Forty-four juvenile thieves: their characters and home backgrounds. London: Baillier, Tindall and Cox, 1946.

Bridges, K. M. B. The social and emotional development of the pre-school child. London: Routeledge, 1931.

Bromberg, W. *The mold of murder; a psychiatric study of homicide.* New York: Grune and Stratton, 1961.

Bronfenbrenner, U. Socialization and social class through time and space. In E. E. Maccoby, T. Newcomb, and E. Hartley (Eds.), *Readings in social psychology.* New York: Holt, Rinehart and Winston, 1958.

Bronfenbrenner, U. Some familial antecedents of responsibility and leadership in adolescents. In L. Petrullo and B. M. Bass (Eds.), *Leadership and interpersonal behavior.* New York: Holt, 1961.

Bronfenbrenner, U., and Ricciuti, H. N. The appraisal of personality characteristics in children. In P. N. Mussen (Ed.), *Handbook of research methods in child development.* New York: Wiley, 1960.

Brown, J. S., and Farber, I. E. Emotions conceptualized as intervening variables— with suggestions toward a theory of frustration. *Psychol. Bull.*, 1951, **48**, 465–

Brown, P., and Elliot, R. Control of aggression in a nursery school class. *J. exp. Child Psychol.*, 1965, **2** (2), 103–107.

Burnstein, E., and McRae, A. V. Some effects of shared threat and prejudice in racially mixed groups. *J. abnorm. soc. Psychol.*, 1962, **64** (4), 257–263.

Burt, C. *The young delinquent*. New York: Appleton, 1929.

Burton, A. The aggression of young children following satiation. *Am. J. Orthopsychiat.*, 1942, **12**, 262–268.

Buss, A. H. *The psychology of aggression*. New York: Wiley, 1961.

Buss, A. H. Physical aggression in relation to different frustrations. *J. abnorm. soc. Psychol.*, 1963, **67**, 1–7.

Buss, A. H., and Durkee, A. Conditioning of hostile verbalizations in a situation resembling a clinical interview. *J. consult. Psychol.*, 1958, **22**, 415–418.

Butcher, J. Manifest aggression: MMPI correlates in normal boys. *J. consult. Psychol.*, 1965, **29**, 446–454.

Capwell, D. F. Personality patterns of adolescent girls: delinquents and non-delinquents. *J. appl. Psychol.*, 1945, **29**, 289–297.

Carpenter, C. R. A field study of the behavior and social relations of howling monkeys. *Comp. Psychol. Monogr.*, No. 48, **10** (2), 1–168.

Chasdi, E. H., and Lawrence, M. S. Some antecedents of aggression and effects of frustration in doll play. In D. McClelland (Ed.), *Studies in motivation*. New York: Appleton-Century-Crofts, 1955.

Child, I. L. Socialization. In G. Lindzey (Ed.), *Handbook of social psychology*. Vol. 2. New York: Addison-Wesley, 1954.

Chittenden, G. E. An experimental study in measuring and modifying assertive behavior in young children. *Monogr. social res. Child Dev.*, 1942, **7** (1).

Chorost, S. B. Parental child-rearing attitudes and their correlates in adolescent hostility. *Genet. Psychol. Monogr.* 1962, **66**, 49–90.

Christie, R., and Jahoda, M. (Eds.) *The authoritarian personality*. Glencoe, Ill.: Free Press, 1954.

Cohen, A. R. Social norms, arbitrariness of frustration, and status of the agent of frustration in the frustration-aggression hypothesis. *J. abnorm. soc. Psychol.*, 1955, **51**, 222–226.

Cohn, F. S. Fantasy aggression in children as studied by the doll play technique. *Child Dev.*, 1962, **33**, 235–250.

Cowan, P., and Walters, R. Studies of reinforcement of aggression: I. Effects of scheduling. *Child Dev.*, 1963, **34**, 543–551.

Crandall, V., Good, S., and Crandall, V. J. Reinforcing effects of adult reactions and non-reactions on children's achievement expectations; a replication study. *Child Dev.*, 1964, **35**, 485–497.

Darve, H. C. An analysis of two hundred quarrels of pre-school children. *Child Dev.*, 1934, **5**, 139–157.

Davidson, M. A., McInness, R. G., and Parnell, R. W. The distribution of personality traits in seven-year-old children; a combined psychological, psychiatric and somatype study. *Br. J. educ. Psychol.*, 1957, **27**, 48–61.

Davis, A. Child training and social class. In R. G. Barker, I. S. Kounin, and H. F. Wright (Eds.), *Child behavior and development*. New York: McGraw-Hill, 1943.

Davis, A. Socialization and adolescent personality. In T. M. Newcomb and E. L. Hartley (Eds.), *Readings in social psychology*. New York: Holt, 1947.

Davis, A. American status systems and the socialization of the child. In C. Kluckhohn and H. A. Murray (Eds.), *Personality in nature, society and culture*. New York: Knopf, 1948.

Davis, A., and Havighurst, R. J. Social class and color differences in child-rearing. In C. Kluckhohn and H. A. Murray (Eds.), *Personality in nature, society and culture*. New York: Knopf, 1948.

Davitz, J. The effects of previous training on postfrustration behavior. *J. abnorm. soc. Psychol.*, 1952, **47**, 309–315.

Delaney, E. J. Parental antecedents of social aggression in young children. *Diss. Abstr.*, 1965, **26** (3), 1763.

DeVore, I. (Ed.) *Primate behavior.* New York: Holt, Rinehart and Winston, 1965.

Dittman, A. T., and Goodrich, D. W. A comparison of social behavior in normal and hyperaggressive preadolescent boys. *Child Dev.*, 1961, **32**, 315–327.

Dollard, J., Doob, L. W., Miller, N. E., Mowrer, O. H., and Sears, R. R. *Frustration and aggression.* New Haven, Conn.: Yale University Press, 1939.

Dollard, J., and Miller, N. *Personality and psychotherapy: an analysis in terms of learning, thinking, and culture.* New York: McGraw-Hill, 1950.

Durbin, E. F. M., and Bowlby, J. Personal aggressiveness and war. In E. F. M. Durbin and G. Catlin (Eds.), *War and democracy.* London: Kegan, Paul, Trench, Trubner, 1938.

Eibl-Eibesfeldt, I. The fighting behavior of animals. *Scient. Am.*, 1961, **205**, 112–122.

Emery, F. E. Psychological effects of the western film: a study in television viewing: II, The experimental study. *Hum. Relat.*, 1959, **12**, 215–232.

Erikson, E. H. *Childhood and society.* New York: Norton, 1950. (Second edition, 1963.)

Eron, L. Relationship of TV viewing habits and aggressive behavior in children. *J. abnorm. soc. Psychol.*, 1963, **67**, 193–196.

Eron, L. D., Walder, L. O., Toigo, R., and Lefkowitz, M. M. Social class, parental punishment for aggression, and child aggression. *Child Dev.*, 1963, **34** (4), 849–867.

Escalona, S. K. The influence of topological and vector psychology upon current research in child development: an addendum. In L. Carmichael (Ed.), *Manual of child psychology.* (2nd ed.) New York: Wiley, 1954.

Fenichel, O. *The psychoanalytic theory of neuroses.* New York: Norton, 1945.

Ferson, J. E. The displacement of hostility. Unpublished doctoral dissertation, University of Texas, 1958.

Ferster, C. B. Withdrawal of positive reinforcement as punishment. *Science*, 1957, **126**, 509.

Feshbach, N. Sex differences in children's modes of aggressive responses toward outsiders. Merrill-Palmer Quart., 1969, **15**.

Feshbach, N., and Feshbach, S. The relationship between empathy and aggression in two age groups. *J. Dev. Psychol.*, in press.

Feshbach, S. The drive-reducing function of fantasy behavior. *J. abnorm. soc. Psychol.*, 1955, **50**, 3–11.

Feshbach, S. The catharsis hypothesis and some consequences of interaction with aggressive and neutral play objects. *J. Personality*, 1956, **24**, 449–462.

Feshbach, S. The stimulating versus carthartic effects of a vicarious aggressive activity. *J. abnorm. soc. Psychol.*, 1961, **63**, 381–385.

Feshbach, S. The function of aggression and the regulation of aggressive drive. *Psychol. Rev.*, 1964, **71**, 257–272.

Feshbach, S. Effects of exposure to aggressive content in television upon aggression in boys. Submitted to the Joint Committee for Research on Television and Children, 1967 (a).

Feshbach, S. The organization and regulation of anger and aggression. Progress Report submitted to N.I.M.H., 1967 (b).

Feshbach, S., and Singer, R. The effects of personal and shared threats upon prejudice. *J. abnorm. soc. Psychol.*, 1957, **54**, 411–416.

Frederickson, N. The effects of frustration on negativistic behavior of young children. *J. genet. Psychol.*, 1942, **61**, 203–226.

Fredericson, E., Story, A. W., Gurney, N. L., and Butterworth, K. The relationship between heredity, sex and aggression in two inbred mouse strains. *J. genet. Psychol.*, 1955, **87**, 121–130.

French, J. Dependency behavior and feelings of rejection in aggressive and non-aggressive boys. *Diss. Abstr.*, 1964, **25** (5).

Freud, A. *The ego and the mechanism of defense.* New York: International Universities Press, 1946 (a).

Freud, A. *The psycho-analytical treatment of children; technical lectures and essays.* New York: International Universities Press, 1946 (b).

Freud, A. *Introduction into the technique of child analysis.* London: Imago, 1948.

Freud, A. Notes on aggression. *Bull. Menninger Clin.*, 1949, **13**, 143–151 (a).

Freud, A. *Aggression in relation to emotional development: normal and pathological.* In A. Freud (Ed.), *The psychoanalytic study of the child.* New York: International Universities Press, 1949 (b).

Freud, A. Notes on aggression. *Yearb. Psychoanal.*, 1950, **6**, 145–154.

Freud, S. *Collected papers.* London: Hogarth, 1925.

Freud, S. *Beyond the pleasure principle.* New York: Boni and Liveright, 1927.

Freud, S. *Civilization and its discontents.* London: Hogarth, 1930. (Second edition, 1957.)

Friedlander, K. Neurosis and home background. In A. Freud (Ed.), *The psychoanalytic study of the child.* New York: International Universities Press, 1949.

Fuller, J. L. Cross-sectional and longitudinal studies of adjustive behavior in dogs. *Ann. N. Y. Acad. Sci.*, 1953, **56**, 214–224.

Gesell, A. L., and Ilg., F. L. *Infant and child in the culture of today; the guidance of development in home and nursery school.* New York: Harper, 1943.

Gluck, M. R. The relationship between hostility in TAT and behavioral hostility. *J. Project. Tech.*, 1959, **23**, 207–213.

Glueck, S., and Glueck, E. *Unraveling juvenile delinquency.* Cambridge, Mass.: Harvard University Press, 1950.

Goldfarb, W. Infant rearing and problem behavior. *Am. J. Orthopsychiat.*, 1943, **13**, 249–260.

Goldfarb, W. Psychological privation in infancy and subsequent adjustment. *Am. J. Orthopsychiat.*, 1945, **15**, 247–255.

Goldstein, A. Aggression and hostility in the elementary school in low socio-economic areas. *Understanding the Child*, 1955, **24**, 20.

Goodenough, F. L. *Anger in young children.* Minneapolis: University of Minnesota Press, 1931.

Goodenough, F. L., and Leahy, A. M. The effect of certain family relationships upon the development of personality. *J. genet. Psychol.*, 1927, **34**, 45–72.

Gordon, J., and Smith, E. Children's aggression, parental attitudes and the effects of an affiliation-arousing story. *J. Pers. soc. Psychol.*, 1965, **1**, 654–659.

Gorlow, L., Zimet, P., and Fine, H. The validity of anxiety and hostility Rorschach content scores among adolescents. *J. consult. Psychol.*, 1952, **16**, 73–75.

Graham, F., Charwat, W., Honig, A., and Welty, P. Aggression as a function of the attack and the attacker. *J. abnorm. soc. Psychol.*, 1951, **46**, 512–520.

Green, E. H. Group play and quarreling among pre-school children. *Child Dev.*, 1933, **4**, 302–307.

Hamblin, R. L. Leadership and crises. *Sociometry*, 1958, **21**, 322–335.

Hamburg, D. A., and Lunde, D. T. Sex hormones in the development of sex differences in human behavior. In E. E. Maccoby (Ed.), *The development of sex differences.* Stanford, Cal.: Stanford University Press, 1966.

Haner, C., and Brown, P. Clarification of the instigation to action concept in the frustration-aggression hypothesis. *J. abnorm. soc. Psychol.*, 1955, **51**, 204–206.

Harlow, H. The heterosexual affectional system in monkeys. *Am. Psychol.*, 1962, **17**, 1–9.

Harris, G., and Levine, S. Sexual differentiation of the brain and its experimental control. *J. Physiol.*, 1962, 42P–43P.

Hartmann, H., Kris, E., and Lowenstein, R. Notes on the theory of aggression. In A. Freud (Ed.), *The psychoanalytic study of the child*. Vol. 3. New York: International Universities Press, 1949. Pp. 9–36.

Hartup, W., and Himeno, Y. Social isolation versus interactions with adults in relation to aggression in preschool children. *J. abnorm. soc. Psychol.*, 1959, **59**, 17–22.

Hathaway, S. R., and Monachesi, E. D. *Analyzing and predicting juvenile delinquency with the M.M.P.I.* Minneapolis: University of Minnesota Press, 1953.

Havighurst, R. J., and Taba, H. *Adolescent character and personality.* New York: Wiley (Science Edition), 1949.

Head, S. W. Content analysis of television drama programs. *Q. Film, Radio and Television*, 1954, **9**, 175–194.

Healy, W., and Bronner, A. F. New light on delinquency and its treatment. New Haven, Conn.: Yale University Press, 1936.

Hewitt, L. E., and Jenkins, R. L. *Fundamental patterns of maladjustment: the dynamics of their origin.* Chicago: State of Illinois, 1946.

Hicks, D. J. Imitation and retention of film-mediated aggressive peer and adult models. *J. Pers. soc. Psychol.*, 1965, **2**, 97–100.

Hollenberg, E. H., and Sperry, M. S. Some antecedents of aggression and effects of frustration in doll play. *Personality*, 1951, **1**, 32–43.

Holton, R. Amplitude of an instrumental response following the cessation of a reward. *Child Dev.*, 1961, **32**, 107–116.

Hops, H., and Walters, R. H. Studies of reinforcement of aggression: II. Effects of emotionally-arousing antecedent conditions. *Child Dev.*, 1963, **34**, 553–562.

Horney, K. *The neurotic personality of our time.* New York: Norton, 1937.

Horney, K. *Our inner conflicts.* New York: Norton, 1945.

Horrocks, J. E., and Gottfried, N. W. Psychological needs and verbally expressed aggression of adolescent delinquent boys. *J. Psychol.*, 1966, **62**, 179–194.

Hoult, T. F. Comic books and juvenile delinquency. *Sociology soc. Res.*, 1949, **33**, 279–284.

Hovland, C., and Sears, R. Minor studies in aggression: VI. Correlation of lynchings with economic indices. *J. Psychol.*, 1940, **9**, 301–310.

Hutchinson, R. R., and Renfrew, J. W. Stalking attack and eating behavior elicited from the same sites in the hypothalamus. *J. comp. physiol. Psychol.*, 1966, **61**, 300–367.

Hutchinson, R. R., Ulrich, R. E., and Azrin, N. H. Effects of age and related factors on the pain-aggression reaction. *J. comp. physiol. Psychol.*, 1965, **59**, 365–369.

Hymann, G. M. Some relationships between hostility, fantasy aggression and aggressive behavior. *Diss. Abstr.*, 1956, **16**, 793–794.

James, W. T. Social organization among dogs of different temperaments, terriers and beagles, reared together. *J. comp. physiol. Psychol.*, 1951, **44**, 71–77.

Jegard, S., and Walters, R. A study of some determinants of aggression in young children. *Child Dev.*, 1960, **31**, 739–747.

Jensen, A. R. Aggression in fantasy and overt behavior. *Psychol. Monogr.*, 1957, **71** (whole No. 445).

Jersild, A. T., and Markey, F. V. Conflicts between preschool children. *Child Dev. Monogr.*, 1935, No. 21.

Kagan, J. The measurement of overt aggression from fantasy. *J. abnorm. soc. Psychol.*, 1956, **52**, 390–393.

Kagan, J. Socialization of aggression and the perception of parents in fantasy. *Child Dev.*, 1958, **29**, 311–320.

Kagan, J. The stability of TAT fantasy and stimulus ambiguity. *J. consult. Psychol.*, 1959, **23**, 266–271.

Kagan, J., and Moss, H. A. *Birth to maturity*. New York: Wiley, 1962.

Kaufmann, H. Definitions and methodology in the study of aggression. *Psychol. Bull.*, 1965, **64**, 351–364.

Kaufmann, H., and Feshbach, S. The influence of anti-aggressive communications upon the response to provocation. *J. Personality*, 1963, **31**, 428–444.

Kenny, D. T. *An experimental test of the catharsis theory of aggression*. Ann Arbor, Mich.: University Microfilms, 1953.

Klapper, J. T. *Children and television: a review of socially prevalent concerns*. New York: Bureau of Applied Social Research, Columbia University, 1954.

Klapper, J. T. The effects of mass communication. Glencoe, Ill.: Free Press, 1960.

Klein, M. *The psychoanalysis of children*. London: Hogarth, 1937.

Koch, H. L. The relation of certain family constellation characteristics and the attitudes of children toward adults. *Child Dev.*, 1955, **26**, 13–40.

Kohlberg, L. Development of moral character and moral ideology. In M. L. Hoffman and L. W. Hoffman (Eds.), *Review of child development research*. Vol. I. New York: Russell Sage, 1964.

Kohn, M. L. Social class and the exercise of parental authority. *Am. Sociol. Rev.*, 1959, **24**, 352–366.

Kohn, M. L. Social class and parent-child relationships: an interpretation. *Am. J. Sociol.*, 1963, **68**(4), 471–480.

Koppitz, E. M. Emotional indicators of human figure drawings of shy and aggressive children. *J. clin. Psychol.*, 1966, **22**, 466–469.

Korner, A. *Some aspects of hostility in young children*. New York: Grune and Stratton, 1949.

Kornrich, M. (Ed.) *Underachievement*. Springfield, Ill.: Thomas, 1965.

Lambert, W. W., Triandis, L. M., and Wolf, M. Some correlates of beliefs in the malevolence and benevolence of supernatural beings: a cross-societal study. *J. abnorm. soc. Psychol.*, 1959, **58**, 162–169.

Langston, R. D. Children's overt and fantasy aggression toward peers as a function of perceived severity of parental punishment. *Diss. Abstr.*, 1961, **21**, 2367.

Lansky, L. M., Crandall, V. J., Kagan, J., and Baker, C. T. Sex differences in aggression and its correlates in middle class adolescents. *Child Dev.*, 1961, **32**, 45–58.

Larder, D. L. Effect of aggressive story content on nonverbal play behavior. *Psychol. Rep.*, 1962, **11**(1), 14–15.

Lefkowitz, M., Walder, L., and Eron, L. Punishment, identification and aggression. *Merrill-Palmer Q.*, 1963, **9**, 159–174.

Lesser, G. S. Maternal attitudes and practices and the aggressive behavior of children. Doctoral dissertation, Yale University, 1952.

Lesser, G. The relationship between overt and fantasy aggression as a function of maternal response to aggression. *J. abnorm. soc. Psychol.*, 1957, **55**, 218–221.

Lesser, G. Application of Guttman's scaling method to aggressive fantasy in children. *Educ. psychol. Measur.*, 1958, **18**, 543–551 (a).

Lesser, G. Conflict analysis of fantasy aggression. *J. Personality*, 1958, **26**, 29–41 (b).

Lesser, G. Population differences in construct validity. *J. consult. Psychol.*, 1959, **23**, 60–65 (a).

Lesser, G. The relationships between various forms of aggression and popularity among lower-class children. *J. educ. Psychol.*, 1959, **50**, 20–25 (b).

Lesser, G. S., and Abelson, R. P. Personality correlates of persuasibility in children. In C. V. Hovland and I. L. Janis (Eds.), *Personality and persuasibility*. New Haven, Conn.: Yale University Press, 1959.

Lesser, L. N. An experimental investigation of the aggressiveness of children's behavior as a function of interpolated activities and individual differences in imaginative productions. *Diss. Abstr.*, 1963, 24(2), 836–837.

Levin, H. The influence of classroom control on kindergarten children's fantasy aggression. *Elementary School J.*, 1955, 55, 462–466.

Levin, H., and Sears, R. R. Identification with parents as a determinant of doll play aggression. *Child Dev.*, 1956, 27, 135–153.

Levin, H., and Turgeon, V. The influence of the mother's presence on children's doll play aggression. *J. abnorm. soc. Psychol.*, 1957, 55, 304–308.

Levy, D. M. On the problem of delinquency. *Am. J. Orthopsychiat.*, 1932, 2, 197–211.

Levy, D. M. Hostility patterns in sibling rivalry experiments. *Am. J. Orthopsychiat.*, 1936, 6, 183–257.

Levy, D. M. The hostile act. *Psychol. Rev.*, 1941, 48, 356–361.

Levy, D. M. *Maternal overprotection*. New York: Columbia University Press, 1943.

Lewin, H. S. Facts and fears about the comics. *Nation's Schools*, 1953, 52, 46–48.

Lewin, K., Lippitt, R., and White, R. Patterns of aggressive behavior in experimentally created social climates. *J. soc. Psychol.*, 1939, 10, 271–299.

Lewis, H. *Deprived children*. London: Oxford University Press, 1954.

Licht, L. A. Direct and displaced physical aggression as a function of self-esteem and method of anger arousal. Unpublished doctoral dissertation, University of California, Los Angeles, 1967.

Lipsitt, L. P., and Levy, N. Electroactual threshold in the neonate. *Child Dev.*, 1959, 30, 547–554.

Livson, N., and Mussen, P. H. The relation of ego control to overt aggression and dependency. *J. abnorm. soc. Psychol.*, 1957, 55, 66–71.

Loewenstein, R. The vital or somatic instincts. *Int. J. Psychoanal.*, 1940, 21, 377–400.

Long, E., and Miezitis, S. Prediction of aggressiveness in school children from clusters of signs on the Rorschach test. *Ont. J. educ. Res.*, 1966, 8, 261–266.

Longstreth, L. E. The relationship between expectations and frustration in children. *Child Dev.*, 1960, 31, 667–671.

Lorenz, K. *On aggression*. New York: Harcourt, Brace and World, 1966.

Lovaas, O. Effect of exposure to symbolic aggression on aggressive behavior. *Child Dev.*, 1961, 32, 37–44 (a).

Lovaas, O. Interaction between verbal and nonverbal behavior. *Child Dev.*, 1961, 32, 329–336 (b).

Lowrey, L. G. Personality distortion and early institutional care. *Am. J. Orthopsychiat.*, 1940, 10, 576–586.

Lowrey, L. G., Zilboorg, G., Bender, L., Brickner, R. M., Reeve, G. H., Lippman, H. S., Slavson, S. R., and Slawson, J. The treatment of aggression. Round Table. *Am. J. Orthopsychiat.*, 1943, 13, 384–441.

MacCasland, B. W. The relation of aggressive fantasy to aggressive behavior in children. *Diss. Abstr.*, 1962, 23 (1), 300–301.

Maccoby, E. E. The taking of adult roles in middle childhood. *J. abnorm. soc. Psychol.*, 1961, 63, 493–503.

Maccoby, E. E., and Gibbs, P. K. Methods of child rearing in two social classes. In W. E. Martin and C. B. Stendler (Eds.), *Readings in child development*. New York: Harcourt, Brace, 1954.

Maccoby, E. E., Levin, H., and Selya, B. M. The effects of emotional arousal on the retention of aggressive and non-aggressive movie content. *Am. Psychol.*, 1955, **10**, 359.

Maccoby, E. E., Levin, H., and Selya, B. M. The effects of emotional arousal on the retention of film content: a failure to replicate. *J. abnorm. soc. Psychol.*, 1956, **53**, 373–374.

Maccoby, E. E., and Wilson, W. C. Identification and observational learning from films. *J. abnorm. soc. Psychol.*, 1957, **55**, 76–87.

Macfarlane, J. W., Allen, L., and Honzik, M. P. A development study of the behavior problems of normal children between 20 months and 14 years. *Univ. Calif. Publs. Child Dev.*, 1954, **2**.

Madsen, J. C. The expression of aggression in two cultures. Unpublished doctoral dissertation, University of Oregon, 1966.

Magee, R. D. Correlates of aggressive-defiant classroom behavior in elementary school boys: a factor analytic study. *Diss. Abstr.*, 1964, **2**(25), 1340–1341.

Malinowski, B. *The sexual life of savages.* New York: Halycon House, 1929.

Mallick, S. K., and McCandless, B. R. A study of catharsis of aggression. *J. Pers. soc. Psychol.*, 1966, **4**, 591–596.

Marquis, J. N. Fantasy measures of aggressive behavior. *Diss. Abstr.*, 1961, **21**(12), 3854–3855.

Maslow, A. H. Deprivation, threat and frustration. *Psychol. Rev.*, 1941, **48**, 364–366.

Maslow, A. H. Conflict, frustration and the theory of threat. *J. abnorm. soc. Psychol.*, 1943, **38**, 81–86.

McCord, I. H. Interparent similarity in patterns of childrearing and its relation to some dimensions of family structure. Unpublished doctoral dissertation, Purdue University, 1964.

McCord, W., McCord, J., and Howard, A. Familial correlates of aggression in non-delinquent male children. *J. abnorm. soc. Psychol.*, 1961, **62**, 79–93.

McKee, J., and Leader, F. The relationship of socio-economic status and aggression to the competitive behavior of pre-school children. *Child Dev.*, 1955, **26**, 135–142.

McNeil, E. Patterns of aggression. *J. Child Psychol. Psychiat.*, 1962, **3**, 65–77.

Mead, M. *Sex and temperament in three primative societies.* New York: Morrow, 1035.

Menlove, F. L. Aggressive symptoms in emotionally disturbed adopted children. *Child Dev.*, 1965, **36**, 519–532.

Menninger, K. A. *Man against himself.* New York: Harcourt, Brace, 1938.

Menninger, K. A. *Love against hate.* New York: Harcourt, Brace, 1942.

Miller, D. R., and Swanson, G. E. *Inner conflict and defense.* New York: Holt, 1960.

Miller, N. E. The frustration-aggression hypothesis. *Psychol. Rev.*, 1941, **48**, 337–342.

Miller, N. E. Experimental studies of conflict. In J. McV. Hunt (Ed.), *Personality and the behavior disorders.* New York: Ronald Press, 1944.

Miller, N. E. Theory and experiment relating psychoanalytic displacement to stimulus-response generalization. *J. abnorm. soc. Psychol.*, 1948, **43**, 155–178.

Miller, N. E. Comments on theoretical models illustrated by the development of a theory of conflict. *J. Personality*, 1951, **20**, 82–100.

Miller, N. E. Liberalization of basic S-R concepts: extensions to conflict behavior, motivation and social learning. In S. Koch (Ed.), *Psychology: a study of a science.* Vol. 2. New York: McGraw-Hill, 1959.

Miller, N. E., and Bugelski, R. Minor studies in aggression: the influence of frustrations imposed by the in-group on attitudes expressed toward out-groups. *J. Psychol.*, 1948, **25**, 437–442.

Miller, N. E., and Dollard, J. *Social learning and imitation.* Published for the Institute of Human Relations by Yale University Press; London: Oxford University Press, 1941.

Miller, N. E., and Stevenson, S. S. Agitated behavior of rats during experimental extinction and a curve of spontaneous recovery. *J. comp. Psychol.*, 1936, **21**, 205–231.

Moore, S. Displaced aggression in young children. *J. abnorm. soc. Psychol.*, 1964, **68**, 200–204.

Moyer, K. E. Kinds of aggression and their physiological basis. Report No. 67–12. Department of Psychology, Carnegie-Mellon University, Pittsburgh, Penn., 1967.

Mulder, M., and Stemmerding, A. Threat, attraction to group, and need for strong leadership: a laboratory experiment in a natural setting. *Hum. Relat.*, 1963, **16**(4), 317–334.

Mullahy, P. *Oedipus myth and complex.* New York: Hermitage Press, 1952.

Munroe, R. L. *Schools of psychoanalytic thought.* New York: Dryden, 1955.

Murphy, L. B. *Social behavior and child personality.* New York: Columbia University Press, 1937.

Murstein, B. (Ed.) *Handbook of projective techniques.* New York: Basic Books, 1965.

Mussen, P. H. Some personality and social factors related to changes in children's attitudes toward Negroes. *J. abnorm. soc. Psychol.*, 1950, **45**, 423–441.

Mussen, P. H., and Jones, M. C. Self-conceptions, motivations, and interpersonal attitudes of late- and early-maturing boys. *Child Dev.*, 1957, **28**(2), 243–256.

Mussen, P. H., and Jones, M. C. The behavior inferred motivations of late and early maturing boys. *Child Dev.*, 1958, **29**, 61–67.

Mussen, P. H., and Naylor, H. The relationships between overt and fantasy aggression. *J. abnorm. soc. Psychol.*, 1954, **49**, 235–240.

Mussen, P. H., and Rutherford, E. Effects of aggressive cartoons in children's aggressive play. *J. abnorm. soc. Psychol.*, 1961, **62**, 461–464.

Muste, M., and Sharpe, D. Some influential factors in the determination of aggressive behavior in pre-school children. *Child Dev.*, 1947, **18**, 11–28.

Nakamura, C. The relationship between children's expressions of hostility and methods of discipline exercised by dominant overprotective parents. *Child Dev.*, 1959, **30**, 109–117.

Noble, G. K. Experimenting with the courtship of lizards. *Nat. Hist.*, 1934, **34**, 1–15.

Noble, G. K. Courtship and sexual selection of the flicker (colaptes auratus luteus). *Auk*, 1936, **53**, 269–282.

Norman, R. D., and Daley, M. F. The comparative personality adjustment of superior and inferior readers. *J. educ. Psychol.*, 1959, **50**, 31–36.

Nunberg, H. *Principles of psychoanalysis.* New York: International Universities Press, 1955.

Oetzel, R. M. The relationship of aggression anxiety to sex typing in ten year old girls. *Diss. Abstr.*, 1964, **25**, 6055.

Oetzel, R. M. Classified summary of research in sex differences. In E. E. Maccoby (Ed.), *The development of sex differences.* Stanford, Cal.: Stanford University Press, 1966.

Olds, J. The influence of practices on the strength of approach drives. *J. exp. Psychol.*, 1955, **50**, 349–353.

Otis, N., and McCandless, B. Responses to repeated frustrations of young children differentiated according to need area. *J. abnorm. soc. Psychol.*, 1955, **50**, 349–353.

Pastore, N. The role of arbitrariness in the frustration-aggression hypothesis. *J. abnorm. soc. Psychol.*, 1952, **47**, 728–731.

Patterson, G. A nonverbal technique for the assessment of aggression in children. *Child Dev.*, 1960, **31**, 643–653.

Patterson, G. R., Littman, R. A., and Bricker, W. Assertive behavior in children: a step toward a theory of aggression. *Monogr. soc. res. Child Dev.*, 1967, **32**(5 and 6).

Patterson, R., and Zeigler, T. W. Ordinal position and schizophrenia. *Am. J. Psychiat.*, 1941, **98**, 455–456.

Penney, R. K. The effects of nonreinforcement of response strength as a function of number of previous reinforcements. *Can. J. Psychol.*, 1960, **14**, 206–215.

Phillips, R. Doll play as a function of the realism of the materials and the length of the experimental session. *Child Dev.*, 1945, **16**, 123–143.

Pintler, M. Doll play as a function of experimenter-child interaction and initial organization of materials. *Child Dev.*, 1945, **16**, 145–166.

Purcell, K. The TAT and antisocial behavior. *J. consult. Psychol.*, 1956, **20**, 449–456.

Rapaport, D. The structure of psychoanalytic theory. In S. Koch (Ed.), *Psychology: a study of a science.* Vol. 3. New York: McGraw-Hill, 1959.

Redl, F., and Wineman, D. *Controls from within: techniques for the treatment of the aggressive child.* New York: Macmillan, 1965.

Richter, C. P. The effects of domestication and selection upon the behavior of the Norway rat. *J. natn. Cancer Inst.*, 1954, **15**, 727–738.

Ricutti, E. A. Children and radio: a study of listeners and non-listeners to various types of radio programs in terms of selected ability, attitudes, and behavior measures. *Genet. Psychol. Monogr.*, 1951, **64**, 69–143.

Riley, M. W., and Riley, J. W., Jr. A sociological approach to communication research. *Publ. Opinion Quart.*, 1951, **15**, 444–460.

Robinson, E. Doll play as a function of the doll family constellation. *Child Dev.*, 1946, **17**, 99–119.

Roff, M., and Roff, L. An analysis of the variance of conflict behavior in preschool children. *Child Dev.*, 1940, **11**, 43–60.

Roland, A. Persuasibility in young children as a function of aggressive motivation and aggression conflict. *J. abnorm. soc. Psychol.*, 1963, **66**, 454–461.

Rosenthal, M. J., Ni, E., Finkelstein, M., and Berkwits, G. K. Father-child relationships and children's problems. *A. M. A. Archs. gen. Psychiat.*, 1962, **7**, 360–373.

Rosenzweig, S. An outline of frustration theory. In J. McV. Hunt (Ed.), *Personality and the behavior disorders.* New York: Ronald Press, 1944.

Rosenzweig, S. The Rosenzweig Picture-Frustration Study, Children's Form. In A. I. Rabin and M. R. Haworth (Eds.), *Projective techniques with children.* New York: Grune and Stratton, 1960.

Rosenzweig, S., and Rosenzweig, L. Aggression in problem children and normals as evaluated by the Rosenzweig P-F Study. *J. abnorm. soc. Psychol.*, 1952, **47**, 683–687.

Ross, A. On the relationship between anxiety and aggression in nine-year-old boys. *Diss. Abstr.* 1964, **24**(12), 5550–5551.

Sanner, E. K. Measurement of aggression in preadolescent boys. *Diss. Abstr.*, 1964, **25**, 4262.

Saul, L. J. *The hostile mind.* New York: Random House, 1956.

Schaar, J. H. *Escape from authority.* New York: Basic Books, 1961.

Schilder, P. The psychogenesis of alcoholism. *Q. J. Stud. Alcohol*, 1941, **2**, 277–292.

Schramm, W., Lyle, J., and Parker, E. B. Television in the lives of our children. Stanford, Cal.: Stanford University Press, 1961.

Scott, J. P. Genetic differences in the social behavior of inbred strains of mice. *J. Hered.*, 1942, **33**, 11–15.

Scott, J. P. Incomplete adjustment caused by frustration of untrained fighting mice. *J. comp. Psychol.*, 1946, **39**, 379–390.

Scott, J. P. "Emotional" behavior of fighting mice caused by conflict between weak stimulatory and weak inhibitory training. *J. comp. Psychol.*, 1947, **40**, 275–282.

Scott, J. P. Dominance and the frustration-aggression hypothesis. *J. physiol. Zool.*, 1948, **21**, 31–39.

Scott, J. P. The process of socialization in higher animals. In *Inter-relations between the social environment and psychiatric disorders*. New York: Milbank Memorial Fund, 1953.

Scott, J. P. The effects of selection and domestication on the behavior of the dog. *J. natl. Cancer Inst.*, 1954, **15**, 739–758.

Scott, J. P. *Aggression*. Chicago: University of Chicago Press, 1958.

Scott, J. P. and Fredericson, E. The causes of fighting in mice and rats. *Physiol. Zool.*, 1951, **24**, 273–309.

Scott, J. P., and Marston, M. V. Nonadaptive behavior resulting from a series of defeats in fighting mice. *J. abnorm. soc. Psychol.*, 1953, **48**, 417–428.

Screven, C. G. The effects of interference on response strength. *J. comp. Physiol. Psychol.*, 1954, **67**, 140–144.

Sears, P. Doll play aggression in normal young children: influence of sex, age, sibling status, father's absence. *Psychol. Monogr.*, 1951, **65**(6).

Sears, R. R. Nonaggression reactions to frustration. *Psychol. Rev.*, 1941, **48**, 343–346.

Sears, R. R. Personality development in the family. In J. M. Seidman (Ed.), *The child*. New York: Rinehart, 1958.

Sears, R. R. Relation of early socialization experiences to aggression in middle childhood. *J. abnorm. soc. Psychol.*, 1961, **63**, 466–492.

Sears, R. R., Maccoby, E. E., and Levin, H. *Patterns of child rearing*. Evanston, Ill.: Row, Peterson, 1957.

Sears, R. R., Rau, L., and Alpert, R. *Identification and child rearing*. Stanford, Cal.: Stanford University Press, 1965.

Sears, R. R., Whiting, J. W. M., Nowlis, V., and Sears, P. S. Some childrearing antecedents of aggression and dependency in young children. *Genet. Psychol. Monogr.*, 1953, **47**, 135–236.

Seay, B., and Harlow, H. F. Maternal separation in the rhesus monkey. *J. nerv. ment. Dis.*, 1965, **140**, 434–441.

Seward, J. P. Aggressive behavior in the rat. *J. comp. Psychol.*, 1945, **38**, 175–197; **39**, 51–76.

Sewell, W. H. Infant training and the personality of the child. *Am. J. Sociol.*, 1952, **58**, 150–159.

Sewell, W. H., and Mussen, P. H. The effects of feeding, weaning, and scheduling procedures on childhood adjustment and the formation of oral symptoms. *Child Dev.*, 1952, **23**, 185–191.

Shaw, M. C., and Grubb, J. Hostility and able high school underachievers. *J. consult. Psychol.*, 1958, **5**, 207–213.

Sheldon, W. H. Constitutional factors in personality. In J. McV. Hunt (Ed.), *Personality and the behavior disorders*. New York: Ronald Press, 1944.

Sheldon, W. H. Varieties of delinquent youth; an introduction to constitutional psychiatry. New York: Harper, 1949.

Sherif, M., Harvey, O. J., White, B. J., Hood, W. R., and Sherif, C. *Intergroup conflict and cooperation: the robbers' cave experiment.* Norman: University of Oklahoma Book Exchange, 1961.

Siegel, A. Film-mediated fantasy aggression and strength of aggressive drive. *Child Dev.,* 1956, **27,** 365–378.

Siegel, A. Aggressive behavior of young children in the absence of an adult. *Child Dev.,* 1957, **28,** 371–378.

Siegel, A. The influence of violence in the mass media upon children's role expectations. *Child Dev.,* 1958, **29,** 35–36.

Siegel, A., and Kohn, L. Permissiveness, permission and aggression: the effect of adult presence or absence on children's play. *Child Dev.,* 1959, **30,** 131–141.

Silverman, M. I. The relationship between self-esteem and aggression in two social classes. *Diss. Abstr.,* 1964, **25**(4), 2616.

Smith, J. R., and Coleman, J. C. The relationship between manifestations of hostility in projective tests and overt behavior. *J. project. Tech.,* 1956, **20,** 236–334.

Smythe, D. W. Dimensions of violence. *Audio-vis. Commun. Rev.,* 1955, **3,** 58–63.

Solomon, R. D. Punishment. *Am. Psychol.,* 1964, **19,** 239–253.

Sones, G. K. Sex differences in adolescents in direct aggression. Unpublished master's dissertation, University of California, Los Angeles, 1968.

Spache, E. D. Personality characteristics of retarded readers as measured by the picture-frustration study. *Educ. psychol. Measur.,* 1954, **14,** 186–192.

Stone, L. J. Aggression and destruction games: balloons. In L. B. Murphy (Ed.), *Personality in young children.* Vol. I. New York: Basic Books, 1956.

Symonds, P. M. *The psychology of parent-child relationships.* New York: Appleton-Century, 1939.

Symonds, P. M. *Adolescent fantasy.* New York: Columbia University Press, 1949.

Terman, L. The measurement of intelligence: an explanation of and a complete guide for the use of the Stanford revision and extension of the Binet-Simon intelligence scale. Boston; New York: Houghton Mifflin, 1916.

Terman, L. Stanford-Binet Intelligence Scale; manual for the third revision form. Boston: Houghton Mifflin, 1960.

Tinbergen, N. The function of sexual fighting in birds; and problem of the origin of territory. *Bird Banding,* 1936, **7,** 1–8.

Tinbergen, N. *The study of instinct.* Oxford: Clarendon Press, 1951 (a).

Tinbergen, N. On the significance of territory in the herring gull. *Ibis,* 1951, **94,** 158–159 (b).

Tinbergen, N. A note on the origin and evolution of threat display. *Ibis,* 1951, **94,** 160–162 (c).

Tinbergen, N. *Social behavior in animals.* New York: Wiley, 1953 (a).

Tinbergen, N. Fighting and threat in animals. *New Biol.,* 1953, **14,** 9–24 (b).

Tinbergen, N. *The herring gull's world.* New York: Basic Books, 1961.

Toews, W. F. Self-esteem, perception of parental control and hostility of adolescents. Doctoral dissertation, Brigham Young University, 1966. University Microfilms, Ann Arbor, Michigan.

Toigo, R., Walder, L., Eron, L. D., and Lefkowitz, M. Examiner effect in the use of a near sociometric procedure in the third grade classroom. *Psychol. Rep.,* 1962, **11,** 785–790.

Ulrich, R. Pain as a cause of aggression. *Am. Zool.,* 1966, **6,** 643–662.

Updegraff, R. L., and Keister, M. E. A study of children's reactions to failure and an experimental attempt to modify them. *Child Dev.,* 1937, **8,** 241–248.

Waelder, R. Critical discussion of the concept of an instinct of destruction. *Bull. Phila. Assn. Psychoanal.,* 1956, **6,** 97–109.

Wagner, A. R. The role of reinforcement and nonreinforcement in an "apparent frustration effect." *J. exp. Psychol.,* 1959, **57,** 130–136.

Walder, L. O., Abelson, R. P., Eron, L. D., Banta, T. J., and Laulicht, J. H. Development of a peer-rating measure of aggression. *Psychol. Reprints,* 1961, **9,** 497–556.

Walker, R. N. Body build and behavior in young children: I. Body and nursery school teacher's ratings. *Monogr. soc. res. Child Dev.,* 1962, **27** (Ser. No. 84).

Walters, J., Pearce, D., and Dahms, L. Affectional and aggressive behavior of preschool children. *Child Dev.,* 1957, **28,** 15–26.

Walters, R. H., and Brown, M. Studies of reinforcement of aggression: III Transfer of responses to an interpersonal situation. *Child Dev.,* 1963, **34,** 563–571.

Walters, R. H., and Brown, M. A test of the high magnitude theory of aggression. *J. exp. Child Psychol.,* 1964, **1,** 367–387.

Walters, R. H., and Demkow, L. F. Timing of punishment as a determinant of response inhibition. *Child Dev.,* 1963, **34**(1), 207–214.

Walters, R. H., Leat, M., and Mezei, L. Inhibition and disinhibition of responses through empathetic learning. *Can. J. Psychol.,* 1963, **17,** 235–243.

Walters, R. H., and Thomas, E. Enhancement of punitiveness by visual and audio-visual displays. *Can. J. Psychol.,* 1963, **17,** 244–255.

Walters, R. H., Thomas, E. L., and Acker, C. W. Enhancement of punitive behavior by audio-visual displays. *Science,* 1962, **136,** 872–873.

Wasman, M. and Flynn, J. P. Directed attack elicited from hypothalamus. *Archs. Neurol.,* 1962, **6,** 220–227.

Waterhouse, I. K., and Child, I. L. Frustration and the quality of performance: III. An experimental study. *J. Personality,* 1953, **22,** 298–311.

Watson, G. A. A comparison of the effects of lax versus strict home training. *J. soc. Psychol.,* 1934, **5,** 102–105.

Watson, G. A. Some personality differences in children related to strict or permissive parental discipline. *J. Psychol.,* 1957, **44,** 227–249.

Weatherley, D. Maternal permissiveness toward aggression and subsequent TAT aggression. *J. abnorm. soc. Psychol.,* 1962, **65**(1), 1–5.

Weiss, W., and Fine, B. J. The effect of induced aggressiveness on opinion change. *J. abnorm. soc. Psychol.,* 1956, **52,** 109–114.

Weller, G. M., and Bell, R. Q. Basal skin conductance and neonatal state. *Child Dev.,* 1965, **36,** 647–657.

Wertham, F. C. *Seduction of the innocent.* New York: Rinehart, 1954.

White, R. K., and Lippitt, R. *Autocracy and democracy: an experimental inquiry.* New York: Harper, 1960.

Whiting, B. B. *Six cultures—studies of child rearing.* (Seven volumes.) New York: Wiley, 1963.

Whiting, J. W. M. and Child, I. L. *Child training and personality.* New Haven, Conn.: Yale University Press, 1953.

Wiggins, J. S., and Winder, C. L. The peer nomination inventory: an empirically derived sociometric measure of adjustment in preadolescent boys. *Psychol. Reprints,* 1961, **9,** 643–677.

Wile, I. S., and Davis, R. The relation of birth to behavior. *Am. J. Orthopsychiat.,* 1941, **11,** 320–334.

Winder, C., and Wiggins, J. S. Social reputation and social behavior: a further validation of the peer nomination inventory. *J. abnorm. soc. Psychol.,* 1964, **68,** 681–684.

Winder, C. L., and Rau, L. Parental attitudes associated with social deviance in preadolescent boys. *J. abnorm. soc. Psychol.,* 1962, **64,** 418–424.

Wittenborn, J. R. *The development of adaptive children.* New York: Russell Sage, 1954.

Worchel, P. Hostility: theory and experimental investigation. In D. Willner (Ed.), *Decisions, values and groups.* Vol. I. New York: Pergamon Press, 1960.

Wright, G. O. Projection and displacement: a cross-cultural study of folk-tale aggression. *J. abnorm. soc. Psychol.*, 1954, **49, 523–28.**

Wright, M. E. Constructiveness of play as affected by group organization and frustration. *Character Person.*, 1942, **11,** 40–49.

Wright, M. E. The influence of frustration upon the social relations of young children. *Character Person.*, 1943, **12,** 111–112.

Yarrow, L. The effect of antecedent frustration on projective play. *Psychol. Monogr.*, 1948, **62**(293).

Young, S. P., and Goldman, E. A. The wolves of North America. Washington, D.C.: American Wildlife Institute, 1944.

Young, W. C., Goy, R., and Phoenix, C. Hormones and sexual behavior. *Science,* 1964, **143,** 212–218.

Zaks, M. S., and Walters, R. H. First steps in the construction of a scale for the measurement of aggression. *J. Psychol.*, 1959, **47,** 199–208.

Zubin, J., Eron, L. D., and Schumer, F. *An experimental approach to projective techniques.* New York: Wiley, 1965.

Zuckerman, S. *The social life of monkeys and apes.* London: Kegan Paul; New York: Harcourt, Brace, 1932.

Zumpe, D. Laboratory observations on the aggressive behavior of some butterfly fishes (Chaetodontidae). *Zur Tierpsychol.*, 1965, **22,** 226–236.

23. Moral Development[1]

MARTIN L. HOFFMAN[2]

Historically three philosophical doctrines bearing on the moral development of the child have held sway. One is the doctrine of "original sin," which assumes early intervention by adults, who represent sacred and secular values, is the only possible salvation of an otherwise lost soul. Another is the doctrine of "innate purity," which holds society, especially adult society, to be a primarily corrupting influence that should be minimized, especially in the early years. The third doctrine assumes that the infant is neither corrupt nor pure but an infinitely malleable *tabula rasa*. Each of these views is represented in the major twentieth-century psychological approaches to moral development. The doctrine of innate purity, one of whose major formulators was Rousseau, has as its main present-day representative Jean Piaget, who has long been director of the institute in Geneva that bears Rousseau's name. According to Piaget, adult-child relations are intrinsically heteronomous and it is only the natural give-and-take that occurs in social interactions among peers that can provide the impetus to moral maturity, by which Piaget means morality guided in the main by higher cognitive processes. The doctrine of original sin is represented in modified form by psychoanalysis. Though highly critical of the

suppressive role of society, Freud nevertheless viewed the young child as a bundle of drives that must be subordinated by adults to societal objectives. This socialization constitutes the moral development process. The third major approach, learning theory, is a descendant of the *tabula rasa* doctrine. It implicitly has much in common with "original sin," however, as evidenced by its stress on the necessity of adult intervention, without which the child's primary motivation would continue to be the gratification of biological drives. It is interesting to note that of these three approaches it is only the one that assumes "innate purity" that places great emphasis on the role of higher mental processes in moral development or in the finished product.

These theoretical approaches and their offshoots have guided the bulk of the moral development research that will dominate the pages of this chapter. Each, in keeping with its philosophical underpinnings, has its own distinctive way of defining what morality is and thus carving out its domain for empirical study. Thus Piaget and his followers define a moral act, in accord with Western views about ethics, as one based on a conscious prior judgment of its rightness or wrongness. Their objective is to study the higher mental processes and thought structures that underlie such judgments, and their research techniques are designed to yield data based on the maximum usage of the child's cognitive processes. According to Freudian theory, moral standards are the largely unconscious products of powerful irrational motives and are based on the need to keep antisocial impulses from conscious awareness. The primary research interest the theory has stimulated concerns the

[1] This paper was prepared in conjunction with a research project entitled "Psychological Processes in Moral Development," conducted under Grant HD 02258 from the National Institute of Child Health and Human Development.
[2] The writer is indebted to Lois Wladis Hoffman and Eleanor Maccoby for their critical reading of earlier drafts of this chapter.

guilt that results when these standards are violated. Learning theory defines morality in terms of specific acts and avoidances which are learned on the basis of rewards and punishments; the typical procedure is to use direct or vicarious reinforcement, with little or no accompanying rationale, to elicit behaviors in the laboratory which are "good" in terms of some culturally shared standard of conduct.

The aim of this chapter is to pull together the major strands of theory and research, raise important issues, and suggest future directions. (Recent papers by Kohlberg, 1963 and 1964; Hoffman, 1963; and Maccoby, 1968 have had similar objectives.) In keeping with the current state of the field the focus will be on processes; and differences between age, sex and sociocultural groups will be brought in only as they bear on this. There are basically two approaches to developmental process. One is Piaget's cognitive-developmental approach, which stresses age and associated cognitive changes as an influence on moral development. The other is social learning—broadly defined to include psychoanalytic as well as the leading theories of learning—which stresses the influence of the social environment, mainly adult socialization techniques. Social learning has focused primarily on the conditions associated with wrongdoing, although there is a recently burgeoning experimental literature on altruism and consideration for others, which will be discussed in detail.

INTERNALIZATION OF MORAL STANDARDS

The guiding concept in most moral development research is the internalization of socially sanctioned prohibitions and mandates. One of the legacies of Freud, and the sociologist Durkheim as well, is the assumption now prevalent among social scientists that the individual does not go through life viewing society's central norms as externally and coercively imposed pressures to which he must submit. Though the norms are initially alien, they are eventually adopted by the individual, largely through the efforts of his early socializers—the parents—and come to serve as internalized guides so that he behaves in accord with them even when external authority is not present to enforce them. That is, control by others is replaced by self-control. Examples of internalization concepts are Freud's "superego" and Durkheim's "collective conscience."

Perhaps the most succinct statement of the assumed societal value of internalization to society has been made by Simmel:

The tendency of society to satisfy itself as cheaply as possible results in appeals to "good conscience," through which the individual pays to himself the wages for his righteousness, which otherwise would probably have to be assured to him in some way through law or custom (Simmel, 1902, p. 19).

Internalization processes may thus serve the social control function of making conformity rewarding in its own right, where rewards for correct behavior and punishments for deviation are not forthcoming from society.

Several social theorists in recent years have challenged the importance of the internalization concept (e.g., Reiss, 1966; Sanford, 1953; Wrong, 1961). They contend that the individual's moral standards are highly vulnerable to internal and external pressures, and must be firmed up by a continuing pattern of social reinforcement and support. Reiss states further that internalization is not necessary for society because of the manifold forms of external surveillance that inevitably exist. He also cites the extensive, society-wide shifts in normative behavior that often occur from one generation to the next as evidence that the parent-child relationship cannot be the major agency of cultural transmission. Rather, standards of conduct are disseminated by institutionally organized systems (e.g., religious, political, legal, and educational agencies) and regulated by collectively enforced sanctions. Innovation, according to Reiss' view, also originates at the social organization level, whereas changes emerging within the family are of minor social consequence. Finally, the parents are seen as less important in determining the values that govern the individual's behavior in adult life than the larger social system, which may counteract the parents at any later point and replace parentally taught values. Reiss concludes that internalization is not a necessary requisite and should not enter into the definition of moral behavior.

These arguments help place internalization in proper perspective. The view that internalization has unlimited influence over behavior is also challenged by laboratory studies in which people behave in ways that contradict their professed and presumably internalized standards; for example, a study by Milgram (1963) shows the possibility that people will sometimes obey outrageous requests when given by respectable authority figures. Also suggestive are the findings of a business survey in which most executives agreed with the statement that businessmen "would violate a code of ethics whenever they thought they could avoid detection" (Baumhart, 1961).

The fact that some people may lack a system of internalized standards and others may have theirs undermined by social pressures in later life, however, does not negate the importance of internalization. Once we discard the simplistic notion that moral standards internalized from parents persist unchanged throughout life, and accept the vulnerability of internalized standards to extreme counterpressures from without, the concept that remains—the acquisition of internal motive force by moral standards which were at first external to the individual—is still an important and viable one. The potential long-range power of this motive force can be seen in the clinical realm, though less durability is ordinarily to be expected. How long an internalized standard will effectively guide behavior depends in part on the amount of pressures against it that the individual encounters.

Reiss' view that the family is rarely the source of normative innovation is compelling, although we would suggest that parents may take a more active role than he indicates. While it is true that the adult's internalized standards may influence his child-rearing behavior and thus serve as a conservative social force, the adult is also aware of social reality and is often capable of subordinating his standards to it. When faced with strong pressures against an internalized standard, he may, with some exertion of will and perhaps a twinge of conscience, suppress the tendency to behave in accord with the standard. In this way new circumstances may have a considerable impact on his behavior, including

his child-rearing practices. He may, for example, hold back and not punish the child for something he himself had been punished for when he was younger. What the child internalizes as a result will be somewhat different from the parent's own internalized standards and closer to the new societal demands. Normative change may be facilitated by this process, in which the adult's internalized standards are filtered through his own cognitive and control systems before finding overt expression in relation to the child. The parent's own standards, though presumably still internalized, may thus give way to societal pressures and the parent may actually contribute to the child's internalization of new norms.[3,4]

With this background we now procede to an examination of internalization and its place in the child development literature. To begin with, several problems of conceptual definition will be cited and an attempt will be made to provide clarification.

1. Objective versus subjective definition. If a person behaved in accord with a moral standard in situations where detection is unlikely, this would meet the requirements for internalization held by most behavioristically oriented researchers: namely, moral behavior which is independent of external sanctions. The behavior might, however, be motivated by irrational fears of ubiquitous authority figures, or retribution by ghosts or gods. It seems clear that the term internalization makes most sense if it refers only to acts which at least meet the requirement of freedom from *subjective* concerns about external sanctions. Behavior based on fear of sanctions, whether realistic or not, should then be considered to be externally motivated.

2. Relevance of cues. In criticizing the internalization concept, Bandura cites the example of a motorist who stops at a traffic

[3] This view is of course directly contrary to the psychoanalytic notion of an internalized superego that does not consist of the parent's conscious moral orientation but his superego which is more rigid and serves as a built-in source of moral conservatism.

[4] For a fuller discussion of the problem of value transmission from one generation to the next, including the question of intergenerational change in moral values, see Maccoby (1968).

light on a lonely dark road and waits patiently for the light to turn green.[5] Bandura argues that while the motorist is exhibiting remarkable control, nevertheless his behavior is clearly externally regulated—by the light. We would apply the subjective criterion here too and distinguish between two kinds of stimuli: those that are responded to as symbols of external sanctions, and those that are not. Only if the light symbolized the law and raised fears of possible detection would the motorist's stopping not qualify as an internalized act. Otherwise it would, even though triggered by an external stimulus.

3. Role of absent reference groups or persons. Several writers, in criticizing the internalization concept, have noted that behavior in accord with a moral standard may merely reflect the norms of an absent reference group or individual (e.g., Brim, 1968; Campbell, 1964; Bandura and Walters, 1963). This problem, too, can be resolved by adhering to a strict subjective criterion. Should the conformity be based on fear of a punitive response from the reference figure if he somehow found out about the actor's behavior, then it would reduce to an externally motivated act. If, on the other hand, the behavior was based on the actor's positive attitude toward the reference figure (love and desire to please him, respect for his judgment, desire to model himself after him) or concern about hurting or disappointing him—without regard for punitive consequences—then the behavior may be appropriately classed as internalized.

By using a subjective criterion of belief in the rightness of an act without regard to sanctions, three types of internalization are possible. The first and most primitive one is based on conditioned fear or anxiety. The individual is repeatedly punished for a deviant act and eventually the kinesthetic and other cues produced by the act arouse anxiety, which may then be avoided by inhibiting the act or engaging in some other corrective action. This, as we shall see, is essentially the concept of internalization held by many learning theorists; and it also has most of the essential ingredients of the psychoanalytic theory of superego formation. In our view it is a borderline

[5] This point was made at the Character Development Conference sponsored by the Social Science Research Council in 1962.

type of internalization, since although the individual is unaware of it, he is motivated by external threat. Furthermore, there is no subjective evaluation of behavior in terms of right and wrong, although, with the advent of cognitive mediation, it may become possible for the individual to apply moralistic labels in the evaluation of behavior with which anxiety has previously become associated.

The second and third types of internalization will be mentioned here only briefly and elaborated upon later. The second is based on the actor's positive orientation toward an absent reference group or person in the manner discussed previously; that is, the actor believes in the standards and employs the moralistic evaluations which have been transmitted by the significant others whom he respects and with whom he identifies. In the third and most advanced type, the individual experiences the standards as an obligation to himself rather than some reference figure. His motives are to avoid self-condemnation and guilt or to attain self-approval. This type of internalization, in addition, typically involves an inner process of thought and judgment concerning right and wrong in which the actor thinks through the standards and accepts them as his own. The second type may at times shade into the third, as when the person comes to feel the moral standards are his own because he has forgotten the reference figure or because there were so many of them that the standard is no longer associated with any particular one. He may then question the standard and finally arrive at a more mature understanding of its worth.

THE COGNITIVE-DEVELOPMENTAL APPROACH TO MORAL IDEOLOGY

The cognitive-developmental approach involves the analysis of thought structures underlying the moral concepts of persons at different age levels in order to define a general direction of movement. These structures, or stages, are characterized as follows. First, each stage is an integrated whole rather than simply the sum of ideas pertaining to isolated bits of behavior. This means the central concept defining a stage is reflected in many acts and there is considerable consistency in level of response among an individual's acts. It also means the stages differ qualitatively and not just quantitatively. Second, in the course of development a given stage is viewed as being integrated into the next and replaced by it. That is, an emerging stage develops out of its predecessor and is thus a synthesis of the old and the new. Third, each individual contributes actively to working out his own synthesis rather than adopting a ready-made one provided by the culture. Fourth, because earlier stages are necessary parts of their successors, the individual must pass through all preceding stages before he can move on to the next one. Thus we come to the most interesting and often debated aspect of the cognitive-developmental approach: the doctrine of invariant sequence, according to which the order of succession of stages is constant and universal. Although the particular age at which a stage appears is influenced by environment and level of cognitive development, either of which can advance or retard—and in the extreme even preclude—the appearance of a stage, the stages will appear in the same order for all individuals and all cultures.

This view of stages contrasts with others, for example, Gesell's (1929), in which stages form an invariant sequence not through an active process of one building upon another but through the maturational unfolding of a series of innate biological patterns, that is, each stage is a direct reflection of the individual's maturational level at the time.

Piaget's Stage Theory

The principal exponent of the cognitive-developmental approach to moral development is Piaget (1932). The essence of morality, according to Piaget, includes both the individual's respect for the rules of social order and his sense of justice, by which Piaget means a concern for reciprocity and equality among individuals. Piaget's interest is in the developmental shift in the basis of these two aspects of morality—from respect and submission to authority, to self-government and control.

In order to reveal in simplest form the developmental processes underlying the shift in orientation toward rules Piaget investigated the attitudes of different-aged children toward the origin, legitimacy, and alterability of the rules in the children's game of marbles. After establishing stages in the meaning of

the rules of marbles, and generalizing to all rules, he elaborated on their further implications for the sense of justice. The sense of justice was also investigated more directly by the technique of telling stories about persons who committed various transgressions and asking children such questions as why the acts are wrong and which of two acts is worse. An example is the item, now well known, in which children are asked to judge who is naughtier, a boy who accidentally breaks fifteen cups as he opens a door or a boy who breaks one cup while trying to sneak jam out of the cupboard.

Through these procedures Piaget evolved a system of two broad stages of moral development which encompass both the respect for rules and sense of justice. In the earlier stage—referred to variously as moral realism, morality of constraint, or heteronomous morality—the child feels an obligation to comply to rules because they are sacred and unalterable. He tends to view behaviors as totally right or wrong and thinks everyone views them in the same way. He judges the rightness or wrongness of an act on the basis of the magnitude of its consequences, the extent to which it conforms exactly to established rules, and whether or not it elicits punishment. He believes in "immanent justice," that is, that violations of social norms are followed by physical accidents or misfortunes willed by God or by some inanimate object.[6]

The child in the more advanced stage—called autonomous morality, morality of cooperation, or reciprocity—in contrast, does not view rules as rigid or unchangeable but as established and maintained through reciprocal social agreement and thus subject to modification in response to human needs or

[6] There is a paradoxical quality to this stage in that the child, for example, may play marbles without any real regard for the details of the rules or for the behavior of the other players, but when he is asked he reports an immutable respect for the rules. Piaget explains this paradox by pointing to the nature of the relationship between the adult and the child at this time, in which there is no mutual exchange or cooperation and which serves to preserve the child's egocentrism. The child's failure to discriminate between his ego and the external world is not corrected by this relationship. Rather, the child and his thought are isolated and the rules for which he feels such obligation remain external to him and do not change his behavior.

other situational demands. The child at this stage gives up his moral absolutism and recognizes a possible diversity in views of right and wrong. His judgments of right and wrong are no longer determined only by the consequences of an act but place great stress on the presence or absence of intention to deceive. And he no longer believes that punishment is impersonally ordained. Another difference is that while the heteronomous child defines duty and obligation largely in terms of obedience to authority, duty and obligation for the autonomous child are more apt to revolve around conforming to peer expectations and considering their welfare, expressing gratitude for past affection and favors, and, above all, putting oneself in the place of others. The child's ideas about how punishment should be administered also change: from the heteronomous advocation of expiatory punishment which is painful, arbitrary, and administered by authority to the notion that punishment should be reciprocally related to the misdeed, for example, through restitution or direct retaliation by the victim.

According to Piaget, both maturation and experience play a role in the transition from one stage to the next. Maturation is important primarily as it affects the child's developing cognitive capacities. Experience is also important, however, and the experiential variable singled out for special attention is the child's shift from interaction primarily with adults, in which socialization consists largely of the imposition of sanctions, to increasing interaction with peers, which has a more mutual give-and-take quality. Although Piaget refers repeatedly to the importance of cognitive development and peer interaction, he does not attempt a systematic explanation of the process by which these two factors interact to move the child through moral realism to moral autonomy. At times he appears to view cognitive development as primary, with moral development being just one derivative of cognitive development and social interaction serving merely as a catalytic agent which advances or retards the operation of a built-in timed mechanism. At other times social interaction appears to play a more central role and it is on these occasions, especially in discussing primitive cultures, that Piaget seems somewhat less inclined to view his moral stages as forming structured wholes that de-

velop universally in a fixed sequence. An attempt to pull together the various threads of Piaget's argument follows.

The two major cognitive limitations that underlie the young child's moral realism are his egocentrism (assumption that other's views of events are the same as his) and "realism" (confusion of subjective and objective aspects of experience as exemplified in the perception of dreams as external events rather than mental phenomena). As a result of these two factors the child assumes there is only one view, which is shared by all, about whether an act is right or wrong, and he sees rules as more like physical regularities which are fixed and unchangeable than as subjective psychosocial expectations which may be changed in the service of human ends. Because of these same cognitive limitations the child also perceives the pain following rule infractions to be the same as the pain that automatically and naturally follows violations of physical law, such as falling from heights or touching fire. That is, he does not realize that the pain following rule infractions is mediated by a human being's judgment that the act warranted punishment. He thus confuses natural catastrophe with moral punishment and believes in "immanent justice." In addition, because the conduct of others appears in its outward shape long before the child has the ability to understand the motives or intentions behind it, the child is apt to compare the outward shape with established rules and judge the act only by this criterion. (He can of course perceive his own inner states and thus he may, for example, minimize the gravity of his own misdeeds when they are unintended or accidental.)

Added to these effects of his cognitive immaturity is the child's heteronomous respect for adults. This is based on a syndrome of feelings toward them which includes inferiority, dependence, affection, admiration, and fear. Commands from parents or other adults whom the child respects are accompanied by a feeling of obligation to comply. This feeling of obligation to adult commands carries over into the realm of rules, which then become not only fixed but also sacred; any attempt to change or modify them is wrong.

It follows that a major cognitive prerequisite for moral growth is the giving up of egocentrism and "realism." This involves the development of a concept of the self as a speaking, perceiving, thinking person, coordinate with other such entities but distinct from them, and the recognition that other individuals may have points of view and perspectives about an event that differ from one's own. The way in which this cognitive shift interacts with and is in part the product of peer relations is suggested in the following quotation from Piaget:

[A]s the child grows up, the prestige of the older children diminishes, he can discuss matters more and more as an equal and has increasing opportunities (beyond the scope of suggestion, obedience, or negativism) of freely contrasting his point of view with that of others. Henceforward, he will not only discover the boundaries that separate his self from the other person, but will learn to understand the other person and be understood by him. So that cooperation is really a factor in the creation of . . . a self that takes up its stand on the norms of reciprocity and objective discussion, and knows how to submit to these in order to make itself respected (1932, pp. 95–96).

In Piaget's discussions of what takes place in peer interactions, two distinct processes seem to emerge. The first pertains to the child's sharing in making decisions and the effects this has on his perspective toward rules and authority. Thus Piaget suggests that by virtue of growing older the child attains greater relative equality with his old interaction partners (parents and older children), which helps lessen his unilateral respect for them. His respect for himself and his agemates is also enhanced, which helps give him the confidence to participate with them in applying rules on the basis of the norms of reciprocity and making decisions about changing the rules. As a direct result of these new modes of social interaction—and aided by parallel developments in cognitive capacities—he arrives at a new conception of rules. They are no longer experienced as coming from above, and the view that they have an infinite past and divine or adult origin is no longer tenable. Instead they are increasingly seen as products of agreement and cooperation based on goals which they serve, and

amenable to change by mutual consent. The experience of interacting with peers thus shakes the child's faith in his earlier views about the source of rules and their social significance. And the natural outcome of the child's efforts to resolve the contradiction is a more mature and broadened perspective on the rules.

The second, and more multifaceted process in interacting with peers deals with the importance of taking alternate and reciprocal roles with them. Such mutual role-taking facilitates the child's developing awareness that he is an individual who is coordinate with but different from others, that is, that he thinks and feels as they do in similar situations, that the consequences of his actions for them and theirs for him are similar, and yet that events seem different when viewed from different vantage points. (Language of course is crucial here in enabling the relevant thoughts and feelings to be communicated.) This awareness in turn helps give rise to mutual respect, which is a necessary condition for respecting the rules as products of group agreement and for gaining a more internalized understanding of what they mean. It also helps sensitize the child to the inner states that underlie the acts of others. This is obviously a major factor in the development of the child's need to treat others as he would have them treat him (i.e., to take his inner states into account). It is also important in contributing the sympathetic attitude needed to make the shift from basing moral judgments of others entirely on the overt aspect of their acts, to taking their intentions into account. "It is only by a continuous effort of generosity and sympathy that we can resist [the tendency to judge acts by their outward shapes] and try to understand other people's reactions in terms of their intentions . . . it is also obvious that to judge [in terms of intentions] will require a greater effort in the case of other people's actions than in that of our own" (Piaget, 1932, p. 180).

While stressing the overriding importance of peer interaction, Piaget, in several rarely cited passages, makes clear his belief that the parent's child-rearing practices might also play a significant role in moral development. According to Piaget, parents tend to be authoritarian in their practices and as a result help consolidate the child's natural tendency toward heteronomy. If instead they would change their ways and provide conditions for the child to interact with them in a reciprocal fashion, this would increase the likelihood of moral autonomy taking root. Thus he states:

In order to remove all traces of moral realism, one must place oneself on the child's own level, and give him a feeling of equality by laying stress on one's own obligations and one's own deficiencies. In the sphere of clumsiness and of untidiness in general (putting away toys, personal cleanliness, etc.), in short in all the multifarious obligations that are so secondary for moral theory but so all-important in daily life (perhaps nine-tenths of the commands given to children relate to these material questions) it is quite easy to draw attention to one's own needs, one's own difficulties, even one's own blunders, and to point out their consequences, thus creating an atmosphere of mutual help and understanding. In this way the child will find himself in the presence, not of a system of commands requiring ritualistic and external obedience, but of a system of social relations such that everyone does his best to obey the same obligations, and does so out of mutual respect (Piaget, 1932, pp. 133–134).

At other points Piaget also indicates that the parent can contribute to the young child's movement toward autonomy by burdening him with fewer demands whose reasons he cannot grasp and which he is therefore apt to place on the same plane as actual physical phenomena (examples are demands regarding cleanliness, food habits, and never telling lies) and by anticipating and creating conditions that prevent misdeeds and thus minimize the child's punishment experiences.

It seems clear from these remarks that Piaget stresses peers only because interactions with them are by nature more likely to be mutual and reciprocal. With enlightenment, parents and presumably other authorities could overcome their natural tendencies to relate heteronomously with children and interact with them in ways that will foster rather than hinder their moral growth.

* * *

It is in discussing primitive cultures both in his earlier work and in a later paper (Piaget, 1947) that Piaget gives fullest reign to his view that social experience is of the utmost importance in moral development. He first points out that in modern society it is in childhood that the greatest degree of intellectual and moral constraint is exercised by the older upon the younger generation. Only as he grows into adulthood does the individual free himself from the bonds of tradition and acquire a personal view of the world. In primitive society, on the other hand, it is the young child who is relatively free because he exists outside the corporate life of the tribe. As he grows older he must become absorbed into the ranks of the tribal initiates. In Piaget's words,

The neophyte must therefore acquire a practical, effective and ideological knowledge of the sacred traditions whose guardians are the Elders. Accordingly, for anything from a few months to two years or more, the adolescent must undergo rites of initiation to whose impressive and sometimes cruel nature all ethnographers bear witness. In the presence of Masters masked to heighten the air of mystery, the young man undergoes every kind of physical test, while at the same time—in an atmosphere of emotional tension and submission to the spirits—he absorbs the body of sacred beliefs and practices which will transform him into an adult member of the clan. Thus, founded as it is on mystical authority, the upbringing of the adolescent in primitive societies ruled by tribal custom tends essentially to conformity. On the one hand, intellectual conformity: there is nothing to induce in him the habit of reflection or the critical spirit, for in every field (from true techniques to mystical representations and from magic to the causal explanation of phenomena) his thoughts are ready-made for him and he bows to the collective notions of the tribe handed down from generation to generation. And, on the other hand, moral conformity: sacred duties and ritual prohibition (taboos) leave only the narrowest margin to action not governed by rules (Havighurst and Neugarten, 1955, pp. 125–126).

Thus the child becomes "progressively enslaved by collective pressure." The first duty of those who are initiated in primitive cultures is "to submit to an already established truth." Piaget concludes that the attitudes of children toward rules in primitive societies should not show a developmental parallel to those in modern society, and thus moral autonomy may not be attained in primitive cultures. He also goes further and suggests the possibility that because such a society exerts more rather than less moral restraint on children as they grow older, their moral orientations may become more rather than less rigid with age. "If the society has a world view which includes a supernatural power that watches over men and rewards and punishes their actions, then belief in immanent justice will probably be as strong in older children as in younger ones, or even stronger." In this suggestion of a possible developmental reversal, and not merely arrest, Piaget comes close to breaking with his notion of invariance of sequence. But clearly he views this as an exception that occurs only under the most extreme conditions.

In summary, Piaget views moral development as the outcome of an active process, involving the development of certain cognitive capacities in conjunction with the exposure to new modes of social experience which provide the basis for a broadened perspective on authority and an enhanced ability to take the role of others. The advances in cognitive development help the child in his efforts to make sense out of new experiences and integrate them with his prior views. The outcome of this struggle is a new and higher level of moral orientation. This process of movement from moral realism to autonomy is seen to occur in all children unless development is arrested, or possibly reversed, by unusual coerciveness of the parents or the culture, which results in extreme deprivation of the experience of mutual and reciprocal social interaction.

It is instructive to contrast Piaget's cognitive-developmental view of the role of social experience with the view of psychoanalytic and social learning theories. According to the latter, as we shall see, the social environment plays a direct molding role and the important social experiences are those in which authorities supply the child with ready-made standards and act in ways that ensure the arousal of motives necessary for adopting the standards. According to the cognitive-developmental approach, new experience is incorporated into existing cognitive structures not in the sense of contributing additional information but through an active process in which the person resolves contradictions between the old and the new and thus creates a new structure. Social experience then does not lead directly to a new moral orientation; its role, rather, is confined to stimulating and challenging the individual to reorganize his pre-existing patterns of moral thought.[7]

Empirical Research on Piaget's Theory

The research on Piaget's theory has typically focused on one or more of the major attributes of his stages, rather than the entire stage sequence in all its complexity. These attributes include the shifts from exclusive concern with consequences (objective responsibility) to concern with intentions; from absolutism to relativism of moral perspective; from support for expiatory and authority-administered punishment to restitutive and reciprocal forms of punishment; from defining obligation in terms of obedience to adult authority, to defining it in terms of conformity to peer expectation; and from immanent justice to a more reality-based view of punishment. The objectives of the various studies have been to see if there is a natural tendency for these attributes to appear in the postulated developmental order, if movement through the stage is accelerated or retarded because of differences in cognitive development or social experience, and if there is consistency across the attributes within a stage.

Universality of Stage Sequence. The research findings on age trends, summarized in Table 1, provide a great deal of support for Piaget's postulated sequence in Western countries (England, United States, and Switzerland), for which the findings were consistently

[7] While not stressed by Piaget, it would follow from his theory that the experience of observing other children whose parents set different rules and other cultural groups with different life styles would provide further stimulation and challenge. Cultural isolation, by the same token, should result in retarded development.

Table 1. Age Trends for Piaget's Moral Attributes in Western Countries

Attribute	Direction of Relation with Age	Reference
Relativism of perspective (vs. absolutism)	+	Lerner (1937a)
	+	MacRae (1954)
Objective view of punishment (vs. immanent justice)	+	Grinder (1964)
	+	Johnson (1962)
	+	Lerner (1937a)
	+	Liu (1950)
	+	MacRae (1954)
	0	Medinnus (1959)
Intentions (vs. consequences)	+	Bandura and McDonald (1963)
	+	Boehm (1962)
	+	Boehm and Nass (1962)
	+	Grinder (1964)
	+	Johnson (1962)
	+	Lerner (1937a)
	+	MacRae (1954)
	+	Whiteman and Kosier (1964)
Restitutive justice (vs. expiative)	+	MacRae (1954)
	+	Harrower (1934)
	+	Johnson (1962)
	+	Schallenberger (1894)
Conformity to peer expectations (vs. obedience to adult authority)	+	MacRae (1954)

in accord with this sequence.[8] In further support of Piaget's view, these findings were obtained with samples drawn from a variety of populations representing both sexes and different levels of intellectual capacity and socioeconomic status. And in one of the studies the subjects were Chinese-American (Liu, 1950). The fact that the same age trends were obtained regardless of class and IQ is especially impressive in view of the finding, to be discussed later, that class and IQ both relate positively to moral judgment.

Despite these clear indications of age trends, however, there is some evidence that even intelligent adults may at times use earlier forms of moral judgment in situations that are conceptually similar though more complex than those used in the child research. In a recent study by Walster (1966) college students judged a hypothetical person to be more responsible for an accident when the

[8] The negative relation between age and reciprocity obtained by Durkin (1959) is not included in this table because the reciprocity indices

used are not in keeping with the spirit of Piaget's concept of a mature morality. That is, the responses coded as reflecting reciprocity include the recommendation that property should not be shared with a child who has previously refused to share; and the belief that whenever one's character has been defamed by another it is just and right to defame that person's character in return. Similarly, the responses taken as counterindicative of reciprocity include the recommendation that one should share with another despite his past unwillingness to share and that one should not defame the character of someone who has previously defamed one's own character.

We have also omitted the findings on age trends for the belief in "collective responsibility" (all members of the group are responsible for the actions of each member) obtained by Johnson (1962) since Piaget makes it clear that the conditions for collective responsibility, i.e., the coalescence of a heteronomous morality of constraint and a deep feeling of individual participation in the collective, occur in primitive but not in modern society. By the time the child in Western society reaches solidarity with peers, according to Piaget, he has given up much of the morality of constraint.

consequences were severe than when they were minor. This occurred despite the fact that the person was described as having taken reasonable and identical safety precautions in both cases.

* * *

If Piaget's stages were universal we would expect to find the same age trends in primitive cultures as in modern society, except perhaps for some retardation or developmental arrest. We should at least find the same sequence. The findings are ambiguous. Jahoda (1958) found the expected decrease in immanent justice with age in West African schoolchildren living in a large city. Dennis (1943) obtained similar results in Hopi Indians. The major contradictory findings come from a study by Havighurst and Neugarten of ten American Indian groups. In four groups there were no age trends but in six the trend was toward *increased* belief in immanent justice with age. These investigators also studied the development of attitudes toward the rules of American games among Indian children from seven tribes who attended American schools. They found a decrease with age in the conception of rules as rigid, fixed, and unchangeable entities, as expected in Piaget's stage theory, in two of the tribes. But there was an increase in three tribes. The remaining tribes showed no change. These findings must be taken as evidence against the universality of Piaget's stages for two reasons. First, these findings cannot be explained by the concept of developmental arrest since in some groups there was actually an increase in "immanent justice" and "fixed rules," that is, a reversal of the sequence. Second, although only two of the stage attributes are involved, at least one of these—the giving up of immanent justice— is assumed by Piaget to be primarily dependent on cognitive development. If such an attribute reversed, it seems likely that there would be an even greater reversal with others which are more dependent on social interaction, such as the preference for expiatory over reciprocal punishment. We would tentatively conclude that sociocultural factors can be highly influential. It remains possible, however, that Piaget's stages are invariant, though only within the confines of the type of social structure that exists in Western society.

Cognitive-Experiential Basis of Moral Development. Since the factors seen by Piaget as responsible for moral development are cognitive development and reciprocal social interaction, it follows that progress through the moral stages is accelerated by advanced cognitive development (IQ), equalitarian child-rearing practices by parents, and intensified interaction with peers. Although the effect of peer interaction has been neglected in the research, this is not true of cognitive development or of child-rearing practices, the findings bearing on which are summarized in Table 2.[9] Clearly the expectations about cognitive development are borne out. The relation between IQ and the moral attributes formulated by Piaget are consistently positive.

The findings for child-rearing practices appear to be far less supportive of Piaget's view. It should be pointed out, however, that the parental indices used have a questionable bearing on Piaget's hypotheses, which we summarized earlier. MacRae (1954) used a measure of parental control over the child's activities (e.g., homework, bedtime, chores, hour of coming home at night) which seems to have some relevance to Piaget's concepts but the data were obtained only from children. The validity of such data, especially those obtained from the younger children studied (the age range was 5-14 years), is questionable. Johnson, on the other hand, obtained data from parents, but he studied their attitudes, not overt behavior. In view of the problems with these measures and the paucity of significant findings in the two studies, we cannot draw any conclusions from the results.

Several studies have been made on the influence of socioeconomic class on Piaget's moral attributes, and the consistent finding is that a positive relation exists (see Table 2). There are several possible explanations for this. One,

[9] Kohlberg has summarized two findings which suggest peer interaction may not contribute to the use of moral judgments based on intentions. Krebs, studying 6-year-olds, found no difference between children who were socially isolated and those who were popular and had reciprocal friendships. And Kugelmass found no difference between kibbutz- and city-reared children in Israel. With respect to his own stage nations (to be discussed later), however, Kohlberg reports that popularity in preadolescent boys is positively related to maturity of moral judgment.

Table 2. Influence of IQ, Child-Rearing Practices, and Social Class on Moral Attributes Formulated by Piaget

Attribute	IQ	Child-rearing Practices	Social Class
Relativism of perspective (vs. absolutism)	+ MacRae (1954)	0 MacRae (1954)	+ MacRae (1950)
Objective view of punishment (vs. immanent justice)	+ Abel (1941) +[a] Johnson (1962) − MacRae (1950)	−[b] Johnson (1962) 0 MacRae (1954)	+[c] Johnson (1962) + Lerner (1937a) + MacRae (1950)
Intentions (vs. consequences)	+ Boehm (1962) + Johnson (1962) +[d] MacRae (1950) + Whiteman and Kosier (1964)	0 Johnson (1962) 0 MacRae (1954)	+ Boehm (1962) + Boehm and Nass (1962) +[e] Johnson (1962) + Lerner (1937a) + MacRae (1954)
Retribute justice (vs. expiative)	+ Abel (1941) +[f] Johnson (1962)	+[g] Johnson (1962) 0 MacRae (1954)	+ Harrower (1934) +[h] Johnson (1962)
Conformity to peer expectations (vs. obedience to adult authority)	+[i] Boehm (1962) − MacRae (1950)	+ MacRae (1954)	0 Boehm (1962) 0 MacRae (1954)

[a] + for 9-year-olds. Curvilinear for 11-year-olds. Zero for 5- and 7-year-olds.
[b] − for 9-year-olds. Zero for 5-, 7-, and 11-year-olds.
[c] + for 9- and 11-year-olds. Zero for 5- and 7-year-olds.
[d] + for middle class. Zero for lower class.
[e] + for 7-, 9-, and 11-year-olds. Zero for 5-year-olds.
[f] + for 5-, 7-, and 9-year-olds. Zero for 11-year-olds.
[g] + for 7-year-olds. Zero for 5-, 9-, and 11-year-olds.
[h] + for 5- and 7-year-olds. Zero for 9- and 11-year-olds.
[i] + for middle class. Zero for lower class.

that the finding is the indirect result of class differences in IQ, is counterindicated by the study by Boehm (1962), in which IQ was partially controlled: a positive relation was obtained for both high- and low-IQ groups. Another explanation, that class differences in moral judgment are mediated by class differences in parental practices, is difficult to evaluate in view of the inconclusive child-rearing results previously reported. A third possibility is that class differences are the result of differences in authority experiences outside the home. Lower-class children have more direct contact with law enforcement agents and other symbols of adult authority, for example, which should retard moral development, according to Piaget's theory. They are also encouraged to spend more time outside the home with peers at an earlier age, however, and this should enhance development. A fourth difference between the two classes that

might be relevant is that though middle-class children spend less time with peers, they very likely receive more help from parents in resolving peer conflicts. Although excessive parental influence over peer interaction may retard moral development such "coaching," if sparingly and judiciously used, might contribute positively to peer interactions of the reciprocal kind Piaget describes. Finally, the possibility of middle-class bias in the content of the items used in the research and even in Piaget's conceptualization must not be overlooked.

The role of social experience is also indicated in a study by Abel (1964) comparing the moral judgments made by two groups of mentally retarded girls, one institutionalized and the other living at home. The institutionalized girls showed consistently greater belief in immanent justice, retributive punishment, and other indices of moral realism. Since IQ was controlled, this finding shows the influence of social experience. That the crucial variable is institutionalization, however, is questionable since Abel also found that length of institutionalization did not relate significantly to the moral indices, that is, girls who had been institutionalized for six or more years obtained no higher scores on moral realism than those who were institutionalized for one year or less. While this may mean that inadequate social relations in the first year of institutionalization is the crucial variable, it is also possible that what is operating instead is the initial shock of institutionalization or perhaps the difference in prior relations with parents who institutionalize their children and those who do not. The relevance of the findings for Piaget's theory is therefore questionable.

The evidence is clear then that cognitive development enhances forward movement along Piaget's moral attributes. There is also general support for the view that social experience makes a similar contribution, although the mechanism by which this occurs is unclear. There is no evidence, for example, that reciprocal interaction—with peers or with parents—is central.

Transitional Processes between Stages. The empirical evidence regarding the process of transition from one stage to the next is unfortunately meager. Several writers (e.g., Johnson, 1962) have commented critically on Piaget's view that each stage involves a cognitive reorganization and that moral development should therefore be saltatory rather than gradual. And they present as evidence findings indicating that the age trends in moral judgment tend to be gradual rather than saltatory. These age trends have all been obtained in cross-sectional studies, however, and we would argue that this method has a built-in bias against the saltatory growth hypothesis. That is, since developmental progress is not tied to particular ages, sudden spurts by individual children will occur at different times, and averaging the scores of groups of children at each age will produce age norms that will appear gradual rather than saltatory. An adequate test of the saltatory growth concept would require careful longitudinal research with testing at frequent intervals so that sudden shifts might be detected. Such research has not yet been done.

An experimental study bearing on transitional processes between Piaget's stages has been done by Bandura and MacDonald (1963). The subjects were boys from 5 to 11 years of age. Those who observed an adult model being reinforced for expressing moral judgments which were more advanced than their own (blaming an actor on the basis of intentions rather than consequences) were found to shift their own moral judgments in the direction of the model. A similar influence was obtained when the model was reinforced for expressing judgments that were less advanced than their own. The shifts occurred immediately after exposure to the model. These findings have been replicated by Cowan, Langer, Heavenrich, and Nathanson (1969) who found, in addition, that the shifts in judgment persisted for two weeks. Even more prolonged effects have been reported by Le Furgy and Woloshin (1969), who used adolescent subjects and models and found the shifts to last as long as three months. The moral dimension in this study was the dichotomy between the view of social and legal norms as inviolable, and the tendency to approve of norm violations in the presence of extenuating circumstances. Long-range effects were obtained only for subjects who were initially strongly committed to the norms and shifted toward flexibility; those who were initially flexible showed only a short-term shift which completely disappeared by the end of the three-month period.

The fact that the children's judgmental responses in these three studies could be modified so readily in either direction would appear to call into question the assumptions both that the stages occur in an invariant and irreversible sequence and that movement through the stages involves a process of successive synthesis. And the fact that shifts in a forward direction were obtained without the benefit of the kinds of social experience postulated by Piaget as necessary for such movement would seem to provide further evidence against his views about the process of transition between stages. More research is needed before these conclusions can be evaluated, however, because of certain limitations in the design of the studies. First, in all the studies the items in the posttest dealt with the same moral dimension and were very similar to those used in the preexposure test. This makes it difficult to know whether the findings reflect an actual change in the children's underlying moral conceptualization or merely a change in surface responses bearing on a particular moral dimension. A more valid test of whether an actual shift in moral structure occurs would be to examine the effects of attempted manipulations of one moral attribute such as concern for intentions on *different* attributes such as belief in expiatory punishment. A second problem in two of the studies is that the model and the experimenter were adults and though they were not the same person, one of them was always present. Thus the children may have been motivated to report the new judgment in order to meet adult expectations (as communicated by the model) in an ambiguous situation; they may not have actually shifted their views.

Le Furgy and Woloshin overcame this problem by having their subjects give the posttest responses in private. Their findings may thus support their conclusion that exposure to advanced moral concepts enhances the child's developmental progression from moral realism to relativism, while exposure to more primitive concepts is less effective because it operates against the normal pressures toward forward movement. Because of the particular moral dimension used and its special meaning to the age group studied (12.6 to 15.6 years), however, an altogether different interpretation is possible. Namely, while the adolescent's adherence to adult social norms is highly vulnerable to counterinfluence from peers, an adolescent who has already rejected the norms is apt to resist any influences in favor of them. We may thus be dealing with an inter-generational conflict variable involving the adolescent's readiness to reject adult values, rather than the difference between a more or less advanced level of morality. (This distinction will be elaborated in our later discussion of the difference between a flexible humanistic morality and one which merely rejects adult norms.) Aside from its surface plausibility, this interpretation is consistent with the evidence to be presented later that observing peers who violate adult norms has a disinhibiting effect on the child.

Consistency across Moral Attributes. The research discussed thus far focuses on one moral attribute at a time. If Piaget's stages are truly structured wholes, a great deal of consistency across these attributes should be found. Children who obtain high scores on one should obtain high scores on the others.

At least two different concepts of consistency have guided the research: consistency across content areas within a given attribute (e.g., is objective responsibility with regard to lying associated with objective responsibility with regard to stealing?); and consistency across different attributes (e.g., is objective responsibility associated with immanent justice?). The evidence tends to be positive, but inconclusively so, for the first type of consistency. Thus high consistency was found within the following attributes by Johnson (1962): immanent justice, objective responsibility, retributive justice, and expiatory punishment; and within immanent justice, objective responsibility, and absolute moral perspective by MacRae (1954). Boehm and Nass (1962), however, found considerable specificity as regards objective responsibility. The evidence for consistency across attributes, which comes from the Johnson and MacRae studies, is less clear-cut. Thus while Johnson reports positive relations among all his moral attributes, MacRae found his attributes to be independent of one another.

The most dramatic finding bearing on consistency was obtained by Havighurst and Neugarten (1955), who asked a group of Navajo Mountain children questions about their attitudes toward both American games and Navajo games. Whereas almost three quarters of the children, who ranged from 6 to 18 years of age, stated that the rules of the American games could be changed, only one in 28 said the rules of Navajo games could be changed. Havighurst and Neugarten suggest the reason is that Navajo children learn American games from older children and adults in the same way that American children do. They also observe rules being changed or adapted to local conditions, such as the size of play space. Navajo games, on the other hand, are not taught. The child observes them until he feels skillful enough to participate in them. Navajo games are also an integral part of the culture of the adult society, and are inextricably tied to religious beliefs. Their legendary origins are repeated on winter nights around the fire, for example, and the supernatural is often associated with them. Havighurst and Neugarten conclude that there is one type of morality for tribal life and one for that part of life in white culture.

This seems to be a reasonable explanation but it does not sufficiently highlight the evidence the findings provide that sociocultural forces must be powerful indeed if they can impose the compartmentalization and specificity that allow the individual simultaneously to maintain two opposed orientations regarding rules, and to alternate between them in accord with the immediate social context. Stated differently, these forces must be powerful if they can perpetuate a heteronomous orientation toward one set of rules after the individual has already attained autonomy with respect to another. These findings would thus seem to be in opposition to the notion that stages are structured wholes which develop in a fixed sequence.

Before appropriate conclusions can be drawn from the findings, however, it is necessary to analyze further the kind and amount of consistency called for in Piaget's theory. According to Piaget, as we have seen, children require certain types of social interaction for moral growth. It is likely that they obtain this interaction in some areas long before others. We should therefore expect the child to repeat the movement from heteronomy to autonomy for each new content area. The child should develop a relatively early autonomous orientation with regard to children's games like marbles, for example, since he participates in these games early and quickly discovers that he and his peers are as much the authority as anyone else. But this may not carry over to rules in other areas until the child has some first-hand experience in these areas. We might also expect him to consider intentions in simple situations involving accidental breakage of objects, long before he is cognitively mature enough to do so with respect to more complex behaviors such as lying. Untrue statements may then continue for a relatively long time to be judged on the basis of the extent of their divergence from reality rather than the presence of intention to deceive. This need for social interaction around individual norms should be especially true of very young children, who cannot specify the criteria (abstract the principle)

they are using in their judgments and therefore cannot apply these criteria to new situations unless they are very similar to the old ones. Older children, because of their greater capacity for abstract reasoning, can more easily specify the criteria (e.g., "in making moral judgments people's intentions must be taken into account"), which can then be applied to a broader range of relevant instances, both new and old. It follows that with young children in particular Piaget's theory calls for consistency across moral attributes only in situations for which there has been the requisite social interaction, or which have stimulus elements in common with these situations. With maturity and the possibility of cognitive mediation, this qualification should become less necessary and consistency across attributes should be higher regardless of content. (These points about moral judgment have a bearing on our later discussion of the generality of moral behavior.)

Another factor making for uneven development that may be introduced is the number and complexity of issues that warrant consideration in making a moral judgment. This will vary with the content area, and children who are advanced in certain areas may be behind in others for which the cognitive prerequisites are more stringent. Judging on the basis of "intentions," for example, may obviously be more mature than judging on the basis of "consequences" with respect to broken or lost objects, but the issue becomes more complex when the harm is done to another person. Mature judgment in this case would require consideration of other aspects of the situation besides intentions and consequences, such as whether the harmful act might have been avoided with reasonable care and forethought. The mature person, for example, might be more critical of the well-intentioned individual who seriously harms another through negligence than he is of someone who intentionally inflicts slight harm.

It follows from these considerations that to test for consistency across stage attributes requires that the attributes be controlled for moral content area and level of complexity. The research to date has not instituted these controls. We must therefore conclude that while the findings generally do not support the notion of stages as structured wholes encompassing all moral areas, the crucial test has not yet been made.

Kohlberg's Extension of Piaget

While accepting the basic cognitive-developmental approach, Kohlberg (1958, 1963a, 1963b) has criticized much of the substance of Piaget's theory and developed his own schema of stages from extensive case analyses of interviews with boys ranging from 10 to 16 years of age. The data were obtained from 2-hour interviews focused on 10 hypothetical moral dilemmas in which acts of obedience to laws, rules, or commands of authority conflict with the needs or welfare of other persons. The subject was asked to choose whether one should perform the obedience-serving act or the need-serving act and then answer a series of questions probing the thinking underlying his choice. Kohlberg's interest was not in the action alternatives selected by the subjects, which presumably reflect the content of their moral values, but in the quality of their judgments as indicated in the reasons given for their choices and their ways of defining the conflict situations.

In developing his stages Kohlberg's aim was to retain the best of Piaget's schema and fit it into a more refined, comprehensive, and logically consistent framework. His final system consists of six developmental stages, each of which is defined in terms of its position on 30 different moral attributes, including those used by Piaget, which the children brought into their thinking. Each moral idea or statement expressed by a child in the course of an interview was assigned to one of 180 cells in the classification system (30 attributes each defined by a 6-point scale corresponding to the 6 stages). This classification yields scores for each subject on each of the moral stages. The score for a given stage was based on the percentage of all his statements which fit that stage. Kohlberg reports interjudge reliability coefficients ranging from .68 to .84.

The six stages are ordered into three levels of moral orientation. The basic themes and major attributes of the levels and stages are as follows.

Premoral Level. Control of conduct is external in two senses: the standards conformed to consist of outer commands or pressures; and the motive is to avoid external punishment, obtain rewards, have favors returned, etc.

Stage 1. Obedience and punishment orientation. Deference to superior power or prestige. Deference is egocentric, not heteronomous in Piaget's sense. Punishment feared like any other aversive stimulus rather than because of its interpersonal implications. Belief in objective responsibility.

Stage 2. Naive hedonistic and instrumental orientation. Acts defined as right which are instrumentally satisfying to the self and occasionally to others. Awareness of relativism of values to each actor's needs and perspective. Naive egalitarianism and orientation to exchange and reciprocity.

Morality of Conventional Role-Conformity. Morality is defined in terms of performing good acts and maintaining the conventional social order or the expectations of other individuals. Definition of good and bad goes beyond mere obedience to rules and authority. Control of conduct is external in that the standards conformed to are rules and expectations held by those who are significant others by virtue of personal attachment or delegated authority. Motivation is largely internal, however. Though based on anticipation of praise or censure by significant others, this differs from the earlier punishment and reward orientation because the child takes the role of the significant others and respects their judgment. Thus the personal reactions of authority, in addition to their purely aversive or pleasant qualities, now also serve as cues to the rightness or wrongness of an act and hence to the moral virtue of the actor.

Stage 3. Good-boy morality of maintaining good relations. Orientation to approval, and to pleasing and helping others. In judging others, considers intentions and has a concept of a morally good person as one who possesses moral virtues.

Stage 4. Authority and social-order maintaining morality. Orientation to "doing duty," and to showing respect for authority and maintaining the given social order for its own sake. Takes the perspective of others who have legitimate rights and expectations in the situation. Believes that virtue must be rewarded.

Morality of Self-Accepted Moral Principles. Morality is defined in terms of conformity to shared or sharable standards, rights, or duties. This level is unlike the previous ones in that the possibility of conflict between two socially accepted standards is acknowledged and attemps at rational decision between them are made. Control of conduct is internal in two senses: the standards conformed to have an internal source and the decision to act is based on an inner process of thought and judgment concerning right and wrong.

Stage 5. Morality of contract, individual rights, and democratically accepted law. Norms of right and wrong defined in terms of laws or institutionalized rules, which are seen to have a rational basis: for example, they express the will of the majority, maximize social utility or welfare, or are necessary for institutional functioning. Though recognized as being arbitrary, sometimes unjust, and only one of many possible alternatives, the law is in general the ultimate criterion of what is right. Duty and obligation similarly defined in terms of abstract concept of contract rather than needs of individual persons. When conflict exists between human need and law or contract, though sympathetic to the former, the individual believes the latter must prevail because of its greater functional rationality for society.

Stage 6. Morality of individual principles of conscience. Orientation not only to existing social rules and standards but also to conscience as a directing agent, mutual respect and trust, and principles of moral choice involving appeal to logical universality and consistency. Conduct controlled by an internalized ideal that exerts pressure toward action that seems right regardless of the reactions of others in the immediate environment. If one acts otherwise, self-condemnation and guilt result. Though aware of importance of law and contract, moral conflict generally resolved in terms of broader moral principles such as the Golden Rule, the greatest good for the greatest number, or the categorical imperative.

Kohlberg's stage 1 is similar to Piaget's heteronomous stage in that both are oriented to obedience. The difference is in the interpretation of obedience. According to Piaget, because of the young child's strong emotional respect for authority he feels unable to judge for himself and tends to rely on adult sanc-

tions and commands to define what is right and wrong. The child is oriented toward the punitive consequences of an act only because punishment serves as a cue indicating the parent's view of its gravity. Kohlberg believes that Piaget reads too much respect for authority and rules into the young child and overlooks the conflict that initially exists between him and the parent. Kohlberg's view is that the young child has no respect for authority in any sense beyond recognizing that parents are more powerful than he is. Responses which are interpreted by Piaget as indicating the young child's deep respect and idealization of authority and rules are interpreted by Kohlberg as indicating cognitive naiveté and often a total lack of any concept of rules. And the young child's definition of wrong in terms of punishment is seen by Kohlberg to reflect a realistic and hedonistic desire to avoid punishment, rather than a deep reverence for the adult's views. Thus whereas Piaget sees the young child's morality as externally oriented in the cognitive sense (the standard conformed to is an outer command or pressure) but not in the motivational sense (the child conforms out of respect, not because he feels compelled to act against his wishes), Kohlberg sees it as external in both the cognitive and motivational sense. In Kohlberg's schema, elements of heteronomous respect for rules and authority are not pronounced until the third and fourth stages.

Kohlberg's stage 2 resembles Piaget's autonomous stage especially with respect to relativism and reciprocity. Kohlberg criticizes Piaget's autonomous stage, however, for imputing too much of these attributes, as well as egalitarianism and utilitarianism, to children who have attained that stage. Kohlberg believes that children of 10 to 12 years of age, who according to Piaget have advanced well into the autonomous stage, are as yet actually far removed from a fully autonomous and mature morality. It is only as the child moves further through Kohlberg's last three stages that such morality develops. In sum, elements of Piaget's heteronomy can be found in Kohlberg's stages 1 to 4 and elements of Piaget's autonomy in Kohlberg's stages 2 to 6.

Kohlberg also takes more literally than Piaget the assumptions of the cognitive-developmental approach to stages mentioned earlier. We have already indicated that Piaget does not press the view that his moral stages fit these assumptions, that is, that they are structured wholes which form an invariant and universal sequence in the direction of increasing maturity.[10] Kohlberg contends that his own stages do fit these criteria but Piaget's do not. In this respect he regards his own stages as closer to Piaget's cognitive than to his moral stages. Kohlberg believes that Piaget's moral stages suffer from too much stress on social determinants and that only the most highly cognitive of his moral attributes satisfy the criteria of stages. In Kohlberg's own thinking, cognitive factors clearly predominate. Thus he views movement from one moral stage to the next as largely a natural outgrowth of cognitive development. The function of environment is to provide the raw material upon which cognitive processes operate. Although the precise nature of these processes is not clear, the following appears to capture the essential features of the theory.

According to Kohlberg, participation in all groups—whether with peers or authority figures—provides the individual with direct experience in taking alternate roles. This in turn gives him a first-hand knowledge about the workings of the actual sociomoral world, including its role system and rules of social order, as well as an appreciation for its essential functional rationality. With such a perspective the individual's view of the social world and its constraining aspects in relation to himself and others—that is, his views about authority and authority relations—change. He is now more likely to take the role of authority and see commonality between its conceptions of what is right and his own. The particular authority to which he responds is determined by the child's comprehension of who is deemed by the social order to be the most relevant or legitimate authority with respect to himself at any given point in his development.

Although participation in all groups is seen by Kohlberg as having these effects, like Piaget, he recognizes that different levels of

participation do exist. Thus some forms of social participation are especially stimulating to moral development because they provide many stage-appropriate opportunities for role taking and gaining understanding of the social order. Other forms which lack these opportunities, or which arouse inhibiting anxieties, will retard progress through the moral stages and perhaps even fix the individual permanently at an early stage. Kohlberg's view on the effects of different levels of participation is most clearly stated in his discussion of the relation between socioeconomic class and the individual's view of the law.

First, Kohlberg's view is that class differences as well as differences between other subgroups reflect differences in social participation patterns rather than institutions and value systems. "The institutions with moral authority (law, government, family, the work order) and the basic moral rules are the same regardless of the individual's particular position in society." The individual's position does influence his interpretation of these institutions and rules, however. Government and the law are perceived quite differently if he feels a sense of potential participation in the social order than if he does not. For the lower-class person who feels little or no sense of participation, the law is simply a constraining thing that is there. The fact that he has no hand in it means that all he can do is obey or disobey it. Lower middle-class individuals may also participate but little in the operations of society, but because of the opportunities it provides them they are more likely to take the perspective of someone with a stake in the social order and to view laws not as arbitrary commands but as the moral basis of that order. Upper middle-class people, who feel a relatively strong sense of participation, are more likely to view laws as the product of various legitimate ideological and interest groups varying in their beliefs as to the best decision in policy matters. The rule of law-obeyer is seen from the perspective of the democratic policy-maker, and the view is that if one does not believe in a law, he should try to get it changed rather than disobey it.

Empirical Evidence. Since Piaget's formulation had a 40-year lead on Kohlberg's, it is not surprising that relatively little research has been done on the latter. In Kohlberg's initial

---

[10] Piaget does believe that these assumptions apply to his stages of intellectual development, however.

study, age trends were found which are consistent with the view that his stages are developmental. Furthermore, two aspects of these trends—earlier stages decrease with age while later ones increase, and the further apart two stages are in the postulated developmental sequence the lower the correlation between them—are cited by Kohlberg as evidence that later stages replace rather than merely add to earlier stages. In our view these conclusions are premature, since they are based on findings obtained in the very same study in which Kohlberg initially constructed his stage schema and the subjects' ages were a known and important factor in this construction.[11] Whether or not the stages occur in the hypothesized developmental sequence is a question that awaits cross-validation in other, more controlled studies in which knowledge of the age of the subject, or of the hypothesized sequence, does not influence the scoring of moral judgment. Kohlberg also found in his initial study that higher moral judgment scores were obtained by middle-class as compared to lower-class boys, and by sociometric "integrates" as compared to sociometric "isolates." Both these findings hold up when IQ is controlled.

In a well designed experimental study, Turiel (1966) attempted a direct test of Kohlberg's stage-theoretical assumptions. Forty-seven seventh-grade boys were assigned stage positions based on their responses to six of Kohlberg's stories about individuals in moral dilemmas. In the experimental condition three different Kohlberg stories were administered; and the subjects were instructed to take the role of the central figure in each of them and "seek advice" from the experimenter. To produce cognitive conflict without suggesting what action the central figure should take, the experimenter's advice consisted of arguments on both sides of the issue. The two arguments were cast in terms of moral concepts at a level which diverged from the subject's own stage position by certain specified amounts—either one or two stages above (+1 or +2) or one stage below (−1). The subjects were retested a week

11 Kohlberg reports that the same age trends have been found by other investigators and in other cultures, but the details needed for evaluating these studies are not yet available.

later on all nine stories: the three used in the experimental condition, which provide an index of direct effects of the experimental treatment; and the six used in the pretest, which provide an index of generalization of the experimental effects and thus of actual change in the thought process rather than mere response shift.

The first of Turiel's two major hypotheses was that a person's existing stage of thought limits how far he can go and therefore the children will be more likely to accept and assimilate moral reasoning one stage rather than two stages above their current level. This hypothesis was confirmed for both the direct and indirect indices of shift. The more crucial second hypothesis was based on the assumption that higher stages are reorganizations and displacements of preceding stages rather than mere additions to them and, furthermore, that there is a tendency toward forward movement through the stage sequence, that is, there is irreversibility. The prediction was that the group exposed to the +1 treatment would shift in the +1 direction to a greater degree that the −1 group would shift in the −1 direction. The findings were just the opposite: the −1 group shifted slightly more in the −1 direction than the +1 group shifted in the +1 direction. This was true for both the direct and indirect shift scores. Furthermore, the experimental groups did not shift to a significantly greater degree than the control group, which had experienced no treatment. The control group, however, for some unknown reason showed considerably more shift in the −1 direction than in the +1 direction. As a result, the net shift (experimental minus control) was greater for the +1 than the −1 group. This difference approached statistical significance and is in the hypothesized direction. Thus it is only if the action of the control group, which is more dramatic than either experimental group, is taken into account that the findings may be interpreted, as they are by Turiel, as supporting the hypothesis.

We may tentatively conclude from the first finding that Kohlberg's stages (at least stages 2, 3, and 4, which were the only ones used in the study) are successively advanced cognitive levels and that children are more likely to progress from one to the next rather than leapfrog any of them; and further that the experience of cognitive conflict (the two contradictory points of view expressed by the experimenter) may be an important factor in moral development. Conclusions cannot be drawn from the second finding until future research confirms Turiel's interpretation of a push toward forward movement and resistance against backward movement. In this connection Rest, Turiel, and Kohlberg (1969) report that when children are presented with statements at different moral levels they tend to prefer those above rather than below their own level. This may indicate that higher-level concepts are more attractive—perhaps because of competence motivation as Turiel suggests (1969)—thus supporting the hypothesis of a push toward forward movement. It may, on the other hand, merely indicate a tendency to reject concepts at lower developmental levels which the individual has already abandoned. A more critical test of Turiel's formulation would require demonstrating that exposure to advanced moral concepts makes the child prefer them to concepts at his own present level.

Motivation, Moral Behavior, and the Cognitive-Developmental Approach

Motivation and affect have not occupied a prominent place in either Piaget's or Kohlberg's thinking; both stress instead the cognitive aspects of moral development. It is true that Piaget occasionally suggests that affective concepts play an important role. In particular he states that sympathy, which is felt in early childhood side by side with moral realism but separate from it because it has little in common with it, becomes an important contributing factor later in the development of moral autonomy. But the process by which sympathy operates is not specified. Motivational concepts are also considered by Kohlberg, as we have seen, but no attempt is made to account for their origins. Furthermore, they constitute only one of the 30 attributes that theoretically describe his stages; and there is no empirical evidence that they actually are a part of the stages.

Two questions bearing on motivation may be asked of both systems. First, what motivates the individual to "try to make sense out of his own experience in a complex social world" and, more importantly, to move ahead in the stage sequence? That is, conceiving of each transition between stages as a choice point, what makes the person (who is, of course, sufficiently developed cognitively to comprehend the alternatives) move forward rather than backward? Why does he feel compelled to take the products of his new experience seriously enough to engage in what must at times be a painful process of thinking through and reorganizing his pre-existing moral structure? Why doesn't he take the simpler way out and reject the new information? Neither Piaget nor Kohlberg seriously considers the possibility that the child might actually resist the impact of the new experience. And deficiency drives like hunger and their reinforcement are viewed by both writers as unnecessary to account for the individual's forward movement. Rather, their view is simply that an intrinsic part of cognitive structures is the need to function; and in functioning these structures repeatedly reach out into the environment and incorporate or assimilate whatever they can. The need to function is strong enough to overpower the security motives that might also be aroused when the person experiences a contradiction between the old and the new, and which might otherwise lead the child to reject the new. This conception of a need to cognize obviously has much in common with current motivational concepts, which stress the importance of curiosity or exploratory drives, activity and sensory needs, effectance and mastery strivings, and needs to reduce dissonance (e.g., Berlyne, 1960; Festinger, 1957; Maslow, 1954; White, 1959).

The second motivational issue bears on the fact that the data used by Piaget and Kohlberg pertain to the individual's judgment of the actions of others. Obviously there is a question here of the relation between one's judgments of others and one's own moral behavior. Because a person has notions of right and wrong and uses them to evaluate the behavior of others, does this necessarily mean he has the capacity to make similar evaluations of his own behavior, blame himself and experience guilt following his own transgressions, and control his future behavior accordingly? Both writers are undoubtedly aware of this problem but neither has addressed himself specifically to it. The problem is less crucial in the early stages of their systems, since a person's own behavior seems as likely as his judgments of others to be influenced by the belief in the infallibility of authority and the orientation toward external sanctions. It is more difficult, however, to see how one's own behavior is influenced in the moral direction by the tendency to consider intentions, since this may help provide excuses for one's own misdeeds or defenses against the awareness of the harmful consequences of one's acts. It is also conceivable that a person could understand the social order and see its functional rationality quite well, discuss moral dilemmas of others intelligently and take the role of most anyone— and still act immorally himself and experience little or no guilt over doing so. Indeed, these social insights might just as readily serve Machiavellian as moral purposes.

The empirical evidence relating Piaget's and Kohlberg's conceptions to the child's own moral behavior is both scarce and inconclusive. Grinder (1964) found that belief in immanent justice and the tendency to consider intentions did not relate to a laboratory measure of resistance to temptation in boys or girls ranging from 7 to 11 years of age (though consideration of intentions did relate positively to rule-conformity in girls). Similarly, Nelson, Grinder, and Challas (1968) report that maturity of moral judgment as assessed in terms of Kohlberg's stages did not relate (though IQ did) to resistance to temptation in seventh-grade boys or girls.[12] On the other hand, Kohlberg reports that moral stages in his initial study related positively to teacher ratings of fairness to peers and adherence to the rules in the absence of authority.[13] Krebs (1968) used Kohlberg's system and found that sixth-grade children at stages 5 and 6 resisted

temptation to a greater extent than children at stages 3 and 4. And, finally, Hoffman (1969 a) found that internal moral judgments related positively to guilt and confession in 13-year-old boys, but not girls.

Aside from the mixed pattern of the results, most of the research just reviewed is limited because any number of motives might underlie resistance to temptation in the experimental situations used. Examples are a blind adherence to meaningless adult commands, which may actually have much in common with Piaget's heteronomous stage; a fear of punishment that might occur despite the absence of authority figures, which fits Kohlberg's first stage; and a mature, responsible reaction to being trusted by the experimenter, which might reflect Kohlberg's most advanced stages. It seems clear that future research would do well to supplement data on overt moral behavior with information on subjective motivation. Should this research demonstrate a lack of relation between moral judgment and moral behavior, it would suggest that these two aspects of morality may develop according to different laws.

All in all, the empirical support for the various aspects of the cognitive-developmental approach to moral development is uneven. The findings on IQ indicate that both Piaget's and Kohlberg's stages are largely cognitively based. The age-differences obtained thus far support the assumption that these stages occur in the expected developmental order, although the findings thus far are convincing only with respect to the type of social structure found in Western society. Crucial studies have not yet been made regarding the assumption that the stages are structured wholes, the theoretical notions advanced about the role of social experience in helping the individual progress through the stages, or the bearing of moral judgment on one's own behavior.

In our view the major contributions of the cognitive-developmentalists thus far have been conceptual and theoretical. These writers have sensitized us to the cognitive dimensions and prerequisites of a mature moral orientation. They have also called attention to the possible importance of the individual's own direct experience as a social participant with peers as well as adults—in contrast to other approaches which view him more as

[12] A limitation of this study is that the moral judgment interviews were given a year after the resistance-to-temptation tests.
[13] At the college level Kohlberg has reported informally that male students rated at stages 5-6, compared with those at stages 3-4, resisted an experimenter's request to administer increasingly more severe electric shocks to another student. In a similar vein Haan, Smith, and Block (1968) have found that college students and Peace Corps volunteers at Kohlberg's higher stages are more apt than those at lower stages to be involved in political protest and hold attitudes to the left of their parents. These authors point out, however, that there is no evidence that the political involvement has a moral basis.

the passive recipient of interventions by authorities.

SOCIALIZATION TECHNIQUES AND MORAL DEVELOPMENT

Piaget and his followers have had little influence on the research dealing with effects of parental behavior on moral development. This is due largely to their commitment to fixed sequences and relative neglect of environmental influences. Furthermore, most of the researchers in the parent-child area have shown little concern with the problem of defining and conceptualizing morality or with the cognitive complexities involved in making moral judgments. They share with Piaget the assumption that mere knowledge of moral standards, which can be acquired passively and at an early age, is no guarantee of a conscience. And their aim, like his, is to understand the processes by which the child who is pleasure dominated and amoral develops moral standards to which he is internally committed. They differ, however, in assuming that since the young child lacks the motivation to control his own behavior external agents must first intervene and the particular forms of adult intervention are the central determiners of the child's moral development. Stressing the emotional and motivational rather than cognitive aspects of morality, these investigators have generally been receptive to the psychoanalytic view of moral development. Like Piaget's theory, psychoanalytic theory was initially intended as a universal explanation of the processes underlying the formation of conscience rather than a source of hypotheses about individual differences. Unlike Piaget, however, psychoanalytic theory puts great stress on the importance of the parent. It has therefore provided the main theoretical inspiration and overall direction for most of the research on the role of parental practices in shaping and determining moral character.

Although the psychoanalytic account of moral development has not been organized into a coherent whole and there is some variation in the approach of the different writers, the central thrust of the theory may be reconstructed briefly as follows. The young child is inevitably subjected to many frustrations, some of which are due to parental inter-

vention and control and some of which, for example, illness and other physical discomforts, have nothing directly to do with the parent. All of these frustrations contribute to the development of hostility toward the parent. Due to anxiety over anticipated punishment, especially loss of love and abandonment by the parent, the child represses the hostility. To help maintain the repression, as well as elicit continuing expressions of affection, the child adopts in relatively unmodified form the rules and prohibitions emanating from the parent. He also develops a generalized motive to emulate the behavior and adopt the inner states of the parent. In addition, he adopts the parent's capacity to punish himself when he violates a prohibition or is tempted to do so—turning inward, in the course of doing this, the hostility that was originally directed toward the parent. This self-punishment is experienced as guilt feelings, which are dreaded because of their intensity and their resemblance to the earlier anxieties about punishment and abandonment. The child therefore tries to avoid guilt by acting always in accordance with incorporated parental prohibitions and erecting various mechanisms of defense against the conscious awareness of impulses to act to the contrary. Some writers (e.g., Freud) see these processes as crystallizing around the child's Oedipal conflicts; others do not. Most are in agreement, however, that the basic processes of conscience formation are accomplished by about 5 or 6 years of age, although later accretions based on the demands of new authority figures may also occur.

Although the researchers disagree with many of the details of psychoanalytic theory, most have accepted its basic premise: at some time in early childhood the individual begins to control his behavior in accord with parental dictates and in the course of this process codes of conduct such as moral standards and values, which were originally externally enforced, become part of the child's own set of standards. Each investigator has focused on one or two concepts stemming from the theory, usually modifying them, however, in line with some of the more recent approaches deriving from academic and experimental psychology. Those who have engaged in the more naturalistic parent-child research have generally focused on the child's anxiety over anticipated loss of parental love. Although

Freud initially conceptualized this as anxiety over separation, it has been given prominence by subsequent writers as the basic punitive element in discipline relevant to long-range character development. The general hypothesis is that moral development is fostered to the degree that the parent's discipline arouses anxiety over loss of love rather than physical pain. The investigators differ as to the precise mechanisms involved and these differences reflect two strands in the psychoanalytic account of moral development. The first, which pertains to the child's adoption of the parent's own motive states including his moral standards, has led to a central concern with identificatory and imitative processes. The second, the introjection by the child of prohibitions emanating from the parent and directed toward him, has fostered interest in reactions to various discipline techniques.

In contrast to the naturalistic studies, most of the experimental research has been guided by social learning theory. The bridge between psychoanalytic and learning theory was provided a number of years ago by Mowrer (1941), who recognized that the psychoanalytic concept of anxiety could be linked to the concept of conditioned fear and that behaviors associated with the termination or reduction of anxiety are reinforced. Mowrer did his research on animals, but his views have recently been adopted nearly intact by Aronfreed and others who have used them as a basis for a series of laboratory experiments with children. Following Mowrer, these investigators have typically dealt with anxiety over physical pain, which is closer to the psychoanalytic concept of castration anxiety, rather than anxiety over loss of love, which is the focus in the more naturalistic research. Recent years have also seen an out-pouring of experimental work on the role of imitation in moral development. Imitation is assumed by these researchers to contain the essential features of identification.

In an earlier review by this writer (Hoffman, 1963a), the following propositions received support: (1) a moral orientation based on the fear of external detection and punishment is associated with the relatively frequent use of discipline techniques involving physical punishment and material deprivation, which we have called power-assertive discipline; (2) a moral orientation characterized by independence of external sanctions and high guilt is associated with relatively frequent use of nonpower-assertive discipline— sometimes called psychological, indirect, or love-oriented discipline. In concluding the review we indicated the need to go beyond empirical generalizations and probe more deeply into the underlying processes by which the parent's practices have the observed effects. The task of ferreting out these processes is difficult, as can be seen by the diversity of suggestions that have already been advanced, each of which focuses on a different aspect of the parent's discipline. Thus Allinsmith and Greening (1955) suggest the significant variable may be the difference in the model presented by the parent during the disciplinary encounter (i.e., parent openly expresses anger versus parent controls anger). The importance of this factor may lie in the model it provides the child for channeling his own aggression. Where the parent himself expresses his anger openly, he thereby encourages the child to express his anger openly; where the parent controls his anger, he discourages the child from openly expressing anger and therefore may promote a turning of the anger inward, which according to psychoanalytic theory is the process by which the guilt capacity is developed.

Another explanation for the differential effects of power-assertive and nonpower-assertive discipline focuses on the duration of punishment. That is, the application of force usually dissipates the parent's anger and thus may relieve the child of his anxiety or guilt rather quickly, thereby reducing his motivation to alter his behavior. Nonpower-assertive discipline, on the other hand, ordinarily lasts a longer and more variable amount of time, so that the child may more often feel compelled to initiate efforts to behave in the parentally desired fashion.

A third possibility, suggested by Sears, Maccoby, and Levin (1957), derives from the psychoanalytic concept of anaclitic identification, which states that the desire to reproduce and stabilize the properties of the "love object" is the major motivation for the child's identification with his parent. According to Sears, Maccoby, and Levin, many attributes of the parent acquire considerable secondary reinforcing value from their prior association with the child's experience of care, affection, and approval from the parent. The child becomes motivated to practice these attributes in order to reproduce the pleasant experience of the mother's nurturant behavior when she is absent. "He wants her to be near him, and when she is not there, he brings her close by imagining her soothing words and actions" (Sears, Maccoby, and Levin, 1957, p. 372). Punishing the child for his misdeeds by withholding love, which is frequently involved in nonpower-assertive discipline, has the effect of making him feel parental loss at the time of subsequent misdeeds. To protect against this loss the child takes on those characteristics of the parent which have become salient at these times. Included are the acts of criticizing, evaluating, punishing, and controlling his behavior as well as the moral values and behavior that have been offered him as replacements for behaviors that are unacceptable to the parent. If the child is thus the criticizer and controller of his behavior, then he is the parent and therefore the parent is not and cannot be lost. In contrast to this response to love withdrawal, the child is more apt to respond to power assertion by simply trying to avoid the parent.

Another formulation has been suggested by Hill (1960), who holds that the crucial underlying factor is the timing of the punishment. Parents who use love withdrawal are assumed to terminate punishment more often when the child engages in a corrective act (e.g., confession, reparation, overt admission of guilt), and thus to reinforce that act. Physical punishment, on the other hand, is more likely to occur and terminate at the time of the deviant act and prior to any corrective act. Corrective acts are thus not reinforced by power assertion.

Another possibility is that the cognitive rather than affective aspects of the parent's discipline are primary. Thus the important variable may be the information often communicated by nonpower-assertive techniques regarding the implications of the child's deviant behavior. For example, Aronfreed's (1961) view is that such information can provide the cognitive and behavioral resources necessary for the child to examine his actions independently and accept responsibility for them.

A final explanation has been advanced by the cognitive dissonance theorists, who focus on the amount of pressure put on the child to comply, in conjunction with the child's need for self-justification of his response (Festinger and Freedman, 1964). According to this view, if the parent succeeds in getting the child to refrain from an act, the child experiences dissonance between the desire to complete the act and the knowledge of not having done so. This dissonance can be reduced in two ways: (1) the child recognizes that he complied only through external pressure; or (2) he comes to believe that he refrained from the act for more intrinsic reasons; for example, he never wanted to do it in the first place because he knew all along that it was wrong. Compliance to power assertion results in condition 1 because the existence of external pressure is too obvious to be denied. Compliance to nonpower-assertive techniques, on the other hand, may result in condition 2 when they are just punitive enough to disengage the child from the act without putting too much obvious pressure on him.

Parent Discipline and Internalization of Prohibitions

To help throw light on which of these hypotheses, if any, are correct, we will in this section review the parent-child research literature very closely. In addition to updating the earlier review, a more precise system of classifying the parent and child variables, suggested by our own research (Hoffman and Saltzstein, 1967), will be used to enable us to test some of the competing notions about processes. Because of our central concern with process, the focus will be on studies in which the variables are defined objectively in terms of fairly specific and overt behavior patterns. Studies that contribute little to an understanding of process because they use global parent concepts (such as strict, punitive, and democratic) or global child concepts (such as leadership and delinquency) are not included (e.g., Peck and Havighurst, 1960; Glueck and Glueck, 1950). The studies relating child-rearing patterns in different cultures to cultural indices of morality (e.g., Whiting and Child, 1953) are also omitted. These studies lack direct relevance to the parent-child area for two reasons: first, because they typically use morality indices not based on child data (e.g., the general prevalence of a self-recriminating response to illness as an index of guilt severity); second, regardless of the measures used, relations obtained with groups as the unit of analysis are not necessarily the same as those obtained with individuals as the unit.[14] Within the limits of these general guidelines and certain more specific criteria to be mentioned later, the attempt is made to pull together all the naturalistic parent-child studies that bear on the topic.

Though the methodological standards of the parent-child research have risen sharply in recent years, it is still possible to find inadequacies in any of the studies reported. Examples are the use of unrepresentative samples, and the collection of both the parent and the child data from the same source, which violates the criterion of independence. Because of such weaknesses generalizations can be made more confidently from groups of studies bearing on the same problem than from individual studies. Where the findings of several studies converge, inferences can be drawn with a fair degree of confidence despite the weaknesses in the individual studies. This is especially true since the nature of these weaknesses tends to vary from study to study and generalizations based on studies using different methods are more soundly grounded than those based on studies using similar methods (Campbell and Fiske, 1959).

It must be recognized at the outset that although this type of research may reveal the relationships that occur in nature, it is not as well suited for analyzing the causal direction of the relationships as the experimental method. Though the laboratory experimental studies often seem contrived and far removed from the effects of discipline in the home, the greater precision and more positive controls they afford make them potentially useful supplements to the more naturalistic studies in the search for important dimensions of socialization practices and the mechanisms underlying their effectiveness. Accordingly, the experimental research bearing on moral development, which has proliferated in recent years, will also be systematically reviewed and related to the parent-child findings wherever possible.

Child-Rearing Concepts. In this review nonpower-assertive discipline is separated into "love withdrawal" and "induction"—giving us a total of three discipline categories instead of the more usual two. These can be briefly described as follows.

Power assertion includes physical punishment, deprivation of material objects or privileges, the direct applications of force, or the threat of any of these. The term "power assertion" is used to highlight the fact that in using these techniques the parent seeks to control the child by capitalizing on his physical power or control over material resources (Hoffman, 1960). Rather than rely on the child's inner resources (e.g., guilt, shame, dependency, love, or respect) or provide him with information necessary for the development of such resources, the parent punishes the child physically or materially, or relies on his fear of punishment.

Nonpower-assertive techniques are more varied, especially in the degree to which love withdrawal either predominates or is a minor part of a technique focused primarily on the consequences of the child's behavior. We define *love-withdrawal* techniques as those in which the parent simply gives direct but nonphysical expression to his anger or disapproval of the child for engaging in some undesirable behavior. Examples are ignoring the child, turning one's back on him, refusing to speak or listen to him, explicitly stating a dislike for the child, and isolating or threatening to leave him. Like power assertion, love withdrawal has a highly punitive quality. Although it poses no immediate physical or material threat to the child, it may be more devastating emotionally than power assertion because it poses the ultimate threat of abandonment or separation. Whereas power assertion ordinarily consists of discrete aversive acts that are quickly over and done with, love withdrawal is typically more prolonged— lasting minutes, hours, or even days—and its duration may be variable and unpredictable. While the parent may know when it will end, the very young child may not since he is

---

[14] For a discussion of the methodological issues involved see Hills (1957) and Kendall and Lazarsfeld (1955). There is also some relevant empirical evidence: Hollenberg (1952) and Faigin (1952) found a lack of agreement between relations obtained cross-culturally and those obtained with parents and children within the same culture.

totally dependent on the parent and more-over lacks the experience and time perspective needed to recognize the temporary nature of the parent's attitude.

Induction includes techniques in which the parent gives explanations or reasons for requiring the child to change his behavior. Examples are pointing out the physical requirements of the situation or the harmful consequences of the child's behavior for himself or others. These techniques are less punitive than power assertion or love withdrawal, and more of an attempt to persuade or convince the child that he should change his behavior in the prescribed manner. Also included are techniques which appeal to conformity-inducing agents that already exist, or potentially exist, within the child. Examples are appeals to the child's pride, strivings for mastery and to be "grown up," and concern for others. The effectiveness of induction as discipline, as compared to power assertion and love withdrawal, appears to be based less on the fear of punishment and more on the child's connecting its cognitive substance with his own resources for comprehending the necessities in the situation and controlling his own behavior accordingly.

One type of induction, called *other-oriented* induction, is singled out for special attention in this review because our own research suggests its importance.[15] The techniques used contain references to the implications of the child's behavior for another person. This may be done by directly pointing out or explaining the nature of the consequences (e.g., If you throw snow on their walk, they will have to clean it up all over again; Pulling the leash like that can hurt the dog's neck; That hurts my feelings.); pointing out the relevant needs or desires of others (e.g., He's afraid of the dark, so please turn the lights back on.); or explaining the motives underlying the other person's behavior toward the child (e.g., Don't yell at him. He was only trying to help.). When the child is young these techniques often focus on the effects of

his behavior on other children. In later years, as more of the child's interactions with peers occur outside the home in the parent's absence, the focus becomes mainly the effects on the parent. Some other-oriented techniques, especially those indicating the effects of the child's behavior on the parent, seem clearly designed to obtain the desired behavior by arousing guilt.

In studies of discipline, investigators are aware that a given technique may encompass any combination of categories. Nevertheless, it is usually possible to classify a technique as predominantly power assertion, love withdrawal, or induction.

Studies on the role of parental affection are also included in this review. Though not a form of discipline, affection looms large in several theoretical accounts of moral development. One is the simple assumption that being well loved provides the emotional security and feeling of confidence in the essential goodness of the world (Erikson's "trust") necessary for considering the needs of others. Another is the view that the affectionate parent becomes a positive object for the child who controls his behavior in order to please her and then, through generalization, controls it out of consideration for others as well. Several other theoretical approaches derive from the psychoanalytic concept of anaclitic identification, in which the child adopts the loving parent's attributes—including evaluative and punitive responses to transgression—so that he can reproduce them and experience the pleasure with which they are associated, even when the parent is absent. This has been most clearly articulated by Sears, Maccoby, and Levin (1957), whose formulation we summarized earlier.

The preceding child-rearing concepts will be used throughout this review.

Internalization Concepts. Earlier we defined an internally based moral act as one that fits a moral standard and subjectively has its source in the actor himself or in some reference group or person, rather than being based on concerns over external sanctions. Four aspects of internalization appear in the parent-child research literature. Two of these reflect the drive or energy the individual commits to the defense and maintenance of a standard even in the absence of external supports or pressures to conform. These are,

---

[15] Other-oriented discipline should not be confused with Riesman's "other direction," which is a broader term including the individual's concern about whether or not he has the approval of others. Other-oriented discipline refers specifically to techniques which point up the effects of the child's behavior on others.

first, the amount of resistance offered to pressures and temptations to behave counter to the standard and, second, the amount of guilt experienced following failure to comply with it. The third pertains to a more cognitive aspect of moral action—the extent to which it is independent of any thoughts about sanctions. The fourth is the tendency to confess and accept responsibility for one's deviant behavior.

Resistance to Pressures to Deviate. From the standpoint of society the most important index of conscience is the degree to which the individual can be counted on to resist pressures to deviate even when the possibilities of detection and punishment are remote. Whether a person resists or yields is a complex matter involving not only his moral standards but also his motives for the rewards attainable by deviating, his system of ego controls (e.g., the ability to defer gratification), and various aspects of the immediate situation. Because of this multidetermination, it is difficult to establish empirically how much of an individual's resistance is due to the strength of his moral standards.

Pressures to deviate may be external (e.g., threats of punishment or disapproval by peers) or internal (e.g., desires for objects which are themselves forbidden or which require forbidden action for their attainment). Perhaps due to psychoanalytic influence, the studies dealing with resistance to deviation pressures have focused on impulse control in the face of inner temptation. They have neglected resistance to external pressure, which may require an even more deep-seated moral commitment. An exception is Milgram's research (e.g., 1965) on the response to an authority's request to do harm to others, but to date the role of antecedent influences on this response has not been a central focus in these studies.[16] Studies of the antecedents of the moral strength or courage necessary to resist social pressures to deviate from one's standards would have obvious bearing on the larger question of how one learns to resolve conflicts between inner- and other-directed pressures (Riesman et al., 1953) as well as

the more specific conflicts that often occur between standards internalized in the home and counterpressures from outside the home.

Some of the resistance-to-temptation research has been guided by a commonsense approach which views resistance as the outcome of a more or less conscious, rational process in which the individual weighs the consequences of one course of action against the other. In the main, however, this research has been heavily influenced by psychoanalytic theory, according to which resistance to temptation is a direct result of the individual's repression of the impulse to deviant action. The repression is motivated by anxiety or guilt avoidance and it may occur the instant the impulse reaches consciousness. Any conscious weighing of alternatives that might occur is fleeting. Strictly speaking, the individual may often be said not to resist temptation at all, since he does not consciously experience temptation.

We need not for present purposes make a choice between these two approaches, since researchers with both views have used comparable methods of assessing resistance to temptation. One study (Allinsmith, 1960) used story completion items in which the hero had not yet transgressed but was tempted to do so. The subject's resistance-to-temptation score was determined by whether or not the hero in his story ending actually transgressed. Usually a more direct behavioral index of resistance to temptation is used: an experimental situation in which the subject is tempted to violate the rules in order to win a prize (Burton, Maccoby, and Allinsmith, 1961; Grinder, 1960, 1962; MacKinnon, 1938; Sears, Rau, and Alpert, 1965).[17] Although it is made clear to the subject that no one knows whether he cheats or keeps score according to the rules, this information is available to the experimenter by one or another devious means, usually observation through a one-way screen. Scores are assigned which indicate whether or not the subject cheats, how long he holds out before cheating, and how much cheating is done. Such

---

[16] Some research has been done on parental antecedents of the child's response to external pressures (e.g., Hoffman, 1953; Mussen and Kagan, 1958) but not where the pressures were opposed to the child's values and standards.

[17] In the MacKinnon study there was no prize. The temptation to cheat was aroused by making the test answers immediately accessible to the subjects and by allowing them to look at certain solutions while prohibiting them from looking at others.

scores appear to satisfy the requirements of an index of resistance to temptation—and not merely rule conformity—since an incentive to deviate is offered.

The measure is limited, however, because it is based on a situation involving success and failure and thus open to the damaging influence of unequal motivation and ability to do well on the task, that is, the temptation to cheat may not be the same for all subjects. Not cheating for some, for example, may signify disinterest in the prize, low achievement strivings in general, or high ability in the task, rather than a strong conscience. And cheating may result from situational factors such as pressure to perform beyond one's ability (Sipos, 1964) and the nature of the task, for example, boys appear to cheat more than girls on masculine tasks (Medinnus, 1959). Another problem, mentioned earlier, is that the motivation underlying resistance to temptation, even when one is left alone, may vary from a morally mature and highly internalized reaction to the experimenter's trust, to a more primitive external notion that the authorities are ubiquitous and will find out if one cheated. It is also possible that resistance is part of a larger pattern of impulse repression which results in the individual's experiencing relatively little temptation in the first place.[18] Despite these problems, the studies using resistance to temptation cannot be ignored because they are the only ones relating discipline to an overt index of resistance to deviation pressures.

Guilt. As an index of internalization the virtues and defects of guilt are in many ways the opposite of resistance to temptation. Experiencing guilt following transgression is not a particular goal of society, which is more interested in overt behavior than intrapsychic responses. Being an emotional response to a completed act, however, guilt is apt to be confounded with fewer nonmoral variables than resistance to temptation and is therefore easier to measure.

As with resistance to temptation, two views of guilt prevail. According to psychoanalytic theory, guilt results from repressed impulses

breaking into awareness and is primarily an unconscious phenomenon. The individual ordinarily experiences guilt dimly, if at all, and only for the brief interval between the initial, fleeting, awareness of the impulse and either the operation of a cognitive defense against the awareness or the occurrence of a moral act. According to the second, more commonsense view, guilt is simply a conscious experience that follows the violation of an internalized standard. Though detection and punishment are unlikely, the individual still feels critical of himself and remorseful because he knows he has done wrong.

Guilt intensity has usually been measured in terms of the subject's responses to deviation story-completion or doll-play situations. The technique presents the subject with a story beginning which focuses on a basically sympathetic child of the same sex and age who has committed a transgression under conditions that minimize the likelihood of detection and punishment. The subject's instructions are to complete the story and tell what the protagonist thinks and feels and "what happens afterwards." The assumption is that the subject identifies with the protagonist and therefore reveals his own internal reactions (although not necessarily his overt reactions) through his completion of the story.

The scoring of guilt has been guided by the two conceptualizations mentioned above. Researchers in the psychoanalytic tradition have sometimes assumed that since detection and punishment are ruled out by the story beginning, any of a large number of painful experiences that follow the transgression (including nightmares, accidents, and unrealistic fears of external punishment) are either direct expressions of guilt or defensive manifestations of guilt (Allinsmith, 1960; Allinsmith and Greening, 1955; Faigin, 1952; Heinicke, 1953; Hollenberg, 1952; Rabin and Goldman, 1966; Shaplin, 1954).[19] The other investigators have tended to define guilt more narrowly as a conscious, self-initiated, and self-critical reaction. As indicated in our earlier discussion of internalization, we believe it is in the interest of conceptual precision to classify exaggerated fears of detection and

---

[18] This suggestion receives some support from the finding by Sears, Rau, and Alpert (1965) that resistance to temptation relates negatively to attention seeking and aggressive behavior in preschool children.

[19] Some nonpsychoanalytic workers have also used measures in which guilt was confounded with fear of external punishment, (Bandura and Walters, 1959; Unger, 1960, 1962).

like responses as external rather than internal. This need not be seen as contradicting psychoanalytic theory since we can agree that guilt may very well underlie these responses. If guilt is involved, however, it is, by definition, only a momentary experience whose function is merely to trigger the person's orientation toward his transgression. This orientation is external when it focuses on punitive consequences. Accordingly, the narrower, nonpsychoanalytic approach is taken in this review, to help assure that generalizations about guilt that may be drawn from the data will bear on truly internalized guilt reactions.

The guilt measures used in four studies fit these criteria quite well (Allinsmith, 1960; Allinsmith and Greening, 1955; Aronfreed, 1961; and Hoffman and Saltzstein, 1967).[20] Usually an overall guilt severity rating is used. In the Hoffman and Saltztein study, however, account was taken of the fact that in some cases a high degree of guilt is sustained throughout the story while in others there is a rapid dissipation of the guilt, the guilt drop usually being accompanied by manifest evidence of the operation of defenses against guilt, for example, the hero comes to think someone else is to blame. Accordingly the procedure used in that study was to compare subjects who obtained high scores on both maximum and terminal guilt with subjects whose scores were low on both indices.

Internal versus External Orientation. The internal-external dimension in relatively pure form, that is, without regard to intensity of commitment to a moral standard, has been used in two studies (Aronfreed, 1961; Hoffman and Saltzstein, 1967). Aronfreed tapped the implicit cognitive basis of moral evaluation with a projective story completion technique in which the central figure commits an act of aggression toward another person. The story endings were coded for degree to which (1) the central figure, without any reliance on external forces or events, accepts responsibility for his action and actively seeks to correct the situation, for example, by making

[20] Although Allinsmith (1960) defines guilt operationally in such a way as to confound it with fear of external punishment, one of his stories produced no externally focused responses. The findings obtained with that story are included in the review.

reparation or modifying his future behavior in the direction of social acceptability; or (2) the events following the transgression are dominated by external concerns, mainly in the form of punishment, or accidents and other unpleasant fortuitous happenings. Hoffman and Saltzstein assessed the explicit cognitive basis of moral evaluation using a measure which was more consciously focused, in the Piaget tradition, and based in part on modifications of some of the items used by Kohlberg (1958). The children were asked to make moral judgments about several hypothetical transgressions. These included judgments about persons committing various crimes (e.g., stealing), choosing which of two crimes was worse (e.g., one involving simple theft and the other a breach of trust), and judgments of crimes with extenuating circumstances (e.g., a man who steals a drug to save his wife's life). In each case the child's response was coded as external (e.g., "you go to jail for that"), internal (e.g., "that's not right, the man trusted you"), or indeterminate.

Confession. The most widely used index of internalization is confessing and accepting responsibility for one's misdeeds even when detection is unlikely. A major limitation of this index is that although confession may be internally motivated—as when a child confesses because he feels guilty for what he did or because he cannot deceive others by denying the act—it may also be nothing more than a learned instrumental act. For example, he may confess in order to be forgiven, because he thinks he might get caught anyway, or because his parents have made confession an end in itself and rewarded him for it in the past. Despite this limitation, confession is worthy of our attention because it is the only internalization index typically based on overt behaviorial data in the natural setting.

Several studies use the parent's report of the child's usual behavior following a misdeed, for example, whether he confesses spontaneously or when asked, as opposed to denying blame (Sears, Maccoby, and Levin, 1957; Levine, 1961; Burton, Maccoby, and Allinsmith, 1961; Hoffman and Saltzstein, 1967). The child's observed behavior in an experimental deviation situation (Sears, Rau, and Alpert, 1960) has also been used, as has the child's fantasy in an experimental doll-play situation (Heinicke, 1953). None of these measures is ideal. In the observational and projective measures there is no assurance that the confession was an internalized moral response. The measures based on the parent's report are flawed because the parent is often the same person providing much of the discipline data. The parent is also likely to be influenced by the desire to make a good impression on the investigator. There is usually no other person, however, with enough background information and close contact with the child to make a knowledgeable estimate of how he acts before detection.

*　*　*

These four dimensions were all used in our review because they clearly bear on morality and because they represent different levels of behavior (affective, cognitive, overt). Each dimension has its advantages and disadvantages, and since a strong case for including one and not the others could not be made we included them all. In doing this our intention was not to treat them as indexes of a single underlying process of "moral development." This would be premature for although the different aspects of morality presumably increase with age (extensive empirical data on age progression are available only for moral judgment), they very likely begin to develop and reach maturity at different ages and progress at different rates, and therefore may reflect different underlying processes. (The question of whether moral development is a unitary process will be discussed in greater detail later).

Relation between Child-Rearing and Internalization of Moral Prohibitions. In reviewing the research, the findings were ordered according to the four internalization indices and four parent practices (three types of discipline plus affection) discussed earlier. That is, the actual empirical findings reported were cast in terms of this framework without regard to the category names used by the investigators and any theoretical interpretations they may have made. It was not difficult to follow this procedure with respect to the morality categories since the investigators' operational definitions were similar to our own. The same was true of power assertion and affection.[21] Classifying the findings on love withdrawal and induction, however, was at times more difficult. The main problem

was that most studies, as already indicated, used only a dichotomy between power-assertive and nonpower-assertive discipline. In these cases it was necessary to decide whether the nonpower-assertive category could more precisely be called love withdrawal or induction. This distinction could sometimes be made directly from the investigator's definition of the category or his description of the kinds of techniques encompassed by it. In one case it was necessary to obtain the raw data, recode them, and run separate analyses for love withdrawal and induction in order to find out which of these categories was actually responsible for the findings.[22] In those cases where the nonpower-assertive category could not be norrowed down to love withdrawal or induction, the findings are included in our review only with respect to their relevance to power assertion.

To make the basis of our love withdrawal and induction coding explicit, detailed descriptions of the measures as defined by the investigators, along with the manner in which we coded them, are presented in the appendix to this chapter.

In Table 3 are summarized the results of the various studies relating the mother's practices to the child's moral development, and Table 4 summarizes the relatively small number of findings bearing on the father's practices. Each finding in the tables gives the following information: direction of the relationship obtained is indicated by plus (significantly positive) or minus (significantly negative); the approximate mean age of the children studied is indicated by the number following the direction of relationship; sex of children studied is indicated by B (Boys), G (girls), M (mixed). The number in brackets corresponds to the number in the References at the end of this chapter. In the induction column, inductions which are pre-

---

[21] The one exception to this was the study by Burton, Maccoby, and Allinsmith (1961). We classified their material deprivation score as power assertion. A score that combined physical punishment and "scolding" was not classified as power assertion, however, since "scolding" is ambiguous and could refer either to power assertion or love withdrawal.

[22] The writer is indebted to Wesley Allinsmith for his cooperation in making his data available for recoding and analysis.

Table 3. Mother's Child-Rearing Practices and Moral Development Indices

Child Morality Index	Power Assertion	Love Withdrawal	Induction	Affection
Internal orientation	− 11 BG [3]		+ 11 BG [3]	
	− 13 G [10]	− 13 G [10]	+ 13 B [10] o	+ 13 G [10]
	− 5 B [7]	0 13 B [10]	0 13 G [10] o	0 13 B [10]
	0 13 B [10]			
Guilt intensity	− 20 B [2]		+ 13 BG [10] o	
	− 13 G [10]		+ 20 B [2] o	
	0 13 B [10]	0 13 BG [10]	0 20 G [2] o	+ 13 B [10]
	0 20 G [2]		0 13 BG [1]	0 13 G [10]
	0 13 BG [1]		0 11 BG [3]	
	0 11 BG [3]			
Resistance to temptation	− 20 B [13]	+ 4 B [4]	+ 13 B [1]	− 4 G [4]
	− 4 G [4]	0 4 G [4]	+ 4 G [17]	0 4 B [4]
	0 4 B [4]	0 11 BG [6]	− 4 M [4]	0 11 BG [6]
	0 4 BG [17]	0 4 BG [17]	0 11 BG [6]	0 4 BG [17]
	0 11 BG [6]		0 4 B [17]	
Confession and acceptance of blame	− 4 M [4]	+ 6 M [16]	+ 6 M [12]	+ 4 M [4]
	− 6 M [16]	+ 13 G [10]	+ 6 M [16]	+ 6 M [16]
	− 13 BG [10]	− 6 M [12]	+ 13 B [10] o	+ 5 B [7]
	0 6 M [12]	0 4 M [4]	− 4 B [17]	+ 13 BG [10]
	0 4 BG [17]	0 13 B [10]	0 13 G [10] o	− 4 B [17]
		0 4 BG [17]	0 4 G [17]	0 4 G [17]
			0 6 M [12] o	0 13 G [10]
			0 4 M [4]	

Key to symbols: +, −, 0:   Direction of relationship obtained.
Numeral: Approximate mean age of subjects.
B, G, M: Boys, Girls, Boys and Girls mixed.
[Numeral]:   Reference number.
o: Predominantly other-oriented.

Table 4. Father's Child-Rearing Practices and Moral Development Indices

Child Morality Index	Power Assertion	Love Withdrawal	Induction	Affection
Internal orientation	− 13 G [10]	0 13 BG [10]	0 13 BG [10] o	+ 13 M [10]
	0 13 B [10]			0 13 BG [10]
Guilt intensity	0 20 BG [2]	0 13 BG [10]	0 20 BG [2] o	0 13 BG [10]
	0 13 BG [10]		0 13 BG [10] o	
Resistance to temptation	− 20 B [13]		0 4 BG [17]	+ 4 B [17]
	0 4 BG [17]			0 4 G [17]
Confession and acceptance of blame	+ 4 B [17]	+ 13 M [10]	0 4 BG [17]	+ 13 G [10]
	− 13 B [10]	+ 13 M [10]	0 13 BG [10] o	+ 4 G [17]
	0 13 G [10]	0 13 BG [10]		0 13 B [10]
	0 4 G [17]			0 4 B [17]

Key to symbols same as Table 3.

dominantly other-oriented are indicated by an "o" placed after the reference number.

The overall pattern of the findings as seen in the tables is as follows. The frequent use of power assertion by the mother is associated with weak moral development to a highly consistent degree. Induction discipline and affection, on the other hand, are associated with advanced moral development, although these relationships are not quite as strong and consistent across the various age levels as the negative ones for power assertion. The two exceptions to this pattern are the negative relationships obtained in the studies of preschool boys dealing with resistance to temptation and confession. A possible explanation is that these children were too young for cognitive processes to influence their motivational systems sufficiently to produce behaviors opposed to their perceived self-interest. In contrast to induction, love withdrawal relates infrequently to the moral indices and the few significant findings obtained do not fit any apparent pattern. Taken as a whole, the importance of the distinction between love withdrawal and induction is clearly demonstrated.

The obtained pattern was most clear-cut for guilt and internal moral orientation. The findings for the two overt indices—resistance to temptation and confession—were more ambiguous, a high degree of consistency being obtained only for power assertion. This may be due to the fact that both these indices refer to responses which often result from a complex decision-making process in which alternative actions, motives, and consequences are weighed. Internal states like guilt and moral judgment, on the other hand, are less subject to such complexities. The resistance to temptation indices have the additional problems mentioned earlier that stem from the use of a cheating situation. The investigators are aware of these problems and some try to take account of them in interpreting their findings, but none of the studies actually controlled the child's general needs for achievement or his desire for the particular prize. Confession, as indicated, may at times be an instrumental response rather than a reflection of moral internalization.

Social Class and the Socialization Process. The subjects in the studies we have reviewed were for the most part from the middle class

or mixed socioeconomic backgrounds. In one study (Hoffman and Saltzstein, 1967 [10])[23], however, a separate analysis was made for lower- and middle-class subjects. Several apparent contrasts were found; foremost is the general paucity of statistically significant relationships in the lower class between the child's performance on the different internalization indices and the parent's discipline. This is especially striking in the case of the mother's discipline. Furthermore, there was no apparent pattern in the few significant relationships obtained and no general conclusion could be drawn from the lower-class data.

This raises the question of why the discipline pattern effective in the middle class should not be effective in the lower class. One possibility is that internalization is a concept which makes little sense in the lower class and should therefore not be expected to relate to parental discipline. This would follow from Kohlberg's view that lower-class people are less likely to attain a mature internal moral orientation because they do not have a stake in the social order. It would also be consistent with Kohn's (1963) view that the lower class has a predominantly external rather than internal orientation—ultimately because lower-class occupations are subject to a great deal of standardization and direct supervision and thus require that one follow explicit rules set down by someone in authority. This is in contrast to middle-class occupations, which foster internalization because they allow more self-direction and make success dependent on one's own actions rather than collective action. The most relevant data on parents are those obtained by Kohn (1959a, 1959b), who found the expressed child-rearing goals of lower-class parents, as compared to those of middle-class parents, were focused more on immediate compliance and less on long-range character development. With seventh-grade children, however, Hoffman and Saltzstein (1967) found that although there was a general tendency for the lower class to be lower on morality than the middle class, the difference was significant only for internal moral judgment and only for girls. The classes did not differ on guilt or confession. We would tentatively conclude that if the level of internalization in lower-class

---

[23] Reference 10 in the tables.

children is lower than that of middle class children, the difference is probably not sufficient to account for the absence of a relation between internalization and discipline.

Another possible explanation is that power assertion is the predominant form of discipline used in the lower class and for this reason all techniques have a power-assertive cast. That is, even when inductions are used the child perceives a power-assertive threat behind them and thus reacts as he would to more openly power-assertive techniques. To the extent this is true, it would reduce the differential effectiveness of discipline techniques and thus lessen the chances of obtaining relations between them and moral development. A predominantly power-assertive child-rearing pattern might be expected in the lower class for several reasons. First, lower-class fathers are apt to experience relatively little power in the occupational sphere; and they may be expected to assert in the home the power that is denied them on the job. Because of the nature of their work, they are also likely to experience considerable psychological distance between themselves and their jobs. As a result, job frustrations are often apt to be felt as due to external forces and thus to produce aggression rather than the more ego-involving (e.g., self-critical) reactions to be expected in occupations allowing more self-direction. This aggression may be displaced and expressed in the home to the mother as well as the children. Furthermore, the mother may be expected to react to her husband's power-assertive and aggressive behavior with anger, but because of his power this is apt to be displaced toward the child in the form of power-assertive discipline, as has been suggested elsewhere (Hoffman, 1963c). For these reasons and also because lower-class parents are typically less influenced by the views of child-rearing experts than middle-class parents (White, 1957), the lower class should use more power assertion and less induction and affection. Analysis of the Hoffman and Saltzstein data indicates this is so, although there is no evidence that the power assertion is salient enough to wash out differences between techniques.

Aside from these possible carry-over effects of power assertion, there are other reasons for expecting discipline to be less crucial in the lower class. First, lower-class mothers more often work full time than do middle-class mothers. Second, the combination of large families and less space may result in the parent and child interacting with many other people besides each other. Third, according to the more traditional family structure usually found in the lower class (e.g., Bronfenbrenner, 1958) the father is more often the ultimate disciplining agent. This is illustrated in the Hoffman and Saltzstein sample in which lower-class boys reported that their mothers had the fathers do the disciplining ("says she'll tell your father") more often than middle-class boys did. Although the father's discipline may not provide a major influence on the child's moral development (as indicated in Table 4), it may suffice to dilute the mother's influence. A fourth factor that may reduce the lower-class mother's influence is that lower-class children are encouraged to spend more time outside the home than middle-class children. For all these reasons the socializing process may be more diffuse in the lower class, that is, it may be more equally shared by the mother with the father, with siblings, members of the extended family, the child's peers, and others.

If discipline is not central and socialization is more diffuse, then what is the basis of internalization in the lower class? We would suggest this as a worthwhile problem for future research. One possibility, in view of the fact that lower-class children generally spend more time with peers, is to follow up Piaget's leads as to the possible influence of peer interaction on moral development.

Role of the Father. In contrast to the mother's, very few relationships were obtained between the father's practices and the child's moral development (Table 4). This was true for boys as well as for girls.

There is some evidence that the father's presence is important, however (Hoffman, 1971). From the initial large sample in the Hoffman and Saltzstein study, a small number of children with no fathers were selected. These were compared to a group matched on IQ and socioeconomic status which was also selected from the larger pool. No differences were found for girls, but the father-absent boys did show consistently lower moral development scores than their counterparts who had fathers. Thus the father does appear to play a necessary role in the boy's moral development, although his discipline methods do not seem to be crucial in this process.

One possible explanation is that the father provides the cognitive content of the child's moral standards by direct instruction in non-discipline situations rather than by his discipline techniques; or his own behavior may serve as a model for the child. These possibilities are suggested by the frequently reported finding that boys show overwhelmingly more identifiation with fathers than with mothers. Further, there is evidence that boys who identify with their fathers tend to make more internal moral judgments than boys who do not identify with them (Hoffman, 1966b). In that same study, however, father identification was not found to relate to guilt, acceptance of blame, and consideration for others. (These findings will be discussed later in connection with the role of identification in moral development.)

A quite different hypothesis is that the father's role is ordinarily latent in its effects and only becomes manifest under exceptional circumstances such as those often associated with delinquency. That is, under normal conditions with the father away working most of the time and the mother handling most of the discipline, the father's importance may lie mainly in providing an adequate role model that operates in the background as a necessary supporting factor. Under these conditions the specific lines along which the child's moral development proceeds may be determined primarily by the mother's discipline; that is, individual differences in children's moral orientations may be due mainly to the mother's discipline. An adequate role model is lacking, however, in extreme cases, as when there is no father, when the father is a criminal, or when the father is at home but unemployed. This may account for the findings in the studies of aggression and delinquency (e.g., Glueck and Glueck, 1950; McCord and McCord, 1958; Miller, 1958), as well as the father-absence findings mentioned earlier, that suggest the father is significant in the development of impulse control in boys.

To give this last interpretation perspective it may be useful to consider another extreme —the frontier father who made most of the major life-and-death decisions, with few if any competing authorities. He was essential to the family's welfare and his everyday activities of providing food, shelter, and protection were highly visible. He could thus command the respect of even the very young child, who would be too immature cognitively to recognize the more abstract symbols of success and importance in modern society. Such a role model would very likely be in the foreground, not the background, and the mother's discipline would probably be no more influential than the father's. The same may be true in primitive cultures which give fathers a kind of sanctity and legitimization in similarly visible ways such as in ceremonials.

Present middle-class American families operate somewhere between the extremes of the absent or ineffectual father and the primitive or frontier father who had visible and, above all, legitimate power, and it may be for this reason that maternal discipline has such pronounced effects in the middle class. Perhaps ours is the only large cultural group for which this is true.

Laboratory Experiments and Other Relevant Research

In this section other research, mainly laboratory experiments, bearing on the preceding generalizations will be discussed. As will be seen, the variables manipulated in the experimental studies do not typically derive from the generalizations obtained in the more naturalistic parent-child research. More often they are a compromise between the dictates of behavior theory and variables thought to be central in real life. The attempt will be made, however, to relate the experimental findings to the parent-child research where possible.

As in our review of the parent-child research, our primary focus will be substantive. Methodological issues and limitations will be stressed, however, to help in the proper interpretation of the findings as well as suggest improvements for future research.

Power Assertion. The most reliable finding in the parent-child research is the negative relation between power assertion and the various moral indices (Table 3). This is the only finding that holds up consistently for both sexes and throughout the entire age range of children studied. The fact that this applies even to preschool children suggests the effects of power assertion operate predominantly through the child's motivational and affective systems and that cognitive processes are relatively unimportant.

The laboratory studies bearing on power assertion have investigated the effects of variations in intensity and timing of punishment as well as the effects of prior nurturant interactions with the socializing adult.

Intensity. In several interrelated studies Parke and Walters (1965) investigated the effects of differing levels of intensity and other aspects of punishment. In each study a multivariate design was used, but our concern here is only with the intensity variable. Six- to eight-year-old boys were given a series of trials on each of which they were required to make a choice between one of two toys. Some toys, they were previously told, were for another boy. Whenever a child either commenced to reach for or touched one of these "forbidden" toys, he was punished. Punishment consisted of a verbal rebuke ("No, that's for the other boy") combined with a loud noise (high-intensity punishment) or a softer noise (low-intensity punishment). Following the punishment trials, the child was left alone for a 15-minute period in a room in which the same toys were displayed. The number of times he touched the forbidden toys, the time that elapsed before his first deviation, and the duration of his deviations were recorded by an observer seated behind a one-way vision screen. In the first study the subjects who received high-intensity punishment were found to deviate less quickly, less often, and for shorter periods of time than those who had been punished mildly. In the second and third studies the findings were generally in the same direction as the first but failed to reach statistical significance.

The intensity variable was also investigated in an experiment by Freedman (1965) conducted within the framework of dissonance theory (Festinger, 1957). Seven- to nine-year-old boys were told not to play with a highly desirable toy, under high or low threat of punishment, and then were left alone with the toy. The children who resisted playing with the toy (95% resisted) were tested again after several weeks and given an opportunity to play with it after the prohibition had been removed. The major finding was that children who had resisted temptation under mild threat in the first session were less likely to play with the toy during the second session than children who had resisted under severe threat. This finding has limited relevance for internalization since an adult was present, though not the same person who was there during the first session. The finding seems important nevertheless because of the long-term effects demonstrated.

Freedman interprets these effects as evidence for greater cognitive dissonance in the mild-threat condition—the dissonance resulting from the knowledge that one wants to play with the forbidden toy but has not done so. The precise way in which dissonance reduction occurs, however, is unclear. Freedman's expectation, that dissonance is reduced by the child's devaluing the forbidden toy, was not supported by his data on the child's actual toy preferences. That is, the children who experienced mild threat were not found to devalue the forbidden toy any more than the children in the high-threat condition. Freedman suggests as an alternative the possibility that the mild-threat children may have reduced dissonance by actually accepting the idea that it is wrong to play with the forbidden toy.[24] An equally plausible explanation that we would suggest assumes that the major influence was not dissonance but the attention focused on the forbidden toy by the experimenter's threats, together with the oppositional forces aroused in the child which might intensify his desire for that toy. Both these effects would be more pronounced under high than low threat, with the result that the value of the forbidden toy may have been raised for the children exposed to high threat.

[24] Freedman defends the dissonance-reduction explanation on the grounds that his high- and mild-threat control groups did not differ in resistance to temptation. His contention is that since the control subjects were accompanied by the experimenter during the free play session following exposure to the threats, unlike the experimental subjects who were left alone, they were minimally tempted to play with the forbidden toy and thus experienced little if any dissonance. This seems reasonable but it also seems likely that with less temptation the control subjects must have more quickly switched their interest to the other toys available, thus reducing their involvement in the forbidden toy. This could explain the lack of difference between the two control groups in resistance to temptation. Thus the control group findings do not provide crucial support for the dissonance interpretation.

Though this view is not supported by Freedman's data on the children's shifts in toy preferences, it is consistent with the findings obtained by Aronson and Carlsmith (1963) and Turner and Right (1965), who found in similar experiments that high threat produced an increase in the child's preference for a forbidden toy, whereas low threat produced a decrease.[25]

Apart from which interpretation is correct, Freedman's finding helps give perspective to the findings obtained by Parke and Walters. Though there may be a tendency for higher intensities of punishment to contribute positively to resistance to temptation immediately following punishment, those who experience mild punishment appear more likely to continue to resist at a later date when the prohibition is removed. This pattern is consistent with the finding in the naturalistic parent-child research of a negative relation between parental power assertion and resistance to temptation (Table 3).

Timing. A natural focus of research interest for learning theorists is the timing of punishment in relation to the child's deviant act. Although the *type* of discipline has not been a concern in these studies, most of them deal with power assertion, probably because these are the only techniques that can be administered quickly and pinpointed in relation to the child's deviant act so as to afford the highly precise variations in timing that are needed.

The basic theoretical framework guiding the research on timing has been provided by Mowrer (1960a, 1960b). According to Mowrer, the execution of an act is accompanied by a sequence of response-produced cues, each providing sensory feedback. Punishment may be administered at any point during this sequence and result in the relatively direct association of a fear-motivated avoidance response with the response-produced cues oc-

curring at that time.[26] Punishment applied at or near initiation of the act will therefore result in a relatively strong association between the deviator's preparatory responses and the emotion of fear, and subsequent initiation of the deviant act will arouse anxiety. The anxiety in turn activates avoidance responses, which are then reinforced by anxiety reduction if they are sufficiently strong to forestall the deviant behavior. In contrast, if the punishment occurs only at completion of the deviant act, anxiety will be most strongly associated with the goal response or immediately subsequent responses and less strongly with stimuli associated with initiation of the act. In addition, the attainment of the goal may be satisfying enough to offset the effects of punishment. This line of reasoning leads to the prediction that the earlier a punishment occurs in a prohibited or disapproved response sequence, the more effectively will it prevent the subsequent commission of the punished behavior.

The only naturalistic study reporting findings on timing of punishment obtained results that contradict this hypothesis (Burton, Maccoby, and Allinsmith, 1961). Mothers of nursery-school children were asked how they trained the child not to play with forbidden objects such as the television set or matches. "If you saw that he was tempted to touch it, would you stop him before he touched it or wait to see if he really played with it and *then* correct him?" The mother's responses were related to indices of the child's resistance to temptation in a laboratory cheating situation (as described previously). Contrary to expectation, children of mothers who said they would wait to see if he actually played with the object were more resistant to temptation than children of mothers who said they would stop him before he touched it. Burton et al. suggest that the question asked the mothers was probably not sufficiently precise to yield information crucial to the timing-of-punishment hypothesis. Their view is that

[25] In these two studies the subjects gave preference-rankings to several toys. They were then allowed to play with all but the *second*-ranked toy, following which they were again asked to rank the toys. Since they had been allowed to play with the first-ranked toys, it seems likely they would tend to lose interest in the second-ranked one—except where the threat against playing with it was strong, which might well have made it more salient and desirable.

[26] Though Mowrer emphasizes the role of kinesthetic and proprioceptive cues arising from the deviant response itself, Walters and Parke (1965) place equal emphasis on perceptual-cognitive factors, which are associated with the functioning of the distance receptors, especially visual and auditory cues accompanying the commission of a deviant act.

since the objects asked about are either dangerous or expensive to repair, very few of the mothers actually allowed the child to play with them for very long. The meaning of "wait till he actually plays with it" was thus that the mother wanted to make sure her intuition about his intentions was correct before applying discipline and that the discipline therefore followed the onset of actual touching fairly closely. If the mother applies discipline when she only *thinks* the child is about to deviate but does not wait to make sure, she will sometimes be right and sometimes wrong, and the result will be poor correlation between the cues the child is actually responding to and the discipline—a relatively inefficient condition for learning. Burton et al. conclude that there is need for more precise data on timing than it may be possible to obtain from interview questions.

Several studies have appeared recently which seem to answer this call for an experimental approach to the study of timing. The first of these, cited by Mowrer (1960b) in support of his theory, was carried out by Black, Solomon, and Whiting. These investigators found that puppies who had been trained to avoid eating horsemeat by tapping them on the nose as they approached it showed more "resistance to temptation" when deprived of food and offered no alternative nutriment than puppies who had been punished only after commencing to eat the horsemeat.

The remaining studies have used children ranging from 6 to 10 years of age. The typical design is to punish or interrupt the children in one group as they commence to reach for a preferred toy (e.g., by removing the toy, depriving them of candy previously given to them, or making a loud unpleasant noise) and to do the same with another group after they have already touched the toy. Shortly afterward, the children are left alone with the prohibited toys and their resisting or yielding to the temptation to play with toys is observed. Significant findings supporting Mowrer's hypothesis were obtained in four of these studies (Aronfreed and Reber, 1965; Walters, Parke, and Cane, 1965; Aronfreed, 1966; Parke and Walters, 1967). Findings in the same direction but not significant were obtained in two studies (Walters and Dembow, 1963; Parke and Walters, 1965). And

in one case an interaction between timing and intensity of punishment was obtained: more resistance to temptation resulted when punishment of high intensity was administered early and punishment of low intensity was administered late (Parke and Walters, 1965).

These studies support the expectation that early punishment contributes to resistance to temptation, yet several questions of interpretation immediately arise. First, is this a specific avoidance of the attractive toy or a generalized inhibition and withdrawal such that the child neglects all toys including the unattractive ones? This is an important question since the aim of socialization in such situations is the avoidance of specific acts, not general inhibition. The only study that provides relevant data suggests that the inhibition may be general: Aronfreed (1966) reports that early punishment contributed to avoidance of all toys, although the forbidden attractive toys were avoided slightly more than the unattractive toys. This is the only study in the group, however, in which the children were given no reason for the punishment. In all the other studies they were told that the forbidden toys were for some other children. Perhaps such a reason is all that is needed for the avoidance to be specific to the forbidden toys. In the absence of evidence, however, it remains possible that these studies bear on a generalized inhibition and not resistance to a particular temptation.

Another, perhaps more basic problem in the timing research is that it ignores the cognitive and verbal abilities of humans. Past 6 or 7 years of age the actual timing of punishment should make little or no difference since it is possible for the connection between punishment and the deviant act to be made cognitively. The children in these studies were all several years older than this minimum and it can therefore be assumed that in the test trials, which usually occurred just ten or twenty minutes after the punishment trials, they knew what they were punished for— reaching for or touching the prohibited toys —*regardless of the timing of the punishment.* As the result of such cognitive mediation of the punishment, all the children should in subsequent situations experience anxiety immediately after the desire for the forbidden toy is aroused. Differences due to timing in the training trials should thus be eliminated.

The differences were not eliminated, however, for which there are several possible explanations. One, which is a variation on the "mediation deficiency" hypothesis, is that though the children have the cognitive capacity under discussion, it is still vulnerable to the emotional effects produced by the punishment trials and the strangeness of the experimental situation. As a result, cognition does not override the more primitive effects of timing on the conditioning of anxiety.[27]

A quite different explanation assumes the cognitive factors do operate and points up a possible flaw in the design of most of the timing experiments. That is, the late-punished subjects were permitted to examine and hold the preferred attractive toy for varying amounts of time before being punished. This interaction with the toy may have increased its attractiveness. The early-punished subjects, on the other hand, who had no chance even to touch the preferred toy, may have more quickly shifted their interest and attention to the other, nonforbidden toys which were available. There is evidence that this shift of interest did occur. In the only two studies reporting relevant data the early-punished subjects are described as either being the only ones to shift their interest to the less attractive toy (Walters, Parke, and Cane, 1965) or as shifting more quickly—thus handling these toys longer—than the late-punished subjects (Aronfreed and Reber, 1965). Furthermore, the one study in which alternative toys were unavailable (Walters, and Dembo, 1963) yielded results which are statistically ambiguous.[28] Thus it appears that the late-punished subjects generally spent more time handling the preferred forbidden toys and the early-punished subjects spent more time handling the alternative toys. Since

neither group had enough time to become satiated, the toy they handled must have become more attractive for them. If so, the experimental manipulations may have altered the attractiveness of the toys for the two groups. The early-punished group did not really show more resistance to temptation; they had less temptation to resist since they had already developed a liking for a substitute.

Pending the satisfactory resolution of these problems, it may be tentatively concluded that power assertion is most effective in getting the child to suppress a deviant act when used at the onset of the act, although the mechanism involved is unknown.

Affectionate Context. Since the relations obtained for power assertion and affection are in the opposite direction (Tables 3 and 4), it would appear that power-assertive parents tend to give the child relatively little affection. Some direct evidence for this is provided in an unpublished finding by Hoffman and Saltzstein: power assertion relates negatively to affection. The possibility therefore exists that power assertion might have more beneficial effects if administered by more affectionate parents. Sears, Maccoby, and Levin (1957) provide some evidence in favor of this proposition. Mothers who were rated by interviewers as warm and affectionate and who made relatively frequent use of physical punishment were likely to say that they found spanking to be an effective means of discipline. In contrast, cold, hostile mothers who made equally frequent use of physical punishment were more likely to report that spanking was ineffective. Moreover, according to the mothers' reports, spanking was more effective when it was administered by the warmer of the two parents. The limitation of these findings is that the mothers' criterion of effectiveness was not based on the child's character development but the extent to which he overtly complied to their standards of behavior and reacted to punishment with hurt feelings rather than anger. An unpublished finding by Hoffman and Saltzstein provides more direct and contrary evidence. Two groups of subjects were selected, one in which the mothers were highly affectionate and the other in which they were not, and relationships were obtained between power assertion and the morality indices in each group. The

[27] The mediation deficiency hypothesis (e.g., Reese, 1962) is that there is a stage in development during which the child does not mediate his overt behavior verbally despite the fact that he is cognitively able to understand and correctly employ the verbal responses necessary for such mediation. We are suggesting that emotional factors also produce this deficiency.

[28] Though the finding is reported as statistically significant, the actual difference was that seven out of nine boys in the early-punishment condition resisted temptation, as compared to four out of eight in the late-punishment condition.

only significant findings obtained in the high-affection group—negative relations between power assertion and guilt, and between power assertion and confession—suggest that affection does not ameliorate the effects of power assertion.

On the other hand, some experimental support for the moderating effect of affection on power assertion is reported by Freedman (1958), who did a resistance-to-temptation study with two groups of puppies. One group, from their third to eighth week of age, experienced two daily 15-minute periods in which they were individually encouraged in any activity they initiated such as play, aggression, and "climbing on the supine handler"; they were never punished. The other group, littermates of the first, "were at first restrained in the experimenter's lap and later taught to sit, to stay, and come upon command. When still older they were trained to follow on a leash." The same experimenter was used for both groups and in all other respects they received identical treatment. At 8 weeks of age each pup was subjected to the following test. Each time he "ate meat from a bowl placed in the center of a room, he was punished with a swat on the rump and a shout of 'no!' After three minutes the experimenter left the room and, observing through a one-way glass, recorded the time that elapsed before the pup again ate." This was done each day for 8 days. The finding was that the more indulged pups took longer to return to the food (resisted temptation longer) than the less indulged pups.[29]

Similar results were obtained by Parke and Walters (1967) with humans. A group of 40 boys experienced two 10-minute periods of positive interaction with the experimenter on two successive days. Attractive constructional materials were provided for the children and, as they played with them, the experimenter provided encouragement and help and warmly expressed approval of their efforts. A second group of 40 boys played, in two 10-minute sessions, with relatively unattractive materials while the experimenter sat in the room without interacting with them. An equal number of children from each group was assigned to

one of four punishment conditions—involving two levels of intensity (a more and a less painfully loud noise) and two levels of timing —which were designed to stop the child from playing with certain attractive toys. The children were then left alone with the toys for 15 minutes and their behavior was observed. The usual measures of the extent to which they resisted or yielded to the temptation to play with the prohibited toys were obtained. Regardless of punishment conditions, children who had experienced positive interaction with the agent of punishment showed significantly greater resistance to temptation than children who had only impersonal contact.

Several explanations are possible. One, offered by Parke and Walters, is that prior nurturance from an adult socializing agent may heighten the love-withdrawal aspect of any discipline technique. According to this view, the inhibitory potential of power assertion is due primarily to its capacity to serve as a dramatic signal of the nurturant adult's displeasure and only secondarily, if at all, to its physically painful qualities. The child complies in order to restore the nurturant relation. This explanation is appealing but it is contradicted by the lack of evidence in our review of the parent-child research that love withdrawal contributes to resistance to temptation.

We suggest an alternative explanation, which, like that advanced by Parke and Walters, plays down the power-assertive quality of the punishment in their experiment. It highlights the cognitive rather than the love-withdrawing aspects, however. First, we note that before the punishment trials commenced the experimenter gave the children an explanation: "Now some of these toys are for another boy, and you are not supposed to touch them." Second, when administering punishment the experimenter also added, "No, that's for the other boy." Ordinarily the latter statement might have an abrupt, perhaps even power-assertive quality, but with the prior nurturant interaction and the experimenter's introductory explanation as background it may provide enough cognitive structure to meet the minimal qualifications of induction. Though it does not point out consequences, it gives the child a reason for prohibiting the act. If so, the finding tells nothing

---

[29] These findings were obtained with four different breeds of puppies, though they were statistically significant for only two of them.

about power assertion but is consistent with the results of the parent-child research: induction plus affection contribute to the internalization of prohibitions.

It is also possible, however, that the finding is an artifact of an experimental design which did not include a control group having a prior *negative* interaction. That is, the prior interaction itself—and not its nurturant quality—may have made the experimenter more salient, and his prohibitions may have been more effective for that reason. Clearly, more research is needed before the possible moderating effects of affection on power assertion can be assessed.

In conclusion, it appears that although the parent-child research indicates power assertion plays a consistently negative role in moral development, the results of the laboratory studies suggest that under certain conditions —high intensity and early timing—power assertion may foster the immediate suppression of pleasure-oriented response tendencies. What accounts for this contradiction? One possibility is that the early-punishment condition used in the laboratory is artificial and that in real life power assertion is usually administered after the act. Another possible explanation is that the resistance to temptation generated in the laboratory studies reflects a more primitive type of internalization than that represented by the moral indices in the parent-child research (see earlier discussion of types of internalization). This primitive internalization is based on response inhibitions, which are quickly conditioned but often short-lived. When they do persist they may actually interfere with later, more advanced types of learning and socialization. For example, they may keep the child from expressing undesirable acts at a later age and thereby deprive him of the experiences needed to learn to control them on a more mature basis.

Love Withdrawal. Perhaps the most surprising result of our research review is the poor showing made by love withdrawal (Table 3). Much of the literature has been predicated on the hypothesis, derived from the psychoanalytic theory of anaclitic identification, that anxiety about possible loss of parental love is the major contributing factor to the child's internalization of parental values

and standards. This hypothesis is seriously called into question by the findings.

A possible explanation is that love withdrawal is only effective in moral development when the parent also freely expresses enough affection to make it obvious to the child that he has something to lose, as suggested by the research of Sears, Maccoby, and Levin (1957). This hypothesis was tested with the Hoffman and Saltzstein data by examining the relation between love withdrawal and several moral indices within groups of subjects who reported that their parents expressed affection frequently or infrequently; that is, within groups which formed the upper and lower quartiles on reported parental affection. The results do not corroborate the hypothesis: in neither group does love withdrawal relate positively to the moral indices.

Some support for a possible relation between love withdrawal and moral development was obtained in an experiment by Parke (1967), who studied resistance to temptation under varying conditions of experimenter nurturance. Parke's subjects, who averaged 7 years of age, first interacted with a highly nurturant experimenter. One group interacted for 10 minutes; another did so for 5 minutes at which time the experimenter abruptly got up, walked to another part of the room and remained there with his back to the child for the remaining 5 minutes. The experimenter then left the room, after first instructing the child not to touch certain toys in his absence and promising to play with him again if he complied. The major finding was that the girls in the nurturance-interrupted condition (the laboratory analogue of love withdrawal) were less likely to touch the forbidden toys than those who had experienced continued nurturance. No differences were obtained for boys. An earlier study of cheating in 4-year-olds by Burton, Allinsmith, and Maccoby (1966) produced dramatically opposite results. Here the girls showed no effects, but the boys did and the direction was the reverse of that obtained by Parke. That is, the boys who were requested by the experimenter to "play the game according to the rules while I'm gone" were *more* apt to cheat when the experimenter's nurturant behavior was interrupted than when it was continued. This finding at first seems to show that love withdrawal leads to *less* resistance to temptation. Burton et al., however, make the plausible suggestion that the boys who had lost the experimenter's attention may have cheated in order to achieve a high score and thereby regain it.

This explanation is consistent with a number of studies indicating that love withdrawal contributes to an intensification of the child's need for adult approval. Thus the use of love-withdrawal discipline by nonpower-assertive parents has been found to relate positively to the child's seeking of nurturance from his nursery school teacher (Hoffman, 1963b). Experimental evidence has also been obtained in a number of studies on social reinforcement in young children (Dorward, Ezerman, Lewis, and Rosenban, 1965; Gewirtz and Baer, 1958a, 1958b; Gewirtz et al., 1958; Hartup, 1958; Lewis, 1965; Lewis et al., 1963; Lewis and Richman, 1964; Stevenson and Odom, 1962; Walters and Karal, 1960; Walters and Parke, 1964a; Walters and Ray, 1960). These studies have generally shown, in one way or another, that when the reinforcement for learning simple discrimination tasks consists of social approval by an adult experimenter, children who had previously experienced a period of social isolation showed more rapid learning than children who had no such experience. Assuming that isolation is an appropriate laboratory analogue of love-withdrawal discipline and that increased learning reflects an increased need for adult approval, these experiments suggest love withdrawal intensifies the need for adult approval.[30]

In one of the studies mentioned (Lewis and Richman, 1964), a probability learning task was used to enable the investigators to determine the type of strategy the children

[30] The researchers who carried out these experiments have different views as to the precise mechanisms by which the isolation increases learning. Thus the findings have been interpreted as supporting the notion that isolation is affective because it arouses dependency needs (Hartup, 1958; Rosenblith, 1959, 1961); produces a general increase in drive level (Gewirtz and Baer, 1958a, 1958b; Gewirtz et al., 1958a, 1958b; Stevenson and Odom, 1962); and arouses anxiety (Walters and Ray, 1960). For our purposes we need not choose among these alternatives, although it is clear that our discussion is most consistent with the anxiety- and dependency-need arousal hypothesis.

used. The results indicate that the control subjects, who were treated in a friendly manner by the experimenter, more often used the strategy of seeking a solution to the problem rather than trying to gain the adult's approval. The subjects who had experienced isolation or a negative encounter with the experimenter, on the other hand, showed less interest in a solution and more interest in obtaining the adult's approval. This strategy worked best because of the particular design of that study, but in most life situations it would probably interfere with an appropriate task orientation and thus diminish learning. This is indicated in a study by Ross (1966), who found dependent children (presumably high on anxiety over possible loss of love) attending more to incidental personal and nontask-relevant cues (mainly stylistic aspects of an adult model's behavior) and less to task-relevant cues than nondependent children. There is also evidence in a recent study by Berkowitz and Zigler (1967) that the increased learning that results from social deprivation is short-lived. These investigators found that a prior period of social deprivation resulted in more rapid learning immediately afterward, but after a 1-week delay it resulted in *less* learning than a prior period of pleasant social interaction.

Some writers have suggested that love withdrawal contributes to a dependent orientation toward the parent, which in turn contributes to moral development (e.g., Sears, Maccoby, and Levin, 1957). The evidence thus far does not support this view. The isolation studies do indicate that love withdrawal may make children more susceptible to adult influence, but only with respect to simple cognitive tasks and in the adult's presence. Further, whether this influence will be consistent with the adult's moral standards is problematic, as indicated in the Burton, Allinsmith, and Maccoby (1966) study cited previously.

Love Withdrawal and Inhibition. There is some evidence that love withdrawal may contribute to the inhibition of anger. Thus it has been found to relate negatively to the expression of overt hostility toward peers (Hoffman, 1963b; Hoffman and Saltzstein, 1967; Sears, 1963). Bandura and Walters (1959) found love withdrawal to relate positively to aggression in adolescent boys, but they suggest this may be due to the fact that their data included the openly rejecting forms of love withdrawal but not the more subtle forms.

Some relevant experimental evidence is also available. Gordon and Cohen (1963) and Gordon and Smith (1965) found that doll play aggression as expressed by children in response to frustration decreased after exposure to a story in which the central figure, a dog, searches unsuccessfully for friends with whom to play. Assuming the story arouses feelings of loneliness and anxiety over separation in the child—feelings akin to the emotional response to love-withdrawal techniques —these findings may be taken as further support for the notion that love withdrawal may contribute to the inhibition of hostility.

Psychoanalytic theory may thus be correct after all in the importance assigned anxiety over love-withdrawal in the socialization of the child's impulses. There is some evidence in the study by Hoffman and Saltzstein (1967), however, against the psychoanalytic view that identification is a necessary mediating process. Whereas love withdrawal related negatively to the child's overt aggression outside the home, neither love withdrawal nor aggression related to identification. This suggests the contribution of love withdrawal to moral development may be to attach anxiety directly to the child's hostile impulses and thus motivate him to keep them under control. It remains possible, however, that a form of unconscious identification which may not be tapped by the more consciously focused measure used in the Hoffman and Saltzstein study serves to mediate between the parents' love withdrawal and the child's inhibition of hostile impulses.

Since hostility is usually expressed toward the parent in situations in which the child's desires conflict with parental demands, the anxiety associated with hostility may generalize to these desires. Thus love withdrawal may contribute to a general anxiety over impulses. This may explain a recent finding by Perdue and Spielberger (1966), who asked college students to recall their childhood and estimate the length of time their parents remained angry after disciplining them. A positive relation was obtained between the duration of the parent's anger, which may be taken as a rough index of love withdrawal, and the

subject's general anxiety level as measured by the Taylor Manifest Anxiety Scale.[31]

These supplementary findings suggest that love withdrawal does make the child more susceptible to adult influence but this has no necessary bearing on moral development. The one contribution to socialization that love withdrawal appears to make is to produce anxiety, which leads to the renunciation of hostile impulses and perhaps other impulses as well. These findings offer no basis for altering the conclusion based on our review of the parent-child research, that love withdrawal alone is an insufficient basis for the development of those capacities—such as guilt and internal moral judgment—which are commonly thought of as critical characteristics of a fully developed, mature conscience.[32]

Induction. The type of discipline most conducive to moral development, according to our review, is induction, especially other-oriented induction. Although in several studies other-oriented induction did not relate to the moral index under investigation, in no case was it found to relate negatively (Table 3).

The effect of pointing out the consequences of the child's behavior has not been investigated in the laboratory. Aronfreed (1966) has recently done a series of studies with young children on the effects of cognitively structuring a prohibited act, and his findings in general are that providing a cognitive structure does increase the likelihood of the child's suppressing the act. This research may have limited relevance to induction since only simple cognitive structurings were used (e.g., calling the act "gentle" or "rough," or referring to it as inappropriate for the child's age). None of the studies involved telling the child the consequences of his behavior. The findings do suggest that giving reasons for prohibiting an act may have an inhibiting effect,

[31] The causality in this study could very well be reversed, however, i.e., high anxiety makes the time elapsed seem longer.

[32] It should be noted that love withdrawal might relate positively to guilt as defined in psychoanalytic terms, i.e., as an irrational response to one's own impulses. As indicated earlier, the concept of guilt used in this paper is quite different from the psychoanalytic, pertaining as it does to a conscious self-critical reaction to the consequences of one's actions.

however, which is contrary to the negative relation obtained by Burton et al. (1961) between induction and resistance to temptation in similar-aged children (Table 3).

The evidence as to whether induction has an inhibiting effect on aggression is also mixed. That it does have an inhibiting effect is suggested in the finding reported by Bandura and Walters (1959) that parents of aggressive adolescent boys use reasoning less often than do parents of nonaggressive boys. On the other hand, in other studies induction has been found to bear no relation to aggression, both in preadolescents (Hoffman and Saltzstein, 1967) and preschool-aged children (Hoffman, 1963b).

Affection. Although the parent-child research indicates that affection contributes positively to moral development the evidence, except for confession, is not as strong as it is for induction. Confession is our weakest index of internalization, for reasons already given, and it seems quite reasonable that a child would be more willing to confess his misdeeds to a loving than a nonloving parent. It is difficult, however, to see how affection can contribute the cognitive prerequisites of internal moral judgments as well as the negative affect and self-critical attitude necessary for guilt.

The laboratory research bearing on affection, which deals mainly with the child's imitation of adult models, also offers little evidence that affection can foster internalization of moral prohibitions. These studies, which will be reported in detail later in this chapter, indicate that a prior nurturant interaction will increase the likelihood of the child's imitation of acts which are neutral and stylistic, but not those which require effort or self-denial. On the other hand, we have already cited the finding by Burton, Allinsmith, and Maccoby (1966) that children showed greater resistance to temptation in a laboratory cheating situation when the experimenter's nurturant behavior was continued than when it was interrupted.

It may be tentatively concluded, though the evidence is by no means clear-cut, that affection does play a role in the internalization of moral prohibitions, but mainly as part of a larger child-rearing pattern. Our view is that affection probably operates mainly as a background or contextual variable, whose function

is to orient the child positively toward the parent and thus make him more receptive to parental influence. This makes it less necessary for the parent to resort to power assertion or love withdrawal and enables him to rely more often on induction.

Laboratory Studies of Self-Criticism. The socialization antecedents of self-criticism, an important ingredient of guilt and other aspects of morality, have been investigated in several recent laboratory studies by Aronfreed and his associates. Aronfreed's theory is that self-criticism is acquired because of its potential as an anxiety-reducing response. Since it occurs at the termination of a deviant act it is, unlike resistance-to-temptation, more likely to be learned when associated with the termination rather than the onset of punishment.

In one experiment Aronfreed (1964) investigated the conditions under which a child would acquire the use of the label "blue" to refer to his own actions, after being repeatedly exposed to the label as a component of punishment. The experiment was conducted with 9- and 10-year-old girls and a female experimenter. The child's task was to guess which of four dolls, none of which she could see, was facing her on each of ten training trials, and to indicate her choice by pushing down one of four levers. On half the trials a buzzer was sounded and she was punished, by disapproval and deprivation of candy previously given her by the experimenter, for the way in which she pushed the levers. No explanation was given for punishing some responses and not others except for the label "blue," which was used by the experimenter to refer to the child's punished response on each trial. The experimenter called it a "blue" response either just at the onset of punishment and buzzer or after the termination of punishment and buzzer. During the test trials, which followed immediately, the buzzer alone (no punishment) continued to be activated as soon as the child pushed a lever. The major finding—consistent with Aronfreed's hypothesis—was that children who had been exposed to the label at termination of buzzer and punishment used the label "blue" to describe the "transgression" which they had just committed, with a much higher frequency than children who were exposed to the label-at-onset condition.

Another experiment, by Aronfreed, Cutick, and Fagen (1963), in which the subjects were grade-school boys, was designed to test the hypothesis that the child's acquisition of a self-critical label is affected by the degree to which the relevant tasks are cognitively structured. The child's task was to knock down some toy soldiers with a "pusher" in order to move a toy nurse to a position of safety. On each of ten training trials, the child was punished by deprivation of some of the candies in a large pile that the experimenter had given him earlier. The number of candies withdrawn was ostensibly determined by how many soldiers had been knocked down (the child could not see how many were actually knocked down). In the high cognitive structure condition instructions and training trials were accompanied by the experimenter's frequent references to the child's performance along the dimensions of "careful-careless" and "gentle-rough." In the low cognitive structure condition these references to the child's use of the pusher were omitted. In the test trial the nurse was made to appear to break after having been pushed by the child. The experimenter then presented "casual," nondirective questions asking why the nurse might have broken. The results supported the hypothesis: children punished under high cognitive structure more often held their own actions responsible for breaking the nurse than children punished under low cognitive structure.

In another closely related experiment (Aronfreed, 1963) the same procedure was used but with one important difference. While some subjects were again punished by the experimenter, who decided how many candies to take and removed them, other subjects evaluated their own performance ("You look at the number of soldiers you knocked down, and you decide how careless and rough you've been") and removed the number of candies they judged appropriate. Their self-deprivation terminated each trial and was followed by the experimenter saying, "Good!" The variations of cognitive structure used in the preceding study were also introduced here. The use of the labels in this study too was found to be proportionate to the amount of cognitive structure given during training. It was unaffected, however, by the child's control over punishment.[33]

The effects of nurturance and its withdrawal were also investigated in the first two studies just discussed, but in neither case were these variables found to affect the child's acquisition of the self-critical label. In a more recent study by Grusec (1966), however, nurturance was found to be highly effective. The subjects, kindergarten children of both sexes, first interacted with a female experimenter in either a high or low nurturance condition. The high condition was deliberately more prolonged than in the Aronfreed studies to maximize the effects of nurturance. The children then played the soldiers-and-nurse game and were (1) criticized for their performance (experimenter calls them a "hurter") and (2) punished by withdrawal of love (experimenter says child's act made her "unhappy" or "disappointed" with him) or withdrawal of previously administered material rewards. Termination of punishment was either contingent or noncontingent on the child's verbalization of the self-critical label. The findings were that high nurturance was more effective in producing the label than low nurturance, regardless of the kind of punishment used. This finding is doubly in opposition to Aronfreed's since the self-critical label was always applied by the experimenter at the onset of punishment. It was also found that high nurturance and contingent reinforcement facilitated the subsequent development of self-criticism only when used in combination with withdrawal of love. With withdrawal of material rewards there was no such effect.

These experiments, taken as a group, indicate that the tendency to criticize oneself for a prohibited act is enhanced when the socialization agent is highly nurturant and provides cognitive labels for the act. If the operational definitions of self-criticism, nurturance, and cognitive structuring are acceptable as rough laboratory approximations of guilt or acceptance of blame, affection, and induction, this series of studies may then be viewed as providing confirming evidence for the results of

---

[33] The child's control of punishment, however, did relate positively to the appearance of reparative tendencies as defined by volunteering methods of repairing the nurse and suggesting alternative ways of continuing the procedure.

our review of the parent-child research. That is, induction and affection contribute positively to internalization. The Grusec study suggests that love withdrawal also contributes, however, which contradicts the review.

We have some reservations concerning the relevance of these self-criticism studies to guilt and internalization. Mainly, it is questionable whether the child who verbalizes the labels actually judges himself as bad and experiences a true sense of wrongdoing. Instead, it seems from the descriptions given in the research reports that the child may merely reproduce the labels used by the experimenter and apply them in parrotlike fashion to his own behavior. This is most evident in the Aronfreed study involving the label "blue," but it also appears to be true in the other studies. Furthermore, the subjects in all the studies were reported as rarely using the labels spontaneously; that is, the bulk of the self-criticism scores came from their responses to the experimenter's questions. The safest view of what took place would therefore seem to be that the experimenter applied the label to a particular behavior and a few moments later, in response to direct questioning, the subject repeated the label since it was the only description of the act given him and thus the only sensible answer available at the time. Furthermore, the parrotlike quality of the self-criticism score was enhanced by the scoring procedure. In all but one of the studies (Aronfreed, Cutick, and Fagen, 1963), for the subject's responses to be scored as self criticism they had to include the precise label used by the experimenter. Similar but nonidentical responses, which might provide a truer index of self-criticism, were not counted. Finally, in all these studies the experimenter was present when the child gave the self-critical response, which further limits its possible relevance to internalization.[34]

Following this line of reasoning, we would suggest that what these studies tell us is that giving and then withdrawing affection may intensify the child's motivation to act in accord with the adult's expectations, and applying a cognitive structure also helps him to do this. The studies then become additional evidence for one of the effects of love withdrawal discussed earlier, that is, intensifying the

child's susceptibility to adult influence in the adult's presence.

The Role of Identification and Imitation

Identification has been viewed, since Freud, as a central and all-encompassing process in the development of a conscience, as well as sex role identity and other important aspects of personality. As already indicated, the psychoanalytic view is that the young child becomes motivated to emulate the parent and adopt his inner states including moral stan-

[34] There are some other technical flaws in the design of these studies. Commenting on her own findings, for example, Grusec (1966) suggests the cessation of material rewards may have had reduced impact because it occurred in the context of visible material rewards that had already been gained. "Although the chip dispenser was turned off, subjects were still being rewarded by the sight of chips, lying on the table in front of them, which they had already won." Another more general problem, that of salience of the experimental manipulations, is illustrated in the study by Aronfreed (1964). The major finding of this study, that labeling at termination of punishment is more effective than labeling at onset of punishment, may have been due to the fact that termination was more salient than onset and not that it produced a stronger association between the label and anxiety reduction. In the label-at-termination condition the child's experience was that a previously pleasant experimenter suddenly and for no apparent reason got up from her seat behind him, walked over to his table, and then took away some of the candy she had given him just a few moments earlier, turned on a loud unpleasant buzzer, and looked with concern at the machine (on which a voltmeter had just begun swinging and a counter had started clicking). All of this took place just before the experimenter applied the label to the child's act. It seems reasonable to assume that by the time the label was uttered, the subject was aroused and his attention fixed on the experimenter. In the learning-at-onset condition, the experimenter's use of the label preceded these dramatic events and may have been drowned out by them. Another reason for questioning Aronfreed's anxiety hypothesis is that the buzzer used to signal a punishment response was loud enough to have aversive qualities of its own. Thus the child may have given the "blue" response to avoid the unpleasantness of the buzzer rather than the anxiety aroused by the buzzer due to its past association with punishment.

dards and the capacity to punish himself and experience guilt when he violates or is tempted to violate them. With this development, he also experiences pressures to act in line with the standards even in the parent's absence. Quite apart from its psychoanalytic origins, it makes good sense logically to assume that some process such as identification operates in moral development. Why should a person criticize and blame himself for not behaving in accord with the standards of another person even in that person's absence, unless he has somehow come to adopt the latter's evaluative role and no longer views his own behavior solely in terms of its relevance to impulse gratification?

While we might conclude from the preceding sections of this chapter that the child comes to criticize and blame himself for violating the parent's standards as a direct result of the parent's discipline techniques, it remains possible that identificatory processes also prevail. Indeed, identification may be the primary mechanism and the child's response to discipline merely an epiphenomenal reflection of this. To gain a fuller understanding of the antecedents of moral development, then, requires that we supplement our examination of the role of discipline with a similar attack on identification.

Two general types of identification are discussed in the literature. In one—referred to as identification with the aggressor or defensive identification—the child, treated punitively by the parent but fearful of further punishment if he fights back, avoids the conflict and gains further parental approval by taking on the characteristics and point of view of the parent (A. Freud, 1946). Although Freud at times seemed to consider this type of identification to be important in moral development, especially in the male, it is now generally thought of as a temporary mechanism or one that leads to an aggressive, hostile outlook toward the world rather than a process that underlies the development of an enduring inner conscience. The other type, referred to as developmental or anaclitic identification, is based on the child's anxiety over the loss of the parent's love. To get rid of this anxiety and assure himself of the parent's continued love, the child strives to become like the parent—to incorporate everything about him including his moral standards

and values. This type of identification, originally seen by Freud as especially characteristic of females, is assumed by most current writers to underlie the development of an inner conscience in both sexes.

Numerous attempts have been made in recent years to clarify these concepts (e.g., Brodbeck, 1954; Bronfenbrenner, 1960; Jacobson, 1954; Mowrer, 1950; Sanford, 1955; Stoke, 1950) and place them within broader theoretical frameworks (e.g., Kagan, 1958; Seward, 1954; Slater, 1961; Whiting, 1960). There are several problems with the identification concept that have generally been overlooked, however. For one thing, the child may not identify in all respects as often assumed by psychoanalytic writers. His striving to emulate the parent may be selective rather than total. Some children may be motivated to adopt certain valued parental characteristics like mechanical skills, social graces, sense of humor, and power; among those the child may not adopt are the parent's values and moral standards.

A second problem is that, apart from the child's motivation, it should be *easier* for him to identify with some parental characteristics than with others. For example, the parent's moral attributes that can readily be manifested in overt behavior (e.g., going out of one's way to help others) or communicated verbally (e.g., moral judgments and moral values) may be easy to emulate. The parent's inner states, however, such as temptation, self-criticism and guilt, which may never be verbalized, should be much more difficult if not impossible to emulate despite the child's motivation to do so.

Despite these problems, children apparently do try to emulate their parents and if we may assume that parents are the children's main socializing agents and, further, that despite the known diversity of moral standards those of most parents derive from the central values of the culture, then it follows that identification is a potentially important process in the internalization of the culture's standards and values. The empirical research throws little light on these issues. Two approaches, both of which assume with Freud that identification is a unitary process, have been dominant. One predicts consistency among different moral attributes. The results, summarized later, are mixed through suggestive of a slight tendency for moral attributes to interrelate. The second approach hypothesizes that if the conscience is a product of identification it should be related to parental discipline in ways predictable from identificaton theory—i.e., positively to power assertion or love withdrawal depending on which concept of identification is used, "defensive" or "anaclitic." Neither pattern was obtained, as we have seen. In general, then, the findings provide little support for the unitary-process view of identification.

In a recent study identification and morality were independently assessed and the relation between them investigated (Hoffman, in press). The identification score was based on the child's conscious admiration and striving to be like the parent. The moral indices were those reported earlier as being related positively to maternal discipline—guilt, internal moral judgments, confession, and consideration for others. The only significant finding was that among middle-class boys father identification related positively to internal moral judgment. Our interpretation is that identification may contribute to the realization that moral principles are the appropriate bases for judging acts as right or wrong, not whether they lead to detection and punishment, but there is no evidence that it contributes to internalization in the sense of using these principles to evaluate one's own behavior. Identification may thus not be the process by which the child adopts the parent's perspective as a basis for self-evaluation. We have suggested the reason is that parents do not often verbalize inner states such as guilt and self-criticism in the child's presence, and as a result do not provide him with a clear and consistent model of these attributes. Even if such a model were provided, in the normal course of development the child may not be highly motivated to adopt these unpleasant states; they may be acquired as part of his reaction to discipline, as indicated earlier, rather than through identification.

Further light on the role of identification in the child's adoption of the adult's inner states may be gained by examining the experimental research on imitative modeling. These studies, as we shall see, have used ingenious techniques to convert what are ordinarily inner states into outer states which can be readily communicated by the model to the child.

Laboratory Experiments on Imitative Modeling and Moral Development

Numerous laboratory studies have attempted to show the influence of imitative modeling on behavior relevant to moral development. Studies bearing on the influence of models on the child's moral judgment and altruistic behavior are discussed elsewhere in this chapter. The vast majority of the imitative modeling and moral development studies are more directly relevant to the internalization of moral prohibitions, which is our concern here. Most of these have been done by Bandura and his associates, and Bandura has advanced the most fully developed theory of the underlying processes involved (Bandura, 1969). First, he argues against the distinctions frequently made between identification and imitation. His major point is that there is no empirical evidence for such distinctions as these: identification involves the adoption of complex behaviors and motive systems, whereas imitation involves only the reproduction of discrete responses; only identification requires an earlier attachment as a precondition; and only identification can lead to performance of the model's behavior in his absence. He concludes that identification and imitation must be viewed as referring essentially to the same behavior phenomena.

Bandura defines an identificatory event as "the occurrence of similarity between the behavior of a model and another person under conditions where the model's behavior has served as the determinative cue for the matching responses." In accounting for identification, Bandura's most recent formulation assigns a prominent role to observational learning (Bandura, 1968). According to this view, matching behavior is acquired as follows: (1) during the period of exposure, modeling stimulus sequences elicit in the observer perceptual responses that become centrally integrated, because of the temporal contiguity of the stimuli, into images which are later retrievable; and (2) the observer verbally codes these observational inputs. The coded observations remain as representational symbolic events which, in conjunction with appropriate environmental cues, may at a later date activate the image. The image then serves as a guide for the overt enactment of appropriate modeling responses. Whether the responses actually are performed, however, is determined primarily by reinforcing events that may be externally applied, self-administered, or vicariously experienced. Bandura also states that the distinctive characteristics of the model may come to function as discriminative stimuli for regulating the generalization of identificatory responses to unfamiliar models, in different social situations, and across different classes of behavior displayed by the same model.

As Bandura points out, this view differs in several important respects from the psychoanalytic view, which depicts identification as a pervasive and more or less unitary modeling outcome that is firmly established early in a child's life, and which results from nurturant and threatening interactions with parental figures. In contrast, according to Bandura's view, identification is a continuous process in which new responses are acquired and existing repertoires of behavior are modified to some extent as a function of both direct and vicarious experiences with not only the parents but a wide variety of actual or symbolic models whose attitudes, values, and social responses are exemplified behaviorally or in verbally coded forms.

According to Bandura and his colleagues, any behavior, including the control of aggression and other impulses, can be acquired through imitation and observational learning. Hence the relevance of their formulations and much of their recent research to moral development.

Resistance to Temptation. In a recent study Stein (1967) tested the prediction that children in a temptation situation would imitate a model who exhibited yielding or resisting behavior. The subjects were fourth-grade boys and the model was an adult male. The experimental temptation consisted of assigning the child to do a boring job while a highly attractive movie was shown just outside his line of vision. The job consisted of watching for a light and pushing a button when the light went on. The prohibition against looking at the movie was established by the experimenter's saying. "The lights probably won't come on very often so you may do whatever you like as long as you stay in your chair. You must stay in your chair, though, so you'll be ready when the lights do come on." The child was scored as yielding to temptation if he left his job to look at the movie.

Before being placed in the temptation situation, the child was exposed to one of three experimental treatments: (1) a resisting model; (2) a yielding model; or (3) no model.[35] In each case the model indicated an interest in the movie through his motor behavior and the comment, "I sure wish I could see the movie." The findings were that the subjects who observed a yielding model showed more yielding when left alone in the room than either those who observed a resisting model or those in the control condition who observed no model. The subjects who observed a resisting model, however, did not show more resistance than the control subjects. Indeed, they showed slightly (though not significantly) less.[36] These results suggest that while observing a model may help disinhibit a prohibited response tendency, it may be ineffective as an agent of inhibition. Other interpretations are also possible. One is that the high level of resistance shown by the control group produced a "ceiling effect" leaving the subjects who observed a resisting model little room for improvement. This possibility does not receive support from the data, as pointed out by Stein, since the resistance scores were actually lower in the resisting-model than in the no-model condition. It is still possible, however, that the deviant response had relatively little salience for the control subjects and consequently their deviation scores were spuriously low. Whichever interpretation is correct, there is no evidence in this study that observing a resisting model contributes to resistance to temptation.

In two other studies dealing with resistance to temptation, the child observes a peer model who deviates from a prohibition and is either punished or rewarded for this. The assumptions are that the consequences to the model

[35] There were actually three different types of resisting-model conditions, but all produced similar results.

[36] Since there were three resisting-model conditions and six resistance-to-temptation indices, and analyses were done separately for the two schools in the study, 36 comparisons were actually made between groups who observed a resisting model and groups who observed no model. The no-model groups were higher on 24 and the resisting-model groups higher on only 3. Nine ties occurred, in which both groups obtained the maximum resistance scores possible.

serve as a cue signifying to the observer the permissibility or nonpermissibility of the punished response; and that the affective expression of models undergoing rewarding or punishing experiences elicit corresponding emotional responses in the observer. These vicariously aroused emotional responses can then become conditioned to the modeled responses or stimuli associated with them. In one such study by Walters and Parke (1964) the subjects, 6-year-old boys, were first shown some toys and forbidden by the experimenter from touching them with the statement, "Now, these toys have been arranged for someone else, so you'd better not touch them." They then observed a 3-minute color film sequence depicting an adult female, presumably a mother, indicate to a small boy that he should not play with toys that had been placed on a nearby table. The "mother" then sat the child down beside the table, handed him an open book, and left the room. After her departure, the child put the book aside and played for approximately 2 minutes with the prohibited toys. For the model-rewarded condition, the last part of the film showed the "mother" return to the child, sit by him, hand him toys, and play with him in an affectionate manner. In contrast, under the model-punished condition the film ending showed the "mother," on her return from the other room, snatch from the child the toy he was then playing with, shake him, and sit him down once more in the chair with the book. For the no-consequence condition the film ceased after the model had played with the toys for 2 minutes, that is, the "mother" did not reenter the room. After the film, the experimenter made an excuse to leave the room, promised to return soon and play a game with the child, and gave him the dull task of "reading a dictionary" while she was gone. The experimenter remained outside the room for a 15-minute period during which an observer recorded the latency of the first deviant response made by each child, the number of times the toy was touched or played with, and the duration of deviation. Children in a control group saw no film but were otherwise treated in the same way as children under the three film conditions.

The findings were as follows: (1) the subjects who observed the model punished deviated less quickly, less often, and for a shorter period of time than subjects under the model-rewarded and no-consequence conditions; (2) they actually deviated slightly (though not significantly) *more* than the control group who saw no film; and (3) the no-consequence condition resulted in as much deviation as the model-rewarded condition.

In an earlier study, similar to the one just described except for the lack of a no-consequences group and other design details which will be mentioned later, Walters, Leat, and Mezei (1963) did find that the children in the model-punished condition showed more resistance to temptation than those in the control group (and more than those who saw the model rewarded). The discrepancy may be accounted for by differences in the two samples. Whereas middle-class children were used by Walters and Parke, those in the Walters, Leat, and Mezei study came from lower-class, immigrant families "known to be somewhat indulgent" in their child-rearing practices. These subjects might be relatively less responsive to (less apt to attend or comprehend) the experimenter's verbalized prohibition than to the clear visual message in the film that deviation will be punished. If so, the two studies may be seen as indicating that observing a model punished for deviating may be a more effective agent of inhibition in the lower than in the middle class.

We would suggest another possibly influential factor based on a subtle difference at the very end of the model-punished films in the two studies. The Walters, Leat, and Mezei film ended as follows: "the mother, in entering the room, shook her head and her finger at the boy who then dropped his toys, jumped into a chesterfield, and held a blanket up to his face." Apart from its dramatic aspects, this ending may have communicated to the observing child that the model felt shame because of his actions. The focus of attention at the end of the Walters and Parke film, on the other hand, was exclusively on the adult's punishment of the child, as described earlier. Depicting the model's displeasure with himself might thus be a more potent stimulus for producing the elements of an internalized inhibitory response than depicting external punishment alone.

It is also possible that the discrepancy is due to the fact that the Walters and Parke study came later and incorporated a number of design improvements, several of which bear on the important issue of the assurance given the subject that he was on his own when the experimenter left the room. In the earlier Walters, Leat, and Mezei study the child interacted with two adults, the experimenter and a film assistant. It was the assistant who, before leaving the experimental room, reminded the child about the experimenter's departure and return and told him that the door would be closed so no one would bother him. Under these conditions the child might well be expected to be somewhat apprehensive about the possible surprise return of at least one of the two adults. And any apprehension about being punished for playing with the toys would be heightened by having just seen another child play with identical toys. The Walters and Parke subjects interacted with only one adult, the experimenter, who told him about her own departure. She also stated that not only would the door be closed but she would knock before she returned. In addition, the toys presented to the subject and model were not identical. While these precautions were probably not foolproof, they very likely resulted in less concern among the Walters and Parke subjects about a surprise visit from an adult, and the findings should thus bear more on internalized resistance to temptation and less on fear. In drawing conclusions we would therefore assign greater weight to the Walters and Parke findings.

Let us now consider the implications of Walters and Parke's findings. First, it is clear that the consequences to the model have a pronounced effect on the observing child. When the model is punished the child is less likely to engage in the prohibited act than when the model is rewarded. The crucial question is whether this means that punishing the model led to inhibition or rewarding the model led to disinhibition of the act. Both conclusions are possible, depending on whether the condition in which there was no model, or the one in which there were no consequences to the model, is used as the control for evaluating the effectiveness of the model-punished condition.

The more obvious and traditional view is that the only legitimate control for evaluating the effectiveness of models is a condition involving no models. Opposed to this is the view that the prohibited act, playing with the toys, has a low probability of occurring because of its novelty and low salience as well as the child's initial reticence in the strange surroundings of the experimental room. The frequency of the act in the no-model condition is consequently too low to be improved upon in the modeling condition. According to this view the subject becomes familiar with the behavior for the first time only after exposure to the model, and the no-consequence group is therefore the appropriate one to use as a control. The evidence against this position is twofold. First, although the deviation scores in the no-model condition were low they did allow room for improvement, yet the deviation scores in the model-punished condition were consistently higher (though not significantly). Especially noteworthy is the fact that although less than half the no-model subjects did not deviate at all, still fewer model-punished subjects met this criterion. Thus the lack of difference between the model-punished and no-model groups cannot be explained entirely as due to a ceiling effect.

Perhaps the most crucial argument against using the no-consequence condition as the control is that as much deviation occurred in it as in the model-rewarded condition, which suggests the two may be psychologically equivalent. This makes sense when they are examined in detail. The medium for both is a 3-minute film in which an adult first issues a prohibition and then puts the child on a chair, gives him a book to read, and leaves the room; the child then plays with the prohibited toys alone for 2 minutes. The only difference is that in the remaining short portion of the film the adult either returns and affectionately enters into the child's play (model-rewarded) or the child continues to play alone (no-consequence). Thus in both conditions the child observes a peer model enjoying play with prohibited toys without being punished. These similarities may be salient enough to override the differences, with the result that the no-consequence film is subjectively as rewarding as the model-rewarded film. It is also possible that the absence of some form of punishment, which the subjects very likely expected because of their prior socialization experiences, served to legitimize the prohibited act in both conditions.

Both points of view have merit and neither condition seems ideal as a control. The case against the no-consequence condition seems stronger to us, however, and on the assumption that this is so we would interpret the Walters and Parke findings as follows. First, the subjects were initially motivated to play with the attractive toys, but deterred by the experimenter's prohibition perhaps because of the general tendency to obey adult authority in strange unstructured situations. Second, watching a peer model play had an initially disinhibiting effect. Third, this disinhibition was sustained in the absence of punishment, that is, in the model-rewarded and no-consequence conditions. (Our analysis thus far may also encompass the Stein findings mentioned earlier since the yielding-model condition there was essentially the same as the no-consequence condition here.) Fourth, the punishment to the model was potent enough to counteract the disinhibition and re-establish the baseline level of inhibition created by the prohibition, but not enough to increase the inhibition beyond that level. Exposure to a deviant model who is punished thus appears to have an inhibiting effect on the response tendency initially aroused by the model's deviant act, but not on that existing before exposure. Stated differently, the effectiveness of a prohibition may be reduced by exposing the child to a model performing the prohibited act; the reduction is temporary if the model is subsequently punished.

This interpretation is tentative and pending further research we would only conclude that the research thus far does not provide evidence for the view that observing a model punished for violating a prohibition has the effect of increasing resistance to temptation.

Inhibition of Aggression. The preceding studies pertain to efforts to get the child to inhibit behaviors that are ordinarily permitted. The effect of observing models on the inhibition of aggression, which is ordinarily not permitted, has been investigated in two studies. Bandura, Ross, and Ross (1963b) exposed nursery-school children to films that depict an adult model employing considerable physical and verbal aggression against another adult in order to amass his possessions. Under a model-rewarded condition the aggressor successfully appropriated these possessions and rewarded himself for doing so; under a model-punished condition the aggressor received severe punishment for his behavior. Two control conditions were included: one in which the children observed the models engage in vigorous but nonaggressive play, and another in which there was no model. In a subsequent free-play situation the children who observed the model punished exhibited significantly less aggression than children who saw him rewarded. They did not show less aggression, however, than the children in either of the control groups.

Three film sequences were utilized by Bandura (1965) in a further study of the influence of consequences to the model on children's aggressive behavior. The major portion of each sequence depicted an adult behaving in an aggressive manner toward an inflated rubber doll. In one sequence the adult was punished for his aggression. In another he was rewarded, and in the third there were no consequences. As in the earlier study, children who saw the model punished for aggression showed less aggressive behavior in a subsequent test situation than children who saw the model rewarded. They also showed less aggression than children in the no-consequence condition. The same amount of aggression was displayed by children in the model-rewarded and no-consequence conditions.

Putting the two sets of findings together, the following pattern emerges: the model-punished condition produced less aggression than either the model-rewarded or no-consequence condition but no less than the no-model (and also the active nonaggressive model) condition; the no-consequence condition produced the same amount of aggression as the model-rewarded condition. This pattern is the same as that obtained in the Walters and Parke study discussed previously, and a similar analysis may be made. First, it is clear that the consequences to an aggressive model have a great influence on the subject's aggression; and whether this signifies an inhibitory effect for the model-punished condition or a disinhibitory effect for the model-rewarded condition depends on whether the no-consequence or no-model condition is chosen for purposes of comparison. Here again our view is that neither is ideal but the no-model condition is the more appropriate, for reasons that follow.

First, any ceiling-effect explanation is doubtful since the aggression scores in the no-model condition were as high as the active-nonaggressive-model condition and high enough for an effective inhibitory agent to have a marked effect, yet the model-punished group tended to show slightly (though not significantly) more rather than less aggression. Second, the fact that the no-consequence and model-rewarded conditions produced the same amount of aggression suggests they were psychologically equivalent and equally rewarding, as in the Walters and Parke study. That is, both films were taken up largely by the model engaged in highly vigorous aggressive behavior against a Bobo doll. The only difference was that in the model-rewarded film another adult praised the model and gave him candy and soft drinks. The model's engaging in freely aggressive action without punishment could well have been the salient aspect of both films. Furthermore, the fact that the aggressive model was an adult may have provided an added element of legitimization of aggression in the two conditions, thus tending to equalize them further.

Our tentative interpretation of the findings is that the low level of aggression in the no-model condition was primarily the result of the child's past socialization experiences. Witnessing a model behave aggressively appears to have a disinhibiting effect, which is sustained if the model is rewarded or merely goes unpunished. (The weakening of inhibitions against aggression by exposure to models has also been demonstrated in several other studies, including those of Bandura and Huston, 1961, Bandura, Ross, and Ross, 1963a, and Kimbrell, 1958.) Punishment to the model has the effect of neutralizing the disinhibition and reducing the aggression to the baseline level—but not below.

A serious limitation of these aggression studies is that the experimenter was present (throughout the entire test session in the Bandura, Ross, and Ross study and during the second half of it in the Bandura study). There was good reason for this since Bandura and his colleagues report that in pretests the children exhibited some anxiety about being left in the room for a relatively long period and tended to leave before the termination of the session. We cannot be certain what effect the adult's presence had on the aggression displayed by the subjects. It might, on the one hand, have heightened their expectation about punishment and thus lowered the frequency of aggression. On the other hand, a study by Siegel and Kohn (1959) indicates that the presence of a permissive, nonsanctioning adult may actually increase a child's aggressive behavior, perhaps, we would suggest because the lack of disapproval of the child's initial aggressive acts resolves the ambiguity in the situation and legitimizes further aggresson. In any case, the experimenter's presence does limit the possible relevance to internalization of any inhibitory effects that might be found.

Our tentative conclusion is that the research does not support the view that the child's inhibitions against the expression of aggression are increased by exposure to aggressive models who are punished.

Self-Denial in Relation to Performance Standards. A number of recent experiments by Bandura, Mischel, and their associates have dealt with the child's adoption of a model's performance standards. In the first of these studies (Bandura and Kupers, 1964) children participated in a bowling game with an adult or peer model. The scores, which could range from 5 to 30, were controlled by the experimenter. At the outset of the game the children and their models were given access to a plentiful supply of candy from which they could help themselves as they wished. Under one experimental condition, the model set a high standard for self-reward—on trials in which he obtained or exceeded a score of 20 he rewarded himself with one or two candies and made such self-approving statements as "I deserve some M and Ms for that high score" or "That's great! That certainly is worth an M and M treat." In contrast, on trials in which he failed to meet the adopted standard he took no candy and remarked self-critically, "No M and Ms for that" or "That does not deserve an M and M treat." In the other experimental condition the model exhibited a similar pattern of self-reward and self-disapproval except that he adopted the standard of 10, a relatively low level of performance. After exposure to their respective models, the children played the bowling game several times in succession. This was done in the absence of the model, although the experimenter and a research assistant were present. During these trials the children received a wide range of scores, and the performances for which they rewarded themselves with candy and self-approval were recorded.

It was found that the children's patterns of self-reward closely matched those of the model to which they had been exposed; moreover they tended to reproduce the self-approving and self-critical comments of their model. Thus, although both groups had access to a plentiful supply of candy, the children who had observed the model apply a high criterion of self-reward helped themselves to the candy sparingly and only when they achieved relatively high levels of performance, whereas children who were exposed to the low-standard model rewarded themselves generously even for minimal performance. A control group of children who were not exposed to models appeared to reward themselves randomly and for minimal performance.

Similar results were obtained more recently by Liebert and Opra (1968). Bandura and Whalen (1966), however, obtained discrepant results in a study using essentially the same procedure as part of a complex multivariate design investigating the extent to which the modeling effect is influenced by the subject's prior experience of success or failure in the game and his perception of the model's relative competence. As in the other studies, the subjects were found to reward themselves more often when their performance equaled or exceeded that of the model and less often if it did not; and this effect was obtained whether the subjects had previously experienced success or failure in the task and regardless of the relative competence of the model in relation to themselves. However, in six separate comparisons, the six experimental groups whose performance did not reach the standards set by the models were found to reward themselves *more* frequently than control groups with comparable performance scores who had observed no model. Two of these differences were statistically significant.

It is clear from these studies that the child's pattern of self-reward can be influenced readily by observation of an adult model, but it is not clear whether the influence is due to the inhibiting effects of the model's high standards or the disinhibiting effects of low standards. In interpreting the discrepant findings, the Bandura and Whalen study should be given considerable weight since the design allowed for six different, independent tests. Also, greater precautions were taken than in the Bandura and Kupers study to reduce situational pressures on the subjects to adopt the model's pattern of self-reward. Whereas Bandura and Kupers had the same experimenter and assistant present throughout, Bandura and Whalen had different adults present during the modeling and self-reward trials and they had no knowledge of the conditions to which the subjects were assigned. The Liebert and Opra study should also be weighed heavily, however, since it was the only one in which the subject was completely alone during the self-reward trials. Our tentative conclusion is that these studies lend slight support to the notion that self-denial may be acquired through the observation of models who adhere to stringent standards of self-reward.

There are two possibly important limitations to this self-denial, however. First, it appears to be fragile and short-lived. Thus Bandura, Grusec, and Menlove (1967) found that the effectiveness of an adult model's stringent standards of self-reward was destroyed when a competing peer model using a more lenient standard was present. This finding is all the more dramatic when we consider that children will generally imitate an adult rather than a peer when the same self-reward criterion is used (Bandura and Kupers, 1964). The fragility of the model-established standard is also indicated in a study by Mischel and Liebert (1966), who found that children will adopt an adult model's stringent criterion of self-reward if in addition the model explicitly and directly imposes the same stringent criterion on the child ("No, no, no, that's not a very good score, I don't want *you* to take a treat for that."); however, when either the model's self-imposed standard or the standard imposed on the child by the model became more lenient, the child adopted the more lenient standard. One finding in this study was especially striking. Although none of the subjects rewarded themselves for performance that failed to reach the model's standard when the same standard was imposed on the subject, over 90% of the subjects rewarded themselves for performance below the model's standard but higher than the imposed standard. The self-denying standards that may be acquired through modeling, then, appear to be highly vulnerable and readily abandoned in favor of other, more lenient standards that might be available.

A second possible limitation is that the effective stimulus may not be the model's behavior but his communication of the performance standard. A unique feature of these self-reward studies is the absence of either an experimental prohibition or relevant background socialization experiences that might guide the subject's behavior. The norm in question—that the amount of candy to be taken should be contingent upon performance —is communicated only as part of the model's behavior. This means the subjects in the no-model control condition did not know there was a norm. We therefore cannot tell if the differences in self-denying behavior between the experimental and control group are due to the modeling process, to the model's communication of the norm, or both. This issue could be resolved by introducing a control condition in which the subjects observe no model but are told what the standard of self-reward is. Very likely, these subjects would reward themselves less often than those who were totally in the dark about the standards. [There is no direct evidence for this but it seems likely in view of Bandura and Perloff's (1967) finding that children who are instructed to set their own performance standards and reward themselves when they attain it tend to set high standards and to adhere to them even in the absence of any social surveillance.] How such a control group would compare with subjects who were exposed to models using stringent standards remains to be seen. Until such a comparison is made, definitive conclusions cannot be drawn.

Deferment of Gratification. Still another aspect of inhibition and self-control that has been studied experimentally in relation to imitative modeling is the ability of the child to defer immediate gratification in favor of more valued long-range satisfactions. In a series of studies by Mischel and his associates (Mischel, 1965) children have been confronted with real choices between immediately available but less valued objects and delayed but more valued ones. These investigations have shown that delay responses are relatively stable, tend to increase with age, and can be increased by decreasing the delay interval or raising the probability that the delayed choice will be forthcoming. Delaying gratification cannot be thought of as a direct indication of moral inhibition, since the motive remains self-gain; that is, the individual simply tolerates temporary frustration for greater pleasure in the future. It is thus more of an ego skill. The self-control involved, however, would clearly appear to be an important ingredient of moral acts requiring inhibition of unacceptable impulses, and there is empirical evidence for this: the ability to defer gratification has been found to relate positively to a laboratory index of resistance to temptation (Mischel and Gilligan, 1964) and a questionnaire measure of social responsibility (Mischel, 1961). Thus it may be viewed as a necessary, though probably not sufficient factor in moral action.

In a study on imitation and deferment of gratification by Bandura and Mischel (1965) fourth- and fifth-grade children were administered a series of 14 paired choices. Each pair consisted of a less valued item that could be obtained immediately or a more valued one that would not be available until 1 to 4 weeks later. The subjects were asked to choose one item from each pair and advised to choose carefully because they would actually receive 1 of the 14 items they selected—either on the same day or after the delay period indicated for their preference. Several weeks later the subjects were exposed to an adult model who made choices in a similar situation though with items more appropriate for adults. With high-delay children, the models consistently selected the immediately available items and in several instances commented briefly according to a prearranged script on the benefits of immediate self-reward (e.g., "Chess figures are chess figures. I can get much use out of the plastic ones right away."). In addition, after the fourth choice, the model casually summarized his immediate-gratification philosophy of life as follows: "You probably have noticed that I am a person who likes things now. One can spend so much time in life waiting that one never gets around to really living. I find that it is better to make the most of each moment or life will pass you by." With low-delay children the model consistently selected the more valued, delayed items. The model likewise commented periodically on the virtues of self-imposed delay (e.g., "The wooden chess figures are of much better quality, more attractive, and will last longer. I'll wait two weeks for the better ones.") and expounded his postponement-of-gratification philosophy of life in the following manner: "You have probably noticed that I am a person who is willing to forego having fewer or less valuable things now, for the sake of more and bigger benefits later. I usually find that life is more gratifying when I take that carefully into account." Immediately after observing the model the children were individually administered another set of 14 choices which differed somewhat from the original set. To test for stability of the altered delay pattern, the children were also readministered the original set of 14 choices between 4 and 5 weeks later.

Substantial modifications were obtained in both the immediate postexposure test and the later test. The effects of the model were most pronounced for the children who initially showed a preference for delayed rewards. These children showed a marked shift toward a preference for immediate and less valued rewards after observing a model who favored immediate gratification. For the subjects who initially exhibited a disposition toward immediate rewards—a more important group for our purposes since they shifted toward increased self-control—the findings are less clear-cut. On the one hand, these subjects did show an increased willingness to wait for more highly valued rewards after observing a model who exhibited such a preference, both immediately after exposure to the model and in the later test, whereas a control group of comparable subjects who did not observe a model shifted significantly only in the postexposure test. On the other hand, when a direct comparison was made, the experimental and control groups did not differ significantly in either the immediate or the later test, a finding which resembles those obtained in the modeling studies already discussed.[37]

Another problem of interpretation in this study stems from the fact that the model gave a convincing philosophy and rationale for his act, which means that the subjects may have shifted their preference because they were persuaded by these arguments. Indeed, a third experimental group which did not see the model but heard his recorded comments shifted just as much as the group that did see the model. The finding is no less interesting if the model's arguments are the important factor, especially in view of the long-range effects demonstrated, but the usual imitative modeling notions would not apply. Still another possibility is that the subjects perceived the model's behavior as defining the socially acceptable norm in such choice-making situations, and then merely shifted their preference accordingly. This is plausible particularly since the experimenter was present while the subjects made their choices (although the model had left).

With these conceptual and methodological qualifications, we would tentatively conclude that observing models can increase the child's willingness to forgo immediate gratification when this is clearly in the interest of still greater gratification in the future. It would be

---

[37] A possible problem in the design of the experiment should be mentioned. In the initial testing, the children were told they would actually receive one of their choices. To maintain the trustworthiness of the experimenter this promise was kept, the payoff item being selected in advance. Thus (assuming some consistency in their choices) most of the low-delay children must have received their choices that same day. By the time several weeks had passed and they were exposed to the model, many of them may have found that their friends in the high-delay group had in the meantime received their choices, *which were more desirable.* The low-delay children would then have entered the modeling situation already favorably disposed to the future orientation espoused by the model, since they knew the experimenter was trustworthy and would keep his promise to give them the more desirable alternative if they chose it. This might account for at least some of their shift. It might also explain the otherwise puzzling finding that the low-delay control subjects, who observed no model, shifted just as much as the experimental subjects in the postexposure test. These control subjects too may have found out that the experimenter kept his promise.

worthwhile to conduct a similar study in which a model gives a well developed rationale for self-denying behavior that does not so clearly serve his own interests.

* * *

The most clear-cut conclusion to emerge from our analysis of the experimental findings on imitative modeling is that the direct observation of a model who yields to temptation and deviates from a social norm or prohibition has a disinhibiting effect on the observer, whether the model is rewarded or not.[38] The evidence is inconclusive, however, as to whether a model who behaves in an inhibitory or self-denying way, or is punished for violating a norm or prohibition, contributes to inhibition or self-denial. Punishment to the model does appear capable of inhibiting the response tendency previously aroused by the model's deviating behavior, but the research to date has not shown that it can raise the child's level of control beyond the baseline that existed before exposure to the model (except possibly when in the service of greater future gratification). Stated differently, there is far more evidence that the observation of models is capable of undermining the effects of the child's past socialization in impulse control and self-denial than that it is an effective means of furthering these aspects of moral development. In brief, it appears that models can more readily reduce than increase the child's inhibition of impulse expression. There is also evidence that inhibitions resulting from modeling influences are highly vulnerable to counterinfluences such as the presence of self-indulging models. If this analysis is correct, the laboratory findings are generally consistent with the few naturalistic findings pertaining to identification, which also provide little support for the view that identification is a significant factor in the development of an internal moral orientation.

We have no ready explanation for these findings. The laboratory research does sug-

gest, however, that the failure to imitate a model's self-denying behaviors is more likely due to motivational factors than to deficiencies in cognitive and other capacities since the subjects were able to imitate the models, sometimes in remarkable detail, when self-denial was not involved. The mere observing of models thus may not be enough to arouse sufficiently powerful motives to overcome the child's tendency toward self-gratification. Furthermore, as will be seen, prior nurturant interactions which may increase imitation of neutral acts are ineffective when it comes to self-denying behaviors. It may well be that identificatory motives powerful enough to overcome self-gratification tendencies cannot easily be produced in the typical laboratory experiment with models who are strangers to the child. Though such motives may exist in relation to the parent, we have suggested earlier that the paucity of relations thus far found between parent identification and morality may be due to the fact that the parents' moral attributes are not ordinarily manifested in actions or in words.

Perhaps the virtues of the experimental and naturalistic approaches can best be combined by adapting Mussen and Parker's (1965) procedure of using the subject's own parent as the model. The parent could then display inhibitory and self-denying behaviors to the child in more sharply defined form than is usually done in the home. He could, for example, communicate the basis of his action choice—perhaps including explicit verbalization of his temptation to deviate, which is rare in the natural setting—in terms that articulate directly with the child's needs. This would provide a relatively clear test of the possible, though not necessarily the actual effectiveness of identification in eliciting self-denying behavior in the child. It would be most illuminating to see if the findings on aggression inhibition and resistance to temptation are different when the child's parent—rather than a stranger—is the model. A still further refinement would be to include an independent assessment of the child's motive to identify with the parent and then see if this affects the extent to which he actually imitates her self-denying behavior in the laboratory. Such a design might allow for the most valid test of the possible effectiveness of a self-denying model.

---

[38] There is also evidence in a study by Kimbrell and Blake (1958) that the disinhibiting effects of models increases with the intensity of the observer's drive. College students who were made very thirsty eating crackers and Mexican hot sauce were found to be influenced by peer models, who violated a sign prohibiting drinking water from a fountain, to a greater extent than students who were made less thirsty.

Regarding punishment to a deviating model, the research thus far has dealt exclusively with power-assertive punishment. As we have seen, the results are unclear as to whether this type of punishment has an inhibiting effect on the observer. We wish to point out that even if the results were clear they would still have little or no bearing on internalization, since the most likely motive for the inhibitory behavior would be the child's fear that he too will otherwise be punished. We would suggest that future investigators take the cue from the naturalistic parent-child research reviewed earlier, and have the model "punished" with inductions rather than power assertions. This should provide a better test of the possible role of imitative modeling in internalization.

Another recommendation for future research is to heighten the motivation to deviate so that even subjects not exposed to models will deviate sufficiently for the effects of modeling to be demonstrated, that is, the "ceiling effect" will be reduced. This might be accomplished by such procedures as preselecting subjects who are relatively uninhibited and making certain they are at ease in the experimental situation, making the rewards of yielding to temptation much greater, and providing instigations to aggression following exposure to the model.

We conclude only that a great deal more research is needed before a definitive statement about the role of identificatory and modeling processes in moral development may be made. We have pointed up some problems in interpreting the laboratory findings. The naturalistic findings are also limited since they are based on only one study and deal with a conscious type of identification. It thus remains possible an unconscious type such as that postulated in psychoanalytic theory does make a significant contribution to moral development. It is also possible that identification relates to moral attributes which have not been studied but are nonetheless important such as resistance to external pressures to deviate from one's standards. Finally, though the evidence thus far suggests that identification and imitation may not play a major role in the self-denying aspects of moral development, it is possible they are important in faciliating the acquisition of behaviors that are in the service of goals which

the child shares with the model such as language and other ego skills as well as certain readily visible attributes of sex roles.[39]

Antecedents of Identification. Any discussion of the antecedents of identification must seem anticlimatic after the preceding section, which suggests the possibility that identification may have little bearing on moral development. Because identification has long been assumed to be important, however, and because it may relate to aspects of morality other than those which have been investigated, we shall withhold final judgment and briefly review the findings bearing on its antecedents.

In the literature the concept of identification as originally defined in psychoanalytic theory has been modified and molded to fit each author's theoretical preference, with the result that a variety of subtly different notions has guided the empirical research. With each investigator stressing one or another aspect of identification, the measures used have been many and varied and there has been little overlap between those used in the different studies.

Studies relating parental practices to the following indices of parent identification are included in this review: actual similarity between parent and child (Payne and Mussen, 1956); similarity as perceived by the child (Faigin, 1952; Hollenberg, 1952); a combination of conscious motivation to emulate and perceived similarity (Hoffman and Saltzstein, 1967). Also included are two studies using a fantasy index of identification—doll play acting out of the parent role (Sears, 1953; Hoffman, 1963b). The subjects in these two studies were preschool children, who are young enough for it to be assumed that taking the parent role in doll play reflects the child's identification with *his* parent and not merely with adult figures in general or with an abstract conception of the parental role. Not included are studies using appropriate sex-typing as an index of identification. These studies assume that sex-typing is a consequent of parent identification and therefore an adequate measure of it (Levin and Sears, 1956; Bronson, 1959; Mussen and Distler, 1959, 1960). This assumption may be criticized on

[39] The impulse denial often associated with masculine development, however, may not be so readily acquired through identification.

the grounds that appropriate sex-typing may result from other developmental processes such as identification with persons of the same sex other than the parent, or even from sex-role defined interaction with the parent of the *opposite* sex (Johnson, 1963).

The variables pertaining to parental practices are the same as those used in the research on moral development reported earlier: power assertion, love withdrawal, induction, and affection.

The results are summarized for mothers in Table 5 and for fathers in Table 6. The findings are fairly clear-cut and consistent. Identification with the mother relates negatively to power assertion and positively to affection. There is also some evidence that boys tend to identify with mothers who use induction discipline and fathers who are affectionate.

This general pattern of a positive relation between affection and identification is consistent with the findings in several laboratory studies of imitative modeling. In the earliest of these a prior nurturant interaction with the model was found to increase the child's tendency to imitate the model's neutral verbal and stylistic acts (Bandura and Huston, 1961). A similar finding was obtained by Mussen and Parker (1965), who used the child's own mother as a model. In this study the mother's general nurturance to the child, as measured by judges' ratings of interview responses, related positively to the child's ten-

dency to imitate certain mannerisms she deliberately expressed in a laboratory situation. Finally, Sgan (1967) found that a continuing nurturant interaction with a model produced more imitation of the model's picture preferences than nurturance followed by its withdrawal.

On the other hand, the children in the Mussen and Parker study did not imitate their mother's more effortful and task-relevant behaviors. Similarly, prior nurturant interactions have been found to have no effect on the child's imitation of aggressive or charitable acts (Bandura and Huston, 1961; Rosenhan and White, 1967), both of which tend to be imitated equally with or without a nurturant interaction. And there is some evidence that nurturance may actually contribute negatively to behavior involving self-denial: Bandura, Grusec, and Menlove (1967) found that a prior nurturant interaction decreased the child's adoption of the model's high standards of performance and self-reward.

Thus the evidence from both the naturalistic and laboratory research is that the child is more likely to emulate an adult who is nurturant than one who is not, but only with respect to behaviors that require little if any effort or self-denial.

Anaclitic Identification and Identification with the Aggressor. In the Hoffman and Saltzstein (1968) study it was possible to make further tests bearing more specifically on the

Table 5. Mother's Child-Rearing Practices and Identification

Power Assertion		Love Withdrawal		Induction		Affection		
−	? M [5]	−	13 G [10]	+	13 B [10] o	+	? M	[5]
−	? M [11]	0	13 B [10]	0	13 G [10] o	+	13 BG	[10]
−	4 M [9]							
−	13 BG [10]							

Key to symbols in Table 3.

Table 6. Father's Child-Rearing Practices and Identification

Power Assertion		Love Withdrawal		Induction		Affection		
0	4 M [9]	0	13 BG [10]	0	13 BG [10] o	+	5 B	[15]
0	13 BG [10]					+	10 B	[8]
						+	15 B	[14]
						0	13 BG	[10]

Key to symbols in Table 3.

concepts of anaclitic identification and identification with the aggressor. According to the theoretical formulation discussed earlier, anaclitic identification should be fostered by love withdrawal from an affectionate parent. This was tested by investigating the relation between love withdrawal and identification for the children whose parents were rated in the upper quartile on affection. No relation was obtained, which casts doubt on the notion that anaclitic identification results from withdrawal of love in the discipline encounter. Perhaps a more extreme form of loss of love such as occurs during prolonged separation is needed, as suggested in Freud's original formulation.

A similar procedure was used for identification with the aggressor, which might be expected to result from the use of power assertion by an affectionate parent. (Power assertion without compensating affection might lead the child simply to avoid and thus not be influenced by the parent.) No relation was obtained between identification and power assertion in the high-affection group, which suggests that identification with the aggressor is not a result of punitiveness in the discipline encounter. There is some contrary evidence, however. Preschool children with power assertive parents have been found to be power assertive toward their peers (Hoffman, 1960). And in a recent laboratory study by Mischel and Grusec (1966), preschool children were found to reproduce the aversive behaviors of an adult model that had been directed toward them initially; they expressed these behaviors toward another child, provided they had a prior nurturant interaction with the model.[40] Perhaps identification with the aggressor does occur as a result of the child's experiences in the discipline encounter, but as a form of subliminal behavioral imitation rather than the conscious emulation process tapped in the Hoffman and Saltzstein study.

Consideration for Others

In contrast to the voluminous research on moral prohibitions, very little has been done on the development of altruism and consideration for others. This disinterest is perhaps a reflection of certain value orientations in Western society. Though the ethical norms of our traditional religions stress the importance of altruism and consideration, the striving individualism of the culture places obstacles in the way of such behavior. Western psychological theory has also evolved along lines antithetical to giving consideration a central place in personality. This is most evident in psychoanalytical theory, which has had the greatest impact on the moral development research. Psychoanalysis has generally assumed that the individual's willingness to give up more than he gains involves the suppression and transformation of primitive impulses and self-oriented motives, all in the service of avoiding guilt or anxiety. This view also fits well with the behavioristic assumption that complex motives such as altruism derive from the operation of more basic biological drives.

Recent years have seen a gradual change in this view, which reflects certain broader changes in psychological theory—mainly the psychoanalytic shift toward ego psychology and the newly won respectability of concepts pertaining to growth and mastery strivings which do not derive from deficiency motives (White, 1959).

Before proceeding to the research on consideration for others, the concept must be defined and its difference from moral prohibitions made clear. It is useful to view consideration for others in the broader existential framework of how one handles the universal conflict between one's own rights and desires, and one's obligations to others. Because the self is not identical with the other, inevitable conflicts arise in which the choice between serving the self or the other must be made. In these situations the individual who has

[40] Two other sets of findings have sometimes been cited as illustrative of identification-with-the-aggressor: (1) the positive relation between power assertion and aggression that has consistently been obtained in the parent-child research (Allinsmith, 1960; Becker et al., 1962; Hoffman, 1960; Hoffman and Saltzstein, 1967); and (2) the modeling studies by Bandura and his associates in which the child has been shown to emulate in fine detail the aggressive behavior of adult models. The problem with (1) is that the relation can just as readily be explained by the notion that power assertion frustrates the child and thus instigates the aggression, which is then displaced to others. And (2) is limited because the model's aggression is not directed toward the subject, that is, the child does not adopt a mode of aggression that was originally directed toward him.

internalized the standard of consideration will be motivated to take the other's welfare into account. On observing someone in need, he feels an urge to help, even though this will cost him more than he will gain and may often require self-sacrifice or deprivation while serving no selfish instrumental purpose. Whether or not he actually resolves the moral conflict by making the necessary sacrifice and acting on the other's behalf is a more complex matter, involving his control system, competing motives, and other situational factors.

The standards of altruism and consideration are similar to moral prohibitions in one important respect: they require a certain amount of self-denial or self-sacrifice. A person who behaves altruistically may not realize this because of a generalized guilt that precludes awareness of his own impulses and desires. To the extent this occurs, his altruism may be, as suggested in psychoanalytic theory, a mere reflection of repression and self-denial or perhaps a means of making restitution for transgressions dimly felt to have been committed in the past. Since some conscious or unconscious self-denial is invariably involved, the process in acquiring altruistic standards should bear some resemblance to the internalization of moral prohibitions. They should also differ, for two reasons. First, the self-denial involved in altruism and consideration is clearly in the service of another's welfare, which is usually not true of prohibitions. Second, altruism and consideration do not refer primarily to orientations toward one's own transgressions but to going out of one's way to help others when one has not been responsible for their plight.

Two empirical studies have attempted to relate parental practices to the child's consideration for others. In one, a study of preschool children (Hoffman, 1963b), parent data were obtained from interviews in which the mother gave a fully detailed account of her interaction with the child the day before the interview. The interviews were coded for the four types of discipline already discussed: power assertion, love withdrawal, induction, and other-oriented induction. The other-oriented induction techniques reported referred most often to the implications of the child's behavior for someone other than the parent— usually the child's sibling (all the children had one younger sibling) or a friend. Scores

were also obtained for affection (the amount of pleasurable, nondisciplinary interaction between parent and child). The measure of consideration for others, based on nursery school observations, was the frequency with which the child gave direct and unsolicited help to another child in distress, or used influence techniques which showed awareness of the other child's needs. The results were that none of the parent measures related to the child's consideration for others. When the sample was dichotomized on the basis of the mother's use of power assertion, however, other-oriented induction was found to be positively related to consideration in the low-power-assertion group, and negatively related in the high-power-assertion group.

The measure of consideration used in this study was a compromise. An ideal index would tap the extent to which the child makes a personal sacrifice, perhaps resists external counterpressures, or at least goes out of his way to help another person. This behavior, moreover, would be motivated internally and not by self-seeking instrumental goals, and it would not merely reflect a general pattern of inhibition and self-denial. Since spontaneous instances of such behavior are rare in young children, it was necessary to use a less strict definition. It was possible, however, to test whether the behaviors coded as consideration were part of a general self-seeking orientation or a pattern of overcontrol and inhibition. This was done by relating the child's consideration score to the frequency with which he spontaneously initiated social contacts, expressed hostility, and sought nurturance from others in the nursery school. No significant relations were obtained in the lower-power-assertion group (though some were in the high-power-assertion group), which suggests the measure of consideration may have been satisfactory for the subsample in which induction related positively to consideration.

In the second study (Hoffman and Saltzstein, 1967) the subjects were seventh-grade children and the data on consideration were provided by nominations made by classmates of the child most likely to "care about the other children's feelings" and "defend a child being made fun of by the group." The parent measures have already been described (see Appendix). The findings for girls fit exactly the pattern obtained for moral prohibitions: consideration related positively to induction and affection, negatively to power assertion, and bore no relation to love withdrawal. This suggests that consideration in girls may often develop as part of a general pattern of internalization of moral prohibitions. There was one additional finding for consideration that was not obtained for prohibitions, however. When separate scores were obtained for other-oriented induction depending on whether the parent pointed up the consequences of the child's behavior for the parent or for the child's peers, the score for peers related positively to consideration only, whereas the score for parents related positively to both consideration and the prohibition indices. Taken together with the findings in the preschool study mentioned earlier, this indicates that inductions regarding the child's peers may play a special role in the development of consideration for others in girls. One possibility is that in using these techniques the mother serves as a considerate model.

The findings for boys were quite different and difficult to comprehend. Consideration related positively to power assertion as well as affection, negatively to love withdrawal, and did not relate to induction. Several explanations are possible. One is that boys are not responsive to the mother as a model of consideration. Another is that consideration is not a likely internalized standard for boys. Some unpublished evidence for this was obtained with a measure of values administered to the children in that same study. The largest sex difference found was on the consideration item ("goes out of his way to help others"); the boys obtained much lower scores than the girls. Still another possibility is that the consideration measure tapped something quite different for the two sexes. Indeed it was found that the part of the measure dealing with defending a child against the group contributed most to the consideration scores obtained by boys, and the part dealing with caring about other children's feelings contributed most for girls. It is possible that defending an underdog has an aggressive anti-authority edge to it, which might result in part from experiencing power assertive discipline in the home. This possibility is also suggested by the finding reported by Elmis and Milgram (1966) that male college stu-

dents who resisted requests by an adult experimenter to apply electric shock to a peer reported that their parents used power-assertive discipline when they were children more often than those who submitted to the experimenter's requests.

Laboratory Studies on Consideration for Others. As with internalized prohibitions, the laboratory studies on consideration deal with variables different from those used in the more naturalistic research. A recent study by Aronfreed and Paskal (1966) used a complex design to test a two-step theory of the process by which children learn to respond sympathetically and come to the aid of someone in distress. According to this theory the child must first have the experience of observing the distress of others in very close association with his own direct experience of distress. This results in his own empathic distress becoming conditioned to cues from others indicating their distress. Then he must acquire specific overt acts which can be used to relieve the distress of others as well as his own empathic distress.

In phase 1 of the experiment 7- to 8-year-old girls were given 12 trials in which they classified a number of small toy replicas of real objects as to whether they were most appropriate for a "house," a "dog," or a "school." To indicate their choice they pushed one of three levers. The middle one, for "dog," was rarely correct. During these trials the subject and the adult female experimenter wore earphones. On half the trials the subject heard a highly aversive noise, which began after she made her classification response and continued for 7 seconds.[41] She had previously been told that the experimenter would hear an even louder noise. To show distress the experimenter held her head starting 3 seconds before and continuing throughout the 7-second period during which the subject heard the noise.

Immediately after the child's empathic distress had thus been conditioned to distress cues from the experimenter, phase 2 began. This was designed to enable the child to acquire a sympathetic act by observing a model perform it. According to Aronfreed, this must

[41] These trials were randomly selected and not contingent on the child's choice, so that they would not be seen as punishment for a particular choice.

be done under conditions in which the child experiences at least a minimal amount of pain reduction as a result of the model's act. Accordingly, phase 2 consisted of another series of 12 classification trials in which the experimenter, no longer wearing earphones, indicated her own classification of each toy immediately after the child classified it. The child had previously been told that the experimenter might in the course of making her own choices turn off the noise in the child's earphones. When the child completed each classification, the experimenter would appear to think for a couple of seconds with her hand poised above one of the two outer levers which the child knew by now were most often correct. The experimenter actually chose one of these on six trials. On the remaining six, however, the child began to hear noise through her earphones as the experimenter began making her choice. The noise lasted only 3 seconds since the experimenter moved farily rapidly to depress the middle lever, which turned it off. At the same time she commented that she chose the middle lever to terminate the noise in the child's earphones. She thus served as a model who clearly surrendered the opportunity to make a correct classification in order to perform a "sympathetic" act.

In the final (test) phase of the experiment the subject did not wear earphones and was given the experimenter's prior role of classifying each toy following its classification by another child. The other child, who wore earphones, was previously trained to show distress by holding her head in her hands on half the classification trials, just as the experimenter did in phase 1.[42]

Four control groups experienced a similar three-phase sequence with certain variations. In the main control group the only difference was that in phase 1 the experimenter showed distress on the six trials in which the subject

did *not* hear the noise, that is, there was no pairing of the subject's distress and the distress cue from the experimenter. In the second control group the noise heard by the subject was reduced in intensity; in the third, the other child in the test phase wore earphones but gave no sign of distress; and in the fourth he neither wore earphones nor showed distress.

The major finding was that in the test phase the subjects in the experimental group were more likely than those in any of the control groups to make the "sympathetic" response of pushing the middle lever. Certain problems of interpretation should be noted before conclusions are drawn. One stems from the experimenter's beginning to show distress, in phase 1, 3 seconds before the subject actually experienced pain. After one or two such trials the subject must have felt some anticipatory anxiety on subsequent trials when the experimenter gave these distress cues—anxiety that would have been felt even if the experimenter had not continued giving the cues for the 7 seconds during which the subject experienced pain. The crucial variable might thus not be the sharing of pain. (To test for this possibility would require another control condition in which the experimenter only gave the distress cues for the 3 seconds before the subject experienced pain.) Another reason why the sharing of pain might not be needed to account for the findings is that the subjects in the main control condition, who alternately experienced pain or distress cues from the experimenter, must have quickly realized that one—and only one—person always experienced pain and that the experimenter's doing so was the precondition for their own being spared. They must therefore have felt some relief whenever the experimenter showed distress. It may have been this, rather than the lack of a shared-pain experience, that led the control subjects to make relatively few sympathetic responses. A further limitation stems from the fact that the experimenter remained in the room throughout the test trials. Thus the children may have operated the middle lever merely for the purpose of doing what the experimenter expected, in order to gain approval. Pending clarification of these issues, this experiment may be viewed as providing suggestive evidence for Aronfreed's hypothesis that

---

[42] If the subject made the sympathetic choice of the middle lever, the other child immediately raised her head in response to the termination of the noise in her earphones, so that the subject's choice actually removed the sign of distress given by the other child. But if the subject made the nonsympathetic, task-oriented choice of one of the two outer levers, the other child did not raise her head until 5 seconds after the subject had operated the lever.

a prior experience of shared pain will help foster the learning of sympathetic behavior.

In another experiment, using 6- to 8-year-old girls and an adult female experimenter, Aronfreed and Paskal (1965) sought to test a related theory of how "altruistic" (as distinguished from sympathetic) behavior might be acquired. According to these writers, altruism or self-sacrificing behavior can be enhanced by first attaching, through contiguous association, positive affect in the child with expressions of joy in the receiver. Expressions of joy on the part of others then become stimuli for the arousal of positive affect in the child and thereby acquire the power to reinforce his altruistic acts. In the training phase, which was designed to produce the necessary association between affect and expressive cues of joy, the experimenter showed the child how to operate two levers of a box. The box was automated to dispense a small candy or turn on a light, on a randomized schedule, depending on which lever was operated. During the initial demonstration the child simply watched while the experimenter varied her choices in an unpredictable sequence. When candy was dispensed the experimenter calmly collected it. When the light was activated, however, she looked at it, smiled, and at the same time used a pleased and excited tone of voice to give one of four exclamations all of which were roughly equivalent to, "There is the light!" Immediately following these expressive cues she gave the child a firm hug and smiled broadly at her, trying to make these acts appear to be a reflection of her own extreme pleasure at seeing the light.

During the test phase that followed immediately, the child operated the levers for many trials. The experimenter now sat across from her, facing the rear of the box, with her gaze fixed on another light. This light was visible to the experimenter only, although its presence was made known to the child. The child was also told (1) that the light would go on whenever she chose the light-producing lever and (2) that she could keep all of the candy which came out of the box (although it was not to be consumed until the task was complete). Whenever the child chose to operate the light-producing lever the experimenter smiled at the light and exclaimed, "There is the light!" The previous conjunction of these expressive cues with the

child's direct experience of affection during the training trials had a marked effect on the child's choices during the test. Children who were exposed to this conjunction were more willing to forgo the candy-producing choice than children who were exposed to either the cues or the affection but not both.

Midlarsky and Bryan (1967) used essentially the same procedure with one important improvement. Following the training and test phases, there was an "anonymous donor" test in which the experimenter was not present. Each subject was asked to donate candy to "needy children whose parents can't afford to buy them any candy" by placing some of her own candy through the slot in a half-filled donation box. The subject was told that the size of donation was her decision and she need not donate any candy if she did not choose to do so. She was also informed that no one would ever know what she decided and the experimenter would wait for her outside of the experimental room.

The first set of findings replicated those obtained in the Aronfreed and Paskal study. Furthermore, the effects carried over into the anonymous phase of the study. That is, the children who had experienced both the experimenter's hugs and expressive cues contributed more candy to charity than the children in the control groups. These findings suggest that an altruistic norm—and not just a specific lever-pushing response—was learned and expressed in the absence of authority. Midlarsky and Bryan, however, after doing some internal analyses of their data and reexamining their procedures, conclude that the mechanism underlying the charitable behavior may have been direct reinforcement rather than secondary reinforcement as postulated by Aronfreed and Paskal. Their argument is as follows. Before the anonymous test the subject's supplies of candies were replenished in order to equate the amount of candy for the different experimental conditions. Naturally, those who had sacrificed candies for the experimenter in the prior test were given more and they may have experienced this as reward for their sacrificing behavior. Furthermore, they may have anticipated further reward for such behavior since the experimenter was outside the room waiting to escort them back to the classroom. Another hypothesis suggested by Midlarsky and Bryan is that the training programs acted to modify the incentive values attached to the candies. That is, the experimenter provided a warm, kind, and nurturant model who virtually ignored the candies and this low incentive value might have been adopted by the children.

A direct attempt to study the influence of a model on the child's altruistic behavior has been made by Rosenhan and White (1967). Fourth- and fifth-grade subjects played a bowling game—in which the scores had been programmed in advance—first taking turns with an adult model and later with no one else present. When the subject or the model obtained high scores he was awarded 5-cent gift certificates from a local department store. Each time the model won gift certificates he donated half of them to charity. The first time he won he said (ostensibly talking to himself), "I won. I believe I will give one certificate to the orphans each time I win." On subsequent winnings he said nothing when making donations. The findings were that almost half the subjects who observed the model contributed in his absence, whereas none of the control subjects who saw no model did so.[43] The occurrence of a prior positive or negative relationship with the model had no effect on the child's altruistic behavior.[44]

The potential importance of this study lies in the demonstration that children can learn in a laboratory setting to donate a valued commodity to charity in the absence of adult authority. This suggests that altruistic be-

[43] A secondary finding of interest was that nearly 90% of the children who contributed in the model's absence had previously done so in his presence. Rosenhan and White conclude from this that rehearsal as well as observation of the model may be necessary for the internalization of the altruistic norm. This seems reasonable, although it is also possible that the subjects who gave in the experimenter's absence would have done so even without the intervening step of giving in his presence. The design of the study did not allow for this possibility.

[44] It was found, however, that more girls who had some kind of a prior relationship (either positive or negative) with the model donated in the model's presence than those who had no relationship. But when the model was absent the findings were reversed: more girls who had *not* had a prior relationship gave than those who had.

havior may be more readily taught than heretofore assumed. Before accepting this conclusion three flaws in the design should be considered and taken into account in any future replication. First, the results could be due to the low salience that the donation box and the possibility of a charitable act may have had for the control subjects. The box, along with an appropriate sign and picture of children in ragged attire, was placed on a table near the bowling game. After explaining the game the experimenter "casually, as if as an afterthought, called the subject's and model's attention to the box, explaining that some gift certificates were being collected for some orphans and if 'either of you would like to give some of your certificates to them you can, but you do not have to.'" This was all that was communicated to the control subjects about giving and it may not have occurred to them as something to consider seriously, which could explain why not one of them made a contribution. Second, the attempt to create anonymity may not have been successful. Though left alone, to make a contribution the subject had to put his donation into a box. Despite the fact that 10 certificates were kept in the box at all times for the express purpose of allaying any suspicion, it seems likely that any child in the age group studied who was suspicious would readily surmise that the adults could figure out whether or not he contributed. Third, there is the question of just how much of a sacrifice the child felt he was making by donating a gift certificate worth only a few cents which had been given to him just a few moments earlier. There was no real loss, as would have been the case, for example, had the child given up a possession of his own which had value to him. This same limitation, of course, also applies to the other studies of altruism discussed in this section.

The preceding experiments are important pioneering efforts that demonstrate children can be trained to perform altruistic and considerate acts in a laboratory setting. They also indicate that traditional learning concepts may be extended to encompass such training and suggest some of the mechanisms that may be involved, for example, primary or secondary reinforcement, observation learning, desire to please an adult. They do not enable us to ascertain which are the mechanisms of central importance, however, nor do they indicate the extent to which the acts become part of the child's internalized moral orientation. These remain as tasks for future research.

Methodological Issues

Our major conclusion—that moral development is associated positively with induction and affection and negatively with power-assertion—derives almost entirely from the naturalistic research. A common problem in this type of research is that no definitive conclusions may be drawn about causal direction of the relations obtained. Any solution to this will have to wait for application of longitudinal studies or the experimental method. Relevant longitudinal studies have not yet been made and, as we have seen, the laboratory studies have not typically followed the leads suggested in the naturalistic research. Nevertheless, there is some scattered support for the proposition that discipline affects moral development rather than the reverse. First, despite the lack of relevant longitudinal studies, a number of the findings reported in Table 3 bear on the parent's reported use of discipline in the past when the child was very young. If these reports are assumed to be reasonably valid, to argue that the child's moral development elicits different discipline patterns (rather than the reverse) necessitates the further assumption that the child's morality has not changed basically from early childhood.[45] This is an unlikely assumption in view of common observations (e.g., about the child's changing acceptance of responsibility for transgression) and the findings about the developmental course of moral judgments obtained by Piaget and his followers. Second,

[45] There is some suggestive evidence for the face validity of these reports in the Hoffman and Saltzstein data in which the parents reported both their current practices (the children were seventh graders at the time) and the practices used when the children were "about five years old." Significant positive correlations were obtained between the techniques reported in the past and the present, yet the parents as a group reported using significantly more power assertion and less induction in the past than in the present. This is precisely the pattern to be expected if the reports were valid.

we may note in the table that whereas the findings for power assertion are consistent across the entire age range studied and include children as young as 4 years of age, the findings for induction are not consistent until after the preschool years. This makes sense when we consider that a certain level of cognitive development is necessary for the child to respond appropriately to induction. Third, there is evidence that the parent's discipline choice is influenced by relatively enduring characteristics of the parent and by the marital relation, neither of which can readily be derived from the child's behavior. Thus in the study by Hoffman (1963) the mother's use of power assertion appeared to be partly a reaction to her husband's power-assertive behavior toward her. And an unpublished finding obtained in the Hoffman and Saltzstein (1967) study was a significant positive relation between the mother's acceptance of humanistic values and her use of induction techniques. Fourth, in one of the studies reporting a positive relation between power assertion and the child's aggressive behavior toward peers (Hoffman, 1960) power assertion did not relate to the child's aggressiveness at home nor was it used any more frequently in response to aggression than to other deviant behaviors, which suggests that power assertion leads to aggression, not the reverse. Fifth, the view that the parent's discipline choice results from the child's moral development rather than the reverse would still leave unanswered the question of what led to the moral development in the first place. One of the most plausible answers to this question is that the parent who uses induction discipline often expresses similar views in the child's presence outside the discipline situation; and the child's identification with the parent in these situations is the important factor rather than the effects of the discipline. This explanation, which cannot be ruled out, appears to be unlikely because the identification and imitation research—both naturalistic and experimental—gives it so little support. As a final point, the possibility that the pattern obtained is the spurious result of IQ or social class, both of which relate to parent discipline and morality, can be tentatively discounted on the basis of findings obtained in the one study which controlled these variables (Hoffman and Saltzstein,

1967).[46] Although none of these points alone is convincing, taken together they constitute a reasonable case for assuming, until more definitive longitudinal and experimental evidence is available, that the direction of causality is from the child-rearing pattern obtained, to the child's moral development.

While the naturalistic research lacks the precision and controls needed for establishing causal direction and also for making a direct study of the psychological processes involved in socializing the child, the experimental research also has its limitations. Because laboratory experiments in this area have not generally been subject to intensive methodological critique, we have pointed up some of the shortcomings of this research throughout our discussion in the hope that this will stimulate improvement in future designs. Some of the more technical criticisms apply to specific studies only; others are more widely applicable. Among the latter are four which we believe should be given special attention.

First, the intensity of the parent-child relation is not adequately captured in the experiments in which the child interacts with a strange adult, nor is parental affection handled by having the adult spend a few minutes in prior nurturant interaction with the child. Second, the moral socialization process is often so drastically telescoped in the laboratory that its essential features appear to be lost. For example, the long-range interaction between parent and child, presumably involved in the acquisition of moral attributes such as self-criticism and resistance to temptation, is often represented by one interaction between experimenter and subject (e.g., some form of punishment followed by resistance to temptation). While a single interaction may be an appropriate way of simulating the child's immediate response to a parental technique, it provides a far less adequate characterization of the entire socialization process. Third, the subjects are typically old enough to possess the moral standards under study. This raises

[46] In this study IQ was found to relate positively to internalized moral judgments and consideration for others, negatively to confession, and negatively to parent identification. The high and low groups for these variables, within each social class group, were therefore matched on IQ. Since IQ did not relate to guilt, there was no need to control IQ in the guilt analysis.

the question of whether the experimental treatment actually produces a change in moral structure or merely serves to activate an already existing norm—a causality problem having much in common with the more visible one in the naturalistic research. Aronfreed is one of the very few investigators who have tried to cope with this problem, by employing a behavior in which the child could not possibly have previously been socialized, but his particular approach (using the label "blue" to refer to an act) is highly artificial and its relevance to the moral concept it was designed to tap (self-criticism) is questionable. A fourth problem, one that is very difficult to resolve, is that the experimental treatments are often more salient than the control treatments. This, of course, throws any theoretical interpretation of the findings into question.

Thus the naturalistic and experimental research both have their limitations. Progress can be expected to the degree these problems are recognized and eliminated, and each method used to its fullest advantage. Naturalistic research keeps us closer to real-life concepts and can perhaps give us a view of the relations that actually exist between antecedent and consequent conditions. Experimental research, on the other hand, may be needed to provide a close look at the processes which underlie transition and growth.

It is beyond the scope of this chapter to suggest experimental designs for the future, but, very generally, it does seem that several of the preceding problems might be handled by combining some of the features of the studies by Mussen and Parker (1965), Midlarsky and Bryan (1967), Bandura and Mischel (1965), and Turiel (1966). Thus the child's parent might be used as the experimental socialization agent, either in the home or laboratory setting; and four distinct phases might be included in the experimental design: (1) an initial one in which subjects are preselected on the basis of their readiness for the new standard or mode of behavior under study (ideally they would not quite be operating at the new level but have the necessary cognitive and other prerequisites); (2) one in which the child is exposed to the experimental treatment (e.g., discipline, punishment, model) designed to advance the child's moral level; (3) one which tests the child's immediate reaction or learning; and (4) a generalization test which is given sometime later and uses different test materials.

Theoretical Implications

If our conclusion that induction is a major contributing factor in moral development is correct, the central question for theoretical analysis to emerge from our review is: What processes underlie the effectiveness of inductions? In attempting to answer this question, the theories mentioned earlier that focus on the love-withdrawal aspect of nonpower-assertive techniques can be ruled out fairly quickly. Included are those theories that stress (1) the intense need for love, evoked by these techniques, which compels the child to behave in the parentally desired fashion or to identify with the parent; (2) the reinforcement of the child's corrective acts that results from the termination of love withdrawal at the onset of these acts. These theories are thrown into question by the absence of a relation between love withdrawal and the various moral indices.

One of the theories mentioned earlier suggests that the significant variable differentiating power-assertive and nonpower-assertive techniques is the difference in the model presented by the parent in using these techniques. Such a modeling effect, specific to the discipline encounter, remains a possibility despite the general findings on identification and imitation that suggest these may not be major processes in moral development. The research on consideration for others, for example, suggests that in using inductions pointing up the effect of the child's behavior on peers the mother may provide an effective positive model. This finding is limited to girls, however. Furthermore, the parent cannot be said to provide such a model when she points out the consequences of the child's behavior for herself, and yet this type of induction was found to relate positively to most of the moral indices. It would appear that modeling is not the basic mechanism through which induction has its effects, although, as will be seen later, we believe it does play a role.

More recent attempts to account for the effectiveness of nonpower-assertive discipline stress the cognitive aspects of the child's reaction to the parent's discipline. Notable among these is dissonance theory. When ap-

plied to discipline, as indicated earlier, the dissonance referred to is the cognitively experienced discrepancy between the child's desires and his overt behavior. The way in which the child reduces dissonance, however, according to the theory, results less from the cognitive or informational aspects of a discipline technique than from its power aspects. The greater the power, the more likely the child is to reduce dissonance by viewing his resolution to the dilemma (i.e., his "good" behavior) as having been imposed by the parent; the less power, the more likely he will be to view it as his own idea.

It is possible to incorporate induction into dissonance theory, however, by viewing it as providing the child with reasons for refraining from the prohibited act, and thus enabling him more easily to view himself as having refrained voluntarily. A problem in this formulation is that for the child to grasp the parent's explanation requires that he actively attend to it; this will make it difficult for him to ignore the fact that it originated with the parent. This problem may be resolved by focusing on the child's cognitive response in situations that occur a long time after the original discipline encounter has ended. That is, when he is faced with the same situation in the future the content of the induction may occur to him as a good reason for refraining from the act; while the fact that the reason originated with the parent in a discipline encounter may be forgotten. This selective memory should be facilitated by the fact that the informational aspect of induction is more salient in the discipline encounter and more easily represented in language than its relatively mild power aspect.

Even this modified formulation has two problems, which are inherent in dissonance theory. One is that it is confined to the impact of discipline which is (1) applied before the child has acted and (2) successful in achieving compliance. It is therefore best suited for explaining the antecedents of resistance to temptation and perhaps helping, sharing, and other considerate acts. It is not equipped to handle responses that occur after the deviant act, especially guilt to which inductions relate quite srongly. A perhaps more important limitation of the theory stems from its requirement that the child must not only comply, but a precarious balance of forces must exist to enable him to submit to parental pressures without knowing he has submitted. This would seem to require that he comply with the parent's first influence attempt because after that parents typically become more power assertive, thus making it more difficult for the child to deceive himself into thinking he complied of his own accord. Children do not ordinarily comply to their parent's initial influence attempts unless the issue is a relatively unimportant one. Despite these limitations we would tentatively conclude that dissonance theory may account in part for the relation between induction and certain aspects of morality but probably not guilt and other reactions to transgression.

To account for guilt, and perhaps the other moral indices as well, we offer an alternative theory which includes an affect-arousal component, empathy, in addition to the view that induction may provide the resources that help the child evaluate the rightness or wrongness of his behavior. This theory is also less sensitive than dissonance theory to the timing of the technique in relation to the child's behavior.

Any theory of discipline and its effects must take account of the fact that all discipline encounters have a great deal in common regardless of the particular technique used and, further, that most techniques are not unidimensional or mutually exclusive as may have been implied in our discussion thus far, but occur in combinations (e.g., love withdrawal plus induction). Thus some mutual influence in their effects is to be expected and all techniques are best viewed as having some power-assertive, love-withdrawing, and inductive qualities. For these reasons our theory will be presented in the framework of an analysis of the discipline encounter into what appears to us to be its most basic cognitive and emotional factors. This analysis is an extension of ideas we have presented elsewhere (Hoffman, 1960, 1963b; Hoffman and Saltzstein, 1967). It is intended not only to help explain the findings reported but to go beyond them to a more general discussion of the role of parental discipline in moral development.

First, any discipline encounter generates a certain amount of anger in the child by preventing him from completing or repeating a motivated act. Techniques with high power-assertive components are most apt to arouse

intense anger because they frustrate the child's need for autonomy as well as to complete the act. They dramatically underscore the extent to which the child's freedom is circumscribed by the superior power and resources of the adult world. This is no doubt exacerbated by the fact that power assertion is often applied abruptly with few explanations or compensations offered to the child. The empirical evidence for a positive relation between power assertion and anger has been summarized by Becker (1964).

Second, a discipline technique also provides the child with a model for discharging the anger, and may provide him with an object against which to discharge it. The disciplinary act itself constitutes the model the child may imitate, especially when it involves relatively direct forms of discharge rather than control of anger.

Third, as much animal and human learning research has shown, what is learned will depend on the stimuli to which the organism is compelled to attend. Discipline techniques explicitly or implicitly provide such a focus. Techniques with dominant love withdrawal or power-assertive components direct the child to the consequences of his behavior for the actor i.e., the child himself, and to the authority or contractual aspect of the parent-child relationship. Techniques in which induction is the salient component are more apt to focus his attention on the consequences of his actions for others—the parent, or some third party. This factor should be especially important in determining the cognitive aspects of the child's standards such as the bases of moral judgments. For example, if transgressions are followed by induction, the child will learn that the act was wrong because it did harm to others.

Fourth, to be effective the technique must enlist already existing emotional and motivational tendencies within the child. The most pervasive of these resources is the child's need for approval. This factor requires a generally high level of affection from the parent. The child who is accustomed to this may generally be unaware of a need for approval, but the disapproval conveyed in any discipline encounter disturbs his complacency and arouses the need at least to show that he is worthy of the parent's approval. The arousal must be sufficient to disengage the child from what he is doing and motivate him to attend and process the information contained in the inductive portion of the technique, as well as other cues in the situation signifying why his behavior is objectionable and what more suitable alternatives exist. Too much arousal, however, may produce intense feelings of anxiety over loss of love which reduce the child's "range of effective cue utilization" (Easterbrook, 1959) and are thus disfunctional to cognitive learning in the situation. The result may be a cognitively primitive response in which the child's act, the hostile impulse that led to it, and the pain cues emitted by the victim are all confounded and associated with anxiety.

All three types of discipline communicate some negative evaluation by the parent and are thus capable of arousing the child's need for approval. Techniques with pronounced love-withdrawing or power-assertive components often may be too highly arousing, however, and it may only be when these components are subdued, as in predominantly inductive techniques, that the need for approval is aroused to an optimal degree.[47] Inductions, furthermore, not only explain the consequence of the child's behavior, which may make the criticism appear to derive from the situation rather than negative parental feeling toward the child, but often also suggest corrective acts such as apology and reparation that give the child a ready means of regaining any lost approval.

Other motives may supplement the need for approval in disengaging the child from what he is doing and directing his attention

to the parent. One is the child's mastery strivings or effectance needs, which may at times be successfully elicited by the use of techniques that point out the behavior in question is the mature or grown-up thing to do. The child's expectations based on past discipline encounters will also play a role. If the parent often uses power assertion or love withdrawal, for example, the child may respond to inductions largely in terms of their implicit threat and thus overlook their cognitive elements. The affectionate parent who frequently uses inductions, on the other hand, may appear as a mediator between the child's wants and reality demands. Assuming the inductions typically do not obviously contradict reality as experienced by the child, he may view requests emanating from such a source as deriving from the requirements of the situation even at times when an explanation is not given.[48] The child's mastery striving may be involved here too; that is, through the frequent use of induction the parent may successfully communicate the expectation that the child is amenable to reason. The child then may experience a need to live up to this expectation.

The second emotional resource, empathy, has long been overlooked by psychologists as a possibly important factor in socialization.[49] Empathy has been observed in children to occur long before the child's moral controls are firmly established (e.g., Murphy, 1937).[50]

[47] The optimal amount of arousal depends on such situational factors as how involved the child is in what he is doing and how close he is to completion. In some cases the arousal needed to disengage the child may be too high for inductions to be effectively used.

This point bears a surface similarity to dissonance theory. The difference is that we refer to the optimal level of pressure for the child to attend and comprehend accurately the parent's message; dissonance theory refers to the optimal level of pressure for the child to comply without awareness of submitting so that he may later feel that he complied voluntarily. Stated differently, whereas the purpose of our optimal level is to maximize the child's cognitive operations in the discipline encounter, that of dissonance theory is to minimize it.

[48] Other factors, such as the legitimacy ascribed to the parent by his spouse and others, may also contribute to the child's view of him as an objective mediator of reality.

[49] As previously indicated, Piaget states that empathy is important in moral development but he does not incorporate it into his theoretical system.

[50] Whether the empathy is typically lost by adulthood is difficult to say. The studies by Berger (1962) and DiLollo and Berger (1965) indicate that college students will respond empathically when witnessing what appears to be the expression of pain in another student. Evidence has been presented by Lerner and Simmons (1966), on the other hand, which suggests that college students tend to reject and devaluate others in distress. Lerner's view is that this is part of a general need to believe in a just world in which individuals receive what they deserve. A possible reason for these discrepant results is that Berger and DiLollo and Berger used psycho-

We believe that it is a potentially important emotional resource because it adds to the aroused need for approval the pain the child vicariously experiences from having harmed another, thus intensifying his motivation to learn moral rules and control his impulses. Of the three types of discipline under consideration, induction—specifically other-oriented induction—seems most capable of enlisting the child's proclivities for empathy in the struggle to control his impulses. In our view, inductions serve two major purposes. First, they direct the child's attention to the other person's distress and explain its nature if this is not obvious (e.g., if it is psychological). This should often elicit an empathic response.[51] Second, they communicate to the child that he was responsible for the distress. How this is done depends on the situation and the child's cognitive capacities at the time. When he is very young it may only be possible to point up the consequences of his act, and this may need to be done immediately. With further cognitive development the parent may in addition explain why the child's behavior was not justified or point up the motives underlying the prior action of the victim, and the elapsed time between act and induction is less crucial. Without some communication of responsibility the child might respond empathically but dissociate himself from the causal act or resort to such defenses as denying it, minimizing its consequences, and imputing hostile intent to the victim in order to justify it. These evasions are especially likely in the young child whose empathy is a direct emotional response to the other's affective state, often with no accompanying understanding of what caused it, and whose cognitive processes are highly susceptible to the disruptive effects of the frustration and emotional involvement that led up to his deviant act. This may be why the preschool child, who frequently responds empathically to other children in distress (Murphy, 1937), rarely does so when he has caused the distress; and, if he does respond empathically, for ex-

ample, by crying along with the victim, he is seemingly oblivious to his own role.

Thus we are proposing that at a fairly young age the child is capable of both empathy and the awareness of being responsible for another's distress. He also knows the difference between accidental and intentional, and provoked and unprovoked acts. These responses do not naturally occur *together*, however, especially in the emotionally charged context of the deviant act. Interventions by an external agent, ordinarily in the form of induction techniques, are necessary. Given the optimum arousal conditions for engaging the child's attention, discussed earlier, the resulting coalescence of empathy and awareness of being the causal agent of the other's distress produces a response having the cognitive (self-critical) and affective properties of guilt. Repeated experiences of this kind help sensitize the child to the human consequences of his behavior, which then come to stand out among the welter of emotional and other stimuli in the situation. With further cognitive development this sensitivity expands from an exclusive focus on physical harm to inclusion of feelings such as embarrassment, pride, and rejection. And the child's capacity for direct empathic response becomes elaborated into a more sophisticated and cognitively based ability to take the other's role in a variety of situations. Eventually he can infer the feelings of others just from knowing the stresses operating on them; direct observation of distress cues emanating from them is unnecessary. Explanations need not be given in detail and behavior changes in the child may be brought about by more indirect and subtle appeals. (Indeed, beyond a certain age the child may need to prove that he can make the appropriate judgments and do what is right with no outside help, and overly elaborate explanations may actually backfire because they communicate a lack of confidence.) Eventually, under optimal conditions, even subtle inductions are unnecessary for the child to assess the consequences of his behavior and react with guilt to the victim's cues of distress.

Thus far we have focused on the child's response following transgressions. It must be assumed, however, since an integral part of the guilt experience as here defined is a conscious self-blame or criticism, that it will often include a resolution to act in a more prosocial

---

galvanic and motoric indices, whereas Lerner dealt with a cognitive-evaluative response to the victim.

[51] Inductions also may contribute to the arousal of empathy by relating the victim's pain to that of the child in similar situations in which he has been the victim of someone else's actions.

manner in the future. The young child may only be able to carry out these resolutions in situations that bear a strong physical resemblance to the earlier ones; or he may overgeneralize. With further cognitive development, however, he is enabled to organize his past experience in terms of psychologically relevant categories, reflect on these categories and match them against new situations, and then act accordingly. Moral considerations may thus become appropriately influential before the act as well as afterwards.[52]

It follows from this analysis that techniques which are predominantly power assertive are least effective in promoting development of moral standards and internalization of controls because they elicit intense hostility in the child and simultaneously provide him with a model for expressing that hostility outwardly as well as a relatively legitimate object against which to express it. Because of fear the hostility may not be expressed to the parent but may later be displaced to peers. Nevertheless, in the discipline encounter it makes the child's need for approval less salient and functions as an obstacle both to the arousal of empathy and the comprehension of any inductive components of the technique. Power assertion, especially in the absence of compensating affection, also fosters the image of the parent as an arbitrary, punitive, and unrewarding person—someone to be avoided rather than approached and emulated, which further diminishes the parent's influence. Finally, it sensitizes the child to the necessity of anticipating the responses of adult authorities in order to avoid punishment, thus making his developing system of controls responsive to external rather than internal forces.

When the child is preverbal, power asser-

[52] There is no empirical evidence that guilt affects the child's future behavior as here suggested. There are several studies, however, all done with college students, indicating that inducing guilt (by making the subject feel he has broken something of value or in some way hurt another) results in an increase in "altruistic" behavior as exemplified by volunteering to participate in an experiment without pay (Freedman, Wallington, and Bless, 1967; Brock and Becker, 1966; Wallace and Sadalla, 1966). And, in a more recent study by Carlsmith and Gross (1969), the subject's altruistic behavior was generalized to others, which suggests it was more than just reparation to the victim.

tion, especially when used at the onset of deviant acts may be the most effective technique for establishing connections between these acts and unpleasant experience and thus producing response inhibitions, as well as gaining immediate compliance. Such inhibitions may serve a useful socialization function pending the acquisition of the cognitive and other prerequisites for a more mature basis of behavior controls. It is also possible, however, as suggested earlier, that these inhibitions may actually interfere with later, mature socialization. Furthermore, there is the danger that because of the absence of cognitive guidance and because the act punished is not the same at different times, the aspect of the discipline situation that is most consistently present is the parent and therefore any conditioning is more to the parent's presence than to a particular act.[53]

Techniques which are primarily inductive tend to avoid these deleterious effects of power assertion in several ways. They help foster the image of the parent as a rational, nonarbitrary authority. They provide the child with cognitive resources needed to control his own behavior. And other-oriented inductions in particular are the techniques most likely to motivate the child optimally to focus his attention on the harm done others as the

[53] It should be clear that the findings and our conjecture about the processes involved pertain to the excessive use of power assertion. There are many situations in which power assertion may be useful, e.g., those involving danger and extreme emotional outbursts where physical restraint may be necessary to provide a sense of security to the very young child who lacks an adequate system of self-control. Even in everyday situations the occasional and appropriate use of power assertion may serve to highlight what is important to the parent and thus communicate his value system. Later in this chapter evidence will be presented which suggests that the occasional use of power assertion when the child openly defies the parent may help maintain the level of motivation necessary for him to attend and be influenced by the parent's inductions. Finally, the appropriate use of power assertion may contribute to a sense of identity; that is, being openly confronted with interpersonal conflict may help foster a heightened sense of self. The total avoidance of power assertion, on the other hand, may contribute to a dulling of the borderline between self and notself. It may also present the child with a model of excessive self-control, as suggested later.

salient aspect of his transgressions, and thus help integrate his capacity for empathy with the knowledge of the human consequences of his own behavior. These techniques should therefore be the most facilitative form of discipline for building long-term controls independent of external sanctions, and the findings would seem to support this view.

Love withdrawal stands midway between the other two techniques in the attributes that promote internalization. Techniques in which love withdrawal is salient provide a more controlled form of aggression by the parent than power assertion, but less than induction. They employ the affectionate relationship between child and parent perhaps to a greater degree than the other two techniques, but in a way more likely than they to produce anxiety in the child. Furthermore, a characteristic of love withdrawal techniques is to separate the parent from the child, thus reducing or stopping communication between them. As a result, they are less effective than inductions because they do not include the cognitive material needed to heighten the child's awareness of wrongdoing and facilitate his learning to generalize accurately to other relevant situations; or, if cognitive material is included, the anxiety aroused disrupts comprehension of the message. Finally, these techniques fail to capitalize on the child's capacity for empathy.

To summarize, all discipline techniques have power assertive, love withdrawal, and inductive components. The primary function of the first two is motive arousal and of the last, providing a morally relevant cognitive structure. When degree of arousal is optimal, the child attends to and is subject to maximum influence by the cognitive material. That is, focusing his attention on the harm done others as the salient aspect of his transgression helps integrate his capacity for empathy with the knowledge of the human consequences of his own behavior. This, we suggest, may be the essential contribution of the discipline encounter to the child's moral development.

MORAL DEVELOPMENT, PERSONALITY STRUCTURE, AND PARENTAL PRACTICES

Although the empirical studies relating parental practices to moral development have been guided in the main by psychoanalytic theory, they have neglected one essential aspect of the theory: that concerning the potentially harmful psychological effects of oversocialization and development of an overly harsh and severe conscience. According to psychoanalytic theory, as we have seen, the repression of impulses is an essential part of the child's identification with the parent and internalization of his standards, and a major function of the conscience or superego is to avoid guilt by keeping the repressed impulses from conscious awareness. Further, the postulated developmental sequence is largely completed in early childhood—before cognitive and other ego processes have sufficiently matured for inner conflicts to be verbalized, for the powerful emotions accompanying frustration to be assimilated and placed under conscious control, and for the reasons underlying parental demands to be understood. The resulting superego therefore operates to a great extent outside conscious awareness and is relatively unaffected by changes in reality conditions. The individual's moral standards must be rigidly adhered to in order to keep the repressed impulses from entering consciousness. If the standards are violated for some reason, say, accidentally or in response to strong external pressures or competing drives, defenses may be activated which serve to diminish the person's awareness of the act or his responsibility for its consequences.

Conceptualizing the development of conscience in this manner, psychoanalysis has traditionally viewed it as a potentially harmful psychological force that may interfere with spontaneity and emotional fulfillment and serves to keep the individual out of touch with his own impulses. Accordingly, these writers have usually treated the superego as something to be tolerated as the price of living in an orderly society but often undesirable from the standpoint of the individual's mental health. This essentially negative attitude toward the superego can be seen in the psychoanalytic view that a major goal of psychotherapy is to reduce the severity of the superego to a bearable level and transfer one of its major functions, impulse control, to more conscious ego processes.

Some of the recent psychoanalytic theorists have shown concern with this preponderantly negative side of the superego in the literature. Lederer (1964) has been perhaps the most sharply critical. In discussing the positive and negative aspects of the superego, those which "define the ideals and values of man" and those which "prevent the expression of forbidden instinctual drives," he states:

[T]hese two faces have received strikingly unequal attention. Of the positive aspect, Freud said once (1923, p. 37): "It is easy to show that the ego ideal answers to everything that is expected of the higher nature of man" . . . He does not actually go on to demonstrate this, but the statement is so sweeping, and by virtue of its reference to what is highest and therefore most valuable in man it is of such importance, that one would expect a flood of literature to have dealt with its amplification. This, to my knowledge, has not happened. . . .

[Despite occasional references by Freud and others to the positive superego functions] the negative aspects . . . have consistently held the limelight. Thus, the adjectives we are most accustomed to hearing in conjunction with the term superego are "strict," "harsh," "demanding," "rigid," "tyrannical," "hostile," "severe," "sadistic," and "corruptible." . . . Its function is to force the individual into compliance with a social order he never made, into obedience toward an alien apparatus that deprives him of his instinctual birthright. "The price we pay for our advance in civilization is a loss of happiness through the heightening of the sense of guilt" (Freud, 1930, p. 134), in other words through submission to the whip of internal authority.

Thus the inner agency which represents the best in man seems also to make him unhappy. A civilization bent on the pursuit of happiness could easily conclude that therefore the less superego the better . . . . At any rate, the superego, in spite of its admitted protective efforts, gets into ill repute and is regarded with cautious hostility (pp. 20–21).

Quite apart from its harmful effects on impulse expression, such a concept of conscience does not provide a satisfactory basis for moral action. For example, it would follow from superego considerations that children who consistently resist temptation may often be incapable of rebelling against social norms even when this is desirable; and altruism may

be nothing more than a reaction against one's hostile impulses. It would also follow that in moral conflict situations the individual is always under internal pressure to defend himself against the awareness of temptations. This self-deception may require a reduction in cognitive and other ego functions (e.g., ability to anticipate consequences, suspend judgment, defer gratification, and consider alternatives), which will not only decrease the chances for a constructive resolution of the conflict but may at times actually contribute to the occurrence of transgressions by permitting them to occur without awareness. If psychoanalytic theory gives a valid account of how the superego develops and functions, we must either question the psychological value of an internalized morality or search for an alternative basis of moral action that accords better with personality needs as well as with societal demands.

Psychoanalytic writings that may be viewed as attempts to cope with these problems and clarify and improve the superego concept fall into three broad categories: (1) those which view the most negative features of the superego as merely precursors which may not exist in the final product; (2) those which postulate a separate structure or a part of the superego that handles the positive moral functions; and (3) those which view the superego as naturally losing much of its destructive force with age and becoming more responsive to reality due to the increased strength of cognitive and other ego capacities. These approaches will now be discussed briefly.

1. A number of writers have attempted to make a distinction between the finally developed stable and autonomous superego and its precursors. Among the precursor concepts to be found in the literature are those of "sphincter morality" (Ferenczi, 1925), "early narcissistic identifications" (A. Reich, 1954), "early transient primitive identifications" (Beres, 1958), "superego primordia" (Spitz, 1958), and "preautonomous superego plan" (Sandler, 1960). More directly relevant to our present purpose is the view expressed by Beres (1958) that identifying with the aggressor, turning aggression toward the self, and reaction formation are precursors of the superego but not functions of the finished structure. Cain (1961), drawing from the animal as well

as the human literature, also concludes that turning aggression inward is not necessarily a superego function. Hartmann and Lowenstein (1962) take a different approach. They suggest that many of the human's inborn structures that serve the ego are of an inhibiting character and therefore the early capacities for inhibiting id impulses are ego rather than superego functions.

According to the just-mentioned writers the forerunners of the superego may continue as part of the finally developed superego system, but in the normal healthy personality the role they play is minimal. Only in pathological cases, in which further superego growth does not occur, do they remain dominant. Many of the most negative features of the superego as conceptualized by Freud are thus relegated to the status of precursors which may or may not exist in the finally developed superego.

2. Freud and others use the term "ego ideal" to refer to the positive aspects of the conscience, but these writers have been unclear as to whether it is part of the superego or a separate structural entity with its own developmental history. Three recent concepts of this type will be discussed briefly. Sandler (1960) uses the concept "ideal self" to refer to the image of the positive aspects of parents which the child incorporates into his perceptual or "representational" world. The standards of other authority figures as well as the positive norms of society are similarly incorporated as the child grows older. The ideal self is seen as being separate from the superego, which is defined more narrowly as the parental prohibitions which the child has introjected during the Oedipal period. The ideal self also lacks the motivational underpinning of the superego, although Sandler does suggest that the admired parental qualities that contribute to it are incorporated, along with the parent's prohibitions, as part of the resolution of the Oedipus complex.

Schafer (1960) suggests that the child identifies not only with the punitive but also with the loving aspects of the parents, including the love, comfort, protection, and guidance which they give him, as well as their ideals and moral structures which are more or less representative of their society. Just as in the "restrictive superego" parent hostility is turned into hostility toward the self, in the "loving superego" parent love is turned into self-love. The "loving superego," in contrast to the more restrictive superego, is ego-syntonic, culture-syntonic, and provides the foundation for positive ideals and moral standards. Despite the extreme differences noted between the loving and restrictive superegos, Schafer sees them both as developing along the lines suggested by Freud in which the resolution of the Oedipus complex is the decisive factor, although he seems to stress somewhat more than Freud the importance of the parent's being gentle and lenient (though not rigidly permissive).

Lederer (1964) describes the healthy superego as one that has a hard, totally ego-syntonic and conflict-free core, in which the "ego and superego are fused." He suggests that such a superego is based primarily on identification with a father (Lederer deals only with boys) who is basically kind and protective but also able to be aggressive and strong when necessary. Signs of aggression and strength are seen as important and positive because they connote safety and protection to the child. Pathology occurs when the father is too severe and repressive (neuroses) or ineffectual and "lacking moral fiber" (delinquency and identity problems). Like Sandler and Schafer, Lederer accepts the basic Freudian notion that the superego emerges from the resolution of Oedipal conflicts. He is closer to Freud than the other writers in his view that the boy's identification with the aggressive aspects of the father provides much of the motivational force for a strong superego.

3. The view that the severity of the superego diminishes with age leaving many of its functions to be taken over by the ego, implied in much of the psychoanalytic literature, has been stated explicitly by Jacobsen (1954) and Hartmann (1960). Jacobsen's view is that the superego mellows with age and loses some of its "exaggerated idealism" as the result of ego maturity, particularly after the "tempest of instinctual conflicts during adolescence has subsided." With the aid of the neutralized energy then available to it, the superego can operate on the basis of more reasonable goals, more mature moral judgments, and more tolerance. Hartmann (1960) also accepts the notion of an early developing superego that is harsh, idealistic, and unrealistic. Moreover, he believes that in normal

development—or else in psychoanalytic treatment—this superego loses some of its destructive force due to the increasing strength of the ego. Here again, there is no basic alteration of Freud's conception of the superego and its development. Moral maturity results from the weakening of the superego and strengthening of the ego; to the extent a person is well oriented in society and aware of the issues entailed in a given situation, he is likely to behave in a reliable manner. A possible argument against this view that ego functions alone can handle the matter of conscience is that they can serve selfish and immoral as well as moral interests. It therefore begs the question of what makes the person utilize his ego capacities for prosocial rather than anti-social ends.

It is clear that the psychoanalytic writers recognize the need for positive moral concepts and have clarified and sharpened some of Freud's notions about the superego. They have not, however, developed any basically new views regarding the processes of moral development nor do they claim to do so. They all accept the core Freudian notion that the superego begins to develop in the course of the child's resolution of Oedipal conflicts during the fifth or sixth year of life, expands later by assimilating other authority figures as well as the value system of the culture, is subjected to conflict with new biological drives in adolescence, and eventually loses much of its power. And they further agree with Freud that despite the resulting changes, the superego's characteristic modes of operation are laid down in the early years and remain substantially unchanged.

Hartmann (1960) comes close to diverging from the usual psychoanalytic view when he states: "We do not expect an analyzed person to have no guilt feelings, but guilt should be more in line with integrated parts of his personality, authentic moral codes, and reality situations." Although many practicing psychoanalysts might subscribe to this statement, it is rare in the literature to find a psychoanalytic writer defending the value of guilt of any kind. Hartmann, however, does not develop the notion of an integrated superego or give any ideas as to how the capacity for constructive guilt might develop, although he seems to imply that this is what is left after

psychoanalysis removes the destructive guilt. The same is true of the neo-Freudian writers like Fromm who use such concepts as "humanistic conscience" to refer to a more positively based morality than one based on the traditional Freudian view of superego dynamics. None of these writers has delineated the properties of a positive conscience, theorized systematically about the antecedent experiences that help foster its development, or investigated its antecedents empirically.

The reason psychoanalytic theory has a well defined and coherent view of the inhibitory functions of moral structures, yet is so incomplete with respect to positive functions, probably lies in the fact that it evolved in the course of treating severely neurotic individuals. The same is true of the early psychoanalytic conception of ego development, which later had to be revised to encompass the coping behaviors and higher mental processes of normal and creative persons. The ego was originally thought to draw its strength from id drives, but to account for conflict-free ego function it was necessary to abandon this notion and postulate the importance of structures which never were part of the id, for example, the sense organs and the brain and the cognitive apparatus based on them. Ego development is now seen as derived from these structures and largely independent of the id. In a similar manner it may be necessary, as currently recognized in "ego psychology" (e.g., Stein, 1966), to reevaluate superego theory and search for structures that form the basis of a positive morality. Since the destructive elements of the superego derive primarily from its repressed-impulse base, a necessary point of departure is to search for an alternative motive base. Our earlier discussion of the parent-child research, all of which was done with nonclinical populations, suggests that one such possibility may be the child's primitive empathic potential.

Some of our own unpublished research which was designed to contribute further along these lines will be summarized here, not so much to provide answers as to raise issues and stimulate further work in which the individual's moral development is viewed within the context of his total personality development. In the interest of brevity our presentation will focus mainly on a discussion of the results. The theoretical rationale and methodological details are presented elsewhere (Hoffman, 1970).

The basic approach was first to identify children having the elements of an internalized conscience which is humanistic, flexible, and well integrated with the rest of the personality and then to begin the search for the antecedents of such a conscience by studying the parental practices used with these children, as compared to another group whose moral structures are equally internalized but more rigidly conventional and presumably based to a greater extent on repression. The two groups were picked from the white, middle-class portion of the large sample of seventh graders used in the Hoffman and Saltzstein study (1967). All were from intact homes and none was rated as a behavior problem by their teachers.

Selection was based mainly on the responses given to several moral judgment items. Two criteria were used. The first was the moral standards or principles given in support of the judgments. Those emphasizing the consequences of behavior for others or stressing certain interpersonal moral values such as mutual trust were coded as humanistic; those phrased in terms of the violation of an institutional norm were coded as conventional. The major item used for this purpose, adapted from Kohlberg (1958), deals with two young men: one breaks into a store and steals $500 and the other obtains an equal amount of money from a known benefactor by pretending that he is ill and desperately in need of it. The subjects were asked to decide who did worse and state their reasons. Responses coded as conventional are exemplified by those stating that breaking into the store was worse because stealing is against the law or may involve property destruction; or that there was no difference because both men stole the same amount, or because both acts are opposed to religious precepts. Responses coded as humanistic, on the other hand, generally stated that the "borrower" was worse because of the violation of a trust and personal deception involved, the possible lessening of the benefactor's faith in people, or the ultimate loss to others who really needed the money. The second criterion was the flexibility with which standards were applied, particularly the extent to which extenuating circumstances were taken into ac-

count. Two items were used to tap flexibility. In one, a boy whose friend is being teased by several of his classmates tells a lie to save the friend from further embarrassment. In another, a man who needs a certain drug to save his wife's life tries every available legitimate means of obtaining it and finally, in desperation, breaks into a store and steals it. In each case the subjects are asked whether the actions were right or wrong and to give their reasons. Responses which justified the acts because of the extenuating circumstances were coded as flexible; responses which criticized them for being against religious precepts or against the law without regard to the extenuating circumstances or simply stated that they should never be done were coded as rigid. In coding, the reasons given were more important than the direction of the choices, and perfunctory responses were not coded at all.

Two internalized groups were selected: one which gave predominantly conventional-rigid responses and another which gave predominantly humanistic-flexible responses. To enable us to view differences between these groups in proper perspective and provide continuity with the previous research, a third group with an externally focused moral orientation was also selected. The external group was lower on IQ, which fits the consistently positive relation between IQ and internal moral judgment found in previous research, but by excluding the subjects with low scores it was possible to effect a very close match between the final three groups.

Evidence that the humanistic-flexible and conventional-rigid groups are internalized was obtained by comparing them with the external group on several independent internalization indices: story completion guilt intensity, teacher ratings of the extent to which the child accepts or denies responsibility for his misdeeds, and parent reports of whether or not he confesses after doing something wrong. The humanistic and conventional groups were similar to each other and consistently higher than the external on all of these indices, which must be kept in mind as we review the differences between them on certain morally relevant personality charactertistics.

Guilt and Repression

Two story-completion items were used to measure guilt. In one (adapted from Allinsmith, 1960) the "hero," who is very unhappy over not winning any contests in an outdoor meet, wins the main event by cheating in a manner that seemingly cannot be detected. He is being cheered and congratulated by his friends at the point where the subject is asked to complete the story. In the other story, the hero is on the way to a ball game with a friend when they pass a small child who seems to be lost. The hero suggests they stop and help, but his friend convinces him otherwise by pointing out that the child's parents will probably find him and that they will miss part of the game if they stop. The next day the hero discovers that the child, after being left alone by his babysitter, had wandered out into the street and was fatally struck by a car. At this point the subject is asked to complete the story. The important difference between these stories, for our purposes, is that in one—the "cheating" story—the focus is on the build-up and expression of an anti-moral impulse; no mention is made of harm done to others and the harm actually done is minor and rectifiable. In the "lost child" story, on the other hand, anti-moral impulse expression is a far less intrinsic part of a transgression which is more an act of omission, i.e., not acting on a prosocial impulse rather than giving vent to an anti-social one. The human consequences, however, are salient as well as extreme and irreversible.

Our hypothesis was that guilt in the humanistic-flexible subjects is primarily a response to the actual harm done others, whereas in the conventional group it is more a response to their own impulse arousal. From this it follows that the humanistic group should show more guilt on the "lost child" story and the conventional group more on the "cheating" story. These expectations were largely confirmed though statistically only for boys. Although there was no difference on the cheating story, the humanistic-flexible boys had higher "maximal guilt scores (defined earlier) on the lost-child story. Moreover, both their maximal and terminal guilt scores were differentially higher on the lost-child than on the cheating story. We also expected the conventional-rigid subjects to show more defenses against guilt on the lost-child story, and it was to test this hypothesis that several possibilities for externalizing blame were built into that story. In actuality they, like the humanistic-flexible

subjects, gave little explicit evidence of defense.[54] While their low overall guilt response to this story may reflect the prior operation of a defense, it is also possible that both the low guilt and low defense merely signify that these subjects were relatively untouched by the story despite the severe consequences.

These findings suggest that the humanistic-flexible subjects may be particularly responsive to the actual human consequences of action, apart from the relevance of these consequences to their own impulses; that is, they can experience guilt primarily as a direct result of the awareness of the consequences of their behavior for others.[55] The conven-

[54] It was the boys in the external group who showed the greatest amount of defense and a corresponding drop from "maximal" to "terminal" guilt. Though their maximal guilt scores were on a par with those obtained by the humanistic boys (actually slightly higher), their terminal guilt was significantly lower. This suggests they may have the capacity for guilt but cannot sustain it and have developed defenses which are activated immediately upon experiencing it. It is also possible that their external, fear-dominated orientation itself may be a defense against guilt—that referred to in the psychoanalytic literature as projection of the superego. In any case, this question of whether an external orientation reflects a lack of internal standards or inability to handle the guilt resulting from a violation of such standards seems worthy of further investigation. If the above finding is replicated it would suggest that the development of an external moral orientation is more complex, at least in the middle class, than might appear from the literature, and perhaps that the concept of an under-socialized person has been used too loosely and needs conceptual refinement.

[55] This view of guilt as a direct conscious response to the awareness of causing another person distress, which might be called "true" guilt, has much in common with the concept of "existential" or "ontological" guilt advanced by some existential psychologists who see all humans as having the potential for guilt once they are mature enough cognitively to be aware of the element of choice in their behavior. These writers suggest that the awareness of choice makes the individual vulnerable to certain problems of human existence, including the moral one of finding a satisfactory balance between one's rights and his obligations to others. The mere knowledge of others in need may thus make the more fortunate individual feel guilty, especially when his own needs are indulged. Further, a

tional-rigid subjects, on the other hand, appear to operate to a greater degree in accord with the Freudian formulation that guilt stems primarily from the awareness of unacceptable impulses in themselves and only secondarily from the amount of harm done to others by their actions. In short, whereas the humanistic-flexible group's conscience seems tuned outwardly (toward consequences for others), the conventional-rigid group's conscience seems tuned inwardly (toward their own impulses).[56]

Another hypothesis was that while the conventional subjects have more guilt over impulses they are also less aware of them. The humanistic subjects, on the other hand, can more readily tolerate their impulses.[57] Our expectation that this would be reflected in the cheating story, where impulse expression is salient, was supported, though again significantly only for boys. That is, the humanistic boys produced more story endings in which the hero is at first happy or proud over winning the race and only *later* shows the guilt

reaction.[58] These responses stand in contrast to those more typical for the conventional subjects, in which the hero feels guilty immediately and never experiences pleasure over winning the race despite the fact that the story beginning clearly indicates he was highly motivated to win.

A final and related hypothesis was that the guilt of the conventional-rigid subjects would have more of a harsh ego-alien superego quality to it than that of the humanistic-flexible subjects. The score for ego-alien guilt was obtained on a third story item, adapted from Allinsmith (1960), in which the child, home alone one day, goes to the closet to get a box which his parents have repeatedly told him never to take down. Responses coded as ego-alien are those in which there is no evidence of conscious guilt but such happenings as the following occur: the child or a pet gets burned by chemicals that spill from the box, the child is accidentally shot with a gun that was in the box, or he falls and breaks a leg while reaching for the box. Such responses suggest a kind of primitive fear of catastrophe that may be associated with the idea of yielding to temptation in violation of parental prohibitions. To the degree the child is deterred from violating parental injunctions by some such primitive (and presumably partly unconscious) fear, his conscience may be described as having an ego-alien quality. When this story was scored on a three-point scale from ego-alien to ego-syntonic (i.e., ego-alien responses lacking conscious guilt; ego-alien responses plus conscious guilt; and conscious guilt lacking an ego-alien quality) the conventional-rigid subjects were found to be higher in the ego-alien direction.[59]

certain amount of such guilt is inevitable because human limitations and the conditions of life prevent one's being totally dedicated to the needs of others. This is seen as a relatively benign kind of guilt, however, which does not necessarily lead to symptom formation. Instead, if faced up to and not evaded, it has constructive effects on the personality; for example, it helps produce an appropriate sense of humility and heightens one's sensitivity in relations with others. Thus it stands in contrast to the psychoanalytic view of guilt, which encompasses more than its direct interpersonal aspects, stresses its unconscious components, and sees it not as a primary response but a derivative of a more basic anxiety over loss of parental love.

[56] This distinction bears a superficial resemblance to Piaget's intentions-consequences dichotomy. The difference is that we deal with the actor's orientation either to his own impulses or to the human consequences of his own act; whereas Piaget deals with the actor's orientation to the intentions underlying or the material consequences of someone else's act.

[57] A reported incident in the life of Mark Twain illustrates this point well. In one of his lectures Twain expressed his dislike for the fact that "a reporter has to lie a little" and gave this as his reason for leaving the profession. Then he added: "I am different from Washington: I have a higher and grander standard of principle. Washington could not lie. I *can* lie, but I *won't*."

[58] In some of these stories the hero is depicted as a basically honest person who makes a mistake under pressure, realizes this, and then tries to rectify his error. In others, a delayed awareness of depriving someone who deserves the prize leads to the hero's moral action. And still others focus on his growing dissatisfaction with the image of himself as a cheater, or deal with his struggle for the courage necessary to confess what he has done. In the latter stories, the hero's struggle and subsequent victory over himself are sometimes explicitly presented as contributing to his moral growth.

[59] It should be noted, however, that ego-alien responses were not frequent and though given

Some evidence for greater repression in the conventional-rigid group was obtained on a 25-item sentence completion test. The conventional-rigid group had higher scores than the humanistic-flexible group on four different repression indices, although the difference was significant for only one: the total number of "blanks" and erased responses on the test.

* * *

Are the humanistic-flexible subjects truly more flexible than the conventional-rigid ones, or merely less concerned with conventional standards? The most relevant finding is that although the humanistic group showed more guilt than the conventional on the story focused on human need (lost child), they also showed as much guilt as the conventional on the story dealing with the more conventional transgression of cheating. Further evidence was obtained on a measure of values on which both groups were found to assign equal importance to conventional values such as obeying parents and attending church, as well as to humanistic values such as going out of one's way to help others. (Both groups, it might be added, placed greater stress on all these values than the external group.) We would tentatively conclude that the humanistic-flexible subjects are like the conventional-rigid in generally upholding conventional standards but are relatively quick to relinquish them in the service of human needs (as in their moral judgment responses). Thus, though conventional standards are shared by the two groups, in the humanistic they appear to be part of a broader morality which gives still higher priority to matters of human concern.

To summarize, the humanistic-flexible and conventional-rigid groups appear to be two variants of an internalized conscience which differ not only in the manifest content but also the hierarchial arrangement and motivational basis of their moral standards. Thus, in making moral judgments about other people's violations, the humanistic-flexible subjects tend to stress the consequences for others and are more likely to take extenuating circumstances into account. Their story completions suggest they are more tolerant and accepting of their

more often by the conventional-rigid subjects, this difference was not statistically significant. Only the continuum ranging from ego-alien to ego-syntonic guilt produced a significant result.

own impulses. That is, though high on guilt and other indices of internalization, they give evidence of being able to contemplate or consider in fantasy behaving in violation of their standards. They also appear to experience guilt primarily as a direct result of harmful consequences of their behavior for others, rather than unacceptable impulses in themselves. The conventional-rigid subjects, on the other hand, are more likely to give a religious or legal basis for their moral judgments and to ignore extenuating circumstances. Their story-completions suggest that they may, to a relatively great extent, operate in accord with the Freudian notion that guilt stems less from the amount of harm actually done others than from awareness of unacceptable impulses; and they tend to avoid expressing these impulses even in fantasy. This pattern, together with the sentence completion findings, suggests that repression may be an underlying mechanism in these subjects. Perhaps impulse intolerance is a way of avoiding moral conflict, i.e., one experiences no conflict if unaware of temptation. Thus, although the two groups were selected on the basis of conscious moral judgments, they appear to reflect moral syndromes which differ beyond the conscious and rational aspects of moral orientations. We now turn to the parent discipline findings.

Parent Discipline

Before comparing the discipline patterns in the two groups it should be noted, in keeping with the findings in our research review, that the parents in *both groups obtained higher scores on induction and affection, and lower scores on power assertion, than those in our external comparison group.* This should be kept in mind as we examine the differences between them.

The most interesting finding was that the parents of the conventional-rigid group more often reported using love withdrawal as a discipline technique, especially in response to the child's anger. Thus, although love withdrawal was not found in our research review to contribute to an internalized moral orientation but only to the inhibition of hostile impulses, it does appear to have a bearing on the type of internalized moral orientation. How might this occur? We would suggest that given the requisite pattern for internalization—low power assertion, high induction and affection—love withdrawal may lead to an intensified inhibition not only of hostility but of other impulses associated with behaviors that have been frowned upon by the parent. That is, the child learns to be good in order to avoid losing the parent's love—and what being good ultimately means, in this case, is controlling impulses. The frequent use of love withdrawal may also color the child's reactions to other-oriented induction techniques so that the harm to others pointed up serves mainly as a signal or confirmation of the fact that he has expressed unacceptable impulses. Subsequently, exposure to pain cues from others may arouse anxiety because of their association with these impulses. The interaction between love withdrawal and other-oriented induction may thus account for the generally inhibited pattern reported earlier for the conventional-rigid group as well as the evidence that impulse rejection may serve as the basis of their moral orientation.

The parents of the humanistic-flexible group show a different pattern in response to the child's anger. Our expectation was that they would handle anger with firmness but relatively little threat, and they give some evidence that this is true. In response to anger directed toward themselves, their techniques were focused more on the issue which led up to the anger (usually something the child wanted which the parent denied him) than the anger itself which was more often the focus of the conventional parents' techniques. This generally serves to keep the original argument going rather than terminate it abruptly. Even when they criticize, yell, or do something more severe like sending the child to his room, this is also done with the instigating disagreement in mind. For example, they may suggest that the child calm down, think it over, and then come back to rediscuss it. This focus on the instigating disagreement rather than the anger would seem to tone down any love-withdrawing quality that the parent's technique might otherwise have, in two ways. First, it communicates that the parent is critical of the child's anger more because it is dysfunctional to the issue at hand than because it is intrinsically objectionable. Second, it places a time limit on the parent's expressed critical feelings toward the child. That is, since it indicates the prior relationship will soon be restored, the child is not left to wonder for very long

whether or not his parent still loves him. In terms of our earlier analysis of the discipline encounter, these techniques would seem to arouse the child's need for approval and thus the motivation to control his anger, but not because of undue anxiety over loss of love.

There is also similar evidence regarding the parents' handling of the child's expressions of anger toward other children. This was obtained on an item in which the child was described as destroying something his friend had built, after verbal provocation by the friend. The parents in both groups indicated that they would express strong disapproval, and most included specific reference to the hurt feelings of the victim. The parents of the humanistic-flexible group included an additional element, however: they more often reported making the child repair the damage or help the friend do so. Here too, then, as when the child expresses anger toward the parent, these parents appear to react as critically as the conventional but they also indicate that one's anger need not necessarily damage his relationship with the person toward whom it is expressed. The act of repairing the damage may also, in addition to suggesting a constructive manner of restoring the relationship, serve to place a finite limit on whatever love withdrawal is communicated by the parent.

Another major difference is that the parents of the humanistic-flexible group more often report using power assertion (though less often than the external group). The excessive use of power assertion, as shown earlier, generally operates against the development of an internalized moral orientation. How then can we account for its greater use by the parents of the humanistic children? Further investigation of this finding provides several leads. First, in the very situation in which the parents report using more power assertion, their children see them as using reasons. Second, and this may explain the first, these parents indicate clearly that they would impose their will only when the child flatly refuses to do something the importance of which has already been explained and which cannot wait. Thus, though they assert power, they do not appear to do so indiscriminately and it may be this to which the children respond. We would conclude that it may be constructive at times when the child is unreasonably defiant, for the parent to follow through on a demand. This may help motivate the child to give up his needs of the moment and attend to the parent when induction techniques are used. He might otherwise simply ignore the parent and not be influenced by inductions; or he might respond inappropriately to them, e.g., by developing a false sense of omnipotence from those that indicate he can hurt the parent. Thus, although excessive power assertion may prevent a constructive response to induction, as suggested earlier, its use at times when the child is overly defiant may constitute an appropriate degree of firmness that actually facilitates a constructive response. Stated differently, some power assertion may be needed for the voice of reason to be heard.

The parents of the conventional-rigid children, in contrast, tend to respond in this situation with either love withdrawal or induction. It appears they do not engage in open conflict with the child even when he is defiant.

In another type of discipline situation, in which the child accidentally damages something of value to the parent, the parents of the conventional-rigid subjects were again more often reported as using love withdrawal. This may be expected to contribute further to the child's anxiety over losing the parent's love. In accident situations, this anxiety would presumably become associated with whatever impulses might underlie the accident, e.g., unconscious hostility to the parent, possibly affection as when the accident occurs while the child is being helpful or simply the child's sheer exuberance and excitement that led to his carelessness. Love withdrawal following accidents may therefore help generalize the child's anxiety and lead to confusion about many feelings—even positive ones—and distrust of them.[60]

In the accidental damage situation the parents of the humanistic-flexible group are more likely to respond in a highly permissive manner, which suggests they view such behavior as lying outside the child's control. Inferring to negative intent, they see no reason for punishment. While this permissiveness makes no direct contribution to moral development, it may communicate the parent's orientation to take the child's point of view, i.e., to be emphatic and supportive rather than materialistic.

We will now pass over the other specific discipline findings to a larger pattern of differences which was found. Namely, the parents in the conventional-rigid group tend to use some variant of love withdrawal regardless of the situation. The discipline used in the humanistic-flexible group, on the other hand, is more varied and discriminating. It ranges, as we have seen, from power assertion to total permissiveness, depending on the situation, and cushions the disciplining of aggression by focusing on the precipitating issues and suggesting reparation where possible. We would suggest this difference reflects a greater tendency in the humanistic-flexible group to look at behavior in its larger context—including the doer's point of view, his intentions, abilities, and limitations, and the pressures operating on him at the time—rather than judge an act in isolation. The conventional-rigid parents, on the other hand, are more likely to ignore contextual factors, to compare specific acts with external standards of good or bad behavior, and act accordingly.

Parent as Model. Though our interest in the parent focused mainly on discipline rather than the parent's own moral orientation, data were available which suggest the possible influence of the parent as a model. First there is some evidence that both the humanistic and conventional groups tend to identify with their parents, and to about the same degree. That is, when asked "Which person do you look up to most?" and "Which person do you want to be like when you grow up?", the subjects in these groups were equally likely, and both to a greater extent than the external group, to mention a parent.

How did they differ? At the simplest level—that of the actual characteristics of the identification model—we might expect the parents of the humanistic and conventional groups to fit the humanistic and conventional patterns. The

---

[60] Another possible explanation, suggested by Lois Wladis Hoffman, is that the particular techniques used in the accidental damage situation, as exemplified by such statements as "Can't you do anything right" and "You ought to be ashamed of yourself," contribute to a negative self-image in the child. The impulses in question might then be avoided because of their association with this self-image rather than with anxiety over loss of love.

discipline findings presented earlier suggest this may indeed be the case. The frequent use of love withdrawal by the conventional parents, together with their seeming reluctance to engage in open conflict even with a defiant child, would appear to provide a model of excessive impulse control which may contribute to the inhibition of impulses underlying the conventional children's moral orientation. The humanistic parents provide quite a different model. Their firm yet relatively nonpunitive manner of reacting to the child's anger, together with their permissive response to accidental damage, suggests a model who is flexible, emphatic rather than materialistic, and accepts and handles his own anger in a constructively modulated fashion. Such a model might be expected to contribute to the impulse tolerance and tendency to consider extenuating circumstances that our findings suggest characterizes the humanistic children.

Apart from the discipline encounter, what kind of models do the parents present? Relevant data were provided by two of the moral judgment items used initially in selecting the groups. No differences were found on the item dealing with the two men who obtained money by theft or deception but on the one in which a boy told a lie to protect a friend who was being teased by his peer group, differences were obtained. Fathers of boys and mothers of girls in the humanistic group were more likely than their conventional counterparts to approve of the lie—which, of course, exactly parallels the children's responses to this item. In response to a probe question about whether they would like the boy who told the lie, most parents in both groups stated that they would. The difference thus seems to be rather narrow: whereas the humanistic parents say they would like the boy and he was right for lying because of the circumstances, the conventionals say they would like him but he was wrong despite the circumstances. The findings obtained on two other probe questions suggest the difference may be important, however. When asked if they thought their own child might do the same thing, the same-sexed parents of the humanistic-flexible children more often said they would.[61] Moreover, when asked what they would do if their child did it, they more often said they would show approval, which suggests these parents will more often encourage the child to go out of his way to help others even if it means violating a conventional norm.

The reasons the parents gave for approving of the lie varied: some stressed the boy's courage in standing up to the group; others mentioned his trying to reduce friction between the other boys; some just stated that he did more good than harm by lying; and some referred explicitly to his lying to save the other boy's feelings. This last type of reason was most prominent among the fathers of the humanistic boys and distinguished them from the conventionals. This suggests that the father's tendency to empathize openly with someone in distress, even if the latter violated a conventional norm, may contribute to his son's humanistic orientation. When such a situation occurs in real life, the humanistic boys may experience conflict between conventional and humanistic norms. The father's unambiguously empathic response may then have an especially powerful effect because he is not just expressing his values didactically, but reinforcing the empathy experienced by the child at the time and helping him resolve his own ambivalence.

On the assumption that the psychoanalytic theory of superego formation is more applicable to the conventional subjects, we expected this group to give more evidence of "positional" identification and the humanistic group more "personal" identification (Slater, 1961). In positional identification, which corresponds roughly to defensive identification or identification-with-the-aggressor, the child identifies with the parental role especially its power aspects. In personal identification, the child seeks to emulate personal attributes of the parent which are not relevant to power. Our expectation was not borne out where we expected it to be, that is, in the reasons the children gave for admiring and wanting to emulate the parent, but it did receive indirect support in two sentence completion items. In response to the item, "the main thing about my father is . . . ," the humanistic boys gave more personal responses (e.g., "good sense of humor," "enjoys driv-

[61] It is possible that wishful thinking is involved here rather than an accurate description of the children, since the results for the opposite-sexed parent, though in the same direction as the same-sexed parent, were not significant.

ing") and fewer power structure responses (e.g., "too strict," "not strict enough," "always says no") than the conventional group. They also gave fewer power-structure responses to a comparable mother item.[62]

It would thus appear that the humanistic boys tend to identify with the personal characteristics of their fathers among which is a relatively direct and visible empathic concern for others. Identification with such a father may provide a motive base, in addition to that suggested in our analysis of the mother-child discipline encounter, which contributes to the willingness of the humanistic boys to relinquish conventional standards in the service of human needs. Perhaps this is necessary in order to help counteract the larger socio-cultural influences which discourage expressions of empathy in males. That is, boys may need the combined effects of the maternal discipline pattern described earlier and the support of an openly empathic father.

IS MORAL DEVELOPMENT A UNITARY PROCESS?

Now that we have critically reviewed the research, we are in a good position to reassess the long-standing issue of whether moral development is a unitary process. The three major theoretical positions differ on this. The Freudian and Piagetian approaches, as we have seen, though vastly different, both view moral development as a completely unitary process. The behavioristic learning theories (e.g., Bandura and Walters, 1963), on the other hand, take the other extreme and view it as but one example of discrimination training, in which some responses become inhibited and others elicited in the presence of certain stimuli as a result of reinforcement contingencies.

The best known and most elaborate empirical study relevant to this issue was carried out by Hartshorne and May in the 1920s (Hartshorne and May, 1928–1930). Over a period of 5 years tests designed to disclose cheating and other forms of dishonesty, along with tests of moral knowledge and other variables, were administered to several thou-

sand children between the ages of 8 and 16. The major findings were that the intercorrelations among tests tended to be low. On the basis of these results Hartshorne and May advanced their doctrine of specificity, which states that neither honesty nor dishonesty is a unified character trait but rather a specific function of life situations. They suggest further that the consistency with which an individual is honest or dishonest in different situations is a function of the extent to which the situations have common elements and the individual has learned to be honest or dishonest in them. Thus any apparent generality of moral behavior is a function of situational similarity, that is, individuals respond similarly to different situations that have stimulus elements in common.

Burton (1963) recently reanalyzed that portion of Hartshorne and May's behavioral honesty data which was based on their six most reliable cheating tests. The findings provide some support for a "generality" dimension underlying honesty in different test-taking situations. Using factor analysis, three components were extracted which account for a substantial portion of the total variance in the scores. Results similar to Burton's have been obtained by Sears, Rau, and Alpert (1965) and Nelson, Grinder, and Mutterer (1968), who collected new resistance to temptation data from preschool children under more controlled conditions than Hartshorne and May. Sears, Rau, and Alpert studied the relation between six different measures of resistance to temptation, all given in a play setting. Evidence for both generality and specificity were obtained. While the correlations between tests ranged from 0 to .45, all but one correlation for each sex was positive and most were statistically significant. Nelson, Grinder, and Mutterer administered six different resistance-to-temptation measures to sixth graders. Various statistical procedures were used including analysis of variance and factor analysis. Depending on the procedure, anywhere from about 15 to 50% of the variance in the test scores appeared to be due to "persons." There was a great deal of similarity in the test situations, however, since although the settings differed, the tests were all administered by the same experimenter over a relatively short period of time.

Though most of the research on the gen-

[62] Most of the nonpower responses to this item refer not to the mother's personal characteristics but to her positive feelings for the subject (e.g., "loves me," "kind and understanding").

erality-specificity issue has dealt with overt behavior, there are also some relevant findings bearing on moral judgment and guilt. The mixed results with Piaget's moral attributes—consistency within an attribute and inconsistency between them—have already been cited. With respect to story-completion guilt Allinsmith (1960) reports that the amount of guilt following one type of transgression does not relate to the amount of guilt following another. In Allinsmith's scoring procedure concerns about punishment and detection were included in the scoring of guilt. Using this same procedure, which might better be viewed as providing an index of total deviation anxiety rather than guilt, we found a similar lack of relation between responses to the "lost child" and "cheating" stories described above. Using the more stringent definition of guilt described earlier, however, highly significant and positive relations were found for boys on all three guilt indices: maximum guilt, terminal guilt, and guilt drop (difference between maximum and terminal). For girls, a significant correlation was obtained only for maximum guilt.[63]

It seems clear from these studies that both specificity and generality can be found in moral behavior as in any other trait. Individuals do vary in their general predispositions toward honesty and dishonesty but their actual behavior in moral conflict situations is not an all-or-none matter. Whether or not one sees generality depends largely on how strict his definition of generality is.

To the extent that any generality occurs, it may be based, as Burton suggests, on two gradients. The first is preverbal and is identical to Hartshorne and May's notion of common stimulus elements in different tests. The other pertains to conceptual similarities and requires cognitive mediation, from which one would expect greater consistency with increasing age and verbal ability. In support of these expectations is Burton's analysis of the Hartshorne and May data, which shows that consistency in test scores increased with age and was greater in the middle than the lower

[63] It is unlikely that halo or contamination effects in the coding of guilt can account for these relations since all the coding was "blind" and only one story was coded at a time, i.e., several hundred "lost child" stories were coded before the coding of the "cheating" story was begun.

class; girls, however, who are more verbal than boys, were not more consistent.

Besides the question of situational generality there is the question of whether different aspects of morality interrelate. We have already mentioned the contradictory findings obtained by Krebs (1968), Grinder (1964), and others relating moral judgment to resistance to temptation. Perhaps more directly to the point is the relation between resistance to temptation and guilt. The studies relating each of these to parental practices, reviewed earlier, were initially guided by the assumption that conscience is a unitary process and therefore the parental antecedents of guilt and resistance to temptation are similar. This assumption has roots in the psychoanalytic view that guilt-prone individuals avoid transgressing in order to avoid guilt. Correspondingly, the person with little guilt potential—or with smoothly functioning defenses against guilt—has little reason to resist temptation. We have already indicated that the parental pattern most highly related to the moral indices related less strongly to resistance to temptation than to guilt. In addition, guilt and resistance to temptation have not been found to relate to each other with any consistency. Thus, whereas MacKinnon (1938) and Grinder (1960) report low positive relations between the two, Allinsmith (1960) and Maccoby (1959) report no relation and Burton et al. (1961) report a negative one.

One possible explanation for these mixed findings is that consistency between resistance to temptation and guilt should be expected only when the same moral standard is involved; this condition was met only in the MacKinnon (1938) study in which both the resistance to temptation and guilt measures dealt with cheating. The graduate student subjects in this study who cheated on a problim-solving task by copying also tended to deny that they had cheated and to report that they would not feel guilty over cheating; the students who did not cheat reported that they would feel guilty if they did. These findings fit the notion of "dynamic consistency" (Hoffman, 1963a) which suggests there is a tendency toward consistency at different personality levels with respect to the same moral standard. The finding in our research review of a common parental pattern for most of the moral indices is also generally supportive of this view, as is that mentioned earlier in which the preadolescent children who showed humanistic concerns in their moral judgments also gave evidence of guilt in transgressions involving harm to others. Obviously more work is needed with a broader age range of subjects and with different types of transgressions before the extent to which dynamic consistency exists can be assessed.

Personality and situational factors which may limit both behavioral generality and dynamic consistency should also be investigated. We can expect generality across different cheating tests to diminish, for example, if such variables as motivation, intelligence and expectations of success or failure in the particular task are not controlled. Similarly, there are many reasons why a person who would feel guilty if he violated a standard might not predictably resist temptation even with respect to the same standard. Thus though a person is highly committed to the standard and motivated to avoid guilt, he might become so involved in striving for highly desired objectives that he fails to discriminate relevant cues and anticipate the consequences of his actions; this is especially likely in young children. Or he might be fully aware of the consequences, yet lack the ego controls necessary to resist gratifying the impulse in question. Another possibility is that he both foresees the consequences and has the controls, yet is quite willing to tolerate guilt in order to attain his immediate objectives. Finally, he might transgress accidentally, or as a result of a temporary lapse of conscious control due to alcohol or drugs, or through the operation of cognitive defenses which enable him to do so without awareness, or to fulfill an unconscious need for punishment. Knowing a person's moral orientation alone then does not enable us to predict with confidence how he will *behave*. Whether he resists or submits to temptation is a function of a complex balance of forces involving his achievement needs and specific goal strivings, guilt and other aspects of his moral structure, his system of ego controls, and various aspects of the immediate situation.

We would tentatively conclude that behavior generality and dynamic consistency both increase with age. The morality of the very young child is very likely a simple matter of the rote learning of specific acts and avoidances, with generalization taking place primarily on the basis of common stimulus elements. After 4 or 5 years of age when cognitive mediation becomes possible, generalization begins to occur on the basis of conceptual similarities. At some later point, perhaps because certain moral principles have been internalized, the individual may also begin to experience strains toward consistency between these principles and his conduct. Whether or not these strains are enough to produce consistent behavior, however, will be influenced in part by other characteristics of the person in interaction with situational factors.

CONCLUSION

In this chapter the major research studies bearing on psychological processes in moral development have been reviewed and the findings used as a basis for evaluating various theoretical positions. It seems clear that no one theory has a monopoly on explanation in this area. Moral development is a complex, multifaceted phenomenon to which several different processes appear to contribute. As an attempt to synthesize the findings and most promising hypotheses, we would tentatively suggest that moral development proceeds along four tracks whose end products are behavioral conformity, perception of authority as rational, impulse inhibition, and consideration for others. Each appears to have its own experiential base, as follows:

1. Social learning theory seems best suited to account for the early forerunners of morality which consist of the expression and inhibition of specific acts defined by socialization agents as good or bad and rewarded or punished accordingly, and other acts having stimulus elements in common. (To this point the process is applicable to animals as well as humans.) With cognitive mediation, generalization based on conceptual as well as physical similarity becomes possible and variables such as timing and intensity of punishment, which were initially important, play a decreasing role. These processes may continue through life as a basis of the individual's moral behavior, and if the same reinforcement contingencies occur with later socialization agents the same behavioral standards

will continue to prevail; otherwise, they are subject to extinction.

In sum, this is essentially an external morality in which the child's motives are hedonistic and which is defined by whatever behaviors are rewarded or punished by authority or have stimulus or conceptual elements in common with them.

2. With further cognitive development the child may re-evaluate and shift his view of authority and rules so that they are no longer external, arbitrary, and constraining but largely objective and rational. Two types of experience help foster this development. One is the interaction with authority figures who are rational in their demands, for example, parents who use inductions which are comprehensible and make sense in terms of the child's own experience, and who do not subject him to excessive surveillance. These parents are apt to be seen as mediators of reality demands who basically sympathize with the child's interests rather than insensitive and powerful figures acting on personal whim; and punishment, though painful, will often be recognized as legitimate. This view of the parent presumably carries over and influences the child's orientation to future socialization agents.

A second factor is the individual's own experience in taking the role of authority. This includes participating in decisions about his behavior in the home, and about rules of games and the like with peers. It may also eventually include taking both authority and subordinate roles in more formally organized groups and organizations. These experiences give the individual direct contact with various factors that must be considered in making decisions about human action and thus make the authority role appear less arbitrary and more functional and rational. (Increased familiarity also exposes the nonrational aspects of social systems and depending on whether they predominate or not the person's view of authority as rational will be either weakened or broadened to encompass human frailty.) This morality, like the first, is defined by the demands of authority, but the individual does not comply merely to avoid punishment. Rather, having interacted with and actually taken the role of rational authority, he has come to view it as legitimate.

3. The preceding two processes are contentless and may encompass many behaviors, both positive and negative. The third stresses the taming of antisocial impulses and builds upon the initial opposition between the child's impulses and the norms of society. Important adults give or withhold love contingent upon the child's behavior and, as a result, painful anxiety states become associated not only with deviant behaviors but also with the impulses underlying them. These impulses are henceforth denied direct expression. Pressures toward conformity are thus assured even in the absence of authority and when, for whatever reason, the norms are violated, anxiety (or guilt) is evoked.

4. A fourth process of moral development builds upon the child's potential for prosocial affect—mainly the capacity for empathy. This may be accomplished by a socialization pattern which facilitates the integration of empathy with appropriate cognitive functioning. We have suggested this pattern includes parental discipline techniques that foster the simultaneous experience of empathy and awareness of the harmful effects of one's actions on others. The result of this experience is a guilt response that is conscious, focused primarily on the victim's inner states rather than the actor's own impulses, and lacks much of the irrationality of the guilt postulated in psychoanalytic theory, as well as efforts to be more considerate in the future. Because of the disruptive emotionality of children in situations involving harm to others, this process ordinarily requires the intervention of an outside person who can be both sympathetic and objective—typically an adult operating as a more or less self-conscious socialization agent and using discipline techniques with high inductive components.

Other experiences in and out of the home supplement induction discipline in the further elaboration and refinement of the child's motivation to consider others. Foremost among these are the processes by which the child acquires a sense of mutuality with peers in-concluding the recognition of shared inner states. Specifically, the taking of reciprocal roles—in which the person alternately affects others and is affected by them in similar ways—may heighten his sensitivity to the inner states aroused in others by his own behaviors, i.e., having been in the other person's place helps him to know how the latter feels in response to his own behavior.

We are suggesting then that both induction by adults and reciprocal role-playing with peers contribute to the simultaneous experience of empathy and awareness of consequences. These effects can be further enhanced by any experience that helps broaden the range of situations in which the child can empathize. Examples are exposure to adults who openly express empathy and compassion—in real life but also perhaps in books and the mass media. The child's empathic range may also be broadened by experiences that help him understand the motives underlying the behavior of others and recognize that he might behave similarly in their place, for example, certain inductions which attempt to do this explicitly, and reciprocal role-playing.

These processes are best viewed not as developmental stages, but as socialization modes which progress independently of one another. They may coexist and interact in a manner which is mutually supportive (e.g., the view of authority as rational may facilitate the child's responding appropriately to inductions) or non-supportive (e.g., early conditioned inhibitions may prevent a behavior from occurring later on when its control might be acquired on the basis of a more advanced mode).

A number of specific directions for further research have been suggested in this chapter. To these we would add the general observation that most of the research to date has investigated either the cognitive determinants of cognitive aspects of moral development, or the emotional determinants of emotional aspects. Our interpretation of how induction and reciprocal role-playing operate suggests this is an artificial separation and fuller understanding of moral development, especially guilt and consideration for others, requires study of the interpenetration of cognitive and affective processes. Research is needed which will tell us, for example, the age at which relevant information about another person's inner states can influence the child's hostility in a conflict situation, and the processes that underlie this influence.

Another area much in need of further work

is the role of models, especially morally acting models. We have suggested certain improvements that might be made in the modeling research. Should future investigations provide convincing evidence that models can play an important role in moral development, a next step would be to study the interaction between the processes involved in modeling and those involved in the administration of discipline. These processes may be mutually facilitative; or they may operate independently, for example, modeling may be especially relevant to overt aspects of moral development and discipline to inner states such as guilt.

Other important questions remain about moral development in the real world. What are the age trends in degree of resemblance between the moral concepts of children and their parents? When do children generally begin to diverge from their parents, and by what processes do they shift their allegiance to other significant figures? Is the concept of internalization viable or is the moral behavior of most people due mainly to conformity pressures? Is it true that today's youth are increasingly tending to discard as trivial many of the conventional moral standards of the older generation, in favor of concerns which are more broadly humanistic and, if so, what processes are involved in the breakdown of the old and emergence of the new? A possible framework for approaching some of these questions, especially the last, is to view the four previously mentioned socialization modes in historical perspective. It is clear from surveys of changes in childrearing practices (e.g., Bronfenbrenner, 1958) that the past two decades have seen a shift, in middle class America at least, from the first and third, to the second and fourth socialization modes. This may be why the middle class youth appear increasingly to resolve moral conflicts in favor of human ends and to raise serious questions about the worth of institutional norms which do not seem to serve these ends. It is also likely that conflicts between humanistic and institutional norms are now salient for relatively more people—and at a younger age, before personal commitments to the institutional norms have been made—owing to social changes which have intensified these conflicts, as well as advances in the technology of mass communication which have made them more visible.

APPENDIX: AUTHORS' DESCRIPTIONS OF DISCIPLINE TECHNIQUES CLASSIFIED IN TABLES 3 TO 6 AS LOVE WITHDRAWAL OR INDUCTION

Techniques Classified as Predominantly Love Withdrawal

Allinsmith, W., and Greening, T. [2]* College students' reports of parent's use of the following technique: "Not punish you directly but ignore you till you were good again," (The raw data were made available by the authors, thus enabling us to recode and reanalyze them in terms of the love-withdrawal and induction categories.)

Burton, R., Maccoby, E. E., and Allinsmith, W. [4] Parent's reported use of "I'm not going to talk to you until you behave better."

Grinder, R. [6] Same as Sears, Maccoby, Levin (below).

Hoffman, M. L., and Saltzstein, H. D. [10] Composite score based on reports by parents and children that the parent uses such techniques as: "Gives you an angry look and walks away," "Does it herself but seems angry and ignores you for a while afterwards," "Asks in an angry voice why you didn't try harder," "Says she doesn't like children who don't show respect for their parents," "Says she won't talk to you or have anything to do with you unless you say you're sorry."

Levine, B. B. [12] Parent's reported use of "I ignore him for a little while."

Sears, R. R., Maccoby, E. E., and Levin, H. [16] "The mother may simply look coldly at the child; she may turn her back, or refuse to listen to what he is saying; she may tell him she does not want to look at him until his face is smiling and pleasant. Or she may put him in a separate room, with the implication that he cannot be accepted in the family circle until he has stopped being 'naughty'! She may use a threat of separation from her, such as that she might have to go away and leave him unless he behaves better, or that she might have to send him away. She may tell him that he is making his mother unhappy, or is hurting her feelings, or is making her want to cry, with the implication that only by being good can he restore the happy loving relationship between them. All these

* Numbers in brackets refer to reference numbers given in tables.

actions, on the mother's part, we regard as manifestations of one underlying process: the mother is indicating to the child that her warmth and affection toward him are conditional on his good behavior."

Sears, R., Rau, L., and Alpert, R. [17] Parent's reported use of "isolation."

Techniques Classified as Predominantly Induction

Allinsmith, W. [1] Parent's reported use of techniques which can be mainly characterized as pointing out the effects of the child's behavior—usually the effects on the child and, less frequently, the effects on the parent (personal communication from the author).

Allinsmith, W. and Greening, T. [2] College students' reports of parents use of the following techniques: "Reason with you calmly in such a way that you felt your mother was hurt or disappointed."

Aronfreed, J. [3] Parent's reported use of the following techniques: "withdrawal of love in the form of rejecting or ignoring the child, indicating disappointment, refusing to speak to the child, or telling the child that he ought to feel bad; techniques influencing the child to assume or examine his own responsibility, such as asking him to report or account for his behavior, insisting upon his making reparation, or encouraging him in various ways to define transgressions for himself or to imitate his own moral responses; explanation of relevant standards (including "reasoning" and "talking things over"), describing the consequences of his actions to the child, suggesting appropriate alternative actions or simply telling the child what aspects of his behavior were unacceptable." (Classified as induction, despite inclusion of love-withdrawal, because they seemed to be far more heavily weighted with induction techniques.)

Grinder, R. [6] Same as Sears, Maccoby, Levin (below).

Hoffman, M. L. and Saltzstein, H. D. [10] Composite score based on (a) reports by parents and children (objective items) that the parent uses such techniques as: "Says she'd do it herself but she's tired or not feeling well," "Looks sad and tells you how much she liked the thing you broke or spoiled," "Reminds you how much it means to them for you to do well," "Says your father will be disappointed," "Says she's hurt or disappointed by what you said"; and (*b*) the parent's reports, on open-ended items dealing with the child's harmful behavior toward peers, that she uses techniques which explicitly point out the harmful consequences of the child's act for the victim, is solicitous of the victim in a manner which clearly communicates her concern to her own child, or suggests that the child engage in some kind of reparative behavior.

Levine, B. B. [12] Parent's report: "I try to explain why what he did was wrong." Also "I reprimand him, saying he disappoints me or hurts me." (The latter item is the one we designated as other-oriented.)

Sears, R., Maccoby, E. E., and Levin, H.

[16] "Reasoning involves not only the mother's labeling of the child's actions and their consequences, but also her drawing of generalizations for the child from things that have happened to him, so that he will be better able to anticipate probable outcomes of various courses of action when similar situations arise in the future. Usually reasoning occurs after a deviation, but sometimes it involves pointing out to the child, in advance, dangers or rewarding situations in his environment of which he would otherwise be unaware."

Sears, R., Rau, L., and Alpert, R. [17] Use of "reasoning" as reported in mother interview or observed in parent-child interaction situation in laboratory setting.

References

Abel, T. Moral judgments among subnormals. *J. abnorm. soc. Psychol.*, 1941, **36**, 378–392.

Adorno, T. W., Frenkel-Brunswick, E., Levinson, D. J., and Sanford, R. N. *The authoritarian personality.* New York: Harper, 1950.

Allinsmith, B. B. Expressive styles: II. Directness with which anger is expressed. In D. R. Miller and G. E. Swanson (Eds.), *Inner conflict and defense.* New York: Holt, 1960. Pp. 315–336.

Allinsmith, W. Moral standards: II. The learning of moral standards. In D. R. Miller and G. E. Swanson (Eds.), *Inner conflict and defense.* New York: Holt, 1960. Pp. 141–176. [1] *

Allinsmith, W., and Greening, T. C. Guilt over anger as predicted from parental discipline: a study of superego development. *Am. Psychol.*, 1955, **10**, 320 (Abstract). [2]

Aronfreed, J. The nature, variety, and social patterning of moral responses to transgression. *J. abnorm. soc. Psychol.*, 1961, **63**, 223–241. [3]

Aronfreed, J. The effect of experimental socialization paradigms upon two moral responses to transgression. *J. abnorm. soc. Psychol.*, 1963, **66**, 437–448.

Aronfreed, J. The origins of self-criticism. *Psychol. Rev.*, 1964, **71**, 193–218.

Aronfreed, J. The internalization of social control through punishment: experimental studies of the role of conditioning and the second signal system in the development of conscience. *Proceedings of the XVIIIth International Congress of Psychology.* Moscow, USSR, August, 1966.

Aronfreed, J., Cutick, R.A., and Fagen, S. A. Cognitive structure, punishment, and nurturance in the experimental induction of self-criticism. *Child Dev.*, 1963, **34**, 281–294.

Aronfreed, J., and Paskal, V. Altruism, empathy, and the conditioning of positive affect. Unpublished manuscript. University of Pennsylvania, 1965.

Aronfreed, J., and Paskal, V. The development of sympathetic behavior in children: an experimental test of a two-phase hypothesis. Unpublished manuscript. University of Pennsylvania, 1966.

* Numbers in brackets refer to reference numbers given in tables.

Aronfreed, J., and Reber, A. Internalized behavioral suppression and the timing of social punishment. *J. Pers. soc. Psychol.*, 1965, 1, 3–16.

Aronson, E., and Carlsmith, J. M. Effect of the severity of threat on the devaluation of forbidden behavior. *J. abnorm. soc. Psychol.*, 1963, 66, 584–589.

Bandura, A. Social learning through imitation. In M. R. Jones (Ed.), *Nebraska symposium on motivation, 1962.* Lincoln: University of Nebraska Press, 1962.

Bandura, A. Influence of models' reinforcement contingencies on the acquisition of imitative responses. *J. Pers. soc. Psychol.*, 1965, 1, 589–595.

Bandura, A. Social-learning theory of identificatory processes. In D. A. Goslin and D. C. Glass (Eds.), *Handbook of socialization theory and research.* Chicago: Rand McNally, 1969.

Bandura, A., Grusec, J. E., and Menlove, F. L. Some determinants of self-monitoring reinforcement systems. *J. Pers. soc. Psychol.*, 1967, 5, 449–455.

Bandura, A., and Huston, A. C. Identification as a process in incidental learning. *J. abnorm. soc. Psychol.*, 1961, 63, 311–318.

Bandura, A., and Kupers, C. J. Transmission of patterns of self-reinforcement through modeling. *J. abnorm. soc. Psychol.*, 1964, 69, 1–9.

Bandura, A., and MacDonald, F. J. Influence of social reinforcement and the behavior of models in shaping children's moral judgments. *J. abnorm. soc. Psychol.*, 1963, 67, 274–281.

Bandura, A., and Mischel, W. Modification and self-imposed delay of reward through exposure to live and symbolic models. *J. Pers. soc. Psychol.*, 1965, 2, 698–705.

Bandura, A., and Perloff, B. Relative efficacy of self-monitored and externally-imposed reinforcement systems. *J. Pers. soc. Psychol.*, 1967, 7, 111–116.

Bandura, A., Ross, D., and Ross, S. A. Transmission of aggression through imitation of aggressive models. *J. abnorm. soc. Psychol.*, 1961, 63, 575–582.

Bandura, A., Ross, D., and Ross, S. A. Imitation of film-mediated aggressive models. *J. abnorm. soc. Psychol.*, 1963, 66, 3–11. (a)

Bandura, A., Ross, D., and Ross, S. A. Vicarious reinforcement and imitative learning. *J. abnorm. soc. Psychol.*, 1963, 67, 601–607. (b)

Bandura, A., and Walters, R. H. *Adolescent aggression.* New York: Ronald Press, 1959.

Bandura, A., and Walters, R. H. *Social learning and personality development.* New York: Holt, Rinehart, and Winston, 1963.

Bandura, A., and Whalen, C. The influence of antecedent reinforcement and divergent modeling cues on patterns of self-reward. *J. Pers. soc. Psychol.*, 1966, 3, 373–382.

Baumhart, R. C. How ethical are businessmen? *Harv. busin. Rev.*, 1961, 39, 6–19; 156–176.

Becker, W. Parent discipline. In M. L. Hoffman and L. W. Hoffman (Eds.), *Review of child development research.* Vol. I. New York: Russell Sage, 1964.

Becker, W. C., Peterson, D. R., Luria, Z., Shoemaker, D. J., Hellmer, L. A. Relations of factors derived from parent-interview ratings to behavior problems of five-year-olds. *Child Dev.*, 1962, 33, 509–535.

Beres, D. Vicissitudes of superego function and superego precursors in childhood. *Psychoanalytic study of the child.* Vol. 13. New York: International Universities Press, 1958.

Berger, S. M. Conditioning through vicarious instigation. *Psychol. Rev.*, 1962, 69, 450–466.

Berkowitz, H., and Zigler, E. Effects of preliminary positive and negative interactions and delay conditions on children's responsiveness to social reinforcement. *J. Pers. soc. Psychol.*, 1965, 2, 500–505.

Berkowitz, L., and Daniels, L. R. Responsibility and dependency. *J. abnorm. soc. Psychol.*, 1963, **66**, 429–436.

Berkowitz, L., and Daniels, L. R. Affecting the salience of the social responsibility norm: effects of past help on the response to dependency relationships. *J. abnorm. soc. Psychol.*, 1964, **68**, 275–281.

Berlyne, D. E. *Conflict, arousal, and curiosity*. New York: McGraw-Hill, 1960.

Boehm, L. The develoment of conscience: a comparison of American children of different mental and socioeconomic levels. *Child Dev.*, 1962, **33**, 575–590.

Boehm, L., and Nass, M. L. Social class differences in conscience develoment. *Child Dev.*, 1962, **33**, 565–575.

Breznitz, S., and Kuglemass, S. Intentionally in moral judgment: development stages. *Child Dev.*, 1967, **38**, 469–480.

Brim, O. G., Jr. Adult socialization. In J. A. Clausen (Ed.), *Socialization and society*. Boston, Mass.: Little Brown, 1968.

Brodbeck, A. J. Learning theory and identification: IV. Oedipal motivation as a determinant of conscience development. *J. genet. Psychol.*, 1954, **84**, 219-227.

Bronfenbrenner, U. Socialization and social class through time and space. In E. E. Maccoby, T. M. Newcomb, and E. L. Hartley (Eds.), *Readings in social psychology*. New York: Holt, Rinehart, and Winston, 1958. Pp. 400–425.

Bronfenbrenner, U. Freudian theories of identification and their derivatives. *Child Dev.*, 1960, **31**, 15–40.

Bronfenbrenner, U. Soviet methods of character education: some implications for research. *Am. Psychol.*, 1962, **17**, 550–565.

Bronson, W. C. Dimensions of ego and infantile identification. *J. Personality*, 1959, **27**, 532–545.

Burton, R. V. The generality of honesty reconsidered. *Psychol. Rev.*, 1963, **70**, 481–499.

Burton, R. V., Allinsmith, W., and Maccoby, E. E. Resistance to temptation in relation to sex of child, sex of experimenter, and withdrawal of attention. *J. Pers. soc. Psychol.*, 1966, **3**, 253–258.

Burton, R. V., Maccoby, R. R., and Allinsmith, W. Antecedents of resistance to temptation in four-year-old children. *Child Dev.*, 1961, **32**, 689–710. [4]

Cain, A. The presuperego "turning inward" of aggression. *Psychoanal. Q.*, 1961, **30**, 171–208.

Campbell, D. T., and Fiske, D. W. Convergent and discriminant validation by the multitrait-multimethod matrix. *Psychol. Bull.*, 1959, **56**, 81–105.

Campbell, E. Q. The internalization of moral norms. *Sociometry*, 1964, **27**, 391–412.

Cava, E. L., and Raush, H. Identification and the adolescent boy's perception of his father. *J. abnorm. soc. Psychol.*, 1952, **47**, 855–856.

Chittenden, G. E. An experimental study in measuring and modifying assertive behavior in young children. *Monogr. soc. res. child Dev.*, 1942, **7**, (No. 1, Serial No. 31).

Cowan, P. A., Langer, J., Heavenrich, J., and Nathanson, M. Social learning and Piaget's cognitive theory of moral development. *J. Pers. soc. Psychol.*, 1969, in press.

Darlington, R. B., and Macker, C. E. Displacement of guilt-produced altruistic behavior. *J. Pers. soc. Psychol.*, 1966, **4**, 442–443.

Dennis, W. Animism and related tendencies in Hopi children. *J. abnorm. soc. Psychol.*, 1943, **38**, 21–37.

DiLollo, V., and Berger, S. M. Effects of apparent pain in others on observer's reaction time. *J. Pers. soc. Psychol.*, 1965, **2**, 573–575.

Dorwart, W., Ezerman, R., Lewis, M., and Rosenhan, D. The effect of brief social deprivation on social and nonsocial reinforcement. *J. Pers. soc. Psychol.*, 1965, **2**, 111–115.

Durkin, D. Children's concepts of justice: a comparison with the Piaget data. *Child Dev.*, 1959, **30**, 59–67. (a)

Durkin, D. Children's acceptance of reciprocity `as a justice-principle. *Child Dev.*, 1959, **30**, 289–296. (b)

Durkin, D. Children's concept of justice: a further comparison with the Piaget data. *J. educ. Res.*, 1959, **52**, 252–257. (c)

Durkin, D. The specificity of children's moral judgments. *J. genet. Psychol.*, 1961, **98**, 3–13.

Easterbrook, J. A. The effect of emotion on cue utilization and the organization of behavior. *Psychol. Rev.*, 1959, **66**, 183–201.

Elmis, A. C., and Milgram, S. Personality characteristics associated with obedience and defiance toward authoritative command. *J. exp. Res. Pers.*, 1966, **1**, 282–289.

Faigin, H. Child rearing in the Rimrock community with special reference to the development of guilt. Unpublished doctoral dissertation, Harvard University, 1952. [5]

Faigin, H. Social behavior of young children in the kibbutz. *J. abnorm. soc. Psychol.*, 1958, **56**, 111–130.

Ferenczi, S. Psychonalysis of sexual habits. *Further contributions to the theory and technique of psychoanalysis.* London: Hogarth Press, 1927.

Festinger, L. *A theory of cognitive dissonance.* Evanston, Ill.: Row, Peterson, 1957.

Festinger, L., and Freedman, J. L. Dissonance reduction and moral values. Symposium of Personality Change. University of Texas. In P. Worchel and D. Byrne (Eds.), *Personality change.* New York: Wiley, 1964. Pp. 220–243.

Fischer, W. F. Sharing in preschool children as a function of amount and type of reinforcement. *Genet. psychol. Monogr.*, 1963, **68**, 215–245.

Flugel, J. C. *Man, morals, and society: a psycho-analytical study.* New York: International Universities Press, 1955.

Freedman, D. G. Constitutional and environmental interactions in rearing of four breeds of dogs. *Science*, 1958, **127**, 585–586.

Freedman, J. L. Long-term behavioral effects of cognitive dissonance. *J. exp. soc. Psychol.*, 1965, **1**, 145–155.

Freud, A. *The ego and the mechanisms of defense.* New York: International Universities Press, 1946.

Freud, S. *Civilization and its discontents.* London: Hogarth Press, 1955. (Originally published, 1930.)

Fromm, E. *Escape from freedom.* New York: Rinehart, 1947.

Geseli, A. Maturation and infant behavior pattern. *Psychol. Rev.*, 1929, **36**, 307–319.

Gewirtz, J. L., and Baer, D. M. Deprivation and satiation of social reinforcers as drive conditions. *J. abnorm. soc. Psychol.*, 1958, **57**, 165–172. (a)

Gewirtz, J. L., and Baer, D. M. The effect of brief social deprivation on behaviors for a social reinforcer. *J. abnorm. soc. Psychol.*, 1958, **56**, 49–56. (b)

Glueck, S., and Glueck, E. *Unraveling juvenile delinquency.* Cambridge, Mass.: Harvard University Press, 1950.

Gordon, J. E., and Cohn, F. Effect of fantasy arousal of affiliation drive on doll play aggression. *J. abnorm. soc. Psychol.*, 1963, **66**, 301–307.

Gordon, J. E., and Smith, E. Children's aggression, parental attitudes, and the effects of an affiliation-arousing story. *J. Pers. soc. Psychol.*, 1965, **1**, 654–659.

Grinder, R. E. Behavior in a temptation situation and its relation to certain aspects of socialization. Unpublished doctoral dissertation, Harvard University, 1960.

Grinder, R. E. Parental childrearing practices, conscience, and resistance to temptation of sixth-grade children. *Child Dev.*, 1962, **33**, 803-820. [6]

Grinder, R. E. Relations between behavior and cognitive dimensions of conscience in middle childhood. *Child Dev.*, 1964, **35**, 881–891.

Grinder, R. E., and McMichael, R. Cultural influences on conscience development: resistance to temptation and guilt among Samoans and American Caucasians. *J. abnorm. soc. Psychol.*, 1963, **66**, 503–507.

Grusec, J. Some antecedents of self-criticism. *J. Pers. scc. Psychol.*, 1966, **4**, 244–252.

Haan, N., Smith, M. B., and Block, J. Moral reasoning of young adults: political-social behavior, family background, and personality correlates. *J. Pers. soc. Psychol.*, 1968, **10**, 183–201.

Haner, C. F., Ellsworth, R. W. Empathic conditioning and its relation to anxiety level. *Am. Psychol.*, 1960, **15**, 493. (Abstract)

Harrower, M. R. Social status and the moral development of the child. *Bri. J. educ. Psychol.*, 1934, **4**, 75–95.

Hartmann, H. *Psychoanalysis and moral values.* New York: International Universities Press, 1960.

Hartmann, H., and Lowenstein, R. Notes on the superego. *Psychoanalytic study of the child.* Vol. 17. New York: International Universities Press, 1962.

Hartshorne, H., and May, M. S. *Studies in the nature of character:* Vol. I, *Studies in deceit;* Vol. II, *Studies in self-control;* Vol. III, *Studies in the organization of character.* New York: Macmillan, 1928–1930.

Hartup, W. N. Nurturance and nurturance-withdrawal in relation to the dependency behavior of preschool children. *Child Dev.*, 1958, **29**, 191–201.

Havighurst, R. J., and Neugarten, B. L. *American Indian and white children.* Chicago: University of Chicago Press, 1955.

Havighurst, R. J., and Taba, H. *Adolescent character and personality.* New York: Wiley (Science Edition), 1949.

Heinicke, C. M. Some antecedents and correlates of guilt and fear in young boys. Unpublished doctoral dissertation, Harvard University, 1953. [7]

Hill, W. F. Learning theory and the acquisition of values. *Psychol. Rev.*, 1960, **67**, 317–331.

Hills, J. R. Within-groups correlations and their correction for attenuation. *Psychol. Bull.*, 1957, **54**, 131–134.

Hoffman, L. W. The father's role in the family and the child's peer-group adjustment. *Merrill-Palmer Q.*, 1961, **7**, 97–105. [8]

Hoffman, M. L. Some psychodynamic factors in compulsive conformity. *J. abnorm. soc. Psychol.*, 1953, **48**, 383–393.

Hoffman, M. L. Power assertion by the parent and its impact on the child. *Child Dev.*, 1960, **31**, 129–143.

Hoffman, M. L. Childrearing practices and moral development: generalizations from empirical research. *Child Dev.*, 1963, **34**, 295–318. (a)

Hoffman, M. L. Parent discipline and the child's consideration for others. *Child Dev.*, 1963, **34**, 573–588. (b) [9]

Hoffman, M. L. Personality, family structure, and social class as antecedents of parental power assertion. *Child Dev.*, 1963, **34**, 869–884. (c)

Hoffman, M. L. Conscience, personality structure, and socialization techniques. *Human Dev.*, 1970, **13**, 90–126.

Hoffman, M. L. Identification and moral development. *Child Dev.* In press.

Hoffman, M. L., and Saltzstein, H. D. Parent practices and the child's moral orientation. Paper read at American Psychological Association, Chicago, September, 1960.

Hoffman, M. L., and Saltzstein, H. D. Techniques and processes in moral development. Mimeographed research report, 1964.

Hoffman, M. L., and Saltzstein, H. D. Parent discipline and the child's moral development. *J. Pers. soc. Psychol.*, 1967, **5**, 45–57. [10]

Hollenberg, E. Child training among the Zeepi with special reference to the internalization of moral values. Unpublished doctoral dissertation, Harvard University, 1952. [11]

Jacobson, E. The self and the object world: vicissitudes of infantile cathexes and their influences on ideational and affective development. *Psychoanalytic study of the child.* Vol. 9. New York: International Universities Press, 1953.

Jacobson, E. Contributions of the metapsychology of psychotic identification. *J. Am. psychoanal. Ass.*, 1954, **2**, 239–262.

Jacobson, E. Superego formation and the period of latency. *The self and the object world.* Part II. New York: International Universities Press, 1964.

Jahoda, G. Immanent justice among West African children. *J. soc. Psychol.*, 1958, **47**, 241–248.

Johnson, M. M. Sex role learning in the nuclear family. *Child Dev.*, 1963, **34**, 319–334.

Johnson, R. C. A study of children's moral judgments. *Child Dev.*, 1962, **33**, 327–354.

Johnson, R. C. Early studies of children's moral judgments. *Child Dev.*, 1962, **33**, 603–605.

Kagan, J. The concept of identification. *Psychol. Rev.*, 1958, **65**, 296–305.

Kaufman, I. (reporter) Panel report on superego development and pathology in childhood. *J. Am. psychoanal. Ass.*, 1958, **6**, 540–551.

Kendall, P. L., and Lazarsfeld, P. F. The relation between individual and group characteristics. In P. F. Lazarsfeld and M. Rosenberg (Eds.), *The language of social research.* New York: Free Press, 1955. Pp. 290–297.

Kimbrell, D. L., and Blake, R. R. Motivational factors in the violation of a prohibition. *J. abnorm. soc. Psychol.*, 1958, **56**, 132–133.

Kohlberg, L. The development of modes of moral thinking and choice in the years 10 to 16. Unpublished doctoral dissertation, University of Chicago, 1958.

Kohlberg, L. Moral development and identification. In H. W. Stevenson (Ed.), *Child psychology. 62nd Yearbook of the National Society for the Study of Education.* Chicago: University of Chicago Press, 1963. (a)

Kohlberg, L. The development of children's orientations toward a moral order: I. Sequence in the development of moral thought. *Vita hum.*, 1963, **6**, 11–33. (b)

Kohlberg, L. Sex differences in morality. In E. E. Maccoby (Ed.), *Sex role development.* New York: Social Science Research Council, 1964.

Kohn, M. L. Social class and parental values. *Am. J. Sociol.*, 1959, **64**, 337–351.

Kohn, M. L. Social class and the exercise of parental authority. *Am. sociological Rev.*, 1959, **24**, 352–366.

Kohn, M. L. Social class and parent-child relationships: an interpretation. *Am. J. Sociol.*, 1963, **68**, 471–480.

Krebs, R. L. Some relationships between moral judgment, attention, and resistance to temptation. Unpublished doctoral dissertation, University of Chicago, 1968.

Lampl de Groot, J. Ego ideal and superego. *Psychoanalytic study of the child.* Vol. 17. New York: International Universities Press, 1962.

Lederer, W. Dragons, delinquents, and destiny. *Psychol. Iss.*, 1964, **4**.

Lefkowitz, M., Blake, R. R., and Mouton, J. S. Status factors in pedestrain violation of traffic signals. *J. abnorm. soc. Psychol.*, 1955, **51**, 704–705.

Le Furgy, W. G., and Woloshin, G. W. Immediate and long-term effects of experimentally induced social influence in the modification of adolescents' moral judgments. *J. abnorm. soc. Psychol.*, 1969, **12**, 104–110.

Lenrow, P. B. Studies of sympathy. In S. S. Tomkins and C. E. Izard (Eds.), *Affect, cognition, and personality*. New York: Springer, 1965.

Lerner, E. *Constraint areas and the moral judgment of children*. Menasha, Wisc.: Banta, 1937. (a)

Lerner, E. The problem of perspective in moral reasoning. *Am. J. Sociol.*, 1937, **43**, 249–269. (b)

Lerner, M. J., and Simmons, C. H. Observer's reaction to the "innocent victim": compassion or rejection? *J. Pers. soc. Psychol.*, 1966, **4**, 203–210.

Levin, H., and Sears, R. R. Identification with parents as a determinant of doll-play aggression. *Child Dev.*, 1956, **27**, 135–153.

Levine, B. B. Punishment techniques and the development of conscience. Unpublished doctoral dissertation, Northwestern University, 1961. [12]

Lewis, M. Social isolation: a parametric study of its effect on social reinforcement. *J. exp. Child Psychol.*, 1965, **2**, 205–218.

Lewis, M., and Richman, S. Social encounters and their effect on subsequent social reinforcement. *J. abnorm. soc. Psychol.*, 1964, **69**, 253–257.

Lewis, M., Wall, A. M., and Aronfreed, J. Developmental change in the relative values of social and nonsocial reinforcement. *J. exp. Psychol.*, 1963, **66**, 133–137.

Liebert, R. M., and Opra, J. P., Jr. Children's adoption of self-reward patterns: incentive level and method of transmission. *Child Dev.*, 1968, **39**, 537–544.

Liu, Ching-Ho. The influence of cultural background on the moral judgment of children. Doctoral dissertation, Columbia University, 1950.

Luria, Z., Goldwasser, M., and Goldwasser, A. Response to transgression in stories by Israeli children. *Child Dev.*, 1963, **34**, 271–281.

Maccoby, E. E. The generality of moral behavior. *Am. Psychol.*, 1959, **14**, 358. (Abstract)

Maccoby, E. E. The taking of adult roles in middle childhood. *J. abnorm. soc. Psychol.*, 1961, **63**, 493–504.

Maccoby, E. E. Moral values and behavior in childhood. In J. A. Clausen (Ed.), *Socialization and society*. Boston, Mass.: Little Brown, 1968.

MacKinnon, D. W. Violation of prohibitions. In H. W. Murray (Ed.), *Exploration in personality*. New York: Oxford University Press, 1938. Pp. 491–501. [13]

MacRae, D. *The development of moral judgment in children*. Unpublished doctoral dissertation, Harvard University, 1950.

MacRae, D., Jr. A test of Piaget's theories of moral development. *J. abnorm. soc. Psychol.*, 1954, **49**, 14–19.

Maslow, A. H. *Motivation and personality*. New York: Harper and Row, 1954.

Maslow, A. H. Deficiency motivation and growth motivation. In R. M. Jones (Ed.), *Nebraska Motivation Symposium*. Lincoln: University of Nebraska, 1955.

McCord, J., and McCord, W. The effect of parental role model on criminality. *J. soc. Iss.*, 1958, **14**, 66–75.

Medinnus, G. R. Immanent justice in children: a review of the literature and additional data. *J. genet. Psychol.*, 1959, **94**, 253–262.

Midlarsky, E., and Bryan, J. H. Training charity in children. *J. Pers. soc. Psychol.*, 1967, **5**, 408–415.

Milgram, S. Behavioral study of obedience. *J. Pers. soc. Psychol.*, 1963, **67**, 371–378.

Milgram, S. Group pressure and action against a person. *J. Pers. soc. Psychol.*, 1964, **69**, 137–143.

Miller, W. B. Lower class culture as a generating mileau of gang delinquency. *J. soc. Iss.*, 1958, **14**, 5–19.

Miller, D. R., and Swanson, G. E. *Inner conflict and defense*. New York: Holt, Rinehart, and Winston, 1960.

Mischel, W. Preference for delayed reinforcement and social responsibility. *J. abnorm. soc. Psychol.*, 1961, **62**, 1–7.

Mischel, W. Theory and research on the antecedents of self-imposed delay of reward. In B. A. Maher (Ed.), *Progress in experimental personality research*. Vol, 2. New York: Academic Press, 1965.

Mischel, W., and Gilligan, C. Delay of gratification, motivation for the prohibited gratification, and responses to temptation. *J. abnorm. soc. Psychol.*, 1964, **69**, 411–417.

Mischel, W., and Grusec, J. Determinants of the rehearsal and transmission of neutral and aversive behaviors. *J. Pers. soc. Psychol.*, 1966, **2**, 197–205.

Mischel, W., and Liebert, R. M. Effects of discrepancies between observed and imposed reward criteria on their acquisition and transmission. *J. Pers. soc. Psychol.*, 1966, **3**, 45–53.

Mischel, W., and Liebert, R. M. The role of power in the adoption of self-reward patterns. *Child Dev.*, 1967, **38**, 673–684.

Morris, J. F. The development of moral values in children. *Br. J. educ. Psychol.*, 1959, **94**, 253–262.

Mowrer, O. H. *Learning theory and personality dynamics*. New York: Ronald Press, 1950.

Mowrer, O. H. Identification: a link between learning theory and psychotherapy. In O. H. Mowrer *Learning theory and personality dynamics*. New York: Ronald Press, 1952. Pp. 573–616.

Mowrer, O. H. *Learning theory and behavior*. New York: Wiley, 1960. (a)

Mowrer, O. H. *Learning theory and the symbolic processes*. New York: Wiley, 1960. (b)

Murphy, L. B. *Social behavior and child personality*. New York: Columbia University Press, 1937.

Mussen, P., and Distler, L. Masculinity, identification, and father-son relationships. *J. abnorm. soc. Psychol.*, 1959, **59**, 350–356.

Mussen P. H., and Distler, L. Child rearing antecedents of masculine identification in kindergarten boys. *Child Dev.*, 1960, **31**, 89–100. [14]

Mussen, P. H., and Kagan, J. Group conformity and perception of parents. *Child Dev.*, 1958, **29**, 57–60.

Mussen, P. H., and Parker, A. L. Mother nurturance and girls' incidental imitative learning. *J. Pers. soc. Psychol.*, 1965, **2**, 94–97.

Nass, M. L. Development of conscience: a comparison of the moral judgments of deaf and hearing children. *Child Dev.*, 1964, **35**, 1073–1080.

Nelson, E. A., Grinder, R. E., and Challas, J. H. Resistance to temptation and moral judgment: behavioral correlates of Kohlberg's measure of moral development. University of Wisconsin. Mimeographed paper.

Nelsen, E. A., Grinder, R. E., and Mutterer, M. L. Sources of variance in behavioral measures on honesty in temptation situations: methodological analyses. *Develop. Psychol.*, 1969, **1**, 265–279.

Nunberg, H. *Principles of psychoanalysis*. New York: International Universities Press, 1955.

Parke, R. D. Nurturance, withdrawal, and resistance to deviation. *Child Dev.*, 1967, **38**, 1101–1110.

Parke, R. D., and Walters, R. H. Some factors influencing the efficacy of punishment training for inducing response inhibition. *Monogr. soc. res. Child Dev.*, 1967, **32**(1).

Payne, D. E., and Mussen, P. H.   Parent-child relations and father identification among adolescent boys. *J. abnorm. soc. Psychol.*, 1956, **52**, 358–362. [15]

Peck, R. F. Family patterns correlated with adolescent personality structure. *J. abnorm. soc. Psychol.*, 1958, **57**, 347–350.

Peck, R. F., and Havighurst, R. J. *The psychology of character development.* New York: Wiley, 1960.

Perdue, O., and Spielberger, C. D. Perceptions of anxious and nonanxious college students of their childhood punishment experiences. *Ment. Hyg.*, 1966, **50**, 390–397.

Piaget, J. *The child's conceptions of the world.* London: Routledge, Kegan Paul, 1928.

Piaget, J. *The moral judgment of the child.* New York: Harcourt, Brace, 1932.

Piaget, J. The moral development of the adolescent in two types of society, primitive and "modern." Lecture given July 24, 1947, at the UNESCO Seminar on Education for International Understanding. UNESCO, Paris. (mimeographed)

Piers, G., and Singer, M. *Shame and guilt: a psychoanalytic and cultural study.* Springfield, Ill.: Thomas, 1953.

Pittel, S. M., and Mendelsohn, G. A. Measurement of moral values: a review and critique. *Psychol. Bull.*, 1966, **66**, 22–35.

Rabin, A. I. Some psychosexual differences between kibbutz and non-kibbutz Israeli boys. *J. project. Tech.*, 1958, **22**, 328–332.

Rabin, A. I., and Goldman, H. Severity of guilt and diffuseness of identification. Paper read at meetings of American Psychological Association, Philadelphia, September 2, 1963.

Rappaport, D. The theory of ego autonomy: a generalization. *Bull. Menninger Clin.*, 1958, **22**, 13–35.

Rebelsky, F. G. An inquiry into the meaning of confession. *Merrill-Palmer Q.*, 1963, **9**, 287–295.

Rebelsky, F. G., Allinsmith, W. A., and Grinder, R. Sex differences in children's use of fantasy confession and their relation to temptation. *Child Dev.*, 1963, **34**, 955–962.

Reese, H. W. Verbal mediation as a function of age level. *Psychol. Bull.*, 1962, **59**, 502–509.

Reich, A. Early identification as archaic elements in the superego. *J. Am. Psychoanal. Ass.*, 1954, **2**, 218–238.

Reiss, A. Social organization and socialization: variations on a theme about generations. Mimeographed paper. Department of Sociology, University of Michigan, 1966.

Rest, J., Turiel, E., and Kohlberg, L. Relations between level of moral judgment and preference and comprehension of the moral judgment of others. *J. Personality*, 1969.

Riesman, D., Denny, R., and Glaser, M. *The lonely crowd.* Garden City, N. Y.: Doubleday Anchor, 1953.

Ritvo, S., and Solnit, A. The relationship of early ego identification to superego formation. *Int. J. Psychoanal.*, 1960, **41**, 295–300.

Rosenblith, J. F. Learning by imitation in kindergarten children. *Child Dev.*, 1959, **30**, 69–80.

Rosenblith, J. F. Imitative color choices in kindergarten children. *Child Dev.*, 1961, **32**, 211–223.

Rosenhan, D., and White, G. M. Observation and rehearsal as determinants of prosocial behavior. *J. Pers. soc. Psychol.*, 1967, **5**, 424–431.

Ross, D. Relationship between dependency, intentional learning, and incidental learning in preschool children. *J. Pers. soc. Psychol.*, 1966, **4**, 374–381.

Sandler, J. On the concept of superego. *Psychoanalytic study of the child*. Vol. 15. New York: International Universities Press, 1960.

Sandler, J., Holder, A., and Meers, D. The ego ideal and ideal self. *Psychoanalytic study of the child*. Vol. 18. New York: International Universities Press, 1963.

Sandler, J., Kawenoka, M., Neurath, L., Rosenblatt, B., Schnurmann, A., and Sigal, J. Classification of superego material in the Hampstead Index. *Psychoanalytic study of the child*. Vol. 17. New York: International Universities Press, 1962.

Sanford, R. N. Individual and social change in a community under pressure: the oath controversy. *J. soc. Iss.*, 1953, **9**, 25–42.

Sanford, R. N. The dynamics of identification. *Psychol. Rev.*, 1955, **62**, 106–118.

Schafer, R. The loving and beloved superego in Freud's structural theory. *Psychoanalytic study of the child*. Vol. 15. New York: International Universities Press, 1960.

Schallenberger, M. Children's rights. *Pedag. Semin. J. genet. Psychol.*, 1894, **3**, 87–96.

Sears, P. S. Child rearing factors related to the playing of sex-typed roles. *Am. Psychol.*, 1953, **8**, 431. (Abstract)

Sears, R. R. Dependency motivation. In M. R. Jones (Ed.), *Nebraska Symposium on Motivation*. Lincoln: University of Nebraska Press, 1963. Pp. 25–36.

Sears, R. R., Maccoby, E. E., and Levin, H. *Patterns of child rearing*. Evanston, Ill.: Row, Peterson, 1957. [**16**]

Sears, R. R., Rau, L., and Alpert, R. *Identification and child rearing*. Stanford, Cal.: Stanford University Press, 1965. [**17**]

Sears, R. R., Whiting, J. W. M., Nowlis, V., and Sears, P. S. Some child-rearing antecedents of aggression and dependency in young children. *Genet. Psychol. Monogr.*, 1953, **47**, 135–203.

Seward, J. P. Learning theory and identification. *J. genet. Psychol.*, 1954, **84**, 201–210.

Sgan, M. L. Social reinforcement, socioeconomic status, and susceptibility to experimenter influence. *J. Pers. soc. Psychol.*, 1967, **5**, 202–210.

Shaplin, J. T. Child training and the identification of preadolescent boys with their parents. Unpublished doctoral dissertation, Harvard University, 1954.

Shoben, E. J. Love, loneliness, and logic. *J. indiv. Psychol.*, 1960, **16**, 11–24.

Siegel, A. E., and Kohn, L. Permissiveness, permission and aggression: the effect of adult presence or absence on aggression in children's play. *Child Dev.*, 1959, **30**, 131–141.

Simmel, G. The number of members as determining the sociological form of the group. *Am. J. Sociol.*, 1902, **8**, 1–46.

Sipos, I. The influence of an induced frustration situation on the stability of honest behavior in pupils. *Čslká. Psychol.*, 1964, **8**, 16–23.

Slater, P. Toward a dualistic theory of identification. *Merrill-Palmer Q.*, 1961, **7**, 113–126.

Solomon, R. L., Turner, L. H. Discriminative classical conditioning in dogs paralyzed by curare can later control discriminative avoidance responses in the normal state. *Psychol. Rev.*, 1962, **69**, 202–219.

Spitz, R. On the genesis of superego components. *Psychoanalytic study of the child*. Vol. 13. New York: International Universities Press, 1958.

Stein, A. H. Imitation of resistance to temptation. *Child Dev.*, 1967, **38**, 157–169.

Stein, M. H. Self-observation, reality, and the superego. In R. M. Loewenstein, L. M. Newman, M. Schur, and A. J. Solnit (Eds.), *Psychoanalysis: a general psychology*. New York: International Universities Press, 1966.

Stevenson, H. W., and Odom, R. D. The effectiveness of social reinforcement following two conditions of social deprivation. *J. abnorm. soc. Psychol.*, 1962, **65**, 429–431.

Stoke, S. M. An inquiry into the concept of identification. *J. genet. Psychol.*, 1950, **76**, 163–189.

Turiel, E. An experimental test of the sequentiality of developmental stages in the child's moral judgments. *J. Pers. soc. Psychol.*, 1966, **3**, 611–618.

Turiel, E. Developmental processes in the child's moral thinking. In P. Mussen, J. Langer, and M. Covington (Eds.), *New directions in developmental psychology*. New York: Holt, Rinehart and Winston, 1969.

Turner, E. A., and Wright, J. C. Effects of severity of threat and perceived availability on the attractiveness of objects. *J. Pers. soc. Psychol.*, 1965, **2**, 128–132.

Unger, S. M. On the development of guilt-response systems. Unpublished doctoral dissertation, Cornell University, 1960. (L. C. Card No. Mic. 60–889.)

Unger, S. M. On the functioning of guilt potential in a conflict dilemma. *Psychol. Rep.*, 1962, **11**, 681–682.

Walster, E. Assignment of responsibility for an accident. *J. Pers. soc. Psychol.*, 1966, **3**, 73–79.

Walters, R. H., and Dembow, L. Timing of punishment as a determinant of response inhibition. *Child Dev.*, 1963, **34**, 207–214.

Walters, R. H., and Karal, P. Social deprivation and verbal behavior. *J. Personality*, 1960, **28**, 89–107.

Walters, R. H., Leat, M., and Mezei, L. Inhibition and disinhibition of responses through empathetic learning. *Can. J. Psychol.*, 1963, **17**, 235–240.

Walters, R. H., and Parke, R. D. Emotional arousal, isolation, and discrimination learning in children. *J. exp. Child Psychol.*, 1964, **1**, 163–173.

Walters, R. H., and Parke, R. D. The role of the distance receptors in the development of social responsiveness. In L. P. Lipsitt and C. C. Spiker (Eds.), *Advances in child development and behavior*. Vol. 2. New York: Academic Press, 1965. Pp. 59–96.

Walters, R. H., and Parke, R. D. Influence of response consequences to a social model on resistance to deviation. *J. exp. Child Psychol.*, 1964, **1**, 269–280.

Walters, R. H., Parke, R. D., and Cane, V. A. Timing of punishment and the observation of consequence to others as determinants of response inhibition. *J. exp. Child Psychol.*, 1965, **2**, 10–30.

Walters, R. H., and Ray, E. Anxiety, social isolation and reinforcer effectiveness. *J. Personality*, 1960, **28**, 358–367.

White, M. S. Social class, child-rearing practices, and child behavior. *Am. Sociol. Rev.*, 1957, **22**, 704–712.

White, R. W. Motivation reconsidered: the concept of competence. *Psychol. Rev.*, 1959, **66**, 297–333.

Whiteman, P. H., and Kosier, P. Development of children's moralistic judgments: age, sex, IQ. and certain personal experiential variables. *Child Dev.*, 1964, **35**, 843–851.

Whiting, J., and Child, I. *Child training and personality: a cross-cultural study*. New Haven, Conn.: Yale University Press, 1953.

Whiting J. W. M. Social structure and child rearing: a theory of identification. Paper read at Tulane University as part of the Mona Brorsman Sheckman Lectures in Social Psychiatry, March 17–19, 1960.

Wright, B. A. Altruism in children and the perceived conduct of others, *J. abnorm. soc. Psychol.*, 1942, **37**, 218–233.

Wrong, D. H. The oversocialized conception of man. *Am. sociol. Rev.*, 1961, **26**, 183–193.

24. Peer Interaction and Social Organization*

WILLARD W. HARTUP

This chapter is concerned with research on peer interactions in childhood. It is based almost entirely upon studies of human children, although recent advances in the comparative study of peer influences are also discussed. An attempt has been made to bring together research on peer influences as this has involved the study of infants, preschool children, elementary school children, and adolescents.

Research evidence concerning peer interactions in infancy does not articulate very well with data concerning group formation and functioning in adolescence. There are numerous gaps and discontinuities in the literature. In some important areas, such as research on small group processes, no attempt to chart developmental trends has ever been made. Nevertheless, a comprehensive picture of peer influences on child behavior can be obtained only by examining the literature on group formation in adolescence as well as the literature on peer interactions in early childhood. The contents of this chapter are diverse, reflecting the diversity of the research in this field.

It is both challenging and difficult to isolate the variance in children's socialization that derives from contact with peers. Peer interactions affect behavior additively or interactively in conjunction with inputs from the inanimate environment and with inputs from parents and other socializing agents. Neither contrived experiments nor experiments of nature provide very good opportunities for studying behavioral changes which derive directly from peer interaction. The investigator must always tease this information from data that also vary as a function of organismic factors, stimulation from the nonsocial environment, and stimulation from adults.

If the world provides virtually no opportunity to study children's socialization occurring solely in the peer group, the world also provides few instances for studying children's development in the absence of peer interaction. There are, of course, many single-child families living in remote habitations. The literature of child psychology, however, contains no reports concerning children who have been deprived of contact with peers. Such reports would probably not be entirely meaningful, in any case, since remote habitation is usually confounded with other biological and environmental anomalies.

It is for these reasons that the field of comparative psychology offers promising assistance to those who wish to examine the effects of peer interaction in the absence of parental influences. This field also provides evidence of the reverse kind—that is, evidence concerning the effects of peer deprivation. Comparative studies, however, cannot answer many of the appropriate questions concerning the effects of peers on the socialization of human children: Do peers contribute to the child's acquisition of social norms? Do peer contacts affect self-attitudes? How are informal peer groups formed? To answer these questions, child psychologists must be content to use multivariate approaches—both differential and experimental—which take into account the nonpeer influences that also contribute to

* The bibliographic assistance of Brian Coates, Elizabeth Konen, and Helen Pitts is gratefully acknowledged. The author also wishes to thank Shirley Moore and John P. Hill for their suggestions and critical comments.

361

childhood socialization. Such studies are given major emphasis in this chapter.

Cross-cultural research shows clearly that the larger social milieu is an important determinant of peer influences on children's development. The impact of the peer group varies enormously from culture to culture. Such variation is found among cultures which employ peers rather incidentally in the child's socialization (e.g., the United States) as well as among cultures which deliberately use peers as socializing agents (e.g., the Soviet Union). In spite of these variations, few attempts have been made to explore peer influence problems cross-culturally. Research concerning peer influences on children's behavior has been most extensive in the case of children living in the United States. It is for this reason that large-scale consideration of the cultural context as a factor in peer relations is not included in this chapter. Since this report emphasizes studies of U.S. children it is, to a considerable extent, culture-specific rather than species-specific.

One of the major themes in this chapter concerns the pervasive role played by situational factors in determining the nature of peer relations in childhood. Even when cultural factors are set aside, few aspects of peer interaction are free from situational influence. Variables such as the nature of the peer group's norms, the difficulty of the group's task, the age of the interacting children, and the personality of the children composing the group are important modifiers of general principles concerning peer interaction.

Two major topics will be discussed:

1. Processes of group formation and group functioning, including those factors that are salient in the emergence of informal peer groups and those personal and situational variables which affect children's groups when such groups are considered as units.

2. Peer influences on the socialization of the individual child, including the manner in which the child evaluates his peers and the influences that peers have upon maintenance and change in his behavior.

This chapter emphasizes the literature on peer relations that has appeared since 1950. A large sampling of material from earlier decades has been included, however, since much of the basic material in this area appeared

well before 1950. Other reviews of methodological problems and research in this area can be found in such sources as the first two editions of the *Manual of Child Psychology* (Carmichael, 1946; 1954); *Handbook of Research Methods in Child Development* (Mussen, 1960); and *Review of Child Development Research* (Hoffman and Hoffman, 1964).

HISTORICAL OVERVIEW

Scientific interest in children's peer relations arose within the context of general interest in the effects of social groups on human behavior. Between 1830 and 1930 there was an outpouring of speculative and theoretical literature that dealt with two major propositions: (1) group experiences are among the most significant determinants of human nature, and (2) social phenomena are amenable to scientific investigation.

During this early period, these propositions were debated by numerous theorists. Some of the most influential were Emile Durkheim, Charles Cooley, George H. Mead, and Sigmund Freud. The data employed by these writers were collected personally and casually. Nevertheless, these insightful men laid out most of the fundamental hypotheses upon which research workers have concentrated their efforts up to, and including, the present time. For example, they were deeply interested in the formation and maintenance of social groups and in the group as an agent of social control. Indeed, a traditional emphasis in social psychology has concerned the role of the group in establishing, maintaining, and changing the behavior of the individual. It is also remarkable that, even in these early writings, it was recognized that early social experience is of central importance to ontogenesis in many species.

Among the early writers, Cooley (1909) probably gave the most explicit attention to the role of peer relations in child development. Even so, he was principally interested in the general effects of group experience on human behavior. The following passages reveal some of the hypotheses that were (and, in some cases, still are) debated in this field:

. . . the view here maintained is that human nature is not something existing separately in the individual, but a group nature or primary phase of society. It is the nature which is developed and expressed in those simple, face-to-face groups that are somewhat alike in all societies; groups of the family, the playground, and the neighborhood. In the essential similarity of these is to be found the basis, in experience, for similar ideas and sentiments in the human mind. In these, everywhere, human nature comes into existence. Man does not have it at birth; he cannot acquire it except through fellowship, and it decays in isolation (pp. 29–30).

In these relations mankind realizes itself, gratifies its primary needs, in a fairly satisfactory manner, and from the experience forms standards of what it is to expect from more elaborate association. Since groups of this sort are never obliterated from human experience, but flourish more or less under all kinds of institutions, they remain an enduring criterion by which the latter are ultimately judged. Of course these simpler relations are not uniform for all societies, but vary considerably with race, with the general state of civilization, and with the particular sort of institutions that may prevail. The primary groups themselves are subject to improvement and decay (pp. 32–33).

There seems to be, among children as among primitive people, a certain reluctance to ascribe laws to the mere human choice of themselves and their fellows. They wish to assign them to a higher source and to think of them as having an unquestionable sanction (p. 45).

Without healthly play, especially group play, human nature cannot rightly develop, and to preserve this is coming to be seen as a special need (p. 49).

Note that in these passages, the child's peer group is given parity with other groups as a source of social norms and as a medium for the gratification of needs. Note that the peer group is recognized as a universal factor in socialization but that the function of such groups may vary across cultures. Note also that the peer group is not presumed to be immutable, even though the factors that lead to change and dissolution are not discussed

in these passages. Note finally that Cooley pointed to a unique quality in the functioning of children's groups—namely, that children ordinarily expect social sanctions to derive from "higher" and more absolute authorities than peers. Piaget (1932) elaborated upon this thesis and he, too, held that reliance on adults for social norms is characteristic of children's play during early childhood.

Another issue that was frequently debated during the early years of this century was whether or not groups constitute legitimate objects of scientific inquiry. As mentioned, most of the early accounts of social influences on behavior were based on casual observation. Adequate methods for carefully observing or manipulating group behavior were virtually nonexistent. There were heated arguments during this period (see Allport, 1954) concerning the "reality" of social phenomena. These arguments swirled around concepts such as "group mind," "collective unconscious," and "institutions." It is not possible to specify the causal factors that finally terminated these debates. Nevertheless, Cartwright and Zander (1960) pointed out that the decline in publications concerning these questions occurred simultaneously, during the 1930s, with the advent of new and improved techniques for gathering "hard data" concerning social behavior.

At least two of the three major advances in the technology of social psychology originated in work with children. The first of these was the invention of controlled methods for observing the behavior of individuals in groups. During the late 1920s and early 1930s categories were devised that were based on overt behavior, sampling techniques were established, and methods developed for obtaining reliable data that could be readily quantified. Many child psychologists contributed to this effort, but major figures included Mildren Parten, Florence Goodenough, and Dorothy Thomas.

A second methodological advance came in 1937 when Lewin and his colleagues began their experimental work on the "social climate" of children's groups. A major purpose of this research was to isolate, by means of experimental techniques, some of the consequences of variations in leadership style. It is true that experimental (i.e., manipulative) strategies were used in group research long before 1937. Most writers cite Triplett's (1897) study as the first experimental study on the topic of peer relations.[1] But the Lewin experiments were begun at a time when observational techniques and quantitative methods were also improving. These improvements, coupled with the subject matter of the experiments, gave this work a catalytic quality that has influenced countless other investigators during the past 30 years.

A third advance that occurred in the 1930s involved the sociometric technique. Although many early investigators had experimented with methods for studying the social choices of children, it was Moreno's (1934) work that popularized the "sociometric test." Moreno began his work with adults, but no invention has had a greater impact on students of the social psychology of childhood. Most commonly, sociometric tests employ subjective data, but such data are readily quantifiable and are particularly appropriate for studies of interpersonal attraction, group cohesiveness, and changes occurring in group functioning. Other investigators have shown that sociograms may be derived from observational data as well as the subjects' own reports. Thus, sociometry is an extremely versatile method. Literally thousands of sociometric studies have been published during the past 30 years.

The scientific study of *children's* groups only partially survived World War II. Thompson (1960) lamented this fact and this state of affairs has changed but little during the past decade. Most of the postwar research concerning group dynamics has involved the study of adults. Work with children has languished except for studies which have been conducted with the purpose of elucidating general problems in this field. There has, and continues to be, relatively little *developmental* research concerning peer relations. It is frustrating, indeed, to report that the major contributions concerning the developmental aspects of peer relations were made 20 years ago. On the bright side, however, is the fact that empirical information concerning many problems in the area of peer influences is increasing.

There is a desperate need for integrative

[1] He found that children were more energetic and performed better at winding fishing reels when they worked in groups than when they worked alone.

theorizing in this area. At the same time, a general theory concerning the development of peer relations may never emerge. Peers are merely a subset among the various social influences to which children are exposed. Peers constitute a special category of socializing agent only because of their chronological age in relation to the chronological age of the child. There may be unique determinants of the peer affectional system (because, for example, peers are ascribed a different status from that ascribed to adults) but we should not expect the laws of peer influence to be entirely orthogonal to the laws governing the child's responsiveness to persons bearing other age, sex, kinship, or ethnic relations to him. On the contrary, it is to be expected that the major elements of a comprehensive theory of children's peer relations will consist of more general and basic principles of behavioral development.

PATTERNS OF INTERACTION WITH AGEMATES

The topography of children's peer interactions changes drastically between infancy and adolescence. The research literature, however, is most complete in documenting those changes that occur during early childhood. Information is sparse concerning peer interactions among children between 18 and 30 months of age, but masses of data have been accumulated concerning the social behavior of children attending nursery schools. The relevant data have been accumulated from observations in both contrived and naturalistic settings. Much of this material was collected during the period between 1930 and 1945 and has been adequately summarized in other publications. The following account is therefore extremely brief.

Primitive responsiveness to peers occurs during the first year of life. The earliest data concerning infant peer relations were derived from observations of institutionalized babies. Bühler (1930) reported that infants were essentially "socially blind" prior to 4 months of age. Bridges (1933) reported, however, that institutionalized babies would orient toward the movements of an infant in an adjoining crib by the age of 2 months. These two investigators agreed that responsiveness to the cries of other babies was not frequent until the fifth month and that, in general, social interest increased slowly until the tenth month. After this point, the vigor of infant-infant interactions was observed to increase more rapidly.

Perhaps the most detailed account of infant-infant interaction is contained in a study by Maudry and Nekula (1939). Babies between the ages of 6 and 25 months were observed using a "baby party" technique. Infants between the ages of 6 and 8 months ignored about half of one another's overtures. The social contacts that occurred were qualitatively similar to contacts made with play materials (i.e., they consisted mainly of exploratory looking and grasping). Fighting (mostly over toys) peaked between 9 and 13 months and decreased after this. Bridges, however, reported that fighting among institutionalized infants peaked at 15 months and did not diminish until after the age of 2 years. This difference in results probably derives from the fact that the "baby party" observations were conducted while the subjects occupied a playpen, whereas Bridges' observations were made in dormitory situations.

All of these early investigators found that, toward the middle of the second year, babies attended positively to peers once conflicts involving play materials were resolved. In other words, toys served as vehicles for both positive and negative social contact. In most instances, the larger infant (even though the subjects were matched in age) proved to be more dominant. It has recently been reported, however, that during co-twin interaction the smaller twin tends to be more successful in confiscating toys (Brown, Stafford, and Vandenberg, 1967). Marked individual differences in peer responsiveness were reported by all of these investigators.

Although responsiveness to peers is evident during infancy, it apparently lags behind responsiveness to adults. This may be due to the fact that other babies are less salient stimuli for the infant than active, mobile adult caretakers. It is also true, however, that the actions of other infants are less familiar stimuli than the sight and sound of adults, even in the case of twins. Furthermore, adults nurture the infant and their activity is likely to be linked to his actions—that is, adults respond to the infant's signals, whereas other infants do this less regularly.

The early development of children's relations with agemates is similar, in some respects, to the sequence with which the peer affectional system develops in Rhesus monkeys (Harlow and Harlow, 1965). The first stage in such development appears to be a "reflex stage," which extends through the first 20 or 30 days of the infant monkey's life. Visual orienting to peers as well as following and other proximity-maintaining behaviors are common. A second stage, the "exploration stage," involves brief periods of gross bodily contact along with oral and manual manipulation of both inanimate and animate objects. Object exploration appears to precede social exploration, but the Harlows believe that similar variables probably determine both types of exploration.

This exploratory stage is followed by a period of "interactive play." Social interaction takes various forms, ranging from rough-and-tumble play to chasing agemates back and forth in the cage. Between the sixth and eighth month, the tempo of such play increases so that play becomes more "integrated" or "mixed." At about one year of age, the infant monkey shows signs of an "aggressive stage" of peer interaction. Genteel rough-housing is replaced by physical contact that includes wrestling, biting, and clasping. These are clearly aversive behaviors. Patterns of dominance can be identified at this time and general social status positions become apparent.

The determinants of these changes in the peer affectional system of the Rhesus have not been thoroughly explored. Total social isolation (including isolation from the mother) for a period of 6 months, as compared to semi-isolation (no contact with other monkeys except for sight and sound), produced an absence of social play with peers for as long as 24 weeks following the termination of the isolation experience. Twelve months of isolation produced even more profound deficits in social behavior.

Deprivation of contact with peers affects social behavior even though the infant monkey is reared with the natural mother. Infants deprived of peer contact (except for sight and sound) during the first 4 months of life developed normal responsiveness to agemates but were more wary and aggressive than infants who had had opportunity for peer contact from 15 days onward. Infants who were deprived of peer contact for 8 months also developed play responses but were even more wary and hyperaggressive than were infants who had been deprived of peer contact for only 4 months. The Harlows concluded that animals who are deprived of the opportunity to form affectional responses to peers during the first year (before the stage of aggressive interaction) fail to acquire the necessary modulating and controlling systems needed later for effective social relations.

The Harlow studies also reveal that contact with peers plays a compensatory role in social development when contact with a mother-figure is lacking or atypical. Whether the infant monkey is reared with the natural mother (either one who has been adequately socialized herself or one who has been reared under "motherless" conditions), an inanimate surrogate mother, or no mother, laboratory-born animals having physical contact with peers during infancy appear to be similar to ferally reared animals in their later social and sexual behavior.

It is difficult to separate the role of social deprivation from stimulus deprivation in some of these studies. Under conditions of social isolation, there was also less frequent exposure to complex and changing patterns of stimulation than in the nonisolation conditions. Sackett (1965) has argued that some of the deficit found in the social behavior of isolated animals may be due to the fact that the postisolation "test" situations involved relatively complex levels of stimulation. Consequently, the test conditions may have been incongruent with the isolated animal's preference for low-complexity stimuli. If isolated animals could be introduced to peers very gradually, the deficits produced by social isolation could conceivably be less pervasive than those reported.

There are several important implications contained in this research. First, there seems to be a stagelike progression in the formation of the peer affectional system in infant monkeys. Second, contact with peers seems to have important compensatory effects when mothering is inadequate. Finally, isolation from peers for prolonged periods, even when mothering is adequate, seems to alter the infant's capacities for subsequently relating to the peer culture. The extent to which these findings may be generalized to the human child is, of course, problematical. There is no reason to assume, however, that these principles do not hold generally in the case of human children.

There is one dramatic study in the literature of child psychology that supports the Harlow results concerning the compensatory value of peer interaction. Freud and Dann (1951) described six German-Jewish children whose parents were killed in concentration camps prior to World War II. These children had arrived at the same camp when they were a few months old and were always in close contact with one another after that. When the children were between 3 and 4 years of age, they were taken to live in England. At this time, their behavior toward adults was bizarre in many ways:

They showed no pleasure in the arrangements which had been made for them and behaved in a wild, restless, and uncontrollably noisy manner. During the first days after arrival they destroyed all the toys and damaged much of the furniture. Toward the staff they behaved either with cold indifference or with active hostility, making no exception for the young assistant Maureen who had accompanied them from Windermere and was their only link with the immediate past. At times they ignored the adults so completely that they would not look up when one of them entered the room (p. 130).

But their extensive contact with each other during their early years had produced a high degree of mutual attachment. This attachment was similar in many respects to the peer attachment shown by infant monkeys who have been reared with peers even though deprived of contact with a mother-figure:

The children's positive feelings were centered exclusively in their own group. It was evident that they cared greatly for each other and not at all for anybody or anything else. They had no other wish than to be together and became upset when they were separated from each other, even for short moments. No child would consent to remain upstairs while the others were downstairs, or vice versa, and no child would be taken for a walk or on an errand without the others. If anything of the kind happened, the single child would constantly ask for the other children while the group would fret for the missing child (p. 131).

The group as a whole was closely knit, there were no clear leaders, and there was almost none of the jealousy, rivalry, or competition shown between siblings in normal families. Sharing was spontaneous; there was much evidence of mutual support.

The whole concentration camp experience, in spite of maintaining an opportunity for the development of social attachments, had effects on behavior that persisted through a year of residence in the therapeutic nursery. At the close of the study, the children were still "hypersensitive, restless, aggressive, and difficult to handle. They showed a heightened autoerotism and some of them the beginning of neurotic symptoms." The major significance of this study, however, is contained in the following words:

But they were neither deficient, delinquent nor psychotic. They had found an alternative placement for their libido and, on the strength of this, had mastered some of their anxieties, and developed social attitudes. That they were able to acquire a new language in the midst of their upheavals, bears witness to a basically unharmed contact with their environment (p. 168).

This study obviously furnishes only limited evidence concerning the variance contributed by peer relations to the social development of the child. Early deprivation and separation were confounded with the unusual peer experiences in this experiment of nature. When combined with data emerging from comparative studies, however, this study persuasively supports the conclusion that early contact with peers contributes significantly to the social development of the human child.

During the years from 2 to 5, social participation changes both quantitatively and qualitatively (Parten, 1932). In nursery school groups, amount of participation is substantially correlated with chronological age (.61), although there is also a slight correlation with IQ (.26). With increasing age, children participate more frequently in parallel, associative, and cooperative activities and less

frequently in idleness, solitary play, and onlooker behavior. Seeking attention and praise from peers increases in absolute frequency during this period (Hattwick and Sanders, 1938; Martin, 1964) and also relative to the frequency with which such overtures are made to adults (Heathers, 1955; Martin, 1964). Positive responses occur much more frequently than aggression (Manwell and Mangert, 1934; Walters, Pearce, and Dahms, 1957).

One observational study has been conducted concerning the frequency of four kinds of generalized positive reinforcement in the peer interactions of nursery school children: *giving positive attention and approval, affection and personal acceptance, submission,* and *tangible objects* (Charlesworth and Hartup, 1967). Such behaviors occurred at a significantly higher rate among 4-year-olds than among 3-year-olds. Situational influences were evident, in that reinforcement rates varied from classroom to classroom and from activity to activity within classrooms. Also, reinforcing rates were reasonably stable over time; a correlation of .51 between fall and spring observations was found for one group of 15 children. Finally, the most reinforcing children were found to scatter their reinforcements widely, and the more reinforcements a child gave to others, the more he in turn received (average $r = .75$). Kohn (1966) has reported similar findings from an observational study of 11 kindergarten children. Rate of positive social initiations was significantly related to positive initiations received ($r = .68$). Thus reciprocity appears to characterize the young child's interactions with his agemates.

Altruism increases only slightly during the preschool years (Gewirtz, 1948; Hartup and Keller, 1960; Stith and Connor, 1962; Walters et al., 1957). Situational factors, such as the range of children's ages in the peer group, are related to the occurrence of such behavior (Murphy, 1937). It is clear, however, that preschool children display helpfulness and sympathy much less frequently than they manifest simple positive social overtures. Thus the basic social orientation at this age was described by Piaget as "egocentric."

Marked increases in sharing behavior occur between the nursery-kindergarten years and preadolescence (Handlon and Gross, 1959;

Ugurel-Semin, 1952). Age differences in social orientation have also been studied. Fry (1967) employed a matching task that required the subject to "take the point of view of his partner." The subjects ranged in age between 9 and 20 years. Performance on this task increased directly with age. Further, the performance of the 9- and 10-year-old children did not improve, above initial levels, when they were shifted to different partners. On the other hand, improvement was apparent for 13- and 14-year-olds and was quite marked in the case of college students. Consistent with these findings are Smith's (1960) results, which show a decline between the preschool years and adulthood in amount of unilateral action occurring in groups of individuals who are working on collaborative projects.

Although social participation and cooperative play increase during the preschool years, competition and rivalry also increase. Leuba (1933) compared performance on a peg-inserting task when the child worked alone with performance when another child was present and also working at the task. First, 2-year-old children were little affected by the presence of the other child. Next, the output of 3- and 4-year-old children was reduced by the distraction and rivalry elicited by the other child's presence. The output of the 5-year-olds, however, was increased by the presence of the second child. Presumably, by this age, children are able to use rivalrous motivation in an adaptive manner. A variation on this interpretation is that inserting pegs is easier for 5-year-olds than for 4-year-olds, so that increased motivation produces a facilitating, rather than interfering, effect on performance. Greenberg (1932) discovered profound differences in amount of rivalrous competition shown by children between the ages of 2 and 7 when the subjects worked under competition-inducing instructions. Ascendant behavior, as contrasted with submissiveness, also increases in peer interactions during the preschool years. In one study (Stott and Ball, 1957), such behaviors reached a peak among 5-year-olds and changed little during the elementary school years.

Quarreling changes in several respects during early childhood (Dawe, 1934). Older preschoolers participate in fewer, but longer quarrels. Disputes occur most frequently between children of the same sex who are of different ages; boys engage in more quarreling than girls.

Age changes in aggressive behavior cannot be described simply. Total frequencies of aggressive peer interaction tend to increase between the ages of 2 and 4 years and then to decline (Walters et al., 1957). On the other hand, sex differences in aggression become more pronounced during the preschool period and modes of aggression also change. For example, screaming, weeping, hitting, and physical attack decline. Relative to physical aggression, verbal aggression increases (Jersild and Markey, 1935). Although the evidence is very sparse, the decline in total aggression, with physical aggression declining relatively more than verbal aggression, appears to continue through middle childhood. Thus qualitative changes may be of greater significance than changes with age in total amount of peer aggression.

There is little doubt that the changes which occur in child-child interactions during infancy and childhood are closely linked with changes in sensory-motor capacities, cognitive skills, and the development of impulse controls. It is well known, for example, that young children have difficulty in "taking the role of another." This capacity increases during middle childhood (e.g., Flavell et al., 1968). Role-taking ability would appear to be one prerequisite for the emergence of many of the social behaviors described in this section. It is inherent, for example, in cooperation and in altruistic interaction. Thus we can speculate that age-changes in altruism and age changes in role-taking derive from a common source. This should not be taken to mean that increased role-taking skill *causes* increases in altruistic behavior. It is just as reasonable to argue that altruistic interchange (perhaps under the control of external reinforcers) contributes to changes in the child's cognitive functioning. It is important to note, however, that these age changes occur in tandem and it is reasonable to speculate that they are functionally related.

Recent experimental work has shown that contingencies of both adult and peer reinforcements affect the frequency with which children display assertive, aggressive, cooperative, and competitive behaviors. Those studies which show that peer responses act as reinforcers of such behavior are reviewed in later sections of this chapter. At this point, however, it should be noted that other research (e.g., Harris, Wolf, and Baer, 1967) shows that contingently presented adult attentiveness increases social participation, modifies frustration reactions, and changes the character of children's play behavior. Such studies do not prove that changes in the frequency with which the environment dispenses reinforcement produce all of the age changes in peer interaction. Quite probably the environment provides more regular reinforcement for social participation as the child grows older but detailed verification of this hypothesis has not yet appeared in the ecological literature. To deny that such reinforcements are operative in producing age changes in peer interaction, however, would be foolhardy indeed.

Finally, some of the age changes occurring in peer interaction probably derive from modeling. Peer modeling is discussed later in the chapter. Nevertheless, we can note here that research has repeatedly shown that adult models can alter the manner in which children behave toward agemates. Rosenhan and White (1967), for example, showed that exposure to charitable adult models produced increases in the extent to which elementary school children donated gift certificates to charity; Midlarsky and Bryan (1967) also demonstrated that adult models were effective in modifying patterns of altruism. Other recent work indicates that the self-reinforcement criteria which a child will display in front of another child can be modified by prior exposure to a self-reinforcing model (Mischel and Liebert, 1966). Bandura's work (see Bandura and Walters, 1963) concerning the imitation of aggression also has implications for theorizing concerning the origins of age changes in peer interaction. These studies, of course, do not show how frequently children of various ages are exposed to altruistic or aggressive models. They show only that modeling can affect agemate interaction. It seems reasonable to conclude, however, that age changes partially derive from variations in experiences with social models.

GROUP FORMATION

The study of children's groups has long been overshadowed by research dealing with the group behavior of adults. Nevertheless, there have been many excellent studies of children's interactions in groups. Bracketing a period of 40 years are the brilliant descriptive accounts of group functioning by Thrasher (1927), Shaw and McKay (1931), and the work of Muzafer and Carolyn Sherif (1964). During this period, other studies appeared that were focused on such problems as behavior contagion and social power. The work of Lewin and his associates has already been cited as a high mark in the study of leadership factors. These examples, however, represent deviations from the norm. Research on children's groups has been sporadic, extremely heterogeneous in theoretical orientation, and diverse with respect to the nature of the problems studied.

It is appropriate that research on children's groups has been heavily influenced by adult studies since many factors influencing group formation should not be age-specific. On the other hand, many qualitative changes in group functioning take place during childhood. For example, the role played by norms in group functioning differs drastically in groups composed of 4-year-olds compared to the operation of norms in groups of 10-year-olds or groups of adolescents. Evidence is very scattered, however, concerning such age changes.

The term *group* should be used with precision. First, we must exclude instances in which children are found together as aggregates or mere conglomerations of individuals. Groups, as opposed to aggregates, are composed of *interacting* individuals. Groups are composed of people who "bear an explicit psychological relationship to one another" (Krech and Crutchfield, 1948); who are "organisms interacting" (Gibb, 1954); or "who stand in more or less definite interdependent status" (Sherif, Harvey, White, Hood, and Sherif, 1961). But interaction alone does not define a group—at least a group that possesses much stability through time. In addition, groups are composed of people who possess common goals or common motives (Sherif and Sherif, 1964).

Other factors which are important in the formation and maintenance of peer groups include norms and status differentiation. Stable groups possess a set of explicit or implicit values (norms) that are shared by the individual members and which, to some extent, set them off from other people. Norms may consist of a group code, but shared interests and common motivations are also normative aspects of group functioning. Status differentiation is also a universal characteristic of groups. Even though an aggregate shares certain motives and certain values, it is not truly a group until leaders and followers have emerged or until labor has been divided in some way.

Each of the factors mentioned in the foregoing paragraphs has been explored in relation to the formation and functioning of children's groups. It is clear that shared goals are key factors in the initial formation and maintenance of children's informal peer groups, at least in middle childhood (Sherif et al., 1961). It is also clear that individual differences inevitably produce differentiation of status positions; children's peer groups always possess a hierarchical structure. Further, new norms are likely to arise through intragroup interaction once a common purpose has been established and status positions have been defined within the group.

The preceding comments apply to both informal ("real") groups and *ad hoc* groups (aggregates brought together for some short-term purpose and when there has not been a history of previous interaction). Some writers (e.g., Stogdill, 1950) have suggested that aggregates which possess clearly defined and stable status positions should be called *organizations*. It may be convenient to refer to certain institutionalized groups (such as school clubs, community groups, and other groups which have a stable existence in spite of changes in membership) as organizations but this distinction is not a particularly useful one since status differentiation is a universal attribute of group functioning.

The term *membership group* is used to refer to any group to which the individual belongs, whether or not he aspires to membership. Certain immutable factors such as sex, age, school status, or ethnicity determine membership in some groups. On the other hand, membership status can be bestowed on the basis of an infinite number of other attributes. Most investigators are agreed, however, that the internal functioning of groups and their impact on the individual child vary according to the degree to which the group serves a *reference function*—that is, according to the strength of the member's identification with the group or desire to belong to it. The nature of this reference function and the plight of the child who lacks affiliation with a reference group is graphically depicted by this excerpt from Carson McCullers' great novel, *The Member of the Wedding:*

The long hundred miles did not make her sadder and make her feel more far away than the knowing that they were them and both together and she was only her and parted from them, by herself. And as she sickened with this feeling a thought and explanation suddenly came to her, so that she knew and almost said aloud: *They are the we of me.* Yesterday, and all the twelve years of her life, she had only been Frankie. She was an *I* person who had to walk around and do things by herself. All other people had a *we* to claim, all others except her. . . . All members of clubs have a *we* to belong to and talk about. The soldiers in the army can say *we,* and even the criminals on chain-gangs. But the old Frankie had had no *we* to claim, unless it would be the terrible summer *we* of her and John Henry and Berenice—and that was the last *we* in the world she wanted (McCullers, 1951, p. 646).

The remainder of this section is devoted to research concerning both spontaneous (informal) and *ad hoc* children's groups. Studies are discussed in which data were collected both in natural conditions and in conjunction with experimental manipulations. The major theme is the *formation* of peer groups. It should be recognized, however, that to separate the process of group formation from other aspects of group functioning is to make an arbitrary distinction. Practically all of the research concerning group formation has involved preadolescent or adolescent subjects and most of the research deals with boys rather than with girls.

Time is one dimension that must be considered in discussing the formation of informal peer groups. Such groups do not emerge instantaneously, even though *ad hoc* groups may become structured and productive within very short periods. The informal peer group, however, becomes organized on the basis of interpersonal observations, interactions, and evaluations that cumulate over time. Even though status positions may become polarized within minutes of initial social contact, the structure of informal groups is likely to change considerably over longer periods.

Time is an important dimension in group formation in yet another sense. Children, initially strangers to one another, do not immediately develop group norms. Again, some norm formation may occur rather quickly. On the other hand, observational studies show that group standards, codes, and goals proliferate and undergo elaboration as time passes. Thus, in order to understand the processes of group formation, it is necessary to study peer interaction over some period of time. Many of the determinants of group formation cannot be deduced from observations of groups that already exist.

Group formation in childhood has been described very clearly in a series of experiments conducted by Sherif and his colleagues. All of these studies involved groups of preadolescent or adolescent boys. In the first of these (Sherif and Sherif, 1953), several major hypotheses were tested: (1) when individual children are brought together in physical proximity and perceive that they share a common goal, the aggregate will acquire a hierarchical structure—leadership and followership positions, friendship patterns, and a division of labor will emerge; (2) the group will acquire a reference function—shared attitudes and values will become evident; (3) if two such groups are brought into a relationship under conditions of competition and frustration, intergroup hostility will occur.

Two groups of middle-class white, Protestant boys were recruited and removed to a summer campsite. The experiment consisted of three phases. During Stage I, the two groups lived apart for 3 days while fluctuations in informal groupings were observed and budding friendships were measured by means of disguised sociograms. Stage II began when the initial groups were split and two new groups formed. The data from Stage I were used to stratify the new groups. For example, friendship combinations were broken up and the two new groups were carefully matched on the basis of ability and personality characteristics. Stage II lasted for 5 days. The groups occupied separate quarters and had their own programs of activities. Adult leadership was relatively unobtrusive; intergroup contact was minimal.

Data from this stage of the research reveal several important aspects of the formative process. First, after 5 days, a clear hierarchical structure emerged in both groups. Positions at the top and at the bottom of the status hierarchy polarized first. In neither group was there a perfect correlation between leadership status and popularity. Important differences existed between the groups in the cohesiveness of the social structure. The "Bull Dogs," for example, appeared more closely knit than the "Red Devils" since the hierarchy in the latter group included only a few high-status boys while the remainder occupied relatively low-status positions.

The next most important finding from this stage of the experiment concerns the emergence of norms. There was much "we-they" talk; each group adopted an identifying color and a group nickname. Rules, sanctions, and punishments were developed by the group members themselves. Intergroup attitudes at this point were competitive and mildly derogatory but not openly hostile. Friendship choices, however, had shifted markedly from Stage I. Such choices were now centered in the new in-groups.

The Sherifs believe that aggregates acquire the foregoing characteristics because the social unit itself becomes, over time, a salient source of satisfaction and frustration to the individual member. Emergent hierarchies and shared norms, however, also maintain the existence of the group. It does not follow that children have a "natural" propensity for forming structured groups or that they need to share norms with peers in order to survive. Rather, it seems that the incentives and punishments arising from peer interaction itself produce these outcomes; these outcomes, in turn, serve to sustain the group.

Later research by these investigators (Sherif and Sherif, 1964) has shown that peer group norms are not perpetuated indefinitely. The individual members, once involved in group interactions, may change their interests or attitudes. Once the group's norms cease to be salient for an individual child, the group may change. Either membership will shift or the group's norms will be modified. Once again, the dimension of time in group formation must be emphasized. Informal peer groups of children or adolescents are not immutable. On the contrary, they undergo constant change (see also Hallworth, 1953).

In the preceding experiment, Stage III began when the camp staff brought the two groups ("Bull Dogs" and "Red Devils") into contact and into direct competition through a series of contests. This competition inadvertently resulted in imbalanced frustration. One group consistently won while the other consistently lost. When the experimenters contrived a frustration experience for the losing group, a series of violent intergroup feuds and antagonisms resulted. The solidarity of the most severely frustrated group disintegrated considerably and the group which had the more democratic organizational structure during Stage II was most concerted in its out-group antagonism. Efforts on the part of the camp staff to establish intergroup solidarity were only partially successful before the experiment was concluded.

The experimental design employed in this study involved a succession of manipulations on only two groups. The data strongly suggest, however, that frustration and competition are major determinants of disharmony in intergroup relations. The role of intergroup antagonism in precipitating change in the structure of the in-group is also revealed, emphasizing the fact that situational or environmental factors are extremely important in the maintenance of cohesiveness within the informal peer group.

A second experiment (Sherif et al., 1961), commonly called the Robbers Cave experiment, replicated and extended the foregoing findings. Twenty-two fifth-grade boys were divided into matched aggregates and were observed during the time in which group formation took place. In this experiment, neither group was aware of the other's presence. Once again, the aggregates became units in a relatively short time; status hierarchies were evident. Leaders were visible, although leadership and ability were not perfectly correlated. Norms emerged, consisting mainly of shared attitudes about individual members themselves, places in the camp, and camp activities. These norms were not as pervasive as in the earlier experiment. When the groups accidentally discovered each other, however, norms proliferated within each in-group.

Contrived instances of intergroup competition and frustration were better controlled in this experiment than in the first study. Success and failure were manipulated so that neither group experienced more frequent failure than did the other. Nevertheless, the introduction of competition produced a marked increase in intergroup hostility. Unlike the earlier results, solidarity within the in-group was promoted by the competition. Signs of internal friction and disintegration were temporary, usually following upon specific instances of failure or frustration. Aggression toward the outgroup seemed to be characteristic of both high- and low-status members even though it had been expected that the low-status boys might manifest more of this behavior.

Although the general solidarity of each group did not decline under conditions of competition and conflict, the internal structuring of both groups underwent change. Different boys became leaders during this stage. In particular, those boys who excelled in the competition rose in the status hierarchy. Thus the vissicitudes of leadership appear to be directly related to changes taking place in the peer group's major goals.

The final episodes in this experiment involved an attempt by the experimenters to engineer instances in which both groups would have to work cooperatively on highly salient problems (such as restoring the water supply). It was predicted that this experience would reduce intergroup conflict, reduce stereotyping in intergroup evaluation, and produce increases in friendship choices across group lines. This proved to be the case.

The experiments described have numerous practical implications. If, for example, the membership of two hostile peer groups can be reshuffled and the newly formed groups induced to function with some common purpose, interpersonal hostility *within* each new group should diminish. Further, if two hostile groups combine to work cooperatively toward a superordinate goal, intergroup hostility should be reduced.

The first of these propositions has been subjected to several tests in which Negro and white children have been brought together for short periods of equalitarian contact in racially integrated summer camps. Mussen (1950) found that such experience did not change significantly the attitudes of white children, as a whole, toward Negro children.

The existence of individual differences in the effects of the camp experience is suggested, however, by the moderate correlation ($r =$ .51) that was found between pretests and posttests of ethnocentrism. Mussen's results indicate that these individual differences in prejudice-change were associated with personality factors. Yarrow, Campbell, and Yarrow (1958) also reported marked individual differences in the effects of an integrated camp experience. In this instance, however, the group contact produced significant reduction of prejudice in the group as a whole. It has also been reported that experience in international summer camps increases cross-national friendship choices while decreasing cross-national sterotypes and ethnocentric attitudes (Bjerstedt, 1961).

The inconsistent outcomes of group contact experiments with children is generally consonant with other studies involving interracial contact (Eisenman, 1965). Such contact, by itself, may not always bring about significant improvement in interracial attitudes. The Sherif studies emphasize that such contact must involve mutually shared norms and cooperative activity in order for reduction in tensions to occur. Ordinary camp programs may or may not emphasize such experiences. It is also possible that those studies showing the most general reduction in ethnocentric attitudes may have included populations who were less prejudiced in the first place (e.g., Bjerstedt). Comparative data are clearly needed concerning the effects of different kinds of interracial camp experience. Programs could be varied experimentally in the degree to which emphasis is placed on norm-sharing, cooperative activity, the formation of small interracial subgroups, and so forth.

A final study by the Sherifs (1964) confirms some of the earlier results. In this instance, however, the subjects consisted of intact peer groups of adolescent boys. First, structurization was visible in all groups; the leadership and lowest status positions were easiest to identify. Further, the relation between leadership and popularity varied considerably across the groups studied. Changes in the group's activities were likely to be accompanied by shifts in the status hierarchy. Group membership was not completely constant. Addition of new members and elimination of old members were relatively frequent

and occurred most often at the lower status levels.[2] Thus these informal adolescent groups seemed particularly "open" at the bottom of the status hierarchy. The functioning of norms in these adolescent reference groups was also clearly visible. Most groups used insignia, shared standards of dress, and adopted consensual rules governing important activities. Loyalty to the peer group was one of the most pervasive of these norms. Application of group rules to individual members was likely to vary, however, according to the importance of the activity and the standing of the individual member in the group.

Once again, the findings suggest that informal peer groups are not organized just so that children can be one of a "set." Admittedly, this generalization is based on studies of boys; girls might be an exception. Nevertheless, it appears that informal peer groups coalesce on the basis of some strong common motivation that is not reduced by other social affiliations. Interactions within the group itself serve as primary sources of such gratification. If satisfaction fails to develop or diminishes, the cohesiveness of the group is likely to be reduced and dissolution may result. Thus intragroup behavior is an interactive function of situational, personal, and interpersonal variables.

Group Norms

Do group norms govern peer interaction at all age levels? If infancy is excluded, the answer to this question is probably yes. There is little question, however, that norms are likely to be less obvious and less pervasive in young children's peer groups than in groups of older children.

Primitive norms were noted by Faigin (1958) in her observations of Israeli 2-year-olds. There were six children in each of these groups and the ages of the children ranged between 19 and 38 months. These children clearly differentiated "we" from "they" and appeared to be strongly identified with the peer group. For example, group members defended each other when quarrels developed with children from an out-group. Within each of the groups, interest in role-playing activities was the most salient norm, but there

2 New children accepted into ongoing groups acquire clearly defined and relatively stable positions rather quickly (Ziller and Behringer, 1961).

were also relatively clear sanctions governing social interaction. It is somewhat difficult, however, to tell how influential the adult caretakers were in establishing these particular norms.

Other data concerning the operation of norms in groups of nursery school children were presented by Merei (1949). This investigator observed 12 4-child groups in day nurseries. Some of these groups consisted of children as young as 4 years of age; others were made up of children as old as 11. Merei did not discuss age differences in norm formation but, in describing *all* of the groups, he states:

The children formed traditions such as permanent seating order (who should sit where); permanent division of objects (who plays with what); group ownership of certain objects, ceremonies connected with their use, expressions of belonging together; returning to certain activities; rituals; sequences of games; forming a group jargon out of expressions accidentally uttered, etc. (p. 24).

These data, inadequate though they are, suggest the following: in relatively small subgroups (three- to six-child groups), the nursery school peer group develops norms, at least in the form of shared interests and common conventions. Subgroups, for example, are likely to be clearly aware that "we are the ones who play cowboys." There is less convincing evidence, however, that peer groups of young children spontaneously produce the wide number of binding conduct-standards that emerge in informal groups of older children. The young child is clearly responsive to rules, particularly those emanating from adults. Nevertheless, as will be shown later, children of this age do not yield consistently to group norms in common conformity tasks.

Intensive study of normative influences in young children's groups is clearly needed. The role played by norms in such groups may differ in degree, or pervasiveness, from the role played by norms in groups of older children. But existing data do not support more specific conclusions concerning normative factors in group functioning during the preschool years.

Groups of kindergarten-primary school children are apparently able to produce much more formal, moralistic norms than are groups of younger children. Documentation is again weak. One descriptive report (Turner, 1957) concerns a group of children of this age who participated in an experiment in self-government. They were able to establish an elaborate code for governing their conduct in school. In this study, the teacher devised a group discussion procedure for handling altercations and other social problems, but the group was left free to devise its own statutes. Over a 3-year period, a quasi legal procedure for handling disputes was developed. The "criminal code" that emerged was remarkably similar to conventional adult sanctions. This account is a fascinating descriptive record. The evidence it offers concerning the formation of norms by groups of young children is confounded, of course, by the teacher's influence. Since she was quite unobtrusive, however, the results suggest that the children themselves and the interactions that occurred within the group were the principal sources of the norms that developed. This account of normative functioning in the peer group contrasts strikingly with the accounts of norm development in preschool groups. Thus the early school years appear to form a transitional period—peer group norms are increasingly manifest.[3]

Numerous studies, in addition to those conducted by the Sherifs, confirm the fact that group norms are salient aspects of peer group functioning during middle childhood (Crane, 1952; Haines, 1953; Hallworth, 1953; Polansky, Lippitt, and Redl, 1950). There is little evidence, however, to suggest that group norms are either more or less pervasive in informal peer groups in adolescence than during middle childhood. The norm taxonomy shifts across this time span, of course, but this taxonomy has been explored only among adolescents. For example, a factor analytic study of the attitudes and activities serving as norms in informal adolescent groups was completed by Phelps and Horrocks in 1958. A large body of questionaire data was obtained from a sample of 200 adolescents in a small Ohio city. The analysis revealed that socioeconomic status and sex were not overriding variables in determining group norms, although both vari-

[3] Piaget (1932) has also emphasized this point; his views will be presented later in this chapter.

ables had significant loadings on several of the factors emerging from this analysis. For example, emancipation from the home and assumption of the adult role (as reflected by wanting to have access to automobile transportation and to get away from adult supervision) were central among adolescents from lower socioeconomic families; pressures in the direction of the school's moral code were central among upper-class adolescents; engaging in a variety of activities within the radius of home or school supervision was characteristic of girls, although the normative activities of upper-class girls (e. g., slumber parties, patronizing high-quality restaurants, dancing, making candy) were not shared by lower class girls; masculine-role activities were central norms for boys. Boys' norms, in general, were somewhat less influenced by variations in social class than girls' norms. In contrast to the foregoing sex- or class-linked norms, concern for social conformity, appearance, and rejection of "immature" behavior was a factor that emerged without appreciable loadings from either sex or socioeconomic status. The descriptive material assembled by Sherif and Sherif (1964) on adolescent groups of boys does not differ markedly from the preceding data.

There is little evidence concerning the stability of group norms during different periods in childhood or variations in the latitude with which norms apply to the behavior of individual members within preadolescent and adolescent groups. Wilson (1963) reported that ethnic attitudes become more stable and less variable from early to late adolescence. On the other hand, as will be discussed later, general conformity to peer pressures actually decreases during adolescence. Once again, there are interesting developmental problems relating to group functioning that need to be explored.

Group Structures

We have stated that all peer groups—both groups of young children and groups of adolescents—are structured. Age changes in the structurization of children's groups, however, are probably not as dramatic as their common stereotypes. In the first place, the characteristics of popular and non-popular older children are not markedly different from the attributes of popular and non-popular younger children. Sociometric fluctuations are somewhat more marked in groups of nursery school children than in groups of older children. But considerable stability exists even in young children's groups. These aspects of group structure will be discussed in a separate section of this report.

Cleavages within informal groups may differ, however, according to the age of the group. Preschool groups show cleavages by sex and by race just as do the peer groups of older children. As will be reported later, these cleavages are only slightly less strong in the young child's peer group. Little evidence can be found, however, to support the notion that such cleavages in young children's groups are based on strong rejection of different-race children or children of the opposite sex.

For example, in studies by Stevenson and Stevenson (1960), McCandless and Hoyt (1961), Campbell and Yarrow (1956), and Lambert and Taguchi (1956) no strong rejection of racial out-groups was reported in integrated groups of young children. This was the case, even though racial cleavage existed as defined by the frequency with which children had play contacts with same- and different-race children. On the other hand, rejection definitely becomes a factor in peer group cleavages as children become older (Campbell and Yarrow). It has been suggested that one determinant of racial cleavages among young children is the comfort that is signalled by the stimulus of a like-race child. There also may be greater norm-sharing between like-sex or like-race children. Such norm-sharing may also function as a determinant of cleavages in older children's groups but rejection appears to function as a more powerful determinant of cleavages in older children's groups than in younger peer groups.

The cohesiveness of informal groups increases, at least from the preschool period to middle childhood. The evidence is diverse, but strong, on this point. Ad hoc groups of elementary school children who are engaged in solving a common problem show more other-directed actions than do groups of preschool children (e.g., Smith, 1960). The sheer tendency to participate in informal peer groups (such as "gangs") is positively related to age. Thrasher (1927) reported that gang formation is most prevalent during early adolescence. Cultural factors, however, may modify the timing of this peak. For example, Wolman (1951) reported that Israeli youth most frequently participated in gangs between the ages of 10 and 12. In this instance, the early decline in gang formation may be related to the increase in the Israeli child's opportunities to join organized youth groups, which occurs at age 13.

Other evidence concerning age factors in group structuring concerns the individual member's participation in coalitions. Vinacke and Gullickson (1964) studied same-sex triads composed of 7- and 8-year-olds, 14- to 16-year-olds, and college students. A task was used that made it necessary for the subjects to bargain and form alliances. There were no significant age differences among the female subjects in the tendency to form coalitions. Girls used essentially accomodative strategies at all levels. There was, however, a significant trend for older boys to form coalitions more frequently than younger boys. The younger boys did not differ from the girls; these males showed accomodative strategies in their bargaining. On the other hand, greater amounts of "exploitive bargaining" were used by the older males. They also showed more frequent competition and intensive effort to defeat their opponents than did the younger boys.

Such age differences suggest that sex-typing has an impact on certain aspects of group structurization. The impact of sex-typing on group behavior may, however, depend on the nature of the group's task. For example, males and females are subjected to different pressures with respect to approval-seeking and task-mastery. Such differences could well produce different kinds of group structures when the task is a competitive one, such as was used by Vinacke and Gullickson. Sex differences in structurization may not be the case, however, when the group's mode of functioning is noncompetitive.

In summary, common goals, interdependent and cooperative interaction, and the existence of norms have a significant impact on the formation of children's groups. These factors appear to be involved in the formation of cohesive peer groups at all age levels. Norms may vary in pervasiveness at different age levels, and the taxonomy of peer group norms may depend on age and cultural setting. Status differentiation is found in all children's groups but the personal and situational variables affecting such differentiation are not strongly age-specific. Time is an important dimension in the formation of informal peer groups. Consolidation of aims, crystallization of a structure, and norms may emerge rapidly but these developments do not occur instantaneously. Further, the equilibrium of children's groups is seldom more than momentary. Flux—in structure, in cohesiveness, in central motives, and in membership—is one of the most common characteristics of children's peer groups.

SITUATIONAL FACTORS IN GROUP FUNCTIONING

The purpose of this section is to review those studies that have dealt with situational determinants of social interaction in groups. This research consists primarily of studies conducted with *ad hoc* groups rather than studies conducted in spontaneously formed groups. Research workers have been unusually ingenious in constructing experimental situations that simulate conditions existing in informal groups. Nevertheless, the student of this literature must be concerned with the problem of generalizing the findings. It is not known whether the results of most of the studies in this area may be applied to group functioning as it occurs in school groups, other formally organized groups, or informal peer groups. This problem exists because there has been relatively little parametric research concerning the effects on group functioning of such factors as group size, the type of activity the group is engaged in, and the composition of the group.

Effects of the Milieu

Both the immediate situation in which interaction takes place and the larger cultural milieu influence the nature of group behavior. Such factors influence peer interaction among very young children. Faigin's (1958) observations in two Israeli nurseries showed that dependent, passive behavior was more common among children who resided in a highly structured nursery than among children who lived in a less highly organized center. In nursery schools, complex social interaction occurs most frequently in the doll corner (Shure, 1963) and in dramatic play (Charlesworth and Hartup, 1967). Play with a single child, as opposed to larger groups, occurs more frequently in block and game areas; parallel play is most common in art and book locations. Jersild and Markey (1935) reported that interpersonal aggression is an inverse function of the amount of space available in the nursery school.

Findings based on observations of preadolescent boys attending summer camps are strikingly similar to the results for nursery school children. Gump, Schoggen, and Redl (1957) reported that "robust" interactions, including assertive behavior, blocking attempts, and attack responses, occurred more frequently during swimming than during crafts. On the other hand, helping reactions occurred more frequently during the latter activity. Also, while expressive actions occurred more frequently in swimming, utilitarian behavior occurred with equal frequency in the two types of activities. When desired goals were delayed or in short supply, competitiveness increased. When the setting directed attention to individual tasks, peer interaction dropped. Blood and Livant (1957) reported that there is a significant relation between the manner in which informal peer groups of adolescents arrange cabin space in summer camps and the sociometric polarizations occurring in the group. In this instance, however, it was undoubtedly the sociometric orderings that determined the milieu arrangements rather than the reverse.

Few parametric studies exist concerning the relation between group size and patterns of interaction in informal children's groups. That this factor affects peer interaction is demonstrated by Hare's (1952) study of discussion behavior in nine 5-member and nine 12-member groups of Boy Scouts. The major effects of group size were as follows: (1) group consensus was greater in the 5-member groups; (2) the leader's skill was a more salient factor in attaining consensus in the 12-member groups; (3) the leader's opinions had more influence in the 5-member groups; (4) members of the larger groups felt that their own opinions were less important; and (5) factions emerged more frequently in the larger groups. Clearly, cohesiveness in children's peer groups is a function of group size.

The influence of the subculture on children's peer interactions is pervasive. Such in-

fluences can be seen clearly in the case of aggressive and competitive behaviors. In one study (McKee and Leader, 1955), preschool children from lower and upper middle-class backgrounds were brought in pairs to a playroom containing two piles of construction blocks. Instances of both aggressive and competitive behavior were more frequent during observation of the children from the lower middle-class. Apparently, at least by inference, children from the lower middle-class are exposed more frequently than upper middle-class children to demands for competition and rewards for such behavior. Anthropological accounts concerning competitive attitudes and behaviors confirm the hypothesis that cultural influences on patterns of peer interaction are pervasive. Zuni and Hopi children, for example, are not competitive in their relations with each other.

Within formally organized peer groups, cultural factors may be associated with the target chosen for aggression as well as with sheer amount of aggression. Maas (1954) found, for example, that lower-class adolescents were more aggressive toward other members of the rank-and-file than middle-class youngsters (thereby confirming the McKee and Leader results). The lower-class subjects, however, were actually *less* aggressive toward the club president than were the middle-class children, and there was no significant difference between the two social class groups in aggressiveness directed toward the adult leaders.

Cultural influences on peer interaction are also apparent with respect to children's attitudes toward members of ethnic minorities (Epstein and Komorita, 1965; Morland, 1966), the types of norms that prevail in informal peer groups of children and adolescents (Phelps and Horrocks, 1959; Sherif and Sherif, 1964), manifestations of self-reliance and nurturance toward other children (Lambert, Triandis, and Wolf, 1959), and conformity to peer influences (Tuma and Livson, 1960). These cultural influences on peer interactions, as well as the relation between cultural factors and peer acceptance, are discussed at greater length in other sections of this chapter. It is by now clear, however, that cultural factors account for a significant portion of the variance in the topography of child-child relations beginning in very early childhood.

Leadership Style

A number of early studies (Chittenden, 1942; Jack, 1934; Page, 1934) demonstrate that adult intervention is effective in modifying the assertive and dominant behavior of children. Chittenden's study is particularly interesting because it demonstrated that experimental modeling sessions modified assertiveness both immediately after the experimental exposure and in the nursery school peer group as long as a month after training.

It remained for Lewin, Lippitt, and White (1939; see also Lippitt and White, 1943; 1958) to extend the study of adult leadership and its effects on children's social behavior within the context of what is called "group atmosphere" or "social climate." These studies, which were conducted in ad hoc groups of 11-year-old boys, demonstrated that varying styles of leadership produced marked differences in social behavior. The effects of three types of adult leadership were examined: "democratic," "authoritarian," and "laissez-faire." The components of these leadership styles are well-known, and thus not reviewed here. It should be noted, however, that the strategy employed in these studies was quite sophisticated, involving control of personality differences among the experimenters as well as examination, within groups, of the effects of shifts in leadership style.

Following is a brief summary of some of the major results of this series of studies:

1. Authoritarian leadership produced two major types of social climate—aggressive or apathetic.

2. In the atmospheres created by authoritarian leadership, as well as in the atmosphere created by laissez-faire leadership, expressions of irritability and aggressiveness toward fellow group members occured more frequently than in the democratic climates.

3. In at least one group, authoritarian leadership created high interpersonal tension and scapegoating; in others, authoritarian leadership produced aggressiveness that was channeled toward out-groups or toward the leader.

4. Requests for attention and approval from fellow members were more frequent in the democratic and laissez-faire climates than in the autocratic climates.

5. Interpersonal friendliness did not vary as a function of leadership style, although "we-feeling" tended to be lower in the authoritarian groups than in the others.

6. Task-related suggestions by the children were less frequent in the authoritarian groups.

7. When the authoritarian leaders were absent for brief periods, work-motivation dropped quickly or did not develop; absence of the democratic leader produced little change in amount of task-oriented effort.

8. There was a wider range of individual differences, particularly in ascendant reactions, in the democratic atmospheres than in the authoritarian or laissez-faire climates.

The data from these studies are, of course, far richer than this brief summary depicts. Of major importance is the general finding that leadership style had a direct bearing on interpersonal behavior in these groups. These studies are somewhat less convincing, however, in specifying the particular outcomes that result from particular styles of leadership. For example, the experimenter-leaders were, as a group, a sample of equalitarian adults. As a consequence, the studies do not furnish information concerning group functioning under authoritarian leadership imposed by committed authoritarian adults. Second, most of the subjects came from "democratic" homes. Thus clues concerning interaction effects between differences in family background of the subjects and differences in leadership style are absent. Finally, it should be mentioned that the studies embraced only a small number of leadership styles. For example, the authoritarian climates involved rather distant, cold leadership. It has long been regretted by students in this field that no good data exist concerning children's social behavior within a "benevolent autocracy."

The foregoing comments refer to limitations of these studies rather than to criticisms. The limitations existing in this research are similar, in many respects, to limitations that are pervasive in experimental social psychology. It is regrettable, however, that parametric extensions of these studies in leadership style have not been carried out. The results of this research have been applied widely, to fields such as education, without full recognition of the limitations mentioned here. Even so, the studies indisputably accomplished their primary objective: they tested the hypothesis that leadership style is one determinant of social interaction in children's groups.

The literature includes several other demonstrations of the fact that styles of adult leadership influence children's group behavior. These include Thompson's (1940) induction of prejudice by means of prejudicial leadership and Wright's (1940) finding that leader-imposed frustration increases cohesiveness in dyads of children. Also, Katz, Blau, Brown, and Strodtbeck (1957) found that status positions in *ad hoc* groups of adolescents were likely to be less stable when choice of task was imposed by an adult leader than when this choice was made by the group itself. Even when the group was antagonistic toward its leader, the leader's position was more stable when the choice emanated from within the group than when imposed by an adult authority-figure.

An experiment showing the effects of two different leadership styles on the behavior of nursery school children was conducted by Thompson (1944). In one group, the teacher used active, intrusive guidance. In the other, she used an impersonal teaching style, giving assistance to the children only when it was requested. Under "active" leadership, as contrasted with "reserved" leadership, instances of ascendance, constructive play, and social participation were more frequent; interpersonal rejection and aggression were less frequent. Here again, only two leadership styles were examined. The personality of the teacher was held constant in this study (she taught *both* experimental groups) but we do not know whether a different teacher could have generated the same results. Recent work suggests that different adults have enormously different effects on children's behavior, even when their interactions with the child are restricted to dispensing simple approving statements (Stevenson, 1961).

Taken as a whole, these early studies indicate that an involved, child-centered, democratic leadership style produces more cohesive group functioning and a higher incidence of socially approved, task-oriented behaviors than does distant or autocratic leadership. Descriptive accounts concerning the outcomes of democratic leadership in classroom situations have confirmed the experimental results (e.g., Spector, 1953; Turner, 1957). Nevertheless, the parametric limitations of this research still stand.

Other studies have been focused on somewhat different dimensions of leadership style as these determine attitude change in children's groups. Hare (1953) found that significant opinion change took place in groups of 13-year-old Boy Scouts under *both* participatory and supervisory leadership. Somewhat greater change was evidenced under participatory leadership but this difference was not statistically reliable. Additional research suggests, however, that the main effects of leadership style on attitude change may be less important than the interaction between leadership style and the type of sanction that the leader employs (Zander and Curtis, 1962). For example, one group of adolescents reported themselves as less responsive to social pressure from coercive leaders than to pressure from individuals with whom a "referent" (participatory) relationship had been established. Coerciveness itself, however, tended to weaken motivation to do well, to reduce actual performance, and to reduce self-ratings of performance, as compared to rewarding feedback.

Kipnis (1958) contrasted the effectiveness of participatory and nonparticipatory leadership, using three different sanction conditions. Fifth- and sixth-grade children were exposed to biased views concerning the desirability of certain comic books. One-third of the subjects in each leadership condition were rewarded for conforming to the propaganda (i.e., they received free movie passes). Another one-third of the children were punished for nonconformity (i.e., they were threatened with withdrawal of the movie passes); no sanctions were imposed on the remaining children. After the exposure period, the subjects rated their comic book preferences. Compliance with the propaganda was similar among the children in the reward and punishment conditions; change in attitudes was greater in each of these conditions than among children in the control group. A check of the children's preferences made a week later, however, revealed a significant interaction between leadership style and sanction condition. In the reward and no sanction conditions, participatory leadership had produced more attitude change than the lecture method. On the other hand, when punishment had been threatened for noncompliance, significantly more change in attitudes occurred through lecture than through participatory leadership. Thus the effects of sanctions on attitude change depended on the locus of the social influence.

Cooperation and Competition

Various studies, both naturalistic and experimental, show that cooperative activity within the peer group contributes to cohesiveness and productivity. These are consistent with the results of research employing adult subjects (e.g., Haythorn, 1953). It should be noted, however, that threat from an external source may sometimes enhance cohesiveness in children's groups.

Stendler, Damrin, and Haines (1951) conducted an experimental study with three groups of 7-year-olds. The manner in which rewards were dispensed to the children varied from day to day. The children painted a mural during the first session and the experimenter emphasized that each child would be awarded a prize if all worked together to make a good picture. During the second and third sessions, a reward was promised to the individual child who completed the best painting. Social behavior was observed both during the painting sessions and in free play. Order of presentation and experimental treatment were confounded in this study, but the results show that positive behaviors (friendly conversation, sharing, and helping) exceeded negative behaviors during all cooperative work sessions. The reverse was true under competition.[4] Also, there was more boasting and deprecation in the competitive sessions and less time was spent on the task. Sociometric measurement of cohesiveness was not completed, but the results suggest that a more consolidated, friendly pattern of peer interactions occurred when individuals were rewarded for the group product rather than for individual products.

Another experimental study of this problem compared the effects of group versus individual rewards on the cohesiveness of small groups of fourth-grade children (Phillips and D'Amico, 1956). Sociometric ratings were obtained prior to the experiment and four co-

---

[4] These results do not necessarily hold when the cooperative situation provides a group reward (e.g., a "class prize") rather than individual rewards (Maller, 1929).

hesive groups and four noncohesive groups (i.e., groups containing few mutual friends) were assembled. The task for each of the groups was to play "Twenty Questions." Two of the cohesive groups and two of the noncohesive groups were told that individuals would share equally in the rewards to be given; the other groups were told that each child would share in the rewards according to the relative contribution made to the game. Significant increases in cohesiveness were found in three of the four groups that worked under cooperative conditions. On the other hand, the effects of competition were notable in their variability. There was no change in cohesiveness in two of these groups, a significant increase in one, and a significant decrease in the remaining group. In the competitive groups that increased in cohesiveness or that did not change, interaction during the game produced a more equitable distribution of rewards than occurred in the group that showed a decrease in cohesiveness. Perhaps the most important aspect of these findings, then, is that the effects of competition and cooperation on group solidarity may depend on the manner in which the group *itself* adjusts to the rules of the game.

In a study conducted in classrooms, Kinney (1953) found that the use of small, cooperating groups produced greater solidarity and greater reduction in the number of isolates and rejected children than when teaching was conducted with the class as a whole or when the class was divided into ability groups. The use of discussion techniques in promoting acceptance within groups of adolescents, however, has produced inconclusive results (Amundson, 1953). The effectiveness of such techniques appears to depend on the skill of the teachers leading the groups.

One other study (Avigdor, 1952) shows the effects of cooperative intergroup experience on attitudes toward the out-group. Groups of lower- and lower middle-class preadolescent girls were placed in cooperative and competitive situations. Cooperative experience tended to produce more favorable descriptions of the out-group than competitive experience; ratings of the out-group also tended to be less variable when the intergroup experience had been cooperative. In no instance, even under competitive conditions, was the out-group described solely in terms of negative or unfavorable characteristics. Further, the criticisms tended to focus on abilities or characteristics related to the activities in which the groups were engaged.

It has already been reported that intergroup conflict which results in unequal amounts of frustration produces reduction in intragroup cohesiveness (Sherif and Sherif, 1953), whereas balanced intergroup frustration may increase solidarity (Sherif et al., 1961). The results of a study by Thibault (1950) suggest that the effects of intergroup frustration depend on whether aggression can be successfully directed toward the perceived source of conflict. If a group feels victimized (or the members believe they have had unfair advantage over a second group), lack of opportunity to express hostility tends to enhance cohesiveness. On the other hand, if hostility is expressed through acts of aggression, the cohesiveness of the group may not rise above its original level. Studies with adults (e.g., Lanzetta, 1955) also suggest that threat or stress situations may enhance interpersonal acceptance and cohesiveness. The children's literature, however, contains little additional information on this point except for Wright's (1940) finding that adult-imposed frustration enhanced solidarity in pairs of preschool children.

Contingencies of Reinforcement

Several studies indicate that cooperative behavior in children can be controlled by the contingent presentation of material rewards. For example, Azrin and Lindsley (1956) selected 10 pairs of children between the ages of 7 and 12 and presented them with a stylus-maneuvering task. Cooperation (simultaneous insertion of styluses in opposite holes) was reinforced by means of a jelly bean that was dropped into a container. The container was accessible to both children. Reinforcement was delivered on a continuous schedule for 15 minutes, or longer if the children had not reached a steady rate of cooperative responding. A 15-minute extinction period followed. The experiment terminated after a second period in which cooperation was continuously reinforced. This period lasted until the children showed a stable response rate for three successive minutes. All pairs acquired the cooperative strategy during the first phase of the experiment—all within 10 minutes. Ces-

sation of reinforcement produced a significant decrement in rate of cooperative responding but reinstatement of the reinforcement produced a significant increase in responding. One particularly interesting finding is that the extinction curves shown by the various pairs of subjects were very different. This variability probably reflects differences between pairs of subjects in the extent to which affective responses were elicited by the cessation of reinforcement.

Weingold and Webster (1964) examined the effects of punishment on cooperation. First, pairs of 10-year-old boys were positively reinforced for pushing levers in a cooperative sequence. One member of each dyad received continuous reinforcement for cooperative responding while the other child received reinforcement on a 50% random schedule. This procedure resulted in significant increases in rate of cooperative responding. Next, punishment was administered to one-half of the subjects. Specifically, one member of each dyad "lost a point" for cooperative responding (on a 50% random schedule) while his partner was placed on simple extinction. Members of the other dyads were both placed on extinction. The results showed that the nonpunished pairs continued to respond cooperatively at a high rate; possibly they were unable to distinguish the extinction period from the acquisition period. On the other hand, the punished pairs showed an immediate and lasting decrement in cooperative responding.

The data from these studies confirm and extend earlier work showing that the interpersonal behavior of children may be functionally related to contingencies of reinforcement (e.g., Wolfle and Wolfle, 1939). The role of reinforcement in the acquisition and maintenance of more complex forms of group influence and behavior has not been extensively explored, although Fischer (1963) reported increases in sharing behavior among preschool children as a function of receiving contingent reinforcement.

Cohesiveness

The relation between a group's cohesiveness and its efficiency as a working unit is not a simple, linear function. For example, Shaw and Shaw (1962) found that cohesiveness (defined sociometrically) was significantly correlated with learning to spell lists of words (average $r = .47$) as measured by a test given immediately after one period of group study. On the other hand, cohesiveness was not correlated significantly (average $r = .01$) with scores obtained on a test given after a second study period. The cohesive groups were found to be more democratic, friendly, and cooperative than the low-cohesive groups and this type of interaction apparently facilitated learning the spelling lessons during the first study session. These groups seemed satiated with the task, however, during the second study period, and they apparently felt comfortable in stopping. On the other hand, the low cohesive groups adopted individualistic, noninteractive study paterns during the first study session and maintained these patterns throughout the second period.

Lott and Lott (1966) found that cohesiveness affected group performance on a verbal learning task according to the ability of the children composing the group. Among high-IQ fourth- and fifth-graders, those in cohesive groups did better than those in non-cohesive groups. Among low IQ children, cohesiveness did not significantly affect group performance. The low IQ children who had been placed in noncohesive groups, however, performed slightly better than those who had been placed in cohesive groups. The authors suggested that incentive motivation derives from the interpersonal attraction existing in cohesive groups. When tasks are relatively easy (as these tasks would have been for the bright children), this motivation could be expected to facilitate performance. Motivation deriving from cohesiveness would be expected to impede performance, however, when the task is more difficult (as would be the case for low-IQ children). Although the Lott study and the Shaw study differ with respect to the main issues examined, both investigations show that group cohesiveness tends to interact with task variables in determining group performance. Research with adults (e.g., Hoffman, 1959; Shaw, 1960) also supports the view that cohesiveness has varying effects on group behavior, depending on task conditions.

The cohesiveness of a group also affects communication patterns. Scofield (1960) found that *ad hoc* groups of seventh graders who were nonfriends spent more time in arriving at a consensus concerning appropriate stories for TAT pictures than did groups of friends. The greater time spent in discussion by nonfriends could mean that they were more task-motivated than the groups of friends. On the other hand, the heterogeneous groups may simply have required a longer time to resolve differences of opinion. The Shaw (1962) study, cited previously, supports the second interpretation.

A different kind of group homogeneity was the independent variable in another study of discussion behavior (Altman and McGinnies, 1960). Five hundred high school boys were assigned to five different kinds of groups on the basis of scores on the California E Scale: (1) all low scorers; (2) all high scorers; (3) low scorers in the majority; (4) high scorers in the majority; (5) an equal number of high and low scorers. The subjects viewed and discussed a film dealing with ethnic minorities. Then they completed an attitude questionnaire. The composition of the group clearly affected discussion behavior. Those groups comprised of equal numbers of high and low scorers (the least homogeneous) were less spontaneous, made fewer comments, and produced fewer opposition-directed communications than did the other groups. Further, the individual members of these groups were less attracted to the group, were least accurate in their perceptions of the opinions held by other members, and were also least attracted to other members who held the same opinions as themselves.

Within cohesive groups, communication tends to flow according to the social structure of the group. Naturalistic studies confirm the hypothesis that flow of information tends to be directed to the higher status group member, although this tendency varies somewhat from group to group (Sherif et al., 1961). Studies of information exchange in small groups have yielded similar findings (e.g., Larson and Hill, 1958).

Communication exchange is more rapid when the roles are not rigidly polarized within the group, even though such exchange tends to occur in concordance with sociometric linkages. Larson and Hill reported that communication is most frequent among group members whose status in the group is changing in the same rather than opposite directions. Finally, the act of transmitting information in small *ad hoc* groups tends to be associated with subsequent increases in social status. That is, those who speak up in such groups are likely to rise in the status hierarchy. Taken as a whole, then, the findings concerning the relation between status and communication in small groups indicate reciprocal causation. Status factors seem to be important determinants of communication in children's groups but the act of communication also affects the status of the initiating agent.

Group Problem Solving

Much evidence suggests that group problem solving is *generally* superior to individual problem solving. It has been argued that this occurs because the presence of one able person in the group ensures that all individuals will be able to perform the task. On these grounds, several investigators have insisted that the adequacy of group problem solving reflects the ability of the most able member (e.g., Lorge and Solomon, 1955). This hypothesis has been questioned, however, with respect to its generalizability across various types of task. On problems calling for an insightful solution, for example, there may be no concordance between the group's ability and the ability of the best member (Hoffman, 1965).

One study with children points to the fact that the group's perceptions concerning the most able member affect the relation existing between that individual's ability and the group's performance. Hudgins and Smith (1966) conducted a group problem-solving experiment with fifth- to eighth-grade children. Two replications of the experiment were completed using arithmetic problems; two other replications involved social studies tasks. *Ad hoc* groups were formed so as to contain one high-ability child and two moderate-ability children. In half of the groups, the high ability child was initially perceived as such (i.e., he was sociometrically judged to be a good student). Group problem solving was not better than the independent problem solving of the most able member *when this child was perceived as most able*. When the high-ability child was not perceived as such, the group did better than the most able child, but only on the arithmetic tasks.

Two points are important here. First, if the individual members of a group are aware that they differ in ability, the group may gear its level of performance to that of the most able member. Second, in the absence of such awareness, the ability of the most capable member affects group output according to the type of task involved. In tasks involving complex, step-by-step problems (such as the arithmetic test used in this study) group interaction may actually produce better average performance than the most able individual working alone. When problems require more insightful solutions (such as the social studies tests), the group may actually not do any better (or may do worse)than the most able member.

Effects of Expectations and Past Experience. The relation between initial expectations and the outcomes of group experience was studied by Borgatta, Cottrell, and Wilker (1959). Subjects were Girl Scouts attending a National Roundup. Those who reported high initial expectations concerning the group experience reported greater satisfaction at the conclusion of the roundup than those who had low initial expectations. Among the girls with low expectations, however, those who held leadership positions were more positive in their assessment of the experience than those who were nonleaders. This differential shift may have derived form the fact that the leaders enjoyed a greater number of positive experiences during the roundup than did the nonleaders. It is also possible, however, that the leadership position simply allowed the child to perceive that her initial expectations were discrepant and to adjust her assessment of the experience accordingly.

Information possessed by group members concerning the expectations of other members also affects group interaction. Morgan and Sawyer (1967) devised a bargaining task for the purpose of studying decisions, made by pairs of children, concerning the distribution of monetary rewards. Various alternative distributions were possible: (1) an equalitarian distribution—both subjects would receive the same amount of money; (2) an equitable distribution—both would receive the same number of coins even though the total value differed; or (3) an inequitable solution—one would receive the maximum money available while the other child would receive none. Pairs of friends and pairs of nonfriends were tested.

The children in some pairs were told privately about the outcome that was expected by the other child. Children in other pairs were not given this information. Among friends, being informed concerning expected outcomes, as compared with being uniformed, produced significantly more equalitarian resolutions. Information had little effect, however, on the kinds of decisions reached by nonfriends—they tended to be equalitarian under both information conditions. On the other hand, the duration of bargaining among nonfriend pairs was shortened significantly when they were informed of each other's expectations.

Generally, the data suggest that equalitarian solutions are the most attractive forms of conflict resolution for 10- to 12-year-old boys, whether they are friends or not. Knowing what the other person expects affects conflict-resolution, but in different ways among friends and among nonfriends. Information concerning expected outcomes appears to permit friends to approach the equality that they *prefer*, but perhaps do not *require*. Among nonfriends, equality appears to be the only acceptable solution; knowing what the other person expects then simply permits such pairs to approach the equalitarian solution more rapidly.

The foregoing results concern the effects of expectations on group functioning as these have been studied in *ad hoc* groups which were brought together for brief periods. Does the child's prior group experience have any bearing on the group's productivity? Will children who have worked in a variety of groups, as compared with children who have worked with the same partners, perform better when transferred to a new group?

Goldberg and Maccoby (1965) hypothesized that stable group membership produces status polarizations that interfere with productivity when the individuals are transferred to new groups. Children who have had experience in several different groups would not be expected to have assumed heavily polarized status positions and they should find transition less difficult. A study of second-grade children showed, however, that this is not the case. Children who spent four sessions working on tower building with the same partners performed better when they were transferred to a new group than did children who had worked on the task in four different groups.

There were no mean differences in the performance of the stable and changing groups during training. It seemed, however, that repeated experience with the same group of partners provided the children with an opportunity to develop smooth, equalitarian interaction techniques. These behaviors apparently generalized when the child was eventually placed in a new group. On the other hand, the changing groups showed frequent instances of dominance and coercion during the training sessions, which prevented them from learning the techniques that would maximize *average* levels of performance in new groups.

Once again, the importance of *time* in the analysis of group functioning is revealed. Children apparently require a certain amount of time, in a stable group, to suppress interpersonal behaviors that interfere with group output. Conversely, time is required to develop cooperative techniques appropriate to the task at hand. Even though total time spent in group activity is equal, repeated shifts in partners may interfere with the development of appropriate patterns of task-oriented social behavior.

Personality Factors. The self-esteem of group members is an important determinant of peer interaction. In one experiment, elementary school boys were placed in competitive situations after having been identified as positive or negative self-evaluators (Rychlak, 1960). The subjects were then given false norms (i.e., some were led to believe they were performing better than most boys, others were told that they were performing at an average level). Negative self-evaluators, regardless of whether they were placed at or above the pseudonorm, increased their performance only during the final portion of the practice series. Positive self-evaluators, however, increased their performance from the beginning of practice, although those placed above the norm maintained their greater increase over the entire testing period. One other investigator found that children who display task-centered and group-supportive behavior are "realistic" in the manner in which they perceive their own role status and they realistically comprehend the important aspects of group functioning (Haines, 1953). Thus self-esteem appears to be a determinant of performance in group situations. This relation is a reciprocal one, however. Successful group experience also produces increases in self-esteem (e.g., Beker, 1960).

Anxiety is another variable that has been studied in relation to group functioning. Zander and Wulff (1966) evaluated the performance of four-member groups of high school students working together on a level of aspiration task. The groups were constituted so as to include either high "fear-of-failure" subjects or high "success-approach" subjects. The anxious groups, as compared to the success-approach groups, reported more frequent feelings of tension during the task, were more variable in their aspiration levels, were more satisfied with their group's performance, and were generally less aware of what was happening during group interaction. Further, individuals in the success-oriented groups tended to be particularly responsive to feedback concerning their performance. Specifically, when performance seemed to be good, these subjects evidenced satisfaction with themselves but they were particularly distressed by indications that they were performing poorly.

The data reviewed here suggest that personality factors such as self-assurance, self-esteem and anxiety are important determinants of group interaction. Most of these findings are based on studies of adolescents and the research does not form a very comprehensive body of evidence. Obviously, the relation between personality factors and group functioning is complex; there are few examples of simple linear functions in the data that we have reviewed. Some of the material to be discussed concerning peer influences on the individual child will, however, help to elucidate the characteristics of individual children that appear to affect group interaction.

STATUS IN THE PEER GROUP

No aspect of children's social behavior has received more research attention than peer acceptance or popularity. The referents of the term *acceptance* include the responses that a child elicits in other children and what other children say about him. The core meaning of the concept, however, consists of the degree to which a child's peers wish to have some form of associative contact with him. Peer *rejection* is a term that is also ubiquitous in

studies of peer interaction. Essentially, this term refers to the avoidance of a child by his peers or to negative evaluations of him. There is ample evidence (e.g., Dunnington, 1957b; Moore and Updegraff, 1964; Sells and Roff, 1967) to suggest that acceptance-rejection is not a unidimensional characteristic of peer interaction. Only moderate negative correlations exist between positive choices and negative choices received on sociometric tests. Low acceptance by the peer group sometimes implies indifference; only in some cases does low acceptance imply negative evaluation.

Other terms that refer to status dimensions in children's groups include *leadership, social power,* and *prestige.* Like acceptance, each of these terms implies positive evaluation of the child by his peers. But the core referent of these terms is the capacity that a child possesses for eliciting behavior change in the peer group. In many groups and in many different situations leadership or social power may be positively correlated with peer acceptance (e.g., Keislar, 1953; Lippitt, Polansky, and Rosen, 1952; Marks, 1957; Rosen, Levinger, and Lippitt, 1961). It is also true that such correlations are never perfect (e.g., Hollander and Webb, 1955; Sherif and Sherif, 1964).

It has become common to refer to all techniques designed for the purpose of measuring peer acceptance as *sociometric* instruments. Sociometry was popularized by Moreno (1934), who devised the widely used "nominations" or partial rank-order technique for measuring peer acceptance. Modifications of Moreno's methods, including paired-comparison techniques (Koch, 1933) and comparisons involving frames of reference that extend beyond the immediate peer group (e.g., Gardner and Thompson, 1959) have been developed. In addition, the reputations of peer group members have been studied by means of "Guess Who" tests which were originated by Hartshorne and May (1928) and later modified by Tryon (1939) and Tuddenham (1951).

Both paper-and-pencil inventories and the observations of trained workers or group leaders have been used to obtain sociometric scores. Most sociometric measurement is based on some frame of reference that is pertinent to the setting in which the informal peer group functions. Some investigators, however, have devised tests for assessing sociometric status that are tangential to the main activities of the peer group. For example, Hagman (1933) furnished children with rewards for performing a task and then asked them to select those peers with whom they would share the rewards.

Thus the frames of reference used in eliciting sociometric choices have varied widely. Choices are sometimes obtained for seating companions, play companions, work partners, or, simply, best friends. It is always necessary to attend closely to the particular frame of reference that has been used for assessing status in the peer group. Research workers have been remarkably ingenious, however, in inventing reliable and valid measures of peer status for groups of children ranging in age from as young as three years (e.g., McCandless and Marshall, 1957a) to adolescence. The reader who is interested in methodological problems in this field has several authoritative reviews at his disposal. Excellent critiques have been published by Criswell (1943), Bronfenbrenner (1945), Loomis and Pepinsky (1948), Thompson, Bligh, and Witryol (1951), Lindzey and Borgatta (1954), Marshall (1957), Thompson (1960), and Moore (1967).

POPULARITY

Stability of Peer Acceptance and Rejection

The stability of friendship choices or peer acceptance is usually assessed by means of successive administrations of sociometric tests. Intervals between testing have ranged from a few days to several years. The test-retest method generally produces a conservative estimate of the stability of social status. This is true because the test-retest procedure confounds fluctuations in the phenomenon being measured (i.e., fluctuations in peer preferences) with imperfections in the reliability of the sociometric test itself. Nevertheless, a large body of data indicates that peer preferences remain relatively stable over time. Such stability characterizes both friendship choices (the particular peers that a child nominates as his friends) and peer acceptance (the status accorded the child by the group as a whole).

Witryol and Thompson (1953) reviewed the literature concerning the stability of social acceptance scores and came to the following general conclusions:

1. Paired-comparison sociometric techniques show somewhat greater stability in peer acceptance than partial rank-order techniques.[5]

2. Test-retest stability, using the partial-rank method, varies inversely with the time interval between tests—stability is highest when the interval is a few days or weeks and lowest when the interval consists of several years.

3. Stability is directly related to the age of the children in the peer group.

4. Stability is directly related to degree of acquaintanceship; that is, fluctuations in social status are more marked during the early stages of group formation than after the group has become established.

5. Both sample size and the number of sociometric criteria employed bear a direct relation to the stability of peer acceptance scores.

6. Use of weighted sociometric scores does not enhance stability estimates.

7. Considerable stability of a child's acceptance exists across groups and sociometric criteria.

8. Fluctuation in status is more marked in the middle positions of the status hierarchy than in either high or low positions.

Data accumulating since Witryol and Thompson published their review have not substantially altered these conclusions. For example, the positive relation between length of acquaintance and the stability of social acceptance scores is confirmed by the Sherif studies (1961, 1964). Next, newer studies (Gronlund, 1955c; Moore and Updegraff, 1964) have confirmed that the weighting of sociometric scores does not affect significantly the stability of such scores. Finally, Gronlund has demonstrated that stability of acceptance scores is directly related to the number of sociometric criteria used (1956) and that stability is not markedly affected by the particular sociometric criterion employed in the test (1955a).

A recent longitudinal study provides definitive evidence concerning the relation be-

5 The number of studies using the former method is quite small.

tween the test-retest interval and the stability of sociometric scores. Sells and Roff (1967) studied social acceptance longitudinally, using a sample of 15,300 school children between the ages of 9 and 12. Test-retest correlations based on 1-year intervals were approximately .50. This coefficient dropped to about .40 when stability was measured over a 3-year interval, a finding that is consistent with the results of Bonney (1943) and Feinberg (1964).

Social rejection is somewhat less stable than social acceptance. Sells and Roff found stability coefficients of about .40 when rejection was measured in succeeding years. These correlations dropped to about .35 when computed over a 3-year interval. Why should social rejection be less stable than social acceptance? The answer is not revealed by the data but one can hypothesize that the social behaviors precipitating rejection by the peer group are less likely to receive consistent reinforcement from environmental sources than are behaviors associated with social acceptance.

Recent results suggest that the stability of peer acceptance scores may not increase with age as dramatically as suggested by Witryol and Thompson (1953). For one thing, social acceptance in peer groups of preschool-aged children is at least moderately stable. McCandless and Marshall (1957a) found stability coefficients that ranged between .41 and .76 in subgroups tested at 20-day intervals. Also, Hartup, Glazer, and Charlesworth (1967) reported a test-retest correlation of .68 for one group of preschoolers retested after a 5-month interval. These findings, which are somewhat inconsistent with earlier results, are based on improved instruments for measuring social acceptance in young children (e.g., the picture sociometric technique) first employed in the mid-1950s. With preschoolers, however, stability of rejection scores is low. Hartup et al. (1967) reported a 5-month stability coefficient of only .29 (not significant) for one group of 4-year-olds.

Although peer acceptance scores are moderately stable among young children, there is still a significant relation between age and fluctuation in friendship choices (Horrocks and Thompson, 1946; Thompson and Horrocks, 1947). In large samples of both urban and rural children, less fluctuation in friend-

ship nominations was found among 16- to 18-year-olds than among 11- to 15-year-olds. These investigators found that the younger children chose the same individual child as a best friend about 50% of the time when sociometric tests were separated by a 2-week interval. The older subjects, however, chose the same best friend between 60% and 90% of the time.[6] Girls showed somewhat fewer fluctuations in their friendship choices than did the boys. This sex difference has also been found among kindergarten children (Speroff, 1955). There were no important differences, however, in developmental trends shown in friendship fluctuations among rural and among urban children.

The data just described were based on children showing essentially normal social adjustment. Davids and Parenti (1958) found much more marked fluctuations in friendship choices among emotionally disturbed children than among comparison groups of normal children. Further, disturbed groups did not show the same developmental decrease in friendship fluctuations as did normal children (Davids, 1964).

Correlates of Peer Acceptance and Rejection

The information summarized in this section concerns the behavioral correlates of sociometric status. It should be recognized at the outset that the characteristics which are associated with sociometric status vary from situation to situation. Furthermore, the sociometric ratings made by teachers or observers may be biased by such factors as the training of the observer (King, Erhmann, and Johnson, 1952), the amount of contact the observer has had with the child (Gronlund, 1955b), the observer's rapport with the child (Bogen, 1954), or the child's own social status (Gronlund, 1950).

The literature concerning the relation between behavioral characteristics of children and their acceptance by the peer group consists almost exclusively of correlational findings. The typical strategy has been to administer sociometric tests concurrently with tests of personality factors or intellectual capacities. The two sets of measures are then correlated. The inferences which may be drawn from

[6] Generally consistent results have also been reported by Davis (1957), Warnath (1957), and Wertheimer (1957).

such findings are extremely limited. Moore (1967) states the problem succinctly:

To know that popular children perform a preponderance of friendly behaviors is not to say that their friendliness is the "cause" of their popularity. It is just as reasonable to hypothesize that being well-liked inspires a child to perform friendly behaviors as it is to hypothesize that performing these behaviors causes the child to be well-liked (p. 236).

Investigators who are interested in the correlates of peer acceptance should make increasing use of research strategies that are different from those that have dominated past studies. One strategy that is applicable to some problems, although not all, is the experimental method. For example, peer interchange can be manipulated and the effects of such manipulations on sociometric choices then ferreted out. Also, children's perceptions of each other can sometimes be manipulated by means of bogus information. Such techniques can furnish valuable clues for interpreting the correlational results we already possess. Another strategy that has been insufficiently exploited is the study of status differentiation occurring in informal groups during the time that such groups are being formed or when they are in transition.

It is important to remember that most investigators have found extremely modest correlations between peer acceptance and behavior. It is therefore obvious that no single trait is of overriding importance in determining children's popularity with their peers. Nevertheless, research presents a consistent picture of those attributes that covary with peer acceptance. This consistency is remarkable in view of the fact that an enormously varied group of tests and situations have been employed in studies in this area.

Friendliness and Sociability. A large group of studies shows that peer acceptance is directly associated with such characteristics as friendliness, sociability, social visibility, and outgoingness. These results are more or less uniform across age levels, since they hold for preschool children as well as for adolescents.

Peer acceptance in groups of nursery school children has been found to be positively correlated with observational measures of "friendly approach" and "associative" behaviors (Marshall and McCandless, 1957b); social visibility, as measured by means of a "Guess Who" test (Clifford, 1963); peer perceptions of friendliness (Moore, 1967); the extent to which nurturance is given to peers (Moore and Updegraff, 1964); and frequency with which the child dispenses positive social reinforcers to the peer group (Hartup et al., 1967).

Measures of social rejection were included in only one of these studies (Hartup et al.). In this instance, friendliness was *not* predictive of peer rejection. Although the nonsociable child may not be popular, he is not necessarily rejected by his peers.

Similar results have been reported for elementary school children. Peer acceptance has been found to be positively related to friendliness, "outgoing" behavior, and amount of social participation (Bonney, 1944; Bonney and Powell, 1953); lack of withdrawal as perceived by peers (Winder and Rau, 1962); the frequency with which "kindness" is expressed to peers (Smith, 1950); willingness both to give and receive friendly overtures, as well as willingness to respond positively to the dependent behavior of peers (Campbell and Yarrow, 1961); friendliness, assurance, and enthusiasm (Pope, 1953); social participation (Baron, 1951); an active field analytic orientation in boys but a more passive, field-dependent orientation in girls (Iscoe and Garden, 1961); certainty in interpersonal relations as revealed by story completions (Commoss, 1962); and sensitivity to the social overtures of other children (Klaus, 1959). In addition, Karen (1965) has shown experimentally that increased sharing of reinforcement increases sociometric evaluation. None of the studies mentioned included data concerning the relation of friendliness to peer rejection.

Data for young adolescents are concordant with the data for younger children. Peer acceptance between the ages of 12 and 16 is positively associated with sociability (Marks, 1954); lack of desire to change the behavior of other members of the peer group (Rosen et al., 1961); being helpful, good-natured, and the "life of the party" (Elkins, 1958); friendliness and enthusiasm (Gronlund and Anderson, 1957); being "good company" and, particularly among children from high income families, participation in school activities (Feinberg, Smith, and Schmidt, 1958).

Two of the foregoing studies furnish information concerning the relation of sociability to peer rejection. First, low sociability was *not* checked as a major reason for rejection in Elkins' sample of 12- to 15-year-olds. Feinberg et al. found that rejection was associated with lack of participation in school activities, but only for subjects from higher income families. Thus, once again, lack of sociability does not seem to be a potent factor in rejection by the peer group.

Among older adolescents, Keislar (1953) reported positive correlations between sociability and both peer acceptance and prestige. For girls, however, sociability was more highly correlated with acceptance than it was with prestige. Prestige, on the other hand, proved to be more highly correlated in both sexes with marks, school effort, and other achievement-oriented behaviors than was peer acceptance. Thus peer acceptance appears to have somewhat different correlates during adolescence than does prestige. Jones (1958) reported that high school students who were frequently mentioned in the school paper (a rough index of social participation) were more popular than those who were mentioned less often and Marks (1957) found that popular adolescents were "more prominent" than less popular individuals.

In summary, then, the literature shows that social participation and peer acceptance are positively related at all age levels. Direction of causality is probably reciprocal. Sociability may lead to acceptance, but acceptance undoubtedly inspires greater sociability. The correlations between social participation and popularity, however, are not generally higher in adolescent samples than in samples of preschool children. One would expect this to be the case if sociability and popularity influence each other in a reciprocal fashion. Evidence for such an effect must be sought, however, with more efficient techniques than comparison of correlation coefficients between sociability and acceptance at different age levels.

Compliance, Cooperativeness, and Acceptance of Others. Data from several studies show that compliance, cooperation, and acceptance of others are correlated with peer acceptance. The relation between these variables is positive and, further, this relation exists in peer groups of very young children as well as in peer groups of adolescents. Peer acceptance in preschool groups is positively correlated with complying to routines and "acceptance of the situation" (Koch, 1933); adjustment to, and cooperation with, group rules (Lippitt, 1941); and peer perceptions of conformity (Moore, 1967). Whether or not noncompliance is characteristic of rejected children is unknown; appropriate data are lacking.

Data concerning the relation between prosocial behavior and peer acceptance are sketchy for elementary school children. Klaus (1959) found that accepted children tend to emphasize such behaviors as being neat and tidy, being a good sport, and being able to take a joke in their descriptions of classmates. Campbell and Yarrow (1961) found that popular children differed from unpopular children in the manner in which they describe other children. Specifically, popular children tended to depict other children by using systematic conceptual categories and they were able to make particularly subtle inferences concerning the causes of other children's behavior. Such results may mean simply that popular children are brighter than unpopular children. But peer leaders apparently have more "socially integrative" (i.e., mature) ideologies than nonleaders (Gold, 1962) and this suggests that popular children are socially sensitive and particularly accepting of other children. One bit of direct evidence concerning the relation between popularity and acceptance of others is contained in a study by Reese (1961). He reported a low, but significant correlation ($r = .20$) between acceptance by others and acceptance of others in a sample composed of 507 fourth-, sixth-, and eighth-grade children.

Scattered data for adolescents indicate that social acceptance is positively related to conformity to peer group mores (Elkins, 1958); to good moral judgment as perceived by peers (Porteus and Johnson, 1965); and to sensitivity to the feelings of others (Loban, 1953). Singer (1951) reported that acceptance by the peer group is associated with the individual's acceptance of the group. Similar results have been obtained with medical students (Fey, 1955) but not with fraternity men (Williams, 1962)!

Thus popularity seems to be linked with the effective internalization of social norms.[7] The data do *not* suggest that the popular child is overly conforming or compliant in social situations. Rather the popular child appears to be willing "to modulate his own behavior and to make necessary compromises toward the peaceful and efficient operation of the group" (Moore, 1967, p. 241).

Self-Esteem. If positive evaluation by the peer group is accomplished by effective socialization, we can hypothesize that self-esteem and peer acceptance should be positively correlated. That is, we would predict that popular children have more positive self-concepts than less popular children. Research evidence does not consistently confirm this prediction.

In at least two studies with adults (Fey, 1955; McIntyre, 1952), no significant relation was found between self-acceptance and acceptance by others. With children, Helper (1958) found that boys having high sociometric status were significantly more self-accepting than boys having low status, but this difference was not significant for girls. Reese (1961) has provided the clearest evidence in support of the hypothesis, but his data show that the relation between self-acceptance and peer acceptance is curvilinear. That is, children with moderately high self-concepts were more accepted by their peers than children with either low or very high self-concepts. The possibility that the correlation between self-esteem and peer acceptance is curvilinear has not been explored by others who have found low, but significant correlations between these two variables (Cox, 1966; Horowitz, 1962b; Perkins, 1958; Sears, 1960). It is possible, of course, that the inconsistencies in these findings stem from the use of different methods for assessing children's self-concepts. Reese's results should be replicated and extended because they suggest that high self-esteem may be associated with certain behaviors which "put off" the child's peers—behaviors such as "cockiness," "self-

satisfaction," or even snobbish withdrawal from peer interaction.

Two other studies underscore the fact that the relation between self-acceptance and peer acceptance is complex. R. J. Marshall (1958) found that self-acceptance was lowered when experimental feedback was furnished to the subject consisting of unfavorable reactions by the peer group. No change, however, followed feedback that implied favorable reactions from the peer group. Further, the extent to which a subject believes his evaluations of others are reciprocated is a positive function of his own self-esteem (Weist, 1965). Obviously, the role of self-attitudes in determining a child's peer status needs more study than it has had up to this point.

Socioempathy. Several studies of peer acceptance have involved measurement of the personality construct known as *socioempathy*. Essentially, this term refers to the individual's ability to perceive correctly the status positions of himself and others. Mead (1934) hypothesized that effective social relations can be established only when one can distinguish oneself from others and "take the role of the other." Using specially constructed tests of socioempathic ability, Ausubel (1955) and Rose, Frankel, and Kerr (1956) were unable to confirm this hypothesis. On the other hand, Goslin (1962) found that children who were not popular, as contrasted with popular children, showed: (1) greater disparity between the individual's self-ratings and peers' ratings of him; (2) greater disparity between the individual's ratings of his peers and ratings made by the group as a whole; and (3) greater disparity between self-ratings and how the individual predicted that the peer group would rate him. Other research (Mouton, Bell, and Blake, 1956) confirms that good role players have higher peer status than children who are less skilled at role-taking activity. Popular children are also more proficient in drawing faces on the *Goodenough Draw-a-Man Test* even though they do not perform better than nonpopular children in drawing the body portion of the human figure (Richey and Spotts, 1959).

In summary, the issue concerning the relation between socioempathy and peer acceptance remains in doubt. As indicated in preceding sections of this report, social sensitivity, compliance, and conformity (which involve

[7] It is not known, however, whether adhering to minority group norms that differ from the values of the core culture is associated in any systematic way with popularity.

recognition of others' needs) are positively associated with success in peer relations. But whether the ability to discriminate the peer group status of others facilitates one's own social acceptance remains an open question.

Anxiety and Adjustment. Significant positive correlations between global measures of "adjustment" and measures of sociometric status have been reported by numerous investigators. Trent (1957) listed six studies, all of which showed that popular children were better adjusted than less popular children. A thorough search of the literature reveals numerous additional studies, both with children and adults, that have yielded similar results. Measurement of adjustment has involved tests such as the *California Test of Personality* (Dahlke, 1953); the *Mental Hygiene Analysis* (Baron, 1951), the *Thematic Apperception Test* (Alexander and Alexander, 1952); a composite index of neurotic traits (Thorpe, 1955), and the *Rorschach Test* (Northway and Wigdor, 1947). Other studies (e.g., Mensh and Glidwell, 1958; Hartup, 1959) have employed observational measures of the child's social or school adjustment. Thus there is clear consensus that a child's general adjustment is related to his popularity with peers.

Perhaps the most intriguing findings contained in these studies are those in which neurotic traits have been assessed by means of instruments that do not refer directly to the child's interpersonal relations. The use of adjustment measures that are derived from observations or tests which are heavily loaded with data concerning social behavior does not provide independent assessment of peer acceptance, on the one hand, and personality dynamics, on the other. It is no surprise, for example, that Hartup (1959) reported significant positive correlations between peer acceptance and scores on the *Early-Adjustment-to-School Scale* (a global measure of the nursery school child's competence in school activities and social relations). The EAS is heavily weighted with items referring to the child's peer interactions. Since many of the studies in this area are not flawed in this manner, however, it is possible to conclude that neurotic disturbance is likely to be associated with low peer evaluation.

All of the investigations cited concern the relation between adjustment and popularity in samples of children who were functioning within the normal range. Other evidence shows that relative degree of maladjustment is also inversely related to popularity in disturbed groups (Davids and Parenti, 1958).

The relation between a specific neurotic component, anxiety, and sociometric status has also been explored. Although there are some variations in the results, the evidence supports the conclusion that anxious children are less popular than nonanxious children. In the earliest study of this problem, McCandless, Castaneda, and Palermo (1956) found correlations ranging from .28 to −.75 between scores on the *Children's Manifest Anxiety Scale* and popularity with same-sex peers in fourth- and fifth-grade children. No significant correlations were found for sixth-grade children. Next, Iscoe and Garden (1961) found significant negative correlations between the CMAS and sociometric status (values were not reported), but only for girls. There was also a positive correlation (.65) between CMAS scores and sociometric rejections for the girls in this study. Horowitz (1962b) did not find sex differences among her fourth- to sixth-grade subjects, but the overall correlation between CMAS scores and sociometric status was −.36. This correlation reduced to −.25 when scores on a self-concept scale were partialled out. A similar correlation (−.29) was reported by Trent (1957) for a sample of institutionalized delinquent boys. Cowen, Zax, Klein, Izzo, and Trost (1965) reported correlations of −.19 and −.16 between CMAS scores and peer nominations for "good guy" roles in a school play; these correlations were .21 and .10 when nominations for negative roles was the criterion measure. There is also one study in which zero-order correlations between CMAS scores and sociometric status were reported (McCandless and Ali, 1966). In addition, Hill (1963) found no significant correlations between the *Test Anxiety Scale* and same-sex peer preferences.

The reader may draw his own conclusions from this compilation of results. Using the CMAS, low negative correlations with peer status have been found in the majority of subgroups studied. In the one study in which the TASC was used, however, anxiety did not prove to be predictive of like-sex peer acceptance.

Hill (1963), however, extended his study

in order to assess the relation between anxiety and status with opposite-sex peers. It was anticipated that, among latency-age children, boys would prefer low-anxious (more "masculine") girls and that girls would prefer high-anxious (more "feminine" boys). The results clearly confirmed this expectation. With IQ and defensiveness partialled out, the correlation between acceptance by opposite-sex peers and TASC scores was −.38 for girls and .29 for boys.

The factors which are responsible for the failure of these findings concerning anxiety and peer status to generalize across all of the peer groups studied are not known. Horowitz's (1962b) approach to this problem, in which the additional variable of self-concept was incorporated into the research design, is a promising one. Examination of numerous other factors, as these interact with anxiety in determining peer acceptance, is clearly needed.

Dependency. The relation between dependency and popularity cannot be described simply. First, dependency on adults may interfere with popularity, but dependency on peers may actually be an attribute of popular children. Second, if the overtures a child makes are socially mature, such as help-seeking and approval-seeking, he may be more popular with peers than if his overtures are immature (e.g., affection-seeking or negative attention-seeking).

Most of the studies supporting these hypotheses have involved preschool-aged children. Marshall and McCandless (1957a) studied this problem through direct observation of social interaction in the nursery school. Dependency on adults was negatively related to social acceptance as measured by picture sociometric tests, observations, and teachers' judgments. In a second study (McCandless, Bilous, and Bennett, 1961) two types of dependence on adults were measured—help-seeking and emotional-support seeking. The latter measure was negatively related to sociometric status, particularly in girls, but the help-seeking variable was not significantly correlated with social acceptance. Consistent with these results are Dunnington's (1957a) findings that popular preschoolers, as compared with unpopular children, were less likely to initiate supportive interaction with the adult experimenter during doll play. Similarly,

Northway and Rooks (1956) found that sociometric scores of kindergarteners were inversely related to the child's tendency to copy the experimenter's example in manipulating formboard materials. Finally, Moore and Updegraff (1964) separately measured dependency-on-adults and dependency-on-peers by means of observations conducted in the nursery school. For younger preschoolers, the correlation between adult dependency and sociometric status was −.55, confirming the McCandless et al. findings. This correlation did not hold for older children, possibly because help-seeking was not separated from support-seeking in the measure of dependence. The correlation between sociometric status and peer dependency was only of borderline significance, but it was positive for both older and younger children. It appears, then, that dependent interactions may interfere with peer relations only if dependence is directed at adults and is immature in form. Appropriate dependent interactions with peers, along with other types of social participation, appear to facilitate peer acceptance during early childhood.

A small amount of data for older children confirms the findings with younger children. In one study (Campbell and Yarrow, 1958), popular children were more likely to give mature dependent overtures to their peers than were nonpopular children. These results are distinctly different, but nevertheless consistent with the findings of Wiggins and Winder (1961) and Winder and Rau (1962) which show significant negative correlations between immature forms of dependence (mainly negative attention-seeking) and peer ratings of the child's "likability."

Aggression. The relation between aggression and sociometric status depends, to a considerable extent, on the measure of peer status that is used. Research results are quite inconsistent concerning the manner in which aggression is related to positive sociometric choice. On the other hand, findings are much more uniform concerning the association between aggression and peer rejection.

In studies of preschool children, three investigators reported no significant correlation between peer acceptance and the child's aggressiveness (Hartup et al., 1967; Lippitt, 1941; Marshall and McCandless, 1957b); one investigator reported aggression to be positively related to acceptance (Marshall, 1961); and one reported the relation to be negative (Koch, 1933). On the other hand, there are three studies in which the rejection status of preschool children was used as the sociometric criterion. In all three cases, significant positive correlations between peer rejection and amount of aggression in peer interaction were found (Dunnington, 1957a; Hartup et al., 1967; Moore, 1967).

The aggressiveness of rejected and nonrejected children may also differ qualitatively (Dunnington, 1957a). Nonrejected preschool children directed their aggressiveness more frequently toward the source of frustration and displayed more "thematic" or provoked aggressive behavior in doll play. Thus the aggressive behavior of popular children, when it occurs, may be more reality-oriented than the aggression of nonpopular children. In general, however, hostile social behavior is more closely related to peer rejection than to peer acceptance in nursery school children.

Studies with older children and adolescents confirm the hypothesis that global measures of aggressiveness are not strongly related to the number of positive sociometric choices a child receives from his peers (e.g., Bonney and Powell, 1953; Pope, 1953). Several investigators have shown, however, that immature, unprovoked, or indirect forms of aggressiveness are characteristics of children who are not accepted by their peers. For example, Lesser (1959) found a mean correlation between popularity and verbal aggressiveness of −.45 and a mean correlation of −.69 between popularity and indirect aggressiveness in fifth- and sixth-grade boys. However, popularity and provoked physical aggression were actually positively correlated ($r = .31$). Winder and Rau (1962) and Goertzen (1959) have also reported negative correlations between likability and inappropriate, disruptive aggressive behavior; two other investigators found rejection to be positively associated with "objectionable behavior" (Davids and Parenti, 1958; Elkins, 1958). But, once again, Campbell and Yarrow (1961) found that popular children showed more friendly aggression than nonpopular children.

Thus there seems to be consistent evidence that unpopular preadolescents may not show greater *total* amounts of aggression than their more popular peers, but the aggressive behavior that they do display is likely to be indirect and less socially acceptable.

The foregoing findings are elucidated by the responses of high-, medium-, and low-popular school children on the *Rosenzweig Picture-Frustration Test* (Coons, 1957). Medium- and low-popular children, as contrasted with high-popular children, were: (1) more readily blocked; (2) more likely to minimize or deny frustration; (3) less likely to direct hostility to the environment, blame others, or direct hostility to others; and (4) more impunitive. Low-popular children were also more likely to absolve others of responsibilty for frustration. The children of middle sociometric status proved to be more intropunitive than either the high- or the low-popular children.

A final, tangential point concerning aggression and popularity: the adequacy of peer relations in childhood appears to be related to antisocial behavior in adulthood. In a sample of servicemen, all of whom were former patients in a child guidance clinic, those receiving bad conduct discharges were significantly more likely to have been rated by their childhood counselors as having poor peer adjustment than those with successful service records (Roff, 1961).

IQ and Academic Achievement. The relation between intelligence and sociometric status has been explored in countless studies, at least one of which was published almost 50 years ago (Almack, 1922). The strategy in most of these investigations has been to correlate IQ scores with sociometric scores in unselected populations of school children. Bonney's investigations (e.g., 1942, 1943, 1944) exemplify this approach. Correlations between IQ and popularity are usually significant, although they may range from relatively low magnitudes (.20) to moderate levels (.65). (See Davis, 1957; Gallagher, 1958b; Gronlund and Whitney, 1958; Hill, 1963; Thorpe, 1955a; Wardlow and Greene, 1952). Other investigators have contrasted groups of children at various IQ levels (e.g., by quartiles) and have confirmed that the relation between intelligence and status in the peer group is a positive one (e.g., Heber, 1956; Grossman and Wrighter, 1958; Peck and Gallian, 1962).

All of these investigations suffer from a

common flaw. That is, correlations have been computed between IQ scores and sociometric scores without partialling out the variance attributable to social class. Since IQ and socioeconomic status are directly related, it is not clear as to whether IQ actually accounts for a significant portion of the variance in children's popularity with their peers.

A recent study supplies corrective evidence concerning this problem (Sells and Roff, 1967). Two replications of the study were conducted—one with a sample of 2800 fourth-grade children residing in a large Minnesota city and the other with 3216 children residing in various Texas communities. The strategy used in the two studies differed considerably. In the Minnesota research, the children were divided into four socioeconomic levels, based on census tract information, and the IQs of popular and nonpopular children were compared. Popular peers were significantly brighter than nonpopular peers within all four socioeconomic levels. The mean IQ differences between the popular and nonpopular children varied from 12 to 20 points. In the Texas study, the samples were comprised of schools serving socioeconomically homogeneous populations of either working-class or middle-class children. Correlations between IQ and popularity were then computed separately by school. This procedure is not as elegant as the Minnesota study, although some control for socioeconomic status was established. The correlations between IQ and peer acceptance were all positive; they ranged between .22 and .39. Interestingly, peer rejection (measured separately from peer acceptance) was also positively correlated with IQ in both socioeconomic groups, although these correlations were somewhat lower (between .14 and .32) than those between IQ and acceptance.

Studies of intellectually exceptional children confirm the results described. Very bright children (the "gifted") are likely to be more popular than their less gifted peers. Also, mentally retarded children attending school in regular classrooms are likely to be less popular than children possessing greater intellectual ability (e.g., Baldwin, 1958; Gallagher, 1958a; Johnson, 1950; Martyn, 1957; Miller, 1956).

Academic performance is also positively correlated with sociometric status. Sells and Roff (1967), using a sample of fourth- to seventh-grade children, found an overall correlation of .33 between school marks and acceptance; the correlation between marks and rejection was .27. Finer-grained analysis revealed two interdependent trends in these data. First, the magnitude of the correlation between school marks and status dropped with increasing age (average correlations: fourth grade, .43; fifth grade, .34; sixth grade, .27; seventh grade, .28). Second, peer status was also predictive of early school drop-out. Other investigators (e.g., Feinberg et al., 1958; Muma, 1965) have also reported significant correlations between school marks and sociometric status.

The relation between specific abilities and peer status depends on the sociometric criterion selected. For example, arithmetic ability and reading skills are associated with general popularity (Davis, 1957; Hudgins, Smith, and Johnson, 1962; Porterfield and Schlichting, 1961), but such skills are most closely related to choice of work partners in tasks requiring excellence in the skill itself. Also, as Keislar (1953) has shown, school marks are more highly correlated with prestige than with popularity. Other studies have shown that competence demonstrated in youth-group projects is significantly correlated with leadership in these same groups (H. R. Marshall, 1958; Polansky, Lippitt, and Redl, 1950).

Achievement motivation also relates to peer acceptance, although in a nonlinear fashion. That is, greater popularity is characteristic of children with medium levels of aspiration than is characteristic of children with either very high or very low levels of aspiration (Cassel and Saugstad, 1952). Research shows, then, that bright children who achieve in school at a realistic level have preferred status in the peer group; the overachieving child, however, may have a less certain position in his peer group.

Physical Factors. Popularity is positively associated with such diverse factors as athletic skill, timing of pubescence, and physical attractiveness. Popularity in boys is correlated, at least to a small degree, with mesomorphic body build (Clarke and Greene, 1963; Hanley, 1951) and with strength and athletic skill (Clarke and Clarke, 1961; Feinberg, 1953; Polansky et al., 1950). Further, early maturing boys possess a variety of traits which are esteemed by the peer-culture and, in early adolescence, are likely to be more popular and high in leadership than late-maturers (Davis, 1957; Jones and Bayley, 1950; More, 1953). Although behavioral differences between early and late-maturing males decrease following the early adolescent years, striking residual differences have been reported for subjects studied longitudinally and who have reached adulthood (Jones, 1957; Jones, 1965). Developmental maturity is also associated with prestige in adolescent girls (Faust, 1960). The importance of physical attractiveness in determining peer status has been demonstrated in several studies (Bonney, 1944; Roff and Brody, 1953).

Interpretation of these results is difficult. It has been commonly assumed that the social advantages enjoyed by the attractive, early maturing, mesomorphic individual derive from the positive evaluation that is placed on such characteristics in U.S. culture. Thus it is posited that socially acquired self-attitudes mediate the relation between physical factors and peer acceptance. The results of at least one study, however, suggest that temperamental factors are salient in the developmental concordance shown among physical, social, and emotional traits in adolescents (More, 1953). Consequently, the possibility exists that the relation between physiological traits and popularity is modulated, in part, by constitutional factors. The general issue, however, remains in doubt. Since the role of physiological factors in peer acceptance has only been examined in samples of preadolescents and postadolescents, longitudinal studies beginning early in childhood are needed before these issues can be clarified.

Birth Order. Schachter (1964) found that later-born college students were more popular than firstborns. Further, the firstborns tended to assign their sociometric choices to fewer individuals and to more popular persons than did later-borns. These findings are consistent with the notion that firstborn individuals are more anxious and dependent than later-borns. (It will be recalled that these characteristics, when measured directly, are negatively related to popularity.) Schachter believes that the sources of these personality differences between firstborn and later-born individuals lie in differential child-rearing experiences. He has argued that parents are less consistent

in their handling of firstborn children than they are in handling later-borns, conditions which should give rise to dependence and uncertainty in interpersonal relations. But firstborn children also have the experience of being superseded or placed in rivalrous positions with siblings. Thus it is reasonable to argue, from this standpoint as well, that anxiety generated within the family generalizes to interactions with peers. Such generalization, if it occurs, could deleteriously affect the firstborn child's status with his peers.

Sells and Roff (1964), in their extensive study of peer acceptance, confirmed Schachter's findings. These authors hypothesized, however, that "only" children do not resemble other firstborn children in that they are not exposed to the same socially debilitating experiences with younger siblings. In particular, "only" children are not superseded in the family by younger children. It was predicted, therefore, that youngest and "only" children should have more favorable peer relations than middle and oldest children. Using sociometric data obtained from 1013 elementary school children, significant birth-order effects in peer acceptance scores were obtained, and borderline effects were found in rejection scores. Youngest and "only children" were accepted by their peers. On the other hand, oldest children and middle children were less well-liked and were more likely to be rejected by the peer group. Elkins (1958) has also reported that highly chosen children tend to be youngest children. Thus birth order appears to account for a significant portion of the variance in children's peer relations. It must be said, however, that the personality factors which mediate this relation have not been studied directly in child populations; hence these factors remain obscure.

Children's Names. One study has concerned the relation between the desirability of children's names and popularity (McDavid and Harari, 1966). A two fold precedure was used:

1. The subjects (10- to 12-year-olds) all gave social desirability rankings to names occurring within their own peer group.
2. An outside group of children ranked these same names.

The social desirability rankings proved to be significantly correlated with popularity.

When the name-ranking was done by the peer group itself, this correlation was .63; when done by the outside group, it was .49. One must wonder about the basis for this relation. Does an "oddball" name handicap a child in his relations with peers or do parents who choose strange names go about socializing their children in atypical ways?

Sex. The existence of a sex cleavage in children's peer relations is much too well known to require extensive comment here. Suffice to say that sociometric studies (including subjects as young as 3 years of age; e.g., Abel and Sahinkaya, 1962; Moore and Updegraff, 1964) provide evidence that children prefer like-sex peers to opposite-sex peers through all of early and middle childhood. Further, best friends chosen by adolescents are also most commonly of the same sex.

Even though a sex cleavage in peer relations exists in early childhood, this cleavage is somewhat less strong than in later childhood. It becomes particularly pronounced in middle childhood, reaching a peak during preadolescence. During adolescence, however, increasing numbers of individuals choose opposite-sex friends and peer relations undergo considerable restructuring with respect to sex membership (Broderick and Fowler, 1961; Broderick, 1966). Patterns of cross-sex sociometric choices during adolescence, however, may be changing over the years. It has been reported that a greater percentage of U.S. adolescents made cross-sex choices in 1963 ($N = 2000$) than in 1942 ($N = 700$) (Kuhlen and Houlihan, 1965).

With specific reference to cross-sex preferences, McCandless and Marshall (1957b) found that preschoolers ascribe girls with slightly greater acceptance than boys. On the other hand, Bonney (1954) found no evidence, based on a large sample of elementary school children, that boys choose girls more often than the reverse.

The status position that a child enjoys with the opposite sex is, however, associated with his status among same-sex peers. Reese's (1962) data for fifth-grade children show this clearly for boys; that is, acceptance by girls was significantly associated with acceptance by other boys. Girls who were least accepted by other girls tended also to be least accepted by boys, but popularity with the opposite sex did not differ for girls who were moderately or highly popular with other girls.

Ethnicity. The social system in all-Negro peer groups tends to be ordered in ways that are similar to all-white peer groups. Many of the factors that are predictive of peer acceptance in groups of white children are also predictive of status in segregated groups of Negro children (Sells and Roff, 1967). In racially mixed groups, however, ethnicity is related to several different aspects of peer acceptance. First, racial cleavages are generally characteristic of such peer groups. Cleavages have been found in peer groups of both younger and older children and when the subculture is well integrated (McCandless and Hoyt, 1961; Springer, 1953) or highly segregated (Jansen and Gallagher, 1966; Morland, 1966; Radke, Sutherland, and Rosenberg, 1950; Stevenson and Stevenson, 1960).

In segregated settings, own-race cleavage appears to be stronger among the majority-group children than among children in the racial minority (Morland, 1966). In areas which are characterized by *de facto* segregation or which are well integrated, results are more variable. For example, in one urban elementary school in which Negro children outnumbered white children 10 to 1, own-race cleavage was stronger among the white children than among the Negro children (Radke et al., 1950). In another study, conducted in a setting in which white children were in the majority, own-race cleavage was stronger in the minority group of Oriental children (Lambert and Taguchi, 1956). It has also been found, however, in both Massachusetts and Hawaii, that own-race cleavage is stronger among majority-group children than among minority-group children (Morland, 1966; Springer, 1953).

Why should the minority group ever show stronger racial cleavage than the majority? Lambert and Taguchi have suggested that when faced with a threatening situation (such as perceiving oneself in a minority status) the child seeks cues which have been associated previously with nurturance and support —namely, like-race persons. The lesser cohesiveness of the majority peer group in such situations may derive from the lack of this threat.

It would be expected that, in general, cleavages should be less marked in integrated subcultures than in segregated cultures. Surprisingly, there is little cross-cultural material bearing on this question. At least one investigator (Morland, 1966) found that cleavages in peer preferences were more pronounced among Southern U.S. children than among Northern children. Radke and Trager (1950), however, did not find that children's preferences varied according to the racial composition of the neighborhood in which the children lived. These neighborhoods ranged from "all white" to "mostly Negro." Nor did Clark and Clark (1952) find differential preferences for same- and different-race children among Northern and Southern Negro children.

Evidence drawn from mixed-race peer groups suggests that the minority-group children are significantly less popular than majority-group children (Morland, 1966; Radke and Trager, 1950).[8] Two studies, both from the Southwestern United States, show that Latin American children are less accepted, although not necessarily more rejected, than Anglo-American children (Peck and Gallian, 1962; Sells and Roff, 1967). This finding held when socioeconomic status and size of the minority representation in the peer group were held constant. It is interesting, however, that in a sample of delinquent girls (all of whom, in a sense, were social rejects) no status differentiation was apparent according to whether the girl was Latin- or Anglo-American (Weber, 1950).

One final, poignant note will close this brief discussion of ethnic factors in peer relations. Kerckhoff and McCormick (1955) reported that U.S. Indian children who were highly identified with the white peer culture and who gave evidence of being sensitive to their marginal status were more likely to be rejected by the white group than Indian children who were not oriented toward their white peers. These data are consistent with Katz' (1955) observations of social interaction in an interracial YMCA group. Thus the climate that is created by the subculture produces racial barriers in peer relations that are extremely difficult for the child to penetrate.

It would be appropriate, at this point, to review the entire literature dealing with the development of ethnocentrism in children. As previously indicated, ethnocentric attitudes are potent factors in children's peer interactions. The topic of ethnocentrism, however, is much broader than the subject of racial cleavage in children's groups. It is for this reason that racial awareness is not discussed further here. There are several recent reviews of this literature that focus on normative studies (Stevenson, 1967); personality factors in ethnocentrism (McCandless, 1967); and the child-rearing antecedents of ethnocentrism (e.g., Epstein and Komorita, 1966a, 1966b). No accounting of the social psychology of childhood is complete without a recognition of this particular literature, and no student of peer relations in childhood can afford to be unfamiliar with this research material.

Social Class. Generally, research supports the conclusion that the lower-class child is less popular in mixed peer groups than the middle- or upper-class child. Good evidence concerning this point, however, is scarce. Cannon (1957) reported that socioeconomic status was directly related to peer acceptance among children living in a small town but that this relation did not hold among rural children. The findings for the town children are suspect, however, because the data were not analyzed separately for children of varying levels of intelligence. The findings for the rural children are suspect for a different reason: it has been exceedingly difficult to develop valid measures of social class for rural populations. Elkins (1958) also reported a direct relation between popularity and socioeconomic status but, once again, the effects of IQ were not partialled out. Even Sells and Roff (1967), who clearly showed that IQ is associated with peer acceptance when socioeconomic status is partialled out, failed to report findings concerning the direct relation of social class to peer acceptance.

Perhaps the best evidence concerning this problem is contained in a study by Grossman and Wrighter (1948). A sample of sixth graders was divided into three IQ levels. The higher the economic level of the father's occupation, the more popular the child at each IQ level. Other data suggest that socioeconomic status is a better predictor of girls' peer acceptance than boys' (Brown and Bond, 1955; Davis, 1957). Further, social class may be less important in the peer relations of high

---

[8] This is also true of physically handicapped minorities (Centers and Centers, 1963) and minorities composed of orphanage children attending a public school (Castle, 1954).

school students (once drop-out of lower-class adolescents has occurred) than in the peer evaluations of younger children (McGuire, Lanmon, and White, 1953).

Empirical information of good quality concerning the relation between socioeconomic status and peer acceptance is, then, in short supply. It is therefore not surprising that data elucidating this relation are also almost non-existent. It is known, of course, that lower-class children are less well-adjusted according to core-culture norms and less likely to do well in school than middle-class children. We have already shown that each of these variables accounts for a portion of the variance in peer acceptance scores. Consequently, mixed peer groups appear to be dominated by middle-class or core-culture values.

The results of one study support the hypothesis that social class differences in values may account for some of the socioeconomic bias in children's acceptance by the peer group. Feinberg et al. (1958) conducted an extensive survey of male adolescents' peer attitudes in lower-, middle-, and upper-income groups. Individuals from all income groups agreed in characterizing accepted peers as intelligent, fair, able to take a joke, good company, athletic, quiet, conscientious, and honest. Furthermore, all income groups agreed that rejected individuals are pesty, noisy, conceited, silly, and effeminate. But adolescent boys from low- and middle-income families also stressed the importance of common interests, ability to talk well, and minding one's own business as factors in acceptance; fighting was given as a common reason for rejection. In contrast, adolescents from high-income groups stressed cooperativeness, leadership, participation in activities, cheerfulness, and scholarship as factors involved in peer acceptance. Attributes associated with rejection included low IQ, lack of leadership, failure to participate in activities, and immaturity.

These data indicate that peer status may be ascribed on the basis of some values which are held in common by lower-, middle-, and upper-class members of children's groups while, at the same time, there is considerable discordance in peer values among various socioeconomic groups. Upper-income adolescents, for instance, placed much heavier stress on achievement, leadership, and mature social skills than the other two groups did. In one

other study, lower-class children were found to make opposite-sex sociometric choices more frequently than middle-class children during the middle childhood years (Kanous, Daugherty, and Cohn, 1962). Value differences such as the ones mentioned here could well produce the bias in peer acceptance that is apparently associated with socioeconomic status.

Success and Failure. We have indicated that popular children are likely to be bright, get good marks, and to be sociable. Such data suggest, but do not firmly support the hypothesis that success and failure experiences are important determinants of peer group status. Children who are liked by their teachers tend to receive higher sociometric scores than those who are not preferred by the teacher (Gronlund, 1953), but such findings do not provide answers to the question raised above. Nor does information which shows that children who fail in school are less well-liked than those who do not fail (Goodlad, 1954).

More convincing are the findings of two experimental studies, both conducted with elementary school children. In one investigation (Heber and Heber, 1957), the objective was to examine the effects of group success and group failure on peer ratings. Some groups constituted for the experiment were composed of high-status children and others of low-status youngsters. Groups of both types were assigned to success, failure, or neutral conditions. Regardless of the initial status of the group, either neutral or successful experience produced more positive peer evaluations. The effects of the success experience, however, were more permanent (as measured by further testing after a two-week interval). The effects of group failure depended on the initial status of the group. Children in high-status groups tended to be less positive about their fellows as a consequence of failure; failure had no effects, however, on peer evaluations in low-status groups. Here, then, is evidence that shared success and failure experiences modify children's evaluations of each other; the nature of these changes, however, depends on the initial status of the children involved.

In the foregoing study, the effects of success and failure on peer relations involved *shared* experiences. That is, the individual's success (or failure) was confounded with simultaneous success (or failure) by his fellows. The effects of individual success experiences were studied by Flanders and Havumaki (1960). The subjects were high school students, divided into 10-member groups for purposes of the experiment. In one condition, the teacher-moderator interacted only with those students sitting in odd-numbered seats. In a second condition, praise was directed toward the whole group. Subsequent sociometric data showed that in Condition I, subjects occupying the odd-numbered seats received significantly more positive choices than those in even-numbered seats. On the other hand, there was no significant difference between the choices given to odd- and even-numbered subjects in Condition II.

Other research has shown that success experiences affect the child's own friendship choices as well as the manner in which he is evaluated by his peers (Lott and Lott, 1960). Third- and fourth-graders were divided into three-child *ad hoc* groups to play a "rocket game." The groups played this game twice during the experiment. One-half of the subjects received attractive rewards for successful performance while the remaining half of the subjects did not. Postexperimental sociometric tests revealed that the proportion of play-group members chosen by the rewarded subjects was significantly greater than the proportion chosen by the nonrewarded subjects. Thus interpersonal attractiveness was increased when the peer's presence was contiguous with the subject's own success. The studies in this area suggest, then, that social attraction varies as a function of both observing rewards being given to others and the extent to which the child himself enjoys pleasant experiences in the presence of his peers.

All of the findings discussed in this section have involved success and failure as manipulated by sources external to the peer group (i.e., an adult). Research also has shown that sociometric choice is directly associated with the extent to which children give reinforcement to each other; this material is discussed later in this chapter.

Child-Rearing Factors

Research concerning the child-rearing correlates of peer acceptance presents a surprisingly consistent picture. Winder and Rau (1962) found that both the mothers and

fathers of "likable" boys expressed low demands for aggression and infrequently used aggressive punishment with their sons. The mothers of high-status boys also infrequently used deprivation of privileges, were high in self-esteem, and evidenced good parental adjustment. The fathers of high-status boys, in addition to fostering nonaggressive behaviors, gave favorable evaluations of their sons' competence. Thus the distinctive aspects of the high-status boy's socialization included parental discouragement of antisocial behavior, low amounts of frustration and punishment, and supportive reinforcement. All of these child-rearing behaviors would be expected to foster the development of positive self-concepts.

Elkins (1958) also found that children whose parents were pleased with them tended to receive higher sociometric scores than children who had dissatisfied parents. Further, absence of family tension coupled with loving and casual parental attitudes are predictive of high peer status (Cox, 1966). Data from children themselves present much the same picture: accepted children are more satisfied with their home lives and describe their families as more cohesive than do less well-accepted children (Elkins, 1958; Warnath, 1955).

The child-rearing antecedents of peer acceptance have also been studied by Hoffman (1961). The parental variables included in this study proved to be more predictive of boys' than girls' peer status. Further, the father's relations with the child seemed to be particularly salient antecedents of boys' peer adjustment. For example, if the mother was dominant in the household, the boy's relations with peers were likely to be aggressive and unfriendly; also, he was likely to be unsuccessful in exerting influence in the peer group. It was not reported that mother-dominant boys were less liked by their peers, but one would suspect that this was the case. When the father was dominant in disciplining his son (not necessarily punitive), the child was likely to be forceful and intrusive in initiating friendships, and to have high power in the peer group. Once again, the findings do not reveal explicitly that dominant fathers had sons who had high peer status, but general peer relations were more effective in such instances.

Affectional interaction between the boy and

his parents also predicted peer adjustment in the Hoffman study. Affection from the father was significantly related to boys' liking of other children, as well as being liked by them. This variable was also positively correlated with self-confidence, assertiveness, and effective skills in peer interaction. Maternal affection was predictive of both liking others and being liked. These relations were not strong among girls, although maternal warmth was significantly associated with good peer adjustment.

The significance of the father's behavior for boys' peer adjustment was also found by Lynn and Sawrey (1959). Norwegian boys whose fathers were absent for long periods had significantly poorer peer adjustment, including fewer friends, than did boys whose fathers were regularly present in the home. Finally, Wyer (1965) reported that children whose fathers avoid communication with them are generally uncertain in social situations. Thus the child-rearing factors associated with good peer relations (at least for boys) include relations with a father who is a visible figure in the household, and who is dominant, warm, and supportive.

Much has been written concerning the effects of nursery school experience on peer adjustment (e.g., Bonney and Nicholson, 1958; Brown and Hunt, 1961). Nevertheless, serious methodological flaws exist in these experiments. There is little question that peer relations improve from the beginning of a nursery school experience to its end. The later peer adjustment of children who have attended nursery school has not yet been assessed, however, using adequate control groups (e.g., non-nursery school children whose parents desired such schooling for their children although they were unable to obtain it).

LEADERSHIP

The terms *leadership, social power,* and *effective initiative* refer to the child's capacity to influence an organized group in its norm-setting efforts and achievement (Sherif and Sherif, 1964; Stogdill, 1950). Prerequisite conditions for leadership behavior include the existence of a group, a common task, and differentiation of responsibility. To a considerable extent those factors that are correlated

with popularity in the peer group are also predictive of social power or leadership. Perhaps the major exception to this statement is that assertiveness and aggressiveness are more closely related to leadership (particularly in boys) than to popularity (Lippitt and Gold, 1959). Otherwise, the personalities of leaders and the personalities of popular children do not differ markedly.

The Generality of Leadership

One would expect considerable cross-situational fluctuation in the leadership status of individual children. To some extent this is true. That is, the power hierarchy in the peer group is different when the group's task consists of completing an English lesson from when the task consists of planning a party. There are numerous reasons for the instability of leadership status. Variations in skill, as perceived by the peer group, are certainly related to such instability. On the other hand, the urgency of the task and the previous relations that have been formed in the peer group also produce fluctuations in leadership status (Shears, 1953; Sherif and Sherif, 1964). Finally, as reported earlier, leadership designations are less stable when the peer group works on tasks assigned to it than when it works on tasks of its own choosing (Katz et al., 1957).

Nevertheless, leadership has some degree of cross-situational stability. Among preschoolers, for example, Gellert (1961) found that the dominant members of two-child dyads tended to be the *same* children during three different testing sessions. The power relations existing in these dyads clearly did not fluctuate extensively from one time to the next.

Most of the data on this problem, however, are derived from adolescent groups. First, adolescents agree among themselves in their rank-ordering of traits that characterize people who can "get other people to do things for them." Trait-rankings given by one group of male adolescents (Rosen, Levinger, and Lippitt, 1961) were as follows: helpfulness, fairness, sociability, expertness, fearlessness, and physical strength. The concordance coefficient for this sample was .60. Next, these traits were ranked as they would apply to six specific situations: organizing a party; conducting a meeting; raising children; organizing a fishing trip; dissuading an angry crowd;

and training commandos. The general trait-rankings (as listed above) correlated with the rankings obtained for the specific situations in the following order: .60, .83, .94, .71, .09, and −.14. Thus the general attributes of social power were perceived in much the same way across four of the situations. Equally important, however, is the fact that fearlessness and physical strength were emphasized *more* strongly in two of the social situations (dissuading a crowd and training commandos) than in the others. The importance of this study consists of the information it reveals concerning the generality of opinions about social power. It does not reveal, of course, the extent to which actual leadership behavior possesses cross-situational generality.

The best direct evidence concerning situational influences on leadership status was provided by Sherif and Sherif (1964). They concluded upon the basis of intensive study of adolescent peer groups:

The leader position is the top rank in the status structure, but the leadership role involves the shared expectations of other members for a particular individual occupying that position. These expectations vary markedly in terms of the kinds of activities the group engages in and the qualities which count in their scheme of things. Invariably, however, they involve the supposition that what the leader approves of, what he suggests himself, or what he decides will be accomplished, will work out well. When his initiations to action and his decisions lead to failure in interteam competition, or result in social gatherings which bore and distress members, or get his fellow members into unnecessary trouble with authorities, then his work ceases to be effective. A new leader takes the initiative or the membership drifts away to other centers of interest (pp. 159–160).

Correlates of Leadership Status

What are the behavioral characteristics of socially powerful children? Comprehensive studies of this problem were conducted during the 1950s at the University of Michigan. Most of this research took place in such settings as camps and classrooms. The following publications are representative: Polansky et al., 1950; Lippitt et al., 1952; Gold, 1958; Zander and Van Egmond, 1958; Lippitt and Gold, 1959; Rosen, Levinger, and Lippitt, 1960; Rosen et al., 1961.

First, there were small but significant correlations between social power and IQ. Second, as mentioned previously, powerful children were also well-liked. The correlations between social power and popularity varied somewhat, but ranged roughly between .50 and .80, with the modal coefficient being in the lower .70s.[9] Disregarding IQ, socially powerful children were perceived by their peers as being able in school and, in camp situations, competent in athletics and campcraft. In one study (Koslin, Haarlow, Karlins, and Pargament, 1968), a multiple correlation of .79 was obtained between campers' expectations concerning performance of group members in four camp activities and participant observers' ratings of "effective initiative."

In the Michigan studies, powerful children were generally more sociable and better adjusted than were children who did not possess the capacity to influence their peers. That is, the powerful children were active and vigorous in participation with their peers and had relatively few mental health problems. The powerful children were also likely to be frequent sources of contagious influence, as well as to be particularly successful in their direct attempts to influence other children.[10] For boys, but not necessarily for girls, aggressiveness was associated with social power. However, Zander and Van Egmond reported that aggressiveness differentiated powerful from nonpowerful boys among low IQ children more clearly than among high IQ children.

Also in the Michigan studies, the socially powerful child was likely to be realistic about his status in the peer group. There was a high degree of association between self-ratings and others' ratings of this attribute. The social realism of powerful children is also revealed by the fact that leaders engage in more self-voting behavior than nonleaders (Trent, 1954). The self-concepts of leaders are likely to be more positive than those of nonleaders (Bordeau, Dales, and Connor, 1963) and

[9] In one interesting study of peer relations in a dual cultural setting (South Africa) the investigator found significantly more outgroup *leadership* choices than outgroup *friendship* choices (Muir, 1963).

[10] Most of the leader characteristics mentioned thus far were also found by Terman (1904).

young adult leaders appear to be more socio-empathic than nonleaders (Trapp, 1955). One study with children, however, does not confirm this finding (Cohn, Fisher, and Brown, 1962).

Leadership is moderately correlated with "followership" (Hollander and Webb, 1955). Terman (1904) also found a positive relation between leadership and suggestibility. The Michigan studies, however, revealed that children possessing high social power tended to resist the *direct* influence attempts of others more frequently than did nonpowerful children.

Thus the composite picture of the powerful child shows him to be intellectually able, actively and appropriately sociable, and, among boys, assertive and aggressive. This constellation of attributes characterizes peer group leaders at virtually all socioeconomic levels. The following vignettes from the narrative accounts of Sherif and Sherif (1964) provide flesh-and-blood pictures of typical peer group leaders. First, with respect to the leader of a high socioeconomic group:

It was Sterling whose word counted most. His father was a dentist; his car a 6-year-old yellow convertible. He had flunked algebra and was taking it over (he passed). But the only time he got into real trouble at school was when he cut a required assembly and was expelled for two days. This was not real trouble, for his father reinstated him. Sterling was aggressive in his relationship with others, but jovially so. He was fun. When he made suggestions they sounded like polite orders, and were received that way. His decisions were usually on matters of substance. . . . It was his idea to get two adjoining motel rooms for an end-of-school party, and he figured the cost at $3.00 a boy. Don and Jack worked out the details, collected the money, arranged for refreshments. Sterling interfered only when he had a better idea: "We need a case of beer for the afternoon to get tanked up for the party" (pp. 12–13).

Then, with reference to the leader of a low socioeconomic group:

. . . Rogelio's words began to count more and more. This erect, self-confident boy had an almost uncanny ability to call plays and make selections which won the game without hurting anyone's feelings. . . . Juan was the best fighter in the group . . . but they knew Rogelio could hold his own, and would not take an insult from an outsider. . . . Wero remarked that Rogelio was the best one to have along to keep them out of trouble. In two months' time, Rogelio was the acknowledged leader, though he had never competed or come into conflict with Juan (pp. 28–29).

These portraits summarize some of the most important findings reviewed in this section. They also illustrate an important precaution to be used in interpreting the data reviewed in the preceding pages. That is, many of the correlations reported in studies of peer status are extremely modest in magnitude. Therefore *all* anxious children are not unpopular, *all* leaders are not the most proficient in athletics, and so forth. Such attributes may, in general, facilitate peer acceptance. "But the leader need not have the best car, be the smoothest operator, the biggest ladykiller, nor the toughest, as the case may be. In fact, usually he is not" (Sherif and Sherif, 1964, p. 159).

FRIENDSHIPS

Many fortuitous factors are involved in children's selections of friends. Clearly, age, sex, and propinquity are determinants of such choices. The role played by personality factors in the formation of friendships, however, is far from clear. One particular question remains unanswered: are friends chosen on the basis of similarity in personality attributes or is complementarity the major determinant of friendship choice?

The similarity existing between children and their sociometric nominees was explored by Davitz (1955). A 20-item, forced-choice inventory concerning preferences for camp activities was given to each subject (children between 6 and 13 years of age). The child rated his own preferences, and also the preferences of those children whom he had nominated first and last on the sociometric test. Perceived similarity was significantly greater between the children and their first-chosen peers than between the subjects and their last-chosen peers. There was no difference, however, in actual similarity between the subjects and their first- and last-nominated peers.

In addition, first-choice peers were perceived as more similar than they actually proved to be. There was no difference between perceived and actual similarity to last-named sociometric choices. Thus perceptions of similarity were exaggerated in the case of high-choice peers but not in the case of low-choice peers. This exaggeration in perceived similarity to preferred peers may be a kind of haloing produced by sociometric preference or, on the other hand, a determinant of such preference. It must be noted, however, that the children were not actually more different from nonpreferred peers than they were from preferred peers.

Somewhat similar findings were reported by Northway and Detweiler (1955) for a group of girls enrolled in a private school. Self-ratings and "other"-ratings were made with respect to a list of socially desirable traits. Positively chosen peers were rated more highly than the girls rated themselves and there was some tendency for low sociometric choices to be rated lower than the subject rated herself. As would be expected, positively chosen peers were depicted differently from low-choice peers. The findings do not bear directly on the similarity issue in friendship formation, but the data show that preferred peers are perceived more positively than the child perceives himself.

The investigators mentioned above did not actually examine behavioral similarity between *mutual* friends, that is, children whose sociometric choices are reciprocal. Unfortunately, research results concerning the similarity of friends are not in full agreement. Haller and Butterworth (1960) found that occupational aspiration and educational aspiration were correlated within pairs of friends at mean levels of .31 and .19, respectively. These values were obtained with IQ, SES, and parental achievement aspirations held constant. But Thorpe (1955b) found no differences in the similarity existing between pairs of friends, pairs of partial friends, and pairs of nonfriends in terms of IQ, neuroticism, or popularity. Earlier studies yielded inconsistent findings with respect to IQ similarity in mutual friends: Bonney (1942) and Barbe (1954) found evidence of such similarity; Furfey (1927) and Challman (1932) did not. General levels of sociability, however, appear to

be greater among pairs of friends than among pairs of nonfriends (Challman, 1932).

The complementarity-congruence issue was explored directly in a group of 54 eighth-grade girls and boys, all of whom were involved in reciprocated sociometric choices (Hilkevitch, 1960). The data from this study were reported rather sketchily, but the peer reputation variables show complementarity to be evident in pairs of male friends, whereas congruence was more characteristic of female pairs. For example, a high proportion of boys who were reputed to be "attention-seeking" interacted with other boys who, conversely, were willing to share the limelight. Furthermore, these attention-seeking boys tended to interact with peers who would be supportive of them. The only reputations variable indicating congruence in boys' friendship pairs was "popularity with the opposite sex."

In contrast to the boys, the pairs of female friends showed little evidence of complementary social behavior. Such pairs proved, however, to be congruent on variables measuring labile, outgoing social behavior (e.g., reputed interest in having a good time, being fun, and being a best friend). Thus common sociobehavioral traits appear to be aspects of friendship choice in girls, whereas complementary qualities seem to be more salient in the friendship patterns of boys. The sample from which these findings were derived was a highly selected one, both in age and social class background. Consequently, these provocative findings need to be extended.

Using a somewhat different approach to the similarity-complementarity problem, Izard (1960) compared the personality profiles of 30 pairs of high school and college friends with the profiles of 30 pairs of randomly selected individuals. Data from the *Edwards Personal Preference Schedule* showed significantly more similar profiles among the friends than among the nonfriends. No evidence of complementarity appeared in the profiles of friends. The intrapair correlations of the friends were significant on three EPPS scales: Exhibition, Deference, and Endurance. On the other hand, none was significant among the pairs of nonfriends. This study, then, supports the thesis that friends are more similar than nonfriends. Elsewhere in this report, the findings of Byrne and Griffitt (1966) are discussed; they show that perceived similarity in attitudes enhances interpersonal attraction. There are also several studies, cited by Izard, which show that similarity is positively associated with friendship ratings in adults.

Is there a significant relation between the sociometric status of the chooser and the status of the chosen? No, according to Sells and Roff (1967). Zero-order correlations were found between the peer status scores of children and those other children whom the subject chose as "liked most." However, the status of children doing the choosing and the status of those whom they chose as "liked least" was correlated −.15 for a sample of 10,742 Minnesota children and −.16 for a Texas sample of 7312. Thus there is a slight tendency for the rejection choices of high-status children to be more similar to the group's consensus than the rejection choices of low-status children. It is clear from these data, however, that there is no substantial correlation between the status of choosers and chosens on sociometric tests.

The chief conflicting evidence concerning this question is contained in a study of 106 private school boys by Tagiuri, Kogan, and Long (1958). These investigators found a positive relation between the status of the chooser and the status of the chosen. This sample, of course, was a highly selected one, and the sociometric criterion consisted of roommate preferences. The ecology of the private school in which Tagiuri et al. conducted their study and the nature of the sociometric criteria used were very different from the conditions prevailing in the Sells and Roff investigation. Consequently, it is difficult to regard these two sets of findings as conflicting.

Several other interesting findings emerged in the Tagiuri study, all of which need further exploration. First, these investigators found that the status of a boy chosen as a prospective roommate, but who was not expected to reciprocate this choice, was significantly higher than the status of boys who were chosen but who were perceived as likely to reciprocate. Lowest sociometric levels were obtained by boys who were perceived as choosing, but whom the subject himself did not choose.

The problem of reciprocity in sociometric choices is exceedingly complex. The data just described are somewhat tangential to the issue concerning the similarity in peer status of mutual friends. Thorpe's data (mentioned earlier) still provide the most direct evidence concerning this problem. Overall, however, there is little support in the literature for the notion that friends occupy similar status levels in the peer group.

In general, the findings concerning friendship in childhood do not present a complete or consistent picture. Most work on the congruence-complementarity problem has been completed with adolescents and this research has not been extensive. The importance of perceived similarity as a determinant of friendship choice is perhaps most clearly indicated in studies of adults. The existing child data do not seriously contradict the adult findings, although the major work in this area of children's peer relations is yet to be accomplished.

PEER INFLUENCES ON THE INDIVIDUAL CHILD

Peer influences on the behavior of individual children have been studied for many reasons. Some investigators have been interested in the substantive contribution to the child's socialization that derives from peer interaction. Others have been interested in peer influences, in contrast to adult influences, on children's behavior. Still other investigators have employed peers as influence sources when their major concern has been with the more general topic of social influence processes in human behavior.

In spite of the disparate reasons for conducting research on peer influences, an illuminating array of studies now exists concerning variations in behavior as these derive from interaction with peers. From the standpoint of developmental psychology, special attention to the problem of peer influences is needed for its own sake. We do not yet know whether there are unique forms of social influence occurring in the interaction of children with agemates. This issue must be clarified. We would argue that no description of children's socialization is complete without accounting for the variance in behavior that is due to inputs from the peer culture.

The discussion contained in the following pages depicts the *manner* in which children influence each other rather than the simple fact that they *do*. This portion of the chapter is not centered on specific theories of social influence and social learning. Consideration is given to theoretical questions, but it is the child who is the focus of this portion of the chapter rather than particular conceptualizations of social influence processes.

Research dealing with peer influences has been dominated by such concepts as *conformity, suggestibility, yielding, persuasibility, imitation, behavior contagion,* and *social facilitation.* All of these terms refer to instances in which the child's behavior becomes, over time, similar to the behavior of some other person. Each of these terms refers to an outcome of social interaction, but this interaction may not have been initiated with the intent of evoking behavior change.

Wheeler (1966) has attempted to clarify the terminology used in research on social influence. He suggests that the term *behavior contagion* should be used to refer to those instances in which: (1) a person is instigated to act in a given manner but does not do so, presumably as a consequence of approach-avoidance conflict; (2) he then observes another person respond in a manner similar to the way he himself wishes to respond; and (3) he subsequently behaves like the model. This use of the term differs from the usage proposed by other writers; in this case, behavior contagion does not refer specifically to a spread of emotional reactions among the members of a group. Wheeler chooses to regard the spread of emotional reactions in groups as merely a special case of behavior contagion.

How, then, do conformity, imitation, suggestibility, and persuasibility differ from behavior contagion? *Conformity* is a relatively elastic term that refers to shifts of attitudes or perceptions in the direction of some socially imposed norm. In conformity situations, conflict is elicited as a *consequence* of observing the behavior of others; in the case of behavior contagion, conflict exists *prior* to the individual's exposure to the behavior of others. *Yielding, suggestibility,* and *persuasibility* are virtually synonymous with conformity, inasmuch as these terms all refer to shifts in behavior occurring as a consequence of conflict induced by exposure to the actions of other people. Persuasibility, however, is a term that is usually applied to conditions involving opinion shifts. *Social pressure situations* involve direct, face-to-face persuasion rather than simple exposure to the behavior of other people.

All of the foregoing forms of social influence refer to instances in which the individual experiences conflict between his own norms and the norms he perceives as governing the behavior of others. In some conformity or yielding experiments, it is assumed that the subject has acquired his own norms through previous experience. In other instances, a training or baseline experience is provided so as to establish such norms before exposure to the behavioral norms of others. The actions of other people, however, may elicit behavior change when the observer possesses no relevant norms at all. For example, observers can acquire norms through modeling concerning how to act in situations that they have not yet encountered. Terms such as *social facilitation* and *modeling* encompass such forms of social influence, although they are not restricted to them.

Ethologists (e.g., Thorpe, 1956) have used the concept of social facilitation to refer to those instances in which the behavior of one member of a species acts as a releaser for the same behavior in another member of the species. Most ethologists are concerned with social facilitation as it originates instinctively. Bandura and Walters (1963), however, described a similar phenomenon when they discussed the eliciting function of social models. This elicitation refers to instances in which a model's actions serve to reactivate or re-evoke previously acquired behavior. A normative frame of reference may not be possessed by the individual and yet such modeling occurs. Consequently, it may be important to distinguish instances of social influence in which normative conflict is minimal from instances in which such conflict is substantial.

Imitation refers to all of those events in which the actions of one person become similar to the actions of some other person as a consequence of either direct or symbolic observation. Used in this manner, imitation is the most general rubric that has been mentioned here. As a matter of fact, it subsumes all of the other terms mentioned.

Thus far we have defined the various forms of social influence in situational terms. Most of these terms have also been used as personality constructs. That is, considerable research has dealt with conformity-proneness, suggestibility, tendency to yield, and responsiveness to social influence. It is assumed that these are stable characteristics of persons and that individuals differ from one another in the extent to which they manifest such characteristics. Terms such as behavior contagion and imitation are used infrequently in this sense, although the literature contains numerous references to "generalized imitative tendencies" and "susceptibility to contagious influence."

The literature concerning peer influences on child behavior contains, then, two major themes: (1) personality correlates of behavior in peer influence situations; and (2) the situational determinants of such influences. At present, research in this field is somewhat fragmented. For one thing, it has been difficult to employ peers as agents of influence in experimental studies. Recent methodological advances (e.g., TV presentation of peer models) are ameliorating this problem.

Many studies of peer influences have been conducted in contrived laboratory or classroom situations. Such results may generalize to occasions in which social influence is exerted in the informal peer group. To a considerable extent, however, we do not know that this is true.

Age Differences

Some early theorists discussed the origins of imitation in the infant and young child within the framework of instinct theory. Others, such as F. H. Allport (1924) and J. B. Watson (1925), recognized that environmental feedback modifies the development of imitative behavior. As Miller and Dollard (1941) pointed out, however, these early theories gave a plausible account for the emergence of imitative response sequences but they did not adequately account for their termination. Also, little attention was given in these theoretical arguments to the factors that produce a generalized disposition in children to imitate many different kinds of people —peers as well as parents and other adults.

The well-known theory of imitation proposed by Miller and Dollard (1941) accounted for the acquisition of imitative behavior in terms of contingent reinforcement.

Other social learning theorists, such as Bandura and Walters (1963), have proposed that imitation is acquired on the basis of contiguity between external stimuli and covert sensory events. None of these theoretical views is concerned, specifically, with the development of generalized imitative tendencies in children. It may be assumed, however, that such an accounting would emphasize the pervasiveness of reinforcement for imitation in early social experience, the operation of stimulus generalization, and the secondary reinforcing properties of behaviors that replicate the actions of other people.

The social learning approach to the development of conformity predicts, only generally, that such dispositions should become increasingly evident during childhood. The theory does not posit a timetable for these developments. If we know that reinforcement for conforming responses increases substantially during the preschool years, then it is possible to predict that imitation will increase during this period. The theory itself, however, does not specify when age changes in such responsiveness will occur. Thus social learning theory furnishes only a loose basis for predicting that being influenced by peers should be an increasing function of age.

Piaget proposed a general theory of social development from which more explicit predictions can be made concerning age changes in responsiveness to peer influence. The most relevant material is contained in *The Moral Judgment of the Child* (1932). In this treatise, Piaget discussed changes in responsiveness to peers within the broader context of changes in the child's conceptions of the "rules of the game." The child's consciousness of social rules was conceived as moving through a sequence of three stages.

The first of these is essentially a presocial, egocentric stage. During this time, the child possesses no clear conception of formal social norms except for the rules and regulations laid down for him by adults. Rules, insofar as awareness of them in social games is concerned, are taken quite casually by children until they are in their sixth year:

During the first of these stages, which we can designate as the stage of *egocentrism*, the children take great pleasure in imitating the ordered doings of their elders, but in practice know nothing of their *raison d'etre*; each plays essentially for himself, just for the fun of running about or hiding . . . (p. 71).

The second stage in the functioning of social rules is marked both by increased social conformity and the increased importance, to the child, of social interactions with peers:

This second stage sets in from the moment when the child, either through imitation or as the result of verbal exchange, begins to want to play in conformity with certain rules received from outside. . . . From the moment that the child begins to imitate the rules of others, no matter how egocentric in practice his play may be, he regards the rules of the game as sacred and untouchable; he refuses to alter these rules and claims that any modification, even if accepted by general opinion, would be wrong (pp. 45–46).

There is certainly a resemblance between segmented or mechanical solidarity and the societies formed by children of 5 to 8. As in the organized clan so in these groups, temporarily formed and isolated in relation to each other, the individual does not count. Social life and individual life are one. Suggestion and imitation are all-powerful. All individuals are alike except for differences of prestige and age. The traditional rule is coercive and conformity is demanded of all (p. 97).

The period of middle childhood is, then, a period of increasingly explicit and rigid conformity to social norms. While there may be some variation between the child's increasing comprehension of formal rules and his actual practice of them, Piaget's theory clearly suggests that conformity is directly related to age during this period.

A marked change in the child's orientation to rules begins to occur at about age 10. He begins to perceive rules as human artifacts, emanating from a variety of persons, including the individual members of his peer group. Further, rules are no longer external and coercive:

In the first place, the child allows a change in the rules so long as it enlists the votes of all. . . . All opinions are tolerated so long as

their protagonists urge their acceptance by legal methods. . . . He no longer relies, as do the little ones, upon an all-wise tradition. In the second place, the child ceases *ipso facto* to look upon rules as eternal and as having been handed down unchanged from one generation to another. Thirdly, and finally, his ideas on the origin of the rules and of the game do not differ from ours: far from having been imposed as such by adults; must have become gradually fixed on the initiative of the children themselves (pp. 57–58).

Piaget is not entirely explicit concerning the determinants of these changes, but it is clear that this developmental account emphasizes the role of cognitive growth and children's more frequent association with peers during preadolescence and adolescence.

Piaget posits, then, a curvilinear relation between chronological age and conformity in children: conformity to peer influences should increase until preadolescence and then decline. Social learning theory furnishes no basis, within the theory itself, for predicting a decline in social conformity beginning at adolescence. In order to predict such a decline, based on learning principles, one would need to know that independence and resistance to "blind obedience" are increasingly valued and reinforced during this period. The stereotyped version of adolescence, of course, is just the reverse. That is, adolescence is assumed to be characterized by an unusually rich schedule of contingent reinforcement for "blind" conformity to peer group norms. Recent evidence, however, suggests that this is not the case (Douvan and Adelson, 1966). Even so, the principles of social learning offer relatively little assistance in arriving at predictions concerning age changes in conformity behavior. Only if we know the manner in which the environment is programmed with respect to reinforcement for conformity can such changes be predicted.

The classic study of age changes in conformity was conducted by Berenda (1950). Four conformity studies were completed, three of which involved peers as the influence source. Conformity was measured in terms of agreement with false judgments concerning the length of a line shown on a card. In the first of these studies, peer pressure was exerted on the child by the eight brightest children in his school class. Thus the situation involved "prestige" suggestion. The conformity behavior of children ranging from 7 to 10 years of age was compared with children ranging between 11 and 13. Major findings were: (1) children in both age groups gave significantly more wrong judgments when exposed to false norms than when judgments were rendered alone; (2) there was more yielding when the comparison was difficult or ambiguous than when the problem was easy; (3) the younger children yielded somewhat more frequently than the older children, but this difference was not significant.

In two other experiments, Berenda examined the influence of a larger (majority) peer group on children who were members of a smaller (minority) group. In one study, the majority children were instructed to overestimate the length of the critical lines, but to vary their overestimates. In the second study, the majority group's judgments were also false, but they were uniform. Age differences were found only when the majority group gave nonuniform overestimates. In this case, the younger children proved to be significantly more susceptible to group influence than the older children, but only on the most difficult problems.

There are two major themes in these findings: (1) conformity to false peer norms is clearly evident during middle childhood; (2) this conformity is somewhat greater during the period from 7 to 10 years than between 11 and 13. It is interesting to compare these results with those of Terman (1904). He found that suggestibility rises between the second and fourth grades, but falls off rapidly after that. The age changes in these studies, then, are generally consistent with Piaget's theory.

It is also worth noting that Piaget's notions concerning the qualitative changes that occur in the child's conceptions of rules are borne out by Berenda's interview data. The conception of norms possessed by the younger children was absolutistic. For example: "They all said the same number; if so many people said it, it might be right" (pp. 27–28). On the other hand, the preadolescent children allowed for individual fallibility; some of their rationalizations for yielding were remarkably similar to the way in which Piaget described

the child's reactions to social pressure during this period.

"I know they were wrong, but it was like a jury—we were nine and I was the only one against eight. The majority wins. Besides, how could I prove I was right?" "I had a funny feeling inside. You know you are right and they are wrong and you agree with them. And you still feel you are right and you say nothing about it. Once I gave the answer they didn't give. I thought they would think I was wrong. I just gave their answers. If I had the test alone, I wouldn't give the answers I gave." "I know Miss ———— knows more. But she might have strained her eyes" (pp. 29-30; 47).

Berenda's study, of course, involved children within a limited age range. Although there was some decline in yielding to peer influences from middle childhood to preadolescence, the study did not provide for comparison with younger children or with adolescents and adults. Hunt and Synnerdale (1959), however, studied 10 kindergarten children in an Asch-type conformity situation. Of 180 judgments given following exposure to group pressure, only 12% were in the direction of the group norm. Although this study was scarcely more than a pilot investigation, the results suggest that preschool-aged children are generally impervious to normative pressure from their peers. Starkweather (1964) also has reported no evidence of conformity to peer norms in a sample of children between the ages of 2–9 and 5–11. Such data strongly support Piaget's description of these years as a presocial, egocentric stage insofar as the child's responsiveness to peer norms is concerned.

Two studies, both with adolescents, support the hypothesis that peer conformity declines after middle childhood. Marple (1933) found that high school students were more likely to conform to the opinions of "experts" than were college students. Patel and Gordon (1960) exposed adolescent subjects to conformity suggestion under conditions of either high or low prestige. High prestige consisted of bogus norms representing the school class that was one year ahead of the subject; low prestige consisted of norms from a class that was one year behind. The ambiguity of difficulty of the task was also manipulated. In general, conformity decreased from the tenth to the twelfth grades. This decline was somewhat less evident when high-prestige norms were involved than when the subjects were exposed to low-prestige norms, although the ambiguity of the task also affected conformity behavior. Very little decline with age was evidenced, for example, in conformity to high-prestige norms when, simultaneously, the task was difficult.

Three peer conformity studies exist in which subjects were employed from the primary grades through the high school years. McConnell (1963) studied suggestibility by exposing his subjects to false norms concerning the discriminability of pairs of geometric figures and pairs of objects. The testing session consisted of two segments. In the first segment, the influence source consisted of the experimenter; in the second segment, the subjects were given fictitious peer norms. Age differences in suggestibility were studied by means of a composite score based on both segments of the test. This relation was curvilinear. Amount of suggestibility did not differ for subjects between the ages of 6 and 13; thereafter, suggestibility declined steadily through age 18. There was no increase in suggestibility between 6 and 9, as might have been predicted, but the adolescent decline in suggestibility was clearly evident.

Two aspects of the methodology employed in this study require comment. First, there was no separate reporting of the peer-suggestion data. McConnell says that the age curves for the separate measures of suggestibility were all descending in slope. It can be concluded, therefore, that the general measure of suggestibility was a valid index of peer suggestibility. The peer suggestibility measure, however, was obtained *after* the prestige suggestibility measure (exposure to the experimenter's norms). Perhaps suggestibility generalized from the first to the second segment of the testing session. If so, it is possible that the age decrease in peer suggestibility was partly a function of decline in prestige suggestibility.

Iscoe, Williams, and Harvey (1963) studied 256 7-, 9-, 12-, and 15-year-old boys and girls. These investigators used a simulated con-

formity situation in which the child counted metronome clicks and was given false peer norms through earphones. The subject believed that he was hearing the judgments of three other children who were taking the test simultaneously. Conformity, measured in terms of counting errors, increased across these age groups, reaching a peak among the 12-year-olds and decreasing thereafter. The age differences, however, were somewhat different for males and females. The decrease in conformity among the oldest subjects was only apparent in the case of girls; the 15-year-old boys were actually somewhat *more* conforming than the 12-year-olds, although this age comparison was not statistically reliable. In a second report, Iscoe, Williams, and Harvey (1964) compared the data from the previous study (which were based on white children who attended segregated schools) with data obtained from Negro children in the same age range who were also attending segregated schools. A significant interaction between age and race was found. Whereas peer conformity among the white children increased between 9 and 12 years and then decreased, conformity among the Negro children increased between 7 and 9 years and decreased steadily thereafter. The white children, as a whole, were also more conforming than the Negro children.

The data from both racial groups are consistent with the Piagetian analysis, at least to the extent that the shape of the age gradient in peer conformity was curvilinear. It is extremely interesting, however, that the peak in peer conformity occurred three years earlier among the Negro children (at age 9) than it occurred among the white children (at age 12). The main effects of racial groups (indicating greater peer conformity among the white children) are also fascinating. These findings indicate that both sheer susceptibility to peer influence and the stages characterizing the child's social development are open to cultural influence.

Piaget, in his treatment of the imitation problem, emphasized the importance of increased peer contact as a determinant of transitions in conformity behavior. It is almost certainly true that the Negro child is sheltered by the family for a shorter period and exposed to peer interaction earlier than most white children. In light of this, it is not surprising to find that the Negro child's period of greatest conformity to peer influences comes earlier than this period does for white children. At the same time, there is probably greater latitude in the Negro peer culture for independent, nonconforming behavior (e.g., less rigid norms for abiding by "the rules of the game"). These factors could account for the general racial difference that was found in amount of peer conformity.

An alternative to this explanation of the racial differences found by Iscoe et al. is the possibility that the Negro subject perceives his peers (i.e., other Negro children) as having less status and power, and feels that their judgments are worth less simply because they are Negroes. Such peer perceptions would account for both the lesser conformity and the earlier decline in conformity noted for the Negro children as compared to the white children. Unfortunately, data are not available in this study for Negro subjects exposed to norms attributed to white agemates.

Costanzo and Shaw (1966) provide additional data that are consonant with the preceding results. A Crutchfield simulated conformity situation was constructed in which erroneous feedback was given to the subject concerning the performance of the three other members of an *ad hoc* peer group. The subjects consisted of 72 elementary school, high school, and college pupils. Again, a curvilinear relation between conformity and age was obtained. Least conformity was shown by the 7- to 9-year-old subjects, greatest conformity by the 11- to 13-year-olds, and decreased conformity through the remainder of the age range. The 19- to 21-year-old group was no more conforming than the 7- to 9-year-olds. The subjects in this study were also asked to give reasons for the discrepancy between their answers and the bogus norms. These answers were classified as "self-blame" or "other-attributed reasons." The biserial correlation between conformity and incidence of self-blame was .87. Thus both conformity to peer norms and the tendency to blame oneself for deviation increased with age during preadolescence and decreased thereafter.

A final study of age differences in peer conformity was reported by Harvey and Rutherford (1960). In this study, opinion shifts (concerning the merit of art work) were studied as a function of the prestige of the influence source at four age levels: third, sixth, ninth, and eleventh grades. The relation between sheer amount of conformity and age was not reported. The difference in children's responsiveness to the opinions of high- and low-status peers, however, did vary as a function of age. The third graders, for example, did not shift their opinions in accordance with the status of the influence source. The sixth graders, on the other hand, shifted their opinions when they found themselves to be in disagreement with high-status peers but in agreement with low-status peers. The ninth graders, like the third graders, were impervious to the status of the influence source. Thus the data for the third-, sixth-, and ninth-grade subjects suggest a curvilinear relation between age and the child's responsiveness to the status of the influence source. The eleventh graders in this study, however, also showed a tendency to conform in accordance with the status of the influencing agent. This reemergence of sensitivity to the prestige of the influence source is a developmental trend that is difficult to explain. This is particularly true since some of the developmental shifts found in this study could be artifacts of sampling. The low sensitivity to peer status found among the ninth graders, for example, may not be a true developmental shift. This group of children had been together as a peer group for less than a year. The sixth graders and the eleventh graders, however, had functioned as groups for much longer periods of time.

Overall, the data reviewed in this section present a consistent picture concerning the relation between chronological age and conformity to peer influences. Such behavior tends to increase following the preschool years and tends to decrease with the onset of adolescence. The precise age at which peer conformity is greatest varies from study to study. In some samples, this peak has occurred as early as 9 years of age, in others as late as 15. As mentioned earlier, there is a strong possibility that cultural or milieu factors may be responsible for these inconsistencies. Also, the possible effects of variations in experimental procedures should not be ruled out; other sections of this chapter show that situational factors are extremely important sources of variance in peer conformity.

Thus it is not surprising that there are some inconsistencies in the data concerning the precise point in childhood at which peer conformity tends to peak. Rather, it is remarkable that the research is so thoroughly consistent in showing that the functional relation between age and peer conformity is curvilinear, and that middle childhood is generally the period of greatest responsiveness to normative influence from peers.

Birth-Order

In a monograph published in 1959, Schachter reported that firstborn young adults changed their opinions under pressure of false group norms more than did later-born subjects of comparable age. These data were interpreted on the basis of the rationale mentioned earlier in this chapter:

1. Firstborn children, as opposed to later-born children, are subjected to more inconsistent caretaking during their early years and this produces greater responsiveness to anxiety or threat.

2. Firstborns are also more closely protected by their parents and frequent reinforcement is given to them for affiliative, conforming, and dependent behavior.

3. Later-borns are subjected to a certain amount of punishment from older siblings, a factor that presumably should reduce affiliation tendencies toward other children.

Much of the recent research concerning this topic has involved adult subjects. Nevertheless, several investigators have explored the problem using children or adolescents as subjects. Becker and Carroll (1962) studied 48 boys (of indeterminate age) who used the same public playground. Thirty of the subjects were native-born boys and the others were Puerto Rican-born. All of the Puerto Rican children indicated strong identification with their mainland-born peers. Conformity was measured by means of an Asch-type task in which mainland-born children served as the influence sources. In the group as a whole, firstborn boys yielded significantly more than later-borns. It was expected, however, that subjects who were striving for membership in a reference group would be more susceptible to social influence from representatives of that group than would subjects who already belonged to the group. Indeed, it was found

that the Puerto Rican-born boys were more conforming than the mainland-born boys. In addition, it was discovered that the influence of birth order on yielding depended on the ethnicity of the subject. In fact, the birth-order difference was significant only for the mainland-born sample.

Certainly, one should hesitate before concluding that this is an example of cross-cultural difference in the effects of birth order on behavior. The sample of Puerto Rican-born children was small and highly select. It is possible, of course, that child-rearing practices do not differ as markedly in the case of firstborn and later-born children within Puerto Rican culture as within mainland U.S. culture. On the other hand, it may well be that reference-group striving, which was characteristic of this Puerto Rican sample, masked the effects of birth order on yielding to peer influences. An extension of the study, in which the influence source consisted of other Puerto Rican-born children, would throw light on this particular question.

In a second study, these investigators (Becker, Lerner, and Carroll, 1964) studied birth-order effects on yielding behavior under varying incentive conditions. The subjects were 15- and 16-year-olds who were caddies at a golf club. One-third of the subjects received no reward for correctly judging the length of lines, one-third was promised (and given) a small payoff (5 cents), and one-third was offered a larger payoff (25 cents). Accomplices were selected from the same population of caddies. No payoff subjects who were firstborns yielded significantly more than later-borns, thus confirming the Schachter findings. The effects of birth order differed, however, under the two payoff conditions. Significantly fewer firstborn subjects yielded under the small payoff condition than under the control condition; the birth-order effect, in fact, disappeared in the small payoff condition. A reversal occurred, however, under conditions of high payoff. Here there was significantly more yielding by later-born boys than by firstborn boys.

It should be noted that the conditions under which conformity behavior was measured differed from the conventional application of the Asch technique—incentives for independent behavior were offered. It thus appears that when achievement-anxiety is not too great (as created by small payoff), firstborn children abandon their reliance on others for support and behave "responsibly, reliably, and independently." This hypothesis is consistent with other data which show that firstborns have greater achievement motivation than later-borns (Sampson and Hancock, 1967). The fact that the later-borns did not also show a corresponding increase in resistance to group pressure when there was a small payoff is probably due to the fact that they showed very little conformity under the control condition; in other words there was a "floor" effect.

The increased yielding by later borns when incentives were high may indicate that these individuals rely on others principally for validation of their beliefs, rather than for emotional support. High-risk conditions may enhance the creditability of the group judgments for persons who have learned to look to peers for reliable information about the world and thus increase yielding. On the other hand, the high-risk conditions for firstborns may only accentuate their desperate, rigid resistance to relying on the beliefs of others. A possible floor effect, however, once again weakens the argument in defense of this hypothesis.

How can the hypothesis that firstborn children are responsive to normative influences, whereas later-borns are particularly susceptible to informational influences be verified? The conformity of high school boys was studied under three conditions: a control condition; a memory condition, in which the stimulus lines were removed before judgments were announced; and a group-reward condition, in which the stimuli were present while judgments were made but the subjects were told that the "winning" group would receive a prize (Becker, Lerner, and Carroll, 1966). Once again, under the control condition, firstborn subjects conformed significantly more than later-born subjects. Under the group reward condition, the firstborn subjects conformed more than in the control condition; little increase in conformity was noted among the later-borns. In the memory condition, however, the later-borns conformed more than they did in the control condition, whereas firstborns showed less conformity than they did in the control condition. Thus it appears that firstborn children are particularly susceptible to peer norms when: (1) the group

pressure situation is unstructured as to the outcomes of conformity; or (2) the group can obtain a reward only when all subjects are in agreement. When individual achievement is stressed, however, firstborns tend to rely less on the informative feedback provided by peer judgments than do later-borns. Overall, then, it appears that firstborns respond more readily to normative peer influences than do later-borns, but later-borns are particularly responsive to informational feedback from their peers.

Male subjects were used in all of the studies by Becker and his associates. Does sex membership interact with birth order in affecting conformity to peer influences? Sampson and Hancock (1967) studied 251 adolescents of both sexes. The conformity test consisted of judging the size of geometric figures both before and after fictitious group norms were given. The instructions stressed individual achievement. First, males were more conforming than females.[11] Next, an interaction of borderline significance was obtained between sex and birth order. Firstborn subjects conformed more than later-borns only in the case of males; only small birth-order differences were found for females.

The preceding results point to two major deficiencies in existing data concerning birth order and peer conformity. First, insufficient work has been conducted with female subjects. Second, in the studies that have involved females, achievement-oriented instructions have been used. Sampson and Hancock (1967) measured n Ach in their study and found this variable, as well as conformity behavior, to be related to birth order *in males*. Achievement motivation may also be higher in firstborn females than in later-borns (as found by Sampson, 1962). Nevertheless, birth-order differences may not be found in the conformity behavior of females when the conformity situation stresses task mastery. Quite different arousal conditions may elicit achieve-

[11] This finding conflicts with other results which show that females are more conforming than males. It should be noted that the instructions stressed the importance of doing well. Such instructions are probably more potent in eliciting achievement behaviors from boys than from girls. It is therefore not surprising that the males showed more conformity in this study than did the females.

ment-striving in females (Crandall, 1963). If this is the case, the conformity behavior of girls may be elicited by different arousal conditions than is the conformity behavior of males. In short, a wider range of incentive conditions needs to be used in studying birth order and yielding in female subjects.

One conformity study has actually been conducted with children of both sexes under conditions of minimal achievement-arousal (Carrigan and Julian, 1966). The subjects (sixth graders) were asked to select the "best" one of four stories to accompany each of 10 TAT pictures. The bogus peer norms consisted of information concerning the preferences of "last year's class." With respect to birth order, firstborns of *both* sexes conformed more than later-borns. Thus under non-achievement oriented instructions, the birth-order effect held for both sexes.

One other finding from this sudy is of tangential interest. Half of the subjects were exposed to an affiliation-arousing experience (completing a sociometric questionnaire) immediately before the conformity test. A significant interaction between sex and affiliation-condition was obtained: females were significantly more conforming when they had been threatened by social rejection than when they were not. This difference was not as large for males, and it is especially noteworthy that the later-born males actually conformed *less* following potential social rejection than under neutral conditions.

In conclusion, then, the relation between birth order and conformity to peer pressure in children is not a straightforward one. Whether firstborn children are more susceptible to peer influence than later-borns is clearly dependent on the child's sex and the context in which group pressure is exerted.

Sex

Among adults, females are more likely to yield to group pressure in conformity situations than are males (Crutchfield, 1955). There is also evidence to suggest that women are more field-dependent than men (Witkin, 1962). Maccoby and Masters have reviewed the evidence concerning sex differences in children's dependency in their chapter in this book. In large measure, the literature on peer conformity in childhood confirms the findings with adults. That is, under most conditions,

girls are more likely to yield to peer pressure than are boys.

Disregarding interaction effects, girls have been found to be more conforming to peer norms than have boys in the following situations: (1) responding with less sex-appropriate behavior in the presence of a peer than when alone—preschool children (Stein, 1967); (2) counting metronome clicks—7- to 15-year-olds (Iscoe et al.,1963); (3) selection of appropriate stories for TAT pictures—sixth graders (Carrigan and Julian, 1966); (4) conforming to hypothetical rules emanating from the peer group—16-year-olds (Tuma and Livson, 1960); (5) selection of appropriate synonyms for a standard stimulus word —high school students (Patel and Gordon, 1960); (6) estimating the number of dots shown in various configurations—high school students (Wyer, 1966). In addition, Schoeppe (1953), in a descriptive study of 30 adolescents, found the girls to be particularly concerned with "outer conformity," whereas the boys were oriented toward "autonomy or self-directiveness." It has also been reported that the carryover of peer conformity from one task to other, similar tasks is greater for girls than for boys (Saltzstein, Rowe, and Greene, 1966).

No significant sex differences were found in two studies of suggestibility (Costanzo and Shaw, 1966; McConnell, 1963). Also, Crandall, Orleans, Preston, and Rabson (1958) did not find significant sex differences in the frequency with which nursery school children and day camp children complied with peer demands. As reported earlier, Sampson and Hancock (1967) found males to be more conforming than females, but this occurred in an Asch-type situation that was embedded in a battery of achievement tests. Other evidence suggests that when the situation arouses motives that are particularly masculine, peer conformity in males is likely to exceed conformity in females. For example, preschool boys showed more imitative aggression following exposure to aggressive peer models than did girls (Hicks, 1965).

Iscoe et al. (1964) found a significant race-by-sex interaction in conformity; although white females conformed more than white males, Negro boys were actually somewhat more conforming than the Negro girls. This finding is consistent with the hypothesis that early socialization in lower-class Negro families, in which fathers are frequently absent, results in less extensive acquisition of independence and social responsibility in boys than in girls.

The findings of Patel and Gordon (1960) also elucidate the sex differences occurring in conformity behavior. They found that, under low-prestige conditions (when the bogus norms emanated from peers one school grade behind the subject), the greater conformity of the females diminished steadily across the high school years; actually, no significant difference in the conformity behavior of the two sexes was found among seniors. On the other hand, under conditions of high-prestige suggestion (peer norms based on a school class one year ahead of the subject), greater female conformity was consistently evidenced throughout all of the high school years. The tendency for females to conform more than males may be enhanced, then, by prestige suggestion which arouses acceptibility needs rather than task motivation.

Maccoby (1961) reported that acceptance of rule enforcement from peers was significantly related to boys' own enforcement of rules over others ($r = .24$). This was not the case for girls ($r = .06$). Such findings suggest that conformity to peer group norms is a reciprocal phenomenon in boys, whereas it is not in girls. It is as if the boys' conformity is part of a complex of behaviors, all of which involve the learning of moral strictures. The correlates of rule acceptance in girls are not revealed by this study, but one would expect them to include need for social approval. Piaget (1932) has emphasized the role of reciprocity in the acquisition of a moral code in boys and Maccoby's data support this hypothesis.

The bulk of the evidence, then, suggests that when sex-typed norms are not involved, females are more conforming than males. It may be argued that this difference reflects the greater strength of needs for social approval in girls than in boys, a finding that is not dissimilar to sex differences found in such areas as dependency and the motivational bases for achievement. The data reviewed here are very consistent in suggesting that situational factors arousing motives that are salient for males (e.g., achievement, aggres-

sion) wipe out or reverse this sex difference in conformity behavior. Thus no simple statement, such as "Females conform more than males," accurately summarizes the facts. Situational factors, if they elicit sex-typed behavior, can serve either to enhance this sex difference or reverse it.

Intelligence

It is widely assumed that conformists are less intelligent and more rigid in their cognitive functioning than nonconformists (e.g., Crutchfield, 1955). Although this may be true of adults, research suggests that intelligence has little to do with peer conformity in children. For example, Crandall et al. (1958) found no significant relation between peer compliance and IQ in either preschool or elementary school children. Iscoe et al. (1963) computed correlations between conformity and IQ separately for different age and sex groups. Ten of the twelve coefficients reported were negative but none was significant (the values ranged from -.39 to .39). In their second study (1964), the procedures employed by these authors were somewhat different but the results were essentially the same. That is, eliminating IQ from among the independent variables used in that study did not significantly change the efficiency of predicting conformity behavior. Berenda (1950) also found that the relation between yielding and IQ was not significant. Thus far, the research shows that in early and middle childhood there is little or no relation between intellectual competence and conformity to peer influences.

Unfortunately, we have been able to locate few studies concerning the relation between IQ and conformity-proneness in adolescence. One might expect the negative correlation between these variables to rise in magnitude during this time.[12] Wilson (1960) presented data concerning this problem for a group of eleventh- and twelfth-grade boys. Over all subjects, conformity on an attitude judgment series was related significantly to IQ ($r = -.37$). On the other hand, this correlation differed for two major subgroups. Among sub-

---

[12] Generally the correlation between IQ and conformity-proneness in adults is about —.50 (Krech, Crutchfield, and Ballachey, 1962).

jects identified as high in "social accommodation" (i.e., those who were concerned with being rejected by an attractive or desired social object), the correlation was $-.68$; for subjects high in "self-correction" (i.e., those who were concerned primarily with discrepancies existing between their own beliefs and the content of persuasive communications) the relation was only $-.19$. Thus the variance in conformity behavior accounted for by IQ may depend on personality factors. In particular, when the subject is concerned about his relations with the influence source, those who are less bright will evidence greater conformity than brighter subjects. The data as a whole, however, suggest that IQ is not a potent factor in peer conformity among children and adolescents.

Personality Factors

A large body of data concerning conformity-proneness in adults (Hoffman, 1953; Crutchfield, 1955; Krech, Crutchfield, and Ballachey, 1962; Barron, 1953a, 1953b) suggests that the conforming adult: (1) is lower in ego-strength and ability to cope with stress; (2) feels inferior and inadequate; (3) is preoccupied with how he is evaluated by others; (4) has low tolerance for impulsive action, handles hostility intropunitively, and manifests conservative, moralistic attitudes and values; and (5) chooses occupations that stress conventional social values. These findings are based on data from both personality tests and observations.

Data concerning the personality correlates of peer conformity in children and adolescents are not as extensive as the material available for adults. Nevertheless, some of these same relations appear in childhood, suggesting that the antecedents of conformity-proneness lie in the vicissitudes of early socialization. It will be shown in the following discussion, however, that personality factors account for only a portion of the variance in peer-conformity in childhood; situational factors clearly modulate the child's responsiveness to peer influences even though substantial personality variance is involved.

Observational data on nursery school children reveal that peer compliance is positively correlated with instrumental help-seeking and emotional support-seeking from peers. At the same time, compliance during these years is also negatively related to aggressive behavior. Variables that are not significantly related to peer compliance, however, include approval-seeking, dominance, withdrawal, and achievement-striving (Crandall et al., 1958). Emmerich's (1966) findings agree with the foregoing results in most respects. First, yielding to other children's demands and avoiding rough activities both loaded *negatively* on an aggression-dominance factor emerging from observations of nursery school children. Seeking recognition from peers, however, loaded positively on this factor, a finding which constitutes the only discrepancy in the results of these two studies. Thus the nursery school child who is compliant with peers is characteristically nonaggressive and dependent in his other interactions with the peer group.

Further information from the Crandall study suggests that this constellation of personality attributes in nursery school children must be very carefully interpreted. Q-sorts were made by the observers and many of these significantly differentiated the peer-compliant children from the noncompliant children. The following statements, which describe the more compliant children, distinguished between the two groups:

1. Opinions are more readily influenced by others.
2. Has a higher energy level.
3. Is more spontaneous and uninhibited.
4. Is more distractible.
5. Is more suggestible.
6. More often seeks attention and praise from others.
7. Is warmer, friendlier.
8. Shows more empathic sensitivity to others' feelings.
9. Appears more relaxed, easy-going.
10. Is less rigid, inflexible.
11. Is less of a perfectionist.
12. Exhibits less self-pity.
13. Finds it less difficult to admit mistakes.

These data most certainly do not depict the peer-compliant nursery school child as passive-aggressive, authoritarian, and "conformity-prone." Rather peer-compliant children seem to be, at this time, "outer-directed" children.

Is is interesting that those children in this

study who were identified as high in *adult* compliance had personality characteristics of the more stereotyped kind. They were, as contrasted with less compliant children:

1. Is more cooperative, eager to please.
2. Reacts less negatively to commands from others.
3. Is more often a chronic worrier.
4. Is more deferential to persons considered superior.
5. Is less easily irritated by minor frustrations.
6. Uses excuses and rationalizations less frequently.
7. Becomes upset and anxious more readily.

The observational data showed that the adult-compliant children were nonaggressive, withdrawn, and achievement-striving. Taken together, then, the Crandall data suggest that peer compliance in young children is a matter of easy-going, relatively nonaggressive give-and-take. Only adult compliance is accompanied by high submissiveness and anxiety.

The correlation between peer and adult compliance in this study rose from .51 among nursery school children to .76 among primary school children. If covariation in these two aspects of compliance increases with age, we would expect increasing concordance among the personality factors associated with each of these variables. The data confirm this. The observational records for 6-, 7-, and 8-year-olds showed that seeking approval from peers was negatively related to peer compliance and that peer compliance was negatively correlated with dominance and aggression at higher levels than among the nursery school children. Aggression and dominance were also significantly related to adult compliance among the elementary school children and the magnitude of these correlations was also greater than among the nursery school children.

There was more overlap for the older children among the Q-sort items that differentiated peer-compliant children from noncompliant children and those items that differentiated adult-compliant children from noncompliant children. During this period, the child who was highly peer-compliant actually appeared to be *less* "healthy" than the adult compliant child! Both peer- and adult-compliant children were nonaggressive and uncomfortable in the presence of aggressive behavior. But the adult-compliant children seemed to be warm toward adults, desirous of pleasing adults, and appeared neither constricted nor dependent. On the other hand, the peer-compliant children were passive and nonassertive, readily influenced by others, and relied heavily on others in making decisions. This picture of the peer-compliant older child is in sharp contrast to the outgoing, effectively modulated social behavior of peer-compliant nursery school children.

The preceding data suggest that some important transformations may occur in the child's social development during the early childhood years. It would appear that good social adjustment with peers begins with general responsiveness and sensitivity to peers, including ready yielding to peer influences. Compliant behavior toward peers during the preschool period is actually associated with many personality characteristics that are associated with *low* peer compliance later in childhood. Such data suggest the hypothesis that a period of high peer compliance in early childhood serves as a precursor to effective peer relations in later childhood and adolescence. Longitudinal study is required to test this intriguing hypothesis.

The Crandall data do not pinpoint those factors which produce the shift in the role played by peer compliance in the child's personality functioning. It is interesting to note, however, that the peer-compliant older child more closely resembles the conformity-prone adult (as described by Crutchfield) than does his nursery school counterpart.

What other evidence suggests that the older child who conforms to peer demands is similar to the conformity-prone adult? Jakubczak and Walters (1959) studied suggestibility in two groups of 9-year-old boys. One was a highly dependent group and the other was a nondependent group; these subgroups were selected on the basis of a semiprojective test. Suggestibility was studied by means of the autokinetic effect. Both adults and peers were employed as influence sources. The dependent subjects proved to be more responsive to social influence emanating from adults than were the nondependent subjects. The same was true with respect to influence emanating from peers, but this difference failed to reach significance.

Lesser and Abelson (1959) did not report findings concerning the personality correlates of peer persuasibility in their studies of yielding behavior in 7- to 13-year old children. In light of the results discussed above, however, it is pertinent to report here that teacher persuasibility was negatively related to aggression in boys (but not girls), negatively related to self-esteem, and positively correlated with social isolation (the degree to which the child was nominated as *neither* liked nor disliked on a sociometric test). Manipulative studies concerning peer conformity as a function of self-esteem have confirmed these results (Gelfand, 1962).

One other finding from Lesser and Abelson's study is also of interest. Among 7-year-olds, there was a correlation of .44 between the Peer Persuasibility scores of children who were friends and a correlation of −.60 between Peer Persuasibility scores of children who mutually disliked each other. Thus among 7-year-olds, the child who seeks agreement with peers generally finds himself positively reinforced by children with the same needs but negatively reinforced by children who are less compliant. These correlations were much lower among the older children studied by these investigators. The results of one other study (Dodge and Muench, 1969) also show no significant relation between conformity and need for approval among sixth-grade children.

Evidence concerning the personality correlates of peer conformity in adolescents was provided by Young and Gaier (1953). Suggestibility was measured by means of the autokinetic effect and social pressure consisted of false peer group norms. Measures of Introversion-Extroversion, Ascendance-Submission, Self-Sufficiency, and Hysteria were obtained by means of the *Bernreuter Personality Inventory* and the *MMPI*. For 20 subjects, the correlations with suggestibilty were as follows: Extroversion, −.36; Submission, .42; Lack of Self-Sufficiency, .40; Hysteria, .43. These correlations are significant only at borderline levels. When the four personality scores were used as predictors of suggestibility in a multiple regression equation, however, the multiple correlation was .69. The investigators next differentiated two additional groups of subjects on the basis of these predictor variables and *then* gave the autokinetic

test. These groups differed in suggestibility as predicted. This study suggests, then, that low ego-strength, inferiority, and social inadequacy are personality attributes of adolescents who evidence high conformity to peer group norms. It should be recalled, at this point, that Costanzo and Shaw (1966) found a correlation of .87 between self-blame and conformity to peer norms across a wide age range. Such evidence is consistent with the material reported here.

Self-confidence may be related to opinion change in social pressure situations. This relation may be different, however, for males and females (Kogan and Wallach, 1966). Specifically, initially confident adolescent boys showed little shift in the direction of group consensus, either during or after a discussion. Confident females, however, shifted their opinions, although this shift was noted only in postdiscussion assessments. When initial confidence was low, however, both boys and girls shifted in the direction of the group's consensus. Kogan and Wallach believe that extremely confident opinions are, in part, compensatory. That is, individuals who manifest unusually strong opinions are, to a degree, uncertain in their beliefs. For females, the peer group appears to offer the social support needed to reduce the compensatory rigidity in opinion—this is reflected by opinion shifts as a consequence of exposure to the group's values. Confident males, whose socialization has stressed independence, seem to be less receptive to the persuasive arguments of their peers. When either males or females consciously admit to uncertainty, however, the group experience confirms, cognitively, the likelihood of making errors if the individual persists in his extreme opinions. This latter finding suggests that uncertainty and lack of self-esteem may be associated with high susceptibility to peer influences.

Two final studies stress a somewhat different set of personality variables which are correlated with conforming behavior among adolescents. McDavid (1959), who worked with males between the ages of 16 and 18, differentiated one group of subjects who were particularly attentive to the *information* contained in socially communicated messages. Another group was identified as particularly oriented to the *source* of such messages. Conformity was measured by click-counting under pressure of bogus peer norms. The source-oriented group, as compared to the message-oriented group, was: (1) more susceptible to peer influence; (2) more affected by large discrepancies between their judgments and the judgments of the group; and (3) less likely to compromise with the false norms than to agree totally with the norms when yielding did occur. These data add to the composite picture of the peer-conforming adolescent—he is concerned with the interpersonal sources of communication, sensitive to variations between his own behavior and the behavior of the peer group, and rigid with respect to the type of yielding that he does show.

Wilson (1960) identified a group of adolescent boys who were high on social accomodation and compared their conformity behavior with subjects who were highly concerned with the accuracy of information. Conformity was measured in: (1) an attitude series, and (2) a click-counting task. Peer pressure emanated from liked peers for half of the subjects and from disliked peers for the other half. The accommodative subjects changed their attitudes more when influence emanated from liked peers than from disliked peers. The group that was concerned with information accuracy did not change their attitudes differentially according to the attractiveness of the influence source. There was no greater overall attitude change, however, by the accommodative group. In the click-counting task, the accommodative group showed similar conformity to the judgments of liked peers and disliked peers. It is difficult to say why the attractiveness of the source failed to influence the accommodative subjects on this task. Perhaps, however, the attractiveness of the influence source is only an important element in conformity when salient issues are involved (i.e., social attitudes may be more salient than click-counting for adolescent boys). The general evidence contained in these adolescent studies clearly points to the fact that personality factors interact in extremely complex ways with situational factors in determining peer conformity. Taken alone, personality measures are likely to be only gross predictors of conformity proneness.

In summary, the literature concerning the personality correlates of yielding to peer influences indicates the following: (1) in early childhood, peer compliance appears to be embedded in a constellation of easy, comfortable, outgoing social behaviors; (2) in middle childhood and adolescence, the peer-conforming child somewhat resembles the conformity-prone adult—he manifests low ego-strength, repression of impulse, low self-esteem, and high social sensitivity; (3) personality attributes such as these, however, interact with situational factors in determining conformity behavior in older children and adolescents.

Situational Factors

An excellent review of the literature concerning situational factors in conformity behavior has been published by Allen (1965). This review, however, includes very few citations to studies of children. Most of what is known concerning situational factors in yielding behavior has been derived from studies of college sophomores. Nevertheless, in opening a discussion of situational factors that determine a child's compliance with peer influences, it is appropriate to quote some of Allen's remarks here:

A subject in a conformity situation has information and beliefs about several important features of the situation; the task, other members of the group, and the experimenter. Moreover, he thinks about how the group and the experimenter are reacting to him and to the task. Superimposed on these aspects of the situation are certain goals of the subject which are created by the relative salience of clues in the experimental situation. We can assume that the subject engages in some type of cognitive weighing of these factors, which determines the resultant response. The outcome of this weighing is presumably the response that maximizes the possibilty of achieving the momentarily most relevant and salient goal (pp. 169–170).

The most extensively explored situational factors in adult conformity include public versus private responding, attractiveness of the group, status of the influence source and of the subject, interdependence of source and subject, perceived competence of the source and of the subject, composition and sex of the group, unanimity of group pressure, extremity of the group norm, and difficulty of the task. Some, but not all of these problems have been examined with respect to children's yielding to peer influences. Consequently, the following discussion is a supplement to the general literature concerning situational factors in conformity.

Size and Unanimity of the Peer Group. We have been able to find only one study concerning the effects of group size on conformity behavior in children. The few adult studies on this topic (e.g., Asch, 1956) show that social influence increases as the size of the pressure group increases from one person to seven persons. More generally, however, the relation between group size and social influence may be curvilinear. This is borne out by Hare's (1953) study with Boy Scouts. The opinions of group members shifted more toward the group's consensus in 5-member groups than in 12-member groups.

Information concerning the effects of unanimity of group pressure can be found in Berenda's (1950) experiments. In one of these, a small minority group of children was pitted against a majority group who gave extreme overestimates, although not uniform ones, concerning the length of three critical lines. There was a strong tendency to follow the majority, at least on the most difficult task, although this was a compromise kind of yielding. In a second experiment, a small minority group was pitted against a larger group who uniformly selected incorrect comparison lines (in an effort to match a standard line). The only evidence of following behavior found in this study involved difficult judgments in which the majority unanimously provided the *correct* answer. In easy judgments, and in all comparisons when the majority was extremely deviant, the minority children firmly resisted the uniform group pressure. They expressed surprise, disbelief, amazement, and belligerence. On the surface, the results of these studies suggest greater yielding to nonuniform pressure than to uniform pressure. This might be a reasonable inference, except that the tasks employed in the two studies were quite different. In the nonunanimous pressure situation, estimates of a single line were called for. This task is probably much more difficult than selecting a correct comparison line, the task which was employed in the second study. Thus the greater conformity evidenced when group

pressure was not uniform may have been a function of task difficulty rather than unanimity of the peer-group influence.

Alexander (1964) has provided some provocative information concerning the unanimity problem by studying a group of 37 adolescent male cliques. The main focus of the study was on drinking patterns and attitudes. First, consumption patterns in cliques in which all members drank were more uniform than drinking patterns in groups in which more than one-half, but not all members drank. Second, attitudes toward drinking were more positive in all-drinker groups than in mixed groups. Boys who were not members of these cliques tended to prefer uniform cliques to nonuniform cliques. Finally, the nondrinking members of mixed cliques occupied lower status in the group than did drinking members. In this instance, then, uniformity of values in the peer group seemed to be associated with conformity.

Task Difficulty. It has already been reported that Berenda found greater yielding on difficult tasks than on easy ones. Contrary to these results, Iscoe et al. (1963) found that there was relatively greater conformity on the easier of two click-counting tasks. McDavid's (1959) data, however, show that the effects of task difficulty varied for different types of individuals. Those identified as message-oriented as opposed to source-oriented yielded more often as the difficulty of the task increased. The source-oriented group, however, did not yield differentially on easy and difficult tasks. We are forced to conclude, then, that the results present no clear picture concerning the effects of task difficulty on peer conformity in children. Stimulus ambiguity (the task difficulty variable employed by Berenda) may be conceptually different for the child from the task of counting clicks. Parametric studies of the task-difficulty problem are obviously needed.

Competence and Attractiveness of the Influence Source. The clearest evidence concerning the competence of the influence source as a determinant of peer conformity is contained in a study by Gelfand (1962). Fifth-grade children were paired with a confederate and each pair completed a series of four tasks. Half of the subjects were given false norms so that the confederate appeared to be highly successful in performing these tasks. At the same time, the subject himself seemed to have performed poorly. The other half of the subjects were led to believe that they had succeeded while the confederates had failed. A persuasibility test was then given, with the confederate serving as the influence source. Subjects who thought they were less successful than the confederate proved to be more persuasible than did the subjects who believed they were more competent than the confederate. There is no information contained in this study concerning relative amounts of persuasibility when the subject perceives *both* himself and the confederate as competent or perceives *both* as incompetent. But the results clearly point to the relevance of source competence as a major situational determinant of conformity in latency-aged children.

"Attractiveness," as applied to sources of social influence, is a global term. In some studies, this refers to the subject's liking for the influence source. In other studies, attractiveness refers to social status or prestige. Studies concerning the influence of source attractiveness on conformity behavior in adults have produced an array of conflicting results. This probably derives from the fact that manipulations or descriptions of attractiveness have varied enormously (Allen, 1965). Some of this inconsistency is also reflected in the research on this problem that has been conducted with children.

Ramirez and Castaneda (1967) found that children more quickly learned consonant sounds associated with the names of high-status peers than sounds paired with the names of low-status peers. But other studies, focusing more directly on yielding behavior, have provided more complex results. As mentioned, Wilson (1960) found no significant difference between yielding to liked and to disliked peers on a click-counting task. On attitude judgments, however, liked as opposed to disliked peers differentially influenced accommodative subjects but not information-oriented subjects. Moreover, Patel and Gordon (1960) reported a general tendency for their high school subjects to be more influenced by high-prestige than by low-prestige peers. The data revealed, however, that high-prestige peers enhanced conformity among tenth- and eleventh-grade subjects, but not among the high school seniors. Further, the prestige sources produced more conformity on

difficult than on easy tasks. In fact, if the task was difficult, there was more conformity to high-prestige peers than to low-prestige peers at all three of the grade levels studied.

A recent study by Wyer (1966) also indicates that motivational factors interact with prestige factors in affecting peer conformity. An incentive to perform well was provided (i.e., the subjects were told that they were being tested on important skills such as leadership and decision-making ability). The adolescent subjects conformed to group norms unless they neither felt accepted by the other group members nor were attracted to these members. When incentives to perform were absent, however, substantial conformity was noted only among subjects who felt that they were rejected by individuals whom they liked.

The Harvey and Rutherford (1960) results, reviewed earlier, should be mentioned again here. In third-, sixth-, ninth-, and eleventh-grade classes, some subjects were told that a peer leader agreed with the subject's own opinions while, at the same time, a low-status peer disagreed. Others were told that a low-status peer was in agreement with the subject but that a high-status peer had disagreed. The high-status disagree–low-status agree subjects showed significantly more opinion change than the low-status disagree–high-status agree group, but among sixth and eleventh graders only. The authors also reported that the leadership status of the influence sources was highly correlated with their popularity. Consequently, these results suggest that attractiveness of the source may affect opinion change, whether attractiveness is defined in terms of leadership or in terms of popularity. This hypothesis should be subjected to a more direct test, however, before its acceptance can be regarded as more than tentative.

The prestige of the influence source has also been studied in relation to conformity behavior in informal peer groups. The best studies of this type are by Polansky et al. (1950) and Lippitt et al. (1952). The data in these two studies were derived from observations of camp groups, one composed of "problem" children and one composed of "normal" children. First, there was high agreement in these peer groups as to which children had the most prestige. Other data, generally consistent across the two studies, showed that high-prestige children, as compared to other members of the group, were more active socially, more likely to initiate behavior contagion, and were more likely to exert direct influence on their peers.

The greater capacity to exert social influence that was shown by the high-prestige children apparently did not derive from their higher levels of social activity. A ratio of number of contagion initiations divided by total social output was as highly correlated with prestige ($r = .58$) as was sheer frequency of attempts to initiate influence. The prestige of the influence source also affected the success on the influence attempt. That is, high-prestige children were particularly successful both as sources of behavior contagion and in direct attempts to influence the behavior of their peers (see also Cohn, Yee, and Brown, 1961).

Some tangential but important data are reported by Lippitt et al. High-prestige boys, as compared with low-prestige boys, did not differ in the success of their influence attempts during the early phases of group formation. That is, no significant correlation between successful influence attempts and prestige was found during the first half of the camp experience. On the other hand, these variables were positively correlated during the second part of the camp session. Apparently, prestige affects conformity in the informal group only after the group has acquired a cohesive structure.

Status of the Individual Being Influenced. We have already shown that the individual's self-perceptions concerning his competence, attractiveness, and position in the peer group account for significant portions of the variance in conformity to peer influence. Specifically, Lesser and Abelson (1959) found that yielding was positively correlated with social isolation (degree to which the child was not nominated as *either* "liked" or "disliked" on a sociometric test). Wilson (1960) has confirmed this latter finding with adolescents. Boys who were either well-liked or who were disliked conformed significantly less than boys of middle social status. Thus two studies have shown that children of middle sociometric rank are particularly responsive to peer influences.

Harvey and Consalvi (1960) have shown that there is one particular middle status position that is associated with high conformity. Subjects were selected from cliques of delinquent boys at a state training school. Those studied included the clique leaders, second-ranking members, and lowest-ranking members. Conformity was measured in a group pressure situation that included additional members of the clique. The most conformity occurred among second-ranking individuals. Least conformity occurred among the leaders, but they did not differ significantly from the lowest-ranking boys. Once again, both extremely high and extremely low status were not associated with yielding; on the contrary, a middle status position seemed associated with maximum yielding to peer influences. The Harvey and Consalvi data suggest, however, that the person "who has almost made it" to the top of the peer group is the middle-status child who is the most conformity-prone of all.

The studies by Polansky et al. (1950) and Lippitt et al. (1952) also focused on yielding behavior as a function of the child's prestige in the peer group. High-status children proved to be more resistant to *direct* influence than did low-status children. Resistance to *contagious* influence, however, was not consistently related to prestige. Among the disturbed children, high-status boys were particularly open to such influence. On the other hand, among the normal children, power in the peer group was not significantly related to responsiveness to contagion. Thus it is not possible to state conclusively that high-status children are less influenced by their peers in natural settings than are middle- or low-status children. This seems to be the case when the social influence is relatively direct. On the other hand, a child's own status may have less to do with yielding to subtler forms of influence, such as those involved in behavior contagion.

Commitment to the Group. The adult literature shows that the strength of the person's commitment to the group acts as a determinant of influencibility (Allen, 1965). Naturalistic studies with children also suggest that the group's influence on an individual child varies according to the degree that the group serves a "reference function" (Sherif and Sherif, 1964). But commitment can also affect influencibility in *ad hoc* groups. Kiesler, Zanna, and DeSalvo (1966) studied the effects of varying degrees of commitment to the group on conformity behavior among adolescents. None of the subjects involved in this study knew each other initially. They were led to believe, however, that they were only marginally accepted by the group and also that they disagreed with the group on an important issue. Some subjects were told that they would have to remain with the same group for three sessions while others were told that they could change groups if they wished and, indeed, "might be changed anyway." During some of the group discussion sessions the marginal subject's opinions were supported by another deviate (i.e., the subject had an ally). When the subject knew that this ally was present there was very little opinion change, except when commitment to membership in the group also existed. These results need to be extended to less formal groups. The experimental findings are provocative, however, because they indicate that the commitment variable is one more important situational aspect of peer conformity.

Incentive Factors. Most of the research concerning the influence of incentive factors on peer conformity has already been discussed. For example, introducing a small payoff for "accurate" responding in an Asch-type situation led to decreased yielding among firstborn subjects, whereas a large payoff produced more yielding among later-born subjects. Also, as reported earlier, potential social rejection produced increases in conformity, although the effects of this manipulation also depended on the birth-order of the subject. And, finally, we have reported that achievement-oriented instructions enhance conformity unless the subject is neither attracted to nor feels accepted by the peer group (Wyer, 1966).

It is pertinent to include, along with the preceding information, a reference to Kelman's (1950) classic study of conformity in groups as a function of success and failure. Junior college students who experienced failure proved to be more suggestible than similar students who experienced success. Sequential effects of success-failure manipulations were also found. Subjects receiving no feedback or who received ambiguous feedback on one task moved toward the confederate's norms when failure occurred on a second task; movement was away from the confederate's norms after success. On the other hand, subjects who

succeeded or who failed in the first task shifted negligibly after success on the second task but shifted both toward and away from the confederate's norms after failure in the second task.

Obviously, then, a variety of incentive factors (e.g., those relating to social approval, affiliation, and material reward) account for significant portions of the variance in children's tendencies to be influenced by their peers. This range of factors, however, needs to be extended and more information is desperately needed concerning the role of incentive factors in yielding to peer influences among younger children.

Peer Modeling

This section will be devoted to a review of the relatively small amount of research that has concerned peer modeling. Although there has been extensive interest in modeling phenomena during recent years, most of the research with children has involved adult models. Peer modeling studies have mainly involved very young children, and age differences have not been studied. In most instances, the primary research objective has been to obtain a better understanding of the general principles governing imitative behavior change. Only in a broad sense, then, have these studies of peer modeling been aimed at *developmental* problems in peer relations.

Existing studies clearly show that young children are responsive to peer models (Bandura, Grusec, and Menlove, 1967; Bandura and Menlove, 1968; Clifford, 1963; Hartup and Coates, 1967; Hicks, 1965). For example, Hicks showed that preschool-aged children will spontaneously reproduce the novel aggressive behaviors that are displayed by a child model projected on film. Such results contrast with those reported earlier by Siegel (1956). She found that the exposure of young children to an aggressive cartoon did *not* affect the level of aggression shown by the children during postexposure interaction with another child. The difference between the results of these studies undoubtedly derives from the different modeling and testing procedures used. First, the film models used by Hicks were children; those used by Siegel were cartoon figures (Woody Woodpecker). Aggressive cartoon figures may produce both imitative aggression and increases in nonimitative aggression, but this has been demonstrated mainly when the testing situation involves the same play materials as those used by the model in the film (e.g., Bandura, Ross, and Ross, 1963). It is noteworthy, then, that Hicks also used materials for the postexposure test that were exactly like the materials that had been used by the model, whereas Siegel did not. These discrepancies suggest that aggressive peer modeling, when exposure consists of a short film, may not produce widely generalized effects on the young child's behavior. Effects may be apparent, however, in situations that are relevant to the filmed material.

It should be mentioned that there was some carry-over of the modeling in Hicks' study to a second testing session conducted six months after exposure to the film. Although the subjects exposed to aggressive peer models did not differ from the no-model controls at a significant level, there was still somewhat greater imitative aggression shown by the first group at the time of the second session.

The work of Hartup and Coates (1967) shows that very young children will modify their prosocial behavior as a consequence of exposure to peer models. Nursery school children watched another child (the experimenter's confederate) display unusually high frequencies of sharing behavior. Those subjects who observed an altruistic model, as compared to subjects who had not observed a model, exhibited greater sharing.

Through modeling, peers are also effective in altering the emotional behavior of preschool-aged children. Bandura, Grusec, and Menlove (1967) selected a group of 48 children between the ages of 3 and 5 years who were rated by their parents as fearful and avoidant of dogs. The subjects were then exposed to one of the following situations: (1) a "fearless" 4-year-old model who exhibited progressively stronger approach responses toward a dog; (2) a dog with no model present; and (3) a play period in which neither the model nor the dog was present. The children who observed the interaction between the nonanxious model and the dog showed reduction in avoidance behavior as measured both one day and one month later. These children were significantly less avoidant than were the children in the other two groups. In a related study, Bandura

and Menlove (1968) contrasted avoidance reduction in dog-phobic preschoolers who were exposed either to: (1) a series of films in which a 5-year-old model displayed progressively more intimate interactions with a dog; (2) a similar set of films showing a variety of models interacting with a number of different dogs; or (3) a movie which did not include animals. The single-model and multiple-model conditions both produced reductions in the children's avoidance behavior. Only the multiple-modeling condition, however, reduced fears sufficiently to enable the children to interact with dogs in potentially threatening ways. Taken together, these studies provide strong evidence that peers may be employed effectively as models in desensitization procedures for very young children who manifest phobic behaviors.

Peer modeling has also been studied with older children. Clark (1965), for example, showed differential imitation of peers according to whether the model was reinforced or not reinforced. The subjects were boys, aged 9 to 11. A button-pressing task was used and increased selection of the model's response was found when the subject had seen the rewarded model. There was a strong tendency to counterimitate nonrewarded models.

Bandura and Kupers (1964), using subjects between 7 and 9 years of age, provided an opportunity for the child to observe either a peer model who adopted a very high criterion of self-reward for performances in a bowling game, or a peer model who adopted a very low criterion of self-reward. The postexposure test showed that the subjects closely matched the patterns of self-reward that had been used by the model. Peer models have also been shown to alter the conditionability of children in a Taffel-type task (Ditrichs, Simon, and Greene, 1967). Here the exposure to models was in the form of listening to tape recordings of a peer being given approval or being given disapproval contingent upon certain word choices in a sentence-construction task. The subject's own conditionability in a postexposure session was influenced by the vicarious experience with the tape-recorded peer. Other data showing the effects of peer models on the behavior of elementary and high school children have been reported by Grosser, Polansky, and Lippitt (1951), Luchins and Luchins (1961), and Rosekrans (1967).

Determinants of Peer Imitation. Each of the studies previously cited had some objective other than demonstrating the simple fact that children imitate their peers. The particular independent variables studied have varied considerably since each investigator was interested in a different theoretical issue. Consequently, these studies form a coherent whole only when they are considered in the context of the entire literature concerning imitation in children. Obviously, complete coverage of this area would be beyond the scope of the present chapter.

Clark (1965) replicated studies of children's imitation of adults which have shown that response consequences to the model significantly alter the child's tendency to reproduce the model's behavior. Ditrichs et al. (1967) showed that vicarious reinforcement affected conditionability primarily during the acquisition phase of the task, as opposed to the extinction phase, and when the density of the critical "hostile" verbs was modelled in ascending frequency rather than descending frequency. It was harder, however, to produce increases in the extent to which hostile verbs were attached to the pronoun "I" than to the pronoun "they." Luchins and Luchins (1961) found that the peer model's behavior facilitated the subject's solution of a concept-formation task primarily when the subject was relatively naive as to what was expected of him. All of these studies suggest that there may be important task-related factors that modify the effects of peer models on children's behavior. Such factors would include individual differences in the cognitive functioning of the subjects, particularly differences that would determine the aspects of the stimulus situation that are selectively perceived and encoded, and how these are interpreted.

Many recent studies of children's imitation have concerned the role of models in producing disinhibitory effects on behavior. Peer models, however, can produce inhibition as well as disinhibition (Grosser et al., 1951). The children in this study were instructed to complete a series of block designs and to engage in a period of relaxation between designs. The subjects were told that they could relax in any way they wished, but if they decided to play with any of the toys during the break, they were to know that half of the toys were forbidden. Thirty-four boys completed the task in the presence of a confederate who had been instructed to remain at his desk and to engage in restrained "relaxation" behaviors during the break. Thirty-two subjects watched a model who got up and played with the toys. Eight control subjects were given the instructions but completed the task when no other child was present. There was significantly less playing with the toys by subjects who watched a passive model than by children in the no-model condition, but more playing with the toys in the active model condition than in the no-model condition. Observation of a deviant peer model who is subsequently punished will also heighten resistance to deviation (Walters, Parke, and Cane, 1965).

The relation of incentive factors to peer imitation has also been studied. In an early treatment of the imitation problem, Mowrer (1950) hypothesized that rewarding models should be imitated to a greater extent than nonrewarding models. In studies of children's imitation of adults, the findings concerning this hypothesis have been mixed. In the Grosser study, some of the models were instructed to make social overtures to the subject (i.e., to be "friendly"); others were instructed to be withdrawn, although not "unfriendly." This manipulation, which must have produced quite variable interaction between the subjects and the models, did not affect the total amount of imitated deviation. However, the extent to which the subject played with the exact toys used by the deviating model was enhanced by the friendliness of the model.

More recently, Hartup and Coates (1967) have found that the nature of the child's interactions in the peer group affect peer imitation. Instances of positive social exchanges were observed in a nursery school. Later, in the laboratory, each child observed another child engage in sharing behavior. Amount of imitative sharing in the postexposure session depended on the child's past history of reinforcement from the peer group as well as upon his past experience with the particular child who served as the model. That is, children who had had frequent reinforcement from their peers imitated a model who had been a source of such rewards more than they imitated a child who had not been a source of reward. On the other hand, children who had received little reinforcement from their peers in school imitated nonrewarding models more than rewarding models. These findings suggest that children who have had much positive interaction with peers may, as Mowrer suggested, have found it reinforcing to reproduce the behavior of children who had been associated with reward in the past. The behavior of the nonrewarded children is puzzling, however. Possibly, the child who does not receive much peer reinforcement is defensive and anxious or sees himself as particularly similar to nonrewarding children. Such conditions could enhance his tendency to imitate nonrewarding as opposed to rewarding peers. In fact, a perceived similarity hypothesis would account for the total pattern of results obtained in the foregoing study. It has been found directly that when preadolescents perceive themselves as similar to a peer model (in terms of membership in the same reference group and a sharing of interests) they are more likely to imitate the model than if perceived similarity is low (Rosekrans, 1967).

Another type of social experience that may be particularly important in imitation is previous opportunity for sharing an affective experience with the model. Aronfreed (1968) studied the extent to which children would imitate a sympathetic response; that is, a response that involved sacrifice of personal gain but reduced the discomfort of a peer. Imitation of this self-sacrificing response occurred only if *two* conditions were present during a prior series of learning trials: (1) the subject must have experienced discomfort contiguously with signals indicating that another person was also undergoing distress; and (2) the other person's behavior must have been instrumental in reducing the subject's own distress. Thus the imitation of sympathetic behavior may require prior conditioning of an empathic emotional response in the child. At the very least, the results show that the child must have observed another's distress at the same time he himself has experienced discomfort in order for the rewardingness of the model to enhance imitative sympathy.

Other studies have focused on the incentives provided by the task, as they may affect peer imitation. Grosser et al. (1951) had their subjects rank order the toys in the experimental room before the experiment began. Half of the subjects who watched a deviating model saw him play with "high-valence" toys; models for the other children played with "low-valence" toys. Imitation did not differ significantly between the two groups of subjects. These investigators also employed an experimental condition that they called *safety*. That is, some subjects were told that half of the toys were forbidden (this condition, described earlier, may be called "low-safety"); some were not told this. Surprisingly, the low-safety manipulation had rather circumscribed effects on the children's imitation. It did not affect the frequency with which the children actively played with the toys. It did, however, reduce the frequency of "handling" behavior —picking the toys up, examining them, and so forth. The importance of incentive and attentional factors in peer imitation is also suggested by Clifford's finding (1963) that young children who are socially active (visible) are modelled more frequently than children who are "invisible" members of the peer group.

Generalized Nature of Peer Imitation. Only one study exists concerning the relation of peer imitation to imitation of other models (Hartup, 1964b). Forced-choice, incomplete stories were administered to nursery school children. The major findings were as follows: (1) preference for like-sex peer models was positively correlated with preference for like-sex parent models, but in boys only; (2) preference for opposite-sex models was not generalized among children of either sex; (3) children preferring to imitate, rather than to avoid imitative responding, would do so whether the available model was a parent or a peer. Thus a small portion of the variance in peer imitation appears to be accounted for by parent imitation. Otherwise, data do not exist concerning the possibility that the tendency to imitate peers is a component of a more generalized disposition to imitate social models.

Peer Reinforcement

There is a vast literature dealing with the modification and maintenance of children's behavior through the use of adult social reinforcement (see Stevenson, 1965). Only recently, however, has the study of peer reinforcement been pursued. Two types of peer reinforcement studies have been conducted. First, there is a small series of laboratory studies, using simple operant paradigms, in which agemates served as reinforcing agents. The purpose of these studies has not been to contrast the effects of adult and peer social reinforcement, but rather to study some of the situational factors affecting the impact of peer reinforcement on the individual child.

A second group of studies provides descriptive information concerning the exchange of social reinforcers in existing peer groups. Numerous earlier studies dealt with variables that may be construed as reinforcing (e.g., social participation, submissiveness, or sympathy). The recent work, however, has been focused more explicitly on the contingencies and outcomes of peer interaction in terms of "reinforcement theory." Most of the existing peer reinforcement studies, like so many others mentioned in this chapter, have had a dual purpose. They have added to knowledge concerning peer influences on child behavior, but they have also contributed to the general literature concerning social learning processes. These studies have usually involved such reinforcers as attention and approval and have not concerned all of the reinforcing events that may emanate from peers.

The effects of peer reinforcement are dramatically illustrated in Cohen's (1966) study of a single 13-year-old boy, "Justin." A laboratory situation was constructed in which cooperative and competitive operant responding could be studied. Justin's responses were examined in relation to reinforcement that was delivered either by his older brother, a friend, a strange boy, his mother, or his sister. Information feedback and schedules of reinforcement were varied during the course of the experiment. The analyses of cumulative records revealed patterns of cooperative and competitive behavior that were veridical with information that had been obtained about Justin's relations with these people from interviews and questionnaires. The main value of this study is that it demonstrated the efficacy of a reinforcement procedure for yielding information of diagnostic value concerning children's relations with peers (as well as adults). More recent studies have also shown low but significant positive correlations between incidence of conduct problems and

change in behavior during an operant task when social approval was dispensed by a peer (Patterson and Anderson, 1964; Patterson and Fagot, 1967).

Several studies have concerned the relation between peer reinforcement and interpersonal attraction. Some investigators have approached this problem by using measures of social attraction as independent variables and measures of reinforcing effectiveness as dependent variables; others have reversed this strategy. It is safe to say that most investigators have been interested in the relation between peer reinforcement and interpersonal attraction because they believe that such reinforcement is a major determinant of attraction. This does not preclude the possibility, however, that children who have acquired prestige in the peer group, as compared to those who possess low prestige, are differentially effective in modifying the behavior of other children through reinforcement techniques.

One of the first studies to apear in this area concerned the value of a friend's photograph as an incentive in an operant task (Horowitz, 1962a). Among 3-year-olds, lever-pulling rates were highest when the subjects were exposed to a picture of a best friend, next highest when they were exposed to photographs of "neutral" peers, and lowest when a blue light was flashed. However, no reliable differences in performance were associated with these conditions among the 4- and 5-year-old subjects. This age difference may mean that photographic representations of peers do not carry generalized incentive value for older, more socially sophisticated children. There is, however, no ready interpretation of this age difference and no replications of this investigation have been completed.

The capacity of 4- and 5-year-old children to reinforce the marble-dropping performance of their peers was assessed by Hartup (1964a). Verbal approval was periodically administered during the task by either a best friend or a disliked peer. The criterion measure consisted of differences between rate of marble-dropping during a baseline period (when the peer was absent) and during a period in which the peer was present and delivering approving statements. Performance proved to be better maintained when approval was dispensed by disliked peers than when given by liked peers. Performance actually declined during the testing session when reinforcement was given by a friend. A similar study (Tiktin and Hartup, 1965) was conducted with second- and fifth-grade children. Some subjects were reinforced by popular peers, some by unpopular peers, and some by middle-rank (isolate) peers. The results were very similar to the results for younger children. Performance tended to improve throughout the testing session when the reinforcing agent was an unpopular child, to decrease when the reinforcing agent was popular, and to change very little when the agent was a social isolate.

The results of the foregoing studies are only partially consistent with the results of a study by Patterson and Anderson (1964). They found that changes in response preference (rather than response rate) were greater among fourth-grade children when social reinforcement was given by nonfriends than when approval was given by friends. Second- and third-grade subjects, however, showed greater changes when reinforced by friends. One major difference in the methodology of this study, as compared with those mentioned previously, concerns the criterion measure that was used. Change in response preference was studied rather than change in rate of response. The implications of this difference in methodology are not clear, however, since very little is known about the effects of task variables on performance under social reinforcement.

If there is a disposition among preschool and school-age children to perform better when reinforcement emanates from nonfriends than from friends, why? The answer remains in doubt. In one study (Hartup, 1964a), it appeared that the children talked more to reinforcing friends (in spite of instructions) than they did to nonfriends. This finding, however, has not withstood replication. Anxiety factors have also been explored. Hartup and Kobasigawa (1964) found no significant difference in response rate change between those children who perceived their reinforcing agents as friendly from those who thought they were being reinforced by an aggressive child. On the other hand, teacher ratings of aggression anxiety were related to the child's responsiveness to peer reinforcement. Among both preschool boys and girls, the perfor-

mance of children rated as nonanxious deteriorated during the testing session (similar to the manner in which performance declined when approval was delivered by friends). For high-anxious girls, performance changed little during the first half of the testing session but increased during the second half. For boys, the high-anxious group performed better than the low-anxious group, primarily during the middle portion of the session.

Taken as a whole, the findings just cited suggest that situations which are unexpected, unfamiliar, or in which the child is anxious produce the best performance under peer reinforcement. Other data are consistent with this hypothesis, although they do not test it directly. Ferguson (1964) conducted a study in which fifth-grade children were positively reinforced by either a fifth- or a second-grade child. Second-grade subjects were also used and they were reinforced either by another second grader or by a fifth grader. Among children at *both* grade levels, those who were reinforced by a nonagemate showed increasingly better performance during the session than did those reinforced by agemates. In the latter instance, performance declined steadily, just as did the performance of children in the earlier studies who were nonanxious or who were reinforced by friends or popular peers. Floyd (1963) also found that children who received unexpectedly large or unexpectedly small amounts of peer reward modified their sharing behavior more extensively than did children whose reward expectancies were not violated. It may well be then, that the most parsimonious explanation of the results presented is in terms of a cognitive-motivational analysis.

While the effectiveness of peers as reinforcing agents seems to be dependent on the social status of the reinforcing agent, the reverse is also true. That is, the attraction of one child for another appears to derive from patterns of reinforcement exchanged between them. Correlational studies (reviewed previously) show that the number of positive sociometric choices received by a child is positively correlated with the frequency of friendly and associative contacts he initiates with other children in the peer group (Marshall and McCandless, 1957b; Hartup et al., 1967). But correlational analysis does not establish definitively that exchange of reinforcement is a direct determinant of social status. Only manipulative studies can provide clear evidence concerning this particular problem.

The experiments bearing on this issue have involved several different kinds of peer reinforcement. Keislar (1961), for example, varied the feedback given to adolescent female subjects concerning the "liking" of two other girls for attitudes and preferences that had been expressed previously by the subject. If the bogus feedback indicated "liking" for the subject's attitudes, as contrasted to "dislike," the subject was more attracted to the girl providing the evaluation. Byrne and Griffitt (1966) demonstrated the reinforcing effects of consensual attitudes for children as young as 9 years of age. Specifically, social attraction (in the form of sociometric preference) increased as a linear function of perceived similarity in social attitudes. This relation typified children between the fourth and twelfth grades, as well as college students.

Perhaps the most direct evidence concerning the effects of peer reinforcement on social attraction stems from a study by Karen (1965). Two triads of elementary school boys exchanged candy, toys, and pennies. This exchange was manipulated by the experimenter so that, during some sessions, the exchange indicated to each subject that one other member of the triad was sharing resources at a high level while a second member was not. During subsequent sessions, sharing was made to appear equal. Sociometric questions, given during the group meetings, indicated that social attraction fluctuated in accordance with the changing levels of reinforcement. For three of the subjects, there was a clear positive relation between receipt of reinforcement and liking for the person "giving" the reward. This relation was also found, less clearly, for two other subjects but was not apparent in the behavior of the one remaining subject. This ingenious paradigm has excellent potential for furnishing information concerning the role of peer reinforcement in determining interpersonal attraction.

In all of the studies mentioned, the term *reinforcement* has been used in a relatively loose sense. Reinforcement was defined *a priori*, based on the assumption that such behaviors as affection and attention, when pre-

sented contingently upon the occurrence of a response, will maintain or increase the tendency for that response to occur. This assumption may be tenable, but research has also shown that there is considerable intersubject variation in the reinforcing value contained in such social experiences. One group of investigators has instituted a search for those peer behaviors that do, in fact, change or maintain aggressive behavior (Patterson, Littman, and Bricker, 1967). Nursery school children's responses to peer aggression were observed and coded as *passive; cries; defensive postures, telling the teacher, recovering property,* and *retaliation.* Three findings are of particular interest. First, during five different observational periods in each of two nursery schools, bodily attack and attacking with objects were positively reinforced by peers (the first three categories above) between 75% and 97% of the time. Second, instances were tabulated which either confirmed or disconfirmed the following predictions: (1) positive reinforcement of an aggressive act would be followed by a similar response directed toward the same victim; (2) punishment (counter aggression) would be followed by a change in response, a change in choice of victim, or both. There were more confirmations of these two predictions in the observational records than would be expected on a chance basis. Third, peer reinforcement increased the frequency of aggression, although only among some children. If a child was victimized, counterattacked, and was then reinforced by his victim, aggression increased over time. On the other hand, children who were not victimized or who were victimized but not successful in counterattacking showed no significant increase in aggression over time.

The results of this study show that it is possible to identify some of the actions of peers which, according to conventional criteria, may be called reinforcers. In so doing, the investigators have contributed important information concerning the social ecology of the nursery school. These nursery schools provided, through interaction with agemates, excellent conditions for maintaining high levels of aggression. The social significance of these findings has been underscored by Buehler, Patterson, and Furniss (1966), who found similar effects of peer reinforcement on socially deviant behavior among institutionalized delinquent girls.

Thus peer reinforcement may serve to maintain or increase aggressive behavior. It has also been shown, however, that extinction of the individual child's aggressive behavior through nonreinforcement by adults is accompanied by concurrent change in peer interaction. These changes in the behavior of the peer group apparently support the extinction of the child's aggression. Indeed, it is sometimes difficult to institute ordinary reversal procedures in behavior modification studies dealing with aggression. These difficulties appear to be due partly to changes that have taken place in contingencies of peer reinforcement (Scott, Burton, and Yarrow, 1967).

Contingencies of peer reinforcement may also be manipulated effectively by the teachers or supervisors of children's groups. Wahler (1967) selected five nursery school children and established baseline rates for a number of different response classes. Response classes associated with high frequencies of contingent peer reinforcement were then identified for three children. Reponses associated with unusually low rates of peer reinforcement were identified for the other two children. Consider, first, the procedure for the "high-rate" children: the experimenter explained to the peer group that he wanted the children to ignore the subject when the selected behavior occurred; the peer group was also told, however, to respond to all other classes of behavior. Observations were conducted during this experimental phase and through a reversal period during which the contingencies prevailing in the baseline period were reestablished. The two "low-rate" subjects were treated somewhat differently. Their peers were instructed to increase the frequency with which they attended to the subject whenever the selected behavior occurred. A reversal phase was attempted with only one of these two subjects.

The results were consistent across the five subjects. First, the children's peers were able to use attention selectively. Second, behavior change in the selected response class occurred during the experimental phase for each of the five subjects. Finally, reversal of this change (instituted for only four subjects) produced a shift toward the rates of responding that had prevailed during the baseline period. Patterson and Brodsky (1966) have described another instance in which the peer group was used to modify the deviant behavior of one 5-year-old boy.

In sum, then, direct reinforcement from peers is a potent form of social influence during childhood. The effects of such social influence are evident in very early childhood. In addition, very young children can serve effectively as the confederates of teachers and experimenters in bringing about behavior change through this medium.

PEER VERSUS ADULT INFLUENCES

How do peer influences and adult influences combine to affect children's socialization? Research suggests that influences from these two sources are both additive and interactive in their effects on children's behavior. In many instances, the norms of the peer group buttress those influences emanating from the adult culture. On the other hand, peer norms are preeminent in some situations and adult influences prevail in others.

The issue of *cross-pressures* has had considerable research attention. Some studies have been addressed to the simple hypothesis that responsiveness to adult influences wanes during childhood as contact with peers increases. This is not the only important question in this area, however. We also need to know how peer and adult influences combine to affect the child's behavior. For example, we need to know how the child's experiences with one source of influence determine the nature of his responsiveness to the other. We also need a much more complete analysis of the manner in which situational factors affect responsiveness to cross-pressures. Research has already shown that the cross-pressures "problem" is not as central in child development as it has been thought to be. Responsiveness to normative influence from peers increases during childhood but it is doubtful that most children experience great conflict as a result; peer values tend to be basically consonant with parental values. Adolescence, in particular, is probably not the stormy period of cross-pressure that tradition suggests.

Research concerning the peer versus adult problem is fragmented. Samples have been drawn from widely differing age groups. There are no longitudinal studies in this area. Piecing the evidence together, however, we arrive at one main conclusion. The child's behavior under cross-pressure from peers and from adults depends on the situation and the social norms in question. It is not correct to speak of "peer-dominated" or "adult-dominated" periods in children's development, at least after early childhood.

The concordance with which children conform to *both* peer and adult influences has been investigated in very few instances. Perhaps the most extensive study of this problem was conducted by Stukát (1958). A battery of tests was administered to two groups of Swedish children, 9 and 11 years of age, as well as to one group of young adults. The battery included tests of auditory, olfactory, visual, and tactile suggestibility; suggestibility in choosing among interpretations of Rorschach cards; body sway; progressive weights; cojudge suggestions of perceptual discriminations; majority suggestions on artistic judgments; perceptual illusions; and so forth. Responsiveness to peer influences was measured in some of the tests, whereas adults served as influence sources in others. The data were then factor analyzed. One factor emerging from this analysis was labeled "primary suggestibility." Although responsiveness to adults was a common element in this type of conformity, all of the behaviors involved responsiveness to unobtrusive and monotonous verbal suggestions. Thus the nature of the behavior, rather than the source of influence, probably determined the emergence of this factor. Indeed, the factor may be called "hypnotizability."

A second factor emerging from this analysis involved yielding to *both* peer and adult sources of social pressure. "Secondary suggestibility" was characterized by a tendency for the subject to yield to more obvious influence from the experimenter, from a cojudge, or from a peer group. The emergence of this factor suggests that responsiveness to peer influences may be part of a generalized constellation of attributes that can be labeled "responsiveness to suggestion" or "conformity-proneness" (Krech et al., 1962). The possibility that susceptibility to peer influences is embedded in a constellation of attributes that also includes susceptibility to adult influences is supported by the data of Crandall et al. (1958). A correlation of .51 was obtained between peer compliance among nursery school children and compliance to adults. This correlation rose to .76 among 6- to 8-year-olds, indicating substantial common variance in yielding to these two sources of social influence.

Evidence concerning the existence of concordance in adult values and peer values is supplied by Langworthy's (1959) study of the relation between the status hierarchy in a community and peer influences in the local high school. Freshmen and juniors were asked to name those students who influenced them most. Then the important status elements in the community were identified. These included social class, ethnicity, and religion. This hierarchy is described by the following rank-ordering: Upper-Class Yankee Protestant, Upper-Class Yankee Catholic, Lower-Class Yankee Protestant, Lower-Class Polish Catholic, and Lower-Class Greek Orthodox. Examination of the social influence data for the high school students indicated significant concordance between the rank-ordering of status factors in the community and the influence hierarchy in the peer group.

Concordant parent and child values are revealed by the results of several other studies. Friends are selected on a basis that is usually consistent with parent attitudes (Westley and Elkin, 1956). Further, Douvan and Adelson (1966) found that when important decisions are involved, most adolescents tend to seek advice and opinions from parents rather than from peers. Job aspirations appear to be influenced concordantly by peers and by parents.

Adolescents appear to desire harmonious relations with adults (Lucas and Horrocks, 1960). A sample of 200 adolescents took a 90-item "needs test." The following results are of major interest: (1) a clearly defined *recognition-acceptance* factor emerged which indicated a broad need for acceptance from both adults and like sex peers; (2) a factor emerged indicating the salience of independence from adults, but still another factor was composed of items reflecting a need to conform to adult expectations. Thus the primacy of the peer group in the need structure of

U.S. adolescents is not clearly confirmed by these data; peers are important, but their influence does not override other social relations during this period.

Age differences in general attitudes toward adults and peers have been studied among elementary and high school boys and girls (Harris and Tseng, 1957). The attitudes of 3000 children, ranging from the third to the twelfth grade, were assessed by means of an incomplete sentence technique. Differences between attitudes toward parents and attitudes toward peers were not computed within age groups. Rather, trends across age groups were studied. First, attitudes toward both parents and peers were more favorable than unfavorable at all ages. The percentage of subjects reporting positive attitudes toward parents declined somewhat during middle childhood, probably due to fewer instances of nonrealistic forms of appraisal (e.g., "my mommy is the greatest mommy in all the world"). There was an increase, however, in the reporting of positive attitudes toward parents during the last three years of high school. This was due primarily to a marked increase in positive attitudes toward fathers. There was no overall increase in favorability of attitudes toward peers. Attitudes toward same- and opposite-sex peers fluctuated, but there is no picture in these results of increasing rejection of parents or increasing general acceptance of peers during the middle childhood and adolescent years.

Some evidence concerning alienation from parents was found by Witryol and Calkins (1958). Responses of 720 rural school children to social value questionnaires revealed an increase, from grade 4 to grade 12, in the frequency with which dares or challenges to authority-figures were endorsed. Peer aggression declined, however, after grade 9. There may be a consistent bias, however, in the extent to which both adults and peers perceive this alienation. Hess and Goldblatt (1957) reported that: (1) adolescents perceived a relatively greater status difference between themselves and adults than did their parents; (2) adolescents believed that the average adult generally deprecates teenagers, whereas parents believed that teenagers have unrealistically high opinions of themselves; (3) the parents also anticipated that teenagers have a selective tendency to undervalue adults.

Thus the extent of adolescent alienation from adults is dependent on the frame of reference of the perceiver.

Neiman (1954) explored the similarities existing between children and their parents and their peers in attitudes toward femininity. Subjects were drawn from urban schools and each furnished information concerning his own attitudes, the perceived attitudes of his parents, and the perceived attitudes of his peers. There was a significant divergence between "own" attitudes and the attitudes of both parents and peers among 11- to 13-year-olds, indicating that the beliefs of neither reference group were completely assimilated. By 15 to 18 years, however, the difference between own- and peer-attitudes was no longer significant, although the difference between own- and parent-attitudes remained so. This suggests a period of conflict in adolescence concerning this type of norm. Young adults (20 to 24 years of age), on the other hand, showed no significant divergence with parents of the same sex nor with peers, even though attitudes remained different from parents of the opposite sex. By young adulthood, then, discordance in values between children and parents is declining, and this trend is consistent with the increased evaluation of parents during late adolescence found by Harris and Tseng (1957).

The foregoing data suggest that even though considerable concordance exists in adult and peer influences on the child, discordance also occurs in some areas. Other research shows that children differentiate between adults and peers as anchoring points for behavior beginning in early childhood. Among elementary school children, both suggestibility in the autokinetic situation and the modeling of self-reward patterns have been found to be greater when the influence source is an adult as opposed to a peer (Bandura and Kupers, 1964; Jakubczak and Walters, 1959). Hicks (1965), however, reported that preschool children more frequently imitated aggressive male peer models than they imitated adult models or aggressive female peers (immediately after exposure). Considering these findings as a whole, it appears that the relative influence of peers, as contrasted to adults, depends upon the type of behavior that is involved. For example, children probably perceive striking a Bobo doll (Hicks) as more appropriate behavior for a child than for an adult and also more appropriate for a boy than for a girl. If so, the effects of adults and peer models on the child's actions should vary accordingly—which they did. On the other hand, when the accuracy of perceptual judgments or resistance to temptation is involved (Bandura and Kupers; Jakubczak and Walters) an older and presumably wiser model appears to be chosen as the anchoring point for the child's actions.

In studies of older children and adolescents, the cross-pressures problem has been most frequently studied by means of inventory or questionnaire procedures. The results, however, follow the pattern described above. In some instances, discordance in adult and peer influences is evident. Differential yielding, however, is likely to be a function of the behavioral norm or the situation that is involved. That is, in some normative areas, children and adolescents yield primarily to adults; in others they yield primarily to peers.

Bowerman and Kinch (1959) explored the child's general "orientation" toward the family and toward peers among students ranging from the fourth to the tenth grade. A shift away from orientation toward the family occurred during these years—87% of the fourth graders were family-oriented, about 50% of the eighth graders, and 32% of the tenth graders. The greatest shift in the direction of peer orientation, however, involved decisions concerning who should be chosen as the subject's friends.

Brittain (1963) developed a 12-item questionnaire in which each item depicted a hypothetical parent-peer cross-pressure situation. One group of adolescent girls took the inventory twice; the parent and peer pressures were associated with *different* norms on the two administrations of the inventory. That is, each norm was associated once with parent pressure and once with peer pressure. A control group also took the test twice but, for this group, the parent and peer pressures were associated with the same norms on both inventories. The shift in choices from first to second test was greater among the experimental subjects than among the controls on 11 of the 12 items. When status-norms and identity issues were salient in the items, shift toward peer-endorsed norms took place; when future aspirations or achievement in school were salient, shifts to-

ward adult-endorsed alternatives occurred. Thus the responsiveness of adolescents to peer influence, as opposed to parental influence, was highly dependent on the area of judgment involved.

The preceding data help to clarify results obtained by Gaier and Collier (1960). Both U.S. and Finnish children reported that peers or siblings share the subject's own story preferences more frequently than do adults. Story preferences are probably perceived by children as norms appropriately governed by the peer group. Indication that the nature of the norm sometimes determines response to cross-pressures was also reported by Rose (1956). Among rural adolescents, social aspirations were regarded as more praiseworthy by friends than by parents, whereas success aspirations were more likely to be praised by parents. With respect to over a dozen other aspirations, however, there was no great discrepancy in the extent to which these adolescents perceived the attributes as more praiseworthy by either group.

Lippitt and Withey (1957) obtained a series of self-ratings from a group of boys, as well as ratings representing how the subjects thought that their parents and their peers would evaluate them. Most boys evaluated themselves more poorly than they thought others would. While the boys' own ratings and perceived father-ratings were not markedly discrepant, perceived mother-ratings were slightly more positive than the self-ratings. But the perceived peer-ratings were the most positive of all. These data suggest that the peer group may serve as a primary locus of self-esteem in children, an inference which is consistent with Brittain's findings concerning the peer group's salience with respect to status and identity issues.

Additive effects of concordance in parent and peer influences have been found by a number of investigators. First, upward mobility is greater when both peer and parent pressures are high than when pressure is high from one source only or low from both (Simpson, 1962). Next, Haller and Butterworth (1960) studied this problem, using all of the 17-year-old boys in Lenawee County, Michigan, as subjects. These individuals were grouped according to whether they reported high, medium, or low amounts of pressure from parents for high-status jobs and continuing education. Correlations were then computed between the aspiration-levels of pairs of best friends, separately according to whether the members of each pair had experienced similar or different degrees of parental pressure. Peer influence is suggested by the fact that 10 of the 12 subgroup correlations were positive. There was a tendency, however, for the friend-pair correlations to be highest when both peers had been subjected to similar amounts of parental achievement pressure. For example, between friends experiencing medium pressure, this correlation was .51 for occupational aspirations and .47 for educational aspirations. Correlations were also of this general magnitude when friends had both experienced high parental pressure. The correlations were sharply reduced, however, among pairs who had both experienced low parental pressure. Hence, behavioral similarity between children who are friends is maximized when they have experienced similar forms of parental influence; shared *absence* of parental pressure, however, does not have this same effect.

Coleman (1961), in his study of high school social systems, reported both consonance and dissonance between parent-child and child-child pressures. Choice of clubs and participation in similar organized functions with peers were not found in the face of parental disapproval. Conflicting cross-pressures also were apparent, however, particularly in the case of bright girls. When the parents and teachers of such girls strongly endorsed doing well in school (as frequently occurred) but the attitudes of the peer culture were such as to equate brilliance in school with "being a drag," the girl's motivation to do well in school was typically lowered. Hallworth (1953) also found that when the norms of the peer group are not compatible with adult norms, a high proportion of absenteeism and school drop-out occurs.

Rosen (1955) studied the attitudes of 50 Jewish adolescents concerning the use of kosher meat. Each subject's major peer group was identified and his intentions to observe the practice of eating kosher meat were ascertained. The observance practices of the subjects' parents and peers were also surveyed. When either the parents or the peer group were observant, there was a greater tendency for the subject to be observant than when both groups were not. The strongest relation between the group norms and the child's attitudes occurred when the attitudes of both parents and the peer group were homogeneous, either for or against the food practice. When the parent and peer group conflicted as to practice, the child was most likely to resemble that group which served him as a reference group. When attitudes conflicted within one group, the adolescent was most likely to agree with the attitudes of the other group; this tendency was stronger when the peer group was not in conflict than when the parent group was consistent. These data clearly show the additive effects of parent and peer pressures on adolescent behavior. They also show, however, that the effects of discordant pressure may be accurately predicted only when the reference relation to the influence source is also known. Rose's (1956) research also indicates the importance of the reference relation in predicting a child's responsiveness to cross-pressure from parents and peers. Rural high school students reported aspirations and values that most closely resembled whichever of these influence sources that constituted his primary reference group.

The child's family history influences his response to parent versus peer cross-pressures. Brittain (1966) studied ninth- and tenth-grade girls, employing age and sex of the child's siblings as independent variables. Using his *Cross-Pressures Test*, he found that sex of sibling had a significant effect on conformity, but birth order did not. Girls with brothers tended toward parent conformity, while girls with sisters tended toward peer conformity. It is possible, of course, to interpret the data as indicating that girls with sisters manifest greater sibling rivalry and hostility to parents than girls with brothers; such conditions could precipitate a greater shift to peers as a primary reference group. The data are also in accord, however, with Parsons and Bales' (1955) hypothesis that family and peer influences are complementary. That is, siblings of the same sex may constitute a closer analogue to the peer group than siblings of the opposite sex. Related data are reported by Schmuck (1963), who found that college women with sisters were more likely to defy conventional social values than were women with brothers. If defiance of ac-

cepted values can be interpreted as indication
of an antiparental orientation, then these results confirm those of Brittain.

Family size also conceivably may affect
children's orientations toward their peers.
Bowerman and Kinch (1959), for example,
found that children from families with more
than four children shifted their orientation
toward peers more rapidly during middle
childhood than did children from small families. In another study (Rose, 1956), rural
high school students who had no siblings or
few siblings were more likely to choose a single chum as a primary referent, whereas
children from large families were more likely
to choose larger, more organized groups of
peers as their primary reference group. Within the family, then, the presence of siblings
(and possibly their sex) seems to serve as
a basis for an orientation toward peers.
Whether the child generalizes his feelings
toward family members to peers or whether
the child in large families orients toward
peers in order to compensate for lack of parental attention is not, of course, revealed by
these data.

The relation between family adjustment
and maintenance of the family as a reference
group was explored by Bowerman and Kinch
(1959). Holding adjustment to the peer
group constant, it was found that degree of
family orientation was directly related to the
adequacy of family adjustment. Thus it would
appear that when adjustment toward the family is favorable, children maintain a close
relation with this group even though the reference function of the peer group and its
influence increases during childhood. Devereux (1965; 1966) also found that adult-
orientation, as opposed to peer orientation,
was positively related to family warmth and
supportiveness. In addition, this investigator
found that both English and U.S. children
who joined gangs came from homes which
were either highly punitive or highly permissive. Children who came from moderately
controlling homes spent relatively more time
with parents, stayed close to home, and preferred the company of one or two friends
rather than the company of gangs.

One determinant of preference for the peer
norm, as opposed to an adult norm, is the
degree of interpersonal attraction existing between the child and his peers. Actually, re-

search on this question is sparse. Kudirka
(1965) found, among college women, that
susceptibility to the influence of a peer confederate who endorsed defiance of authority
depended on the subject's liking of the confederate. Further, Gragey (1960) has reported that the social power of the influence
source determines the extent to which resistance to authority will be expressed. In his
study, fifth graders were exposed to a peer
confederate who responded to the control
techniques of a new teacher by being either
defiant or submissive. When the confederate
submitted to the teacher's requests, the other
children perceived the new teacher as more
capable, more powerful, and fairer than when
the confederate was defiant. But most important, the magnitude of these effects varied
directly with the social power of the confederate. That is, the effects of defiance produced significantly less positive evaluations
of the teacher when the peer possessed high
social power than when he was known to
possess low power in the peer group.

The cultural milieu may also be a determinant of differences in the extent to which
adults and peers influence the behavior of
the child. Boehm (1959) contrasted 29 Swiss
with 40 U.S. children and found that the
Swiss children had less confidence in their
peers and were generally less dependent on
them than were the U.S. children. Further,
the Swiss subjects continued, until a later age,
to believe in the omniscience of adult authorities and generally did not desire independence from adult supervision as early as
did their U. S. counterparts. One would imagine that this difference may derive from earlier
peer contacts among the American children.

Spiro's (1958) description of socialization
in an Israeli *kibbutz* supports the hypothesis
that age of contact with peers may enhance
the responsiveness of children to peers relative to their responsiveness to adults. First,
the institutional use of the nursery in very
early infancy promoted early reaction to peers
(contagious laughing and babbling by 5
months of age). But Spiro also reports that
peer esteem was the strongest incentive for
producing social conformity in the older *kibbutz*-reared child. The peer group was described as having a major sanctioning function
and, relative to adults, was particularly potent in influencing behavior through praise

for good behavior and through modeling. Spiro's account, however, contains no evidence, even in this peer-oriented culture, of antagonism or conflict produced by peer-parent cross-pressures. Perhaps this culture does not promote a strong early identification with parents and hence no intergeneration rivalry emerges. Extensive cross-cultural evidence concerning this hypothesis, however, is lacking.

A series of cross-cultural comparisons of responsiveness to cross-pressures has been conducted at Cornell University (Devereux, 1965, 1966; Bronfenbrenner, Devereux, Suci, and Rodgers, 1965; Bronfenbrenner, 1967). A "dilemmas test" was devised which consisted of 30 conflict situations, each of which pitted an adult-endorsed norm against peer pressure to deviate from this norm. This test was given to samples of sixth-grade children in England, Germany, the Soviet Union, and the United States. Cultural differences were marked in children's responses on the dilemmas test. For example, the greatest resistance to deviant peer pressure occurred among the Russian children, significantly less resistance was shown by the U. S. and German children, while the English children proved to be most peer-oriented of all. In all of these cultures, boys showed less conformity to the adult-norms than did girls.

The sources of these differences are not entirely clear, but further analyses showed that, compared to U. S. children, the English sixth-graders spent less time with their parents, less time alone, and more time with their peers. The argument that amount of peer contact is a determinant of peer-orientation is strengthened, too, since in England, Germany, and the United States there was a negative correlation between time spent with peers (particularly time spent with gangs) and level of adult orientation.[13] Other cultural differences in childhood socialization also seem to be related to the manner in which the child responds to cross-pressures. For example, guilt and anxiety were positively correlated with adult-orientation within the German, American, and English samples. Further, the English children, as a whole, reported feeling less guilty when they deviated as a result of

peer pressure than did the American or German subjects. Therefore it would appear that high contact with peers and absence of guilt operate additively to produce ready conformity to peer influences during adolescence.

One limitation to these particular studies is that the dilemmas test always pits the peer group against generally accepted cultural values. One would suppose, based on Brittain's findings, that the results might be different if based on dilemmas that pitted *approved* adult and peer norms against each other or that pitted *disapproved* norms against each other.

The Cornell studies, however, reveal certain cultural differences in the way that the situation affects responses to these particular dilemmas. The Russian and U. S. children took comparable test items under three different conditions: (1) a base condition, in which the children were told that their answers would be kept strictly confidential; (2) an adult-exposure condition, in which they were told that their responses would be posted on a chart to be seen later by their parents and teachers; (3) a peer-exposure condition, in which the subjects were told that their responses would be posted for viewing by their classmates. In both cultures, the adult-exposure condition produced more conformity to the socially approved norm than was evident in the base condition. On the other hand, the peer-exposure condition produced shifts in *different* directions in these two cultures. U. S. children moved in the direction of greater conformity to the deviant peer norms. The Russian children, however, exhibited increased adherence to the socially approved, adult-endorsed values. In addition, the Russian children shifted more under the adult-exposure condition than the American children; the amount of shift under peer-exposure, however, was greater among the U. S. children. Brofenbrenner (1967) suggests that these cultural differences in responsiveness to adult versus peer pressure may reflect the greater autonomy of the peer group in U. S. culture and the fact that the peer group represents a direct extension of adult socialization influences in Russian society.

In all of these studies, the composition of the school classroom was a determinant of response to the dilemmas test. Some classrooms appeared to be more peer-oriented than

---

[13] Corresponding data are lacking for Soviet children.

others; these differences were most clearly apparent when the dilemmas test was given under either base or peer-exposure conditions. Devereux (1965) also reported that classrooms with strict teachers appeared to be more peer-oriented than classrooms with more permissive and supportive teachers. Further, the relation between peer conformity and amount of contact with peers was strongest in those classrooms that were peer-oriented. Finally, adult-orientation was lowered when the test was given with the teacher absent rather than when he was present. Taken together, then, these data suggest that both the type of adult influences that are present and the prevailing norms of the peer group are determinants of how a child responds to cross-pressures for conformity.

The subcultural milieu may also alter the relative impact of peers and adults on the child's behavior. Maas (1951) has reported, for example, that surveillance of and interest in children declined earlier among lower-class parents than among parents who are members of the "core culture" (a finding which has been widely replicated). The types of social interactions with peers also differed in the two groups of preadolescents studied: the peer relations of the lower-class children were marked by intense security-seeking. Either the child seemed to identify with the power needs of his peers in order to establish his own status or he seemed to be excessive and desperate in his dependence on the physical presence of peers for succorance and direction.

In sum, research does not indicate that adult influences and peer influences on children's behavior never come into conflict. Close inspection, however, reveals that the determinants of the way in which children respond to cross-pressures are diverse. In some instances, the values and behaviors which are salient in the situation appear to be crucial. In other instances, the attractiveness of the peer influence, the amount of contact with peers, the extent to which the peer group serves a reference function, and the adequacy of family adjustment are key factors. The broader milieu, through the timing and extensiveness with which peer contacts are provided, may also enhance the salience of peer influences.

In general, however, peer influences are not likely to generate unremitting conflict for children. This conception of the child appears to have been exaggerated in both the popular and the scientific literature. Douvan and Adelson (1966) have offered several hypotheses concerning why the cross-pressures problem has been overemphasized:

To begin with, the observer's attention is likely to be captured by the more conspicuous enclaves of adolescent culture: to the lower class youngster, who is quickly alienated from the family . . . and to the upper-middle class group. . . . In the "core culture," parental authority is in greater evidence.

Another reason may lie in the fact that the adolescent culture has undergone genuine changes in recent years, most of these in the direction of increased influence and visibility. Many writers, lay and professional alike, have exaggerated the extent of these changes in the very process of highlighting and documenting them. . . . What we have here, we believe, is something in the nature of a cultural antilag, that is, an alertness to the recent or emergent, an otherwise laudable quickness of vision which may lead the social scientist not only to accentuate the new, but also to exaggerate its scope, power, and significance.

Finally, we may be finding it hard to appraise the actual nature and degree of peer group influence because our perception of it is affected and distorted by the kinds of attention given to adolescence in the mass media. . . . The mass media, by highlighting the simple or spectacular issues and instances, make the central issues of the dispute that much harder to recognize or understand (1966, pp. 198–199).

No one would seriously suggest that there is never dissonance between adult and peer influences on children's behavior. On the other hand, considerable consonance is evident. Many factors, including the nature of the child's early socialization and the characteristics of the influence situation itself, must be taken into account in order to assess the impact on the child of the dissonance that exists.

CONCLUSION

Several general comments can be made concerning the status of research on peer interaction and social organization. First, empirical work has been fragmented. Emphasis on certain problems has been disproportionately heavy; other problems have almost been ignored. For example, the factors associated with sociometric status have probably been overstudied, but the topography of peer-group interaction among 6-, 7- and 8-year-olds has not been thoroughly explored. Group formation has been studied extensively with preadolescents and adolescents, but hardly at all with first-graders. The relative impact on the child of peer influences, as compared to adult influences, has not had the concentrated research attention that this problem deserves. Research on problem-solving in children's groups is scarce. Our knowledge of peer influences and group behavior among girls is appallingly weak. Systematic research concerning play behavior is badly needed. The functional contributions of play to children's development have been emphasized within several theoretical frameworks (e.g., Erikson, 1950; Gilmore, 1967; Maccoby, 1959; Piaget, 1951). Empirical studies have been primarily descriptive (see, for example, Millar, 1968; and Sutton-Smith, 1967), however, and we know relatively little about either motivational factors in play behavior or the role of play in socialization.

Second, there has been a preoccupation with a relatively narrow range of methods. The informal peer group is almost always approached with differential research strategies; the most widely used weapon in this field is the correlation coefficient. It goes without saying that correlational data have clarified many issues concerning children's behavior with their peers. Nevertheless, the extent to which research in this field has been dominated by differential methods is troublesome. There is no reason, presently, why many issues of causation in the field of peer relations would not yield to the experimental method.

Third, laboratory experiments are rarely replicated or extended to the informal peer group. The settings employed in peer influence research have been lifelike and appropriate to the problems studied, but it is clear that peer behavior is enormously susceptible to situational variation. It is not easy to establish, *a priori*, the limits within which findings may be generalized.

Fourth, peer relations research has paid little attention to developmental problems. Conformity behavior is probably the best-understood area in peer relations when considered from a developmental standpoint. Even here, however, the data consist almost entirely of age differences. Information concerning the inputs that are responsible for age differences in conformity behavior consists mainly of fragments. Consequently, there is urgent need for integrating broad-based theories of behavioral development—be they cognitive, psychodynamic, or learning theories —with the classic theories of group dynamics in future studies of peer interaction in childhood.

Fifth, the theorizing that characterizes this field is heterogeneous. There is no parsimonious set of principles which can provide a basis for integrating all of the facts we have mentioned. There is no paucity of relevant theorizing but enormous effort is needed to extend and give order to the present findings.

Finally, an integration of the literature in several other areas would help to clarify the current status of research on peer influences in childhood. For example, anthropological studies contain extensive amounts of descriptive data concerning peer relations in other cultures. This information, however, is scattered in the ethnographic archives and no one has attempted to bring it all together. It is clear to the most casual student of this literature that peer influences impinge upon children at different times and with differing extensiveness across cultures (see Bronfenbrenner, 1962). At present, however, it is impossible to make precise normative statements concerning the cross-cultural variations that exist in children's encounters with peers. It is reasonable to expect that cultural differences in peer socialization should be associated with variations in children's personality and social development. We do not know however, that this is so. A compilation of existing ethnographic material would serve two purposes. It would furnish a broader perspective for assessing the material reviewed in the present chapter, and, more, importantly, it might stimulate cross-societal studies, which are badly needed.

The literature concerning responsiveness to agemates in infrahuman organisms also needs to be subjected to large-scale integration and analysis. Some of the recent work with the Rhesus monkey has been cited in the present chapter. The comparative literature, however, contains many detailed accounts of agemate interaction, particularly in the area of play behavior (see Jewell and Loizos, 1966). Again, the data are primarily descriptive. Assessment of these findings, however, would constitute a giant step toward understanding the unique behavioral consequences of the young organism's contact with agemates.

There is the need, then, both for an intensification of creative research on developmental problems in children's peer relations and for data which will furnish a broader perspective on these problems. This latter objective can be achieved only by examining peer influences within many different cultural and species contexts.

References

Abel, H., and Sahinkaya, R. Emergence of sex and race friendship preferences. *Child Dev.*, 1962, **33**, 939–943.

Alexander, C. N. Consensus and mutual attraction in natural cliques: a study of adolescent drinkers. *Am. J. Sociol.*, 1964, **69**, 395–403.

Alexander, T., and Alexander, M. A study of personality and social status. *Child Dev.*, 1952, **23**, 207–213.

Allen, V. L. Situational factors in conformity. In L. Berkowitz (Ed.), *Advances in experimental social psychology*. Vol. 2. New York: Academic Press, 1965. Pp. 133–175.

Allport, F. H. *Social psychology*. Cambridge, Mass.: Houghton Mifflin, 1924.

Allport, G. W. The historical background of modern social psychology. In G. Lindzey (Ed.), *Handbook of social psychology*. Vol. 2. Cambridge, Mass.: Addison-Wesley, 1954. Pp. 3–56.

Almack, J. C. The influence of intelligence on the selection of associates. *Sch. Society*, 1922, **16**, 529–530.

Altman, I., and McGinnies, E. Interpersonal perception and communication in discussion groups of varied attitudinal composition. *J. abnorm. soc. Psychol.*, 1960, **60**, 390–395.

Amundson, C. L. Increasing interpersonal relations in the high school with the aid of sociometric procedures. *Group Psychother.*, 1953, **6**, 183–188.

Aronfreed, J. *Conduct and conscience: the socialization of internalized control over behavior.* New York: Academic Press, 1968.

Ausubel, D. P. Socioempathy as a function of sociometric status in an adolescent group. *Hum. Relat.*, 1955, **8**, 75–84.

Avigdor, R. The development of stereotypes as a result of group interaction. Unpublished doctoral dissertation, New York University, 1952.

Azrin, N. H., and Lindsley, O. R. The reinforcement of cooperation between children. *J. abnorm. soc. Psychol.*, 1956, **52**, 100–102.

Baldwin, W. K. The social position of the educable mentally retarded child in the regular grades in the public schools. *Except. Child.*, 1958, **25**, 106–108.

Bandura, A., Grusec, J. E., and Menlove, F. L. Vicarious extinction of avoidance behavior. *J. pers. soc. Psychol.*, 1967, **5**, 16–23.

Bandura, A., and Kupers, C. J. Transmission of patterns of self-reinforcement through modeling. *J. abnorm. soc. Psychol.*, 1964, **69**, 1–9.

Bandura, A., and Menlove, F. L. Factors determining vicarious extinction of avoidance behavior through symbolic modeling. *J. pers. soc. Psychol.*, 1968, **8**, 99–108.

Bandura, A., Ross, D., and Ross, S. A. Imitation of film-mediated aggressive models. *J. abnorm. soc. Psychol.*, 1963, **66**, 3–11.

Bandura, A., and Walters, R. H. *Social learning and personality development.* New York: Holt, Rinehart and Winston, 1963.

Barbe, W. B. Peer relationships of children of different intelligence levels. *Sch. Society,* 1954, **80,** 60–62.

Baron, D. Personal-social characteristics and classroom social status: a sociometric study of 5th and 6th grade girls. *Sociometry,* 1951, **14,** 32–41.

Barron, F. An ego-strength scale which predicts response to psychotherapy. *J. consult. Psychol.,* 1953, **17,** 327–333. (a)

Barron, F. Some personality correlates of independence of judgment. *J. Personality,* 1953, **21,** 287–297. (b)

Becker, S. W., and Carroll, J. Ordinal position and conformity. *J. abnorm. soc. Psychol.,* 1962, **65,** 129–131.

Becker, S. W., Lerner, M. J., and Carroll, J. Conformity as a function of birth order, payoff, and type of group pressure. *J. abnorm. soc. Psychol.,* 1964, **69,** 318–323.

Becker, S. W., Lerner, M. J., and Carroll, J. Conformity as a function of birth order and type of group pressure: a verification. *J. pers. soc. Psychol.,* 1966, **3,** 242–244.

Beker, J. The influence of school camping on the self-concepts and social relationships of sixth grade children. *J. educ. Psychol.,* 1960, **51,** 352–356.

Berenda, R. W. *The influence of the group on the judgments of children.* New York: King's Crown Press, 1950.

Bjerstedt, A. Informational and non-informational determinants of nationality stereotypes. *Acta Psychol.,* 1961, **18,** 11–16.

Blood, R. O., and Livant, W. P. The use of space within the cabin group. *J. soc. Iss.,* 1957, **13,** 47–53.

Boehm, L. The development of independence: a comparative study. *Child Dev.,* 1957, **28,** 85–92.

Bogen, I. Pupil-teacher rapport and the teacher's awareness of status structures within the group. *J. educ. Sociol.,* 1954, **28,** 104–114.

Bonney, M. E. A study of the relation of intelligence, family size, and sex differences with mutual friendships in the primary grades. *Child Dev.,* 1942, **13,** 79–100.

Bonney, M. E. The relative stability of social, intellectual, and academic status in grades II to IV, and the interrelationships between these various forms of growth. *J. educ. Psychol.,* 1943, **34,** 88–102.

Bonney, M. E. Relationships between social success, family size, socioeconomic home background, and intelligence among school children in grades III to V. *Sociometry,* 1944, **7,** 26–39.

Bonney, M. E. Choosing between the sexes on a sociometric measurement. *J. soc. Psychol.,* 1954, **39,** 99–114.

Bonney, M. E., and Nicholson, E. L. Comparative social adjustments of elementary school pupils with and without preschool training. *Child Dev.,* 1958, **29,** 125–133.

Bonney, M. E., and Powell, J. Differences in social behavior between sociometrically high and sociometrically low children. *J. educ. Res.,* 1953, **46,** 481–495.

Bondeau, E., Dales, R., and Connor, R. Relations of self-concept to 4-H club leadership. *Rur. Sociol.,* 1963, **28,** 413–418.

Borgatta, E. F., Cottrell, L. S., and Wilker, L. Initial expectation, group climate, and assessment of leaders and members. *J. soc. Psychol.,* 1959, **49,** 285–296.

Bowerman, C. E., and Kinch, J. W. Changes in family and peer orientation of children between the fourth and tenth grades. *Social Forces,* 1959, **37,** 206–211.

Bridges, K. M. B. A study of social development in early infancy. *Child Dev.,* 1933, **4**, 36–49.

Brittain, C. V. Adolescent choices and parent-peer cross-pressures. *Am. Sociol. Rev.,* 1963, **28**, 385–391.

Brittain, C. V. Age and sex of siblings and conformity toward parents versus peers in adolescence. *Child Dev.,* 1966, **37**, 709–714.

Broderick, C. B. Socio-sexual development in a suburban community. *J. Sex Res.,* 1966, **2**, 1–24.

Broderick, C. B. and Fowler, S. E. New patterns of relationships between the sexes among preadolescents. *Marr. family Liv.,* 1961, **23**, 27–30.

Bronfenbrenner, U. The measurement of sociometric status, structure and development. *Sociomet. Monogr.,* 1945, No. 6.

Bronfenbrenner, U. Soviet methods of character education: some implications for research. *Am. Psychol.,* 1962, **17**, 550–564.

Bronfenbrenner, U. Response to pressure from peers versus adults among Soviet and American school children. *Int. J. Psychol.,* 1967, **2**, 199–207.

Bronfenbrenner, U., Devereux, E. C., Suci, G. J., and Rodgers, R. R. Adults and peers as sources of conformity and autonomy. Unpublished manuscript, Cornell University, 1965.

Brown, A. M., Stafford, R. E., and Vandenberg, S. G. Twins: behavioral differences. *Child Dev.,* 1967, **38**, 1055–1064.

Brown, A. W., and Hunt, R. G. Relations between nursery school attendance and teachers' ratings of some aspects of children's adjustment in kindergarten. *Child Dev.,* 1961, **32**, 585–596.

Brown, W. H., and Bond, L. B. Social stratification in a sixth grade class. *J. educ. Res.,* 1955, **48**, 539–543.

Buehler, R. E., Patterson, G. R., and Furness, J. M. The reinforcement of behavior in institutional settings. *Behav. res. Therapy,* 1966, **4**, 157–167.

Bühler, C. *The first year of life.* New York: John Day, 1930.

Byrne, D., and Griffitt, W. B. A developmental investigation of the law of attraction. *J. pers. soc. Psychol.,* 1966, **4**, 699–702.

Campbell, J. D., and Yarrow, M. R. Personal and situational variables in adaptation to change. *J. soc. Iss.,* 1958, **14**, 29–46.

Campbell, J. D., and Yarrow, M. R. Perceptual and behavioral correlates of social effectiveness. *Sociometry,* 1961, **24**, 1–20.

Cannon, K. L. The relationship of social acceptance to socioeconomic status and residence among high school students. *Rur. Sociol.,* 1957, **22**, 142–148.

Carmichael, L. (Ed.) *Manual of child psychology.* New York: Wiley, 1946.

Carmichael, L. (Ed.) *Manual of child psychology.* (2nd ed.) New York: Wiley, 1954.

Carrigan, W. C., and Julian, J. W. Sex and birth-order differences in conformity as a function of need affiliation arousal. *J. pers. soc. Psychol.,* 1966, **3**, 479–483.

Cartwright, D., and Zander, A. *Group dynamics.* (2nd ed.) Evanston, Ill.: Row, Peterson, 1960.

Cassel, R. N., and Saugstad, R. N. Level of aspiration and sociometric distance. *Sociometry,* 1952, **15**, 319–325.

Castle, M. Institution and non-institution children at school: the effects of social stresses on their relationships. *Hum. Relat.,* 1954, **7**, 349–366.

Centers, L., and Centers, R. Peer group attitudes toward the amputee child. *J. soc. Psychol.,* 1963, **61**, 127–132.

Challman, R. C. Factors influencing friendships among preschool children. *Child Dev.,* 1932, **3**, 146–158.

Charlesworth, R., and Hartup, W. W. Positive social reinforcement in the nursery school peer group. *Child Dev.*, 1967, **38**, 993–1002.

Chittenden, G. E. An experimental study in measuring and modifying assertive behavior in young children. *Monogr. soc. res. Child Dev.*, 1942, **7**, (1).

Clark, B. S. The acquisition and extinction of peer imitation in children. *Psychonom. Sci.*, 1965, **2**, 147–148.

Clark, K. B., and Clark. M. K. Racial identification and preference in Negro children. In G. E. Swanson, T. M. Newcomb, and E. L. Hartley (Eds.), *Readings in social psychology.* (2nd ed.) New York: Holt, 1952. Pp. 551–560.

Clarke, H. H., and Clarke, D. H. Social status and mental health of boys as related to their maturity, structural, and strength characteristics. *Res. Q. Am. Ass. Hlth. phys. Educ.*, 1961, **32**, 326–334.

Clarke, H. H., and Greene, W. H. Relationships between personal-social measures applied to 10-year-old boys. *Res. Q. Am. Ass. Hlth. phys. Educ.*, 1963, **34**, 288–298.

Clifford, E. Social visibility. *Child Dev.*, 1963, **34**, 799–808.

Cohen, D. J. Justin and his peers: an experimental analysis of a child's social world. *Child Dev.*, 1962, **33**, 697–717.

Cohn, T., Fisher, A., and Brown, V. Leadership and predicting attitudes of others. *J. soc. Psychol.*, 1961, **55**, 199–206.

Cohn, T., Yee, W., and Brown, V. Attitude change and interpersonal attraction. *J. soc. Psychol.*, 1961, **55**, 207–211.

Coleman, J. S. *The adolescent society.* Glencoe, Ill.: Free Press, 1961.

Commoss, H. H. Some characteristics related to social isolation of second grade children. *J. educ. Psychol.*, 1962, **53**, 38–42.

Cooley, C. H. *Social organization.* New York: Scribner, 1909.

Coons, M. O. Rosenzweig differences in reactions to frustration in children of high, low, and middle sociometric status. *Group Psychother.*, 1957, **10**, 60–63.

Costanzo, P. R., and Shaw, M. E. Conformity as a function of age level. *Child Dev.*, 1966, **37**, 967–975.

Cowen, E. L., Zax, M., Klein, R., Izzo, L. D., and Trost, M. A. Relation of anxiety in school children to school record, achievement, and behavioral measures. *Child Dev.*, 1965, **36**, 685–695.

Cox, S. H. Family background effects on personality development and social acceptance. Unpublished doctoral dissertation, Texas Christian University, 1966.

Crandall, V. J. Achievement. In H. W. Stevenson (Ed.), *Child psychology. The sixty-second yearbook of the National Society for the Study of Education.* Chicago: University of Chicago Press, 1963. Pp. 416–459.

Crandall, V. J., Orleans, S., Preston, A., and Rabson, A. The development of social compliance in young children. *Child Dev.*, 1958, **29**, 429–443.

Crane, A. R. Pre-adolescent gangs: a topological interpretation. *J. genet. Psychol.*, 1952, **81**, 113–124.

Criswell, J. H. Sociometric methods of measuring group preferences. *Sociometry*, 1943, **6**, 398–408.

Crutchfield, R. S. Conformity and character. *Am. Psychol.*, 1955, **10**, 191–198.

Dahlke, H. O. Determinants of sociometric relations among children in the elementary school. *Sociometry*, 1953, **16**, 327–338.

Davids, A. Stability of personal and social preferences in emotionally disturbed and normal children. *J. abnorm. soc. Psychol.*, 1964, **69**, 556–559.

Davids, A., and Parenti, A. N. Time orientation and interpersonal relations of emotionally disturbed and normal children. *J. abnorm. soc. Psychol.*, 1958, **57**, 299–305.

Davis, J. A. Correlates of sociometric status among peers. *J. educ. Res.*, 1957, **50**, 561–569.

Davitz, J. R. Social perception and sociometric choice in children. *J. abnorm. soc. Psychol.*, 1955, **50**, 173–176.

Dawe, H. C. Analysis of two hundred quarrels of preschool children. *Child Dev.*, 1934, **5**, 139–157.

Devereux, E. C. Socialization in cross-cultural perspective: a comparative study of England, Germany and the United States. Unpublished manuscript, Cornell University, 1965.

Devereux, E. C. Authority, guilt, and conformity to adult standards among German school children: a pilot experimental study. Unpublished manuscript, Cornell University, 1966.

Ditrichs, R., Simon, S., and Greene, B. Effect of vicarious scheduling on the verbal conditioning of hostility in children. *J. pers. soc. Psychol.*, 1967, **6**, 71–78.

Dodge, N., and Muench, G. A. Relationship of conformity and the need for approval in children. *Dev. Psychol.*, 1969, **1**, 67–68.

Douvan, E., and Adelson, J. *The adolescent experience.* New York: Wiley, 1966.

Dunnington, M. J. Behavioral differences of sociometric status groups in a nursery school. *Child Dev.*, 1957, **28**, 103–111. (a)

Dunnington, M. J. Investigation of areas of disagreement in sociometric measures of preschool children. *Child Dev.*, 1957, **28**, 93–102. (b)

Eisenman, R. Reducing prejudice by Negro-white contacts. *J. Negro Educ.*, 1965, **34**, 461–462.

Elkins, D. Some factors related to the choice status of ninety eighth-grade children in a school society. *Genet. psychol. Monogr.*, 1958, **58**, 207–272.

Emmerich, W. Continuity and stability in early social development. *Child Dev.*, 1964, **35**, 311–332.

Epstein, R., and Komorita, S. S. Parental discipline, stimulus characteristics of outgroups, and social distance in children. *J. pers. soc. Psychol.*, 1965, **2**, 416–420.

Epstein, R. C., and Komorita, S. S. Childhood prejudice as a function of parental ethnocentrism, punitiveness, and outgroup characteristics. *J. pers. soc. Psychol.*, 1966, **3**, 259–264. (a)

Epstein, R. C., and Komorita, S. S. Prejudice among Negro children as related to parental ethnocentrism and punitiveness. *J. pers. soc. Psychol.*, 1966, **4**, 643–677. (b)

Erikson, E. H. *Childhood and society.* New York: Norton, 1950.

Faigin, H. Social behavior of young children in the kibbutz. *J. abnorm. soc. Psychol.*, 1958, **56**, 117–129.

Faust, M. S. Developmental maturity as a determinant of prestige in adolescent girls. *Child Dev.*, 1960, **31**, 173–184.

Feinberg, M. R. Relation of background experiences to social acceptance. *J. abnorm. soc. Psychol.*, 1953, **48**, 206–214.

Feinberg, M. R. Stability of sociometric status in two adolescent class groups. *J. genet. Psychol.*, 1964, **104**, 83–87.

Feinberg, M. R., Smith, M., and Schmidt, R. An analysis of expressions used by adolescents of varying economic levels to describe accepted and rejected peers. *J. genet. Psychol.*, 1958, **93**, 133–148.

Ferguson, N. Peers as social agents. Unpublished masters thesis, University of Minnesota, 1964.

Fey, W. F. Acceptance by others and its relation to acceptance of self and others: a re-evaluation. *J. abnorm. soc. Psychol.*, 1955, **50**, 274–276.

Fischer, W. F. Sharing in preschool children as a function of amount and type of reinforcement. *Genet. psychol. Monogr.*, 1963, **68**, 219–245.

Flanders, N. A., and Havumaki, S. The effect of teacher-pupil contacts involving praise on the sociometric choices of students. *J. educ. Psychol.*, 1960, **51,** 65–68.

Flavell, J. H., Botkin, P. T., Fry, C. L., Wright, J. W., and Jarvis, P. E. *The development of role-taking and communication skills in children.* New York: Wiley, 1968.

Floyd, J. M. Effects of amount of reward and friendship status on the frequency of sharing in children. Unpublished doctoral dissertation, University of Minnesota, 1964.

Freud, A., and Dann, S. An experiment in group upbringing. In R. Eisler et al. (Eds.), *The psychoanalytic study of the child.* Vol. 6. New York: International Universities Press, 1951. Pp. 127–163.

Fry, C. L. A developmental examination of performance in a tacit coordination game situation. *J. pers. soc. Psychol.*, 1967, **5,** 277–281.

Furfey, P. H. Some factors influencing the selection of boys' "chums." *J. appl. Psychol.*, 1927, **11,** 47–51.

Gaier, E. L., and Collier, M. J. The latency-stage story preferences of American and Finnish children. *Child Dev.*, 1960, **31,** 431–451.

Gallagher, J. J. Peer acceptance of highly gifted children in elementary school. *Elem. sch. J.*, 1958, **58,** 465–470. (a)

Gallagher, J. J. Social status of children related to intelligence, propinquity, and social perception. *Elem. sch. J.*, 1958, **58,** 225–231. (b)

Gardner, E. F., and Thompson, G. G. Measuring and interpreting social relations. *Test service notebook*, No. 22. Yonkers, N. Y.: World Book, 1959.

Gelfand, D. M. The influence of self-esteem on rate of verbal conditioning and social matching behavior. *J. abnorm. soc. Psychol.*, 1962, **65,** 259–265.

Gellert, E. Stability and fluctuation in the power relationships of young children. *J. abnorm. soc. Psychol.*, 1961, **62,** 8–15.

Gewirtz, J. L. Succorance in young children. Unpublished doctoral dissertation, State University of Iowa, 1948.

Gibb, C. A. Leadership. In G. Lindzey (Ed.), *Handbook of social psychology.* Vol. 2. Cambridge, Mass.: Addison-Wesley, 1954. Pp. 877–920.

Gilmore, J. B. Play: a special behavior. In R. N. Haber (Ed.), *Current research in motivation.* New York: Holt, Rinehart and Winston, 1967. Pp. 343–355.

Goertzen, S. M. Factors relating to opinions of seventh grade children regarding the acceptability of certain behaviors in the peer group. *J. genet. Psychol.*, 1959, **94,** 29–34.

Gold, H. A. The importance of ideology in sociometric evaluation of leadership. *Group Psychother.*, 1962, **15,** 224–230.

Gold, M. Power in the classroom. *Sociometry*, 1958, **21,** 50–60.

Goldberg, M. H., and Maccoby, E. E. Children's acquisition of skill in performing a group task under two conditions of group formation. *J. pers. soc. Psychol.*, 1965, **2,** 898–902.

Goodlad, J. I. Some effects of promotion and non-promotion upon the social and personal adjustment of children. *J. exp. Educ.*, 1954, **22,** 301–328.

Goslin, P. A. Accuracy of self-perception and social acceptance. *Sociometry*, 1962, **25,** 283–296.

Gragey, W. J. Effects on classmates of a deviant student's power and response to teacher-exerted control techniques. *J. educ. Psychol.*, 1960, **51,** 1–8.

Greenberg, P. J. Competition in children: an experimental study. *Am. J. Psychol.*, 1932, **44,** 221–248.

Gronlund, N. E. The accuracy of teachers' judgments concerning the sociometric status of sixth grade pupils. *Sociometry*, 1950, **13**, 197–225; 329–357.

Gronlund, N. E. Relation between sociometric status of pupils and teachers' preferences for or against having them in class. *Sociometry*, 1953, **16**, 142–150.

Gronlund, N. E. Generality of sociometric status over criteria in measurement of social acceptability. *Elem. sch. J.*, 1955, **56**, 173–176. (a)

Gronlund, N. E. The relative ability of home-room teachers and special-subject teachers to judge the social acceptability of pre-adolescent pupils. *J. educ. Res.*, 1955, **48**, 381–391. (b)

Gronlund, N. E. The relative stability of classroom social status with unweighted and weighted sociometric choices. *J. educ. Psychol.*, 1955, **46**, 345–354. (c)

Gronlund, N. E., and Anderson, L. Personality characteristics of socially accepted, socially neglected and socially rejected junior high school pupils. *Educ. Admin. Supervis.*, 1957, **43**, 329–338.

Gronlund, N. E., and Barnes, F. P. The reliability of social-acceptability scores using various sociometric choice limits. *Elem. sch. J.*, 1956, **57**, 153–157.

Gronlund, N. E., and Whitney, A. P. The relation between teachers' judgments of pupils' sociometric status and intelligence. *Elem. sch. J.*, 1958, **59**, 264–268.

Grosser, D., Polansky, N., and Lippitt, R. A laboratory study of behavioral contagion. *Hum. Relat.*, 1951, **4**, 115–142.

Grossman, B., and Wrighter, J. The relationship between selection-rejection and intelligence, social status, and personality among sixth-grade children. *Sociometry*, 1948, **11**, 346–355.

Gump, P., Schoggen, P., and Redl, F. The camp milieu and its immediate effects *J. Soc. Iss.*, 1957, **13**, 40–46.

Hagman, E. P. The companionships of preschool children. *U. Iowa Studies in Child Welfare*, 1933, **I**, No. 4.

Haines, A. C. Children's perception of membership roles in problem-solving groups: an exploratory study of interaction process in a third grade. Unpublished doctoral dissertation, University of Illinois, 1952.

Haller, A. O., and Butterworth, C. E. Peer influences on levels of occupational and educational aspiration. *Social Forces*, 1960, **38**, 289–295.

Hallworth, H. J. Group relationships among grammar school boys and girls between the ages of eleven and sixteen years. *Sociometry*, 1953, **16**, 39–70.

Handlon, B. J., and Gross, P. The development of sharing behavior. *J. abnorm. soc. Psychol.*, 1959, **59**, 425–428.

Hanley, C. Physique and reputation of junior high school boys. *Child Dev.*, 1951, **22**, 247–260.

Hare, A. P. A study of interaction and consensus in different sized groups. *Am. Sociol. Rev.*, 1952, **17**, 261–267.

Hare, A. P. Small group discussions with participatory and supervisory leadership. *J. abnorm. soc. Psychol.*, 1953, **48**, 273–275.

Harlow, H. F., and Harlow, M. K. The affectional systems. In A. M. Schrier, H. F. Harlow, and F. Stollnitz (Eds.), *Behavior of nonhuman primates.* Vol. 2. New York: Academic Press, 1965. Pp. 287–334.

Harris, D. B., and Tseng, S. Children's attitudes towards peers and parents as revealed by sentence completions. *Child Dev.*, 1957, **28**, 401–411.

Harris, F. R., Wolf, M. M., and Baer, D. M. Effects of adult social reinforcement on child behavior. In W. W. Hartup and N. L. Smothergill (Eds.), *The young child.* Washington, D. C.: National Association for the Education of Young Children, 1967. Pp. 13–26.

Hartshorne, H., and May, M. A. *Studies in the nature of character*. Vol. I: *Studies in deceit*. New York: Macmillan, 1928.

Hartup, W. W. An evaluation of the Highberger early-adjustment-to-school scale. *Child Dev.*, 1959, **30**, 421–432.

Hartup, W. W. Friendship status and the effectiveness of peers as reinforcing agents. *J. exp. child Psychol.*, 1964, **1**, 154–162. (a)

Hartup, W. W. Patterns of imitative behavior in young children. *Child Dev.*, 1964, **35**, 183–191. (b)

Hartup, W. W., and Coates, B. Imitation of a peer as a function of reinforcement from the peer group and rewardingness of the model. *Child Dev.*, 1967, **38**, 1003–1016.

Hartup, W. W., Glazer, J. A., and Charlesworth, R. Peer reinforcement and sociometric status. *Child Dev.*, 1967, **38**, 1017–1024.

Hartup, W. W., and Keller, E. D. Nurturance in preschool children and its relation to dependency. *Child Dev.*, 1960, **31**, 681–690.

Hartup, W. W., and Kobasigawa, A. Aggression anxiety and the effectiveness of peers as reinforcing agents. Unpublished manuscript, University of Minnesota, 1964.

Harvey, O. J., and Consalvi, C. Status and conformity to pressures in informal groups. *J. abnorm. soc. Psychol.*, 1960, **60**, 182–187.

Harvey, O. J., and Rutherford, J. Status in the informal group: influence and influencibility at differing age levels. *Child Dev.*, 1960, **31**, 377–385.

Hattwick, L. A., and Sanders, M. K. Age differences in behavior at the nursery school level. *Child Dev.*, 1938, **9**, 27–47.

Haythorn, W. The influence of individual members on the characteristics of small groups. *J. abnorm. soc. Psychol.*, 1953, **48**, 276–284.

Heathers, G. Emotional dependence and independence in nursery school play. *J. genet. Psychol.*, 1955, **87**, 37–57.

Heber, R. F. The relation of intelligence and physical maturity to social status of children. *J. educ. Psychol.*, 1956, **47**, 158–162.

Heber, R. F., and Heber, M. E. The effect of group failure and success on social status. *J. educ. Psychol.*, 1957, **48**, 129–134.

Helper, M. M. Parental evaluations of children and children's self-evaluations. *J. abnorm. soc. Psychol.*, 1958, **56**, 190–194.

Hess, R. D., and Goldblatt, I. The status of adolescents in American society: a problem in social identity. *Child Dev.*, 1957, **28**, 459–568.

Hicks, D. J. Imitation and retention of film-mediated aggressive peer and adult models. *J. pers. soc. Psychol.*, 1965, **2**, 97–100.

Hilkevitch, R. R. Social interactional processes: a quantitative study. *Psychol. Rep.*, 1960, **7**, 195–201.

Hill, K. T. Relation of test anxiety, defensiveness, and intelligence to sociometric status. *Child Dev.*, 1963, **34**, 767–776.

Hoffman, L. R. Homogeneity of member personality and its effect on group problem-solving. *J. abnorm. soc. Psychol.*, 1959, **58**, 27–32.

Hoffman, L. R. Group problem solving. In L. Berkowitz (Ed.), *Advances in experimental social psychology*. Vol. 2. New York: Academic Press, 1965. Pp. 99–132.

Hoffman, L. W. The father's role in the family and the child's peer-group adjustment. *Merrill-Palmer Q.*, 1961, **7**, 97–105.

Hoffman, M. L. Some psychodynamic factors in compulsive conformity. *J. abnorm. soc. Psychol.*, 1953, **48**, 383–393.

Hoffman, M. L., and Hoffman, L. W. (Eds.) *Review of child development research*. New York: Russell Sage, 1964.

Hollander, E. P., and Webb, W. B. Leadership, followership and friendship: an analysis of peer nominations. *J. abnorm. soc. Psychol.*, 1955, **50**, 163–167.

Horowitz, F. D. Incentive value of social stimuli for preschool children. *Child Dev.*, 1962, **33**, 111–116. (a)

Horowitz, F. D. The relationship of anxiety, self-concept, and sociometric status among fourth, fifth and sixth grade children. *J. abnorm. soc. Psychol.*, 1962, **65**, 212–214. (b)

Horrocks, J. E., and Thompson, G. G. A study of the friendship fluctuations of rural boys and girls. *J. genet. Psychol.*, 1946, **69**, 189–198.

Hudgins, B. B., and Smith, L. M. Group structure and productivity in problem-solving. *J. educ. Psychol.*, 1966, **57**, 287–296.

Hudgins, B. B., Smith, L. M., and Johnson, T. J. The child's perception of his classmates. *J. genet. Psychol.*, 1962, **101**, 401–405.

Hunt, R. G., and Synnerdale, V. Social influences among kindergarten children. *Sociol. soc. Res.*, 1959, **43**, 171–174.

Iscoe, I., and Garden, J. A. Field dependence, manifest anxiety, and sociometric status in children. *J. consult. Psychol.*, 1961, **25**, 184.

Iscoe, I., Williams, M., and Harvey, J. Modification of children's judgments by a simulated group technique: a normative developmental study. *Child Dev.*, 1963, **34**, 963–978.

Iscoe, I., Williams, M., and Harvey, J. Age, intelligence, and sex as variables in the conformity behavior of Negro and white children. *Child Dev.*, 1964, **35**, 451–460.

Izard, C. E. Personality similarity and friendship. *J. abnorm. soc. Psychol.*, 1960, **61**, 47–51.

Jack, L. M. An experimental study of ascendant behavior in preschool children. *U. Iowa Studies in Child Welfare*, 1934, **9**, No. 3.

Jakubczak, C. F., and Walters, R. H. Suggestibility as dependency behavior. *J. abnorm. soc. Psychol.*, 1959, **59**, 102–107.

Jansen, V. G., and Gallagher, J. J. The social choices of students in racially integrated classes for the culturally disadvantaged talented. *Except. Child.*, 1966, **33**, 221–226.

Jersild, A., and Markey, F. Conflicts between preschool children. *Monogr. soc. res. Child Dev.*, 1935, No. 21.

Jewell, P. A., and Loizos, C. (Eds.), *Play, exploration and territory in mammals.* New York: Academic Press, 1966.

Johnson, G. O. A study of the social position of mentally handicapped children in the regular grades. *Am. J. ment. Defic.*, 1950, **55**, 60–89.

Jones, M. C. The later careers of boys who were early- or late-maturing. *Child Dev.*, 1957, **28**, 113–128.

Jones, M. C. A study of socialization patterns at the high school levels. *J. genet. Psychol.*, 1958, **93**, 87–111.

Jones, M. C. Psychological correlates of somatic development. *Child Dev.*, 1965, **36**, 899–911.

Jones, M. C., and Bayley, N. Physical maturing among boys as related to behavior. *J. educ. Psychol.*, 1950, **41**, 129–148.

Kanous, L. E., Daugherty, R. A., and Cohn, T. S. Relation between heterosexual friendship choices and socioeconomic level. *Child Dev.*, 1962, **33**, 251–255.

Karen, R. L. Operant conditioning and social preference. Unpublished doctoral dissertation, Arizona State University, 1965.

Katz, E., Blau, P. M., Brown, M. L., and Strodtbeck, F. L. Leadership stability and social change: an experiment with small groups. *Sociometry*, 1957, **20**, 36–50.

Katz, I. *Conflict and harmony in an adolescent interracial group.* New York: New York University Press, 1955.

Keislar, E. R. A distinction between social acceptance and prestige among adolescents. *Child Dev.,* 1953, **24,** 275–284.

Keislar, E. R. Experimental development of "like" and "dislike" of others among adolescent girls. *Child Dev.,* 1961, **32,** 59–66.

Kelman, H. C. Effects of success and failure on suggestibility in the autokinetic situation. *J. abnorm. soc. Psychol.,* 1950, **45,** 267–285.

Kerckhoff, R. C., and McCormick, T. C. Marginal status and marginal personality. *Social Forces,* 1955, **34,** 48–55.

Kiesler, C. A., Zanna, M., and DeSalvo, J. Deviation and conformity: opinion change as a function of commitment, attraction, and presence of a deviate. *J. pers. soc. Psychol.,* 1966, **3,** 458–467.

King, G. F., Erhmann, J. C., and Johnson, D. M. Experimental analysis of the reliability of observations of social behavior. *J. soc. Psychol.,* 1952, **35,** 151–160.

Kinney, E. E. A study of peer-group social acceptability at the fifth grade level in a public school. *J. educ. Res.,* 1953, **47,** 57–64.

Kipnis, D. The effects of leadership style and leadership power upon the inducement of an attitude change. *J. abnorm. soc. Psychol.,* 1958, **57,** 173–180.

Klaus, R. A. Interrelationships of attributes that accepted and rejected children ascribe to their peers. Unpublished doctoral dissertation, George Peabody College for Teachers, 1959.

Koch, H. L. Popularity in preschool children: some related factors and a technique for its measurement. *Child Dev.,* 1933, **4,** 164–175.

Kogan, N., and Wallach, M. A. Modification of a judgmental style through group interaction. *J. pers. soc. Psychol.,* 1966, **4,** 165–174.

Kohn, M. The child as a determinant of his peers' approach to him. *J. genet. Psychol.,* 1966, **109,** 91–100.

Koslin, B. L., Haarlow, R. N., Karlins, M., and Pargament, R. Predicting group status from members' cognitions. *Sociometry,* 1968, **31,** 64–75.

Krech, D., and Crutchfield, R. S. *Theory and problems of social psychology.* New York: McGraw-Hill, 1948.

Krech, D., Crutchfield, R. S., and Ballachey, E. L. *Individual in society.* New York: McGraw-Hill, 1962.

Kudrika, N. Z. Defiance of authority under peer influences. Unpublished doctoral dissertation, Yale University, 1965.

Kuhlen, R. G., and Houlihan, N. B. Adolescent heterosexual interest in 1942 and 1963. *Child Dev.,* 1965, **36,** 1049–1052.

Lambert, W. E., and Taguchi, Y. Ethnic cleavages among young children. *J. abnorm. soc. Psychol.,* 1956, **53,** 380–382.

Lambert, W. W., Triandis, L. M., and Wolf, M. Some correlates of beliefs in the malevolence and benevolence of supernatural beings: a cross-societal study. *J. abnorm. soc. Psychol.,* 1959, **58,** 162–169.

Langworthy, R. L. Community status and influence in a high school. *Am. Sociol. Rev.,* 1959, **24,** 537–539.

Lanzetta, J. T. Group behavior under stress. *Hum. Relat.,* 1955, **8,** 29–52.

Larsen, O. N., and Hill, R. J. Social structure and interpersonal communication. *Am. J. Sociol.,* 1958, **63,** 497–505.

Lesser, G. S., and Abelson, R. P. Personality correlates of persuasibility in children. In C. I. Hovland and I. L. Janis (Eds.), *Personality and persuasibility.* New Haven: Yale University Press, 1959. Pp. 187–206.

Lesser, G. S. The relationships between various forms of aggression and popularity among lower-class children. *J. educ. Psychol.,* 1959, **50,** 20–25.

Leuba, C. An experimental study of rivalry in young children. *J. comp. Psychol.*, 1933, **16**, 367–378.

Lewin, K., Lippitt, R., & White, R. K. Patterns of aggressive behavior in experimentally created "social climates." *J. soc. Psychol.*, 1938, **10**, 271–299.

Lindzey, G., and Borgatta, E. F. Sociometric measurements. In G. Lindzey (Ed.), *Handbook of social psychology.* Vol. 1. Cambridge Mass.: Addison-Wesley, 1954. Pp. 405–448.

Lippitt, R. Popularity among preschool children. *Child Dev.*, 1941, **12**, 305–322.

Lippitt, R., and Gold, M. Classroom social structure as a mental health problem. *J. soc. Iss.*, 1959, **15**, 40–49.

Lippitt, R., Polansky, N., and Rosen, S. The dynamics of power: a field study of social influence in groups of children. *Hum. Relat.*, 1952, **5**, 37–64.

Lippitt, R., and White, R. K. The "social climate" of children's groups. In R. G. Barker, J. S. Kounin, and H. F. Wright (Eds.), *Child behavior and development.* New York: McGraw-Hill, 1943. Pp. 485–508.

Lippitt, R., and White, R. K. An experimental study of leadership and group life. In E. E. Maccoby, T. M. Newcomb, and E. L. Hartley (Eds.), *Readings in social psychology.* New York: Holt, 1958. Pp. 496–511.

Lippitt, R., and Withey, S. *Flint youth study: progress report on analysis of data from the first year of field work.* Ann Arbor: Institute for Social Research, University of Michigan, 1957.

Loban, W. A study of social sensitivity (sympathy) among adolescents. *J. educ. Psychol.*, 1953, **44**, 102–112.

Loomis, C. P., and Pepinsky, H. B. Sociometry, 1937–1947: theory and methods. *Sociometry*, 1948, **11**, 262–286.

Lorge, I., and Solomon, H. Two models of group behavior in the solution of Eureka-type problems. *Psychometrika*, 1955, **20**, 139–148.

Lott, A. J., and Lott, B. E. Group cohesiveness and individual learning. *J. educ. Psychol.*, 1966, **57**, 61–73.

Lott, B. E., and Lott, A. J. The formation of positive attitudes towards group members. *J. abnorm. soc. Psychol.*, 1960, **61**, 297–300.

Lucas, C. M., and Horrocks, J. E. An experimental approach to the analysis of adolescent needs. *Child Dev.*, 1960, **31**, 479–487.

Luchins, A. S., and Luchins, E. H. Intentional and unintentional models in social learning. *J. soc. Psychol.*, 1961, **54**, 321–335.

Lynn, D. B., and Sawrey, W. L. The effects of father-absence on Norwegian boys and girls. *J. abnorm. soc. Psychol.*, 1959, **59**, 258–262.

Maas, H. S. Some social class differences in the family systems and group relations of pre- and early adolescents. *Child Dev.*, 1951, **22**, 145–152.

Maas, H. S. The role of members in clubs of lower-class and middle-class adolescents. *Child Dev.*, 1954, **25**, 241–251.

Maccoby, E. E. Role-taking in childhood and its consequences for social learning. *Child Dev.*, 1959, **30**, 239–252.

Maccoby, E. E. The taking of adult roles in middle childhood. *J. abnorm. soc. Psychol.*, 1961, **63**, 493–503.

Maller, J. B. Cooperation and competition: an experimental study in motivation. *Teachers College Contributions to Education*, 1929, No. 384.

Manwell, E. M., and Mengert, I. G. A study of the development of two- and three-year-old children with respect to play activities. *U. Iowa Studies in Child Welfare*, 1934, **9**, No. 3.

Marks, J. B. Interests, leadership, and sociometric status among adolescents. *Sociometry*, 1954, **17**, 340–349.

Marks, J. B. Interests and leadership among adolescents. *J. genet. Psychol.*, 1957, **91**, 163–172.

Marple, C. H. The comparative susceptibility of three age levels to the suggestion of group versus expert opinion. *J. soc. Psychol.*, 1933, **10**, 3–40.

Marshall, H. R. An evaluation of sociometric-social behavior research with preschool children. *Child Dev.*, 1957, **28**, 131–137.

Marshall, H. R. Prediction of social acceptance in community youth groups. *Child Dev.*, 1958, **29**, 173–184.

Marshall, H. R. Relations between home experiences and children's use of language in play interactions with peers. *Psychol. Monogr.*, 1961, **7** (Whole No. 509, 5).

Marshall, H. R., and McCandless, B. R. Relationships between dependence on adults and social acceptance by peers. *Child Dev.*, 1957, **28**, 413–419. (a)

Marshall, H. R., and McCandless, B. R. A study in prediction of social behavior of preschool children. *Child Dev.*, 1957, **28**, 149–159. (b)

Marshall, R. J. Variation in self-attitudes and attitudes toward others as a function of peer group appraisals. Unpublished doctoral dissertation, University of Buffalo, 1958.

Martin, W. Singularity and stability of profiles of social behavior. In C. B. Stendler (Ed.), *Readings in child behavior and development*. New York: Harcourt Brace, 1964, Pp. 448–466.

Martyn, K. A. The social acceptance of gifted children. Unpublished doctoral dissertation, Stanford University, 1957.

Maudry, M., and Nekula, M. Social relations between children of the same age during the first two years of life. *J. genet. Psychol.*, 1939, **54**, 193–215.

McCandless, B. R. *Children: behavior and development*. New York: Holt, Rinehart and Winston, 1967.

McCandless, B. R., and Ali, T. Relations among physical skills and personal and social variables in three cultures of adolescent girls. *J. educ. Psychol.*, 1966, **57**, 366–372.

McCandless, B. R., Bilous, C. B., and Bennett, H. L. Peer popularity and dependence on adults in pre-school-age socialization. *Child Dev.*, 1961, **32**, 511–518.

McCandless, B. R., Castaneda, A., and Palermo, D. S. Anxiety in children and social status. *Child Dev.*, 1956, **27**, 385–391.

McCandless, B. R., and Hoyt, J. M. Sex, ethnicity and play preferences of preschool children. *J. abnorm. soc. Psychol.*, 1961, **62**, 683–685.

McCandless, B. R., and Marshall, H. R. A picture sociometric technique for preschool children and its relation to teacher judgments of friendship. *Child Dev.*, 1957, **28**, 139–148. (a)

McCandless, B. R., and Marshall, H. R. Sex differences in social acceptance and participation of preschool children. *Child Dev.*, 1957, **28**, 421–425. (b)

McConnell, T. R. Suggestibility in children as a function of chronological age. *J. abnorm. soc. Psychol.*, 1963, **67**, 286–289.

McCullers, C. The member of the wedding. In C. McCullers, *The ballad of the sad cafe*. Boston: Houghton Mifflin, 1951. Pp. 595–791.

McDavid, J. W. Personality and situational determinants of conformity. *J. abnorm. soc. Psychol.*, 1959, **58**, 241–246.

McDavid, J. W., and Harari, H. Stereotyping of names and popularity in grade-school children. *Child Dev.*, 1966, **37**, 453–459.

McGuire, C., Lanmon, M., and White, G. D. Adolescent peer acceptance and valuations of role behavior. *Am. Psychol.*, 1953, **8**, 397.

McIntyre, C. J. Acceptance by others and its relation to acceptance of self and others. *J. abnorm. soc. Psychol.*, 1952, 47, 624–625.

McKee, J. P., and Leader, F. B. The relationship of socioeconomic status and aggression to the competitive behavior of preschool children. *Child Dev.*, 1955, 26, 135–142.

Mead, G. H. *Mind, self, and society.* Chicago: University of Chicago Press, 1934.

Mensh, I. N., and Glidewell, J. C. Children's perceptions of relationships among their family and friends. *J. exp. Educ.*, 1958, 27, 65–71.

Merei, F. Group leadership and institutionalization. *Hum. Relat.*, 1949, 2, 23–39.

Midlarsky, E., and Bryan, J. H. Training charity in children. *J. pers. soc. Psychol.*, 1967, 5, 408–415.

Millar, S. *The psychology of play.* Baltimore, Md.: Penguin Books, 1968.

Miller, N. E., and Dollard, J. *Social learning and imitation.* New Haven, Conn.: Yale University Press, 1941.

Miller, R. V. Social status and socioempathic differences among mentally superior, mentally typical and mentally retarded children. *Except. Child.*, 1956, 23, 114–119.

Mischel, W., and Liebert, R. M. Effects of discrepancies between observed and imposed reward criteria on their acquisition and transmission. *J. pers. soc. Psychol.*, 1966, 3, 45–53.

Moore, S. G. Correlates of peer acceptance in nursery school children. In W. W. Hartup and N. L. Smothergill (Eds.), *The young child.* Washington, D. C.: National Association for the Education of Young Children, 1967. Pp. 229–247.

Moore, S. G., and Updegraff, R. Sociometric status of preschool children as related to age, sex, nurturance-giving, and dependence. *Child Dev.*, 1964, 35, 519–524.

More, D. M. Developmental concordance and discordance during puberty and early adolescence. *Monogr. soc. res. Child Dev.*, 1953, 18, (56).

Moreno, J. L. *Who shall survive?* Washington, D. C.: Nervous and Mental Disease Publishing Company, 1934.

Morgan, W. R., and Sawyer, J. Bargaining, expectations and the preference for equality over equity. *J. pers. soc. Psychol.*, 1967, 6, 139–149.

Morland, J. K. A comparison of race awareness in northern and southern children. *Am. J. Orthopsychiat.*, 1966, 36, 22–31.

Mouton, J. S., Bell, R. L., and Blake, R. Role playing skill and sociometric peer status. *Group Psychother.*, 1956, 9, 7–17.

Mower, O. H. *Learning theory and personality dynamics.* New York: Ronald Press, 1950.

Muir, R. K. Leadership in a dual cultural setting: a sociometric study of cleavage between English and African-speaking school children and the role of leaders in bridging it. *Br. J. educ. Psychol.*, 1963, 33, 253–264.

Muma, J. R. Peer evaluation and academic performance. *Personn. guid. J.*, 1965, 44, 405–409.

Murphy, L. B. *Social behavior and child personality; an exploratory study of some roots of sympathy.* New York: Columbia University Press, 1937.

Mussen, P. H. Some personality and social factors related to changes in children's attitudes toward Negroes. *J. abnorm. soc. Psychol.*, 1950, 45, 423–441.

Mussen, P. H. (Ed.) *Handbook of research methods in child development.* New York: Wiley, 1960.

Neiman, L. J. The influence of peer groups upon attitudes toward the feminine role. *Social Problems*, 1954, 2, 104–111.

Northway, M. L., and Detweiler, J. Children's perception of friends and non-friends. *Sociometry*, 1955, 18, 527–531.

Northway, M. L., and Rooks, M. M. Creativity and sociometric status in children. *Sociometry*, 1956, **19**, 450–457.

Northway, M. L., and Wigdor, B. T. Rorschach patterns related to the sociometric status of school children. *Sociometry*, 1947, **10**, 186–199.

Page, M. L. The modification of ascendant behavior in preschool children. *U. Iowa Studies in Child Welfare*, 1936, **12**, No. 3.

Parsons, T., and Bales, R. F. *Family, socialization and interaction process.* Glencoe, Ill.: Free Press, 1955.

Parten, M. B. Social participation among preschool children. *J. abnorm. soc. Psychol.*, 1932–1933, **27**, 243–269.

Patel, H. S., and Gordon, J. E. Some personal and situational determinants of yielding to influence. *J. abnorm. soc. Psychol.*, 1960, **61**, 411–418.

Patterson, G. R., and Anderson, D. Peers as social reinforcers. *Child Dev.*, 1964, **35**, 951–960.

Patterson, G. R., and Brodsky, G. A behavior modification program for a child with multiple problem behaviors. *J. Child Psychol. Psychiat.*, 1966, **7**, 277–295.

Patterson, G. R., and Fagot, B. I. Selective responsiveness to social reinforcers and deviant behaviors in children. *Psychol. Rec.*, 1967, **17**, 369–378.

Patterson, G. R., Littman, R. A., and Bricker, W. Assertive behavior in children: a step toward a theory of aggression. *Monogr. soc. res. Child Dev.*, 1967, **32** (113).

Peck, H. F., and Gallian, C. Intelligence, ethnicity, and social roles in adolescent society. *Sociometry*, 1962, **25**, 64–72.

Perkins, H. V. Teachers' and peers' perceptions of children's self-concepts. *Child Dev.*, 1958, **29**, 203–220.

Phelps, H. R., and Horrocks, J. E. Factors influencing informal groups of adolescents. *Child Dev.*, 1958, **29**, 69–86.

Phillips, B. N., and D'Amico, L. H. Effects of cooperation and competition on the cohesiveness of small face-to-face groups. *J. educ. Psychol.*, 1956, **47**, 65–70.

Piaget, J. *The moral judgment of the child.* Glencoe, Ill.: Free Press, 1932.

Piaget, J. *Play, dreams, and imitation in childhood.* New York: Norton, 1951.

Polansky, N., Lippitt, R., and Redl, F. An investigation of behavior contagion in groups. *Hum. Relat.*, 1950, **3**, 319–348.

Pope, B. Socioeconomic contrasts in children's peer culture prestige values. *Genet. Psychol. Monogr.*, 1953, **48**, 157–220.

Porterfield, O. V., and Schlichting, H. F. Peer status and reading achievement. *J. educ. Res.*, 1961, **54**, 291–297.

Porteus, B. D., and Johnson, R. C. Children's responses to two measures of conscience development and their relation to sociometric nomination. *Child Dev.*, 1965, **36**, 703–711.

Radke, M., Sutherland, J., and Rosenberg, P. Racial attitudes of children. *Sociometry*, 1950, **13**, 154–171.

Radke, M. J., and Trager, H. G. Children's perception of the social roles of Negroes and whites. *J. Psychol.*, 1950, **29**, 3–33.

Ramirez, M., and Castaneda, A. Paired-associate learning of sociometrically ranked children's names. *Child Dev.*, 1967, **38**, 171–179.

Reese, H. W. Relationship between self-acceptance and sociometric choice. *J. abnorm. soc. Psychol.*, 1961, **62**, 472–474.

Reese, H. W. Sociometric choices of the same and opposite sex in late childhood. *Merrill-Palmer Q.*, 1962, **8**, 173–174.

Richey, M. H., and Spotts, J. V. Relation of popularity to performance on the Goodenough Draw-a-Man test. *J. consult. Psychol.*, 1959, **23**, 147–150.

Roff, M. Childhood social interactions and young adult bad conduct. *J. abnorm. soc. Psychol.*, 1961, **63**, 333–337.

Roff, M., and Brody, D. S. Appearance and choice status during adolescence. *J. Psychol.*, 1953, **36**, 347–356.

Roff, M., and Sells, S. B. The relation between the status of chooser and chosen in a sociometric situation at the grade school level. *Psychol. Schools*, 1967, **4**, 101–111.

Rose, A. M. Reference groups of rural high school youth. *Child Dev.*, 1956, **27**, 351–363.

Rose, G., Frankel, N., and Kerr, W. Empathic and sociometric status among young teen-agers. *J. genet. Psychol.*, 1956, **89**, 277–278.

Rosekrans, M. A. Imitation in children as a function of perceived similarity to a social model and vicarious reinforcement. *J. pers. soc. Psychol.*, 1967, **7**, 307–315.

Rosen, B. C. Conflicting group membership: a study of parent-peer group cross-pressures. *Am. Sociol. Rev.*, 1955, **20**, 155–161.

Rosen, S., Levinger, G., and Lippitt, R. Desired change in self and other as a function of resource ownership. *Hum. Relat.*, 1960, **13**, 187–193.

Rosen, S., Levinger, G., and Lippitt, R. Perceived sources of social power. *J. abnorm. soc. Psychol.*, 1961, **62**, 439–441.

Rosenhan, D., and White, G. M. Observation and rehearsal as determinants of prosocial behavior. *J. pers. soc. Psychol.*, 1967, **5**, 424–431.

Rychlak, J. F. A sociopsychological theory of performance in competitive situations. *Hum. Relat.*, 1960, **13**, 157–166.

Sackett, G. P. Effects of rearing conditions upon the behavior of Rhesus monkeys (Macca Mulatta). *Child Dev.*, 1965, **36**, 855–868.

Saltzstein, H. D., Rowe, P. B., and Greene, M. E. Spread of social influence on children's judgments of numerosity. *J. pers. soc. Psychol.*, 1966, **3**, 665–674.

Sampson, E. E., and Hancock, T. An examination of the relationship between ordinal position, personality, and conformity: an extension, replication, and partial verification. *J. pers. soc. Psychol.*, 1967, **5**, 398–407.

Schachter, S. *The psychology of affiliation.* Standford, Cal.: Stanford University Press, 1959.

Schachter, S. Birth order and sociometric choice. *J. abnorm. soc. Psychol.*, 1964, **68**, 453–456.

Schmuck, R. Sex of sibling, birth order position, and female dispositions to conform in two-child families. *Child Dev.*, 1963, **34**, 913–918.

Schoeppe, A. Sex differences in adolescent socialization. *J. soc. Psychol.*, 1953, **38**, 175–185.

Scofield, R. W. Task productivity of groups of friends and non-friends. *Psychol. Rep.*, 1960, **6**, 459–460.

Scott, P. M., Burton, R. V., and Yarrow, M. R. Social reinforcement under natural conditions. *Child Dev.*, 1967, **38**, 53–63.

Sears, P. S. Pursuit of self-esteem: the middle childhood years. Address presented at meetings of the American Psychological Association, 1960.

Sells, S. B., and Roff, M. Peer acceptance-rejection and birth order. *Psychol. Schools*, 1964, **1**, 156–162.

Sells, S. B., and Roff, M. Peer acceptance-rejection and personality development. Final Report, Project No. OE 5-0417, United States Department of Health, Education, and Welfare, 1967.

Shaw, C. K., and McKay, H. D. *Social factors in juvenile delinquency.* Vol. 2. Washington, D. C.: U. S. Government Printing Office, 1931.

Shaw, M. E. A note concerning homogeneity of membership and group problem solving *J. abnorm. soc. Psychol.*, 1960, **60**, 448–450.

Shaw, M. E., and Shaw, L. M. Some effects of sociometric grouping upon learning in a second grade classroom. *J. soc. Psychol.*, 1962, **57**, 453–458.

Shears, L. W. The dynamics of leadership in adolescent school groups. *Br. J. Psychol.*, 1953, **44**, 232–242.

Sherif, M., Harvey, O. J., White, B. J., Hood, W. R., and Sherif, C. W. *Intergroup conflict and cooperation: the Robbers Cave experiment*. Norman: University of Oklahoma Press, 1961.

Sherif, M., and Sherif, C. W. *Groups in harmony and tension*. New York: Harper, 1953.

Sherif, M., and Sherif, C. W. *Reference groups*. New York: Harper and Row, 1964.

Shure, M. B. Psychological ecology of a nursery school. *Child Dev.*, 1963, **34**, 979–992.

Siegel, A. E. Film-mediated fantasy aggression and strength of aggressive drive. *Child Dev.*, 1956, **27**, 365–378.

Simpson, R. L. Parental influence, anticipatory socialization, and social mobility. *Am. Sociol. Bev.*, 1962, **27**, 517–522.

Singer, A. J. Certain aspects of personality and their relation to certain group modes, and constancy of friendship choices. *J. educ. Res.*, 1951, **45**, 33–42.

Smith, A. J. A developmental study of group processes. *J. genet. Psychol.*, 1960, **97**, 29–30.

Smith, G. H. Sociometric study of best-liked and least-liked children. *Elem. sch. J.* 1950, **51**, 77–85.

Spector, S. I. Climate and social acceptability. *J. educ. Sociol.*, 1953, **27**, 108–114.

Speroff, B. J. The stability of sociometric choice among kindergarten children. *Sociometry*, 1955, **18**, 129–131.

Spiro, M. E. *Children of the kibbutz*. Cambridge, Mass.: Harvard University Press, 1958.

Springer, D. National-racial preferences of fifth-grade children in Hawaii. *J. genet. Psychol.*, 1953, **83**, 121–136.

Starkweather, E. K. Conformity and nonconformity as indicators of creativity in preschool children. Cooperative Research Project No. 1967, United States Office of Education, 1964.

Stein, A. H. The influence of peers on sex-inappropriate behavior in preschool children. Unpublished manuscript, Cornell University, 1967.

Stendler, C. B., Damrin, D., and Haines, A. C. Studies in cooperation and competition: I. The effects of working for group and individual rewards on the social climate of children's groups. *J. genet. Psychol.*, 1951, **79**, 173–198.

Stevenson, H. W. Social reinforcement with children as a function of CA, sex of E, and sex of S. *J. abnorm. soc. Psychol.*, 1961, **63**, 147–154.

Stevenson, H. W. Social reinforcement of children's behavior. In L. P. Lipsitt and C. C. Spiker (Eds.), *Advances in child development and behavior*. Vol. 2. New York: Academic Press, 1965. Pp. 97–126.

Stevenson, H. W. Studies of racial awareness in young children. In W. W. Hartup and N. L. Smothergill (Eds.), *The young child*. Washington, D. C.: National Association for the Education of Young Children, 1967. Pp. 206–213.

Stevenson, H. W., and Stevenson, N. Social interaction in an interracial nursery school. *Genet. Psychol. Monogr.*, 1960, **61**, 37–75.

Stith, M., and Connor, R. Dependency and helpfulness in young children. *Child Dev.*, 1962, **33**, 15–20.

Stogdill, R. M. Leadership, membership and organization. *Psychol. Bull.*, 1950, **47**, 1–14.

Stott, L. H., and Ball, R. S. Consistency and change in ascendence-submission in the social interaction of children. *Child Dev.*, 1957, **28**, 259–272.

Stukát, K. G. *Suggestibility: a factorial and experimental analysis.* Stockholm: Almquist and Wiksell, 1958.

Sutton-Smith, B. The role of play in cognitive development. In W. W. Hartup and N. L. Smothergill (Eds.), *The young child.* Washington, D. C.: National Association for the Education of Young Children, 1967. Pp. 96–108.

Tagiuri, R., Kogan, N., and Long, L. M. K. Differentiation of sociometric and status relations in a group. *Psychol. Rep.,* 1958, **4,** 523–526.

Terman, L. M. A preliminary study of the psychology and pedagogy of leadership. *Pedag. Semin.,* 1904, **2,** 413–451.

Thibaut, J. An experimental study of the cohesiveness of underprivileged groups. *Hum. Relat.,* 1950, **3,** 251–278.

Thompson, G. G. The social and emotional development of preschool children under two types of educational program. *Psychol. Monogr.,* 1944, **56,** No. 5.

Thompson, G. G. Children's groups. In P. H. Mussen (Ed.), *Handbook of research methods in child development.* New York: Wiley, 1960. Pp. 821–853.

Thompson, G. G., Bligh, H. F., and Witryol, S. L. A critical examination of several methods of determining levels of social status. *J. soc. Psychol.,* 1951, **33,** 13–32.

Thompson, G. G., and Horrocks, J. E. A study of the friendship fluctuations of urban boys and girls. *J. genet. Psychol.,* 1947, **70,** 53–63.

Thompson, M. M. The effect of discriminatory leadership on the relations between the more and less privileged subgroups. Unpublished doctoral dissertation, State University of Iowa, 1940.

Thorpe, J. G. An investigation into some correlates of sociometric status within school classes. *Sociometry,* 1955, **18,** 49–61. (a)

Thorpe, J. G. A study of some factors in friendship formation. *Sociometry,* 1955, **18,** 207–214. (b)

Thorpe, W. H. *Learning and instinct in animals.* London: Methuen, 1956.

Thrasher, F. M. *The gang.* Chicago: University of Chicago Press, 1927.

Tiktin, S., and Hartup, W. W. Sociometric status and the reinforcing effectiveness of children's peers. *J. exp. child Psychol.,* 1965, **2,** 306–315.

Trapp, E. P. Leadership and popularity as a function of behavioral predictions. *J. abnorm. soc. Psychol.,* 1955, **51,** 452–457.

Trent, R. D. Some individual and group differences in voting for self. *J. soc. Psychol.,* 1954, **39,** 61–65.

Trent, R. D. The relationship of anxiety to popularity and rejection among institutionalized delinquent boys. *Child Dev.,* 1957, **28,** 379–400.

Tripplett, N. The dynamogenic factors in pacemaking and competition. *Am. J. Psychol.,* 1897, **9,** 507–533.

Tryon, C. M. Evaluations of adolescent personality by adolescents. *Monogr. soc. res. Child Dev.,* 1939, **4,** No. 4.

Tuddenham, R. D. Studies in reputation: III. Correlates of popularity among elementary-school children. *J. educ. Psychol.,* 1951, **42,** 257–276.

Tuma, E., and Livson, N. Family socioeconomic status and adolescent attitudes to authority. *Child Dev.,* 1960, **31,** 387–399.

Turner, M. E. *The child within the group: an experiment in self-government.* Stanford, Cal.: Stanford University Press, 1957.

Ugurel-Semin, R. Moral behavior and moral judgment of children. *J. abnorm. soc. Psychol.,* 1952, **47,** 463–474.

Vinacke, W. E., and Gullickson, G. R. Age and sex differences in the formation of coalitions. *Child Dev.,* 1964, **35,** 1217–1231.

Wahler, R. G. Child-child interactions in five field settings: some experimental analyses. *J. exp. child Psychol.,* 1967, **5,** 278–293.

Walters, J., Pearce, D., and Dahms, L. Affectional and aggressive behavior of pre-school children. *Child Dev.*, 1957, **28**, 15–26.

Walters, R. H., Parke, R. D., and Cane, V. A. Timing of punishment and the observation of consequences to others as determinants of response inhibition. *J. exp. child Psychol.*, 1965, **2**, 10–30.

Wardlow, M. E., and Greene, J. E. An exploratory sociometric study of peer status among adolescent girls. *Sociometry*, 1952, **15**, 311–318.

Warnath, C. F. The relation of family cohesiveness and adolescent independence to social effectiveness. *Marr. fam. Liv.*, 1955, **17**, 346–348.

Watson, J. B. What the nursery has to say about instincts. *Pedag. Semin.*, 1925, **32**, 293–326.

Weber, L. C. A study of peer acceptance among delinquent girls. *Sociometry*, 1950, **13**, 363–381.

Weingold, H. P., and Webster, R. L. Effects of punishment on a cooperative behavior in children. *Child Dev.*, 1964, **35**, 1211–1216.

Wertheimer, R. R. Consistency of sociometric status position in male and female high school students. *J. educ. Psychol.*, 1957, **48**, 385–390.

Westley, W., and Elkin, F. The protective environment and adolescent socialization. *Social Forces*, 1956, **35**, 243–249.

Wheeler, L. Toward a theory of behavioral contagion. *Psychol. Rev.*, 1966, **73**, 179–192.

Wiest, W. M. A quantitative extension of Heider's theory of cognitive balance applied to interpersonal perception and self-esteem. *Psychol. Monogr.*, 1965, **79**, 1–20.

Wiggins, J. S., and Winder, C. L. The peer nominations inventory: an empirically derived sociometric measure of adjustment in preadolescent boys. *Psychol. Rep.*, 1961, **9** (Monograph Supplement No. 5), 643–677.

Williams, J. E. Acceptance by others and its relationship to acceptance of self and others: a repeat of Fey's study. *J. abnorm. soc. Psychol.*, 1962, **65**, 438–442.

Wilson, R. S. Personality patterns, source attractiveness, and conformity. *J. Personality*, 1960, **28**, 186–199.

Wilson, W. C. Development of ethnic attitudes in adolescence. *Child Dev.*, 1963, **34**, 247–256.

Winder, C. L., and Rau, L. Parental attitudes associated with social deviance in preadolescent boys. *J. abnorm soc. Psychol.*, 1962, **64**, 418–424.

Witkin, H. A., Dyk, R. B., Faterson, H. F., Goodenough, D. R., and Karp, S. A. *Psychological differentiation: studies of development.* New York: Wiley, 1962.

Witryol, S. L., and Calkins, J. E. Marginal social values of rural school children. *J. genet. Psychol.*, 1958, **92**, 81–93.

Witryol, S. L., and Thompson, G. G. A critical review of the stability of social acceptability scores obtained with the partial-rank-order and the paired-comparison scales. *Genet. Psychol. Monogr.*, 1953, **48**, 221–260.

Wolfle, D. L., and Wolfle, H. M. The development of cooperative behavior in monkeys and young children. *J. genet. Psychol.*, 1939, **55**, 137–175.

Wolman, B. Spontaneous groups of children and adolescents in Israel. *J. soc. Psychol.*, 1951, **34**, 171–182.

Wright, M. E. The influence of frustration upon the social relationships of young children. Unpublished doctoral dissertation, State University of Iowa, 1940.

Wyer, R. S. Effect of child-rearing attitudes and behavior on children's responses to hypothetical social situations. *J. pers. soc. Psychol.*, 1965, **2**, 480–486.

Wyer, R. S. Effects of incentive to perform well, group attraction, and group acceptance on conformity in a judgmental task. *J. pers. soc. Psychol.*, 1966, 4, 21–26.

Yarrow, M. R., Campbell, J. D., and Yarrow, L. J. Acquisition of new norms: A study of racial desegregation. *J. soc. Iss.*, 1958, 14, 8–28.

Young, N., and Gaier, E. L. A preliminary investigation into the prediction of suggestibility from selected personality variables. *J. soc. Psychol.*, 1953, **37**, 53–60.

Zander, A., and Curtis, T. Effects of social power on aspiration setting and striving. *J. abnorm. soc. Psychol.*, 1962, **64**, 63–74.

Zander, A., and Van Egmond, E. Relationship of intelligence and social power to the interpersonal behavior of children. *J. educ. Psychol.*, 1958, **49**, 257–268.

Zander, A., and Wulff, D. Members' test anxiety and competence determinants of a group's aspirations. *J. Personality*, 1966, **34**, 55–70.

Ziller, R. C., and Behringer, R. D. A longitudinal study of the assimilation of the new child in a group. *Hum. Relat.*, 1961, 14, 121–133.

25. Social Class and Ethnic Influences upon Socialization*

ROBERT D. HESS

The social and physical circumstances in which man lives are primarily of his own making. He is responsible for magnificent cities and monstrous slums, massive projects of water control and widespread water pollution, powerful automobiles and chronic air pollution, mass media of communication and individual isolation. Within a major urban area are to be found extremes of personal trauma and personal comfort, deprivation and affluence, social cohesion and anomie. Man must adapt individually to the surroundings he has created collectively. It shapes his behavior and the behavior of his young. The study of socialization is the study of the effects of man-made environments upon man.

As used in this chapter, *class* and *socialization* are heuristic concepts. Socialization refers to the patterns of antecedent variables which shape behavior and tie it to the social system in which an individual lives; social class indicates significant hierarchical differentiations within the society. Great differences exist among the societies of the world in types of behavior transmitted and procedures used to socialize the young. Such diversity of cultural learning and teaching is discussed elsewhere in this book; here the focus is on the variations of socialization and related behavior in children among different socioeconomic and ethnic groups within American society. This is a more restricted coverage than would be required to deal with the full range of theory and research; a number of sources offer more inclusive discussions of socialization (Clausen and Williams, 1963; Zigler and Child, 1968.

American society, as most behavioral scientists agree, has a social stratification that carries with it connotations of social inequality. There is much less agreement among scholars as to the nature of social differentiation, the ease of movement from one social level to another, the criteria to be used in identifying different social strata, and the meaning of terms in current literature. It is generally accepted, however, that members of the society differ with respect to the prestige of their occupations, power to influence the institutions of the community, economic resources, and the availability of educational and occupational opportunity, and that different levels of socioeconomic status offer children experiences which are both different and unequal with respect to the resources and rewards of the society.[1]

In this discussion, no attempt will be made to distinguish among terms used in current literature to indicate social differentiation, except to clarify an author's intent or retain his specific use of a term. This is not to suggest

* I wish to acknowledge with thanks the contributions of Dr. Maria D. Tenezakis, who assisted in the summary research and preparation of this chapter, Mrs. Elizabeth Holstein Delgass, who aided in abstracting publications and provided editorial service, Mrs. Constance Putnam, who helped with typing, proofreading, and other services required in putting together final copy, Dr. Ralph Tyler and the staff of the Center for Advanced Study in Behavioral Sciences, Stanford, California, for providing some of the necessary time and facilities.

[1] The issues involved in conceptualization and measurement of socioeconomic differentiation in this society are discussed in several sources (Barber, 1957; Bendix and Lipset, 1953, 1966; Davis, Gardner and Gardner, 1941; Kahl, 1953; Reisman, 1959; Warner et al., 1949)

that such distinctions are not important. On the contrary, research on how these social variables affect the behavior of children probably suffers from insufficient clarity and specificity about the features of the social system and social levels which we use as independent variables. However, the social status definitions used in the reported research are usually imprecise, making it impossible in this summary to convey consistent meaning by the use of terms such as *social class, occupational level, social status,* or *socioeconomic status.* For the most part, these terms should be regarded as synonymous, referring to a general socioeconomic stratification of society.

Because the term social class includes a complex range of behavior and circumstances, it is more an indication of probability than a variable. To designate the social status of an individual is to identify generally the social and economic context in which he operates and give useful information about experiences that he is likely to encounter. To be useful to students of child psychology, however, social class (or its many synonyms) must be translated into more discreet terms which specify the interactions that occur between the individual and the social context. The experiences that members of any social class enjoy or suffer depend upon both their relative positions within the society and the characteristics of the society itself. *Working class,* as a term, would encompass quite different behavior and experience in the United States than it would, for example, in South Africa, although similar in its connotation of relative status in the two societies. In short, social class must be redefined as specific experimental events which can be measured and used as variables.

In its usual sense, socialization is the acquisition of behavior congruent with group norms and values. As typically defined, it assumes a relevant reference group whose norms are to be transmitted to the new member through an agent or agents acting for the group. Socialization is often used to refer to learning in preadults, but the process it describes continues in various contexts throughout the life of individuals who live in a complex society, so the distinction between preadult and adult socialization is artificial and unnecessary (Brim and Wheeler, 1966).

The concept of socialization implies that the indoctrinating group also takes responsibility for providing a useful role in the group (K. Davis, 1940b; Eisenstadt, 1956); this aspect of socialization is currently of particular relevance. National concern about education and unemployment of the urban poor has led to proposals that both public and private sectors of the economy accept responsibility for finding useful jobs, rather than welfare payments, for youths reaching adult status in the society (Pearl and Riessman, 1965).

Most frequently, references to socialization suggest a process by which children are oriented and trained to operate as members of an established adult community. This also assumes a relatively stable body of information, values, preferences, laws, concepts, rituals, manners, and morals associated with adequate and acceptable adult functioning, and deviation from these norms is regarded as illegal, immoral, or neurotic. Underlying this image of the socializing process is a concept of adult life as a relatively monolithic structure of norms and sanctions with adequate power to impress its expectations upon the developing child.

Although this concept of stable, cultural, adult norms may apply to certain rather closed social and ideological societies or subgroups within the nation (the Amish of Pennsylvania provide a favorite example), considerable difficulty is encountered in attempting to apply it to a complex, differentiated, pluralistic society undergoing rapid social change. At the present time in the United States, there is enormous variety among norms of adult reference groups toward which children are trained; and there is considerable tolerance for subgroup variations in values, behavior, morals, and attitudes. Consensus of the adult community explicit in the concept of socialization is achieved, apparently, on a number of matters of behavior and manners; but on many others, the adults in the community are divided. These divisions are frequently represented by organized groups of one sort or another—religious, political, professional, economic, service, and social.

This pluralism in American society raises issues with respect to the concept of socialization and practical problems of research into relationships between social structure and behavior. One difficulty lies in defining a reference group which can be usefully regarded as a socializing unit. For example, the question of whether the new member of a juvenile gang is socialized to group norms raises issues of the size, organization, and permanence of the socializing group; the question of whether children in slum areas are socialized into a culture of poverty (O. Lewis, 1959) raises other theoretical points. One way to avoid these difficulties is to regard as socializing agents only formal organizations and institutions of the society (family, school, etc.), but this limits the concept severely. These issues are methodological in that they define relevant social units to employ in studies of the relationship between the behavior of parents and other socializing agents and behavioral outcomes in children.

These concerns of theory and method extend beyond the domain of research, carrying implications for the operation and maintenance of social institutions and systems and individual learning. Historically, differentiation within the society was perpetuated in part by physical and geographical distance and a relatively low level of communication. Contemporary society, however, contains communication networks which increasingly bring into confrontation groups with differing norms, values, and convictions about the appropriate techniques for socializing children and the values that should be transmitted. The mass media are central arenas for dispute among groups, with networks and agencies under attack from one group or another which has been, or imagines it has been, insulted or ignored by performers or program; newspapers and publishers are targets of similar objections. This makes available to the object of socialization some of the variety of norms in the society and may offer implicit permission to adopt values and behavior that differ from those of the adults in his immediate community. Its effect is to make the socialization impact more diffuse by creating awareness of multiplicity of norms.

Socialization, which in the modal case tends to resist social change, innovation, and conflict, in a pluralistic society actively acts to create or maintain divisiveness. At the least, it encourages differentiation and differences among individuals based not on biological potential or resources but on induced behavior. From this perspective, then, the question of ethnic and social class variations and differences in socialization is of import to the structure of the society and to the harmony or conflict that exists and develops among the subgroups of the nation. Socialization is of concern to students of political science and sociology as well as psychology because it becomes an instrument for effecting social change, for accelerating or discouraging mobility, both social and geographical, and for altering the structure of competing or disharmonious units within the nation. The "melting pot" concept of Americanization is a statement of socialization towards a presumably single dominating pattern of norms of the nation; it does not encourage maintenance of permanent, pluralistic social, cultural, and political structures. Indeed, the history and social studies textbooks of the public schools have mirrored this attempt to reduce cultural heterogeneity by underplaying the role and significance of ethnic groups, although much of the actual history of the United States has been the history of ethnic groups and their impact upon the nation (DeCharms and Moeller, 1962). Perhaps one of the most significant features of socialization is that the process itself implies or encourages both an affiliation with the socializing groups and the development of allegiance and alignments which tend to persist throughout the life span of the individual. An example is socialization into religious affiliation and into political affiliation, both of which have a high degree of stability over time in comparison with the transmission of concepts and ideologies (Hyman, 1959). These attachments are largely affective in nature and, if not opposed to rational processes, at least are not altogether dependent on them (Tajfel, 1969).

Reviews of research on socialization often include observations on the need for more adequate theory—a theme most explicitly expressed by Sewell (1961). In part, the need arises from the interplay of cultural, social, and psychological principles involved in the process; each discipline views the process in its own terms. In part, it follows from difficulty of defining the concept and specifying groups that act as effective socializing reference units. There is some reason to expect, however, that both theory and research methods will become more useful and more sophisticated.

METHODOLOGICAL PROBLEMS IN THE STUDY OF CLASS-RELATED BEHAVIOR

The present state of research on social status and behavior of children is such that even the few definitive statements that can be made are usually in imprecise terms. This follows in part from lacunae in theory, yet it also results from a lack of clarity and methodological discipline in the studies themselves. Although each study encounters design problems peculiar to its objectives, in this review, comments about method are directed to the difficulties involved in the use of social class or socioeconomic status as an independent variable and the consequent interpretation of research findings.

In reviewing 50 studies, an attempt was made to categorize briefly the techniques employed by the researchers to obtain information about social class background and to group these data in some way suitable for research purposes. Two aspects were noted:

1. *The criteria and categories used for assigning subjects to social class or social status levels.* Researchers have followed any one of several widely known procedures for defining and estimating social class position, such as Warner's Index of Status Characteristics (1949), Hollingshead's Two Factor Index of Social Position (1957), Sim's Social Class Identification Scale (1952a), or they have followed their own inclinations in defining categories and assigning subjects to them.

2. *Source of information,* whether data were taken from school or other records, obtained from mothers or other family members or from the children themselves, and whether the information was gathered through interviews, questionnaires, or by direct observation of neighborhood or house.

Although there is general agreement among social scientists that American society is differentiated on dimensions which reflect economic and social inequality, there is considerably less agreement about the nature of the differentiation and the criteria which most efficiently and faithfully indicate the position of an individual within the social hierarchy

(Bendix and Lipset, 1953; Kahl, 1953; Kahl and Davis, 1955). Disagreement as to the most appropriate indicators of social status is aggravated by different ideas about the nature of social stratification itself. While it is obvious that differences exist among individuals in the population, the salience and significance of the differences for the system and to the individuals themselves is, to a degree, a matter of preference. Two divergent but not conflicting views are most often presented: (1) the emphasis upon social and psychological features, such as prestige, social acceptance, and reputation; and (2) a stress upon economic circumstances and resources, represented by occupational level and access to resources of the society.

Although divergencies in conceptions of the relative importance of various aspects of social stratification cannot be easily dismissed, they do not pose serious methodological barriers for students of social status and childhood behavior. Many indices of social status position have been devised, but there is sufficient agreement among many of these to serve most research purposes. Kahl and Davis (1955) report a study in which a factor analysis of 19 stratification indices for 219 men disclosed a dominant factor which is best conceived of as occupational level, with variables closely related to occupation, such as education. A second factor was represented most saliently by ecological variables, such as area of residence and house type, together with measures of the status of the subject's parents and his spouse's parents. On the first factor, Warner's occupational rating showed the highest correlation with the factor scores. It is of interest that income was the least effective of the 19 variables in indicating socioeconomic status, as evaluated by agreement with other well-known measures. This study is only one of several dealing with the problem of measuring social status, and the reader who wishes to explore this field more thoroughly is referred to these additional studies: Kahl, 1953; Warner, Meeker, and Eels, 1949; Reiss et al., 1961; Bendix and Lipset, 1953; Reisman, 1959; and Barber, 1957.

Among the studies reviewed for this chapter, there was great variation in the procedures used to obtain information on which to base an assignment of social status position, in the number and boundaries of categories

Table 1. Variations in the Use of Social Status Indicators as Independent Variables in Research

Number of SES Study Groups	Groups by Occupation or Index Used
A. Five	I. Professional; II. Semiprofessional; large business; III. Skilled workers; IV. Semiskilled workers; V. Unskilled laborers.
B. Ten	Index based on combination of North-Hatt and Smith occupational prestige scales, then grouped into ten strata; cutoff points of the strata not indicated.
C. Two	Middle class composed of subjects whose father were salesmen, office workers, owners, and managers, professionals. Working class composed of subjects whose fathers were service and maintenance workers, factory workers, manual laborers.
D. Four	1. Professional and technical workers; 2. Clerical workers; 3. Skilled workers; 4. Semiskilled and unskilled workers.
E. Three	"Upper" composed of professional and managerial; "middle" composed of lower level white collar and skilled blue collar; "lower" composed of semiskilled and unskilled workers.
F. Three	I. Wage earner is unemployed or has an unskilled or semiskilled job, eighth grade or less; II. Wage earner with semiskilled clerical or sales job, with education ranging from about ninth grade to high school graduate; III. Professional, managerial.

used, and in the clarity of reporting what had been done. Some researchers obtained data from the children themselves, using questionnaires or other limited-choice self-report techniques. Others gathered data from school records or used the school district itself to define social status, ignoring the possibility that the classes were not homogeneous with regard to socioeconomic origin.

Perhaps the most serious difficulty in the methods used to assign social status to research subjects is in the variety and disparity of categories of classification and in the labeling of these categories. Different researchers use procedures ranging from *ad hoc* judgments of what constitutes middle and lower class to attempts to follow the relatively elaborate techniques for estimating class position offered by Warner's Index of Status Characteristics (ISC). The difficulty involved in the use of different techniques for classification is compounded by a marked inconsistency in the use of cutoff points for separating "middle" from "low" groups.[2] Often the cutoff

point was not indicated. Where the occupational levels were mentioned, they often overlapped. Skilled workers may fall into an intermediate level or occasionally into a "high-status" group. The examples presented in Table 1 indicate the variety of procedures followed by researchers in some of the studies reviewed. These examples are taken from studies in which the procedures are described to some degree. In others, the terms "middle" and "lower" or "working" are used with no further explanation.

One of the issues involved in the problem of categories and cutoff points in assigning persons to high and low groups is whether social status is a continuum that can be treated as a linear scale with equidistant points which can be manipulated statistically. There is reason to question this assumption. Kohn (1963) argues that there is a dividing line between the manual and nonmanual workers which affects the child-rearing practices of parents. Information about this will be incomplete until a procedure is developed to identify underlying dimensions of socioeconomic differentiation which can be used to stratify subjects. If, for example, the behavioral variables under study would be expected to correlate with the degree of autonomy or restriction of parents' occupational

[2] Indeed, the number of groupings is highly variable. Some researchers use two groups; others use five or more. Various labels given to groups reveal differing views of what is middle and what is lower class.

situation, the SES grouping of children should consider parental occupation the basic dimension of categorization, and information would be needed about the number of levels in the chain of command at the father's place of work and his place in the hierarchy.

Inherent in the attempt to identify specific effects of social class experience and differences in the environment is the problem of interaction between social class and other mediating variables which may interact with SES position. Perhaps the most troublesome issue is the relationship between social class and performance on intelligence tests. While it is an established fact that intelligence tests scores differ from one social class to another (Eells et al., 1951), few of the studies reviewed attempted to control for the effects of intelligence in the social class differences reported. Differences between social status levels sometimes disappear if children are grouped by IQ; sometimes both IQ and social status differences are present (Hess and Torney, 1965, 1967). One may take the view that differences in IQ should be regarded as a social class phenomenon and no attempt should be made to control for intelligence. Another view, however, is that social status differences that remain after adequate control for effects of IQ indicate types of variability in behavior that can more reasonably be regarded as social and cultural effects. It may be true, however, that IQ itself is modified by social class experience and that sorting by IQ takes out more class-related variance than is desirable. Perhaps this is a problem on which methodological decisions can be made only with knowledge of the variables involved. It does pose difficulties of interpretation; conclusions based on gross SES differences may be modified when socioeconomic data are analyzed with education or IQ controlled to some degree (Lipsitz, 1965).

One of the most persistent problems in research on class differences in behavior is the interpretation of significant differences in means and percentages between different class groups as class-specific or class-limited characteristics. These interpretative conclusions are often phrased to suggest that all or most of the members of the "middle class" or the "working class" hold similar attitudes or behave in similar ways, differentiating them from members of other social class levels.

Although these statements are usually qualified in original articles, the image presented may easily assume the nature of a stereotype. Secondary sources are particularly likely to drop the qualifying cautions and present a profile of a social class group that portrays each social class as distinct in values or behavior when, in fact, the original data show a high degree of similarity between the groups and a distribution of characteristics that clearly overlaps class lines (Johnsen and Leslie, 1965). For example, if 60% of mothers from middle-class backgrounds express an opinion which is expressed by only 50% of mothers from a lower-class level, this relatively small difference in percentage of response may be described as differentiating the two social class groups. In this way, a number of class profiles have appeared in the literature which are at best simplistic and at worst misleading. An additional source of distortion is the tendency to emphasize social class differences and ignore or deemphasize similarities in responses and behavior. A researcher who finds no differences in class behavior is not likely to emphasize this fact; indeed, it is probably less likely to be published. If the similarities in behavior between different classes are part of a larger project, such similarities are not often presented in a prominent way. The descriptions and reviews of literature of class differences, including this one, are not typically concerned with presentation of overlap and similarities but with points of differentiation.

An additional source of confusion is the effect of the wording of an item upon the distribution of response. Variability arising from interviewer technique or bias and from item wording is, of course, well known. To the extent that phrasing of an item may influence results, possibly through greater exposure to verbal messages and interviews on the part of middle-class subjects, differences that have been described as rising from socioeconomic status experience may have been introduced by the research procedures themselves. This type of error is especially likely to occur when a simple item is used to measure complex values and attitudes.

In summary, the research and method problems now prevalent in the field which limit the usefulness of some of the published studies are these:

1. Lack of uniformity in techniques used for assigning individuals to socioeconomic categories.

2. Grouping SES levels so that they overlap with categories in other studies, that is, occupational levels which are classified as "middle class" are included in a "working class'" category in another study.

3. Use of broad categories such as "working class," which often does not permit distinctions among skilled worker level and unskilled or unemployed occupational classifications, or "middle class," which does not distinguish among professionals and white collar clerical workers or other occupational types whose conditions of work and community life are quite dissimilar.

4. Failure to distinguish between social class and other associated variables, such as IQ and ethnicity.

5. Acceptance of indirect, unverified sources of information about occupational level of subjects, or failure to specify and to attempt to measure those elements of the social context which are presumably related to the behavior under study.

6. Analysis of data which emphasizes the central tendencies of class behavior rather than the variability within each SES grouping, giving rise to stereotyped images of social class.

CONCEPTUALIZATIONS OF THE RELATIONSHIP BETWEEN SOCIAL STRUCTURE AND LEARNING

As a term useful in its perspective but vague in its connotation, socialization has been used in social science literature to refer to such diverse processes as the taming of a young human animal (Freud, 1930) and the preparation of the young for societal roles and their absorption into the society (K. Davis, 1940b). The second approach is typically taken by anthropologists and sociologists; the earlier literature in child psychology (the 1940s and early 1950s) more frequently represented the task as a taming process. Child's review of socialization in the *Handbook of Social Psychology* (Lindzey, 1954) is such a representation of concern for the management of basic physical impulses and needs. This is indicated not so much in Child's definition of socialization as in the

categories of dependent variables of behavior needed to describe the studies reviewed— orality, excretion, sexuality, aggression, dependence, achievement, affection, reproduction, and fear. Congruent with this orientation, the literature in child psychology concentrated upon the analysis of the effects of parental behavior upon acquisition of behavior in children; social class differences were analyzed by examining class differences in parental behavior. Given this approach, the mechanism by which parental behavior is linked to social institutions and larger configurations of society received less attention. Another factor which may have retarded the development of interest among psychologists in the impact of social class was the restricted socioeconomic range of subjects in many research populations used by child psychologists. The ready access to research facilities in university-operated or university-connected nursery and elementary schools led to the use of research groups less heterogeneous than the total population. The fact that most of the major research stations and institutes had few if any children from visible ethnic groups or from urban slums restricted opportunities to observe and study the full range of cultural and socioeconomic differences in the United States.

Whatever the previous circumstances, many child psychologists are now deeply involved in research and experimental programs of intervention with children from urban slum populations. Progress is being made to fill in the gaps in theory about relationships between social structure and the acquisition of behavior in children.

What are the connections between social systems and early learning, and how are they conceptualized to facilitate more definitive research? Perhaps a general paradigm will serve as a reference point for the discussion of different approaches in the current literature. An implicit pattern is expressed in these questions: What are the *conditions* of the external social and cultural world in which the child lives? What are the *adaptive consequences* which adults in the environment acquire in their interaction with the system? *In what specific forms do these adult orientations appear in interaction with children?* What are the *behavioral outcomes* of these experiences in children? This outline assumes a linkage between the society, its institutions and conditions of life, and the behavior of adults who then act as socializing and teaching agents for their children.

In addition to this paradigm is another type of learning which is also class-linked: children interact directly with the environment, and even when no socializing agent is intentionally involved in these points of interaction, the child absorbs information about the norms and values of the social system of which he is a part and develops a pattern of response to it. In some of our studies, for example, mothers in slum areas report that their young children are fearful, citing examples that are realistic for this part of the population—fire, rodents, dark areas, attack by someone stronger, etc. The older child in the slum community becomes aware of the rewards and achievements available to others in the society as he acquires information about society and his own place in it. To the degree that this type of experience conveys a view of the society and its contemporary inequalities and differences, it transmits norms of the system and is part of the process of socialization.

The points of contact between the child and the environment are thus mediated through parents, siblings, other adults or agents (not excluding mass media) or are direct experiences with the social and cultural surroundings. It is not clear whether the behavioral outcomes of direct contact are essentially dissimilar from those mediated through parents; studies of parent-child similarity show parental attitudes and values in many areas account for only a part of the behavior of children and in others, very little at all (Jennings and Niemi, 1968; Reiss, 1965). Perhaps we have underestimated the extent to which diffuse but direct experience with the environment, through interaction with peers, television, newspapers, popular music, observation of life in the community, awareness of social and economic inequality, and other points of contact, directly shapes the child's cognitive and behavioral strategies and resources.

It may be noted in passing that the locus of concern in this chapter is upon the mechanisms of exchange between the environment and the child rather than upon the relative effects of genetic and environmental sources of influence.[3] This interest in specific process of the ecology of human learning rather than the relative impact of experience seems to this reviewer to reflect contemporary pursuits in socialization research.

What are the natures of the environments of children from different sectors of American society? A complete answer to this question would include descriptions of rural and urban groups and so is not within the scope of this chapter. However, to illustrate the types of transmission that occur and to indicate how the circumstances of the environment are translated into child-rearing practices, this discussion will use as a descriptive framework some recently available ethnological and sociological information about the urban poor in the United States.

THE CIRCUMSTANCES OF LOWER-WORKING-CLASS LIFE IN METROPOLITAN SOCIETY

In recent years, the problems of education, housing, crimes, communication, and survival of people in the slum areas of the large cities have drawn national attention and led to a number of empirical social scientific investigations (Clark, 1965; Cloward and Ohlin, 1960; Cohen and Hodges, 1963; Conant, 1961; Ferman et al., 1965; Gordon, 1965; Harlem Youth Opportunities Unlimited, 1964; Harrington, 1964; H. Lewis, 1965; Myrdal, 1962; Rainwater, 1966; Shostak and Gomberg, 1964). The life circumstances of lower-class urban poor may help illustrate some of the central and critical dimensions of American social structure that may be significant in the early acquisition of behavior. The extreme contrasts with middle-class suburban life may also give some impression of the

[3] Although socialization theory assumes modifications and changes in behavior as the result of environmental influences, it does not rule out the possibility that some social class differences may be associated with genetic substructure. A number of scientists have emphasized this possibility recently and have called for more research to evaluate the relative contributions of genetic and nongenetic factors in the development of human behavior. A recent statement by the Academy of Sciences in response to these calls for new research takes the position that the complexity of the problem makes it extremely unlikely that research would produce useful information (Science, 158(3803), Nov. 1967).

disparity in poor communities between society's two major socializing institutions—the family and the school. This discussion will draw heavily upon these writings, particularly the paper by Cohen and Hodges.

Roughly one-sixth of the population of the United States, 34 million persons, have family incomes of $3000 or less or individual incomes of $1500 or less (Keyserling, 1964). The *economic poverty* of familes in urban slums is, of course, the most visible and most pervasive feature of life. Their percentage of national income has changed very little since the early part of the century, although in absolute terms it has improved (Kolko, 1962). While poverty is a basic condition of lower-class life, patterns of socialization of lower-class children would probably not be solved by a sharp increase in family income. In studies of criteria of socioeconomic status (Kahl and Davis, 1955), income does not emerge as a variable of central significance. It is, perhaps, a necessary but not sufficient condition for basic changes in family living patterns and acquisitions of education, prestige, and other rewards of the society. Without denying in any way the importance of economic resources, the emphasis of this review is upon the social and psychological dimensions with which status in the socioeconomic hierarchy is associated.

One significant dimension of social class and structure in the United States is the *extent to which an individual can exercise power* through status, prestige, or affiliation with an institution or organization. (The exercise of power may range from political or corporate decision making or involvement with major civic or regional projects and issues to avoiding arrest through professional connections or, more modestly, dealing with attempts at economic exploitation and obtaining a positive answer to a complaint about goods and services.) A sense of power has much in common with a sense of efficacy; the development of a sense of efficacy helps shape the types of social interaction that develop between the individual and his community. This helplessness encourages a dependence on luck, rather than upon one's own efforts, for economic gain in such long-shot ventures as the numbers games. Powerlessness is one of the central problems of the poor. They are more likely to be arrested without justification and detained without adequate regard for individual rights. In mental health clinics, patients from working-class areas may be diagnosed as more maladjusted with poor prognoses than are their middle-class counterparts with essentially similar records (Haase, 1956; Riessman, 1964). Health services are often inferior although not substantially less expensive (Strauss, 1967); in emergency wards of hospitals, the poor get less adequate emergency treatment (Sudnow, 1967) and are kept on waiting lists longer (Sabagh, Eyman, and Cogburn, 1966); and in many areas of their lives they have more difficulty defending themselves against invasions of privacy by welfare agents (Cloward and Piven, 1967).

Closely related to the conditions of poverty and powerlessness is a *vulnerability to disaster*. The poor are typically not only without financial reserves of their own, but are most likely to be given little advance notice when laid off from work, to be victims of legislative and bureaucratic delay or interruptions of welfare service. They possess little credit or borrowing power and are less likely to have friends with resources (Cloward and Elman, 1966a, 1966b). Life is lived on the edge of incipient tragedy which they are powerless to avert. In disaster situations they are less able to cope and recover (Koos, 1950).

The circumstances of life of the poor combine to *restrict the range of alternatives of action*. Lack of economic resources, lack of power, lack of education, and lack of prestige drastically reduce physical mobility and the opportunity for different options concerning areas of residence, housing, employment and most of the areas of their lives. As a group they are subject to economic control by federal, state, and local public health and welfare agencies who supply them with services, as well as to the public health policies and resources of the community. Their range of medical services is severely restricted, and their bodies are more likely to be exploited for medical education and research as an explicit or implicit contingency for medical services at low cost. The low level of literacy and education and lack of information about how to obtain information make it difficult to discover and use those alternatives that may be technically available.

A central dimension in social structure and

social class differentiations is the *disparity in prestige* enjoyed by members of different levels. The poor are without prestige and status in the society. Their awarness of their position in the society is in itself a fact of life and a mediating screen through which perceptions and information are filtered. This awareness is probably transmitted to children directly through their own observations and indirectly through adults who define for their children their relative position in the community; its effect is part of the socialization process.

Another feature of a lower-class person's life is the *relatively small overlap between his experiences and those of the majority,* that is, the few experiences that the poor have in common with the upper working class or the middle class. Although there is sufficient contact and visibility to make the poor aware of the values of the middle class, their range of experience is quite different. The circumstances of home life are vastly different; the conditions of work for lower- and middle-class persons are discrepant even (or perhaps especially) when they work in the same factory, school building, or university. The contact the poor have with the middle class is from a subordinate position; middle-class persons typically have little exposure to the home and family life of the poor. Whether or not appropriately called a culture of poverty (Lewis, 1959), lower-class life differs dramatically from that of the middle class, especially where it is also influenced by ethnic culture.

In poor neighborhoods, a number of adaptations and consequences emerge, partly as attempts to deal with the problems of survival, but also as inner consequences of the external conditions of life. Because all poverty necessarily contains certain common elements, there may arise a pseudoculture growing out of attempts to deal with a hostile, depriving environment. However, in several significant ways, this "culture" will be different primarily in degree from other segments of the society since certain elements of social conditions and structure apply throughout the system: degree of power, availability of alternatives of action and thought, availability of resources to deal with disaster, and the extent to which experience is shared by other members of the society.

THE ADAPTIVE CONSEQUENCES OF POVERTY

The relevance to this discussion of the circumstances of the external environment lies both in their direct effects upon children and in their transformation into socializing behavior of parents. Although the effects of social class experience are mediated only in part through adults, socialization literature is overwhelmingly concerned with adults' role in the emergence of behavior patterns in children. This discussion of adaptation to poverty therefore is primarily concerned with the consequences of social class environments for adults. In discussing these consequences, it is recognized that the great variation among individuals in modes of response to socioeconomic disadvantage is obscured, and that there is also considerable overlap in experience with other segments of the population. The poor are neither as homogeneous nor as separate from the rest of the society as discussions of this type suggest. There is great overlap with other levels of society and the adaptations that one member makes may be fundamentally different from those of his neighbor.

Among the working class, *relationships tend to be structured in terms of power.* This orientation toward power has been noted and described in a number of studies. Maas (1953) observed it in the relationship between members of adolescent clubs and their club leaders; Christie and Jahoda (1954) describe it as a mark of authoritarian personality; Lipset (1960) regarded it in part as a tendency for working-class individuals to select the least complex alternative. In their study of maternal influences upon cognitive development in children, Hess and Shipman (1967) see it as a preference for the normative, rule-oriented controls, such as phrasing comments and instructions as imperatives, intended to govern the behavior of children; Whyte (1955) observed this tendency to structure social interaction in terms of power in his work with "street corner society"; it may underlie the greater frequency of physical punishment in working class families (Bronfenbrenner, 1958). This orientation to power would seem to follow from the lower-class person's position in the society, in his occupation, and in his interaction with community institutions (Archibald, 1953). In jobs he is likely to hold, instructions are given as specific commands. He has little opportunity to help make decisions which determine the conditions of his work. The central issue is: "Who is in charge?" In other situations, as well, particularly in those that involve interaction with bureaucratic structures (welfare, police, hospitals, credit agencies), the low-status person has relatively little voice in the decisions that affect his daily life; his most characteristic and most adaptive response is to comply and carry out instructions. The distinctions between power and status that middle-class and more highly trained workers can make (e.g., a qualified technician may acquire more status because of his specialization and skill but hold little formal power within the occupational unit) mean little to him. As he perceives it, to have status and authority is to have power (Cohen and Hodges, 1963). In line with this orientation, the lower-class father tends to equate respect from children with their compliance and obedience to his wishes and commands (Cohen and Hodges, 1963; Kohn, 1959a).

This orientation to authority may be responsible in part for the tendency to select authoritarian response [although this generalization is disputed by Lipsitz (1965) and by Becker and Krug (1964)] and to be extra-punitive in management of blame. Not only does he simplify life by a stereotyped, blunt, authoritarian statement, but, as the object of authority, which must occasionally appear to be arbitrary, he shifts easily to the role of authoritarian in matters of value judgment. A comparable logic applies to extra-punitive expressions. If others control his life, then others must be responsible and, of course, to blame for the problems that may beset him. "As the role of others in the determination of behavior increases, the right to blame others for unfortunate consequences also increases" (Henry and Short, 1954). Indeed, this view *is* a somewhat realistic appraisal of his state in life.

One of the consequences of lower-class life is a cluster of attitudes that express *low self-esteem, a sense of inefficacy, and passivity.* The view taken here is that these are not as much stable personality traits as they are adaptive responses to frustration and unpredictability, to being acted upon, to being forced to wait for someone in authority to act. Contingencies linking action to outcome in the relation of middle-class behavior to community institutions are frequently missing or intermittent in the slums. The relatively dependent position of the lower working-class adult in the social structure—his powerlessness—induces magical thought and a tendency to look to superhuman sources for support and assistance. This appears in exercising discipline within the family, when religious sanctions and deity are invoked to help enforce parental demands (Nunn, 1964). There is a view of the environment as not responsive to individual effort (Inkeles, 1960; Hyman, 1953) and, perhaps consequently, a greater tendency to accept events with resignation. This stance may also be involved in the tendency to lower aspirations and expectations in educational and economic areas (Hess and Shipman, 1965, 1968; Hyman, 1953).

One adaptation to this is to elect short-term goals, seeking more immediately predictable gratification (Davis, 1948) and even to use illicit means (delinquent behavior) in achieving rewards usually not available (Cloward and Ohlin, 1960).

The life style of the poor seems to show a *preference for the familiar and a simplification of the experience world.* In the study by Cohen and Hodges (1963) of workers from different socio-economic class levels, lower blue-collar workers were found more likely to agree with statements such as "I'm not the sort of person who enjoys starting a conversation with strangers on the bus or train," and "It is easier not to speak to strangers until they speak to you." To the open-ended question, "What things bother you most in everyday life?" they were most likely to answer that things and people are unpredictable and they prefer familiar and routine events (p. 316). This is not an expression of indifference to popularity, but an indication of lack of confidence and of fear of a social mistake. The workers apparently tend to level the contours of cognitive awareness and understanding and to interpret life in stereotypes, clichés, and familiar phrases (Bernstein, 1961).

Associated with this tendency is a *rejection*

of intellectuality (Cohen and Hodges, 1963), following in part from a mistrust of the unfamiliar—a sense of not understanding nor being able to compete in modes of reasoning not familiar to them—and in part from a reluctance to accept standards of evaluation which would be to their disadvantage if applied to them. Also, the life circumstances of the poor orient them to practical action. Their participation in occupational arenas has not typically been that of policy making, their gratification, not that of considering means and of developing ideas to guide action (Miller and Riessman, 1961).

A second consequence of lower-class life is *the restriction of language and linguistic modes of communication.* The interlacing of language and other forms of social behavior has been brilliantly stated by Bernstein (1962a, 1964). (His theoretical contributions are discussed later in this chapter.) Language serves behavior; to the extent that the life of the lower working class is restricted and lacks opportunities for action and for selection of alternatives, its language of interaction has less need to be complex and differentiated. This does not suggest that there is less communication in terms of frequency of speech or readiness to exchange messages but that the patterning of speech differs in response to the nature of the interaction among participants (Schatzman and Strauss, 1955).

Another adaptive consequence of lower-class life is the *reliance upon nonwork-related friendships and kinship contacts* for social support and resources. One expression of these sociometric choices is a lack of interaction with voluntary organizations with its consequent isolation from the institutions of the community (Wright and Hyman, 1958). Family life and social interaction outside the family are composed of a network of friends and kin to whom one can turn for assistance and support, which, though limited, are significant. Nonparticipation in organizations may follow from the inability of the lower-class adult to see the relationship between the events and needs of his own life and the goals of the organization, with the exception of the union. Skills called for (verbal facility, administrative skill, knowledge of procedures, ability to organize groups in pursuit of goals) are not likely to be developed. Since he can contribute little and has only a dim view of

what he can gain, there is little point to his joining (Cohen and Hodges, 1963). The world of social contacts is divided into friends and strangers. From strangers he has no reason to expect fair or benign treatment; friendships are salient.

The relative isolation of the lower-class person from the paths of experience of the dominant middle class is one antecedent of his relatively *low level of skill and experience in obtaining and evaluating information about events and resources* that affect or might affect his life. To put it more crudely, he often doesn't know what to do and doesn't know how to find out. This ignorance makes him susceptible to exploitation by members of his own social community and by "con men," unscrupulous repairmen, loan agencies, and other individuals, agencies, and groups. It may be, as Cohen and Hodges (1963) argue, that this lack of information makes him more inclined to be credulous, especially of the printed word, and more likely to believe TV commercials: "[the lower-blue-collar worker] has *few independent criteria for evaluating the content of the message, little awareness of specific alternatives, and little disposition to weigh evidence*" [italics theirs]. They comment that the field of his experience is unstructured, increasing suggestibility and gullibility as well as the possibility of eventual disappointment, frustration, and the feeling that life is unpredictable and long-term probabilities of gratification modest at best.

MEDIATING OPERATIONS BETWEEN SOCIAL ECOLOGY AND BEHAVIOR

Against the background of the circumstances and adaptive consequences of life in the lower working class, it may be useful to review several ideas about the processes linking social structure to behavior.

Perhaps the most popular view among writers who have dealt with this topic is that *there is a functional tie between economic activities and child-rearing practices of adults,* either directly or through the salience of values rewarded on the job and therefore in the home. Barry, Child, and Bacon (1959), using 104 societies distributed over the world, examined the proposition that societies which must accumulate and store food (agricultural, dependent on animal husbandry) will place a premium on obedience to experienced and old members of the group, on responsibility in following the accepted routines in connection with economic activities (conscientious, complaint, conservative); societies which engage primarily in hunting and fishing with no means for extended storing of food thus obtained would reward variations in participants' resourcefulness and skill in obtaining food and place high value on individual initiative and skill (individualistic, assertive, venturesome). The results of their investigation show significant association between the type of subsistence economy and patterns of child rearing. They believe this connection applies also to areas of behavior related to economic activites. Other researchers find this general line of argument convincing. Kohn (1963), in interpreting the relationship between social class and parental values, offers the view that there are three basic differences between middle and working classes, over and above the differences in income, prestige, and security. One is that middle-class occupations are more likely to deal with symbols, ideas, interpersonal relations, whereas working-class jobs entail manipulation of things. Second, middle-class occupations permit and may demand more policy making, self-direction, and autonomy; working-class occupations are more likely to be supervised, administered, and routinized. Third, success on the job for the middle class is more likely to be the result of one's own initiative and skill, whereas success or advancement in rank or wages for the working-class person is more frequently tied to group efforts, particularly the union's. The significant axis, for Kohn, is self-direction versus compliance to rules of others. These values and patterns of response appear in the techniques of control exercised by parents over children, in their attitudes toward which characteristics are ideal and which undesirable, and in their orientation toward the importance of external demands rather than inner subjective states. The occupational orientations of adults of the different social classes are applicable primarily to fathers. Indeed, women of a wide range of social-class background employed outside the home are likely to have jobs (secretarial, clerical, sales) more characteristic of working-class occupations.

Occupational diversity also occurs within both working- and middle-class levels. Miller and Swanson (1958) propose a distinction between bureaucratic and entrepreneurial patterns of employment, suggesting that parents who are affiliated with bureaucratic economic structures value and reward social skills and accommodation in their children rather than the self-reliance valued by entrepreneurial parents. Subsequent research has not always supported the difference they found between these groups (Kohn, 1963; Maccoby, unpublished analysis of data from Patterns of Child Rearing Study.) It may be that this distinction gives too little recognition to the self-direction (within broad policy) that the administrative and executive personnel of large corporate bodies must possess. They operate under the direction of higher levels of authority and may have little voice in policy and decision making, but the specifications of the task are much more general and leave much more to their imagination and resourcefulness than do those of blue-collar jobs.

These linkages between the social and occupational structure and parental child-rearing behavior are formulated in a similar fashion by Inkeles (1960). In his view, the emerging industrial society brought with it a role-structure that demanded and presumably rewarded patterns of behavior appropriate (and in this sense necessary) to industrial occupations, including acceptance of an authority hierarchy, standardization and order, regard for time, and cooperative activity. Moreover, industrial job differentiation apparently has somewhat similar effects in different countries, cutting across cultural differences to some degree, even where the absolute level of income and style of life is quite different (Inkeles, 1960). Although it is not clear whether the nature of industrial structure is responsible, there is a good deal of inter-nation congruence in the public ranking of occupational prestige, highly similar to that in the United States. The position a worker holds in the occupational structure does not substantially affect the way he evaluates the prestige of occupations (Inkeles and Rossi, 1956). This pattern of connection between the job and parental values is bolstered by other aspects of social class differentiations, especially level of education, which gives middle-class parents a greater facility in dealing with ideas and verbalizing motives. A later paper (Inkeles, 1966) extends the model of socialization toward adult roles beyond the occupational and industrial arenas to the development of competence for social roles throughout the society. Although Inkeles' formulations emphasize the outcomes of socialization rather than the process, they provide an orientation for considering social class and ethnic differences in both. If society demands differentiated roles, individuals must be trained to fill them. Although it may be difficult to accept the assumption that parents are intentionally acting in service of the total system, it seems likely that the availability of roles and the visibility of established statuses and positions in the occupational and social structure do make children and adolescents aware of the possibilities. Moreover, the school system and, to a degree, parents attempt to provide training oriented toward roles in the system. In part, the process is a matter of practicality; children are oriented toward visible opportunities in the economy. In part, however, it is mediated by values developed in different segments of the society. Dissimilar experience of persons at unequal positions in the sociocultural systems will lead to differences in values and in socializing efforts. Children and, presumably, parents from high socioeconomic levels have more information about occupations and rank their prestige more accurately than children from working-class levels (DeFleur and DeFleur, 1967). Inkeles also argues that socialization should not only take into account roles now available in society but should prepare the individual for defining and developing new roles if they become needed. The mediating agent, in his opinion, is the parent, consciously preparing his children for demands that society will place on him.

With respect to the view of socialization as a response to societal needs, it may be argued that parents tend to socialize their children toward desirable roles rather than take responsibility for meeting the personnel needs of the community. For example, there is a critical need for agricultural workers, particularly at harvest time, in various parts of the United States, but it seems unlikely that parents will socialize their children to meet such a need. Perhaps the concept of deliberate socialization of the child to fill a given role in society applies to certain levels of the social and economic structure but not to others. As a model for understanding the socializing practices of parents in lower SES levels and in ethnic groups (e.g., American Indians), it is perhaps less useful.

The view of an autonomy-compliance axis in occupational structure as an explanatory link between social structure and parental values is persuasive and suggests several lines of research, but with a number of reservations. Certain working-class members would appear to have a great deal of autonomy—farmers, policemen, foremen on construction crews, cabdrivers, for example. Parents who are in occupations which presumably do not follow the pattern of compliance described by Kohn, Inkeles, and others, should hold somewhat different values and select patterns of child rearing more similar to middle- than to lower-class groups. Small businessmen also appear to have occupational requirements that would be reflected in values and techniques of child care. Perhaps occupations such as these account for some of the great variability within the working and middle classes. Perhaps neighborhood homogeneity in connection with occupational experience plays a role in shaping values. However, the specification of structural variables (job autonomy versus compliance; orientation to ideas versus orientation to physical objects; individualistic versus collective efforts for advancement) offer concepts that may make the relationship between input variables and behavioral outcomes more amenable to research.

Another conceptualization of the process which mediates social structure is the view that individuals in different social-class groups hold different values, which are, to a degree, autonomous and persistent (Hyman, 1953; Rosen, 1959).

Hyman's summary of evidence (1953) on social-class differences in values deals with the value placed on formal education, motivation to advance in the economic structure, the relative desirabilities of a secure job with low pay versus a higher paying job with greater risk, beliefs about the possibility of economic advancement, the relative efficacies of hard work versus social skills in job advancement, and occupational goals. In these value areas, working-class persons have lower levels of striving and expectations and are less likely to see economic advancement as something they can effect by hard work. These attitudes, in Hyman's interpretation, are in part realistic responses to the experience of the participants, but they also limit the possibility of change since they represent an acceptance of a relatively poor position in the society.

Another route of transaction between the social system and individual behavior is the *awareness that may develop in an individual about his relative position in the hierarchy and the degree of prestige and opportunity that persons who possess his characteristics and live in his community can command in the society at large.* The central principle involved in this transaction follows from Mead, Cooley, and others in sociological tradition who see self-concept as arising in part from the expectations, attitudes, and behavior of others. Awareness of one's position may come from observation and from impersonal sources—that is, mass media. Self-concept may be affected by specific experiences, particularly those occurring in the family, with much the same results. Social structure here refers to prestige and status components of social stratification, which are explicit or implicit in social class evaluations, and the generalization of status cues to expectations of individual merit. This mechanism socializes to the degree that self-concept and awareness of the evaluation of others considered significant in turn affect the quality of the individual's performance, attitudes, values.

Awareness of social class distinctions appears by the fifth or sixth grade of elementary school, as demonstrated in the study by Neugarten (1946) of sociometric choices of children from varying social class backgrounds. In schools heterogeneous with respect to social status, responses to questions about which of their classmates would be selected as the most desirable friends, as more attractive, and as possessing other positive characteristics, showed that children in both high- and low-status groups selected or nominated more frequently children in high-status groups. Such awareness of differential prestige occurs particularly early if the characteristics which signal the difference in status are more readily visible, as in the case of skin color (Clark and Clark, 1947).

The distinctions of social class and ethnicity

and the generalization of low (or high) group prestige to the self through identification and other processes appear to affect academic performance and to play a role in the effectiveness of interpersonal relationships. The work of Katz and his associates (Katz, Goldston, and Benjamin, 1958; Katz and Cohen, 1962) on the effects of race on productivity and interaction shows that in mixed race teams, Negroes performed less well on tasks for which they have ability equal to that of their white teammates. In one of a number of studies, groups of four college-level students, two Negro and two white, were asked to work together on several cognitive and motor tasks. Negroes tended to defer to their white teammates, to direct interaction toward them, to perform less well, and, in subsequent reports, to minimize and underestimate their own contributions. The perception of inferiority thus appears to lower performance, through expectation of relative failure and, possibly, through a desire not to arouse disapproval of a high-status person by appearing to equal or surpass him in situations that could be regarded as competitive. An attempt to alter the status positions in such face-to-face relationships would be interpreted as aggressive. The role of expectations attached to ascribed status and the function of class-linked cues is elaborated in the formulations of Berger, Cohen, Conner, and Zelditch, (1966). The status-envy concept of Burton and Whiting (1961) is another formulation of the influences that differentials in prestige and status have upon behavior and self-concept. Low self-esteem also may affect the performance of parental roles in various ways. Perhaps, as McKinley (1964) argues, low status in occupational areas creates frustrations which fathers are likely to express in aggression or stern behavior at home; it may also appear in tendencies to restrict the initiative and assertive behavior of children or may possibly be transmitted as a more diffuse sense of depression and inability to cope with environmental problems.

A third conceptualization of social class influences upon behavior is that *deprivation of essential experience,* especially in early childhood, is a central element in creating differences in performance between social status groups (Deutsch, 1963, 1965; Deutsch and Deutsch, 1968). The mediating process in deficit theory is lack of stimulation of cognitive processes, especially verbal, in the family environment and a lack of salience or selective reinforcement of relevant behavior and attention to relevant cues by others. This idea agrees somewhat with the review of longitudinal data by Bloom (1964) and his conclusions that an impoverished environment may retard mental development drastically and keep an individual from attaining the potential possible from an abundant environment. This concept emphasizes quite different environmental elements than formulations which stress the situational and structural factors in shaping behavior. However, it is a central concept of much of the governmental intervention programs, such as Head Start, and many privately financed compensatory programs.

Another suggested route of transmission for social class differences is *through traditional cultural and religious values, which lead to different types of child-rearing practices.* The prestige and position of ethnic minorities in the society is, of course, one aspect of the social structure. To the extent that immigration brought ethnic groups who entered the occupational system at working-class levels and who, to a great extent, remained there, these ethnic influences operate to perpetuate social class patterns of child rearing and performance. Differences in values of ethnic groups have been regarded as relevant for differential achievements (Strodtbeck, 1958; Rosen, 1959), although our information about the extent to which this operates throughout the country is limited. The persistence of ethnic identification and of ethnic voting in adult populations is documented (Wolfinger, 1965) and suggests that ethnic influences may contribute to social class differences in socialization in other behavioral areas as well. In the instance of American Indians, the ethnic and cultural differences are compounded by isolation, powerlessness, and low esteem, producing patterns of behavior and adaptation dramatically incongruous with the norms of our society.

A fourth conceptualization of the mechanisms of transfer between social structure and behavior is emerging from the formulations and research of Bernstein (1961, 1962a, 1962b, 1964) and of Hess and his associates (Hess, 1964; Hess and Shipman, 1965, 1967,

1968). In their view, the child is socialized into modes of communication and strategies of thought which develop as patterns of response to specific interactions with the salient parental figures, especially the mother. Adaptive consequences developed by the mother are transmitted through her linguistic modes, regulatory strategies, cognitive styles, and self-esteem. These early modes of dealing with the child induce similar adaptive consequences in the child. This type of socialization is not a direct teaching of valued behavior, as formulations of linkages to occupational experience argue, but emerges from responses elicited from the child to parental behavior, which itself is linked to social structure. It is not that the low-status child is taught to be passive; rather, the unpredictability of his life and the lack of orderly contingencies in his experience with his environment induce caution and apathy. The sense of powerlessness and of lack of alternative for thought and action that adults in his environment experience are not transmitted as values but are expressed through parenting styles that induce corresponding responses in him. Mothers in slum areas, for example, orient their children toward the public school in terms of the problems of dealing with the authority system of the school rather than toward problems of learning (Hess and Shipman, 1968). This follows in part from the sense of inefficacy in relation to the school, the expectation (or fear) of failure, and prolonged experience in community and occupational spheres of being acted upon rather than acting. The resulting responses in children are either to be compliant or, one of the few known alternatives available, to resist the system by antisocial behavior, either violent or evasive (Cloward and Ohlin, 1960). This view of the interaction between the cultural system and individual adaptive behavior derives from the formulations of Davis on the effects of experience in social-class environments (Davis, 1948).

Conceptualizations of the process of socialization differ with respect to several other issues. One of these is the extent to which the impact of the reference group (social class, ethnic community, etc.) is interpreted either in terms of the situational and structural constraints (e.g., Cohen and Hodges, 1963; Cloward and Ohlin, 1960) or in terms of modal personality characteristics which are transmitted through child-rearing techniques of the parents (Inkeles, 1960; Sears, Maccoby and Levin, 1957). These two points of view represent a disagreement not about the social conditions involved in the experience of the individual nor in the nature of the outcome but in the complexity and nature of the influence. This is a divergence of considerable theoretical and practical significance, particularly with reference to research and to implementation of programs of intervention in the socialization sequence, as well as for urban planning and other forms of social engineering. A second dimension on which studies vary is the selection of different parts of the process for study and concern. Socialization can be regarded as multiple influences and types of input which are channeled through institutions and individuals to a chain of interaction between an adult and a child. Some students of this process orient their research and inquiry to the points of interchange between adult and child, viewing social-class differences in learning in terms of the differences in these specific interactions. Other scholars see as most salient the linkages between the adult and the institutions and wider community in which he is engaged (Kohn, 1963). A third dimension by which studies can be arranged is their interest in the effects of a single socializing agent or context, especially the relative impacts of parental or nonfamily influences (teacher, peers, mass media). The assumptions about the relative role of parents are expressed also in the view that early learning is more significant and permanent than later learning. These assumptions have been challenged from time to time (e.g., Reiss, 1965) and are likely to provide issues for research in the future, particularly on the development of social concepts. Recent studies of political socialization, for example, suggest that the school may be more significant for political learning than the home (Hess and Torney, 1967; Jennings and Niemi, 1968).

SOCIAL CLASS DIFFERENCES IN INTRA-FAMILY PSYCHOSOCIAL OPERATIONS

The study of socialization is a search for contingencies between individual behavior and elements of the environment (Gewirtz, 1966; Hess and Shipman, 1965). In many

respects, the family is a filter through which the young child begins to comprehend the stimuli which come to him from external and internal sources. Members of his family transmit to him, through various processes, schemata of apperception which identify stimuli as salient or unworthy of attention. They also offer constructs and symbols with which to organize and communicate experience (Schachtel, 1949). From this perspective, the cultural and socioeconomic environment in which the family lives touches the child indirectly through values, taboos, aspirations, patterned interaction and other belief systems of his family and directly in that the family itself is a part of its social and cultural surround. The impact of the total social and physical community, however, is increasingly free of mediation through family members as the child grows older and acquires information, values, and other patterns of behavior through more direct, although diffuse, contact with peers, adults in the community, mass media, and observations of his own. Even then, the early patterning of expectations and responses through experience with his family and home continues to filter, order, distort, and interpret the points of interchange with his world and, unless modified by subsequent experience, project the effects of early family interaction into his future matrix of behavior.

In this section will be discussed features of parental values and reported behavior (obtained by self-report) toward and about children that show systematic variation along SES lines; types of parental behavior that have been observed and measured in natural, quasi-natural, and laboratory conditions, and for which SES groups have been compared; and the empirical evidence that class-typed parental values and behavior are associated with the emergence of behavior in their children.

Parental Belief Systems about Children: Reported Child-Rearing Behavior and Values

The research literature on social-class differences in child-rearing behavior is dominated by two types of data: parents' reports of their values about child and parental behavior and parents' reports of what they do in interaction with the children. These two types represent, to somewhat different degrees, the value systems of parents which may or may not represent actual behavior. The assumption that there is a connection between the reports by parents and their behavior has been challenged by a number of studies which tend to show some distortion in self-reports, particularly in the direction of socially desirable behavior (including norms of parenting endorsed by Dr. Spock), as well as considerable disagreement among members of the same family in reporting information about decision making and distribution of power (Crandall and Preston, 1955; Zunich, 1962; Mednick and Shaffer, 1963; Wenar and Coulter, 1962; Robbins, 1963; Hess and Torney, 1963; McCord and McCord, 1961; Hefner, 1963; Yarrow, 1963). The distinction made here between maternal reports of behavior and behavioral data gathered by more direct observational or recordable procedures is more than a methodological nicety.

A widely quoted summary of the relationship between socioeconomic status and maternal reports of child-rearing practices in American families is the review and interpretation by Bronfenbrenner (1958) of studies of childrearing in this country between 1928 and 1957 (Anderson, 1936; Dollard, 1937; Benedict, 1938; Davis, Gardner, and Gardner, 1941; Warner and Lunt, 1941; Baldwin, Kalhorn, and Breese, 1945; Duvall, 1946; Davis and Havighurst, 1946; Warner, Meeker, and Eells, 1949; Stendler, 1950; Spinley, 1953; Wolfenstein, 1953; Maccoby, Gibbs, and staff of the Laboratory of Human Development at Harvard University, 1954; Havighurst and Davis, 1955; McClelland, Rindlisbacher, and DeCharms, 1955; Bayley and Schaefer, 1957; Boek, Lawson, Yankauer, and Sussman, 1957; Clausen, 1957; Klatskin, 1952; Kohn, 1957; Littman, Moore, and Pierce-Jones, 1957; Sears, Maccoby, and Levin, 1957; Spock, 1957; White, 1957; Miller and Swanson, 1958; Strodtbeck, 1958; Miller and Swanson, 1960). Since this report is extensive and detailed, this chapter will summarize it only briefly and then supplement it by reporting relevant studies appearing since 1957.

The research literature to 1957 showed a tendency for mothers to become more relaxed in their attitudes toward breast feeding and toilet training practices in the early years of the child's life. Class differences also appear to have altered somewhat over the period covered by Bronfenbrenner's review. Before World War II, middle-class mothers were less likely than working-class mothers to breast feed, to prolong breast feeding once begun, or to feed on demand. Since the early 1940s, a reverse in class difference is noted, although the patterns are not entirely consistent. Changes in maternal behavior occur most quickly in sectors of the society which have access to and use institutional instruments of change and advice—educational media, professional advice, etc.

Middle-class mothers report that they have more tolerance for the expression of drives and impulses (oral behavior, toilet accidents, sex, and aggression) and that they are less likely to punish occasional lapses of self-control. There is less restriction of movement outside the home in the middle-class families, although there has been a class reversal on this point since the early 1940's. In this reviewer's opinion, the usefulness of this measure of parental behavior may be compromised by the probable difference in physical neighborhoods represented not only by the different studies but by the middle-and-lower class groups within each study. The tendency to restrict movement of children outside the home would seem to be related to the parents' perceptions of the possible hazards. Restricting the movement of a child in a quiet, relatively safe, suburban community is hardly comparable to restricting and supervising the freedom of a child in a slum community or a community of mixed social-class composition with a relatively high crime rate. One might expect large differences between middle-class parents who live in suburban neighborhoods and middle-class parents who live in urban areas. Another qualification on the question of freedom of movement is the study of Psathas (1957) which idicates that lower-class parents grant greater freedom from parental control and supervision with increase in age, a finding congruent with the study of Maas on social-class differences in family system (1951).

In Bronfenbrenner's review, quite clear class differences appear in expectations of independent behavior and achievement. Middle-class parents expect more in these areas than do lower-class parents. The various interview items used in the studies reported by Bronfenbrenner touch different types of mastery, ranging from the child's ability to feed and dress himself, to responsibility for tasks around the home, to caring for personal possessions, to achieving in school and attending college.

One of the most significant generalizations in Bronfenbrenner's review is the conclusion that middle-class parents use "love oriented" discipline (withdrawal of affection, disapproval, shame, guilt), whereas lower-class parents more often use coercive punishment. The terminology in this comparison may seem to some to be prejudicial, suggesting, perhaps, that middle-class parents believe in love and lower-class parents in punishment. The actual contrast, however, is between two different types of punishment, one more likely to be physical, the other psychological.

The interaction that is expressed by the reports of the mothers in most of the studies reviewed by Bronfenbrenner is that middle-class mothers are more responsive to inner states, have a more acceptant and "democratic" relationship with their children; lower-class mothers are more concerned with external standards of conduct and adherence to norms of the community (respectability), illustrated by their tendency to stress the importance of obedience and respect for authority and lower tolerance of aggression directed toward themselves. In certain respects, these general features appear in studies conducted after Bronfenbrenner's review. Social-class difference among parents with respect to control and coercion also appear in two major studies—the Fels and Berkeley longitudinal groups (Bayley and Schaefer, 1960; Kagan and Freeman, 1963; Kagan and Moss, 1962). In both, there was a negative relationship between maternal education and maternal restrictiveness and a small or nonsignificant relation between maternal education and maternal expression of affection during the school years.

A fair degree of agreement emerges from studies of parental values about children and parenting styles. The study of Duvall (1946) is one of the early reports on social-class differences in parental values. She identified as "traditional" the desire on the part of parents that their children be neat and clean, that

they obey and respect authority figures and accept the norms of the adult world. Middle-class families were more likely to hold "developmental" views, preferring that children be eager to learn, cooperative, confiding in parents, happy, and healthy. Subsequent studies reiterate these findings and supplement them with others. Rosen (1959) found mothers from middle-class levels to be more interested in independence training and encouragement of ambition than were working-class mothers. Parental values of middle-class fathers as described by Aberle and Naegele (1952) reflect similar conceptions of the ideal child. A sequence of papers by Kohn and colleagues (1959a, 1959b, 1960) support and supplement these earlier papers. Kohn found that working-class parents are slightly more likely to stress obedience to parents and other adults as well as neatness and cleanliness than are middle-class parents. Parents from middle-class backgrounds tend to place higher priority on curiosity, happiness, consideration, and self-control. Nevertheless, middle- and working-class groups have great overlap in values in the sense that the percentage of differences is not always large and there is considerable agreement in other areas (Johnsen and Leslie, 1965; Kamii and Radin, 1967).

The greater emphasis upon educational achievement by middle-class adults is evident in surveys (Hyman, 1953) and is supported by questionnaire and interview data directed to attitudes about children and participation in schools. Cloward and Jones (1963) studied 998 randomly selected adults from the Lower East Side of Manhattan and found middle-class adults to be more concerned than working- or lower-class groups with the importance or necessity of education. In evaluating the schools, middle-class adults tend to be concerned with the physical plant and adequacy of facilities; lower- and working-class parents, with discipline and teachers. However, lower- and working-class parents who participate, as in membership in PTA, show a similar interest in facilities.

Class differences in reported use of authority in direct confrontation with children are congruent with attitudes described in other studies. Hoffman's description (1960) of influence techniques employed by parents includes a category he calls *unqualified power assertion,* defined as direct commands, threats, deprivations, or physical force intended to put direct pressure on a child to change his immediate course of behavior or action. In a study of 10 working-class and 12 middle-class families, he found that both fathers and mothers from working-class levels used unqualified power assertion more than did middle-class parents according to their taped reports of specific encounters with children.

Values which mothers held with respect to their own roles are part of the pattern of beliefs that contributes to their child-care behavior. In Swinehart's study (1963) of 252 mothers of third graders, values about their roles and their primary child-rearing objectives differed by class. Upper- and middle-class mothers are less accepting of the "service" aspects of the maternal role than are working-class mothers. Middle-class mothers express greater concern about the adequacy of their maternal role behavior, a finding of interest in view of Gildea's conclusion (1961) that middle-class mothers were more certain about their expectations for their own and the child's behavior.

Perhaps the most extensive recent literature on parental attitudes toward children comes from research using the Parent Attitude Research Instrument (PARI) devised by Schaefer and Bell (1958). A review and critique of the research generated by their work and questionnaire has been prepared by Becker and Krug (1965).

The two major factors of the PARI are labeled by the authors of the instrument as "approval of maternal control of the child" and "approval of maternal expression of hostility," and by Zuckerman et al. (1958) "authoritarian-control" and "hostility-rejection." Authoritarian-control attitudes are negatively related, in various studies, to occupation of father and educational level of mother (Becker, Peterson, Hellmer, Shoemaker, and Quay, 1959; Zuckerman, Barrett, and Bragiel, 1960) and to measures of social class (Garfield and Helper, 1962). Within social class, level of education correlates negatively with the scores on control factor (Becker and Krug, 1965; Marshall, 1961), and studies have shown that responses on this factor are changed positively by training and educational experience. These studies of the PARI have also

been consistent in finding the hostility-rejection factor *not* to be related to educational level. Becker and Krug (1965) note that the correlation between education and responses to the PARI is highest for content areas dealing with control of sex, aggression, and lying, a finding also reported by Schaefer and Bell (1958) and Garfield and Helper (1962). One factor that may affect the association between educational level and control scores is the tendency of mothers of lower SES levels (and lower education) to be more moralistic in their verbal comments (and test response?) about sex and aggression. The possibility that a connection exists between response tendencies and item format and content for questions dealing with maternal acceptance of sexual play in children is supported by the findings of Johnsen and Lesile (1965). They offer data indicating that the tendency of mothers to accept expressions of sexual feelings in children varies considerably with the type of item used. As part of their study of the consistency of maternal attitudes, they intercorrelated mothers' responses to items inquiring about tolerance for nudity, masturbation, and sex play. The responses between items dealing with nudity and sex play was .26; between nudity and masturbation, .34; and between sex play and masturbation, .53. The differences in responses according to the type of item show clearly in 6 items on sex permissiveness presented to these mothers. Only 1.8% agreed with the statement: "A mother should teach her children that curiosity about sex should not be satisfied in play with other children," but 87% disagreed with the statement: "A mother should teach her children that it is wrong to be curious about sex."

Another factor may be the tendency of better educated parents (also of higher SES) to reject the extreme statements which are used in authoritarian scales such as "Masturbation is the *worst* habit a child can form." The willingness of working-class mothers to accept this type of statement is, perhaps, a variation of the desire for lower-class persons to simplify experience and not to make as many discriminations or to express qualifications.

As part of a study of the relationship between maternal attitudes and mental health of children, a research team in St. Louis

(Gildea, Glidewell, and Kantor, 1961) examined, by questionnaire and structured home interview, social class differences in attitudes of mothers of a group of 826 third-grade children in St. Louis County, Missouri, using 17 items selected from a pilot study pool of 80 items. These items on face validity criteria were grouped into three dimensions: *responsibility, uncertainty of own judgment, and rejection.*

On items dealing with sense of parental responsibility for the behavior of children, the mothers from high-status groups reported more responsibility for and personal involvement in the behavior problems of their children. However, there was great difference in the magnitude of social-class discrepancy among the three items. In the social-class distribution of three groups (upper, middle, lower; no criteria stated), the discrepancy between upper- and lower-status levels ranged from 7% on one item to 32% on another. Of the four items dealing with discipline, two showed social-class differences. Again, the extent of difference varied widely from item to item. Generally the lower-class mother appeared more strict in obedience training and more concerned about compliance to authority.

Four items were used to assess attitudes of rejection. The social-class differences in pattern of response were not clear. No association was found between maternal attitudes and maternal or teacher reports of the presence of severe behavior problems.

Factor analysis revealed two factors, one which combined the items dealing with discipline and rejection and was interpreted as a measure of attitude toward the need for parental control, the other expressing the mothers assessment of the degree to which the children try to cope with their environment. Social class differences appeared on the first of these factors (lower-class mothers saw children as needing more control) but not on the second. Neither factor showed a significant relationship with teacher or mother reports of presence of disturbance in the children.

Another factor coming from the analysis was interpreted as a mother's feelings of uncertainty in her treatment of the child. Social class differences appeared on four of the six items on this attitude-cluster, with lower-class mothers expressing less confidence in their child rearing practices.

In a study of four social status groups of urban Negro mothers (upper-middle, skilled work level, unskilled work level, and dependent on public assistance) and their 4-year-old children, Hess and Shipman (1965, 1967, 1968; Hess et al., 1968) found SES differences on a wide range of reported as well as observed behavior. Middle-class mothers have slightly higher educational and occupational aspirations for their children and much higher expectations that these aspirations will be reached; they also see themselves as more effective in dealing with the school than do women from working-class levels. Mothers from working-class levels indicate that they would use more imperative commands and instructions (comparable in some sense to Hoffman's Unqualified Power Assertion) in preparing their children for experience in school; they report fewer memberships in organizations and less participation in activities outside the home, along the lines described by Cohen and Hodges (1963). As in other studies, however, the overlap between the upper middle and other groups is considerable. Of particular interest is their finding that the large SES difference on most items appeared between the upper middle and the other three groups, with much less discrepancy among the means of the three working-class groups. Differences, to be reported later, were also found in observed behavior of mothers.

Social Class Differences in Observed Parental Behavior

Perhaps the most troublesome problem in studies of socialization behavior of parents is the enormous difficulty involved in obtaining valid data. Although much of the data published comes from parents' accounts through interviews about their behavior or from self-report obtained through interviews or questionnaires, several studies have attempted to obtain measures of actual behavior from groups of mothers of dissimilar socioeconomic background. These studies have the methodological advantage of bypassing the mothers' or fathers' descriptions of their own behavior, but they encounter other serious problems. The first is that the situations in which parents and children are observed in actual interaction are almost of necessity artificial and contrived, often placing the parents in unfamiliar physical surroundings and requiring them to perform tasks and to engage in behavior not representative of interaction at home. Tape recorders, videotapes, and other recording equipment are now of a quality, size, and versatility to make home observation by machine possible, and it seems likely that studies of parent behavior will use these data-gathering equipment. However, the introduction of recording equipment into the family setting will also distort, to an unknown degree, the data obtained. These techniques of research may affect the quality of data by distorting the behavior of lower-class mothers in different ways and to different degrees than that of middle-class mothers. One would expect both groups of mothers to behave, and to try to get their children to behave, in what they regard as socially desirable ways in the presence of the researcher, teacher, or other figure of institutionalized authority.

The patterns of maternal behavior appearing in reports of observed interaction between mother and child are often different from the patterns reported by parents. This is not altogether a matter of disagreement between behavior and report, although there are discrepancies in this regard; rather, the differences lie primarily in the type of behavior elicited in the observational and quasi-experimental situations. It is relatively difficult to obtain longitudinal observations on child-rearing activities such as *breast versus bottle feeding, toilet training,* etc., which can be easily included in interview and attitudinal studies. Neither are there likely to be enough events which call for discipline to give adequate observational information about norms of physical versus psychological punishment and control. There is likely to be little or no sexual play or interest expressed by the child; the mother's tendency to restrict freedom of movement is usually not elicited in the experimental situation. The categories of behavior that emerge represent types of communication which do not fit nicely into the familiar pigeonholes of *warmth, permissiveness, control,* or *rejection;* they represent a mother-child interaction of maternal techniques of child care.

The first major observational study of pa-

rental behavior was conducted at Fels, using scales developed by Champney (1941) and applied extensively by Baldwin and his colleagues (1945, 1948, 1949). Data obtained by observation in the home and conversations with the mother were summarized on rating scales designed to measure such clusters of behavior as democracy in the home, acceptance of the child, indulgence-protectiveness, degree of control, and activity level. A report of the longitudinal study at Fels indicated social-class differences in degree of coerciveness which is higher in lower-status mothers (Waters and Crandall, 1964). However, the relationship between social class as indicated by mother's educational level and maternal behavior as judged by observations and verbal reports was uneven and low.

Data showing correlational association between some environmental variables during early years of life and subsequent cognitive growth, such as IQ, come from the longitudinal analysis of Guidance Study and the Berkeley Growth Study conducted by the Institute of Human Development at the University of California, Berkeley (Bayley and Schaefer, 1964; Honzik, 1957, 1967).

Correlations from the Berkeley Growth Study, reported by Bayley and Schaefer (1964), show systematic shifts in pattern as children grow older. Age differences in pattern also differ by sex. Boys' intelligence was strongly related to the love-hostility dimension of maternal behavior, with mothers noted as *hostile* having sons who score high in intelligence in the first year but have low IQs from 4 through 18 years, whereas the slow, inactive, but "happy" male babies of mothers rated as *loving* grew into intellectually alert, friendly boys and extroverted adolescents. The girls' IQ scores, on the other hand, were less related to maternal behavior and attitudes and more to parental education and to estimates of mothers' IQs. It was concluded that the impact of the environment on boys' behavior and intellectual functioning is fixed early (by the third year) and persists at least through the age of 18, while the girls' intellectual functioning is more genetically determined.

Relationships between educational level of parents and achievement behavior in childhood and adulthood were reported by Kagan and Moss (1962). Mastery behavior during the first 3 years of life was not related to parental educational level, but substantial associations between achievement scores were noted for both sexes in adulthood. Between the ages of 10 and 14, on the other hand, the association between achievement scores and parental educational level was significant only for boys (the correlations between maternal educational level and girls' intellectual achievement scores were negative but nonsignificant).

Several observational studies of maternal behavior have been specifically directed toward analysis of social-class differences. One of the earliest of these was conducted by Zunich (1961), who modified the observational procedures and categories used by Merrill (1946) and Bishop (1951). Forty middle- and 40 lower-class mothers were observed through a one-way mirror in 30 minutes of relatively free interaction with one of their children in a laboratory equipped with toys, books, etc. The categories used to summarize the mothers' behavior included *contacting, directing, observing attentively, remaining out of contact, teaching.* Nine of 17 categories showed significant differences between social classes. Mothers from middle-class backgrounds were higher on *contacting, directing, helping, interfering by structuring, observing attentively, playing interactively.* Lower-class mothers were higher on *remaining out of contact.* Lower-class mothers did not as often engage in behavior rated as *uncooperative, criticizing, giving permission, interfering, interfering by structuring,* and *playing interactively.* In a later report (Walters, Connor, and Zunich, 1964), mothers were told that the child had not performed adequately, with the suggestion that the child was not mature. Lower-class mothers changed less in response to this (artificial) information, suggesting more concern in middle-class mothers about the negative evaluation of the investigator. It is difficult to argue that in this situation, middle-class mothers were more permissive.

Another group of studies has been conducted by Radin and Kamii on social class differences in maternal attitudes and behavior using the PARI (Kamii, 1965; Kamii and Radin, 1967; Radin and Kamii, 1965). They suggest that middle-class mothers and lower-class mothers activate different types of identification processes in their children. Following statements of theory of Miller and Swanson (1960) and Bronfenbrenner (1961), they hypothesize social class differentiation in the development of *anaclitic* identifications, which they see as fitting the middle-class parental behavioral pattern of threats of withdrawal of love and approval, and *identification with the aggressor,* which they suggest fits the patterns of lower-class parents, typified by more coercion, external controls, and discipline, and less tendency to respond to implicit needs for affection, contact, and reassurance. Twenty middle-class and 20 lower-class Negro mothers were observed in their behavior with their children, at least one of whom was enrolled in a preschool program. Particular attention was given to behavior that met *explicit* needs of the children, that met the *implicit* needs of the child for affection, reassurance, etc., and behavior that attempted to persuade the child to change his actions in some way.

Analysis of maternal behavior in response to the child's explicit requests for attention (by requesting water, milk, or food, showing something to the mother, initiating a conversation, etc.) showed that middle-class mothers were responsive to requests of the child much more (73%) than lower-class mothers (46%), a difference all the more significant since the middle-class children were observed to express needs significantly more often than lower-class children. Middle-class children not only have a higher proportion of their explicit needs satisfied by their mothers but also seek maternal attention much more. The resulting ratio of maternal gratifying responses is about four times as many per unit time for middle-class as for lower-class subjects. The differences between the two groups applied to *implicit* needs, defined as needs for affection and companionship, were also observed. During the 30-minute period of observation, more than half of the lower-class mothers initiated no interaction; only one middle-class mother failed to interact in this way. More than half of the middle-class mothers initiated four or more interactions and were significantly above the lower-class mothers in both nonverbal and verbal communication of affection.

Analysis of the mothers' behavior when they wished to influence the child, rather than merely respond to his explicit or implicit needs, showed lower-class mothers to be somewhat more active (217 attempts for the 20 mothers) than middle-class mothers (187 attempts for 20 mothers). Within these totals, the techniques used by lower-class mothers were to give orders without explanation (35%), request gently without explanations (23%), coax (10%). Middle-class mothers used gentle requests without explanation (22%) as their most frequent style, consulting (14%), gentle requests with explanation (12%), and ordering without explanation (12%). In comparing the pattern of mothers' influence techniques, Kamii found that there was a tendency for middle-class mothers to use psychological techniques more frequently but not at a significant level. Neither was there a significant difference in behavior rated as "coercive," although lower-class mothers tended to be somewhat higher. Of interest in this connection was the finding that most of the mothers of both groups did not engage in coercive behavior, possibly in recognition of the presence of the interviewer in the home. A final class difference was the greater tendency of the middle-class mothers to reward desirable behavior on the part of the child.

In connection with a study of maternal socialization of cognitive behavior in young children, Hess and his colleagues observed interaction between Negro mothers and their 4-year-old children (Hess and Shipman, 1965, 1967, 1968). The mothers came from four different social status levels, ranging from upper middle-class to families on public assistance. In the interaction sessions, mothers were asked to teach their children three simple tasks that they had previously been taught by a staff member. The verbal interaction between mother and child was recorded; a running description of the nonverbal interaction was recorded on a parallel tape. The transcripts were analyzed for the ability of the mother to define the task for the child and to motivate him to work toward solution and for related aspects of teaching strategy of the mothers. Middle-class mothers were more likely to provide an orientation to the task for the child, to request verbal feedback rather than physical compliance, to be specific in their instructions, to use motivation techniques that in-

volved explicit or implicit reward, and, on a number of measures, to provide the child with information he needed to complete the task and to monitor his performance.

These studies of observed maternal behavior agree in their portrayal of middle-class mothers as more attentive and more responsive to their children, and apparently more aware of their children's feelings and perspectives on the activities in which they are engaged. It may be this quality of attention, with its greater degree of communication and apparent interest, that has been called a "warmer" and "closer" relationship by previous studies. They also tend less to use power-oriented punishment in influence techniques, are more likely to explain to the child the rationale involved in a request and to provide ideas and words through which maternal control can be mediated. The differences that emerge seem to show not so much that one group of mothers is more or less controlling than the other, but that the differences are in the types of control used, with the lower-class mothers oriented to the power inherent in their status and to normative-imperative appeals rather than to rationales that let the child avoid confrontation with parental power (Hess and Shipman, 1968). The greater use of language by middle-class mothers evident in these studies can thus be seen to flow from the nature of the interaction and of the regulatory processes the mothers have developed in their relationships with their children. These patterns of interaction represent the accumulation of mutual response experiences. To this reviewer, the behavior of these mothers from lower-class background in interactive situations reflects their adaptation to the social structure in which they live. It is not that they do not wish to perform adequately as mothers or that they prefer punishment as a control strategy. Preliminary reports from research conducted by Bernstein indicate that children adopt the control strategies of their mothers. This early orientation toward authority transmits and reinforces the orientation of adults to the economic and social system of which they are a part. They lack alternatives of action in their own exchanges with the institutions of the community and with other members of their communities and are poorly motivated to seek other techniques because there is little reason to expect reward. It does appear, however, that much of the behavior which distinguishes middle- from lower-class mothers is within the lower-class mother's intellectual range and thus not primarily a function of IQ differences. Hess' data show great variation among working-class groups with respect to these categories of behavior.

Association between Socializing Beliefs and Practices and Behavior of Children

In view of the effort devoted to studies of parental socializing behavior, the predictive power of the data gathered about parents has been disappointingly low or uneven. Results of studies attempting to relate parental values or reports of child-rearing behavior of parents to outcomes in their children show uneven and often contradictory results. The national survey study of political values, reported by Jennings, and Niemi (1968), used interview techniques with a national probability sample of 1669 high school seniors and at least one parent of 94% of the students. While there was considerable agreement between parents and children with respect to party affiliation as in much previous research on more limited groups (Hyman, 1959), on many issues and attitudes there was very little correlation between parents and children. Similar patterns were found with regard to religious attitudes. Children, in general, feel affiliated with the same religious denomination as their parents (74%), but on ideological questions there was much less agreement. In political and other attitudes, the relationships beween family members did not change significantly by sex of parent or child or along parental control dimensions, "democratic," "autocratic," or "close." This finding was not affected by source of information, that is, whether they used the child's or the parents' report about the relationship. They conclude, "it is . . . clear that any model of socialization which rests on assumptions of pervasive currents of parent to child value transmissions of the types examined here is in serious need of modification." The study of Jennings et al. is especially significant in view of the documented social differences in political interest, party identification, and participation.

Other reviews of research in related areas show little reason to rely heavily on expressed parental values and attitudes as antecedents of attitudes and behavior of children. Sewell (1961), in his review of social class and childhood personality, reports data that show virtually no relationship between maternal reports of specific infant-training practices (feeding, weaning, nursing schedule, bowel training, bladder training, and punishment for toilet accidents) and personality characteristics of children (measured on both paper-and-pencil tests and projective tests of personality and ratings of the children's behavior by their mothers and teachers). He also reports low correlation among measures of strictness in several areas of child rearing. Becker and Krug's review of research (1965), which has used the PARI, summarizes the relationships between this instrument and children's behavior. Becker and Krug show that when used with homogeneous groups, the authoritarian control scale of PARI shows relationships to aggressive behavior. In a number of studies, little or no association has been found between the PARI and several measures of achievement, adjustment, self-rating, etc. Gildea's report (1961) of the study of child-rearing attitudes of 830 mothers of upper, middle and lower class and the behavioral problems of their third-grade children includes the finding that the attitudinal differences among the mothers of different social classes (with respect to sense of *responsibility, discipline, rejection*) did not differentiate between groups of children evaluated as "disturbed" and those evaluated as "not disturbed" whether the evaluations were done by teachers or by mothers.

Other studies report findings that support the argument that maternal behavior and attitudes which differ by social class do affect child behavior (Becker and Krug, 1964). Hoffman (1960), in his study of the effects of unqualified power assertion, finds that mothers who are relatively high on this influence technique induce hostility, power needs, and heightened autonomy strivings toward peers. Hess, Shipman, Brophy, and Bear (1968) found observed maternal teaching styles and use of imperative-normative control techniques to be related to cognitive measures of children (IQ, sorting behavior, concept development) for their total sample and within the groups of working-class mothers. These relationships also appeared between maternal behavior when the child was 4 years old and the child's reading readiness test scores 2 years later. The significant dimensions of maternal behavior that emerge in this study were not the strict-permissive or the warmth-hostility factors but such behavior as the mother's tendency to anticipate the child's needs, to give him information necessary for solving tasks, to give him feedback and specific information during test performance, her feelings of efficacy in relation to institutions of the community and participation in the activities outside the home. Most important, then, is the type of appeal used in controlling or regulating the child's behavior, that is, whether she appeals to rules or norms; issues imperative commands ("Do this because I said so"); or uses appeals which take into account subjective states of the child or herself ("How do you think your teacher will feel or you will feel if you don't do your lesson?") or which offer a rationale in terms of the long-term consequences of the act ("If you are late to school you'll miss part of the lesson and not do well on the test.") Some of the findings of Hess and his colleagues have been supported by studies on other working-class Negro groups which relate maternal behavior to performance on scholastic measures (Slaughter, in press).

SOCIAL-CLASS DIFFERENCES IN CHILDREN'S PERSONALITY AND BEHAVIOR

In addition to the studies which attempt to relate the values and behavior of parents to the behavior of their own children, there is a large number of empirical studies of social-class differences in children's personality characteristics and patterns of behavior which report little or no relevant parental behavior. Although these studies add little information about socialization in relation to social stratification, they offer an opportunity to examine in a crude way the plausibility of some of the conceptualizations of socialization described in the preceding pages. These findings are summarized in this section. On topics for which data about children's personality and behavioral characteristics is meager, some evidence on social class differences in the adult population has been included in order to present a more complete picture. On other topics adult data are introduced to show that

trends evident in the pre-adult population are congruent with established differences among adults. The categories within which the empirical evidence is described reflect research interest on the topic in question and are selected more for convenience than to offer a conceptual framework for the study of social class differences.

Self-Concept and Self-Esteem

In a highly competitive society, it is inevitable that self-esteem will derive in part from an individual's perception of his ranking and prestige within relevant groups. To the extent that the symbols and realities of socioeconomic status, membership in a minority group, and other indicators of social structure carry such implication of status, they may be expected to affect the development of self-regard and identity. Furthermore, this impact is relatively difficult to modify; unlike some attitudes that might be amenable to change by education and training, the awareness of social status comes from a structural reality which probably cannot be altered by dealing with the individual only. Research evidence which is relevant to social-class differences in self-concept and self-esteem is thus of particular importance to the organizing concepts of this chapter—that there are functional relationships between social structure and individual behavior and that the acquisition of behavior in childhood is patterned by social and cultural realities.

There is a considerable amount of research available on the child's awareness of his position in the social stratification and his ethnic group membership, much of it stimulated by interest in understanding the origins of attitudes toward minority groups and their relationship to intergroup conflict. Awareness of ethnic group membership appears to begin during the nursery school years, perhaps as part of the process through which the child's self-concept is established. Studies of Negro and white nursery school children attending either interracial or segregated schools have shown that racial awareness appears as early as the age of 4 and increases with age, irrespective of the kind of school the child attends (Ammons, 1950; Clark and Clark, 1947; Goodman, 1952; Horowitz and Horowitz, 1938; Landreth and Johnson, 1953; Morland, 1958; Stevenson and Stevenson,

1960; Stevenson and Stewart, 1958; Vaughn, 1964). Studies with several racial, religious, and national groups of children between the ages of 3 and 10 have shown that membership in an ethnic minority is a predisposing factor in the early development of ethnic awareness (Goodman, 1952; Hartley et al., 1948; Porter, 1963; Radke et al., 1949).

In Negro children, race awareness is apparently accompanied by preference for the white race and ambivalence toward their own; this tendency appears to vary with the age of children, racial and social structure of the geographic area of their residence, and technique used to assess such reactions. A number of studies in which children of nursery school and the lower grades of elementary school were asked to indicate their preferences for dolls, storybook characters, or playmates report that the Negro children show significantly less pronounced ingroup preferences than their white agemates (Clark and Clark, 1947; Goodman, 1952; Landreth and Johnson, 1953; Morland, 1958, 1962; Radke et al., 1949; Stevenson and Stewart, 1958). These studies also showed that responses indicating depreciation by the Negro child of his own racial group decrease with age. On the other hand, characteristics of the stimuli used to assess children's attitudes toward their own and other racial groups account to some extent for the responses given. Negro children's misidentification is reduced when they are given the opportunity to choose between three instead of two differently colored dolls (including white, dark-brown, and mulatto dolls) with which to identify (Greenwald and Oppenheim, 1968). Using a white and a chocolate colored doll, Gregor and McPherson (1966) also found no differences in the degree to which 6- and 7-year-old Negro and white children identified with their own racial group and expressed preference for it. The major difference between the two groups was that a large majority of the white group (93%) expressed outgroup negative bias (only one white S failed to identify either doll as "looking bad") while only 8 out of 92 Negro Ss expressed such bias.

The extent to which white children reject Negroes or express hostility toward them increases with age (Horowitz, 1936; Radke et al., 1949). Deutsch (1960) found that far more negative self-conceptions characterize lower-class Negro elementary school children than low SES white children. Rejection and depreciation of his own racial group have been found to be accompanied in the young Negro child by self-doubt, self-rejection, anxiety, insecurity, fearfulness, and passivity (Clark and Clark, 1947; Goodman, 1952; Morland, 1958; Stevenson and Stewart, 1958; Palermo, 1959; Deutsch, 1960). Comparisons of TAT responses given by white and Negro lower-class boys, aged from 9 to 14, showed that Negroes tend to perceive the world as hostile and threatening, whereas whites tend to see it as warm and friendly (Mussen, 1953).

Although the sources of ethnic attitudes and the processes through which they are acquired may be multiple, these attitudes are learned and are functional for the individual. The congruence of findings of studies conducted in different regions of the U.S. and over many years points to the normative character of ethnic attitudes (Proshansky, 1966) despite some recorded regional and social class-linked variations (McDaniel and Babchuck, 1960; Noel, 1964). Clark (1955) and Sherif et al., (1961) view ethnic prejudice as a problem rooted in social stratification and functioning rather than in pathologies of individuals. The behavior of socializing agents and legalized or de facto segregation of ethnic groups in various social contexts create a social reality for the child, in which direct and indirect adult teaching, as well as the mass media, shape the child's conceptions of his own subcultural group as compared to others. Ethnic group attitudinal norms, as reflected in the values and behavior of his parents, neighbors, teachers, and minister, are experienced early by the child. Whether or not these important others also explicitly or implicitly demand that the child think about and act toward members of various ethnic groups in ways consonant with their attitudes, adult pressures are effective, even in their most subtle forms (Goodman, 1952; Trager and Yarrow, 1952). There is also some evidence that parents are the primary source of their children's ethnic attitudes (Bird, Monachesi, and Burdick, 1952; Goodman, 1952; Radke and Trager, 1950). The younger children tend to be aware of the parental origin of their attitudes, but the older are more likely to forget the source and present various rationalizations (Horowitz, and Horowitz, 1938). Direct acceptance of parental attitudes has been reported more often by prejudiced than by nonprejudiced college students (Allport and Kramer 1946), a finding congruent with those reported by Frenkel-Brunswik and Sanford (1945) and Rosenblith (1949).

Although acquisition of intergroup attitudes does not depend only on direct or indirect transmission of the parental attitudes to children but also on the teaching of the facts of outgroup life by schoolteachers, neighbors, peers, etc., little research has focused on the influence of these other socialization agents. Findings collected through sociometric techniques regarding the influence of racial membership on friendship preferences and ties among peers are conflicting. Criswell (1939), for example, did not find racial cleavages until children were 8 to 10 years old, but Lambert and Taguchi (1956) and McCandless and Hoyt (1961) have detected evidence of such cleavage in preschool years.

Awareness of his social class position seems to be established in the child later than awareness of his racial or ethnic group membership. Polis (1962) found that 95% of a sample of Melbourne school children, aged 13, could say what social class they belonged to while only $\frac{1}{3}$ of a group 2 years younger could do so. Similar findings were reported by Middleton (1954).

Comparing responses of 5- to 8-year-old children on how people get rich and why some are rich and some are poor, Danziger (1958) found that the younger children give fantasy answers ("stealing," "digging up gold," "from God"). Although children of all ages spoke of degrees of work, only in the 8-year-olds did the notion of capital appear even in rudimentary forms, such as saving money left by relatives or selling things. Danziger suggested that economic concepts develop in set stages and that first-hand experience of buying things leads most children to understand exchange relationships better than production ones. If direct experience is a mediating factor in learning economic attitudes and behavior, the differences in income to spend, range of materials purchased, and different types of transaction (cash, charge, stamps, credit, etc.) are obvious SES effects upon economic socialization.

To investigate differences in the ways upper- and lower-class children look at poverty, Estvan (1952) presented a picture of a very poor household to 10- and 11-year-olds in a Midwestern town and asked them what they saw in it, what they felt about it, and how many people (locally, in America, and in the world) lived like this. Upper-class children more often used the word *slum* and talked more about poor jobs and schooling and the lack of playthings; lower-class children talked more about unemployment, illness, lack of clothing, quarrels, and drunkenness. Most other reactions were similar, with children agreeing about the proportion of poor people, the main consequences of poverty, and how they felt about it. Lower-class children were more inclined to see poverty as a neighborhood (or world) problem, whereas upper-class children viewed it as a national one.

The findings of the foregoing studies indicate that the awareness of elementary school children of social stratification and of the relative position of their families in it is emotional-experiential rather than cognitive-rational. Middle- and upper-class elementary school children are more likely than their lower-class agemates to grasp the economic notions underlying social stratification. Such rudimentary awareness of the social stratification and of the child's own relative position in it should be expected to have subtle but powerful effects on his self-concept and self-esteem. These effects, unlike those of racial awareness, seem to be directly measurable only in adolescence.

Studying estimates by primary school boys and girls (grades 7, 8, and 9) of their school work ability as a function of sex, race, and socioeconomic level (defined by the Hollingshead-Redlich occupation scale), Wylie (1963) found more modest self-estimates of ability in girls than boys, Negroes than whites, and low SES than higher SES. The group as a whole showed, however, a relatively high "self-favorability bias."

The effects of low self-esteem upon the personality and behavior of elementary school children are reflected in the poor academic performance of the lower-class and the Negro child in elementary school. The increasing disparity in performance, compared to middle-class norms, which characterizes lower-class and Negro children as they grow older in standard intelligence and achievement tests may reflect (at least in part) a complex process in which low test performance or academic achievement and increasing awareness of failure result in a vicious circle in which self-esteem and level and quality of actual performance interact inseparably.

Teachers' expectancies about the intellectual attainments of their pupils may be externally manipulated and in turn influence the actual performance of the pupils. The effects of these expectancies may be more operative among the younger children (Rosenthal and Jacobson, 1966).

In a study of subjective class identification in high school and college students in relation to several other psychological and sociological characteristics, Sims (1952b) found that the status which students assign themselves in the social hierarchy is related to, but not identical with, their objective social status. Class identification was found to be positively related to general mental ability (particularly verbal).

To specify the impact of various social factors on self-esteem and evaluate the influence of self-esteem on socially significant attitudes and behavior, Rosenberg (1965) collected data from 5024 high school juniors and seniors from 10 randomly selected public high schools in New York State. The sample included "various social classes, religious groups, rural and urban communities and nationality groups." The results showed: (1) that social prestige of a nationality or religious group is unrelated to the self-acceptance of its members; (2) Ss from higher social classes are more likely than those from lower social classes to have high self-esteem. The differences, however, are not large, they are not the same for boys and girls, and they appear to be due in part to certain kinds of parent-child relationships. Rosenberg thought that, among adolescents, subcultural norms or other characteristic aspects of experience deriving from cultural factors are more important determinants of self-esteem than class-linked social prestige. Further analysis of the data in terms of the effects of being raised in dissonant cultural contexts, namely, religious contexts, showed that (1) Catholics being raised in Jewish areas had lower self-esteem than Catholics being raised in Protestant areas, (2) Protestants being raised in Jewish areas had lower self-esteem than Protestants in Catholic areas; and (3) that Jews being raised in Catholic areas had lower self-esteem than Jews in Protestant areas.

Self-esteem was found by Rosenberg to be related to achievement in school and to occupational expectations. Subjects with low self-esteem much less often thought they had the qualities and characteristics required for success in the jobs of their choice. Low self-esteem was also strongly, though complexly, related to interpersonal competence. Adolescents with low self-esteem tended to describe themselves as withdrawn, excessively sensitive, and suspicious. They also tended to provoke problems with peers and so to confirm their fears and suspicions about social relationships.

In an attempt to discover whether people from similar social class levels would also evidence a homogeneity in self-concept, Klausner (1953) studied 106 white males within a year of 17 years of age, using a 60-item questionnaire about the self including 3 self-concept factors: reactive aggression, adjusted inferiority, and social isolation and self-aggression. The results showed that members of different socioeconomic groupings have modally different self-concepts. There is more aggression against the self and more psychosocial isolation in members of the upper socioeconomic groupings. Lower socioeconomic groups reply to feelings of insecurity and inferiority with aggression.

Differences in Personality and Mental Health

The study of functional connections between SES and mental health is complicated by the uncertain distinction between social deviance and psychopathology. For example, in many studies of children, the terms "adjustment" and "maladjustment" signify both mental health and social functioning, suggesting the interlacing of underlying operations. An individual in a social matrix confronts institutions, rules, norms of the society with which he must deal; the ease or difficulty of this adjustment to society would seem to depend, to some measure at least, upon the congruence of patterns of behavior and schedules of social re-enforcement between the institution in which he spends his early years and institutions of the society to which he must later adjust. Such congruence is in part a question of compatibility among institutions and therefore a structural matter; interinstitutional discontinuities may easily become identified in terms of mental health (i.e., truancy in the ghetto) and are often treated as if the origin and locus were primarily within the individual or his family. From this view, the emotional and cognitive stresses involved in transition from the home as the early socializing unit in the lower working-class levels to the school, which as a middle-class institution represents the dominant norms of society, are enormous. This transition to school is not easy even for children of middle class, who go to middle-class schools and are met by teachers who are often friendly, supportive, understanding, and compatible; it is considerably more stressful for children from slum areas. Many other cultural disparities exist in the society, but, for the child, the major institutions are the home and the school, and lack of congruence between these two initiates much of the cognitive and emotional stress that later in his life may be described in clinical terminology. This definitional problem, of course, cannot be resolved in this chapter.

Perhaps one may gain perspective on the problem by examining the areas of behavior in which social class differences in personality features presumably relevant to mental health are most evident in the literature. The degree of agreement among studies on types of social class differences found and theoretical explanations advanced for empirically established differential rates of mental health should also be examined.

Given the extreme differences among social classes in physical environment, economic resources, occupational activities, housing, crowding, power, and prestige, it seems reasonable to expect SES differences in the types of behavior that reflect effective ego functioning and mental health. Research appears to support this expectation. Unfortunately, research literature on this topic is inconclusive. The magnitude of SES differences in frequency of mental illness in adults varies with the SES range and representativeness of the sample studied. The latter factors also influence findings on types of mental diseases or personality maladjustments reported to be predominant in different social classes. In studies of children, both the SES and age

range sampled and the technique used for personality assessment seem to affect the degree of SES differences in overall indexes of personality adjustment and in patterns of traits or personality factors contributing to the overall differences. Moreover, correlations recorded between social class and measures of personality adjustment in children are low, although in many studies they have been statistically significant (Sewell, 1961). Researchers admit that methodological limitations exist with respect to attempt to measure "deeper" personality features (Proshansky, 1963).

1. Indices of SES Differences in Morale and Mental Health. Social class differences in the psychological features of the adult environment are particularly relevant to the development of children's personality structures and consequent class-linked differentials in their mental health. From a simplistic assumption of generational transmission, the perceptions that adults have of themselves and external social conditions of their lives reflect mental health differentials which conceivably influence the personality adjustment of children. The simplest and perhaps most obvious indicator of social class-linked differences in an adult's perception of the environment is the sense of pleasure or gratification he finds in his work. Job satisfaction is related to SES level. Survey research data have shown that, in the U.S. as well as cross-nationally, the proportion of those who report job satisfaction varies directly with position on the standard occupational hierarchy (Inkeles, 1960). An additional finding is that, in the United States, unskilled workers cite job security (in comparison with possible, less secure advancement) as the basis for choosing a job significantly more often than those in more favored occupations. Moreover, measures of optimism, as reflected in the belief that human nature can be changed and in the faith in the meaningfulness of efforts to master one's physical and social environment, were also found to be more typical of high SES levels. In Inkeles' view, it is reasonable to assume that superior intellectual equipment, advanced training, and actual experience produce and maintain a view of the world as a less mysterious and threatening place than it appears to those who face life without these advantages. Survey data have shown, for example, that predictions of the long-run effects of man's mastery of atomic energy become increasingly less optimistic with decrease in educational level (Inkeles, 1960). The lower-class person is also more likely to face life without a clear sense of direction and purpose. The relationship between socioeconomic status and anomie has been demonstrated in several studies; it is inversely related to socioeconomic status, measured by either individual or neighborhood variables, and directly related to social isolation (Bell, 1957).

2. Studies of Social Class Differences in Mental Health and Types of Mental Disturbances in Adults. Analyzing differences in the types of symptoms which predominate in neurotic disorders of patients from different social classes, Freedman (1962) contends that it is not poverty itself but discontent that relates the objective fact of being poor to psychopathology. The meaning and function of neurotic disorders may differ from one person to another depending on an interaction between his self-image and his perception of outer reality. Freedman found that neuroses which are expressed behaviorally or somatically have the highest prevalence in the lower socioeconomic groups, whereas neuroses with subjective symptomatology such as anxiety, depression, or defense other than somatization and socially deviant behavior are significantly more frequent among the upper income groups. Viewed in the perspective of their social significance, the expressions of neuroses ranged through a regular progression from introversive, intimate personal symptoms in the upper socioeconomic groups to the wider, increasingly community-centered collisions in the lower socioeconomic groups. On the basis of these findings, Freedman suggested that class-linked differences in neurotic symptoms reflect differential defense mechanisms acquired during the early stages of personality development.

Studies drawing their samples from psychiatric services' records (Hollingshead and Redlich, 1958; Myers and Roberts, 1959) have reported social class differences in prevalence of treated mental illness, with psychoses, particularly schizophrenia, appearing to be more frequent in the lowest social strata. These studies, however, do not provide valid bases for generalizations to the total population. Recorded or treated frequency and overall (untreated and treated) frequency of personality impairment or mental illness are very different measures of morbidity (Srole et al., 1962). The higher frequency of hospitalization in the lower class might be explained by less access to private therapy or by higher frequency of acute episodes resulting in higher rates of hospitalization. Different rates of hospitalization may also be related to class-linked differential symptomatology of the same mental illness or to the fact that access to therapy during the early stages of the disease varies by social class (Van den Haag, 1966).

Inquiries on the connections between SES and overall prevalence of psychiatric disability in adults, covering a general population rather than samples of treated psychiatric patients, have also yielded contradictory findings. Thus a national Selective Service investigation conducted in 1943 on male registrants, with rejections for "mental and personality disorders" as the criterion of morbidity, yielded almost zero correlations between psychiatric rejection and SES determined on the basis of occupation, excluding students, farmers, and unemployed (Rowntree, McGill, and Hellman, 1945). In a National Health Survey conducted in 1936, the correlation found between SES and incidence of nervous and mental disease was zero for females but positive for males, the white-collar rate of mental disease exceeding that of the blue-collar category (Hailman, 1941). Similar findings were reported in the Baltimore study of 809 men and women (30% of whom were nonwhites). In this study the mental disorder rates by income level were reported only for whites and nonwhites combined. Assuming that the nonwhites of Baltimore were highly concentrated in the lowest of the four income brackets defined and that the three other income groups were predominantly whites, Srole et al. (1962) estimated that among whites the relationship between psychiatric morbidity and income was positive, that is, the highest morbidity rate was found in the top-income category. In contrast, the Boston Selective Service survey yielded inverse correlations between psychiatric rejection rates and SES of the registrants (as indexed by area of residence) with morbidity rates being higher among lower SES Ss (Hyde and Kingsley, 1944). In the Midtown Manhattan home survey (Srole et al., 1962), the relationship between adult mental health and social class was evaluated in terms of both SES-origin (or parental SES) and own-SES of the Ss. On the parental SES range, the frequency of impairment varied inversely and the frequency of "well" rate varied directly. The trends for increasing frequency of impairment and decreasing frequency of sound mental conditions as one descended the scale of parental SES characterized all four age groups into which the age range of the total sample (20 to 59) was divided. This finding suggested that parental SES differentials in mental health implant varying potentialities for mental health during childhood, which under the influence of precipitating factors during adolescence and adulthood result in overt morbidity among the more vulnerable people of all strata of parental SES. This study showed no significant differences between the various SES-origin groups in the frequency of schizophrenic signs, anxiety-tension symptoms, and excessive intake behaviors. All the other pathogromonic dimensions covered[3] were inversely correlated with the Ss' parental-SES. That is, with decline in the parental-SES, the symptomatic tendencies indicating disturbances in intellectual, somatic, affective, characterological and interpersonal functioning increased. The Manhattan Study also showed that the Ss' own SES was even more closely related to their mental health than was their parental-SES.

3. **SES Differences in Measures of Children's Personality Adjustment.**[4] The effects of social-class position on measures of overall personality adjustment of children and specific factors accounting for variance in responses to personality tests seem to depend not only on the width of SES range sampled and the criteria used to determine SES (Auld, 1952), but also on the Ss' age (Sew-

ell, 1961). Whether or not the results are expressed in terms of a gross index of personality adjustment or in terms of traits or factors seems to depend on the technique used for personality assessment.

Studies in which the sample covers a narrow SES range usually yield minimal and often nonsignificant SES differences in the results, regardless of the age of Ss and technique used for personality assessment. Thus no striking social class or ethnic differences were found in college students tested with the Bernreuter Personality Inventory (Minitzer and Sargent, 1939; Sumner, 1948) and the Rorschach (Weatherley et al., 1964). Burchinal (1959) also reported a very low correlation between measures of social status of 176 girls of grades 4 to 10 in 4 rural central Iowa schools and their personality adjustment scores derived from the Mental Health Analysis Test. The negative results of these studies have been attributed to the relative homogeneity of the samples in terms of SES.

The importance of criteria used to determine the Ss' social-class position is illustrated by results of studies based on the same technique for personality assessment and covering approximately the same age range. In a study aimed at standardizing his Personality Inventory, Brown (1934) estimated the social class position of 9- to 15-year-old Ss on the basis of the Sims Score Card (which places more emphasis upon economic than social aspects of status) and found a very small relationship between the Ss' scores on personality adjustment and the Sims Score Card. With same age range children, whose social class position was inferred from the neighborhood in which they lived, Brown (1936) and Springer (1938) found significant SES differences in the Brown Personality Inventory, with lower-status children scoring higher in neuroticism than the higher-status children. Brown also reported that SES differences were more pronounced on the physical symptoms, insecurity, and irritability scales. Using the American Home Scale (which also places more emphasis on economic than social aspects of status), Gough (1946) also reported no significant SES differences in the Brown Personality Inventory scores of sixth-grade children.

The relationship between scores on the

---

[3] These were somatization, neurasthenic symptoms, depression, hostile suspiciousness, self-isolating tendencies, rigidity, immature impulse control, and mental retardation.

[4] Since it is necessary to view the results of personality studies in direct reference to the instrument used, this section will avoid broad, general assertions in favor of more detailed descriptions of specific studies.

California Test of Personality and Ss' social class position has also been found to vary as a function of the criteria used to determine SES. Comparing adolescents of farm and nonfarm families, Stott (1945b) found farm Ss to obtain significantly better self-adjustment scores on the CTP than nonfarm Ss. The range, however, of occupational status differences among the nonfarm families was too narrow to yield significant variations in the Ss' CTP scores. In addition, of two aspects of the socioeconomic status of the farm families, economic and cultural, determined by Ingersoll's Levels of Living Scale, the cultural aspect of status differentiated Ss' self-adjustment scores better than did the economic aspect of status. Adolescents from families with higher cultural level obtained higher self-adjustment scores on the CTP than those from families with lower cultural level (Stott, 1945a). Similarly, Haller and Thomas (1962) found a nonsignificant positive correlation between total adjustment score on the CTP and the Sewell Economic Status Scale score of 441 male 17-year-old high school students in Michigan.

Considering the total number of studies reviewed, one would be inclined to conclude that—provided that a large SES range is sampled—studies with adolescents yield results indicating stronger relationships between Ss' social-class position and their overall index of personality adjustment. In addition, more studies with adolescents than with younger children have shown significant social-class and/or ethnic differences on patterns of personality characteristics.

The following five studies report significant social class or ethnic differences in personality adjustment or in patterns of personality characteristics of elementary school children. Sixth-grade children of professional backgrounds, compared to children of semi-skilled workers, obtained higher scores on dominance, extroversion, and emotional stability as measured by the Pintner's Aspects of Personality Inventory. They also reported fewer worries on the Pressey X-O Test (Maddy, 1943). These differences were small but statistically significant. An important aspect of these findings is that the subjects, especially girls, tended to have personality scores more like those of the occupational group predominant in their neighborhood

than those of their fathers' occupational group.

Fifth-grade rural and small town residents, whose family SES was estimated on the basis of both parents' education and father's occupation and whose personality was assessed through the Rogers' Test of Personality Adjustment, gave evidence that inferiority feelings are inversely related to social class as measured by fathers' occupation. Mean adjustment scores were directly related to social class as determined by fathers' educational and occupational level, except that children whose fathers had done postgraduate study were more maladjusted than children of less educated fathers. The direct relationship between adjustment scores and SES level was also supported when the mother's educational level was used as a measure of social class (Burchinal et al., 1958).

Using the California Test of Personality with a large sample of fourth- to eighth-grade children, Sewell and Haller (1956) found a low but significant association between social status of the family and the child's factor-weighted CTP score of personality adjustment. The lower the SES of the child's family (as determined by the father's occupation and a rating of the family's prestige in the community), the less favorable his score of personality adjustment. In a further exploration of the relationship between SES and personality adjustment through a factor analysis of the 30 items of CTP which (in the previously cited study) had been found to be most highly correlated with the Ss' SES, Sewell and Haller (1959) found that four factors explained approximately 90% of the common variance among the items. Each of these factors—*concern over status, concern over achievement, rejection of family,* and *nervous symptoms*—correlated negatively with SES (their respective correlations being $-.31$, $-.18$, $-.12$, and $-.26$) "indicating that the lower the status of the child the greater the tendency to score high (unfavorably) on each of the factors." Intercorrelations among the factors ranged between $+.25$ and $+.59$. Children concerned about their social status tended to "worry about their achievements, their families, and to display nervous symptoms." Although this is one of few studies in which social class differences in children's personality appeared to be somewhat specific, the magnitude of the correlations between SES and personality characteristics gives little encouragement for considering social class as a major determinant of personality pattern (Sewell, 1961).

Comparisons between Negro and white 5- to 10-year-old boys and girls on Rorschach variables yielded substantial differences between the two race groups on all measures, except F+ percent. With only minor exceptions the scores of Negro children indicated less productivity, less creativity, less emotional responsiveness, and more restriction. No differences between the two groups were apparent at age 5. With increasing age, however, the differences increased. Negro children appeared to maintain a high level of perceptual accuracy (high F+ percent), but at the expense of productivity and originality (Ames and August, 1966). Judging from differences in content of TAT stories of Negro and white, 9- to 14-year-old, lower-class boys, matched for age and of at least normal intelligence, Mussen (1953) also reported significant differences between the two racial groups. Significantly more Negro than white boys told stories in which the hero is hated or reprimanded, but their own aggression seemed more often to take mild (verbal) forms than did aggression in the stories of white boys. Negroes also showed less interest in establishing and maintaining friendly relations with others or in being kind to or respectful of others. White boys, on the other hand, appeared to have more feelings of rejection in the family, evidenced more often than Negro boys fantasy hostility, but tended to view the social environment as more favorable, with others respecting them and following their leadership. White boys also evidenced a higher need for achievement, more thoughtfulness toward others, and a higher tendency for establishing friendly relations.

Studies of adolescents show consistent evidence of social class or ethnic differences, not only on gross personality adjustment scores but on more specific personality dimensions.

From a study of relationships among the California Psychological Inventory, social class, intellectual ability, and leadership talent, Liddle (1958) reported significant positive correlations between social class and measures of socialization, maturity, and responsibility of male and female high school students and a significant positive correlation between social class and measures of poise, ascendancy, and self-assurance of same-age female students (the correlation for males was also positive but not significant). Self-reports of adolescents on the CPI were also closely associated with teachers' and peers' ratings of their psychological adjustment. The higher the Ss' social status, the higher their scores on measures of psychological adjustment, leadership ability, and intelligence.

Significant relationships between social status of high school sophomores and measures of dominance, affiliation, and nurturance obtained through the Edwards' Personal Preference Schedule have also been reported (Mehlman and Fleming, 1963). High-status students compared to those of middle and lower classes were relatively low on affiliation, high on dominance, and lower than all other SES groups on nurturance. A statistically significant interaction between sex and SES was found for aggression and autonomy.

Eight of the personality variables of the Sixteen Personality Factors Test of Cattel were found to have low but significant correlations with social class position of 17-year-old males: cyclothymia (+.11), emotional stability (+.11), character or superego strength (+.12), adventurousness (+.18), sophistication (+.17), will control and character stability (+.10), and nervousness (−.12). In addition, four of the five factors on Cattell's second-order factor of anxiety-integration were significant, with the middle-class students being less anxious and more integrated (Haller and Thomas, 1962). From a study of relationships between social-class position and anxiety, Endler and Bain (1966), using the S-R Inventory of Anxiousness with male and female university freshmen (whose social class position was defined through the Blishen scale of occupational class), found significant SES differences in anxiety related to situations of interpersonal stress. The lower the S's social class, the more signs of anxiety he evidenced in response to situations of interpersonal stress. The relationship did not apply to females, however. No SES difference appeared with respect to anxiety in the face of physical danger for either sex. The authors tentatively concluded that in interpersonal stress situations, the lower-class student feels less confident because he has more at stake and is less well prepared than the middle-class student to meet the challenge that such situations present.

In a study of 223 high school seniors whose personality was assessed through the Minnesota Multiphasic Personality Inventory, Gough (1948a) found 34 out of 550 items of the MMPI to differentiate significantly high- and low-status students. Although none of the 13 MMPI scales showed significant SES differences, the differentiating items were found to form a pattern suggesting that students of higher socioeconomic levels have fewer fears and anxieties, display more social poise, security, confidence in themselves and others and more "emancipated" and "frank" attitudes in moral, religious, and sexual matters; they also tend to be more positive, dogmatic, and self-righteous in their opinions. Gough (1948b) grouped these 34 MMPI items into a "status scale." Personality status scores of a new sample of 263 students, computed on the basis of this scale, correlated .50 with objective status scores based on characteristics of family background. The correlations of the personality status scores with each of a number of other variables (such as MMPI scales, other personality test scores, intelligence and achievement test scores, and academic grades) closely paralleled the pattern of family status scores with the same variables. On the basis of these combined measures, Gough depicted the high-status student's personality as showing "a general attitude of defensiveness and reserve in regard to personal affairs and problems (K scale), greater conventionality (F scale), fewer somatic complaints (Hs scale), more satisfactory overall adjustment (D or depression scale), less tendency toward serious personality disturbances as reflected by Pd and Sc scales, less insecurity, greater intelligence, higher scholastic aptitude, greater skill in mathematics and English, superior academic achievement and less social introversion" (Gough, 1948b, p. 537).

Comparing MMPI profiles of Southern Negro and white high school seniors of both sexes and of varying SES, McDonald and Gynther (1962) found substantial racial dissimilarities for each sex, indicating that separate norms should be developed for male and female Negroes. Ball (1960) also reported significant differences in MMPI responses of ninth-grade Negro and white, male and female students (of two Kentucky integrated high schools), indicating a higher incidence of neurotic tendencies among the Negro males and more introversion and withdrawal tendencies in Negro females. Some of the differences, however, may be attributable to the Ss' social class, since Negroes were predominantly lower class, while whites were mostly from high-status families. In a subsequent study, where the effects of age, sex, and SES were controlled in evaluating racial differences in MMPI characteristics of college students, Butcher, Ball, and Ray (1964) found significant racial differences independent of sex and SES. Negroes of both sexes (matched or nonmatched on SES with whites of both sexes) scored higher than whites on the L (lie) scale, while whites scored higher on the Pa (paranoia) scale. Racial differences not independent of the Ss' sex indicated that Negro males scored higher on the Ma (hypomania) scale and that white females scored higher on the Mf (masculinity-femininity) scale (higher in the "feminine" direction).

A comparison of the Rorschach scores of adolescent males—whose protocols were collected by Hertz (1942) and Glueck and Glueck (1950)—provide indications that those from middle class are more imaginative, more mature, more responsive to the environment, and emotionally warmer and better controlled (Auld, 1951, 1952). Similar findings have been reported by Schachtel (1950) on the basis of the Rorschach Test.

In studies based on projective techniques, the Ss' perception of the testing situation may have an important influence upon his reactions. Considering factors that possibly determine rejections of Rorschach cards—a finding sometimes interpreted by Rorschach specialists as indicating intellectual inability to respond to the stimulus and sometimes as reflecting SES differences in motivation to cope with it—Thorpe and Schwartz (1963) used the Holtzman Inkblot Technique with pre-adolescents stratified into three levels of intelligence and three levels of socioeconomic status. Both intelligence and SES were found to be significantly related to the incidence of card rejections. The lower the Ss' intelligence and SES level, the higher the incidence of rejections. Higher incidence of rejections in lower-class children, indicating less interest and more apathy for the task, may follow from poorer achievement motivation and stronger experiences of stress during the testing situation. Such stress may result from less familiarity with and skill in test taking, a lack of appropriate rapport with the middle-class examiner, or from more experiences of failure than success in terms of academic performance.

On the basis of their responses to the Guilford-Simmerman Temperament survey, male high school seniors from families of manual workers have been described as less emotionally stable, less objective, less friendly, and less thoughtful than those from parents with nonmanual occupations (Singer et al., 1958).

Studies of SES differences in Ss' responses on the Thematic Apperception Test use mostly adult samples (Korchin, Mitchell, and Meltzoff, 1950; Mitchell, 1950). Using the TAT stories to determine differences in motives and values between upper- and middle-class high school students, MacArthur (1955) found consistent differences between the two SES groups, the value of work (and achievement) being the key differentiating factor. In stories told by upper-class Ss, work is accepted when it leads to interesting experiences. In the middle-class group, work is perceived as a means to glory, to autonomy, and to financial improvement, and higher education is viewed as a way to reach these ends. Parental domination is a more frequent theme among the middle-class group, and the mother appears to be a pressure agent. Parents seem less significant in the stories of the upper-class students, a finding that possibly reflects less actual contact of children with parents in the upper class.

Review of the foregoing studies gives the impression that SES differences in personality adjustment, or in patterns of personality dimensions, are less apparent in childhood than in adolescence; it also seems to be difficult to establish statistically significant relationships between SES and personality, when the SES groups are not sufficiently contrasted, particularly in terms of social rather than economic aspects of status. Many of the existing studies suffer from a lack of methodological and conceptual clarity. However, even studies fulfilling the necessary methodological requirements show SES differences which could hardly be considered as reliable early signs of differences in mental illness rates in adults of different social strata. Moreover, SES differences in indices of personality adjustment do not seem to reflect the tremendous gap between the extreme social class levels in terms of environmental conditions assumed to influence personality formation and mental health. Differences found in rates of mental illness and level of effective ego functioning during late adolescence and adulthood may constitute a break up of accumulated predisposing factors to which the techniques used for personality assessment are not sufficiently sensitive. Equally defendable, perhaps, is the hypothesis that the impact of SES differences on childhood personality is more apparent on those ego functions placed under particular stress during the early phases of the developmental process, namely, the cognitive functions. Social class and ethnic differences in this dimension of personality are apparent very early, and their magnitude increases with age.

Differences in Patterns of Interpersonal Behavior

Studies of interpersonal behavior have detected social-class differences in styles or patterns of responses both intergenerational (i.e., in the relationships between adults and children) and intragenerational (i.e., in peer-to-peer relationships). The types of response considered in this section are peer interaction, aggression, compliance, sex behavior, and moral conduct. The relative influence of peer and adult socializing forces on behavior and attitudes of children and adolescents is of some considerable practical and theoretical significance (Coleman, 1961; Eisenstadt, 1956; Sullivan, 1953). The degree to which peer groups are salient in a given society or social subgroup and the extent to which they are recognized by adults and are used as agents of socialization varies (Campbell, 1964). Rapid social change tends to create or enlarge a gap between generations, which, in turn, increases the influence of peers in the socialization process (K. Davis, 1940a; Keniston, 1962). Heterogeneity of cultural values, which characterizes large urban settings, has also been related to the facts that during preadolescence and adolescence peers tend to replace parents as interpreters and enforcers of moral principles, and that values of youth acquire a broader base (Ausubel, 1958). Finally, ethnographic information suggests that youth groups are most likely to develop in "societies in which the family or kinship unit cannot ensure the attainment of full social status on the part of its members" (Eisenstadt, 1962). This may also apply to the development of extended, age-graded gangs in lower-class urban areas (Cloward and Ohlin, 1960; Short and Strodtbeck, 1965). The influence of peers may be socialization of a particular sort, perhaps more directly linked to the circumstances of the external environment than is socialization through parental intervention.

1. SES Differences in Peer Interaction and Friendship Choice. Subcultural variations affect the impact and relevance of the peer group. Parents of lower SES levels, compared to those of higher position, show less concern about and exercise less control over their children's activities outside the home in the later years of childhood (Psathas, 1957). Social class differences in extracurricular activities seem to create different styles of life which influence peer relations (Sherif, 1962). Participation, for example, in organized extracurricular activities within the school and in the community is less likely to be found among high school students as one descends the social class scale (Coster, 1959). Social class differences in degree of involvement in extracurricular activities and in types of these activities have also been found for 10- to 12-year-old children. Those of middle class were more often involved in YMCA and Scouts activities, while the lower-class children took part mainly in clubs for underprivileged children (MacDonald, McGuire, and Havighurst, 1949). Additional congruent evidence has been provided by a national survey conducted by the Institute for Social Research (1956). Not only does the tendency to join clubs show a social-class difference (roughly a third of children from unskilled occupational levels belong to no club; only an eighth of middle-class children have no club membership) but the pattern of club participation also varies along socioeconomic lines. Lower-class children are more likely to belong to Boys Clubs, 4-H, and Y clubs; higher-status children are more likely to belong to different kinds of clubs (e.g., Boy Scouts) and to hold club office (Hess and Torney, 1965).

Friendship ties also appear to be class-bound, although the existing evidence contains some contradictory results. Friendship preferences and reputations as measured by sociometric choices among elementary and high school children were found to favor Ss from higher social class positions. Friendship data for the older group show a relationship between social class and rates on positive items, but there is no apparent relationship between social class and rates on negative items. Only among the younger children was social class position clearly related to rejection of peers (Neugarten, 1946). Sociometric preferences of eighth graders were also found to correlate significantly with the Ss' social class position (Elkins, 1958); and Bonney (1946) argued that the role of social class position in determining friendships, although small, is consistent across a wide age range (including age levels from elementary school to college). Two community studies with adolescents yielded different results. In a Midwestern town, clique membership has been found to be homogeneous with respect to social class (Hollingshead, 1949). However, in a new suburban community in southern California with sufficiently large SES range, but where three-fourths of the sample had lived in the community less than four years, the tendency of junior high school students to choose friends from their own social class was negligible (Udry, 1960).

In American society, the impact of social-status differences on peer relations is in part a matter of ecological segregation (Warner and Lunt, 1941), which reinforces class differences in children's values, interests, and aspirations (Wilson, 1959) and "limits and patterns [their] learning environment" (Martin and Stendler, 1953) in a way which has been denounced as "increasingly irreversible" (Ausubel, 1958). However, even when ecological segregation is not marked, differential associations, behavior, and values appear to be related to status variations, at least among elementary school children (MacDonald, McGuire, and Havighurst, 1949; Neugarten, 1946). Among older children, neither prestige and recognition among peers nor criteria for accepting or rejecting peers are markedly related to parental socioeconomic status

(Jones, 1958; Feinberg, Smith, and Schmidt, 1958). Sex and grade in school appear to be important determinants of children's clique membership (Hollingshead, 1949).

2. Aggression and Conformity. The extent to which children use and value particular interpersonal modes of action is also linked to SES membership. Using a "Guess Who" technique describing 25 social behavior traits, Pope (1953) found restlessness and fighting behavior to be less acceptable among higher-class than among lower-class children. Higher-class groups of both sexes expect their members to conform to adult standards within the classroom. Aggressive and belligerent peers were the most influential among lower-class boys while higher-class boys valued the active, skillful, and daring.

The pattern of evidence on SES differences in aggression of preschool children is not consistent. In a study conducted in the mid-1930s, Jersild and Markey (1935) found children from lower socioeconomic groups to have more conflicts, to engage more often in overt attack, and to display more aggression against persons and use more profanity than children in middle-class groups. However, they were observed to express sympathy more often as well. A study by Roff and Roff (1940) of two nursery schools found that children from working-class homes showed less attention-getting behavior, less resistance to suggestions of the teachers, more willingness to share than did the children in Jersild's middle-class group. Differences between middle- and lower-class groups in type of aggressive outlet were found by Appel (1942) who reported that high SES children fought more often over disagreements about tasks in which they were engaged, while children from low SES levels were more often in conflict over property. In a later study, lower-class preschool children were found to be physically more aggressive and display more competitive behavior (McKee and Leader, 1955). Myrdal (1944) and Deutsch (1960) provided evidence indicating that compared to whites Negro children are more likely to express aggressiveness in covert forms.

More recent work scarcely sets things in order. Goldstein (1955) and Stoltz and Smith (1959) report children from low SES families to be more aggressive. Eron, Walder, Toigo, and Lefkowitz (1963), in a study of third graders, found that middle-class children were nominated as aggressive more often than lower SES classmates on a peer nomination technique. Eron and his colleagues (1963) also found that children from all status levels report with about equal frequency that they are punished for aggression against parents; middle-class girls tend to see themselves as punished for aggression against peers more often than do girls from working-class homes. There was no difference in reports of the frequency of physical punishment by parents, a finding in conflict with many reports in the literature.

One of the problems inherent in the analysis of class-typed aggression is that the definition of aggression is relative to the context, the intent of the aggressor, and the perception of the victim. The tendency to confuse aggression with assertiveness, on the one hand, and hostility with violence, on the other, compounds the problem. In studies of SES and aggressive behavior and of parental sanctions against aggression, a distinction between types of aggressive activity may be useful. Verbal aggressiveness is tolerated, sometimes rewarded, in girls and in middle-class families, where physical aggression or destruction of property might not be (Kamii and Radin, 1967). Aggression may thus be defined by its consequences and the response of the social context. An act that is not given negative sanctions (e.g., omitting a friend from a birthday party list) may cease to be regarded as aggressive if ignored by adults, although the consequences for others may be quite painful. In this sense, the definition of aggression should take into account the ability of the actor to anticipate the consequences to others. If it is true that this type of sensitivity (monitoring inner states of others by observation or empathy) is more prevalent in the middle-class home (Zunich, 1961, 1962; Kamii and Radin, 1967; Hess et al., 1968), the same act by a middle-class child should be regarded as more aggressive than it would if performed by a lower-class child from circumstances which provide him with less insight into the feelings of others.

Nonconformity is aggression against (acts tending to destroy or mitigate effectiveness of) authority figures or against a system of rules or publicly sanctioned norms. The evidence of SES differences in conformity is mixed. Much of the relevant research is reported late in this section in a discussion of delinquency and moral conduct. Although Hess, Shipman, Bear, and Brophy (1968) report slightly more cooperative behavior from working-class than from middle-class preschool children in interaction with their mothers, others have found somewhat different results (Tuma and Livson, 1960); and studies of public schools indicate that this early conforming behavior of working-class children may be a function of age and of the unfamiliarity of the testing situation (Havighurst, 1964).

Somewhat different relationships with authority have been obtained for children of high and low status, following in general outline the findings reported early in the chapter about orientation toward authority of working-class adults and differences between social class groups in emphasis upon external as compared with internal controls. Observational data from adolescent middle- and lower-class members in clubs showed no SES difference in total amount of aggression. Middle class, however, appeared to sanction less aggression and digression in member-with-member interaction. In middle-class groups, more aggression is directed to the club president; in lower-class groups, it is directed toward the adult leader (Maas, 1953).

Investigating social behavior of preadolescents and early adolescents in lower- and middle-class families, Maas (1951) interviewed 10- to 15-year-old boys and girls in 5 different youth groups and found data patterns which suggest that in lower-class families there is a psychologically closed, hierarchical, and quite rigid parental relationship with children compared to the middle class, where there is more open, ostensibly equalitarian, and flexible relationship. Children from high-status homes see their fathers as more powerful in the family authority structure and also see policemen as more powerful than do working-class children; more low-status than high-status children report that their mothers are the central authority figure in the family (Hess and Torney, 1965, 1967).

3. SES Differences in Sex Role Differentiation and Sexual Activity. Studies of sex-typed standards of behavior as reflected in game choices of children reveal social class differences which are congruent with findings on SES differences in parental values and reported behavior. Preferences of toys expressed by lower-class 3- to 8-year-old children of both sexes conform more closely to traditional sex-typed standards than preferences expressed by middle-class children. Lower-class children adopt sex-typed behavior earlier and with greater consistency than do middle-class children, the difference between the two classes being more pronounced for girls than for boys (Rabban, 1950). These findings, which suggest that differentiation of sex roles is sharper in lower- than in middle-class families, are congruent with other evidence; lower-class mothers make a greater distinction between boys and girls in their reported views of what is desirable for children of each sex (Kohn, 1959). There is also evidence that involvement of girls in masculine activities is positively correlated with the educational level of the family (Kagan and Moss, 1962). Information on children's peer-culture prestige values (Pope, 1953) also suggests that social-class differences in sex-role standards of behavior do exist. Both lower- and middle-class boys reject the effeminate boy with nonmasculine interests, but the academically oriented boy is more often accepted by middle- than by lower-class boys. It should be recalled, however, that values of high school peer groups vary from one school to another (Coleman, 1961). Presumably, similar interschool differences appear at elementary school levels. Among girls, the active, noisy, and openly aggressive "tomboy," who in lower class is more likely to associate with boys, seems to enjoy as much prestige from lower-class peers as the ladylike, studious, conforming girl who is less likely to relate with boys. Middle-class girls, however, reject the "tomboy" type of girl but accept the type of "little lady" who in middle class is described as more outgoing and friendly and more likely to associate with boys than the "little lady" of lower class (Pope, 1953).

Hall and Keith (1964) also reported data indicating that masculine sex-role preference is demonstrated more clearly by lower- than upper-class elementary school boys, while upper-class girls tend to receive higher feminine scores than lower-class girls (the SES differences among girls being smaller than those among boys, however).

The best available data on SES differences in sexual behavior in adolescence are those of Kinsey and his associates (1948, 1953). Given that the Kinsey data are based on anamnestic reports of adults, the breakdown of responses by age does not correspond to an easily identifiable population, particularly for the adolescent age range. The Kinsey data regarding adolescence (age range 16 to 20) indicate that male subjects who attained a maximum education of 9 to 12 years of schooling and semiskilled laborers show the highest total sexual outlet. Lowest in total sexual outlet are Ss who had more than 13 years of total schooling and those of skilled labor occupational level. Subjects who had more than 13 years of total schooling and professionals showed the highest incidence of masturbation, nocturnal emissions, and petting to climax. Lowest in these sexual practices were subjects who had 0 to 8 years of total schooling and day laborers or semi-skilled laborers. Subjects with 0 to 8 years of total schooling and semiskilled laborers showed the highest mean frequencies of total premarital intercourse, while those who had 13 years of schooling or more and those classified as lower and upper white collar and professionals showed the lowest mean frequencies in total premarital intercourse. In view of the data on frequency of masturbation, this cannot be taken as evidence of delay of gratification. Subjects who had 9 to 12 years of total schooling and day laborers showed the highest accumulative incidence of homosexual outlet, while subjects who had 13 years of schooling or more and professionals showed somewhat lower incidence, but above that of the lowest educational group.

The data concerning sexual behavior of females were based on 5940 white females divided in groups on the basis of their fathers' occupations classified according to the same occupational scale used for males. Sample divisions based on amount of education were based on the characteristics of the Ss themselves. Most indices of sexual behavior in females had little or no relationship with parents' occupational level. For some of the indices, the differences by Ss' educational level were associated with differences in age

at marriage, which is related to Ss' educational level. Premarital petting, for example, when examined in terms of simple correlations with the Ss' educational level, showed slight differences in accumulative incidence of petting experience, with Ss who had more than 12 years of schooling showing higher percentage of petting during the age period between 15 and 20 than Ss from lower educational levels. However, when groups of different educational levels are compared holding age constant and considering age at marriage, the percentages of those who had engaged in petting to orgasm before marriage in each educational level appear to be almost equal. Similar relationships between age at marriage and Ss' educational level appeared to influence the frequency of incidence of premarital coitus in females. For example, Ss with grade school education appear to start coitus 5 or 6 years before Ss who graduate from college. Percentages of different educational level groups having premarital intercourse were 26 for Ss with grade school education, 47 for those with high school education, and 60 for college graduates. However, the percentages who had premarital coitus were about equal for all educational level groups by the age of 20, and comparisons between educational level groups within age levels at marriage showed no differences in incidence of premarital coitus related to the Ss' educational level.

Among women, active incidence of masturbation was low among grade school graduates but high in college graduates. Active incidence of homosexual responses and contacts was higher among the less educated before 20 years of age and higher among the better educated after 20 years of age. Little or no relationship was found between homosexuality and parental occupational level. Kinsey and his associates also reported that for single females the Ss' educational level had no consistent effect on total sexual outlet except on masturbation and homosexual contacts. The level of parental occupation had no effects, either, except during the younger ages of the Ss.

4. SES Differences in Moral Conduct and Moral Judgment. Evidence on SES differences in children's morality appears to be inconclusive. This is apparently due to differences in measures used for determining children's level of morality. It should be stressed at once that, in studies using behavioral indices of honesty (such as resistance to temptation to cheat) or measures of development of moral judgment (such as those based on Piaget's theory of moral development), the results appear to be consistently and significantly differentiated on the basis of social class background of the Ss. Compared to lower-class Ss, middle-class Ss usually earn better scores on measures of honesty and moral judgment. However, guilt over hostile thoughts and disobedience measured through a story completion technique did not appear to be related to Ss' social class (Allinsmith, 1960).

Using experimental measures of resistance to temptation to cheat, Hartshorne and May (1928–1930) found that by their definition of cheating the lower-class child was more "deceitful." Cheating was negatively correlated with parental educational and occupational level (−.45). When intelligence was partialed out, the correlation was still significant (−.30). The differentiating powers of the experimental measures of honesty which were used by Hartshorne and May are all the more remarkable in view of the low correlation between cheating in one situation and cheating in another and the finding that Ss' tendencies to cheat depended upon the degree of risk of detection and the effort required. Thus Ss could not be reliably divided into "cheaters" and "noncheaters" across situations. From these findings it was concluded that moral conduct, as reflected in measures of resistance to temptation, is in large part the result of individual decisions in specific moral conflict situations. The evidence for altruistic service, however, shows a curvilinear relationship with SES; the group composed mostly of subjects from the middle range of social class showed more altruistic behavior than the upper middle- or lower-class group. Over the whole sample, the correlation between the attempt to be of service and socioeconomic position was almost zero (Hartshorne and May, 1928–1930). Although a factor analysis of Hartshorne and May data by Burton (1936) showed that there is a general factor in the various experimental tests used indicating stable individual differences in attitudes toward classroom cheating, this factor is relatively small compared to variation in cheating coming

from individual situations. This factor may represent differential cautiousness or sensitivity to possible punishment for cheating, an interpretation already suggested by Hartshorne and May.

Havighurst and Taba (1949) chose to use reputation measures of character rather than actual conduct, because these had been found by Hartshorne and May to be more reliable. The ratings they obtained from teachers, other adults, and peers of 112 16-year-old students in "Prairie City" indicated a consistent trend downward in the reputation scores as one went from upper class to lower-lower class. The differences between upper and upper-middle class and the other four lower classes was statistically significant. The items on which Ss were rated were the traditional traits associated with morality; honesty, moral courage, friendliness, loyalty, and responsibility. It is noteworthy that although the correlations of character reputation scores with variables such as social class, intelligence, religious activity, etc., were generally low, there was one exception—Ss' school achievement as indicated by school grades, which correlated .74.

Studies of the cognitive aspects of morality (most of which follow more or less closely Piaget's [1948] theory of stages in the development of moral judgment) have shown that social-class differences in maturity of moral judgment are due to differences in rate of development rather than to class-linked differences in basic moral values. Children's moral judgments develop in the same direction regardless of social class; but, at each age level, middle-class and brighter children appear to be more advanced than lower-class and less intelligent children (Kohlberg, 1963a, 1964).

In a study of 6- to 12-year-olds, Lerner (1937) found that persistence of moral realism among older children was significantly more frequent in the group of lower-class children than in their upper-class agemates. He also found that the lower-class children suggested imminent punishment about 18% more frequently than did the upper-class group, regardless of age. Johnson's study (1962) of fifth-, seventh-, ninth-, and eleventh-grade boys and girls showed that chronological age, IQ, and parental occupation were closely related to several dimensions of development of moral judgment. Social-class differences in maturity of moral judgment were also reported by Kohlberg (1958) for Ss aged 10 to 16. Boehm and Nass (1962), however, found that working class children (ages 6 to 11) did not differ significantly from their upper-middle-class agemates in responses indicating maturity of moral judgment, such as distinctions between intention and outcome of an action. However, comparisons between upper-middle- and working-class children (ages 6 to 9), divided into groups of average and above average intelligence, showed that gifted children and upper-middle-class children mature earlier than children of average intelligence and working-class children when maturity of moral judgment is evaluated on the basis of Ss' ability to make the distinction between actor's intention and action's outcome. The difference in maturity of moral judgment between gifted children and those of average intelligence was greater for the upper-middle-class group. Piaget's assertion that maturity of moral judgment is not attained until peer reciprocity and independence from adult authority are established was not confirmed. As predicted by Boehm (who questioned Piaget's assertion), peer reciprocity and independence from adult authority in making moral judgments appeared earlier in the responses of working-class than those of upper-middle-class children at both levels of intelligence (Boehm and Nass, 1962). These findings indicate that differences in level of intellectual development of SES groups used contribute to a great extent to the observed variations by social class in children's moral judgments. Kohlberg (1964) argues that involvement in social activities which develop role-taking skills also contributes to an earlier maturation of moral judgment.

If one accepts Kohlberg's view (1964) that moral judgment has central cognitive components, some of which emerge from experiences which give the individual practice in role-taking, the social class differences in maternal strategies of control (Hess and Shipman, 1967) and in participation in social organizations would be a source of differences in moral judgment. This position challenges the hypothesis that SES differences in moral judgment are derived from class dif-

ferences in values. The finding that children who participate in social clubs and organizations tend to give more advanced moral judgment responses than those who do not, regardless of social class, is congruent with this view. Experience in different groups and with different individuals with divergent standards gives a perspective that permits individuals to see behavior from several viewpoints and thus enhances the development of cognitively advanced concepts of morality (Kohlberg, 1958, 1964). It may not follow that conduct is also influenced by this type of experience. The discrepancy between cognitive perspective and actual behavior is one of the central problems of theory and research on morality and moral judgment. It may be useful to consider morality not only in superego or cognitive terms but as behavior regulated by the willingness of the individual to accept the goals and norms of the group or institution as his own. Attachment to, or affiliation with, an ideological or institutional system may be more predictive of conformity to the norms of that institution than measures of conscience or moral judgment. If this view of commitment to the norms of the institution or group is valid, SES differences in moral conduct are understandable in terms of allegiance to groups. Conflicts and differences among the demands and expectations of different groups and individuals constitute for the child a basis for discernment and development of both moral values and group allegiance. In this respect, social-class position and ethnic group membership may influence and direct the child's ties to social institutions and his interpretation of the importance of their rules and norms.

Social class differences in moral conduct and moral judgment are especially complicated when studies on delinquency are considered. Ecological findings showing a relationship between delinquency rates and poverty, and studies on delinquent youths point to social class as an important variable in the etiology of delinquency (Short, 1966). Evidence based on field observation and self-reports as well as official records suggests that, in large cities, involvement in delinquency is more likely for lower- than for middle-class children (Short and Strodtbeck,

1965). However, studies conducted in small cities and in rural areas do not show a higher rate of delinquency among lower- than middle-class youths(Clarke and Wenninger, 1962; Erickson and Empey, 1965; Himelhoch, 1964; Nye, Short, and Olson, 1958; Polk, 1963).

Incidence of delinquency by socioeconomic area of urban regions and other background factors has been cited as indicating SES differences in aggression (Healy and Bronner, 1936; Kobrin, 1951; McCord, McCord, and Zola, 1959; Shaw and McKay, 1942) but the validity of these delinquency statistics as an indication of actual antisocial behavior has been questioned (Burgess, 1952; Cohen, 1955; Mehanovitch, 1947; Murphy, Shirley, and Witmer, 1946; Robinson, 1936; Sheldon, 1955); and a study based on anonymous self-reports from samples of high school students in western and midwestern communities revealed relatively little SES difference in frequency of behavior usually considered delinquent if it occurs in lower-class neighborhoods (Nye, Short, and Olson, 1958). However, reports on classroom behavior and data on damage to school property show considerable differences between the responses of lower- and middle-class children to the rules of the educational institutions about property and classroom behavior (Havighurst, 1964). These reports are often confounded with ethnic factors, including conflict between subgroups in the community, and must be seen in the historical perspective of problems of ethnic assimilation into the main culture of the society.

Data relating delinquency and broken homes have been used to support the argument that delinquency is more frequent in the lower class than in middle class, since families broken by divorce and separation and common-law marriages appear to be more common in lower class and in minority groups. However, the relationship between broken homes and delinquency has been found to be very small when ethnicity is controlled (Shaw and McKay, 1931). Moreover, unbroken but unhappy families appear to produce more delinquency than broken but happy homes (Nye et al., 1958). A study of suburban runaways in the 1960s showed that more than one-half of the reported cases of children (age 10 to 17) who voluntarily ran away from their homes came from middle-income families, 15% came from higher-income families, and only 28% came from low-income families. Runaways come essentially from families marked by conflict. Twice as many "repeaters" (i.e., children having run away from home more than one time, whether the incidence was reported by the family or not) as "one-timers" came from middle- and higher-income families. It was also estimated that the reported runaways in this study represented a very small proportion (one-sixth) of the total number of those who may have run away from their homes during the time period included in this study (Shellow et al., 1967). Protection offered by well integrated families as opposed to disorganized families is more effective for girls and pre-adolescents than for adolescent boys (Toby, 1957, 1965).

W. B. Miller (1958) and W. Kvaraceus (Kvaraceus and Miller, 1959) argued that the greater frequency of delinquency among lower-class adolescents is related to a greater frequency in this social class of families dominated by females and lacking a stable father-role incumbent. Socialization in such a family structure creates particular problems for boys in establishing a masculine identity. The tendency of lower-class boys to associate with one-sex peer groups is related to these problems. Miller contends that the bearing of peer group relations on delinquency and particularly on gang delinquency is very important. Because the "street-corner group" fulfills important individual needs, maintenance of membership and achievement of status in it depend on demonstration by the individual that he possesses the qualities and shares the "focal concerns" of the lower-class way of life—trouble, toughness, smartness, excitement, fate, autonomy, and concerns with belonging and with status. The argument that aggressive behavior is functional to the group in several ways (Miller, Geertz, and Cutter, 1961) appears to be supported by findings showing that adolescent gang members display aggressive acts mostly within the gang. Short (1966), commenting on these findings, stressed that "a form of organization indigenous to areas considered disorganized by the criteria of conventional institutional values is found to produce, in some measure, the very behavior by which judgments of disorganization often are made."

One of the variables which have been pointed out as favoring advance in moral judgment and acquisition of moral autonomy is the ability to delay gratification (Kohlberg, 1968). Studies on this variable and its relation to social class yield contradictory results. It seems that age is an important factor, as well as the measures used to investigate this variable. In a recent study of young Negro children from different social-class backgrounds, those from working class were less likely to delay in order to obtain a larger (candy) reward (Hess et al., 1968).

Using a sample of 2500 high school students, divided into four classes according to supervisory "power" of their fathers' occupations, to test the hypothesis that a class-related delay of gratification pattern (DGP) does exist, Schneider and Lysgaard (1953) reported that their results generally give good support to the hypothesis that a "class-related DGP pattern [sic] exists, *especially when the self-identification of class is used.*" To test hypotheses about the relations among DGP, social class, and social mobility, Straus (1962) tested 338 male high school students. Scales with reproducibilities from .92 to .96 were developed to assess the deferment of five needs (affiliation, aggression, consumption, economic independence, and sex). The hypotheses of positive relationships between DGP and achievement role-performance and role-orientation received support. The hypothesis, however, of positive correlation between socioeconomic status and DGP was not supported.

Miller, Riessman, and Seagull (1965) question the way in which the deferred gratification pattern has been used in studies including social class as an independent variable. They argue that delay of gratification or action is related to the probabilities of reward and satisfaction in the environment. The concept of DGP as a personality trait is based on evidence that does not adequately consider the influence of situational factors. This view is congruent with the position taken in this chapter and suggests several lines of inquiry about the possibilities in experimental situations, discriminating between those in which delay of impulse pays off and those in which it does not.

Differences in Educational and Occupational Aspirations and Achievement Orientation

One of the most salient features of American society is the opportunity for social mobility. Not only are routes to more advantageous social and economic positions available, but in all sectors of the society there are values expressed which explicitly encourage individual efforts to achieve. Although individual talent is usually essential for success, other factors which contribute, such as motivation to achieve, an accumulation of knowledge and skills, and the conviction that one has the ability to reach his aspirations are, in part, outcomes of socialization. The notion that success is the result of individual initiative, with its implication that the poor are without ambition, is often used to explain or attempt to justify economic inequality in the society. This is, in another form, a statement of the issue of the extent to which there is a restraining effect of social structure: to what degree do socioeconomic inequalities continue to exist because of the constraints and socializing impact of the social structure, rather than follow from individual differences? The relationship of social stratification to level of aspiration and achievement motivation is thus of considerable theoretical and practical significance.

1. **Children's View of the Educational and Occupational Systems.** Analysis of educational and occupational aspirations if possible only if there is some agreement (among adults) that an occupational hierarchy exists in the society. There is considerable evidence that this is so for adults both in the United States (National Opinion Research Center, 1947) and in other countries (Hodge, Siegel, and Rossi, 1964; Inkeles, 1960; Inkeles and Rossi, 1956). Adult rankings of the prestige of occupations do not differ appreciably by SES (Inkeles, 1960). However, substantially more lower- than middle-class adults recommend skilled labor positions for young people; and college education is emphasized much less among lower- than middle- and upper-class adults (Hyman, 1953). There is also evidence that job preferences of lower-class adults are related to economic and security

considerations (including wages, subsidiary benefits, and steadiness of employment) rather than personal (such as congeniality of the work to the individual's interests, qualifications, and personality pattern), the latter being emphasized more among middle and upper classes (Hyman, 1953; Inkeles, 1960).

Prestige rankings of occupations by elementary school children vary with Ss' age, IQ, and social-class position. Older and brighter children and those more advantaged in terms of family social-class position tend to rank occupations more like adults than do younger, less bright, and lower SES children (Nelson, 1963). Knowledge about characteristics and consequences of occupational roles and statuses increases with age and is more substantial among upper- and middle-class than lower-class children, whether their source of learning is personal contact, television, or general culture (DeFleur and DeFleur, 1967).

Research findings concerning the impact of social-class position upon career-related interests of elementary school children appear to be conflicting. A number of studies report no appreciable SES differences in the occupational interests of elementary school children (Davis, Hagen, and Strouf, 1962; Middleton, 1954; Tyler, 1964). Other investigators found SES differences. When asked to state the reasons for their future vocational choices, middle-class elementary school boys are more likely than their lower-class agemates to offer rationales based on the intrinsic interest of the occupation preferred and on altruistic motives (Galler, 1951). Comparing lower- and middle-class fifth-grade boys with respect to occupational attitudes and interests, Stewart (1959) found no SES differences in the ways they evaluated pictures of a series of occupations in terms of income, importance in the community, or quality of home that holders of various occupations would be likely to have. However, when asked to state their vocational preferences, upper-class children chose almost exclusively upper-class occupations, while a substantial percentage of lower-class Ss chose middle- rather than upper-class occupations.

The relationships between social-class position and vocational aspirations appear to be more clear among adolescents than among younger children. Vocational choices of adolescents from different social strata are usually confined to occupations typical of their particular subculture (Hollingshead, 1949). The impact of parents' occupational values upon the vocational aspirations of adolescents has been documented by several studies. Adults of lower SES emphasize college training much less than those of middle and upper classes; the value systems of adolescents from different social strata regarding college education parallel those of their parents (Hyman, 1953). Similar findings have been reported by Empey (1956), who found that the "American tradition of wanting to get ahead" is shared more by upper- and middle-class than by lower-class high school students. An exploration of relationships between vocational aspirations of adolescent males of similar levels of intelligence and social class (upper-lower) and the core values espoused by their families reveals that parents espousing the core value of "getting ahead," unlike those espousing the value of "getting by," tend to train their children to perceive and use education as a means to reach middle socioeconomic status. Adolescents learn to view the occupational system from their parents' perspective, not only in terms of desirability and possibility of change of status but also in terms of opportunities available, techniques to be used, and appropriate educational goals (Kahl, 1953).

2. SES Differences in Children's Actual Educational and Occupational Choices. An important aspect of children's vocational orientations is realism of choice. Readiness for vocational planning increases with age; there is also some evidence that it is associated with the SES level of the occupation chosen and not with the SES level of the S's family (Gribbons and Lohnes, 1964). Other evidence indicates that lower-class ninth-grade students, compared to their middle-class agemates, show a greater discrepancy between their vocational preferences (i.e., aspirations) and their actual plans (i.e., expectations). No appreciable SES differences were found among these students' vocational preferences. However, stating their occupational plans, lower-class students, unlike their upper-class agemates, lowered their aspirations considerably and said they planned to enter occupations closely approximating those of their fathers (Stephenson, 1955). Similar findings have been reported by Youmans (1956) from a study with twelfth graders, designed to investigate which factors found to be associated with occupational selection contribute most to realism of vocational choice. He found that fathers' occupational level is more highly related to the formulation of realistic occupational choices than are type of community, school curriculum, the youth's work experience, or family background factors (such as work of the mother, educational level of the father, size of family, work done at home by the S, type of allowance received, and S's position among siblings). Other evidence indicates that the influence of the family's SES level upon educational decisions of twelfth graders is nonspecific. While the educational aspirations of middle-class Ss are generally of a higher level, those of lower-class Ss reflect a composite effect of a number of variables including father's and mother's educational level, father's and mother's occupational history, and intentions of school peers and older siblings (Kraus, 1964). Other data from a large sample of ninth- to twelfth-grade Negro and white students of both sexes have also indicated that the mother's influence upon career choice and planning is stronger than the father's among the lower classes regardless of race (Bennet and Gist, 1964).

3. Mechanisms Underlying SES Differences in Educational and Occupational Aspirations and Choice. Few of the relevant studies have been designed to analyze the specific ways in which social stimulus variables associated with social-class position operate in the formation of educational and vocational aspirations and actual plans. In some studies, socioeconomic status is not singled out as the dominant influence upon vocational aspiration and choice.

It has often been argued that differences in level of educational and occupational aspirations are related to intellectual ability since high-aspiring subjects are usually those with higher IQs. However, when the effects of IQ on the preferences of high school seniors were controlled in a study of 4167 high school seniors by Sewell, Haller, and Straus (1957), social class was still found to be significantly associated with occupational aspirations. A study of the relationships be-

tween socioeconomic status and general academic ability as predictors of entrance to college showed that the probability of entering college for a grade 11 male student in the top 25% of academic ability varies from .48 (low SES) to .87 (high SES). For female students this probability varies from .34 to .82. For students in the lowest 25% of academic ability, the probabilities of entering college vary from .06 (low SES) to .26 (high SES) for males and from .07 to .20 for females. (Flanagan and Cooley, 1966). Similar findings have been reported by Mueller and Mueller (1953) and by Wolffe (1961).

Apart from findings supporting the notion that knowledge about occupational roles and status increases during the elementary school years and that the Ss' IQ and SES level have a bearing upon such knowledge, the importance of this age period lies in findings suggesting that the child often moves toward vocational choice through a process marked by premature and perhaps unconscious elimination of many fields of work. Vocational interests seem to be patterned through an early development of sets of dislikes rather than a clustering of preferences emerging against a neutral background (Tyler, 1955). This view is supported by other findings as well. Nelson (1963) found that the process of occupational foreclosure starts early (by the third grade). The reasons for the establishment of this process are not apparent. Moreover, little is known about the implications of early occupational rejections for lower-class children, who have been found to possess less information about the occupational world than their middle-class agemates.

Another element of the process of selection may be that the preferences of middle-class children for middle-class occupations may be accounted for on the basis of preferences for authority roles presumably reflecting middle-class values. Questionnaire data from sixth-grade boys suggest that middle- and upper-class children do not choose "higher" occupations simply because of the greater prestige and economic advantages of these occupations, but also because such children have the opportunity to acquire interests in occupations which involve training, supervising, or controlling others (Maccoby, 1962).

In adolescents, situational and fortuitous

circumstances, such as the type of part-time job a student finds or the particular teacher to whom he is exposed, may have a decisive effect on vocational plans (Edlefsen and Crowe, 1960; Slocum 1956; Slocum and Empey, 1956). Other findings indicate that parental advice is an important factor in the upward mobility of middle- as well as lower-class boys (Kahl, 1953; Simpson, 1962). An additional finding that upwardly mobile lower-class boys had middle-class friends and were members of a number of extracurricular clubs suggests that a working-class boy is most likely to aspire to a high-ranking occupation if he has been influenced in this direction by both parents and peers (Simpson, 1962). School districting (which segregates youths from different social strata) may result in high school populations with modally different values and climates of aspiration. The values of the bulk of students in a high school may have a significant normative influence on the values and educational aspirations of individuals within the school. Data from male students attending high schools characterized by different climates of aspiration show that the ethos of the school does affect aspirations as well as academic achievement, when relevant personal variables are controlled (Wilson, 1959).

A notion often used to conceptualize social class or ethnic group differences in educational and vocational aspirations is that of achievement orientation or achievement syndrome (Heckhausen, 1967; McCelland et al., 1953; Rosen, 1956), consisting of a motivational component (need achievement) and a pattern of specific values presumably related to achievement training and to educational and occupational aspirations. There is some evidence that SES and ethnic differences in educational and occupational aspirations as well as attainments are related to differences in values underlying achievement training and achievement motivation. Belief in the world's orderliness and amenity to rational mastery (the feeling that a person can and must make plans to control his destiny); willingness to leave the family to make one's own way in life; and a preference for individual rather than collective credit for work done are values found to enhance achievement orientation. Most of the variance between two groups of Jewish and Italian adolescents

compared on school performance, parental SES, and values espoused by their families was attributable to the family's social class position (Strodtbeck, 1958).

Analyzing ethnographic and social information indicating different upward mobility rates for different ethnic and religious groups in the U.S., Rosen (1959) hypothesized that dissimilarities in social mobility rates would be attributable to different emphases placed by each group upon independence training given to the child, different value orientations regarding achievement, and different vocational and occupational aspirations of his parents for him. Data collected from 427 pairs of mothers and their sons, aged 8 to 14, drawn from "new-immigration" groups of French-Canadians, southern Italians, Greeks, east European Jews, and from groups of northeastern U.S. Negroes and of native-born white Protestants, supported Rosen's hypotheses. Mothers of each ethnic group placed different emphases upon independence training, with Jewish mothers expecting earlier evidence of self-reliance from their children (mean age 6.83 years) followed by the Protestants (6.87), Negroes (7.23), Greeks (7.67), French-Canadians (7.99), and Italians (8.03). Concomitantly, the groups of Greek, Jewish, and white Protestant boys gave evidence of higher achievement motivation than did Italian, French-Canadian, and Negro boys. Mothers of the former ethnic groups were also more likely to espouse activistic, future-oriented and individualistic values and demonstrated higher educational and occupational aspirations for their sons than did Italian and French-Canadian mothers. The Negro mothers expressed values and educational aspirations comparable to those of Jews, Greeks, and white Protestants, but the level of their occupational aspirations for their sons was the lowest of all ethnic groups, possibly indicating maternal awareness of the severely limited occupational opportunities for Negroes. It was also found that social class and ethnicity interact in influencing motivation, values, and aspirations. Ethnic differences persisted when SES was controlled; some of the ethnic differences seem, however, to reflect differences in the SES composition of these ethnic groups. In a subsequent study analyzing the effects of family structure on achievement motivation,

Rosen (1961) concluded that it is unwise to single out any one demographic factor to explain differences in achievement motivation. Although social class was found to be consistently related to achievement motivation in the expected direction, other factors, such as family size and ordinal position among siblings, acted interdependently and were difficult to assess individually.

The degree to which family values have an impact on the child's value orientations appears to be associated with early independence training and "love-oriented" methods of discipline. Independence training begins earlier and use of "conditional love" discipline by parents is more frequent in middle- than in lower-class families. Also, higher value similarity has been found among middle-class than among lower-class mothers and sons (Rosen, 1964a).

Other results fail to confirm the relationships found by Rosen. No consistent association was found between mobility aspirations of Negro and white high school students, matched for age, sex, intelligence, and SES, and their family experiences, measured by the Dynes et al. questionnaire of affectional patterns in the family and dichotomized into *satisfactory* and *unsatisfactory*. Although achievement value orientation of whites was significantly higher than that of Negroes, Negroes had significantly higher educational and vocational aspirations and, in contrast to whites, valued success in their careers more than happiness. It was suggested, however, that the higher educational-vocational aspirations of Negroes compared to whites might be on a fantasy rather than a reality level (Smith and Abramson, 1962).

Questionnaire findings from white high school seniors suggest that high ambition and a relative emphasis on the educational rather than material component of ambition are associated with (1) high education of the breadwinner in the family relative to his occupation; (2) mother's education higher than father's; and (3) small size. Level but not emphasis of ambition may be related to family stability. Position among siblings and sex of siblings are unrelated to ambition when controls are introduced for family size (Turner, 1962).

An individual's concept of success, including criteria of success, conditions for attaining it, and his personal model of success may provide suggestive information about his aspirational frame of reference. Evidence provided by Katz (1964) indicates no social class differences in the frequency of high school students' identifying wealth and possessions, attributes of personality, job security, and social relationships within the family unit as criteria of success; middle-class adolescents cited status more frequently as a criterion of success. Personal worthiness and effort was cited more often by middle-class than lower-class adolescents as means for attaining success; children of unskilled and skilled workers more frequently mentioned conditions dependent on factors over which the individual has no control. Another interesting finding of this study was that more middle- than lower-class children cited a member of their immediate family as their model of success. Twelve percent of children of unskilled laborers did not mention any individual as their model of success, possibly indicating an absence of "success" in their frame of reference.

Upward mobility aspirations are associated with effective, autonomous ego functioning, whereas downward mobility reflects demoralization. Analyzing interview responses of adolescents of different social strata, Douvan and Adelson (1963) sought to identify personality correlates of mobility strivings. They classified the Ss as upward mobile, stable, or downward mobile, depending upon whether their occupational aspirations were higher than, similar to, or lower than their father's occupation. The upward-aspiring boys were described as being unusually energetic and confident about their personal effectiveness in reaching goals, concerned with the intrinsic interest of their future work, and possessing an extended time perspective in considering occupations. They faced conflicting pressures with internalized moral values and standards of personal behavior rather than with external controls; they also showed more independence from the family, and more realism in assessing themselves and social situations. Upward aspiring boys were also found to have parents who were more likely to employ mild and essentially verbal discipline and use physical punishment infrequently. Their independence from the family did not reflect rebellion against or rejection of their parents.

Another personality pattern often evoked to explain SES differences in upward mobility rates is ability of self-imposed postponement of gratifications. Findings from high school male students show that learning to defer gratification of various adolescent needs is associated with achievement role performance (as reflected to academic grades) and role disposition (i.e., occupational aspirations) but not with the Ss' social-class position (Straus, 1962).

The notion that SES differences in motivation do exist receives some support from laboratory findings indicating that different reinforcing conditions contribute to improvement of performance of various learning tasks in lower and middle class children. Lower-class elementary school children were found to learn a discrimination learning task faster with a material reward (candy), whereas a nonmaterial reward (flashing light) was more effective for middle-class children (Terrel, Durkin, and Wiesley, 1959). Retarded and lower-class elementary school children were also found to learn concept-switching more effectively with tangible reinforcers (e.g., paper coins exchangeable for toys) than without such reinforcers, while middle-class children learn better under the opposite reinforcing conditions (Zigler and deLabry, 1962). Other experiences using verbal versus nonverbal reinforcing conditions failed to show SES differences in performance of a discrimination learning task by elementary school children (Spence and Segner, 1967) and by preschool children (Spence and Dunton, 1967). However, there is some evidence that lower-class elementary school children, when faced with middle-class people and institutions, may feel more uncomfortable than their middle-class agemates. In laboratory settings, identical reinforcers such as approval or disapproval (i.e., the words *right* or *wrong* on the part of the experimenter) have differential effects upon performance of a binary game, depending on the Ss' social class. Under conditions of approval, the performance of lower-class children improved more than that of middle-class children. Under conditions of disapproval, lower-class children performed more poorly than their middle-class peers. No racial differences appeared within the lower-class group (which was composed of Negro and white children), indicating that

"social differences are more potent determiners of behavior than are racial differences" (Rosenhan, 1966).

An important antecedent of an individual's belief that one can control his own destiny is the perception he has of opportunities to obtain rewards offered by his culture. A study of Negro and white lower- and middle-class sixth- and eighth-graders indicates that lower-class children, particularly Negroes, are much less inclined than middle-class children of both races to believe in the possibility of personal control of reinforcers. An additional finding (which, however, should be taken with caution because of low N), that among children with high IQ, lower-class Negroes are more inclined than middle-class whites to believe that reinforcements are externally controlled, suggests that brighter children of lower class may be more sensitive to the perception of reduced chances for cultural or material rewards (Battle and Rotter, 1963).

However, a study of children's beliefs in their own control of reinforcements in intellectual-academic situations (grades 3 to 12) showed that the Ss' scores on an Intellectual Academic Responsibility scale were moderately related to intelligence, ordinal position among siblings, and size of family, and inconsistently to social class (Crandall et al., 1965). Perhaps the differences in findings between this study and that of Battle and Rotter are due to the fact that in classroom situations children of all social strata have more opportunities to experience the effectiveness of personal efforts to achieve and to develop a feeling of responsibility for their own academic attainments. The bearing of such feelings upon behavior is illustrated by the findings of an experiment with adults, in which artificial social classes were created in order to observe the degree and type of upward communication by those who believed themselves to be of low status in the experimental situation. It was found that those Ss in the condition of low status who were told they might become high status tended to communicate in ways designed to establish good relations with high-status persons. However, those of low status who were told that they could not become high status showed less desire to communicate in a friendly, constructive fashion with persons of high status (Cohen, 1958).

Differences in Cognitive Behavior

1. SES Differences in Global Estimates of Intelligence. The empirical finding of a relationship between scores obtained by children on intelligence tests and their social class membership has been recognized since the first intelligence scale developed by Binet and Simon began to be used for research purposes (Binet and Simon, 1916; Stern, 1914; Terman et al., 1915, 1917; Yerkes and Anderson, 1915; Yerkes et al., 1915). Perhaps no relationship in psychology has been more extensively documented. Critical reviews of the "nature-nurture" issue and the evidence available have been presented in two yearbooks by the National Society for the Study of Education, prepared by Terman et al. (1928) and Stoddard et al. (1940), and in six issues of the *Review of Educational Research* (Vol. III, 1933; Vol. VI, 1936; Vol. IX, 1939; Vol. XI, 1941; Vol. XIV, 1944; Vol. XVII, 1947). In addition, Burks and Kelley (1928), Davis (1948), Davis and Eells (1953), Dreger and Miller (1960), Eells (1948, 1953), Eells, Davis, Havighurst, Herrick, and Tyler (1951), Haggard (1954), Jones (1946), Loevinger (1940), Lorimer and Osborn (1934), Murphy, Murphy, and Newcomb (1937), Murray (1947), Schieffelin and Schwesinger (1930), Shuey (1958), Sorokin, Zimmerman, and Galpin (1932), and Stoddard and Wellman (1940) reviewed research on SES differences and discussed the relationship between intelligence and social class and race. Of particular importance to the issue of environment versus genetic effects is the recent monograph of Skeels (1966) describing the impact of early experience on the adult behavior of the group of infants he studied in the early 1930s. After a time lapse of 21 years, Skeels conducted a follow-up study of 25 Ss. Thirteen Ss had comprised an experimental group of children, originally classified as mentally retarded, who were shifted from an orphanage first to an institution with more developmental stimulation and, finally, to adoptive homes. The control group of 12 Ss, initially higher in intelligence, remained in a less stimulating orphanage environment for a prolonged period. The two groups showed divergent patterns of competence, intelligence, education, and occupation, with the experimental group attaining significantly higher levels in all categories.

In a major study of SES and IQ, Eells et al. (1951) approached the problem through an analysis of the relation between social status and IQs (or percentile ranks) secured from nine widely used group intelligence tests[5] and an analysis of individual item responses categorized in several ways (by test, position of the correct response among the distractors, form of symbolism in which the item is expressed, type of question asked, and difficulty of the item). Their sample included approximately 5000 white pupils of ages 9, 10, 13, 14—nearly all white pupils of these ages in a Midwestern industrial community of 100,000 population. One set of four tests was given to the 9- and 10-year-olds and one set of five tests was given to the 13- and 14-year olds. The socioeconomic status of the Ss' families was determined through a modification of Warner's ISC including ratings of the occupation and education of parents, type of house, and dwelling area. This SES index was validated in terms of social-class participation and status on the basis of field data available for this community. These SES groups were selected on the basis of the SES index, one high status and two low status, the latter subdivided by ethnicity.

The evidence reported by Eells et al. (1951) deals with the size of differences among SES groups, its relationship to the Ss' age, the amount of variability within each SES group, the amount of overlapping between groups, and the relationships between these factors and the specific tests or categories of test items used.

Correlation coefficients between IQ or percentile ranks and the SES scores of white

[5] These tests were: (1) Otis Quick-scoring Mental Ability Tests, Alpha Test, Form A; (2) Henmon-Nelson Tests of Mental Ability, Form A, Elementary School Examination—Grades III-VIII; (3) Kuhlmann-Anderson Intelligence Tests, Fifth Ed., Grade III and VI; (4) Terman-McNemar Test of Mental Ability, Form C; (5) Otis Quick-scoring Mental Ability Tests, Beta Test; Form Cm, for Grades IV-IX; (6) California Short-form Test of Mental Maturity, Intermediate S-Form, Grades VII-X; (7) Chicago Tests of Primary Mental Abilities for Ages 11-17; (8) Thurstone Spatial Test; and (9) Thurstone Reasoning Test.

children summarized across many studies (Eells et al., 1951) are moderate in size but statistically significant. The magnitude of correlation varies with the test used and the age level tested; half range between .25 and .50. In Eells' study, using standard group tests and age levels of 9, 10, 13, and 14 years, correlations ranged betwen .20 and .40 and were linear for the two older groups but non-linear for the two younger groups (where the relationship was linear only for groups below upper-middle class). The mean IQ differences between high and low SES groups ranged from 8 to 23 IQ points, the amount of IQ difference varying from test to test and by age level of the Ss. This study also confirmed previous results indicating a large amount of overlapping at all SES levels. Many high SES Ss received low scores and many low SES Ss obtained high scores.

The evidence on effect of the child's age upon the magnitude of the relationship between SES and IQ scores is not consistent, at least for school-age children. Early studies by Yerkes et al. (1915) indicate that SES differences increase with age, but Terman (1915, 1917) found that the correlation between IQ and SES decreased with age. On the basis of a review of literature and their own research findings, Eells et al. (1951) concluded that there is no evidence that SES differences in IQ increase or decrease with increase in age of subjects. Although there were larger SES differences in overall performances for the higher age groups, these differences were found only for certain types of items. The greater discrepancy of IQs by SES for the older groups was related to differences in the proportion of verbal versus nonverbal items used at the higher age levels. A more recent study by Deutsch and Brown (1964) comes to the same conclusion, although Deutsch finds that Negro-white differences do increase between the first and fifth grades.

Roberts, Dickerson, and Horton (1966) reported that age did not appear to be a significant factor in the Stanford-Binet performance of Negro children from ages 7 through 10, while marital status of the mother and her educational level exhibited important relationships with the children's performance. These environmental factors appeared to be more crucial at ages 9 and 10 than for younger children. However, Kennedy et al. (1963) reported Stanford-Binet test results for 1800 Negro children in elementary school in the Southeastern United States which show a decline in mean score with age. Again, it is difficult to assess the effect of differences in type of test item with increasing age upon the test results.

2. SES Differences in the Profile of Cognitive Operations. An item analysis of the IQ test differences between SES groups might be expected to be informative about the environmental conditions that might have been responsible. Findings that bear on this question are not entirely consistent. Evidence was provided in studies reported by Stern (1914), Weintrob and Weintrob (1912), Bridges and Coler (1917), Burt (1922), Stoke (1927), Long (1935), Saltzman (1940), and Murray (1947). Eells et al. (1951), reporting on these studies, concluded that, despite many inadequacies of procedure and some inconsistency of results, there appears to be a common tendency in the findings indicating that "test items which are essentially linguistic or scholastic in nature show comparatively large differences in favor of children from high socio-economic backgrounds, while test items which are primarily perceptual or 'practical' in nature show either smaller differences or differences in favor of children from the lower socio-economic backgrounds."

An item analysis undertaken by Eells and his associates (1951) showed significant differences between high- and low-status groups for half the items in the tests for 9- and 10-year-olds and nearly 85% of the items in the tests for the 13- and 14-year-olds. Mean SES differences were largest for verbal and smallest for picture, geometric-design, and stylized-drawing items, with SES differences showing greater dispersion for verbal and for picture items. Within these categories, the item type (e.g., analogies, opposites) was not consistently related to SES.

Analysis of the types of incorrect responses showed that low SES Ss tended more often than high SES Ss to omit items, but only to the extent that they also marked the answer incorrectly more frequently. Nearly one fourth of the items showed significant SES differences in the pattern of errors. Several of these differences could be attributed to SES differences in opportunity for familiarity with certain objects, words, or processes. On many other items, the errors of high SES Ss were of the type of a near-correct or next-best answer, while the errors of low SES Ss tended to be dispersed over all available distractors, indicating that low SES Ss are more likely to resort to random guessing than are high SES Ss.

Havighurst and Breese (1947), comparing the test scores of 13-year-olds in terms of Primary Mental Abilities (Thurstone and Thurstone, 1943, 1958) found that although high-status children scored higher on all variables, social-class differences were greatest for the Verbal, Word-Fluency, and Number variables and less pronounced for Space, Reasoning, and Memory. Roberts and Robinson (1952) and Mitchell (1956), studying the factorial organization of mental abilities of high and low SES children aged 11 and 12, found the same factors (Number, Verbal Meaning, Space, Word-Fluency, Reasoning, and a general Test Factor) for both SES groups. The organization of mental abilities was, however, much less differentiated for the low-status children, whose pattern reflected a larger general intellective factor (Spearman's g) and less differentiation of the other factors. On the assumption that SES differences in IQ are primarily verbal, Mitchell suggested that this result was partly attributable to the greater saturation of the general factor with verbal components. The lower-class child has not the necessary verbal competence to perform without a particular effort the verbal tasks involved even in nonverbal tests. Therefore all mental tests whether verbal or nonverbal in form are more verbally weighed for the lower-class than for the middle-class child. This point has been elaborated more recently by Jensen (1968).

There is a limited amount of information about the intelligence test performance of ethnic groups (other than Negro) in this country. On performance tests American-Indian children are closer to the norms of white children but do less well on verbal tests (Anastasi and Foley, 1949). They may equal or exceed whites on tests of drawing ability (Dennis, 1942; Russell, 1943; Havighurst, Gunther, and Pratt, 1946). Although it seems plausible, there is little evidence on the possibility of differences among American-Indian tribes. A similar pattern has been found for Mexican-American children (Garth, Elson, and Morton, 1936) and for Italian-American children (Held, 1941). Differences have been found between the pattern of abilities of Japanese-American children and white children, with Japanese groups earning higher scores on tests of visual perception, spatial orientation, and sustained attention but lower on verbal tests and arithmetic (Darsie, 1926).

In a study significant for both methodological design and substantive findings, Lesser et al. (1965) designed a project to analyze the relative impact of social class and ethnicity on intellective functioning. Using tests and testing conditions devised to minimize bias, they examined four mental abilities (verbal ability, reasoning, number facility, space conceptualization) of 320 first-grade children from four ethnic groups (Chinese, Jewish, Negro, and Puerto Rican), with each ethnic group divided into middle and lower class.

The major findings of the study were that both social class and ethnic group membership have strong but different effects upon performance on the tests covering the four mental abilities. Ethnicity affects the pattern or profile of performance; social class affects the level of achievement. Among the four ethnic groups, the rankings on the four test areas were as follows: *Verbal ability:* Jews, Negroes, Chinese, Puerto Ricans; *Reasoning:* Chinese, Jews, Negroes, Puerto Ricans; *Numerical Ability:* Jews, Chinese, Puerto Ricans, Negroes; *Space:* Chinese, Jews, Puerto Ricans, Negroes. Social class differences were greatest for the Negro group, suggesting relatively greater socioeconomic disadvantage for the lower-class Negroes. In interpreting their data, Lesser and his associates concluded that the natural selection argument for social class effects upon mental abilities "seems weakened by the fact that, once the ethnic pattern of mental abilities emerges, no further alteration in the pattern occurs under the influence of differing social class conditions." They also argued that other explanations of social class effects upon mental abilities (motivation, impulse control, problem-solving tactics) gain greater credence from their results.

In other studies the most extensive ethnic comparisons are between Negro and white children. Intelligence test scores of Negro children are typically lower, on the average, than those of white children. Shuey (1958) surveys research literature of approximately 240 studies including roughly 60 tests and thousands of children and adults from all sections of the country. Most of these studies have serious methodological flaws, however. In only 17 of the studies is social class position of the subjects taken into consideration in some way. The distribution of SES within the U.S. Negro population is very different from that of Caucasians. At this point in history there is a disproportionate number of Negroes at low SES levels. Social class and race are thus confounded in many comparisons. Shuey (1958) reported that investigators agree that Negroes do "relatively well in tests that are purposeful, practical, concrete and those that involve rote memory; and perform less efficiently in tests that are relatively abstract in nature and in tests involving certain perceptual-motor functions (e.g., Kohs Block Design)." There is disagreement between investigators as to the difficulty Negroes have with verbal compared with nonverbal test material. Shuey (1958) reports that on the Wechsler-Bellevue, the WISC, and the California Test of Mental Maturity, Negro children and adults achieved higher scores or IQs on the verbal than on the performance sections and that Negro school children scored no higher on the average on the nonverbal than on the verbal group tests. Coleman's report (1966) shows a similar pattern. Also, Lesser (1965) found that Negro children performed better on *verbal* than on *reasoning, number,* and *space* sections of the tests he administered.

Comparing Negro and white children of first and fifth grades divided into three social class levels, Deutsch and Brown (1964) found (by using the Lorge-Thorndike Intelligence Test) a linear relationship between SES and performance level for both Negro and white groups; within this linear relationship, the absolute increase in IQ is greater for the white group than it is for the Negro. Deutsch and Brown concluded that the influence of race tends to increase as the social class level rises and interpreted these results as indicating less participation in the cultural mainstream by the middle-class Negro, while the lowest class status operates similarly for the white as well as for the Negro. Deutsch and Brown argue that "it is more difficult for the Negro to attain identical middle- or upper-middle class status with whites, and all the social class gradations are less marked because Negro life in a caste society is considerably more homogeneous than is life for the majority group." The mean IQ (102) of the upper-middle-class Negro group in Deutsch's study may be atypically low in view of the higher mean (109) reported by Hess and his colleagues for upper-middle-class Negro preschool children on the Stanford-Binet. They also found the WAIS IQ of the upper-middle-class Negro mothers to be 109. In their data, there was no mean difference between middle-class mothers and children in IQ, while the mean scores of children from working-class groups exceeded the mean IQ of their mothers by 13 points (Hess and Shipman, 1967).

3. Interpretations of SES and Ethnic Differences in IQ and Attempts to Reduce Bias in Testing. Two major interpretations have been advanced regarding the mediating causes of SES differences in IQ. One is that natural selection occurs, resulting in a gradual hereditary differentiation. The other is that working-class background does not provide the child an environment most beneficial for maximum development of his intellectual potentialities. Davis and Havighurst (1946) presented a third point of view which sidesteps the hereditary-environment controversy and questions instead whether differences in average IQ found for high- and low-status children represent real differences in intelligence as assumed. They argued that children from different social groups "have substantially different kinds of cultural experiences, different in the kinds of things with which the children deal, in the vocabulary and language with which the children will be familiar, and in the attitudes and values which determine what problems seem important to the children." They then argued that "the usual intelligence tests draw more heavily from the content, the language and the attitudes and values of the high status culture than they do from the low status culture. From this point of view the differences in IQ's or scores on the tests may be a reflection merely of this bias in the test materials, and not of basic differences in the real abilities of children from the different backgrounds." These arguments apply, in some degree, to ethnic differences as well.

Several attempts have been made to deal with the possibility of bias in some tests and testing conditions. To equalize the Ss' attitudes toward taking intelligence tests, their familiarity with test instructions, and their experience with solving types of problems included in intelligence tests and with generalizing solutions to new problems, Haggard (1954) used a pretest and posttest design in which 11-year-old students were given a daily 50-minute practice period for 3 days following the initial testing. In addition, the verbal items and test instructions used in the retest were rewritten. The findings of this study indicated that practice facilitated gain in performance of the high-status students who took the standard forms of the retest and of the low-status children who took the revised forms of the retest; low-status children, where motivated, did better than if not motivated on the standard forms of the retest; high-status children showed a greater gain when they took the revised retest in a silent manner while low-status children showed additional gain in performance when the revised retest was read aloud to them. There was no significant difference between the two SES groups in ability to learn to solve intelligence test problems; and the mere revision of the test items was not sufficient to reduce the difference in performance between the two SES groups. The discrepancy decreased significantly when motivation and practice were also present.

Investigators trying to eliminate cultural bias in test items often assumed that nonverbal items and tests requiring perceptual and motor functions would yield more valid results with children from different ethnic and socioeconomic groups. Using the Davis-Eells Games—a nontimed and nonverbal test of problem-solving ability based on theory and research by Davis and Eells (1953)— with 313 elementary school children, Noll (1960) reported zero correlations between the Ss' SES and their scores on the Davis-Eells Games and a high correlation between their SES and the Otis Quick-scoring Mental Ability Test. However, Stablein, Willey, and Thomson (1961), comparing the performance of Spanish- and Anglo-American children on the Davis-Eells Games, a battery of Metropolitan Achievement Tests (a vocabulary test), and the SRA Primary Mental Abilities Test, found that the mean scores of Spanish-American children were lower than those of Anglo-Americans on all measures, including the Davis-Eells Games.

With the aim of identifying and evaluating tests with reduced dependence on acquired knowledge and thus contributing to the improvement of mental testing for children from different ethnic and social class backgrounds, several investigators compared children's performance on the Progressive Matrices Test of Raven—a nonverbal test with a high loading in g factor—with their performance on other standard intelligence tests. Knief and Stroud (1959), for example, tested 344 fourth-grade low- and middle-class students from a Midwestern town of 80,000, using the Lorge-Thorndike verbal and nonverbal intelligence tests, the Davis-Eells Games, and the Town Test of Basic Skills. One year later, 164 pupils of the initial sample were tested by the Progressive Matrices of Raven. The results indicated that the pupils' ISC scores correlated significantly and to approximately the same extent with their scores on all tests used except the Progressive Matrices. MacArthur and Elley (1963) also analyzed the scores of a representative sample of 271 12- and 13-year-olds to "nine promising culture-reduced tests and subtests."[6] Analysis of the Ss' scores in relation to their scores on measures of SES, verbal intelligence, achievement and school marks, as well as in comparison to their scores in the same tests in previous years, indicated that the Progressive Matrices Test was the best in the battery in terms of "high g loading, consistent and minimal relation with socio-economic status, no evidence of cultural bias by items and moderate correlations with school marks." This study also indicated that the Cattell test of g and the Lorge-Thorndike Figure Analogies subtest were the

[6] Among these tests were Raven's Progressive Matrices, Cattell's Test of g, and specific subtests of the Lorge-Thorndike Non-Verbal Intelligence Test (level 4), the California Test of Mental Maturity Non-Lang, short form, elementary, and the Holzinger-Crowder Uni-Factor Test.

next best tests in the battery, while the California Test of Mental Maturity showed a significantly increasing relationship with SES over 4 years, and verbal items in it indicated a greater variation in item discrimination between different SES levels than did items of the Progressive Matrices Test.

However, when Higgins and Sivers (1958) tested 789 Negro and white 7- to 10-year-old pupils from public schools in the lowest socioeconomic areas of a northwestern city, using the Stanford-Binet and the Colored Raven Progressive Matrices, they found no significant differences between Negro and whites in average IQ obtained through the Stanford-Binet and no significant difference for white children between their performances in the Stanford-Binet and the Progressive Matrices Test. Significant differences were found, however, between the two racial groups; when scores on Progressive Matrices were compared, the Negro mean scores were lower than the white mean scores. The Negro children performed significantly better on the Stanford-Binet than on the Progressive Matrices. These investigators suggested that the Progressive Matrices Test should not be considered as a test of general mental ability (g) but as a measure of special skill. Commenting on the Higgins and Sivers findings, Jensen (1968) suggested that children from low-class environments should be expected to have a "higher threshold for the elicitation of spontaneous verbalization in nominally non-verbal problem situations," and that verbal factors may permeate even the nonverbal tests.

Comparing the performance of Southern white and Negro 7- to 9-year-olds on the Colored Progressive Matrices Test of Raven and the WISC, Semler and Iscoe (1966) found that Negro children compared to their white agemates obtained significantly lower IQs at all age levels. No significant differences appeared, however, on Progressive Matrices scores obtained by Negro and white children at the ages of 8 and 9, while, at the age of 7, Negro children obtained significantly lower scores on this test.

The results of these studies indicate that experiential and motivational factors which influence performance on standard intelligence tests may also be involved in tests considered to be culture-fair. Testing is, itself, an unfamiliar experience for the lower-class child and irrelevant to much of his behavior. Indeed, since interests, work habits, and problem-solving attitudes originate largely from cultural conditions and influence the development of special abilities (Anastasi, 1965), it should not be assumed that nonverbal tests more nearly approach culture-fairness than do verbal tests. As Levinson (1963) pointed out, the constellation of factors resulting from analyses of tests measuring intellectual traits often reflects the values of a particular culture. The finding, for example, that both Jewish and Negro children function more poorly on performance tests than on verbal tests has stimulated entirely different interpretations, verbal learning being stressed as an explanation in one group, and in the other a more passive approach to problem solving which impedes the child's performance when speed is demanded. Anastasi (1961) and Wrightstone (1963) also explained the poorer performance of Negro children on perceptual and spatial tasks on the basis of the detrimental effects of time limits upon motivation.

4. SES Differences in Educational Achievement. The distinction between IQ tests and scholastic achievement or aptitude tests is not clear, particularly when one recalls that Binet originally devised tests to predict school success. In this sense, school achievement tests are the criteria and IQ tests are estimates. As in IQ tests, SES differences in school performance are well known. It is not feasible or useful to review all the research bearing on SES disparity in educational attainment as indicated by tests. Several examples will serve to document the difference and indicate its magnitude. The correlation between scholastic ability and IQ scores would in itself be expected to produce differences in educational achievement among different SES levels.

The extent of this divergence is shown by a survey of the school system of Chicago (Havighurst, 1964). The 21 districts were ranked by an index which combined the median family income and median level of education of adults in the area, based on census data, and a gross index, based on combined scores on two reading tests and two arithmetic tests at grade six. The top third of districts in the SES ranking ranged from achievement at grade level to achievement one grade above norms. The bottom third, with one exception, were all about one year below expected grade level. A similar pattern was apparent from reading readiness scores for first-grade children. In the bottom third of ranking, only 40% were up to standard in this crucial set of skills. These differences also apply to socioeconomic differentials between the districts with substantial numbers of middle-class Negroes and those with predominately working-class Negro populations. The technique for assigning SES ranking is, of course, gross; differentials would probably have been greater if more individualized SES information had been available.

A summary of research data, giving more differentiation among scholastic skills, is reported as the result of a study of socioeconomic status and school achievement (California Elementary School Administrators Association, 1962). This study covered 26 schools in Alameda County, California. By using Hollingshead's Two-Factor Index of Social Position, four SES groups of both Negro and white pupils were included; the scholastic measures were the Sequential Tests of Educational Progress (STEP) covering *reading, writing, social studies, mathematics, science,* and *listening.* Ss were asked to request their parents to fill out the forms needed for assigning social status. The responses of parents and, perhaps, their acceptance of the goals of the school are themselves of interest; only 62% of parents in low SES schools returned the questionnaires while 85% of parents in highest SES levels did so. In terms of the children's achievement scores, the differences among the four SES groups varied considerably from one subject to another. The greatest discrepancies occurred in science where the percentile range was from 83 for the highest SES group to 14 for the lowest. The smallest difference between high and low SES groups was in writing (75 and 37) with differences in reading scores showing next smallest range.

A third study, the most comprehensive, was that supervised by Coleman (1966). This major national study, commissioned by the U.S. Office of Education, was directed particularly to the analysis of scholastic achievement of minority groups and the factors which contributed to educational attainment. The sample was not divided by social class. Thus comparisons of ethnic groups with the majority group do not permit analysis of variability between social class levels within each ethnic group. Comparisons between ethnic groups and whites are confounded with SES, since the proportion of lower and middle class within each ethnic group differs. The comparison, for example, of the average test scores of the Negro and the "majority" group is questionable as a measure of the effect of ethnicity alone, since the proportion of lower class is significantly higher among Negroes than among the white group. Such differences in proportion of lower and middle class probably exist for other ethnic groups as well.

The data reported by Coleman indicate that, with the exception of Oriental American, minority groups, that is, Negroes, Indian-Americans, Mexican-Americans, and Puerto Ricans score distinctly lower on the standard achievement tests than the average white pupils. Their scores are approximately one standard deviation below the majority pupils' scores in the first grade. At grade 12, the scores of minority groups on tests of the same types of skills, verbal and nonverbal, are farther below the majority group than at grade one. Comparison between the groups' average scores for the five achievement tests used at grade 12 showed that Negroes differed from the majority group most, followed by Puerto Ricans, Mexican-Americans, Indian-Americans, and Oriental Americans (who showed the least difference from the majority groups). Coleman concluded that "whatever may be the combination of nonschool factors —poverty, community attitudes, low educational level of parents—which put minority children at a disadvantage in verbal and nonverbal skills when they enter the first grade, the fact is the schools have not overcome it."

Regional differences also appear in the Coleman data. In the South, both white and Negro twelfth graders scored lower than their agemates, white and Negro, in the North. This regional difference was more pronounced for Negroes than for whites, Southern Negroes scoring farther below Southern whites than Northern Negroes did below Northern whites. This regional difference did not exist at the beginning of schooling. However, Coleman points to the fact that "in the metropolitan North and West, 20 per cent of the Negroes of ages 16 and 17 are not enrolled in school—a higher dropout percentage than in either the metropolitan or nonmetropolitan South." If some or many of the Northern dropouts performed poorly when they were in school, Negro achievement in the North may be higher only because some of those who performed poorly have left school.

As already noted, data on achievement scores were not differentiated by social class within each minority group. However, a number of background variables of the pupils were used in computing their contribution to the total variance as compared to school variables. These background variables of the pupils were: urbanism of background (for students of grades 9 and 12), migration (for sixth graders), parents' education, structural integrity of the home, size (smallness) of the family, items in the home indicating its economic standing, reading material at home (such as encyclopedia, etc.), parents' interest (talking about school matters with the pupils, reading to them when they were small, etc.), and parents' educational desires for their children. Coleman found that, at grade 6, economic level of the family (based on the child's report) had the highest relationship to achievement scores for all the minority groups, while the parents' educational level had the highest relation to achievement scores for the majority group of whites. In later years, however, parents' education had the highest relation to achievement scores of the pupils for nearly all groups.

For Negroes of grade 12, the length of time in an urban environment and the (small) size of their families had approximately the same importance as their parents' education. The structural integrity of the home (presence or absence of the father) showed very little relation to achievement for Negroes. It had, however, a strong relation to achievement for other minority groups.

Comparing the performance of a large sample of Southern Negro and white students of grades 4 through 12 in reading achievement tests, Cooper (1964) found that white students at all grades demonstrated higher levels of vocabulary and comprehension proficiency than did Negroes and that the retardation of Negroes increased with added age. Similar findings have been reported by Osborne (1960) from a longitudinal study of 815 white and 446 Negro students whose reading skills (vocabulary and comprehension), arithmetic skills (reasoning and fundamentals), and mental maturity—assessed through the California Achievement and Mental Maturity Tests—have been compared in 1954, 1956, and 1958, when the children were in grades 6, 8, and 10 respectively. Osborne's finding that the discrepancy of Negroes compared to whites increased progressively from grade 6 to 10 not only on vocabulary, reading comprehension, and arithmetic reasoning but also on arithmetic fundamentals—a subtest considered to be less culturally weighted—suggests that an important variable often neglected in racial comparisons is experience, which in most cases depends on the social class position of the family. However, from a study with sixth-grade pupils tested by the California Test of Mental Maturity and the California Arithmetic Test, it was concluded that the effect of socioeconomic conditions on scholastic achievement increases as the intellectual ability decreases. SES affects primarily language, achievement in arithmetic being relatively free of the influence (Curry, 1962). These findings must be regarded with caution, however, in view of other data available.

The position that social class-linked family experience heavily influences Ss' performance on reading tests receives support from the findings of Weiner and Feldman (1963; Feldman and Weiner, 1964), who reported that two reading tests in a standard battery yielded distinctly different score distributions by social class within the same school. The scores of lower-class children of grades 3 through 8 on the Gates Advanced Primary Reading Test were spread over a substantially wider range than were their scores on the Gates Basic Reading Test, Level of Comprehension; the opposite was true for the scores of middle-class children. Negative effects of social and emotional impoverishment on school attainments of lower-class Negro and white children have also been described by Deutsch (1960). The performance of both racial groups on the Stanford Achievement Test was significantly lower than the national norms for this test. Academic retardation of both groups increased with age. For the Negro children, this retardation was, however, significantly more pronounced than for white children. Deutsch suggested that this difference between Negro and white lower-class Ss may stem from the negative feelings that Negro children develop toward themselves, partly in response to the low expectations of their teachers. The detrimental effects of racial segregation and other school qualities upon the scholastic achievement of Negro students have been documented by Hansen (1960), who reported that in an integrated school system the scores of Negro pupils on the Stanford Achievement Test increased steadily. Stallings (1960) reported similar results for 5 years following integration, with most marked progress in the scores of Negro pupils appearing in areas related to reading.

One of the most specific and dramatic statements of the relatively low educational achievement of Negro pupils in northern urban areas is found in a report on education in Harlem, *Youth in the Ghetto* (HARYOU, 1964). The pupils in Harlem schools are almost all Negroes, primarily from low socioeconomic backgrounds. More than half of the students in academic high schools and over 60% of those in vocational schools dropped out without receiving a diploma. The performance of children in Harlem schools, at the time of the report, showed substantial decline with increase in grade. As shown in Table 2, Harlem pupils were 2½ years or more behind national norms in reading comprehension, word knowledge, and arithmetic. IQ scores followed a similar pattern, with average ranging from 91 at grade 3 to 88 at grade 8 for Harlem school pupils, compared to roughly 100 from New York City and, presumably, the rest of the nation. Such data have made the problem of education of minority pupils a matter of national concern.

5. **SES Differences in Other Cognitive Operations.** Some recent studies have provided more detailed information about SES differences in cognitive functioning. Deutsch and

McArdle (1967) are investigating the hypothesis that there are SES differences in auditory discrimination for white and Negro children. If such a difference is found, however, it will be relevant to recall the findings of Lesser et al. (1965) of SES differences in four ethnic groups regardless of the differences in profile of performance, a caution that applies, of course, to much of the current work on SES and ethnic differences in cognitive functions. Deutsch (1960) found lower-class children were less able than a comparable group of middle-class children on tasks requiring concentration and persistence; further, they displayed a tendency to ignore difficult problems. Differences between low- and middle-class children also appear on techniques designed to assess developmental changes in drawing characteristics (Eisner, 1967).

Recent information on the relationship between aspects of cognitive development and maternal behavior as well as other features of the social and cultural environment (Getzels and Jackson, 1961; Kagan and Moss, 1962; Bing, 1963; Hunt, 1964; Dyk and Witkin, 1965; Busse, 1967) has created keen interest in the degree to which manipulation of the learning situation might affect the relative performance of children from different SES levels. Jensen (1963a, 1963b) and John (1963), working independently and with different approaches, concluded that the disparity between lower-, middle-, and upper-class children in language is not simply one of amount of vocabulary but of use of language as a cognitive tool. Their research is extensively reported in the language section of this chapter. Jensen (1961, 1963a, 1963b) also found that when lower-class children were trained to use verbal mediators in learning situations, their performance was improved.

A series of laboratory studies of learning ability of low- and middle-class children indicate that they perform equally well on

Table 2. Median Achievement Scores

Grade	Reading Comprehension			Word Knowledge			Arithmetic		
	Harlem	N.Y.C.	U.S.A.	Harlem	N.Y.C.	U.S.A.	Harlem	N.Y.C.	U.S.A.
3	2.5	3.6	3.7	2.7	3.6	3.7	X	X	X
6	4.1	6.1	6.2	4.1	6.1	6.2	5.0	6.4	6.5
8	6.0	8.1	8.5	6.0	8.1	8.5	5.8	8.1	8.5

complex concept attainment problems (Osler, 1967; Osler and Kofsky, 1965, 1966). Similarly, no SES differences were found in learning paired-associate tasks (Rohwer, 1967), discrimination learning tasks (Zigler and deLabry, 1962; Spence and Segner, 1967), or concept tasks (Siller, 1957). Discussing these findings, Osler (1967) suggested that the fact that many of the lower-status children "fail to acquire the skills and knowledge which their more privileged peers succeed in mastering . . . constitutes no proof of their incapacity to do so."

The fact that laboratory conditions appear to equalize the performances of children of different SES backgrounds in learning complex tasks involving conceptual thinking suggests that there probably are substantial differences not only in the cognitive backgrounds of children in terms of previously acquired knowledge, work habits, and language skills but also in their cognitive styles, a label used to signify differences in both cognitive processes and motivation.

6. The Quest for Contingencies between Culture and Cognition. In more recent years, laboratory studies focus with increased frequency on specific variables which affect development of cognitive processes underlying the performances of children on more global intelligence tests and in scholastic achievement tests.

The studies conducted by Bernstein, Caldwell, Deutsch and Deutsch, Gray, Hess, Jensen, John and Osler among others represent more recent efforts on the part of these investigators to use laboratory and sampling techniques to tease out the background variables related to working-class children's cognitive styles and processes. Older studies of this type by Burks (1928), Cuff (1933), and Osborn (1943) had shown that the level of education of the parents, their interests in reading, their income, and the housing conditions in which they lived tend to be significantly related to differences in the performance of children in intelligence tests, and more recent results confirm this picture (Dave, 1963; Wolf, 1964).

The more significant theoretical and research problem, however, is to specify contingencies between the environment and the developing cognitive styles and operations of

the child and the degree to which these styles can be modified by intervention (Caldwell, 1968, Deutsch and Deutsch, 1968; Gray and Klaus, 1968; Glick, 1968; Hess, 1968). Deutsch (1963, 1965) has suggested that environmental and developmental factors interact and influence intellectual maturation through their influences on the development of the child's perceptual abilities and his language. Interrelationships between language measures and selected demographic variables, based upon the assessments of 292 children of first and fifth grades, led Deutsch to argue that environmentally deprived children are susceptible to a "cumulative deficit phenomenon," which affects both the linguistic and cognitive development by inhibiting the development of "abstract and categorical" use of language.

The research of Hess and his colleagues (1965, 1967, 1968) pursues the argument that early social experiences which are part of mother-child interaction shape thought and cognitive styles of problem solving. Studying mother-child interaction styles on the basis of data gathered from 163 Negro families representing four social status levels ranging from families with mother on public welfare to families with college-educated fathers, they attempted to identify the cognitive environment to which lower-status children are exposed. Of particular relevance for the development of cognitive functioning in the child are the mother's strategies for orienting the child toward selected cues in the environment, the types of regulatory or control techniques she uses, and her patterning of stimuli to organize information for the child. The control techniques call attention to status or normative components in the situation, paraphrased as "You should do this because someone in authority has told you to do it. It is a rule," or "It is the way someone your age or sex should behave," or to subjective personal states, in which the appeal is to how one's actions will make other people feel, or to the consequences of action apart from rules or feelings. These different techniques of control evoke different cognitive responses on the part of the child and are based on dissimilar reinforcement patterns. The orientation of adults from working-class backgrounds toward external control and authority, discussed earlier in the chapter, are congruent with Hess' findings that working-class mothers use normative control to a greater extent than do mothers from the middle class and that this type of control is related negatively to the development of verbal behavior, performance on cognitive tasks, and to reading readiness, as measured by standard tests (Hess et al., 1968). The ability of mothers to organize and sequence material for their children in face-to-face teaching of simple tasks by appropriate orientation and pretask information feedback, motivating specificity of language, and monitoring behavior, are also related both to the mother's social class and to the child's performance in cognitive and school-related tasks.

Working with a subset of the larger sample of Hess and his colleagues, Stodolsky (1965) found significant social-class differences in the children's scores on the Peabody Picture Vocabulary Test, which were related to a particular set of maternal variables— specifically, the mother's score on the vocabulary part of the WAIS and the "discrimination index" of her teaching style, a measure of the extent to which the mother uses specific language when requiring discrimination of task-specific properties of the environment. The higher the mother's social class position, the higher her score on the vocabulary subtest of the WAIS. Although in Stodolsky's data no social class differences appeared in the mothers' "discrimination index," both these maternal variables (i.e., vocabulary scores and "discrimination index") were positively and significantly correlated with the children's vocabulary scores. This finding suggests that children whose mothers both provide rich and precise language models and interact with them appropriately perform better linguistically and conceptually, regardless of whether the mothers' qualities are directly or indirectly related to their social class position.

The literature on cognitive behavior and SES, both theoretical and empirical, is increasing rapidly as a result of large government appropriations and foundation grants for research on U.S. lower-class populations. In addition, major research programs have been established by Project Head Start, Office of Economic Opportunity, and the National Laboratory on Early Education of the U.S. Office of Education, which are oriented toward more intensive examination of many of the issues discussed in this section. These studies and programs encompass many different ethnic groups, thousands of white and nonwhite children, use many existing and newly developed tests, and attempt, among other goals, to relate teacher and parent behavior and characteristics to pupil behavior. There is a growing body of evidence on the effects of integration on school achievement and experimental studies of attempts to alter the deleterious effects of SES and racial bias. A major study of educational attainment of American Indian children is planned, and several national testing programs are accumulating data which will yield more definitive information on SES and test scores.

Differences in Language and Communication

Numerous distinguished theorists have argued that language and culture are intimately and functionally related, and there is perhaps no more obvious hypothesis than to suggest that we should find social class differences among children in both structure and use of language. Our knowledge is somewhat incomplete, however, about the process by which language is acquired in different cultural and social class groups and the relation of language to dissimilarities in cognitive functioning that are known to exist. These issues, however, are discussed elsewhere in this book. As new information is obtained on both the acquisition of language and its interaction with cognition, the linkage between language and social class will also become more clear.

Studies of the effects of social class membership and ethnic background on the verbal behavior of children follow three main lines of interest. In a first category may be grouped those that focus upon deviations from standard English in the language used by subcultural groups of adults and the social liability that such deviations presumably constitute for the speaker. Investigators attempting to identify ethnic- and social class-linked differences in the phonological and morphological components of children's language seem to assume that deviations from standard English are learned early and affect the child's cognitive development. However, studies focusing on deviations from standard English have not been able to explain fully the nature of the assumed relationship between linguistic and cognitive development in children from working-class levels.

Another group of investigators goes beyond the description of ethnic or social class differences in the structured system of verbal symbols and the rate at which parts of that system are learned to the functions of verbal behavior per se. Viewing verbal behavior as a means of communication, both inter-individual and intra-individual (i.e., a system of symbolic mediators, that may facilitate not only communication between individuals but also thinking and action for the individual himself [Carrol, 1964]), these investigators assume that subcultural differences in verbal behavior reflect differential use of these two major functions.

In a third category may be grouped studies that attempt to identify and evaluate the role of several "mediating process" variables, through which the environment influences the development of the child's verbal behavior. It is suggested that environmental features which shape verbal behavior may be grouped in terms of context, that is, the nonverbal setting in which the language occurs, amount and quality of verbal stimulation provided by the environment, and types of responses given to the child's speech (Cazden, 1966).

1. Variations in the Use of Standard English. For comparing nonstandard to standard English, the method most frequently used consists of counting "errors or deviations from standard English" and expressing the sum as a percentage of total use of a particular part of speech (e.g., pronouns) or as a percentage of total words used (Cazden, 1966).

Investigators who have used this descriptive method in comparing same-age groups of children from different social strata and ethnic backgrounds found that, among preschool and elementary school children, most errors occur in verb usage. Deviant use of auxiliary verbs (particularly among Negro children from families who have migrated from the rural South), violation of subject-verb agreement, use of present for past tense, deviant use of pronouns and double negatives have been mentioned as the most frequent errors (Templin, 1957; Thomas, 1962; Loban,

1963).[6] In a study of verbal learning from kindergarten through the end of high school, Loban (1965) reported some additional measures of language development which are related to social class: use of subordination to increase coherence, and proportion of noncommunicative utterances occurring in speech, such as false starts and word fragments.

The argument that use of nonstandard English creates a social liability for the adult speaker has been advanced by Fries (1940) and substantiated by Putnam and O'Hern (1955) and Harms (1961a, 1963), who showed that listeners from different social strata were able to rate with considerable agreement the social status of an individual after hearing his tape-recorded speech. Harms (1961b) also showed that speakers of standard English possess a more effective means of communication in an experiment where listeners from different social statuses were asked to hear short messages recorded by speakers of different social statuses and then replace words systematically deleted from written versions of the messages. It was found that, although listeners understood better the speakers of their own social status, high-status speakers were the most comprehensible to listeners of all social backgrounds.

Evidence as to whether the use of nonstandard English by children impedes their cognitive development can hardly be drawn from studies describing ethnic and class-linked differences in language development. Studies in which language development in children of different social strata and ethnic backgrounds was compared showed that in all measures used—pronunciation, vocabulary, and sentence structure—children of higher-status families were more "advanced" than children from lower-status families. For example, cultural differences in phonological development were found to start early. Comparing the frequency of phonetic types (i.e., "elemental speech sounds listed in the International Phonetic Alphabet") produced by infants of working- and middle-class families, Irwin (1948a, 1948b) found no social class

[6] Goodman (1966) criticizes the conclusions drawn by Templin and Thomas. In an analysis of the data reported by Thomas, he argues that children studied by these authors show differences but not a deficiency in language development.

differences before 18 months of age. Between 18 and 30 months, however, infants of middle-class families received significantly higher scores than did those from lower-class families. McCarthy (1930), who reported in detail the verbal behavior of 140 children—divided into 7 age groups ranging from 18 to 44 months—found that in each age group, children from upper-class families showed more advanced linguistic development than did children from lower-class families.

Templin (1957), D. R. Thomas (1962), and Loban (1963) found subcultural differences in children's vocabulary; McCarthy (1952) and Jahoda (1964) reported poorer performances in vocabulary tests by lower-class than by middle-class samples. Jahoda (1964) found SES differences increased in boys between ages 10 and 14.

Additional evidence about the relationship between SES, linguistic, and cognitive development is provided by studies involving language comprehension in children. Peisach (1965), for example, used the Cloze technique to determine the extent to which information is communicated from the teacher to students of different social levels and ethnic origins and the degree to which children from different social strata communicate effectively with each other. Children were asked to replace words deleted from samples of teachers' and peers' speech using words that made semantic and/or grammatical sense. The major findings of this study, which compared Negro and white first- and fifth-grade pupils of lower and middle class showed no racial difference in any of these receptive language skills. There was a social class difference in understanding the teacher's speech, which was larger among fifth graders than among first graders; this difference disappeared when intelligence was statistically controlled. However, the superiority of middle-class fifth graders in understanding both lower- and middle-class peers' speech was maintained even when intelligence was controlled: lower-class fifth graders had more trouble in understanding middle-class peers' speech than middle-class fifth graders had in understanding speech of lower-class peers. Cazden (1966) commented on these findings that "dialect differences are confounded with other linguistic variables such as vocabulary load and utterance complexity."

The study by Lesser, Fifer, and Clark (1965) also provides evidence on the relationships between verbal and other mental abilities. Language, as measured by a vocabulary test, was examined as one of four mental abilities (verbal, reasoning, numerical, and space) in terms of patterns and relative levels in first-grade pupils from four ethnic backgrounds (Chinese, Jewish, Negro, and Puerto Rican), each divided into lower and middle social class subgroups. The most salient finding of this study was the different effects of ethnic background and social class. Ethnic background affects the *pattern* of verbal and other mental abilities, while social class affects primarily the *level* of scores across the mental abilities. On verbal ability Jewish children ranked first, followed by Negroes, Chinese, and Puerto Ricans; middle-class children in all ethnic groups were significantly superior to lower-class children. It was also found that social class position is more highly related to mental abilities for Negro children than for other ethnic groups. Also on each mental ability test the scores of the middle-class children from all ethnic groups studied were more similar to each other than were the scores of the lower-class children. The interpretations suggested by Lesser and his associates of their findings are covered in the section on cognitive development. Where they overlap with other research, most of their findings agree with results of other investigators. However, studies of language proficiency of Puerto Rican children in New York show somewhat inconsistent results.[7] Anastasi and deJesus (1953) found young Puerto Rican children to exceed white norms on several measures, but older Puerto Rican children were significantly below test norms (Anastasi and Cordova, 1953).

[7] The effects of early bilingualism upon language and cognitive development are discussed in many studies and papers. In a recent review and critique, Diebold (1966) argues for the possibility that bilingualism may have positive rather than detrimental effects. The bilingual child develops a flexibility and versatility of communication and conceptual skills from the necessity of selecting from a wider range of alternative symbols in speech and thought. This greater diversity of linguistic abilities may give rise to conceptualizing environments in terms of more general principles as well as their specific linguistic symbols.

The existing evidence on subcultural differences in sentence structure or grammatical patterns used, reflecting superiority of middle-class children, is scarce and inconclusive. Loban (1963), for example, analyzing utterances of oral language of children in informal interviews, found that important differences between low and high social class groups lay not in frequency of their use of certain structural patterns but in their ability to make substitutions within the patterns. "The important differences show up in the substitution of word groups for single words, in the choice and arrangements of movable syntactic elements, in the variety of nominals, and in strategies with prediction."

A similar conclusion was reached by Fries (1940), who, analyzing language samples taken from the correspondence of American citizens with agencies of the federal government, found that "vulgar English seems essentially poverty stricken. It uses less of the resources of the language, and a few forms are used very frequently."

Despite these findings, there is some question whether use of nonstandard dialects necessarily reflects impoverishment (Robinson, 1965a, 1965b). In an attempt to test Bernstein's (1962a, 1962b) hypotheses concerning elaborated and restricted language codes, namely that (1) there are differences in vocabulary between the two codes and (2) the structural elements of the restricted code are more predictable than those of the elaborated code, Robinson used the Cloze technique with working- and middle-class boys and obtained results that confirmed both hypotheses. Working-class boys used a more limited vocabulary than did middle-class boys and the structural elements of working-class language were more predictable than those of middle-class language. Robinson, however, raised the question of whether lower-class boys use restricted codes out of necessity or by preference. To test this question, he established a testing situation in which lower- and middle-class boys were asked to write a formal and an informal letter. According to Bernstein's theory, the lower-class Ss should be at a greater disadvantage in writing a formal letter, because of their restricted code. This study showed fewer language differences in formal letters than in informal letters written by lower- and middle-class boys (Robin-

son, 1965b). In other words, the use of nonstandard English may not indicate linguistic or mental impoverishment. However, subjects who, despite unconventional usage of language, exhibit high linguistic skills are rather exceptional; there is a relationship between sensitivity to linguistic conventions and proficiency in language (Loban, 1963). Quantitative measures of vocabulary which consistently show social class differences, however, do not further our understanding of the deficiency-difference issue and may confound wide variations in overlap between children from different ethnic backgrounds (Cazden, 1966).

Studies on social class and sentence structure yield conflicting results and cast doubt upon the usefulness of the measures commonly used in such studies, that is, the mean length of response in words. Regard for this measure rests on the widespread finding that mean sentence length increases with age (Brown & Frazer, 1964; Cowan et al., 1967) and that there exists "a close correspondence between mean length and the emergence of specific grammatical features in the speech of children under 4 years of age" (Cazden, 1966).

Comparing 5-year-old Negro and white children living in uniracial and in interracial neighborhoods, Anastasi and D'Angelo (1952) found no significant race differences for mean sentence length. However, more "mature" sentence types—functionally and structurally complete and elaborated—were found among white children than among Negro children. Studying the relationships between socioeconomic status and acquisition of grammar by children of grades 2, 4, and 6, LaCivita et al. (1966) found no social class differences. In this study six sentences, each containing nonsense words, were presented individually to the Ss. Syntactic position and grammatical signals (such as -ed ending) provided cues to suggest three parts of speech—nouns, verbs, and modifiers. The responses were classified as homogeneous or heterogeneous. No difference was found between the two social classes in terms of homogeneity of responses.

The study of Cowan et al. (1967) with 96 children 5, 7, 9, and 11 years old, divided into equal sex and SES subgroups within each age level and tested by one of

two different experimenters, showed that the
mean length of responses was influenced by
the stimulus, that is, the picture to which the
Ss responded. Age, sex, and SES effects interacted; the experimenter effect also interacted with age and sex of the Ss. The authors
concluded that although age is a main factor
influencing the length of responses of the
children and sex and SES interact with age,
"the magnitude of developmental changes,
and the precise nature of individual differences cannot be described precisely . . . without specifying the particular examiner, stimulus and child."

In conclusion, although the reviewed research evidence shows that a relationship
between social class and the use of nonstandard English does exist, the degree to which
this suggests linguistic impoverishment is not
clear.

**2. The Intrapersonal and Interpersonal
Functions of Verbal Behavior.** The studies in
which ethnic and class-linked differences in
language are assessed as reflecting different
modes of communication, interindividual and
intraindividual, are primarily concerned with
verbal behavior per se, that is, with speech
as a means of interindividual communication
and with verbal mediators as means of shaping thinking and action. Though it is not
clear how the use of language for interindividual communication affects its use as an
intraindividual cognitive tool (Cazden, 1966),
the importance of their relationship has been
strongly emphasized, particularly in the case
of the growing child (Cazden, 1966; Jensen,
1968; John, 1964) and theories have been
proposed to explain the findings which indicate social class-linked differences in both
these functions of verbal behavior. Description of subcultural differences in the use of
language in interindividual communication
have been contributed by Milner (1951),
Khater (1951), and Keller (1963), focusing
on communication between children and
adults, and Schatzman and Strauss (1955),
focusing on communication between adults.
Bernstein (1958, 1959, 1960, 1961, 1962a,
1962b), Loban (1963), Lawton (1964) and
Hess et al. (1965, 1967, 1968) have studied interindividual communication among adults and
between adults and children and have been
concerned with the way the modes of communication which prevail in different social

strata shape children's cognitive functioning.
Milner (1951) and Keller (1963) found that
children from higher-status families are more
likely to participate in whole-family mealtime
conversations than children from lower-status
families, who eat alone or with siblings rather
than with adults in the family.

Evidence of the existence of different patterns of verbal behavior in kindergarten children has been provided by Khater (1951).
He reported that in verbal interactions with
peers, lower-class children appear to be withdrawn; during discussions of a particular
topic they tend to deviate from the assigned
topic to discuss themselves; in speaking about
their experiences they draw from the present
or project themselves to the future. In contrast, middle-class kindergarten children interact freely among themselves, are more able
to concentrate in discussion of an assigned
topic and, when reporting personal experiences, draw from both immediate and remote
in place and time. Furthermore, pronunciation and sentence structure are more "mature" in middle- than in lower-class children.

Differences in the communicative styles of
varying SES levels are more than differences
in intelligibility, grammar, and vocabulary.
Using language in crisis as a data source,
Schatzman and Strauss (1955) reported that
analysis of interviews gathered from lower-
and middle-class natives of Arkansas (after
a tornado) showed a "considerable disparity
in (a) the number and kinds of perspectives
utilized in communication; (b) the ability to
take the listener's role; (c) the handling of
classification; and (d) the framework and
stylistic devices which order and implement
the communication." The authors suggested
that the upper-status subject's superiority in
making his meaning explicit is due to a more
frequent exposure to situations requiring it.
In contrast, lower-class subjects are not accustomed to talking about their experiences
with people with whom they do not share
previous experience and symbolism. The experience of the upper-class speaker not only
teaches him how to encode more information,
but also provides him with a larger variety
of rules and conventions for organizing
speech and thought.

There may be SES differences in styles of
communication. On the basis of three experiments, in which lower- and middle-class

boys played statues, painted, and solved a spatial puzzle, Miller and Swanson (1960) argue that lower-class individuals express themselves most effectively through nonverbal means, essentially by manipulating the voluntary muscles of the body, while middle-class persons express themselves best verbally, through the manipulation of ideas.

In a series of publications focusing on relationships among social structure, language, and behavior, Bernstein (1958, 1959, 1960, 1961, 1962a, 1962b, 1964) suggested that social class differences in child's cognitive functioning result from social class-linked differences in the orientation of parent-child relationships and modes of communication. In some of his early formulations, Bernstein distinguished between two types of families: (1) those oriented toward control through appeal to status or norms related to ascribed roles, in which the personal characteristics of the child, his feelings, preferences, and subjective states, have little influence on the family's decision-making process and parents demand that he regulate his behavior in accordance with status and role expectations; (2) those oriented toward persons, in which status demands are modified by consideration of the unique personality characteristics of the participants, communication is less regulated by status or role ascriptions, decisions are more individualized, and personal or subjective states, feelings, and preferences are considered as important in justifying behavior.

In Bernstein's view, different linguistic codes prevail in the communication among members of these two types of families, restricted in the case of status-oriented families, elaborated in the case of families oriented to persons.[8] Restricted codes are characterized by simple, short, and often unfinished sentences and by only rare use of subordinate clauses which contribute to an elaboration of the sentence content. Lacking in specificity and exactness needed for precise conceptualization and differentiation, restricted codes result in a highly condensed

and rather stereotyped language resorting heavily to structural elements of implicit meaning. With statements usually made in general terms, commonly shared and easily understood, this language is often used in impersonal situations when the speaker's intent is to promote solidarity and reduce tension. This "sociocentric" language "restricts," however, the range of details of information communicated and the exactness of concepts involved.

By contrast, communication through elaborated codes is highly individualized, and the messages it uses tend to be specific to the particular situation, the topic, and the persons involved, both speaker and listeners. This language seeks to express a wider and more complex range of thought and to make precise its nuances. Speakers using this language tend to discriminate between cognitive and affective content. Elaborated language seeks—and facilitates—verbal elaboration of the speaker's intent (and is thus characterized as "egocentric"), while restricted (or sociocentric) language limits the "verbal explication of intent."

The type of verbal exchange within his family to which the child is exposed during the early stages of his development conditions and structures what he learns and how, thus setting limits within which future learning may take place. Speech progressively molds the child's perception and shapes his experiences through emphasizing and structuring specific elements of the environment. Responses evoked from the infant by the speech of adults surrounding him are progressively coordinated, differentiated, and stabilized in parallel to the development of his own speech.

Bernstein reported an experiment in which he analyzed the verbal behavior of 16-year-old lower- and middle-class boys, grouped so that their speech patterns could be compared with social class and their verbal and nonverbal intelligence held constant. An unstructured discussion provided speech samples of the boys (1962a). Verbal planning functions associated with speech were assessed through Goldman-Eisler's (1958) measures of hesitation phenomena during speech. Goldman-Eisler had previously shown that, in fluent speech consisting of habitual and more or less automatic combinations of words, gaps in its continuity are short, determined mostly by

---

[8] In fact, Bernstein stresses, in middle-class families, where the person-oriented relationships encourage—and demand—the development of elaborated codes, children become able to use both modes of communication or linguistic codes, whereas lower-class children are limited to the restricted code above.

breathing, the motor dimension of speech. Hesitations or pauses, which are longer, are related to the symbolic dimension of speech and appear when its sequence is not a matter of common learning, and choice of words is highly individual and unexpected. Bernstein tested three hypotheses related to restricted and elaborated codes as measured through the hesitation phenomena: that the codes can be distinguished; that their use is associated with social class; and that their use is independent of measured intelligence. Analysis of the recorded group discussions confirmed all three hypotheses. The language of middle-class children compared with that of working-class subjects was marked by more complex syntactic structures and less common lexical items. Also, working-class speech had a greater incidence of words of the pronoun class, a further finding taken as symptomatic of a restricted code.

Lawton (1963, 1964), analyzing the oral speech and written work of lower- and middle-class boys, reported results supportive of Bernstein's restricted-elaborated code distinction. In oral speech, lower-class boys used fewer "uncommon" adjectives and adverbs, fewer personal pronouns and passive verbs, and simpler syntactic structures than did middle-class boys. In written essays, the lower-class boys used a narrower vocabulary and simpler sentence structures.

However, similar findings have been interpreted in different though not contradictory ways by Bernstein (1962b) and Loban (1963). Both found that the ways through which middle- and lower-class speakers deal with uncertainty are different. Loban found that middle-class elementary school children as compared with lower-class children more frequently used language expressing "tentativeness" (e.g., expressions like "I think," "I am not exactly sure,") and interpreted this finding as an indication of greater cognitive flexibility in middle-class speakers. Bernstein —who also found that middle-class speakers more often use "I think" sequences, whereas lower-class speakers more often use terminal sequences (e.g., "isn't it," "you know," "ain't it," "wouldn't he")—considers the former as "egocentric" and the latter as "sociocentric" or "sympathy circulatory sequences," since they "invite implicit affirmation of the previous sequence [and] tend to close communi-cation, rather than to facilitate its development and elaboration." In Bernstein's view "the 'I think' sequence [which] allows the listener far more degrees of freedom and may be regarded as an invitation to develop the communication on his own terms" is an egocentric sequence.

The work of Hess and his associates (Hess and Shipman, 1965; Olim, Hess, and Shipman, 1967) constitutes an effort to relate linguistic modes of Negro mothers to the cognitive development of their preschool children. As part of this effort, an analysis was made of social class differences in language of the mothers in their research group. The greatest differences among the four groups (upper-middle, skilled workers, unskilled workers, families on public welfare) was between the upper middle class and the other three groups. The most obvious difference was in total amount of verbal output in response to questions and tasks asking for verbal response to the staff member or in her presence. This may reflect the impact of situational contexts on verbal behavior and, if so, support Bernstein's description of greater linguistic versatility in middle-class persons. Differences also appeared on other measures of linguistic complexity, such as the tendency of mothers to use abstract words and complex syntactic structures (coordinate and subordinate clauses, unusual infinitive phrases, infinitive clauses, and participial phrases).

Data supporting the theory that social class differences in styles of intrafamilial relationships foster differences in problem-solving ability were also reported by Straus (1968) from a study including samples of middle- and working-class families in the United States, India, and Puerto Rico. In all three national samples, working-class family groups were less successful in solving a laboratory problem than were their middle-class compatriots. Tests of possible factors contributing to the observed SES differences showed that differences in motivation did not account for the lower problem-solving ability of working-class families. Significant SES differences were found, however, in amount of intrafamily communication and creativity. It was also found that the less industrialized and urbanized the society from which the sample was drawn, the larger the SES differences observed.

Several studies have dealt with the relationship between measures of linguistic development and the child's ability to use language as a cognitive tool. Jensen (1968), in an extensive discussion of this topic, stressed that the use of language to mediate cognitive activity depends upon the existence within the individual of a hierarchical verbal network affected by environmental stimuli, both verbal and nonverbal. "A great deal of what we think of as intelligence, or as verbal ability or learning ability can be thought of in terms of the extensiveness and complexity of this verbal network and of the strength of the interconnections between its elements." We need further knowledge not simply about the total repertoire of verbal elements that a child of a certain age possesses, but also about the structure of relations between these elements, the strength of their association, the level of their hierarchical organization, and the conditions underlying the individual's use of the verbal network he possesses.

It is possible that there are social class or ethnic differences in the threshold for the elicitation of spontaneous verbalization in presumably nonverbal as well as verbal problem situations. Jensen (1968) advances this argument on the basis of results of Higgins and Sivers (1958) that lower-class white and Negro children with very similar Stanford Binet IQs differed significantly on the Progressive Matrices, with Negro children obtaining lower scores. Jensen suggests that Negro children may have showed less spontaneous verbal behavior than white children while taking the Progressive Matrices test (Jensen, 1968).

Children may have to learn to use verbal mediators in problem-solving situations. In support of this notion, Jensen (1963a) reported an experiment in which junior high school students, mostly of middle class, classified as gifted, average, and retarded, were presented with multiple stimulus-response problems. Only students in the gifted and average groups gave evidence of learning during the first phase of the experiment, in which no reinforcement procedures were used. On subsequent days, the retarded children were given additional trials, during which a variety of reinforcement procedures was used: verbal reinforcement by the experimenter; stimulus naming by subject prior to responding; stimulus naming while learning; enforced delay of response following reinforcement. When the performance of retarded children rose above the chance level of correct response, all three groups were tested on a similar but harder task. Although the difference between the three groups was still significant, the retarded group showed marked improvement. It was also found that the retarded group, although as homogeneous in IQ as the other two groups, was more heterogeneous than the former in learning ability. After verbalization training, several of the "retarded" children learned faster than the average and did as well as gifted children. These "retarded" children who performed well after training were from lower-class backgrounds. This pattern was confirmed in a follow-up study (Jensen, 1968).

In an experiment based on Jensen's (1968) proposition that paired-associate learning depends on available relevant verbal mediators, while serial learning is relatively unaffected by the Ss' previous verbal experience, Rapier (1968) explored variations in the learning ability of 80 intellectually normal and retarded elementary school children of low and high social class. After having learned a serial list and a paired-associate list in the first phase of the experiment, the Ss were divided into an experimental and a control group on the basis of CA, IQ, and SES. In a second phase of the experiment one day later, sentences linking the pairs presented in the first phase were given to the experimental group. A second list of paired-associates, but no instructions in mediation, was given to the control group. One week later, another list of paired associates was learned by both groups.

The results indicated that learning under conditions of mediation was significantly faster than learning with no mediation. No transfer of mediation effect was observed one week later in the learning of any group. However, the low social class retardates showed an increasing superiority to the high social class retardates in learning the three successive lists of paired associates; their performance in the third list was almost as good as that of the normal Ss. Observed differences in learning ability of high and low SES retardates may follow from the fact that the latter, having a limited previous familiarity with different stimuli, can profit most from "learning how to learn." Rapier concluded that "I.Q. is a better predictor of learning ability in the high SES than in the low SES."

Experiments using measures of *word association* may clarify several characteristics of the verbal network a child possesses and observed differences in cognitive abilities among children from different social classes and ethnic groups. Speed of response, for example, is a sensitive measure of the associative strength between the elements of the verbal network, while the type of associative response indicates the quality of rational links between the elements.

Entwisle (1966a, 1966b) found that "paradigmatic responses," that is, "response words that are the same part of speech as the stimulus word," increase with age (from 5 to 10). Linguistic development as measured by the number of paradigmatic responses given to words of different form classes and frequencies is invariant (i.e., the number of paradigmatic responses increases with age for all form classes). However, the rate of growth is different for different subcultural groups. Amish children develop more slowly than rural Maryland children, and the latter group develops more slowly than urban Maryland children when all groups are matched on intelligence. Only slight differences in linguistic development were associated with SES origin among urban Maryland children. These negligible differentials between SES groups may be related to the fact that none of Entwisle's lower SES urban subjects resembled slum dwellers in terms of economic deprivation.

Measures of the associative network, based on distinctions between common and idiosyncratic responses, appear also to be sensitive to developmental changes, perhaps because commonality of responses increases with age. Negro children are less able to give a common specific reaction (e.g., *chair* to the stimulus *table*) than white children of the same age and correspondingly more inclined to give idiosyncratic reactions (Mitchell, Rosanoff, and Rosanoff, 1919). This finding led Jensen (1968) to suggest that the responses of Negro children probably reflect social class differences between the groups in develop-

ment of intrinsic rational links between the elements of their verbal repertoire. A study by John (1963) gives support to this hypothesis. Word associations of first- and fifth-grade Negro children of lower-lower, upper-lower, and middle class were evaluated on the basis of whether their class of grammatical form corresponded to that of the stimulus word. In this measure of word association, which is highly related to mental age, the lower-lower-class group had the poorest performance. In terms of speed of response, this group was also the lowest. Both these measures of word associations yielded larger social class differences in the first than in the fifth grade. Additional tests performed by John revealed social class differences in the structure of verbal associations. John used a verbal identification test consisting essentially of sets of pictures of various objects. In a first phase of the test, the child was asked simply to name the objects pictured in each set (e.g., doll, ball, rocking horse, and blocks). In a second phase, the child was asked to give a single name for each group of pictorial stimuli. While the first part of the task calls for S-V (pictorial stimulus-verbal) behavior only, the second requires hierarchical verbal associations. The results indicated no social class differences in the simple S-V labeling task in the first grade, but fifth graders, although they did markedly better overall than the first graders, showed significant social class differences. In the second task, which calls for higher-order associations, there were social class differences at both the first and the fifth grades.

Commenting on John's experiments, Jensen stressed that "in order to understand these findings we must recognize the hierarchical nature of the verbal associative network." Jensen speaks of a hierarchy of verbal associations and maintains that these levels of the associative network correspond to the degree of abstraction and generality, and the strength and richness of the associative connections involved in this hierarchical structure are intimately related to the person's capacity for a host of behaviors that are recognized under such names as abstract thinking, concept formation, ability to categorize and generalize, and so on. It is in the development of hierarchical associations, more than of direct S-V and V-V [verbal-verbal] associations, that social class differences seem to be most prominent" (Jensen, 1968).

A follow-up study by John (1964; John and Goldstein, 1964) with an experimental sorting task devised to elicit *classificatory* behavior, showed that while 45% of the middle-class fifth graders performed the task according to concepts, only 13% of the lower-lower-class children did so. At the first grade, very few children of any social class group performed in a hierarchical fashion and no social class differences were observed. Also, significantly fewer verbalizations of their sorting behavior were given by lower- than by middle-class children. These studies indicate the usefulness of experiments designed to elicit clues of covert verbal associations and the relevance of such experimentation to the study of SES differences in language development.

Vocabulary tests have been used to indicate whether specific items are part of an individual's verbal network and to give an estimate of its total size. Northern white, Northern Negro, and Southern Negro (recent immigrants) children of grades four to six were matched by Carson and Rabin (1960) on the Full Range Picture Vocabulary Test and were administered a different word vocabulary test. Grouping the definitions obtained into six levels: categorization, synonym, essential description, essential function, vague description or function, and complete error, they found that definitions from levels one to three on the vocabulary tests were given by the Northern white children most and by the Southern Negro children least.

Word definitions given by elementary school children grouped as "deprived" and "nondeprived" were classified by Spain (1962) as: generic (superordinate), descriptive, and functional. The findings showed that functional definitions remained predominant for deprived children of all ages. Descriptive and generic definitions increased with age for both groups. However, while the rate of increase with age of the descriptive definitions was similar for both groups, the increase of generic definition was marked for the nondeprived group but significantly slower for the deprived group. By the end of elementary school, the deprived group was 4 years behind the nondeprived group in this type of response. The research carried out by Deutsch and his colleagues (1965) shows that lower-class and minority group children are more likely to use language in a denotative and labeling rather than an abstract and categorizing manner. Results of this kind led Deutsch to regard this inhibition of linguistic and cognitive development as a "cumulative deficit phenomenon."

3. Mediating Contextual Variables in the Emergence of SES Differences in Language. Given the uncertainty now existent among theorists with respect to the processes by which language is acquired, any generalizations about specific environmental elements which produce the discrepancies among different SES levels described earlier are necessarily tentative. It may be useful, however, to summarize the ideas which have been suggested and some of the empirical findings thought to be relevant to class variations in language.

A number of studies show institutionalized children to develop speech and vocalization later than children living with their parents (Brodbeck and Irwin, 1946; Goldfarb, 1945; Kellmer-Pringle and Bossio, 1958; Provence and Lipton, 1962). These studies, together with the finding of Rheingold and Bayley (1959) that children who had a single mothering experience excelled in vocalization compared to children who had six to eight mother surrogates, are sometimes used as a basis for arguing that maternal affection and care are conducive to early development of speech in infants. There is some reason to question the extent to which these results can be generalized, especially in view of the noncomparability of institutionalized and noninstitutionalized children. If the conclusions are valid, however, there is very little information in the studies on specific environmental elements producing the differences between groups. Perhaps the amount of speech to which the child was exposed is relevant. It has also been suggested that the tendency of parents and siblings to engage in verbal play to reinforce verbal behavior of the child promotes early speech development. Unfortunately, our information about the speech behavior of lower-class families is exceedingly limited and, while it seems plausible to argue that lower-class families have limited verbal exchange with infants and that there is less encouragement of early vocalization, there are few if any sound data on communication patterns of lower-class families in the home.

The influence of peers on language development may be an important source of social class variation. There is some agreement that children speak more like their peers than like their parents (Jesperson, 1922; Hockett, 1950). Stewart (1964) noted that "it is easy to find cases involving second- or third-generation Washington (D.C.) Negro families in which the parents are speakers of a quite standard variety of English, but where the children's speech is much closer to that of the newer immigrants [from the South]" and this observation led him to the conclusion that children learn more language behavior from their peer group than from their parents. Other findings suggest that conversation with parents, as compared to conversation with peers, contributes to better development of language in young children. Koch (1954) found a birth-order effect on language development with a first-born child whose next sibling arrives 2 to 4 years later showing the greatest proficiency in verbal skills. Nisbet (1961) reported similar findings. In support of this generalization also is a study of preschool children matched by age, sex, intelligence, and family background but differentiated by the fact that one group lived with their families while a second group lived in a residential nursery. Measures of vocabulary and sentence structure obtained under controlled and spontaneous conditions and ratings of expressive ability in social discourse showed that children living in the nursery showed some retardation in all language skills compared with those living with their families (Kellmer-Pringle and Tanner, 1958). This finding points to the importance of parental rather than peer influence. In another study of factors influencing language development and related mental functions, kindergarten orphanage children were given speech and language training on weekends for a total of 92 hours over a period of about 7 months (Dawe, 1942). At the end of the program which included training in the understanding of words and concepts looking at and discussing pictures, listening to poems and stories, and going on short excursions, the experimental group was found to be su-

perior to a matched control group on tests of vocabulary, general information, IQ, and reading readiness. Improvement was also found in language ability as measured by mean sentence length and sentence complexity.

The process of generalization and discrimination involved in learning the meaning of more abstract words may not come about simply through receptive exposure to many examples (as in listening to radio or TV) but through participation with another person. Lower-class preschool Negro children have trouble on the Peabody Picture Vocabulary Test with action words such as *digging* and *tying*, not because they have less experience with the referent, but because they cannot easily fit the label to the varying forms of action experienced (John and Goldstein, 1964). First-grade Negro children scoring high in reading readiness were found to be from upper-lower-class backgrounds while the low-scoring children were from lower-lower-class (Milner, 1951). The high-scoring children were surrounded at home by a richer verbal environment, including more available books, more reading of these books by adults to children, and more opportunities for emotionally positive interaction, with parents favoring language development (e.g., through a tendency to talk with children during meals).

In an effort to explain the specific effect of SES upon language development, Deutsch (1963) argues that language is influenced by the overall *signal-to-noise ratio* prevailing in the child's daily environment. Children developing in slums, characterized by a high noise level both in the literal sense and in the sense of minimum noninstructional conversation directed toward them, may acquire the habit of inattention toward both meaningless noise and meaningful stimuli so that a general decrease in effective stimulation results.

Children in both middle- and lower-class families are exposed to standard English through the mass media, especially television. There are few SES differences in the pattern of televiewing; children from all levels watch TV roughly 20 hours a week (Schramm, Lyle, and Parker, 1961). The viewing preferences of children are not greatly influenced by parental evaluation of shows or parental intervention (Ainbinder, 1967). This suggests that children from both middle- and lower-class levels have a great deal of exposure, under conditions of attention and involvement, to standard English and to a range of vocabulary that exceeds at least that of the preschool and primary school child. This contact seems to have very little effect on the development of standard language skills in lower-class children. Perhaps it is the emotional relationship to the persons who are the sources of language and the consequent reinforcement which affective ties can generate through approval, attention, and other social reinforcement which are critical to development of communicative skills.

The value of language stimulation is difficult to assess. To compare the effects of adult expansions and adult modeling of well formed sentences, Cazden (1965) exposed a group of 4 urban Negro children, 28 to 38 months old, attending a day-care center to 40 minutes a day of intensive and deliberate expansion, that is, adult responses to the child's incomplete utterances by the nearest complete sentence fitting with the particular situation; a second group of 4 same-age children was exposed for 30 minutes a day to an equal number of well formed sentences, which deliberately were not expansions. Expansions and modeling were provided to the children by two trained tutors who talked with each child of the two groups in individual play sessions daily for 3 months. The experimental groups were compared to a control group receiving no special treatment. A structured sentence imitation test and 5 measures of spontaneous speech used to assess children's language development showed that those who received nonexpanding but modeling language stimulation gained the most. To interpret her data, Cazden suggested that expansions, by definition contingent on the child's speech both in content and timing, are less effective because they provide less variety of vocabulary and grammatical patterns than the adult's nonexpanding speech normally contains. She concludes that "it is the amount and richness of language stimulation available in the context of face-to-face interaction which is most important."

The theoretical formulations and research of Bernstein and of Hess and his colleagues

suggest that the language facility of the child develops in response to the need for verbal communication in the early interaction of the child with others in the environment, especially the mother. If there is less inclination on the part of the mother to communicate *verbally* with her child, as the work of Zunich (1961), Kamii and Radin (1967) and Hess and Shipman (1967) indicates, and to use language to respond to the child's explicit needs (Kamii, 1965), this early interaction offers the lower-class child less stimulation, less exposure to models, and less reinforcement, that is, less corrective feedback, from an adult on whom he is dependent. The strategies that lower-class mothers use to regulate the behavior of their children not only utilize fewer verbal exchanges but are also more likely to be imperative rather than instructive or oriented to subjective states of mother and child. Imperative-normative language type of control tends to cut off response and thought in the child and makes dialogue both unnecessary and, perhaps, unwelcome. Verbal communication thus develops in service of the interpersonal relationships which it helps mediate. SES discrepancies may usefully be regarded as growing out of differences in patterns of interaction and influence (Hess and Shipman, 1967).

SES Differences in Political Learning

Among the emerging interests in empirical analysis of processes by which children are inducted into roles in institutions of the society and are taught appropriate behavior for such roles, the study of political socialization is one of the most recent and the most active. The nature of political behavior makes it a particularly useful topic for examining social class differences in socialization, in part because of the obvious relationship between the social structure—which is to a great degree political—and socialization. Research on both young and older adult populations shows well documented differences among social class and ethnic groups in political behavior, suggesting that these differences begin in preadult life.

There is a large and growing body of research and theoretical literature on social class differences in political behavior (Campbell et al., 1960; Key, 1961; Lipset et al., 1954; Lane, 1959; Berelson et al., 1954) which can only be summarized briefly here. These studies describe lower-class adults as favoring social welfare programs and other economically liberal policies and organizations. They show less enthusiasm than do upper-middle-class levels for liberal programs affecting civil liberties and civil rights, less tolerance toward minorities, less support for foreign aid aspects of foreign policy. Low-status adults also tend to support more policies of rigid political and administrative control, sometimes interpreted as authoritarianism, in dealing with noncompliance and crime and to be more strict generally in applying rules to others, including disciplinary measures in child rearing. They, themselves, tend to show more immediate deference to authority. There is a contradictory mingling of liberal and conservative orientations at both upper and lower social status levels, with high-status persons showing more liberal attitudes in social tolerance for minorities and civil matters and more conservatism in economic spheres, and lower-status persons displaying more liberal attitudes on economic issue and less liberal on questions of individual liberty versus group rights.

Differences between social classes in party affiliation are also well documented. Party attachment is transmitted from one generation to another. A number of studies, beginning as early as 1928 with the study of Dartmouth College undergraduates by G. Allport, show high similarities between parents and children in party preferences. Of Allport's research group of 340 college students, 79% reported that they agreed with their father's voting preference. Hyman (1959) reviews research on intrafamily resemblance and transmission of party allegiance, concluding that "These and other studies establish very clearly a family correspondence in views that are relevant to matters of political orientation" (p. 72). Quite apart from this, however, one would expect socioeconomic differences to emerge if only for the reason that attitudes toward political authority are related to other areas of socialization. Since adult political orientations involve affiliation, dependency, aggression, regard for rules and norms, and other attitudes toward authority, it may be expected that children's political socialization will show similar differences among the various socioeconomic levels.

Studies of political socialization represent a departure from the mainstream of research on socialization. They offer a type of analysis which views a child's behavior through the organizational networks of the society, focusing interest on his response patterns of interaction or potential interaction with institutions of the community—the school, the church, medical facilities, economic units, government, etc.

The first such experience, of course, is with his family, where the roles of son or daughter, of brother or sister, are taught both explicitly and implicitly. Some of this early experience in the family may be seen as role learning, not only through the management of biosocial characteristics or ascribed statuses (age, sex, age relationship, and kinship) which he has at birth but also through training from older members of the group and his own ability and efforts (K. Davis, 1940b). The role learning in nonfamily arenas includes that of member in religious organizations and contexts, of citizen in the community, of patient in interaction with the medical professions, and of pupil in school. Some indication of the social class differences among urban Negro mothers in their techniques for teaching young children the role of pupil in the public school appears in the work of Hess and Shipman (1968), who describe working-class mothers as stressing the need to deal with the school as an institution of authority, urging their children to be compliant and cooperative and to avoid trouble, in contrast with upper-middle-class mothers, who are more likely to orient their children toward other aspects of school experience, such as classroom learning and sociability. It is useful to view learning as an induction to social systems at times when the child is required in the normal course of his life to interact with organizations having formal expectations and regulations and when continued interaction with the system is dependent upon some degree of acceptance of it. This view of socialization as the development of roles in society in interaction with the needs of social and economic systems has been formulated in various ways by Inkeles (1966), Clausen and Williams (1963), Elkin (1960), and Brim and Wheeler (1966) and is particularly relevant for analysis of political socialization (Hess and Torney, 1967).

Although children cannot participate in elections, they are involved in the political life of the nation both *subjectively*, as they express concern about national affairs and elections, and *actively*, by wearing buttons, passing out handbills, talking about political matters, marching in protests and demonstrations (Greenstein, 1965; Hess and Torney, 1967; Hyman, 1959). This type of behavior is regarded as anticipatory socialization (Easton and Hess, 1961; Hess and Easton, 1960) and, to a great extent, takes place at the elementary school level (Greenstein, 1965; Hess and Torney, 1967). The relative effectiveness of the family, the school, and peers as agents of socialization and sources of information is a matter of some disagreement; Hyman (1959), on the basis of several studies, regards it as crucial. Others disagree, however, arguing that, except for socialization into party affiliation, the role of the family has been overestimated (Hess and Torney, 1967; Jennings and Niemi, 1968). Children from working-class homes are more likely to view the teacher as a major source of political learning and counsel (Greenstein, 1965; Hess and Torney, 1967), suggesting that the relative roles of family and school may vary by social class (Greenstein, 1965; Hess and Torney, 1967). The evidence on this comparison, however, is sparse.

Social class differences in political or quasi-political attitudes of children in the United States have been reported from time to time in the past 40 years (Meltzer, 1925; Allport, 1929). Often these have been based on questions included as part of a larger survey such as the Purdue Opinion Panel (1951), conducted with approximately 3,000 adolescents from high schools throughout the United States under the direction of Remmers; the work of Centers (1950); or studies of civic education and information (Burton, 1936) or of children's heroes and exemplars (Hill, 1930). Much of the early research on socioeconomic differences in political attitudes was oriented to issues of "liberalism" versus "conservatism." A study in 1939 by Davidson (1943) of 102 New York City children of high intelligence (mean IQ 143) ranging in age from 9 to 13 showed that children from low-income families were more liberal than the more affluent children on a variety of social attitudes. The relationship as reported was curvilinear with middle-income groups holding the most liberal attitudes. Centers' data (1950) showed that children from semi-skilled and unskilled occupational levels were more inclined to express pro-labor orientation and approval of collectivism than were children from business, executive, and professional backgrounds. Studies of authoritarianism also express interest in the liberal-conservative axis as a conceptual basis for analysis of political behavior. Remmers' results from the 1951 Purdue Opinion Poll (No. 30) reveal more "implicit" authoritarianism among children whose mothers completed no more than grade school than among those whose mothers completed college. Scale items regarded by Hyman (1959) as approximating certain items on the F scale designed to measure authoritarian inclinations (Adorno, 1950) are: "There will always be strong groups and weak groups, and it is best that the strong continue to dominate the weak" (grade school 24%, college 16%); "Obedience and respect for authority are the most important virtues that children should learn" (83%, 66%). Level of political interest has also been a favorite topic for inquiry. In later polls (No. 33), Remmers' data show a higher percent of noninterest on the part of lower SES groups as measured by the item "How closely have you been following the political conventions and speeches this year?" Using two levels of maternal education, grade school completed and college completed, Remmers found that more than twice as many teens from homes of low educational levels reported little interest in the convention and election speeches (36% to 16%). Even greater difference appeared when the data were grouped by level of family income.

Except for studies of factors influencing choice of party, carried out for the most part with young adults (e.g., Maccoby et al., 1954), interest in direct and systematic studies of political socialization developed in the late 1950s, expressed in the review of literature by Hyman (1959), the research of Greenstein (1960, 1965) on children in grades 4 through 8 in New Haven, and the studies of Easton, Hess, and their associates, Torney and Dennis, of 12,000 school children in grades 2 through 8 in 8 cities selected from 4 regions of the United States (Easton and Dennis, 1965, 1967; Easton and Hess, 1962;

Hess and Easton, 1960; Hess and Torney, 1963, 1967; Torney, 1965). With respect to social class differences, their results generally agreed. Greenstein, defining socioeconomic levels on the basis of blue-collar versus white-collar occupation levels, found that upper-class children made more reference to political issues and were more likely to think in political terms than working-class children, a tendency which increased between grades four and five for upper-class children and a year later for lower class children. This difference may be related to variations in educational attainment and intelligence which Greenstein did not explore. There was little difference between upper- and lower-status children in level of interest in party identification (as against having no party preference), but the children from middle-class homes have more information about the parties, more opinions about how the parties differ, and more knowledge about names of leaders of the parties. Whether or not a child develops identification with a party appears, in Greenstein's data, to be related to opinions about political leaders; for example, children who thought of themselves as Republicans were more likely to report that they thought President Eisenhower had been doing a good job. In more general ratings, however, lower SES groups gave both Eisenhower and Stevenson higher ratings than did middle SES children. This early subjective party affiliation may be limited to election and candidate matters, according to Hess and Torney (1967), who found little relationship between party preference in children and political attitudes other than candidate choice. More upper- than lower-status children in Greenstein's group regarded themselves as "independent" in party affiliation, a finding supported by the study conducted by Hess and Easton (Hess and Torney, 1967). Lower-status children rely less on parents than on teachers as sources of political advice and less frequently report that they would make up their own minds about election contests. They tended to view political figures, including the policeman, more favorably, a finding also reported by others (Hess and Torney, 1967).

The studies of Hess and Easton and their associates, Dennis and Torney, offer the following pattern of social class differences.

Their analyses assigned social status on the basis of children's report of their fathers' occupational levels using three levels: *low status*—unskilled workers; *middle status*—skilled workers, clerical workers, sales workers and owners of small businesses; and *high status*—executives, professionals, and owners of large businesses. This analysis of social status differences is based on differences within IQ groups, giving some opportunity to inspect the relative impact of these two sources of variation. Differences reported here are those remaining after the effects of IQ difference have been taken into account.

Children from the high-status group acquire political attitudes and, presumably, information as well at an earlier age than do those from lower-status levels, although the tendency to acquire these attitudes is positively related to intelligence within each social status level. The affective attachment of children to the nation, as measured by items offering opportunity to express nationalistic feelings ("America is the best country in the world," etc.), shows few social class differences; nor is the child's expectation of assistance, help, and protection from government and the President strongly influenced by social class membership. The child's feeling of affiliation toward the President, measured by such items as "I like him," "He is my favorite," varies only slightly by intelligence but is more frequently expressed in very positive terms by children from working-class homes. Children from unskilled and skilled working-class background have less positive attitudes toward their own fathers and more positive attitudes toward the President of the United States than do high-status children. Social class differences do not appear in opinions about the role qualities of the President, as indicated by such items as "He makes important decision," "He knows more than most other men."

Children's views of law and of policemen vary by social status. Children from lower-status backgrounds perceive laws in more idealized and unquestioning terms, more frequently selecting alternatives such as "All laws are fair." The policeman is viewed more positively by children from working-class areas, perhaps as part of a general tendency to hold high regard for extrafamilial authority. However, there are no social class differ-

ences in the childrens view of the power of
the policeman to "make people do what he
wants" or in their opinion about the likelihood
of punishment as a consequence of law-
breaking.

One of the greatest discrepancies in the
political attitudes of children from different
social class levels is in their feeling of security
in the system and their feelings of efficacy in
relation to it. Social class differences appeared
on items dealing with the competence of the
government, but IQ differences account for
most of the divergence. There is no social
class difference in children's opinions about
the importance of a citizen's interest or in
their own interest in the government and
voting, a finding in agreement with Greenstein's data on the children's prediction that
they would vote when they become adults.

Feelings of efficacy in relation to the system are stronger in children from middle-
status backgrounds and, within status levels,
in children of high intelligence. These two
variables combine to produce large differences in response from children of divergent
social backgrounds. In view of their greater
feelings of efficacy, it is not surprising that
children of high social status participate more
frequently, by their own report, in political
discussion than do children of low status.
There are no status differences in report of
the level of one's own interest in political
matters; however, this may reflect differences
in reinforcement by their social contexts.
Children from low socioeconomic homes are
less likely to report that their parents are
highly interested in political matters than are
children from high-status backgrounds.

Social class differences among adults in
preference for a given political party have
been a feature of American political life for
many years. For children who express preference, a similar differentiation by social class
in choice of party begins to appear at about
the fifth-grade level and is more marked by
the end of elementary school. However, they
do not regard their own party as essentially
different from the other major party. At this
age, they can provide little rationalization
for their partisanship. There is some tendency,
however, for low-status children to see Demo-
crats in more positive terms than do middle-
status children, especially in eighth grade.
Children from middle-status levels value in-

dependence from political parties more than
children from lower-class backgrounds, but
the differences by IQ levels within social
class appear to account for most of the inter-
class variations. Although party affiliation is
not strongly differentiated by social class
until after grade five, emotional response to
the outcome of the 1960 election (Kennedy
versus Nixon) varied greatly by social status
background at the early grades, suggesting
that affiliation to party may be mediated by
identification with a candidate and consequent polarization of allegiance in the election conflict.

Class differences evident in political interests, participation, and orientation of preadults are, in general, comparable to the
participation and attitudes of adults from
similar social class backgrounds.

SUMMARY

An unfortunate side effect of research on
social class and ethnic differences is that it
focuses attention upon discrepancies between
groups and ignores the areas of overlap and
similarity. This creates a distorted and incomplete picture and impedes the development of adequate theory about the effects
of cultural and social experience upon behavior. The categories of social class grouping used in most research studies are based
on a concept of group (population) differences, which perhaps unwittingly are often
presented as gross, pervasive characteristics
of distinctly different sectors of the society.
In this regard, the influence of the null hypotheses approach (i.e., do these groups
come from different populations?) has been
a disservice to this field. The interaction between behavior and environment takes place
according to laws of learning and contingencies which apply in all parts of the society;
the distribution of antecedent socializing behavior is different for various areas of action
and belief. A theory of the influence of social
class and ethnicity should be derived from
a comprehensive analysis of the points of contact and exchange between the external environment and human development and behavior, rather than upon a body of research
which deals in false dichotomies for the sake
of methodological and conceptual convenience. SES differences in behavior can then

usefully be understood first as the effects of the fixed structural features of a social system (prestige, power, access to information, etc.), and, second, in terms of the distribution within the total population of other environmental features which influence behavior but which are not necessarily a part of the socioeconomic system. It is possible that some types of parental behavior may, through historical, ethnic, or religious tradition, occur more frequently in one social status than in another, giving rise to class-related behavior not linked to the larger elements of social structure and, in a sense, a by-product of the influence of social class upon learning.

Researchers in socialization may have underestimated the extent of the nonfamily environment's role in the socialization of the child compared to that of parental values. The external configuration of the physical and social environments shows more variation from one social class to another than do the expressed values. Following a model of assumed intrafamilial transmission of values, attitudes, and behavior, a number of studies have found relatively low correlations between parents' attitudes and behavior and patterns of behavior in their children. Social class differences are similar for adults and children in many instances, however, suggesting that the acquisition of behavior in childhood takes place to a considerable extent outside the family. This raises a question about the effectiveness of parental values (at least as expressed in research contexts) in molding the behavior of children. While it is true that the social classes differ with respect to certain values, these are not as impressive or persistent as the differences in physical condition, esthetic beauty, space, comfort, and resources in the home and in the community, in the display of order and routine as against disorder and unpredictability, in children's exposure to physical and verbal exchanges that occur between adults and between adults and children. Perhaps values arise from the conditions of the environment. There is an enormous gap within the society in the external features and the physical and human behavior to which the child is exposed, quite apart from any direct socializing impact of the values of his own family. The notion that the poor and the disadvantaged continue to be so because they

maintain a pattern of existence congruent with their values and lack of initiative may be a comforting thought to more affluent members of society because it places upon the poor the responsibility for their own condition. With respect to the role of values in this type of socialization, however, it should be remembered that the lower segments of society occupy a place in the structure where individuals are lacking in freedom of choice or in the resources to carry out aspirations for changing their way of life, should they have motivations to do so. It may be that in lower-class communities, expressed values, insofar as they differ, are a result of circumstances. From the point of view of the conditions that tend to maintain and reinforce human behavior, it would be most unusual to discover that adults or children in disadvantaged areas maintained a confidence in the reasonableness of long-term rewards, continued to regard their life as subject to their own control and efforts, and looked upon education as the route to success.

The question of degree of parental influence upon children may turn out to be a function of relative effectiveness of parental versus nonfamily models, reinforcements schedules, authority figures, mass media, etc. The parent has options on socialization and control which, if not exercised, will increase nonfamily influence upon behavior. The degree to which parents monitor the parent-child interaction and other child behavior may be a central variable in the relative influence of home and nonhome factors. The monitoring is less close in the working class homes (does this suggest it is more permissive?), and it is possible that parental influence is less powerful there.

As already noted, methodological weakness of research in the field is such that relatively few of the accumulated research results can be regarded as definitive. Often the weight of conviction follows not from the rigor of design and concept but from the fact that on certain topics many studies have shown roughly similar relationships, providing a crude sort of increased confidence by imprecise replication. An aspect of the problems of design and method which is not mentioned elsewhere, however, is the probable influence and contribution to this field of several research organizations and enterprises which touch large groups occasionally as samples, and which accumulate in data storage banks information of diversity and quantity that may eclipse many of the small studies that we have relied on in the past for information.[9] Reviews of the type represented in this chapter will probably no longer be feasible, given the huge number of reports and studies soon to be available and the emergence of data storage and information retrieval systems which will perform summary and review functions and provide bibliographic and survey services to the field. These new developments will raise problems of editorial policy of journals, since efficient retrieval systems can make papers and data available more quickly than they can be published by professional journals, and introduce problems of quality control of the data fed into storage and retrieval systems. Whatever the issues and the adequacy of solution, there are likely to be dramatic impacts of these developments upon research on socialization.

One feature of the research in this area is the expanding range of theoretical viewpoint evident in both research design and interpretation of results. Many of the studies included in the preceding pages are not, strictly speaking, studies of socialization. Often socioeconomic status was included as a cutting parameter with little apparent relevance to socialization theory. Many of the projects designed to examine socialization processes themselves are based on a limited range of theory, for example, dealing only with transmission processes between parent and child, with little reference to the connections between the parents and larger segments of the society. A corollary to this view is the growing attention toward socialization of children into patterns of interaction with institutions

of the community and into other forms of behavior comprising much of adult life.

A more comprehensive theory will possibly stimulate research which uses more of the diversity of socioeconomic and ethnic backgrounds in the United States. Much of the available research is based on a narrow SES range and upon Caucasian parts of the population. A great deal of methodological power could be gained from greater heterogeneity of population parameters. Successful replication of correlational or more experimental studies in widely different types of groups would immediately rule out alternative explanations of factors associated with cultural and socioeconomic differences, and patterns of stimulus input could be studied which are not available in middle- and upper-working-class parts of the community. In terms of input in the study of socialization, we have been working with a highly restricted range.

There has been a shift in areas of research interest in the past decade. No recent studies of any scope deal with the questions of social class differences in patterns of child rearing. The familiar variables—toilet training, feeding, concern about sex play, and the like— no longer dominate the research stage. These are specific behavioral items which have not been particularly useful in explaining the emergence of response patterns in children. Some global variables are of less interest or may soon disappear as mediating variables, for example, permissibility, strictness, control, warmth. The specifics of behavior concealed by these terms are beginning to be identified with observable patterns of behavior (such as degree of monitoring) that are, perhaps, more useful. Type of control and the cognitive appeal on which it is based are now of more concern than a gross measure of the amount of parental control.

The expanding areas are those amenable to relatively direct forms of data gathering and examination and given high priority by funding agencies. Values, attitudes, personality tendencies, except in relatively new areas of research such as socialization into system-relevant behavior or in experimental manipulation are less active. It is perhaps not accidental that the rapidly growing areas in social class and socialization research are relevant to the practical and theoretical problems of learning in urban children.

[9] These include the Evaluation and Research Centers of Project Head Start of the U.S. Office of Economic Opportunity; Project Follow Through of the U.S. Office of Education and Project Head Start; Project Talent; the study of equality of educational opportunity of the U.S. Office of Education conducted by Coleman; the National Laboratory in Early Education, with its centers in several universities in this country; and a number of research corporations which are gathering data on children's behavior and learning.

References

Aberle, D. F., and Naegele, K. D. Middle class fathers' occupational role and attitudes toward children. *Am. J. Orthopsychiat.*, 1952, **22**, 366–378.

Adorno, T. W., Frenkel-Brunswick, E., Levinson, D. J., and Sanford, R. N. *The authoritarian personality*. New York: Harper, 1950.

Ainbinder, H. G. Attitude transmission in the family. Unpublished doctoral dissertation, University of Chicago, 1967.

Allinsmith, W. A. Moral standards: II. The learning of moral standards. In D. R. Miller and G. E. Swanson (Eds.), *Inner conflict and defense*. New York: Holt, 1960. Pp. 141–176.

Allport, G. W. The composition of political attitudes. *Am. J. Sociol.*, 1929–1930, **35**, 220–238.

Allport, G. W. and Kramer, B. M. Some roots of prejudice. *J. Psychol.*, 1946, **22**, 9–39.

Ames, L. B., and August, J. Rorschach responses of Negro and white 5- to 10-year olds. *J. genet. Psychol.*, 1966, **109**, 297–309.

Ammons, R. B. Reactions in a projective doll-play interview of white males, two to six years of age, to differences in skin color and facial features. *J. genet. Psychol.*, 1950, **76**, 323–341.

Anastasi, A. Psychological tests: uses and abuses. *Teachers College Record*, 1961, **62**, 389–393.

Anastasi, A. Culture-fair testing. *Educ. Dig.*, 1965, **30**, 9–11.

Anastasi, A., and D'Angelo, R. Y. A comparison of Negro and white preschool children in language development and Goodenough Draw-a-Man IQ. *J. genet. Psychol.*, 1952, **81**, 147–165.

Anastasi, A., and deJesus, C. Language development and nonverbal IQ of Puerto Rican preschool children in New York City. *J. abnorm. soc. Psychol.*, 1953, **48**, 357–366.

Anastasi, A., and Cordova, F. A. Some effects of bilingualism upon the intelligence test performance of Puerto Rican children in New York City. *J. educ. Psychol.*, 1953, **44**, 1–19.

Anastasi, A., and Foley, J. P., Jr. *Differential psychology*. New York: Macmillan, 1949.

Anderson, H. E. (Chrmn.) *The young child in the home*. Report of the Committee on the Infant and Preschool Child, White House Conference on Child Health and Protection. New York: Appleton-Century, 1936.

Appel, M. H. Aggressive behavior of nursery school children and adult procedures in dealing with such behavior. *J. exp. Educ.*, 1942, **11**, 185–199.

Archibald, K. Status orientations among shipyard workers. In R. Bendix and S. Lipset (Eds.), *Class, status and power*. Glencoe, Ill.: Free Press, 1953.

Auld, B. F., Jr. Cultural influences on personality test responses. Paper read at Eastern Psychological Association, Brooklyn, March 1951.

Auld, B. F., Jr. Influence of social class on personality test responses. *Psychol. Bull.*, 1952, **49**, 318–332.

Ausubel, D. P. *Theory and problems of child development*. New York: Grune & Stratton, 1958.

Baldwin, A. L. Socialization and the parent-child relationship. *Child Dev.*, 1948, **19**, 127–136.

Baldwin, A. L. The effects of home environment on nursery school behavior. *Child Dev.*, 1949, **20**, 49–62.

Baldwin, A. L., J. Kalhorn, and F. H. Breese. Patterns of parent behavior. *Psychol. Monogr.*, 1945, **58**(3), 1–75.

Ball, J. C. Comparison of MMPI profile differences among Negro-white adolescents. *J. clin. Psychol.*, 1960, **16**, 304–307.

Barber, B. *Social stratification: comparative analysis of structure and process.* New York: Harcourt-Brace, 1957.

Barry, H., Child, I. L., and Bacon, M. K. Relation of child training to subsistence economy. *Am. Anthrop.*, 1959, **61**, 51–63 .

Battle, E. S., and Rotter, J. B. Children's feeling of personal control as related to social class and ethnic groups. *J. Personality*, 1963, **31**, 482–490.

Bayley, N., and Schaefer, E. S. Relationships between socio-economic variables and the behavior of mothers toward young children. Unpublished manuscript, 1957.

Bayley, N., and Schaefer, E. S. Relationships between socioeconomic variables and behavior of mothers toward young children. *J. genet. Psychol.*, 1960, **96**, 61–77.

Bayley, N., and Schaefer, E. S. Correlations of maternal and child behaviors with the development of mental abilities: data from the Berkeley growth study. *Soc. res. child dev. Monogr.*, 1964, **29** (Serial No. 97).

Becker, W. C. Consequences of different kinds of parental discipline. In M. L. Hoffman and L. W. Hoffman (Eds.), *Review of child development research.* Vol. 1. New York: Russell Sage, 1964. Pp. 169–208.

Becker, W. C., and Krug, R. S. A comparison of the ability of the PAS, PARI, parent self ratings and empirically keyed questionnaire scales to predict ratings of child behavior. Urbana: University of Illinois. Mimeographed report available on request. January 1964.

Becker, W. C., and Krug, R. S. The parent attitude research instrument—a research review. *Child Dev.*, 1965, **36**, 329–365.

Becker, W. C., Peterson, D. R., Hellmer, L. A., Shoemaker, D. J. and Quay, H. C. Factors in parental behavior and personality as related to problem behavior in children. *J. consult. Psychol.*, 1959, **23**, 107–118.

Bell, W. Anomie, social isolation, and the class structure. *Sociometry*, 1957, **20**, 105–116.

Bendix, R., and Lipset, S. M. (Eds.) *Class, status and power. A reader in social stratification.* Glencoe, Ill.: Free Press, 1953.

Bendix, R., and Lipset S. M. (Eds.) *Class, status and power. Social stratification in comparative perspective.* (2nd ed.) New York: Free Press, 1966.

Benedict, R. Continuities and discontinuities in cultural conditioning. *Psychiatry*, 1938, **1**, 161–167.

Bennet, W. S., Jr., and Gist, N. P. Class and family influences on student aspirations. *Social Forces*, 1964, **43**, 167–173.

Berelson, B., Lazarsfeld, P., and McPhee, W. *Voting.* Chicago: University of Chicago Press, 1954.

Berger, J., Cohen, B., Conner, T., and Zelditch, M., Jr. Status characteristics and expectation states. In J. Berger, M. Zelditch Jr., and B. Anderson (Eds.), *Sociological theories in progress.* Boston: Houghton-Mifflin, 1966.

Bernstein, B. Some sociological determinants of perception. *Br. J. Sociol.*, 1958, **9**, 159–174.

Bernstein, B. A public language: some sociological implications of a linguistic form. *Br. J. Sociol.*, 1959, **10**, 311–326.

Bernstein, B. Language and social class (research note). *Br. J. Sociol.*, 1960, **11**, 271–276.

Bernstein, B. Social class and linguistic development: a theory of social learning. In A. H. Halsey, J. Floud, and C. A. Anderson (Eds.), *Economy, education and society.* New York: Free Press, 1961. Pp. 288–314.

Bernstein, B. Linguistic codes, hesitation phenomena and intelligence. *Language and Speech,* 1962, 5, 31–46. (a)

Bernstein, B. Social class, linguistic codes and grammatical elements. *Language and Speech,* 1962, 5, 221–240. (b)

Bernstein, B. Elaborated and restricted codes: their social origins and some consequences. In J. Gumperz, and D. Hymes (Eds.), The ethnography of communication. *American Anthropologist Special Publication,* 1964, 66, 55–69. (Reprinted in A. G. Smith (Ed.), *Communication and Culture.* New York: Holt, Rinehart & Winston, 1966. Pp. 427–441.)

Binet, A. and Simon, T. The development of intelligence in children. E. S. Kite, trans. Baltimore, Md.: Williams & Wilkins, 1916. (Consists of translations of five articles published in *L'Annee Psychologique,* 1905–1911.)

Bing, E. Effect of childrearing practices on development of differential cognitive abilities. *Child Dev.,* 1963, 34, 631–648.

Bird, C., Monachesi, E. D., and Burdick, H. Infiltration and the attitudes of white and Negro parents and children. *J. abnorm. soc. Psychol.,* 1952, 47, 688–699.

Bishop, B. M. Mother-child interaction and the social behavior of children. *Psychol. Monogr.,* 1951, 65, 1–34.

Bloom, B. *Stability and change in human characteristics.* New York: Wiley, 1964.

Boehm. L.. and Nass. M. L. Social class differences in conscience development. *Child Dev.,* 1962, 33, 565–574.

Boek, W. E., Lawson, E. D., Yankauer, A., and Sussman, M. B. *Social class, maternal health, and child care.* Albany: New York State Department of Health, 1957.

Bonney, M. E. A sociometric study of the relationship of some factors to mutual friendships on the elementary, secondary, and college levels. *Sociometry,* 1946, 9, 21–47.

Bridges, J. W., and Coler, L. E. The relations of intelligence to social status. *Psychol. Rev.,* 1917, 24, 1–31.

Brim, O. G., Jr., and Wheeler, S. *Socialization after childhood.* New York: Wiley, 1966.

Brodbeck, A. J., and Irwin, O. C. The speech behavior of infants without families. *Child Dev.,* 1946, 17, 145–156.

Bronfenbrenner, U. Socialization and social class through time and space. In E. E. Maccoby, T. M. Newcomb, and E. L. Hartley (Eds.), *Readings in social psychology.* New York: Holt, 1958.

Brown, F. A psychoneurotic inventory for children between nine and fourteen years of age. *J. appl. Psychol.,* 1934, 18, 566–577.

Brown, F. A comparative study of the influence of race and locale upon emotional stability of children. *J. genet. Psychol.,* 1936, 49, 325–342.

Brown, R., and Fraser, C. The acquisition of syntax. In U. Bellugi and R. Brown (Eds.), The acquisition of language. *Soc. res. child dev. Monogr.,* 1964, 29 (Serial No. 92), 43–79.

Burchinal, L. G. Social status, measured intelligence, achievement, and personality adjustment of rural Iowa girls. *Sociometry,* 1959, 22, 75–80.

Burchinal, L. G., Gardner, B., and Hawkes, G. R. Children's personality adjustment and the socioeconomic status of their families. *J. genet. Psychol.,* 1958, 92, 149–159.

Burgess, E. W. The economic factor in juvenile delinquency. *J. crim. Law, Criminol. pol. Sci.,* 1952, 43, 29–42.

Burks, B. S. A summary of literature on the determiners of intelligence quotient and the educational quotient. In *Twenty-seventh Yearbook of the National Society for the Study of Education.* Bloomington, Ill.: Public School Publishing Co., 1928. Pp. 248–350.

Burks, B. S., and Kelley, T. L. Nature and nurture: their influence upon intelligence. In *Twenty-seventh Yearbook of the National Society for the Study of Education*. Bloomington, Ill.: Public School Publishing Co., 1928. Pp. 9–38.

Burt, C. *Mental and scholastic tests*. London: P. S. King & Sons, 1922. Pp. 190–199.

Burton, R. V., and Whiting, J. W. The absent father and cross-sex identity. *Merrill-Palmer Q.*, 1961, 7, 85–95.

Burton, W. H. *Children's civic information*. Los Angeles: University of Southern California Press, 1936.

Busse, T. Child rearing correlates of flexible thinking. Unpublished doctoral dissertation, University of Chicago, 1967.

Butcher, J., Ball, B., and Ray, E. Effects of socio-economic level on MMPI differences in Negro-white college students. *J. counsel. Psychol.*, 1964, 11, 83–87.

Caldwell, B. M. The fourth dimension in early childhood education. In R. D. Hess and R. M. Bear (Eds.), *Early education*, Chicago: Aldine, 1968.

California Elementary School Administrators Association. *The neighborhood and the school: a study of socio-economic status and school achievement*. Burlingame, Cal.: Author, 1962.

Campbell, A., Converse, P., Miller, W., and Stokes, D. *The American voter*. New York: Wiley, 1960.

Campbell, J. D. Peer relations in childhood. In M. Hoffman and L. W. Hoffman (Eds.), *Review of child development research*. New York: Russell Sage, 1964. Pp. 289–322.

Carrol, J. B. *Language and thought*. Englewood Cliffs, N.J.: Prentice-Hall, 1964.

Carson, A. S., and Rabin, A. I. Verbal comprehension and communication in Negro and white children. *J. educ. Psychol.*, 1960, 51, 47–51.

Cazden, C. B. Environmental assistance to the child's acquisition of grammar. Unpublished doctoral dissertation, Harvard University, 1965.

Cazden, C. B. Subcultural differences in child language: an inter-disciplinary review. *Merrill-Palmer Q.*, 1966, 12, 185–219.

Centers, R. Children of the New Deal: social stratification and adolescent attitudes. *Int. J. Opin. att. Res.*, 1950, 4, 315–317; 322–35.

Champney, H. The measurement of parent behavior. *Child Dev.*, 1941, 12, 131–166.

Child, I. L. Socialization. In G. Lindzey (Ed.), *Handbook of Social psychology*. Vol. II. Cambridge, Mass.: Addison-Wesley, 1954.

Christie, R., and Jahoda, M. (Eds.) *Studies in the scope and method of "The authoritarian personality."* Glencoe, Ill.: Free Press, 1954.

Clarke, J. P., and Wenninger, E. P. Socioeconomic class and area as correlates of illegal behavior among juveniles. *Am. Sociol. Rev.*, 1962, 27, 826–834.

Clark, K. B. *Prejudice and your child*. Boston: Beacon Press, 1955.

Clark, K. B. *Dark ghetto: dilemmas of social power*. New York: Harper, 1965.

Clark, K. B., and Clark, M. P. Racial identification and preferences in Negro children. In T. M. Newcomb and E. L. Hartley (Eds.), *Readings in social psychology*. New York: Holt, 1947. Pp. 169–178.

Clausen, J. A., and Williams, J. R. Sociological correlates of child behavior. In H. Stevenson (Ed.), *Child psychology. The Sixty-Second Yearbook of the National Society of the Study of Education*. Chicago: University of Chicago Press, 1963. Pp. 62–107.

Cloward, R. A., and Elman, R. M. Poverty, injustice, and the welfare state. *The Nation*, Part 1, February 28, 1966, 148–151. (a)

Cloward, R. A., and Elman, R. M. Poverty, injustice, and the welfare state. *The Nation,* Part 2, March 7, 1966, 264–268. (b)

Cloward, R. A., and Jones, J. A. Social class: educational attitudes and participation. In A. H. Passow (Ed.), *Education in depressed areas.* New York: Teachers College, Columbia University, 1963. Pp. 190–216.

Cloward, R. A., and Ohlin, L. E. *Delinquency and opportunity.* Glencoe, Ill.: Free Press, 1960.

Cloward, R., and Piven, R. F. The weapon of poverty: birth of a movement. *The Nation,* May 8, 1967, 582–588.

Cohen, A., and Hodges, H. Characteristics of the lower-blue-collar class. *Social Probs.,* 1963, **10**(4).

Cohen, A. R. Upward communication in experimentally created hierarchies. *Hum. Relat.,* 1958, **11**, 41–53.

Cohen, A. K. *Delinquent boys.* Glencoe, Ill.: Free Press, 1955.

Coleman, J. S. *The adolescent society.* Glencoe, Ill.: Free Press, 1961.

Coleman, J. S. Equality of educational opportunity. Washington, D.C.: U.S. Government Printing Office, 1966. (Monograph produced under a grant from the U.S. Office of Education.)

Conant, J. B. *Slums and suburbs.* New York: McGraw-Hill, 1961.

Coster, J. K. Some characteristics of high school pupils from three income groups. *J. educ. Psychol.,* 1959, **50**, 55–62.

Cowan, P. A., Weber, J., Hoddinott, B. A., and Klein, J. Mean length of spoken responses as a function of stimulus, experimenter and subject. *Child Dev.,* 1967, **38**, 191–203.

Crandall, V. C., Katkovsky, W., and Crandall, V. J. Children's beliefs in their own control of reinforcements in intellectual-academic achievement situations. *Child Dev.,* 1965, **36**, 91–109.

Crandall, V. J., and Preston, A. Patterns and levels of maternal behavior. *Child Dev.,* 1955, **26**, 267–277.

Criswell, J. H. Social structure revealed in a sociometric retest. *Sociometry,* 1939, **2**, 69–75.

Cuff, N. B. Relationship of socio-economic status to intelligence and achievement. *Peabody J. Educ.,* 1933, XI, 106–110.

Curry, R. L. The effect of socio-economic status on the scholastic achievement of sixth-grade children. *Br. J. educ. Psychol.,* 1962, **32**, 46–49.

Danziger, K. Children's earliest conceptions of economic relationships. *J. soc. Psychol.,* 1958, **47**, 231–240.

Darsie, M. L. Mental capacity of American-born Japanese children. *Comp. psychol. Monogr.,* 1926, **3** (Serial No. 15).

Dave, R. H. The identification and measurement of environmental process variables that are related to educational achievement. Unpublished doctoral dissertation, University of Chicago, 1963.

Davidson, H. *Personality and economic background.* New York: King's Crown, 1943.

Davis, A. *Social class influences upon learning.* (The Inglis Lecture.) Cambridge, Mass.: Harvard University Press, 1948.

Davis, A., and Eells, K. W. *Manual for the Davis-Eells test of general intelligence or problem-solving ability manual.* Yonkers-on-Hudson, N. Y.: World Book, 1953.

Davis, A., Gardner, B. B., and Gardner, M. *Deep South, a social anthropological study of caste and class.* Chicago: University of Chicago Press, 1941.

Davis, A., and Havighurst, R. J. Social class and color differences in child rearing. *Am. Sociol. Rev.,* 1946, **11**, 698–710.

Davis, D. A., Hagen, N. and Strouf, J. Occupational choice of twelve-year olds. *Personnel guid. J.*, 1962, **40**, 628–629.

Davis, K. The sociology of parent-youth conflict. *Am. Sociol. Rev.*, 1940, **5**, 523–535. (a)

Davis, K. The child and the social structure. *J. educ. Sociol.*, 1940, **14**, 217–229. (b)

Dawe, H. A study of the effects of an educational program upon language development and related mental functions in young children. *J. exp. Educ.*, 1942, **11**, 200–209.

DeCharms, R., and Moeller, G. H. Values expressed in American children's readers: 1900–1950. *J. abnorm. soc. Psychol.*, 1962, **64**, 136–142.

DeFleur, M. L., and DeFleur, L. B. The relative contribution of television as a learning source for children's occupational knowledge. *Am. Sociol. Rev.*, 1967, **32**, 777–789.

Dennis, W. The performance of Hopi children on the Goodenough Draw-a-Man Test. *J. comp. Psychol.*, 1942, **34**, 341–348.

Deutsch, C. P. Auditory discrimination and learning: social factors. *Merrill-Palmer Q.*, 1964, **10**, 277–296.

Deutsch, C. P., and McArdle, M. The development of auditory discrimination: relationship to reading proficiency and to social class. *Project Literacy Reports.* Ithaca, N. Y.: Cornell University, 1967.

Deutsch, M. Minority group and class status as related to social and personality factors in scholastic achievement. *Monogr. Soc. Appl. Anthropol.*, 1960, No. 2.

Deutsch, M. The disadvantaged child and the learning process. In A. H. Passow (Ed.), *Education in depressed areas.* New York: Columbia University, 1963. Pp. 163–179.

Deutsch, M. The role of social class in language development and cognition. *Am. J. Orthopsychiat.*, 1965, **25**, 78–88.

Deutsch, M., and Brown, B. Social influences in Negro-white intelligence differences. *J. Soc. Iss.*, 1964, **20**, 24–35.

Deutsch C. P., and Deutsch M. Brief reflections on the theory of early childhood enrichment programs. In R. D. Hess and R. M. Bear (Eds.), *Early education.* Chicago: Aldine, 1968.

Diebold, A. R. The consequences of early bilingualism in cognitive development and personality formation. Paper read at symposium at Rice University, Houston, Texas, November 1966.

Dollard, J. *Caste and class in a Southern town.* New Haven, Conn.: Yale University Press, 1937.

Douvan, E., and Adelson, J. The psychodynamics of social mobility in adolescent boys. In W. W. Charters and N. L. Gage (Eds.), *Readings in the social pschology of education.* Boston: Allyn & Bacon, 1963. Pp. 21–35.

Dreger, R. M., and Miller, K. S. Comparative psychological studies of Negroes and whites in the United States. *Psychol. Bull.*, 1960, **57**, 361–402.

Duvall, E. M. Conceptions of parenthood. *Am. J. Sociol.*, 1946, **57**, 193–203.

Dyk, R. B., and Witkin, H. A. Family experiences related to the development of differentiation in children. *Child Dev.*, 1965, **36**, 21–55.

Easton, D., and Dennis, J. The child's image of government. *Ann. Am. Acad. Polit. soc. Sci.*, 1965, **361**, 4057.

Easton, D., and Dennis, J. Regime norms and political efficacy. *Am. Polit. Sci. Rev.*, April 1967.

Easton, D., and Hess, R. D. Youth and the political system. In S. M. Lipset and L. Lowenthal (Eds.), *Culture and social character.* Glencoe, Ill.: Free Press, 1961.

Easton, D., and Hess, R. D. The child's political world. *Midwest J. Polit. Sci.*, 1962, **6**, 229–246.

Edlefsen, J. B., and Crowe, M. J. *Teenagers' occupational aspirations.* Pullman, Wash.: Bull. 618, Agricultural Experimentation Station, State College of Washington, 1960.

Eells, K. W. Social status factors in intelligence test items. Unpublished doctoral dissertation, University of Chicago, 1948.

Eells, K. W. Some implications for school practice of the Chicago studies of cultural bias in intelligence tests. *Harvard educ. Rev.*, 1953, **23**, 284–297.

Eells, N. W., Davis, A., Havighurst, R., Herrick, V., and Tyler, R. *Intelligence and cultural differences.* Chicago: University of Chicago Press, 1951.

Eisenstadt, S. N. *From generation to generation.* Glencoe, Ill.: Free Press 1956.

Eisenstadt, S. N. Archetypal patterns of youth. *Daedalus*, Winter 1962, 28–46.

Eisner, E. W. A comparison of the developmental drawing characteristics of culturally advantaged and culturally disadvantaged children. Project Number 3086. Final Report. Stanford, Cal.: Stanford University, 1967.

Elkin, F. *The child and society: the process of socialization.* New York: Random House, 1960.

Elkins, D. Some factors related to the choice-status of ninety eighth-grade children in a school society. *Genet. Psychol. Monogr.*, 1958, **58**, 207–272.

Empey, L. T. Social class and occupational aspirations: a comparison of absolute and relative measurement. *Am. Sociol. Rev.*, 1956, **21**, 703–709.

Endler, N. S., and Bain, J. M. Interpersonal anxiety as a function of social class *J. soc. Psychol.*, 1966, **70**, 221–227.

Entwisle, D. R. Developmental sociolinguistics: a comparative study in four sub-cultural settings. *Sociometry*, 1966, **29**, 67–84. (a)

Entwisle, D. R. Form class and children's word associations. *J. verb. Learn. verb. Behav.*, 1966, **5**, 558–565. (b)

Erickson, M. L., and Empey, L. T. Class position, peers, and delinquency. *Sociol. soc. Res.*, 1965, **49**, 268–282.

Eron, L. D., Walder, L. O., Toigo, R., and Lefkowitz, M. M. Social class, parental punishment for aggression and child aggression. *Child Dev.*, 1963, **34**, 849–867.

Estvan, F. J. The relationship of social status, intelligence and sex of ten and eleven year old children to an awareness of poverty. *Genet. Psychol. Monogr.*, 1952, **46**, 3–60.

Feinberg, M. R., Smith, M., and Schmidt, R. An analysis of expressions used by adolescents at varying economic levels to describe accepted and rejected peers. *J. genet. Psychol.*, 1958, **93**, 133–148.

Feldman, S., and Weiner, M. The use of a standardized reading achievement test with two levels of socio-economic status pupils. *J. exp. Educ.*, 1964, **32**, 269–274.

Ferman, L., Kornbluh, J. L., and Huber, A. (Eds.) *Poverty in America*: a book of readings. Ann Arbor: University of Michigan Press, 1965.

Flanagan, J. C., and Cooley, W. W. *Project talent one-year followup studies.* Cooperative Research Project Number 2333, University of Pittsburgh, 1966.

Freedman, L. Z. Psychopathology and poverty. Paper read at Thirteenth Annual Human Development Symposium at the University of Chicago, April 1962.

Frenkel-Brunswik, E., and Sanford, R. N. Some personality factors in anti-Semitism. *J. Psychol.*, 1945, **20**, 271–291.

Freud, S. *Das Unbehagen in der Kultur.* Vienna: 1930. (English translation: *Civilization and its discontents.* London: 1930. Collected works of Sigmund Freud, standard edition, Vol. 21.)

Fries, C. C. *American English grammar.* New York: Appleton-Century, 1940.

Galler, E. H. Influence of social class on childrens choices of occupation. *Elem. Sch. J.*, 1951, **51**, 439–445.

Garfield, S. L., and Helper, M. M. Parental attitudes and socioeconomic status. *J. clin. Psychol.*, 1962, **18**, 171–175.

Garth, T. R., Elson, T. H., and Morton, M. M. Administration of nonlanguage intelligence tests to Mexicans. *J. abnorm. soc. Psychol.*, 1936, **31**, 53–58.

Getzels, J. W., and Jackson, P. W. Family environment and cognitive style: a study of the sources of highly intelligent and highly creative adolescents. *Am. Sociol. Rev.*, 1961, **26**, 351–359.

Gewirtz, J. On conceptualizing of the functional environment: the roles of stimulation and change in stimulus conditions in effecting behavior outcomes. Prepared for inclusion in a volume on individual and group caretaking functions, Early Child Care Reexamined Committee, February, 1966.

Gildea, M. C.-L., Glidewell, J. C., and Kantor, M. B. Maternal attitudes and general adjustment in school children. In J. C. Glidewell (Ed.), *Parental attitudes and child behavior*. Springfield, Ill.: Thomas, 1961.

Ginzberg, E. Towards a theory of occupational choice. *Occupations*, 1952, **30**, 491–494.

Glick, J. Some problems in the evaluation of pre-school intervention programs. In R. D. Hess and R. M. Bear (Eds.), *Early education*. Chicago: Aldine, 1968. Pp. 215–221.

Glueck, S., and Glueck, E. *Unraveling juvenile delinquency*. New York: Commonwealth Fund, 1950.

Goldfarb, W. The effects of psychological deprivation in infancy and subsequent stimulation. *Am. J. Psychiat.*, 1945, **102**, 18–33.

Goldman-Eisler, F. Speech analysis and mental process. *Language and Speech*, 1958, **1**, 59–75.

Goldstein, A. Aggression and hostility in the elementary school in low socioeconomic areas. *Understanding the Child*, 1955, **24**, 20.

Goodman, K. S. Research critique on D. R. Thomas, Oral language sentence structure and vocabulary of kindergarten children living in low socio-economic urban areas. *Elem. Eng.*, 1966, **43**, 897–901.

Goodman, M. E. *Race awareness in young children*. Cambridge, Mass.: Addison-Wesley, 1952.

Gordon, J. *The poor of Harlem: social functioning in the underclass*. Welfare Administration Project 105, Office of the Mayor, Interdepartmental Neighborhood Service Center, 145 West 125 Street, New York, July 1965.

Gough, H. G. The relationship of socio-economic status to personality inventory and achievement test scores. *J. educ. Psychol.*, 1946, **37**, 527–540.

Gough, H. G. A new dimension of status: I. Development of a personality scale. *Am. Sociol. Rev.*, 1948, **13**, 401–409. (a)

Gough, H. G. A new dimension of status: II. Relationship of the St scale to other variables. *Am. Sociol. Rev.*, 1948, **13**, 534–537. (b)

Gray, S. W., and Klaus, R. A. The early training project and its general rationale. In R. D. Hess and R. M. Bear (Eds.), *Early education*, Chicago: Aldine, 1968. Pp. 63–70.

Greenstein, F. I. The benevolent leader: Children's images of political authority. *Am. Polit. Sci. Rev.*, 1960, **54**, 934–943.

Greenstein, F. I. *Children and politics*. New Haven, Conn.: Yale University Press, 1965.

Greenwald, H. J., and Oppenheim, D. B. Reported magnitude of self-misidentification among Negro children—artifact? *J. Pers. soc. Psychol.*, 1968, **8**, 49–52.

Gregor, A. J., and McPherson, D. A. Racial attitudes among white and Negro children in a Deep-South standard metropolitan area. *J. soc. Psychol.*, 1966, **68,** 95–106.

Gribbons, W. D., and Lohnes, P. R. Relationships among measures of readiness for vocational planning. *J. counsel. Psychol.*, 1964, **11,** 13–19.

Haase, W. Rorschach diagnosis, socio-economic class, and examiner bias. Unpublished doctoral dissertation, New York University, 1956.

Haggard, E. A. Social-status and intelligence: an experimental study of certain cultural determinants of measured intelligence. *Genet. psychol. Monogr.*, 1954, **49,** 141–186.

Hailman, D. E. *The prevalence of disabling illness among male and female workers and housewives.* Public Health Bulletin 260. Washington, D.C.: United States Public Health Service, 1941.

Hall, M., and Keith, R. A. Sex-role preference among children of upper and lower social classes. *J. Soc. Psychol.*, 1964, **62,** 101–110.

Haller, A. O., and Thomas, S. Personality correlates of the socioeconomic status of adolescent males. *Sociometry,* 1962, **25,** 398–404.

Hansen, C. F. The scholastic performances of Negro and white pupils in the integrated public schools of the District of Columbia. *Harvard Educ. Rev.,* 1960, **30,** 216–236.

Harlem Youth Opportunities Unlimited, Inc. *Youth in the ghetto.* New York: Century Printing Co., 1964.

Harms, L. S. Listener comprehension of speakers of three status groups. *Language and Speech,* 1961, **4,** 109–112. (a)

Harms, L. S. Listener judgments of status cues in speech. *Qly. J. Speech,* 1961, **47,** 164–168 (b)

Harms, L. S. Status cues in speech: extra-race and extra-region identification. *Lingua,* 1963, **12,** 300–306.

Harrington, M. *The other America.* New York: Macmillan, 1964.

Hartley, E. L., Rosenbaum, M., and Schwartz, S. Children's use of ethnic frames of reference: an exploratory study of children's conceptualizations of multiple ethnic group membership. *J. Psychol.,* 1948, **26,** 367–386.

Hartshorne, H., May, M. A., Mallee J. B., and Shuttleworth F. K. *Studies in the nature of the character.* Vols. I-III. New York: Macmillan, 1928–1930.

Havighurst, R. J. *The public schools of Chicago.* Chicago: The Board of Education of the City of Chicago, 1964.

Havighurst, R. J., and Breese, F. H. Relation between ability and social status in a Midwestern community. III. Primary mental abilities. *J. educ. Psychol.,* 1947, **38,** 241–247.

Havighurst, R. J., and Davis, A. A comparison of the Chicago and Harvard studies of social class differences in child rearing. *Am. Sociol. Rev.,* 1955, **20,** 438–442.

Havighurst, R. J., Gunther, M. K., and Pratt, I. E. Environment and the Draw-a-Man Test: the performance of Indian children. *J. abnorm. soc. Psychol.,* 1946, **41,** 50–63.

Havighurst, R. J., and Taba, H. *Adolescent character and personality.* New York: Wiley, 1949.

Healy, W., and Bronner, A. F. *New light on delinquency and its treatment.* New Haven, Conn.: Yale University Press, 1936.

Heckhausen, H. *The anatomy of achievement motivation.* New York, London: Academic Press, 1967.

Hefner, L. T. Reliability of mothers' reports on child development. Unpublished doctoral dissertation, University of Michigan, 1963.

Held, O. C. A comparative study of the performance of Jewish and gentile college students on the American Council Psychological Examination. *J. soc. Psychol.*, 1941, **13**, 407–411.

Henry, A. F., and Short, J. F. *Suicide and homicide*. Glencoe, Ill.: Free Press, 1954.

Hertz, M. R. Personality patterns in adolescence as portrayed by the Rorschach ink-blot method: I. The movement factors. *J. gen. Psychol.*, 1942, **27**, 119–188.

Hess, R. D. Early education as socialization. In R. D. Hess and R. M. Bear (Eds.), *Early education*. Chicago: Aldine, 1968.

Hess, R. D. Education and rehabilitation: the future of the welfare class. *Marr. fam. Liv.*, 1964, **26**, 422–429.

Hess, R. D., and Bear, R. M. (Eds.) *Early education*. Chicago: Aldine, 1968.

Hess, R. D., and Easton, D. The child's changing image of the president. *Publ. Opin. Q.*, 1960, **24**, 632–634.

Hess, R. D., and Shipman, V. C. Early experience and the socialization of cognitive modes in children. *Child Dev.*, 1965, **34**, 869–886.

Hess, R. D., and Shipman, V. C. Cognitive elements in maternal behavior. In J. P. Hill (Ed.), *Minnesota Symposia on Child Psychology*. Vol. I. Minneapolis: University of Minnesota Press, 1967.

Hess, R. D., and Shipman, V. C. Maternal attitudes toward the school and the role of the pupil: some social class comparisons. In A. H. Passow (Ed.), *Developing programs for the educationally disadvantaged*. New York: Teachers College, Columbia University, 1968.

Hess, R. D., Shipman, V. C., Brophy, J., and Bear, R. Cognitive environments of urban preschool Negro children. Report to the Children's Bureau, Social Security Administration, HEW, 1968.

Hess, R. D., and Torney, J. V. A comparison of methods used to measure family power structure. Paper delivered at the Symposium on Family Structure and Socialization, Society for Research in Child Development, Berkeley, Cal., April 1963.

Hess, R. D., and Torney, J. V. The development of basic attitudes and values toward government and citizenship during the elementary school years. Part 1. Cooperative Research Project 1078. Unpublished report to the U.S. Office of Education. University of Chicago, 1965.

Hess, R. D., and Torney, J. V. *The development of political attitudes in children*. Chicago: Aldine Publishing Company, 1967.

Higgins, C., and Sivers, C. H. A comparison of Stanford-Binet and Colored Raven Progressive Matrices IQs for children with low socioeconomic status. *J. consult. Psychol.*, 1958, **22**, 465–468.

Hill, D. S. Personification of ideals by urban children. *J. soc. Psychol.*, 1930, **1**, 379–392.

Himelhoch, J. Socioeconomic status and delinquency in rural New England. Paper read at American Sociological Association, 1964.

Hockett, C. F. Age-grading and linguistic continuity. *Language*, 1950, **26**, 449–457.

Hodge, R. W., Siegel, P. M., and Rossi, P. H. Occupational prestige in the United States, 1925–63. *Am. J. Sociol.*, 1964, **70**, 286–302.

Hoffman, M. L. Power assertion by the parent and its impact on the child. *Child Dev.*, 1960, **31**, 129–143.

Hollingshead, A. B. *Elmtown's youth*. New York: Wiley, 1949.

Hollingshead, A. B. *Two factor index of social position*. New Haven: privately printed, 1957.

Hollingshead, A. B., and Redlich, F. C. *Social class and mental illness: a community study*. New York: Wiley, 1958.

Honzik, M. P. Developmental studies of parent-child resemblance in intelligence. *Child Dev.*, 1957, **28**, 215–228.

Honzik, M. P. Prediction of differential abilities at age 18 from the early family environment. In *Proceedings, Seventy-Fifth Annual Convention, American Psychological Association: 1967.* Vol. 2. Washington, D.C.: American Psychological Association, 1967. Pp. 151–152.

Hyman, H. H. The value systems of different classes. In R. Bendix and S. Lipset (Eds.), *Class, status and power.* Glencoe, Ill.: Free Press, 1953. Pp. 426–442.

Hyman, H. H. *Political socialization. A study in the psychology of political behavior.* Glencoe, Ill.: Free Press, 1959.

Inkeles, A. Industrial man: the relation of status to experience, perception, and value. *Am. J. Sociol.*, 1960, **66**, 1–31.

Inkeles, A. Social structure and the socialization of competence. *Harvard educ. Rev.*, 1966, **36**, 265–283.

Inkeles, A., and Rossi, P. H. National comparisons of occupational prestige. *Am. J. Sociol.*, 1956, **61**, 329–339.

Institute for Social Research, Survey Research Center, University of Michigan. *A study of adolescent boys: a report of a national survey of boys in the fourteen to sixteen year age range.* New Brunswick, N.J.: University of Michigan and Boy Scouts of America, 1956.

Irwin, O. C. Infant speech: the effect of family occupational status and of age on use of sound types. *J. Speech Hear. Disorders*, 1948, **13**, 224–226. (a)

Irwin, O. C. Infant speech: the effect of family occupational status and of age on sound frequency. *J. Speech Hear. Disorders*, 1948, **13**, 320–323. (b)

Jahoda, G. Social class differentials in vocabulary expansions. *Br. J. educ. Psychol.*, 1964, **34**, 321–323.

Jennings, M. K., and Niemi, R. G. The transmission of political values from parent to child. *Am. Polit. Sci. Rev.*, 1968, **62**, 169–184.

Jensen, A. R. Learning abilities in Mexican-American and Anglo-American children. *Calif. J. educ. Res.*, 1961, **12**, 147–159.

Jensen, A. R. Learning ability in retarded, average, and gifted children. *Merrill-Palmer Q.*, 1963, **9**, 123–140. (a)

Jensen, A. R. Learning in the preschool years. *J. Nursery Educ.*, 1963, **18**, 133–139. (b)

Jensen, A. R. Social class and verbal learning. In M. Deutsch, I. Katz, and A. R. Jensen (Eds.), *Social class, race, and psychological development.* New York: Holt, Rinehart & Winston, 1968.

Jersild, A., and Markey, F. Conflicts between preschool children. *Child Development Monographs*, No. 21. New York: Teacher College, Columbia University, 1935.

Jesperson, O. *Language: its nature, development and origin.* London: Allen & Unwin, 1922.

John, V. P. The intellectual development of slum children: some preliminary findings. *Am. J. Orthopsychiat.*, 1963, **33**, 813–822.

John, V. P. Position paper on preschool programs. Unpublished manuscript for Commissioner Keppler, Yeshiva University, 1964.

John, V. P., and Goldstein, L. S. The social context of language acquisition. *Merrill-Palmer Q.*, 1964, **10**, 265–275.

Johnsen, K. P., and Leslie, G. Methodological notes on research in child-rearing and social class. *Merrill-Palmer Q.*, 1965, **11**, 345–358.

Jones, M. C. A study of socialization patterns at the high school levels. *J. genet. Psychol.*, 1958, **93**, 87–111.

Kagan, J., and Freeman, M. Relation of childhood intelligence, maternal behaviors, and social class to behavior during adolescence. *Child Dev.*, 1963, **34**, 899–911.

Kagan, J., and Moss, H. A. *Birth to maturity: a study in psychological development.* New York: Wiley, 1962.

Kahl, J. A. Educational and occupational aspirations of the "common man" boys. *Harvard Educ. Rev.*, 1953, **23**, 186–203.

Kamii, C. K. Socio-economic class differences in the preschool socialization practices of Negro mothers. (Doctoral dissertation, University of Michigan.) Ann Arbor, Mich.: University Microfilms, 1965.

Kamii, C. K., and Radin, N. L. Class differences in the socialization practices of Negro mothers. *J. Marr. Family*, 1967, **29**, 302–310.

Katz, F. M. The meaning of success: some differences in value systems of social classes. *J. soc. Psychol.*, 1964, **62**, 141–148.

Katz, I., and Cohen, M. The effects of training Negroes upon cooperative problem solving in biracial teams. *J. abnorm. soc. Psychol.*, 1962, **64**, 319–325.

Katz, I., Goldston, J., and Benjamin, S. Behavior and productivity in bi-racial work groups. *Hum. Relat.*, 1958, **11**, 123–141.

Keller, S. The social world of the urban slum child: some early findings. *Am. J. Orthopsychiat.*, 1963, **33**, 823–831.

Kellmer-Pringle, M. L., and Bossio, V. A study of deprived children. Part II: language development and reading attainment. *Vita hum.*, 1958, **1**, 142–170.

Kellmer-Pringle, M. L., and Tanner, M. The effects of early deprivation on speech development: a comparative study of 4 years olds in a nursery school and in residential nurseries. *Language and Speech*. 1958, **1**, 269–287.

Keniston, K. Social change and youth in America. *Daedalus*, Winter 1962, 145–171.

Kennedy, W. A., Van de Riet, V., and White, J. C. A normative sample of intelligence and achievement of Negro elementary school children in the southeastern United States. *Monogr. Soc. Res. Child Dev.*, 1963, **28**, (112 pp.).

Key, V.O., Jr. *Public opinion and American democracy.* New York: Alfred Knopf, 1961.

Keyserling, L. H. *Progress on poverty.* Washington, D.C.: Conference on Economic Progress, 1964.

Khater, M. R. The influence of social class on the language patterns of kindergarten children. Unpublished doctoral dissertation, University of Chicago, 1951.

Kinsey, A. C., Pomeroy, W. B., and Martin, C. E. *Sexual behavior in the human male.* Philadelphia, Pa.: Saunders, 1948.

Kinsey, A. C., Pomeroy, W. B., Martin, C. E., and Gebhard, P. H. *Sexual behavior in the human female.* Philadelphia, Pa.: Saunders, 1953.

Klatskin, E. H. Shifts in child care practices in three social classes under an infant care program of flexible methodology. *Am. J. Orthopsychiat.*, 1952, **22**, 52–61.

Klausner, S. Z. Social class and self-concept. *J. soc. Psychol.*, 1953, **38**, 201–205.

Knief, L. M., and Stroud, J. B. Intercorrelations among various intelligence, achievement, and social class scores. *J. educ. Psychol.*, 1959, **50**, 117–120.

Kobrin, S. The conflict of values in delinquency areas. *Am. Sociol. Rev.*, 1951, **16**, 653–661.

Koch, H. The relation of "primary mental abilities" in five and six year olds to sex of child and characteristics of his siblings. *Child Dev.*, 1954, **25**, 209–223.

Kohlberg, L. The development of modes of moral thinking and choice in the years ten to sixteen. Unpublished doctoral dissertation, University of Chicago, 1958.

Kohlberg, L. Moral development and identification. In H. Stevenson (Ed.), *Child psychology. 62nd Yearbook of the National Society for Studies in Education*. Chicago: University of Chicago Press, 1963. Pp. 277–332. (a)

Kohlberg, L. The development of children's orientations toward a moral order: I. Sequence in the development of moral thought. *Vita hum.*, 1963, **6**, 11–33. (b)

Kohlberg, L. Development of moral character and moral ideology. In M. Hoffman and L. W. Hoffman (Eds.), *Review of child development research*. New York: Russell Sage, 1964. Pp. 383–431.

Kohlberg, L. Moral development. In D. L. Sills (Ed.), *International Encyclopedia of the social sciences*. Vol. 10. New York: Macmillan and Free Press, 1968 Pp. 483–494.

Kohn, M. L. Social class and parental values. Paper read at American Sociological Society, Washington D. C., August, 1957.

Kohn, M. L. Social class and the exercise of parental authority. *Am. Sociol. Rev.*, 1959, **24**, 352–366. (a)

Kohn, M. L. Social class and parental values. *Am. J. Sociol.*, 1959, **64**, 337–351. (b)

Kohn, M. L. Social class and parent-child relationships: an interpretation. *Am. J. Sociol.*, 1963, **68**, 471–480.

Kohn, M. L., and Carroll, E. E. Social class and the allocation of parental responsibilities. *Sociometry*, 1960, **23**(4), 372–392.

Kolko, G. *Wealth and power in America*. New York: Praeger, 1962.

Koos, E. L. Class differences in family reactions to crisis. *Marr. family Liv.*, 1950, **12**, 77–78.

Korchin, S. J., Mitchell, H. E., and Meltzoff, J. A critical evaluation of the Thompson Thematic Apperception Test. *J. project. Techn.*, 1950, **14**, 445–452.

Kraus, I. Sources of educational aspirations among working-class youth. *Am. Sociol. Rev.*, 1964, **29**, 867–879.

Kvaraceus, W., and Miller, W. B. *Delinquent behavior: culture and the individual*. Washington, D.C.: National Education Association of the United States, 1959.

LaCivita, A. F., Kean, J. M. and Yamamoto, K. Socio-economic status of children and acquisition of grammar. *J. educ. Res.*, 1966, **60**, 71–74.

Lambert, W. E., and Taguchi, Y. Ethnic cleavage among young children. *J. abnorm. soc. Psychol.*, 1956, **53**, 380–382.

Landreth, C., and Johnson, B. C. Young children's responses to a different skin color. *Child Dev.*, 1953, **24**, 63–80.

Lane, R. *Political life: why people get involved in politics*. Glencoe, Ill.: Free Press, 1959.

Lawton, D. Social class differences in language development: a study of some samples of written work. *Language and Speech*, 1963, **6**, 120–143.

Lawton, D. Social class language differences in group discussions. *Language and Speech*, 1964, **7**, 183–204.

Lerner, E. *Constraint areas and the moral judgment of children*. Menasha, Wisc.: Banta, 1937.

Lesser, G. S., Fifer, G., and Clark, D. H. Mental abilities of children in different social class and cultural groups. *Monogr. Soc. Res. Child Dev.*, 1965, **30**, (Serial No. 102).

Levinson, B. M. The WAIS quotient of subcultural deviation. *J. genet. Psychol.*, 1963, **103**, 123–131.

Lewis, H. Child rearing among low-income families. In L. Ferman, Kornbluh, J. L., and A. Huber (Eds.), *Poverty in America*: A book of readings. Ann Arbor, Mich.: University of Michigan Press, 1965. Pp. 342–353.

Lewis, O. *Five families*. New York: Basic Books, 1959.

Liddle, G. The California Psychological Inventory and certain social and personal factors. *J. educ. Psychol.*, 1958, **49**, 144–149.

Lindzey, G. (Ed.) *Handbook of social psychology.* Vol. II. Cambridge, Mass.: Addison-Wesley, 1954.

Lipset, S. M., Lazarsfeld, P. F., Barton, A. H., and Linz J. The psychology of voting: an analysis of political behavior. In G. Lindzey (Ed.), *Handbook of social psychology.* Vol. II. Cambridge, Mass.: Addison-Wesley, 1954. Pp. 1124–1175.

Lipsitz, L. Working-class authoritarianism: a re-evaluation. *Am. Sociol. Rev.*, 1965. **30**(1), 103–109.

Littman, R. A., Moore, R. A., and Pierce-Jones, J. Social class differences in child rearing: a third community for comparison with Chicago and Newton. *Am. Sociol. Rev.*, 1957, **22**, 694–704.

Loban, W. D. *The language of elementary school children.* Champaign, Ill.: National Council of Teachers of English, 1963.

Loban, W. D. Language proficiency and school learning. In J. D. Krumboltz (Ed.), *Learning and the educational process.* Chicago: Rand McNally, 1965. Pp. 113–131.

Loevinger, J. Intelligence as related to socio-economic factors. In the *Thirty-ninth Yearbook of the National Society for the Study of Education. Part I.* Bloomington, Ill.: Public School Publishing Co., 1940. Pp. 159–210.

Long, H. H. Test results of third-grade Negro children selected on the basis of socio-economic status. *J. Negro Educ.*, 1935, **4**, 192–212; 523–552.

Lorimer, F., and Osborn, F. Variations in cultural-intellectual development among groups classified by occupation or social status. In *Dynamics of Population.* New York: Macmillan, 1934. Pp. 157–176.

Maas, H. S. Some social class differences in the family systems and group relations of pre and early adolescents. *Child Dev.*, 1951, **22**, 145–152.

Maas, H. S. The role of member in clubs of lower-class and middle class adolescents. In J. M. Seidman (Ed.), *The adolescent.* New York: Holt, Rinehart & Winston, 1953. Pp. 294–304.

MacArthur, C. Personality differences between middle and upper classes. *J. abnorm. soc. Psychol.*, 1955, **50**, 247–254.

MacArthur, R. S., and Elley, W. B. The reduction of socio-economic bias in intelligence testing. *Br. J. educ. Psychol.*, 1963, **33**, 107–119.

Maccoby, E. E. Class differences in boys' choices of authority roles. *Sociometry*, 1962, **25**, 117–119.

Maccoby, E. E., Gibbs, P. K. and the staff of the Laboratory of Human Development at Harvard University. Methods of child rearing in two social classes. In W. E. Martin and C. B. Stendler (Eds.), *Readings in child development.* New York: Harcourt, Brace, 1954. Pp. 380–396.

Maccoby, E. E., Matthews, R., and Morton, A. Youth and political change. *Publ. Opinion Q.*, 1954, **18**, 23–39.

MacDonald, M., McGuire, C., and Havighurst, R. J. Leisure activities and the socioeconomic status of children. *Am. J. Sociol.*, 1949, **54**, 505–519.

Maddy, N. R. Comparison of children's personality traits, attitudes, and intelligence with parental occupation. *Genet. Psychol. Monogr.*, 1943, **27**, 3–65.

Marshall, H. R. Relations between home experience and children's use of language in play interactions with peers. *Psycholog. Monogr.*, 1961, **75**, No. 509.

Martin, W. E., and Stendler, C. B. *Child development: the process of growing up in society.* New York: Harcourt, Brace, 1953.

McCandless, B. R., and Hoyt, J. M. Sex, ethnicity, and play preferences of pre-school children. *J. abnorm. soc. Psychol.*, 1961, **62**, 683–685.

McCarthy, D. The language development of the preschool child. *Inst. Child Welfare Monogr. Ser.*, 1930, No. 4.

McCarthy, D. Factors that influence language growth: home influences. *Elementary English*, 1952, **29**, 421–428; 440.

McClelland, D. C., Atkinson, J. W., Clark, R. A., and Lowell, E. L. *The achievement motive.* New York: Appleton-Century-Crofts, 1953.

McClelland, D. C., Rindlisbacher, A. and DeCharms, R. Religious and other sources of parental attitudes toward independence training. In D. C. McClelland (Ed.), *Studies in motivation.* New York: Appleton-Century-Crofts, 1955. Pp. 389–397.

McCord, J., and McCord, W. Cultural stereotypes and validity of interviews for research in child development. *Child Dev.*, 1961, **32**, 171–185.

McCord, W., McCord, J., and Zola, I. K. *Origins of crime.* New York: Columbia University Press, 1959.

McDaniel, P. A., and Babchuk, N. Negro conceptions of white people in a northeastern city. *Phylon*, 1960, **21**, 7–19.

McDonald, R. L., and Gynther, M. D. MMPI norms for southern adolescent Negroes. *J. soc. Psychol.*, 1962, **58**, 277–282.

McKee, J. P., and Leader, F. B. The relationships of socio-economic status and aggression to the competitive behavior of preschool children. *Child Dev.*, 1955, **26**, 135–142.

McKinley, D. G. *Social class and family life.* Glencoe, Ill.: Free Press, 1964.

Mednick, S. A., and Shaffer, J. B. P. Mothers' retrospective reports in child rearing research. *Am. J. Orthopsychiat.*, 1963, **33**, 457–461.

Mehanovitch, C. S. Who is the juvenile delinquent? *Social Science*, 1947, **22**, 45–50.

Mehlman, M. R., and Fleming, J. E. Social stratification and some personality variables. *J. gen. Psychol.*, 1963, **69**, 3–10.

Meltzer, H. *Children's social concepts: a study of their nature and development.* New York: Teachers College, Columbia University, Contributions to Education No. 192, 1925.

Merrill, B. A. A measurement of mother-child interaction. *J. abnorm. soc. Psychol.*, 1946, **41**, 37–49.

Middleton, M. R. Class and family. In O. A. Oeser and S. B. Hammond (Eds.), *Social Structure and personality in a city.* New York: Macmillan, 1954. Pp. 256–258.

Miller, D. R., and Swanson, G. E. *The changing American parent.* New York: Wiley, 1958.

Miller, D. R., and Swanson, G. E. Expressive styles: III. Two styles of expression: motoric and conceptual. In D. R. Miller and G. E. Swanson (Eds.), *Inner conflict and defense.* New York: Holt, Rinehart & Winston, 1960. Pp. 337–352.

Miller, D. R., and Swanson, G. E. (Eds.) *Inner conflict and defense.* New York: Holt, Rinehart & Winston, 1960.

Miller, S. M., and Riessman, F. The working class subculture: a new view. *Social Problems*, 1961, **9**, 86–97.

Miller, S. M., Riessman, F., and Seagull, A. A. Poverty and self-indulgence: a critique of the non-deferred gratification pattern. In L. Ferman, J. K. Kornbluch, and A. Huber. (Eds.), *Poverty in America: A book of readings*, Ann Arbor: University of Michigan Press, 1965. Pp. 285–302.

Miller, W. B. Lower class culture as a generating milieu of gang delinquency. *J. Soc. Iss.*, 1958, **14**, 5–19.

Miller, W. B., Geertz, H., and Cutter, H. S. G. Aggression in a boys' street corner group. *Psychiatry*, 1961, **24**, 283–298.

Milner, E. A study of the relationship between reading readiness in grade one school children and patterns of parent-child interaction. *Child Dev.*, 1951, **22**, 95–112.

Minitzer, S., and Sargent, S. S. The relationship between family economic status and some personality traits of college students. *School and Society*, 1939, **49**, 322–324.

Mitchell, H. E. Social class and race as factors affecting the role of the family in Thematic Apperception Test stories. *Am. Psychol.*, 1950, **5**, 299–300. (Abstract)

Mitchell, J. V. A comparison of the factorial structure of cognitive functions for a high and low status group. *J. educ. Psychol.*, 1956, **47**, 397–414.

Mitchell, I., Rosanoff, I. R., and Rosanoff, A. J. A study of association in Negro children. *Psychol. Rev.*, 1919, **26**, 354–359.

Morland, J. K. Racial recognition by nursery school children in Lynchburg, Virginia. *Social Forces*, 1958, **37**, 132–137.

Murphy, G., Murphy, L. B., and Newcomb, T. M. *Experimental social psychology*. New York: Harper, 1937. Pp. 27–75.

Murphy, F. J., Shirley, M. M., and Witmer, H. L. The incidence of hidden delinquency. *Am. J. Orthopsychiat.*, 1946, **16**, 686–696.

Murray, W. The intelligence-test performance of Negro children of different social classes. Unpublished doctoral dissertation, University of Chicago, 1947.

Mussen, P. H. Differences between the TAT responses of Negroes and white boys. *J. consult. Psychol.*, 1953, **17**, 373–376.

Myrdal, G. *An American dilemma: the Negro problem and modern democracy.* New York: Harper, 1944.

Myrdal, G. *Challenge to affluence.* New York: Pantheon Books 1962.

National Academy of Science. Racial studies: Academy states positions on call for new research. *Science*, 1967, **158**(3803), 892–893.

National Opinion Research Center. Jobs and occupations: a popular evaluation. *Opinion News*, 1947, **9**, 3–13.

National Society for the Study of Education. Intelligence: its nature and nurture. In *Thirty–ninth Yearbook of the National Society for the Study of Education, Part I and Part II.* Bloomington, Ill.: Public School Publishing Co., 1940.

National Society for the Study of Education. Nature and nurture. In the *Twenty–seventh Yearbook of the National Society for the Study of Education, Part I and Part II.* Bloomington, Ill.: Public School Publishing Co., 1928.

Nelson, R. C. Knowledge and interests concerning sixteen occupations among elementary and secondary school students. *Educ. psychol. Measur.*, 1963, **23**, 741–754.

Neugarten, B. L. Social class and friendship among school children. *Am. J. Sociol.*, 1946, **51**, 305–313.

Nisbet, J. Family environment and intelligence. In A. H. Halsey, J. Floud, and C. A. Anderson (Eds.), *Education economy and society.* New York: Free Press of Glencoe 1961. Pp. 273–287.

Noel, D. L. Group identification among Negroes: an empirical analysis. *J. Soc. Iss.*, 1964, **20**, 71–84.

Noll, V. H. Relation of scores on Davis-Eells games to socioeconomic status, intelligence tests results, and school achievement. *Educ. psychol. Measur.*, 1960, **20**, 119–129.

Nunn, C. Z. Child control through a "Coalition with God." *Child Dev.*, 1964, **35**, 417–432.

Nye, F. I., Short, J. F., and Olson, V. J. Socioeconomic status and delinquent behavior. *Am. J. Sociol.*, 1958, **63**, 381–389.

O'Connor, P. Ethnocentrism, "intolerance of ambiguity," and abstract reasoning ability. *J. abnorm. soc. Psychol.*, 1952, **47**, 526–530.

Olim, E. G., Hess, R. D., and Shipman, V. C. Role of mother's language styles in mediating their preschool children's cognitive development. *School Review*, 1967, **75**, 414–424.

Osborn, R. C. How is intellectual performance related to social and economic background? *J. educ. Psychol.*, 1943, *XXXIV*, 215–228.

Osborne, R. T. Racial differences in mental growth and school achievement: a longitudinal study. *Psychol. Rep.*, 1960, **7**, 233–239.

Osler, S. F. Social class effects on concept attainment. Paper read at APA Symposium on Cognitive Development in Special Populations, September 1967.

Osler, S. F., and Kofsky, E. Stimulus uncertainty as a variable in the development of conceptual ability. *J. exp. Child Psychol.* 1965, **2**, 264–279.

Osler, S. F., and Kofsky, E. Structure and strategy in concept learning. *J. exp. Child Psychol,.* 1966, **4**, 198–209.

Palermo, D. S. Racial comparisons and additional normative data on the Children's Manifest Anxiety Scale. *Child Dev.*, 1959, **30**, 53–57.

Pearl, A., and Riessman, F. *New careers for the poor.* New York: Free Press, 1965.

Peisach Cherry, E. Children's comprehension of teacher and peer speech. *Child Dev.*, 1965, **36**, 467–480.

Piaget, J. *The moral judgment of the child.* Glencoe, Ill.: Free Press, 1948.

Polis, T. Choices of political authority in middle childhood. Unpublished B. A. thesis, University of Melbourne, 1962.

Polk, K. An exploration of rural juvenile delinquency. Mimeographed paper from Lane County Youth Study Project, University of Oregon, 1963.

Pope, B. Socio-economic contrasts in children's peer culture prestige values. *Genet. psychol. Monogr.*, 1953, **48**, 157–220.

Porter, J. D. Racial concept formation in preschool age children. Unpublished masters thesis, Cornell University, 1963. Cited in M. E. Goodman, *Race awareness in young children* (rev. ed.). New York: Crowell-Collier, 1964.

Proshansky, H. M. (Ed.) *Linking social class and socialization: towards a framework for analysis and research.* Ann Arbor, Mich. Institute for Social Research, 1963.

Proshansky, H. M. The development of intergroup attitudes. In L. W. Hoffman and M. L. Hoffman (Eds.), *Review of child development research*, Vol. 2. New York: Russell Sage, 1966.

Provence, S., and Lipton, R. C. *Infants in institutions.* New York: International Universities Press, 1962.

Psathas, G. Ethnicity, social class and adolescent independence from parental control. *Am. Sociol. Rev.*, 1957, **22**, 415–423.

Purdue Opinion Panel. Reports XXX and XXXIII. Lafayette, Ind.: Purdue University Division of Educational Reference.

Putnam, G. N., and O'Hern, E. The status significance of an isolated urban dialect. Language Dissertation No. 53. *Language*, 1955, **31**,(4), Whole Part 2.

Rabban, M. Sex-role identification in young children in two diverse social groups. *Genet. psychol. Monogr.*, 1950, **42**, 81–158.

Radin, N., and Kamii, C. The child-rearing attitudes of disadvantaged Negro mothers and some educational implications. *J. Negro Educ.*, 1965, **34**, 138–146.

Radke, M. J., and Trager, H. G. Children's perceptions of the social roles of Negroes and whites. *J. Psychol.*, 1950, **29**, 3–33.

Radke, M. J., Trager, H. G., and Davis, H. Social perceptions and attitudes of children. *Genet. psychol. Monogr.*, 1949, **40**, 327–447.

Radke-Yarrow, M. R., Trager, H. G., and Miller J. The role of parents in the development of children's ethnic attitudes. *Child Dev.*, 1952, **23**, 13–53.

Rainwater, L. Crucible of identity: the Negro lower class family. In T. Parsons and K. Clark (Eds.), *The Negro American*. Cambridge, Mass.: Riverside Press, 1966. Pp. 183–184.

Rapier, J. L. Learning abilities of normal and retarded children as a function of social class. *J. Educ. Psychol.* 1968, **59**, 102–110.

Reisman, L. *Class in American society*. Glencoe, Ill.: Free Press, 1959.

Reiss, A. J. Social organization and socialization; variations on a theme about generations. Working paper No. 1. Center for Research on Social Organization. Ann Arbor: University of Michigan 1965. (Multilith)

Reiss, A. J., Duncan, O. D., Hatt, P. K., and North, C. C. *Occupation and social status*. New York: Free Press of Glencoe, 1961.

Review of Educational Research. Growth and development. *Rev. Educ. Res.*, 1941, XI; 1944, XIV; 1947, XVII.

Review of Educational Research. Mental and physical development. *Rev. Educ. Res.*, 1933, III; 1936, VI; 1939, IX.

Rheingold, H. L., and Bayley, N. The later effects of an experimental modification of mothering. *Child Dev.*, 1959, **30**, 363–372.

Riessman, F. *New approaches to mental health treatment for labor and low income groups*. New York: National Institute of Labor Education, Mental Health Program, 250 West 57th Street, New York 19, New York, February 1964.

Robbins, L. C. The accuracy of parental recall of aspects of child development and of child rearing practice. *J. abnorm. soc. Psychol.*, 1963, **66**, 261–270.

Roberts, S. O., Dickerson, A. E., and Horton, C. P. Performance of Negro American children ages 7-10 on the Stanford-Binet by selected background factors. Paper read at the American Psychological Association, New York, September 1966.

Roberts, S. O., and Robinson, J. M. Intercorrelations of the Primary Mental Abilities Test for ten-year-olds by socioeconomic status, sex, and race. *Am. Psychol.*, 1952, **7**, 304–305.

Robinson, S. M. *Can delinquency be measured?* New York: Columbia University Press, 1936.

Robinson, W. P. Cloze procedure as a technique for the investigation of social class differences in language usage. *Language and Speech*, 1965, **8**, 42–55. (a)

Robinson, W. P. The elaborated code in working class language. *Language and Speech*, 1965, **8**, 243–252. (b)

Roff, M., and Roff, L. An analysis of the variance of conflict behavior in preschool children. *Child Dev.*, 1940, **11**, 43–60.

Rohwer, W. D. Social class, race, genes and educational potential. Paper read at Annual Meeting of American Educational Research, Association, New York, February, 1967.

Rosen, B. C. The achievement syndrome: a psychocultural dimension of social stratification. *Am. Sociol. Rev.*, 1956, **21**, 203–211

Rosen, B. C. Race, ethnicity, and the achievement syndrome. *Am. Sociol. Rev.*, 1959, **24**, 47–60.

Rosen, B. C. Family structure and achievement motivation. *Am. Sociol. Rev.*, 1961, **26**, 575–585.

Rosen, B. C. Family structure and value transmission. *Merrill-Palmer Q.*, 1964, **10**, 59–76. (a)

Rosen, B. C. The achievement syndrome and economic growth in Brazil. *Social Forces*, 1964, **42**, 341–354. (b)

Rosen, B. C. Some structural sources of achievement motivation and values: family and society. Paper read at the Conference on the Socialization of Competence, Puerto Rico, March 1965.

Rosenberg, M. *Society and the adolescent self-image.* Princeton, N. J.: Princeton University Press, 1965.

Rosenblith, J. F. A replication of "some roots of prejudice." *J. abnorm. soc. Psychol.,* 1949, **44,**, 470–489.

Rosenhan, D. L. Effects of social class and race on responsiveness to approval and disapproval. *J. Pers. soc. Psychol.,* 1966, **4,** 253–259.

Rosenthal, R., and Jacobson, L. Teachers' expectancies: determinants of pupils' IQ gains. *Psychol. Rep.,* 1966, **19,** 115–118.

Rowntree, L. G., McGill, K. H., and Hellman, L. P. Mental and personality disorders in selective service registrants. *J. Am. Med. Assn.,* 1945, **128,** 1084–1087.

Russell, R. W. The spontaneous and instructed drawings of Zuni children. *J. comp. Psychol.,* 1943, **35,** 11–15.

Sabagh, G., Eyman, R. K., and Cogburn, D. N. The speed of hospitalization: a study of a preadmission waiting list cohort in a hospital for the retarded. *Social Problems,* Fall 1966, **14,** 119–128.

Saltzman, S. The influence of social and economic background on Stanford Binet performance. *J. soc. Psychol.,* 1940, **12,** 71–81.

Schachtel, E. G. On memory and childhood amnesia. In P. Mullahay, *A study of interpersonal relations.* New York: Hermitage Press, 1949.

Schaefer, E. S., and Bell, R. Q. Development of a parental attitude research instrument. *Child Dev.,* 1958, **29,** 339–361.

Schatzman, L., and Strauss, A. Social class and modes of communication. *Am. J. Sociol,* 1955, **60,** 329–338. (Reprinted in A. G. Smith (Ed.), *Communication and culture.* New York: Holt, Rinehart & Winston, 1966. Pp. 442–455.)

Schieffelin, B., and Schwesinger, G. C. Heredity and environment. In *Mental tests and heredity.* Part II. Eugenics Research Association Monograph Series. New York: Galton, 1930. Pp. 19–58.

Schneider, L., and Lysgaard, S. The deferred gratification pattern: a preliminary study. *Am. Sociol. Rev.,* 1953, **18,** 142–149.

Schramm, W., Lyle, J., and Parker, E. B. *Television in the lives of our children.* Stanford, Cal.: Stanford University Press, 1961.

Schwesinger, G. C. *Heredity and environment: studies in the genesis of psychological characteristics.* New York: Macmillan, 1933 Pp. 165–351.

Sears, R. R. Relation of early socialization experiences to aggression in middle childhood. *J. abnorm. soc. Psychol.,* 1961, **63,** 466–492.

Sears, R. R., Maccoby, E. E., and Levin, H. *Patterns of child rearing.* Evanston, Ill.: Row, Peterson, 1957.

Semler, I. J., and Iscoe, I. Structure of intelligence in Negro and white children. *J. educ. Psychol.,* 1966, **57**(6), 326–336.

Sewell, W. H. Social class and childhood personality. *Sociometry,* 1961, **24,** 340–356.

Sewell, W. H., and Haller, A. O. Social status and the personality adjustment of the child. *Sociometry,* 1956, **19,** 114–125.

Sewell, W. H., and Haller, A. O. Factors in the relationship between social status and the personality adjustment of the child. *Am. Sociol. Rev.,* 1959, **24,** 511–520.

Sewell, W. H., Haller, A. O., and Straus, M. A. Social status and educational and occupational aspiration. *Am. sociol. Rev.,* 1957, **22,** 67–73.

Shaw, C. R., and McKay, H. D. Social factors in juvenile delinquency; study of the community, the family, and the gang in relation to delinquent behavior, for the National Commission on Law Observance and Enforcement. Vol. II. Washington, D. C.: Government Printing Office, 1931.

Shaw, C. R., and McKay, H. D. *Juvenile delinquency and urban areas.* Chicago: University of Chicago Press, 1942.

Sheldon, H. D. Problems in statistical study of juvenile delinquency. Quoted in E. H. Sutherland and D. R. Cressey, *Principles of criminology.* Chicago: Lippincott, 1955.

Shellow, R., Schamp, J. R., Liebow, E., and Unger, E. Suburban runaways of the 1960's *Monogr. Soc. Res. Child Dev.,* 1967, **32**(No. 3).

Sherif, M. The self and reference groups: meeting ground of individual and group approaches. *Ann. N. Y. Acad. Sci.,* 1962, **96**, 797–813.

Sherif, M., Harvey, O. J., White, B. J., Hood, W. R., and Sherif, C. W. *Intergroup conflict and cooperation: the robbers cave experiment.* Norman: University of Oklahoma, Institute of Group Relations, 1961.

Short, J. F., Jr. Juvenile delinquency: the sociocultural context. In L. W. Hoffman and M. L. Hoffman (Eds.), *Review of child development research.* Vol. 2. New York: Russell Sage, 1966. Pp. 423–468.

Short, J. F., Jr., and Strodtbeck, F. L. *Group process and gang delinquency.* Chicago: University of Chicago Press, 1965.

Shostak, A. B., and Gomberg, W. (Eds.) *Blue-collar world: studies of the American worker.* Englewood Cliffs, N. J.: Prentice-Hall, 1964.

Shuey, A. M. *The testing of Negro intelligence.* Lynchburg, Va: Bell, 1958.

Siller, J. Socioeconomic status and conceptual thinking. *J. abnorm. soc. Psychol.,* 1957, **55**, 365–371.

Simpson, R. L. Parental influence, anticipatory socialization, and social mobility. *Am. Sociolog. Rev.,* 1962, **27**, 517–522.

Sims, V. M. *SCI Occupational rating scale.* New York: Harcourt, Brace & World, 1952. (a).

Sims, V. M. Some correlates of social-class identification among high-school and college students. *School Rev.,* 1952, **60**, 160–163. (b)

Singer, S. L., Stefflre, B., and Thompson, F. W. Temperament scores and socioeconomic status. *J. counsel. Psychol.,* 1958, **5**, 281–284.

Skeels, H. M. Adult status of children with contrasting early life experiences. *Monogr. Soc. Res. Child Dev.,* 1966, **31** (No. 3., Serial no. 105).

Slaughter, D. T. Maternal antecedents of academic achievement behavior in Negro Head Start children. Unpublished doctoral dissertation, University of Chicago, 1968.

Slocum, W. L. *Occupational and educational plans for high school seniors from farm and non-farm homes.* Pullman: Bulletin 564, Agri. Exper. Sta., State College of Washington, 1956.

Slocum, W. L., and Empey, L. T. *Occupational planning by young women.* Pullman: Bulletin 568, Agri. Exper. Stat., State College of Washington, 1956.

Smith, H. P., and Abramson, M. Racial and family experience correlates of mobility aspiration. *J. Negro Educ.,* 1962, **31**, 117–124.

Sorokin, P. A., Zimmerman, C. C., and Galpin, C. J. *A systematic source book in rural sociology.* Minneapolis: University of Minnesota Press 1932. Pp. 226–351.

Spain, C. J. Definition of familiar nouns by culturally deprived and non deprived children of varying ages. Unpublished doctoral dissertation, George Peabody College for Teachers, 1962.

Spence, J. T., and Dunton, M. C. The influence of verbal and non verbal reinforcement combinations in the discrimination learning of middle and lower-class children. *Child Dev.,* 1967, **38**, 1177–1186.

Spence, J. T., and Segner, L. L. Verbal versus nonverbal reinforcement combinations in the discrimination learning of middle- and lower-class children. *Child Dev.*, 1967 **38**, 29–38.

Spinley, B. M. *The deprived and the privileged: personality development in English society.* London: Routledge & Kegan Paul, 1953.

Spock, B. *Baby and child care.* New York: Pocket Books, 1957.

Springer, N. N. The influence of general social status on the emotional stability of children. *J. genet. Psychol.*, 1938, **53**, 321–328.

Srole, L., Langner, T. S., Michael, S. T., Opler, M. K., and Rennie, T. A. C. *Mental health in the metropolis: the midtown Manhattan study.* Vol. I. New York: McGraw-Hill, 1962.

Stablein, J. E., Willey, D. S., and Thomson, C. W. An evaluation of the Davis-Eells (culture-fair) test using Spanish and Anglo-American children. *J. educ. Sociol.*, 1961, **35**, 73–78.

Stallings, F. H. *Atlanta and Washington racial differences in academic achievement.* Southern Regional Council Report No. L-16. Atlanta, February 1960.

Stendler, C. B. Sixty years of child training practices, *J. Pediatrics*, 1950, **36**, 122–134.

Stephenson, R. M. Occupational aspirations and plans of 443 ninth graders. *J. educ. Res.*, 1955, **49**, 27–35.

Stern, W. *The psychological methods of testing intelligence.* Translated by G. M. Whipple. Baltimore, Md.: Warwick & York, 1914. Pp. 50–57.

Stevenson, H. W., and Stevenson, N. G. Social interaction in an interracial nursery school. *Genet. Psychol. Monogr.*, 1960, **61**, 37–75.

Stevenson, H. W., and Stewart, E. C. A development study of racial awareness in young children. *Child Dev.*, 1958, **29**, 399–409.

Stewart, L. H. Relationship of socioeconomic status to children's occupational attitudes and interests. *J. genet. Psychol.*, 1959, **95**, 111–136.

Stewart, W. A. Foreign language teaching methods in quasi foreign language situations. In W. A. Stewart (Ed.), *Non-standard speech and the teaching of English.* Washington, D.C.: Center for Applied Linguistics, 1964. Pp. 1–15.

Stoddard, G. D., and Wellman, B. L. Environment and the IQ. In *Thirty-ninth Yearbook of the National Society for the Study of Education.* Bloomington, Ill.: Public School Publishing Co., 1940. Pp. 405–442.

Stodolsky, S. S. Maternal behavior and language and concept formation in Negro preschool children: an inquiry into process. Unpublished doctoral dissertation, University of Chicago, 1965.

Stodolsky, S. S., and Lesser, G. Learning patterns in the disadvantaged. *Harvard Educ. Rev.*, 1967, **37**, 546–593.

Stoke, S. M. Occupational groups and child development. *Harvard Monographs in Education*, No. 8. Cambridge, Mass.: Harvard University Press, 1927.

Stoltz, R. E., and Smith, M. D. Some effect of socio-economic, age, and sex factors on children's responses to the Rosenzweig Picture-Frustration Study. *J. clin. Psychol.*, 1959, **15**, 200–203.

Stott, L. H. Family prosperity in relation to the psychological adjustments of farm folk. *Rur. Sociol.*, 1945, **10**, 256–263. (a)

Stott, L. H. Some environmental factors in relation to the personality adjustments of rural children. *Rur. Sociol.*, 1945, **10**, 394–403. (b)

Straus, M. A. Deferred gratification, social class, and the achievement syndrome. *Am. Sociol. Rev.*, 1962, **27**, 326–335.

Straus, M. A. Communication, creativity, and problem solving ability of middle and working class families in three societies. *Am. J. Sociol.*, 1968, **73**, 417–431.

Strodtbeck, F. L. Family interaction, values and achievement. In A. L. Baldwin,

D. C. McClelland, U. Bronfenbrenner, and F. L. Strodtbeck (Eds.), *Talent and society*. Princeton, N. J.: Van Nostrand, 1958. Pp. 135–194.

Sudnow, D. Dead on arrival. *Transaction*, 1967, **5**, 36–43.

Sullivan, H. S. *The interpersonal theory of psychiatry*, New York: Norton, 1953.

Sumner, F. C. Neurotic tendency and socio-economic status of Negro college women. *J. soc. Psychol.*, 1948, **28**, 291.

Swinehart, J. W. Socio-economic level, status aspiration, and maternal role. *Am. Sociol. Rev.*, 1963, **28**, 391–399.

Tajfel, H. The formation of national attitudes: a social psychological perspective. In M. Sherif and C. W. Sherif (Eds.), *Interdisciplinary relationships in the social sciences*. Chicago: Aldine, 1969.

Templin, M. Certain language skills in children: their development and interrelationships. *Inst. Child Welfare Monogr. Ser.*, 1957, No. 26.

Terman, L. M., Lyman G., Ordahl, G., Ordahl, L. E., Galbreath, N., and Talbert, W. *The Stanford revision and extension of the Binet-Simon scale for measuring intelligence*. Baltimore, Md.: Warwick & York, 1917.

Terrel, G., Jr., Durkin, K., and Wiesley, M. Social class and the nature of the incentive in discrimination learning. *J. abnorm. soc. Psychol.*, 1959, **59**, 270–272.

Thomas, D. R. Oral language sentence structure and vocabulary of kindergarten children living in low socio-economic urban areas. Unpublished doctoral dissertation, Wayne State University, 1962.

Thorpe, J. S., and Schwartz, J. D. The roles of intelligence and social status in rejections on the Holtzman Inkblot Technique. *J. project. Tech.*, 1963, **27**, 248–251.

Thurstone, L. L., and Thurstone, T. G. *The Chicago tests of primary mental abilities*. Chicago: Science Research Associates, 1943.

Thurstone, L. L., and Thurstone, T. G. *SRA primary mental abilities*. Chicago: Science Research Associates, 1958.

Toby, J. The differential impact of family disorganization. *Am. Sociol. Rev.*, 1957, **22**, 505–512.

Toby, J. An evaluation of early identification and intensive treatment programs for predelinquents. *Social Problems*, 1965, **13**, 160–175.

Torney, J. Structural dimensions of children's political attitude-concept systems: a study of developmental and measurement aspects. Unpublished doctoral dissertation, University of Chicago, 1965.

Trager, H. G., and Yarrow, M. R. *They learn what they live: prejudice in young children*. New York: Harper, 1952.

Tuma, E., and Livson, N. Family socioeconomic status and adolescent attitudes toward authority. *Child Dev.*, 1960, **31**, 387–399.

Turner, R. H. Some family determinants of ambition. *Sociol. soc. Res.*, 1962, **46**, 397–411.

Tyler, L. E. The development of "vocational interests": I. The organization of likes and dislikes in ten-year-old children. *J. genet. Psychol.*, 1955, **86**, 33–44.

Tyler, L. E. The antecedents of two varieties of vocational interests. *Genet. Psychol. Monogr.*, 1964, **70**, 177–227.

Udry, R. J. The importance of social class in a suburban school. *J. educ. Sociol.*, 1960, **33**, 307–310.

Van den Haag, E. On diagnosed mental illness and social class (I). *Am. Sociol. Rev.*, 1966, **31**, 544.

Vaughn, G M. Ethnic awareness in relation to minority group membership. *J. genet. Psychol.*, 1964, **105**, 119–130.

Walters, J., Connor, R., and Zunich, M. Interaction of mothers and children from lower class families. *Child Dev.*, 1964, **35**, 433–440.

Warner, W. L., and Lunt, P. S. *The social life of a modern community*, New Haven, Conn.: Yale University Press, 1941.

Warner, W. L., Meeker, M., and Eells, K. *Social class in America*. Chicago: Science Research Associates, 1949.

Waters, E., and Crandall, V. J. Social class and observed maternal behavior from 1940–1960. *Child Dev.*, 1964, 35, 1021–1032.

Weatherley, J. K., Corke, P. P., and McCary, J. L. A comparison of Rorschach responses between Negro and white college students. *J. project. Tech.*, 1964, 28, 103–106.

Weiner, M., and Feldman, S. Measurement of reading skills in lower socio-economic status children. New York: New York University School of Education, 1963.

Weintrob, J., and Weintrob, R. The influence of environment on mental ability as shown by Binet-Simon tests. *J. educ. Psychol.*, 1912, III, 577–583.

Wenar, C., and Coulter, J. B. A reliability study of developmental histories. *Child Dev.*, 1962, 33, 453–462.

White, M. S. Social class, child rearing practices, and child behavior. *Am. Sociol. Rev.*, 1957, 22, 704–712.

Whyte, W. F. *Street corner society; the social structure of an Italian slum.* (2nd ed.) Chicago: University of Chicago Press, 1955.

Wilson, A. B. Residential segregation of social classes and aspirations of high school boys. *Am. Sociol. Rev.*, 1959, 24, 836–845.

Wolf, R. M. The identification and measurement of environmental process variables related to intelligence. Unpublished dissertation, University of Chicago, 1964.

Wolfenstein, M. Trends in infant care. *Am. J. Orthopsychiat.*, 1953, XXIII, 120–130.

Wolfinger, R. E. The development and persistence of ethnic voting. *Am. Polit. Sci. Rev.*, 1965, 59, 896–908.

Wolfle, D. Educational opportunity, measured intelligence and social background. In A. H. Halsey, J. Floud, and C. A. Anderson (Eds.), *Education, economy and society.* New York: Free Press of Glencoe, 1961. Pp. 216–240.

Wright, C., and Hyman, H. Voluntary association memberships of American adults: evidence from national sample surveys. *Am. Sociol. Rev.*, 1958, 23, 284–294.

Wrightstone, J. W. Relation of testing programs to teaching and learning. In W. G. Findley (Ed.), *The impact and improvement of school testing programs. The Sixty second Yearbook of the National Society for the Study of Education,* Part II. Chicago: University of Chicago Press, 1963. Pp. 45–61.

Wylie, R. C. Children's estimates of their schoolwork ability, as a function of sex, race, and socioeconomic level. *J. Personality*, 1963, 31, 203–224.

Yarrow, M. R. Problems of methods in parent-child research. *Child Dev.*, 1963, 34, 215–226.

Yerkes, R. M., and Anderson, H. M. The importance of social status as indicated by the results of the point-scale method of measuring mental capacity. *J. educ. Psychol.*, 1915, 6, 137–150.

Yerkes, R. M., Bridges, J. W., and Hardwick, R. S. *A point scale for measuring mental ability.* Baltimore, Md.: Warwick & York, 1915. Pp. 75–88.

Youmans, E. G. Occupational expectations of twelfth grade Michigan boys. *J. exp. Educ.*, 1956, 24, 259–271.

Zigler, E., and Child, I. L. Socialization. In G. Lindzey and E. Aronson (Eds.), *The handbook of social psychology.* Vol. III. Reading, Mass: Addison-Wesley, 1968.

Zigler, E., and deLabry, J. Concept-switching in middle-class, lower-class and retarded children. *J. abnorm. soc. Psychol.*, 1962, **65,** 267–273.

Zuckerman, M., Barret, B. H., and Bragiel, R. M. The parental attitudes of parents of child guidance cases: I. Comparisons with normals, investigations of socioeconomic and family constellation factors, and relations to parents' reactions to the clinics. *Child Dev.*, 1960, **31,** 401–417.

Zuckerman, M., Ribback, B. B., Monashkin, I., and Norton, J. A., Jr. Normative data and factor analysis on the parental attitude research instrument. *J. consult. Psychol.*, 1958, **22,** 165–171.

Zunich, M. A study of relationships between child-rearing attitudes and maternal behavior. *J. exp. Educ.*, 1961, **30,** 231–241.

Zunich, M. Relationship between maternal behavior and attitudes toward children. *J. genet. Psychol.*, 1962, **100,** 155–165.

26. Cross-Cultural Study in Child Psychology

ROBERT A. LeVINE[1]

THE CROSS-CULTURAL RESEARCH STRATEGY

No animal lives under more diverse conditions than man, and no species exhibits more behavioral variation from one population to another. Cross-cultural study in child psychology, as in developmental psychology generally, is a research strategy for using measurable variations among human populations (in behavior patterns, environmental conditions, gene frequencies) to search systematically for the causes of individual behavior and development. From this perspective, cross-cultural study should serve child psychology as social epidemiology serves pathology in medicine, by expanding the range of observable variation (given ethical restraint on experimental intervention by investigators), by discovering the limits of this range for the human species, by identifying extreme or unusual populations in which experimental or quasi-experimental studies (e.g., longitudinal studies) would shed especially crucial light on etiological issues. As Graham (1964) has pointed out for epidemiology, cross-group comparisons of frequency often suggest etiological hypotheses when medical researchers are at a loss to explain why some persons get a disease and others do not, but the ultimate explanation must be in terms of the immediate biochemical or biophysical agent inducing tissue damage. In other words, knowing that the frequency of a given disease varies with nationality, social class, ethnicity, or occupation is the beginning but not the end of investigation; the question of what it is about that social category, group, or role that increases or decreases the probability of

one's incurring the disease must eventually be answered. This is similar to the argument by J. S. Bruner (Bruner, Olver, and Greenfield, 1966, pp. 2-3) that "a child does not perform a certain act in a certain way at a certain age *because* the culture he lives in exhibits that pattern. . . . What is needed for a psychological explanation is a psychological theory. *How* does a culture in which a child lives affect his way of looking at the world?"

This emphasis on proximate or efficient causes implies not only a certain sequence of research goals but also a certain form of interaction between investigators of different training and experience. Just as the pathologist or biochemist needs someone acquainted with the occupational structure to suggest plausible hypotheses about the differential distribution of disease by occupational role, or someone acquainted with the history and customs of European countries to imagine why Scandinavians contract a certain disease more frequently than Italians, so the child psychologist needs someone acquainted with a culture to tell him what it is about that culture that may act on children to produce a distinctive cognitive or motivational disposition. In the early stages of comparative research, when the goal is primarily to detect similarities and differences, it may suffice to concentrate on children drawn from popula-

[1] While working on this article the author was recipient of a Research Scientist Development Award from the National Institute of Mental Health; support for clerical and research assistance was provided by a grant from the United States Office of Education to the Early Education Research Center, University of Chicago.

559

tions differing so grossly in nationality, religion, economic and educational development, community structure (e.g., rural-urban), or other pronounced environmental characteristics (e.g., father-absent families of seamen, collective settlements with communal child care) that no specialized information on the cultures involved appears necessary. Even at this stage the adequacy of interpretation of findings is contingent on the amount of cultural and social-structural information about the populations that is available to the investigator. As his studies become more refined and aim to test etiological hypotheses, however, ethnographic information is essential in all phases of the research process, and the child psychologist must be prepared to make background field investigations himself, depend heavily on native informants from the various groups to be compared, or collaborate with anthropological specialists on the relevant populations. If he neglects this background information, the entire study will be called into question and he will find it impossible to dispel legitimate doubts raised concerning his research design, data collection procedures, and interpretation of findings. In other words, in order to know *how* a culture affects the development of behavioral dispositions in a child, one has to know about the culture as well as about the child. This applies as well to determinants such as nutrition and genes; these classes of variables must be understood in their own terms (i.e., their range of variation, their relations with one another, their usual mode of affecting organisms) in order to hypothesize plausibly about their possible effect on child development. Just as the epidemiologist seeks the juncture at which social participation, diet, or genetic inheritance results in tissue damage, so the cross-cultural child psychologist must seek the points at which environmental or constitutional factors become determinants of behavioral dispositions in the child. And this requires simultaneous attention to the child's capacities for responding to stimulation, on the one hand, and to the kinds of stimulation impinging on him, on the other.

A hypothetical illustration may make clearer the implications of this point for the cross-cultural research to be reviewed in this chapter. Suppose it had been fairly well established, through a series of careful comparative studies, that children in industrial societies score significantly higher on the average on measures of intellectual functioning at several age levels than do children from peasant and tribal societies. How are these findings to be interpreted etiologically, that is, what do they tell us about the causes of intellectual growth? First, it should be noted that the acceptance of such findings as facts about differences between populations involves a complex inferential procedure in itself: it means we reject the hypotheses that the findings were due to bias in sampling the populations, or to response sets (e.g., passive acquiescence, fear of foreign investigators or of adults in general) more characteristic of one population than another, or to differential familiarity with the testing situation, the tasks, or the investigator as a type of person, or to misinterpretation of the tasks in some cultural contexts and not others. But suppose we had satisfied ourselves that the findings did not reflect transient responses to the measurement conditions or errors in selecting subjects from the various populations, how then would we explain them?

In attempting such an explanation, we would be confronted with the fact that the populations of the industrial and nonindustrial societies differ from one another in numerous ways, each one of which could conceivably account for the differences in intellectual functioning. This confounding of possible determinants in our cross-cultural comparison leaves open several divergent lines of explanation.

1. The lower intellectual performance of the children in the nonindustrial societies is due to the protein-calorie malnutrition widespread in those societies and rare among the industrialized peoples; this malnutrition affects brain function in children and retards or arrests a variety of developmental processes.

2. There is a genetic basis for the differences in intellectual performance, as indirectly indicated by the fact that the industrial populations measured happen to be predominantly white caucasoids of European stock, sharing a number of visible morphological characteristics that are not found among the nonindustrial peoples, who are Asians, Africans,

and indigenous peoples of the Pacific and the Americas. If the populations differ in some obviously inherited characters, they may differ in others that determine intellectual development and performance.

3. The differences are attributable to differences in early cognitive stimulation and experience, with children in the nonindustrial societies being cognitively impoverished, whereas their industrialized counterparts are cognitively enriched. This depends on the behavior of the children's caretakers and playmates in stimulating the child, engaging him in certain types of verbal exchange, providing him with toys, puzzles, games, or other implements that might foster intellectual development, encouraging his intellectual mastery of parts of his environment so that he acquires certain symbolic skills along with physical skills. Later on, it involves experience in nursery school and regular primary schools.

4. The measured differences have their basis in the social motives the children have acquired through the socialization process, that is, the children in the industrial societies have been trained in self-reliance, achievement, and the delay of gratification in the service of long-range goals—all of which promote active intellectual development and performance—whereas the nonindustrial peoples foster dependence and passive obedience in their children and fail to train them in postponement of satisfaction and active mastery in the face of environmental challenge.

5. Broad differences in cultural milieu, not reducible to specific child-training or early stimulation practices, account for the gap in intellectual functioning. In this perspective, it is the child's early and pervasive exposure to his culture's beliefs and values that determines his mode of intellectual functioning and his performance on measures derived from the industrial culture of the investigator. The *ideational context* provided by the culture is more important as a determinant than identifiable dimensions of early experience that might vary from one individual to another within the same cultural group; industrial cultures provide a different ideational context for cognitive development than do folk and peasant cultures.

To these five contrasting lines of explanation could be added others based on other differences somewhat more removed, but which nevertheless also tend to be confounded in any broad comparison of industrial and nonindustrial societies—for example, climate, urbanization, the presence or absence of economic institutions directly related to industrial technology, gross national product or per capita income, educational development, and literacy rates. How should we decide which of these many plausible explanations to accept or reject, or what is the relative contribution of their alleged determinants to the observed cross-cultural variance in intellectual performance? Most generally, by investigations of such variance in which each of the hypothesized causes varies while the others are held constant. More specifically, through comparative, quasi-experimental, and experimental studies designed to achieve this manipulation of variables.

The term "comparative" in the present context is not limited to cross-cultural studies, for correlational studies of individual differences, of variations between groups defined by age, sex, demographic variables, and subcultural boundaries, are also comparative and seek in similar ways to test developmental hypotheses with synchronic data. A comparative attack on our hypothetical research problem could begin by extending the comparison to include a Japanese sample, so that there would be representation of an industrialized population that was not European in its genetic, linguistic, or cultural origins; this would allow a preliminary examination of the questions raised by the genetic and cultural-milieu hypotheses. If the Japanese scored as high as other industrial populations, it would not prove that the difference between them and the nonindustrial, non-Western groups were not caused by gene frequencies or cultural milieu, but it would demonstrate that a people and its culture did not have to be derived from European sources in order to show a high average score. The more general comparative strategy, however, would consist of making comparisons of subgroups and individuals *within* each of the populations, both industrial and nonindustrial. Comparisons of this type have the advantage of holding language, cultural milieu, other milieu variables (climate, socioeconomic environment, etc.) and (sometimes) gene pool more or less constant, while allowing some of the more specific factors to vary. Thus subgroups varying in nutrition, cognitive stimulation of children, and training in obedience, self-reliance, and achievement would provide opportunities for studying the effects of these factors (and, negatively, the effects of genetic and milieu factors) within a population and of replicating such studies across several populations.

The first step in a given population might be to identify subgroups varying conspicuously on dimensions related to the dichotomy of industrial and nonindustrial societies: occupational role, degree of urbanization, literacy and schooling, socio-economic status, "modern" versus "traditional" life-style. A large-scale comparative survey of children drawn from such varying segments would at least indicate whether intellectual performance and development as measured in the original contrast of industrial and nonindustrial societies vary at the intrapopulation level concomitantly with factors conceptually related to that contrast. If they do not, we would conclude that the original contrast happened to coincide with cross-cultural differences in more subtle cultural or biological factors that vary independently of socioeconomic differentiation within populations. Exploratory research into culture, child-rearing practices, diet, and disease would be required to discover what these factors might be and how they have been retained in the relatively "industrialized" segments of predominantly nonindustrial populations. Some studies of overseas immigrants from nonindustrial to industrial populations might also be helpful, to see if more radical changes affect the dependent variables. If intellectual performance does covary with obvious socioeconomic and acculturative groupings within populations, we might be tempted to accept this as presumptive evidence of the environmental etiology of the intellectual behavior variables, although it would not in fact rule out the possibility of differential selection into social groupings on the basis of genetically determined aspects of behavior. More important in terms of immediate research goals, such findings often confound several environmental determinants. In other words, those subgroups, particularly in the nonindustrial societies, that are more modernized in occupation and life-style and higher in socioeconomic status tend to give their children a better diet

and also more cognitive stimulation, achievement training, and schooling, not to mention numerous other advantages in life. Which of these advantages has an effect on intellectual development?

There are two strategies available to answer this question more decisively in comparative research. If the samples in the original survey were large enough and heterogeneous enough, then statistical analyses could be made that allowed examination of the relations of each independent variable with intellectual performance holding constant one or more of the other independent variables. For a recent 12-country survey that analyzes cross-national and intranational variation in the mathematics achievement scores of adolescents this way, see Husén (1967); although the focus of the study is not psychological, it illustrates the problems and methods of disentangling by statistical procedures variables affecting intellectual performance that have been confounded by the natural operation of social and cultural processes. If this kind of analysis is impossible or inconclusive, then it is necessary to find natural variation across subgroups or at the level of individual differences, in which one of these factors varies while the others are held constant, and to conduct new investigations. For example, Greenfield (in Bruner et al., 1966) was able to find among the Wolof of Senegal (West Africa) a cluster of villages in which some children go to school and others do not, and she was able to ascertain through Wolof informants that children "are *not* chosen to go to school on the basis of their intelligence" (Bruner et al., 1966, p. 229). Thus in comparing the two groups on measures of cognitive development, factors of diet, general cultural and community milieu, and perhaps more specific preschool child-training practices were held constant, and only schoolgoing varied systematically. In western Nigeria there are villages of the same cultural and linguistic group, at similar levels of Westernization, that have diets differing drastically in protein content because of local differences in ecology and degree of involvement in cocoa production. In such a setting it would be possible to examine the effects of nutrition on intellectual development, holding other factors constant. The more intensive the available ethnographic, ecological, and economic information on the local scene, the better the chances of detecting such opportunities for controlled comparison—and the poorer the chances of overlooking a hidden confounding of relevant variables. The discovery of opportunities for significant studies of individual differences, for example, of the effects of specific child-rearing practices on intellectual development, are even more dependent on ethnographic information concerning the distribution and range of variation of such practices in a given segment of the population. The art of designing significant comparative studies lies in matching intensive local knowledge with knowledge of the factors held to be causal in relevant theoretical formulations.

There can be no question that an extensive set of comparative studies like the ones mentioned above, replicated where possible in both industrial and nonindustrial populations, could tell us a great deal about the determinants of intellectual development. But there are limits to the comparative strategy for developmental studies. It is difficult to dispel lingering doubts about the concealed confounding of variables. Can we be certain, for example, that there were no preschool differences between the schooled and unschooled Wolof children, differences that might have fostered or retarded school-going and that also are relevant to intellectual performance? And in our proposed comparison of Nigerian villages varying in diet, can we be sure that endemic malnutrition does not affect parents' child-rearing practices (e.g., cognitive stimulation patterns) as well as acting directly on the child? In addition to these uncertainties, there are those more familiar to child psychologists concerning developmental inference from the cross-sectional samples to which one-shot comparative studies are limited. Finally, it seems likely that the confounding of many more factors might be missed if the dependent variable were a social or motivational disposition rather than a cognitive one, because of the larger number of theoretically conceivable determinants in social structure and culture. Ultimately, the only way to resolve such doubts is through diachronic study, experimental or quasi-experimental, in which the child's behavior is sampled over time, either before and after the intervention of a specific independent variable or during the course of a hypothesized

developmental process, and he is compared with himself at two or more points in time as well as with putative counterparts who may or may not resemble him in all ways save those under study.

Quasi-experimental study in this context usually means the longitudinal study of children before and after some naturally occurring experience of theoretical relevance and includes the use of repeated measurements in a developmental time series. For our hypothetical problem of intellectual development, it could mean measuring the intellectual performance of children before, during, and after the onset of schooling or some other educational or cognitive exposure that had been introduced into the community but was not yet universal within it. Although children would not be randomly assigned to exposure and nonexposure groups as in a true experiment, this quasi-experiment has the advantage over comparative study of being able to hold constant genetic factors and most environmental influences while allowing the educational exposure to vary from one point in time to another. Since intellectual maturation might produce an effect on intellectual performance in the absence of training (especially in a long time series), it would be necessary to have a nonexposed group measured at the same points in time for comparison, and perhaps a previously untested group at each age level as well to avoid practice effects. (These and other problems of control are thoroughly discussed in Campbell and Stanley, 1967.) Some cultural settings provide even more types of relevant comparisons than the investigator himself might think of. For example, in communities of northern Nigeria and other parts of West Africa where both Islam and European institutions have had their effects, there are children from the same villages and even families attending European schools, Koranic schools (in which children are often taught to pronounce and write Arabic without understanding it), and no school. Longitudinal comparison of these three groups might help specify the particular elements in school-going or the acquisition of literacy that affect cognitive development. Quasi-experimental studies are not limited to educational interventions, however; longitudinal comparisons of fraternal with identical twins in several cultures would allow the influence of genetic factors on intellectual performance to manifest themselves, and the investigator might find situations in which some children were going to be sent away from their parents or otherwise exposed to more or less cognitively enriching environments, while others were not. Furthermore, quasi-experimental study is suitable for examining the effects of changing diet or parental child-training practices if and when the investigator knows in advance that these changes will take place (e.g., as the result of a government information or action program).

Experimental study could also help identify etiological factors. Despite ethical and practical constraints on the manipulation of children, it is possible for the investigator to experiment with education and nutrition by providing some children with *more* than the amount children usually receive in that community or region and then examining the result. The great advantage here is that the investigator can select what (training routines or nutritional supplements) to add and which children to add it to, enabling him to study the effects of interventions that would never occur naturally in the societies he is investigating. By providing protein and other food supplements to some but not all of the malnourished children in a particular local area, it would be possible to examine the effect of nutrition on intellectual performance, just as supplementary education such as nursery school stimulation or special task training could be added selectively in a given community or cluster of communities. For supplementary training, random assignment of children to experimental and control groups is possible. Experiments in inducing additional parental child stimulation and training also could be designed, assuming that the intervention would entail procedures judged by the experimenter to be beneficial to the children and that a high degree of parental cooperation could be established. Furthermore, it is by no means inconceivable that investigators in some areas could do better than manipulating one variable at a time, for example, giving one group of children additional protein, parental cognitive stimulation, *and* special nursery school training, another group none of these three, and applying the six remaining combinations of treatments to six other experimental groups. Alternatively, a similar design might be more feasible through combining comparative and experimental approaches, for example, allowing diet to vary naturally across villages (as in the western Nigerian illustration given earlier), parental stimulation to vary naturally at the level of individual differences within each village, and intervening only to provide nursery school training to experimental groups that include children varying in diet and parental stimulation (to be contrasted over time with a control group of children varying similarly but with no exposure to nursery school). The more knowledge of local variation that is built into such field experiments, the more powerful are the inferences that can be drawn from them.

If the results of such field experiments showed that an environmental factor (singly or in combination with others) was capable of raising the average intellectual performance level of children from low-scoring populations up to the average for high-scoring populations (with regression artifacts eliminated), and if the results could be replicated in a variety of low-scoring groups, then the validity of the genetic and milieu-type hypotheses would be seriously damaged. This would particularly be the case if the experimental interventions could convincingly be shown to be equivalent to conditions that were present in the high-scoring industrial groups of the original comparison. A less powerful effect of experimental intervention would suggest untapped interaction among factors, the effects of genetic or milieu variables, or the operation of other unmeasured variables, and might necessitate another round of exploratory research before more precise studies could be designed. It should be emphasized, however, that no matter how positive and replicable the findings of a single experimental study, it is unlikely to be a "crucial experiment" that will fully explain the dependent variable in question (see Campbell and Stanley, 1967, p. 3). For example, even if our hypothetical experiment in augmenting intellectual performance showed an environmental variable to have an effect powerful enough to eliminate the difference between industrial and nonindustrial societies, we would not be justified in concluding that variations in intellectual development were thereby fully accounted for. One fallacy in such a claim lies in the fact that the experiment dealt only with children in the lower range on both independent and dependent variables; it may well be that a different set of determinants operate at the higher range. Thus protein supplements might dramatically raise the average scores of malnourished children, but amount of protein intake seems unlikely to account for the considerable variations in intellectual performance among populations where childhood diet is nutritionally adequate. In the latter populations, genetic and child-rearing variables might account for larger portions of the variance. Another fallacy is the implicit assumption that the experimental intervention is itself adequately specified in the experiment. It is more probable that the independent variable—for example, cognitive stimulation by parents or nursery school experience— would be comprised of numerous elements, some of which are causes of intellectual performance, while others are accidentally confounded with the causes. Other experiments based on more precise hypotheses would be necessary to examine separately the effects of each of the elements comprising the independent variable in the study in question. Like less controlled investigations, field experiments in cross-cultural child psychology should be seen not as producing definitive solutions but as part of a process of progressive refinement of research studies and their findings.

In this hypothetical example we have seen that an attempt to explain a psychological difference between populations led us to consider a variety of contrasting explanations, each one of which provided a plausible basis for relating the difference in question to another observed difference between the populations. Since none of these causal hypotheses could be empirically falsified with available facts, and since the relative contribution (if any) of the hypothetical causes to the observed psychological variations was in question, it was necessary to obtain more relevant facts. The search for facts relevant to each of the hypotheses required a series of studies examining differences comparatively both within and between populations, and using longitudinal study and field experiment to observe individuals and their reactions over time. Much of the information value of these studies was dependent on the creative use of local background information to design research that was of special relevance to certain hypotheses and that advanced the specification of proximate causes beyond the terms set forth in the original explanations. In the end, if these investigations generated a set of mutually consistent findings, we might well have been able to explain with some accuracy the initial cross-population difference in the context of the developmental processes that lay beneath it. Through this research other more precise and more general questions concerning intellectual development would have arisen for future investigation. Taken as a whole, the research process outlined hypothetically is parallel in many respects to the kind of medical and epidemiological research that generates a wide range of correlational and experimental data relevant to the etiology of a particular disease.

If the research strategy of the hypothetical example is taken as one model (though not necessarily the only one) of the way cross-cultural study can contribute to child psychology, then it has a number of implications for the evaluation of extant findings and the design of future studies.

1. The Dependent Variable as Starting Point. Research into causal relations can begin with dependent or independent variables, that is (in the present context), with aspects of child behavior and development or presumed causes of child behavior and development like child rearing or nutrition.[2] Starting with independent variables entails the risk that their effects will turn out to be trivial, irrelevant, or otherwise uninteresting according to the external criteria by which the scientist evaluates his research. To a certain extent much of the research on collective child-rearing in the *kibbutz* communities of Israel falls into this category: the unusual child-care practices are assumed to have some sort of impact on personality development and then an empirical search is carried out to detect the hypothesized effects. Although it could be claimed (as the author does later) that even negative findings on this issue are significant, it may eventually turn out that the

[2] The distinction between dependent-variable-centered research and independent-variable-centered research in comparative study was suggested by M. Brewster Smith (personal communication).

differences in childhood experience between the kibbutz and conventional communities account for few of the variations in which students of personality development are centrally interested. Beginning with dependent variables guarantees the scientist that his efforts will be directed toward explaining a phenomenon he considers important or interesting. This could be thought of as the etiological approach, in which a well-documented variation of definite interest to the investigator and perhaps broader social significance poses an explanatory problem for research, that is, a search for causes.

Contemplation of etiological research in this field, however, exposes the greatest weakness of the psychological sciences in general and cross-cultural studies in particular: there is a lack of a body of well-documented variations to explain, a lack which in turn rests on disagreement among behavioral scientists about how to measure behavioral dispositions. The epidemiologist (of nonpsychiatric diseases) has diagnostic tools of generally accepted validity for ascertaining whether or not a given individual has cervical cancer, elevated blood pressure, etc., and his surveys of frequency in population have as their foundation the knowledge of a scientific consensus concerning individual diagnosis. In cross-cultural studies of behavioral dispositions, however, measurement of the individual is so problematical that it is a rare set of findings that cannot be challenged by critics purely on the basis of the reliability and validity of the instruments and indexes used. This dissensus concerning measurement creates a dilemma for the investigator: if he uses an instrument that has been used previously, he does so in full awareness that it is regarded with suspicion by part of the relevant scientific community; if he attempts to devise a new and better instrument (as many do), he destroys comparability of results with previous studies. For most cross-cultural studies the problem is further compounded by the issue of cultural comparability: even if an instrument is regarded as valid and reliable for intracultural comparison, its use in a culturally differing population raises serious doubts concerning whether it is measuring the same disposition in the context of a different language and system of conventionalized meanings, and there are no generally accepted or

followed rules for allaying these doubts. The consequence is that we do not have comparable developmental data for children the world over or even for a diverse sample of societies, and much of the cross-cultural data we do have are of dubious quality because of questions concerning the validity and/or comparability of the data collection procedures.

Having not yet collected a body of solid evidence concerning cross-cultural variations in child development, we are therefore in a weak position to explain them. The studies reviewed in the following section suggest to the present author that major aims of future research should be (a) the development of more valid and widely accepted measuring instruments and research designs for cross-cultural psychological study of children and adolescents, and (b) the accumulation in diverse societies of comparable data on aspects of psychological development that represent a common denominator of scientific interests in personality, cognition, and the formation of social dispositions.

2. Coordination and Continuity among Studies. The complexity of our hypothetical example was due to the assumption that no single study, however broad or narrow its scope, could adequately account for the variation we sought to explain. The studies focused on the interaction of different variables in relation to the dependent variable, they held different factors constant, and they examined differing segments of the range of variation of the dependent variable. It was emphasized that a creative process was involved in designing research that optimally exploited the constancies and variations of natural conditions for explanatory information. This model of research assumes that within the framework of a single explanatory goal, a multiplicity of experimental, longitudinal, and comparative studies are required to test the variety of alternative hypotheses offered in explanation of the original findings. Some studies sacrifice generality of scope for control; in others, generality and replicability under diverse conditions assume primacy as research questions. The findings of different studies are fitted together like pieces of a jigsaw puzzle, each one of which contributes a limited piece of information to the increasingly coherent whole.

If this model is accepted as being appropriate to developmental psychology, then several implications flow from it. One is that more communication and coordination are needed among investigators who use diverse approaches to explain variation in the same dependent variables, not only in order to improve the comparability of measuring instruments but, even more importantly, to identify the questions that each type of research is best equipped to answer and to relate the answers to each other within a common explanatory framework. Overly ambitious studies that attempt to be definitive are unlikely to be fruitful, but so are large numbers of specialized investigations designed without reference to their appropriate place in the overall search for explanation. It is thus possible for the scientific literature to grow, as it has in cross-cultural child psychology, without a corresponding growth in the kind of information from which theoretical conclusions can be drawn. Cross-cultural studies must be integrated with other developmental research not simply in order to test the same hypotheses that are being tested on other kinds of variations, but to answer relevant research questions that cannot otherwise be answered. A review of data in a given research area should be able to sweep continuously across intracultural and cross-cultural studies, accumulating unique as well as replicative findings and a complementary as well as consistent pattern of results. To put it another way, every study reviewed in this chapter should be essential to include also in a topical chapter where it would contribute either some unique information on relations between variables of interest or a significant replication under genuinely diverse conditions; insofar as the studies reviewed here can be dispensed within their respective topical chapters, they were not well designed to provide information vital to a larger explanatory framework in child psychology.

Another implication of the multiple-study model of etiological research concerns sequence. Research coordination should extend not only across space and cultural boundaries but over time as well; in other words, some kinds of studies should precede others. Campbell and Stanley (1966, p. 64) argue that "the relatively inexpensive correlational approach can provide a preliminary survey of hypotheses, and those which survive this can then be checked through the more expensive experimental manipulation." Their argument is based on the premise that since causal hypotheses necessarily imply correlation, correlational studies can be used to eliminate those alternative hypotheses relating variables that turn out not to be even correlated, and then experimental studies can be used to eliminate those remaining hypotheses whose correlations are noncausal. There are, as our hypothetical example showed, other reasons for using comparative surveys before controlled experiments; for example, the breadth and heterogeneity of the cross-cultural comparison allow us to discover how great is the range of variation on factors of interest and which ones are naturally confounded, suggesting thereby the kinds of experiments or quasi-experiments that are feasible and that need to be done. When a controlled field experiment is done, it may be possible to tease out experimentally effective independent variables not previously anticipated; these results in turn should lead to new surveys that seek to find, in Campbell and Stanley's terminology, whether or not the internally valid experiment has external validity, that is, generalizability. Regardless of whether one conceives of the process as moving toward increasing specification and precision or as a cycle alternating between breadth and control, a strategy of cross-cultural research involving a rational ordering of types of studies over time would improve the cumulativeness of data collection in this field.

3. **The Importance of Local Information.** The hypothetical example showed the relevance of the data usually collected by anthropologists to longitudinal and experimental investigations of child development. The implication is that such data are essential in both the design and interpretation phases of the research process. If this is not apparent to child psychologists in most of the studies they do, it is because they know enough about their own society and culture to take account of it without resorting to specialized sources of information or they make errors in design or interpretation that are never brought to their attention. When the investigator moves outside his own culture, his dependence on sociocultural information becomes or should become more apparent.

To design an effective intracultural study,

the investigator needs ethnographic information on at least three points. First is the distribution of potential independent and dependent variables, and whether the variation occurs at the level of individual differences or subgroups. The study by Greenfield (in Bruner et al., 1966) of school-going and non-school-going children from the same village cluster is a good example of utilizing this kind of information in a research design, but the information utilized required only superficial knowledge from an ethnographic standpoint. Somewhat more to the point is Ainsworth's (1967) frank revelation concerning her intent to study the effects of mother-infant separation and weaning among the Ganda (of East Africa).

As an "experiment of opportunity," the project was originally intended to investigate the responses of very young children to separation from their mothers under conditions in which this response was not confounded by the effects of a depriving institution or of traumatic influences such as illness or the breakup of the family. Since the Ganda were reputed customarily to separate infants from their mothers at the time of weaning and to send them to be reared by grandmothers or other relatives, this society appeared to be a good setting for such a natural experiment. Furthermore, it was generally understood that weaning was, by ancient custom, sudden and traumatic among the Ganda. Therefore, it seemed likely that this society would also provide a good opportunity to contrast the effects of customarily abrupt weaning with the effects of gradual weaning practiced by those who had abandoned old customs.

My original plan was to select a sample of unweaned babies who could be expected to undergo the process within a few months and observe them in their relations to their mothers and to other members of their families; my hope was to establish a base line of behavior before the disruption that weaning might be expected to bring. It was anticipated that some would be weaned abruptly according to ancient custom whereas others would be weaned gradually and the responses of the two groups were to be compared. Furthermore, it was thought that some would be separated from their families at weaning according to old custom whereas others

would not be, and the comparison of the separated and non-separated groups could possibly throw light on the breach of ties implicit in "pure" separation unconfounded by other traumatic or depriving conditions.

. . . Long before the sample was complete, information obtained from our first participants suggested that an insufficient number of babies were likely to be separated from their families for mother-child separation to remain the focus of the research. It became apparent that the "experiment of opportunity" was not going to materialize. Furthermore, inquiries about weaning plans yielded the information that abrupt weaning was *not* customary among the Ganda, contrary to the impression that Europeans had gained, and thus we could not expect to make a comparison between abrupt and gradual weaning (Ainsworth, 1967, pp. 3-4).

If accurate ethnographic information concerning actual infant- and child-care practices and their distribution among the Ganda had been available to her, Ainsworth would not have made the mistake of designing a study that could not be carried out. Unless such information is available, child psychologists working in exotic cultures can expect frustrations similar to hers, particularly if they are seeking to exploit the natural experiments that offer the most dramatic rewards in cross-cultural research.

The second point on which the investigator needs ethnographic information in designing an intracultural study is that of constants across individuals or groups in the population. When factors that tend to vary in his own society are held constant in an exotic culture, he is thereby afforded a unique opportunity to examine other variables with more clarity. The relatively greater social and cultural homogeneity presumed for "traditional" societies has long been seen as an advantage for the psychological researcher, enabling him to assume that family life-styles and exposure to cultural influences are held constant for children from a given community of such a society. The same holds more specifically for institutionalized patterns regarded as mandatory for all children or adolescents in a society—initiation ceremonies or vision quest, task demands, participation in formal peer groups, preparation for certain kinds of marital or occupational roles—assuming they are held constant across individuals, they constitute a controlled frame for the observation of factors that vary in that situation. Homogeneity specific or general, however, cannot be assumed without detailed empirical evidence, for even in a small community there is often differential participation, access, or exposure to institutional patterns. Ethnographic investigation, in addition to revealing whether or not a conspicuous institutional pattern is as universal as it appears in a community, also uncovers less obvious constancies that might go unnoticed in a straightforward psychological study. In exploring the normative context of behavior in population, the ethnographer naturally becomes aware of those social expectancies, cultural beliefs, and conventional meanings that are unchallenged among its members; some of these universals could become genuine constants in a developmental study of individual differences. He might find, for example, that although there were few behavioral manifestations of belief in witchcraft and sorcery, the existence of witches and efficacy of sorcerers were taken for granted throughout the community; once he had satisfied himself concerning the absence of skeptics, he (or his psychologist-collaborator) would have the opportunity to study the development of interpersonal attitudes and views of the world where such beliefs were both present and held constant —a condition not obtainable in communities ordinarily accessible to him.

Finally, ethnographic information is essential to the design of exotic developmental studies for anticipating the confounding of variables and devising appropriate controls. In any attempt to divide children into groups receiving different treatment—school-going versus nonschool-going, separated-from-mother versus stay-at-home—there is the possibility that subsequent differences in observable behavior between the two groups may be due to preexisting differences beside the one selected as independent variable. Only intensive knowledge of the families and communities involved can help detect possibilities for contaminating influences. In the school comparison, it would be important to know whether or not, apart from going to school, the pupils were acquainted with a greater range of objects and experiences than nonpupils, or whether, regardless of sophistication, school-goers tended to come from wealthier families with higher status in the community and differing family composition and life-styles. In the Ganda infant study, even if Ainsworth had found that some children were sent away and others were not, the question of whether all the separations represented conformity to customary norms or whether some families who otherwise would not have conformed to custom did so because of pressing economic or domestic reasons would have had to be answered. If the answer to the second question were positive, she might have designed her study to include only custom-conforming separations in the separation group or to include a third group of coercive separations. It would also have been important to know whether there were differences in status or life-style that coincided with separation versus nonseparation (quite likely if nonseparation was the product of acculturation) and if these other differences involved aspects of the infant's environment that might affect his behavior and be mistakenly interpreted as effects of separation. The more detailed the ethnographic acquaintance with the community, the more controls can be built into the design to prevent contamination of the independent variables. Far from being an alternative to the systematic psychological study of children in exotic setting—as it has sometimes been presented—intensive ethnography is a prerequisite to systematic comparisons of individual differences.

Local information, so important in design, is essential in the interpretation of results both cross-cultural and intracultural, particularly if the findings reveal group differences or deviations from expectation. Any finding of group difference, as in our hypothetical example, can open up a Pandora's box of competing explanations, and it is only the investigator with intensive knowledge of characteristics differentiating the populations involved who can generate plausible alternative hypotheses that fit the data at hand and deserve more controlled research. Ethnographic ignorance can lure the researcher into false conclusions. Suppose he were doing a cross-national study of European populations and included an Arab sample solely because he suspected the psychological dependent variable might be affected by the direction in which a child has learned to read script. If he found that the Arab children differed from the others, it would be tempting to conclude that this was due to the attribute for which they were included—reading from right to left (even though such a conclusion would be a violation of Campbell's [1961, p. 344] rule for cross-cultural studies: *"No comparison of a single pair of natural objects is interpretable"*). The investigator with no knowledge of the Arab population and its culture apart from the way they read would be more tempted toward this fallacy than one whose intensive acquaintance would suggest to him a variety of rival explanations. At the intra-cultural level, ethnographic information is vital for explaining deviant cases, negative results, and serendipitous findings as well as for generating interpretations of differences between groups defined by age, sex, status, and group membership variables. The ethnographic experience, in its breadth of scope and richness of detail, provides an irreplaceable reservoir of information about factors potentially accounting for measurable psychological variation. Interpretation of quantitative variation on the basis of ethnographic evidence lends to findings plausibility and meaning rather than certainty. In this respect it is identical to psychological interpretations of sex differences among American children using commonly known aspects of American boys' and girls' experiences. Although not "proving" anything, such interpretations point the way to future investigation and constitute vital connective tissue between one study and another.

This long review through hypothetical example of the cross-cultural research strategy in child psychology has shown that if the etiological model of research is adopted, there are obstacles of measurement to be faced and overcome, that cross-cultural studies cannot be fruitfully separated from other developmental studies, that anthropological data should attend the research process in all its phases. From the perspective of this model and the methodological implications drawn from it, the cross-cultural literature in child psychology appears deficient in so many respects that a review of established facts and principles is not possible at this time. A review will nevertheless be attempted, extracting from the large number of diverse studies the

data, generalizations, and methodological experiences that seem to be helpful for future research. In line with this objective, the etiological model will serve as an organizing framework, so that the review will begin with what we know about constancies and variation in the psychology of infants and children, proceed to what is known about the environments in which children are raised, and thence to studies linking environmental variation with variation in development or its outcomes. The omission of cross-population differences in genetic factors and their impact on behavioral development is not an exclusion on principle but is due to the lack of information on this neglected subject.

Other limitations of this chapter should be noted. It is restricted to quantitative studies, that is, studies in which individuals or societies were aggregated for induction in accordance with standard psychological practices, however assailable those practices have been (see Bakan, 1967). To include anecdotal, ethnographic, or clinical studies would have constituted a discontinuity with the other chapters in this book which is contrary to the approach taken here. I have also tried to avoid covering the same ground as several recent or forthcoming surveys: DeVos and Hippler (1968) on cross-cultural differences in all aspects of behavior and psychological development, Zelditch (1964) on the cross-cultural study of family structure (see also Marsh, 1967), and Chapter 25 of this book, Social Class and Ethnic Group Influences on Socialization by Hess. The last limitation is of course arbitrary in terms of my view that intrapopulation and cross-population comparisons *should* be continuous and coordinated, but at present it represents a realistic and convenient division of labor.

CROSS-CULTURAL CONSTANCIES AND VARIATIONS IN THE BEHAVIOR OF INFANTS AND CHILDREN

This section is devoted to a review of cross-cultural studies that are primarily descriptive in the sense that they compare the responses of samples of children drawn from different populations or subpopulations *without* attempting to measure directly at the level of individual differences within the same samples any factor believed to produce or influence the responses. In other words, this is research that seeks to demonstrate psychological similarities and differences between groups, and to explain differences that manifest themselves solely in terms of group characteristics known to the investigator from sources outside the study.

Publications in this category are numerous and becoming more so. Our bibliographic search[3] *excluded* all studies limited to the continental United States unless they involved an American Indian sample, and it could hardly be considered an exhaustive inventory, but it turned up 77 such studies in the 9-year period 1959-1967. If one takes into account neglect of foreign-language sources, the local unavailability of some publications, and inevitable omissions in the search, it seems probable that the true number for that period would exceed 90, or more than 10 publications per year.

Our search revealed several chronic deficiencies in the literature, the most glaring being the prevalence of the two-group comparison which is so resistant to valid interpretation, the relative infrequency of the subgroup comparisons that would allow an assessment of replicability across universal demographic divisions, the even greater rarity of age comparisons—making developmental inferences impossible, and the tendency to rely on a single instrument. Although there are a number of well-designed and carefully executed studies, the coherent picture one would expect from such an extensive literature does not emerge. Altogether the impression is one of wasted effort, especially because so many of the studies of extremely dubious validity could have been respectable contributions to knowledge if another instrument and a few more subgroups had been intelligently added. Ironically, many of the studies attempting ambitious cross-cultural comparisons are weaker than those conducted in a single non-Western society. Such studies are more likely to include age comparisons *within* each of several demographically defined subgroups and to

have been conducted by investigators whose superior local knowledge guided sample selection and interpretation of findings. If there were agreement on the instruments and procedures to be used, the single-culture study with multiple subgroups and age comparisons would be much more valuable for the accumulation of cross-cultural information than the wide-ranging but superficial comparative study.

There is an interpretive fallacy common to many of the quantitative comparisons reviewed that deserves emphasis, especially because (according to Bakan, 1967, p. 20) it is so widespread in psychological research that it has attained a certain legitimacy. This is the assumption that the demonstration of a statistically significant difference in means between groups necessarily supports the investigator's hypothesis concerning the causes or cosymptoms of the difference. As Bakan points out, such reasoning confounds the inference from sample difference to population difference with the inference from the population difference to the nature of the behavioral phenomenon; the test of significance bears on the first inference but not the second. Many an investigator takes the p-value of the t-test as the probability that his general hypothesis is true, whereas it represents the probability of a mean difference between populations that might be predictable from many hypothetical premises. This misinterpretation is particularly tempting in cross-cultural research because, as pointed out in the previous section, the investigator's knowledge of the populations may be limited to those factors his hypotheses lead him to deem significant, and he is therefore unaware of confounding factors that would suggest alternative hypotheses. Indeed, he may choose particular populations for comparison on the basis of some striking or theoretically significant cultural difference to which he later attributes psychological differences that are hypothetically related and show themselves to be statistically significant. Having successfully "predicted" the significant difference, he leaps to the conclusion that his theoretical basis for prediction has a probability signified by the p of the statistical test. In so doing he confuses the tasks of description and explanation and sometimes offers a fallacious interpretation as established fact.

[3] For the bibliographic research I am indebted to Carolyn Jirari, Joseph Kotzin, Lillian Lahr, Lauren Langman, Winnie Ngcobo, Beba Varadachar, Louis Varga, Carol Ziegler, and Mrs. Barbara Kosarko, who also prepared early versions of the manuscript.

Two-group comparisons, so common in this literature, are especially vulnerable to this fallacy since they are, as Campbell has argued, basically uninterpretable in explanatory terms. The irony is that this fallacy is promoted by the otherwise commendable tendency of researchers to treat culturally differing populations as representing different points on a transcultural dimension rather than as unique and incomparable entities. In selecting a particular dimension for comparison and remaining ignorant of other ways in which the groups differ, the researcher jeopardizes the validity of the very explanation he seeks to establish. In consequence, cross-cultural publications accumulate that are inadequate as psychological description or explanation.

It could be argued that the cross-cultural literature as a whole is not relevant to scientific advancement since one really sound and imaginative large-scale comparative study each decade is worth more than a dozen routine data-collection efforts every year. But the advancement of cross-cultural knowledge requires large amounts of data from diverse populations living under diverse conditions, particularly if investigations are seen as mutually complementary and additive over time rather than as "crucial experiments" that provide definitive solutions to major research problems. Each badly designed small-scale study that might easily have been improved to the point of contributing some theoretically significant information represents a missed opportunity to collect data from which the field might have benefited, an opportunity that might not soon recur because it might be some years before a psychological investigator willing and able to do the study would be located at that place again. The harnessing of these unpredictable research efforts for the goal of cumulative understanding is overdue. It could be accomplished through a field manual for the cross-cultural psychological testing of children, written by a group of internationally respected child psychologists, which would establish guidelines for research design, sample selection, developmental comparisons, reliability and validity checks, and procedures for the collection, analysis, and presentation of data, including advice on the use of various instruments cross-culturally. The goal of such a field manual would be to maximize the validity and hence scientific utility of findings from studies conducted all over the world. The guidelines would probably be welcomed by most investigators moving into this field for the first time, and they might become standards of acceptability for journals publishing cross-cultural studies so that the comparability of scattered investigations might be influenced in a relatively short time. If there were ten or more studies meeting agreed-upon research standards being published every year, the cross-cultural branch of child psychology could progress more rapidly and contribute more effectively to the mainstream of psychological research.

In the present state of this literature it has seemed appropriate to present a selective overview of major studies or those of particular theoretical interest rather than attempting a genuine inventory of dependable findings. Hardly any well-known studies in this field, including those of its most reputable contributors, have failed to provoke serious methodological criticism profoundly challenging the validity of the results. Insofar as the results of some cross-cultural studies have gained acceptance by child psychologists, they have become incorporated into the literature of their respective topical specialties and are discussed in the chapters on those topics along with other studies of noncomparative nature. Thus the present section of this chapter concentrates on issues and findings peculiar to cross-cultural study. It is from this perspective that four aspects—infant motor development, perception, cognitive development, and social and motivational development—are reviewed.

Infant Motor Development

There have been relatively few cross-cultural studies of infant motor development; DeVos and Hippler (1968) have reviewed these along with studies comparing ethnic groups in American and European populations. In general, the earlier studies showed few major group differences even when comparing white Americans with Balinese or with Indians of the southwestern United States. From the studies by Dennis (1940) and Mead and MacGregor (1951), it appears that the general stages of motor development and the timing of these stages are fairly uniform across the diverse populations observed, although with some noteworthy exceptions: Dennis found that the American Indian children walk alone at a later age than white Americans, and Mead and MacGregor showed the following:

Where the American children go from frogging to creeping on all fours, then to standing and walking, with squatting coming after standing, the Balinese children . . . combine frogging, creeping, and all-fours simultaneously in a flexible, interchangeable state, from which they go from sitting to squatting to standing (1951, p. 181).

They also found what Gesell calls a "meandering tonus," characteristic of motor organization in American neonates, which persisted beyond infancy, so that low tonal organization could be termed "a crucial feature of the behavior of these Balinese children" (1951, p. 182). Mead and MacGregor attribute the deviation of Balinese infants from Gesell norms to the customary way in which Balinese adults carry and handle their infants, who spend more time than American infants being carried or sitting, and, specifically, being carried in a loose sling and held astride the caretaker's hip. They argue that adults foster the persistence of low tonal organization by a passive and noninteractive way of handling the infant and that in learning situations "the low tonus becomes high flexibility, capable of absorbing the pattern of activity that the teacher is imparting" (1951, p. 183). This in turn is seen as culturally adaptive for the "kinesthetic learning," "whole-body learning," and "total skin contact" which Bateson and Mead (1942) had earlier argued was crucial for Balinese character formation in their *Balinese Character: A Photographic Analysis*. Mead and MacGregor explicitly consider genetic and nutritional hypotheses to account for Balinese differences and propose research on them. Although they do not suggest that motor development differs radically from one population to another, Mead and MacGregor, and the photographs they present, do make a plausible case for somewhat differing patterns of motoric organization that can be related to modes of learning and interaction prevalent in a cultural group. Their study was based on only eight children and lacked the detailed longitudinal data necessary to test the

hypothesized linkages between adult handling and infant motoric activity and between the latter and receptivity to culturally valued learning. It showed, however, that a microscopic analysis of infant behavior combined with detailed knowledge of the cultural context could reveal cross-cultural differences in motor development of possible psychological significance. Unfortunately, the interesting questions raised by Mead and MacGregor have not been examined empirically in larger-scale studies during the ensuing 17 years.

The possibility that there are gross differences across populations in the timing of infant motor development has been raised by the African studies of Faladé (1955), Geber (1958, 1960, 1961), Geber and Dean (1957a, 1957b, 1958), and Ainsworth (1967). Except for the research of Faladé, which was done in Dakar, Senegal, all of the studies were conducted among the Ganda people in and around Kampala, Uganda. In general, they consistently point to precocity of motor development for Africans, especially during the first year of life, but declining so sharply during and just after the second year that after age 3 they are below rather than above European and American norms. From a psychological point of view, it is particularly significant that this early motor precocity is associated with intellectual and social precocity, which also appears to diminish over time.

Figure 1, reproduced from Geber and Dean (1957b, p. 1060) shows the Gesell development quotients for 56 Ganda children, 51 of whom were tested twice and the rest three times. These are general development quotients, which combine scores for motor and manual activity with those for "adaptivity," language, and personal-social behavior. The average quotient for American and European children at each age level is 100. In their cross-sectional studies Geber and Dean saw a total of 252 Ganda children whose average performance approximated the trends of Fig. 1 and supported the finding of precocity in the first 2 years of life.

Ainsworth (1967, pp. 319-330) also worked among the Ganda, making careful systematic observations on 28 children in home settings; 13 of these children were tested by Geber in the clinic. Since her observational data and interviews with mothers

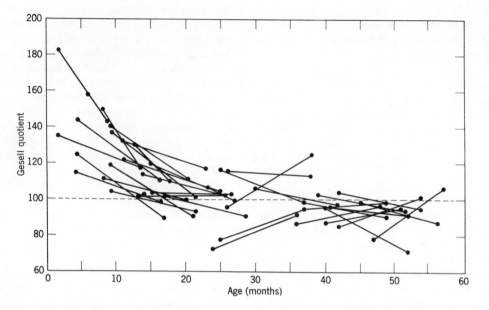

Figure 1. Gesell quotients for general development of children who were tested in successive years. The quotients usually fell as age increased.

contained information on the timing of events in motor development, Ainsworth was able to compare them to European norms on the Griffiths Infant Intelligence Scale. The general trend of her findings is evident in the following excerpts:

> Most of the babies in this sample were clearly accelerated in their rate of sensorimotor development. The rate of their physical growth, as checked by measurements of height and weight upon visits to the clinic, was not accelerated. On the contrary, most of the babies were average in height and weight when compared with Western norms. But they sat and crawled and stood and walked much earlier than the average baby in Western societies. Although the focus of my interest was upon the development of interpersonal relations, the striking acceleration of these Ganda babies in sensorimotor development merits consideration (1967, p. 319).

> The mean age of "crawling" from the mothers' reports was 5.6 months; that from our own observations 6.6 months. The mean age of "creeping" from our own actual observations was 7.5—but this could not refer to the very onset of creeping. All we knew

was that the child was able to creep on the occasion of one visit and we had not seen him do so on an earlier visit. On the basis of our own observations *crawling occurred about two and a half months earlier than the Griffiths' norms and creeping about three and a half months earlier* (1967, p. 325, italics added).

> . . . Limiting ourselves to those babies in which standing alone could be pinpointed by our own observations, the mean age of achieving the milestone was eleven months —two months in advance of the Griffiths' norms. Moreover, the intermediate stages in development of standing were observed to be well in advance of the Griffiths' norms. Standing firmly when supported was observed to occur at about seven months (Griffiths' eleven months); being able to pull oneself to a standing position while holding onto furniture was observed at about seven or eight months (Griffiths' eleven months) (1967, p. 325).

Walking is an important landmark in present-day Ganda society because it is, more often than not, the signal that a child is old enough to be weaned. Fourteen of the sample were able to walk, and with one exception

. . . we were on hand to witness the event. The mean age of achievement of walking was eleven months . . . We used as our criterion for walking the ability to take a few steps before falling. Griffiths places this item at fourteen months. For those whom we observed long enough to ascertain when they could "trot about well," we found this to occur at about twelve months whereas Griffiths places it at sixteen months (1967, p. 326).

I recorded four-syllable vocalization in the case of nine infants, but there is no reason to suppose that my record caught anything approximating a first achievement. The mean age at which I observed this type of vocalization was thirty-eight weeks; Griffiths places this item at the beginning of the ninth month (1967, p. 367).

Thus Ainsworth's observations in the home support Geber's testing in the clinic. Although the documentation is far from conclusive, there is the strong suggestion of considerable precocity in sensorimotor attainments and concomitant social-intellectual capacities in infancy. The findings from Geber's original study were striking enough and raised enough important issues concerning the impact of early precocity on subsequent development so that if it had been conducted in America rather than Uganda numerous replications would have been attempted over the last decade. At present, however, we still stand in need of more evidence on larger African samples of infants growing up under diverse environmental conditions.

Both Geber and Ainsworth favor an environmental explanation of the motor precocity of Ganda infants. Geber emphasizes the availability, nurturance, and physical closeness of the mother to the infant, and she attributes the decline after the second year to the emotional rejection of weaning. Ainsworth stresses the absence of infant confinement, freedom to move about and interact with others, and "postural adjustments to being held and carried during the earliest months" (1967, p. 328). This is supported, although weakly because of a small and selective sample, by the lack of precocity in highly acculturated Ganda who treat their infants like Europeans (Geber, 1958). But

the environmental line of explanation is called into question by the findings of Geber and Dean (1957a, 1957b) who, in examining 113 newborn Ganda children by a standard method for determining the degree of muscular tone and the eliciting of "primitive" reflexes, found a high degree of precocity present *at birth*. They summarize their findings by saying:

They (the Ganda neonates) showed development that is, to say the least, highly unusual in European children at birth or in the first weeks of life, and the African children in fact behaved much like European children 3 to 4 weeks of age. They were not only less hypertonic in their flexion, but had a remarkable control of the head, and many of them could even raise the chin completely free of the table when they were lying on their fronts. Few showed the primitive reflexes after the first day or so of life, even the near-convulsive Moro reflex—usually a very consistent finding in European children —being found in only 6 of the 79 children more than 24 hours of age. The well-known grasp reflex, which enables the European child to suspend himself from a stick in a somewhat simian manner, was feebly and poorly sustained, and automatic walking was rare. Children only 2 days old were able to follow movement with their eyes, and some appeared to be able to focus.

A study of the African child at birth, more detailed and exact than was possible for this series, would probably show a large number of other points of difference from European children. *No explanation was offered for the precocity, but it was fairly clear that it had a genetic basis* (1957b, p. 1061, italics added).

If the precocity at birth is to be regarded as a genuine precursor of the subsequent precocity of Ganda infants, then the handling of the child and other environmental events might be less important than they have appeared to Geber and Ainsworth. Future research on sensorimotor development in Africans as compared with others should be concentrated on the establishment of a body of reliable facts regarding the timing of developmental events for various populations so that it is clear what differences there are that require explanation in environmental, genetic, or nutritional terms.

Indications of group differences in early motor behavior are not limited to the deviation of Africans from European and American norms. The preliminary report by Caudill and Weinstein (1966) on 30 Japanese and 30 American infants who are part of a longitudinal study also shows strong differences. Time-sample observations were carried out in the homes of the infants, who were in all cases first-born, normal, 3 to 4 months old, and from middle-class families (in both countries). One category used was "active," which means "gross repetitive bodily movements, usually of the arms and legs, and does not include minor movements such as twitches or startles." The agreement of Caudill, who observed in both Japan and the United States, with the local observers, was relatively low (64%) for this category, but the discrepancies were due to his recording fewer active observations than either of the two local observers, so that the authors regard this low reliability as not affecting the cross-cultural comparison itself. In 800 observations, the American infants were found to be so much more active than the Japanese that virtually all the American cases are above the median of the combined sample and all the Japanese cases below it; probability using the Mann-Whitney U Test is less than .0001. The authors explain this striking difference in environmental terms, involving some of the equally striking differences in maternal treatment and infant living conditions between the two groups (these are discussed later in this chapter). Whether it is accounted for in environmental or genetic terms, however, such a major difference in gross activity level at 3-4 months must be taken into consideration in attempting to assess the impact of subsequent child-rearing practices. In other words, even at this early age one cannot assume a behaviorally constant organism across these two populations. And if it cannot be assumed for middle-class Japanese and Americans, are we safe in assuming it for any other pair of populations of diverse origins?

Perceptual Development

There is an extensive literature, beginning a century ago, on cross-cultural differences in perception; it has been reviewed at length by Segall, Campbell, and Herskovits (1966, pp. 23-68). Although few of these studies have involved children, most of them are addressed to developmental problems. The present review will discuss a few of the most recent studies. Concerning the larger literature, Segall, Campbell, and Herskovits conclude:

It thus appears that at this point in the history of psychological and anthropological concern for this problem there is little unequivocal evidence of cultural influence on perception. On the other hand, for all its inherent ambiguity, the evidence certainly points in that direction. In sum, the materials reviewed here suggest that while additional methodologies and instrumentations may be required, there is considerable likelihood of documenting authentic perceptual differences across cultures. In addition, the literature seems to us to suggest that if cultural differences in perception are to be found, they are likely to be the result of culturally mediated differences in experience, rather than manifestations of biological differences among cultural groups (1966, p. 68).

Subsequent studies have supported this conclusion and gone beyond, to identify environmental parameters that produce cross-population differences in perception and to propose adaptive functions for these differences. Some of the recent data are strikingly convincing and the explanatory hypotheses highly plausible, but there is a notable lack of data on children in the very years (1 to 6) during which the perceptual differences are hypothesized to be formed by environmental factors. The largest scale and most fully reported research to date, that of Segall, Campbell, and Herskovits (1966) illustrates this quite explicitly. These investigators hypothesized that the visual environment of a population encourages the development in children of inference habits—ways of making perceptual judgments from visual cues—that are adaptive in that visual environment but not necessarily in others. These inference habits are based on relatively frequent aspects of the environment that must be taken into account for effective adaptation in that environment, but they lead one to misjudge visual cues when "ecologically unrepresentative" settings for visual performance are provided—as in an optical illusion experiment. In the "carpentered world" of modern cities, it is highly adaptive—ecologically valid on a probabilistic basis—to judge acute angles as being right angles tilted and extended in space, but the unvarying application of such an inference habit makes one more susceptible to the Müller-Lyer and Sander parallelogram illusions, that is, to misjudgments of the length of lines in an atypical visual context. This "carpentered world hypothesis" led the investigators to predict that Western subjects would display these illusions more frequently than non-Western subjects, especially when the latter inhabited noncarpentered visual environments. Data on these and other illusions were collected from 1878 persons in 13 non-Western ethnic groups (12 African, from various parts of the continent, and 1 from the Philippines), South African Europeans, and inhabitants of Evanston, Illinois. In the design, administration, and analysis, a great deal of care was taken (and is reported) to insure the validity of the measures. Although it was not possible to predict a group's exact rank on illusion susceptibility from the information on visual environments, the data as a whole strongly supported the "carpentered world" hypothesis in particular and the general environmental theory of perceptual development as well. The study contains many pieces of evidence favoring the presumption of early visual experience as the determining factor. For example, Evanston adults who spent their childhood in the city showed significantly more of the Müller-Lyer illusion than those raised in the country, even though they were currently inhabiting a similar visual environment (Segall, Campbell, and Herskovits, 1966, p. 205).

But the data on children themselves are less conclusive. The Müller-Lyer illusion *decreases* with age (at least after age 4) for *both* Western and non-Western samples. As the authors state:

Why the illusion-producing habits should be acquired at all in noncarpentered worlds and why they should subsequently decline are questions for which an answer at the present time would be premature. . . . Data collected from children under age 4 are required before the hypothetical details concerning the acquisition of the inference habits postulated above can be put to test (Segall, Campbell, and Herskovits, 1966, p. 199).

A recent study by Berry (1966) comparing the Temne of Sierra Leone (West Africa) with Canadian Eskimo and Scottish subjects reveals some of the same strengths and weaknesses. Berry also believes that perceptual skills (as he calls them) have adaptive value in terms given by the local ecology and its visual environment, but he argues for cultural mediation, with language and arts and crafts operating to develop (presumably in children) discriminations and spatial skills that will prove adaptive later in life. His ecological comparison of the Temne and Eskimo is a compelling one:

The Temne land is covered with bush and other vegetation providing a wealth of varied visual stimulation. Color is also abundant. . . . On the other hand, the Eskimo environment is bleak at any time of the year. . . . The Eskimo, when compared to the Temne, inhabits a world of uniform visual stimulation. . . . The Temne are farmers who work land near their villages and rarely have to leave the numerous paths through the bush. The Eskimo, on the other hand, are hunters who must travel widely on the sea and land, and far along the coasts in search of game and trap animals.

It is evident that the Eskimo must develop certain perceptual skills, merely to survive in their situation, which the Temne are not called upon to do:

1. He must first of all in order to hunt effectively develop the ability to isolate slight variation in visual stimulation from a relatively featureless array; he must learn to be aware of minute detail.

2. Secondly, in order to navigate effectively in this environment he must learn to organize these small details into a spatial awareness, an awareness of his present location in relation to objects around him (Berry, 1966, pp. 211-212).

Thus Berry goes farther than Segall, Campbell, and Herskovits in presenting evidence for the survival relevance of perceptual skills. He also performs an analysis of geometrical-spatial terms in the Temne and

Eskimo languages, showing that the Eskimo make more distinctions, and that if one includes Eskimo "localizers" (affixes indicating the spatial location of objects), "it is possible that the Eskimo possess a geometrical-spatial term system as complex as that of Western technical man" (1966, p. 213). More impressionistically, he compares Eskimo and Temne arts and crafts, indicating more elaboration and intricate detail for the Eskimo. In his psychological comparisons, Berry demonstrates that in a tachistoscopically administered closure task the Eskimo see more gaps and smaller gaps than the Temne, suggesting finer perceptual discrimination. To assess spatial skills, he used a battery of four tests: Kohs Blocks, Witkin Embedded Figures Test, Morrisby Shapes, and Raven Matrices, which on the whole correlated highly in the six samples. Without going into the details of the results, which include controlled comparisons of subgroups and individuals varying in degree of Westernization, we can say simply that the Eskimos scored consistently higher than the Temne and the differences were substantial; Eskimo-Scottish differences were slight or nonexistent. The findings are particularly important because they rule out the possibility that group differences are simply a function of Western contact. Western education heightens scores, but even the traditional Eskimo sample scores much higher than the Temne samples and closely resembles the Scottish group. Thus Berry's ecological and cultural-mediation hypotheses appear confirmed. The absence of subjects under 10 years of age, however, leaves open to question the causes of these divergences in perceptual development and the ages at which they first appear. From the viewpoint of child psychology, the evidence for environmental determination in individual development (as opposed to natural selection having produced a different genetic base in the Eskimo and Temne populations) is circumstantial rather than direct.

Some data relevant to this point have been produced by D'Andrade (1967), using the Kohs blocks among the Hausa of Northern Nigeria, a farming people similar in some respects to the Temne. He found that, although first-grade children did poorly compared to Western norms, he was able—by careful observation of the kind of mistakes made—to design a "programmed instruction" procedure that could bring them up to Western norms. Although the experiment was carried out with only six subjects, the results were strikingly uniform and suggested that the skill involved, whether regarded as perceptual or cognitive, is "rapidly modifiable when the proper conditions for new learning are found" (D'Andrade 1967, p. 15). The genetic hypothesis was rejected. The investigator was able to draw further conclusions from the improved performance of the Hausa children when they were given the task of copying a design from another set of blocks rather than from a drawing:

Looking back on the results of the testing and training procedures among Hausa children, it seems to fit the data to suppose that the children's initial poor performance on the Kohs block test was due to a lack of familiarity with drawings and, in general, with any type of pictorial representation. In rural Hausa villages children rarely see pictures or drawings of any type, and even more rarely use any kind of pictorial representation as a "blueprint" for action. Maps, building diagrams, etc., leave even adults baffled. At Ahmadu Bello University, in Zaria, instructors from the Faculty of Engineering report that students experience unusual difficulty in the mechanical drawing class. Many adults cannot even identify the contents of ordinary photographs (D'Andrade 1967, p. 15).

This conclusion is congruent with the findings of Hudson's (1960) study of pictorial depth perception in South Africa. Eleven samples of subjects varying in educational level, race, and ethnicity (Europeans and Africans of presumably mixed Bantu-speaking origins), and age (from 6 or 7 to over 40 years) were tested with a specially constructed series of pictures that can be interpreted meaningfully in two- or three-dimensional terms, although to anyone experienced in interpreting perspective in pictures, the three-dimensional judgment is obvious. In comparing proportions of the samples that made three-dimensional judgments, Hudson found a powerful relationship of education or even current school-group with a higher frequency of pictorial depth perception in both European and African groups. The lowest frequencies were found in illiterate and slightly schooled African mine laborers, but white European laborers, most of whom were over 20 and had some primary schooling, scored far below African schoolchildren in the 14-20 age range. Hudson's use of readily available "captive populations" for study does not allow factors of family background, early environment, and educational selection to be disentangled from that of the subjects' own educational experience, but his findings nevertheless suggest that pictorial depth perception, although almost absent in "traditional" Africans and weak in less educated Europeans, is readily developed through training and exposure in school. If this is so, it has important implications for the interpretation of performance on perceptual and cognitive tests that require familiarity with two-dimensional pictures as representations of three-dimensional objects. The most important implication, as indicated by D'Andrade (1967), is that poor performance may represent an easily reversible lack of acquaintance and training rather than a stable deficit in perceptual or cognitive capacities. Just how reversible at various ages and with what general effects is open to question and research, as is the issue of what the early determinants are and how they affect initial performance.

A related study that deserves mention is that of Suchman (1966), who analyzed data on color-form preferences of 119 Hausa children ranging in age from 3 to 15; the children were pupils of Koranic schools in Zaria, Northern Nigeria, a few miles from the village in which D'Andrade worked. Although three nonverbal measures using abstract forms were administered and careful checks showed that the tasks were understood, the Hausa children showed no tendency to shift from color to form preferences, as Western children do from kindergarten age onward. Here is a case in which there are data on the relevant age groups and it is clear that a developmental transition found in the West does not occur. It seems at least possible that some aspects of school experience promote the shift in Western children, whereas in Hausa Koranic schools, where children are taught to recite and memorize the Koran in Arabic and to pronounce and write Arabic characters without understanding them, these aspects are missing.

This interpretation is supported by the analysis of Greenfield, Reich, and Olver (in Bruner et al., 1966, p. 270-318) of data from another West African people, the Wolof of Senegal. Unschooled Wolof children were asked to group familiar objects that had similiarities and differences of color, form and function.

For all practical purposes children at all ages base their groupings exclusively on the attribute of color. The percentage of subjects using color attributes as a basis for grouping were, respectively:

70% of the six- and seven-year-olds
40% of eight-year-olds
80% of ten- to sixteen-year-olds (Bruner et al., 1966, p. 286).

This was not true of Wolof children going to school either in a "bush" village or in the city, which leads the investigators to a cognitive interpretation of perceptual patterns:

Bush children who do not go to school rely on color attributes at every stage of development; school children, in contrast, move away from an initial reliance on color—the bush children mainly toward form, the city children, toward form and function. Thus the school appears to favor the growth of a certain type of perceptual equivalence, namely, equivalence based on form. . . . It must be stressed, however, that . . . this perceptual development is basically a conceptual one. Likely as not, this development is also closely tied to language. By conceptual we mean that school is teaching European habits of perceptual *analysis*. An analysis into parts is plainly crucial to concepts based on the multidimensional attribute of form, whereas unitary global perception could suffice for color grouping. Similarly, the breaking up of innate shape constancies into their component parts of retinal image and angle of view is basic if one is to understand two-dimensional conventions for three-dimensional representation. And we have seen that schooling is required for recognizing objects represented in this way, although not necessarily for dealing with less analytic pictorial representations (Bruner et al., 1966, p. 315–316).

The authors go on to argue that schooling makes its impact through forcing children to practice language independent of familiar, automatically given contexts; it teaches them to regard words as labels that can be assigned to objects in a variety of contexts, thus giving them the analytic tools to "see" form rather than merely color. This view is consistent with that of Segall, Campbell, and Herskovits (1966) that perception, rather than being given in experience, requires the development of inference habits for the interpretation of visual cues, but it emphasizes the presence or absence of context-free verbal mediation (more loosely, abstract thinking) as the factor that accounts for major cross-cultural differences in perceptual development and especially for the arrested development (as they see it) of those who do not go to school.

To summarize, recent research on the cross-cultural study of perception has succeeded in raising a series of sharply focused developmental questions without having collected the relevant data from children, especially very young children, that would help answer them. The present state of knowledge can be represented conservatively by the following propositions:

1. There are substantial differences in optical illusion susceptibility, pictorial depth perception and color-form preferences across culturally distinct human populations.

2. The differences found so far do not conform to any simple concept of more and less advanced peoples, nor do they simply reflect a Western bias in testing procedures; on the contrary, "traditional" peoples in Africa and the Philippines are *less* susceptible to certain standard illusions than Westerners, and the Eskimos—a hunting people at a low level of development in terms of sociocultural evolution—show a high level of perceptual skill on ordinary European tests.

3. Plausible hypotheses have been advanced relating cross-cultural differences in perception to concomitant variations in environmental parameters affecting entire populations—typical visual environment, survival relevance of perceptual skills, presence or absence of two-dimensional pictures, geometrical-spatial lexicon of the language, presence or absence of crafts requiring fine perceptual discrimination. The evidence is uneven but tends to support these ecological hypotheses.

4. There is a general presumption that these environmental parameters affect the early experience of children but little evidence is available concerning how this happens or the age at which divergent perceptual development begins.

5. The consistent improvement of some perceptual abilities with level of schooling within culturally defined populations, although based on cross-sectional studies only, and the improvement achieved through experimental training, suggest that the cross-cultural differences in perception may reflect primarily a lack of familiarity with certain types of visual cues and inference procedures, easily reversed under the proper conditions.

Developmental research in this field is now ready to begin. The cross-cultural measuring instruments exist and have shown differences across populations. There is an abundance of theory about the environmental origins of the differences, and the environmental factors identified are ones that vary naturally *and can be manipulated experimentally*. The time is ripe for cross-cultural studies of perceptual development, following infants and young children over time in longitudinal designs, observing the effects of schooling and experimentally introducing training in or exposure to pictorial representation of objects, experience with right-angled objects, etc., especially in populations low on pictorial depth perception and illusion susceptibility. A few well-designed developmental studies along these lines, combining experiment with longitudinal observation and systematically exploring for possible effects of perceptual adaptation on cognitive performance (as well as for effects of verbal and literacy training on perceptual performance), in populations shown to diverge perceptually from our own, might have an important impact on our understanding of early development.

Cognitive Development

This category contains more cross-cultural studies of children than any other, particularly if its boundaries are defined broadly enough to include intelligence testing, studies addressed to Piaget's developmental formulations, and other research on cognitive processes in children. There are, for example, cross-cultural studies using the Goodenough

Draw-A-Man-Test from 1926 to the present (see Johnson, Johnson, and Price-Williams, 1967, for a review), and publications examining the universality of Piaget's findings beginning more than 35 years ago (see Mead, 1932). In recent years, as cognitive development has become the major research interest of American child psychologists, cross-cultural publications on this topic have increased apace, although studies of more than routine interest remain few and far between.

It is difficult to summarize what is known in this area because the divergence among investigators in theory, method, and interpretation of findings is very wide. The sources of this divergence in the area of cognitive development and the controversies proceeding from it are discussed at length in other chapters of this book. Suffice it to say here that an investigator's position on the nature-nurture problem and the type of environmental determinism he hypothesizes usually accounts for his cross-cultural research strategy. Those inspired by Piaget and Werner tend to posit invariant developmental sequences for the human species and to approach cross-cultural studies with a replicative intent, to demonstrate the universality of stages, although sometimes with the additional notion that not all populations reach the final stage. Conversely, critics of Piaget particularly attempt to explode his stage formulations by showing they do not hold in a particular exotic group. Moderate environmentalists (e.g., Bruner et al., 1966) approach cross-cultural comparison with the intent to find environments varying in their capacity to elicit development to the next higher stage in an invariant sequence; they are more interested in environmental conditions and how they interact with cognition in a given stage to produce developmental advance. Extreme environmentalists like behaviorists and linguistic adherents of the Sapir-Whorf hypothesis are often motivated to demonstrate maximum plasticity of organism through documenting maximal differences across populations and showing how the response patterns of a given population reflect distinctive environmental features of that population (the ecologically or socially determined reward structure, the rules of speech, or normative patterns of stimulating infants and young children). Such environ-

mentalists often pay more attention to the environmental conditions than they do to the individual except insofar as his behavior is isomorphically responsive to those conditions. In other words, the lack of agreement on theory and method extends to whether or not cross-cultural study is worthwhile and if so, what its purpose should be. These divergent approaches to cognitive development produce cross-cultural data addressed to different issues, and they cannot be fruitfully integrated or even encompassed in this chapter, so the present section is devoted to a discussion of findings that may contribute to an eventual resolution of the controversies in this field.

DeVos and Hippler (1969) have reviewed cross-cultural studies of intelligence and cognitive processes, and the reader is referred to their article for a more comprehensive account than this one.

Some years ago, a cross cultural discussion of standard intelligence tests might have argued at length that they are geared to Western middle-class values and biased against persons not exposed to those values early in life, that is, non-Western peoples and the lower classes in our own society; it might have ended with an evaluation of the relative merits of "culture-free" intelligence tests such as the Porteus Maze Test, Goodenough Draw-A-Man Test, and the Raven Progressive Matrices. We now can take the bias of the tests as established fact and go beyond to see if we can learn something more from them, as DeVos and Hippler do.

What we learn is that standard intelligence tests measure the current capacity of individuals to participate effectively in Western schools, which are a worldwide feature of "modernization." Average scores for populations or subgroups tend to reflect the degree of modernization in their life situations or backgrounds, as measured by urbanism, involvement in bureaucratic or industrial occupations, education of parents, and other economic indexes and aspects of life-style. It is not surprising that the Japanese, who have the most modern industrial economy outside Europe and the United States, score particularly high on Western intelligence tests (DeVos, personal communication), for educational development along Western lines has been a major aspect of modernization in Japan. From this perspective, intelligence test scores measure a population's degree of intellectual adaptation to a modernized socioeconomic environment that includes Western-type educational institutions; they tell us little or nothing about the population's intellectual adaptations to other aspects of its environment past or present. For the least modernized peoples in the world, the intelligence tests tend to yield negative information, indicating what we already know, that they are not adapted to the intellectual norms of modern institutions, to which they have been recently or only partly exposed. There is no reason to believe that this information indicates a lack of long-run potential for making such an adaptation under the right educational and economic conditions; on the contrary, the diffusion of Western education provides numerous examples of large-scale adaptive changes within a few generations. In the case of the Japanese, as reported in the international study of mathematics achievement (Husén, 1967), change has involved surpassing European and American norms.

There is much to be learned from inquiring into how and why children in a given population do poorly on a standard intelligence test; their mistakes can be used as clues to their habitual mode of cognitive functioning. In such an inquiry, factors of response set and familiarity effects—usually regarded as test artifacts to be eliminated —become the primary objects of attention. We have already noted D'Andrade's (1967) discovery that the poor performance of Hausa children on the Kohs block test was due to their general lack of familiarity with pictorial representation and that their performance could be improved by having them use another set of blocks, rather than a picture, as a model. Another factor affecting test performance has been suggested by Johnson, Johnson, and Price-Williams (1967), who administered the Draw-A-Man Test (DAMT) to 256 school children aged 6 to 16 in highland Guatemala and found that the mean IQ was 85.08 compared with means of 102 to 117 for North American Indian children on the same test. In North America, girls usually score higher than boys on the DAMT, but this was strongly reversed among the Guatemalan children, which the investiga-

tors attribute to the sex roles in Guatemala, where girls are expected "to defer to others, to be passive, and to avoid the appearance of intellectual ambitions" (1967, p. 154). Looking more closely at their results, they found that although there were no significant differences in IQ between Indian and Ladino boys, Indian girls scored far below Ladino girls ($t=3.61$; $p<.001$). Their observations in the testing situation are relevant here:

During the DAMT administration, attempts to trace from the backs of school books were fairly frequent, especially among the girls. These children were demonstrating the fact that they were never asked for an original solution to a problem. Ordinarily, classroom questions came supplied with ready-made answers. The children, especially the girls, expected to be told what the answer was, and then to memorize it. . . . In the case of the Indian girls passive learning was so much the order of the day that a Ladino girl would occasionally burst into the testing room, take the pencil from the Indian girl's hand, and attempt to make her drawing or to answer questions for her. Indians were more passive learners than Ladinos, and Indian girls were the most passive of the four groups (Johnson, Johnson, and Price-Williams, 1967, p. 153).

In this case, then, it would seem that the social expectation of compliance and rote learning, especially strong for girls and reinforced in classroom experience, made the testing procedure with its demand for active and original response particularly unfamiliar and helped account for poor performance. This raises the more general questions of whether preschool training in social habits such as obedience might affect performance on cognitive tasks, and whether such effects occur through a simple generalization of the habit (from the original interactive situation in the family to the interactive situation of intelligence testing) or through an arrest in cognitive development itself. In other words, does severe obedience and compliance training produce an inhibition of cognitive performance or a deficit in cognitive capacity?

A similar problem was raised by Greenfield (in Bruner et al., 1966) concerning the responses of Wolof children in Senegal, West

Africa, to a Piaget conservation task (conservation of a continuous quantity). The Wolof children who had been to school did almost as well as American children on the task, but those who did not go to school were far behind and did not improve markedly at all after age 9. They did improve markedly, however, if they were allowed to pour the water in the experiment themselves rather than watching the experimenter do it:

Magical-action reasons, which constituted a quarter of all reasons when an adult pours, are non-existent when the unschooled older children themselves pour. Responses like, "The water is not the same because you poured it," disappear (Bruner et al., 1966, p. 250).

Greenfield explains this as follows:

The intervention of an authority figure in the standard experiment attracts attention; whatever that person does is important, even if irrelevant to the solution of the problem. . . . Only when the authority figure withdraws does the child turn fully to the logically essential parts of the action . . . (Bruner et al., 1966, p. 250).

Why do Wolof children have this reaction to an adult experimenter? The answer may be found in the background information:

The experimental situation, in so far as it consists of an interview of one child by one adult, is unheard of in the traditional culture, where almost everything occurs in groups, and adults command rather than seek the opinions of children (Bruner et al., 1966, p. 230).

That the factor of habitual compliance and awe in the presence of an adult may explain the poor performance of the unschooled Wolof children is given support by Price-Williams' (1961) finding that unschooled Tiv children in Nigeria, all of whom showed conservation by age 8, performed the experimental operations themselves spontaneously and on their own initiative, whereas the Wolof children never did so. Greenfield (Bruner et al., 1966, p. 249) interprets this as evidence that "Tiv culture is quite different from the Wolof one in promoting an active manipulative approach to the physical world." Such an explanation, like the one adduced in the Guatemalan study, suggests that early childhood experience—perhaps differential reinforcement for manipulative and compliant behavior in the presence of adults, perhaps more general features of parent-child or authority relations—strongly influences initial response to experimental and testing situations designed to measure intellectual performance in the child.

Gay and Cole (1967), working with the Kpelle, an agricultural group in Liberia, independently arrived at similar conclusions:

We see this lack of analysis, this unquestioning acceptance of authority, as the primary stumbling block to the Kpelle child's progress in school. For him the world remains a mystery to be accepted on authority, not a complex pattern of comprehensible regularities (1967, p. 94).

The child must never question those older than himself. If he is told to do a chore in a certain way, he must do it in that way, and no other. If he asks "Why," or acts in a manner unsanctioned by tradition, he is likely to be beaten (1967, p. 16).

Although the evidence to date may be regarded as no more than suggestive, cross-cultural investigators of cognitive processes in children would be well advised to find out the extent to which these initial test responses reflect a general disposition of unthinking compliance in response to tasks set by adults.

Despite the effects of preschool socialization, schooling—even a few years of it—has been found to improve performance on a variety of cognitive tasks in a striking way. Greenfield (in Bruner et al., 1966, pp. 225-257, 283-314), as noted earlier, found large differences between schooled and unschooled Wolof children from the villages on the Piaget conservation task and on the shift from color to form preference in grouping objects as equivalent; the school-going children were closer to their American or European counterparts than they were to unschooled children from their communities. Gay and Cole (1967, pp. 54-56) show similar results for the Kpelle in a task involving the identification of geometrical shapes and in the learning of logical rules (1967, pp. 80-82):

. . . The schoolchildren are clearly the best performers in all of the problem solving tasks we have used. Obviously, the first two years of schooling have more effect on the child than our survey of their mathematics learning would indicate. The children appear to be learning the ability to use generalizing verbal labels about a wide range of things (1967, p. 88).

Greenfield, Reich, and Olver (in Bruner et al., 1966) also regard the school's primary contribution to cognitive growth (in the West African setting) in terms of verbal mediation, more particularly giving the child practice in using words isolated from their usual context, and they see the learning of writing as particularly influential in this regard. It should be emphasized, however, that neither Greenfield nor Gay and Cole argue that the school is any less authoritarian than the preschool environment; on the contrary, from an American point of view, West African schools are repressive and emphasize passive rote-learning. This strongly suggests that instructional content (e.g., context-free use of words) can improve cognitive performance without seriously altering the habitual passivity, obedience, and deference to adult authority produced by prior socialization. Unthinking compliance may still contribute somewhat to depressing performance below the level of populations in which active mastery is fostered in children, but the instructional factors appear to have an independent effect of major proportions on fostering development to qualitatively different levels of cognition.

But Gay and Cole (1967) resist the notion that verbal mediation is due entirely to the influence of Western schooling. Replicating the Kendler experiment on verbal mediation in the concept acquisition of fast and slow learners with 64 preschool Kpelle children, they found the same difference between fast and slow learners—fast initial learners shift within dimensions more rapidly, whereas slow initial learners shift across dimensions more rapidly than fast learners—which had been explained in terms of the use of verbal mediation by 5-year-old fast learners but not slow learners in America. Gay and Cole conclude that "sim-

ple forms of verbal mediation develop in the Kpelle child at about the same time that they appear in American children" (1967, p. 87). This finding contributes to their general view that a simple dichotomy of concrete and abstract is inadequate for understanding their material on the Kpelle. Their monograph presents substantial ethnographic and linguistic data along with systematic psychological studies, and it provides a picture of the contexts in which Kpelle adults use concepts of number, space, and measurement and the relevant vocabulary and syntax in the Kpelle language. Kpelle intellectual development is seen as adapted to the environmental demands for conceptualization in various domains of that cultural-ecological setting. There is no denial of "concreteness" as an emphasis in Kpelle thinking; on the contrary, the authors report that children learn (outside of school) almost exclusively by imitation and correction of mistakes, with no general lectures and a minimum of verbalization. They further state:

One of the ubiquitous findings in our experiments is that Kpelle subjects had great difficulty when asked to explain the reason for an answer or to state the general rule underlying the solution of a problem (1967, p. 84).

But knowing the linguistic and ecological settings of Kpelle thought leads the investigators beyond the concrete-abstract dichotomy. Instead of merely stating that Kpelle thinking is generally context-dependent, they have conducted research on thinking in the specific contexts typical of the culture. They find, for example, that Kpelle do better than Americans at estimating the number of cups of rice in a container (something they habitually do at the market) and the number of stones in a pile (stones are used as markers), and in solving a problem using the logical connective of disjunction (their language distinguishes inclusive from exclusive disjunction more explicitly than English). These tasks, like the ones in which Americans exceed Kpelle, vary in their degree of concreteness or abstractness and so do the means of solving them. Some Kpelle solutions do involve verbal mediation, within the conceptual capacities provided by their language and habitualized by their customary life. At this highly specific level of discourse about cognition, it is impossible to ignore the linguistic resources available to the individual as a determinant of success or failure in solving certain types of problems.

This lengthy discussion began with the importance of inquiring into why some groups of children do poorly on intelligence tests. The point was that the tasks posed for them by intelligence tests, or other measures of cognitive performance, were to some degree unfamiliar, and that the unfamiliarity is worthy of investigation in its own right. Three determinants of unfamiliarity were revealed:

1. Habitual unthinking obedience and awe in the presence of adults.
2. Lack of experience in verbal mediation, verbal labeling, or dealing with words independently of the contexts in which they are customarily used.
3. Culture-specific cognitive patterns differing from Western ones and acquired as habits adaptive for conformity to economic role demands or to syntactical rules of the vernacular language.

Each of these factors was seen to influence the cognitive functioning of children in a direction typical for this population but incompatible with performing well on at least some of the tests and measures of thinking devised by Western psychologists. Thus their poor performance, if followed to its roots, is an indicator of the kind of cognitive functioning and development characteristic of the population studied. A major research question raised was the stability and persistence of these cognitive patterns; it was observed that even a few years of schooling and particularly learning to write seems to remove the most pronounced effects of inexperience with context-free verbal labels and to raise performance on some tests up to Western levels. The evidence suggests a powerful influence of literacy on cognitive development, which was partly hidden when cognitive studies were limited to populations in which all children went to school. But there is little evidence to date on the reversibility of the habitual compliance or economically and linguistically adaptive cognitive patterns that also decrease performance level

on some Western tests. It is abundantly clear that investigators need to pay a great deal of attention to the ecological, economic, interactive, cultural, and linguistic contexts in which cognitive development takes place in other societies. More specifically, they need to find out enough about variations in and apparent effects of such factors to design studies in which they are systematically varied, as school-going has already been varied in African studies. It is only through such studies that we will be able to discover the varieties of cognitive development patterns in human populations rather than seeing some populations as inexplicably deficient.

The careful reader will have noticed that, in order to draw some general methodological conclusions from the studies discussed, this reviewer has had to combine investigations using diverse performance measures as if they were all measuring a unitary entity of cognition. Strictly speaking, this is unjustified and is partly due to the lack of consensus in this field about what to measure and how to measure it. The number of research instruments purportedly measuring a cognitive capacity in children and applicable cross-culturally is potentially vast, and there is a tendency for different investigators to use different instruments but to draw general conclusions about cognitive development. In attempting to limit the resultant intellectual chaos, it will be necessary for cross-cultural investigators to begin with a more coherent approach to cognitive development than the single instrument itself provides. There are four different approaches or research strategies suggested by the literature to date.

1. The approach of Gay and Cole (1967), which is to begin with an ethnographic and linguistic description of cognition in a cultural group, in terms of the modes of thought conventionally used by adults for adaptation, the ways in which logical relationships are expressed in the vernacular language, the ways children seem to acquire knowledge and conventional cognitive patterns, and the nature of local classroom instruction and children's reaction to it. Research instruments specifically aimed at tapping the differences in cognitive functioning between the population under study and Western populations —some selected from Western psychology,

others devised in the field—are administered to children and adults in the field and in Western contrast groups to yield differential profiles of cognitive capacities. Age comparisons are made to arrive at some conclusions concerning the direction of development over time in the local context of the population studied.

2. The approach used by Kohlberg (1966) in his noncomparative studies, which takes seriously Piaget's concept of developmental structures of thought in its implication of consistency of response level across different tasks at the same structural level. Each structural level is operationalized into a number of tests or tasks that are administered repeatedly to children as they grow older, and their performance is compared to their performance on a battery of the usual psychometric tests of intellectual abilities. The degree of cross-task consistency of performance indicates the validity of assuming some general cognitive structures, and the correlation of psychometric test scores with the Piaget tests indicates the relation of structural levels to conventional measures of intellectual competence. A wide variety of inferences about cognitive development is possible using this approach. Previous cross-cultural studies of Piaget tasks have typically involved administering one or two tasks to children of different ages in another culture, observing whether or not Piaget's sequence of stages was reproduced, noting the ages at which a stage was typically attained, and relating observed deviations from the sequence or age of attainment of Western children to environmental conditions in the culture under study. Kohlberg's (1966) own cross-cultural study of the development of dream concepts in American and Atayal (a Malaysian aboriginal group in Taiwan) children differs from this pattern, though not radically; he shows that Atayal children go through the same stages as American children, although more slowly, until the age of 11, when training in the religious beliefs of their culture—involving dreams as soul-wanderings caused by ghosts—reverses their tendency to think of dreams as subjective phenomena. But the advantages of Kohlberg's approach for cross-cultural studies will only be realized when his full research design is replicated in drastically different cultures, so that an assess-

ment of developmental structures rather than task-specific responses can be made comparatively.

3. In the approach of Bruner et al. (1966), a general theory of cognitive development is advanced in which cognition is explicitly viewed as a means of interacting with an environment, and stages are described—enactive, ikonic, symbolic representations of experience—that are seen as partly produced by that environment and adaptive in it. This differs from the theory of Piaget in emphasizing the adaptive values of different modes of representing experience in different environmental contexts. Cross-cultural investigation is conducted not merely with the replicative intent of discovering universal sequences of cognitive development but in order to find cultural environments varying in their general adaptive demands and the particular conditions of childhood experience in ways hypothesized to affect the development from one stage of representing experience to another. This approach can stand for that type of theory that includes a cross-culturally applicable concept of environmental conditions in its conceptualization of cognitive development.

4. The final approach to be mentioned is a less theoretical one in which developmental trends and cross-cultural differences are allowed to emerge from the application of fairly standard psychological instruments rather than being hypothesized a priori or defined in terms of culture-specific criteria of adaptation. This would involve a concept of mental abilities as varied types of intellectual competence (e.g., verbal, numerical, spatial) that can be found in all human populations to some degree but not necessarily the same degree, with the expectation that a population might be relatively high in one type and low in another (see Lesser, Fifer, and Clark, 1965, for an example of this model). For cross-cultural investigation, a number of different measures of each mental ability would be carefully selected to vary the response biases contributed by each instrument and aim for convergent validation. Each instrument used either would be well known to Western psychologists in terms of its correlations with various independent measures of performance or would be run against such measures prior to cross-cultural work. For

optimal results, this kind of study should involve large samples from a large number of diverse populations so that multivariate analysis could be applied both within and between populations. Within such an overall strategy, even conventional psychometric methods could contribute much more to the comparative understanding of cognitive development than is represented in the literature to date.

Social and Motivational Development

It is the opinion of this reviewer that cross-cultural uniformities and variations in the social dispositions and motives of children cannot be adequately summarized at this point. One reason for this is that five major comparative studies promising to surpass anything done to date are currently in progress or being written up, and it is reasonable to expect that their results will render obsolete any statements that could be made on the basis of presently available evidence. The first of these is the observational data on 134 children from the Six Cultures Study (B. B. Whiting, 1966) covering 12 variables of interpersonal behavior in natural settings in the Philippines, Okinawa, Mexico, New England, and Africa (see Longabaugh, 1966, for a factor analysis of these data). Second is the study of compliance behavior of schoolchildren in five diverse societies by R. D. Hess, L. Minturn, and their collaborators. Third is the study of coping behavior in children and adolescents in the United States, Latin America, and Europe by R. J. Havighurst, R. Peck, R. Diaz-Guererro, and their associates. Fourth, the study of sex identity in children drawn from a number of groups in Africa and the Americas by J. W. M. Whiting and his collaborators. And, finally, the study of moral development in Taiwan, Turkey, Yucatan, and the United States by L. Kohlberg and his associates. All of these studies will produce age and sex comparisons as well as cross-cultural ones, and at least one study is longitudinal. A great deal of thought has gone into the selection and development of instruments, and in most cases ethnographic material for interpretation is being supplied by members of the research team who were raised in the culture studied or anthropologists who have worked there. When these results are in, we shall be in a better position to generalize about similarities and differences in social and motivational development across the species.

One large-scale study of social development that has been published and deserves review here is the Lambert and Klineberg (1967) study of national stereotypes in children. The sample consisted of 3300 children at 3 age levels (ages 6, 10, and 14) from schools in 10 nations selected for general diversity and availability: the United States (Watertown, Massachusetts), South Africa (Zulu and Sotho children in Johannesburg), Brazil (Recife), Canada (English-speaking and French-speaking children in Montreal), France (Paris), Germany (West Berlin), Israel (children of European and Oriental origins in Jerusalem and Tel Aviv), Japan (Kyoto), Lebanon (Christians, Moslems and Druzes in Beirut), and Turkey (Istanbul). The open-ended interview procedures were organized and administered by investigators of local origin in each case. Quantitative comparison revealed a great many similarities and differences across groups defined by nationality, sex, and social class. Some developmental trends were common to most of the groups. For example:

. . . At the 6-year age level many different national groups of children made overgeneralized statements about the personality traits of their own group at the same time as they described foreign peoples in more factual, objective terms. Thus, the stereotyping process itself appears to get its start in the early conceptions children develop of their own group, and it is only much later, from 10 years of age on, that children start stereotyping foreign peoples. By the time they are 10 and 14, children apparently become concerned with foreign peoples as something more than comparison groups (Lambert and Klineberg 1967, pp. 223–224).

The authors interpret this evidence as requiring modification of the view presented by Piaget and Weil (1951), in which concepts of our own and foreign people develop simultaneously as part of the shift away from egocentric thinking. Lambert and Klineberg favor a view emphasizing environmental factors which facilitate the acquisition of certain information. They also found that ten-year-olds were generally more favorable to foreign peoples than children older or younger and that boys were more favorable than girls.

Some of the factors accounting for differences across national and other groups are explored, particularly gross aspects of national geography and recent international relations. But there is only a minimal attempt to interpret the findings in terms of a comparative analysis of the different sociopolitical environments of the samples of children studied or in terms of differences in child training; the authors recommend future research on these topics. The study as a whole, although it presents profiles of results for each sample, provides little information on the cultural contexts in which the national stereotypes develop, which severely limits the possibilities for understanding the results. Like the international study of mathematics achievement (Husen, 1967), this internationally coordinated study seems to leave many of the most intriguing variations unaccounted for because they would involve detailed local knowledge which the coordinating analysts of the study did not possess. Even so, when we are able to examine these results alongside the results from the five other comparative studies mentioned above, it should be possible to draw some conclusions about the psychological processes involved in social development.

The other reasons for not summarizing the literature to date are indicative of the nature of research on this subject. The most significant studies by far are those that do not limit themselves to merely documenting differences in children's social behavior or motives between populations but attempt to account for the differences in terms of variations in childhood experience; for this reason, they are summarized in the section on antecedent-consequent relationships rather than the present section. Many investigators of social and motivational development are environmentalists seeking in early experience the roots of adult personality and social behavior patterns which are assumed to have their precursors in children's behavior and attitudes. Their goal is to test hypotheses linking antecedents and consequents, and they take the associations and correlations their data reveal as contributing information concerning the validity of the theoretical constructs that inspired their research. The focus on construct validity,

to the neglect of other types of validation of the psychological measures employed, leads to some consequences that are unfortunate from a comparative point of view. For one thing, hardly any two investigators use the same research instruments, so that results of different studies are not comparable. Many devise their own instruments to accord with the hypotheses they are testing and the key concepts of those hypotheses, and most of the others alter previously used techniques in attempting to improve them. Although these investigators undoubtedly view their more precise operationalism as far superior to using "canned" techniques like standard psychometric tests, their procedures (taking different studies together) lack not only the comparability of such tests but also the reliability and validity, which for new techniques are often unknown and unreported. Their assumption is of course that if their techniques were excessively lacking in reliability and validity (apart from face validity), they would not be able to show antecedent-consequent relationships. Be that as it may, this approach simply does not produce a cumulative body of descriptive evidence concerning similarities and differences among human populations. No such body of evidence will be able to accumulate until there is more agreement among investigators on the research instruments to be used.

The focus on antecedent-consequent relationships has also operated to diminish attention to age trends; few studies in this area are developmental in the sense of measuring the same disposition over time, even in a cross-sectional design. The bulk of the research reports involve findings that children of a *given* age in two or three cultural or national groups, usually selected by convenience rather than on a theoretical basis, have different attitudes, expectations, or aspirations and that these are plausible in terms of concomitant differences (not quantitatively measured) in value system, family structure, or other aspects of culture. Unless set in the context of a larger institutional or psychological comparison, such findings are of limited information value, particularly when—as is often the case—the attitude investigated is little more than the child's report that he is aware of some aspects of his social and cultural environment.

In this selective survey of cross-cultural psychological data on infant motor development, perceptual development, cognitive development (postponing social and motivational development to a later section), we have encountered some of the difficulties and shortcomings discussed earlier. Foremost among them has been the increasing disagreement on what to measure and how to measure it as one moves from the Müller-Lyer illusion to more elusive aspects of behavior and development. Another finding is that relatively little real developmental information is available after the first few years of life. It is hoped that this painful exposure of deficiencies in our knowledge has identified and emphasized researchable areas and problems sufficiently to stimulate future work.

CROSS-CULTURAL CONSTANCIES AND VARIATIONS IN THE ENVIRONMENTS OF INFANTS AND CHILDREN

In the 15 years since Whiting and Child (1953, pp. 63-105) summarized and illustrated child-training variations among societies the world over that had been described in ethnographic publications, anthropologists and other students of socialization processes have amassed an enormous amount of documentation on this subject. The emphasis has been on variation; the environment of the human individual has been shown to vary from birth in amount of mother-infant contact, nutrition and feeding practices, sleeping arrangements, caretaking patterns, number of caretakers and others with whom he interacts, age at weaning from the breast, toilet training, and other early disciplines; verbal stimulation, contact with father, exposure to adult behavior in various settings, method and severity of punishment, age at induction into economic roles, values inculcated by reinforcement and direct tuition, method of teaching, transition rituals and other separation experiences, etc. No matter how the environment of infancy and childhood is defined —in terms of meeting organic needs, in terms of social interaction and sociospatial context, in terms of culturally mediated meanings and values, or all three—there are significant variations across human populations. Environments vary on so many dimensions concurrently that the exact nature of their

causal impact on behavioral variations is by no means self-evident; sophisticated research designs are required to disentangle naturally confounded influences.

On the whole, less attention has been paid to constancies or uniformities in environments. Whiting and Child stated:

. . . Child training the world over is in certain important respects identical . . . in that it is found always to be concerned with certain universal problems of behavior. Parents everywhere have similar problems to solve in bringing up their children. In all societies the helpless infant, getting his food by nursing at his mother's breast and having digested it, freely evacuating the waste products, exploring his genitals, biting and kicking at will, must be changed into a responsible adult obeying the rules of his society. . . . There is no clear evidence in any case that any of these basic problems are in fact absent from the life of any people. Child training everywhere seems to be in considerable part concerned with problems which arise from universal characteristics of the human infant and from universal characteristics of adult culture which are incompatible with the continuation of infantile behavior (1953, pp. 63-64).

In addition to the universal functional problems of socializing the impulse life of children, it has been suggested that childhood environments have a structural universal in the nuclear family of wife, husband, and children (with sexual relations permitted only between husband and wife) and other functional universals in insuring infant survival and giving children positive competence and role training for future social participation. Such suggestions have for the most part been theoretical, and empirical research has been focused on exploring the range of environmental diversity in the belief that any statements of universals must take account of this extraordinarily broad range. Few have concerned themselves with actually researching species-specific universals or those derived from our primate heritage. The techniques of Ainsworth (1967) for observing mother-infant interaction and the development of attachments may, if applied cross-culturally, yield some precise evidence concerning species universals of early care and social interaction that are adapted to the human organism and its unique capacities and weaknesses. Our present empirical knowledge of universals, however, is generated primarily from the study of variations and tends to be formulated as rather vague limits on a broad range of variation.

In reviewing some illustrative aspects of cross-cultural variations in environments, the problem of their psychological relevance should be borne in mind. Developmental psychologists sometimes turn to other cultures for "normal" examples of what is found only in deviant cases in their own culture; this is a major argument for cross-cultural studies. It often turns out, however, that the initial ethnographic account either was not accurate (as in Ainsworth's instance of weaning and mother-infant separation, described earlier) or did not take into account a variety of contextual factors that mitigate the developmental event and make it questionable to use as a parallel to the original pathogenic pattern. Thus, although it is possible to find cultures in which children are cared for by nonparents, where children regularly observe parental sexual relations, where a variety of separation experiences are institutionalized, the investigator is well advised to approach such ethnographic cases not with the assumption of traumatic impact carried over from the clinic but with the assumption that a population-wide pattern that has survived cannot be totally maladaptive and may not be identical to the one he has observed at home. It is his task to find out whether the environmental parallel is really apt and, if it is, how the pathogenic character of the event observed in our culture is avoided, diminished, or concealed in another population.

This review is limited to examples of cross-cultural differences in early environments that have been demonstrated quantitatively. In searching for such illustrative data, we discovered that although the interview designed by Sears, Maccoby, and Levin (1957) for their study of mothers in the Boston area had been adapted for use in a number of studies—for example, in the Six Cultures Study (see Minturn and Lambert, 1964), in Puerto Rico by Landy (1959), in Lebanon by Pro-

thro (1962), and in the Philippines by Guthrie and Jacobs (1966)—each investigator had so altered the interview schedule or manner of reporting results that there were no comparable findings across the full range of published studies. This sad state of affairs is no doubt contrary to the intent of the investigators, but it indicates that greater efforts at comparability are required if environmental survey data are to be cumulative. It was nevertheless possible to find examples of quantitative comparisons in a more limited range of populations.

The first example concerns the size and composition of the primary groups in which the child grows up, which can reasonably be expected to have an effect on the social interaction in which he becomes engaged. B. Whiting (1966) presents the figures on household and "courtyard" (i.e., a domestic unit of close interaction but larger than the individual household) for the six communities involved in the Six Culture Study (Table 1).

On interpersonal density of household, the greatest contrast is between India and New England, with households in the former averaging more than twice as many persons in each category. The Kenya community has the most children per household but the fewest men, since in this polygynous community each wife has her own house with her children; for this group it is the "courtyard," the polygynous extended family, that is the effective domestic unit. At the "courtyard" level, New England has less than half the average number of persons (total) of any community except the Okinawan. The New England community also has the smallest average number of children by far, reflecting differences in birth rates between industrial societies like the United States and the nonindustrial peoples of Asia, Africa, and Latin America, among whom many infants are born though a smaller proportion live to maturity. The variation in the interpersonal environments of children indicated by these figures is very great indeed.

Similar variations in household density are shown by Whiting et al. (1966) for three of the groups of the Harvard Values Study —the Zuni, Mormons, and Texans—all living in discrete communities in the same part of New Mexico. The Zuni average three persons

Table 1. Composition of Households and Courtyards in Six Communities

	Taira (Okinawa)	Tarong (Philippines)	Khalapur (India)	Juxtlahuaca (Mexico)	Orchard Town (New England)	Nyansongo (Kenya)
Household Average no. of adult males	1.3	1.4	2.6	1.3	1.0	.87
Average no. of adult females	1.8	1.7	2.4	1.2	1.0	1.0
Average no. of children	3.5	3.5	5.7	4.0	2.8	5.8
Courtyard Average no. of adult males	1.4	3.2	2.9	2.9	1.1	2.1
Average no. of adult females	1.8	4.3	2.6	3.0	1.2	3.2
Average no. of children	3.9	7.9	5.9	6.7	2.8	7.1
Total	7.1	15.4	11.4	12.6	5.1	12.4

B. Whiting, 1966.

per room, the Mormons two, and the Texans one, suggesting major differences in the psychological ecology of early life.

Another aspect of psychological ecology concerns sleeping arrangements—which family members sleep together? Whiting and Whiting (1959) point out that in most societies, unlike the middle-class norm in our own, infants sleep with their mothers. The most careful large-scale study of sleeping arrangements in a single population is that of Caudill and Plath (1966), who surveyed 323 households in 3 Japanese cities. Their results deviate so sharply from what we know to be typical of our own society that comparative figures are unnecessary to show American-Japanese differences.

Until the age of 15 (years) a child has about a 50 per cent chance of sleeping with one or both parents. From birth to age 15, a child's chances of co-sleeping with a sibling gradually increase; and before age 15 only a few children are likely to sleep alone (1966, p. 359).

There is little change in access to a parent in sleeping arrangements during the transition from infancy to childhood. In contrast, there is a sharp physical separation from the parents during this transition in the urban American family, if indeed such a separation had not already been made in infancy. . . . In Japan, the path seems to lead toward increasing interdependence with other persons, whereas in America the path seems to lead toward increasing independence from others. . . . From the age of 16 to 26 (years) or more, roughly 20 per cent of the children continue to co-sleep in a two-generation group, mainly with a parent; and about 40 per cent co-sleep in a one-generation group, mostly with a sibling (1966, p. 361).

In summary, then, an individual in urban Japan can expect to co-sleep in a two-generation group, first as a child and then as a parent, over approximately half of his life. This starts at birth and continues until puberty; it resumes after the birth of the first child and continues until about the time of menopause for the mother; and it reoccurs for a few years in old age. . . . Sleeping arrangements in Japanese families tend . . . to underplay (or largely ignore) the potentiality for the growth of conjugal intimacy between husband and wife in sexual and other matters in favor of a more general familial cohesion (1966, p. 363).

Evidence of this kind shows how variable is the gross, observable context of experience in infancy and early childhood. Mother-infant interaction is also variable. On the comparison of 30 American and 30 Japanese infants of 3-4 months old referred to in an earlier section, Caudill and Weinstein (1966) report:

Turning now to the difference between the two cultures in the caretaker's behavior, we believe that the key categories are talks to and rocks. The American mother is significantly ($p < .02$) talking to her baby more, while the Japanese mother is rocking ($p < .005$) her baby more. Thus, the style of the American mother seems to be in the direction of stimulating her baby to respond by use of her voice, whereas the style of the Japanese mother seems to be more in the direction of soothing and quieting her baby by non-verbal means (1966, p. 18).

In the Harvard Values Study, Whiting et al. (1966, pp. 90–92) were able to show major differences in infant care among the three groups surveyed (see Table 2).

Although these data are taken from retrospective interviews with mothers and hence of doubtful reliability, the differences they show are consistent with each other and with the respective values of the three groups as described by anthropologists: the Texans

Table 2. Group Differences in Infant Care

	Child Breast Fed Only	Median Age of Weaning (Months)	Median Age of Onset of Toilet Training (Months)
Texans (N = 16)	44%	9	9
Mormons (N = 15)	68%	11	12
Zuni (N = 15)	86%	24	18

Whiting et al., 1966.

Table 3. Proportion of Time Mother Cared for Infant in Six Cultures

	Percent of High Scores
Orchard Town (New England)	92
Taira (Okinawa)	58
Tarong (Philippines)	50
Juxtlahuaca (Mexico)	50
Khalapur (India)	46
Nyansongo (Kenya)	38

Minturn, Lambert, et al. 1964, p. 97.

breast-feed least frequently and began weaning and toilet training earliest, the Zuni are at the opposite end on all three variables, and the Mormons fall in the middle. A variety of less directly comparable evidence seen by this reviewer suggests that in these aspects of infant care and training, the Texans are roughly representative of the populations of northern Europe and the United States, the Zuni of folk and peasant populations of the New World, Asia, and Africa, and neither is particularly extreme. In other words, these New Mexico communities illustrate a major tendency in cross-cultural variation but they do not represent its entire range.

In the factor analysis of the retrospective mother interviews from the Six Cultures Study by Minturn, Lambert, et al. (1964), Proportion of Time Mother Cared for Baby emerged as a separate factor, showing large intersociety variance, most of it due to the fact that only in the Orchard Town (New England) sample did mothers of infants spend most of their time in infant care. In the other five cultures, mothers had other adults or children to take over care of their infants while they attended to other important chores. Table 3 shows the relative position of the six samples on the variable with the highest loading ($+.72$) on this factor.

The difference between Orchard Town and Okinawa is statistically significant ($x^2 = 7.11$, $p < .01$), as is the distribution as a whole $x^2 = 15.66$, $p < .01$). These data indicate major cross-cultural variations in sheer amount of mother-infant contact in the daytime and that, in this comparison, the American group is unique in the exclusiveness of mother's role as infant caretaker. There are few non-Western societies in which infant care and associated household tasks are regarded as constituting a full-time job for a woman, but in most societies other caretakers are more readily available.

Without going further into the abundant evidence, we can conclude that cross-cultural variations in the environments of infants appear large and manifold, even if one's view is limited to available quantitative data. Infants in culturally different populations vary in the household density, sleeping arrangements, amount of contact with mother, amount of verbal and motoric stimulation by mother, probability of being breast-fed, and age of weaning and toilet training to which they are subjected.

Variations in childhood environment are equally great or more so. The data presented previously on size and composition of households and other domestic groups and on sleeping arrangements must be seen as evidence for cross-cultural differences in the interpersonal environments of children as well as infants. And it is not only the number of persons and the age and sex composition of units that varies, but the kinship, authority, and functional relations in the units, producing variations in the standards of behavior children must learn to conform to and variations in the models for behavior they are exposed to. Out of the vast amount of data on socialization of the child, a few quantitative examples will be presented.

The handling of aggression in children is a prominent topic in the literature. Minturn, Lambert, et al. (1964) found two aggression factors in the factor analysis of the Six Culture Study mother interviews, one concerning the mother's reaction to aggression directed toward her and one concerning her restrictive and punitive handling of aggression against other children. The second factor showed large differences between societies (Table 4).

The Mexican sample is by far the most restrictive of children's fighting and other expression of aggression, while the New England sample deviates from all the rest in its permissiveness, even encouraging children to retaliate when attacked. Turning to the Harvard Values Study, we find a similar range of variation: of the Zuni mothers, 77% were rated high on intolerance of aggression among peers; the corresponding figures were 69% for the Mormons and 6% for the Texans (Whiting et al., 1966, p. 101). The Texans, like the New Englanders, stand out for their tolerance of children's fighting.

In a large-scale survey of child-rearing

Table 4. Percent of Cases with Positive Factor Scores on Maternal Restriction of Peer-Directed Aggression in Six Cultures

	Percent of + Cases
Juxtlahuaca (Mexico)	91
Taira (Okinawa)	63
Khalapur (India)	63
Nyansongo (Kenya)	63
Tarong (Philippines)	57
Orchard Town (New England)	8

practices in Lebanon, Prothro (1962, p. 157) found that more "modern" mothers, that is, Christian middle-class mothers of Beirut, were more likely to believe that a child should learn how to fight when necessary than rural Moslems, particularly peasant farmers. He saw this as part of a modern-traditional difference in child rearing. Some data collected among the Yoruba in Nigeria in a project directed by the present reviewer (see LeVine, Klein, and Owen, 1967, for a description of the project) point in the same direction. Interviews were conducted in the city of Ibadan with 31 Yoruba mothers characterized by a relatively traditional life-style and 35 Yoruba "elite" mothers with a secondary school education and something like a modern, suburban life-style. Applying the scale from Sears, Maccoby, and Levin (1957, p. 246), "Mother strongly discourages aggression against other children (excluding siblings)," it was found that 87.4% of the traditionals and 42.9% of the elites could be so characterized. In these and other data, contemporary Western child-rearing values seem to entail tolerance of children's fighting and other aggressive encounters, and it looks as if Westernization among nonindustrial agricultural peoples involves relaxation of traditional constraints on childhood aggression. Minturn, Lambert, et al. (1964) and Whiting et al. (1966) argue that the psychological effect of overcrowding in household and courtyard is the crucial ecological variable accounting for severe aggression training. Referring to the Zuni, Whiting et al. state:

We presume that crowded living conditions required an emphasis on harmony and strict control of aggression. We believe this to be a consequence, not so much of the sheer number of people living under one roof, as of the requirement that several women share in the running of a household (1966, p. 113).

In regard to the process of Westernization, perhaps it would be most correct to state that if the traditional society was highly intolerant of aggression in children, which is not true of all non-Western groups by any means, then Westernization in life-style would be accompanied by reduction in severity of aggression training. It is not clear whether this is due to changes in household size (or complexity) or independent attitude change, but it is clear that there are large differences in aggression training among contemporary peoples of the world. It does not seem too far-fetched to propose that these differences might be related to the differences in compliance and active mastery noted previously in the section on cognitive development. In other words, the severe aggression training of some traditional African, Latin American, and other peoples may be part of a larger tendency to make children orderly, obedient, and pacific, producing an inhibitedness that manifests itself in performance on cognitive tasks.

Teaching methods and instructional content also vary widely across cultures. In some groups that have no schools, as mentioned in the section on cognitive development, there is no explicit teaching, only observation and imitation by children and correction of mistakes by their elders, without any statements of general principles—an instructional procedure that differs greatly from our own. In such folk and peasant societies, children often begin adult tasks as early as they are physically capable and can make themselves useful by so doing; they can usually perform adult subsistence roles quite competently before puberty, which puts a very different cast on adolescence as a stage of life from the one to which we are accustomed. The ecological pressures on the society as a whole make themselves felt more directly in childhood.

A major interest of cross-cultural researchers in the last 10 years has been in attempting to demonstrate that child-rearing practices and other aspects of infant and child experience are caused or influenced by social-structural, economic, and ecological factors, as suggested earlier by Kardiner and Linton (1939) and Whiting and Child (1953). For example, Barry, Child, and Bacon (1958) showed relations between subsistence economy (hunting and gathering, agriculture, pastoralism) and the training of children in achievement, obedience, self-reliance, and responsibility in a large sample of societies; Whiting (1961) showed a relation between household size and infant indulgence; and (as mentioned earlier) both Whiting et al. (1966) and Minturn, Lambert, et al. (1964) have argued with evidence that household size is related to severity of aggression training. The causal directions hypothesized in these correlational studies may be open to doubt, but they have at least demonstrated that aspects of infant care and child training covary cross-culturally with a larger institutional and ecological context.

ANTECEDENT-CONSEQUENT RELATIONS: EFFECTS OF ENVIRONMENT ON INFANT AND CHILD BEHAVIOR

The primary interest in cross-cultural studies of child development has always been to find environmental causes of subsequent behavioral development. In putting this section at the end this reviewer is reversing the usual priorities in order to suggest that there are many prior questions that need to be answered before we can ask what the antecedents in early experience of later behavior and development are. From the viewpoint of the etiological model proposed here, we need to know more about the developmental variations we are trying to account for before launching a full-scale search for causal factors. In other words, we need to have more comparable information on children and their behavior and how it changes over time in different human populations before we begin the real work of explaining it in environmental or any other terms. But the lure of cross-cultural research related to development has always been that of the dramatic environmental variations sampled in the foregoing section, so we have a body of cross-cultural literature on the effects of early experience on personality development. This literature has two distinct parts: cross-cultural surveys using societies rather than individuals as units and involving secondary analysis of ethnographic data, and individual differences studies carried out either in a population differing culturally from our own or in two or more culturally distinct populations.

Cross-Cultural Surveys

In their book *Child Training and Personality*, Whiting and Child (1953) adapted the method of cross-cultural survey—the quantitative analysis of ethnographic materials from a large sample of societies—to the study of antecedent-consequent relations in individual development. Previous surveys (e.g., Murdock, 1949) had regarded the associations and correlations shown among cultural characteristics as revealing the functional order in cultures and social structures as well as trends in sociocultural evolution. The ingenious adaptation of Whiting and Child was based on an analogue with learning experiments, in which correlational analysis is applied to data on differential treatment and differential subsequent behavior of animals in standard situations, indicating the predictive value of hypotheses linking treatment variables with performance variables in a causal sequence. Whiting and Child argued that if cross-cultural variations in child-training customs could be regarded as treatment variables, and customary beliefs and practices (hypothetically influenced by unconscious motives) as performance variables, the observed associations and correlations would reflect on the possibility of universal connections between the two in individual development. Correlation would not demonstrate causal connection, but lack of observed relation would disconfirm causal hypotheses, allowing research attention to be focused on hypotheses that had survived the correlational test.

The research reported by Whiting and Child (1953) themselves remains the largest single study of this type carried out and reported in the literature. The most striking of its findings, taken as a whole, is that severe or punitive training in a given motivational system (e.g., dependence, aggression) tends to be related cross-culturally to beliefs reflecting anxious preoccupation in that motivational system, whereas relative indulgence tends not to be related to relevant cultural beliefs. In the causal interpretation of Whiting and Child, this was taken to indicate, among other things, that the psychoanalytic concept

of fixation as due to excessive frustration *or* indulgence at a given psychosexual stage needs to be modified, since indulgence showed no discernible effect. In their volume, hypotheses concerning the role of identification in the development of guilt and the relation of aggression training to the projection and displacement of aggression in sorcery and other magical and religious beliefs are also examined in great detail.

The Whiting and Child study was a major landmark in cross-cultural research on child development; it lifted the field out of the case study phase into systematic hypothesis-testing and it established once and for all the relevance of anthropological data on the full range of human variation to the concerns of developmental psychology. It became a methodological model for many other hypothesis-testing studies. In 1961, Whiting reviewed those done from 1953 to 1960, showing relations between child training variables and male initiation ceremonies (Whiting, Kluckhohn, and Anthony, 1958), menstrual taboos (Stephens, 1962), kin avoidance customs (D'Andrade in Stephens, 1962), decorative art, mourning customs, and malevolence-benevolence of gods (Lambert, Triandis, and Wolf, 1959). His review article presents Whiting's later views on the relation between childhood experience and religion, art, and folklore, his interpretation of empirical studies on the subject, and a method for extracting causal inferences from correlational data. Theoretically, there is a shift away from the behaviorism of the Whiting and Child volume (1953) toward a more psychoanalytic position. Except for his discussion of aggression training, there is less emphasis on parental reinforcement during the years of socialization between 2 and 6 and more on patterns of indulgence, dependence, and control in infancy as independent variables. This shift coincides with greater attention to social-structural variables, notably those of household living and sleeping arrangements, which are seen as shaping the infant's earliest interpersonal experience and determining his initial identifications with human objects.

Whiting's social-structural theory of identification, based on assumptions concerning the child's envy and desire to be like those whom he views as controlling crucial resources, is spelled out in his study with Burton (Burton and Whiting, 1961) and has influenced other cross-cultural investigators, particularly with respect to the origins of cross-sex identity in males. For example, Bacon, Child, and Barry (1963) show that crimes of violence have some of the same cross-cultural correlates in infant care as male initiation ceremonies (Burton and Whiting, 1961), and both crimes and ceremonies are accounted for in terms of the prevalent male identity problems stemming from infantile experience. In a more recent cross-cultural study, Whiting (1964) pushes back the causal sequence from male initiation ceremonies to exclusive mother-child sleeping arrangements to the postpartum sex taboo favored by polygyny to the high infant mortality rate of low-protein populations, to the crops grown in areas high in rainfall and temperature. In other words, peoples inhabiting tropical areas with high rainfall are likely to have little protein food available to curtail fatal nutritional disorders in children; their cultural adaptation is to prolong lactation by marital arrangements in which husbands have several wives and cohabit with the nonlactating ones. The resulting exclusive mother-infant sleeping arrangements favor the development of a feminine identity in boys that can (in some social structures) cause difficulties in adapting to adult male sex role demands, and initiation ceremonies are an attempted cultural solution, or resolution. The developmental hypotheses in this theory are currently being subjected to psychological tests of individual differences by Whiting and his co-workers (see D'Andrade, 1966).

In the years since Whiting's (1961) review article, some dozen or more articles attempting to test antecedent-consequent relations through cross-cultural surveys have been published; several of them have already been mentioned. Most have used child-training measures derived either from the original Whiting and Child study (1953), that is, initial indulgence or socialization anxiety in one of several behavior systems, or from the subsequent studies of Barry, Bacon, and Child (1957) and Barry, Child, and Bacon (1958), that is, training in obedience, responsibility, nurturance, achievement, self-reliance, independence; some have used measures of mother-infant closeness and separation de-

rived from the later work of Whiting discussed earlier. The child-rearing antecedents have been found to be positively related to cultural variables such as female initiation ceremonies (Brown, 1963), the couvade (Burton and Whiting, 1961), games and folktale themes (Roberts and Sutton-Smith, 1962; Roberts, Sutton-Smith, and Kendon, 1963), love magic (Shirley and Romney, 1962), sibling terminology (Nerlove and Romney, 1967), drinking behavior (Bacon, Barry, and Child, 1965), and romantic love (Rosenblatt, 1966). Some of these studies, for example, the work of Roberts et al. on games and the monograph by Bacon, Barry, and Child on drinking behavior, represent major efforts at understanding psychologically significant aspects of culture regardless of whether their developmental hypotheses hold up in further replication. The use of the cross-cultural survey has even gone beyond culture to relate early treatment of infants to adult stature (Landauer and Whiting, 1964; Gunders and Whiting, 1968). This extensive literature deserves full-scale review of its own, in which the results of 15 years of research activity are examined in relation to one another. Such a review would range beyond the bounds of child psychology.

The research tradition initiated by Whiting and Child (1953) has generated an active opposition in those who accept the cross-cultural survey as a hypothesis-testing method but are skeptical of the psychological interpretation of culture or critical on methodological grounds. For example, the studies of male initiation ceremonies by Whiting, Kluckhohn, and Anthony (1958) and Burton and Whiting (1961) have stimulated two book-length counterstudies by Young (1965) and Cohen (1964), who show the ceremonies to be related to variables of social structure that do not require hypothetical links to infantile experience. Bock (1967) has challenged the Shirley and Romney study (1962) on grounds of areally biased sampling of societies. Young and Bacdayan (1965) have produced a sociological counterstudy of menstrual taboos to contradict Stephens' (1962) castration-anxiety argument. Cohen (1966) has attacked the reasoning in the Landauer and Whiting study (1964) of stature.

From the accumulating evidence on both sides it is clear that customs like child-rearing practices and the variety of cultural behavior patterns with which they have been hypothetically linked tend to be associated with many other customs, and these multiple associations lend themselves to a variety of interpretations, some of them sociological or ecological rather than psychological. This calls into question the adequacy of the analogy with learning experiments and the methodological model of searching for correlations between one or two treatment variables and one or two performance variables on the basis of a priori causal hypotheses. In the welter of multiple connections exhibited by cultural variables it is all too easy to find support for simple causal hypotheses by limiting one's investigation to a few variables rather than looking at the larger structure of relations in which they are embedded. A theoretical model that can handle complex multivariate relations would be more appropriate and is readily available in the functional-evolutionary formulation of Murdock (1949), which Whiting and Child (1953) recast in more causal terms. But the methodological implication of accepting a view of culture as "an interdependent causal network" evolving in *reciprocal* adaptation over time is, as Barkow (1967) points out, that cross-cultural surveys can yield only limited inferences about specific causal sequences like the possible effect of early experience on later individual development. To test generalizations about change, it is necessary to study organisms or societies during the process of change.

From the view point of child psychology, cross-cultural surveys, however suggestive and stimulating, are inadequate because they involve no direct measures of individuals as children or adults. In other words, the cross-cultural survey attempting to link early experience patterns with a cultural index of personality shares all the deficiencies and inferential gaps of cross-sectional designs in general plus a few of its own—the undemonstrated links between training and child behavior, between child behavior and personality as an adult, and between adult personality and culture pattern. Whiting and Child were keenly aware of these gaps, as indicated by the direct measures of child behavior in the Harvard Values Study (J. M. W. Whiting et al., 1966) and the Six Cultures Study of

Socialization (B. B. Whiting, 1966), but they have not given up the cross-cultural survey as a supplementary device for testing hypotheses.

Antecedent-Consequent Studies of Individual Differences

The cross-cultural investigator seeking to find invariant causal sequences between the antecedent experiences of individuals and their consequent behavior is faced with an inevitable quandary of practical limitations: if he attempts to work on individual differences within a single population, the generality of his findings are in doubt; whereas if he wants to test his hypotheses cross-culturally as well as at the level of individual differences, he cannot in a reasonable length of time accumulate data from enough populations for a genuine statistical comparison of societies. One of the main reasons that Whiting and others have retained the cross-cultural survey of ethnographic materials despite its obvious deficiencies is that, in effect, it is the only method that allows the use of systematic inductive procedures at the cross-cultural level. The Six Cultures Study of Socialization was designed as both a cross-cultural and individual-differences study, but six groups are not adequate for generalizing about humankind, especially when five of them are of one ecological type (agricultural). It could conceivably be replicated by a few dozen other investigators in other settings well distributed around the world, but the time and effort involved in the original study makes this highly unlikely.

Another approach to the problem of generality is to seek a population representing a type of environmental treatment or a range of treatments not available in our own society. This is the "crucial experiment" approach which the pioneering work of Margaret Mead in Samoa (1928) and New Guinea (1930) suggested. As a strategy in child psychology, it involves replicating the collection of individual data on environmental antecedents and behavioral effects in a setting deviating from our own in specified ways believed likely to shed particularly crucial light on how environment affects development. It is based on the same reasoning that leads investigators of normal children to seek institutionalized children and other deviant and pathological cases in order to better understand normal development and what keeps it from becoming pathological. Thus investigators interested in the effects of parent-child relations on personality development in children become interested in the Israeli kibbutzim, where parents do not raise their own children (Spiro, 1958; Rabin, 1965; Neubauer, 1965). Thus Ainsworth (1967), interested in the effects of mother-infant separation on development, decides to work among the Ganda, who are reputed to send infants away normally rather than because of family pathology and breakdown as in our own society. Thus Greenfield (in Bruner et al., 1966), interested in the effects of schooling on cognitive development, goes to the Wolof because some of their children do not go to school. As noted earlier, this reviewer believes that the "crucial experiment" is rarely as crucial as anticipated. At best, if it affords a type of comparison not available at home—like schooled versus unschooled children—it still must be fitted into a body of other evidence.

The kibbutz studies just cited, for example, have been relatively uninformative regarding the effect of living with parents on personality development for a number of reasons. For one thing, kibbutz children are not raised in total isolation from their parents even though they do not occupy the same house, eat together, or live in a situation of normal (Western) dependence of child on parents or normal discipline of parent over child. They know who their parents are and see and visit them regularly, with an apparently significant permanent attachment beginning in early life. Thus the parallel with orphans in our culture is a poor one, and the environmental deviations of kibbutz infancy and childhood from Western norms are more subtle than they seem at first. Second, many environmental factors other than parent-child contact vary between kibbutz samples and usual Western middle-class samples, a fact that becomes obvious when one thinks of a kibbutz as an agricultural community of 400-500 persons. Rabin (1965) handled this appropriately by comparing kibbutz children with children in *moshav* communities that are also small, agricultural, and in Israel, but not communal in economy or child-rearing practices. Third, in the absence of massive defects or other powerful effects obvious to the casual ob-

server, behavioral science techniques of systematic observation, testing, and clinical assessment have not yet produced unequivocal evidence on the psychological characteristics of kibbutz-raised children as contrasted with children raised by their parents. It is fairly clear that most of the kibbutz children are within the normal range in intelligence and mental health, but other developmental conclusions are subject to dispute. They may possibly be less intense in their Oedipal rivalries, more superficial in their object relations, more controlled by peer sanctions, and better adapted to army life, but behavioral scientists and clinicians have not reached agreement on these points, nor on more global issues of the superiority or inferiority of their psychological adjustment. Although the subject has not received the systematic research attention it deserves and further evidence may produce important insights, the kibbutz case is a good example of the risks involved in choosing a population for developmental study on the basis of striking environmental variations in the expectation of finding consequent psychological differences, instead of adopting the etiological strategy outlined earlier in this chapter.

Although the kibbutz studies have not yet deepened our detailed understanding of the effect of parents on personality development, they have contributed to knowledge of human development in the broader sense. They have shown that collective infant and child rearing need not inflict obvious damage on the intelligence and mental health of individuals. They have shown that a group of utopians could, on the basis of ideological principles, construct a new environment for children that, at least in the short run, produces individuals who personally support the principles of the founders, contribute to the maintenance of the community in its original form, and have some adaptive capacities that reflect their upbringing. The far-reaching implications of these facts for sociological theories of human development have not yet been fully digested, but from our point of view it is doubtful that specialized psychological research was needed to establish them.

In this section we shall examine a few promising examples of antecedent-consequent studies of individual differences. A genuine review seems premature at this point, particularly since the antecedent-consequent data are not yet available from the Six Cultures Study, the Whiting sex identity study, and the other ongoing projects mentioned in the section on social development. The cognitive development section included a discussion of several studies that compared performance of children undergoing different treatments—for example, schooled and unschooled—but those will not be reexamined here.

The most extensive effort to date to apply the etiological model cross-culturally in developmental psychology is represented by the literature on achievement motivation, which is reviewed elsewhere in this book. The study of n Achievement began as a problem of individual differences among American college students manifested in an experimental setting. Once the validity of these differences was established, a developmental dimension was added through the search for child-rearing antecedents (Winterbottom, 1958; Rosen and D'Andrade, 1958; McClelland et al., 1958), with simultaneous attention to ethnic differences and their antecedents. Correlational studies in the United States indicated that a pattern of maternal independence and achievement training, applied early and with a minimum of paternal interference, predicted subsequent n Achievement in boys. The next step was to discover whether this pattern was associated with differences in n Achievement between national populations. In the most thorough integration of cross-cultural research with personality psychology so far, McClelland (1961) reported some confirmation of the American results in a cross-cultural comparison of samples from Brazil, Germany, and Japan, but revealed a curvilinear relationship between age of independence training and achievement motivation, with an optimum average of a little over 8 years. Subsequent studies by Rosen (1962) and Bradburn (1963) have lent cross-cultural support to the pattern of child-rearing determinants emerging from U.S. studies. Rosen used a TAT measure of achievement motivation with 346 Brazilian boys aged 9 to 11 and 794 boys of roughly the same age from the Northeastern United States; data on perception of parents was collected from the boys, and a sample of their mothers was interviewed. Dividing the

boys' families into five social class groups, Rosen reported predominantly linear negative relations of social class with mean age of achievement training ($F = 29.2$; $p < .001$) and mean age of independence training ($F = 15.7$; $P < .001$) in both Brazil and the United States. Although n Achievement scores showed a somewhat similar distribution, except positively related to social class, the mean level of achievement motivation among Brazilian boys of all classes was so much lower than that of the boys in the U.S. sample that social class accounted for a smaller proportion of the variance. Rosen attributes the cross-national differences to the stronger presence in Brazil of an authoritarian, "father-centered" family structure in which the father, "far from encouraging independence, tends to thwart his son's efforts to be self-reliant and autonomous" (1962, p. 623). This finding is supported at an intracultural level by Bradburn (1963), who reports that in a Turkish sample, also characterized by an authoritarian, father-centered family structure and also scoring lower than Americans on n Achievement, men who had been raised apart from their fathers showed a significantly higher mean level of n Achievement than those raised at home with their fathers present. Taken together, these studies present a consistent picture of antecedent-consequent relations with respect to achievement motivation that is rare in cross-cultural studies; whether it will hold up in larger scale comparisons and longitudinal studies remains to be seen.

A number of studies reversing the etiological strategy have taken the antecedent variable of father absence as their point of departure and examined its hypothesized consequents in sex identity (D'Andrade, 1966), delinquency (see Burton and Whiting, 1961, for a review of the literature from a cross-cultural perspective), and delay of gratification (Mischel, 1961). Mischel's comparison of children in Trinidad and Grenada is particularly noteworthy, not merely for showing a relation between father-absence and delay of gratification in another culturally differing population, but in indicating how ethnic differences can be accounted for by structural effects in a cross-cultural comparison. Among both Trinidad and Grenada Negro children (aged 8-9), father-absence was associated with preference for immediate reinforcement, and the Trinidad group was significantly higher on delayed reinforcement when the whole groups and only father-present subjects were compared. The Trinidad East Indian children also scored higher on delayed reinforcement than the Trinidad Negro children, but the difference disappeared when only father-present subjects were compared. The suggestion is that the cultural factors determining the difference between Trinidad and Grenada Negro children cannot be reduced to the effects of father-absence, whereas father-absence accounts for the Negro-Indian difference in Trinidad. In a sample of Trinidad Negro children aged 11-14, no relation between father-absence and preferred type of reinforcement was found, raising the possibility that the observed effects are not permanent. This is the kind of antecedent-consequent research that raises important questions for future research. One of its implications— that father-absence does not have the same psychological meaning and consequence in all cultural contexts—must be taken into consideration by future investigators of the subject, regardless of the studies so far indicating that father-absence frequently affects psychological development.

If the hypothesized child-rearing antecedents of achievement motivation *seem* more strongly supported by research to date than the hypothesized consequents of father absence, it is not only because of a more comparable literature and mutually consistent body of findings but also because of face validity: the intervening variables between independence and achievement training and *n* Achievement scores are fewer and less open to dispute than those between father-absence and its alleged effects in sex identity, delinquency, and delay of gratification. In correlational studies involving identification and other complex processes more attention is required to the intervening variables.

The studies reviewed so far tested hypotheses of antecedent-consequent relations through statistical comparisons of individuals and groups on whom both antecedent and consequent measures were taken at a single point in development. This is the prevalent method in psychology, but it has the disadvantages that accrue to a purely cross-sectional approach and the retrospective account of antecedent variables. A radically different approach to environmental effects on behavioral development is based on ethology and attempts to observe a behavior pattern from its inception, taking account of environmental inputs and the unfolding of developmental phases along the way. In this vein, Ainsworth (1967) studied attachment behavior in 28 Ganda infants over a period of up to 32 weeks, during which time she visited their homes approximately every 2 weeks for a 2-hour visit and somewhat more frequently for briefer visits. When her observations began, the infants ranged in age from 2 days to 80 weeks, with a median of 24 weeks; her study involved an overlapping longitudinal design. During her visits, Ainsworth made detailed naturalistic observations of child and mother and also interviewed the mother. Her book presents extremely detailed evidence on every aspect of the research, including case summaries. On the basis of her notes she developed a catalog of sixteen patterns of attachment behavior and describes their change through a series of five phases she observed: the undiscriminating phase, differential responsiveness, differential responsiveness at a distance, active initiative, and stranger anxiety. Concerning this developmental pattern and its implications for the study of attachment, Ainsworth concludes:

Even though this study of Ganda babies does not enable us to answer some of the most crucial questions about attachment, it has highlighted several very significant points: attachment develops in an orderly way; a number of patterns of behavior have been identified as attachment behavior and emerge in orderly sequence over time; separation anxiety and stranger anxiety also undergo a developmental sequence, and although interlocked with the development of attachment, neither seems to be an adequate sole criterion for attachment; attachment to familiar figures other than the mother can emerge very soon after attachment to the mother (if not simultaneously), and this is particularly noteworthy in a society in which there is an especially close and intimate infant-mother relationship (1967, pp. 384-385).

Although Ainsworth discovered that a number of children became attached to persons other than the mother, including persons who did not feed or care for them, she used the criteria of strength and security of attachment to mother to classify all 28 into three groups: secure-attached, insecure-attached, and nonattached. She could not distinguish the three groups on the basis of maternal warmth, and although the mothers of all nonattached infants shared their mothering duties with others, enough of the mothers of attached infants did so that there was no statistically significant difference. Three variables did differentiate the three groups: (1) amount of care given by the mother (median test shows $p < .05$), (2) mother's excellence as an informant ($p < .05$), and (3) mother's reported enjoyment of breast-feeding ($p < .01$). Ainsworth interprets all three antecedents as reflecting more significant underlying variables; for example, the mother's excellence as an informant reflected her interest in and attention to the child, so that she was able to report a great deal about his behavior; enjoyment of breast-feeding appeared to be part of a broader set of attitudes toward contact with the infant. Although Ainsworth could have carried out this study in America and is currently doing so, the great differences in environmental context between the Ganda and the U.S. will make a replication of these results much more significant.

One of the most interesting implications of Ainsworth's study concerns weaning and is not based on statistical evidence since only eight children were weaned from the breast during the period of observation; three of them had been fed on schedule and five on demand. The latter showed considerably more disturbance than the former: "To the schedule-fed babies, weaning seems to cause little or no change in the baby's relationship with his mother. To the demand-fed babies, weaning seems to imply rejection by and separation from the mother" (1967, p. 412). The author hypothesizes that in demand feeding, in which the infant takes the initiative in feeding and has some control over it, "feeding behavior becomes an integral part of the whole organization of attachment behavior" (1967, p. 413), whereas for the schedule-fed child, who is allowed neither to take initiative in feeding nor to gain control over it, feeding response remains relatively independent of his relationship to his mother

as a person, and weaning does not affect that relationship. "The argument here is that attachment does not grow through receiving but through actively reaching out and attaching oneself" (1967, p. 413); since the activity of the schedule-fed child toward his mother does not involve the initiation of feeding, weaning can be carried out without threatening attachment. This subtle and testable hypothesis could have been based only on observations in a society in which breast-feeding is continued well into the period of full attachment (none of the Ganda infants was weaned earlier than 8 months) and in which both demand and schedule feeding occur. Ainsworth's work exemplifies the role of intensive observation in generating useful hypotheses for future research.

We have seen that antecedent-consequent studies of psychological development cross-culturally can be based on the model of experimental studies of learning, as in the n Achievement and father-absence studies, or on the model of ethological observation, as in Ainsworth's infant study. This does not exhaust available models of research. The work of Caudill in Japan represents an eclectic approach that begins with anthropological field study of a particular culture, its patterns of personality development and psychopathology, and its indigenous psychotherapy, and then borrows the methods of social survey, epidemiological survey, and longitudinal child study to provide quantitative data for the generation and testing of hypotheses. The survey data on Japanese sleeping arrangements by Caudill and Plath (1966) have been cited earlier in this chapter, as has the infant study of Caudill and Weinstein (1966), which is unique in psychological anthropology as a longitudinal comparison of Japanese and American samples. Caudill uses his knowledge of Japanese culture to make sense of the data collection, which has been going on for more than a decade, and continues. From different parts of the project, antecedent-consequent relations are emerging, for example in the analysis of data on 717 patients admitted in 1958 to four psychiatric hospitals in the Tokyo area. Caudill (1963) reports that among the psychotics, but not neurotics, eldest sons and youngest daughters are significantly overrepresented, particularly in the more traditional families in which children remain dependent on family resources until late in life. He is able to relate this to traditional parent-child relationships for children of different birth order and their maladaptive nature under contemporary socioeconomic conditions. This long-term project represents a model of research in which systematic methods from a variety of behavioral sciences are imported into an ethnographic study to yield meaningful data on antecedent-consequent relations in development.

SUMMARY

This chapter has been based on the view that cross-cultural study is a research strategy available to child psychology rather than a separate field of substantive interest; a parallel with social epidemiology in medicine was drawn and an etiological approach was proposed. From this viewpoint the reviewer believed this chapter could make a more lasting contribution by considering methodological problems and proposing methodological guidelines for cross-cultural study in child psychology rather than by attempting to summarize the early, fragmentary findings of a large but diffuse literature. Findings have been reviewed, but without the thoroughness that such a survey usually entails; relatively few of the items in the bibliography have been cited or discussed in the text, and the reader is invited to use the bibliography for purposes beyond those of the present chapter. It is nonetheless possible to provide a crude summary of cross-cultural knowledge of child development as it has appeared in this review.

Cross-cultural data of interest were divided into three types: those concerning the behavior and development of infants and children in human populations, those concerning the environments in which children are raised, and those relating environmental variations to behavioral variations as cause and effect. In all three types the emphasis, following that of the literature, was on variation across human populations rather than on constancies or universals. In the behavior and development of immature humans, investigators have succeeded in uncovering a great many dimensions of variation, although some of these may turn out to be due to the research instru-

ments rather than to the dispositions studied. The few available studies of infant motor behavior and development indicate that although universal features are most conspicuous, careful observation (among the Balinese, Ganda, and Japanese) uncovers marked deviations from Western norms. The precocious motor skill of Ganda infants, which diminishes drastically after the second year of life, appears to be present at birth and has given rise to speculation regarding prenatal determinants. The field of perception offers the most reliable data on cross-cultural differences (in illusion susceptibility, pictorial depth perception, and color-form preferences), which are substantial, but none of the data are on small children, so their developmental origins remain obscure. Perceptual differences between populations have been shown to correspond to their differing ecologies, lending support to theories of ecological determinism, and within populations some of them correlate with amount of schooling, suggesting that the dispositions involved can be modified by experience. Although differences between modern urban populations and traditional agriculturalists predominate in the literature, striking differences have also been shown between the latter and specialized hunters like the Eskimos, so that perceptual differences do not appear to be merely a function of degree of modernization.

Many of the same statements could be made about cognitive development but with less confidence and with some special problems about response set. One reason for this similarity is that some of the tests used to measure early cognitive performance depend heavily on perceptual skills. On the whole, children with no formal schooling in nonindustrial societies do poorly on tasks requiring verbal fluency, familiarity with pictorial representation of three-dimensional objects, abstract thinking, or active problem-solving skills—although some groups are notable exceptions. This means that they tend to score low on intelligence tests and to attain levels of development more slowly on Piaget tasks. It is not simply a question of Western tests with non-Western children, since the Japanese tend to score higher than Western populations on Western intelligence tests, but there are some important indications that the differences are less stable than they seem; for example, the performance levels of children in nonindustrial societies with only 2 years of schooling is much higher than that of their agemates who do not go to school and minor alterations in the tasks elevate performance drastically. The general drift of evidence is toward the conclusion that the largest differences between industrial and nonindustrial peoples are due to familiarity effects that are easily eliminated with practice in school or elsewhere. Other evidence suggests that early, severe training in obedience and compliance interferes with the capacity for active mastery involved in solving novel problems and has a permanently adverse effect on intellectual performance. The effects of such nonintellectual factors on intellectual performance constitute a promising topic for research. Another conclusion emerging from cross-cultural studies of cognitive development is that culture-specific cognitive skills can be found in the children of a given population if the investigator is well enough acquainted with the language, culture, or ecology of that population to know what modes of thinking it favors.

There are numerous cross-cultural differences in children's social attitudes, motives, and other social dispositions, which are shown by studies in the bibliography. Many of these differences may be explained in terms of knowledge of the cultures studied, but until currently ongoing studies publish their data on the development of such dispositions, their relation to factors varying across individuals and groups, and their variation across more than two groups at a time, the extant literature is hard to evaluate. Suffice it to say that the literature implies that whenever a psychological investigator has had the idea of an attitudinal difference between groups he has been able to devise an instrument that will demonstrate it. Although this is probably not the actual state of affairs, there is immense diversity in the attitudes and values that children acquire.

Recent years have seen the amassing of much evidence supporting the contention of anthropologists that infants and children are raised under extremely variable conditions. Quantitative data are now available and have been sampled in this chapter. Although cultural diversity is worldwide, there appear to be a number of especially sharp discontinuities in the treatment of infants and young children between Western cultures, particularly those of northern European origin, and non-Western cultures, especially those of agriculturalists. The Western groups isolate infants more spatially, wean and toilet-train them earlier, give less childhood training in specific economic tasks, and are much more tolerant of their aggressive behavior. The modernized segments of some of the Asian and African populations deviate from their own backgrounds toward Western practices, and there is a possibility that the future will see a worldwide division between the childhood environment of the modern middle classes and that of traditional farmers and workers. Since modernization—in terms of educational level and socioeconomic participation—seems to account for major differences in the perceptual-cognitive performance of children as well as in the immediate environments in which they develop, studies of antecedent-consequent relations along a meaningful modernization gradient should assume a high priority for future research.

The review of antecedent-consequent studies uncovered few relationships that have been strongly substantiated through cross-cultural research so far. Cross-cultural surveys have demonstrated that child-rearing customs are embedded in a network of other culture patterns including household structure, subsistence economy, and magico-religious systems, but they have not resolved disputes over causal directions in these relations. Comparative studies of individual differences and group means point to a pattern of child-rearing antecedents for achievement motivation and to various personality consequences for father-absence. Alternative models for studying antecedent-consequent relations, based on ethology and social epidemiology, have been illustrated.

It is virtually mandatory to say that more data are needed, but in this chapter the need speaks for itself. Even apart from the issues of data quality raised earlier, we must have more data—particularly on young children and in longitudinal measurement—before we can show what cross-cultural study can do for child psychology.

References

Abiola, E. T. The nature of intellectual development in Nigerian children: a comparison study between two groups of Yoruba children. *Teach. Educ.*, 1965, **6**, 37–58.

Ainsworth, M. D. *Infancy in Uganda: infant care and the growth of love.* Baltimore, Md.: John Hopkins University Press, 1967.

Albino, R. C., and Thompson, V. J. The effects of sudden weaning on Zulu children. *Br. J. med. Psychol.*, 1956, **29**, 177–210.

Allen, M. G. Childhood experience and adult personality: a cross-cultural study using the concept of ego strength. *J. soc. Psychol.*, 1967, **71**(1), 53–68.

Allport, G. W., and Pettigrew, T. F. Cultural influence on the perception of movement: the Trapezoidal Illusion among Zulus. *J. abnorm. soc. Psychol.*, 1957, **55**, 104–113.

Anderson, G. L., and Anderson, H. H. A cross-national study of children: a study in creativity and mental health. In Ira J. Gordon (Ed.), *Human development.* Chicago, Ill.: Scott, Foresman, 1965. Pp. 307–314.

Anderson, H. H., and Anderson, G. L. Social values of teachers in Rio de Janeiro, Mexico City, and Los Angeles County, California: a comparative study of teachers and children. *J. soc. Psychol.*, 1962, **58** (2), 207–226.

Anderson, H. H., Anderson, G. L., Cohen, I. H., and Nutt, F. D. Image of the teacher by adolescent children in four countries: Germany, England, Mexico and U.S. *J. soc. Psychol.*, 1959, **50**, 47–55.

Antonovsky, H. F. Cross-cultural consistency of children's preferences for the orientation of figures. *Am. J. Psychol.*, 1964, **77**, (2), 295–297.

Bacon, M. K., Barry, H. H., III, and Child, I. L. A cross-cultural study of drinking. *Q. J. Stud. Alcohol*, 1965, **26** (Supplement 3).

Bacon, M. K., Child, I. L., and Barry, H., III. A cross-cultural study of correlates of crime. *J. abnorm. soc. Psychol.*, 1963, **66** (4), 291–300.

Bakan, D. *On method: toward a reconstruction of psychological investigation.* San Francisco, Cal.: Jossey-Bass, 1967.

Barker, R. G., Wright, H. F., Barker, L. S., and Schoggen, M. *Specimen records of American and English children.* Lawrence: University of Kansas Publications, 1961, IX.

Barkow, J. H. The causal interpretation of correlation in cross-cultural studies. *Am. Anthrop.*, 1967, **69** (5), 506–510.

Barry, H. H., III, Child, I. L., and Bacon, M. K. Relation of child training to subsistence economy. *Am. Anthrop.*, 1958, **61**, 51–63.

Barry, H. H., III, Bacon, M. K., and Child, I. L. A cross-cultural survey of some sex differences in socialization. *J. abnorm. soc. Psychol.*, 1957, **55**, 327–332.

Bateson, G., and Mead, M. *Balinese character: a photographic analysis.* New York: New York Academy of Sciences, 1942.

Bern, D. The influence of certain developmental factors on fostering the ability to differentiate the passage of time. *J. soc. Psychol.*, 1967, **72** (1), 9–17.

Berry, J. W. Temne and Eskimo perceptual skills. *Int. J. Psychol.*, 1966, **1** (3), 207–229.

Bjerstedt, Å. "Ego-involved world-mindedness" nationality, images, and methods of research: a methodological note. *J. Conflict Resolution*, 1960, 4, 185–192.

Bloch, H. A., and Neideshoffer, A. Adolescent behavior and the gang: a cross-cultural analysis. *J. soc. Ther.*, 1957, 3, 174–179.

Bock, P. K. Love magic, menstrual taboos and the facts of geography. *Am. Anthrop.*, 1967, **69** (5), 506–510.

Boehm, L. The development of conscience of preschool children: a cultural and subcultural comparison. *J. soc. Psychol.*, 1963, **59** (2,) 355–360. (a)

Boehm, L. Independence in Swiss and American children. In W. Dennis (Ed.), *Readings in Child Psychology*. 2nd ed., Englewood Cliffs, N.J.: Prentice-Hall, 1963. (b)

Boehm, L. Moral judgment: a cultural and subcultural comparison with some of Piaget's research conclusions. *Int. J. Psychol.*, 1966, **1** (2), 143–150.

Bradburn, N. M. *N* Achievement and father dominance in Turkey. *J. abnorm. soc. Psychol.*, 1963, **67**, 464–468.

Brown, J. A cross-cultural study of female initiation rites. *Am. Anthrop.*, 1963, **65**, 837–853.

Bruner, J. S., Olver, R. R., and Greenfield, P. *Studies in cognitive growth*. New York: Wiley, 1966.

Burton, R., and Whiting, J. W. M. The absent father and cross-sex identity. *Merrill-Palmer, Q.*, 1961, **7**, 85–97.

Butcher, H. J., Ainsworth, M. and Nesbitt, J. E. A comparison of British and American children. *Br. J. educ. Psychol.*, 1963, **33** (3), 276–285.

Campbell, D. T. The mutual methodological relevance of anthropology and psychology. In F. L. K. Hsu (Ed.), *Psychological anthropology*. Homewood, Ill.: Dorsey Press, 1961.

Campbell, D. T., and Stanley, J. S. *Experimental and quasi-experimental designs for research*. Chicago: Rand-McNally, 1967.

Carney, R. E., and Trowbridge, N. Intelligence test performance of Indian children as a function of type of test and age. *Percept. Mot. Skills*, 1962, **14**, 511–514.

Caudill, W. Social background and sibling rank among Japanese psychiatric patients. *Paper for Second Conference on the Modernization of Japan*, 1968.

Caudill, W., and Plath, D. W. Who sleeps by whom? Parent-child involvement in urban Japanese families. *Psychiatry*, 1966, **29**, 344–366.

Caudill, W., and Weinstein, H. Maternal care and infant behavior in Japanese and American urban middle class families. In R. König and R. Hill (Eds.), *Yearbook of the International Sociological Association*, 1966.

Chatterjee, N. A comparison of performance of tribal and nontribal boys of Tripura (India) on five performance tests. *J. Psychol. Res.*, 9 (3), 151–158.

Clignet, R. Reflection on problems in psychology in Africa. *Bull. Inst. natl. Etude Trav. Orient. Prof.*, 1962, **18** (2), 86–94.

Cohen, Y. *The transition from childhood to adolescence*. Chicago: Aldine, 1964.

Cohen, Y. On alternative views of the individual in culture-and-personality studies. *Am. Anthrop.*, **68** (2), 355–361.

Coombs, L. M., Kron, R. E., Collister, E. G., and Anderson, K. E. The Indian child goes to school: a study of interracial differences. *U.S. Department of Interior, Bureau of Indian Affairs*, 1958, Washington, D.C., 249 pp.

Cowley, J. J., and Murray, M. Some aspects of the development of spatial concepts in Zulu children. *J. soc. Res.*, 1962, **13**, 1–18.

D'Andrade, R. G. Paternal absence and cross-sex identification. Unpublished manuscript, 1966.

D'Andrade, R. G. Testing and training procedures at Bassawa, Paper 4. *Institute of Education, Ahmadu Bello University*, 1967. (Mimeographed.)

Danziger, K. Independence training and social class in Jawa, Indonesia. *J. soc. Psychol.*, 1960, **51**, 65–74. (a)

Danziger, K. Parental demands and social class in Jawa, Indonesia. *J. soc. Psychol.*, 1960, **51**, 75–86. (b)

Dawson, J. T. Cultural and physiological influences upon spatial-perceptual processes in West Africa: I. *Int. J. Psychol.*, 1967, **2** (2), 115–128.

Demos, G. Attitudes of student ethnic groups on issues related to education. *Cal. J. educ. Res.*, 1960, **11**, 204–206.

Dennis, W. Are Hopi children non-competitive? *J. abnorm. soc. Psychol.*, 1955, **50**, 99–100.

Dennis, W. A cross-cultural study of the reinforcement of child behavior. *Child Dev.*, 1957, **28**, 431–438. (a)

Dennis, W. Performance of Near Eastern children on the Draw-A-Man Test. *Child Dev.*, 1957, **28**, 427–430. (b)

Dennis, W. Uses of common objects as indicators of cultural orientations. *J. abnorm. soc. Psychol.*, 1957, **55**, 21–28. (c)

Dennis, W. Environmental influences upon motor development. In *Readings in child psychology*, 2nd ed. Englewood Cliffs, N.J.: Prentice-Hall, 1963. Pp. 83–94. (a)

Dennis, W. Values expressed in children's drawings. In *Readings in child psychology*, 2nd ed. Englewood Cliffs, N.J.: Prentice-Hall. Pp. 265–271. (b)

Dennis, W. Goodenough scores, art experience, and modernization. *J. soc. Psychol.*, 1966, **68**, 211–228. (a)

Dennis, W. *Group values through children's drawings.* New York: Wiley, 1966. (b)

Dennis, W., and Najarian, F. Infant development under environmental handicap. *Psychol. Monogr.*, 1957, **71** (7).

Devereux, E. C., Jr., Bronfenbrener, U. and Suci, G. J. Patterns of parent behavior in the United States of America and the Federal Republic of Germany: a cross-national comparison. *Int. soc. sci. J.*, 1962, **14** (3), 488–506.

DeVos, G., and Hippler, A. Cultural psychology: comparative studies of human behavior. In G. Lindzey and E. Aronson (Eds.), *Handbook of social psychology.* Vol. IV. Cambridge, Mass.: Addison-Wesley, 1969.

Doob, L. Eidetic imagery: a cross-cultural will-o'-the-wisp? *J. Psychol.*, 1966, **63**, 13–34.

Egawa, R. Intellectual differences between rural children and city children: a factor analytic study. *Jap. J. educ. Psychol.*, 1956, **4**, 102–109.

Faladé, S. Le developpement psycho-moteur du jeune Africain originaire du Senegal au cours de sa premiere annee. Paris: Foulon, 1955.

Fancher, E. C. A comparative study of American and Hungarian developmental trends with the Szondi Test. *J. genet. Psychol.*, 1962, **101**, 229–253.

Fancher, E. C., and Weinstein, M. A Szondi study of developmental and cultural factors in personality: the seven-year-old. *J. genet. Psychol.*, 1956, **88**, 81–88.

Fenz, W. D., and Arkoff, A. Comparative need patterns of five ancestry groups in Hawaii. *J. soc. Psychol.*, 1962, **58** (1), 67–89.

Field, P. B. A new cross-cultural study of drunkenness. In D. J. Pittman and C. R. Snyder (Eds.), *Society, culture and drinking patterns.* New York: Wiley, 1962.

Frijda, N., and Jahoda, G. On the scope and methods of cross-cultural research. *Int. J. Psychol.*, 1966, **1** (2), 109–127.

Gaier, E. L., and Collier, M. J. The latency-stage story performances of American and Finnish children. *Child Dev.*, 1960, **31**, 431–451.

Gay, J., and Cole, M. *The new mathematics and an old culture.* New York: Holt, Rinehart & Winston, 1967.

Geber, M. The psychomotor development of African children in the first year and the influence of maternal behavior. *J. soc. Psychol.*, 1958, **47**, 185–195.

Geber, M. Gesell and Terman-Merrill test applied in Uganda (Scientific Films). In A. Merminod (Ed.), *Modern problems in pediatrics: the growth of the normal child during the first three years.* The Proceedings of a Seminar organized by International Children Center, Zurich, 1960.

Geber, M. Longitudinal study of psychomotor development among the Baganda children. *Proceedings of the 14th International Congress of Applied Psychology,* 1961.

Geber, M., and Dean, R. F. A. The state of development of newborn African children. *Lancet,* 1957, **1,** 1216. (a)

Geber, M., and Dean, R. F. A. Gesell tests on African children. *Pediatrics,* 1957, **30,** 1055–1065. (b)

Geber, M., and Dean, R. F. A. Psychomotor development in African children: the effect of social class and the need for improved tests. *Bull. World Health Org.,* 1958, **18,** 471–476.

Goodman, M. E. Values, attitudes, and social conceptions of Japanese and American children. *Am. Anthrop.,* 1957, **59,** 979–999.

Goodman, M. E. Japanese and American children: a comparative study of social concepts and attitudes. *Marr. fam. Living,* 1958, **20,** 316–319.

Goodnow, J. J. A test of milieu effects with some of Piaget's tasks. *Psychol. Monogr.,* 1962, **76** (36) (Whole number 555.)

Goodnow, J. J. Cultural variations in cognitive skills. In D. Price-Williams (Ed.), *Cross-Cultural Studies.* Harmondsworth, England: Penguin Books, 1969.

Goodnow, J. J., and Bethon, G. Piaget's tasks: the effects of schooling and intelligence. *Child Dev.,* 1966, **37** (3), 574–582.

Graham, S. Sociological aspects and health and illness. In R. E. L. Faris (Ed.), *Handbook of Modern Sociology.* Chicago: Rand-McNally, 1964.

Greenfield, P. M., and Bruner, J. S. Culture and cognitive growth. *Int. J. Psychol.,* 1966, **1** (2), 89–107.

Gunders, S. M., and Whiting, J. W. M. Mother-infant separation and physical growth. *Ethnology,* 1968, **7,** 196–206.

Guthrie, G. M., and Jacobs, P. J. *Child rearing and personality development in the Philippines.* University Park: Pennsylvania State University Press, 1966.

Harari, H., and McDavid, J. W. Cultural influence on retention of logical and symbolic material. *J. educ. Psychol.,* 1966, **57** (1), 18–22.

Harrison, D. M., and Chagnon, J. G. The effect of age, sex and language on the Minnesota Percepto-Diagnostic Test. *J. clin. Psychol.,* 1966, **22** (3), 302–303.

Honigman, J. J., and Carrera, R. N. Cross-cultural use of Machover's Figure Drawing Test. *Am. Anthrop.,* 1957, **59,** 650–654.

Hudson, W. Pictorial depth perception in sub-cultural groups in Africa. *J. soc. Psychol.,* 1960, **52,** 183–208.

Hudson, W. Pictorial perception and educational adaptation in Africa. *Psychol. Afr.,* 1962, **9,** 226–239.

Hudson, W. The study of the problem of pictorial perception among unacculturated groups. *Int. J. Psychol.,* 1967, **2,** 90–107.

Husén, T. *International study of achievement in mathematics: a comparison of twelve countries.* Vol. I. New York: Wiley, 1967.

Jahoda, G. Assessment of abstract behavior in a non-Western culture. *J. Abnorm. Soc. Psychol.,* 1956, **53,** 237–43.

Jahoda, G. Child animism: I. A critical survey of cross-cultural research. *J. soc. Psychol.,* 1958, **47,** 197–212. (a)

Jahoda, G. Child animism: II. A study in West Africa. *J. soc. Psychol.,* 1958, **47,** 213–222. (b)

Jahoda, G. Immanent justice among West African children. *J. soc. Psychol.,* 1958, **47,** 241–248. (c)

Jalota, S. A comparative study of intelligence scores by rural and urban school children. *J. voc. educ. Guidance, Baroda,* 1961–62, **8,** (2–3), 6–7.

Jensen, B. L. Left-right orientation in profile drawings. *Am. J. Psychol.,* 1952, **65,** 80–83.

Johnson, D. L., Johnson, C. A., and Price-Williams, D. R. The Draw-A-Man Test and Raven Progressive Matrices performance of Guatemalan boys and Ladino children. *Rev. Interam. Psicol.*, 1967, 1, 143–157.

Kaplan, B. (Ed.) *Primary records in culture and personality.* Vol. II. Madison, Wisc.: Microcard Foundation, 1957. (209 microcards.)

Kardiner, A., and Linton, R. *The individual and his society.* New York: Columbia University Press, 1939.

Kaye, B. *Bringing up children in ghana.* London: Allen & Unwin, 1962.

Kreitler, H. and Kreitler, S. Children's concepts of sexuality and birth. *Child Dev.*, 1966, 37 (2), 363–378.

Kuwata, Y. Report on comparative study in mentality of Formosan and Japanese children. *Jap. J. Psychol.*, 1926, 1, 46–48.

Lambert, W. E., and Klineberg, O. A pilot study of the origin and development of national stereotypes. *Int. soc. Sci. J.*, 1959, 11, 221–238.

Lambert, W. E., and Klineberg, O. Cultural comparisons of boy's occupational aspirations. *Br. J. soc. clin. Psychol.*, 1963, 3 (1), 56–65.

Lambert, W. E., and Klineberg, O. *Children's views of foreign peoples; a cross national study.* New York: Appleton-Century-Crofts, 1967.

Lambert, W. W., Triandis, L. M., and Wolf, M. Some correlates of beliefs in the malevolence and benevolence of supernatural beings: a cross-societal study. *J. abnorm. soc. Psychol.*, 1959, 58, 162–169.

Landauer, T., and Whiting, J. W. M. Infantile stimulation and adult stature of human males. *Am. Anthrop.*, 1964, 66, 1007–1028.

Landy, D. *Tropical childhood: cultural transmission and learning in a rural Puerto Rican village.* Chapel Hill: University of North Carolina Press, 1959.

Leblanc, M. African adaptation and intercultural comparison of a projective test: the Rosenzweig Test. *Rev. Psychol. Appl.*, 1956, 6, 91–109.

Leichty, M. M. Family attitudes and self-concept in Vietnamese and U.S. children. *Am. J. Orthopsychiat.*, 1963, 33 (1), 38–50.

Lesser, G. S., Fifer, G. and Clark, D. H. Mental abilities of children from different social-class and cultural groups. *Monogr. Soc. Res. Child Dev.*, 1965, 30 (4, Serial no. 102), 1–115.

Lester, D. Antecedents of the fear of the dead. *Psychol. Rep.*, 1966, 19, 741–742.

LeVine, R. A., Klein, N. H. and Owen, C. Father-child relationships and changing life-styles in Ibadan, Nigeria. In H. Miner (Ed.), *The city in modern Africa.* New York: Praeger, 1967.

Lloyd, B. B. Choice behavior and social structure: a comparison of two African societies. *J. soc. Psychol.*, 1968, 74, 3–12.

Lloyd, F., and Pidgeon, D. A. An investigation into the effects of coaching on verbal test material with European, Indian and African children. *Br. J. educ. Psychol.*, 1961, 31, 145–151.

Longabaugh, R. The structure of interpersonal behavior. *Sociometry*, 1966, 29, 441–460.

Louttit, C. M. Racial comparisons of ability in immediate recall of logical and nonsense material. *J. soc. Psychol.*, 1931, 2, 205–215.

Lovell, K., Healey, D., and Rowland, A. D. Growth of some geometrical concepts. *Child Dev.*, 1962, 33, (4), 751–767.

Luria, Z., Goldwasser, M., and Goldwasser, A. Response to transgression in stories by Israeli children. *Child Dev.*, 1963, 34 (2), 271–280.

Madsen, M. C. Cooperative and competitive motivation of children in three Mexican subcultures. *Psychol. Rep.*, 1967, 20, 1307–1320.

Marsh, R. *Comparative sociology.* New York: Harcourt, Brace & World, 1967.

Matsumoto, M., and Smith, H. T. Japanese and American children's perception of parents. *J. genet. Psychol.*, 1961, 98, 83–88.

McClelland, D. C. *The achieving society,* Princeton, N.J.: Van Nostrand, 1961.

McClelland, D. C., Baldwin, A. L., Bronfenbrenner, U., and Strodtback, F. L. *Talent and society: new perspectives in the identification of talent.* Princeton, N.J.: Van Nostrand, 1958. Pp. 135–194.

Mead, M. *Coming of age in Samoa.* New York: Morrow, 1928.

Mead, M. *Growing up in New Guinea.* New York: Morrow, 1930.

Mead, M. An investigation of the thought of primitive children, with special reference to animism. *J. R. Anthrop. Inst.,* 1932, **62**, 173–190.

Mead, M., and MacGregor, F. C. *Growth and culture: a photographic study of Balinese childhood.* New York: Putnam, 1951.

Mercado, S. J., Diaz Guerrero P., and Gardner, R. W. Cognitive control in children of Mexico and the U.S. *J. soc. Psychol.,* 1963, **59** (2), 199–208.

Minturn, L., and Lambert, W. W. *Mothers of six cultures: antecedents of child rearing.* New York: Wiley, 1964.

Mischel, W. Father absence and delay of gratification: cross-cultural comparisons. *J. abnorm. soc. Psychol.,* 1961, **63**, 116–124.

Mundy-Castle, A. Pictorial depth perception in Ghanaian children. *Int. J. Psychol.,* 1966, **1**, 290–300.

Muir, R. K. Leadership in a dual cultural setting: a sociometric study of cleavage between English and African-speaking school children and the role of the leaders in bridging it. *Br. J. educ. Psychol.,* 1963, **33** (3), 253–264.

Munroe, R. L., Munroe, R. H., and Daniels, R. E. Effect of status and values on estimation of coin size in two East African societies. *J. soc. Psychol.,* 1969, **77**, 25–34.

Murdock, G. P. *Social structure.* New York: Macmillan, 1949.

Murphy, R. M., and Nolan, E. G. Irrelevant goal-seeking behavior as a function of culture. *Psychol. Rep.,* 1963, **13** (2), 449–450.

Mussen, P. H., Young, H. B., Gaddini, R., and Morante, L. The influence of father-son relationships on adolescent personality and attitudes. *J. Child Psychol. Psychiat.,* 1963, **4** (1), 3–16.

Najarian-Svajian, P. H. The idea of immanent justice among Lebanese children and adults. *J. genet. Psychol.,* 1966, **109** (1), 57–66.

Nanda, P. C., Das, J. P., and Mishra, H. K. Discrimination of geometrical patterns in tribal, rural and urban children. *J. soc. Psychol.,* 1965, **67**, 197–200.

Nerlove, S., and Romney, A. K. Sibling terminology and cross-sex behavior. *Am. Anthrop.,* 1967, **69**, 187.

Neubauer, P. B. (Ed.) *Children in collectives; child-rearing aims and practices in the kibbutz.* Springfield, Ill.: Thomas, 1965.

Nissen, H. W., Kinder, S., and Machover, F. E. A study of performance tests given to a group of native African Negro children. *Br. J. Psychol.,* 1934, **25**, 308–355.

Ombredane, A., Bertelson, P., and Beniest-Moirot, E. Speed and accuracy of performance of an African native population and of Belgian children on a Paper-and-Pencil Perceptual Task. *J. soc. Psychol.,* 1958, **47**, 327–337.

Pareek, U. N. *Developmental patterns in reactions to frustration.* Bombay, India: Asia Publishing House, 1964.

Pasricha, P. A tryout of abstract reasoning test with school children of Baroda. *J. Voc. Educ. Guidance,* 1963, **9** (5), 118–121.

Patel, K. A comparison of English speaking and non-English speaking nursery children in English medium schools in India. *J. Psychol. Res.,* 1965, **9** (3), 103–108.

Personke, C. Spelling achievements of Scottish and American children. *Elementary School J.,* 1966, **66** (6), 337–343.

Piaget, J., and Weil, A. M. The development in children of the idea of homeland

and of relations with other countries. *Int. Soc. Sci. Bull.*, 1951, 3, 561–578.

Price-Williams, D. R. A study concerning concepts of conservation of quantities among primitive children. *Acta Psychol.*, 1961, 18, 297–305.

Price-Williams, D. R. Abstract and concrete modes of classification in a primitive society. *Br. J. educ. Psychol.*, 1962, 32, 50–61.

Price-Williams, D. (Ed.). *Cross-cultural studies*. Harmondsworth, England: Penguin Books, 1969.

Prothro, E. T. Patterns of permissiveness among preliterate peoples. *J. abnorm. soc. Psychol.*, 1960, 61:151–154.

Prothro, E. T. *Child rearing in the Lebanon*. Cambridge, Mass.: Harvard University Press, 1962.

Rabin, A. I. Comparison of American and Israeli children by means of a sentence completion technique. *J. soc. Psychol.*, 1959, 49, 3–12.

Rabin, A. I. *Growing up in the Kibbutz*. New York: Springer, 1965.

Rabin, A. I., and Timuaco, J. A. Sexual differentiation of American and Filipino children as reflected in the Draw-a-Person Test. *J. soc. Psychol.*, 1959, 50, 207–211.

Ramsey, C. E., and Smith, R. J. Japanese and American perceptions of occupations. *Am. J. Sociol.*, 1960, 65, 475–482.

Rapp, D. W. Child rearing attitudes of mothers in Germany and the United States. *Child Dev.*, 1961, 32, 669–678.

Rathbun, C., di Virgilio, L. and Waldfogel, S. The restitutive process in children following radical separation from family and culture. *Am. J. Orthopsychiat.*, 1958, 28, 408–415.

Richelle, M. Use of a text of voluntary restraint of a graphic movement with a group of Moroccan children. *Schweiz. Z. Psychol. Anwend.*, 1955, 14, 309–313.

Roberts, J. M. and Sutton-Smith, B. Child training and game involvement. *Ethnology*, 1962, 1, 160–186.

Roberts, J. M., Sutton-Smith, B., and Kendon, B. Strategy in games and folklore. *J. soc. Psychol.*, 1963, 61, 185–199.

Rosen, B. C., and D'Andrade, R. G. The psycho-social origins of achievement motivation. *Sociometry*, 1959, 22, 185–218.

Rosen, B. C. Socialization and achievement motivation in Brazil. *Am. Sociol. Rev.*, 1962, 27 (5), 612–624.

Rosenblatt, P. C. Functions of games: an examination of individual difference hypotheses derived from a cross-cultural study. *J. soc. Psychol.*, 1962, 58 (1), 17–22.

Rosenblatt, P. C. A cross-cultural study of child rearing and romantic love. *J. Pers. soc. Psychol.*, 1966, 4, 336–338.

Sandiford, P., and Kerr, R. Intelligence of Chinese and Japanese children. *J. educ. Psychol.*, 1926, 17, 361–367.

Sarason, S. B., and Gladwin, T. Psychological and cultural problems in mental subnormality: a review of research. *Am. J. Ment. Defic.*, 1958, 62, 1115–1307.

Sarnoff, J., Lighthall, F., Waite, R., Davidson, K., and Sarason, A. A cross-cultural study of anxiety among American and English school children. *J. educ. Psychol.*, 1958, 49, 129–136.

Scofield, R. W., and Sun, C. W. A comparative study of the differential effect upon personality of Chinese and American child training practices. *J. soc. Psychol.*, 1960, 52, 221–224.

Seagoe, M. V., and Murakami, K. A comparative study of children's play in America and Japan. *Cal. J. Educ. Res.*, 1961, 12, 124–130.

Sears, R. R., Maccoby, E. E. and Levin, H. *Patterns of child rearing*. Evanston, Ill.: Row, Peterson, 1957.

Segall, M. H., Campbell, D. T. and Herskovits, M. J. Cultural differences in the perception of geometric illusions. *Science*, 1963, **139**, 769–771.

Segall, M. H., Campbell, D. T. and Herskovits, M. J. *The influence of culture on visual perception*. Indianapolis, Ind.: Bobbs-Merrill, 1966.

Shirley, R. W., and Romney, A. K. Love magic and socialization: a cross-cultural study. *Am. Anthrop.*, 1962, **64**, 1028–1031.

Smit, C. Comparative analysis of results from Kraus-Weber Test of minimum muscular fitness in South African children. *J soc. Res.* (Pretoria), 1961, **12** (1), 1–20.

Spiro, M. E. *Children of the Kibbutz*. Cambridge, Mass.: Harvard University Press, 1958.

Stephens, W. *The Oedipus complex: cross-cultural evidence*. New York: Free Press, 1962.

Storm, T., Anthony, W. S., and Porsolt, R. D. Ethnic and social class differences in performance for material and non-material rewards: New Zealand children. *J. Pers. soc. Psychol.*, 1965, **2** (5), 759–762.

Suchman, R. G. Cultural differences in children's color and form preferences. *J. soc. Psychol.*, 1966, **70** (1), 3–10.

Takala, A., and Takala, M. Finnish children's reactions to frustration in the Rosenzweig Test: an ethnic and cultural comparison. *Acta Psychol.*, 1957, **13**, 43–50.

Talerico, M., and Brown, F. Intelligence test patterns of Puerto Rican children seen in child psychiatry. *J. soc. Psychol.*, 1963, **61** (1), 57–66.

Tanaka, Y., Oyama, T., and Osgood, C. E. A cross-culture and cross-concept study of the generality of semantic spaces. *J. verb. Learn. verb. Behav.*, 1963, **2** (5–6), 392–405.

Terhune, K. W. An examination of some contributing demographic variables in a cross-national study. *J. soc. Psychol.*, 1963, **59** (2), 209–219.

Thomas, R. M., and Surachmad, W. Social-class differences in mother's expectations for children in Indonesia. *J. soc. Psychol.*, 1962, **57**, 303–307.

Torrance, E. P. Cultural discontinuities and the development of originality in thinking. *Except. Children*, 1962, **29**, 2–13.

Valantin, S., and Collomb, H. Psycho-sociological study of the educational situation in Senegal. In Frederic R. Wickert (Ed.), *Readings in African Psychology from French Language Sources*. East Lansing: Michigan State University, African Studies Center. 1967. Pp. 325–330.

Vaughan, G. M. The effect of the ethnic grouping of the experimenter upon children's responses to tests of an ethnic nature. *Br. J. soc. clin. Psychol.*, 1963, **3** (1), 66–70.

Vernon, P. *Intelligence and cultural environment*. London: Methuen, 1969.

Wallis, R. A. The overt fears of Dakota children. *Child Dev.*, 1954, **25**, 185–192.

Walters, R. The intelligence test performance of Maori children: a cross-cultural study. *J. abnorm. soc. Psychol.*, 1951, **57**, 107–114.

Whiting, B. B. (Ed.), *Six cultures series*. Volumes I–VII, New York: Wiley, 1966.

Whiting, J. W. M. Sorcery, sin, and the superego: a cross-cultural study of some mechanisms of social control. In M. R. Jones (Ed.), *Nebraska symposium on motivation*. Lincoln: University of Nebraska Press, 1959.

Whiting, J. W. M. Totem and taboo: a re-evaluation. In J. Masserman (Ed.), *Psychoanalysis and human values*. New York: Grune & Stratton, 1960.

Whiting, J. W. M. Socialization process. In F. L. K. Hsu (Ed.), *Psychological anthropology: approaches to cultures and personality*. Homewood, Ill.: Dorsey Press, 1961.

Whiting, J. W. M. Effects of climate on certain cultural practices. In W. H. Good-enough (Ed.), *Explorations in cultural anthropology.* New York: McGraw-Hill, 1964.

Whiting, J. W. M., et al. The learning of values. In E. Z. Vogt and E. M. Albert (Eds.), *People of Rimrock: a study of values in five cultures.* Cambridge, Mass.: Harvard University Press, 1966.

Whiting, J. W. M., and Child, I. *Child training and personality,* New Haven, Conn.: Yale University Press, 1953.

Whiting, J. W. M., Child, I. L., and W. W. Lambert, et al. (1966), *Field Guide for a Study of Socialization,* John Wiley: New York.

Whiting, J. W. M., Kluckhohn, R., and Anthony, A. A. The function of male initiation ceremonies at puberty. In E. E. Maccoby, T. M. Newcomb, and E. L. Hartley (Eds.), *Readings in social psychology.* New York: Holt, 1958.

Whiting, J. W. M., and Whiting, B. B. Contributions of anthropology to methods of studying child rearing. In P. H. Mussen (Ed.), *Handbook of research methods in child development.* New York: Wiley, 1959.

Winterbottom, M. R. The relation of need for achievement to learning experience in independence and mastery. In J. W. Atkinson (Ed.), *Motives in fantasy, action and society.* Princeton, N.J.: Van Nostrand, 1958. Pp. 453–478.

Wright, G. O. Projection and displacement: a cross-cultural study of folk-tale aggression. *J. abnorm. soc. Psychol.,* 1954, **49,** 523–528.

Young, F. W. The function of male initiation ceremonies: a cross-cultural test of an alternate hypothesis. *Am. J. Sociol.,* 1962, **67,** 379–396.

Young, F. W. Initiation ceremonies. Indianapolis, Ind.: Bobbs-Merrill, 1965.

Young, F. W., and Bacdayan, A. A. Menstrual taboos and social rigidity. *Ethnology,* 1965, **4** (2), 225–240.

Young, J. A., and Jenkinson, M. D. An objective comparison of achievement in the basic subjects for matched groups of children in Manchester, England and Edmonton, Alberta. *Alberta J. educ. Res.,* 1963–64, **9–10,** 59–66.

Zaccone, F. D. Cultural values and development of motivations: the need for achievement and need for affiliation in a study of 281 subjects. *Riv. psicol. Soc.,* 1952, **29** (1), 101–111.

Zaidi, S. M. H. A study of cultural orientation of Pakistan children through their use of common objects. *J. soc. Psychol.,* 1960, **52,** 41–49.

Zelditch, M. Cross-cultural analyses of family structure. In H. T. Christensen (Ed.), *Handbook of marriage and the family.* Chicago: Rand-McNally, 1964.

PART V

PSYCHOPATHOLOGY

27. Mental Retardation

H. B. ROBINSON and N. M. ROBINSON

More dramatic than even the recent surge of interest in developmental psychology has been the new burgeoning of attempts to understand the processes which produce mental retardation and to develop programs that will ameliorate this problem. After a long period of gross neglect of the retarded and emphasis on their institutional custody (Kanner, 1964), a deepening concern is evident in public support of programs for education and rehabilitation, in numerous measures for the "culturally disadvantaged," whose ranks include a large proportion of the borderline and mildly retarded, and in wide-ranged research attacks which are being focused on almost every facet of the complex problem of mental retardation. Among developmental psychologists, attention has centered in large part on the cognitive functioning of the retarded and upon the prevention and remediation of intellectual deficit through programs for young children of high-risk, culturally disadvantaged families.

PROBLEMS OF DEFINITION

In the light of continuing controversy about the nature of intelligence, its organization, its predictability, and its susceptibility to change, it is not surprising that controversy has surrounded the matter of defining mental retardation. Earlier attempts at definition, founded largely on the concept of unitary mental ability which is impervious to change, usually focused upon the adult retardate's incapacity and his inability to achieve social competence (Benda, 1954; Doll, 1941; Kanner, 1957; Tredgold, 1937). Some workers recognized the dependence of any definition

upon the particular norms of the society in which the retardate attempted to become adequate and independent (Kanner, 1957), but most conceived of mental retardation (variously labeled *mental deficiency, feeble-mindedness, amentia,* and a host of other terms) as an incurable, severe disorder, one that should be carefully distinguished from emotional disturbance. The older definitions, as they were applied to the diagnosis of children, required not a description of the child's present behavior, but rather a prediction about his eventual status as an adult.

A striking new development occurred in 1959 with the publication of a definition of mental retardation by the American Association on Mental Deficiency (Heber, 1959). This definition states that "Mental retardation refers to subaverage general intellectual functioning which originates during the developmental period and is associated with impairment in adaptive behavior" (Heber, 1961, p. 3). More revolutionary than this succinct declaration are the definitions of terms which accompany it. "Subaverage general intellectual functioning" is to be regarded as performance on a recognized test of general intelligence which falls only one standard deviation or more below the population mean. "Impairment in adaptive behavior" is seen as the individual's ineffectiveness in adapting to the demands of his environment and is viewed from a developmental standpoint. It may be reflected during infancy and early childhood mainly by impairment in maturation manifested by retarded development in sensory motor behavior, self-help skills, and language. During the school years, the predominant area of impairment is in learning the skills that are of special importance in the academic setting. At the adult level, impairment in adaptation is reflected primarily in social adjustment, specifically in the ability of the individual to maintain himself economically and to meet and conform to the standards of the community.

The implications of this definition reflect a changing view of mental retardation. First, the definition makes clear that diagnosis of mental status must be only a description of present behavior and can be neither an uncertain estimate of untapped potential functioning nor a prediction of later intelligence. While there does indeed tend to be considerable stability of IQ level over time, the process of prediction of later status is seen as separate from the process of diagnosis. Second, specific reliance is placed upon objective, individually administered tests of general intelligence in conjunction with numerous other sources of information, recognizing the contribution of mental testing to the description of the behavior of retardates. Third, the definition is specifically developmental in approach, tying diagnosis to behavioral descriptions appropriate to the individual's own age level.

Fourth, much greater stress is placed upon the borderline and mild intellectual handicaps. Those whose measured intelligence falls only one standard deviation below the population mean may be categorized as mentally retarded if their social adjustment is likewise significantly below the population mean; that is, anyone with a tested IQ of about 85 or less may be included. This recommendation stands in great contrast to former rules of thumb and, indeed, to most of the currently valid legal and administrative guidelines which set the cutting point at or near IQ 70. According to the A.A.M.D. definition, about one person in six may be regarded as retarded; according to former definitions, only about one person in 33 should be considered as falling into the retarded range of measured intelligence. This shift, which is open to some dispute, recognizes the high standards of intellectual performance which an industrialized, technologically sophisticated society requires of its schoolchildren and its adult citizens. Although the shift properly calls attention to the significant adjustment problems attendant on even a mild intellectual

deficit, it is regarded as arbitrarily overinclusive by many workers who feel it both impractical and possibly damaging to those of borderline intelligence who would be labeled retarded. This shift has made little impact on such criteria as selection for special classes or admission to residential institutions, but it has been adopted by the Vocational Rehabilitation Administration.

Finally, the new definition avoids both the notion of incurability and the necessity for distinguishing between mental retardation and other problems of childhood, such as emotional disturbance and cultural deprivation, which are often associated with limitations of intellectual functioning. Mental retardation is seen as no more or less than a behavioral symptom, not necessarily stable from one time of life to another, and accompanied or caused by any of a number of genetic, physiological, emotional, and experiential factors.

Despite efforts to the contrary, however, the new definition of mental retardation tends to place very heavy emphasis upon obtained measures of intellectual functioning. Although the definition specifies retarded functioning as measured by both tests of intelligence and assessments of social adequacy, there presently exists no well-standardized instrument for the assessment of nonintellective adaptive behavior. Many workers, moreover, including those who respect the value of intelligence tests now in use, are somewhat impatient with the unidimensional, or even bidimensional diagnosis of mental retardation. They have suggested that, for example, profiles of deficit in specific cognitive areas (e.g., self-help, occupational skills, independence within the community), in personality variables (e.g., dependence, impulse control, egocentrism), and possibly in other areas be developed at least as a supplement to the use of the IQ. While such multidimensional systems would introduce difficult technical problems and the necessity for more complex assessment of the individual and his adjustment, rebellion against the "tyranny of the IQ" is widespread and probably justified. The new definition of mental retardation represents a step in this direction, by providing for the coordination of measures of intellectual and behavioral adequacy, but unless appropriate measures are developed in a variety of behavioral areas, the practical application of the definition will continue to give undue emphasis to scores on tests of general intelligence.

LEVELS OF RETARDATION

Five levels of retardation are described by the A.A.M.D. manual (Heber, 1961), each level encompassing a spread of one standard deviation on the normal curve. Rough descriptions of the behavior of adults at each of these levels (Cassel, 1961; Heber, 1961; Sloan and Birch, 1955) indicate the extreme diversity among individuals who fall into the retarded group.

Borderline Mental Retardation (Binet IQ 68 to 83). Adults are frequently able to achieve social and vocational adequacy if they have proper training and job opportunities. Most blend with the normal population, although they typically can maintain no more than a low socioeconomic existence. An increasing percentage are unemployed as the result of automation of unskilled jobs. Most are capable of marriage and of having and raising children. During the school years, they are found in low ability groups and are candidates for programs for "slow learners." Their retardation tends to be most handicapping in academic pursuits and a very large percentage fail to complete high school. Many individuals, particularly adults, whose IQs fall within this range are not properly designated "retarded"; only if there is evidence of impairment in adaptive behavior to the extent of one standard deviation or more should the diagnosis of borderline retardation be applied (Heber, 1962).[1] Nevertheless, this group constitutes by far the largest proportion of the retarded population, indeed many more than all the rest combined. It should be noted that for many purposes (e.g., admission to institutions or special classes), this group is often regarded as not sufficiently retarded to be eligible for the specialized services designed to meet the needs of those with more marked deficiencies.

Mild Mental Retardation (Binet IQ 52 to 67). The mildly retarded represent almost 90% of those at this and all lower levels

[1] The lack of a well-standardized instrument for the assessment of adaptive behavior constitutes a major problem in diagnosis at this level.

(President's Committee on Mental Retardation, 1967). Adults are likely to be capable of maintaining themselves in unskilled laboring jobs but will frequently need supervision in handling their social and financial affairs (Charles, 1957; Collmann and Newlyn, 1956, 1957). Their low-level skills leave them particularly vulnerable to unemployment (Channing, 1932). Many of their problems are more properly attributable to ethnic and socioeconomic status than to their retardation per se (Keeler, 1964; Kennedy, 1948). The women, more than the men, may be capable of adequate married life because home-making skills are less demanding than public work (Bijou, Ainsworth, and Steckey, 1943). Sheltered workshops are often appropriate, especially for the more retarded segment of this group. Mildly retarded schoolchildren are usually eligible for special classes for the educable mentally retarded, although only about one in three is so placed (Mackie, 1965). Across the United States, only about 1% of mildly retarded individuals are institutionalized, and then most often during the adolescent years due to behavior problems rather than to limitations of intelligence (Hobbs, 1964; Maney, Pace, and Morrison, 1964; Tarjan, Wright, Kramer, Person, and Morgan, 1958). The great majority of the mildly retarded are properly diagnosed as cultural-familial (Stein and Susser, 1963); they exhibit no recognizable symptoms of brain injury and come from families low in intelligence and in socioeconomic status. There are, however, others at this level, representing a wide socioeconomic spectrum, with emotional disorders or with central nervous system impairment. A great many of the mildly retarded are not identified as handicapped at all until the rigorous demands of school make apparent their deficiencies in verbal-abstract intellectual capacity.

Moderate Mental Retardation (Binet IQ 36 to 51). Approximately 6% of the retarded (excluding the borderline) fall within this range. Adults are usually found living dependently within the family setting, though a sizable proportion are institutionalized (Delp and Lorenz, 1953; Saenger, 1957; Visier, 1965). Few hold jobs except within the confines of sheltered workshops or family businesses; most can do useful work within the household and can be left without supervision for several hours. Marriage is rare; the majority have little heterosexual social contact and few friends of their own. During the childhood years, most are eligible for special classes for "trainable" retardates; emphasis is upon the development of self-care rather than academic achievement. Brain damage, mongolism, and other pathological conditions are frequent, and identification of the child as retarded is more likely to occur during infancy or early childhood, when distinct impairment of motor, verbal, and social development is noted.

Severe Mental Retardation (Binet IQ 20 to 35). About 3½% of those mildly or more retarded are represented in this group. Adults and children are often institutionalized, though some remain within the family setting; they usually require constant supervision. Language and the self-care skills require prolonged training; appropriate training is not ordinarily provided in "trainable" classes within school systems except for the upper portion of this range. Very little independent behavior is observed; lethargy and apathy are frequent but may be largely a product of unstimulating life circumstances and interpersonal relationships (McKinney and Keele, 1963). Some adults are friendly and affectionate, but in the main they can communicate only on a momentary, concrete level. Genetic disorders and environmental insults resulting in neurological damage, and perhaps severe emotional disturbances (Woodward, 1963) account for almost all mental retardation in this group.

Profound Mental Retardation (Binet IQ below 20). Only approximately 1½% of the retarded population mildly or more retarded is included in this group. Total supervision is required for these individuals, who usually cannot protect or care for themselves. They may learn to walk and to vocalize a greeting and other simple phrases, and some can be trained to use the toilet and feed themselves. Many, having sustained severe neurologic damage, are confined to a bed or wheelchair. Little learning of any kind is exhibited, but the individual is by no means impervious to his surroundings (Berkson and Mason, 1963). The mortality rate during childhood is very high.

It must be noted that the A.A.M.D. def-

inition and classification system, while gaining rapidly in acceptance, is used mainly by professional workers in the United States. Throughout the world, there is considerable variation in terminology, in classification, and indeed in overall major orientation in the field of retardation (Scheerenberger, 1964). Within the English language alone, there are no fewer than 23 systems of classification (Gelof, 1963). Even within the same American community, variations in terminology are likely to coexist, the most important variant being the widely employed system of distinctions between "slow learning," "educable mentally retarded," "trainable mentally retarded," and "custodial" children as commonly applied within school systems.

PREVALENCE OF MENTAL RETARDATION

Although there is no doubt that the incidence of intellectual deficit is a major problem throughout the world, it is almost impossible to arrive at precise estimates of the extent of this disorder. The proportions of children who are regarded as intellectually subnormal vary greatly in different countries according to the definition of retardation and the adequacy of the survey techniques utilized (World Health Organization, 1954). Even surveys within a single country, the United States, conducted since 1894, have reported prevalence rates from 0.05 to 13% of the population (Wallin, 1958).

It is clear that no definitive answers can be expected to statistical questions concerning the worldwide prevalence of intellectual subnormality. Indeed, the question itself may be meaningless. Mental retardation is not a disease entity like measles or pneumonia; a person is judged retarded only in the context of the community in which he lives, and in relation to the precise demands which are placed upon him.

Within the United States, a consensus has emerged that approximately 3% of the population should be regarded as retarded (Scheerenberger, 1964). It is, one should note, clear that the A.A.M.D. definition is being ignored in such estimates. Even so, in a population of 200,000,000 persons, using a cutoff point of IQ 70, 6,000,000 individuals would be retarded. As a major health problem, this figure is exceeded only by mental illness, cardiac disease, arthritis, and cancer (President's Panel on Mental Retardation, 1962). This 3% estimate exceeds slightly the 2.15% to be expected if intelligence were distributed precisely according to the normal curve. The excess is concentrated in the more severe levels of retardation (Dingman and Tarjan, 1960). It reflects the effects of pathological processes which are so severely crippling that they override the normal variation in intelligence which results from the interplay of a large number of sources.

Despite the severe national problem inherent in the existence of any handicap in 6,000,000 citizens, the total 3% estimate must be taken as minimal. It fails to consider the very real nature of a handicap of borderline intelligence. That this is no idle matter is indicated by the fact that, in some states, nearly half of peacetime draft selectees have failed to be inducted for reasons of intellectual deficit; the national average is about one in six (Ginzberg, 1965). Poor academic achievement and failure to develop minimal conceptual skills characterize the majority of our nation's children who are of borderline intelligence.

Handicaps of borderline and mild retardation, moreover, take their toll differentially at different ages. There is, for example, a trend for more individuals to be identified as retarded during the school years than during any other period. There follows a sharp drop beginning in the late teens and extending into adulthood (Akesson, 1961; Dingman, 1959; Gruenberg, 1964; New York State Department of Mental Hygiene, 1955). Apparently, for many retarded children, the years of school present the most difficult tasks to be met at any time in life (Dexter, 1964). After an initial spurt in the primary school years, a marked increase in reported cases occurs in adolescence, probably due to an interplay of factors including more complex learning tasks in school, the greater foresight and control required by society, and physical maturity, which is upsetting both to the child himself and to adults who grow apprehensive about possible sexual and aggressive misbehavior. Once the critical period of adolescence and school attendance is passed, however, many of the more mildly handicapped blend into society and become at least marginally adequate citizens (Charles, 1957; Collmann and Newlyn, 1956, 1957; Kennedy, 1948).

Currently, there are strong trends toward social change in the United States, some of which may be expected to decrease the prevalence and others of which may be expected to increase the prevalence of the retarded. On the one hand, strides are being made to improve medical care, especially for lower socioeconomic groups; to improve educational efforts at all levels, but especially at the preschool levels for the culturally deprived; to expand the number and to increase the effectiveness of special education classes in the public schools; to improve the capacities for work of undereducated and underemployed; and so on. In many ways, the entire "War on Poverty" can be conceived as the broadest attack ever mounted on the problems of the borderline and mildly retarded.

In contrast, rapid movement within Western societies toward industrialization and automation tends to bode ill for the borderline and mildly retarded individuals who are capable only of minimally skilled occupations. Life in an urban, specialized environment requires more general "know how" and tends to decrease the opportunity for dependence upon the extended family group and sympathetic individuals in a cohesive neighborhood. Higher achievement demanded of schoolchildren places even more pressure upon the marginal and retarded student. Considerable ingenuity will be required to maintain roles for retarded children and adults which carry with them opportunities for feelings of competence, success, and dignity (Fischer, 1962; Ginzberg, 1965). The growth of service industries with many jobs requiring minimal conceptual skills can be viewed as a somewhat optimistic note in an otherwise dismal picture.

Although the incidence of severe handicap is much less than that of mild degree, at least 0.25% of the population of the United States falls within the moderately to profoundly retarded group (IQs below about 50), a minimum of 500,000 persons (Dingman and Tarjan, 1960). These severely handicapped children and adults would be recognizable in any society as incapable of independent existence. Their cognitive and often their physical handicaps are such that they can function in school or in a work situation under only protected conditions, and some require such intensive care that institutionalization becomes almost imperative.

ETIOLOGY

Mental retardation, as we have seen, does not constitute a syndrome in the usual sense, but rather a symptom which can stem from a wide variety of disorders. As such, it is in some ways an artificial and oversimplified category, misleading because of its apparent objectivity. Not only does the category encompass enormous differences in degree (including as it does both the borderline retardate, who is barely differentiable from the low-normal, and the individual so profoundly handicapped that he remains throughout life in the status of a helpless infant) but also wide differences in etiology. The retardation of some children is the result of pathological gene alleles (single dominants or paired recessives); others clearly suffer errors in chromosomal make-up; still other children presumably suffer an unfortunate selection among hundreds, perhaps thousands of pairs of genes, no single pair of which would produce noticeable deficit. Other retardates suffer from no inherited disorder but have experienced a traumatic injury or damage to the brain. For a great many children, the primary etiological factors must be found in the socialization situation, including extremely complex and little-understood processes which determine learning ability and personality formation.

It must be clear, therefore, that no single theoretical model will suffice to "explain" retardation (Bijou, 1963). Although some workers search for a general model, representing retardation as, for example, a simple slowing of development or a set of specific deficits (e.g., Weir, 1967; Zigler, 1966, 1967a), their searches are not likely to be very fruitful. Presumably, advances in diagnosis and behavioral observation will reveal homogenous subgroups of the retarded who exhibit characteristic behavior patterns. We cannot, however, expect to find pervasive traits or dimensions common to all retardates but not to normal children, other than their

relative deficit in general mental ability and its direct consequences.

In any given child, it is often impossible to diagnose the etiological factors responsible for his retardation. Even when it is possible, on the basis of medical and behavioral evidence, to categorize the child as "brain-injured" or "cultural-familial," the precise deleterious agents are still likely to remain obscured. There are many reasons for this state of affairs, among them the following:

1. So many factors, known and unknown, may interfere with normal development, at any time from the formation of the reproductive cells through postnatal growth, that the task of isolating their effects is an enormous one.

2. Prenatal history of the child is often unobserved, especially during the crucial first trimester, and parents are notoriously poor informants about any unusual circumstances or symptoms which might provide clues.

3. The results of the disorder, whether of genetic or environmental nature, are often not evident until long after the point of origin, as, for example, when the mildly retarded child enters school.

4. The armamentarium of medical and behavioral diagnostic techniques is limited; neurological and psychological diagnoses, for example, are often crude and nonspecific, and sometimes insensitive to deficits that actually exist (Goldfarb, 1961).

5. Apparently identical symptoms may result from dissimilar causes; microcephaly, for example, may result from genetic sources (Komai, Kishimato, and Ozaki, 1955) or from prenatal damage (Murphy, 1928), and genetic hydrocephalus is known to result from at least three different types of mutant genes (Fraser, 1965). Furthermore, it is often the timing of the damage rather than the specific agent that determines the deficits which will result (Wilson, 1965).

6. Dissimilar symptoms may result from the same source; congenital rubella, for example, may produce growth retardation in different parts of the body (Naeye and Blane, 1965) and a wide variety of symptoms, not all of which are present in any given victim (Lindquist, Plotkin, Shaw, Gilden, and Williams, 1965).

7. It is often extremely difficult to distinguish cause from effect; damage to a premature child, for example, may result not from his prematurity per se but primarily from the same source as the prematurity (Wilson, Parmalee, and Huggins, 1963).

8. A great many disorders stem from an interaction of special conditions: epilepsy, for example, appears to require both a genetic and an environmental component, each varying somewhat inversely with the other (Donsted, 1955), and even clearly genetic metabolic disorders such as phenylketonuria will not always wreak havoc with the child if diet is suitably controlled.

9. Finally, the retardation of so many children, especially those who are born to families of the lower socioeconomic groups, apparently stems from such a multitude of sources in the genetic-physiological-social-emotional complex that attempts at isolating "primary" factors are fruitless.

Despite this difficulty in identifying precise etiological factors, help may often be offered to a child and his family. In the brain-injured child, for example, it makes little difference what the destructive agent was; the important task is to assess the capabilities and deficits of that child and to help him develop to the limit of his capacities. When, however, continuing deleterious agents are suspected (e.g., metabolic deficiency, brain tumor, emotionally disordered family, lack of stimulation or attention) it is important to formulate the constellation of agents and to proceed toward their remediation. It is in this context that careful etiological diagnosis is called for, but the worker must be prepared for the high degree of likelihood that many important questions will remain unsolved.

For heuristic purposes, it is valuable to distinguish among several etiological categories. These include both single-factor pathological states, such as clear genetic anomalies and severe brain injury, which account for most cases of very marked retardation, and other multiple-factor interactions, such as the complex of handicaps typical in families of low socioeconomic status, who tend to produce children whose retardation is mild in degree.

Genetic Factors[2]

The potential contribution of the field of genetics to the understanding of mental retardation probably cannot be overestimated. Astounding strides have been made in recent years in screening techniques to detect amino acids and enzyme deficiencies, in staining and observation techniques to detect chromosomal anomalies, in biochemical discoveries regarding the essential nature of the genetic code and its mutations, and in other areas of inquiry within the field. These discoveries have already markedly affected our understanding of the mechanisms by which some children become retarded, and have permitted beginnings at prevention of retardation in some cases. By 1964, more than 200 recessive disorders had been identified (Beadle, Tatum, McKusick, Hsia, and Sager, 1964), many of which produce retardation, and additional disorders are rapidly being isolated. A great many questions remain unanswered, of course, particularly those relating to polygenic combinations which are assumed to produce retardation only through the combined efforts of numerous genes. To the field of genetics we can look in the future for further dramatic insights into the extremely complex and, in many ways, miraculous mechanisms by which the development of the organism is governed.

Genetic factors which contribute to mental retardation vary from deleterious single gene pairs, to gross abnormalities in the chromosomal complement, and to elusive polygenic combinations. Interactions between genetic and environmental factors occur, of course, at all developmental stages. Genetic mutations and chromosomal anomalies are produced even before conception by environmental factors such as radiation (Muller, 1927), viral infections (Robinson and Puck, 1965), and chemicals (Ingalls, Ingenito, and Curley, 1963; Tough and Brown, 1965). In some disorders, special treatment begun very soon after birth can prevent brain damage resulting from genetic metabolic and endocrine disorders. Genetically determined fac-

[2] See also Chapter 2. For other discussions of genetic factors and syndromes in mental retardation, see Anderson (1964), Carter (1966), Gottesman (1963), Robinson and Robinson (1965a), and Waisman and Gerritsen (1964).

tors such as sex and race interact with a variety of environmental variables at later stages in life to produce psychologically important differences among people. It is clear that at no point in the life process can either "nature" or "nurture" be considered to operate alone; in every range of intelligence, and in every phase of development, their interaction must be considered (Anastasi, 1958; Liverant, 1960).

Recessive Gene Disorders. The great majority of genetically determined syndromes associated with mental retardation are caused by the unfortunate pairing of two recessive alleles. Such a recessive gene pair produces a faulty patterning for the formation of an enzyme necessary for an important metabolic process. In this sense, all genetically determined abnormalities are associated with faulty metabolic processes. These disorders can, however, be classified into various subgroups characterized by faulty metabolisms of carbohydrates, fats, or proteins; disorders in the storage of biochemical substances in the cells due to overproduction or to a slowing of metabolic breakdown; faulty or missing endocrine secretions; anomalies in the structure of brain and cranium; etc. By far the greatest number of identified recessive disorders have been shown to involve the faulty metabolism of amino acids, both because of the complexity of these metabolic processes and because of recent advances in the biochemical understanding and identification of them. Among the more common recessive disorders are galactosemia, phenylketonuria, a group of related disorders known as amaurotic familial idiocy, cretinism, and a number of anomalies of cranial formation.

Galactosemia, one of the first recessive syndromes to be identified, results from the absence of the enzyme required to metabolize galactose, a carbohydrate constituent in milk (Isselbacher, Anderson, Kurahashi, and Kalckar, 1956). Early removal of milk from the diet is often effective in preventing retardation (Mason and Turner, 1935). Even without treatment, however, there is wide variability in the clinical symptoms (Hsia, Inouye, and Walker, 1961), and some untreated children with this disorder have developed normal intelligence (Baker, Mellman, Tedesco, and Segal, 1966).

Phenylketonuria (commonly known as PKU) results from the absence of an enzyme necessary for the conversion of the amino acid phenylalanine to tyrosine, which leads to the build-up of substances toxic to the developing central nervous system. Phenylketonuria is one of the more frequent recessive disorders, appearing in about one of every 10,000 births. It has also been one of the most thoroughly investigated, although it is still not completely understood. Apparently, more than one type of phenylketonuria exists (Medical World News, 1965). Although dietary treatment can prevent the usual severe retardation (Bickel, Girrard, and Hickmans, 1954; Sutherland, Umbarger, and Berry, 1966), even those affected children whose treatment is begun in early infancy tend not to equal the developmental progress of their unaffected siblings (Berman, Waisman, and Graham, 1966). Some affected children who have had no treatment have unaccountably not been notably retarded (Allen and Gibson, 1961; Mabry and Podoll, 1963; Tapia, 1961).

Amaurotic familial idiocy is a group of disorders resulting from faulty metabolism of the lipids, a wide spectrum of fatty compounds which play an important role in the development of the brain. A number of these diseases lead not only to mental retardation but to early death.

Cretinism is a general term which covers several different disorders resulting in an absence, insufficiency, or error of production of the thyroid hormone. The most common form of cretinism is not genetic but rather stems from either iodine insufficiency or from antibodies in the mother. There are, however, at least three separate inherited types of cretinism (Stanbury and McGirr, 1957), each of which constitutes a distinctly different interference with one of the major enzyme systems involved in the synthesis and liberation of the thyroid hormone. Early administration of thyroid hormone is often effective in reducing the degree of retardation (Bruch and McCune, 1944; Smith, Blizzard, and Wilkins, 1957).

There are a number of anomalies of cranial formation, which in at least some instances are genetically transmitted. Gene defects can lead to premature closing of the apertures of the skull, to biochemical abnormalities in the bones which make them either underresponsive or overresponsive to normal pressures, to abnormal growth or fluid within the cranium, which exerts pressure, and to a number of other anomalies. Among the best identified of these is microcephaly (Komai et al., 1955), which invariably leads to severe mental subnormality in its genetic form (Brandon, Kirman, and Williams, 1959).

Dominant Gene Disorders. Syndromes associated with mental retardation caused by a dominant gene are extremely rare. Almost all such disorders produce marked abnormalities and the persons affected tend either to be sterile or to be socially removed from opportunities to reproduce, so that the hereditary line dies out rather quickly. Only when the disorder is not invariably associated with severe mental defect or sterility is it likely to occur with any frequency.

One example of such a disorder is tuberous sclerosis (Bourneville's disease) (de la Cruz and LaVeck, 1962), characterized by multiple hardened areas of the cortex, a variety of skin manifestations, and tumors in various internal organs and throughout the central nervous system. A similar disorder is neurofibromatosis (von Recklinghausen's disease), which is characterized by light brown patches on the body and tumors of the skin and nerves. Neither of these disorders is invariably associated with mental retardation, although in some instances the retardation is very profound. The relationship between skin disorders and mental retardation is due to the fact that the ectoderm, the outer layer of the embryo, furnishes the protoplasm from which the skin and the central nervous system as well as the eyes, the tooth enamel, and the lining of part of the mouth, nose, and anus, all develop; a genetic disorder with skin manifestations is thus also likely to involve the central nervous system.

Chromosomal Aberrations. Variations from the normal human complement of 46 chromosomes usually, but not invariably, produce gross abnormalities in the developing child. Chromosomal anomalies account for a very large proportion of spontaneously aborted fetuses (Carr, 1963, 1965; Szulman, 1965; Thiede and Salm, 1964). Most of the anomalies discovered in living children have consisted of extra chromosomes.[3] Another variant which does not cause abnormalities in the carrier, but may in his offspring, is a translocation of chromosomes in which one becomes hooked to another, leaving, however, the actual amount of genetic material unaffected (Carter, Hamerton, Polani, Gunlap, and Walker, 1960).

Aberrations in sex chromosomes occur in about 0.2% of a normal population (Maclean, 1964) and can be detected by fairly simple microscopic examination of stained cells (Barr and Bertram, 1949; Davidson and Smith, 1954). The normal complement of sex chromosomes is, of course, XY for the male and XX for the female. Phenotypic males are found, however, with XXY combinations, or less commonly with XXXY or XXYY combinations. The presence of at least one Y chromosome is almost always apparent if the individual is male (Bergstrand and Lindsten, 1965). Extra Y chromosomes are rare (Muldal and Ockley, 1960), but of special interest because they have been implicated in a syndrome associated with criminal behavior (Telfer, Baker, Clark, and Richardson, 1968). Phenotypic females are sometimes found who have XO, or XXX, or some other abnormal pattern of X chromosomes. The two most frequent syndromes are Turner's syndrome (XO) in females, about 20% of whom are mentally retarded (Haddad and Wilkins, 1959), and Klinefelter's syndrome (usually XXY) in males, of whom approximately 25% are retarded (Barr, et al., 1964).

Aberrations in autosomal chromosomes produce a number of rather rare and severe syndromes in which there is usually an extra amount of chromosomal material. Most of those discovered in living children are examples of trisomy of the smaller chromosomes (e.g., Butler, Snodgrass, France, Sinclair, and Russell, 1965; Hecht, Bryant, Motuisky, and Giblett, 1963; Jongbloet, 1965).

---

[3] Principle exceptions are females having only one X chromosome (Grumbach, van Wyk, and Wilkins, 1955) (the Y chromosome, which is very small, being absent in all females in any event) and deletion of portions of other chromosomes (Dyggve and Mikkelsen, 1965; Hijmans and Shearin, 1965; Lejeune, 1964). Absence of chromosomal material is usually incompatible with life.

By far the most common of these disorders is Down's syndrome, commonly known as mongolism, in which there is an extra chromosome of the smallest class, usually labeled chromosome #21. Mongolism is of special interest because its many symptoms are usually clear cut although seldom are all present in any given mongoloid child, because it is so frequent, and because after years of puzzlement the chromosomal anomaly has so recently been discovered (Lejeune, Gautier, and Turpin, 1959). Almost all mongoloids possess 47 instead of the normal 46 chromosomes.[4] From 10 to 20% of moderately and severely retarded children are mongoloid (Masland, 1958). The risk of having a mongoloid child varies greatly with the age of the mother. Between the maternal ages of 15 and 24 years, for example, the risk is less than 1 in 1500 births, but in the mother who is older than 45, the risk is as high as 1 in 38 (Knobloch and Pasamanick, 1962).

Most surveys of the intellectual level of institutionalized mongoloid children have obtained mean IQs of approximately 25 (Johnson and Barnett, 1961; Nakamura, 1961; Sternlicht and Wanderer, 1962). Home-reared mongoloid children tend to perform significantly higher than those institutionalized early (Centerwall and Centerwall, 1960; Shipe and Shotwell, 1965; Stedman and Eichorn, 1964) but usually remain in the severely and moderately retarded ranges. The individual differences among mongoloids are, however, quite considerable. In fact, two pub-

---

[4] In the approximately 3% of mongoloids who have only 46 chromosomes, there is a translocation of one chromosome upon another (typically, #21 is attached to #15). This type is not related to the age of the mother, since the translocation is frequently passed down through phenotypically normal generations, but in each meiotic cell division there is one chance in three that the chromosomes will fail to divide properly and the embryo will actually possess two #21 chromosomes. In still other cases, an error in mitotic cell division has taken place after conception, producing an individual with trisomy-21 in one strain of cells but with a normal complement of chromosomes in others. Symptoms of mongolism are particularly variable in such cases. This condition, known as *mosaicism,* as well as the condition produced by translocation, are also known to occur in other chromosomal disorders.

lished diaries of mongoloid youths (Hunt, 1967; Seagoe, 1964) demonstrate vividly that some mongoloid children, under intense stimulation, may develop intelligence up to and even above the mildly retarded range.

Genetic Susceptibility to Environmental Effects. By still unidentified mechanisms, the genetic constitution of an organism is known to affect his susceptibility to potentially harmful environmental events. In mice, for example, some strains are extremely susceptible to intrauterine damage by specific agents, whereas others are much less susceptible (Fraser, 1964). A variety of relatively minor prenatal factors may cross what seem to be genetically determined threshholds of vulnerability, so that some genotypes are more likely than others to suffer damage.

A similar situation is thought to occur in human beings with regard to epileptic seizures, which may be a symptom of brain damage but may also themselves cause further mental deterioration (Pond, 1961). Studies of epileptic patients and their families have furnished strong evidence that susceptibility to epilepsy is inheritable, with the evidence for genetic factors strongest in persons who have experienecd no apparent brain damage (Lennox, 1951, 1960; Lennox, Gibbs, and Gibbs, 1940). In addition, a dozen or so agents of brain injury have been implicated in the etiology of seizure patterns (Chao, Druckman, and Kellaway, 1958). It seems altogether possible that inherited predispositions affect to a marked degree the individual's response to a wide range of environmental circumstances.

Polygenic Inheritance. The conditions which have been described in the preceding discussion deal with discrete syndromes which, although they may vary in phenotypic severity, are either present or absent in a given individual. These syndromes (with the exception of epilepsy) are primarily the result of chromosomal errors or the action of "major" dominant or single pairs of recessive genes.

Most human traits, including intelligence, however, cannot be characterized as either present or absent; rather, they vary continuously over a range, and often follow a normal curve of distribution. Individual genes act on a unitary, either-or basis, and thus a genetic theory is needed to account for the continuous distribution of intelligence and yet to retain the unitary action of individual gene pairs. Such a theory is the multiple-factor hypothesis, or the concept of polygenic inheritance. According to this theory, the genes are acknowledged to occur in discrete pairs, but combinations of numerous pairs are said to bear upon the same characteristics. The genes involved in such polygenic groups are very elusive because each pair produces only a small increment or decrement, the sum total of which has an effect on intelligence (Anderson, 1964; Fuller, 1954; Snyder, 1955). If discrete pairs of genes, working in combination with one another, each contribute slightly to the eventual outcome, then, as in the coin-tossing games played by students of probability, a distribution will be produced in which most fall more or less toward the middle, but some by chance fall toward the extremes because of fortunate or unlucky combinations of genes (McClearn, 1962). Similarly, environmental influences which may be positive or negative also contribute to this normal distribution.

Most workers tend to regard cultural-familial mentally retarded individuals as simply the lower extreme of the normal distribution produced by small, incremental factors which are both genetic and environmental in origin (Anderson, 1964). These individuals constitute the largest single group of retardates and usually exhibit a fairly uncomplicated picture of borderline to mild mental subnormality. They tend to have retarded parents and siblings and to live in lower socioeconomic circumstances (either as cause or effect of their condition). Evidence for the heritability of intelligence is so strong that it is almost imperative to assume that some genetic factors are operating in conjunction with environmental factors in the etiology of the cultural-familial group. The multiple-factor hypothesis, although by no means clearly proved, remains our best guess about the gross nature of this mode of inheritance.

Brain Injury[5]

The complexity of the developing organism and complete dependence on its environment for nurturance leaves children vulnerable to

[5] For another discussion of brain injury and associated syndromes see Robinson and Robinson (1965a).

organic insult from the moment of conception onward. That so few children suffer damage serious enough to produce mental retardation is, indeed, to be wondered at. It has been widely held that brain injury is most commonly seen in children with the more severe degrees of retardation. It is far more likely, however, that mild degrees of brain injury are to be found throughout the entire range of intelligence, and that a great number of mildly handicapped children, including those whose disorders seem to result from emotional disturbance or from cultural deprivation, actually have suffered minor degrees of injury.

Perhaps the most important idea to be developed about brain injury in retarded children is that brain-injured children do not constitute a homogenous group, from the points of view of etiology, behavior, or treatment. Indeed, the complexities of the central nervous system, the wide variations in the timing of damage, the differences between diffuse damage and relatively circumscribed lesions, and the individual differences among children in genetic constitution and their psychosocial environments, should make it clear that the category of "brain-injury" is a misleading oversimplification.

It is generally accepted (e.g., Yannet, 1957) that of the retarded children with major brain injury most sustained damage during the prenatal period, an additional smaller group suffers from the effects of a stressful birth, and a still smaller group sustained damage during childhood. Experimental work in the development of the embryo and fetus, reviewed by Fraser (1964) and Norris (1965), suggests that in many instances it is the timing of the assault rather than its precise nature which determines the type of maldevelopment, although most agents of damage also have specific biologic effects which may produce characteristic malformations. A great many agents of damage in the prenatal period have been identified, among them a wide variety of maternal nutritional deficiencies (Culley, 1965; Harrell, Woodyard, and Gates, 1955; King, 1965); viral infections (Hardy, 1965a; Mitchell and Woodside, 1967) such as rubella (eg., Plotkin and Vaheri, 1967; Sever, Nelson, and Gilkeson, 1965), cytomegalic inclusion disease (Rosenstein and Navarete-Reyna, 1964), and possibly with lesser frequency, influenza

(Coffey and Jessop, 1959); bacterial infection by congenital syphilis (Bass, 1952); the fungus toxoplasmosis (Gard, Magnusson, and Hagberg, 1952); maternal sensitization to Rh-positive blood type (Zimmerman and Yannet, 1935); maternal hypertension (Chesley and Annetto, 1947); maternal diabetes (Dekaban and Magee, 1958); anoxia (Warkany, 1958); a variety of drugs (Apgar, 1964); radiation (Murphy, Shirlock, and Doll, 1942); a complex of as yet incompletely understood factors related to social class and background of the parents (Baird and Scott, 1953); maternal age (Battaglia, Frazier, and Hellegers, 1963; Lilienfeld and Pasamanick, 1956); paternal age (Yerushalmy, quoted by Penrose, 1955); parity (Masland, 1958); and maternal emotions (Sontag, 1941).

Stressful conditions surounding the birth process are also known to lead to brain damage (Hardy, 1965b). Prematurity (low birth weight) has been much studied, but seldom with adequate social-class controls; although the majority of studies following premature children tend to show reduction in IQ (e.g., Wiener, Rider, Oppel, Fischer, and Harper, 1965), especially when birth weight is very low, some carefully controlled studies have failed to find such effects (Robinson and Robinson, 1965b). Neonatal anoxia (Graham, Ernhart, Thurston, and Craft, 1962), neonatal hypoglycemia (Haworth and McRae, 1965); mechanical injury through increased pressure (Benda, 1954), precipitous birth (Yacorzynski and Tucker, 1960), or breech birth (Morgan and Kane, 1964); prolonged pregnancy (Mead and Marcus, 1964); and other factors are involved. Signs of stress measured immediately after birth are often indicative of brain injury (Apgar, 1965; Kennedy, Drage, and Schwartz, 1963). Following birth, the antigenic processes begun by exchange of maternal and fetal blood may culminate in severe jaundice (hyperbilirubinemia) and kernicterus, with resulting damage (Boggs, 1963; Van Camp, 1964). Damage during the period of childhood is much more rare, the chief postnatal hazards being head injury (Fabian, 1956; Hjern and Nylander, 1964); malnutrition during infancy (Cravioto and Robles, 1965); brain tumors (Guvener, Bagchi, Kooi, and Calhoun, 1964); intracranial malformations (Weaver, 1965); toxins, especially lead (Aronson, 1965) and insecti-

cides (McIntire, Angle, and Maragos, 1965); demyelinating diseases (Rapin, 1965); and infections of the brain including, most importantly, encephalitis (Greenbaum and Lurie, 1948; Matejcek, Doutlik, and Janda, 1964) and, to a lesser extent, meningitis (Lawson, Metcalfe, and Pampiglione, 1965). Genetic metabolic diseases, such as PKU, should also be mentioned, for in most instances the child is born essentially normal, having depended before birth on his mother's metabolic system.

The preceding list should make clear the astonishing diversity of possible antecedents of brain damage, and the consequent difficulties in arriving at definitive diagnoses. The list also presents a challenge, because so many of the items can potentially be controlled. No pregnant mother need, for example, suffer dietary deficiencies, no child need ingest lead from flaking paint; older mothers can be discouraged from having children; many infections now can, or shortly will be preventable by appropriate vaccines. As long as we fail to control these potentially controllable precursors of damage, we may expect a toll in stillbirths and spontaneous abortions, in mild as well as severe retardation, and in many specific learning disabilities and unhealthy behavior traits in children whose intelligence is in the normal range (Lilienfeld and Parkhurst, 1951).

Psychosocial Factors[6]

Long before birth, the psychosocial environment intrudes on the development of the child, even as remotely as the mother's experiences during her own childhood, which are reflected in her ability to bear healthy children (Baird and Scott, 1953; Drillien, 1957). During the gestational period, factors connected with low socioeconomic status, such as medical care, maternal nutrition, infections, fatigue, and general health of the mother, all intrude upon the embryo and fetus.

Of at least equal importance, however, are the child's experiences in the psychosocial environment, his family, school, and community. Throughout this book, so much attention has been accorded the relationship between

[6] See also reviews by Freeberg (1967), Hunt (1961), McCandless (1964), and Robinson and Robinson (1965a).

intelligence and the experiences of the child that no attempt will be made here to summarize the many known and suspected relationships involved. It should be made clear, however, that all those factors which effect cognitive development within the normal range also affect the mentally retarded. Even the most profoundly retarded child is capable of response to his environment (Fuller, 1949; McKinney and Keele, 1963).

Cultural-Familial Mental Retardation. The diagnostic criteria by which a child is judged to exhibit cultural-familial mental retardation are threefold (Heber, 1959). First, the child must be mildly retarded; second, there must be no reasonable indication of a cerebral pathologic condition; and third, there must be evidence of retarded intellectual functioning in at least one of the parents and in one or more of any siblings. Thus the diagnosis rests on the absence of neurologic signs and on family background; it is a presumptive rather than a positive diagnosis.

The dismal picture of the family circumstances of the cultural-familial mentally retarded child has been documented in a variety of research investigations (e.g., Kugel and Parsons, 1967). Benda, Squires, Newell, Ogonik, Wise, and Akin (1964) found generalized deprivation in the backgrounds of 250 institutionalized cultural-familial retardates they studied.[7] The homes were characterized by family disintegration, mental retardation, mental illness, and emotional instability. Emotional mothering, nonverbal codes of communication, and verbal communication were all severely reduced in this group's experience. In another study which sampled mentally retarded children in British schools (Stein and Susser, 1963), the majority of educable retarded children without clinical signs of organicity were found to come from homes classified as "demotic," that is, homes in which the father was a manual worker and no member of the family had attended grammar school. Selective service rejectees in this country likewise tend to come from homes characterized by poverty, large numbers of children, and poor education (Pres-

It must be kept in mind, of course, that the 1% of mildly retarded children who are to be found in institutions constitute a negatively selected group.

ident's Task Force on Manpower Conservation, 1964).

Nowhere is the nature -nurture controversy still so alive as with respect to the etiology of this disorder, which has been an important focus of disagreement since the famous study by Dugdale (1877) of the pseudonymous Jukes family. By-and-large, however, the cultural-familial diagnosis, which characterizes by far the majority of retardates, can probably best be seen as multifactorial in etiology, combining the deleterious effects of polygenic inheritance with unlucky circumstances *in utero* and at birth, together with environments which are unable to meet physiological or psychological needs or to foster a high level of cognitive growth. That the numbers of cultural-familial retardates can be accommodated within the normal distribution of intelligence leads credence to the belief that no single factor can be incriminated, but that many determinants, each slight in its own effect, militate against the intellectual growth of these children. It seems probable, too, that in any given child, genetic or environmental factors may predominate; there is no reason to suspect identical or even similar patterns of etiology in this heterogeneous group. In this context, it should be pointed out that a great many so-called "cultural-familial" retardates exhibit abnormal EEG patterns and other signs of neurological damage (Kugel, 1963; Kugel and Parsons, 1967).

A great many psychosocial factors have been considered important in the etiology of cultural-familial retardation. Among the more important are emotional inadequacy of the parents; low level of achievement motivation of the family and the subculture of which it is a part; poor structure and limited elaborateness of the language patterns; racial and other differences which lead to discriminatory responses by individuals in the larger society; marginal financial status of the family; inaccessibility of special preventive or remedial instruction; nonadjustive family goals for children in areas of dependency, passivity, aggression, and self-control; father absence or uninvolvement; parental rejection and ignoring; inaccessibility of adults to reinforce and facilitate new behavior patterns; and so on (Chilman, 1965; Robinson, 1967b). In fact, in all the studies of social class differences conducted in the past decade, it is difficult to identify any factors in which lower socio-economic class families, from which these children come, produce a situation more favorable to the growth of intelligence in children than do middle-and upper-class families. Presumably, there are in addition genetic factors and physiological damage which are unfavorable to children from the lower socioeconomic class; the sum total is a dismal picture.

In line with current thinking about this group, Zigler (1967a, 1967b) has described the cultural-familial retarded child as an essentially normal individual of low intelligence, in whom no special defects are to be expected. He maintains that "the familial retardate's cognitive development differs from that of the normal individual only in respect to its rate and the upper limit achieved." On this basis, he predicts that groups of normals and cultural-familial retardates matched on mental age should not differ with respect to "formal cognitive processes related to I.Q." (1967a, p. 294). In general, as long as these cognitive processes have been measured in formal ways (e.g., those suggested by Piaget), mental age indeed appears to be the most salient yardstick, although there may be early leveling off by retardates (Jackson, 1965). Nevertheless, it must be remembered in investigating the psychological abilities, motivational variables, and achievement of retarded children that not only have they a longer history of experience (and thus, for example, a wider vocabulary in the horizontal sense [Spreen, 1965] than normal children of the same MA), but also that they come from a specific segment of society. It is necessary, therefore, although in practice unusual, to compare them with children of higher intelligence who come from the same social stratum. To find, for example, that cultural-familial children are differently affected by success and failure than are normal children (Heber, 1957) does not warrant the conclusion that the behavior of the cultural-familial children is a function of their low intelligence rather than the result of those general experiences having to do with the culture in which they have lived and learned.

Emotional Disturbance. There is little doubt that the incidences of emotional disturbance among the mentally retarded, and retardation among the emotionally disturbed, are higher than the incidence of either in the general population (Beier, 1964; Gardner 1961; Garfield, 1963; Philips, 1966). Among severely and profoundly retarded children there is an especially high incidence of psychotic behavior (O'Gorman, 1954). The concomitance results from a variety of complex relationships between these two somewhat arbitrarily defined aspects of human behavior. In many instances, it is likely that the retardation and emotional disturbances stem more or less directly from the same causes, whether these are primarily physiological or psychological, or both combined. Once they are present, it is probable that in most instances each tends to intensify the other to the further detriment of the child and his family.

Retarded children appear to be especially vulnerable to emotional stress because of deficiencies in judgment and anticipation which lead to repeated experiences of frustration and failure to meet the demands of the environment, and because of reduced capacity for sophisticated psychological defenses. Handicapped children are of necessity more dependent upon their families than are non-handicapped children. The parents of retarded children are, however, often retarded themselves and ill-equipped to meet the needs of children. The presence in a normal family of physically unattractive or markedly retarded child often engenders strong feelings of ambivalence and guilt in the parents. For children predisposed to disturbances in impulse control because of damage to the central nervous system or other causes (Philips, 1966), family and school life is likely to become a series of battles, the child in essence creating for himself a hostile world. Certainly discrepancies in the rates of physical, intellectual, and emotional growth can combine over time to produce an asynchrony of motivations, capabilities, and societal demands which exert additional pressures on the retarded child and his family.

Given the current state of our knowledge, it is clearly impossible in most instances to separate emotional maladjustment from mental retardation in children. Children tend to respond totally to a stress or defect in any sphere of life, and most emotionally disturbed and mentally retarded children tend therefore to show mixed symptoms in all spheres (Benda, Farrell, and Chipman, 1951). It a favorable development that the A.A.M.D. definition of mental retardation frees the clinician from the necessity of making an "either-or" decision between retardation and emotional disturbance, and enables him to concern himself with how best to help the child.

Childhood Schizophrenia.[8] On even an *a priori* basis, it is clear that the gross disturbances of reality contact, emotional lability, and social relationships exhibited by psychotic children are capable of interfering with processes that are basic to cognitive development. Indeed, well over half of the psychotic children who have been tested have been judged to be borderline or subnormal in intelligence (Pollack, 1958). Except in isolated islands of competence which sometimes appear, most children who have been psychotic from an early age exhibit varying degrees of cognitive deficit even when evaluated in the fairly propitious conditions of the individual testing situation; their functioning level is probably ordinarily at an even lower level.

A number of recent studies (e.g., Goldberg and Soper, 1963; Goldfarb, 1961; Hinton, 1963; Webster, 1963) have identified large numbers of children, competently adjudged psychotic, who exhibited upon close and prolonged examination a number of signs of organic central nervous system damage. The possibility appears strong, as Goldfarb (1961) has suggested, that some children are subjected to such overwhelming psychopathogenic factors that no organic substrate need be involved, but in other children organic factors are highly predisposing and produce deviant behavior in interaction with family settings which would have been adequate under normal circumstances.

Neurotic and Character Disorders. There is considerable evidence that, as a group, retardates tend to exhibit a rather high rate of neurotic and conduct disorders. To cite but two examples, Weaver (1946) found that of 8000 U. S. military recruits of subnormal intelligence, 44% of the men and 38% of the women, all of whom were adjudged acceptable at the time of induction, exhibited psychiatric or psychosomatic problems or repeatedly misbehaved. Similarly, Dewan (1948) found that during induction

assessment of a sample of Canadian recruits nearly half of the retarded were seen as emotionally unstable, compared with only about 20% in the group of normal intelligence.

There is less reason in the milder and often later-appearing forms of disturbance than in the case of childhood schizophrenia to expect strong causal effect of emotional disturbance upon intellectual functioning. While the possibility of such a relationship is not denied, as yet there is little firm evidence to support such a conclusion (Beier, 1964). On the other hand, it should again be pointed out that the basis for a diagnosis of mental retardation rests not upon intellectual factors alone, but upon a variety of gross measures of behavioral adequacy (Heber, 1959). In this sense, it can be said that neurotic maladjustment and character disorders do play a causal role, for in a sizable proportion of mildly retarded individuals, especially adults, a more adequate personal adjustment would preclude the diagnosis. In fact, surveys of adult retardates in work situations clearly indict personality problems rather than inability to perform the work as the chief reason for failure. Success in obtaining and keeping a job is related to many variables, including initiative, self-confidence, cooperation, cheerfulness, social mixing with other employees, respect for the supervisor, responsibility, promptness, temperamental stability, and efficiency in work habits (Cohen, 1960; Collman and Newlyn, 1956, 1957; Goldstein, 1964; Kolstoe, 1961; Neuhaus, 1967; Warren, 1961).

Institutionalization. Among the first demonstrations of the importance of very early childhood experiences in determining intelligence and adjustment were widely publicized studies of infants reared in institutions (Goldfarb, 1955; Spitz, 1945; Skeels and Dye, 1939). Later studies of children reared in institutions have tended to demonstrate that the important factor is not institutionalization per se but rather the nature of the care received (Dennis, 1960; Rheingold, 1960; Skeels and Dye, 1939; Skeels, 1966), although even "enriched" institutional programs are not usually as favorable to development as an adequate home (Stedman and Eichorn, 1964).

It should be clear that any study of the effects of institutionalization upon retarded

---

[8] See also Chapters 28 and 29 in this book.

children must take into account the quality of the care offered in relation to the child's needs. Within a single institution, there are often marked differences among programs; even in institutions with excellent reputations for remedial programs, there may be custodial wards in which retarded children receive only minimal attention.

Studies of retarded children in institutions are very difficult to decipher because of the strong selective influences which surround admission. Children who enter institutions very early in life are likely to be severely or profoundly retarded, to have medical problems and physical handicaps, and to exhibit behavior problems, especially hyperactivity, which interfere with family management (Graliker, Koch, and Henderson, 1965; Olshansky and Schonfield, 1964). These children come from adequate as well as inadequate homes. Children in the mildly retarded range are usually institutionalized at a later age and for a shorter time (Dingman, 1959), and behavior problems and delinquency tend to play a much more important role in precipitating their institutionalization (Benda et al., 1964; Graliker et al., 1965; Maney, Pace, and Morrison, 1964). These children tend to come from much less adequate homes (Hobbs, 1964; Olshansky and Schonfield, 1964).

Mildly retarded children actually constitute a minority of institutionalized children (Scheerenberger, 1965), and thus most studies of institutionalization have dealt with the more severely retarded. Moreover, typical studies in this area have compared children in at least average homes with those in institutions who are from homes which must be judged far below average. Some studies, which deserve special attention, have evaluated children before and after admission to institutions, the children thus serving as their own controls (Clarke, Clarke, and Reiman, 1958). A few other well-controlled studies have compared mongoloid children reared in their own homes with those from equivalent families who have been institutionalized on routine medical advice (Centerwall and Centerwall, 1960; Shipe and Shotwell, 1965; Stedman and Eichorn, 1964).

By far the greatest attention has been paid the social deprivation aspects of institutionalization. Very early admission to an institu-

tion apparently prevents the establishment of meaningful and deep ties to other people (Goldfarb, 1943; Matejcek and Langmeier, 1965). Moreover, the institutionalized retardate develops a wariness of interacting with strangers on a meaningful level, presumably because of a history of painful experiences (Zigler, 1967a). It has been clearly documented, however, that despite this wariness in strange relationships, institutionalized retarded and normal children are highly motivated to seek and maintain interactions with supportive adults. Institutionalized children will persist, for example, in performing a simple, uninteresting task for a significantly longer period than will noninstitutionalized children when an experimenter is present (Green and Zigler, 1962; Stevenson and Fahel, 1961). This persistence has been related to the degree of the child's social deprivation prior to institutionalization (Zigler and Williams, 1963), and to the degree of deprivation within the institution itself (Butterfield and Zigler, 1965a).

In the typical institution there is some indication that the child initially is highly motivated to seek supportive adult interactions, but that as his reaching out is unreinforced, he tends to withdraw from susceptibility to the kind of support which is available in an experimental session (McConnell, 1965; Stevenson and Knights, 1962), so that responsiveness is inversely related to length of institutionalization. With increasing length of institutionalization, retarded children not only cease to persevere at simple tasks, but they become less outer-directed in general (less suggestible, less imitative, less sensitive to verbal cues, less visually alert to their environment) than noninstitutionalized retarded children, who, lacking confidence in their abilities, tend to rely on others for solutions to their problems (Zigler, 1966). In general, it is clear that the typical institutional setting is poorly suited to maintain healthy social relationships, but it is encouraging to note that an enriched social climate within an institution is able to counteract this state of affairs to some extent, at least (Butterfield and Zigler, 1965a).

Few of the many possible personality variables possibly affected by institutionalization have been studied very objectively, and it is in this general area more than any other that the poorer adjustment of retardates prior to admission must be considered. A substantial improvement in social adjustment, for example, was found by Clarke, Clarke, and Reiman (1958) following institutionalization of adolescents from very adverse backgrounds. On the other hand, mildly retarded adolescent girls evaluated by Guthrie, Butler, and Gorlow (1963) tended to regard themselves as more worthless and to be more self-oriented than did noninstitutionalized girls matched for age, IQ, and economic background. The finding that these institutionalized girls seldom admitted to feelings of anger is particularly interesting in view of institutional codes, which are probably more repressive and authoritarian than those in own homes (Stein and Longenecker, 1962).

As shown by the studies of mongoloid children, those institutionalized very early tend not to develop at a rate equivalent to those in their own homes. However, there is evidence (Clarke and Clarke, 1954; Clarke et al., 1958) that removal from a very inadequate environment to an institution in adolescence may be accompanied by a distinct rise in tested intelligence.

There are some indications that verbal development is especially vulnerable to retardation when children grow up in an institutional setting (Lyle, 1961; Schlanger, 1964; Sievers and Essa, 1961; Skeels, Updegraff, Wellman, and Williams, 1938). On the other hand, occasional studies have found little indication of this differential, and a few have even found its reversal (Mueller and Weaver, 1964; Wachs and Butterfield, 1965).

It has also been suggested that the retarded child outside the institution is buffeted by the demands of normal society so that he is deprived of feelings of success, whereas the institution makes more reasonable demands. Noonan and Barry (1967), for example, reported that noninstitutionalized retardates worked longer and faster in an experimental situation than did either normals or institutionalized retardates when, and only when, they were given considerable verbal encouragement. Clearly more research is needed, since there is some indication that parents of retardates in a private school actually have lower standards for their children's achievement than do the attendants

working with the children (Stein and Longenecker, 1962).

Although the evidence is not clear that institutionalization need always have deleterious effects upon the adjustment and achievement of children, it certainly is clear that better institutions are needed. Far too many are understaffed, underequipped, and in general far below the standards acceptable for child care. In order to retain the solution of institutional care for some children, substantial improvements are required. As society is presently organized, institutionalization presents a reasonable alternative to many adequate families, whose children require intensive medical attention, or whose presence within an ordinary home setting is extremely disruptive. For other children from inadequate homes, the institution may be the only alternative to foster-home care, which is often very difficult to obtain for retarded children with behavior problems.

It is therefore unfortunate that the consensus has become so firm that institutionalization is always an inferior alternative to home care. This consensus has served to effectively discourage attempts to discover innovative improvements in methods of institutional care, so that the institution has in essence been isolated from community solutions, and has received much less than its share of research support. Although some recent attempts to provide such innovative efforts have received support from the federal government (Secretary's Committee on Mental Retardation, 1967), considerable further work is needed in this area.

LEARNING BY RETARDATES[9]

In the past several years, there has been an unusual proliferation of studies of the learning behavior of retardates. In general, the studies have had at least one of three aims: (1) to demonstrate that the laws of learning established with lower animals and

[9] Because there exist careful reviews of the literature to the mid-1960s (Astrup, Sersen, and Wortis, 1967; Denny, 1964; Ellis, 1963a, Chaps. 2-5 and 11-13; Robinson and Robinson, 1965a; Watson, 1967; Watson and Lawson, 1966) no attempt will be made here to review comprehensively the extensive literature on learning by retardates.

other human beings also apply to the mentally retarded; (2) to demonstrate specific although not necessarily unique deficits in learning by retardates who are compared with normal children of the same chronological or mental age; and (3) to discover specific teaching techniques which are especially effective with retarded children.

By and large, the first aim has been reached; it has been demonstrated that retardates' learning is determined by the same laws as are the behaviors of other children and subhuman species (Watson and Lawson, 1966). The same dimensions of the learning process and of performance which have proved relevant to other groups are relevant also to the behavior of retardates.

The second aim, the demonstration of specific deficits in learning common to, but not necessarily unique to retardates, has tended to lead to research endeavors which have been minimally fruitful. A number of theorists have, however, advanced hypotheses about retardate learning deficits (e.g., Zigler, 1967a). Actually, there is little reason to suspect that special deficits should be shown by all or even most retardates matched with normals for mental age. As we have seen, retardates constitute a very heterogeneous group, ranging in IQ from zero to 85, in mental age from zero to above 13 years, and with vast differences in etiology, in neurological integrity, in life experiences, in physical capacities, in motivation, in adjustment, and so on. Compounding this situation, researchers have tended not to be careful in describing subject groups, or in attempting to select homogeneous or contrasting groups. Even when cultural-familial children have been contrasted with "organics" of equivalent MA, previous learning histories of both groups have been ignored and the brain-injured have tended to be grossly neurologically handicapped. This state of affairs probably has stemmed in part from a lack of sophistication by learning theorists uninformed about mental retardation and in part from the assumption by a few workers that retardation in any context should be characterized by particular defects in learning. As has been indicated, not only the retardate's ability to learn but his motivation to perform are highly dependent upon many factors, including his history of relationships with others. It is clear that if investigations

of special defects are to aid in our understanding of the learning processes of mentally retarded individuals, great care must be given to the design of these investigations and great caution must be applied in generalizing from specific results with specific subgroups.

With respect to the final aim, the discovery of effective teaching methods, the most successful work has dealt with the application of operant conditioning techniques to learning in the retarded. Primarily by demonstrations of such techniques in a variety of situations, by the development of techniques of programmed instruction, and by increased understanding of reinforcement principles by teachers, can the field of learning theory be said to have contributed to practical work with retarded children. Additional contributions have, of course, occurred in such other areas as the delineation of factors relevant to visual discrimination learning by trainable retardates, but in none of these areas has so enthusiastic or fruitful an application of laboratory findings taken place.

Attention and Distractibility. A number of research studies point to the importance of attention to relevant cues in learning by retardates. An extensive set of studies which have considered the slope of learning curves in moderately and severely retarded institutionalized children has been reported by Zeaman and House (1963; Zeaman, 1965). The experimental task usually involved a two-choice discrimination, using the Wisconsin General Test apparatus. These authors have shown that the most important differences in simple discrimination learning between normals and these retardates appeared in the earliest stages of the learning, and constitute a slowness among the retarded subjects in "zeroing in" on the relevant cues in the situation (Zeaman and House, 1958a, 1958b). In addition, ability to maintain concentration was often poorer in these subjects than in normal children. The length of the initial phase of the learning curve, which appears flat because essentially only chance successes are occurring, varied widely in the retarded subjects. Lower-MA subjects (MA 2–4) took much longer to begin to show improvement than did higher-MA subjects (MA 4–6). Once improvement began, however, both groups learned rapidly and attained equal levels of mastery. Zeaman and House contend that the initial, flat stage corresponds with the period of developing attention to the relevant cues, while the steeper rate, which appears rather suddenly, is indicative of the active stage of instrumental discriminative learning. Particularly concerning the facilitation of learning in the severely handicapped, these studies point to the importance of setting up learning situations so that relevant cues are of maximum salience. The roles of motivation, reinforcement, and understanding of the task as other determinants of the shape of the learning (performance) curve must not, of course, be overlooked.

The complaint is often voiced that retarded children are more "distractible" than are normal children, by which it is usually meant that the presence of a distracting stimulus is thought to be more disruptive to the performance of retardates. Indeed, retarded children do tend to have more difficulty in maintaining concentration and in attending to relevant stimuli, but it should be pointed out that these deficits may stem from internal factors rather unrelated to the presence or absence of distracting stimuli in the external environment. As a matter of fact, the weight of the evidence from studies of both brain-injured and cultural-familial groups tends to indicate that the presence of external distracting stimuli is no more disruptive to these individuals than to normals of comparable MA, and may in some instances even enhance performance for all groups (Baumeister, 1963; Brown, 1964a, 1964b; Cromwell and Foshee, 1960; Ellis, Hawkins, Pryer, and Jones, 1963; Gardner, Cromwell, and Foshee, 1959; Girardeau and Ellis, 1964; Schlanger, 1958; Spradlin, Cromwell, and Foshee, 1960). Most of the studies show no more tendency toward distractibility, in this sense, among brain-injured than among cultural-familial retardates, except perhaps in brain-injured children with very severe organic injuries (Cruse, 1961).

It seems clear that many severely and moderately retarded children do have difficulty in attending to a task, but that this distractibility usually stems from internal disruption and lack of focus. While casting doubt on the theoretical assumptions underlying the design of teaching techniques and materials for use with brain-injured children (e.g.,

Strauss and Kephart, 1955; Strauss and Lehtinen, 1947), which simplify the environment and minimize the presence of distracting stimuli, such techniques and materials may still be useful in facilitating organically impaired children's return to the central task after internally based disruptions have occurred.

Classical Conditioning. Classical conditioning has not been a popular focus of Anglo-American research, but it has been an important vehicle for research with retardates in the Soviet Union (e.g., Luria, 1963). Denny (1964) and Astrup, Serson, and Wortis (1967), summarizing work in this area, conclude that retardates, especially the less severely handicapped, condition about as rapidly as do normal subjects matched for CA. It should be noted, however, that rapid conditionability is not necessarily a sign of developmental maturity. More severely retarded and brain-injured subjects tend to condition somewhat more slowly than do normal individuals (e.g., Franks and Franks, 1950). As soon as verbal signals and symbolic systems become involved, even the mildly retarded begin to show deficits in conditioned learning.

In addition, retardates consistently extinguish classically conditioned responses more slowly than do normal subjects. To Denny (1964) and to Astrup et al. (1967), this finding seems to fit into a wider pattern of a deficit of inhibition. The finding may also be related to the Zeaman-House suggestion that the retardate is slow to center on relevant cues (i.e., inhibit responses to irrelevant cues), and possibly also to Zigler's (1962) findings of heightened motivation to persevere in simple tasks by socially deprived, institutionalized children motivated only by the generalized reinforcement of the presence of the experimenter. The Russian studies and, for the most part, American studies have, however, investigated classical conditioning primarily in brain-damaged subjects. It may be suspected that the disinhibition and distractibility prominent in some brain-injured children are specific to a subgroup and cannot be applied to the entire range of the retarded.

Operant Conditioning. It has been clear for some time (Mitrano, 1939) that retarded children, like others, are responsive to techniques of operant conditioning and that they are capable of response-shaping and of predictable increments and decrements in desirable and undesirable responses. Moreover, they are capable of responding differentially to the four basic schedules of reinforcement (Bijou and Orlando, 1965). There are, however, some behavioral differences which are probably related to low intelligence, brain damage, or both.

As in classical conditioning, extinction of established responses appears to be slower in individuals of low mental ability. This slower extinction may stem from a variety of sources: from impairment of inhibitory capacity, from retarded information-processing, from a reduced repertoire of alternative strategies or competing responses, from incidental reinforcement (such as the attention of the experimenter) inherent in the experimental situation (Green and Zigler, 1962), and so on. Oatley, Bryant, and Tinson (1965) found that severely retarded children were slow to modify their responses in the face of nonreinforcement, but that the shift could be speeded by preventing the operation of the previous response. Little investigation has been made of patterns of extinction of operant responses in the retarded, but it appears that extinction is less closely related to the schedule of reinforcement under which the response was acquired than in normal children (Spradlin, 1962), and there is often a high resistance to schedule shifting after variable interval training (Orlando and Bijou, 1960).

Variability from session to session may be more extreme than is typical of other subjects (Barrett and Lindsley, 1962), and the more retarded subjects tend to show erratic pauses (Ellis, Barnett, and Pryer, 1960) but, in general, higher MA groups show a higher overall rate of response (Barnett, Ellis, and Pryer, 1960). It may be more difficult to establish secondary reinforcers with severely retarded subjects (Girardeau, 1962), although this clearly can be accomplished (Watson, Lawson, and Sanders, 1965). Predictable relationships between these variables and age, IQ, verbal ability, diagnosis, or length of institutionalization have not been consistent (Barrett, 1965).

Operant conditioning techniques have been very successfully applied to the amelioration of a wide range of behavior problems in re-

tarded subjects. Even the most profoundly retarded subjects have been found capable of learning under these conditions (Fuller, 1965). The use of positive reinforcers and, less frequently, negative reinforcers in the control of self-help, social, and educational behaviors in the severely and profoundly retarded has been an enthusiastic focus of research (Ullman and Krasner, 1965; Watson, 1967). Toilet training, for example, has been shown to be amenable to operant conditioning techniques (Hundziak, Maurer, and Watson, 1965; Watson, 1965), as has training for a variety of other patterns of desired behavior (Bensberg, Colwell, and Cassel, 1965; Girardeau and Spradlin, 1964). Birnbrauer and Lawler (1964), for example, used token reinforcements, both immediate and delayed, in classes of severely retarded institutionalized subjects to obtain not only acceptable social and self-help behavior within the classroom, but also persistent independent work on programmed lessons. Mildly retarded children, too, are responsive to such techniques; the hyperactivity of a mildly retarded boy with minimal brain damage, for example, responded readily to their use (Patterson, 1965).

Although it has been clearly established that the armamentarium of operant conditioning techniques is applicable to the behavior of retarded children, it is still not clear how transfer of skills may be best engineered (Baumeister and Klosowiski, 1965; Sidman, 1966), how skills may be maintained after a return to nonexperimental reinforcement schedules (Watson, 1967), and how carefully engineered experimental techniques can best be adopted for use by nonspecialists such as ward attendants, teachers, and parents.

Discrete-Trial Discrimination Learning. Studies of discrimination learning in retardates are abundant, dating back at least to studies by Kuhlmann published in 1904. The abundance of these studies is in part attributable to ease and neatness of available experimental designs and to the fact that problems may be made simple enough to fall well within the capabilities of retarded children. In most studies the subjects have been vaguely discribed, and details of procedure have varied widely.

Several studies have not, in fact, found significant differences between retardates and normal children of comparable mental age

(Ellis and Sloan, 1959; Kass and Stevenson, 1961; Martin and Blum, 1961; Plenderleith, 1956; Stevenson, 1960; Stevenson and Zigler, 1957), but a larger number of studies have found retardates inferior, sometimes dramatically inferior, to matched-MA normal controls (Girardeau, 1959; House and Zeaman, 1958a, 1958b; Hetherington, Ross, and Pick, 1964; Rudel, 1959; Stevenson and Iscoe, 1955). The seeming contradiction between these two sets of studies apparently depends upon the manipulation of a number of factors in the experimental situation, and to some extent upon the degree and kind of intellectual handicap of the retarded subjects. Mildly retarded cultural-familial children tend to show less deficit than do brain-damaged retardates or those with mental ages below about 5 years. It is clear, also, that retardates are likely to show a marked tendency for a position effect in choosing between stimuli; studies which have employed three concurrent stimuli rather than two have, therefore, less strongly reinforced the position effect and have tended to show less deficit in retardates' responses (Denny, 1964).

Moderately retarded subjects have difficulty, as we have seen, in attending to the relevant dimensions of the problem and appear to focus, when they do at all, on broad classes of stimuli rather than on specific cues (Zeaman, 1965). Studies which have involved the direction of attention of subjects by such techniques as introducing novel stimuli into a series of trials (Zeaman, House, and Orlando, 1958), increasing proximity in space of stimulus to reward (Zeaman and House, 1963), using familiar objects rather than simplified visual patterns (Zeaman et al., 1958) and eliminating delay of reinforcement (Schoelkopf and Orlando, 1965) have tended to facilitate learning. The presence of an experimenter has also appeared to help direct attention to the task at hand (Denny, 1965). On the other hand, as would be expected, retardates tend to show increased deficit when the discrimination task is difficult or the success criterion very high, and when changes in difficulty are introduced during a series of discrimination trials (Katz, 1967).

Among the moderately and severely retarded, at least, verbal mediation plays a less important role in discrimination learning than does attention (Milgram and Furth, 1964,

1967; Zeaman, 1965). The deficits in verbal mediation processes have also been confirmed in other aspects of learning, such as verbal conditioning (Metzger, 1960; Shipe, 1959) and verbal and abstract learning (Berkson and Cantor, 1960; Griffith and Spitz, 1958; Griffith, Spitz, and Lipman, 1959; Stacey and Cantor, 1953; Weatherwax and Benoit, 1958). Luria (1959) has emphasized the poor verbal regulation of motor behavior in the organically retarded child. When such control exists, it tends to be more concretely related to the physical properties (sound) of the word, rather than its meaning (Luria and Vinogradova, 1959). Children who can spontaneously name stimuli tend to learn more rapidly (Zeaman et al., 1958) and teaching retarded subjects names for the stimuli also tends to aid discrimination accuracy (Barnett, Ellis, and Pryer, 1959; Cantor and Hottel, 1957), although response latencies may be increased (Rieber, 1964).

In line with the observation of a deficit in verbal mediation is the finding that retarded children sometimes actually show less deficit in discrimination reversal than do normal subjects (O'Connor and Hermelin, 1959; Penney, Croskery, and Allen, 1962), and are less disrupted by conflict situations such as choosing between two previously negative cues (Heal, Ross, Sanders, and Scholwalter, 1965). If verbal mediational cues were being employed, original sets to respond should be more persistent. Conflicting evidence in this area, however, is substantial (Gardner, 1948; Milgram and Furth, 1964; Plenderleith, 1956; Stevenson and Zigler, 1957).

Paired-Associate and Serial Learning. A number of investigators have employed paired-associate learning and serial-learning techniques with retarded subjects, despite the rather high demands made by these methods for sustained attention and symbolic skills. The experimental evidence suggests that retardate performance is often inferior to that of matched-CA controls but not necessarily to that of matched-MA controls. As the learning tasks become more difficult and verbal mediators become more important, retarded subjects are increasingly at a disadvantage.

Studies of paired-associate learning which have employed familiar pictures rather than printed words, however, have not consistently demonstrated a significant advantage for normal subjects of like CA except when they were very bright (Akutagwa and Benoit, 1959; Berkson and Cantor, 1960; Lott, 1958; Podolsky, 1965). Contrary evidence was, however, obtained by J. Robinson (1965) with mildly retarded and normal girls. On the other hand, with subjects below IQ 50, there does appear to be impairment even in tasks employing familiar pictures, when subjects are compared with controls matched for MA (Podolsky, 1965).

With paired-associate tasks employing nonsense syllables (Ahmad, 1963; Jensen, 1965; Johnson and Blake, 1960), numbers (J. Robinson, 1965), or paired visual and auditory stimuli (Blue, 1963) mildly retarded individuals have tended to be at a disadvantage. Within the narrow IQ-range of the mildly retarded group, however, IQ may not be related to associative learning ability (Kingsley, 1964).

In the more difficult serial verbal learning tasks, retardates have tended to fare even less well (Ellis, Pryer, Distephano, and Pryer, 1960; Jensen, 1965; Pryer, 1960). The experimental results are not entirely consistent (Cassel, 1957; Johnson and Blake, 1960), but the weight of the evidence indicates that under most experimental conditions, retarded subjects do rather poorly compared with normal subjects of their own MA, and that the more abstract and verbal the task, the more clearly this disadvantage appears (Lipman, 1963).

Stimulus Generalization and Transfer of Training. Teachers and parents frequently observe that retarded children fail to apply in new contexts what they already know, that, in other words, they fail to generalize from one stimulus situation to another, or to infer general rules on the basis of learning in a specific context (Bryant, 1964). There is little experimental work in this important area. The few available studies suggest that there is essential equivalence between normal and retarded groups of equal MA when only simple stimulus generalization is involved (Barnett, 1958), but that in complex situations, normal subjects tend more frequently to utilize learned cues in generalizing their responses. For example, Bialer (1961b) devised a rather complicated procedure in which transfer on the basis of concrete stimulus similarity could be distinguished from

transfer on the basis of learned equivalent names for dissimilar stimuli. To a greater extent than the mildly retarded subjects, normal subjects of the same CA tended to utilize the learned name in attacking the problem. Other studies (Bryant, 1965; Singler, 1964) have suggested that severely subnormal subjects tend to transfer on the basis of relatively general, conglomerate, "peanut brittle" learning, whereas normal subjects are better able to select specific learned cues on which to base transfer. In simple conditioning situations, for example, the subjects often either concentrate poorly or fail to discriminate the original stimulus, responding perhaps to the overall demand for some action, and thus producing overgeneralization to similar cues (Astrup et al., 1967).

While there may be such deficits in retarded children, the trend of studies tends to suggest that they, like normal children, exhibit transfer when the experimenter has paid careful attention to the variety of stimulus presentations in original learning (Watson, 1964), when he has provided for sufficient repetition and positive reinforcement, and when he has made an effort to teach by understanding rather than by rote memory (Katz, 1964).

Learning Set. Closely related to the problems of stimulus generalization and transfer of training are the problems concerning the ability to form learning sets, that is, to improve with practice on a series of similar discrimination learning problems. A number of studies have found that the rate of improvement during successive problems is associated with MA (Berkson and Cantor, 1960; Ellis, 1958; Harter, 1967; Kaufman and Peterson, 1958; Stevenson and Swartz, 1958). Of greater relevance is the finding that the more severely retarded subjects do not establish learning sets as effectively as do normal children matched for MA (Girardeau, 1959; Harter, 1967; House, 1964; Katz, 1967; Prysiazniuk and Wicijowski, 1964; Wischner and O'Donnell, 1961). In some situations moderately and severely retarded children exhibit, in fact, an even weaker tendency to establish learning sets than do lower primates (House and Zeaman, 1958), possibly because of marked perseveration in responding to the position rather than to the nature of the stimuli (Ellis, Girardeau, and Pryer, 1963).

The child's pattern of previous experience apparently is an important ingredient in his ability to establish learning sets. Noninstitutionalized retardates, for example, appear to establish learning sets more effectively than do matched institutionalized subjects (Harter, 1967; Kaufman, 1963). The subject's experience of success or failure in this type of situation is also important (House and Zeaman, 1960; Kass and Stevenson, 1961). Zeaman and House (1960), for example, found that moderately retarded subjects who had experienced prolonged failure on a difficult problem were then unable to solve much simpler problems, although they had previously been able to do so, possibly because their attention to relevant aspects of the stimuli had been extinguished, or possibly because of their expectancy of failure.

Memory: Long-Term Versus Short-Term.
The observation has often been recorded that retarded children do not seem to remember very well what they have learned. There is plentiful evidence to the contrary, however; retarded children who have learned a response to the same degree of mastery as have normal children of the same CA remember that response equally well over a protracted period of time (Cantor and Ryan, 1962; Delker, 1965; Johnson and Blake, 1960; Lance, 1965; Lott, 1958; Vergason, 1964). Several factors are probably at work in the observation that retardates do not *seem* to remember well. First, it is likely that because original learning is more difficult for them, retardates do not sufficiently master the responses in the beginning. Second, it is likely that the recall situations are not often identical to that in which the responses were learned, and that retardates are actually being asked to generalize from original learning; this is a task which, as we have already seen, is a more difficult one. Finally, when forgetting does occur, it may be the result of a reduction in interim-rehersal due to retardates' restricted opportunities to have put to use the skills and information so laboriously acquired, or due to the irrelevance of the learning to the childrens' everyday experiences. It is clear that management of the original learning situation and the provision of opportunities for continuing applications of the learned material are important aspects of the educator's task in helping retarded children to utilize their apparently normal ability to remember over a protracted period.

The situation with respect to short-term memory may not be as favorable to the retarded child. Short-term memory involves the type of temporary storage that enables one to remember a telephone number while making call, without actually learning it. It has been suggested by a number of researchers (e.g., Peterson, 1966) that short-term memory does not involve the same kind of structural changes in the central nervous system that occur with long-term memory (learning), but rather it depends upon a stimulus trace, or reverberatory neuronal mechanism, which persists for only a very short time, measured in seconds rather than hours or days. Ellis (1963b) has postulated that an essential short-term memory defect accounts for many of the learning difficulties of retardates. He sees most retardates as suffering subnormal integrity of the central nervous system. With regard to individuals with such neuropathology and/or immaturity, Ellis hypothesizes that the stimulus trace is both shortened in duration and lessened in intensity. This reduction hampers short-term storage needed in the processes of establishing long-term memory. It also makes it more difficult for the retardate to see separate events as contiguous, or related, because the trace of the first has disappeared when the second event occurs.

Ellis has, in fact, been able to marshal considerable evidence to demonstrate the inadequacy of short-term memory in retardates. His evidence has been culled from studies of serial verbal learning, delayed responses, brain-wave characteristics, reaction-time studies, fixed-interval reinforcement studies, and from factor-analytic treatment of intelligence-test results. A number of other workers have found corroborative data in experiments designed specifically to test the stimulus-trace hypothesis by comparing retardates with normal controls (e.g., Baumeister, Smith, and Rose, 1965; Blue, 1965; Hermelin and O'-Connor, 1964).

As convincing as are Ellis' theory and its supporting data, his contentions have not invariably been confirmed by experimental results (e.g., Belmont, 1967; Cantor and Ryan, 1962; Hawkins, 1963; Headrick and Ellis, 1964). As Ellis himself suggests, the theory should be considered at this point no more than a set of provocative hypotheses.

STUDIES OF PERSONALITY IN MENTALLY RETARDED CHILDREN

It should not, perhaps, be surprising that so few empirical studies of personality development and functioning in retarded children are to be found in the literature. Very few lines of research have been followed with any persistence or success in this area, and contrasted with studies of cognitive functioning in retardates, our evidence concerning personality is meager and often contradictory.

It is not difficult to find explanations for this state of affairs. To begin, the IQ is, in practice, used as almost the only basis for distinguishing the retarded from the normal population of children. This most often applies to the mildly retarded, who usually do not exhibit blatant physiological symptoms and who generally pass the early developmental milestones within the normal range. Most of them are not identified as retarded until they are confronted with the rigorous intellectual requirements posed by the schools. Thus categorized primarily on the basis of deficient cognitive abilities, it is to be expected that they would show much greater diversity in personality than in intellectual functioning. It is similarly to be expected that retarded children should be amenable to description according to the same personality variables that vary among normal children (Cromwell, 1959).

An equally potent reason for the paucity of important research in this area is the lack of appropriate research tools. Personality research is difficult enough with normal and superior children. It is much more difficult with retarded children, who tend to give rather barren responses to most projective materials, and who frequently cannot respond appropriately to group tests which require reading, sustained attention, self-evaluation, and an understanding of complex relationships.

Investigations of personality in retarded children are certainly not, however, a matter of indifference. Personality functioning is intimately related to social adjustment, achievement, and even to the development of intelligence. Among mildly retarded adults, as we have seen, success in obtaining and keeping a job is much more closely related to personality and work-habit variables than to ability to learn the simple job skills demanded. Achievement in school is also clearly correlated with adequacy of personal adjustment among retardates (Snyder, 1964; Snyder, Jefferson, and Strauss, 1965). It is unfortunate then, that many writers have so freely described the personality handicaps of the retarded in the almost total absence of corroborating evidence (Heber, 1964).

Emotional Disturbance. The relatively high incidence of emotional disorders among retarded children has been discussed in a previous section, and some of the reasons for the frequent concomitance of retardation and emotional disturbance have been examined. It is probably that most retarded children face unusual hazards in personality development, and that the more severe forms of emotional disturbance play a causative role in producing intellectual deficit. For all retarded children, whatever the source of their retardation, problems of living are made more stressful by difficulties in problem solving and foresight, by limited repertoires of behavioral alternatives, by experiences of failure, and by a number of other factors which are associated with both limited intelligence and with being unable to satisfy fully the demands of family and society.

Lewinian Concept of Rigidity. It is chiefly of historical value to mention, among studies of personality in retardates, the Lewin-Kounin hypothesis developed to explain differences between cultural-familial retarded and normal individuals. Lewin (1935) made use of two concepts of development: increasing differentiation, or the numbers of regions within the personality and in the perceived environment; and increasing rigidity, or reduction in the permeability of boundaries between regions. He assumed that the former is related to mental age, and the latter to chronological age. It should be noted that the concept of rigidity, as Lewin used the word, did not apply to behavior, and did not, in fact correspond with many other ordinary connotations of the word. A rigidity of boundaries might result in perseveration and stereotyped behavior in some situations, but in others it might enable the individual to begin a new activity more easily without interference from a previous pattern related to a different region of the personality.

Using various satiation and classification-shifting techniques, Kounin (e.g., 1941a, 1941b) gathered apparently confirming evidence with older and younger mental retardates and normal subjects, all groups equal in mean MA but differing in mean CA and IQ. These studies, although widely accepted for a time, came under increasing criticism concerning their methodology and interpretation (e.g., Zigler, 1962). By far the most concerted attack on the Lewin-Kounin work came from a series of recent experiments by Zigler, Stevenson, and their colleagues (e.g., Stevenson and Fahel, 1961; Stevenson and Zigler, 1957; Zigler, 1961; Zigler and de-Labry, 1962; Zigler, Hodgen, and Stevenson, 1958; Zigler and Unell, 1962). They have taken the position, for which they have amassed considerable evidence, that differences in Kounin-like tasks between subjects of the same MA are due entirely to motivational factors. Institutionalized children, for example, both normal and retarded, tend to show no satiation effects (i.e., to show high "rigidity") on Zigler's simple tasks, evidently as a product of their very high degree of motivation for the social reinforcement of the examiner's presence.

Cognitive flexibility in object-sorting activities of the type investigated by Kounin can evidently be learned almost as well by retardates as by normal subjects. Corter and McKinney (1966), who studied educable retardates and normal children of the same MA, found the normal children only slightly better at such tasks when first tested, and found the groups making the same amount of improvement during training.

Tempering these findings somewhat is a study of speed and accuracy in complex card-sorting tasks (Backer, 1965), in which not only motivational factors but hypotheses consistent with a Lewinian formulation were substantiated. This view is not widely held, however, and it may be concluded that the Lewin-Kounin hypothesis was important chiefly for the intensive lines of research which it generated.

Motivation. Heber (1964) has reviewed the existing literature on the experimental manipulation of motivation in retarded subjects. Studies in this area have usually at-tempted to vary incentives and reinforcers rather than to manipulate need or excitation level. This variable has received considerable attention precisely because it is subject to experimental test. Although some experimenters have not found retardates' performances to vary significantly with differences in the nature of reinforcement or incentive (e.g., Cantor and Hottel, 1955; Evans, 1964; Wolfensberger, 1960), it seems probable that in these studies the experimental differences were not meaningful to the children, or that they were overridden in importance by other variables such as the simple attention of the experimenter. In fact, most studies have demonstrated that even severely retarded children are sensitive to most kinds of variation in reinforcers, both positive and negative, social and nonsocial, material and nonmaterial, primary and secondary, smaller and larger, more and less favored, and so on (Heber, 1964). It is of little value to demonstrate the obvious fact that motivational variables are important in retarded children, but there is considerable practical value in exploring whether there are reinforcers which tend to be particularly potent for retarded children as a group or, more likely, whether there are reinforcers which are especially potent for subgroups and individual children, and which may be utilized in enhancing their learning in real-life situations at home and school. Material reinforcers, for example, have appeared to be more effective with retarded than with non-retarded individuals (Perry and Stotsky, 1965). It should be pointed out, however, that there is considerable variation from group to group and individual to individual in the potency of various reinforcers, apparently dependent upon the child's history of experience with different classes of reinforcers, his success-failure ratio, sex, age, mental age, and so on.

Few studies have investigated specific types of motivation. In the important area of achievement motivation, for example, only two important studies can be found. Retarded children apparently tend to express lower achievement motivation as measured by Mc-Clelland techniques than do normal children (Jordan and DeCharms, 1959), and brain-injured children may be less willing to compete than are cultural-familial retardates, probably expressing the results of long-standing frustration, differences in parental expectations, or both (Tolman and Johnson, 1958).

Expectancy and Locus of Control. Another sizable body of literature has stemmed from the work of Rotter (1954). Studies in this area have been concerned with retarded children's expectations of success and failure. According to Cromwell and his co-workers, who have conducted most of the relevant research, a child's previous history of reinforcement and his developmental level are among the chief determinants of his expectations concerning a novel situation and of his reactions to success and failure.

First, it has been reasoned that the retarded child's reactions to reward and punishment differ from those of the normal child, in large part because of the retardate's frequent encounters with failure. Success should have a more distinctive and enhancing effect on a retarded child's behavior than on that of a normal child, because success is more unusual for the retarded child, while the reverse should be true for punishment. Studies with retarded and normal children of the same MA have tended to confirm these notions (Cromwell, 1959; Gardner, 1958; Heber, 1957; McManis, 1965; Stevenson and Zigler, 1958), although a few studies have found the opposite to be true (Sprague, Binder, and Silver, 1964) or have found success and failure to produce similar effects in normal and retarded subjects (Blackman and Kahn, 1963; Butterfield and Zigler, 1965b). On the whole, it seems reasonable to assume that retarded children experience considerably more failures than do children of normal or superior mental ability, and that failure experiences probably color a number of areas of personality, including overall self-concept, feelings of competence, achievement motivation, attitudes toward school and community, willingness to try new tasks, and so on.

A second assumption investigated by some workers is that the ability to conceptualize success and failure as the outcome of one's own efforts is a developmental phenomenon, more closely attuned to mental age than to chronological age. Bialer and Cromwell (1960) allowed retarded children to complete one puzzle but interrupted them before they finished a second. They found that the younger and less intelligent children were more likely to return to the completed puz-

zle, while the older and brighter ones tended to return to the interrupted puzzle. Subsequently (1965), they found that mentally retarded children who preferred to return to the interrupted puzzle ("success-strivers") showed a greater increment in performance after a failure experience than did those who preferred to return to the completed puzzle ("failure-avoiders").

A few studies have extended investigations of conceptualized locus-of-control to retarded populations. These studies have ordinarily utilized a questionnaire designed to tap a child's tendency to see the outcome of events as being under his own control rather than under the control of others or a function of luck. Bialer (1961a) found that mental age was more closely related than chronological age, in both normal and retarded subjects, to the development of convictions of internal locus of control, to the tendency to return to the interrupted puzzle, and to delay of gratification. Similarly, Miller (1961) found that under success-reward conditions, retarded subjects who saw the locus of control as external performed equally well as subjects who saw the locus of control as internal, but under nonrewarding conditions they were much less able to withstand failure or a lack of reinforcement.

Self-Concept. Working on the assumption that the retarded child's interactions with his environment are largely unsuccessful and therefore unlikely to promote self-acceptance, a number of workers have become interested in measuring the self-concept of retarded children in a variety of settings. Measurement problems have been formidable. The usual method of assessment has been the questionnaire, an experimental device which poses difficulties, as has been pointed out, when used with retarded subjects. Retarded children tend to have some difficulty in responding to new tasks in a differential way, and it is possible that they respond more frequently in accordance with what they see as a general rule (e.g., "say something nice") than according to differentiated, honest self-perceptions.

Some workers have, as one would expect from this hypothesis, found more positive self-concept scores for retarded children and, indeed, higher self-concept scores by retardates than can be considered realistic (Fine and Caldwell, 1967; Knight, 1967; Perron and Pecheux, 1964). Ringness (1961) compared self-concept responses of retarded, normal, and superior children with their achievement scores, sociometric measures, and teachers' ratings. The retarded children tended to overestimate their status and to be less realistic and less reliable in responding than did the other groups. Several other studies have, in contrast, found more negative self-concept responses in educable retardates than in normal children (Curtis, 1964; Lambeth, 1966; Piers and Harris, 1964).

A majority of the self-concept studies have centered around the question of the effects of special placement for retarded children. Some have found no significant differences between borderline and retarded children in institutions and those in special classes in their communities (Lambeth, 1966), but others have found higher self-concepts in students in special school placement (Kern and Pfaeffle, 1962) or in institutional placement (Guthrie, Butler, and Gorlow, 1967). Variables related to social adjustment rather than personal adjustment tend to lead to the more positive findings. Two conflicting studies have measured self-concepts during the early period of special class placement. Meyerowitz (1962, 1967) found that retarded children who had been randomly selected for placement in special education classes gave lower self-concept scores at the end of first grade than did retarded children randomly retained in regular classes, both groups being lower than the normal controls. By the end of second grade, however, the special-class retardates obtained lower mean scores than did either of the other groups, the retardates in regular classes obtaining scores similar to the controls. In contrast, Towne and Joiner (1966) reported that self-concept scores obtained from somewhat older children just before special placement, and measured repeatedly during the first year of placement, showed a steady rise over this period. Mayer (1966) found for junior high special students no relationship between age of special placement and self-concept scores.

Self-concept responses among retardates appear to be correlated with IQ (Gorlow, Butler, and Guthrie, 1963; Lambeth, 1966), absence of speech defects (Lambeth, 1966), and academic achievement (Brookover, Erick-

son, and Joiner, 1967; Snyder, Jefferson, and Strauss, 1965).

It now seems clear that various self-concept inventories can be used with fair reliability with mildly retarded children. Further research should help to clarify some of the complex issues raised in this important area of personality development. Substantial refinements in methodology and assessment techniques will be necessary, however, before any definitive answers will be forthcoming. Badly needed are longitudinal research projects in which carefully drawn samples are equated on a number of variables other than the one being tested. Because of the diverse and serious methodological handicaps of measurement and population sampling which have plagued studies in this area, little faith can be placed in any of the data obtained thus far.

Anxiety. Although a number of scattered studies have dealt with other personality traits (Heber, 1964), the only one of these areas which has been explored with retardate-subjects by a sizable group of investigators is that of anxiety. This is, in part, explainable by the fact that the Children's Manifest Anxiety Scale (CMAS) (Castaneda, McCandless, and Palermo, 1956) is one of the few objective measures of personality which is relatively easy to apply to groups of mentally retarded subjects. It should be noted again, perhaps, that there are reasons to question the usefulness of any paper-and-pencil test with retarded children.

In this area there is again conflicting evidence. Scores on the CMAS appear to be unrelated to scores on standard intelligence tests (Kitano, 1960), and some studies (e.g., Lipman, 1960) have failed to find significant differences in performance on the CMAS by educable retardates and equal MA normal controls. On the other hand, many workers (Cochran and Cleland, 1963; Feldhusen and Thurston, 1964; Malpass, Mark, and Palermo, 1960) have found retarded children to obtain higher scores on the CMAS. In some instances, high achievement has appeared to be related to low test anxiety rather than to low general anxiety (Wiener, Crawford, and Snyder, 1960), whereas in other studies achievement, particularly school achievement, has been found to relate to low general anxiety among retardates (Lipman and Griffith,

1960; Reger, 1964). It is obvious that considerably more work is needed to clarify issues in this area.

Personality Patterns in Specific Groups. A very few studies have been concerned with descriptions of the personal adjustment of specific subgroups of retarded children.

The personality of mongoloid children has received special attention because they have a reputation for being happier, more friendly, and more easily managed than other equally retarded children, although they are also seen as stubborn at times. In fact, this stereotype has been, for the most part, upheld by objective studies (Domino, 1965; Domino, Goldschmid, and Kaplan, 1964; Lyle, 1961; Silverstein, 1964; Wunsch, 1957). These characteristics are by no means invariable, however, and the adjustment of the mongoloid child, like that of other children, depends in large measure upon the quality of his environment.

Among brain-injured children, there are some whose behavior corresponds with what has come to be known as the "Strauss syndrome." Alfred Strauss and his co-workers described all, or most, brain-injured children as "erratic, uncoordinated, uncontrolled, uninhibited, and socially unaccepted" (Strauss and Lehtinen, 1947, p. 84). Aside from their difficulties with perceptual and conceptual tasks, these children were said to be unable to inhibit sensations and actions, to be unable to develop organized behavior patterns, to be assailed by chaotic sensations, and therefore to be especially dependent upon routine. The behavior of such children had a push and a persistence which made them particularly difficult to manage and at times almost unbearable to live with. Gallagher (1957) found that brain-injured children more frequently exhibited unfavorable personality characteristics, and were more frequently rated as hyperkinetic, lacking attention, fearful, and inhibited than the cultural-familial controls with whom they were matched. Likewise, Strauss and Kephart (1955) found that teachers designated the brain-injured group as more erratic, uncoordinated, uncontrolled, uninhibited, and socially unacceptable than cultural-familial retardates matched for MA and IQ. Other investigators (Hanauer, 1952; Semmel, 1960) have failed, however, to find evidence of instability or maladjustment when brain-injured children have been compared with others who were similarly retarded. Although no one seriously doubts that some brain-injured children do exhibit the Strauss syndrome, in recent years it has been recognized that numerous other brain-injured children do not demonstrate this hyperkinetic, impulsive activity.

Future Research. It should be clear that the important area of personality development in the retarded has barely been touched by the available studies. Not one of the studies reviewed, for example, touches upon important antecedent variables in parent-child relationships, nor have there been any longitudinal studies of retardates which could shed light upon such important factors as the stability of personality traits. The simple questions regarding the levels of anxiety or self-concept in retardates, in general, versus those of normal children, are but a beginning, and they suffer, in their generality, not only from methodological difficulties but from sampling problems as well. Too frequently, retardates have been studied without reference to very basic variables such as the social class and ethnic group in which they live, without regard to etiology of their disorder, and with only minimal attention to CA-related and MA-related variables. The very contradictions in the findings of different investigators substantiate the complexity of this heterogeneous group designated "retarded."

REMEDIATION AND PREVENTION

The decade of the 1960s has witnessed a dramatic growth in programs of service to the retarded. By 1967, more than $400 million per year was being appropriated by the federal government, and more than twice that amount by states, localities, and private organizations for activities directly benefitting the retarded (President's Committee on Mental Retardation, 1967). When there is added to this amount the appropriate part of the sums spent in the War on Poverty, which directly benefit the borderline and mildly retarded who are economically handicapped, the financial investment in this area can be seen as enormous.

Most of the money spent in these programs is designed to remediate deficiencies of academic achievement, vocational skills, and emotional adjustment, and to provide residential arrangements for retardates whose families cannot provide a home for them. In 1967 there were 201,000 institutionalized retardates in the United States, and 81,000 full-time staff in public facilities for the retarded. At the same time, there were, in public school special classes, 588,000 educable-level children and 89,000 trainable children, a marked increase over the corresponding 109,000 and 5,000 chidren so accommodated in 1953. These programs, together with diagnosis and medical treatment, vocational rehabilitation, recreation, semi-supervised boarding homes, foster parent care, day care, remediation in areas such as speech and physical therapy, and psychotherapy, are receiving by far the bulk of the sums appropriated for the retarded. Efforts at prevention are, in contrast, very meager.

Remediation

It is abundantly clear by now that most of the mildly retarded, and nearly all of the borderline retarded group, are capable of adequate, fairy independent, and productive citizenship even in a complex industrial society, providing that they are given good preparation for this role, and providing that the society takes into account their needs for jobs which require low-order skills. It is this hope which lies behind the provision of such diversified services for the retarded.

Education. By far the major effort has centered in providing educational experiences for retarded children (usually those with IQs below 75 and above 50) which minimize academic training to the level necessary for functioning in society (e.g., handling money, reading newspapers and telephone directories, basic health science) and maximize training for vocational skills and general citizenship. These classes for the educable mentally retarded (EMR) have been enthusiastically endorsed by a great many school systems, although even now the majority of educable mentally retarded remain in regular classrooms or have left school.

Studies of the effectiveness of special classes have been handicapped by the ordinary processes of selecting children for these classes. Children recommended for special-class placement naturally tend to exhibit more emotional problems, lower academic achievement, and in general more deviant social behavior than do those equally retarded children who are not nominated for special placement. Moreover, special-class teachers tend to place more emphasis on personal and social adjustment of their pupils, and to be less academically demanding than do teachers in regular classes (Fine, 1967; Johnson, 1962).

It is not surprising, therefore, that comprehensive reviews of the academic achievement of EMR special-class pupils consistently find these pupils trailing behind equally retarded children in regular classes (e.g., Kirk, 1964; Quay, 1963; Thurstone, 1959; Stanton and Cassidy, 1964). A more positive picture of social adjustment generally obtains, with the special class pupils, despite their negative selection, showing at least as positive social adjustment as their regular class peers. In the one carefully designed study in which children with IQs below 85 were screened prior to first grade and randomly assigned to special classes or regular classes, Goldstein, Moss, and Jordan (1965) found that there were few differences among the high-IQ ("slow learner") groups related to special class placement, but that for the low-IQ (EMR) groups, there were in some areas data that supported the higher academic achievement of children in special classes. For both "slow learner" and EMR groups, social and personal adjustment appeared to be favorably influenced by special-class placement. The weight of the evidence, then, appears to be in favor of special-class placement for at least many EMR children, with perhaps the recommendations that special attention be given to the development of suitable curricula, and that teachers be encouraged to raise their expectations regarding the possibility of somewhat higher academic attainment by their pupils.

Research on the efficacy of special classes for trainable mentally retarded (TMR) children has, in general, been very discouraging (Cain and Levine, 1963; Kirk, 1957, 1964; Warren, 1963). Academic gains, which receive little emphasis in such classes, have been almost negligible. Occasionally, special programs for TMR children have been found to produce gains in nonacademic areas such as social adjustment, self-care, language, and economic usefulness (Peck and Sexton, 1961). These programs have demonstrated the utility of careful preparation of teachers, materials, and curricula. Because studies of learning in retarded children have demonstrated that substantial gains are possible, there is reason to believe that attention to the improvement of TMR programs in the schools is called for (McCarthy and Scheerenberger, 1966).

A number of specialized curricula have been proposed for retarded children, beginning with the famous efforts of Itard in 1799 to convert the "Wild Boy of Aveyron" to an educated, civilized man. Most of the study plans proposed prior to the 1960s were general adaptations of curricula in the regular classroom and were intended for all EMR or TMR children (Kirk and Johnson, 1951). There was, in addition, emphasis on vocational and social rather than academic goals. A review of more recent proposals (Erdman and Olson, 1966), however, reveals a trend toward specialized curricula to deal not only with vocational and social goals but also with personality and learning problems of more selected groups of children, based on understanding of specific handicaps and specific needs. Among these curricula are, for example, special programs for remediation of inadequate motor development (Kephart, 1960) and specific language disabilities (Smith, 1962; Wiseman, 1965), and programs proposed for specific deficits due to brain injury (Cruickshank, Bentzen, Ratzeberg, and Tannhouser, 1961; Frostig and Horne, 1964; Gallagher, 1960). The rapid growth of attention to "learning disorders" (Bateman, 1966) reflects increased interest in the specific deficits of children of normal or borderline intelligence who are thought to exhibit the effects of minimal brain damage and/or specific handicapping learning experiences. This trend is being extended to the education of EMR children, but clear evidence is lacking as to the efficacy of any of the new curriculum proposals.

Other Services. A wide range of services to retarded children and their families is slowly becoming available throughout the United States. To a large extent, these services are fragmented and uncoordinated, but the very existence of experimental and pilot service programs is an encouraging development.

Diagnostic services are, in general, more readily available to families than are follow-up treatment or enrichment programs. By 1966, for example, there were almost 200 mental retardation clinics in the country, over half of them supported wholly or in part by federal funds (Secretary's Committee on Mental Retardation, 1967), and many other clinical facilities offered diagnostic services suitable to the needs of mentally retarded children.

Residential institutional care, while undergoing some expansion, is increasingly being utilized for more severely retarded, multiple-handicapped children. With the expansion of community facilities, especially educational facilities, for mildly retarded children, increasing efforts are being made to maintain retarded children in their own homes, or in foster homes in the community. A limited number of preschool classes, recreation programs, and day-care facilities for the more severely retarded are making broadening of these efforts more feasible. Specific therapeutic programs such as parental counseling, speech therapy, physical therapy, and psychotherapy are slowly becoming available, but it remains difficult to obtain such services for retarded children in view of the heavy demand for remediation of problems in children of normal intelligence.

For the mentally retarded adolescent and adult, the Vocational Rehabilitation Administration is rapidly expanding its program of services. It is estimated that during the year ending June 30, 1968, 24,000 retardates would receive services through this program (Secretary's Committee on Mental Retardation, 1967). Vocational training classes in the schools, and sheltered workshops for the handicapped (Cohen, 1966) also provide for the need of the retarded to become economically self-sufficient. Special provision can be made in some instances, through the Secretary of Labor, to enable the individual with severely impaired earning capacity to be employed at less than the legal minimum wage. Many states and communities are also establishing boarding homes for retarded adults who are capable of economic independence but not of managing their entire living pattern.

Unfortunately, these and other efforts have seldom been accompanied by empirical evaluation of their efficacy. It is, however, evident that without such efforts at remediation and service, little progress can be made. It is also quite evident that the needs of retarded children and adults are far greater than those ordinarily met in the community or in the better institutions.

Prevention

A wide variety of preventive efforts can and should be established to prevent mental retardation in as many children as possible. Despite unquestioned advances in medical sophistication and technology, and unprecedented interest in preschool education, the United States is not an important world leader in the delivery of these services to its populace, particularly not to the high-risk segments from which the majority of the retarded come. To cite but one example, in the United States in 1964, the mortality rate in the first year of life was approximately 24.8 per 1000 live births (U. S. Children's Bureau, 1964), a figure which places the United States approximately twelfth to fifteenth among the industrialized nations of the world. Rates for nonwhites and for poor urban neighborhoods were much higher than this. Delivery of adequate prenatal supervision to all mothers by obstetric personnel, even with reorganization of services, would require at least a doubling of the number of obstetricians presently in practice. Only 6% of children age 3, and only 62% of those age 5, were in 1967 afforded organized experiences, such as in nursery school, outside their homes (Schloss, 1967), and there are group day-care facilities for only about 2% of children under school age whose mothers work (U. S. Children's Bureau and U. S. Women's Bureau, 1965).

As can be seen from the complexity of the brief review of the etiology of mental retardation and lesser forms of intellectual handicap, both in this chapter and elsewhere in this book, the problems of prevention are diverse and enormous in magnitiude. Among the possible avenues of prevention already feasible are provision of birth control methods for high-risk groups such as the culturally deprived, and the older potential mother who is likely to bear a mongoloid child; genetic counseling services to families; prenatal medical services to all pregnant women; nutritional supplements to pregnant mothers and

children; development and administration of vaccines against damaging infectious diseases; liberalized abortions for pregnancies in which there is strong suspicion of a damaged fetus; biochemical screening of newborns for metabolic and endocrine disorders; training in homemaking and parental skills for young adults, and so on. As research reveals new and practicable methods of prevention, this list will surely expand.

An example of a rapid, perhaps overenthusiastic, acceptance of a preventative measure was the adoption of screening techniques for phenylketonuria. At least 37 states have legislation concerned with such screening, most of them making screening for PKU mandatory, and in other states such screening is widely practiced. With this exception, however, the task of preventing mental retardation has not received much public acceptance as a major goal. Some support, but little in comparison with other programs, is given by the federal government (Secretary's Committee on Mental Retardation, 1967) for prenatal care, and scattered programs in other phases of this program area do exist. Free preventive health clinics for infants, for example, have been widespread for some years, and in general good medical care is available even to the indigent family possessing the wit, wisdom, and fortitude to demand it.

Of equal importance is the provision of an optimal environment for learning, particularly during the crucial period of infant and preschool years when intellectual growth is most rapid and most malleable (Bloom, 1964; Robinson, 1968b). One of the most widely quoted studies in the early education of the mentally retarded (Kirk, 1958) provided preschool experience for 1-3 years prior to first grade for mentally retarded children in a community and in an institution. Kirk's findings presaged a number of later attempts to provide enrichment experiences for culturally deprived children. He found that during the preschool years, both experimental groups showed significant improvement in comparison to their control groups, but that once the children entered public school the control group tended to catch up with the community group. In the institutional setting, however, the experimental group tended to retain its lead. The experience of an initial spurt of development for retarded and/or culturally deprived preschool children in experimental programs, with a subsequent "washing out" of the differences between experimentals and controls after both groups enter public schools in the community, has been shared by a number of studies (e.g., Blatt and Garfunkel, 1967; Klaus and Gray, 1967; Spicker, Hodges, and McCandless, 1966; Weickart, 1967). It is possible that genetic and physiological differences among children override preschool educational efforts, that the efforts have not been well geared to the enduring needs of the children, that too little follow-up in the elementary school years has been carried out, or, finally, that efforts at providing optimal environments have started too late and should have been begun during infancy, when children first begin to respond to their varied environments (Robinson, 1968a, 1968b). There is much reason to be encouraged with the results of experimental preschool programs with culturally deprived and retarded children, although due caution is necessary in view of the apparent lack of stability of results. This is an area of prevention which is relatively untapped but which, like most others, would if successful repay many times over the preventive investment.

Still another area of importance is the integration of the many disparate services which are offered to families in this society. The capable, middle-class family may not suffer so acutely from the splintering of services in health care, education, enrichment, and so on, because of its relative freedom to act and its acceptance of the importance of such services, but the less capable and less affluent family, with parents of limited intellect and competence, is often at a loss to subcontract for these services in any meaningful way. It will be increasingly necessary to integrate services and to provide comprehensive and easily available programs for all retarded or potentially retarded children and their families (Robinson, 1967a).

Finally, it should be said that in prevention there lies the major hope for the reduction of our retarded population. Without belittling the often startling successes of remediation programs in enhancing the adjustment of retarded children, even the best of these programs can hope only for a modest rise in intellectual competence, together with the development of social skills. The best and most comprehensive programs of prevention can, with much less effort per child and with much more optimism, hope to avoid having to deal with the problems of retardation at all. Preventive efforts will never, of course, succeed in every instance. It will always be imperative to offer a wide range of remediation programs to retarded children and adults. On the other hand, it is unquestionably foolhardy not to emphasize broad-gauged efforts at prevention of retardation, whatever the immediate cost.

References

Ahmad, S. K. Paired associate verbal learning by normals and mentally retarded under stimulus and response meaningfulness. *Diss. Abstr.*, 1965, **25**, 5433. (Abstract)

Akesson, H. O. Epidemiology and genetics of mental deficiency in a southern Swedish population. Translated by R. N. Elston. Uppsala, Sweden: The Institute for Medical Genetics of the University of Uppsala, 1961.

Akutagwa, D., and Benoit, E. P. The effect of age and relative brightness on associative learning in children. *Child Dev.*, 1959, **30**, 229–238.

Allen, R. J., and Gibson, R. M. Phenylketonuria with normal intelligence. *Am. J. Dis. Child.*, 1961, **102**, 115–123.

Anastasi, A. Heredity, environment, and the question "how?" *Psychol. Rev.*, 1958, **65**, 197–208.

Anderson, V. E. Genetics in mental retardation. In H. A. Stevens and R. Heber (Eds.), *Mental retardation: a review of research*. Chicago: University of Chicago Press, 1964. Pp. 348–394.

Apgar, V. Drugs in pregnancy. *J. Am. med. Ass.*, 1964, **190**, 840–841.

Apgar, V. Perinatal problems and the central nervous system. *Phys. Ther.*, 1965, **45**, 357–358.

Aronson, S. M. Lead encephalopathy. In C. H. Carter (Ed.), *Medical aspects of mental retardation*. Springfield, Ill.: Thomas, 1965. Pp. 878–903.

Astrup, C., Sersen, E. A., and Wortis, J. Conditional reflex studies in mental retardation: a review. *Am. J. ment. Defic.*, 1967, **71**, 513–530.

Bacher, J. H. The effect of special class placement on the self-concept, social adjustment, and reading growth of slow learners. *Diss. Abstr.*, 1965, **25**, 7071. (Abstract)

Backer, M. H. An experimental investigation of the motivational hypothesis of rigidity in retardates, a comparison of retardates and normal performance on a series of card sorting tasks. Unpublished doctoral dissertation, University of North Carolina at Chapel Hill, 1965.

Baird, D., and Scott, E. M. Intelligence and childbearing. *Eugen. Rev.*, 1953, **45**, 139–154.

Baker, L., Mellman, W. J., Tedesco, T. A., and Segal, S. Galactosemia: symptomatic and asymptomatic homozygotes in one Negro sibship. *J. Pediat.*, 1966, **68**, 551–558.

Barnett, C. D. Stimulus generalization in normals and retardates on a visual-spatial task requiring a voluntary response. Unpublished doctoral dissertation, George Peabody College for Teachers, 1958.

Barnett, C. D., Ellis, N. R., and Pryer, M. W. Stimulus pretraining and the delayed reaction in defectives. *Am. J. ment. Defic.*, 1959, **64**, 104–111.

Barnett, C. D., Ellis, N. R., and Pryer, M. W. Learning in familial and brain-injured defectives. *Am. J. ment. Defic.*, 1960, **64**, 894–901.

Barr, M. L., and Bertram, E. G. A morphological distinction between neurones of the male and female, and the behavior of the nucleolar satellite during accelerated nucleoprotein syntheses. *Nature*, 1949, **163**, 676.

Barr, M. L., Carr, D. H., Soltan, H. C., Weins, R. G., and Plunkett, E. R. The XXYY of Klinefelter's syndrome. *Can. med. Asso. J.*, 1964, **90**, 9, 575–580.

Barr, M. L., Shaver, E. L., Carr, D. H., and Plunkett, E. R. The chromatin-positive Klinefelter syndrome among patients in mental deficiency hospitals. *J. mental Defic. Res.*, 160, **4**, 89–107.

Barrett, B. H. Acquisition of operant differentiation and discrimination in institutionalized retarded children. *Am. J. Orthopsychiat.*, 1965, **35**, 862–885.

Barrett, B. H., and Lindsley, O. R. Deficits in acquisition of operant discrimination and differentiation shown by institutionalized retarded children. *Am. J. ment. Defic.*, 1962, **67**, 424–436.

Bass, M. H. Diseases of the pregnant woman affecting the offspring. *Adv. internal Med.*, 1952, **5**, 15–58.

Bateman, B. Learning disorders. *Rev. educ. Res.*, 1966, **36**, 93–119.

Battaglia, F., Frazier, T., and Hellegers, A. Obstetric and pediatric complications of juvenile pregnancy. *Pediatrics*, 1963, **32**, 902–910.

Baumeister, A. A., and Ellis, N. R. Delayed response performance of retardates. *Am. J. ment. Defic.*, 1963, **67**, 714–722.

Baumeister, A. A., and Klosowski, R. An attempt to group toilet train severely retarded patients. *Ment. Retardation*, 1965, **3**, 24–26.

Baumeister, A. A., Smith, T. E., and Rose, J. D. The effects of stimulus complexity and retention interval upon short-term memory. *Am. J. ment. Defic.*, 1965, **70**, 129–134.

Beadle, G. W., Tatum, E. L., McKusick, V., Hsia, D. Y., and Sager, R. Genes take on added meaning. Recent insights into heredity promise improved tools for clinical use. *Med. W. News*, 1964, **5**(22), 95–100.

Beier, D. C. Behavioral disturbances in the mentally retarded. In H. Stevens and R. Heber (Eds.), *Mental retardation: a review of research*. Chicago: University of Chicago Press, 1964. Pp. 453–487.

Belmont, J. M. Perceptual short-term memory in children, retardates and adults. *J. exp. Child Psychol.*, 1967, **5**, 114–122.

Benda, C. E. Psychopathology of childhood. In L. Carmichael (Ed.), *Manual of Child Psychology* (2nd ed.) New York: Wiley, 1954. Pp. 1115–1161.

Benda, C. E., Farrell, M. J., and Chipman, C. E. The inadequacy of present-day concepts of mental deficiency and mental illness in child psychiatry. *Am. J. Psychiat.*, 1951, **107**, 721–727.

Benda, C. E., Squires, N. D., Ogonik, J., Wise, R., and Akin, R. The relationship between intellectual inadequacy and emotional and sociocultural privation. *Compreh. Psychiat.*, 1964, **5**(5), 294–313.

Bensburg, G. J., Colwell, C. N., and Cassel, R. H. Teaching the profoundly retarded self-help activities by behavior shaping techniques. *Am. J. ment. Defic.*, 1965, **69**, 674–679.

Bergstrand, C. G., and Lindsten, J. Male phenotype without demonstrable Y-chromosome. *Acta Paediat., Scand., Supplement*, 1965, **159**, 46–47.

Berkson, G., and Cantor, G. N. A study of mediation in mentally retarded and normal school children. *J. educ. Psychol.*, 1960, **51**, 82–86.

Berkson, G., and Mason, W. A. Stereotyped movements of mental defectives: III. Situation effects. *Am. J. ment. Defic.*, 1963, **68**, 409–412.

Berman, P. W., Waisman, H. A., and Graham, F. K. Intelligence in treated phenylketonuric children: a developmental study. *Child Dev.*, 1966, **37**, 731–747.

Bialer, I. Conceptualization of success and failure in mentally retarded and normal children. *J. Personality*, 1961, **29**, 301–333. (a)

Bialer, I. Primary and secondary stimulus generalization as related to intelligence level. In R. Cromwell (Ed.), *Abstracts of Peabody studies in mental retardation*. Nashville, Tenn.: George Peabody College for Teachers, 1961. (b)

Bialer, I., and Cromwell, R. L. Task repetition in mental defectives as a function of chronological and mental age. *Am. J. ment. Defic.*, 1960, **65**, 265–268.

Bialer, I., and Cromwell, R. L. Failure as motivation with mentally retarded children. *Am. J. ment. Defic.*, 1965, **69**, 680–684.

Bickel, H., Girrard, J., and Hickmans, E. M. The influence of phenylalanine intake on the chemistry and behavior of a phenylketonuric child. *Acta Paediat.*, 1954, **43**, 64–77.

Bijou, S. W. Theory and research in mental (developmental) retardation. *Psychol. Rec.*, 1963, **13**, 95–110.

Bijou, S. W., Ainsworth, M. H., and Stockey, M. R. The social adjustment of mentally retarded girls paroled from the Wayne County Training School. *Am. J. ment. Defic.*, 1943, **47**, 422–428.

Bijou, S. W., and Orlando, R. Rapid development of multiple-schedule performance with retarded children. In L. P. Ullman and L. Krasner (Eds.), *Case studies in behavior modification*. New York: Holt, Rinehart, & Winston, 1965. Pp. 339–347.

Birnbrauer, J. S., and Lawler, J. Token reinforcement for learning. *Ment. Retardation*, 1964, **2**, 275–279.

Blackman, L. S., and Kahn, H. Success and failure as determinants of aspirational shifts in retardates and normals. *Am. J. ment. Defic.*, 1963, **67**, 751–755.

Blatt, B. The physical, personality, and academic status of children who are mentally retarded attending special classes as compared with children who are mentally retarded attending regular classes. *Am. J. ment. Defic.*, 1958, **62**, 810–818.

Blatt, B., and Garfunkel, F. Educating intelligence: determinants of school behavior of disadvantaged children. *Exceptional Children*, 1967, 33, 601–608.

Bloom, B. S. *Stability and change in human characteristics.* New York: Wiley, 1964.

Blue, C. M. The role of short-term memory in the paired-associate learning of normal and retarded subjects. Unpublished doctoral dissertation, George Peabody College, 1962.

Blue, C. M. Performance of normal and retarded subjects on a modified paired-associate task. *Am. J. ment. Defic.*, 1963, 68, 228–234.

Boggs, T. R. Preliminary data with respect to the relationship of highest serum bilirubin to certain other findings in the collaborative project. Paper presented at the spring scientific meeting of the Collaborative Perinatal Project, National Institute of Neurological Diseases and Blindness, Washington, 1963.

Brandon, M. W. G., Kirman, B. H., and Williams, C. E. Microcephaly. *J. ment. Sci.*, 1959, 105, 721–747.

Brookover, W. B., Erickson, E. L., and Joiner, L. M. Self-concept and achievement. Vol. 3. U. S. Office of Education, Cooperative Research Project No. 2831 East Lansing: Michigan State University, 1967.

Brown, R. I. The effect of visual distraction on perception in subjects of subnormal intelligence. *Br. J. soc. clin. Psychol.*, 1964, 3, 20–28. (a)

Brown, R. I. Distraction in subnormals. In J. Øster (Ed.), *International Copenhagen Congress on the scientific study of mental retardation,* 1964. Vol. 1. Pp. 351–358. (b)

Bruch, H. and McCune, D. J. Mental development of congenitally hypothyroid children. *Am. J. Dis. Child.*, 1944, 67, 205–224.

Bryant, P. E. Verbalisation and flexibility in retarded children. In J. Øster (Ed.), *International Copenhagen Congress on the scientific study of mental retardation,* 1964. Vol. 1. Pp. 359–365.

Bryant, P. E. The transfer of positive and negative learning by normal and severely subnormal children. *Br. J. Psychol.*, 1965, 56, 81–86.

Butler, L. J., Snodgrass, G. J., France, N. E., Sinclair, L., and Russell, A. E. (16–18) trisomy syndrome: analysis of 13 cases. *Archi. Dis. Child.*, 1965, 40, 600–611.

Butterfield, S. C., and Zigler, E. The influence of differing institutional social climates on the effectiveness of social reinforcement in the mentally retarded. *Am. J. ment. Defic.*, 1965, 70, 48–57. (a)

Butterfield, E. C., and Zigler, E. The effects of success and failure on the discrimination learning of normal and retarded children. *J. abnorm. Psychol.*, 1965, 70, 25–31. (b)

Cain, L. F., and Levine, S. Effects of community and institutional school programs on trainable mentally retarded children. Washington, D. C.: The Council for Exceptional Children, NEA, CEC Research Monograph, 1963, Series B, No. B-1.

Cantor, G. N., and Hottel, J. V. Discrimination learning in mental defectives as a function of magnitude of food reward and intelligence level. *Am. J. ment. Defic.*, 1955, 60, 380–384.

Cantor, G. N., and Hottel, J. V. Psychomotor learning in defectives as a function of verbal pretraining. *Psychol., Rec.*, 1957, 7, 79–85.

Cantor, G. N., and Ryan, T. J. Retention of verbal paired-associates in normals and retardates. *Am. J. ment. Defic.*, 1962, 66, 861–865.

Carr, D. H. Chromosome studies in abortuses and stillborn infants. *Lancet*, 1963, 2, 603–606.

Carr, D. H. Chromosome studies in spontaneous abortions. *Obstet. Gynec.*, 1965, 26, 308–326.

Carter, C. H. *Handbook of mental retardation syndromes.* Springfield, Ill.: Thomas, 1966.

Carter, C. O., Hamerton, J. L., Polani, P. E., Gunlap, A., and Weller, S. D. V. Chromosome translocation as a cause of familial mongolism. *Lancet,* 1960, **2,** 678–680.

Cassel, R. H. Serial verbal learning and retroactive inhibition in aments and children. *J. clin. Psychol.,* 1957, **13,** 369–372.

Cassel, R. N. Expected educational, occupational, and personal development for five discernible groups of "educable but mentally handicapped students." *Am. J. ment. Defic.,* 1961, **65,** 801–804.

Castaneda, A., McCandless, B. R., and Palermo, D. S. The children's form of the manifest anxiety scale. *Child Dev.,* 1956, **27,** 317–326.

Centerwall, S. A., and Centerwall, W. R. A study of children with mongolism reared in the home compared to those reared away from the home. *Pediatrics,* 1960, **25,** 678–685.

Chao, D. H., Druckman, R., and Kellaway, P. *Convulsive disorders of children,* Philadelphia: Saunders, 1958.

Charles, D. C. Adult adjustment of some deficient American children: II. *Am. J. ment. Defic.,* 1957, **62,** 300–304.

Chesley, L. C., and Annetto, J. E. Pregnancy in the patient with hypertensive disease. *Am. J. Obstet. Gynec.,* 1947, **53,** 372–381.

Chilman, C. S. Child-rearing and family relationship patterns of the very poor. *Welfare in Review,* 1965, 9–19.

Clarke, A. D. B., and Clarke, A. M. Cognitive changes in the feebleminded. *Br. J. Psychol.,* 1954, **45,** 173–179.

Clarke, A. D. B., Clarke, A. M., and Reiman, S. Cognitive and social changes in the feebleminded—three further studies. *Br. J. Psychol.,* 1958, **49,** 144–157.

Cochran, I. L., and Cleland, C. C. Manifest anxiety of retardates and normals matched as to academic achievement. *Am. J. ment. Defic.,* 1963, **67,** 539–542.

Coffey, V. P., and Jessop, W. J. Rubella and incidence of congenital abnormalities. *Ir. J. med. Sci.,* 1959, **397,** 1–11.

Cohen, J. S. An analysis of vocational failures of mental retardates placed in the community after a period of institutionalization. *Am. J. ment. Defic.,* 1960, **65,** 371–372.

Cohen, J. S. The sheltered workshop. *Ment. Retard. Abstr.,* 1966, **3,** 163–169.

Collmann, R. D., and Newlyn, D. Employment success of educationally subnormal ex-pupils in England. *Am. J. ment. Defic.,* 1956, **60,** 733–743.

Collmann, R. D., and Newlyn, D. Employment success of mentally dull and intellectually normal ex-pupils in England. *Am. J. ment. Defic.,* 1957, **61,** 484–490.

Corter, H. M., and McKinney, J. D. Cognitive flexibility training with educable retarded and bright normal children of the same mental age. *N. Carol. J. Publ. Hlth.,* 1966, **2,** 4, 30–42.

Cravioto, J., and Robles, B. Evolution of adaptive and motor behavior during rehabilitation from kwashiorkor. *Am. J. Orthopsychiat.,* 1965, **35,** 449–464.

Cromwell, R. L. A methodological approach to personality research in mental retardation. *Am. J. ment. Defic.,* 1959, **64,** 333–340.

Cromwell, R. L., and Foshee, J. G. Studies in activity level: IV. Effects of visual stimulation during task performance in mental defectives. *Am. J. ment. Defic.,* 1960, **65,** 248–251.

Cruickshank, W. M., Bentzen, F., Ratzeberg, F. H., and Tannhouser, M. T. *A teaching method for brain-injured and hyperactive children.* Syracuse, N.Y.: Syracuse University Press, 1961.

Cruse, D. B. Effects of distraction upon the performance of brain-injured and familial retarded children. *Am. J. ment. Defic.*, 1961, **66**, 86-92.

Culley, W. J. Nutrition and mental retardation. In C. H. Carter (Ed.), *Medical aspects of mental retardation.* Springfield, Ill.: Thomas, 1965, Pp. 88-111.

Curtis, L. T. A comparative analysis of the self-concept of the adolescent mentally retarded in relation to certain groups of adolescents. *Diss. Abstr.*, 1964, **25**, 2846-2847. (Abstract)

Davidson, W. M., and Smith, D. R. A morphological sex difference in the poly-morphonuclear neutrophil leukocytes. *Br. Med. J.*, 1954, **2**, 6-7.

Dekaban, A. S., and Magee, K. R. Occurrence of neurologic abnormalities in infants of diabetic mothers. *Neurology*, 1958, **8**, 193–200.

de la Cruz, F. F., and LaVeck, G. D. Tuberous sclerosis: a review and report of eight cases. *Am. J. ment. Defic.*, 1962, **67**, 369–380.

Delker, H. A. H. The relationship between memory and intelligence among junior high school students. *Diss. Abstr.*, 1965, **25**, 5107–5108. (Abstract)

Delp, H. A., and Lorenz, M. Follow-up of 84 public school special class pupils with I.Q.'s below 50. *Am. J. ment. Defic.*, 1953, **58**, 175–182.

Dennis, W. Causes of retardation among institutional children: Iran. *J. genet. Psychol.*, 1960, **96**, 47–59.

Denny, M. R. Research in learning and performance. In H. Stevens and R. Heber (Eds.), *Mental retardation: a review of research.* Chicago: University of Chicago Press, 1964. Pp. 100–142.

Dewan, J. G. Intelligence and emotional stability. *Am. J. Psychiat.*, 1948, **704**, 548–554.

Dexter, L. A. *The tyranny of schooling.* New York: Basic Books, 1964.

Dingman, H. F. Some uses of descriptive statistics in population analysis. *Am. J. ment. Defic.*, 1959, **64**, 291–295.

Dingman, H. F., and Tarjan, G. Mental retardation and the normal distribution curve. *Am. J. ment. Defic.*, 1960, **64**, 991–994.

Doll, E. A. The essentials of an inclusive concept of mental deficiency. *Am. J. ment. Defic.*, 1941, **46**, 214–219.

Domino, G. Personality traits in institutionalized mongoloids. *Am. J. ment. Defic.*, 1965, **69**, 568–570.

Domino, G., Goldschmid, M., and Kaplan, M. Personality traits of institutionalized mongoloid girls. *Am. J. ment. Defic.*, 1964, **68**, 498–502.

Drillien, C. M. The social and economic factors affecting the incidence of pre-mature birth Part I: Premature birth without complications of pregnancy. *J. Obstet. Gynec., Br. Commonw.*, 1957, **64**, 161–184.

Dugdale, R. L. *The Jukes: a study of crime, pauperism, disease, and heredity.* New York: Putnam, 1877.

Dyggve, H. V., and Mikkelsen, M. Partial deletion of the short arms of a chromo-some of the 4–5 group (Denver). *Arch. Dis. Childh.*, 1965, **40**, 82–85.

Ellis, N. R. Object-quality discrimination learning sets in mental defectives. *J. comp. physiol. Psychol.*, 1958, **51**, 79–81.

Ellis, N. R. Amount of reward and operant behavior in mental defectives. *Am. J. ment. Defic.*, 1962, **66**, 595–599.

Ellis, N. R. *Handbook of mental deficiency.* New York: McGraw-Hill, 1963. (a)

Ellis, N. R. The stimulus trace and behavioral inadequacy. In N. R. Ellis (Ed.), *Handbook of mental deficiency.* New York: McGraw-Hill 1963. Pp. 134–158. (b)

Ellis, N. R., Barnett, C. D., and Pryer, M. W. Operant behavior in mental defec-tives: exploratory studies. *J. exp. Anal. Behav.*, 1960, **3**, 63–69.

Ellis, N. R., Girardeau, F. L., and Pryer, M. W. Analysis of learning sets in normal and severely defective human beings. In R. L. Cromwell (Ed.), *Abstracts of Peabody studies in mental retardation*, 1963, **2**, 53. (Abstract)

Ellis, N. R., Hawkins, W. F., Pryer, M. W., and Jones, R. W. Distraction effects in oddity learning by normal and mentally defective humans. *Am. J. ment. Defic.*, 1963, **67**, 576–583.

Ellis, N. R., Pryer, M. W., and Barnett, C. D. Note on habit formation in normal and retarded subjects. *Psychol. Rep.*, 1960, **6**, 385–386.

Ellis, N. R., Pryer, M. W., Distefano, M. K., Jr., and Pryer, R. S. Learning in mentally defective, normal, and superior subjects. *Am. J. ment. Defic.*, 1960, **64**, 725–734.

Ellis, N. R., and Sloan, W. Oddity learning as a function of mental age. *J. comp. physiol. Psychol.*, 1959, **52**, 228–230.

Erdman, R. L., and Olson, J. L. Relationships between educational programs for the mentally retarded and the culturally deprived. *Ment. Retard. Abstr.*, 1966, **3**, 311–316.

Evans, R. A. Word recall and associative clustering in mental retardates. *Am. J. ment. Defic.*, 1964, **69**, 413–418.

Fabian, A. A. Prognosis in head injuries in children. *J. nerv. ment. Dis.*, 1956, **123**, 428–431.

Feldhusen, J. F., and Thurston, J. R. Personality and the adjustment of high and low anxious children. *J. educ. Res.*, 1964, **57**, 265–267.

Fine, M. J. Attitudes of regular and special class teachers toward the educable mentally retarded child. *Exceptional Children*, 1967, **33**, 429–430.

Fine, M. J., and Caldwell, T. E. Self evaluation of school related behavior of educable mentally retarded children—a preliminary report. *Exceptional Children*, 1967, **33**, 324.

Fischer, J. The stupidity problem. *Harper's Magazine*, 1962, **225**, 14–24.

Franks, V., and Franks, C. M. Conditioning in defectives and in normals as related to intelligence and mental deficit: the application of a learning theory model to a study of the learning process in the mental defective. *Proceedings of the London Conference of the Scientific Study of Mental Deficiency*, July, 1950.

Fraser, F. C. Teratogenesis of the central nervous system. In H. A. Stevens and R. Heber (Eds.), *Mental retardation: a review of research*. Chicago: University of Chicago Press, 1964. Pp. 395–428.

Fraser, F. C. Some genetic aspects of teratology. In J. G. Wilson and J. Warkany (Eds.), *Teratology—principles and techniques*. Chicago: University of Chicago Press, 1965. Pp. 21–56.

Freeberg, N. E., and Payne, D. T. Parental influence on cognitive development in early childhood: a review. *Child Dev.*, 1967, **38**, 65–87.

Frostig, M., and Horne, D. *The Frostig Program for the development of visual perception*. Chicago: Follett, 1964.

Fuller, J. L. Nature and nurture: a modern synthesis. *Doubleday papers in psychology*, No. 4. Garden City, N. Y.: Doubleday, 1954.

Fuller, P. R. Operant conditioning of a vegetative human organism. *Am. J. Psychol.*, 1949, **62**, 587–589.

Gallagher, J. J. A comparison of brain-injured and non-brain-injured mentally retarded children on several psychological variables. *Monogr. Soc. Res. Child Dev.*, 1957, **22**, 2, (No. 65).

Gallagher, J. J. *The tutoring of brain-injured mentally retarded children*. Springfield, Ill.: C. Thomas, 1960.

Gard, S., Magnusson, J. H., and Hagberg, E. Congenital toxoplasmosis. *Acta Paediat.*, 1952, **41**, 15–31.

Gardner, P. L. The learning of low grade aments. *Am. J. ment. Defi.*, 1948, **50**, 59–80.

Gardner, W. I. Reactions of intellectually normal and retarded boys after experimentally induced failure—a social learning theory interpretation. Unpublished doctoral dissertation, George Peabody College for Teachers, 1958.

Gardner, W. I. Personality concomitants of mental retardation. In R. K. Wilcox (Ed.), *Strategies for behavioral research in mental retardation.* Madison: University of Wisconsin Press, 1961. Pp. 86–98.

Gardner, W. I., Cromwell, R. L., and Foshee, J. G. Studies in activity level: II. Effects of visual stimulation in organics, familials, hyperactives, and hypoactives. *Am. J. ment. Defic.*, 1959, **63**, 1028–1033.

Garfield, S. L. Abnormal behavior and mental deficiency. In N. R. Ellis (Ed.), *Handbook in mental deficiency: psychological theory and research.* New York: McGraw-Hill, 1963, Pp. 574–601.

Gelof, M. Comparisons of systems of classifications relating degrees of retardation to measured intelligence. *Am. J. ment. Defic.*, 1963, **68**, 297–317.

Ginzberg, E. The mentally handicapped in a technological society. In S. F. Osler and R. E. Cooke (Eds.), *The biosocial basis of mental retardation.* Baltimore, Md.: Johns Hopkins Press, 1965. Pp. 1–15.

Girardeau, F. L. The formation of discrimination learning sets in mongoloid and normal children. *J. comp. physiol. Psychol.*, 1959, **52**, 566–570.

Girardeau, F. L. The effect of secondary reinforcement on the operant behavior of mental defectives. *Am. J. ment. Defic.*, 1962, **67**, 441–449.

Girardeau, F. L., and Ellis, N. R. Rote verbal learning by normal and mentally retarded children. *Am. J. ment. Defic.*, 1964, **68**, 525–532.

Girardeau, F. L., and Spradlin, J. E. Token rewards in a cottage program. *Mental Retardation*, 1964, **2**, 345–351.

Goldberg, B., and Soper, H. Childhood psychosis or mental retardation: a diagnostic dilemma. I. Psychiatric and psychological aspects. *Can. med. Ass. J.*, 1963, **89**, 1015–1019.

Goldfarb, W. Emotional and intellectual consequences of psychologic deprivation in infancy: a reevaluation. In P. H. Hoch and J. Zubin (Eds.), *Psychopathology of childhood.* New York: Grune and Stratton, 1955. Pp. 105–119.

Goldfarb, W. *Childhood schizophrenia.* Cambridge: The Commonwealth Fund and Harvard University Press, 1961.

Goldstein, H. Social and occupational adjustment. In H. A. Stevens and R. Heber (Eds.), *Mental retardation: a review of research.* Chicago: University of Chicago Press, 1964. Pp. 214–258.

Goldstein, H., Moss, J. W., and Jordan, L. J. *The efficacy of special class training on the development of mentally retarded children.* Urbana: University of Illinois Press, 1965.

Gorlow, L., Butler, A., and Guthrie, G. M. Correlates of self-attitudes of retardates. *Am. J. ment. Defic.*, 1963, **67**, 549–555.

Gottesman, I. Genetic aspects of intelligent behavior. In N. Ellis (Ed.), *Handbook of mental deficiency.* New York: McGraw-Hill, 1963. Pp. 253–296.

Graham, F. K., Ernhart, C. B., Thurston, D., and Craft, M. Development three years after perinatal anoxia and other potentially damaging newborn experiences. *Psychol. Monogr.*, 1962, **76** (Whole No. 522).

Graliker, B. V., Koch, R., and Henderson, R. A. A study of factors influencing placement of retarded children in a state residential institution. *Am. J. ment. Defic.*, 1965, **69**, 553–559.

Green, C., and Zigler, E. Social deprivation and the performance of retarded and normal children on a satiation type task. *Child Dev.*, 1962, **33**, 499–508.

Greenbaum, J. V., & Lurie, L. Encephalitis as a causative factor in behavior disorders of children: an analysis of seventy-eight cases. *J. Am. med. Ass.*, 1948, **136**, 923–930.

Griffith, B. C., and Spitz, H. H. Some relationships between abstraction and word meanings in retarded adolescents. *Am. J. ment. Defic.*, 1958, **63**, 247–251.

Griffith, B. C., Spitz, H. H., and Lipman, R. E. Verbal mediation and concept formation in retarded and normal subjects. *J. exp. Psychol.*, 1959, **58**, 247–250.

Gruenberg, E. M. Epidemiology. In H. A. Stevens and R. Heber (Eds.), *Mental retardation: a review of research.* Chicago: University of Chicago Press, 1964. Pp. 259–306.

Grumbach, M. M., van Wyk, J. J., and Wilkins, L. Chromosomal sex in gonadal dysgenesis (ovarian agenesis): relationship to male pseudo-hermaphroditism and theories of human sex differentiation. *J. clin. Endocr. Metab.*, 1955, **15**, 1161.

Gula, H. Paper given at Conference on Group Care for Children, U. S. Children's Bureau, January 1965.

Guthrie, G. M., Butler, A., and Gorlow, L. Patterns of self-attitudes of retardates. *Am. J. ment. Defic.*, 1961, **66**, 222–229.

Guthrie, G. M., Butler, A., and Gorlow, L. Personality differences between institutionalized and non-institutionalized retardates. *Am. J. ment. Defic.*, 1963, **67**, 543–548.

Guvener, A., Bagchi, B. K., Kooi, K. A., and Calhoun, H. D. Mental and seizure manifestations in relation to brain tumors. A statistical study. *Epilepsia*, 1964, **5**, 166–175.

Haddad, H. M., and Wilkins, L. Congenital anomalies associated with gonadal aplasia, review of 55 cases. *Pediatrics*, 1959, **23**, 885.

Hanauer, K. An experimental study using the Marble Board test as a tool for diagnosing brain injury in mentally retarded children. Unpublished master's thesis, University of Denver, 1952.

Hardy, J. B. Viral infection in pregnancy: a review. *Am. J. Obstet. Gynec.*, 1965, **93**, 1052–1065. (a)

Hardy, J. B. Perinatal factors and intelligence. In S. F. Osler and R. E. Cooke (Eds.), *The biosocial bases of mental retardation.* Baltimore, Md.: Johns Hopkins Press, 1965. Pp. 35–60. (b)

Harrell, R. F., Woodyard, E., and Gates, A. I. *The effect of mothers' diets on the intelligence of offspring: a study of the influence of vitamin supplementation of the diet of pregnant and lactating women on the intelligence of their children.* New York: Bureau of Publications, Teachers College, 1955.

Harter, S. Mental age, I.Q., and motivational factors in the discrimination learning set performance of normal and retarded children. *J. exp. Child Psychol.*, 1967, **5**, 123–141.

Hawkins, W. F. The effects of stimulus asynchrony in compound trial-and-error learning by normals and retardates. Unpublished doctoral dissertation, George Peabody College for Teachers, 1963.

Haworth, J. C., and McRae, K. N. The neurological and developmental effects of neonatal hypoglycemia: a follow-up of 22 cases. *Can. med. Ass. J.*, 1965, **92**, 861–865.

Headrick, M. W., and Ellis, N. R. Short-term visual memory in normals and retardates. *J. exp. Child Psychol.*, 1964, **1**, 339–347.

Heal, L. W., Ross, L. E., Sanders, F., and Scholwalter, M. E. Motor conflict in mental defectives and normal children of a comparable mental age. *Abstracts of Peabody Studies in Mental Retardation*, 1962–1964, **3**, No. 35. (Abstract)

Heber, R. Expectancy and expectancy changes in normal and mentally retarded boys. Unpublished doctoral dissertation, George Peabody College for Teachers, 1957.

Heber, R. A manual on terminology and classification in mental retardation. *Am. J. ment. Defic.*, 1959, **64** (Monogr. Suppl.). (Rev. ed., 1961.)

Heber, R. Mental retardation: concept and classification. In E. R. Trapp and P. Himelstein (Eds.), *Readings on the exceptional child.* New York: Appleton-Century-Crofts, 1962. Pp. 69–81.

Heber, R. Personality. In H. A. Stevens and R. Heber (Eds.), *Mental retardation: a review of research.* Chicago: University of Chicago Press, 1964. Pp. 143–147.

Hecht, F., Bryant, J. S., Motuisky, A., and Giblett, E. R. The No. 17–18 trisomy syndrome. *J. Pediat.*, 1963, **63**, 605–621.

Hermelin, B., and O'Connor, N. Short term memory in normal and subnormal children. *Am. J. ment. Defic.*, 1964, **69**, 121–125.

Hetherington, E. M., Ross, L. E., and Pick, H. L., Jr. Delay of reward and learning in mentally retarded and normal children. *Child Dev.*, 1964, **35**, 653–659.

Hijmans, J. C., and Shearin, D. B. Partial deletion of short arms of chromosome No. 5. *Am. J. Dis. Child.*, 1965, **109**, 85–89.

Hinton, G. Childhood psychosis or mental retardation: a diagnostic dilemma. II. Pediatric and neurological aspects. *Can. med. Ass. J.*, 1963, **89**, 1020–1024.

Hjern, B., and Nylander, I. Acute head injuries in children: traumatology, therapy, and prognosis. *Acta Paediat.*, 1964, Supplement 52.

Hobbs, M. T. A comparison of institutionalized and noninstitutionalized mentally retarded. *Am. J. ment. Defic.*, 1964, **69**, 206–210.

House, B. J. Oddity performance in retardates: I. Acquisition and transfer. *Child Dev.*, 1964, **35**, 635–643.

House, B. J., and Zeaman, D. A comparison of discrimination learning in normal and mentally defective children. *Child Dev.*, 1958, **29**, 411–415. (a)

House, B. J., and Zeaman, D. Visual discrimination learning in imbeciles. *Am. J. ment. Defic.*, 1958, **63**, 447–452. (b)

House, B. J., and Zeaman, D. Transfer of a discrimination from objects to patterns. *J. exp. Psychol.*, 1960, **59**, 298–302.

Hsia, D. Y. Y., Inouye, T., and Walker, F. A. Galactosemia. *J. Am. med. Ass.*, 1961, **178**, 944.

Hundziak, M., Maurer, R. A., and Watson, L. S., Jr. Operant conditioning in toilet training of severely mentally retarded boys. *Am. J. ment. Defic.*, 1965, **70**, 120–125.

Hunt, J. M. *Intelligence and experience.* New York: Ronald Press, 1961.

Hunt, N. *The world of Nigel Hunt.* New York: Garrett Publications, 1967.

Ingalls, T. H., Ingenito, E. F., and Curley, F. J. Acquired chromosomal anomalies induced in mice by injection of a teratogen in pregnancy. *Science*, 1963, **141**, 810–812.

Isselbacher, K. J., Anderson, E. P., Kurahashi, K., and Kalckar, N. M. Congenital galactosemia, a single enzymatic block in galactose metabolism. *Science*, 1956, **123**, 635–636.

Itard, J. M. G. *The wild boy of Aveyron.* Translated by G. and M. Humphrey. New York: Appleton-Century-Crofts, 1932.

Jackson, S. The growth of logical thinking in normal and subnormal children. *Br. J. educ. Psychol.*, 1965, **35**, 255–258. (Abstract)

Jensen, A. R. Rote learning in retarded adults and normal children. *Am. J. ment. Defic.*, 1965, **69**, 828–834.

Johnson, C. D., and Barnett, C. D. Relationship of physical stigmata to intellectual status in mongoloids. *Am. J. ment. Defic.*, 1961, **66**, 435–437.

Johnson, G. O. Special education for the mentally retarded—a paradox. *Exceptional Children*, 1962, **29**, 62–69.

Johnson, G. O., and Blake, K. A. Learning performance of retarded and normal children. *Syracuse University Special Education and Rehabilitation Monographs*, 1960, No. 5.

Jongbloet, J. Trisomie D_1 avec translocation D/D. (Trisomy D with D/D translocation.) *Acta Paediat., Belg.*, 1965, **19**, 64–65.

Kanner, L. *Child psychiatry*. (3rd ed.) Springfield, Ill.: Thomas, 1957.

Kanner, L. *A history of the care and study of the mentally retarded*. Springfield, Ill.: Thomas, 1964.

Kass, N., and Stevenson, H. W. The effect of pretraining reinforcement conditions on learning by normal and retarded children. *Am. J. ment. Defic.*, 1961, **66**, 76–80.

Katz, P. Another look at transfer of learning and mental retardation. *Mental Retardation*, 1964, **2**, 177–183.

Katz, P. Acquisition and retention of discrimination learning sets in lower-class preschool children. *J. educ. Psychol.*, 1967, **58**, 253–258.

Kaufman, M. E. The formation of a learning set in institutionalized and noninstitutionalized mental defectives. *Am. J. ment. Defic.*, 1963, **67**, 601–605.

Kaufman, M. E., and Peterson, W. M. Acquisition of a learning set by normal and mentally retarded children. *J. comp. physiol. Psychol.*, 1958, **51**, 619–621.

Keeler, K. F. Post-school adjustment of educable mentally retarded youth educated in San Francisco. (Research Study No. 1.) *Diss. Abstr.*, 1964, **25**, 936–937.

Kennedy, C., Drage, J. S., and Schwartz, B. K. Preliminary data with respect to the relationships between Apgar score at one and five minutes and fetal outcome. Paper presented at the spring meeting of the Collaborative Perinatal Project, National Institute of Neurological Diseases and Blindness, Washington, D. C., 1963.

Kennedy, R. J. R. The social adjustment of morons in a Connecticut city. Hartford, Conn.: State Office Building, 1948.

Kephart, N. C. *The slow learner in the classroom*. Columbus, O.: Merrill, 1960.

Kern, W. H., and Pfaeffle, H. A comparison of social adjustment of mentally retarded children in various educational settings. *Am. J. ment. Defic.*, 1962, **67**, 407–413.

King, L. S. Intrauterine malnutrition. *J. Am. med. Ass.*, 1965, **191**, 1077–1079.

Kingsley, R. F. The relationship of the primary mental abilities, sex, and social class to associative learning ability in educable mentally handicapped children. *Diss. Abstr.*, 1964, **25**, 324.

Kirk, S. A. *Public school provisions for severely retarded children*. Albany: New York State Interdepartmental Health Resources Board, 1957.

Kirk, S. A. *Early education of the mentally retarded: an experimental study*. Urbana: University of Illinois Press, 1958.

Kirk, S. A. Research in education. In H. A. Stevens and R. Heber (Eds.), *Mental retardation: a review of research*. Chicago: University of Chicago Press, 1964. Pp. 57–99.

Kirk, S. A., and Johnson, G. O. *Educating the retarded child*. Cambridge, Mass.: Houghton Mifflin, 1951.

Kitano, H. L. Validity of the children's manifest anxiety scale and the modified revised California inventory. *Child Dev.*, 1960, **31**, 67–72.

Klaus, R. A., and Gray, S. W. *The early training project for disadvantaged children: a report after five years*. Nashville, Tenn.: George Peabody College for Teachers, 1967.

Knight, O. B. The self concept of educable mentally retarded children in special and regular classes. Unpublished doctoral dissertation, University of North Carolina at Chapel Hill, 1967.

Knobloch, H., and Pasamanick, B. The developmental behavior approach to the neurologic examination in infancy. *Child Dev.*, 1962, 33, 181–198.

Kolstoe, O. P. An examination of some characteristics which discriminate between employed and not-employed mentally retarded males. *Am. J. ment. Defic.*, 1961, 66, 472–482.

Komai, T., Kishimoto, K., and Ozaki, Y. Genetic study of microcephaly based on Japanese material. *Am. J. hum. Genet.*, 1955, 7, 51–65.

Kounin, J. Experimental studies of rigidity. I. The measurement of rigidity in normal and feebleminded persons. *Character Person.*, 1941, 9, 251–273. (a)

Kounin, J. Experimental studies of rigidity. II. The explanatory power of the concept of rigidity as applied to feeblemindedness. *Character Person.*, 1941, 9, 273–282. (b)

Kugel, R. B. Familial mental retardation: some possible neurophysiological and psychosocial interrelationships. In A. J. Solnit and S. Provence (Eds.), *Modern perspectives in child development*. New York: International Universities Press, 1963. Pp. 206–216.

Kugel, R. B., and Parsons, M. H. *Children of deprivation: changing the course of familial retardation*. Children's Bureau Publication No. 440. Washington, D.C.: U. S. Government Printing Office, 1967.

Kuhlmann, F. Experimental studies in mental deficiency. *Am. J. Psychol.*, 1904, 15, 391–446.

Lambeth, H. D. The self concept of mentally retarded children in relation to educational placement and developmental variables. Unpublished doctoral dissertation, University of North Carolina at Chapel Hill, 1966.

Lance, W. D. Effects of meaningfulness and over-learning on retention in normal and retarded adolescents. *Am. J. ment. Defic.*, 1965, 70, 270–275.

Lawson, D., Metcalfe, M., and Pampiglione, G. Meningitis in childhood. *Br. Med. J.*, 1965, 1(5434), 557–562.

Lejeune, J. A new syndrome of physical and mental deficiency related to a partial autosomal deletion. Paper presented at Joseph P. Kennedy, Jr., Foundation Scientific Symposium on Mental Retardation, New York, February, 1964.

Lejeune, J., Gautier, M., and Turpin, R. Le mongolisme. Premier example d'aberration autosomique humaine. *Annls. Génet.*, 1959, 1, 41.

Lennox, W. G. The heredity of epilepsy as told by relatives and twins. *J. Am. med. Ass.*, 1951, 146, 529–536.

Lennox, W. G. *Epilepsy and related disorders*. Boston: Little, Brown, 1960. 2 vols.

Lennox, W. G., Gibbs, E. L., and Gibbs, F. A. Inheritance of cerebral dysrhythmia and epilepsy. *Arch. neurol. Psychiat.*, 1940, 44, 1155–1183.

Lewin, K. *A dynamic theory of personality*. New York: McGraw-Hill, 1935.

Lilienfeld, A. M., and Parkhurst, E. A study of the association of factors of pregnancy and parturition with the development of cerebral palsy. A preliminary report. *Am. J. Hyg.*, 1951, 53, 262–282.

Lilienfeld, A. M., and Pasamanick, B. The association of material and fetal factors with the development of mental deficiency: II. *Am. J. ment. Defic.*, 1956, 60, 557–569.

Lindquist, J. M., Plotkin, S. A., Shaw, L., Gilden, R. V., and Williams, M. L. Congenital rubella syndrome as a systemic infection. Studies of affected infants born in Philadelphia, U. S. A. *Br. med. J.*, 1965, 2(5475), 1401–1406.

Lipman, R. S. Learning: verbal, perceptual-motor and classical conditioning. In N. R. Ellis (Ed.), *Handbook of mental deficiency*. New York: McGraw-Hill, 1963. Pp. 391–423.

Lipman, R. S. Children's manifest anxiety in retardates and approximately equal MA normals. *Am. J. ment. Defic.*, 1964, **65**, 342–348.

Lipman, R. S., and Griffith, B. C. Effects of anxiety level on concept formation: a test of drive theory. *Am. J. ment. Defic.*, 1960, **65**, 342–348.

Liverant, S. Intelligence: a concept in need of re-examination. *J. consult. Psychol.*, 1960, **24**, 101–110.

Lott, B. S. Paired associate learning, generalization, and retention as a function of intelligence. *Am. J. ment. Defic.*, 1958, **63**, 481–489.

Luria, A. R. Experimental study of the higher nervous activity of the abnormal child. *J. ment. defic. Res.*, 1959, **3**, 1–22.

Luria, A. R. (Ed.) *The mentally retarded child.* Translated by W. P. Robinson. New York: Pergamon Press, 1963.

Luria, A. R., and Vinogradova, O. S. An objective investigation of the dynamics of semantic systems. *Br. J. Psychol.*, 1951, **50**, 89–105.

Lyle, J. G. The effect of an institution environment upon the verbal development of imbecile children (ii) speech and language. *J. ment. defic. Res.*, 1960, **4**, 1–13.

Lyle, J. G. Some personality characteristics of "trainable" children in relation to verbal ability. *Am. J. ment. Defic.*, 1961, **66**, 69–75.

Mabry, C., and Podoll, E. Above average intelligence in untreated phenylketonuria. *J. Pediat.*, 1963, **63**, 1038–1040.

Mackie, R. P. Spotlighting advances in special education. *Exceptional Children*, 1965, **32**, 77–81.

Maclean, N. Sex-chromosome abnormalities in newborn babies. *Lancet*, 1964, **1**, 286–290.

Malpass, L. F., Marks, S., and Palermo, D. S. Responses of retarded children to the Children's Manifest Anxiety Scale. *J. educ. Psychol.*, 1960, **51**, 305–308.

Maney, A. C., Pace, R., and Morrison, D. F. A factor analytic study of the need for institutionalization: Problems and populations for program development. *Am. J. ment. Defic.*, 1964, **69**, 372–384.

Martin, W. E., and Blum, A. Interest generalization and learning in mentally normal and subnormal children. *J. comp. physiol. Psychol.*, 1961, **54**, 28–32.

Masland, R. L. The prevention of mental subnormality. In R. L. Masland, S. B. Sarason, and T. Gladwin, *Mental subnormality.* New York: Basic Books, 1958. Pp. 11–141.

Mason, H. H., and Turner, M. E. Chronic galactosemia. Report of case with studies on carbohydrates. *Am. J. Dis. Child.*, 1935, **50**, 359–374.

Matejcek, Z., and Langmeier, J. New observations on psychological deprivation in institutional children in Czechoslovakia. *Slow Learning Child*, 1965, **12**, 20–37.

Mayer, C. L. The relationship of early special class placement and the self-concepts of mentally handicapped children. *Exceptional Children*, 1966, **33**, 77–81.

McCandless, B. R. Relation of environmental factors to intellectual functioning. In H. A. Stevens and R. Heber (Eds.), *Mental retardation: a review of research.* Chicago: University of Chicago Press, 1964. Pp. 175–213.

McCarthy, J. J., and Scheerenberger, R. C. A decade of research on the education of the mentally retarded. *Ment. Retard. Abstr.*, 1966, **3**, 481–501.

McClearn, G. E. The inheritance of behavior. In L. Postman (Ed.), *Psychology in the making.* New York: Knopf, 1962. Pp. 144–252.

McConnell, T. R. Outerdirectedness in normal and retarded children as a function of institutionalization. *Abstracts of Peabody Studies in Mental Retardation, 1962–1964*, 1965, **3**, No. 80.

McKinney, J. P., and Keele, T. Effects of increased mothering on the behavior of severely retarded boys. *Am. J. ment. Defic.*, 1963, **67**, 556–562.

McManis, D. L. Pursuit-rotor performance of normal and retarded children in four verbal-incentive conditions. *Child Dev.*, 1965, **36**, 667–683.

Mead, P. B., and Marcus, S. L. Prolonged pregnancy. *Am. J. Obstet. Gynec.*, 1964, **89**, 495–502.

Medical World News. Tests find two PKU types—and a dilemma. *Med. Wld. News*, 1965, **6**(46), 38–39.

Metzger, R. Probability learning in children and aments. *Am. J. ment. Defic.*, 1960, **64**, 869–974.

Meyerowitz, J. H. Self-derogations in young retardates and special class placement. *Child Dev.*, 1962, **33**, 443–451.

Meyerowitz, J. H. Self-derogation and special classes. Baylor University College of Medicine, personal communication, 1967. (Mimeographed)

Milgram, N. A., and Furth, H. G. Position reversal vs. dimension reversal in normal and retarded children. *Child Dev.*, 1964, **35**, 701–708.

Milgram, N. A., and Furth, H. G. Factors affecting conceptual control in normal and retarded children. *Child Dev.*, 1967, **38**, 531–543.

Miller, M. B. Locus of control, learning climate, and climate shift in serial learning with mental retardates. Ann Arbor, Mich.: University Microfilms, 1961.

Mitchell, S. C., and Woodside, G. L. Virus etiology of congenital malformations. *Science*, 1967, **157**, 1337–1338.

Mitrano, A. J. Principles of conditioning in human goal behavior. *Psychol. Monogr.*, 1939, **51**, No. 230.

Morgan, H. S., and Kane, S. H. An analysis of 16,327 breech births. *J. Am. med. Ass.*, 1964, **187**(4), 262–264.

Mueller, M. W., and Weaver, S. J. Psycholinguistic abilities of institutionalized and non-institutionalized trainable mental retardates. *Am. J. ment. Defic.*, 1964, **68**, 775–783.

Muldal, S., and Ockley, C. H. The double male: a new chromosome constitution in Klinefelter's syndrome. *Lancet*, 1960, **2**, 493.

Muller, H. J. Artificial transmutation of genes. *Science*, 1927, **66**, 84.

Murphy, D. P. Ovarian irradiation: its effect on the health of subsequent children. *Surgery Gynec. Obstet.*, 1928, **47**, 201–215.

Murphy, D. P., Shirlock, M. E., and Doll, E. A. Microcephaly following maternal pelvic irradiation for the interruption of pregnancy. *Am. J. Roentg. rad. Ther.*, 1942, **48**, 356–359.

Naeye, R. L., and Blanc, W. Pathogenesis of congenital rubella. *J. Am. med. Ass.*, 1965, **194**(12), 1277–1283.

Nakamura, H. Nature of institutionalized adult mongoloid intelligence. *Am. J. ment. Defic.*, 1961, **66**, 456–458.

Neuhaus, E. C. Training the mentally retarded for competitive employment. *Exceptional Children*, 1967, **33**, 625–628.

New York State Department of Mental Hygiene, Mental Health Research Unit. *Technical report: a special census of suspected referred mental retardation. Onondaga County, New York.* Syracuse, N.Y., 1965.

Noonan, J. R., and Barry, J. R. Performance of retarded children. *Science*, 1967, **156**, 171.

Norris, A. S. Mental retardation associated with conditions due to trauma or physical agents in the prenatal period. In Charles H. Carter (Ed.), *Medical aspects of mental retardation.* Springfield, Ill.: Thomas, 1965. Pp. 248–260.

Oatley, K. G., Bryant, P. E., and Tinson, C. Non-reinforcement and the emission of alternative responses by severely subnormal children. *J. ment. Defic. Res.*, 1965, **9**, 191–200.

O'Connor, M., and Hermelin, B. Discrimination and reversal learning in imbeciles. *J. abnorm. soc. Psychol.*, 1959, **59**, 409–412.

O'Gorman, G. Psychosis as a cause of mental defect. *J. ment. Sci.*, 1954, **100**, 934–943.

Olshansky, S., and Schonfield, J. Institutionalization of preschool retardates. *Mental Retardation*, 1964, **2**, 109–115.

Orlando, R., and Bijou, S. W. Single and multiple schedules of reinforcement in developmentally retarded children. *J. exp. Anal. Behav.*, 1960, **3**, 339–348.

Ounsted, C. Genetic and social aspects of the epilepsies of childhood. *Eugen. Rev.*, 1955, **47**, 33–49.

Patterson, G. R. An application of conditioning techniques to the control of a hyperactive child. In L. P. Ullman and L. Krasner (Eds.), *Case studies in behavior modification*. New York: Holt, Rinehart, & Winston, 1965. Pp. 370–375.

Penney, R. K., Croskery, J., and Allen, G. Effect of training schedules on rigidity as manifested by normal and mentally retarded children. *Psychol. Rep.*, 1962, **10**, 243–249.

Penrose, L. S. Parental age and mutation. *Lancet*, 1955, **1**, 312–313.

Perron, R., and Pecheux, M.-G. Les debiles mentaux percoivent-ils leur handicap? Donnes experimentales sur l'auto-estimation de l'equipment personnel. In J. Øster (Ed.), *International Copenhagen Congress on the Scientific Study of Mental Retardation*, Vol. 2. Proceedings of the 1964 Copenhagen Congress. Copenhagen, Denmark: Det Berlingske Bogtrykkeri, 1964. Pp. 620–622.

Perry, S. L., and Stotsky, B. A. Type of reward, incentive, and incentive-sequence as factors in the motor performance of mentally retarded, physically handicapped, and college students. *J. Psychol.*, 1965, **60**, 55–65.

Peterson, L. R. Short-term memory. *Scient. Am.*, 1966, **215**(1), 90–95.

Philips, I. Children, mental retardation, and emotional disorder. In I. Philips (Ed.), *Prevention and treatment of mental retardation*. New York: Basic Books, 1966. Pp. 111–112.

Piers, E. V., and Harris, D. B. Age and other correlates of self-concept in children. *J. educ. Psychol.*, 1964, **55**, 91–95.

Plenderleith, M. Discrimination learning and discrimination reversal learning in normal and feebleminded children. *J. genet. Psychol.*, 1956, **88**, 107–112.

Plotkin, S. A., and Vaheri, A. Human fibroblasts infected with rubella virus produce a growth inhibitor. *Science*, 1967, **156**, 659–661.

Podolsky, C. The relation of chronological age and mental age to the performance of school age normals and retardates in selected learning tasks. *Diss. Abstr.*, 1965, **25**, 7085.

Pollack, M. Brain damage, mental retardation, and childhood schizophrenia. *Am. J. Psychiat.*, 1958, **415**, 422–428.

Pond, D. A. Psychiatric aspects of epileptic and brain damaged children. *Br. Med. J.*, 1961, **11**, 1377–1382, 1454–1459.

President's Committee on Mental Retardation. *MR 67: a first report to the President on the nation's progress and remaining great needs in the campaign to combat mental retardation*. Washington, D.C.: U.S. Government Printing Office, 1967.

President's Panel on Mental Retardation. *A proposed program for national action to combat mental retardation*. Washington, D.C.: U. S. Government Printing Office, 1962.

President's Task Force on Manpower Conservation. *One-third of a nation*. Washington, D.C.: U. S. Government Printing Office, 1964.

Pryer, R. S. Retroactive inhibition in normals and defectives as a function of temporal position of the interpolated task. *Am. J. ment. Defic.*, 1960, **64**, 1004–1015.

Prysiazniuk, A. W., and Wicijowski, P. J. Learning sets in mongoloid and non-mongoloid children: a replication. *Am. J. ment. Defic.*, 1964, **69**, 76–78.

Quay, L. C. Academic skills. In N. R. Ellis (Ed.), *Handbook of mental deficiency*. New York: McGraw-Hill, 1963. Pp. 664–690.

Rapin, I. The demyelinating diseases proper. In C. H. Carter (Ed.), *Medical aspects of mental retardation*. Springfield, Ill.: Thomas, 1965. Pp. 737–759.

Reger, R. Reading ability and CMAS scores in educable mentally retarded boys. *Am. J. ment. Defic.*, 1964, **68**, 652–655.

Rheingold, H. L. The measurement of maternal care. *Child Dev.*, 1960, **31**, 565–575.

Rieber, M. Verbal mediation in normal and retarded children. *Am. J. ment. Defic.*, 1964, **68**, 635–641.

Ringness, T. A. Self concept of children of low, average, and high intelligence. *Am. J. ment. Defic.*, 1961, **65**, 453–461.

Robinson, A., and Puck, T. T. Sex chromatin in newborns: presumptive evidence for external factors in human nondisjunction. *Science*, 1965, **148**(3666), 83–85.

Robinson, H. B. Growing up replete. Paper presented to the Conference on Foster Care, Child Welfare League of America, New Orleans, October, 1967. (a)

Robinson, H. B. Social-cultural deprivation as a form of child abuse, Governor's Council on Child Abuse, Raleigh: North Carolina State Board of Health, 1967. (b)

Robinson, H. B. Early childhood. In L. L. Dittmann (Ed.), *New perspectives in early childhood*. New York: Atherton Press, 1968. (a)

Robinson, H. B. The problem of timing in preschool education. In R. Hess and R. Bear (Eds.), *Early education*. Chicago: Aldine Press, 1968. (b)

Robinson, H. B., and Robinson, N. M. *The mentally retarded child: a psychological approach*. New York: McGraw-Hill, 1965. (a)

Robinson, N. M., and Robinson, H. B. A follow-up study of ex-premature and control children at school age. *Pediatrics*, 1965, **35**, 425–433. (b)

Robinson, J. The effects of familiarity and delay upon the performance of a paired-associates learning task by normal and retarded girls. *Abstracts of Peabody Studies in Mental Retardation 1962–1964*, 1965, **3**, No. 40.

Rosenstein, D., and Navarete-Reyna, A. Cytomegalic inclusion disease—observation of the characteristic inclusion bodies in the placenta. *Am. J. Obstet. Gynec.*, 1964, **89**, 220–224.

Rotter, J. B. *Social learning and clinical psychology*. New York: Prentice-Hall, 1954.

Rudel, R. G. The absolute response in tests of generalization in normal and retarded children. *Am. J. Psychol.*, 1959, **72**, 401–408.

Saenger, G. *The adjustment of severely retarded adults in the community*. Albany, N. Y.: Interdepartmental Health Resources Board, 1957.

Scheerenberger, R. C. Mental retardation: definition, classification, and prevalence. *Ment. Retard. Abstr.*, 1964, **1**, 432–441.

Schlanger, B. B. Environmental influences on the verbal output of mentally retarded children. *J. Speech Hear. Disorders*, 1954, **19**, 339–343.

Schlanger, B. B. Results of varying presentations to brain damaged children of an auditory word discrimination test. *Am. J. ment. Defic.*, 1958, **63**, 464–468.

Schloss, S. Nursery-kindergarten enrollment of children under six: October, 1966. Washington, D.C.: U. S. Government Printing Office, 1967.

Schoelkopf, A. M., and Orlando, R. Delayed versus immediate reinforcement in simultaneous discrimination problems with mentally retarded children. Psychol. Rec., 1965, 15, 15–23.

Seagoe, M. V. Yesterday was Tuesday, all night and all day. Boston: Little, Brown, 1964.

Secretary's Committee on Mental Retardation. Mental retardation activities of the U. S. Department of Health, Education, and Welfare, January, 1967. Washington, D.C.: U. S. Government Printing Office, 1967.

Semmel, M. I. Comparison of teacher ratings of brain-injured and mongoloid severely retarded (trainable) children attending community day-school classes. Am. J. ment. Defic., 1960, 64, 963–971.

Sever, J. L., Nelson, K. B., and Gilkeson, M. R. Rubella epidemic, 1964: effect on 6000 pregnancies. Am. J. Dis. Child., 1965, 110, 395–407.

Shipe, D. M. A comparison of probability learning in mentally retarded and normal children. Minor Research Project. George Peabody College for Teachers, 1959.

Shipe, M. D., and Shotwell, A. M. Effects of out-of-home care on mongoloid children: a continuation study. Am. J. ment. Defic., 1965, 69, 649–652.

Sidman, M. Programming perception and learning for retarded children. Paper read at annual meeting of the American Association on Mental Deficiency, Chicago, May 1966.

Sievers, D. J., and Essa, S. H. Language development in institutionalized and community mentally retarded children. Am. J. ment. Defic., 1961, 66, 413–420.

Silverstein, A. B. An empirical test of the mongoloid stereotype. Am. J. ment. Defic., 1964, 68, 493–497.

Singler, R. V. Incidental and intentional learning in retarded and normal children. Diss. Abstr., 1964, 25, 652.

Skeels, H. M. Adult status of children with contrasting early life experiences. Monogr. Soc. Res. Child Dev., 1966, No. 105.

Skeels, H. M., and Dye, H. B. A study of the effects of differential stimulation on mentally retarded children. Proceedings and Addresses of the American Association on Mental Deficiency, 1939, 44, 114–136.

Skeels, H. M., Updegraff, R., Wellman, B. L., and Williams, H. M. A study of environmental stimulation, an orphanage preschool project. University of Iowa Studies on Child Welfare, 1938, 15, No. 4, 129–145.

Sloan, W., and Birch, J. W. A rationale for degrees of retardation. Am. J. ment. Defic., 1955, 60, 258–264.

Smith, D. W., Blizzard, R. M., and Wilkins, L. The mental prognosis in hypothyroidism of infancy and childhood. Pediatrics, 1957, 19, 1011–1020.

Smith, J. O. Effects of a group language development program upon the psycholinguistic abilities of educable mental retardates. Peabody College Research Monograph Series in Special Education, 1962, No. 1.

Snyder, L. H. Human heredity and its modern applications. Am. Scient., 1955, 43, 391–419.

Snyder, R. T. An investigation of personality variability as a major determiner of the degree of academic attainment among educable retardates. Diss. Abstr., 1964, 25, 3409. (Abstract)

Snyder, R. T., Jefferson, W., and Strauss, R. Personality variables as determiners of academic achievement of the retarded. Mental Retardation, 1965, 3, 15–18.

Sontag, L. W. The significance of fetal environment differences. *Am. J. Obstet. Gynec.*, 1941, **42**, 996–1003.

Spicker, H. H., Hodges, W. L., and McCandless, B. R. A diagnostically based curriculum for psychosocially deprived, preschool, mentally retarded children: interim report. *Exceptional Children.* 1966, **33**, 215–220.

Spitz, R. A. Hospitalism; an inquiry into the genesis of psychiatric conditions in early childhood. *Psychoanalytic study of the child.* I. New York: International Universities Press, 1945. Pp. 53–74.

Spradlin, J. E. Effects of reinforcement schedules on extinction in severely mentally retarded children. *Am. J. ment. Defic.*, 1962, **66**, 634–640.

Spradlin, J. E., Cromwell, R. L., and Foshee, J. G. Studies in activity level: III. Effects of auditory stimulation in organics, familials, hyperactives and hypoactives. *Am. J. ment. Defic.*, 1960, **64**, 754–757.

Sprague, R. L., Binder, A., and Silver, R. Learning factors in the responses of the retarded to ambiguous stimuli. *Am. J. ment. Defic.*, 1964, **68**, 722–733.

Spreen, O. Language functions in mental retardation: a review. I. Language development, types of retardation, and intelligence level. *Am. J. ment. Defic.*, 1965, **69**, 482–494.

Stacey, C. L., and Cantor, G. N. The use of Zaslows' test of concept formation on a group of subnormals. *J. clin. Psychol.*, 1953, **9**, 51–53.

Stanbury, J. M., and McGirr, E. M. Sporadic or non-endemic familial cretinism with goitre. *Am. J. Med.*, 1957, **22**, 712–723.

Stanton, J. E., and Cassidy, V. M. Effectiveness of special classes for educable mentally retarded. *Mental Retardation*, 1964, **2**, 8–13.

Stedman, D. J., and Eichorn, D. H. A comparison of the growth and development of institutionalized and home-reared mongoloids during infancy and early childhood. *Am. J. ment. Defic.*, 1964, **69**, 391–401.

Stein, J. F., and Longenecker, E. D. Patterns of mothering affecting handicapped children in residential treatment. *Am. J. ment. Defic.*, 1962, **66**, 749–758.

Stein, Z., and Susser, M. The social distribution of mental retardation. *Am. J. ment. Defic.*, 1963, **67**, 811–821.

Sternlicht, M., and Wanderer, Z. W. Nature of institutionalized adult mongoloid intelligence. *Am. J. ment. Defic.*, 1962, **67**, 301–302.

Stevenson, H. W. Learning of complex problems by normal and retarded Ss. *Am. J. ment. Defic.*, 1960, **64**, 1021–1026.

Stevenson, H. W., and Fahel, L. S. The effect of social reinforcement on the performance of institutionalized and noninstitutionalized normal and feebleminded children. *J. Personality*, 1961, **29**, 136–147.

Stevenson, H. W., and Iscoe, I. Transposition in the feebleminded. *J. exp. Psychol.*, 1955, **49**, 11–15.

Stevenson, H. W., and Knights, R. M. The effectiveness of social reinforcement after brief and extended institutionalization. *Am. J. ment. Defic.*, 1962, **66**, 589–594.

Stevenson, H W., and Swartz, J. D. Learning set in children as a function of intellectual level. *J. comp. physiol. Psychol.*, 1958, **51**, 755–757.

Stevenson, H. W., and Zigler, E. F. Discrimination learning and rigidity in normal and feebleminded individuals. *J. Personality*, 1957, **25**, 699–711.

Stevenson, H. W., and Zigler, E. F. Probability learning in children. *J. exp. Psychol.*, 1958, **56**, 185–192.

Strauss, A. A., and Kephart, N. C. *Psychopathology and education of the brain-injured child.* Vol. 2. New York: Grune & Stratton, 1955.

Strauss, A. A., and Lehtinen, L. E. *Psychopathology and education of the brain-injured child.* New York: Grune & Stratton, 1947.

Sutherland, B. S., Umbarger, B., and Berry, H. K. The treatment of phenyl-ketonuria. *Am. J. Dis. Child.*, 1966, **3**, 505–523.

Szulman, A. E. Chromosomal aberrations in spontaneous human abortions. *New Eng. J. Med.*, 1965, **272**, 811–818.

Tapia, F. Phenylpyruvic oligophrenia: report of a case with normal intelligence. *Dis. Nerv. Syst.*, 1961, **22**, 465–466.

Tarjan, G., Wright, S. W., Kramer, M., Person, P. P., and Morgan, R. The natural history of mental deficiency in a state hospital. I. Probabilities of release and death by age, intelligence quotient, and diagnosis. *Am. J. Dis. Child.*, 1958, **96**, 64–70.

Telfer, M. A., Baker, D., Clark, G. R., and Richardson, C. E. Incidence of gross chromosomal errors among tall criminal American males. *Science*, 1968, **159**, 1249–1250.

Thiede, H. A., and Salm, S. B. Chromosome studies of human spontaneous abortions. *Am. J. Obstet. Gynec.*, 1964, **90**, 205–215.

Thurstone, T. G. An evaluation of educating mentally handicapped children in special classes and in regular classes. U. S. Office of Education Cooperative Research Program, Project No. OE-SAE 6452. University of North Carolina, 1959.

Tough, I. M., and Brown, W. M. C. Chromosome aberrations and exposures to ambient benzene. *Lancet*, 1965, **1** (7387), 684.

Towne, R. C., and Joiner, L. M. The effect of special class placement on the self concept of ability of the educable mentally retarded child. U. S. O. E. Cooperative Research Project No. 06001. East Lansing: College of Education, Michigan State University, 1966.

Tredgold, A. F. *A textbook of mental deficiency.* Baltimore, Md.: William Wood, 1937.

Ullman, L. P., and Krasner, L. (Eds.) *Case studies in behavior modification.* New York: Holt, Rinehart, & Winston, 1965.

U. S. Children's Bureau. *Infant mortality: a challenge to the nation.* U. S. Department of Health, Education, and Welfare, 1966.

U. S. Children's Bureau and U. S. Women's Bureau. *Child care arrangements of the nation's working mothers, 1965.* U. S. Department of Health, Education, and Welfare and U. S. Department of Labor. Washington, D.C.: U. S. Government Printing Office, 1965.

Van Camp, D. Psychological evaluation of children who had neonatal hyper-bilirubinemia. *Am. J. ment. Defic.*, 1964, **68**, 803–806.

Vergason, G. A. Retention in retarded and normal subjects as a function of amount of original training. *Am. J. ment. Defic.*, 1964, **68**, 623–629.

Visier, J. P. A propos du devenir des debiles profonds. (Concerning the future of severely retarded.) *Sauvegarde de l'Enfance*, 1965, **20**, 292–295.

Wachs, T. D., and Butterfield, E. C. The effects of institutional environment and length of institutionalization on the verbal productivity of retardates. *Abstracts of Peabody Studies in Mental Retardation, 1962–1964*, 1965, 3 (No. 64). (Abstract)

Waisman, H. A., and Gerritsen, T. Biochemical and clinical correlations. In H. A. Stevens and R. Heber (Eds.), *Mental retardation: a review of research.* Chicago: University of Chicago Press, 1964. Pp. 307–347.

Warkany, J. Effects of anoxia in early gestation. In W. F. Windle (Ed.), *Neurological and psychological deficits of asphyxia neonatorum.* Springfield, Ill.: Thomas, 1958. Pp. 130–140.

Warren, F. G. Ratings of employed and unemployed mentally handicapped males on personality and work factors. *Am. J. ment. Defic.*, 1961, **65**, 629–633.

Warren, S. A. Academic achievement of trainable pupils with five or more years of schooling. *Training School Bulletin*, 1963, **2**, 75–86.

Watson, L. S., Jr. Application of operant conditioning techniques to institutionalized severely and profoundly retarded children. Paper presented at the annual convention of the American Psychological Association, Chicago, 1965. (Mimeographed)

Watson, L. S., Jr. Application of operant conditioning techniques to institutionalized severely and profoundly retarded children. *Ment. Retard. Abstr.*, 1967, **4**, 1–18.

Watson, L. S., Jr., Clevenger, L. J., and Hundziak, M. Transfer of word recognition performance by brain-injured mentally retarded children. A paper presented at the convention of the Great Lakes Region American Association on Mental Deficiency, Columbus, O., 1964.

Watson, L. S., Jr., and Lawson, R. Instrumental learning in mental retardates. *Ment. Retard. Abstr.*, 1966, **3**, 1–20.

Watson, L. S., Jr., Lawson, R., and Sanders, C. Generalized or token reinforcement with severely and profoundly retarded children. Paper presented at the annual convention of the American Association on Mental Deficiency, Miami, Fla., 1965.

Weatherwax, J., and Benoit, E. P. Concrete and abstract thinking in organic and non-organic mentally retarded children. *Am. J. ment. Defic.*, 1957, **62**, 548–553.

Weaver, E. N. Hydrocephalus, intracranial aneurysms, intracranial vascular malformations, cerebral cysts, intracranial tumors, premature craniosynostosis. In C. H. Carter (Ed.), *Medical aspects of mental retardation*. Springfield, Ill.: Thomas, 1965. Pp. 297–357.

Weaver, T. R. The incidence of maladjustment among mental defectives in military environment. *Am. J. ment. Defic.*, 1946, **51**, 238–246.

Webster, T. G. Problems of emotional development in young retarded children. *Am. J. Psychiat.*, 1963, **120**, 37–53.

Weikart, D. P. Results of preschool intervention programs. In D. P. Weikart (Ed.), *Preschool intervention: a preliminary report of the Perry Preschool Project*. Ann Arbor, Mich.: Campus Publishers, 1967. Pp. 117–159.

Weir, M. W. Mental retardation (letter). *Science*, 1967, **157**, 576–577.

Wiener, G., Crawford, E. E., and Snyder, R. T. Some correlates of overt anxiety in mildly retarded patients. *Am. J. ment. Defic.*, 1960, **64**, 735–739.

Wiener, G., Rider, R. V., Oppel, W. C., Fischer, L. K., and Harper, P. A. Correlates of low birth weight: psychological status at six to seven years of age. *Pediatrics*, 1965, **35**, 434–444.

Wilson, J. G. Embryological considerations in teratology. In J. G. Wilson, and J. Warkany (Eds.), *Teratology—principles and techniques*. Chicago: University of Chicago Press, 1965. Pp. 251–257.

Wilson, M. G., Parmalee, A. H., and Huggins, M. H. Prenatal history of infants with birth weights of 1500 grams or less. *J. Pediat.*, 1963, **63**, 1140–1150.

Wiseman, D. E. A classroom procedure for identifying and remediating language problems. *Mental Retardation*, 1965, **3**, 20–24.

Wolfensberger, W. Differential rewards as motivating factors in mental deficiency research. *Am. J. ment. Defic.*, 1960, **64**, 902–906.

Woodward, M. Early experience and behavior disorders in severely subnormal children. *Br. J. soc. clin. Psychol.*, 1963, **2**, 174–184.

Wunsch, W. L. Some characteristics of mongoloids evaluated at a clinic for children with retarded mental development. *Am. J. ment. Defic.*, 1957, **62**, 122–130.

Yacorzynski, G. K., and Tucker, B. E. What price intelligence? *Am. Psychol.*, 1960, **15**, 201–203.

Yannet, H. Classification and etiological factors in mental retardation. *J. Pediat.*, 1957, **50**, 226–230.

Zeaman, D. Learning processes of the mentally retarded. In S. F. Osler and R. E. Cooke (Eds.), *The biosocial basis of mental retardation*. Baltimore, Md.: Johns Hopkins Press, 1965. Pp. 107–127.

Zeaman, D., and House, B. J. Approach and avoidance in the discrimination learning of retardates. In D. Zeaman et al., *Learning and transfer in mental defectives*. Progress report No. 2, National Institutes of Mental Health, 1960. Pp. 32–70.

Zeaman, D., and House, B. J. The role of attention in retardate discrimination learning. In N. Ellis (Ed.), *Handbook of mental deficiency*. New York: McGraw-Hill, 1963. Pp. 159–223.

Zeaman, D., House, B. J., and Orlando, R. Use of special training conditions in visual discrimination learning with imbeciles. *Am. J. ment. Defic.*, 1958, **63**, 453–459.

Zigler, E. Social deprivation and rigidity in the performance of feebleminded children. *J. abnorm. soc. Psychol.*, 1961, **62**, 413–421.

Zigler, E. Rigidity in the feebleminded. In E. P. Trapp and P. Himelstein (Eds.), *Research readings on the exceptional child*. New York: Appleton-Century-Crofts, 1962. Pp. 141–162.

Zigler, E. Mental retardation: current issues and approaches. In L. W. Hoffman and M. L. Hoffman (Eds.), *Review of child development research*. Vol. 2. New York: Russell Sage, 1966. Pp. 107–168.

Zigler, E. Familial mental retardation: a continuing dilemma. *Science*, 1967, **155**, 292–298. (a)

Zigler, E. Mental retardation (letter). *Science*, 1967, **157**, 578–579. (b)

Zigler, E., and deLabry, J. Concept-switching in middle-class, lower-class, and retarded children. *J. abnorm. soc. Psychol.*, 1962, **65**, 267–272.

Zigler, E., Hodgen, L., and Stevenson, H. W. The effect of support and non-support on the performance of normal and feebleminded children. *J. Personality*, 1958, **26**, 106–122.

Zigler, E., and Unell, E. Concept-switching in normal and feebleminded children as a function of reinforcement. *Am. J. ment. Defic.*, 1962, **66**, 651–657.

Zigler, E., and Williams, J. Institutionalization and the effectiveness of social reinforcement: a three-year follow-up study. *J. abnorm. soc. Psychol.*, 1963, **66**, 197–205.

Zimmerman, H. M., and Yannet, H. Cerebral sequelae of icterus gravis neonatorum and their relation to kernicterus. *Am. J. Dis. Child.*, 1935, **49**, 418.

28. The Behavior Disorders of Childhood

E. JAMES ANTHONY

THE RELATIONSHIP BETWEEN NORMAL AND ABNORMAL BEHAVIOR

Abnormal behavior has been regarded by some as a departure from the normal, differing from it in kind; others consider it an extension of the habitual range, distinctive only in degree; and a third point of view holds that all forms of behavioral deviancy express both qualitative and quantitative changes. The consideration has some operational importance since the extent to which the two modes of behaving are judged conterminous may help the clinician and investigator decide how far they can go in applying the theories and methods of Normal Psychology directly to behavior pathology. It may also determine the degree to which the area of study is looked upon as "absurd, unpredictable, irregular and unnatural" (Cameron, 1947) and treated as though it somehow lay outside the bounds that enclosed the legitimate behavioral sciences. Cameron has been a strong protagonist of the quantitative approach and has put forward a "principle of continuity" that stated that abnormal behavior should not be alienated from the spectrum of normal behavior and that "all attitudes and responses found in behavior pathology (were) in some way related to and derived from normal biosocial behavior" (1947).

The relationship is still far from resolved, and, in the words of Lapouse and Monk (1959, p. 803), "One of the psychiatric dilemmas of our time is the decision as to what is normal and what is abnormal in human behavior." There is, however, an increasing tendency to consider the two behavioral modes on a continuum so that it would no longer represent an act of extreme alienation to progress from one form to the other. For example, Buckle and Lebovici (1960) emphasize that *all* children show signs and symptoms of disturbed behavior at some time, and Kanner (1960) is of the opinion that the recognition of the abnormal may be more closely related to the "annoyance threshold" of the environment than to any intrinsic, differentiating quality in the activity. He goes on to say that "a multitude of early breath-holders, nail-biters, nose-pickers and casual masturbators" develop into reasonably happy and efficient adults because of tolerant and resourceful parental attitudes; in the absence of these, he feels it is more than likely that the children will be referred to clinics where such symptoms will be accorded a prominence "far out of proportion to their role as everyday problems of the everyday child" (1960, p. 19). His conclusion is that there is no absolute criterion for the normalcy of any of the common forms of behavior problems and that the judgment of normality and abnormality is bound up with the attitude of the evaluating agent. Shepherd, Oppenheim, and Mitchell (1966) also lend support to this point of view, finding, in a survey, that clinic children did not differ from supposedly normal children in their symptomatic behavior but the clinic parents were more anxious, more easily upset, less able to cope with their children, and much more likely to consult with others on their problems. All these factors predisposed them to seek clinical help.

When large-scale epidemiological studies are carried out, the differentiation of normal from abnormal becomes even more obscure. Lapouse and Monk (1958) found a high prevalence of behavior characteristics, commonly considered indicative of psychopathology, in a general population of children and concluded that this wide variety of behavioral symptoms represented manifestations of developmental stress occurring in essentially normal children. At certain critical stages of development, there was apparently a transient tendency for many children to develop symptomatic behavior.

Fashionable trends could also be held responsible for determining what should or should not be regarded as abnormal. Kanner (1960) offered a capsular history of nail biting from the literature over a period of 25 years. In 1908, nail biting was regarded as "a stigma of degeneration;" in 1912 it was seen as "an exquisite psychopathic symptom"; and in 1931 it was described as "a sign of an unresolved Oedipus complex." Following this, a survey indicated that 66% of school children had been nail-biters at some time or another, which led Kanner to remark that it was "hardly realistic to assume that two-thirds of our youth are degenerate, exquisitely psychopathic or walking around with an unresolved Oedipus complex" (1960, p. 18).

In addition, therefore, to the predominant trend in regarding abnormal behavior simply as an extension of normal behavior, there was a further inclination to reduce the difference between the two to a value judgment or to an accident of the referral procedures. A more moderate attitude was held by those who still felt the need to segregate the two behaviors on the grounds that an accumulation of quantitative factors could eventuate in qualitative differences. Pathological behavior could thus be differentiated not only by its greater intensity, frequency, and persistence but also because it was experienced by both patient and clinician as "different." It was also more likely to be associated with other symptoms and to be embedded in an overtly pathogenic environment.

In summary, there would seem to be appreciably more support for the "continuous" over the "discontinuous" hypothesis with the added qualification that more radical discrepancies could emerge at higher intensities. The dividing line between normal and disordered behavior was far from fixed, fluctuating with different social and cultural settings. It would appear, therefore, that the behavior of any individual, whether normal or abnormal, was ultimately "cribbed, cabinned and confined" within the limits of his culture (Frank, 1939).

DEFINITION OF THE BEHAVIOR DISORDERS

The earliest concept of "behavior disorders" was largely descriptive and referred to aberrations from the behavioral norm manifested by the growing child and stemming from the way in which his relationship to himself and to his environment brought about difficulties in adjustment. His responses were thought to be conditioned by both biological and environmental factors and their symptomatic expression was dependent on the individuality of the child and on the individual vicissitudes of his life. The abnormal behavior itself was regarded as a symptom rather than as an entity.

The term received further definition and delineation when Brown, Pollock, Potter, and Cohen (1937) included it in their general classification of psychiatric disorders in childhood and outlined its tripartite constitution of habit dysfunction, conduct disorder, and neurotic traits. They emphasized the fluid nature of the disturbance, its lack of internalization, and its developing status that had yet to crystallize into elements of the personality. Each part of the disorder represented a transition: the habit dysfunctions, mostly preschool phenomena, could be regarded as forerunners of later psychosomatic illness; neurotic traits were thought to be prepsychoneurotic; and the disturbances of conduct were on their way to becoming character disorders and psychopathies. This hypothetical development would suggest that the reactive and situational disturbances of early childhood gradually harden over time into the more persistent patterns of adolescent and adult life. Whether the connections are as straightforward as this remains to be demonstrated.

A further definition of the condition was made by Van Ophuijsen (1945), who regarded it as a primary environmental reaction that tended to become persistent and patterned without transforming into psychoneurosis or psychopathy, although there was some measure of overlap. He described it as a "character disorder" having its onset before the age of 3 years. Habit dysfunctions were always in the picture and frequently associated with neurotic traits. In a more dynamic appraisal, he noted the concurrence of aggressiveness, narcissism, the absence of guilt feelings, and the invariable rejection by one or both parents.

Blau and Hulse (1956) resuscitated Freud's early concept of "actual neurosis" to explain the primary behavior disorders. According to them, the symptoms representing "pure anxiety" were physiopathological responses to conflict and not defensive transformations of anxiety as are the psychoneuroses. The anxiety was expressed in acting out, and the acting out could end in delinquency.

Anthony (1967) suggested that there were two types of behavior disorders: a phase-specific, circumscribed variety, corresponding to the psychoneuroses and localized to a particular stage of development when particular developmental problems needed to be solved; and a diffuse variety, corresponding to the primary behavior disorders and frequently invading every stage of development. In the former condition, the influence of the environment was relatively benign and constitutional factors conspicuously absent. The child was generally able to cope with his difficulties, defend himself against his anxieties, and internalize the external threats successfully. In the latter, the environment tended to be both pathological and pathogenic and the constitution disposing to greater vulnerability. The history recorded a series of adaptive failures that reflected the child's incapacity to deal internally with anxiety. Habit dysfunctions were joined in turn by neurotic traits and conduct disorders and the triad of disturbances gradually settled into chronicity.

In one of the official definitions of behavior disorder (Hinsie and Campbell, 1960), the primary disorders are defined as not being secondary to somatic diseases or defects, to convulsive disorders, or to the psychoses or psychoneuroses. They are considered to be reactions to an unfavorable environment and may appear as problems of personality development (as persisting undesirable traits or habits), as conduct disorders (involving a large number of antisocial tendencies), and as neurotic traits and school problems.

There is some justification for including "behavior disorders" as a coordinate term and to consider it in its broadest sense of behavior pathology, subsuming both the primary disorders and those secondary to psychosis, psychopathy, psychoneurosis, and organic damage, defect, or disease. The reasons for so doing were summarized by Hunt (1944), who expressed his preference for the term "behavior disorder" as opposed to "mental disorder" with its implied dualism. It was his conviction that a monistic approach was more likely to lead eventually to "a systematic science of molar behavior in which the individual organism would be the focus of concern" (Hunt, 1944, p. V). The monism, embracing primary and secondary, would also include the continuum of normal and abnormal so that the fundamental dynamic laws of behavior and personality development can be applied to all four elements of the disorder.

In summary, the term "behavior disorder" for the purpose of this chapter will be taken to include all forms of disturbed behavior, irrespective of etiological factors which may be, as Mathers (1931, p. 21) once expressed it with regard to normal behavior, "multiform, variable, vague and subtle, rooted widely and deeply in the very fundamentals of life and society."

CLASSIFICATION OF THE BEHAVIOR DISORDERS

The Problem of Variability

The question of continuity versus discontinuity previously raised in relation to normality and abnormality becomes a matter of equal concern with respect to classification. The manifestations of abnormal behavior are highly varied and the approach to a scientifically useful nomenclature must seek to contain this variety.

It has been said that the ultimate task of science is to account for variation, and this statement seems specially pertinent to the field of abnormal behavior. A scientific study of behavior pathology should involve the analysis of variation and covariation along dimensions of environmental effects, behavioral responses over time, and differences in reaction between individuals. The phenotypic variance in behavior can be ascribed to genetic factors, environmental factors, and to the interaction between these two.

The variations may be viewed as either discontinuous or continuous. In the discontinuous type, the individuals are assigned to a class and measurement consists of counting the frequency with which different individuals are assigned to separate classes. In the continuous type, on the other hand, individuals are allocated according to the grade of expression of a particular trait and it becomes necessary to use statistical quantities like means and variances and appropriate scales of measurement.

A common characteristic of the class-oriented method is the use of dichotomous classifications in place of continuous gradations so that individuals are, for example, classified as either introverted or extroverted. There is a tendency for the discontinuous method to deal with ends and to ignore means or processes so that the ways in which a person may shut himself off or open himself up to his social environment is neglected or ignored by the classification. Also, since the individual is absorbed into a class, his individual characteristics are lost within the abstract statistical averages, and if, by chance, he falls into neither the one nor the other class but proves an exception to the rule, his uniqueness is given no consideration so that nothing is learned from him as a special case. Instead of obtaining description in terms of his own special quality, he is given a blanket endowment of class properties.

In its traditional taxonomy, psychiatric diagnosis has been based on the discontinuous system, but, lacking a full knowledge of etiological factors, the system has had to rely on the consensus of experts, who, out of their experience, cluster certain symptoms and create a diagnostic syndrome. It is not altogether surprising that when the system is used by others, there is a minimal degree of reliability in the assignment of cases to particular categories.

Diagnostic Models

The traditional diagnostic model has passed through a number of stages, as discussed by Anthony (1965). The earliest model in child psychiatry, when it was still not yet officially child psychiatry (the label was first coined by Tramer of Switzerland 35 years ago) was,

in the main, a biological one: abnormalities in behavior were correlated with structural changes in the brain. On the European continent, the child psychiatrists are still faithful to this model, as are adult psychiatrists. Encephalopathy and encephalitis are the powerful twin determinants of undesirable or deviant behavior. The concept of "reproductive casualty" has reactivated this model in the United States, but it is less completely dedicated to a monocasual position.

With the flowering of the child guidance movement, the model underwent a drastic change with the psychological factors gaining predominance, at first with an appreciable contribution from the social and cultural environment, but later, as psychoanalytic thinking achieved primacy, with an almost exclusive focus on intrapsychic events.

The social model was brought into action to combat the structural theory of mental illness with its emphasis on disease entities and to stress the importance of the environment in causing, maintaining, and patterning of psychiatric states. If the individual was sick, it was society that made him so, and the structure of his response reflected the structure of the social conditions to which he was reacting. There is a certain value in taking up extreme positions of this kind and in exaggerating the significance of the somatic, the psychological, and the social layers of the human organism since it stimulates a great deal of investigation for and against the model until eventually the limitations of a particular model become apparent, both in research and in clinical application, and it is scrapped or modified.

There has been a general proclivity over the past decade to construct a model more representative of the complex notions that have come into being in the field of psychological medicine. The interaction between medical and psychiatric thought led first to the elaboration of a psychobiological model and, when this proved not wholly adequate, to the subsequent building of a sociopsychobiological one. Since child psychiatry was dealing with a developing organism, the feature of time was added as a necessary dimension to the general picture. On inspecting this final diagnostic model more closely, one can observe it to be made up of a population of symptoms stemming from somatic, psychological, and social sources. The clusters or constellations in any developing individual undergo changes with time, both in the components of the cluster and in the nuclear or primary symptom involved. For example, enuresis and encopresis would tend to be at the center of such a cluster during the early stages of childhood and to be associated with other immaturities; later, they are likely to yield the nuclear position to learning disabilities, and still later to delinquent behavior. Occasionally the primary symptom, for instance bed wetting, retains its nuclear position throughout development, and the child's personality, often a passive-aggressive one, is built up around it.

A more recent clinical research model has been proposed by Haggard (1962) in which an energetic system *A* is brought into contact with the environment system *C* by a mediating or ego system *B*. There is much to be

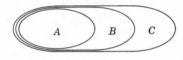

said for this model since it puts a needed focus on the interface problems encountered by the individual in his pursuit of satisfaction, interest, and safety. Under *B* is subsumed the ego functions, the defense measures, the coping devices, and the contact and communication skills.

Reductive and Constructive Explanations

Diagnosis is a scientific explanation, and all such explanations can be regarded as descriptions of functional relationships between variables at different levels of discourse. Two major kinds of scientific explanation can be differentiated. In the reductive type, a particular set of phenomena (a cluster of symptoms) is functionally related to another set of phenomena along hierarchical levels of description. Thus the symptom may be placed in the context of society, of individual personality, of an organ system, of a tissue, of a cell, or in terms of physiology, biochemistry, biophysics, etc. At the same time, it can be thought of as something in the process of being (structure), becoming (development), and behaving (function).

Along another axis, one can elaborate con-

structive explanations, by means of which the phenomena or symptomatology are described in terms of higher order constructs and abstractions as found in the behavior sciences.

Examples of both types of explanation can be given. A disturbance in feeding behavior might be related to an absence of stomach contractions or to certain neurophysiological events, which in turn occur because of certain biochemical conditions, etc. On the other hand, the feeding disturbance might be because of food deprivation, leading to a certain habitual mode of feeding behavior or conditioning, or to certain oral fixations and regressions stemming from deprivation. The reductive explanations in terms of physiology, biochemistry, and biophysics would find favor in the medical disciplines, whereas the more constructive hypotheses would obtain a better hearing from the behavioral sciences. The state of the art at the present time limits the amount of reductive explanation possible and, as a consequence, drives the child psychiatrist and psychologist to pursue constructive explanations within the behavioral field. It is convenient to regard the two types of explanations as complementary rather than mutually exclusive, especially since the only biological reductionism possible currently is in the form of analogy with little support from scientific evidence.

The Process of Decision-Making in Psychiatric Diagnosis

The growing complexity of the diagnostic model over the past 50 years has led to a steady expansion of case records so that the diagnostician may be confronted with comparatively huge accumulations of data—social, psychological, psychiatric, and pediatric—which he is required to digest before he can reach a decision.

Fifty years ago when the model was simpler and the case records correspondingly thinner a record might consist of a single sheet on which was inscribed (often in illegible handwriting) a few relevant statements running to at most thirty or forty sentences. Today the average number of sentences in a case record from clinics where child psychiatrists are being trained varies between 200 and 800 sentences and can frequently reach the dimensions of a short novel. Between 8 and 15% of the statements have proved on investigation (Eiduson, Trinidad, Johnson, and Rottenberg, 1965) to be redundant, but it is extremely difficult to decide beforehand which statements are necessary and which are redundant. Redundancy is a function of the science in question, its stage of evolution, and the rigor it has managed to develop.

Eiduson et al. (1965) have analyzed clinic records in terms of length, the distribution of information, the amount and kind of invariant, common and unique information, and occurrence of omissions and details, making use of an interesting "event system." Total information is conceived of as a series of events that take place in the life of the patient or his close family members. Events are made up of actual happenings—illness, the birth of a sibling, failure in school—that have a physical or outside validity but also include psychological phenomena that can only be inferred and have poor outside validity such as fears, fantasies, impressions, values, and other subjective or judgmental phenomena. The Event Concept, guiding the process, stipulates that *everything* that occurs to a patient or to a significant person in his life is an event. This is the common unit in terms of which all information in the record is transcribed with the help of a special lexicon. Once the data are partitioned into such a series, programming permits a wide diversity of information—hard and soft—to be sorted, arranged, and searched in a systematic fashion. The Event Concept is general enough to permit all data in a record to be encompassed in the same conceptual framework and put into the computer in the same form. Factual and impressionistic data are both given equivalent information-producing status. Of particular significance to the clinician is the fact that no restraints at all are placed on the history-taking and examination. It is too early to judge to what extent collection procedures influence the data obtained and consequently the diagnosis made, but the approach will undoubtedly shed fresh light on the complex process of clinical diagnosis.

The Traditional Classifications

The traditional classification of behavior disorders was based entirely on the clinical experiences of individual practitioners. A surprising fact that emerges from an inspection

Table 1. Some Clinical Approaches to the Classification of Behavior Disorders[a]

Author	Classification
Miller (1936)	A. Objective disorders (habit and conduct disorders)
	B. Subjective disorders (neurotic traits)
	C. Mixed disorders (neurotic delinquency)
Gerard (1947)	A. Disturbances in body function
	B. Disturbances in behavior (aggression, inhibition, hypersexuality)
	C. Disturbances associated with conscious anxiety
Louttit (1947)	A. Direct primary behavior disorders (environmental type)
	B. Indirect primary behavior disorders (intrapsychic type)—aggression
	C. Indirect primary behavior disorders (intrapsychic type)—withdrawal
Ackerman (1953)	A. Conflict with environment expressed in habit disorders
	B. Conflict with environment expressed in conduct disorders
	C. Conflict with self expressed in neurotic traits
Cameron (1955)	A. Primary habit disorder (eating, eliminating, sleeping)
	B. Secondary habit disorder (Conduct disorder, tension and gratification disorder, speech disorder)
	C. Other reactive disorders (motor, learning, neurotic traits)
Chess (1959)	A. Reactive behavior disorders
	B. Neurotic behavior disorders
	C. Neurotic character disorders

[a] Psychoneurotic, psychosomatic, psychotic and organic disturbances are not included in these classifications which mainly confine themselves to the Primary Behavior Disorder Group.

Table 2. Taxonomy of Behavior Disorders of Childhood

Class	Subclass	Items of Disordered Behavior
I. Functional behavior	A. Eating	Anorexia, bulimia, food fads, pica, rumination
	B. Eliminating	Enuresis, encopresis, constipation, diarrhea, vomiting
	C. Sleeping	Nightmares, night terrors, sleepwalking, insomnia
	D. Moving	Hyperkinesis, tics, rocking, head banging, incoordination
	E. Speaking	Retarded speech, mutism, lisping, stammering
II. Cognitive behavior	A. Thinking	Prelogical, magical, concrete, amorphous, confused
	B. Remembering	Amnesia, forgetful, reduced memory span
	C. Learning	General and specific learning disability, psuedo-retardation
	D. Orienting	Disorientation in space, time, and identity
	E. Reality testing	Confusion of internal-external, subjective-objective
III. Affective behavior	A. Fearfulness	Single and multiple fears, cowardice, flight reactions
	B. Anxiety	Agitation, apprehension, panic, separation anxiety, tension habits
	C. Depression-elation	Sadness, grief, euphoria, clowning, nostalgia, despair
	D. Shame-guilt	Inferiority, inadequacy feelings, retribution, restitution
	E. Disgust	Anticontamination behavior
IV. Social behavior	A. Attacking	Aggressive, homicidal, suicidal, destructive
	B. Avoiding	Withdrawal, self-isolation, autism, daydreaming
	C. Oppositional	Negativism, noncooperation, wilfulness, contrariness
	D. Dominance-submission	Bossy, controlling, egocentric-dependent, clinging
	E. Abnormal sexual	Masturbation, homosexuality, promiscuity, transvestitism
V. Integrative behavior	A. Poor impulse control	Hyperkinetic, undisciplined, incorrigible, impulsive
	B. Low frustration tol.	Demands for immediate gratification
	C. Rigid-stereotyped	Perseverative, repetitive, compulsive, stimulus-bound, inhibited
	D. Inadequate coping	Sense of helplessness
	E. Disorganized	Chaotic, aimless, disorderly, unplanful

of these classifications is that a certain consensus exists between the authors despite differing theoretical approaches. There is rough agreement that the behavior disorders can manifest themselves in bodily disturbances, in inhibited, anxious, neurotic reactions and in active, outgoing, aggressive conduct. Chess (1959) has related her system elegantly to the degree to which the deviant behavior becomes internalized and part of the habitual reaction of the individual, irrespective of the situation.

The G.A.P. (Group for the Advancement of Psychiatry) Report has tried to move away from classifications built on the adult terminology. It includes a diagnosis of normality, thereby bringing the normal and abnormal together in the same system and it includes a whole group of developmental deviations in the areas of sensorimotor, cognitive, social, sexual, and affective development, which emphasizes for the first time that departures from normal behavior may occur at a time, in a sequence, or to a degree not expected for a given age level. The reactive disorders represent a mild excess over the transient, normal symptoms and their character is largely governed by the stressful situation that occasions them as well as the age at which they occur. The normal, reactive, and developmental disorders are all relatively extraneous, whereas the psychoneurotic, personality, and psychotic disorders have invaded the inner psychic structures of the individual.

In Table 2, an attempt has been made to construct a taxonomy of behavior disorders based on the main facets of normal behavior. The items of disordered behavior represent a sample of symptoms associated with each

Table 3. Distribution of Characteristics by Typology Groups

Characteristics	I	II	III	IV
Intelligence (WISC)				
Under 70	86%	22%	0%	9%
—70-90	14%	71%	58%	55%
Over 90	0%	7%	42%	36%
E.E.G.				
Abnormal	0%	10%	10%	0%
Questionable	100%	50%	10%	43%
Normal	0%	40%	80%	57%
Paranatal trauma	16%	50%	0%	9%
Global rating of security				
Mild	0%	0%	2%	0%
Moderate	0%	24%	17%	20%
Severe	15%	6%	8%	4%
Improvement with drugs				
Chlorpromazine	80%		60%	
Benadryl	50%		0%	
Placebo	0%		43%	

After Fish (1964).

subclass and could clearly be extended to include every known symptom.

The symptom pictures of childhood are not stable and consistent and may shift with the social setting and life situation. A child who has one set of symptoms at one period may develop a completely new set of symptoms at another. One sees overwhelming acute anxiety reactions with dramatic disorganizations of personality functioning which are completely reversible. Nor are the lines between normal and abnormal as clearly defined or maintained as with adults. Everyone who is concerned with children clinically is aware of the importance of having a developmental frame of reference. It could be said that clinical syndromes are shaped by the age and stage of the child, the level of his personality organization at the particular time of his development, and by the dynamic equilibrium between his growing needs and the potentiality of his environment to satisfy them (Langford, 1964).

Classifications Derived for Research Purposes

Fish (1964) aimed at establishing diagnostic categories that could be used in research, that is, by different observers, To do this, degrees of integrative impairment were translated into descriptive statements of the child's current adaptive patterning, focusing on critical aspects of behavior and thinking. She found, as other clinicians have found, that the cases did not fit into a single linear continuum of severity, but that they fell into four fairly clearly defined types. The type I case was predominately psychotic and termed autistic-disjunctive; type II was predominately borderline and termed immature-labile; type III was mostly neurotic and termed anxious-neurotic; and type IV contained children manifesting antisocial behavior, the type being termed sociopathic-paranoid. Type II was regarded as a transitional type with the subjects developing into one of the other three types as they grew older.

The patients were classified on their observable behavior with respect to speech, affect, motility, adaptive function, and the ways in which they related to the examiner, to their peers, and to different environments. It was also possible to correlate the types with intelligence, E.E.G. findings, birth injuries,

Table 4.   Some Actuarial Approaches to the Classification of Childhood Behavior Disorders

Author	Classification
Ackerson (1942)	A. Personality-total (sensitive, neurotic, worrisome, seclusive) B. Conduct-total (violent, destructive, abusive, thieving, truanting)
Hewitt and Jenkins (1946) and Jenkins (1964)	A. Overinhibited (shy-seclusive and overanxious) B. Aggressive (hyperactive, undomesticated, and socialized delinquency)
Collins and Maxwell (1962)	A. Anxiety factor (anxious, timid, nervous) B. Rebellious factor (aggressive, destructive, oppositional) (Plus a rootless factor, to do with parent loss and a school problem factor for girls)
Dreger (1964)	A. Relatively immature (nonsociable, semisurgent egocentricity) and sociable anxiety B. Egocentric antisocial aggressivness (Plus semisociable, nonanxious, desurgent, retardation, and relatively mature, semisociable egocentricity)
Achenbach (1966)	A. Internalizing (anxious, phobic, compulsive, somatic, withdrawn) B. Externalizing (aggressive, delinquent, social)

and response to drugs. If we set aside the psychotic and borderline categories, we once again find ourselves with a classification of anxious, neurotic, and inhibited patients contrasted with acting out, antisocial, aggressive ones.

Rutter (1967) has also made a plea for a more adequate classification, pointing out that this lack has been a severe obstacle to progress in child psychiatry since without a common language, studies at different clinical and research centers cannot be compared with one another. To achieve this, he has postulated three principles of classification: that it be defined in operational terms and based on facts not concepts; that it conveys information relevant to the clinical situation and has predictive value; and that it is aimed to classify disorders *not* children. On the basis of this, he has outlined a "purely phenomenological" classification for which he feels operational definitions could easily be provided. Rutter's own interest in it lies in its usefulness as a means of scientific communication and of ordering material. His classification was commented on favorably by Eisenberg (1967), who felt that we needed to recognize that behavior disorders represented a final common pathway for the

expression of a diverse matrix of causes and that Rutter's schema was workable, acceptable to clinicians with varying orientations, and formulated in such a manner as to be testable for reliability and validity. Anthony (1967), on the other hand, felt that the classification did not offer anything new that would facilitate communication and that taxonomy was not one man's business but required a coordination of views if it was to escape a biased viewpoint.

Classifications Based on a Statistical Approach

Empirical studies of child symptom groupings have used the actuarial approach.

Ackerson (1942) pioneered this field by setting up an exploratory, atheoretical study with the disinterested objective of finding out how 125 behavior problems intercorrelated with one another. It has been quite properly described as "a monumental undertaking that could have deterred a less intrepid and preserving investigator." There is no doubt that he encountered huge difficulties in translating case data from the files of the Chicago Institute of Juvenile Research into statistically manipulable categories since case records are notoriously vague, nebulous, inconsistent, and impressionistic, however much they make rich clinical reading. From his massive number of correlations, Ackerson managed to extract two sets of total scores representing unweighted summations of the specific personality and conduct problems noted for each 2113 boys and 1181 girls. The personality total score was highly correlated with mental conflict, changeable moods, depression, an unhappy appearance, and "queer" behavior and less highly correlated with sensitivity, worrisomeness, nervousness, daydreaming, and feelings of inferiority. The conduct total score, in fairly sharp contrast, was highly correlated with truancy, disobedience, destructiveness, cruelty, lying and swearing, stealing automobiles, and staying out late.

It was possible from the data to construct certain syndromes such as *hypophrenia* in which the correlations brought together the picture of a slow, dull child, retarded at school and manifesting listlessness, lack of initiative, apprehensiveness, bashfulness, and follower tendencies. He was likely to have a mentally retarded sibling and to show a preference for playing with younger children. There was also a syndrome of *normality* which correlated well with popularity, leadership qualities, feeding habits (sic), altruistic leanings, and a denial of any sexual misbehavior.

In the area of prognosis, there were certain correlations pointing to an ominous future and these included an unfavorable prognosis by the staff, expulsion from school, pathological lying, fire setting, emotional instability, marked negativism, gross sexual problems, violence, and "sneakiness" (sic). Rather surprising and contrary to many other findings, there were low or negligible correlations with "vicious" or disturbing home conditions.

Hewitt and Jenkins (1946) recorded the presence or absence of 94 symptomatic traits occurring in each of 500 child guidance clinic case histories. Of the 94 traits, 45, chosen because of either high frequency or "obvious clinical importance," were crosstabulated with the whole series of traits. By inspection, three clusters of traits, resembling three behavior syndromes previously suggested by a committee of consultants, were found. From 10 to 12 traits in each cluster,

6 or 7 were chosen to form the final three clusters by which cases were to be classified. For each cluster, traits were chosen which correlated at least .30 with most of the other traits in the cluster and which fitted the clinical picture suggested by the cluster. The clusters thus formed were interpreted as representing the overinhibited child, the unsocialized aggressive child, and the socialized delinquent child. Later, the overinhibited category was subclassified into the shy-seclusive and the overanxious types and another common factor of aggressiveness was subdivided into hyperactive, undomesticated, and socialized delinquent types.

The various subgroups are shown in Table 5 analyzed in terms of boy-girl ratios, the typical ages at which they tend to occur, the predominant symptomatology, and the type of family background with which they tend to become associated.

This study, however, included several highly similar symptom categories which could explain the separation of aggressiveness into socialized and unsocialized clusters not found in other studies. In addition, the clustering process appeared to involve a certain degree of "clinical" judgment, and the clusters found conformed without exception to the judges' expectations. Another consideration is that the authors employed a heterogeneous population and failed to make comparisons among homogeneous segments of their sample. The cluster analysis used might have produced fewer and more general groupings than rotated factor methods.

Collins, Maxwell, and Cameron (1962, 1963) submitted an "item sheet" of child psychiatric clinic data to a principal component analysis to discover whether there were any major components inherent in the intercorrelation of the items. Feeling that a certain homogeneity in the children forming the sample was desirable, they delimited the age range to subjects between their eighth and tenth birthdays as representative of middle childhood and excluded, in pursuance of homogeneity, those regarded as epileptic, retarded, or psychotic. The final sample was made up of 268 boys and 98 girls, considered separately, and the final list of items totaled 59 for the boys and 64 for the girls.

Relatively little intercorrelation and common variance was found in the data. Factors

Table 5. Five Symptomatic Groups

Primary Groups	M/F Quot.	Typical Ages	Symptomatology	Family Background
Inhibited				
Shy-seclusive	3.8	9–14	Timid, sensitive, underactive, apathetic, depressed, friendless	Mother handicapped by mental or physical illness
Overanxious-neurotic	1.7	9–12	Fearful, nervous, over-imaginative, sleep-disturbed, feeling inferior, easily upset, tending to frequent illness	Neurotic, overanxious mother with close tie to patient
Aggressive				
Hyperactive	5.3	9–11	Mischievous, bashful, over-dependent, unable to concentrate, difficulty with peers	Moderate tendency to maternal rejection
Undomesticated	3.2	11–14	Negativistic, defiant, hostile, vengeful, sullen, malicious quarrelsome, rude	Marked maternal rejection, irresponsible, unstable mother, unwanted child, openly hostile to mother
Socialized delinquent	10.1	12–15	Stealing, absconding, truanting, staying out late, associating with bad companions	Gross parental neglect, inadequate or absent father, poverty

After R. Jenkins (1966).

of "rebelliousness," "rootlessness," and "anxiety" were identified among the boys. The girls were different in having "rebelliousness" and "rootlessness" appearing as a single factor and also an additional factor of "school failure, with timidity" that did not emerge for the boys. The process of extracting the factors insured that they were independent, that is, orthogonal, so that in the boys the "rebelliousness" factor was practically uncorrelated with the "rootlessness" factor. As an advance on the Hewitt-Jenkins study, the sexes were considered separately and the age range did not mix prepubertal and postpubertal children. The findings, in implying that there were features of childhood disturbance particularly associated with age and sex, supported the correctness of this procedure.

In the second Collins-Maxwell-Cameron study, boys and girls between 5 and 7 years of age were considered, using the same item sheet as previously and again making use of items occurring in at least 10% and in not more than 90% of cases. Although the study, as before, aimed at maximum homogeneity, the sample still appeared to be quite heterogeneous so that clinical "types" of children did not emerge. There was a general similarity between the factors for the younger and older groups of children, although "rebelliousness" in boys was now associated with such items as absence of father and nocturnal enuresis. However, by and large, it would appear that the syndromes of behavior to which such labels as rebelliousness, rootlessness, cossettedness, anxiety, and social maladaptation were attached when describing the results for 8- to 10-year-old children were seen in embryo, if not explicitly, in the data for the younger children. There was therefore a developmental trend in symptomatic expression.

Dreger (1964) had parents or parent surrogates of child clinic patients sort 229 discrete behavioral items according to whether or not the child had manifested them in the previous 6 months. The intercorrelations of 142 behavior items and demographic variables were analyzed by the principal-factor method with an oblimin rotation of the 10 largest factors. The rotated factors were left unlabeled but their descriptions suggest that some of them resembled the general clusters found by Hewitt-Jenkins and others, while others vaguely resembled discrete syndromes. A cluster analysis of factor scores revealed five types of clinical cases, one of which (Egocentric Antisocial Aggressiveness) seemed to match the Hewitt Jenkins Unsocialized Aggressiveness, and two others (Relatively Immature, Nonsociable, Semisurgent, Egocentricity and Sociable Anxiety) appeared to be related to overinhibition. Apart from the barbarous nomenclature, Dreger's study, although not biased by psychiatric stereotypes, showed poor interrater agreement between parents rating the same child (a mean agreement of 36%) and the nonpsychiatric control subjects were found to exhibit more sadistic behavior than reported for the clinic children. Moreover, his use of "first order" behavior items rather than more general symptom categories, although increasing objectivity, may have resulted in low frequency of responding in many categories with the production of clusters at a level too molecular to allow useful interpretation. Dreger does make an appropriate comment on the comparison of factor analytic studies, which he says is fraught with danger, "for what may appear to be matching variables from one study to the next sometimes turn out empirically to be very much different. Only if two studies use identical variables, can the matching of factor for factor from one study to the next be safe."

Achenbach (1966) has not only furnished a good review of the various factor analytic approaches to classification but has also tried to elucidate the relationship between the general sympton clusters found, for example, in the Hewitt-Jenkins study and the specific functional syndromes employed in adult psychiatry. His aim was to obtain, for research purposes, a more differentiated empirical classification of child psychiatric cases than at present available. He was interested in finding out to what extent cases classified according to factors represented types of cases and whether the classifications derived from the factor analysis of symptoms or significant relationship to biographical variables. Five principal-factor analyses were performed on the symptoms and biographical data from the case histories of 300 male and 300 female child psychiatric patients. The symptoms were intercorrelated and factor analyzed, separately for each sex, by the principal-factor method and the factors were rotated to the varimax, quartimax, and oblimin criteria for simple structure.

The first principal factor for both sexes was bipolar, with antisocial behavior ("externalizing") at one end and neurotic symptoms ("internalizing") at the other end. For the boys alone a factor labeled sexual problems and for the girls alone factors labeled depressive symptoms, anxiety symptoms, neurotic and delinquent behavior, enuresis and other immaturities, and obesity were found. The parents of externalizers were found to have significantly more overt social problems and to be rated less concerned with their child's difficulty than the parents of internalizers. The obesity factor classified only girls aged 10 to 14 and the neurotic and delinquent behavior factor found between the ages of 12 and 15 suggested that these were phenomena belonging to a specific developmental stage and not to be expected in patients from other age groups. It would appear that the internalizing-externalizing dichotomy could be readily used for classifying case histories and live patients using as a criterion point 60% or more coming from one or other category. If subtle differences were being investigated, a more rigorous criterion (75% plus) could be employed.

In summary, the crucial question posed by any classification is its purpose—clinical, investigative, or actuarial. In the past, clinical nomenclature tended to reflect the idiosyncrasies of particular centers so that scientific communication was beset with misunderstanding and misinterpretation. More recently, under the aegis of the W.H.O., an attempt has been made to obtain international consensus on the diagnostic labeling of a sample of selected case records. A further step forward toward a more rational usage was taken by the G.A.P. Committee on Child Psychiatry (1966) with its effort to base its proposed classification on theoretical considerations involving such important concepts as stress, conflict, crisis, vulnerability. It also pioneered the novel category of "healthy reaction" in order to confront clinicians with the obvious but often overlooked fact that not everyone coming to see them is necessarily sick. Even more important is the Committee's reference to sociocultural influences on the diagnostic picture in view of the fact that recent studies have linked mental illness and symptom tolerance with social and ethnic factors. On the whole, clinicians lean more favorably toward complex categorizations that appear to acknowledge the richness and complexity of the case record. They are, therefore, especially predisposed toward the *diagnostic profile* that adds further dimensions of etiology, prognosis, and therapeutic potential to the single diagnostic label.

Researchers, on the other hand, have tended toward greater parsimony and have reduced their classifications to the level of dichotomies. Langfeldt (1959) has emphasized the usefulness of dichotomous categorization as a means of sharpening knowledge when etiology is still unknown and multiple classes only add confusion to the field. The internalizing-externalizing dichotomy has been as valuable as the endogenous-exogamous dichotomy in segrating basic ingoing from outgoing tendencies. However, it should be recognized that its early advantages could well be offset by premature and fixed theorizing unless it gave place to the heuristically more valuable dimensional approach in which falsely isolated polarities could be brought onto the same continuum. The third alternative, the typical Linaean classification, must also be regarded as a transitional device, otherwise it could become stifling, self-defeating, and a source of sterile semantic controversy.

The statisticians are not much better off at the present time. Factor analysis is still a subject of dispute within their own ranks, its correct application requiring the truth of assumptions underlying a certain type of statistical model. Moran (1966) has some doubts about its capacity to establish psychiatric syndromes and suggests that component analysis might be better for the purpose and "more natural." He raises the important question as to whether it is at all feasible to construct, within the scope of statistical theory and on the evidence provided by a single sample (and not two samples known beforehand to come from two different populations) a discriminant function that would demonstrate that subjects belonged to two different groups manifesting different collections of symptoms, and which would be as closely descriptive of the clinician's subjective judgment as possible. Moran concludes that while there have been instances in which a frequency distribution carried out on scores resulting from a multiple regression analysis has turned out to be strongly bimodal and therefore suggestive of two groups within the sample, there was as yet no mathematical theory available for the construction of this kind of discriminate function. Bechtoldt (1964) has also been critical of the use of factor analysis in classificatory studies raising questions as to whether the results could not be obtained more economically by simple item analysis or item clustering methods followed by factor analysis. For him factor analysis was "an exploratory procedure at the borderline of science" (1967), helpful in setting up initial operational definitions of behavioral variables. Its drawbacks were that it was a within-group procedure used with a single group, that no distinction between dependent and independent variables were made, and that there was none of the controls used in everyday experimental work.

What appeared manifest from a survey of the work being done was that classification was a thriving field and that adequate nosologies were essential if a science of behavior disorders was ever to be built. It is possible that as our clinical skills grow in sophistication and subtlety, our classifications will improve in concert with them. However impressive our statistical techniques, there is no substitute in this area for clinical acumen, knowledge, and experience. The crudities in some classifications reflect this fact.

There has been one recent development, still in the pilot stage, of categorizing entities in terms of the predominant defense mechanisms involved. This has necessitated the ordering of the various mechanisms along a developmental scale somewhat loosely linked to the psychoanalytic psychosexual stages.

Eventual syndromes are derived from various combinations of defenses, some primitive and some mature, the admixture reflecting the character and strength of the defense organization, and, to some extent, the adaptive capacity of the individual (Table 6). For example, the category of obsessional neurosis would be made up largely of defense responses within stage 2 (reaction formation, undoing, isolation, etc.) but mechan-

Table 6. Classification of Defense Mechanisms

Stage 1	Stage 2	Stage 3	Stage 4
Avoidance	Reaction	Repression	Intellectualization
Withdrawal	formation	Regression	Estheticism
Introjection	Undoing	Somatization	Falling ill
Projection	Isolation	Sublimation	Bulimia
Massive denial	Displacement	Identification	Altruistic surrender
Blocking	Detachment	Counterphobia	Clowning
Inhibition	Ritualization	Desexualization	Acting out
Depersonalization	Rationalization		
Splitting	Magical		
	thinking		
	Controlling		

isms from the other stages would be added in varying amounts from case to case and contributing to the individuality of any particular case. The arrangement is still tentative and included in this section to indicate a different but interesting approach to the subject.

THE INCIDENCE, PREVALENCE, AND FATE OF THE BEHAVIOR DISORDERS

The number of terminations from clinic service by age group and sex in the United States for the year ending June 30, 1961, provide a very accurate estimate of admission rates because of the short duration of clinic care for most patients. These rates do not represent the incidence or prevalence of mental disorders because of the many selective factors that determine clinic admission, but they do provide a "bird's-eye view" of the general situation in the country. The clinic

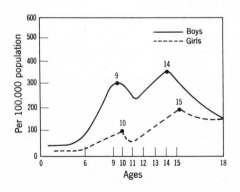

Fig. 1. The clinic termination rate for children in the U.S.A. (From Rosen, Bahn, and Kramer, 1964).

termination rate for children (persons under 18 years of age) was 212 per 100,000 population, which was 16% higher than that for adults (Rosen, Bahn, and Kramer, 1964). The termination rate for boys (277) was almost twice that for girls (145) and the rates were highest for boys between 10 and 14 years (434) and for girls between 15 and 17 years (262). When the figures are broken down for each year of age, an interesting finding emerges. Rather than a continual rise in clinic rates, two distinct periods of increased clinic usage appear: for boys, a decided peak at around age 9 and again at 14; for girls, a slight rise to age 10 and a marked increase at 15. For both sexes the rates were relatively low at 11 to 12 years. The nonwhite rates were lower throughout childhood in contrast to the higher nonwhite rates at almost all other ages, but there is a sharper rise in the nonwhite rate during middle adolescence. The commonest diagnosis for the children of school age was transient situational personality disorder. For every major diagnostic group, the rates for boys exceeded those for girls. Among the psychoneuroses, anxiety reaction was predominant for both boys and girls, but depressive reactions rose in adolescence, particularly for girls. These data provided by Rosen, Bahn, and Kramer (1964) provide the most extensive description yet available nationally on the utilization of psychiatric clinics by various segments of the population and demonstrates the striking fact that children 10 to 14 years have the maximum clinic usage rate in the country with peaks at 9 to 10 (preadolescence) and at 14 to 15 (middle adolescence).

In support of this finding, the mental

health survey of Los Angeles County (1960), based on teacher evaluations, also indicated higher proportions of emotionally disturbed children in the fourth and fifth grades than in all other grades. Among the factors responsible for this have been mentioned scholastic, family, and other social pressures, psychosocial developmental problems, and variation in adult tolerance of behavior and therefore referral tendency.

There have been a number of important studies on the incidence, prevalence, and fate of childhood behavior disorders, both in Europe and in the United States. The studies have been of several kinds: longitudinal, cross-sectional, and follow-up and have involved surveys of general or clinic populations and comparisons between clinic and control groups.

Longitudinal Studies

The Berkeley study by Macfarlane, Allen, and Honzik (1954) represented a developmental study of the behavior problems of normal children between 21 months and 14 years. The sample was made up of every third child born in Berkeley over a period of 18 months between the years 1928 to 1929 and there was a slight shrinkage over time in the lower socioeconomic section of the sample.

Figure 2 is a paradigm of the proclivities of various symptoms and symptom groups during development, some tending to decline with age, some to increase with age, some to increase and then decline with age, some to decline and then increase with age, and some to show no change at all with age (see Table 8).

Table 7. Studies on the Incidence, Prevalence and Fate of Childhood Behavior Disorders

Type of Study	Chief Investigator	Population Area	Sample (N, Onset, Age Range F.U. Period)
A. Longitudinal prospective	MacFarlane	Berkeley, USA	116 Onset 1928
	Douglas	Britain (National)	5362 Onset 1946
	Hindley-Moore	London, England	164 Onset 1952
	Thomas	New York, USA	128 Onset 1956
B. Cross-sectional contemporaneous	Lapouse	Buffalo, USA	482 (6–12)
	Bremer	Norway	
	Brandon	Newcastle, England	1000
	Shepherd	Buckinghamshire, England	6287 (5–15)
	Ryle	London, England	159 (5–12)
	Stennet	Minnesota, USA	1500 (9–11)
	Rutter	Isle of Wight, England	284 (10–11)
C. Follow-up retrospective	Pasamanick	Baltimore, USA	1151 902 Control
	Wolff	Edinburgh, Scotland	100 Clinic 100 Control (5–12)
	Renaud	Berkeley, USA	100
	Robins	St. Louis, USA	524 (30 years)
	Pritchard	London, England	64 (10.8 mean years)
	Wolff	London, England	43 (3–6 years)

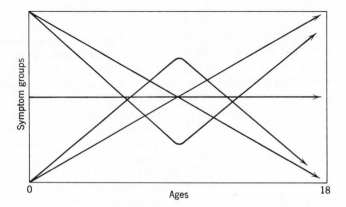

Fig. 2. Paradigm of symptomatic behavior during childhood.

The method involved simple over-ended inventory questioning of mothers and therefore depended on what they were able to observe, likely to distort, and willing to report. The investigators referred to it with candor as a "not-going-beneath-the-surface" approach, at the same time insisting that it nevertheless was able to secure some interesting and significant facts.

The data were organized along empirically derived scales of descriptive continua, which have been used in the same or modified form by other epidemiological investigators. The findings with regard to sex and ordinal position were not striking. First-born boys seemed to show a special predisposition to withdrawal and internalization, later-born boys being more overt, aggressive, and competitive. Life seemed "more difficult" for first-born girls, who were also more withdrawn, manifested more problems, and seemed less capable of aggression. One would expect that if these "normal symptoms" became exaggerated into "clinical symptoms," there would be a tendency for first children to have internalizing disorders, and children other than firstborns, externalizing disorders.

The study was able to demonstrate that most problems occurring during normal development tended not to persist and that, generally speaking, symptoms occurred in clusters rather than independently. For example, irritability, moodiness, negativism, somberness, reserve, and overdependence, more or less together, tended to occur in girls of preschool age and in boys at pre-

Table 8. Five Developmental Trends in the Expression of Symptoms

	Type of Trend	Behavioral Item
I.	Symptoms declining with age	Enuresis, encopresis, speech problems, fears, thumbsucking, overeating, temper tantrums, destructiveness
II.	Symptoms increasing with age	Nail biting
III.	Symptoms declining and then increasing with age	Restless sleep, disturbing dreams, timidity, irritability, attention-seeking, dependence, jealousy, food finickiness (boys), somberness
IV.	Symptoms increasing and then declining with age	Poor appetite, lying
V.	Symptoms unrelated to age	Oversensitivity

After Macfarlane.

puberty. These age differences for the sexes may well reflect varying degrees of cultural pressure and inhibition of overt expression for the two sexes.

The investigators, at the end of their investigation, stressed the multifactorial nature of personality and behavior dynamics and the necessity of avoiding overgeneralization at the present state of limited knowledge. Looking backward over the long years of the many childhoods that they had investigated, they had this to say about the resilience of their subjects:

May we pay our respects to the adaptive capacity of the human organism, born in a very unfinished and singularly dependent state into a highly complex and not-too-sensible world. Unless handicapped by inadequate structure and health and impossible and capricious living situations, he threads his way to some measure of stable and characteristic patterning. When we look at the hazards of the course, we are not sure that we have begun to understand how or why.

Macfarlane ends by quoting from the last sentence of a very inadequate master's thesis which ran as follows: "This thesis can be regarded as successful as it will be stimulating to further research in others, since it leaves so many questions unanswered." The Berkeley study has left many questions unanswered and subsequent longitudinal studies have not done much better. The international child development study, operating from various cities in different countries, has come up with surprisingly little in the field of psychological development and has been heavily grounded by detail and data.

The British national survey of health and development has been following 5362 children born in the first week of March, 1946 (Douglas and Mulligan, 1961), disturbances being assessed from material gathered by health visitors and schoolteachers. The findings have emphasized how small a proportion of children showing evidence of psychiatric disturbances are actually under psychiatric care. The losses in this research population have been comparatively small. After 20 years, 98% of the sample are still known and 90% are still actively cooperating.

In a recent analysis (Douglas, 1966) the school progress of some nervous and troublesome children is traced. About 15% of the boys in the sample (288) had been "cautioned" by the police or brought up before the courts, 4.2% for trivial offenses, 10.4% for indictable offenses; moreover, 4% were recidivists. The 288 delinquents were compared with 942 nondelinquents. The delinquents came from large families living in overcrowded conditions and lacking amenities. Their parents were generally semiskilled workers with a poor standard of education and there was a greater tendency for the family to be "broken." The delinquents had more difficulty in bowel and bladder training than the controls and throughout their school careers were recognized as troublesome children with poor attitudes to work, obedience, and discipline and were badly rated by their teachers, who picked them out as being both nervous and aggressive. The national study was also able to support the Berkeley findings that boys and girls who are early in reaching sexual maturity are also superior to the late-maturing children in tests of mental ability and school performance, although it has yet to supply the evidence that they have fewer adjustment problems.

At the Center for the Study of Human Development in London, a sample of children, recruited before birth and studied longitudinally with contact not less than once a year, were observed with respect to maladjustments as they passed through school. Disturbances were investigated with regard to reluctance to go to school, difficulties in relationships to teachers, peers, and the school program and environment. The disturbances were graded in terms of severity and persistence. About 80% of the children were found to experience difficulties in early school life, nearly one-half of moderate or marked severity. The number of difficulties decreased slightly in the latter period at elementary school, but a substantial number still showed more than mild disturbances. Boys showed more difficulties than girls and boys who were only children tended to have the most problems of adjustment to school. The commonest and most persistent type of difficulty experienced by these normal children was a general reluctance to go to school. Although the children adapt progressively during these first 6 years, 18% never become reconciled to school. It should be borne in mind that the evidence is based not on verified happenings at school but on the perceptions of children and parents when interviewed at the Development Center; however, perceptions determine attitudes and behavior and the parents' attitudes to school certainly affected those of their children (Moore, 1966).

The longitudinal study conducted by Thomas, Birch, Chess, and others (1960, 1964) in New York on 128 children followed from infancy has paid special attention to the later development of behavior disorders. Earlier, Fries and Woolf (1953) had suggested that the constitutional level of activity present from birth, which they referred to as the "congenital activity type," had a particular relevance for later developments in personality as well as personality disorders. The New York workers also concluded that behavior disorders such as acting out, antisocial activity, or inhibition might be determined by congenital patterns. The sample under study came from a preponderantly middle-class Jewish professional family background and were selected for their relative social homogeneity. When joining the project, all parents were informed that psychiatric advice would be freely available at any point should problems arise in connection with their child. Of the 92 children aged at least 3 years in the study, 21 had had psychiatric referral by the age of 6 years. Of these, 3 were placed in psychiatric treatment elsewhere, 6 presented disorders of some severity, and 11 had lesser behavioral disturbances. The children, as infants, had been rated on a three-point scale for nine characteristics of behavior: regularity, adaptability, mood, intensity, approach-withdrawal, persistence, distractability, activity, and threshold. The scores for all categories were so distributed that there was a pronounced skew toward one of the polar scoring positions and, in all but the last two categories, the middle position was rarely used. Accordingly, each category had a most frequently occurring or modal score position and a least frequent or amodal score position and the subjects were ranked according to the proportion of amodal responses in each category. This simple ratio score was employed because of the infrequent use of the middle point on the scale for most categories, and a ranking procedure modal was chosen be-

cause of the positively skewed distribution of ratio scores. By this method, the children were characterized in terms of the relative frequency with which they exhibited a particular score on any behavioral variable.

It was found that these quantitative measures of behavioral styles, made as early as the first and second year of life, were able to differentiate to a significant extent those children who were later referred for psychiatric evaluation. *The differences in normal behavior antedated the onset of symptomatic behavior* and the differentiation was more efficient when patterns of functioning were considered than when individual categories were examined. The clinical cases could be differentiated similarly from their siblings raised in the same home but not presenting problems of behavior. The investigators were, of course, aware that the behavioral style represented only one important factor for the developmental course and that it was the interaction between the child and his environment that was relevant. However, the fact that the association between the temperamental characteristic and the later psychiatric referral came through even when the other variables had not been systematically excluded suggested that it represented a powerful determinant in itself. Nevertheless, *not all children with amodal patterns on intensity, adaptability, regularity, and mood (the strongest clinical predictors) developed behavioral disorders, nor did all children with such disorders have this pattern. An important factor which seemed to modify or alter the influence of the behavioral characteristic was the parental reaction to the child,* and it was noticeable that the few markedly amodal children whose parents had a high tolerance of "difficult" behavior seemed to have less persistent problems. On the other hand, mild and undemanding children with calm and unresponsive parents sometimes developed disturbances of behavior associated with the ignoring of their mildly expressed legitimate demands. Thus neither the parental characteristics nor the temperament of the child was found to be an independent influence on the child's development; rather they are interdependent. There needed to be a fit between the child's behavior and the parental response. The best way of coping with one child might well be the worst with one of dissimilar temperament. However, the majority of children, being adaptable, are likely to develop normally in many different sorts of homes and the unadaptable child may run a high risk of behavioral disorder with many varieties of parental care.

In contrast to the Shepherd, Oppenheim, Mitchell (1966) findings, the investigators were of the opinion that their findings did not represent referral artifacts, where the differences between children were actually differences between complaining and uncomplaining mothers. Their reasons for this belief were dependent on the fact that the scores derived from maternal reports had a high measure of agreement with scores derived from direct observation of the child's behavior. There also seemed to be no systematic bias in maternal reporting of behavior and this was investigated with regard to other siblings in the family. However, there were two factors that might have been responsible for the high referral rate: the type of sample (middle-class Jewish professional) and the open offer for psychiatric advice made to every parent in the study. Despite some loosenesses in methodology, the study represented an advance on other longitudinal studies in that it developed concepts as it moved along and was not simply a data-collecting process. Further, unlike many conceptual frameworks, these authors did not regard their ideas as immutable and their characteristics as absolute and archetypal. Their flexible point of view was alive to the fact that changes in the characteristics would continue throughout development. Perhaps the most significant feature about the categories was that they were derived from an inductive analysis of the child's *overt* patterns of behavior in his everyday *normal* life rather than from restricted experimental situations which might have rendered generalization more debatable.

Cross-Sectional Studies

Retrospective and prospective studies of personality development each have their own strengths and weaknesses, but the biases of parental recall do place the retrospective approach at a disadvantage. However, the longitudinal study is also loaded with inherent problems—the maintenance of samples, the methodological difficulties involved with the use of tests at different stages of development,

and, most disturbing, the way in which scientific advances tend to render one's concepts and methods unfashionable and unmeaningful. There is a built-in obsolescence principle at work in all longitudinal studies. The epidemiological approach is relatively free from these two disadvantages, but it is a massive instrument lacking the support of direct observation and therefore susceptible to all the problems inherent in the indirect, questionnaire techniques.

The Buffalo study carried out in the spring of 1955 by Lapouse and Monk (1958) made use of mothers as the source of information, although the investigators were fully cognizant of the hazards entailed in the matter of reliability because of such variables as standards, sensitivity, ability to comprehend and communicate, maintenance of interest, and anxiety after being interviewed. The interview took about 1½ hours and required the completion of 200 items on the schedule involving census data, the rating of various behavioral functions on a continuous 5-point scale, the evaluation of symptoms in terms of intensity and frequency, and any additional comment that the mother wished to make. This was a careful study based on random sampling (with 94% success), the careful training of interviewers through a training manual, the objective selection of the index child (by Kish's method), the weighting of interviews to ensure adequate representation when children came from larger households, the spot-checking of coding reliability, the computing of sampling errors, and the testing of the soundness of data by means of reliability (interview-reinterview of 10% of the cases) and validity (involving the correlation of mother and child responses in a sufficient number of cases).

It was found that about half this representative sample of apparently normal children aged 6 to 12 manifested many fears and worries and had frequent temper tantrums; that about one-third experienced nightmares and bit their nails; and that 10–20% wet their beds, sucked their thumbs, and showed tics and other evidences of tension. The investigators questioned whether this high prevalence represented a large amount of psychiatric disorder in the general population or whether it simply signified *a tendency for most children to undergo transient develop-*

mental stresses as a result of pressures inherent in Western societies. They feel that one way to anwer this would be to determine whether the children in fact functioned efficiently in their home and school environments in spite of these symptoms.

An expectable facet of the validity study was the demonstration that mothers are much more accurate in reporting the presence or absence of well-defined manifest behavior than they are regarding the occurrence of subjective symptoms. For example, there was an 84% consensus between mother and child with respect to bed wetting and only 54% when it came to nightmares, fears, and worries. In keeping with the national study of psychiatric outpatient clinics for children, Lapouse and Monk demonstrated that rate of behavior deviations was higher in boys than in girls. They also found that the prevalence of deviations is markedly affected by age, but in place of a critical peak around 9–10, their findings showed that younger children (6–8) far exceeded older children (9–12) in the amount of deviant behavior. Deviations were also found to be more frequent in Negro children so that the vulnerable group was made up of younger children, Negro children, and boys.

The Buckinghamshire survey (Shepherd, Oppenheim, and Mitchell, 1966) attempted to face two fundamental questions: first, the extent to which the behavior of the clinic child was distributed in the general population; and second, the part played by key adults in the interpretation of that behavior. The survey was able to demonstrate that a supposedly normal population included children with behavior disturbances comparable to those of patients at a child guidance clinic and that referral was related chiefly to parental reactions. The mothers of clinic children were anxious and nervous women who sought consultation. The survey also concluded, on the basis of a 2-year follow-up, that treatment made no apparent difference to this "large pool of morbidity in the community," 63% of the clinic cases improving as against 61% of the matched controls who had not attended the clinics. Like Lapouse and Monk, these investigators felt that many disturbances of behavior are *no more than temporary exaggerations of widely distributed reaction patterns* and that such behavior can-

not be deemed morbid without some knowledge of its frequency, intensity, duration, association with other forms of behavior, and the setting in which it occurs. The limits of deviance have to be closely defined in this field.

Brandon (1960), investigating a sample of families in the Newcastle One Thousand Families Survey, came up with evidence of behavior disturbance in 20% of the children by the age of 11. She found that nearly all "abnormal" symptoms (rated on modified Macfarlane scales) were significantly more common in children independently rated as maladjusted than in controls.

Ryle, Pond, and Hamilton (1965) attempted to describe the prevalence and patterns of emotional disorder in a sample of children unselected on psychiatric grounds. The children, 79 boys and 80 girls, ranged in age from 5 to 12. Their symptoms and behavior, as described by their parents, were rated against scales slightly modified from those used by Macfarlane. Twenty-two five-point scales were used, each providing detailed examples of the type, severity, and frequency of the characteristic being rated. Interrater disagreements never exceeded three per case and were never more than one point on the scale. Since the Macfarlane scales did not record psychosomatic symptoms, an arbitrary score of 2 was allotted where these were reported and the combined Macfarlane and psychosomatic scores were taken as a measure of severity of disturbance. In addition to deriving a total symptom score from the Macfarlane ratings, problem items were classified on clinical grounds into six groups, yielding six subscores: habit disorders (including tension and psychosomatic symptoms), inhibited behavior, compliant behavior, antisocial behavior, acting out behavior, and "unclassified."

The results confirmed the conclusions of Lapouse, Shepherd, and Bremer (1951) that *a large proportion of supposedly normal children exhibit symptoms or behavior of a type which would be judged "pathological" in a clinic setting.* The parental but not the teachers' recognition of disturbance correlated closely with the Macfarlane rating score, which may have been due either to the uncertain validity of the teacher's form or to the fact that children behave very differently at home and at school. Few age or sex differences were observed.

The Minnesota survey (Stennett, 1964) made use of Bower's identification process based on ability, achievement, teacher ratings, and peer- and self-perception, as a screening device .The Bower battery was found to be a reliable system capable of detecting up to 85% of emotionally handicapped children (EHC) and of excluding 82% of those not considered EHC.

It was found that between 5 and 10% of the total sample of 1500 children between the ages 9 and 11 had "adjustive difficulties" of sufficient severity to warrant professional attention and that 22% could be labeled EHC either in a moderate or severe form. (For those in the remedial reading class, the EHC incidence was as high as 30%.) Of the EHC students, 78% of the boys and 66% of the girls had learning disabilities and were charasterized by being absent more frequently, not doing as well academically, and being either older or younger than their class group. Girls in this category resorted to "feeling sick" and boys to aggression. In contrast to the conclusions of Lapouse, Stennett considered that the children with EHC were *not simply going through a phase which they would outgrow, but were actually suffering from a "disease."* Some did recover spontaneously, but in general the group tended to get stuck on a track leading to increasingly severe educational deficit as demonstrated on the Academic Progress Chart (Stringer, 1962). About 8½% of the EHC retain the diagnosis after 3 years, but the study was not able to make clear ways of differentiating between the self-healing and the chronic child.

In the Isle of Wight survey (Rutter and Graham, 1966), two psychiatrists agreed well in their independent, overall ratings of children for psychiatric disturbance on the basis of semistructured interviews. Children given high symptom rating counts by parents or teachers were independently judged to be psychiatrically disturbed by the psychiatrists. In a sample of 284 10- and 11-year-old children, the investigators attempted to ascertain the prevalence of actual psychiatric disorders, not simply behavioral deviances, and they used as the criteria the presence of suffering in the child or distress in the community. The

behavioral disturbances diagnosed in this study therefore were "handicapping disorders" of the kind seen by psychiatrists. The screening device used was a behavioral inventory given to teachers and parents. The test-retest reliability over 2-3 months was .74 for mother, .89 for the same teacher, and .72 for different teachers. The father-mother correlation was .64. The questionnaire was shown to reliably discriminate children under psychiatric care with a critical score of nine on the teacher's scale and thirteen on the parents' scale. It was able to differentiate 72-82% of clinic boys and 50-70% of clinic girls and could differentiate 72-92% of neurotic from antisocial types of disorders.

Of the 284 children in the total study, 13% were studied more intensively through interviews with parent and child, a teacher's report, and a short psychometric examination (a brief version of the W.I.S.C. and Neal's Reading Test). Of the smaller sample, 48% were classified as possibly abnormal and 20% as definitely abnormal. Of the total research population of 2193 subjects, 138, or 6.3%, were thought to have definite psychiatric disorders. Of course, 90 probably required psychiatric referral: 48 for diagnosis and advice, 46 for possible treatment, and 44 for probable treatment. Actually, only 15 children (or 16% of those who required it) were attending child guidance clinics, which would suggest that the referral system was far from meeting the need.

Wolff (1967) has been conducting a comparative study of Edinburgh primary school children referred to a psychiatric department with behavior disorders and of a matched control group of nonreferred children. The aim of the study was to determine in what way clinic children differed from nonclinic children in the community and, at the same time, to explore the relationship between childhood behavior disorders and gross, easily recognizable adverse events occurring in the lives of the children and in the childhod of their parents. Of three possible indices of psychiatric illness—presence of symptoms, overall impairment of functioning, and psychiatric referral—the first two have been studied intensively, but surprisingly little attention has been paid to referral, although it is the most objective of all and the one selected for this investigation. Of course, in the absence of enough service facilities to satisfy public demand, referral rates cannot be used as a measure of the prevalence of psychiatric disorders in childhood, but Wolff has attempted to study the factors that determine referral—the types of behavior difficulties that alarm or irritate parents sufficiently for them to seek psychiatric help.

Once again, mothers were chosen as the main informants on the grounds that they were more with their children and knew more about their children than anyone else, and that although their retrospective accounts tended to be inaccurate, the information they supplied about current behavior usually agreed well with independent observations of the children themselves, *provided that the parents are asked not for judgments but for descriptions of what their children actually do in response to specific situations* (Thomas et al., 1963). In this study, to minimize the effect of interviewer bias, a method of focused interviewing was used. Standard questions were asked in a uniform order, but the interviewer was free after every set of questions to explore each area of inquiry according to the individual mother's responses. During the interview, a precoded behavior inventory was completed based on the rating scheme devised by Macfarlane. These scales have been used in several studies, but they have a number of disadvantages. For example, no standard method of interviewing is specified so that ratings assigned to several types of behavior varied according to the intensity with which the mothers are interviewed. The more time an interviewer spends with a mother, the more likely is the child to be given a normal rather than an abnormal rating. Further, the ratings are not scaled, but instead for each type of behavior one or more ratings are empirically designated as abnormal. An additional problem is that some scales are one-tailed and others two-tailed. Finally, many of the ratings were so defined as to force both mother and interviewer into making judgments. It was found that the

mean test-retest reliability of 55 testable scales was .73. The 30 scales for "objective" items at a greater test-retest reliability (.83) and the 25 scales for "subjective" items (.62). This is in keeping with other workers who have found agreements between mothers and fathers to be high for what they call "open behavior" but low for "internalized difficulties" whose assessments involved judgments (Peterson et al., 1959). Behavior scales can never be completely validated since children do not necessarily behave at school as they do at home. (In the Rutter and Graham study, the psychiatrists' assessments of impaired functioning agreed both with teachers' and mothers' total ratings of behavior disturbances in the children, *but there was little overlap between those children who were identified as disturbed at home and those identified as disturbed in school.*) Psychiatric interviews can provide validating data for only some aspects of behavior. The Rutter behavior questionnaire was also included in the Edinburgh study.

The data were analyzed in terms of behavioral items occurring very rarely, rarely, or commonly in the control group as compared with the clinic group. The items that occurred very rarely or rarely in the control group, and therefore differentiated clinic from nonclinic children, were *conduct disorders, enuresis, encopresis, discontent, and symptoms indicative of unhappiness, anxiety, and poor relationships with other people.* The control group of children was chosen to match the clinic group and not to be representative of the general childhood population of Edinburgh. Nevertheless, there was a close concurrence between the prevalence of behavior symptoms in this group and those for general childhood populations established by other workers.

The sex differences in Wolff's study were in keeping with those found by Macfarlane and by Lapouse and Monk; boys tending to be more outwardly aggressive and girls manifesting more anxious and inhibited behavior

Table 9. **Prevalence of Behavior Symptoms for Childhood Populations in Different Areas**

Area	Stammering	Enuresis	Tics	Temper Tantrums	Thumb Sucking	Nail Biting
Buffalo, USA	4%	17%	12%	80%	10%	27%
Edinburgh, U.K.	4%	14%	18%	82%	12%	34%

From Lapouse and Monk, and Wolff.

indicative of greater internalization. Similarly, there was altogether a greater prevalence of symptoms in children under 8, the only symptoms commoner in older children being tics, stammering, and excessive modesty. In general, *clinic girls were more different from control girls than clinic boys from control boys, and older clinic children were more different from older control children than younger clinic children from younger control children.* As in the Isle of Wight study, Wolff found that psychiatrically disturbed children obtained high scores on teachers' *or* parents' behavior rating scales but rarely on both.

There have been some interesting studies attempting to relate the occurrence of behavior disorders to the obstetrical history of the children. Rogers, Lilienfeld, and Pasamanick (1955) established the fact that among children with behavior disorders, a significantly greater proportion were premature or had been exposed to complications of pregnancy and delivery than among a control group of children. Since then the view has been expressed repeatedly (Stott, 1962; 1965) that childhood behavior disorders in general are based on some ill-defined, congenital vulnerability to which birth injury makes a major contribution. Pasamanick (1956) has hypothesized a "continuum of reproductive casualty" leading to the notion that in childhood every disorder is related to every other one and that birth injury, constitutional vulnerability, social deprivation, and emotional traumata all make significant but nonspecific contributions to psychiatric morbidity.

Pasamanick's retrospective studies did seem to demonstrate an association between brain damage and the complications of pregnancy, particularly the chronic-anoxia producing ones of bleeding in the third trimester, toxemia, and prematurity. The socioeconomic variations in the incidence of these complications could help to explain the increased incidence of neurpsychiatric disability in the lower sections of society as a consequence of organic brain damage. The findings also appeared to demonstrate a seasonal variation in the complications of pregnancy and in the births of abnormal babies, correlating the facts of poverty and climatic conditions with the greater liability of the disadvantaged groups. In the absence of organic factors, it was differences in the socio-

cultural milieu that produced significant differences in behavior, although the relative weights of the two influences were not too clear. For example, *the differences in frequency of perinatal complications between Negro and white sections of the population were far greater than the perinatal differences between the behaviorally disturbed and nondisturbed children.* Although the differences between the experimental and control groups were statistically significant, each type of obstetric complication occurred only in an eighth or less of disturbed white children and in a third of the white and in about two-thirds of was only when obstetric complications were totaled for each case that one or more complications were found to have occurred in a third of the white and in about two-thirds of the Negro disturbed subjects. When this procedure of adding complications was used, no less than a quarter of the white and a half of the Negro control children had also been exposed to one or more obstetric complications. The disturbed group of children included all those with behavior disorders who had been referred to the Division of Special Services of the Baltimore Department of Education and who were not mentally retarded. They were presumably mainly children identified as disturbed in the school setting rather than by their parents at home. When children classified as "confused, disorganized, and hyperactive" were looked at separately, it was found that the difference in frequency of obstetric complications between these children and their controls was even greater than between the experimental and control groups as a whole suggesting that *birth injury may contribute more to some types of behavior disorders than to others.*

In a smaller study, Wolff (1967) took another look at the contribution of obstetric complications to the etiology of behavior disorders in childhood. Her results did not contradict the findings of others that complications could predispose children to later behavioral disturbances, but she did reiterate the important point that perinatal factors can be causally related with any confidence to only certain types of behavior disorders, that is, those manifesting overactivity, restlessness, and distractability. She felt that it would not be surprising if other behavior problems were found to have a more reactive nature dependent on environmental experiences. It was therefore understandable that when special risk groups of children were examined, relationships between specific hazards and subsequent behavior disturbances were found which disappeared when they were looked for in a more general childhood population. *This would seem to indicate that the hazardous events were rare and could not account for the majority of behavior disorders found in children.* When large populations were examined, statistically significant relationships could be found between behavior disorders and traumatic antecedent events, when, in fact, such events were causally operative in only a minority of disturbed children. It was clear from Wolff's study that prematurity and obstetric complications did not contribute significantly to the etiology of behavior disorders in a population of psychiatrically referred primary school children from whom those with constitutional disorders had been excluded. This group had been identified as in need of treatment by their parents and not by teachers or outside agencies and Wolff recognized the fact that possibly children identified as disturbed at school by teachers might contain a greater number exposed to obstetric hazards. Her findings, however, are similar to Brandon's (1960) since he too was unable to find significant differences in obstetric histories when comparing a group of children identified as maladjusted with a group of controls. In Wolff's study, there were also no significant differences between the clinic and control groups with regard to maternal age, birth weight, complications of pregnancy and delivery, and the postnatal condition of the child.

Follow-Up Studies

Renaud and Estes (1961) attempted to explore the question whether a significant number of mentally healthy adults, adequately functioning and symptom free, have had pathogenic childhoods. The subjects were military officers with an average age of 33 and they were considered "above normal" with regard to occupation, education, income, mental stability, and mental ability. It was concluded that the childhood biographies did not differ especially, if at all, from those of psychiatric patients with respect to the amount of childhood exposure to events and conditions considered to be precursors of maladjustment. The parents ranged from the dependable and considerate to the ineffectual and authoritarian, and included in abundance were overt and covert parental discord, rigid and indulgent patterns of discipline, unresolved sibling jealousies, repressive and unrealistic approaches to sexual information and practice, mothers with chronic physical complaints, etc. The investigators were of the opinion that *if many of these subjects had complained of gross inhibitions, incapacities, phobias, or psychosomatic illness, "background factors" would have been available to account for them.* It would seem that detailed studies of control populations of normal and superior subjects are required to eliminate overgeneralizations regarding the biographical correlates of mental illness.

There have been several studies in which children with a special psychiatric disturbance have been followed up but only two studies in which children with a variety of childhood conditions have been followed into adult life for purposes of intergroup comparisons. These are the studies by O'Neal and Robins (1958, 1959, 1960, 1962) and Pritchard and Graham (1966).

For the purpose of comparing the incidence of psychiatric disorder in the adult life of disturbed children with that of normal children, the control follow-up study is the only satisfactory technique.

In the St. Louis study (O'Neal and Robins, 1958), the follow-up was 526 children who were seen 30 to 35 years earlier in a child guidance clinic where they were carefully evaluated but seldom treated. The study also included 100 control subjects selected from the public school records. The children, when first seen, were 17 years or less, had IQs over 80, and had been referred because of problem behavior. They were all Caucasian. The controls were matched with respect to sex, race, year of birth, place of residence, IQ, and by an absence of behavior disturbances as indicated by school records. No less than 90% of the total sample was eventually located and 82% were examined psychiatrically as adults.

The emphasis of the study was upon the sociopaths, describing their characteristics as child guidance patients and their later development into adult life. It provided the long-needed account of the natural history of the sociopathic individual. As was to be expected, children referred as antisocial problems provided a high rate of antisocial adults, a quarter of them being finally diagnosed as sociopaths, but they also showed a tendency toward deviant behavior in "every area in which society sets norms" (Robins, 1966,) so that deviance seemed to be a "unitary phenomenon." The control group, on the other hand, was found to produce extraordinarily well adjusted adults despite similar unfavorable early social environments. Those referred for other than antisocial reasons tended to be intermediate between the antisocial referrals and controls in most areas of adult maladjustment. The antisocial child was shown to carry the worst prognosis and to be most urgently in need of attention, whereas symptoms such as shyness, nervousness, irritability, tantrums, insomnia, fears, speech defects, hypersensitiveness, and tics were all unrelated to psychiatric outcome. The Dallas study (Morris, Soroker, and Burruss, 1954) had also demonstrated that shy and withdrawn children do not turn out too badly as adults, especially if they marry dependable spouses, although at least a half dozen studies on the childhood adjustments of later schizophrenics have incriminated shyness and withdrawal in the child as significant developmental antecedents (Anthony, 1968).

Apart from the symptomatic behavior of the child, in the St. Louis study, the father who was alcoholic or sociopathic appeared to be the most ominous factor for both boys and girls, even if they had never lived with him or had been removed from him in infancy, which was, according to the author, suggestive of genetic influence. The investigation as a whole is highly supportive of the "disease' hypothesis for the reason that sociopathy is seen to occur in families for gen-

erations, follows a predictable course, and appears primary rather than secondary to unfavorable environmental influences.

The Maudsley Investigators (Prichard and Graham, 1966) had the logistical advantage over the St. Louis group of being able to conduct a follow-up study entirely on the hospital premises since they were dealing with patients who had "graduated" from child guidance to the adult clinic. The records of such patients were filed together in the same folder for the convenience of the clinician. The arrangement facilitated the work of the investigators since it helped in the location of subjects, but for the purpose of "blind" camparison, the notes were kept separate and all analyses were conducted separately.

The sample was a small one (75) in comparison to that of St. Louis, and the findings had much in common although there were some important divergences. For example, none of those diagnosed as schizophrenic in adult life fell into the childhood group of "behavior disturbances without court appearance," which is in contrast to the St. Louis finding of a striking association between adult psychosis and a history of delinquency without court appearance in childhood. The Maudsley Investigation also found a statistically significant association between childhood delinquency (especially theft) and adult sociopathy, and there was also a consistent tendency for affective disorders in later life (anxiety and depression) to be associated with neurotic symptoms in childhood, and particularly for adult anxiety states to be associated with childhood anxiety states or phobias. There was a striking absence of patients diagnosed as having an antisocial personality disorder as adults in the childhood neurotic group.

Another short-term follow-up study was conducted by Wolff (1961) on preschool

Table 10. Comparison between the Maudsley and St. Louis Follow-Up Studies

	Child Category			
Adult Category	Delinquent		Neurotic and Conduct	
	M.	S.L.	M.	S.L.
Neurotic	19%	20%	51%	51%
Psychotic	23%	12%	15%	14%
Sociopathic	35%	40%	6%	8%

After Pritchard and Graham (1966).

children with behavior disorders attending the Maudsley Child Guidance Clinic. The family background was generally characterized by a high incidence of psychiatric disturbance with a history of early parental deprivation in the parents of the children. The outcome, 3 to 6 years later, showed that boys did worse than girls, and that children, in general, did less well when they came from broken homes, where there was open marital strife between the parents and when the parents themselves had been treated for psychiatric disorders in the past.

In summary, these longitudinal, cross-sectional and retrospective studies all point to the fact that there is a fairly sizable pool of disturbance in the general children's population, varying in amount with such factors as class and culture. Certain ages make a larger contribution to the pool and boys in general add more than their share. The pool is in a constant state of flux, with symptoms coming and going, and certain stages of development seem more prone to certain constellations of symptoms. Apart from intensity and persistence, there are certain types of symptoms that are far more likely to be found in clinical subjects. Although symptom tolerance is undoubtedly a factor affecting the referral, the making of a child patient is not entirely a function of the complaining parent. Certain transformations take place in the child—internalizations, identifications, defense organization—and render him diagnosably different from children undergoing a transient developmental stress with the manifestation of transient symptoms.

ETIOLOGICAL FACTORS IN THE DEVELOPMENT OF BEHAVIOR DISORDERS

The Concept of Risk

The concept of risk is central to any consideration regarding the transmission of behavior disorders across generations. On the one side, it is linked to certain inherent preconditions such as vulnerability and predisposition, and on the other side, to stress, trauma, and adverse influences in the environment. Vulnerability has been defined as the individual's capacity to deal actively with affective arousal; it is represented as a balance between the assets and the weaknesses of the constitutional equipment (or the "management processes," as Lazarus refers to them) and the environmental variables. It is usually appraised in terms of its level and locus. It may express itself as a general manifestation or as a localized effect limited to certain functional areas such as speech, motor activity, autonomic functioning, perceptual clarity, sleep-wakefulness, and spatial orientation.

The malfunctioning of the individual may terminate with the disappearance of stress or may continue, where there is a latent tendency to maladjustment, in the usual environment. As Moliere remarked, "A healthy person is nothing but an unrevealed patient," and the joke contains an important truth. The hidden traits that stem from the genetic makeup are of crucial concern in the understanding of disease ecology and have frequently been neglected in favor of what is merely visible. The subclinical occurrence of disorders, the so-called iceberg effect, has assumed great significance to the epidemiologist of physical illness since the discovery of "carrier" states. It is possible that new developments in the field of mental illness may make the concept equally meaningful and available to psychiatrists and psychologists. The problem of vulnerability and resistance has been summed up in a striking analogy by Jacques May, the disease ecologist: "It is as though," he says, "I had on a table three dolls, one of glass, another of celluloid, and a third of steel, and I chose to hit the three dolls with a hammer, using equal strength. The first doll would break, the second would scar, and the third would emit a pleasant musical sound." A student of abnormal psychology today would be as interested in the doll that emitted the "pleasant musical sound" as he was in the ones that broke down or scarred. He might even go further. The maintenance of normality under abnormal circumstances is interesting, but certain individuals, under heavy stress, respond with highly superior modes of behavior such as creativity, productivity, and constructiveness. (One is reminded here of Toynbee's "challenge and response" formulation in his analysis of social growth and decay.) Jacques May's analogy is an oversimplified account of the psychological traumatic situation where many more variables than he has considered are involved. These would include the pre-traumatic adjustment, the age and sex of the individual, the presence or absence of helpful people, the previous experience of similar stress, the intensity and duration of the trauma, and the availability of after-care. These and other factors enter into the element of risk, the study of which, because of the new interest in preventive psychiatry, has undergone rapid growth in the last decade.

In any appraisal of risk, it is important to distinguish between high-risk heredity (the level of genetic expectation), high-risk constitutions (activity and reactivity patterns), high-risk environments (familial, institutional, poverty), high-risk situations and experiences (separation, hospitalization, illness, and other psychological traumata), and high-risk points in development (critical periods and critical stages).

Genetic Risk. To help in tracing the effect of genetic elements, Kallmann (1964) elaborated a pluridimensional model of sequential levels of integration and interaction in which there are molecular chromosomal and cellular levels prior to the stage where a behavioral deviation resulting from a mutational change in the chromosome material becomes clinically recognizable. Following penetrance to the stage of clinical expression in the phenotype, the total adjustment level of the perfected individual and the levels of the family and the population become discernible. The model has some heuristic value in reminding us about the many levels at which causes, effects, and interactions must be studied, each level representing a different universe of discourse (psychiatric, psychological, social, biochemical, cytological).

However, there is no doubt that the genes-to-behavior pathway involves a very complex chain of events. Strictly speaking, there are no genes for behavior, but only genes that exert their influence on behavior through their effects at a more molecular level of organization. Enzymes, hormones, and neurons mediate the path between the genes and behavior. Although human behavioral genetics is still relatively young, and, as Gottesman (1966) points out, "fraught with disconcerting vagueness," some rudimentary work on the genetic mode of transmission of personality traits has been carried out. Personality test data from C.P.I. on a sample of 147 pairs of normal twins, 79 identical and 68 fraternal

but same-sex, were evaluated within the framework of evolutionary biology. All 18 of the trait intraclass correlation coefficients for the identical twins were significant at less than the .01 level compared to 9 for the fraternals. When heritability of the traits was estimated from the intrapair variances, 7 had one-third or more of the within-family variance significantly associated with genetic factors.

Shields (1954), in a study of 36 uniovular and 26 binovular twins among South London school children, found a greater concordance for child psychiatric disturbances among uniovular than among binovular twins. Complete concordance was found in none of the dizygotic pairs but was present in 36% of the monozygotic pairs; 69% of the dizygotic and 17% of the monozygotic were discordant. Other pairs were partially concordant. However, among the concordant pairs, twins showed similar symptoms in different contexts or at different times, so that qualitative concordance was greater than quantative concordance. Environmental variables often appeared important. It was concluded, on the basis of this study, that genetic factors determined the physical basis of personality and that genetic effects upon neurosis were mediated through this influence of personality. Disorders not closely related to personality, for example, juvenile delinquency, were less influenced by genetic factors than were disorders more closely related. *The vulnerability was determined genetically, but the disturbance was often precipitated by environmental circumstances.*

Slater (1953) had observed that in binovular adult twins with psychosis, the more severely affected twin also had a history of having been the more neurotic child of the pair. He thought that this implied that the constitutional make-up predisposing to psychosis in the adult helps to cause neurotic symptoms in childhood and that these were therefore of genetic determination.

In his study of psychiatric illness in parents and their children, Rutter (1966) reached the conclusion, after careful consideration of the genetic influence, that environmental factors were "of considerable importance" in the association, since he had observed that death and chronic illness in the parent also conduced to psychiatric disorder in the child and genetic factors could in no way be held responsible for these connections. In addition, the lack of relationship between the type of parental disorder and the type of disorder in the child argued strongly against a genetic link, as did the very heterogeneity of disorders found in association with parental illness.

Anthony (1968) reported on childhood antecedents of adult schizophrenia. Dealing with a high-risk sample of children, one or both of whose parents are schizophrenic, he calculated from the genetic expectation furnished by various investigations that about 18% of the sample were fated to become schizophrenic, and that these were sometimes recognizable during childhood by the transient appearance from time to time of "micropsychotic episodes of withdrawal, suspiciousness and sudden massive regression."

Constitutional Risk. Each individual is born with a unique constitutional make-up, possessing at birth a combination of physical features which constitute one important aspect of his individuality. These physical and morphological attributes may influence other aspects of his development such as the quality of the parent-infant interaction (Blauvelt and McKenna, 1961) as well as other significant relationships throughout childhood.

The importance of physique in relation to adjustment has long been recognized. Burt (1938) had found correlations, albeit low, between plumpness and cheerfulness in children, on the one hand, and between thinness and inhibition, on the other. Davidson, McInnes, and Parnell (1957) investigated the body build of 7-year-old children and discovered that ectomorphy was associated with anxiety and restlessness in the group as a whole and with meticulous, fussy, and conscientious traits in the girls. On the Rorschach Test the ectomorphic children tended to give an excess of movement responses, but not at a significant level. Parnell (1957) observed that ectomorphic students with poor muscular development and below average in fat were six times more likely to seek psychiatric help. Even in younger children, the ectomorphs were a risk. Walker (1962, 1963), in his study of 125 nursery school children, using somatotyping photography (front, side, and rear views) and Sheldon's 7-point scale, had the children rated by their nursery school

teachers on a specially prepared behavior-rating scale. A number of significant relationships between physique components and specific behavior items were found, and some interesting relationships also appeared for the total cluster scores. Endomorphy, for example, showed least relationship with behavior clinical. Mesomorphy, on the other hand, correlated significantly with aggressiveness, assertiveness, energy, and activity. One might expect mesomorphic children, therefore, to develop externalizing syndromes. Ectomorphic children were those whom parents usually complained about because they were shy, sensitive, irritable, and unfriendly, nervous, fearful, and anxious. This disposed them to the development of internalizing syndromes.

There is a fair degree of evidence to support the view that the autonomic nervous system, like body build, bears a significant relationship to certain forms of behavior, particularly behavior associated with affective experiences (Wenger, 1947). The S child (sympathetic predominant) tends to be emotionally unstable, tense, and restless, impulsive, overactive, insecure, and dependent upon affection and approval from others. The P child (parasympathetic predominant) is altogether more stable, stolid, secure, independent, self-sufficient, dominant, and individualistic. It would seem, therefore, that the S child would be far more likely to develop behavior pathology.

The relationship of the behavior disorders to physical growth and hormonal changes has not as yet been delineated with precision. According to Tanner (1947), there is a midgrowth spurt between $5\frac{1}{2}$ and $7\frac{1}{2}$ years and an adolescent spurt beginning in prepuberty, and it is hypothetically possible that these accelerations may help to overload the adjustment capacity of the child. On the temporal scale, the spurts tend to anticipate the peak ages for referral to the clinic. There is strong evidence for the impact of physical maturation upon adaptation. Early maturers tend to be better adjusted and more confident and relaxed, whereas late maturers show evidence of maladjustment in having more feelings of inadequacy and rejection and more need for belonging and being supported. The late maturers also displayed greater aggression in the psychiatric sense of wanting to deprive others by belittling attacks, a trait which was found to correlate highly with maladjustment (Mussen and Jones, 1957; Jones and Mussen, 1958). These differences might well be explained on the basis of late maturers being predominantly ectomorphic, since ectomorphic behavior, according to Walker (1963), is made up of aggressive fault finding, anxious dependency, fears of failure, and feelings of being unloved. To add to the difficulties of the late maturer, particularly if he is a boy, either he or his parents may become considerably worried, consciously or unconsciously, by his as yet deficient development of masculinity.

Too little as yet is known of the complicated changes in hormone production and their effect on behavior during the child's development. Hormonal assays have not established norms of production at different developmental levels, but what work there is suggests a gradual rise in androgens, estrogens, and 17-ketosteroids throughout the developing period with small, ill-defined peaks at mid-childhood and a fairly sharp rise at puberty. The excretion of hormones during the earlier period is thought predominantly adrenal rather than pituitary or gonadal, as it becomes later on. It is known on experimental grounds that estrogens lower the threshold response, but the effect on human behavior is still to be explored.

Another "constitutional" attribute is the original temperamental tendency in children. Fries and Wolff (1953), on the basis of activity, muscle tonus, and crying attempted to relate five infantile activity types (hyperactive, active, moderately active, quiet, and inactive) to subsequent behavior disorders. They regarded the variable as constitutional in basic nature, but congenital rather than hereditary in that it is a joint production of genes, intrauterine influences, and birth experiences. Activity type was estimated by means of the startle response to sudden sound and to the frustration response with the removal of the bottle or breast. It was found that the child's activity type may significantly influence the quality of the parent-child relationship, the quiet reaction, for example, predisposing toward the establishment of a dependent relationship. Some activity patterns fit the child better than others. Because of cultural mores, a quiet girl and an active boy tend in general to have an easier adjustment respectively to their sex roles. Very early on, the children, as soon as they are mobile, tend to cope with environmental difficulties in accordance with their activity pattern; the active child tries to master the situation through his own efforts, whereas the quiet child is more likely to appeal to and to depend upon adults. The patterns also dispose the child to adopt certain defense and escape mechanisms, the active child acting out and the quiet child withdrawing into fantasy. It may also predispose the child to develop particular symptom formations and whereas all types seem capable of developing any of the behavior disorders, the two extreme types—the excessively quiet and the excessively active—seem more vulnerable to psychological illness. A study of Escalona and Heider (1959) has thrown some doubt on the stability of congenital activity characteristics, about 67% remaining true to type. These investigators concluded that variability and range in bodily activity and such characteristics as restlessness or the capacity to remain quiet are relatively more stable than is activity level as such.

It would seem that congenital predispositions, however strong, are susceptible to modification by parental handling and various other environmental situations through which the child is exposed during his early years. This is also true of the congenital characteristics of reactivity which has been the concern of the longitudinal study by Thomas et al. (1963). These investigators clearly recognized the importance of congenital predispositions in relation to later behavior development, normal and abnormal, and personal affectiveness. In terms of the total pattern of reactivity (especially with regard to activity level, threshold, intensity of reaction, mood, and distractibility) each infant was unique and statistical analysis contributed evidence that identifiable characteristics of reactivity are persistent features of the child's behavior at least through the first two years of life. The work of Rutter et al. (1964) indicating the part played by these early temperamental characteristics in the later development of behavioral disorders has already been mentioned.

Reproductive Risk. A reference has already been made to the Baltimore Study on the connection between obstetrical experiences and subsequent behavioral disorders which represented the benign role of the "continuum of reproductive casualty" (Pasamanick et al., 1956). Criticism has already been offered regarding this formulation and the difficulty in controlling for factors of class and race. In addition, two British surveys were also mentioned which failed to substantiate the finding with regard to behavior disorders as a group and had suggested that the obstetrical etiology might be specifically related to the hyperactive syndrome or the disturbing behavior in the classroom associated with restlessness and inattention. It would be an impossible task for epidemiological research to recognize such distinctions between primary and secondary types of behavior disorders, but the inclusion of a children's clinician in such research might have prevented the application of a monocausal hypothesis to the whole field of childhood behavior disorders.

The significance of the prenatal environment in the genesis of later abnormal behavior has been stressed, without too much objective evidence, since primitive times. It was strongly believed that the thoughts, desires, and emotional experiences of the mother could "mark" her unborn child and that any shock to her would communicate itself unchanged to the fetus.

Recently, the matter has been put on a more scientific footing and there is growing evidence that chemical irregularities in the mother's blood brought about by drugs, alcohol, nicotine, dietary deficiencies, or endocrine imbalances may have repercussions on the unborn child. It was also felt that severe emotional tensions, continued over long periods, may also affect the chemical balance of the mother's blood and, by placental transmission, influence the level of fetal activity. There is some evidence this may carry over into infancy and later in the form of adjustment difficulties. Stott (1957) has offered some proof that "pregnancy stresses" may leave their mark on the adjustment and learning capacities of the future child.

The concept of "birth trauma" has been considered, therefore, in several different etiological ways. For Rank, it represented a lifelong psychological inquiry so that all subsequent anxieties were repercussions of this first traumatic separation; for Freud, the birth

process brought into being a model for the expression of later anxious behavior; for Greenacre (1945), the trauma was a sort of physiological crisis in which the gross imbalance between the sensory experience of birth and the infant's restricted capacity to do anything about it generated an overwhelming sense of helplessness in the face of threat; for Bender (1954), the sharp break in living conditions with the completion of birth made inordinate demands on the adaptive capacity of certain predisposed infants in whom it could precipitate psychotic developments; and for Pasamanick (1956) it was a major factor in the production for a wide range of neuropsychiatric disorders, including the behavior disorders of childhood.

Stott (1959), who shares Pasamanick's view on the importance of prenatal, natal, and postnatal physical damage and disturbance, has investigated the aftermath of these stresses on the later functioning of the individual. He has shown that infection (respiratory and gastrointestinal, especially) in the postnatal period can produce a particular kind of syndrome—a "convalescent" syndrome—which was characterized by a personality that was "unforthcoming and associated with a learning disability." It has also been demonstrated that early brain damage was significantly high in groups of delinquents and psychopaths (Rogers et al., 1956).

Illegitimacy was also found to play a part in the genesis of later antisocial and delinquent behavior (Craft, 1961; Kelmer-Pringle, 1962), but there have been varying reports on its effect on the birth process itself in the way of difficult delivery, damage, and premature delivery on subsequent morbidity and mortality rates.

A low birth weight (less than 3 pounds) has been indicated in the production of a discouragingly high incidence of developmental handicaps: subaverage intelligence: 90%; slower than other siblings: 73%; behavior problem: 78% (Drillien, 1961). Behavior and personality disorders also appear to be common in children born prematurely. The circumstances of nursery care in the neonatal stage and of home care thereafter conspire against the development of a normal mother-child relationship and this may be aggravated by the oversolicitude that may persist as a parental attitude long after the premature infant has caught up with his peers. A special "Prematurity Syndrome" was described by Shirley (1939) in which the children characteristically showed a retarded language and motor development, a high sensory acuity, delayed bowel and bladder control, a short attention span, and an increased susceptibility to infection. Psychiatrically, they were regarded as highly emotional, tense, anxious, and shy with a disposition to developing feeding problems and behavior disorders.

Environmental Risk

Nonfamilial Environments. In the year 1760, a Spanish bishop made the following entry in his diary: "En la Casa de Ninos Expositos el nino se va poniendo triste y muchos de ellos mueren de tristeza."[1] Judging from this comment made over 200 years ago, the adverse effect of institutional care on children has been recognized for a long time, but it is only recently—since the matter was documented by Spitz (1945), Bowlby (1951), and Goldfarb (1944)—that the dimensions of the problem have been truly recognized. In spite of careful hygiene and precautions against contagion, the infants and younger children show extreme susceptibility to infection and illnesses of all kinds and the mortality rate at the end of the second year after admission varies between 30 and 75%. In addition, the children are backward in their development. In the Foundling Home, described by Spitz, the corridor into which the children's cubicles open is bleak and deserted except at feeding time. Most of the day, nothing goes on to attract the babies' attention. Each child lies in a cot which, when bed sheets are hung over the railings, screens him effectively from the world. Since he is also completely separated from the other cubicles, he is condemned to solitary confinement until he is able to stand up in his cot. The characteristics of institutional care were summed up by David and Appell (1961) in the following observation: There is a multiplicity of caretakers, a minimum of social contact together with long periods of isolation during waking time, and a poverty

of interchange between attendant and infant during the contact period. The institutional routine ensures that the attendant cannot get to know any particular infant or his needs or establish a warm relationship with him.

These various descriptions point to one form of deprivation which is a general term that includes, in addition to institutional upbringing and separation from parents, the effects of poverty and malnutrition, the absence of sensory stimulation, social isolation, and cultural lack. These economic, physical, social, cultural, and emotional factors have been confused in many studies and, in recent years, early deprivation has been used synonymously with separation and the latter has gained in significance as a key explanatory concept in psychopathology. According to Bowlby (1951), the prerequisite for normal mental health is the experience in infancy and early childhood of a warm, intimate, and continuous relationship with a mother or mother surrogate in which both mother and child find satisfaction and enjoyment. Within the scope of such a relationship, the emotions of anxiety and guilt, which in excess characterize mental ill health, have a chance of developing in a moderate and organized way. The crucial factors relevant to the deprivation experience include its duration, its intensity, the age at which it occurs, the presence or absence of previous experiences of the same kind, the quality of the prior relationship, the constitutional vulnerability and resilience, and the experiences following deprivation. Different aspects of the personality may be damaged by different experiences at different stages of development (Clarke and Clarke, 1960). For these reasons, it is not possible to generalize about income and some of the conflicting results obtained are no doubt related to the difficulty in controlling for the large number of variables involved.

The long-term effects of institutional care have occasioned a great deal of controversy. The critics have questioned whether the ultimate states of backwardness in psychopathy, among other disturbances, are as inevitable, as invariable, as permanent, and as irreversible as the early group of investigators had suggested. The work of Spitz on the effects of hospitalism (1945) was called in question because of methodological looseness (Pinneau, 1955), and Goldfarb has been criticized

---

[1] Quoted by Rene A. Spitz (1945): "In the orphanage, children become sad and many of them die of sadness."

because of the subjective nature of many of his ratings (O'Connor, 1956).

Confronted with this conflicting body of evidence, Bowlby was led to revise his earlier conclusions in the following statement: "Outcome is immensely varied, and of those who are damaged only a small minority develop those very serious disabilities of personality which first drew attention to the pathogenic nature of the experience" (1956, p. 240). The revision would be in keeping with the increasing recognition of the complexity and multifactorial nature of human development with the constant interplay of individual differences and environmental events. "The institution is not simply an environment lacking in a mother-figure . . . . [I]nstitutional environments tend to be deviant in many other respects, such as in the amount, the quality, and the variety of sensory and social stimulation, and in the kind of learning conditions provided" (Yarrow, 1964, p. 99).

Familial Environments. It is difficult to conceive of the child or his behavior outside of his family setting. The family, according to Lewis (1956), provides "the matrix within which the individual is moulded and developed, the area where his strongest emotional ties are formed, the background against which much of his most intense personal life is enacted." It is the first dynamic group to which the child is exposed and in it, he has his earliest experiences of interpersonal transactions. Like the child, the family grows

and organizes itself and develops structure. It creates history and traditions for its membership and establishes norms of behavior appropriate to class and culture. It is the primary institution that teaches the basic psychological and social lessons to the young child and it supplies him with his initial models for appropriate and affective behavior. When the family is disturbed, it also supplies him with pathological identifications and learning experiences. It would not be surprising, therefore, to find that the attitudes and behavior of the parents as well as their mental and physical health may have a decisive impact on the adjustment of the child.

Parent-Child Pathology. Parental attitudes and behavior, like parental deprivation, have come in for a fair share of etiological blame. It became explicit in the 1930s that problem children frequently had problem parents and had become problems mainly because of this fact. There followed a spate of dimensional studies regarding parental attitudes and many oversimplified schemata were constructed to demonstrate the sequence of relationship between specific parental attitudes and childhood behavior disorders. An example of this is given in the next table.

It will be observed that there are two types of overprotection syndrome, a dominated and an indulged type (Levy, 1943). The behavior of the indulged group was featured by disobedience, impudence, tantrums, excessive demands, and varying de-

Table 11. Parental Attitudes and Childhood Behavior Disorders

	Accepting			Rejecting		
	Autocratic	Democratic	Laissez-faire	Autocratic	Democratic	Laissez-faire
	Overprotection syndrome (dominated type)	Normal reactions of childhood or situational disorders	Overprotection syndrome (indulged type)	Authoritarian syndrome-antisocial disorders	Primary behavior disorder-Neurotic type	Neglect syndrome-Socialized delinquency
Care	++	+	++	0	0	0
Contact	++	+	++	0	0	0
Control	++	+	0	++	+	0

grees of tyrannical behavior, all thought to represent accelerated growth of the aggressive components of the personality and related directly to maternal indulgence. Levy refers to this type of child, in the fully developed form, as "an infant-monster or egocentric psychopath" and points out that in addition to the low frustration tolerance, the child gradually evolves into an exploitative character using every device, through charm, wheedling, coaxing, and bullying, in order to get his own way. Unless this is stemmed by reality experiences, he will continue into adult life to play the part of the beloved tyrant of an ever-responding mother. The maternal infantilizing behavior may leave the *enfant terrible* with a permanent illusion of omnipotence.

The dominated type of overprotection leads to excessive submissiveness, obedience, timidity, dependence, passivity, orderliness, and poor peer relationships. The dominated child lets his mother think and act for him and feels lost and homesick in her absence. He is ready to cry at the slightest provocation and inevitably comes in for teasing as a "mamma's boy." The inseparability of mother and child conduces to the development of school phobias, especially on first admission to school. Boys in this category seem effeminate and girls seem shy and inhibited. The amount of care and contact is excessive in both cases, but whereas the mother is overcontrolling in the dominated type, she appears completely permissive in the indulged type.

Rejecting behavior tends to stimulate acting out. Care and contact with the child are minimal or absent, but this situation may be coupled with an extreme degree of strictness leading to the development of various kinds of authoritarian syndromes characterized by hyperaggressiveness and antisocial tendencies. Where neglect is total, even to the point of exercising no control over the child, the deviations take the form of asocial behavior, hypochondriasis, and socialized delinquency. When the parents are rejecting but attempt to deal fairly with the child, he may show a primary behavior disorder with a predominance of habit dysfunctions and neurotic traits. It will be noted that delinquency in part may be caused by too much as well as by too little parental discipline when this is associated with outright rejection of the child.

Family Pathology. It is becoming customary today, when speaking of childhood behavior disorders, to incriminate the family as a whole generating its own pathology as a function of the interaction of the individual members. The structure of the family helps to determine its reactions, bringing about distinctive differences between small families versus large families, short spacings between siblings versus long spacings, one-sex sibships versus mixed sibships, younger parents versus older parents, and nuclear family groups versus extended family groups. The consideration of these factors has led to the formulation of the concept of family equilibrium related to a model type of structural arrangement that might conduce, theoretically at least, to balance or homeostasis.

The natural history of a family group extends from the mating of the parents, through the development of the children, the mating of the children, and the emergence of new families. The notion that parents undergo developmental stages with respect to the stages passed through by their children has led to a more complex viewpoint of the parent-child relationship. The capacity of parents to cope with children competently at various ages demands a certain depth, maturity, and flexibility of personality. The failure of individuals to develop psychologically as parents, although procreating, may end in a psychopathology of parenthood constituting a distortion of what Wolman (1956) referred to as the vectorial relationship. Parents create life, protect it and care for it, regardless of any attributes of the child. The weaker the child, the more they protect it. To be an adequate parent, one needs to be strong, friendly and willing to give and be ready to take care without asking anything in return. To give without asking is the essence of vectorialism, that is, parenthood. In any family, there is a balance between giving, taking, and reciprocating. In this context, there are parents who neglect themselves and worry constantly about the children, parents who make infantile, selfish demands on their children, and parents who insist on an exaggerated mutuality. All these responses can bring about maladjustments in the children. Families may also vary in the degree to which the members may communicate with one another, influence one another, express feelings to one another, or sensitively perceive one another. Families differ with respect to their tolerance of abnormal behavior, internalizing or externalizing, and they differ in the extent to which they keep their pathology encapsulated or open to the environment.

The family has been long regarded as a transmitter of cultural values and standards from one generation to the next, but more recently the transmitting function has been considered with regard to psychiatric disorders, over and above genetic transmission. Ehrenwald (1958) has described several generations of families in which neurotic modes of behavior have been passed presumably from person to person in a sort of pseudoheredity, and several authors have described the spread of feeling "by contagion" from mothers to infants and from parents to children. In many respects, the family offers optimal conditions for the spread of infection, both physical and psychological.

The Influence of Sick Parents—The Physically Ill. Physical illness, like psychiatric illness, tends to affect families as a whole so that they show similar illness rates over a 3-year period and the illness of one child tends to be reflected in the state of health of the other children in the family (Downes, 1945). There was also an excess rate of illness in members coming from families in which there was a chronically ill person.

The children from such families also tend to show a high rate of delinquency, behavior problems, and difficulties with their parents. The Gluecks (1950) found that 39.6% of the fathers of institutionalized delinquents had a "serious physical ailment" and that 48.6% of the mothers were physically ill. These figures were significantly different from those of a control group at the 1% level. Litauer (1957) similarly noted that parental physical illness was much more frequent in the so-called "clinical offender," that is, the delinquent referred to the psychiatric clinic. In another study by Bennett (1960), high rates of chronic physical illness in the parents, as well as physical deformity, occurred frequently in the families of both neurotic and delinquent children. Craig (1956), investigating 200 children with behavior disorders, observed that parental physical illness sometimes precipitated or contributed to the child's maladjustment. It appeared that illness impaired the energy of the parents and made them irritable with the children.

The children of parents with multiple sclerosis, examined on the Rorschach Test, as compared with a control sample, showed more responses indicative of bodily concern, dysphoria, hostility, dependency longings, constraint in interpersonal relations, and "false maturity." There were also higher scores on "diffuse anxiety" in children under 13 years.

Ekdahl made a study of 28 families where a parent was admitted to hospital because of tuberculosis. The disruption in living arrangements was greater when the mother had been hospitalized, but the care and disposition of the children was always a problem and led to bitter family arguments which added to the children's distress.

Anthony (1968) also made a study of families in which a parent was ill with tuberculosis, and pointed out that the "distancing," necessitated by disease precautions, often led to marked disturbances in the parent-child relationships, especially with the younger children who least understood the reason for the various contact prohibitions. In some sensitive children, a contamination phobia could arise, whereas in others, with a large element of suggestibility, hypochondriasis could be generated.

The evidence would point in the direction that chronic physical illness in a parent may be associated with the development of various types of psychiatric disorder in the children.

The Effect of Sick Parents—Psychiatric Illness. There has been some argument in the literature regarding the comparative pathogenic strengths of neurosis, psychopathy, and psychosis in a parent. For example, Post (1962) found a lower incidence of psychopathology in the children of psychotic parents (14.3%) as compared with the children of nonpsychotic, but psychiatrically ill parents (42.8%).

Downes (1942), in a longitudinal morbidity study of families in Baltimore, discovered an excess rate of illness as compared with the general population when there was a parent suffering from chronic psychoneurosis or "nervousness," even when the factor of social conditions was kept constant. Neurotic mothers seemed to have a more deleterious effect than neurotic fathers, the children of the former tending to have significantly higher rates of behavioral and psychosomatic disorders. The differences between the neurotic and non-neurotic parental groups were large and could not be ascribed to such contaminating factors as the varying interest of the mothers or physicians in psychiatric illness. The findings obtained further support from Kellner (1963), who was also able to demonstrate a higher rate of psychiatric disorder in the children of neurotic parents. There were two findings of particular interest in this study: there was an association between neurotic disorders between the parents in the family and between mothers and children, but not between fathers and children; and secondly, the illnesses in a family often came in pairs or clusters. However, Hare and Shaw (1965) found that physical and mental ill health in fathers was also associated with an increased rate of behavior disorder in the children.

Huschka (1941), in an investigation based on the clinical records of children with behavior disorders, found that 41.6% of the mothers suffered from neurotic symptoms, depression, suicidal impulses, or paranoid trends and concluded that the mother's condition influenced the child at every stage of his development although not conducing to any specific types of disturbance.

Depressed mothers (Fabian and Donohue, 1956) as well as mothers whose depressions or obsessions overlay murderous impulses or feelings toward their children (Anthony, 1959) were prone to have devastating clinical influences on their children, who could be passive and fearful, withdrawn, infantile, ailing, overidentified with the parents' pathological attitudes, or manifesting some type of behavior disorder.

Lewis (1954) found that neurotic reactions were particularly common in the children of neurotic and psychopathic parents, the association being statistically significant. About 26% of juvenile delinquents have psychiatrically ill parents, generally neurotic mothers (Litauer, 1957).

The influence of parental psychosis on the development of children has been receiving increasing attention in the past few years. The results from various investigations with respect to the incidence of disorder in the offspring have been contradictory, but Anthony (1968) has suggested that this is, in part, at least a function of the psychological distance at which the investigator studies his subjects. The closer one gets to the child, in terms of intensive and repeated interviewing and testing, the more disturbed do the children begin to appear. This may also be due to a striking tendency in families with a psychotic parent to keep the matter secret, masked or encapsulated within the orbit of the family so that the children may lead lives dictated by a double standard of reality—one for home consumption and the other for presentation to the external environment. The children, for example, may "go along" with delusional beliefs within the family in a type of *folie à deux*, while maintaining a rational perspective at school or elsewhere. There were other factors that also had bearing on the degree of adjustment or maladjustment of the children. These included the health of the spouse, the nature of the psychosis, whether process or reactive, the continuity of home life, the adequacy of surrogation, the sex of the child (mothers and daughters seem especially prone to "share" their disturbance), and, most important, the degree of involvement of the child in the parent or his illness. Anthony also found that the attacking types of psychoses tended to generate more disturbance than the avoidance variety.

Rutter (1966) argued against a specific genetic link between the disorders in parent and child because of the lack of correlation between type of parental illness and the type of illness in the child. Unlike Anthony, he made no distinction between the process and reactive psychoses, and the study of the children involved simply routine examination without any attempt to study them in depth or over time. In fact, the subjects were studied only from records. Such a procedure would certainly guard against the influence of preconceptions, but it would be unlikely to come up with anything more than pedestrian conclusions. (There is a general tendency for British psychiatric investigators to confine themselves to down-to-earth, pragmatic actuarial studies and this leads to a certain monotony in the findings and presentation.)

In concluding this section, it could be claimed that children, seen at close quarters, are more sensitive to the variations of illness in the parent than has been previously supposed. As a general rule, it could be said that the younger ones in the family tend to react to the "culture of illness," whereas the older ones may show more illness-specific effects. In some cases, the response may be simply to the "climate" generated by disturbed or disturbing parents, although even then the more particular effects of imitation and identification may play a part. It would seem that sick parents often have sick children, the sickness in the child being reactive rather than "neurotically conflictual." All this would lend support to Ackerman's claim (1958) that a psychosocial diagnosis of the family could always be made, that psychiatric illness as a single or isolated instance does not occur in family life and that the sick behavior of the various members are interwoven and mutually reinforcing. This has also been emphasized by Pollack (1952) among others.

Situational Risk

This type of risk has already been mentioned with reference to the effects of institutional life on the behavior and development of young children.

Although the methodology used in separation research is loose and open to many criticisms, there still remains a solid body of clinical findings that cannot be lightly dismissed, although they have suffered from overstatement. The retrogressive stages of "anaclitic depression" have been well documented by Spitz (1946) and further support came from Bowlby and his co-workers (1960), who also described stages of protest, despair, and resignation. The immediate effects of separation as described in a large number of children has been generally accepted, but a great deal of controversy has fastened onto the long-term outcome. Wootton (1959) stated that no decisive study has been carried out yet to demonstrate unequivocally that delinquents as a group have experienced greater maternal or parental separation or that separated children are disproportionately delinquent. Lewis (1954) actually felt that children who had been long exposed to the dislike or indifference of their natural mothers may become *less* deprived when separated and treated with consideration. She was unable to find any evidence from her own data

that delinquency or affectionless psychopathy was a significant aftermath in separated children.

Studies of childhood bereavement have also produced some contradictory findings which could be even more perplexing if one did not remember that the concept of death undergoes various stages of development from fantasy-based to reality-based. It suffers from the deficiencies of all single explanations put to the service of complex phenomena, and as a long-term explanation, it is bedevilled by an infinite number of possibly mutative events that intervene at all points and in all forms between cause and event.

Nevertheless, it has been put forward as a monocausal hypothesis to account, in part or whole, for adult depressive illness, schizophrenia, suicide, marital disharmony, criminality, personality disorder, neurosis, and occupational maladjustment. Arguing from Freud's thesis in *Mourning and Melancholia* (1917) and from the observation that children, especially younger ones, do not appear to mourn, some theorists have suggested that bereaved children may postpone their mourning into adult life and therefore become predisposed to depressive illness and other related disturbances.

The follow-ups of cases of childhood bereavement have produced the following significant connections: delinquency in boys with father loss (Gregory, 1958); male and female criminality with father loss (16.5%) and to a lesser extent mother loss (10.9%) (Brown, 1966); reactive depression with loss of the opposite-sex parent, marital disharmony with loss of both parents, occupational maladjustment in men with father loss, personality disorder, reactive depression, and neurosis with mother loss (0 to 5 years) and father loss (5 to 15 years) (Gay and Tonge, 1967); male depression with father loss and female depression with mother loss and depression in both sexes with parent loss (10 to 15 years), male and female schizophrenia with mother loss (0 to 5 years), male schizophrenia with father loss (5 to 10 years), male alcoholism with parent loss, female alcoholism with mother loss, male drug addiction with father loss, female drug addiction with mother loss.

It has also been found that over twice as many children attending a psychiatric clinic had lost a parent through a death as would be expected from comparable death rates in the general population. Children with psychiatric disorder were most often bereaved between the ages of 2 and 5 years, but the psychiatric disorder was frequently not manifest until early adolescence. Almost a third of the children showed no sign of disorder until at least 5 years after the parent's death (Rutter, 1966).

In psychoanalytic theory, the concept of trauma has undergone many revisions. From being a single all-embracing cause of mental illness (e.g., Freud's original seduction hypothesis), the concept of trauma was for a while in disrepute and disregarded until it was rehabilitated both in psychoanalysis and in the stress and disaster literature. Trauma was seen to produce a traumatic neurosis, which was a period of maladaptation often characterized by striking symptoms and signs of acute anxiety or panic which could settle down into a more chronic form with recurrent nightmares. The individual set about mastering this anxiety by means of repetition, constantly returning, as it were, to the "scene of the crime." As mentioned with reference to May's analogy of the three dolls, resilience varies considerably in a given population of children or even in a given family or with the stage of development. The individual's interpretation or understanding of the trauma may determine the intensity of his reaction. In the framework of psychoanalytic theory, for example, a castration threat, which may have marked effects when given at the height of the Oedipal phase, may fall on relatively deaf ears during the anal stage of development. It is this phase-specific characteristic of trauma that must be considered in every context.

Developmental Risk

According to psychoanalytic theory, the different developmental stages may each make a partial or complete contribution to the clinical picture, depending on the degree of fixation at or regression to a particular stage. For example, children deprived of adequate oral satisfaction as infants would need and seek oral satisfactions as older children. As one consequence, they might become finger suckers. According to psychoanalytic theory, therefore, babies who have had less sucking would tend to suck more as children, which is in contrast to learning theory, according to which one would expect that babies who had been given considerable oral reinforcement would tend later to acquire the generalized oral habits and thus become habitual finger suckers (O'Connor and Franks, 1961).

Levy (1928) found that a finger-sucking group had been nursed less often and for briefer periods in infancy than a nonfinger sucking group, and that puppies that had little opportunity to suck during feeding sucked excessively between meals at each other's bodies as contrasted with breast-fed puppies that showed none of this whatsoever (1934). These findings were confirmed by Roberts (1944) and Goldman-Eisler (1951). *There thus seems to be some support for the view that oral deprivation in infancy may help to determine oral habit patterns and personality reactions in later life.* There is, however, less support for the assumptions that the type of feeding (e.g., breast or bottle), its duration, or the type of scheduling is also related to later adjustment. The Rogersons (1939) did find that bottle-fed, as compared with breast-fed babies, tended to be more neurotic later on and to make poorer school progress. They also showed a higher incidence of eating disturbances and did not appear to be as physically healthy. Holway (1949) also found a positive relationship between the duration of breast feeding and later adjustment, although neither Peterson and Spano (1941) or Sewell and Mussen (1952) were able to confirm this.

Toilet training has been regarded by learning theorists as a sequence of learned responses (Mussen and Conger, 1956) so that anything that interfered with the learning process (starting before the child was physiologically mature, capable of understanding the situation, or able to sit in comfort) might eventuate in bowel or bladder dysfunction. According to psychoanalytic theory, excessive coercion or indulgence during the anal phase might lead to fixation and predispose to the later development of an anal character or anal symptomatology. Anthony (1957) attempted to correlate certain types of bowel dysfunction, such as encopresis and constipation, with the pressure of toilet training. A high-pressure type of training tended to have its onset at under 8 months, be completed under 18 months, and be enforced by physical and psychological coercion; a low-pressure type, on the other hand, had its onset after 2 years and would make use of inconsistent or neglectful techniques with little involvement on the part of the mother. He also concluded that training pressures had a long history and were rooted in the deeper psychopathology of the mother. He next attempted to correlate the degree of pressure and the "level of aspiration" in the mother with regard to toilet training. He found that the high-pressure group responded to failure in training by a certain age by an increase in their aspiration level, whereas this was the reverse for the low-pressure group. He also found that the continuous type of encopresis in which bowel control had never been established was associated in 66.7% of cases with neglectful modes of training, whereas the discontinuous type of encopresis, in which bowel training was established early but followed later by incontinence, was associated in 63.3% of cases with a coercive training. Children with marked constipation were also coercively trained in 75% of cases. Anthony was able to demonstrate that children subjected to coercive and early training were inclined to exhibit compulsive and rigid personalities later on, a finding in keeping with that of Despert (1944).

There was some evidence to indicate that harsh toilet training was related to negativism and aggression (Sears, Whiting, Nowlis, and Sears, 1953; Macfarlane, Allen, and Honzik, 1954), but a recent study by Beloff (1957) appeared to militate against the relationship between anal character formations and early toilet training. The characteristic traits manifested by the subjects, such as parsimony, punctuality, procrastination, pedantry, and preciseness, showed more association with the personality of the mother than with her method of toilet training. However, it would not be difficult to suppose that the personality of the mother would also correlate with her behavior in a specific situation.

The relationship between the infantile experience and later behavior in childhood or adult life is clearly a difficult one to establish by the present means at our disposal, but there would seem to be enough looser types of evidence that would support an association. This would be meaningful within the context of psychoanalytic theory, already discussed, as well as learning theory as discussed by Hebb (1949): "If the learning we know and can study, in the mature animal, is heavily loaded with transfer effects, what are the properties of the original learning from which these effects come? How can it be possible even to consider making a theory of learning in general from the data of maturity alone. . . . Transfer from infant experience may be much greater and more generalized" (1949, p. 13).

Critical Periods of Development

Developmental psychologists, who subscribe to "stage" theory, constantly struggle with the problem of transition and adaptation to new stages while leaving the earlier one behind; further, they are concerned with the effects of this on the development of the personality. This was pointed out first by psychoanalysts and later by others, but conclusive, empirical data have only accrued within recent years. Hebb (1949) had indicated that later stages of development depended on the integrity of preceding ones, while ethologists, studying the early life of animals, postulated the existence of critical periods of development during which the future of later patterns of behavior were determined. Animals have relatively short periods of immaturity and because of this are profoundly vulnerable to early deprivation of constituents important for their growth. The prolongation of development in man appears to have endowed him with a greater capacity for compensation, sometimes even up to the age of 30 years, after which, as William James put it, his personality is set hard, like a plaster cast.

There is some evidence to suggest that there are certain "natural" stages and transitions that interrupt the course of development and give rise to temporary imbalances or maladaptations which might grow, in susceptible individuals, to psychiatric disorder.

The periods 4-7 years, 9-11 years, and 14-16 years tend to be peak times for psychiatric referrals. They are also linked with accelerations in physical development and, according to Piaget, with radical changes in the modes of thinking. In the educational system, the child graduates to a new educational environment at these times.

In a developmentally oriented psychopathology, the influence of such critical epochs will receive greater recognition in the genesis of behavior disorders, especially when taken in conjunction with the physical and psychological changes occurring at the same time.

In summary, it is clear that the work of a psychiatric clinic could be greatly enhanced by the careful consideration of the part that these various hazards might play in the production of psychopathology in any particular case and perhaps point to the possibility of preventive or therapeutic measures. There is some, albeit slight evidence to suggest that a summation of risks might take place and help to explain the perplexing differential vulnerability of siblings within a family. Being born of certain parents, under certain traumatic conditions, and living in certain disadvantageous surroundings with exposure to certain stresses may lead at certain critical periods to the expression of abnormal behavior—but then again it may not. There remain as yet inexplicable, unstudied, perhaps ineluctable factors, which unexpectedly and surprisingly make an individual, at high risk, respond "with a pleasant musical note."

THEORIES OF THE BEHAVIOR DISORDERS

In the previous section on etiology, a considerable body of research data of various kinds was assembled; little was done to it except the organization of the data within the concept of *risk*. The methodological rigor of many of these studies left much to be desired, especially in the way of controls, but the massive accumulation of even doubtful data pointing in one direction, as in the separation research, eventually begins to sound convincing even in the absence of scientifically acceptable and decisive work.

Curiously enough, there has been very little reference to hard or soft etiological data in relation to theory building in psychopathology, the more popular source of evidence being that derived from treatment, whether psychoanalytic, operant, social learning, or drug.

Neuropsychological Theory

Certain behavior disorders, as already noted, fall into a borderline category which is not convincingly organic nor obviously psychological, but contains elements from both sides. The theory of the secondary be-havior disorders quite understandably is a mixture of neurological hypothetical constructs and psychological hypotheses, the latter providing the more speculative aspects, although, in fairness, it should be added that current-day neurology also provides a fertile field for speculators. Krech (1950) reminds the neuropsychologist of two important points that must be held in mind: it is the psychological data, in the last analysis, which must provide the tests of the adequacy of any theory of brain action; and the unified point of view will not be achieved by *reducing* psychological principles to neurological ones and neurological to physical ones, but by making them each *congruent* with the other, the test of congruence being the extent to which the data are encompassed most conclusively.

If one were to extend Pasamanick's hypothesis of reproductive casualty, it could be assumed that every individual is to a greater or lesser extent a birth casualty and, under normal circumstances, suffers from minimal damage which he quickly overcomes or compensates for. This could account for the pervasiveness of behavioral symptoms in the general population of children. The environmental influence could be added to the organic one, either helping or hindering the expression of symptomatic behavior, the rate in "bad" subcultural environments being higher.

Stott (1962) would hold the entire reproductive period, stretching from conception to the postnatal stage, causally responsible and would link the childhood behavior disorders as a group to a poorly defined "congenital vulnerability."

Most theorists, holding to an organic point of view, have fallen back upon a concept of "immaturity" or "developmental lag" in which the normal maturation of the brain is delayed. The evidence for much of this has been based on the E.E.G. (Hill, 1952). Over the years, there have been many studies of the E.E.G. in the behavior disorders in childhood and an overall finding has been a high incidence of electroencephalographic abnormality from 40 to 75% of instances. In general, this abnormality has been the appearance, randomly or even paroxysmally, of slow waves (in the theta and delta frequency ranges) which would be normal at a much younger age. It is, therefore, quite nonspecific and may occur in such different types of behavioral disturbances as nocturnal enuresis, progressive antisocial behavior, and stammering.

This theory of cortical immaturity is far too simple, at least in its present form, to account for the complex variability of the "functional" behavior disorders. Moreover, the fact that some of this abnormal behavior can be modified by the use of such drugs as the amphetamines still does not tell us much about the processes at work.

The research program conducted by Levine and his associates (1960) on the long-term effects of early handling or "gentling" of animals has helped to extend the organic hypothesis. Levine has shown how the changing pressures and sudden challenges of the early environment may influence both the physiology and the behavior of the adult. One of the more surprising discoveries is that whereas electrically shocked infants did not differ from unshocked controls as adults, a group of infants who had been left alone, unshocked but also unhandled, exhibited a marked degree of emotional disorder at adulthood as measured operationally by objective responses to given situations. This would suggest that the pathogenic factor was not early stressful experience but *the absence of experience*. What tied this work firmly to the organic hypothesis was the finding of concomitantly high cholesterol in studies of brain tissue in the unstimulated animals, suggesting that maturation of structure ran parallel to the maturation of function. In all respects, the manipulated infants achieved a more rapid rate of development and Levine has suggested that perhaps some degree of stressful experience in infancy is necessary for the successful adaptation of the individual to the environment that he will encounter in later life. It may well be that what conduces to pathology is "too little" as well as "too much" and that what constitutes stress should be redefined to include both.

Psychoanalytic Theory of the Behavior Disorders

As mentioned earlier, Blau and Hulse have conceived of childhood behavior disorders as "actual neuroses" similar to what was described by Freud in his early work. According to this theory, the symptoms of anxiety-neurosis were, in some measure, surrogates for the specific activity which should have followed upon excitation of a sexual kind but did not do so. The symptoms of the anxiety attack mimic the excitation process. The nervous system, says Freud, reacts to an internal source of excitation with a neurosis just as it reacts to an analogous external one with a corresponding effect. It is again difficult to believe that this relatively simple formulation can account for all the complex phenomena subsumed under the label of behavior disorder. However, accepting the view that the family behavior disorders have not undergone internalization, it is possible to see them as dammed-up or discharging phenomena, lacking a conflict structure. In more recent psychoanalytic terms, they would be predominantly a pregenital syndrome in which the pathology is focused on the dyadic relationship with the mother and involves the twin problems of symbiosis and separation. Like other pregential syndromes, aggressiveness would be to the forefront and narcissism a prominent characteristic.

The comprehensive nature of psychoanalytic theory, as it is presently constituted, provides a greater explanatory strength over a wider spectrum of phenomena than any other contemporary theory. There is also no other set of constructions as clinically useful in elucidating different aspects of personality development. Added to the stage concept or the theory of infantile sexuality, are the rich repertoire of defense mechanisms and its interrelation within the same framework of both normal and pathological functioning. If behavior pathology is regarded as one end of a continuum alongside normal behavior, it is obviously useful to have a theory that encompasses both and allows the passage from the pathological to the normal side as required by the idea of cure or recovery.

The central and crucial problem for psychoanalytic theory, as Baldwin has pointed out (1967), is essentially a "theory about what people think, feel, dream, and fancy, rather than about how they behave" (p. 376). One would therefore assume that it would be more effective in explaining the psychoneuroses than it would be the behavior disorders and this is certainly true. The theory is at its best when showing how instinctive motivation operates in the production of thoughts and feelings and it contains an elaborate and sophisticated theory regarding the ways in which the instincts lead to thoughts and feelings and then on to behavior.

A further advantage of psychoanalytic theory is that it deals with trivia with the same interest that it affords the more serious problems of life. This concern with the "psychopathology of everyday life" permits it to cover a range from the mild and transient disorder to the gross psychoses.

However, its emphasis on intrapsychic processes of the individual has also implied some neglect of the actual and the environmental and especially in the ways in which thoughts and feelings are transformed into behavior. The understanding of this process is important for an understanding of a period of behavior.

In summary, psychoanalytic theory is unrivaled in its capacity to further understanding of the psychoneuroses. For the reasons given, it has been less successful in explaining the psychoses and the wide variety of conditions generically labeled the behavior disorders. Nevertheless, it is, to date, the most complete theory of human behavior that we have and, in many ways, most satisfying to the clinical mind.

LEARNING THEORY AND THE BEHAVIOR DISORDERS

Learning theory has the advantage that it is relatively straightforward and uncomplicated, but its theoretical use in the explanation of maladaptive behavior has run it into some problems. The matter has been examined in some detail by Wolf (1966). He points out that it is a characteristic feature of ontogenetic and even of phylogenetic learning that responses, no longer adaptive and enhancing the needs of the organism, tend to be discarded, and the survival of the individual and his species in a varied environment is dependent on the flexible capacity to extinguish patterns of behavior no longer appropriate to changed conditions as well as on the capacity to acquire and retain appropriate ones. This is in full keeping with the reward-punishment model of learning: adaptive behavior being reinforced by its own rewarding outcome is retained, whereas unadaptive behavior which cannot be rein-

forced by its own harmful outcome is cast off and extinguished.

However, in applying this "instrumental" (operant) model of learning to human psychopathology, we are confronted by "the disconcerting paradox," as Wolf puts it, that maladaptive patterns may be retained for years in spite of their unrewarding and even incapacitating outcome. Learning theorists have explained this contradiction by suggesting that a symptom, such as a phobia, is essentially an avoidance response to a feared stimulus or situation. Even though it is no longer appropriate, by continuing to avoid the stimulus, the organism deprives itself of further opportunities to unlearn an inappropriate response.

The pertinent question that arises is how, if avoidance behavior is designed to avoid suffering, can this apply to the suffering patient, and if the disorder really protects the patient from suffering, why call any kind of procedure that deprives him of such protection "therapeutic"? In the avoidance hypothesis, the persistence of the morbid pattern is ascribed to the absence of reexposure and, therefore, opportunity not only for further reinforcement but also for extinction through nonreinforcement. Another explanation is that the patterns persist because they are being constantly reinforced by their own rewarding outcomes, which may be pleasurable.

Is this not a further contradiction in terms? Why call a pattern that is rewarding to the organism "maladaptive," and why cure patients of patterns that are beneficial to them? The clinical reason for doing so is clear. Illness is always a "bad thing" in its consequences for the patient whatever the secondary and partial gains accruing from the illness may be. The disorder may prove to be the lesser of two alternative evils available to the patient, but if the totality of satisfactions of mental health did not outweigh those of illness, the patients would never ask to be relieved of their conditions.

The crucial problem here for psychopathology is whether learning theory is prepared to extend itself in the face of greater complexity. *Man is not only a learning creature like an animal but also, whether investigators like it or not, a thinking creature in the Pascalian sense, who not only benefits from previous relevant experience but also profits from the experiences of others, and who before finally deciding how to respond to a stimulus often prefers to take his time and weigh his action in the light of past experience. He may also explore the available knowledge in his environment and pool the experience of contemporaries and even past generations. He is, therefore, able to learn not only from firsthand experiences but also from secondhand ones, and a maladaptive response that has grown out of his own experiences can be unlearned by exposure to new, disconfirming, firsthand experiences* (Wolf, 1966).

According to psychoanalysis, the unlearning requires an emotional experience in addition to the intellectual insight imparted to the patient. Learning theorists, dealing with human behavior, normal or abnormal, and wishing to influence it, must take note of this "higher" learning capacity of man. In the same context, Soviet psychologists have struggled beyond the classical Pavlovian model and are making use of "higher" order conditioning principles involving the use of language.

Wolf is surprisingly hopeful about a possible future synthesis between the two major theories currently in use for the understanding of abnormal behavior:

The learning theory model and the psychoanalytic model are by no means incompatible alternatives. On the contrary, they bear out each other's most important contributions, and interdisciplinary integration of the two models is likely to open up sharper insights into the genesis and treatment of psychogenic disorders. I submit that their integration is sooner or later inevitable, however passionately some or many of us may choose to resist it. Psychoanalysis cannot remain for much longer outside the behavioral sciences, nor can the sciences of human behavior for much longer ignore the body of knowledge amassed by the psychoanalytic schools of thought (1966, p. 9).

Learning theories start with simpler, molecular ideas of behavior to explain complex behavior, and psychodynamic ideas start with complex, molar behavior and analyze its components. Each is useful and necessary, and they have a common meeting point where the language of each can be translated into the other, especially in describing behavior during psychotherapy. Disagreements occur when theories are overgeneralized and when the same data accord equally well with either approach. The simple symptoms can be reasonably described as faulty habits in the language of learning theories, but more complex symptoms have less value in this respect (Marks and Gelder, 1966). Both psychoanalytic and learning theorists, in spite of Freud's prediction that abnormal behavior will eventually require biochemical understanding, are currently of the opinion that behavior pathology will shift gradually in emphasis from speculations about "a psyche in a somatic container" to the study of the operations of human individuals in a social field.

In summary, the applicability of instrumental conditioning to the socialization or malsocialization of a child is fairly clear. The child undoubtedly undergoes a process definable in terms of "shaping" as the regime of parental approval and disapproval is gradually modified in the strictness of its requirements during the course of development. There is no question that a child's actions, whether social or antisocial, are reinforced and that some learning occurs by way of it, but it is difficult to specify just how much.

The fact of extinction poses a problem. Many of the behavior patterns are obviously reinforced when they occur but do not seem to be reinforced afterward. How to account for the apparent permanence of some learning is by no means easy. *Partial reinforcement* can help to account for some long-lasting effects, especially for the persistence of behavior that parents would like to extinguish. For example, temper tantrums can be reinforced both by reactions of solicitude and annoyance; the parents, on advice to ignore the behavior, tend to break down at times and respond, thus establishing a pattern of partial reinforcement highly resistant to extinction. Probably no more than 10% reinforcement could lead to recalcitrance. *Secondary reinforcements* may also gradually be superimposed on the primary ones, so that new values get attached to old behavioral responses and consolidate them.

Clinicians have been critical of S-R theory because of its comparative neglect of the actual process of thinking which is considered by them as imperative to the business of psychopathology and cure. Recently Berlyne (1965) attempted to introduce a more complicated picture of the "central" process by postulating a system of "transformational thoughts" interposed between stimulus, situational thought, and response, representing overt action. This is somewhat similar to Freud's "secondary process" and Piaget's "operations" and adds needed "depth" to S-R theory.

Social Learning Theory and the Behavior Disorders

One attempt to bring psychoanalytic and S-R theory together within the same framework was provided by Miller and Dollard (1941) among others, making use of explanatory principles derived from both Freud and Hull. It has therefore been said that social learning theory was nothing more than Freudian theory dressed up in the language of stimulus-response. Missing, however, from the reformulation are such cardinal psychoanalytic concepts as primary instinctual drives, the psychosexual development, and, above all, the repressed Unconscious.

The basic elements of this theory focus on infantile dependency and its concomitant anxieties. Dependency is seen as the root of nearly all socialization—the gradual transformation of aggression into socially acceptable form, the appearance of various adult behavior patterns instilled through the fear of punishment and the appearance of identification and conscience. These concepts of dependency, identification, imitation, and resistance to temptation are seen not as units but as sets of partially independent specific behavior patterns whose organization varies from individual to individual depending on the particular child-rearing experience.

Certain aspects of social-learning theory are very pertinent to the understanding of the genesis of behavior disorders. For example, one quite consistent finding in studies of the effects of child-rearing practices is the way in which parental aggressiveness is associated with greater aggressiveness in the child, this being especially true where it is a question of physical punishment. In terms of theory, the parent is said to provide a model which the child imitates. Thus the parent who is overtly aggressive toward people in general, and toward the child in particular, provides a model of aggressive, uninhibited behavior at the same time that he frustrates and angers the child. It often follows that the child's own overt aggression is counteracted by parental punishment, which may help to fix the child in an aggressive set. The inconsistency of the parent's punitive response further aggravates the situation.

The social-learning theorists, before the concept of modelling was introduced, attributed all aggressive behavior to frustration, although Freud had already examined and discarded this hypothesis. Severe aggressive and antisocial behavior is often seen in the absence of any frustration. In many instances it also appears to bring little but unhappiness to the aggressor, but, far from attenuating the response, it seems rather to be consolidated by the harsh consequences. Further, it observably begins very early in life in the form of anger even before there is anything specific at which to be angry. The anger is an aroused state. Later, it becomes more object directed and motivated. The anger may then rid the child of the annoyance and, what is more important, bring help from the mother. It does, however, create more problems than it solves and this is what leads it to become a prime ingredient in the behavior disorders. A conflictual "double-bind" communication comes into being, the parent's anger, in response to the child's anger, serving both as a model and as a warning. Conflicts around the expression of aggression are currently viewed as crucial in the production of psychopathology.

A study of children with aggressive behavior disorders, compared with a control group of nonaggressive subjects, showed that the aggressive children were more directly aggressive toward adults outside the home and toward peers than they were toward their parents. There were, however, greater feelings of hostility toward their fathers. The most striking source of difference between subjects and controls lay in the reaction of the parents. The parents in the aggressive group encouraged their children to be aggressive and resorted more frequently to physical modes of punishment. They were also less tolerant of dependency behavior.

Sociological Theories of the Behavior Disorders

The sociological theories of abnormal behavior attempt to study it in terms of transactions between the individual, his family, his school, his work, and his recreational group, as it takes place in the confines of a certain geographical space. Within this framework, the idea of role is basic to the understanding of the interrelationship between two systems—the psychological system of the group. The child's behavior is structured by his role and his role to a large extent is institutionalized by his age, sex, ordinal position in the family, etc. His personality has been described by Sarbin (1954) as the action systems arising out of the interplay of self and role, some behavior being ascribed to self-action and other behavior to role-determined action.

All these considerations are especially significant in understanding deviant and psychopathological behavior. The ego can carry out its function of perceiving, conceiving, organizing, and maintaining integrative and predictive stability and carrying out effective and resourceful action if it has faithfully learned how the system in which it exists transacts its business of giving and gaining information. When the environment, under conditions of disorder, appears ambiguous, incongruous, or lacking in lucidity, the ego is confronted with too many problems to solve and too complex a conceptual organization to master so that anxiety intervenes. From the medical point of view, psychiatric illness is a happening that is "intrinsic"; from the point of view of the individual, it is a "self-perceived uneasiness"; and from the point of view of dynamic psychiatry, it is a process.

The child, when he is brought to the clinic, has to learn to conceptualize himself as ill, that is, someone who is himself suffering or is causing others to suffer. It is not enough, however, for him to perceive himself as sick; it takes a doctor to make him formally sick, that is, to validate him in his sick role and thus assure him of the help, the indulgences, and privileges, and the responsibilities of the sick role (Stainbrook, 1965). Children, in general, have a special difficulty in understanding the conception of psychiatric illness and in developing a desire to "get well" or "cooperate" with the psychiatrist. The child cannot seem to assume the institutionalized norms characteristic of sick people in our society, according to Parsons' formulation (1951). A sick child is therefore something of a "nuisance" until he learns how to be sick in a particular society so that his behavior becomes diagnosable within the conventional nomenclature of disorders.

The conditions under which a characteristic pattern of behavior may be defined as "ill" varies with the time and circumstance, in particular, the locus of the child on the developmental continuum and the degree to which his behavior fits or misfits his organizational role and position. His locus in geographical or social space is equally a matter of fit, so that residential or social mobility, by adding novelty in excess to his life space, may impose a strain on his interpersonal strategies so that they no longer will be able to cope with the demands made on them. In a new setting or circumstance, the child may strive to become either unduly placating or defiantly aggressive, very similar, in fact, to Levy's (1950) well-known demonstration of the effects of introducing a new hen into an established group of hens. For the new hen, whether it came in fighting or flighting, it always represented a phase of acute maladjustment and it was attacked by the group throughout the period of its "newness," approximately seven days.

Ethology and the Behavior Disorders

The ethologists thus far have contributed less to the theory of behavior than to the description of its nuances. Ethologists have made a remarkable series of observations on mobile and expressive behavior in species ranging from fish to man likely to become of increasing value to the student of abnormal behavior. The repertoire of observed phenomena includes a wide range of rituals, gestures, signals, displacement and territorial behavior, courtship and parental patterns, and group identities and organizations. In essence, the phenomena are studied under various circumstances, both in the natural setting and in the laboratory. The raw data are subjected to a dissecting out process, an approach alien to the experimental psychologist who preferred to test hypotheses under controlled conditions. The work of the ethologist is therefore more in the tradition of the naturalist.

They have discovered that many complex activities are innate or unlearned. These inherited "fixed-action patterns" are not, however, as rigid as the definition implies since they can be modified by experience or learning. They are not unlike some of the basic activity patterns and reaction patterns described by investigators of infant behavior (see section on etiology), although the focus in these infant studies has been on individual differences rather than species similarities.

Ethologists have also been responsible for the delineation of critical periods early in life during which primary social relationships are established with peers and families. In some species, a "fear" period also develops toward the end of the critical period and strange or novel stimuli suddenly evoke avoidance and panic. This fear period may actually help to consolidate the attachment established earlier between the parent figure and the offspring. Similar observations have also been made by the observers of development in the human infant. On the basis of these innate patterns, the developing individual learns what to approach or avoid on future occasions. It therefore would seem that disturbances of social behavior, both asocial and antisocial, may have their origins in this early vulnerable phase.

Another example of the phenomena revealed by ethologists is displacement behavior, which can be defined as a behavior pattern performed out of the particular functional context of behavior to which it is normally related. When a drive is activated, modes of response related to it tend to be evoked, but if the drive becomes overstrong, other modes of response related to other drives may make their appearance. These responses can be regarded as substitute means of discharging excitation when discharge through the normal channels of adaptive activity is prevented. When discharged vicariously, excitation may be reflected in activity which is inefficient, diffuse, and poorly organized but which forms part of behavior patterns more or less closely associated with the drives that have been frustrated. Children, under conditions of frustration of activity, may scratch their heads, pick their noses, pull at their clothes, and shake their legs rhythmically. Such displacement activity is often seen in excess in classrooms of younger children toward the end of the day but may also be observed in gross form in institutional settings where stimulation is diminished or meaningless. In some residential units, disturbed children have been observed to display such phenomena as "pecking order," "territoriality," and fight-flight conflicts.

In summing up, it would seem that there are many ways of conceptualizing abnormal behavioral phenomena depending on the etiology concerned. When, for example, there is organic derangement, the condition can be helpfully viewed within the spectrum of sublethal casualties; with cases of primitive ego defect when the patterns of behavior have been grossly simplified and the training program disturbed, the various types of learning theory provide a suitable theoretical framework; with complex neurotic disorders, the most satisfying set of theories to date has been the psychoanalytical; and, when it is a question of delinquency or sociopathy, necessitating social action, it appears most pertinent to make use of sociological theory. Each viewpoint represents a segmental aspect of a multidimensional process and therefore, to some extent, proves less than satisfactory in explaining the total clinical picture.

The problem that arises in using systematic theory, naïve learning or psychoanalytic, has to do with taking the system in all-or-none fashion. Systems, in general, do not mix together well and representative theorists from different systems do not take kindly to eclecticism. The Freudian unconscious has also proved a hurdle for those psychologists who respect the "psychic surface" of life and do not feel impelled to penetrate into the depths or trace the origins of conduct back to the earliest formative stages.

Zigler (1963) has complained that the "grand designs" that attempt to explain everything actually succeed in explaining very little and he feels that many of the theoretical systems are heavily loaded with constructs that are either tied to the observable and reportable, and therefore are little more than "shorthand," or are related to the abstract with only a remote connection to empirical operations. He is of the opinion that there is a place for an intermediate group of constructs that are neither pretentiously overexplanatory nor simply direct translations of raw data.

It is questionable whether an integrated theory can be derived from the patchwork quilt of the already existing systems. Baldwin (1967) has suggested that such a unified theoretical framework would need to pay proper respect to both behavioral and mental events, would need to recognize more than one level of functioning, would need to include concepts of motivation, learning, and affect, and, above all, would require to be set within the context of maturation and development.

Given systems or integrated systems or intermediate constructs, a further problem lies in the "explanation" that is provided. A theory is intended to provide an explanation for some class of events and the explanation can be more or less satisfactory and more or less complete. However, a large part of many theories is more descriptive than explanatory and the two are sometimes confused. Where there is a large element of description, the theory gains in interest rather than truth and validity is overlooked in favor of breadth, depth, uniqueness or elegance. In addition to explanation, there is also the problem of prediction, which can be defined as an accurate empirical statement whose accuracy can be checked. Prediction, however, is not everything and a vague, incomprehensible hunch, even if it leads to accurate prediction, will not be of much use to other scientific workers.

To place the science of behavior pathology on a sound footing, all these factors in theory-making must be considered. It may be premature to use systematic theory in our present state of ignorance, but one must remember that the clinician and his patients cannot wait indefinitely while an integrated, powerfully explanatory, and predictive theory is fabricated. They must do the best they can with what they have at present, which is, for clinical purposes, surprisingly satisfactory.

THE CLINICAL ENCOUNTER

The child patient is brought, often unwillingly and apprehensively, to the clinic center where the diagnostic team prepares to meet him and his family in an inevitably stressful series of interchanges. The duration of time spent on the waiting list determines to some extent the amount of catharsis generated by the clinical encounter. Cases-in-waiting sometimes develop adaptations both to their disorder and to the impending process of investigation. Symptoms may be relieved and families on the verge of breaking up may be reconstituted. Each movement in the total process may bring about its own mitigation; the application for help, the time on the waiting list, the diagnostic interviews, the postdiagnostic communication of salient findings may all conduce to change for the better in ways not yet clearly understood.

A large number of families "drop out" from the clinic before therapy is instituted because of apparent improvement in the presenting complaint or in their way of looking at it. The clinic encounter thus may induce behavioral changes, sometimes of a lasting nature, at any point in the referral-diagnosis-treatment sequence. This fact makes for one of the difficulties in finding suitable control subjects in researches testing the efficacy of any particular form of treatment. Because of this "Western Electric" effect, it is not possible to specify when and how the therapy begins to exert its influence so that the control subjects can be said only to have received less treatment or different treatment rather than no treatment at all.

The Problem of Interdisciplinary Communication. The study of behavior pathology has become more promising with the use of interdisciplinary clinical teams with members from both the behavioral and biological sciences. These specialists bring with them their own special techniques and orientation, and it is often left to the least specialized member of the team, the psychiatrist, to synthesize the diverse findings from the various examinations—physical investigations, psychiatric observations, psychological evaluations, speech and language assessment, developmental history, and appraisal of the psychosocial environment, particularly the familial part of it.

A constant problem of such multidisciplinary investigation lies in communication. The different participants do not speak the same language and, what is more serious, may not share the same theoretical frame of reference.

The difficulty has been eloquently described by Piaget (1960):

Let us imagine that some poor child has been studied by each of us for a month or a year and that we need to coordinate our results. We would know its brain rhythm, the rates of physical growth, the family conflicts, the relations with its social environment, its reactions to problems of intelligence, the extent of its vocabulary, its drawings, etc. etc. However, and this is the tragedy of present studies, we would be incapable without a common language of achieving anything other than an enormous dossier consisting of a series of chapters complete with a concluding essay on the "personality" of the child. . . . [E]ach would continue, in the absence of a common language, to tell his own separate story in his own separate language without there being any real synthesis (1960, p. 5).

The size of our clinical dossiers represent a striking testimony to the hard work that clinics put in to the understanding of the individual case, but the language barrier intrudes into every record. Whether it is possible to find a common language is still a moot point since none of the suggested ones have been put to use.

For Piaget, the most appropriate common language is probabilistic in which the information and communication framework are supplemented by concepts of strategy and the theory of gains. He feels that the generality of such a language would make it possible to establish fairly direct correspondence between the physical and physiological models and the various forms of behavior, both normal and abnormal. A core concept of equilibrium within the language would enable isomorphisms to be found between models of intraindividual and interindividual operations. As an alternative to this, Bertalanffy (1960) has suggested the language of general system theory which would provide "explanations in principle" without promising qualitative solutions for behavioral phenomena where the complexity of the process and the lack of definition of the relevant parameters were overwhelming. In place of equilibrium, which appeared to have a special meaning for Piaget alone, he suggested the concepts of open systems and steady states in which the individual is regarded, much more realistically, as an essentially active system.

Both these "languages" are too generalized and abstract for day-to-day use by clinicians, even those who are anxious to learn a common language. Here, for example, is Piaget's attempt to transpose the Oedipus Complex into the language of probabilism:

The Oedipus stage represents a certain form of affective equilibrium, characterized by a maximization of the "gains" expected from the mother and by a minimization of the "losses" expected from the father. In this connection, it would be of interest to examine whether the equilibrium point corresponds merely to a Bayes strategy, the criterion of which would be a simple maximum of "gain minus loss," or whether it corresponds to a minimax strategy, with a search for the minimum loss which the subject supposes a hostile environment is trying to inflict on him (1960, p. 8).

This is clearly not feasible as a common language, since it reduces a powerful and emotionally loaded concept to an intellectual abstraction with little of the original dynamism left. It would be harder to prevail upon clinicians to talk the language of Boolean algebra, although this has also been tried—not too successfully.

The language of operant theory has been used and is being increasingly used since behavior therapy came into vogue. Operant theory deals with the problem of conflict not as a special topic involving new principles but as it would with any situation involving operants, except that the operants are applied in more complex combinations. Here is a sample of the language:

When a child is placed in a situation where a response will have stimulus consequences with opposing functions (i.e., a situation of emotional conflict), he may show a certain amount of "emotional" behavior. . . . Much of this follows from the fact that very often in conflict situations, the child must accept negative reinforcement in order to get more powerful positive reinforcement, or, he must lose positive reinforcement in order to escape or avoid more powerful negative reinforcements. The presentation of negative reinforcers, or the loss of positive reinforcers has a close connection with what is usually called "emotional" behavior (Bijou and Baer, 1961, p. 70).

The tendency here is to reduce the inherently complex to a set of simple statements each of which are testable. Clinicians, however, do not generally conduct their inquiries in a rigorous scientific form. Their preference is to accumulate a melange of subjective statements from which they ultimately extract intuitive generalizations that fit the dynamic model.

Psychoanalytic language can provide clinicians with a heavy load of usable concepts built into a fairly logical and comprehensive superstructure. Over the past few decades, it has become the *lingua franca* of clinical practice and is not likely to be displaced too easily from this position since several generations have already grown up speaking it. Like any other mother tongue, it has become vulgarized in use and concepts have degenerated into cliches and been brandished as shibboleths. However, its explanatory power remains strong. Here is a description of a mother-child relationship stated with the characteristic candor, intimacy, and intensity of this communicative mode:

It is, however, difficult to evaluate whether anything fundamental was accomplished with Brad whether through therapy with him or through his mother's treatment. We probably underestimated the mutual seduction in which Brad and his mother were involved, the mutual sadistic satisfaction obtained from each other and the mutual feeding of each other's guilt feelings. The parallelisms in this mother and her child are obvious—the primitive and unattenuated sexuality and aggression, the need to split off a part of the personality to inanimate objects or to each other, the reliance on magic controls, the intense anxiety lest these fail and retaliation in kind follow; the feelings of worthlessness and of being undeserving, the guilt and expectation of punishment, the sense of fatalistic discouragement; and, as a protection against all this, denial, omnipotent fantasies, and withdrawal into daydreams (Pavenstedt, 1955, p. 400).

Whether the same mother-child relationship would be described by another clinician in approximately the same terms is, of course, very much open to question. No interviewer reliability studies have been carried out and this is something that very much needs to be done in the clinical field.

The Physical Investigation. A thorough physical examination of the child is becoming a routine procedure in most psychiatric clinics for children, and there is also increasing use of special physical measures. The physical status is described in terms of height, weight, state of health, and neurological integrity. In addition, the more enterprising clinics attempt to determine the bone age, the dynamometer strength, the sex type (buccal smear), the body build (simple inspection), and EEG. The last is perhaps the most frequently used of the special investigations. From what has already been said in the section on etiology and in the section relating to the mind-body relationship, it would seem that clinics of the future will develop sophisticated batteries of physical tests to parallel the sophisticated batteries of psychological tests that they now possess. Hormonal studies are still difficult to include as routine measures, because they need special laboratory facilities and also because the lack of normative data limits its usefulness.

The presence of nonspecific EEG abnormalities in children with behavior disorders has been observed since the early years of EEG research, but significant correlations between EEG findings and behavior have not been confirmed by all investigators, nor could the occurrence of specific EEG patterns with isolated behavior disturbances be demonstrated. Gross and Wilson (1966) described a syndrome of "subconvulsive cerebral dysrhythmia" involving a triad of behavior disorder, learning disability, and abnormal EEG, in the absence of neurological signs or overt seizures. In their experience (which must have involved a biased sample of cases), "half of the children having a significant behavior disorder or learning disturbance in school show abnormalities in the EEG and many of these can be definitely improved by proper anticonvulsant therapy." It is also their opinion that the EEG should be done routinely in all cases of behavior disorder and learning disability. Loomis (1936), on the other hand, found no significant correlation between EEG abnormalities and delinquent behavior in institutionalized male adolescents and thus felt that "undue emphasis" had been placed on the role of cerebral pathology in theories of delinquent behavior.

Hughes (1961) was able to classify children with behavior disorders referred by the court into three EEG groups: "spike" cases with long histories of significant medical and social factors dating from infancy, "vegetative" types of symptoms, sudden aggressive impulses against people, and lack of guilt and remorse following such attacks; "nonspecific abnormal cases" with a history of temper tantrums, postnatal head injury, low IQ, and significant reading retardation; and "normal rhythm" cases with a history of absconding and truanting.

Itil, Rizzo, and Shapiro (1966) carried out a quantitative study of 20 children and adolescents, ages ranging from 11 to 17, admitted to an in-patient unit with behavior disturbances. The subjects were selected on the basis of having EEG abnormalities such as paroxysmal activity, dysrhythmic patterns, spikes, sharp waves and focal disturbances. The patients were then treated with diphenylhydantoin and thioridazine after an interim period of placebo treatment. The behavior was rated before and after the treatment for frustration tolerance, hyperactivity, aggressive-destructive behavior, impulsivity, poor school performance, antisocial acts, sexual acting out, irritability, and stubbornness. Out of 20 patients, 15 showed moderate to marked improvement in behavior after 3 months of combined drug treatment. Abnormal EEG findings, such as burst activity and dysrhythmic patterns, decreased after drug treatment, and in some subjects the inhibition of abnormal activity due to treatment was remarkable. However, there was no adequate control group for a comparative estimation. Nevertheless, the significance of the study lay in the demonstration that significant correlations between behavior alterations and EEG changes can be defined if certain behavior characteristics and various EEG components are collected systematically, treated individually, and analyzed quantitatively.

The bias toward psychogenesis in most child guidance clinics results in neglecting or ignoring physical factors, either causal or associated, overlooking them, or explaining them away in psychodynamic terms. Koupernik (1960) showed how an appreciation of the organic side can bring a better understanding of the complex interaction between psychogenic and physiogenic influences. He reported the case of a 5-year-old boy with a previously normal development apart from an instrumental delivery at birth. Quite unexpectedly, the child began to display attacks of terror, crying out that he was afraid of the Baby Jesus, epigastric pain, agitated behavior, and bouts of difficult breathing. His mother was described as anxious. The family history was negative. A careful physical investigation revealed the following: an abnormal EEG (outbursts of spike-and-wave activity, and sometimes slow waves, mainly on the left side and persisting during sleep); an abnormal induced hypoglycemia curve; an inversion of the respiratory rhythm; and a 7% eosinophilia.

As a result of the investigation, several possible explanations for the anxiety attacks could be considered:

1. They were psychogenic in origin; he was a sensitive child exposed to some frightening experience or presentation (T.V., pictures, films). Klackenberg and Melin (1953) found that children exposed to frightening films showed EEG abnormalities, mainly the appearance of theta and delta waves. Eosinophilia has been shown to be a concomitant of stress. The context of the "day terror" might be ascribed to retaliatory fears arising from sibling jealousy.

2. They were epileptic in origin; evidence lay in the abnormal EEG, the recurrent epigastric pain (abnormal epilepsy), and the "visual hallucinations" of the Baby Jesus (temporal lobe involvement). The epilepsy could be secondary to a scar resulting from the instrumental delivery.

3. They were hypoglycemic in origin; spontaneous hypoglycemia from pancreatic hyperinsulinism can cause anxiety attacks and can bring about epileptic-type abnormalities in the EEG. Garland (1958) has claimed that most hypoglycemia attacks are in fact psychogenic in origin.

4. They were asthmatic in origin; this would be supported by the inversion of the respiratory rhythm and the eosinophila. Asthma has been regarded as an expression of anxiety related to the mother (the child would run to the mother during his attacks)

—separation anxiety, associated with participant anxiety on the part of the mother (although her anxiety could also be secondary to the child's attacks).

Linking these findings together, Koupernik came up with an intriguing, if speculative, polygenic theory. The painful psychological stress stimulates the subcortical structures, especially the reticular formation, the thalamus, the hypothalamus, and the rhinencephalon. The intensity of this summating effect varies from subject to subject depending on past conditioned experience and on "emotional resonance;" it is probably more active in children in whom the neocortex is able to inhibit the response. In turn, the reaction will cause peripheral phenomena either through Selye's stress mechanism or through the orthosynthesis or ergotropic system described by Hess. In some cases, it is the impairment of the intermediary agency, for example, the subcortical centers that could be held responsible.

This type of theorizing gives the term "psychosomatic" a much wider meaning, at the same time giving full credit to the reverberations that a somatic illness can have on the mother-child relationship. However, it should be remembered that the brain mechanisms described are still largely speculative in nature.

In summary, with regard to physical findings in behavior disorders, it would be fair to say that the field is still relatively new and that adequate normative studies are lacking so that the significance of various findings is difficult to assess. Because of the complexity of the interrelationships involved, it is unlikely that single physiological factors could be held responsible for a whole range of varied and subtle disorders of behavior. It is also difficult to isolate the effects of physiological or biochemical dysfunction from other emotional and social factors and this is best demonstrated in the case of diabetic children in whom a maladjustment rate of 40-60% has been found. However, it would appear that children with early diabetes accept its bondage as part of growing up and in general do better than those who acquire it after the age of 7 or 8 years. A specific crisis often appears with the development of puberty when the diabetic regime is rejected along with other restrictions imposed by the parents. Because of the medical factor, the adolescent crisis in diabetic individuals must be treated with greater concern and caution, since the acting-out of the diabetic can take specifically dangerous forms such as overeating, undereating, and refusal of insulin shots.

Psychiatric Observation. The data derived from observation have been much questioned, especially in the case of the clinical observer who works alone and has no ancillary observer with whom to match observations. In an investigation carried out by Miller (1964) based on a "blind" Q-sort of 80 statements regarding manifest behavior by 5 types of observers—fathers, mothers, teachers, psychologists, and psychiatrists—it was found that the parents were the only judgmental pairs who showed consistent agreement. The clinicians showed least consensus. The data indicated that the interjudge agreement on the manifest personality of the children was low. One interesting finding in the study was that there was a high degree of agreement among judges with respect to the healthy child as contrasted with the disturbed child. In the Midtown Manhattan study (Srole, 1962), two psychiatrists were able to agree on the behavior of individuals who were markedly disturbed or markedly healthy, but could not agree on pathology at the intermediate levels. Miller thoughtfully concluded that an observation could not be communicated with any confidence beyond the person making the observation.

Anthony (1968) has discussed the problem of subjective versus objective clinical observation and the advantages and disadvantages of the two perspectives. The subjective observer is a participant observer in that he is involved in the situation under observation and is interpreting it in terms of his idiosyncratic frame of reference. The subjective observer recognizes the fact that he cannot put his own reactions to an event completely "between brackets" and that to some extent the observed situation is invested with additional elements deriving from the observer. In child psychiatry, there has been a recent trend toward the purely factual observation on which a plurality of observers can reach agreement. According to this viewpoint, the first duty of the clinical observer is to record the facts as they occur and to phrase the language of the record in the simplest, most concrete language with a minimum of adjectival embellishments or qualifying clauses. The behavior to be observed should be characteristic of the overall functioning of the child and obtained from activities in routine, everyday situations. The sequence of events should be allowed to speak for itself without interpretation or comment.

The protocols are deliberately maintained at a factual level and are descriptive of visible and audible behavior. The approach would seem especially appropriate for children still predominately in the sensorimotor stage of development before complex motivations intervene. Here is an example from the records of a severely disturbed child who is mute:

Mary picks up the ball from the floor. She puts the ball to her mouth. She licks the ball. She lets the ball fall on the floor. She goes to the chair and sits down. She drums on the table with her fingers. She looks at the mirror on the wall and smiles. She gets up and goes to the mirror. She puts her face close to the mirror and licks it. She goes to the table. She looks at the picture on the table. The picture is of a child sitting on a chair blowing bubbles through a pipe. She makes a sucking movement of her mouth. She puts her finger in her mouth and sucks on it. etc. etc.

This flat, dull, monotonous "raw" description is characteristic of such protocols. There is no depth, perspective, and meaning and there is not meant to be. The self-effacing clinical observer is nowhere to be seen, although we presume he is somewhere in the room.

Anthony questions whether the clinician can ever encompass both the subjective and objective points of view or use them at different times to enhance the scope of his observations. Observer-training, using videotape, is now being developed at several child psychiatric centers where a step-by-step analysis of the observational process is carried out. Anthony (1968) has provided several paradigms of observational analyses with the hope of making clinical data more available to the researcher.

Psychological Evaluation. Psychological testing is carried out in children's clinics in various ways. It may be requested as a laboratory investigation by the physician in charge of the case, or it may be part of the routine diagnostic process carried out by the three members of the child guidance team. The tests used may be selected on the basis of the child's condition, or a group of tests are administered routinely to every case irrespective of the problem involved. The argument for using a regular battery is that the psychologist becomes familiar with the dimensions of the test and can therefore interpret with greater assurance. There is, nevertheless, something pedestrian and limiting in restricting the evaluation to five or six standard tests when such a huge number of varied and subtle procedures have been devised to illuminate different aspects of personality and cognition. Within the last few years, psychologists have suggested that instead of the psychiatrist referring a patient for testing, he should, on the basis of his understanding of the child's problem, set forth a number of questions that are perplexing in the case. The psychologist would then transform these questions into specific hypotheses and proceed to test them by means of standard or contrived measures. In this way, each case becomes in itself a scientific project that permits the psychologist to be used as a scientist rather than as a technician. The approach is also effective in relieving the monotony of routine test administration.

Barendregt and his associates (1961) have demonstrated how effectively and scientifically psychodiagnostic investigations can be carried out, exploring, for example, such important issues as the clinical method of predicting behavior or the factors involved in judging behavior. An important finding that has bearing on battery size is that the accuracy of predictions at first increased with the increasing number of data, but an optimal point was soon reached after which a systematic decline set in. In the investigation of judgment, it was shown that some subjects are judged more accurately than others and more accurately on one aspect of behavior and not another; further, there was no demonstrable relationship between the accuracy of a judgment and the confidence with which it was made. It was also proven that the halo effect played a significant role in the judgment process, causing a shift in the direction of the social appreciation of the judged trait. This again has an important bearing on child guidance practice where clinical psychologists often insist on having background data before determining the meaning of their results. Teachers who have prior knowledge of IQs of children show bias in their assessment of test results and clinical psychologists who have prior knowledge of the case history of their subjects can produce formulations very much in keeping with the life history of the patient.

Some Implications for the Mind-Body Relationship in Childhood Disorders

The "mysterious leap" from mind to body and body to mind in psychosomatic illness has its counterpart in all forms of mental and physical disorder, suggesting a mutually interacting system in which mind and body habitually suffer together but to different degrees in different conditions. The total picture of illness, therefore, as it is perceived today, is that it is brought about by the cooperation that still remains so mystifying.

Under conditions of stress, children develop a wide variety of disorders ranging from fears and nightmares to ulcers and colitis, and the older they get, the more likely are they to make "meaningful connections" between the mental and the physical. The 5-year-old child attending kindergarten may produce cyclical vomiting on a school morning and make nothing of the coincidence; at 8 or 9, he may develop abdominal pain and regard his condition, with the help of a physician and parents, as a "grumbling appendix" resulting from school cooking; at 14 or 15, he may begin to suffer from severe migrainous headaches during school term and ascribe these to the tensions generated by academic pressures. As he grows further in sophistication, he may see the whole somatic tendency as a reflection of a chronic relational disturbance with his mother. Mention has already been made to the learning of the role of patient during the child's development. This implies his increasing capacity to understand the process of illness. Before his conceptions achieve biological clarity, being sick may be associated with such reactions as guilt, fear, shame, depression, and even disgust. In time, he may come to enjoy the secondary benefits

such as the increased contact with his mother and the relief from daily obligations.

Where there are sick models in the immediate household, or parents with a personal or professional investment in illness (nurses or doctors), the role assumption may be markedly facilitated and become, after a while, a style of life. In hypochondriasis, such antecedent circumstances may play an important part in consolidating the "sick" outlook.

A chronic hypochondriacal attitude in the child is made up of current complaints of vague ill health and anxious anticipation of future illness. A variety of factors in the child, the family, and the caring physician may contribute to the genesis of hypochondriasis. Factors in the child include identification with ill parents and siblings and the adoption of familial somatization techniques for dealing with stress; self-mothering in the absence of parental figures; attention-seeking aimed at obtaining a greater acceptance and approval within the family; a "flight into sickness" to avoid threatening situations or pressures; reactivation of the sickness role which once obtained for the child a suspension from regular routine and the loving solicitude of the parents; a compensation for social and educational failure linked to a lowering of self-esteem; a need to ward off indefinite, formless anxiety by the adoption of a definite form of sickness that might be cured; the effect of naïve infantile theories of disease that "logically" systematize bodily discomforts; and above all the atonement for guilt feelings in relation to hostile and sexual impulses and acts.

The parents of such children, particularly the mothers, may be grossly hypochondriacal themselves and may treat the child as a somatic extension of themselves. Their oversolicitude and protectiveness may thinly veil strong feelings of rejection, but, more frequently, the dislike and hostility is relatively unmasked. From time to time the overprotective mother may "decompensate," giving the child a glimpse of her real attitudes and feelings, and these exposures may in turn set off a reaction of invalidism.

Where there is much family history of disease, the anxious anticipation of the parents may fill the child with foreboding about his "inheritance." There is no doubt that some mothers, not necessarily nurses by profession, are at their best in the sickroom and enjoy the acts of ministration. The child's "sickness" then becomes an essential part in the relationship with the mother and he literally becomes her "patient." A sickroom atmosphere is created around him almost from birth, and he may never have seen himself as a healthy child. Hypochondriasis is very much a family disturbance, and the various members seem to understand unconsciously the child's need to be surrounded by as much somatic anxiety as possible. The family may react, in fact, calmly and unconcernedly in the presence of actual illness.

The child's reaction to illness depends on his developmental level, his previous adaptive capacity, the prior nature of the parent-child relationship, the existing family equilibrium, the nature of the illness in terms of pain or limitation, and the fantasied meaning of the illness to the child (Prugh, 1967).

The behavior of the child changes even before his physical illness is recognized and diagnosed. Commonly, there is restlessness, listlessness, irritability, loss of appetite, negativism, insomnia, and nightmares or night terrors. Somewhat later, regression may occur, perhaps more strikingly in the younger children, but in the older ones depression is more frequent. Still later, lags in perceptual-motor functions may develop, especially after such systemic illnesses as pneumonia. These difficulties may become chronic, resulting in resistance to learning or other behavioral disturbances. Stott (1959) has described a convalescent type of personality development that occurs following illness; this is characterized chiefly by "unforthcomingness." Strong dependency reactions may also date from serious illness.

If mind and body are so closely associated, especially during the period of childhood, the question arises as to whether children with behavior disorders are more likely to suffer from an excess of physical illness or psychosomatic conditions, and, conversely, whether sickly children show an increased tendency to . emotional disturbances. The question has become of more than practical importance since Hinckle and Wolff (1957, 1961) developed

a general theory of illness subsumed under four main hypotheses stating:

1. That illnesses do not occur at random in the life of an individual but in temporal "clusters" separated by periods of well-being, the average duration of a cluster being approximately seven years.

2. That these clusters commonly correspond to periods of environmental stress.

3. That a minority of "susceptibles" account for most of the morbidity in any given population over a long period of time, the individuals at risk tending to show a higher incidence of illness.

4. That during a cluster, the individual shows an increased susceptibility to all forms of illness, regardless of nature or etiology, so that there is a parallelism between the occurrence of psychiatric disorders and the occurrence of bodily illness.

Various investigators (Shepherd et al., 1964; Fraser, 1947; Hare et al., 1965; Downes and Simon, 1953) have reported an association between physical and psychiatric illness, although some others have not been able to confirm this (Kreitman et al., 1966; Kessel, 1960).

It should not be too difficult to test these hypotheses in children, and there is a certain amount of evidence already available to suggest some degree of support for them.

The Psychopathology of the Behavior Disorders

In various classificatory attempts throughout this chapter, the internalizing-externalizing dichotomy has been mentioned, distinguishing between the vector of disturbance running within the individual in the one instance and out into the environment in the other. Anxiety states, phobias, depressions, and obsessions involve suffering mainly for the individual, whereas delinquency, truancy, aggressive behavior, and destructiveness inflict suffering on the environment. A fairly similar dichotomy classifies the disorders into inner-directed disturbances involving the concomitant experience of guilt and the outer-directed disturbances involving the experience of shame. A psychoanalytically oriented classification would refer to the first as genital syndromes and to the second as pregenital syndromes, the criterion of difference being the setting up of an internalized superego within the psychic apparatus. A still further division in the psychopathology would lie between disturbances energized by anxiety and the defensive transformations in response to anxiety, on the one side, and disturbances energized by depression and the defensive transformations in response to depression on the other (Anthony, 1967).

From a descriptive point of view, psychopathology can be considered in two ways, transactional and developmental. The former considers the individual disturbance as part of a general matrix of disturbance involving the total responding environment, which includes such factors as family pathology and community tolerance. Developmental psychopathology, on the other hand, is concerned with changes over time in individuals and their symptoms or in the developmental antecedents of later adult disorders. The transactional approach is mainly cross-sectional and attempts to build up the concerted picture of the developed syndrome from a sample of cases manifesting the syndrome. The developmental approach tries to trace the "natural history" of the disturbance from its earliest onset to its termination without therapeutic intervention.

Transactional Psychopathology

Transactional psychopathology attempts to follow the repercussions of a behavior disorder through the several environments in which an individual lives. In ecological terms, it tries to delineate the ecosphere item by item and the movements of the individual within this total environment in response to this total environment over a measurable period of time, such as a day. It represents a cross-sectional way of looking at the patient.

Following the child through his "behavioral day," one can begin to map out the size of his world, the various geographical elements that structure it, and the gradations of familiarity with which he knows it. His degree of adjustment within the different regions of this world may vary considerably, and there are parts that constitute "trouble spots," where his behavior seems distinctly maladapted, and areas where he "feels at home," where behavioral deviances are minimal.

These would be for the most part descriptive, since the science of the human psychological environment is not yet advanced enough to carry out factor or cluster analyses as biological ecology can currently do.

However, the psychologist has the advantage in being able to extract from the individual a biased picture of his environment, the bias itself providing significant information. For example, if children are asked to map out their world on an elementary grid system, one may find an amplification or elimination of significant parts. In Fig. 3 a 7-year-old girl has mapped her world as she lives in it and experiences it. The disproportionately large unnamed structure in the middle of the grid represents a bridge under which, a year previously, she had been sexually assaulted by a man under very distressing circumstances.

Reactions to and interactions with meaningful people in this total environment are then elicited and illustrative transactions from remembered specific encounters are then recorded. The transactions are samples from the immediate and remote parts of the environment with home as the point of departure. They take place with parents, with siblings, with relatives, friends, and neighbors, with teachers and schoolmates, with pediatricians, dentists, shopkeepers, and others.

Parents with a serious physical illness such as tuberculosis may also occasion a series of reactive disorders in the children, but once again if the identification-involvement process is powerful enough, the child may show curious parasomatic symptoms suggestive at times of conversion states and at others of hypochondriasis. The symptoms may simulate those of the sick parent, but because of the child's naive medical knowledge may caricature the original illness in bizarre ways. When the illness is infectious, as is tuberculosis, the requirement of the parent to keep a safe distance from the child and to refrain from such intimacies as kissing and hugging may be particularly upsetting for the younger child who cannot understand the need for distancing and segregation. A dangerous image of the parent may be inculcated so that some children eventually do show reactions of fear when brought into contact with the parent.

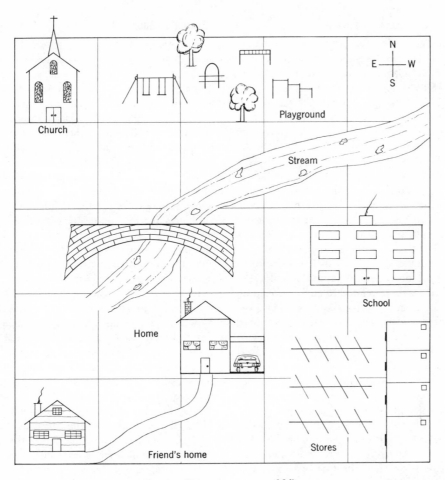

Fig. 3. "Mapping my world."

Parental Attitudes and Childhood Disorder

The influence of solicitous, indulging, permissive, authoritarian, neglecting, and rejecting parents on the various disorders promoted in their children has already been discussed. It is, however, important to keep the relative nature of such transactions in mind since they vary with the situation. Anna Freud (1955) has pointed out that a mother may reject a child at one stage of development and not at another, at one time of the month (during the menstrual phase) and not at another, at one time of the day and not at another, and in relation to some activities and not to others. Although some attitudes have a characterological, predictable, and fairly permanent quality to them, there are many others that are situationally determined and are reversible or modifiable.

The subtle influence of a mother on her younger children often seems to act like a contagion (Escalona, 1953) so that if fears of the child are check-listed alongside those of the mother, many of the reactions can be seen to be shared. On the psychosomatic level, depressive illness in the mother has been found to have a significant association with feeding difficulties, vomiting, and rumination in her infant. The paramenstruum in the mother (Dalton, 1966) has been shown in one study to be closely linked with the incidence of acute coryza in her preschool children. (The influence of the menstrual period on behavior disorders in girls has also been demonstrated by Dalton. She found that 45% of misdemeanors in school, 46% of acute psychiatric disorders, 52% of accidents occurred during the paramenstruum.)

The Hyperaggressive Parent

Hyperaggressiveness, when it occurs as a central feature of parental psychopathology, may be associated with grave disturbances in the child ranging from hyperaggressiveness to an almost complete inhibition of all aggressive responses. In its extreme murderous form in the mother, it has been referred to as the Medea complex (Wittles, 1933), dynamically understood by Stern (1948) as a displacement of death wishes from the father. Anthony (1957) described a group of "murderous mothers" whose aggressive psychopathology extended from the overt murderously intended act to subtle and covert wishes to attack the child. Each mother was referred to this sample with an irresistible impulse to kill one of her offspring and this cold, encapsulated wish, unrelated to any provocation, was differentiated by the mothers themselves from provoked aggression with subsequent punitive action. The encapsulated wish clearly represented a transferred or displaced affect since it was dissociated from any explicable cause-and-effect aggressive sequence. In this sense, it could be regarded as an obsessional thought and the gap between the thought and the act of killing related to differences in the nature of the parent's psychopathology. Filicidal and infanticidal acts were psychotic; primitive, brutal behavior was mostly psychopathic; encapsulated ideas and impulses were mostly depressive and obsessional. Whereas the obsessional parents are characteristically overcome with guilt, the battering parents show little or none, and their relationship learning seems fixed at the level of brutal experiences with their own parents without modification from subsequent relational experiences. The "scarlet thread" of aggression running through the generation, according to Sears (1957), is certainly there, but the modeling or shaping process is not always visible and overt so that hyperaggressiveness may at times appear to skip a generation. Hyperagressiveness in the child may stem from hyperagressiveness in the parent ("identification with the aggressor") from erotic overstimulation by the parents, from emotional deprivation, and from (presumably) constitutional factors as in the case of the hyperkinetic, anxiety-driven child.

Sibling Jealousy

Transactional psychopathology involving siblings may take the form of jealousy, envy, bullying, teasing, aggressive attacks, cruelty, sexual exploration, and various forms of scapegoating. In the miniature society of the family, the siblings may separate out as a subgroup, particularly when the parents are habitually unavailable or busy. Within the subgroup, many of the parental functions are duplicated and substitute parental relationships may be established. In its extreme form, the "pecking order" of the siblings may create problems for the more stress-sensitive of the children, since sibling government is usually less merciful in its operations. In other families, territoriality may become so extreme that a child, sharing a room with another child, may have his floor space reduced to a bare minimum with dire threats of punishment. When certain of the children, the smaller or handicapped ones, are given "diplomatic immunity" by the parents, the sibling reaction may become exaggerated and acted out in antisocial ways in school or on the playground on other children.

The family may be split into subgroups along the age axis or the sex axis so that younger and older, or male and female, may become embroiled in internecine warfare. In such cases, the behavior disorders of the children are often kept strictly within the family so that the school reports nothing but good behavior. Under authoritarian or inhibitory conditions at home, the reverse may be true; the school may refer the child to the clinic and the parents come unwillingly, wondering what the problem is. As might be expected, teachers are sensitive to the more externalizing types of disorders with high annoyance value for a classroom, and although they are now more sensitive to the disturbances of the "model" child than they used to be 20 years ago, they are still more prone to refer disturbing rather than disturbed children.

Sex Differences and Psychopathology

Up until puberty, it is extremely difficult to find a pathological condition in which the incidence among girls is greater than among boys, and some authors have spoken of the "handicap" of being male. The developmental rates are markedly different, judging from bone age, dental age, and the development of the reproductive system. At the age of 6, girls are already a developmental year ahead and this becomes 18 months by age 9. The greater vulnerability to stress on the part of the male begins during pregnancy and birth, when he shows a much higher fetal, neonatal, and stillbirth rate; this extends into the whole of the first year. During the first grade, the boy is referred eleven times as often as a girl for social and emotional immaturity, a syndrome characterized by a high rate of absenteeism, fatigability, inability to attend and concentrate, shyness, poor motivation for work, underweight, inability to follow directions, slow learning, infantile speech patterns, and problems in the visual-motor and visual-perception areas. As a school child, he is referred to the school clinic for stuttering (four to one), reading difficulty (five to one), speech, hearing and eye problems (four to one), and eventually to the psychiatric clinic for personality disorders (2.6 to 1), behavior problems (4.4 to 1), school failure (2.6 to 1), and delinquency (4.5 to 1).

Bentzen (1963) emphasizes the snowballing of events which eventually brings boys in such a preponderance into the child guidance clinics. She says that "a society which recognizes only covertly the possibility of such a relationship between a biologically-determined developmental differential between the sexes and the male predominance in learning and behavior disorders may itself precipitate stress and trauma thereby initiating the deviant behavior response patterns that society has come to expect as 'normal' for boys."

The effect of sex differences probably depends largely on whatever cultural factors are currently determining sex roles. The sexes are less differentiated in school in terms of their abilities than in the clinic in terms of their symptoms. Many of the behavioral traits that tend to show up at an early age, such as aggressiveness and activity, might be more related to physical and hormonal factors, but it is unlikely that any of them is determined by physical factors alone. The fact that girls tend to develop internalizing syndromes more often than boys might be inferred from several studies, including Terman's (1925), which indicated that girls had the edge over boys in terms of fearfulness, timidity, and a tendency to worry. School studies in general report more problem behavior among boys, but the undesirable behavior in question is invariably of the aggressive kind involving disobedience, defiance, destructiveness, and cruelty. Studies have invariably reported a much greater frequency of quarrelsome behavior among boys.

The Ordinal Position and Psychopathology

A good deal of folklore has grown up around ordinal positions and clinical investigators appear to have been influenced by some of it. Long ago, Stanley Hall made the comment that "being an only child is a disease in itself" and this began a large number of studies purporting to demonstrate that a lack of "corrective sibling experience" during development was sufficient in itself to generate pathological attitudes and behavior. Burt (1925) found that the proportion of only children in a delinquent group was greatly in excess of that found among nondelinquent controls (12.2% to 1.7%). The emphasis on "the dangers of being an only child" (Hooker, 1931) led inevitably to a consideration of the dangers involved in being a child in any one of the ordinal positions. And it took a careful study by Goodenough and Leaky (1927) to make the point that any position in the family involved certain problems of adjustment.

In a sample of 400 consecutive cases at a children's clinic for "problem children," Reynolds (1925) found that oldest children made up 27% of the sample, youngest, 20.8%, only, 11.8%, and adopted, 6%. In Goodenough's study at about the same time (1924), in a sample of 322 consecutive cases, oldest children comprised 30.4%, youngest, 25.5%, only, 12.7%, and middle, 31.7%, the ratio of boys to girls being 2:1. With regard to specific behavioral problems, she found that oldest children had the highest rate for temper tantrums (this was especially so for girls), that only children were highest for rebellious attitudes, neurotic traits (nervousness, timidity, sleep disturbances, fearfulness, and feeding problems), and enuresis; middle children predominated in the conduct disorders; but youngest children showed no outstanding symptomatic characteristics. If anything, only children show a somewhat greater tendency to develop an overprotection syndrome, either of the indulgence variety when they are aggressive, domineering, quarrelsome, selfish, egoistical, unpopular, exhibitionistic, and "spoilt" or the dominated variety when they are shy, seclusive, sensitive, overimaginative, and asocial. More rigorous studies are certainly called for in this area, with greater appreciation of the "dynamics" of the ordinal positions. In future studies, the character of the ordinal "sandwich" must be brought out, that is, whether a particular child is flanked by two boys, two girls, by a boy and girl or by one child only as in the oldest and youngest positions.

Another as yet inadequately investigated psychological factor that might bear interestingly on the development of psychopathology in the child was termed "the margin of safety" by Katz (1951). The concept has to do with the amount of precautionary measures an individual feels that he must use in order to feel comfortably safe during an undertaking, and has a direct relationship to risk-taking.

In adult life, there are people who arrive at stations an hour before the train must leave and spend the time anxiously checking and rechecking their tickets and baggage; there are others who just make it "by the skin of their teeth" and enjoy the elation of almost missing it. Anxious, fearful, phobic, obsessional children tend to operate with wide margins of safety, whereas acting-out, impulsive, accident prone, hyperactive, and delinquent children function with often

frighteningly narrow margins, apparently undelivered by the past experiences of "not making it." In testing maneuvers (such as carrying a full glass of water over a measured distance, the hand pressure being transmitted to a measuring device) the difference between children can be marked. In many cases, the past history of the child—chronic oversolicitude on the part of a mother or a protracted and painful hospital experience— appears to have a close bearing on the response.

Antisocial Psychopathology

Careful developmental studies of the antisocial characters have not been carried out, so that most appraisals are cross-sectional and transactional. Since these individuals are also resistant to psychotherapy and do not tolerate the procedure for any sufficient length of time, there has been a vast accumulation of social information but very little in depth.

Delinquency, since it is relatively easy to recognize and gives the illusion of being a homogeneous condition, has been more investigated than other psychiatric syndromes. With the use of factor analytic techniques, it has been categorized in several ways by several authors as indicated in Table 12. It will be seen from this table that there is a rough agreement on the existence of categories of sociopath, psychopath, and neuropath, although Beck has also included an organic group.

The conditions for delinquency are created by the nature of the parent-child relationship, by defects and disturbances in the parent, and by conditions of the environment. As compared with nondelinquent children, who

Table 12. Categories of Delinquency

Hewitt and Jenkins (1941)	Riess (1952)	Beck (1958)	Petersen (1959)
1. Socialized	1. Integrated	1. Social	1. Inadequate
2. Unsocialized, aggressive	2. Superego defect	2. Asocial	2. Psychopathic
3. Maladjusted, withdrawing	3. Ego defect	3. Neurotic	3. Neurotic
		4. Accidental, organic	

Table 13. Conditions for Delinquency

Parent-Child Relationship	Parental Quality	Habitual Haunts
1. Overstrict paternal discipline	1. Criminality (both)	1. Distant neighborhoods
2. Unsuitable maternal supervision	2. Mental disturbance (both)	2. Street corners
3. Paternal indifference or hostility	3. Mental retardation (especially mother)	3. Vacant lots
4. Maternal indifference or hostility	4. Drunkenness (especially father)	4. Railway yards
5. Unintegrated family	5. Serious physical ailment (both)	5. Waterfronts, cheap poolrooms, dance halls

After Glueck and Glueck (1950).

tend to remain at home or in official play-grounds, the delinquent invariably finds his way to unsavory haunts. The Gluecks (1950) have been able to use the characteristics of the parent-child relationship as predictors of future delinquency (Table 13). In Table 14, McKegney (1967) has attempted to isolate significant behavioral variables within a de-linquent population, and again one can per-ceive the components of fight and flight with an intermediate component of apparent adap-tation to the situation. When all the condi-tions mentioned in Table 14 are satisfied, de-linquency becomes a way of life that is "natural" to the delinquent. In order to change, the delinquent must meet an experi-ence sufficiently moving to force him to re-orient himself and modify his delinquent techniques. Recent work would suggest that this experience is more likely to succeed if the delinquent can be approached through interest in himself.

Toward a Developmental Psychopathology

An integrated theory of the behavior dis-orders of childhood needs, above all, to be developmental so that the occurrence of pathology can be seen against the orderly progression of the nonpathological spheres. To create a genuine developmental psycho-

pathology, the concomitant developments in psychophysiology and psychology should form a background for the evolving disturbance, sharing in it in certain ways. It would there-fore seem appropriate to examine this sup-porting structure in further detail.

Developmental Psychophysiology. Stern and his co-workers (1968) are currently studying the effective developmental factors on spontaneous fluctuations, habituation, and conditionability of physiological response sys-tems and are making use of these measures: (1) to define "critical periods" of develop-ment during which the child must be exposed to a more or less specific series of life experi-

Table 14. Composition of Behavior Traits within a Delinquent Population

Trait	Incidence
1. Aggression	13%
2. Isolation	10.5%
3. Flight	17%
4. Conformity	12%
5. Socialization	24%
N = 200	

After McKegney (1967).

Note: The Ss were considered to manifest that trait by the criterion of possessing two-thirds of significant variables in that trait.

ences in order to develop normally; (2) to predict the development of later pathology, both somatic and psychopathologic; and (3) to relate the psychophysiological findings to the development of such psychological variables as trust and cooperativeness.

The developmental hypotheses under experimental scrutiny suggest that lability in physiological systems varies systematically as a function of age-related factors as part of the general tendency for lability to decrease with age; that changes in lability in given physiological measures will be correlated with alterations in psychological development, and since the latter is a function of environmental factors, it is felt that these factors will also influence the physiological measures during development; and that the maintenance or development of high levels of lability in a given physiological system will predispose the organism to later developments of disturbance in that system. There is already much research evidence to indicate that undue lability in a physiologic system of process is an important indication of vulnerability to disease.

Stern (1968) has been especially concerned with the Sokolovian Model of the orienting response and its habituation and especially to the terminal orienting responses occurring toward the end of a stimulus provided it persists sufficiently long. This terminal phenomenon is also subject to the process of habituation. It has so far been demonstrated that younger children, in comparison with older children and adults, show more terminal orienting responses and a slower rate of habituation to such responses.

In addition to lability studies, Stern has been investigating differentiation at a physiological level, making the useful distinction between stimulus and response differentiation. Contrary to expectation, recent data would suggest that the presence of manifest psychopathology may under certain conditions accelerate the differentiation, comparable to the precocious ego development occurring in certain obsessional children. In a psychophysiological study attempting to determine differences between the children of psychotic as compared with physically ill parents in terms of parameters of plethysmographic and electrodermal responsiveness, the general expectation was that children of mentally disturbed

parents, who themselves show marked disturbances (see later section), would manifest a more immature pattern of responsiveness than the controls. Figure 4, taken from Anthony (1968), demonstrates a surprising reversal of expectation.

One explanation of why children differ so clearly from adults in terms of their response to the termination of a stimulus complex is that because of their shorter attention span, they may be less able to form an image of a stimulus as a single event and so respond to its onset and offset as two distinct events.

It is difficult, at the present state of knowledge, to be sure how much the "microgenesis" observed in the psychophysiological laboratory represents a "slice of life" and a miniaturization of a long-term tendency. Is the electrophysiological "maturity" or "immaturity" that shows itself a reaction stemming from a chronic, ingrained tendency, or is it a response to the here-and-now provocations of the peculiar environment of the laboratory?

The same is true of the EEG where artifacts of various kinds are very likely to intrude because of the nature of the apparatus and the situation. If one follows a child through a particular session, he may recapitulate his EEG progress through life, especially if he falls asleep during the session. At the beginning of life, one sees the slow activity seen later only in sleep, and it clearly has to do with the inactivity of the infant. As the child gets older, this delta activity becomes intermittent and declines gradually until the tenth year. The theta rhythms reach a peak around 5 years and then subside into adolescence. The alpha rhythms are first seen at about 9-11 and persist as the dominant rhythms into adult life. As the child becomes drowsy and falls asleep, this sequence reverses itself.

The slow rhythms, as already mentioned, can be observed in delinquent children, especially those who are docile and easily led into trouble (Grey Walter, 1953). Next, there is an "astonishing correspondence" between the age of frequencies of theta rhythms and temper tantrums in children. Finally, around age 9 there is a differentiation in alpha rhythm into those whose alpha persists even in an alert, attending situation and those in whom there is little or no alpha at any time. There has been some suggestion that this

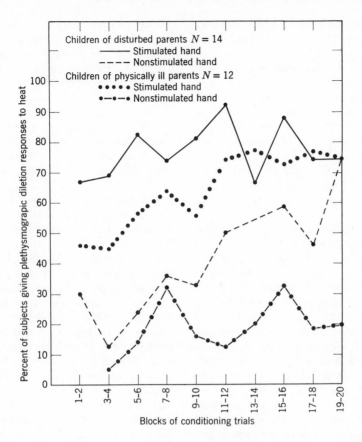

Fig. 4.

division at this age may be significantly related to the appearance of reading disabilities.

A great deal of work remains to be done in the psychophysiological area and its prime importance may lie in helping in the differentiation of externalizing and internalizing syndromes. It has already been shown that children who give minimal expressive response to an emotional stimulus may still show a considerable P.G.R. response and vice versa, but autonomic "flatness" may also be linked to a flat effect. The relationship of EEG (alpha) reactivity and P.G.R. reactivity has not as yet been clarified.

Developmental Psychology. Werner (1957) postulated an orthogenic, regulative principle which stated that development proceeded from a state of relative globality and lack of differentiation to a state of increasing differentiation, articulation, and hierarchic integration. According to this principle, which, of course, also implies directiveness, a relative lack of differentiation between subject and object was developmentally prior to one in which there was a subject-object polarity. The increasing differentiation also involved the corollary that the organism became increasingly less dominated by the immediate concrete situation, less stimulus-bound, and less impelled by his own affective states.

As a consequence of this freedom, there was a clearer understanding of goals, a possibility of employing substitutive means and alternative ends, and, hence a greater capacity for delay and planned action. The individual can exercise choice, willfully rearrange a situation, and manipulate the environment rather than respond passively to it. In Piaget's terms, the child was less egocentric and less given to interpreting the external world solely in terms of his own subjective needs and feelings. According to him, there is a major developmental revolution from preoperational to postoperational thinking between the years of 6 and 8, and, at the same time, there is also an interesting shift on the Rorschach from undifferentiated, diffuse global responses to small, detailed responses (Friedman, 1952).

Differentiation, in this developmental context, means horizontal differentiation or more differentiated functioning within a circumscribed developmental stage. Vertical differentiation implies that the maturer individual will manifest a wider range of genetically different operations, that is, he will be able to perform at genetically different levels. This would imply a certain degree of mobility as opposed to the greater fixity of the more immature individual.

Psychological differentiation, as a function of the complexity of a system's structure, has been systematically and experimentally explored by Witkin (1962), who has further refined the principle by relating it to the concept of field dependency and independency. Witkin notes that at each level of differentiation varied modes of integration are possible and that adjustment is mainly a function of effectiveness of integration. However, it is possible for a poorly developed differentiation as a result of an inadequately formed nervous system to become a primary source of psychopathology. The capacity for differentiation and its rate of progress is dependent on the constitutional characteristics of the child and the particular circumstances under which he grows up, which may either foster or hinder this development.

The concept of field dependence emerged initially from studies of perception of the upright in space in which several ingenious perceptual tests were employed. An analytical and a global mode of perceiving were isolated in these studies, the one representing a tendency to experience items as discrete from their backgrounds and the other, in contrast, representing failure to overcome the influence of an embedding context. Witkin feels that a tendency toward an analytical or global way of perceiving characterizes a person's perception and shows a marked individual self-consistency.

Working with disturbed children, Pollack and Goldfarb (1962) found that performances ranged over the entire perceptual continuum, but that there was a tendency to cluster toward the extremes of the distribution, suggesting that psychopathology is less likely to develop among the "intermediates" than among the "extremes." Individuals with a global field approach tended to suffer from identity problems, poor ego controls, strong feelings of inadequacy, passivity, and helplessness. Patients with an analytic approach, on the other hand, were outwardly aggressive, isolated, and overideational in their thinking. Marked field dependency was also found in clinical groups with serious dependency problems, such as asthmatic children (Fishbein, 1958). In general, individuals who have been clinically evaluated as less differentiated tend to be significantly more field dependent than more differentiated groups. More differentiated patients would be those with organized symptoms and reasonably well-developed defensive structures, whereas undifferentiated patients would be likely to have

Table 15. A Perceptual Approach to Psychopathology

Degree of Psychological Differentiation	Ability to Overcome Embedding Context	Articulation of Experience	Clinical Picture
Undifferentiated children	Field dependent	Global approach	Poor impulse control; Serious identity problem; Marked dependency; Passivity; Lack of responsibility and initiative; Feelings of inadequacy and helplessness; Poor ego resources
Differentiated children	Field independent	Analytic approach	Well-organized neurotic defenses; Rigid controls; Overintellectualization; Circumscribed interpersonal relations; Emotionally distant; Paranoidal tendency

From Witkin.

Table 16. "Contrary Imaginations"

The Converger	The Diverger
1. Scores high on IQ tests and low on open-ended tests	1. Scores low on IQ tests and high on open-ended tests
2. Has a nonverbal bias and uses words carefully and economically	2. Has a verbal bias and tends to be articulate and communicative
3. Is consistently accurate	3. Is erratic and only intermittently accurate
4. Has interests that are technical, mechanical, and action-oriented	4. Has interests that are cultural, artistic, contemplative
5. Is likely to be a physical scientist	5. Is likely to be an artist, historian, or linguist
6. Drawings are less likely to include people	6. Drawings are more likely to include people
7. Tends to give common or expected responses	7. Is more likely to give rare (less than 1% sample) responses
8. Responses are down-to-earth and in keeping with facts (occasionally there is a violent response that is ghoulish)	8. Responses tend to include the fantastic, the bizarre, and the violent
9. Shows a tendency to reflect majority openness	9. More likely to take minority positions on religious and political questions
10. Defenses lie in the direction of inhibition	10. Defenses lie in a subtle distortion of true openness

From Hudson.

inadequate and unstable personalities given to impulsive acting out and emotional discharge. This would roughly correspond to the division into internalizers and externalizers.

Witkin's evidence so far suggests that when they become psychologically ill, individuals with contrasting modes of field approach are likely to develop different kinds of psychopathology. Children with a global approach have problems of impulse control, a poorly developed sense of responsibility, and a lack of resources and initiative, as opposed to children with an analytic approach where the problems are more likely to stem from rigidity, emotional distance, overintellectualization, and a circumscription of interpersonal relations.

Witkin was alive to the possibility that these individual differences in the area of perception might also have their counterpart in intellectual functioning and that, for example, the basic ability to "break up" a configuration might equally well show itself in a problem-solving situation. An analysis of the subtests of the WISC indicated that effective performance on block design, picture completion, and object assembly required the overcoming of an embedding context. The analytic ability was not unlike the adaptive flexibility isolated by factor analysis by Guilford et al. (1957) using insight problems similar to those derived by Duncker in his classical studies and other problem-solving tests. Hudson (1966) has followed through on the work of Guilford and has extracted two "contrary imaginations," labeled converger and diverger, which represent the extremes of a normal distribution curve

(Table 16). These two types are fairly similar to Witkin's analytic and global and to Wynne's (1967) analytic and amorphous, which he feels may be a determining factor as to whether a schizophrenic develops a hebephrenic or paranoid type of illness.

There would be little reason not to suppose, although there is no evidence yet to support it, that these contrary imaginations would give rise to contrary psychopathologies in the manner suggested by Witkin. It might also be proved that the more open, global, amorphous, divergent thinker would give high penetration scores on Fischer's system of Rorschach analysis, whereas the other prototype would be more likely to create barriers. Piaget's classification of children into autonomous and heteronomous is also based on the differentiation principle and, like Witkin, Piaget attempts to relate the response to the extent of the influence exercised by the field. Piaget, however, sees the heteronomous child

Table 17. Schema for a Developmental Psychopathology

Ages	Educational Status	Psychosexual Stages (Freud)	Psychosocial Stages (Erikson)	Psychocognitive Stages (Piaget)	Psychoaffective Stages (Jersild)	Psychopathology
0-18m	(Infancy)	Oral	Basic Trust vs. Mistrust	Sensori-motor	Fears of Dark, Strangers, Aloneness Sudden noise Loss of support	Autism Anaclitic depression Feeding and sleeping problems Colic Failure to thrive
18m-3	(Nursery)	Anal	Antonomy vs. Doubt, Shame	Symbolic	Fears of Separation, Desertion, Sudden movements	Symbiosis Negativism Constipation Shyness and withdrawal Fearfulness Night terrors
3-5	Pre-school and Kindergarten	Genital Oedipal	Initiative vs. Guilt	Intuition, Representational	Animals Imaginary creatures Injury	Phobias Nightmares Speech problems Enuresis Encopresis Masturbation Anxiety states
6-11	Elementary School	Latency	Industry vs. Inferiority	Concrete Operational	School failure Ridicule Loss of possessions Disfigurement Disease Death	School problems School phobias Obsessive reactions Conversion symptoms Tics Depressive equivalents
12-17	High School Junior & Senior	Adolescent recapitulation	Identity vs. Role Confusion	Formal Operational	Being different physically, socially, intellectually, Sexual fears Loss of face	Identity diffusion Anorexia Nervosa Delinquency Acting out disorders Schizophrenia

Table 18. Primary Behavior Disorder

	Primary Behavior Disorder (Nuclear Syndrome)		
	Habit Disorder ↓	Neurotic Traits ↓	Conduct Disorder ↓
Syndromes	Psychophysical Disorders	Psychoneurotic Disorders	Personality Disorders
School refusal	Separation anxiety "Bilious attacks" Vomiting Abdominal pain Migraine	Specific phobias re: teachers, work, environment Anxiety Depression Obsessional state	Character disorder Borderline psychosis Psychosis
Anorexia Nervosa and Obesity	Obesity Bulimia Anorexia Vomiting	Hysteria Depression Obsessional state Anxiety state	Character disorder Borderline psychosis Psychosis
Tics	Motor restlessness Transient tics Mannerisms Habit spasms	Psychogenic tics Hysteria Obsessional state	Multiple tic syndrome Character disorder Borderline psychosis Psychosis
Delinquency	Enuresis Encopresis, Motor restlessness Food thieving	Neurotic delinquency Anxiety state Phobias Obsessional state	Psychopathic delinquency Character disorder Borderline psychosis Psychosis

merging through gradual developmental steps into the autonomous one with a strong sense of equality, justice, self-reliance, and self-determination. It could be that under pathological conditions, such development might fail to occur with the result that the child remains an undifferentiated, heteronomous individual, highly dependent on external authority for his attitudes and behavior. Mentally retarded children have been shown to remain at this first level.

It would appear that differentiation may be able to provide a unifying principle that might apply to all stages of development, both normal and abnormal. Piaget's assimilation-accommodation mechanisms seem less potent in the sphere of clinical development but the balance of the two mechanisms can be used to illuminate certain types of psychopathology.

Developmental Psychopathology

Developmental Psychopathology has so far been understood mainly in the context of psychoanalytic theory, but more recently, attempts are being made to link it with developmental psychology. The frames of reference, other than psychoanalytic, are still little more than skeletal, but a juxtapositioning of theoretical points of view does indicate some interesting convergences that might help to stimulate research, especially in the area of "intermediate" theorizing (Zigler, 1964). In Table 17, a schema is put forward for a possible developmental psychopathology, the aim being to understand the various disorders in terms of the psychosexual, psychosocial, psychocognitive, and psychoaffective operations at work during any particular stage. At the present time, this could not be expected to do more than generate hypotheses, but it could break ground in an important but un-researched area.

The Primary Behavior Disorders

As a further heuristic exercise, it is possible to look upon the primary behavior disorders of childhood as a nuclear syndrome with internalizing, externalizing, and somatic components. As the child develops, and the pressures that confront him become more specific and classifiable, the three nuclear components, depending on their preponderance in the original syndrome, may begin to produce differential effects so that more specific syndromes begin to emerge out of the diffuse primary behavioral background. In Table 18, examples are given of this in relation to school refusal, anorexia nervosa, obesity, tics, and delinquency.

Depending on the original preponderance and later treatment by the environment, different types of the same disorder present themselves. For example, school refusal at first-grade level may be obviously a separation anxiety with much clinging to the mother and a large psychophysical display. In the latency child, the separation anxiety may be less easy to detect and the phobic displacement onto teachers or school in general may be very marked, as might be the associated anxiety, depression, or obsessiveness. In the adolescent, the refusal becomes associated with severe character disorders or borderline psychosis, so that the reasons for refusal may seem quite inexplicable or bizzare. The same is apparent with the feeding disturbances and the motor disorders. In its simplest form, any one of these may represent a simple amplification and elaboration of the primary habit disorder. In its intermediate development, the anxiety is dealt with along characteristic psychoneurotic defensive lines and at a later stage the symptom is attached to a serious personality disorder in which treatment is difficult and the prognosis grave.

Two authors, Wertz (1962) and Anderson (1962), have attempted to follow the behavior disorders, both primary and secondary types, through childhood into adolescence. According to Wertz, there is a constant ebb and flow of behavior disorder symptomatology until the child enters adolescence, with usually a preponderance of one type, the other types playing a secondary role. From an in-spection of his clinical data, Wertz feels that his findings support the following clinical beliefs: (1) van Ophuijsen's contention that behavior disorders had their onset before the age of 3; (2) that the best way a disturbed child had of coping with his internal and external problems was to develop a conduct disorder; (3) that the type of behavior disorder that first appears in early childhood tends to persist as the major form until adolescence; (4) that the more "congenital activity" (Fries, 1957) that the child has available to him, the more likely is he to "thrust" into the environment and develop a conduct disorder, and, in contrast, the less he has, the more will his predominant pathology tend to take the form of a habit disorder or neurotic trait formation. The question, therefore, of which child internalizes and which externalizes may be a function of "motor energy"; (5) that the habit disorders are not "minor and transient" with only a slight emotional component, since they can be followed into adolescence and contribute a share to the upheaval at that time; and (6) that it is the child with conduct disorder, and not the quiet, withdrawn child, who is most likely to develop schizophrenia in maturity. This is in keeping with the views of O'Neil and Robins (1959) and Morris et al (1954), who may well have confused, through not taking it into account, the development of a process schizophrenia with its quiet, unobtrusive earlier history with the reactive schizo-affective disorder with its long history of turbulence and acting out.

Wertz conceives of the behavior disorders "as a barometer of the child's development as seen against the background of his mind-body complex and environment." Under relatively normal conditions, the symptoms ebb and flow, but when conditions become pathological, the type of behavior disorder remains more or less fixed, although even then it may transiently give place to some other type during latency. It is because of the child's essential nature—his constant growth and development, his malleability, his adaptive capacities, his psychological fluctuations—that his mode of symptomatic expression takes this characteristic form of the "behavior disorders." The translation from childhood to adult psychopathology begins to take place at adolescence mainly because of the greater need for a tightening of security measures against the increased aggressive and sexual drives that follow puberty.

Wertz presents his case very clearly and concisely when he says: "It is well to bear in mind that the psychological substratum of clinical behavior is a continuum from birth to death. The apparent differences between the problems of one age group as compared with another have a strikingly similar basis. The unresolved problems are being continuously re-presented for ongoing solution throughout an entire lifetime. The difference is found in the forces rather than the identity."

Whether or not the predominant type of behavior disturbance during childhood is of the habit, neurotic, or conduct type or a mixture of all three in varying proportions, there are often periods of quiescence, and almost invariably an acute exacerbation in adolescence. At this time, the condition may settle down into a chronic character disorder or erupt further into a psychosis.

The Secondary Behavior Disorders

The secondary behavior disorders have a different "natural history" with hardly any of the ebb and flow, the variability, or the periods of quiescence. Different authors have given them different names, for example, "the hyperkinetic behavior disorders" (Bradley, 1957), "the neurophrenias" (Doll, 1953), "the postencephalitic behavior disorders" (Levy, 1959), "brain damage" (Strauss and Lehtinen, 1947), "the association deficit pathology" (ADP) (Anderson, 1962). They have also been referred to in the literature under the headings of the Minimal Brain Damage Syndrome and Organic Brain Syndrome. Anderson has attempted to study the behavioral characteristics throughout the life span of the individual with this disorder, and she has observed very little change over time.

The manifestations vary somewhat from individual to individual depending on the original intellectual potential, the time, extent, and degree of sustained damage to the brain, and the life experiences subsequent to the damage, but the basic characteristics are present in all such individuals at all times of their history. These salient features are immaturity, poor interpersonal relationships, impulsivity, difficulty with change or shift in perspective, low frustration and stress tol-erance manifested in incongruous worries, temper tantrums, rages, panics, or major catastrophic reactions often indistinguishable from schizophrenic episodes.

In investigating a particular case, the following are the usual findings: a lifelong pattern of maladjustment; a history of birth injury or later infectious illness; a clinical combination of perseveration, stereotypy, and rigidity of response, associated with a difficulty in perceiving relationships (spatial, figure-ground, part-whole); a tendency to concreteness in thinking; and a lack of empathy in feeling. There are no pathognomonic tests that would allow a weight of positive or negative evidence to be accumulated for each case. The *WISC* may show patterns of scatter and a high performance low verbal discrepancy; the *Bender* may point to a disturbance in meaningful organization; the *Beery* may complement this finding and offer normative data in addition; the *TAT* may reveal an overall immaturity with a paucity of imagery, shallowness, stereotypy, and emphasis on concrete details; the *Rorschach* may be of poor quality, perseverative, and lacking in human movement; the *Sentence Completion* may offer an abundance of clichés, stereotypes, poor ideation, and inconsequential detail; and the *Draw-a-Person* may give evidence of general immaturity. The EEG is likely to show some abnormality in more than half the cases.

The natural history of the two types of behavior disorder is illustrated in Table 19.

The developmental antecedents of many adult psychiatric conditions have not been closely investigated by prospective studies; a fair indication of the childhood adjustment has been gained from several retrospective investigations. As already mentioned in earlier sections, psychopathy and criminality have their antecedents in conduct disorders during all phases of childhood; anxious adults have been anxious children; and obsessional adults have, in a majority of cases shown obsessional traits in earlier life; manic depression can have antecedents in earlier mood swings and hypochondriacal concerns (Anthony and Scott, 1960); and schizophrenia may show process or reactive precursors (Anthony, 1968).

In summing up, it would seem that there exist enough conceptual thinking and initial

Table 19. The Natural History of the Primary and Secondary Behavior Disorders

Class of Disorder	Preschool	Latency	Early Adolescence	Late Adolescence
Primary behavior disorder	Feeding problems Negativism Temper tantrums Sleep disturbance Enuresis Encopresis Demanding	Insomnia Nightmares Fears Depression Nail biting Nervousness Sibling jealousy	Truanting Lying Stealing Destructiveness Rages Poor scholastic achievement	School refusal Chronic depression Feelings of inadequacy and inferiority Mistrustfulness Sexual problems
Clinic diagnosis	P.B.D. predominantly habit	P.B.D. predominantly neurotic	P.B.D. predominantly conduct	Severe character disorder or early psychosis
Secondary behavior disorder	Restless "Driven" Distractible Impulsive Insensitive Low frustration tolerance Poor coordination Absence of guilt and shame	No essential change in clinical practice	No essential change, but less manageable because of explosive behavior and paranoid ideation	May either settle down into a shallow, egocentric, insensitive, impulsive adult with poor judgment or decompensate into psychosis under stress
Clinic diagnosis	Organic brain syndrome (Hyperkinetic)	Organic brain syndrome	Organic brain syndrome	Organic brain syndrome

data to set up an ongoing research program in developmental psychopathology which should be of inestimable worth to the clinical world, especially if based firmly on a developmental triad of neurology, psychophysiology, and psychology. It would certainly add a firm scientific structure to the practice of child psychiatry, which is, at present, lacking.

THE EXPERIMENTAL APPROACH TO THE PSYCHOPATHOLOGY OF CHILDHOOD

Clinicians, as a group, are inclined to be both skeptical and disapproving of the experimental approach, and since they are not profoundly concerned with the process of validation, they seem unable to see the role experiments might play in this regard. The developmental theories upon which clinical practice is based have been built largely upon observations which have never been submitted to experimental investigation. How

then, asks Zigler (1963), does one ever choose between systems when no criterion of validity exists independent of the system? In the absence of such a criterion, all such systems must be equally "true," and therefore the choice of a system must be largely personal. He points out that "observation is not what is at fault, but the failure of developmentalists to appreciate the importance of maximizing the stability of observation. Such stability and objectivity are maximally provided by the experiment" (p. 351).

He then goes on to describe two kinds of experiments: one, an extension of natural observation in which the natural situation is duplicated in the laboratory and a number of controls are exerted to discover the relationship between particular variables; the other, phenomena which would be unlikely to exist in the outside world are created in the laboratory. Herein lies the quandary: it is difficult, in fact, to establish "natural" conditions in the laboratory, and when conditions are highly artificial, it is difficult to generalize the findings outside the laboratory. Thus it is easy to understand the predilection of clinicians for natural observation.

The inherent difficulties of the experimental approach in clinical studies have also been discussed by another clinical investigator whose wide frame of reference allowed him to explore all available research avenues. Levy (1963) has this to say about the ideal of the controlled experiment in the study of the mother-child dyad:

The most convincing evidence in science is that derived by experiment. Under certain given conditions certain results will follow. Anyone skilled enough to reject the experiment will, if the evidence is true, come out with the same result. But our material does not ordinarily lend itself to the controlled conditions required by laboratory procedures. A study of mothers who have marked difficulties with their children is best checked against a study of mothers who have little or no difficulties with their children. But mothers do not present themselves for study unless they have difficulties, and although willing to answer superficial questions or even fill out questionnaires, they are not ready to submit to the intensive examinations required for thorough investigation. Difficulties in acquiring normal samples as controls may be solved some future day (p. 13).

In the last two decades, "normal" controls have been acquired by payment, by the promise of pediatric care, and by appeals to humanitarian values such as "helping science." Unfortunately, the volunteers often turn out to be something less than controls activated by doubtful motives. Nevertheless, by perseverance, an acceptable control group can now frequently be built up even though "drop-outs" are not infrequent.

Levy feels that control of all conditions for the purpose of an experiment would require complete isolation of mother and child. Even if this were possible, uncontrolled factors would always complicate the procedure. He concludes that "we try to do the best with what we have," and his "best" method is to study the factor under investigation in its most exaggerated or "pure" form so that it can be seen more clearly and in relation to all pertinent data. The selection of such cases affords an opportunity for approximating, he

Table 20. Clinical Groupings of Children Who Later Became Schizophrenic

Author	N	Grouping
Kunkel (1920)	?	I. Quiet, shy; II. Nervous, excitable; III. Inactive, apathetic; IV. Docile, "model"
Kasanin (1932)	49	I. Odd, peculiar (22.2%); II. Mildly maladjusted (29.6%); III. Average adjustment (9.3%); IV. Outstanding (11.1%); V. "Shut in" (27.8%)
Birren (1944)	53	I. Apathetic (15.1%); II. Excitable (1.9%); III. Normal rapport (11.3%) (based on test behavior)
Wittman (1944)	86	I. "Shut in" (50%); II. Excitable (0%); III. Timid, immature ("a fair number"); IV. Friendly, pleasant ("very few")
O'Neal and Robins (1959)	524	I. Delinquent (6%); II. Antisocial (30%); III. Neurotic (15%); IV. Normal controls (3%) (refers to later "psychotic reactions" not specifically schizophrenia)
Morris (1954)	606	I. Introverts (0.16%); II. Ambiverts (0.99%); III. Extroverts (0.49%)
Bower (1960)	44	(Using Kasanin's groupings) I. (20.5%); II. (43.2%); III. (20.5%); IV. (6.8%); V. (9.0%)
Gardner (1967)	60	Distribution of neurotic symptoms for boys and girls: I. Anxious (58%, 65%); II. Phobic (18%, 17%); III. Obsessive-compulsive (30%, 27%); IV. Hysterical (3%, 12%)

feels, "the requirements of ideal human experiments" (p. 19).

Luria (1932) offered a mode of approach that constituted a characteristic expression of the Russian school of laboratory work into the clinical field and the effort was warmly welcomed in America by Adolf Meyer, among others, who saw it as "a true psychobiology and not largely neurologising tautologies" (1932).

Luria was successful in obtaining artificial models simulating actual effects but the conflicts and experimental neuroses that he was able to establish prevailed within the borders of a very limited system and did not extend into the entire personality. His ultimate aim was to produce stable and enduring affective disturbances.

Earlier, Lewis (1929) had also occupied himself with the problem of "the serious experiment" in which "the failure in the experiment begins with the failure in life," and he was the first experimental psychologist who succeeded in artificially producing changes not limited to the role of the experiment but making contact with the personality itself.

Spurred on by such considerations, Luria undertook and carried out the task of producing synthetically a complete model of a stable and intense disorganization of behavior in adult neurotics, but, perhaps for ethical reasons, his clinical experimental studies of children were restricted to the investigation of coping and organizational behavior in the normal and retarded. For example, he studied the motor responses that were made indicating a choice (pointing) on reception of a stimulus. The complicated trajectory was registered by means of a small light fastened to the extended finger. In this way a cyclogram was obtained showing simple, delayed, irregular, and chaotic patterns of movements. The younger and more retarded children tended to give undifferentiated and diffuse responses in a direct, impulsive manner.

Eysenck (1960) has criticized the traditional paradigm of psychiatric research in which two groups are compared and contrasted for significant differences as summarized in the mathematical statement that X members of class Y show behavior Z and suggested instead the paradigm of the experimental psychologist, summarized in the statement that change in the independent variable X produces a change Y in the function Z, where change Y might be in the direction of making function Z more or less "abnormal." He does not attempt to tackle the problem of "the serious experiment," and his whole approach with its characteristically cold, detached, and distant quality would be doomed to failure with children since it would be unable to efface the border between life actions and the artificial response obtained in the laboratory. The clinicians would therefore be less likely to accept its authenticity or applicability, whereas they are prone to acknowledge the relevance of Lewin's "miniature life situations." Nevertheless, Eysenck's suggested framework should receive the serious consideration of every clinical investigator who is becoming disenchanted with the limited research goals provided by the repetitive exploration of intergroup differences.

Levy (1937) was on the way to following the Eysenck paradigm when he carried out an interesting investigation of sibling jealousy using the so-called amputation doll technique, which utilized dolls to represent the mother, a baby, and an older brother or sister. The child was exposed to a provocative situation—the baby at mother's breast—and his response was then categorized in several ways: an unwanted display of affection or helpfulness, a tendency to destructiveness, or varying forms of competitiveness. He may be subdued in his behavior as though he were grieving, or he may resort to vindictive action or fantasies of self-glorification. Children who suffer from the pathological jealousy may show quite contrasting behavior at different times and in different situations, and their reactions to the same person at different times may range from attacks to attempts to curry favor. The laboratory situation suggests that the repertoire of the jealous child may resemble that of any other disturbed person who tries many different techniques on meeting a problem.

The anthropologist Henry (1940) made use of the same technique to study Pilaga Indian children who, generally speaking, experience a great amount of affection and attention during early life and are then increasingly ignored and neglected until, with the coming of a new child, they are left entirely to their own resources. As a consequence, the little Pilaga Indian becomes a "poor, hostile, little flounderer for many years." The hostility was very obvious in the play.

A play situation with dolls was also used by Heinicke (1956) with a more elegant scoring device to study the aggressive responses of children who have been subjected to separation from the mother. Others (Paruch, 1941; Fite, 1940; Korner, 1947) have also made use of the same fruitful technique to explore aggressive reactions in children.

Frankel-Brunswik (1948) carried out an unfinished study of the perceptual and conceptual study of children with "authoritarian" personalities and prejudice. These children were, in many ways, disturbed children with strong sadomasochistic and obsessive-compulsive tendencies. This meant that they were rigid in their responses, unable to shift their attitudes with changing circumstances, intolerant of ambiguity, given to all-or-none dichotomized thinking, troubled by disorder and untidiness, and anxious to bring about closure.

In a series of little experiments, they differed significantly from freer, more liberal children. The experiments included the following types of situations: as a photograph that was gradually being brought into focus was still out of focus, the children were asked to guess what it was. The liberal children were able to alter their diagnosis with the changing data provided by the percept; the rigid children, having adopted a position, were unable to reorient themselves flexibly. Conditions of maximal ambiguity could produce almost catastrophic reactions in these subjects. Another situation would depict a zoo in which a small area was left untidy; the prejudiced children would not be satisfied until they had restored order in the smallest detail. A card would be presented depicting a group of zebras with one zebra isolated from the group with his stripes running in the opposite direction. The prejudiced children understood at once that the zebra on his own had been excluded because he was different.

Psychosomatic behavior lends itself to experimental investigation because of the objective indices of change provided by the condition itself. Asthmatic subjects respond asthmatically to the provocation of artificial flowers and to the suggestion of dust in the room. The respiratory records of children with asthma may change significantly as they listen to taped voices of their mothers, fathers, and neutral observers reading them a story. The voice of the mother brings about maximal changes in the breathing while that of the father hardly brings about more change than that of a neutral stranger. This would suggest that the psychopathology of the asthmatic child was more closely linked with the relationship with the mother than to the father, which would support the theory of separation anxiety as causative (1963).

Noting that many asthmatic children are relieved of their asthma when separated from their mothers and relapse when brought into contact with them again, Purcell (1962) has attempted to evaluate the separation factor by keeping the children in their normal environment at home and sending the parents away to a motel. According to him, asthmatics can be classified into psychogenic and physiogenic types, the latter also referred to as steroid-dependent, and it is those of the psychogenic variety who are sensitive to psychological precipitants, brought about in the first place by psychological causes, and relieved by largely psychological measures.

Anthony, a clinical investigator, returned from working with Piaget with the firm intention of approaching the psychopathology of childhood in an experimental way. In an overall review (1956), he attempted to outline the various ways in which Piaget's developmental psychology might help the clinical investigator to explore the abnormal developmental responses of children manifesting a wide range of disorders.

Encopresis and Enuresis (1957)

Anthony began his studies investigating the reaction of disgust in children with bowel incontinence. From a prior analysis of the background material, he dichotomized the subjects into two groups, the one in which the childhood incontinence was continuous with the infantile state of incontinence so that no bowel control had ever been established, and the other, the discontinuous type, in which toilet training had been successful and had broken down at some later date. From the clinical data, the continuous type was associated with a neglectful child-rearing experience, whereas the discontinuous cases gave a history of highly coercive techniques employed by the mother. It was predicted that the aversion reaction would distinguish between these two types and that it would also bear a direct relation to the duration of continence, the intensity of the "reaction formations," the degree of training pressure, and the social status.

To test these hypotheses, a perceptual battery was elaborated, each subtest involving one of the sensory modalities. The stimulus range was from pleasant to unpleasant, as graded by adult responses, and the subjects were rated on a 7-point scale with strong attraction and repulsion poles with a neutral response at point 4. In addition to verbal responses, motor and autonomic components of disgust behavior were noted. In only one case did vomiting occur in the test situation. On the basis of the ratings, the subjects were classified into strong, intermediate, weak, and unclassifiable reactors, first with respect to the individual subtests, and finally with respect to the battery as a whole. Attempts to assess retest reliability after periods of 3 and 6 months proved impractical since experience in this particular type of testing situation provided children with such vivid recollections of their first encounter with it that the two situations were not at all comparable. The perceptual battery consisted of a range of odors, a range of colors, a range of tactile experiences, and a word association test in which half the stimulus words had some reference to dirt and feces, the galvanic skin responses also being recorded. Also included was a visual test in which two illuminated disks were to be compared; one was a fixed size and the other could be made larger or smaller by means of a camera shutter device. Within the circle of the fixed

disk, there was a photographed scene depicting some toilet event. The subject was asked to adjust the movable disk to match exactly the fixed one and was rewarded for accuracy. This represented a modification of the original method of Bruner and Goodman (1947).

Long reaction times in the word association subtest and underestimation in the comparometer test were interpreted as aversion tendencies. The aversion reaction for the different sensory modalities are shown in Table 21. The ability of the different subtests to discriminate between the two functional tests was by no means the same. In this respect, they could be divided into good discriminators such as smell, intermediate discriminators such as touch, and poor discriminators such as sound and sight. The intercorrelations between smell and touch and smell and sound were fairly high, but those between moderate and poor discriminators were low or absent.

If any system of "perceptual defense" (Postman, 1953) was operating in these experimental situations, it was differentiating between presumably more threatening and less threatening sensory modalities. If Angyal's (1941) theory that the disgust reaction was an attempt to ward off the ingestion of excretory material was true, then the differential perceptual behavior is more understandable in that smell and touch can be fought off as constituting the more immediate

Table 21. Strong Aversion Reaction for Different Sensory Modalities

Perceptual Battery	"Continuous" Type (%)	"Discontinuous" Type (%)	Level of Confidence (%)
Smell	7	90	0.3
Colour	17	14	Not sig.
Touch	21	53	1
Sight[a]	43	67	10
Sound[a]	37	60	10

[a] Long reaction time in the word association subtest and underestimation in the comparometer test have been interpreted as aversion tendencies.

threat. With vision and hearing, there is warning of a possible threatening situation at a distance so that withdrawal can take place in time. The aversion reaction was also found to bear a fairly constant relationship to the period of bowel continence and to the extent of "reaction formation" established in the children.

Sleep Disturbances (1959)

A group of children suffering from sleep disturbances of a specific kind—night terrors, nightmares, and sleep walking—were compared with a control group of subjects also derived from the clinic population but with no history of significant sleep disturbance. A series of test situations explored the excitability, tenseness, emotionality, fearfulness, egocentrism, suggestibility, and imagination, significant differences being found in the areas of tension, fearfulness, and suggestibility. There was borderline support for the experimental group being more imaginative as well.

Comparisons were then made of the tendency to visualize (Lowenfeld's battery), to perceive eidetic imagery (the Jaensch technique), and to substantialize and reify (Piaget). The groups were also compared with regard to the frequency, recency, and vividness of their dream imagery. Significant differences were found for the eidetic and visualizing tendency between the night terror and nightmare subgroups and the controls, but this did not hold for the sleep walkers, who reported significantly less dream imagery. When plotted against age, there was a gradual diminution in eidetic imagery and dream realism, with the visualizing capacity holding up throughout the age periods explored.

On the basis of the clinical and experimental findings, two nocturnal syndromes were isolated, a visual and a motor type. The visual syndrome was characterized by night terrors, nightmares, hyponogogic hallucinations, day terrors, and phobias. The subjects showed a strong visual and eidetic tendency and had frequent and vivid dreams. On intelligence tests, they were better on the verbal side, and the EEG showed little or no alpha rhythm. The motor syndrome, on the other hand, included symptoms of sleep walking, tics, stammering, and general restlessness. The subjects were generally haptic, and their dreams were poorly remembered and vague. On intelligence testing, they were better on the performance side, and their EEG showed persistent and prominent alpha rhythm. It would seem that the experimenter was exploring a constitutional tendency that determined the character of the sleep disturbance and in the light of this he quoted an aphorism from Galen that said: "Always this is to be remembered, that no cause is efficient without an aptitude of the body." A worthwhile reminder to the clinical investigator of the psychosomatic unity.

Family Relationships (1954)

In a third study, Anthony and Bene investigated the problem of ambivalence in children by means of a specially designed test called The Family Relations Test in which the subject posted predetermined "messages" into figures of various ages, shapes, and sizes, sufficiently stereotyped to stand for members of his family. The advantage of the test is that the child is not asked to verbalize analytically his many complex feelings for his family since this would probably lie outside his inclination and ability. He is only expected to make choices between preselected emotional attitudes which are general enough to fit into the frame of reference of any child and moreover are expressed in his language. In addition to the family representatives, another important figure is incorporated into the test, labeled "Mr. Nobody." This helps to accommodate those items which are not felt to apply to anyone in the family.

The "feeling" recorded in the message is inserted into a figure and immediately vanishes from sight, leaving no incriminating traces behind. As there is no visible reminder to the child of his distribution of love and hate, there is less guilt to interfere with his freedom of expression. The feelings, positive and negative, are divided into those that the child feels for his family and those that he thinks that his family feel for him. The ambivalence is measured by the ratio of positive and negative feelings posted into any particular figure.

The test has been used to explore family feeling in children suffering from various clinical conditions. It is equipped with devices for appraising egocentric attitudes and the strength of defenses against emotional expression. The results can also indicate the degree of ambivalence in the involvement with different family members, the extent to which positive and negative feelings have undergone inhibition or release, and the presence of discrepancies between incoming and outgoing feelings which may be of diagnostic importance. Comparisons of test results with case history and questionnaire material showed reasonably good agreement, and the odd-even reliability coefficients obtained for various parts of the test were around .80.

Autism (1958)

The fourth study in the series exploring clinical differences from an experimental point of view focused on autism or withdrawal. Once again, the clinical cases were dichotomized into continuous and discontinuous types depending on whether the onset occurred during infancy or later.

Since the phenomenon of attention was thought to be a crucial factor in the development of autism, it was studied in a stimulus-response setup, the stimulus being a graded series of sound produced by the dropping of a graded series of weights at a fixed distance from the respondent. The responses were rated on a scale ranging from a fully developed startle to a complete absence of attention and orientation. In a second experiment, the graduated series was replaced by a single loud sound, and the test was repeated every day for 8 days. The withdrawn children were matched against neurotic ones for age and sex. The characteristics of a fully developed autistic pattern were the complete absence of any startle response at any time, the lack of preparatory set after the first experience, the turning away from the stimulus source, an accelerated adaptation to the situation, and a large number of zero responses in which no attention was obtained.

Following this, the capacity for perceptual discrimination was investigated by means of an apparatus constructed for social conditioning and modeled on that of Smolensky. The unconditioned stimulus was a chocolate ball that ran down a trough and presented itself alluringly on a small stage facing the child. The conditioning stimulus was either a light or a buzzer and subsequently both. The reaching behavior of the child was recorded

on a continuously revolving drum by the breaking of three photoelectric circuits. The results were as follows: none of the autistic children could be conditioned with a light stimulus; there was some conditioning with sound but less than with the controls. Lack of reinforcement brought about quicker extinction in the autistic group, and thereafter the tendency seemed completely and permanently lost. One interpretation of these findings was that the rapid adaptation to the unexpected stimulus combined with the rapid extinction of the unrewarding stimulus helped to dissociate the individual from his environment and thereby conduced to autism.

In a third experiment, Piaget's study of the searching behavior of infants was standardized for use with older subjects. Each subject was given an "organismic" age derived from its chronological, mental, social, and bone age. When the autistic group was regarded as a whole, the peak behavior correlated roughly with organismic age and showed the same sequential trends as a normally developing infant.

A final investigation explored the egocentricity of the autistic child by means of a little experimental situation devised by Piaget and called by him "The Test of the Three Mountains." This consisted of a series of toy mountains of different configuration and height. A toy child was manipulated into climbing the mountains one after another. At the top of each he was reported to have taken a photograph of the landscape in front of him. These photographs were then presented to the subjects, and they were then asked to identify the position from which the picture was taken. To do so with any degree of accuracy, the subject had to be able to put himself in the position of the perceiving toy child and perceive the situation from his point of view.

Piaget found that children under the age of 7 had difficulty in overcoming their subjective perspective, and he termed this the child's egocentricity. It was predicted that the autistic children would score highly on this perceptual test for egocentricity, and the percentage of responses did show a difference with some significance in the capacity of the autistic children to take up a normal perspective. The test was repeated after 7 days, and correlations for the test-retest scores were .92 for the neurotic group and .47 for those with autism.

Perceptual Anomaly—Micropsia (1960)

In the fifth experimental approach, the unusual psychiatric syndrome of micropsia was investigated. Micropsia is a perceptual syndrome in that the experience is almost entirely visual. The descriptions given of the microptic attack are usually similar: "Things become small and move far away; everything and everyone suddenly seem to get smaller and smaller and to go further and further away; it's like looking through the wrong end of the telescope."

There again appear to be two main varieties: psychogenic and physiogenic. In the former, the attack comes on gradually, lasts only a short time, seems to be confined to the diminution of people mainly and is associated with "hysterical" personality features and a psychogenic precipation. The physiogenic type has a sudden onset and is often prolonged. Consciousness is somewhat diminished and there may be associated epileptic attacks, a family history of epilepsy, and a dysrhythmia on the EEG.

The experimental approach included tests of size constancy and perceptual tests of size-distance discrepancies. The small numbers (17) did not lend themselves very comfortably to statistical analysis. Nonparametric methods were considered, but, because of the number of ties, were not used. It was postulated that there would be significant differences between the microptic and control groups in the degree of object constancy for short, fixed distance (Cambridge technique) as reflected in the Brunswick ratio, in the degree of size constancy over a wide range of distances (Holway-Boring technique), and

in the rating of perceptual awareness of size-distance discrepancies on a perceptual card test. The findings are summarized in Table 22.

From the clinical findings and experimental investigations, the group of microptic children emerge as introspective, sensitive, and unstable, with a tendency toward experiencing unusual subjective sensations and reacting inordinately to them. They tended to show a low constancy in size judgments, a poor appreciation of size-distance relationships which builds them to gross artificial discrepancies, and a "realism" (in a Piaget-type of inquiry) that causes them to interpret as actual the apparent shrinking of the object with distance. As the distance of the object from them increases, their misinterpretation of size increases, and their viewpoint becomes increasingly dominated by "the law of the visual angle." If one is to place any credit on the statements of the children indicating object size during the microptic attacks, it would appear that their estimates would bring them very close to the theoretical condition in which perceived size is predicted on the basis of geometrical optics. The microptic subjects at these times seem to be perceiving their unchanged retinal images.

The Children of Psychotic Parents (1968)

In a sixth investigation dealing with an experimental approach to the developmental antecedents of schizophrenia, Anthony investigated the childhood premorbid states of high-risk children and the correlations between specific psychotic disturbances in schizophrenic parents and response behavior in their children. As a general hypothesis, it was postulated that the children of psychotic parents would tend to overdifferentiation or underdifferentiation as compared with con-

Table 22.

Investigation	M_e	$\triangle_e$	M_c	$\triangle_c$	D	C.R.	Level of Sig.
Size constancy (B.R.)[a]	46	9.78	56	12.38	10	2.62	.01
Perceptual cards	2.1	.68	2.6	.48	.5	2.46	.05
Piaget interview	2.3	.67	2.8	.38	.5	2.67	.01

[a]Brunswik Ratio (B.R.) $= (P\text{-}S)/(R\text{-}S)$, where $P =$ phenomenal size
$R =$ real size
$S =$ "stimulus" size

trols (the children of physically ill parents). Subsidiary hypotheses were related to possible influences of abnormal psychopathology in the parent (thought disorder, affective blunting, "double-bind communication," etc.) on offspring at various stages of their development. The battery of investigations included the following five.

The Affect Discrimination Test. In this test the children were asked to select from a series of photographs depicting different emotional displays, a named affect that would match the facial expression, and a named affect that would match a specific situation that might occasion a particular facial expression. In a normative study preceding the main investigation, it was shown that affect discrimination developed evenly with chronological age. The experimental subjects have so far shown at times a tendency to grossly mis-

read the affect displayed as compared with control subjects whose errors of judgment were of a lesser degree.

The "Double-Bind" Communication Test. Here a male adult voice is fed into one ear and a female adult voice into the other ear simultaneously, each suggesting a separate task for the child to perform. The child is instructed to ignore one voice and follow the instruction dictated by the other. The experimental group showed less capacity to attend completely to one communication to the exclusion of the other.

The Expectation of Benevolence or Hostility Test. This was derived from Baldwin and modified radically for the present research. The subject plays the game with a stranger, who is labeled as such, and he is asked to anticipate the stranger's reactions to him in terms of good or bad feeling toward the child

Table 23. Experimental Approaches to the Psychopathology of Childhood

Behavior Disorder	Experimental Techniques	Groups Differentiated
Encopresis (1957)	Perceptual battery (smell, sight, sound, touch); Comparometer—size matching; Autonomic (GSR) reactions with word association	Continuous vs. discontinuous
Ambivalence (1957)	Family figures; Sorting of "messages" of input and output; Feelings—positive/negative ratio	
Autism (1958)	Stimulus-adaptation; Social conditioning (Smolensky apparatus); Searching behavior (Piaget); Three mountains test (Piaget)	Primary vs. secondary
Sleep disturbances (1959)	Lowensfeld battery; Eidetic imagery (Jaensch); Dream study (Piaget); E.E.G.; Depth of sleep study	Visual vs. motor
Micropsia (1960)	Object constancy, short range (Cambridge); Object constancy, long range (Holway-Boring); Size-distance discrepancy; Piaget inquiry	Psychogenic vs. physiogenic
Minimal brain damage (1964)	Standard play situation; Autonomic reactions	Anoxia vs. controls
Prepsychosis parapsychosis (1968)	Affect discrimination; "Double-bind communication" test; "Broken bridge" (Piaget); Three mountains (Piaget); Prediction of benevolence-hostility (Baldwin); Witkin perceptual battery; Autonomic responses	Mentally-ill parents vs. physically-ill parents

Anthony (1957–1968).

and the way in which this is affected by the stranger's self-interest. The experimental child is more likely to anticipate malevolence on the part of the stranger, although he is offered no data on which to base such a supposition.

The "Broken Bridge" Test. This was adapted from an open-ended story by Piaget and deals with the child's expectation that wrongdoing is punished by the nature of things, the "immanent justice" latent in the universe. Some boys steal apples and are chased by the farmer. They escape over a bridge, which is old and rotten and breaks as they cross. The critical question is: Would the bridge have broken if the boys had not been engaged in delinquent activity?

The Three Mountains Test. This test, also derived from Piaget, has been described previously.

In these two last tests, the experimental group showed itself as more magically disposed in its judgments and more egocentric. The factor of differentiation was investigated by means of the Witkin battery (the Children's Embedded Fgure Test, the Rod and Frame, and the Draw-a-Person Test).

The different approaches to different clinical syndromes in this series of studies are summarized in Table 23.

In summary, although the experimental approach to the psychopathology of childhood promises a sharper delineation of the clinical states, it has been a relatively neglected field, but with the entry of experimental psychologists into the clinical field in increasing numbers, a new era of scientific accomplishment can be expected. Clinicians themselves still tend to eschew the experimental method, some for vaguely felt ethical reasons, others for reasons suggesting disbelief that the laboratory procedure could ever be, in Lewis' term, a "serious experiment" in touch with real life. Time alone will tell whether these objections are sufficiently valid to impede further developments in this field.

THE TREATMENT AND FOLLOW-UP OF THE BEHAVIOR DISORDERS

Individual Psychotherapy

This has been the "treatment of choice" for some decades now in most child guidance clinics, where it usually forms part of a collaboration approach in which the parents are also seen in single or joint therapy. The difficulties with regard to collaborative treatment reside in the "team discomforts" occasioned by status and role problems on the part of team members from the different disciplines, sometimes resulting in a disruptive rivalry which fails to gain a direct and overt expression.

There is no doubt that the child in psychotherapy begins to regard his sessions as something special, different, and private and it seems to be universal that children do not spontaneously or even under questioning discuss the context of their sessions with their parents, as if this were primarily their own concern. Those few who do are typically grossly immature and particularly girls who have not outgrown their early attachment to their mother.

This special "therapeutic alliance" makes subtle demands on the capacities of the children and those below a certain level of intelligence, comprehension, verbal skill, self-awareness, and potential for relationship or "transference," in psychoanalytic terms, may not be able to take full advantage of the situation. As a consequence, it has been shown that children who obtain psychotherapy in clinics tend to come from better socioeconomic and cultural environments.

Play therapy takes into account that the younger children have difficulty in communicating their ideas and fantasies directly, but can do so in the language of play. Through the symbolic route, they can abreact their anxieties of the past, prepare for anxieties of the future, and "play out" their anxieties of the present.

Family Therapy

Family therapists, in general, adopt the transactional point of view, which postulates that events involving the family occur within a total system of interdependent subsystems, any one of which may temporarily become a focus of observation. The "world" being observed includes the observing therapist and his observing (Bell, 1962). The relationships that develop involve three levels of systematic concept formation: the intrapsychic (using psychoanalytic concepts), the interpersonal (using the concepts derived from small group dynamics—role and role-conflict resolution), and the cultural (using culture-values concepts). The family therapists have a group rather than an individual-oriented perspective, attending to what goes on *between* people in their interactions and communications.

Analysis of the communication system in the family focuses on symptoms as communications, on nonverbal communications, on the breakdown of verbal communications, on the discrepancies and contradictions between verbal and nonverbal comunications, and on the private language established in some families.

With this emphasis on the family as a group, the therapist attempts to form a type of group with the family in which he can play a planned, controlled, and communicated role. He also establishes a subgroup with each member, which can demonstrate to the rest of the family the rich potentialities of the dyadic relationship. As an outsider, he calls into being family patterns of response that are meant for public occasions and situations. One of his major therapeutic responsibilities is to ensure the participation of all family members, which necessitates limiting the family group to children over the age of 9 years.

Family therapy, like individual therapy, depends on the personal and social skills of the therapist, which help him to make manifest through his own behavior in the group the increased fluidity in communication, flexibility in roles and functions, and freedom in the choice of relationships, that it is possible for the family to achieve.

Group Therapy

Slavson (1964) and Anthony (1957) have both described in some detail the techniques used in the treatment of children at different stages of development in groups. Slavson has concentrated his therapeutic attention on the *activity* of the children and on the *individual* in the group; Anthony, on the other hand, has focused on the verbal communications and on the group as a whole. The former holds that children talk in actions as in play and that these are susceptible of interpretation, whereas the latter believes that if the therapist can create a suitable therapeutic environment, the children can quite adequately speak for themselves in words. The technical problem is to convert action into

speech by limiting the possibilities of action and encouraging the use of speech.

It is more difficult to talk therapeutically to children than to adults, because it requires more radical change in one's normal talking habits. Since most adult communications to children take the form of information, advice, and prohibition, they are largely one-way channels allowing for minimum feedback. To establish a two-way communicative process with the child usually necessitates a complete change of attitude and behavior in the average adult. He must become interested in what the child has to say to him, and since factual information is not the child's strong point, he has to relinquish some of his propinquity for "data-gathering." To develop the necessary empathy for this task requires some degree of reactivation of the adult's own childhood experiences and recollections. To talk to a child without talking down to him is by no means an easy matter for many adults. Successful talking with children above all implies reciprocal communication (Anthony, 1964).

Anthony has described a "small table" technique for doing group work with pre-school children, making use of play material to stimulate "collective fantasies." He also uses a "small room" technique with latency children and exploits the problems of closeness and movement restriction as experienced by the group. Finally, his approach with adolescents involves a "small circle" with a premium on verbal interchange. He has also spoken of making a "therapeutic contract" with the young patients so that a period of "talking time" is exchanged for a period of "doing time," which allows for the sampling of both verbal and activity patterns.

Family and group therapy have now been added to many clinic programs and offer an alternative or addition to individual psychotherapy. The selection of cases for the three modes of therapy, individual, family, and group, has become an important part of the diagnostic process but the criteria are still far from clear. Where family pathology is very much in evidence or where disturbing family interactions are conducing to the child's pathology, family therapy would seem to be the treatment of choice. However, the range of family therapy is extending, since it has been found that children expected to make progress in psychotherapy failed to do so because of inherent attitudes in the parents not necessarily manifested in a recognizable psychopathology. Family therapy is then undertaken to facilitate the treatment of the child, or it may be limited to conjoint therapy with the parents. Many therapists believe that family therapy will eventually establish a primacy in the clinic since the increased understanding of the interlocking relationships within the family would make it virtually impossible for pathology to reside uniquely in the child.

Hypnotic Therapy

Hypnosis has not been used to any extent in the treatment of children except in the relief of extremely painful conditions. Bernstein (1963) has described the management of burned children with the aid of hypnosis, in which an attempt is made to achieve anesthesia during the changes of dressing. The child is told that hypnosis does not mean going to sleep, that it provides a special kind of relaxation which would help him to bear pain better. Trance inductions are then induced gradually over a period of sessions. The children are able to relax and focus their thoughts on pictures of a happy time and place. The need for rescue in these children is so great that it neutralizes any panic they might experience from submitting to the hypnotist. Undue anxiety during the induction phase is a warning signal to be especially careful. At the end of the hypnotic relationship children inevitably show resentment toward the therapist.

Behavior Therapy

A learning-oriented approach to behavior disorders has begun to enter the practice of some clinics, replacing, though still to a very small extent, the explicit assumption that the main therapeutic task is to resolve conflicts. In the newer therapy, an attempt is made to relate the way in which the behavior has been learned to techniques for unlearning it. From this point of view, a neurosis is just a bad habit—a persistent habit of unadaptive behavior, acquired by learning. Instead of regarding the symptoms, as in the psychoanalytic view, as an index of deeper and less tractable psychopathology, a neurosis is regarded as nothing but its own symptoms;

thus when the symptoms are eliminated, so is the neurosis. The dynamic view is that unless you get rid of the hidden conflicts as well, they will only produce other symptoms in place of the eliminated ones.

According to learning theory, maladaptive behavior may occur as a result of a failure in acquiring learned patterns of behavior, often the learning of behavior inappropriate to the patient's environment or to the learning of conflict (Pick, 1961). Phenotypically similar behaviors may either be directly learned, or established and maintained by conflict, or established by conflict but no longer maintained by it, or determined by more than one of these factors.

Dollard and Miller (1950) have summed up the learning conditions of therapy as follows: Permissiveness leading to anxiety-reduction, the consistent failure to punish leading to the extinction of fears, discrimination between the conditions in which the fears were first learned and the present conditions, trial of new modes of adjustment that are awarded and gradually become established.

Therapeutic change can be brought about by conditioning, by gradual learning, by sudden insight, by identification, and by the resolution of transferred conflicts. The classical uses of conflict-resolving therapy, insight therapy, and abreactive therapy are giving place to graded learning, relearning, and unlearning.

The therapy by negative practice and conditioned inhibition has been applied to relatively simple monosymptomatic conditions, such as phobias and tics, but more recently there have been more ambitious attempts to modify multiple problem behaviors. It is now generally accepted that manipulation of reinforcement contingencies has a significant impact upon behavior, reiterating the importance of the Law of Effect. In the earlier studies, dramatic changes in mild or single classes of deviance were described. After the classic study by Jones (1924) on children's fears, there followed Williams (1959) on temper tantrums, Harris et al. (1964) on crawling, Mowrer (1938) on enuresis.

Walton (1961) attempted to eliminate tics in an 11-year-old boy in whom the symptom had been present for over 6 years. The tics were regarded as tension-reducing phenomena that tended to occur when the patient got

excited or encountered new situations. Theoretically, they could be viewed as originally
unconditioned tension reducers that had become elaborated as drive-reducing conditioned responses, once evoked in a variety of
situations arousing intense emotion. When
such movements either produced or coincided with a reduction or cessation of the
tension, the tics would become stronger by a
process of reinforcement by means of stim-
ulus-generalization, a variety of stimuli similar to these original stimuli would then evoke
the tic, which would become further reinforced, thus leading to the development of a
powerful positive habit.

On the basis of this theoretical model, it
was argued that it should be possible to extinguish the tics by building up negative
habits of "not performing the tics." If the
patient were to be given massed practice in
the tic, then reactive inhibition should build
up rapidly. When this reached a certain critical point, the patient would be forced to
"rest" or not perform the tic. This habit of
not performing the tic would then be associated with drive-reduction due to the dissipation of reactive inhibition, and hence would
be reinforced with repetition, a negative
habit would be built up incompatible with
the positive habit of doing the tic.

Following this argument, a treatment program was established for the child in which
he spent sessions practicing his tic. There
was a gradual but striking decline in the
patient's ability to imitate his tic voluntarily,
which was associated by the generalization
of this improvement to his involuntary tics.
These improved very much with respect to
both frequency and intensity, and he went for
periods of up to three or four days with little
evidence of their presence, something un-
heard-of before his treatment.

Patterson and Brodsky (1966) broke new
ground by instituting a behavior modification
program for a child with multiple problem
behaviors consisting of hyperaggression, fearlessness, and negativism. The 5-year-old patient had been rejected by his peer group.
The parents, teachers, peer group, and experimenters served as treatment agents. One
program counterconditioned the fear reactions; a "time-out" procedure was used to
alter the assaultive behavior, and an operant
conditioning technique was used to increase

cooperative behaviors. Finally, a conditioning
program was initiated which altered the
interaction between child and his peers.

There is no doubt that the effect of the
conditioning produces a reprogramming of
the social environment. The altered program
of positive and negative reinforcers maintains
the effect of the initial behavior modification.
The peer group often takes over by dispensing more social reinforcers. Attempts to
reprogram the social environment are only
just beginning. In some instances, the parent
and child have been observed interacting
under relatively controlled laboratory conditions. The parent is reinforced for appropriately reinforcing the child and programmed teaching manuals have been developed
for use by parents and teachers. Whole
families are now being included in the behavior modification program, the observation
data in the home and the school being used
for retraining the parents in the home.

As already mentioned, one could wish that
the evaluation of the results of psychotherapy
were more reliable and this is equally true of
the reports published by the behavior therapists. These have also lacked comprehensive,
long-term follow-ups, independent outside
ratings of patients before and after treatment,
and untreated control groups for comparison.
The behavior therapists claim between 80
and 90% successes with as few as 30 therapeutic sessions. However, the criteria used
are practically unquantifiable and may involve
the uses of such terms as "improved interpersonal relationships."

Already there have been attempts to draw
behavior and analytic therapy together, analytic therapy being considered a form of corrective deconditioning and reconditioning.
Behavior therapists have also pointed out that
patients undergoing behavior therapy spontaneously made emotionally insightful statements about themselves as they became de-
sensitized.

A further extension of reinforcement procedures has been the establishment of token
exchange systems for children who are hyperactive, hyperaggressive, or hyperwithdrawn.
Using the parents as therapeutic aids has
helped in generalization and this type of technique has been especially effective in controlling negative behavior.

Drug Therapy

Eisenberg (1968) has said that the medical evaluation of drugs follows the familiar sequence of initial enthusiasm, growing disenchantment, and reports of toxicity, premature calls for discard, and a final sober view with appreciation of indications and precautions in use. They are, he says, neither "the passport to a brave new world nor the gateway to the inferno" (p. 640). This "sober view" indicates that with careful selection and regulation drugs can add "a significant dimension to patient care."

The careful practitioner will understand clearly the indications for use and the penalties for abuse in the way of toxic symptoms, also bearing in mind that what works for the adult need not necessarily work for the child. Drugs can be effective in controlling symptoms not amenable to other treatments and can synergistically facilitate other methods of psychiatric treatment, including psychotherapy. Because they are given by the therapist to his patient, they may become inverted with emotional feelings for the relationship, which may add to or subtract from their efficacy. It represents an important transaction between doctor and patient and an important communication to the patient and his family. "Skill in the use of drugs requires, in addition to knowledge of their pharmaceutical properties, sensitivity to their psychological implications" (Eisenberg, 1968, p. 639).

Tranquilizers, such as the *phenothiazines*, have proved effective in the management of overactive children, but they can have some disturbing side effects. Sedatives, such as *diphenylmethane* derivatives, have been used with a variety of behavior disorders with success and their side effects are limited to drowsiness (Freedman, 1955). *Phenobarbital* has proved a cheap and relatively safe sedative for children, although it tends to excite hyperkinetic children. When a behavior disorder is associated with EEG abnormalities in the temporal lobe, it can be benefited by the use of *anticonvulsants. Stimulant* drugs (e.g., amphetamines) can be used with great advantage in the hyperkinetic syndrome.

The Evaluation of Psychotherapy

The concept of multicausation poses many problems for treatment. The concept signifies that no one of many contributing causes is the *sine qua non*. The multiple causes may be interchangeable or additive and vary from time to time as to the part they play in final expression of the behavioral disorder. Multicausation has often been contrasted with specificity, but, in itself, it is no more than a specificity of multiple structure. Thus a combination of certain hereditary, psychological, and social factors can be regarded as specific. In a behavior disorder, the subject may demonstrate causative factors, some of which are specific and some nonspecific. When it comes to the treatment situation, attempts may be made in some cases to uncover and remove the specific factors with the hope that the nonspecific background factors would then subside of their own accord. In other treatment situations, no such attempt is made to differentiate between the two sets of causal agents.

There have been over 80 studies of the effects of various psychotherapeutic techniques in which some form of control procedure or comparison has been made. Of these about 17 have had to do with child psychotherapy. Heinicke and Goldman (1960) carried out a review of these studies in all of which some type of eclectic psychotherapy was used, and where at least three criteria of outcome status were employed during the follow-up study. A pooling of these studies revealed that in approximately 80% of the cases, psychotherapy was found to be either completely or partially successful at follow-up.

Of the 17 studies, the authors then selected 10 which met the following criteria: the follow-up study involved direct contact with the child or his family; the criteria of evaluation were clear-cut and comparable to those used in the classical studies by Lehrman and Witmer; the sample covered a fair range of clinical cases and was not restricted to only one type of case; and the type of help given could be clearly labeled psychotherapy. The outcome status of these 10 studies is shown in Table 24.

Although such results seem extremely favorable, the question is whether these children would have changed as much without therapy. Favorable environmental influences or normal maturational processes could have led to the disappearance of the difficulties. Therefore it was clearly not sufficient to pronounce in favor of psychotherapy without comparing

Table 24. Average Values on Follow-Up
Results of Ten Studies

Outcome Status	Median	Mean
Successfully adjusted	55%	57%
Partially improved	26%	24%
No improvement	16%	18%

From Heinicke and Goldman (1960).

the degree and quality of change in children equivalent in all respects except that they do not receive psychotherapy.

Levitt, Beiser, and Robertson (1959) investigated the effects of treatment on children who attended a child guidance clinic. These were compared with others who were accepted for treatment but "voluntarily terminated contact with the clinic without ever having received any treatment interviews." In the treatment group, at least one member of the family had five one-hour or longer sessions. On follow-up 5-6 years later, 237 treated children and 93 defectors were tested. Out of a total of 26 variables, no significant differences were found between the treated and untreated group.

A number of factors may have been responsible for the lack of significant differences between the two groups (Kellner, 1967). The children were examined 5-6 years later after treatment and some of them had only a very brief course of therapy. The longer the follow-up, the more likely the specific effects of treatment are to be overshadowed by life experiences so that the differences between treated and untreated are likely to decrease with the passage of time. Again, the children followed-up and tested were only a small proportion of the initial sample and therefore may not have been representative. However, an average of 18% of parents gave improvement in the child as one of the reasons for defection and therefore the defectors may have had a larger proportion of remissions before they were due for treatment. It is thus doubtful whether defectors can be regarded as a suitable control group.

Shouksmith and Taylor (1964) investigated the effects of nondirective counseling in high-ability, underachieving pupils. These were 12- and 13-year-olds with IQs of 116 or higher, falling two deciles below expectancy. Thirty-six children were divided into three groups and matched for IQ, age, and

achievement. The experimental group received individual nondirective counseling every two weeks, the "placebo" group took the same psychological and achievement tests as those in the experimental group, and the control group took only the initial screening and final appraisal test. The children in the study were not conspicuously distressed. After six months, achievement tests indicated a significant degree of improvement in the experimental as compared with the placebo and control groups. The experimental group also showed improved peer acceptance, readier cooperation, and improved social adjustment as contrasted with the placebo and control groups, which did not show these improvements.

Eisenberg, Conners, and Lawrence (1965) investigated the effects of psychotherapy in neurotic children, excluding any with brain damage, psychopathy, psychosis, or intelligence levels less then 80. Children in the psychotherapy group received five treatment interviews in addition to the four intake ones, whereas the control children received only the intake interviews followed by a consultation interview. The Clyde Mood Scale ratings by parents show that children in the psychotherapy group became significantly less "aggressive" and more "friendly" after treatment than children in the control group and teachers' ratings also significantly favored the children in the psychotherapy group.

Lehrman et al. (1949) found that at the 1-year follow-up, children who had received psychotherapy had a significantly higher incidence of successful adjustment ratings and a lower incidence of partially improved ratings than the children who had not received treatment. They concluded that "the positive effect of the treatment . . . was established beyond a doubt."

Witmer carried out a carefully executed study (1933) and also made a comparison of treatment results in various types of child guidance clinics (1935). She is not as positive as Lehrman in her concluding remarks about the effects of therapy, but she does think that it is likely to be an "auxiliary factor . . . which can come into effective operation under certain circumstances."

An analysis of the Lehrman and Witmer studies indicates that the percentage in the successful category increases significantly from the evaluation at the closing of the case to the evaluation at follow-up, while the percentage in the partial improvement category decreases. It would thus seem that a significant amount of improvement takes place after the treatment is ended. In both studies, the controls have "serious flaws" (Heinicke and Goldman, 1960). It would seem that they differed from the group receiving therapy in certain important prognostic respects and that, furthermore, many of the children in the so-called control group did in fact receive some sort of help. In Lehrman's study, although the treated and untreated groups were equated in terms of age and sex, they were nonetheless different with respect to severity of the referral problem and the adequacy of the home background. The treatment group contained a significantly greater number of diagnoses in the area of psychoneurosis and severe psychopathic cases as opposed to the milder behavior disorders and also had significantly lower ratings in terms of parental adequacy. These differences would all favor the progress of the control group. According to Lehrman (1949), "the characteristics of the children in the control group were such as to bias them in the direction of a more favorable outcome than was true of the treatment group." A similar examination of Witmer's control group reveals that they also received help and that they were more favorably situated in terms of parental background. Despite this "favoring" of the control group at follow-up, the treatment groups showed a significantly higher percentage of successful adjustments and fewer partial improvements. The various studies have also shown what clinicians have often reported, that many of the most significant changes take place after the termination of treatment.

Various factors complicate the assessment of controlled trials of psychotherapy. Many patients improve, remit, or apparently recover without formal psychotherapy and hence a large proportion of control patients do improve. This improvement occurs largely in the first few months following the onset of the disorder and therefore it is easier to demonstrate the effects of a treatment variable in conditions of long standing and a tendency to improve without treatment is less marked or when there are fewer fluctuations in the severity of symptoms. Nondirective verbal methods appear to be highly effective in some types of cases and ineffective in others and, unfortunately, the mismatching of patient and treatment is only too common. The improvement criteria are often inadequate, and in a number of studies, questionnaires and personality inventories were used, which may have been unsuitable to measure changes. Symptom checklists are unstable and often do not contain the patient's most important symptoms. Improvement is not a unitary process and there is sometimes no correlation in the changes of scores on different measures. Furthermore, psychotherapy tends to increase the variability of a treated group and therefore the comparison of mean scores may hide changes which have occurred. The evidence also would suggest that patients with different personalities may change in different ways and that the personality, experience, and technical competence of the therapist may be a major factor.

In summing up, it is clear that psychotherapy research has been carried out on samples which have varied greatly, and the techniques of treatment and assessments employed have been so diverse that some of the studies have very little in common. The evidence would suggest that the various methods of psychotherapy with children are effective and that different techniques lead to changes of a different kind (Kellner, 1967).

Amble and Moore (1966) feel that it is impossible to blind the rater to the fact that the patient has had treatment, and since it is possible that this information could significantly affect the rater's judgment, they consider it necessary to assess the influence of this knowledge on the rater. They found, from investigating this factor, that experienced professional workers were not significantly influenced in their ratings by information that the patient had been in treatment and apparently evaluated the progress or lack of progress with considerable objectivity.

THE PREVENTION OF CHILDHOOD BEHAVIOR DISORDERS

Prevention, in the field of abnormal psychology, can take two forms: primary prevention denotes measures employed to reduce the incidence of a disorder in the general population by attempting to reduce the incidence of new cases of the disorder; secondary prevention, in contrast, aims at lowering the frequency of the disorder at any particular time by successful treatment of established cases prior to that time, thus reducing the number of old cases in the population (Caplan, 1968).

There has been a resurgence of interest in preventive intervention at premorbid or early stages in the evolution of a psychiatric disorder. Primary prevention requires adequate predictive instruments and secondary prevention requires adequate screening devices.

Predictive Devices

Mention has already been made of the Gluecks' parental attitude and behavior indices, which they have used with a fair degree of success. Kvaraceus (1961) has some doubts about the various instruments used in forecasting delinquency (social indices, questionnaires, sentence completion, open-ended stories, etc.) and concludes that "the behavior ratings of experienced teachers showed more promise than the Kvaraceus Delinquency Proneness Scale."

Jenkins and Blodgett (1960) have tried to predict success and failure in the management of delinquent boys from a sentence completion test. Positive signs included increased acceptance of others and assumption of personal responsibility and negative signs, increased rejection of others, and rejection of personal responsibility. Further negative prognostic signs would be a persistently low self-concept, a dedifferentiation of responses, and developing confusion. Truancy (Williams, 1947) emerges from a situation where there is poor parental control, no realistic goals for the children to attain, poor socioeconomic conditions, a tendency to join gangs, a history of past illnesses, low intelligence, an increasing dislike of teachers, and inconsistently punitive parents.

All studies, almost without exception, show "broken homes" in the background of delinquency, but it is not the "brokenness" as such but the various associated factors of tension, neglect, and poverty that predispose to delinquent behavior. From a predictive point of view, the Gluecks' tables offer the most promise since they are broadly based and include psychological test factors, personality traits, character structure, and the social factors already mentioned. The Gluecks do not feel that the influence of the neighborhood or of the more inclusive environmental conditions presents a fruitful target for exploration and their approach has come in for some criticism on the grounds that it tends to ignore significant dynamic and ecological factors which need recognition for an achievement of fuller understanding.

Screening Devices

With regard to early detection of emotional illnesses in schoolchildren, mention has already been made of a screening instrument called the Academic Progress Chart or APC by its authors (Stringer and Glidewell, 1967). It was based on the assumption that one of the major determinants of efficiency in children's academic learning is adequacy of ego development and functioning. If this were true, then faults in ego structure, or aberrations in ego functioning, amounting to emotional disturbance, could be expected to impair efficiency in academic learning.

The APC is a simple grid with chronological age on the horizontal axis, grade level on the vertical axis, and an expected-progress line so drawn as to cover one grade per school year. For any individual child an actual-progress line can be constructed relative to the expected-progress line by using the data (the central tendency scores) of his achievement test scores as he moves from one grade to the next. Each child's achievement can thus be measured along three main dimensions: *level*, in terms of grade equivalent at a given point in time; its *slope* or rate of achievement, a measure of change in level of achievement relative to the amount of time involved in such change; and its *change of slope* or change in rate of achievement, the difference obtained by algebraic subtraction of one slope from the next slope following.

From a normal school population, the APC was able to select 22% of the children as disturbed and in need of help and 78% as not disturbed. This correctly identified 41% of the children adjudged by the caseworkers to be disturbed and 73% of the children adjudged by the caseworkers to be healthy. Thus, although the instrument missed 59% of the disturbed children and erroneously selected 43% as disturbed, its total valid-

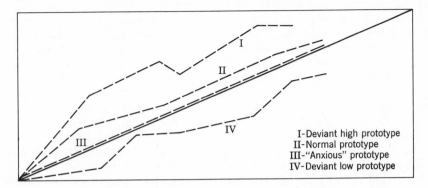

Fig. 5.   Academic progress chart. (Schematized from Stringer and Glidewell, 1967.)

decision rate was 73%, a 12% improvement over chance expectancy.

The relationship between APC identification and identification by other criteria such as a symptom inventory was low but stable and reliable. Both a resources inventory and the symptom inventory were more efficient in screening than the APC on generalized criteria, the symptom inventory producing a valid-decision rate as high as 84%, but both these require individual interviews with mothers and considerable psychiatric sophistication on the part of the interviewer, and they are therefore not as practicable as the APC for maintaining mental health surveillance of a total elementary school population.

Stringer and Glidewell come up with an interesting and pertinent analogy when they compare education in the mental health field to immunization in the field of physical health. Education, as immunization, "begins in the home, in the family, with that kind of training that develops a child's psychosocial resources and coping strengths to the point where he can enter school well prepared to benefit by the process of elementary education. Given this kind of start, any reasonably good school will stimulate further development of resources and coping strengths, thus providing continuing effective immunization against mental illness. The children with whom education does not 'take' remain vulnerable to illness and can gain immunity only through suffering illness and recovering from it—a risky proceeding, at best. The children with whom education does 'take' are significantly less liable to illness and more resilient in recovery from it."

Reference has already been made to Rut-

ter's screening device in his epidemiological study in the Isle of Wight. It was based on a straightforward behavioral inventory and given to both teachers and parents with a reasonable degree of success, although there was a surprising absence of overlap between parent and teacher assessments.

Bower (1960) has also developed instruments for the early identification of the emotionally handicapped children in school and related it to primary prevention (1961). Bower found that children in the fourth, fifth, and sixth grades who were identified clinically as emotionally disturbed were achieving at a lower level in arithmetic and reading, were manifesting greater self-dissatisfaction on an instrument he developed to measure self-perception, and were rated negatively by peers on a sociometric instrument.

Eighty-nine percent of the children selected randomly from a group scoring highest in the negative direction on a combination of self and peer perception ratings and a teacher's adjustment rating were found on individual clinical examination to have moderate to severe clinical problems. The self-perception test, "Thinking About Yourself" (TAY), consists of a series of descriptions of concrete attributes of young children. The child is asked to indicate those he feels actually describe himself (self-concept) and those he feels he would like to possess (desired self). The discrepancy between these two estimates is taken as an index of satisfaction with self. The class play is a two-part test and presumes for the child a series of specific roles in a play to be conducted by the class. Half the roles are negative, half positive. In Part I, which is a type of sociometric estimate, each child nominates as many of his classmates as he wishes for each of the roles in the play. In Part II, the child indicates which parts he would like to play and those for which he thinks he might be chosen by peers and teachers. In Part I, the measure is the percentage of negative role choices and in Part II the percentage of negative roles indicated by the child.

Zax, Cowen, Izzo, and Trost (1964) made use of the Bower measures in addition to other measures. They gave achievement and aptitude tests and extracted an achievement-aptitude discrepancy index. A special teacher's rating form was also developed in which the teacher checked characteristics from a list and indicated their intensity on a three-point scale. An overall adjustment scale was also derived simply by having the teacher rate the child on a five-point scale ranging from very well adjusted to very poorly adjusted. Their findings confirmed and to some extent expanded those reported by Bower. They found that intropunitive patterns in children are more highly related to successful adjustment than are denial patterns, and it was their opinion that the class play was an especially useful device for the early detection of emotional disturbance.

Lindemann and Ross (1955) developed a screening method of Interaction Process Analysis based on protocols taken by the psychologist during doll play sessions. Four variables were rated by the clinician on the basis of the total doll play situation: the ease with which the child separated from the mother, the extent to which the child controlled his emotions, the amount of unusual behavior, and the number of special demands made on the experimenter. All variables were adjudged in terms of a four-point adjustment rating scale ranging from good to poor. In addition, some of the Sears categories and the method of Interaction Process Analysis devised by Bales were also tried out. The authors felt their predictive test of social adaptation demonstrated the feasibility of evaluating the degree of personality integration in populations of young children. The technique did help to distinguish children into good and poor adjustment groups.

In summary, it would seem that both these approaches, predictive and screening, are valuable from an epidemiological point of view in describing populations, but their fallibility becomes apparent when reduced to the consideration of a single case. The screening devices are not predictive and vice versa so that it is not possible to say whether a particular case screened as emotionally disturbed is "normally" disturbed, as are many others in the general population, or psychiatrically disturbed and whether the disturbance is transient or chronic. Clinical intervention in a "normally" disturbed state may exaggerate the significance of it and even help to perpetuate it. Finding large numbers of cases requiring clinical help without having such help available would not further the cause of prevention at all unless new community resources are created to match the screening efforts.

THE PRESENT STATE OF THE SCIENCE

A resurgence of psychological interest in this area of behavior pathology has led to some hopeful developments and already one can point to various advances that have been made over the past two decades. O'Connor and Franks (1960, p. 393), however, have been less impressed, as evident in the following statement: "A review of our knowledge in any field other than the field of delinquency does not support the view that the psychology or psychiatry of abnormality in children has made notable progress. In learning studies, motivation and knowledge of social behavior, evidence is accumulating, but where neurosis and psychosis are concerned we are scarcely able to offer even a definition." In view of the fact that this is a relatively young discipline, this is somewhat hypercritical. The abnormal psychology of childhood is still far from being an experimental or a predictive science, although it is moving gradually toward the point when significant elements of past and present history, taken in conjunction with test responses, might be able to forecast the type of behavior disorders that will eventually develop; this has already been carried out with some success in the case of delinquency.

It must be confessed, however, that the practice of child psychiatry and clinical child psychology has been and still is predominantly undertaken with traditional diagnostic, prognostic, and therapeutic tools. The experimental approach has been largely neglected and epidemiological studies have been conducted by investigators from outside disciplines. The traditional approach to behavior pathology is largely built on a medical disease model in which emotional and mental illness is classified into separate, discrete categories of disorder and in which the clinical data are made up of an accumulation of heterogeneous and often unrelated facts. Research into such disorders consists of the comparison of groups with and without the disorder.

Since this approach has not proved fruitful, the psychopathologist should pay some attention to the alternative approach of Eysenck (1960), who has suggested, first, the replacement of the disease concept by a concept of defective functioning within certain psychological systems; second, the replacement of the traditional psychiatric classificatory system of abnormality by the use of a dimensional framework produced by a combination of factors or continua; third, the replacement of the traditional paradigm of psychiatric research by the paradigm of the experimental psychologist (discussed earlier in the experimental section); and fourth, replacing the accumulation of heterogeneous, unrelated facts which weigh down textbooks of psychiatry by the process of generalization from the available data with the establishment of well-substantiated laws.

The psychopathologist, as Jaspers advises (1962), must move beyond the particular preoccupations of the clinician to the general case and develop an orderly scheme of communicable concepts. But whereas Eysenck's body of knowledge is built up on the basis of experimental data, Jaspers' psychopathology is founded on a "psychology of meaningful connections" and the convincing experience that comes with understanding. Since he places an emphasis on understanding, Jaspers is of the opinion that the primary task for the psychopathologist is to differentiate the various modes of understanding, clarify them, and embody them in all the factual content available to him.

Psychopathology can therefore be constructed on a broad theoretical system like Freud's, on a rigorous experimental approach like Eysenck's or on the understanding of phenomenological experiences as in the case of Jaspers. As in normal child development, there is an unfortunate cleavage between applied and basic research, slight though this is, and conceptualization. The "academic" child psychopathologists tend to focus upon the study of specific behaviors as a function of age; theirs is largely an atheoretical and empirical approach as contrasted with the systematic and theoretically loaded methods employed by students of Freud, Erikson, and Piaget.

In order to advance further, it would seem imperative for psychopathology to vary its ideas and methods over a broad range so that optimal conditions for diagnosis and treatment can be studied. The stereotypics of approach, developed and practiced and embalmed in the clinic, need to be broken down and transformed into fresh and flexibly manipulated techniques that can be carefully appraised in regular follow-ups. The future depends on the building up of a developmental psychopathology based on sound research, including experimental methods. To what extent the inner psychological events belonging, as Hume put it, to "the theater of the mind" can be properly depicted by the variety of concepts accumulated in this chapter remains to be seen. As Freud (1895) once said with the brighter optimism of his earlier days: "In spite of everything, the hope is always justified that there may be some degree of correspondence between the real processes and our idea of them "

References

Achenbach, T. M. The classification of children's psychiatric symptoms: a factor analytic study. *Psychol. Monogr.*, 1966, **80** 6.

Ackerman, N. W. *Psychodynamics of family life.* New York: Basic Books, 1958.

Ackerson, F. *Children's behavior problems.* Chicago: University of Chicago Press, 1942.

Amble, B. R., and Moore, R. The influence of a set on the evaluation of psychotherapy. *Amr. J. Orthopsychiat.*, 1966, **36**, 50–56.

Anderson, C. M., and Plymate, H. B. Management of the brain-damaged adolescent. *Amr. J. Orthopsychiat.*, 1962, **32**(3), 492–500.

Anthony, E. J. The significance of Jean Piaget for child psychiatry. *Br. J. med. Psychol.*, 1956, **29**(1), 20–34.

Anthony, E. J. An experimental approach to the psychopathology of childhood: encopresis. *Br. J. med. Psychol.*, 1957, **30**(3), 146–175.

Anthony, E. J. An experimental approach to the psychopathology of childhood: autism. *Br. J. med. Psychol.*, 1958, **31**(3 and 4), 211–225.

Anthony, E. J. An experimental approach to psychopathology of childhood: sleep disturbances. *Br. J. med. Psychol.*, 1959, **32**(1), 18–37. (a)

Anthony, E. J. A group of murderous mothers. 2nd Int. Congr. Group Psychother. Zurich. *Acta Psychother.*, 1959, **7**, Suppl. p. 1–6. (b)

Anthony, E. J. An experimental approach to the psychopathology of childhood: micropsia. *Psychiatric Research Reports* #13, Dec., 1960.

Anthony, E. J. The talking doctor has begun to shoot. *Bull. Chicago Inst. Med.* Proceedings of the Int. Med. Chicago, Vol. 25, No. 10, July, 1965.

Anthony, E. J. Psychoneurotic disorders of childhood. In *Comprehensive textbook of psychiatry* A. Freedman and H. Kaplan (Eds.), Baltimore, Md.: Williams & Wilkins, 1967, 1387–1406.

Anthony, E. J. Classification and categorization in child psychiatry. *Int. J. Psychiat.*, 1967, **3**(3), 173–178.

Anthony, E. J. On observing children. In R. Miller (Ed.), *Foundations of child psychiatry.* London: Pergamon Press, 1968. (b)

Anthony, E. J. Developmental antecedents of schizophrenia. In S. Katz and D. Rosenthal (Eds.), *Transmission of schizophrenia.* London: Pergamon Press, 1968. (c)

Anthony, E. J., and Bene, E. A technique for the objective assessment of the child's family relationship. *J. ment. Sci.*, 1957, **103**(432), 541–555.

Anthony, E. J., and Scott P. Manic depressive psychosis in childhood. *J. child Psychol. Psychiat.*, 1960, **1**, 53–73.

Appell, G., and David, M. A study of nursing care and nurse-infant interaction. In B. M. Foss (Ed.), *Determinants of infant behavior.* London: Methuen, 1961.

Angyal, A. (1941), Disgust and related aversions. *J. abnorm. soc. Psychol.*, 1941, **36**, 393–412.

Baldwin, A. L. *Theories of child development.* New York: Wiley, 1964.

Barendregt, J. T. *Research in psychodiagnostics.* Paris: Mouton, 1961.

Bechtoldt, H. P. Diagnostic classification in child psychiatry R. L. Jenkins and J. Cole (Eds.), *Psychiatric research reports of the Amer. Psychiat. Assoc,* 1964.

Bell, J. E. Recent advances in family group therapy. *J. child Psychol. Psychiat.*, 1962, **3**, 1–16.

Beloff, H. The structure and origin of the anal character. *Genet. Psychol. Monogr.*, 1962, **55**, 275–278.

Bennett, I. *Delinquent and neurotic children.* London, 1960.

Bentzen, F. Sex ratios in learning and behavior disorders. *Amr. J. Orthopsychiat.*, 1963, **3**, 92–98.

Berlyne, D. E. *Structure and direction in thinking.* New York: Wiley, 1965.

Bertalanffy, L. von, J. M. Tanner and B. Inhelder (Eds.), In *Discussions on child development.* New York: International Universities Press, 1960.

Blau, A., and Hulse, W. C. Anxiety (actual) neuroses as a cause of behavior disorders in children. *Amr. J. Orthopsychiat.*, 1956, **26**, 108–118.

Bender, L. Childhood schizophrenia: a clinical study of 100 schizophrenic children. *Amr. J. Orthopsychiat.*, 1947, **17**, 40–56.

Bijou, S. W., and Baer, D. M. *Child development.* Vol. I. New York: Appleton-Century-Crofts, 1961.

Blauvelt, H., and McKenna, J. Mother-neonate interaction. In B. M. Foss (Ed.), *Determinants of infant behavior.* London: Methuen, 1961.

Bower, E. M. *Early identification of emotionally disturbed children in school.* Springfield, Ill. Thomas, 1960.

Bower, E. M. Primary prevention in a school setting. In G. Caplan (Ed.), *Prevention of mental disorders in children.* New York: Basic Books, 1961.

Bowlby, J. *Child care and the growth of love.* London: Penguin Books, 1951.

Bowlby, J. Processes of mourning. *Int. J. Psychoanal.*, 1961, **42**, 314–340.

Bowlby, J., Ainsworth, M., Boston, B., and Rosenbloth, O. The effects of mother-child separation: a follow-up study. *Br. J. med. Psychol.*, 1956, **29**, 211–249.

Bradley, C. Characteristics and management of children with behavior problems associated with organic brain damage. *Pediat. Clin. N. Amr.*, 1957, **4**, 1049–1060.

Bradley, J. V. Direction of know-turn stereotypes. *USAF WADC Tech. Rep.*, 1957, **57**, 388–399.

Brandon, S. *An epidemiological study of maladjustment in childhood.* Thesis for the degree of Doctor of Medicine. University of Durham.

Brown, F. W. Childhood bereavement and subsequent psychiatric disorder. *Br. J. Psychiat.*, 1966, **112**(491), 1035.

Brown, S., Pollock, H. M., Potter, H. W., and Cohen, D. W. *Outline for the psychiatric classification of problem children.* Utica, N. Y.: State Hospital Press, 1937.

Bruner, J. S., and Goodman, C. C. Value and need as organizing factors in perception. *J. abnorm. soc. Psychol.*, 1947, **42**, 33–44.

Buckle, D., and Lebovici, S. *Child guidance centers.* Geneva: World Health Organization, 1960. P. 87.

Burt, C. *The young delinquent.* New York: Appleton-Century-Crofts, 1925.

Burt, C. The analysis of temperament. *Br. J. med. Psychol.*, 1938, **17**, 158–188.

Cameron, K. Diagnostic categories in child psychiatry. *Br. J. med. Psychol.*, 1955, **28**(1), 67-71.

Cameron, N. *The psychology of behavior disorders.* Boston: Houghton Mifflin, 1947.

Caplan, G. Opportunities for school psychologists in the primary prevention of mental disorder in childhood. In E. Miller (Ed.), *Foundations of child psychiatry.* London: Pergamon Press, 1968.

Chess, S. *An introduction to child psychiatry.* New York: Grune and Stratton, 1959.

Clarke, A. D. B., and Clarke, A. Some recent advances in the study of early deprivation. *J. child Psychol. Psychiat.*, 1960, **1**, 26–36.

Collins, L. F., Maxwell, A. E., and Cameron, K. A factor analysis of some child psychiatric clinic data. *J. ment. Sci.*, 1962, **108**, 274–285.

Collins, L. F., Maxwell, A. E., and Cameron, K. An analysis of the case material of the younger maladjusted child. *Br. J. Psychiat.*, 1963, **109**(463), 758–765.

Craft, M., Stephenson, G., Fabisch, W., and Burnand, G. 100 Admissions to a psychopathic unit. *J. Ment. Sci.*, 1962, **108**, 504.

Craig, W. The child in the maladjusted household. *Practitioner*, 1956, **177**, 21.

Dalton, K. The influence of the mother's health on her child. *Proc. R. Soc. Med.*, 1966, **59**, 1014.

Despert, L. Urinary control and enuresis. *Psychosom. Med.*, 1944, **6**, 294–307.

Davidson, M. A., McInnes, R. G., and Parnell, R. W. The distribution of personality traits in seven-year-old children: a combined psychological, psychiatric, and somatotype study. *Br. educ. Psychol.*, 1957, **27**, 48–61.

Doll, E. A. Mental deficiency versus neurophrenia. *Amr. J. ment. Defic.*, 1953, **57**, 477–480.

Dollard, J., and Miller, N. E. *Personality and psychotherapy.* New York: McGraw-Hill, 1950.

Douglas, J. W. The school progress of nervous and troublesome children. *Br. J. Psychiat.*, 1966, **112**(492), 1115–1116.

Douglas, J. W. B., and Mulligan, D. G. Emotional adjustment and educational achievement—the preliminary results of a longitudinal study of a national sample of children. *Proc. R. Soc. Med.*, 1961, **54**, 885–891.

Downes, J. Illness in the chronic disease family. *Amr. J. Publ. Hlth.*, 1942, **32**, 589.

Downes, J. Sickness as an index of the need for health supervision of the school child. *Amr. J. Publ. Hlth.*, 1945, **35**, 593.

Downes, J., and Simon, K. Psychoneurotic patients and their families. *Psychosom. Med.*, 1953, **15**, 463.

Dreger, M. A progress report on a factor-analytic approach to classification in child psychiatry. In R. L. Jenkins and J. O. Cole (Eds.), *Diagnostic classification in child psychiatry.* Psychiatric Research Reports of the American Psychiatric Association. Vol. 18, pp. 221–258.

Drillien, C. The incidence of mental and physical handicaps in school age children of very low birth weight. *Pediat.*, 1961, **27**, 452.

Ehrenwald, J. Neurotic interaction and patterns of pseudo-heredity in the family. *Amr. J. Psychiat.*, 1958, **115**, 134.

Eiduson, B. T., Trinidad, C. M., Johnson, M. A., and Rottenberg, D. Use of psychiatric case records as information vehicles. *Reiss-Davis Clin. Bull.*, 1965, **2**(2), 59–68.

Eisenberg, L. Classification and categorization in child psychiatry. *Int. J. Psychiat.*, 1967, **3**(3), 149–181.

Eisenberg, L. Pharmacology in childhood: a critique. In E. Miller (Ed.), *Foundations of child psychiatry.* London: Pergamon Press, 1968.

Eisenberg, L., Connors, K. C., and Lawrence, S. A controlled study of the differential applications of out-patient psychiatric treatment for children. *Jap. J. child Psychiat.*, 1965, **6**(3), 125–132.

Ekdahl, M. C., Rice, E. P., and Schmidt, W. M. Children of parents hospitalized for mental illness. *Amr. J. Publ. Hlth.*, 1962, **52**, 428.

Escalona, S. Emotional development in the first year of life. In M. Senn (Ed.), *Problems of infancy and childhood.* New York: Josiah Macy Foundation, 1953.

Escalona, S., and Heider, G. *Prediction and outcome.* New York: Basic Books, 1959.

Eysenck, H. J. Classification and problem of diagnosis. In *Handbook of abnormal psychology.* London: Pitman Medical Pub. Co., 1960.

Eysenck, H. J. A note on "Impulse repressions and emotional adjustment." *J. consult. Psychol.*, 1961, **25**(4), 362–363.

Fabian, A. A. and Donohue, J. F. Maternal depression: a challenging child guidance problem. *Amr. J. Orthopsychiat.*, 1956, **26**, 400.

Fish, B., and Shapiro, T. A descriptive typology of children's psychiatric disorders: II: A behavioral classification. In R. L. Jenkins and J. O. Cole (Eds.), *American Psychiatric Association Psychiatric Research Reports* #18, 1964.

Fishbein, G. M. Quoted in H. A. Witkin, R. B. Dyk, H. F. Faterson, D. R. Goodenough, and S. A. Karp, *Psychological Differentiation* New York: Wiley, 1962.

Fite, M. D. Aggressive behavior in young children and children's attitudes toward aggression. *Genet. Psychol. Monogr.*, 1940, **22**, 151–319.

Frank, L. Cultural coercion and individual distortion. *Psychiatry*, 1939, **2**, 11–24.

Frankel-Brunswik, E. *Prejudice in children: an experimental approach.* Unpublished address, 1957.

Fraser, R. The incidence of neurosis among factory workers. *M. R. C. Indust. Health Res. Board Rep. #90*, 1947.

Freud, A. Safeguarding the emotional health of our children. An inquiry into the concept of the rejecting mother. *Child Welfare*, 1955, **34**, 3, 1–4.

Freud, S. *Studies in hysteria.* New York: Avon Books, 1895. P. 295.

Freud, S. Mourning and melancholia. In *Collected Papers.* Vol. IV. London, 1917.

Friedman, H. Perceptual regression in schizophrenia. *J. Genet. Psychol.*, 1952, **81**, 63–98.

Fries, M. E., and Woolf, P. J. Some hypotheses on the role of the congenital activity type in personality development. *Psychoanal. Study of the Child.* Vol. VIII. New York: International Universities Press, 1953. Pp. 48–62.

Gay, M. J., and Tonge, W. L. The hate effects of loss of parents in childhood. *Br. J. Psychiat.* 1967, **113** (500), 753–760.

Glueck, S., and Glueck, E. *Unraveling juvenile delinquency.* Cambridge, Mass.: Harvard University Press, 1950.

Goldfarb, W. Infant rearing and problem behavior. *Am. J. Orthopsychiat.*, 1943, **13**, 249.

Goldfarb, W. Infant rearing as a factor in foster home replacement. *Am. J. Orthopsychiat.*, 1944, **14**, 162.

Goldfarb, W. Psychological privation in infancy and subsequent adjustment. *Am. J. Orthopsychiat.*, 1945, **15**, 247.

Goldfarb, W. Effects of psychological deprivation in infancy and subsequent stimulation. *Am. J. Psychiat.*, 1946, **102**, 18–33.

Goldman, A. E. Symbolic representation in schizophrenia. *J. Personality*, 1960, **28**, 293–316.

Goldman-Eisler, F. The problem of "orality" and of its origin in early childhood. *J. ment. Sci.*, 1951, **97**, 765–782.

Goodenough, F. L., and Leahy, A. M. The effect of certain family relationships upon the development of personality. *Ped. Sem.*, 1924, **34**, 45–71.

Gottesman, I. Genetic variance in adaptive personality traits. *J. child Psychol. Psychiat.*, 1966, **17**, 199–208.

Greenacre, P. The biologic economy of birth. *Psychoanalytic study of the child.* Vol. I. New York: International Universities Press, 1945.

Gregory, I. Studies of parental deprivation in psychiatric patients. *Am J. Psychiat.*, 1958, **115**, 432.

Grey, W., In J. M. Tanner, and B. Inhelder, (Eds.), *Discussions on child development* New York: International Universities Press, 1953.

Gross, M. D., and Wilson, W. C. Treatment of minimal brain dysfunction in childhood. *Current Psychiat. Ther.*, 1967, **7**, 7–14.

Guilford, J. P., Frick, J. W., Christenson, P. R., and Merrifield, P. R. A factor analytic study of flexibility in thinking. *U. S. S. Calif. Lab. Rep. #18*, 1957.

Haggard, E. Diagnostic models in psychological research. Report given at Int. Conf. on "Adaptation to Change," June, 1968, sponsored by F.F.R.P.

Hare, E. H., and Shaw, G. K. A study in family health: a comparison of the health of fathers, mothers and children. *Br. J. Psychiat.*, 1965, **111**, 467.

Harris, F. R., and Johnston, M. K., Kelley, C. S., and Wolf, M. M. Effects of positive reinforcement on regressed crawling on a nursery school child. *J. educ. Psychol.*, 1964, **55**, 1, 35–41.

Hebb, D. O. *The organization of behavior.* London: Chapman and Hall, 1949.

Heinicke, C. M. Some effects of separating two-year-old children from their parents. *Hum. Relat.*, 1956, **9**, 105–176.

Heinicke, C. M., and Goldman, A. Research on psychotherapy with children: a review and suggestions for further study. *Am. J. Orthopsychiat.*, 1960, **30**, 483.

Henry, J. Some cultural determinants of hostility in Pilaga Indian children. *Am. J. Orthopsychiat.*, 1940, **10**, 111–122.

Heron, M. J. A note on the concept of endogenous-exogenous. *Br. J. med. Psychol.*, 1965, **38**, 241.

Hewitt, L. E., and Jenkins, R. L., *Fundamental patterns of maladjustment: the dynamics of their origin.* Springfield: State of Illinois, 1946.

Hill, D. E.E.G. in episodic psychiatric and psychopathic behavior. *Electroenceph. Clin. Neurophysiol.*, 1952, **4**, 419.

Hinkle, L. E., and Wolff, H. G. The nature of man's adaption to his total environment and the relation of this to illness. *Archs. Int. Med.*, 1957, **32**, 1.

Hinsie, L., and Campbell, R. *Psychiatric dictionary.* New York: Oxford University Press, 1960.

Holway, A. R. Early self-regulation of infants and later behavior in play interviews. *Am. J. Orthopsychiat.*, 1949, **19**, 612–623.

Hooker, H. F. A study of the only child at school. *J. genet. Psychol.*, 1931, **39**, 122–215.

Hudson, L. *Contrary imaginations: a psychological study of the young student.* New York: Schocken Books, 1966.

Hughes, J. R. Electro-clinical correlations in the positive spike phenomenon. *Electroenceph. Clin Neurophysiol.*, 1961, **13**, 399–605.

Hunt, J. McV. (Ed.) *Personality and the behavior disorders,* New York: Ronald Press, 1944.

Huschka, M. Psychopathological disorders in the mother. *J. neuro. ment. Dis.*, 1941, **94**, 76.

Itil, T., Rizzo, A., and Shapiro, D. Quantitative study of behavior and E.E.G. correlation during treatment of adolescents. *Diseases nerv. Syst.*, 1967, **28**, 731–736.

Jaspers, K. *General Psychopathology.* (H. J. Tians, and M. W. Hamilton, Eds.) Manchester University Press.

Jenkins, R. L. Diagnosis, dynamics and treatment in child psychiatry. In R. L. Jenkins, and J. Cole, (Eds.), *Diagnostic classifications in child psychiatry.* Psychiatric Research Reports of the American Psychiatric Association. Vol. 18, pp. 91–120.

Jenkins, R. L., and Blodgett, E. Prediction of success or failure of delinquent boys from sentence completion. *Am. J. Orthopsychiat.*, 1960, **30**, 741–756.

Jones, M. C. The elimination of children's fears. *J. exp. Psychol.*, 1924, **7**, 382–390.

Jones, M. C., and Mussen, P. H. Self-conceptions, motivations, and inter-personal attitudes of early- and late-maturing girls. *Child Dev.*, 1958, **29**, 491–501.

Kallmann, F. J. The genetic theory of schizophrenia. *Am. J. Psychiat.*, 1966, **3**, 309–322.

Kanner, L. Do behavior symptoms always indicate psychopathology? *J. child Psychol. Psychiat.*, 1960, **1**, 17–25.

Katz, D. Presidential Address. *Proceedings of the International Congress of Psychology.* Stockholm, 1951.

Kellmer, Pringle, M. L. The incidence of some supposedly adverse family conditions. *Br. J. educ. Psychol.*, 1961, **31**, 183.

Kellner, R. *Family ill health.* London, 1963.

Kellner, R. The evidence in favor of psychotherapy. *Br. J. med. Psychol.*, 1967, **40**, 341.

Kessel, W. Psychiatric morbidity in a London general practice. *Br. J. prev. soc. Med.*, 1960, **14** (5), 16–22.

Klackenberg, G. and Melin, Karl Axel. Crisis of anxiety in the child and his E.E.G. *Rev. Neuro-psychiat. Inf. hyg. Ment. Enf.*, 1953, **4** (7–8), 199.

Koupernik, C. Epileptic paroxysm of a vegetative and anxious nature in children. *J. child Psychol. Psychiat.*, 1960, **1** (2), 146–155.

Kreitman, N., Pearce, K., and Ryle, A. The relationship of psychiatric, psychosomatic, and organic illness in a general practice. *Br. J. Psychiat.*, 1960, **112**, 487–569.

Krech, D. Behavior and neurophysiology. In M. H. Marx (Ed.), *Theories in contemporary psychology.* New York: Macmillan, 1964.

Kvarceus, W. C. Forecasting delinquency: a three year experiment. *Except. Children.*, 1961, **27**, 429–435.

Langfeldt, G. The significance of a dichotomy in clinical psychiatry. *Am. J. Psychiat.*, 1959, **116** (6), 537–539.

Langford, W. Reflections on classification in child psychiatry as related to the activities of the committee on child psychiatry of the group for the advancement of psychiatry. In R. L. Jenkins, and J. O. Cole (Eds.), *Diagnostic classification in child psychiatry.* American Psychiatric Association Psychiatric Report #18.

Lapouse, R., and Monk, M. An epidemiologic study of behavior characteristics in children. *Am. J. Publ. Hlth.*, 1958, **48**, 1134–1144.

Lapouse, R. and Monk, M. Fears and worries in a representative sample of children. *Am. J. Orthospychiat.*, 1959, **29**, 803–818.

Lehrman, L. J., Sirluck, H., Black, B. J., and Glick, S. J. Success and failure of treatment of children in the child guidance clinics of the Jewish Board of Guardians. New York City: *Jewish Board of Guardians Research Monograph, No. I.*, 1949.

LeVine, S. Stimulation in infancy. *Sci. Amer.*, 1960, **202**, 80–86.

Levitt, E. E., Beiser, H. R., and Robertson, R. E. A follow-up evaluation of cases treated at a community child guidance clinic. *Am. J. Orthopsychiat.*, 1959, **29**, 337–349.

Levy, D. M. Finger-sucking and accessory movements in early childhood. *Am. J. Psychiat.*, 1928, **7**, 881–918.

Levy, D. M. Experiments on the sucking reflex and social behavior of dogs. *Am. J. Orthopsychiat.*, 1934, **4**, 203–224.

Levy, D. M. Studies in sibling rivalry. *Res. Monogr. Am. Orthopsychiat. Ass.* 1937, **2**, 1–96.

Levy, D. M. *Maternal overprotection.* New York: Columbia University Press, 1943.

Levy, D. M. The strange hen. *Am. J. Orthopsychiat.*, 1950, **20**, 335.

Levy, S. (1959), Post-Encephalitic Behavior Disorder—A Forgotten Entity: A Report of 100 Cases. *Am. J. Psychiat.*, **115**, 1062–1067.

Lewis, A. Preface to *Children of Sick Parents* by M. Rutter. London: Oxford University Press, 1966.

Lewis, H. *Deprived children.* London: Oxford University Press, 1954.

Lewin, K. Field theories and experiment in social psychology. Concepts and methods. *Am. J. Sociol.*, 1929, **46**, 368–396.

Lindemann, E. G., and Ross, A. C. A follow-up study of a predictive test of social adaption in pre-school children. In G. Caplan (Ed.), *Emotional problems of early childhood.* New York: Basic Books, 1955. Pp. 79–83.

Litauer, W. *Juvenile delinquency in psychiatric clinics.* London, 1957.

Loomis, A. L., Harvey, E. N., and Hobart, G. Electric potentials of the human brain. *J. exp. Psychol.*, 1936, **19**, 249.

Luria, A. R. *The nature of human conflicts.* New York: Liveright, 1932.

MacFarlane, J. W., Allen, L., and Honzik, M. P. *A developmental study of the behavior problems of normal children.* Berkeley: University of California Press, 1954.

Marks, I. M., and Gelder, M. G. Common ground between behavior therapy and psychodynamic methods. *Br. J. med. Psychol.*, 1966, **39**, 11–23.

Mathers, A. T. Difficulties and problems in the program for the prevention of mental disease. *Can. Publ. Hlth. J.*, 1931, **22**, 10.

McKegney, F. P. Psychological correlates of behavior in seriously delinquent juveniles. *Br. J. Psychiat.*, 1964, **113**, 781–792.

Medawar, P. Onwards from Spencer: evolution and evolutionism. *Encounter*, 1963, **21**, 35–43.

Mental Health Survey of Los Angeles County. 1960.

Miller, L. C. Q-Sort agreement among observers of children. *Am. J. Orthopsychiat.*, 1964, **34**, 71–75.

Miller, N. E., and Dollard, J. *Social learning and imitation.* New Haven, Conn.: Yale University Press, 1941.

Moore, T. Difficulties of the ordinary child in adjusting to primary school. *J. child Psychol. Psychiat.*, 1966, **7** (1), 17–38.

Moran, P. A. The establishment of a psychiatric syndrome. *Br. J. Psychiat.*, 1966, **112**, 1165–1171.

Morris, H. H., Jr., Escoll, P. J., and Wexler, R. Aggressive behavior disorders of childhood—A follow-up study. *Am. J. Psychiat.*, 1956, **112**, 991–997.

Morris, D. P., Soroker, E., and Burruss, G. Follow-up studies of shy withdrawn children—I. Evaluation of later adjustment. *Am. J. Orthopsychiat.*, 1954, **24**, 743–754.

Mowrer, O. H. Enuresis. A method for its study and treatment. *Am. J. Orthopsychiat.*, 1938, **8**, 436–459.

Mussen, P H., and Conger, J. J. *Child development and personality.* New York: Harper, 1956.

Mussen, P. H., and Jones, M. C. Self-conceptions, motivations and interpersonal attitudes of late and early maturing boys. *Child Dev.*, 1957, **28**, 243.

O'Connor, N. The evidence for the permanently disturbing effects of mother-child separation. *Acta. Psychologica*, 1956, **12**, 174.

O'Connor, N. and Franks, C. Childhood upbringing and other environmental factors. In H. J., Eysenck (Ed.), *Handbook of abnormal psychology*, London, 1960.

Olson, W. Developmental theory in education. In D. B. Harris (Ed.), *the concept of development.* Minneapolis: University of Minnesota Press, 1957.

O'Neal, P., and Robins, L. N. The relation of childhood behavior problems to adult psychiatric status: a thirty year follow-up study of 150 subjects. *Am. J. Psychiat.*, 1958, **114**, 961–969.

O'Neal, P., and Robins, L. N. Childhood patterns predictive of adult schizophrenia: a thirty year follow-up study. *Am. J. Psychiat.*, 1959, **115**, 385.

O'Neal, P., and Robins, L. N. Parental deviance and the genesis of sociopathic personality. *Am. J. Psychiat.*, 1962, **118**, 1114–1124.

Parnell. R. W. Physique and mental breakdown in young adults, *Br. Med. J.*, 1957, **1**, 1485–1490.

Parsons, T. Illness and the role of the physician; a sociological perspective. *Am. J. Orthopsychiat.*, 1951, **21**, 452.

Pasamanick, B., Rogers, M. E., and Lilienfield, A. M. Pregnancy experience and the development of behavior disorders in children. *Am. J. Psychiat.*, 1956, **112**, 613–618.

Patterson, G. R., and Brodsky, G. A behavior modification program for a child with multiple problem behaviors. *J. child Psychol. Psychiat.*, 1966, **7**, 277–295.

Pavenstedt, E. History of a child with atypical development. G. Caplan, (Ed.), *Emotional problems of early childhood*, New York: Basic Books, 1955.

Peterson, D. R., Quay, H. D., and Cameron, G. R. Personality and background factors in juvenile delinquency as inferred from questionnaire responses. *J. consult. Psychol.*, 1959, **23**, 395–399.

Peterson, C. H., and Spano, F. Breast feeding, maternal rejection and child personality. *Charact. Pers.*, 1961, **10**, 62–66.

Piaget, J. *Discussions on child development.* (J. M. Tanner, and B. Inhelder, Eds.) New York: International Universities Press, 1960.

Pick, T. Behavior theory and child guidance. *J. child Psychol. Psychiat.*, 1961, **2**, 136–147.

Pinneau, S. R. The infantile disorders of hospitalism and anaclitic depression. *Psychol. Bull.*, 1955, **52**, 429–452.

Pollak, O. *Social science and psychotherapy for children. New York*, 1952.

Post, F. Family neurosis and family psychosis. *J. ment. Sci.*, 1962, **108**, 147.

Postman, L. Perception, motivation, and behavior. *J. Personality*, 1953, **22**, 17–31.

Pritchard, M., and Graham, P. An investigation of a group of patients who have attended both the child and adult departments of the same psychiatric hospital. *Br. J. Psychiat.*, 1966, **112**, 487–603.

Prugh, D. Children's reaction to illness. In A. M. Freedman and H. I. Kaplan, (Eds.), *Comprehensive textbook of psychiatry.* Baltimore, Md.: Williams and Wilkins, 1967.

Purcell, K., and Melz, J. R. Distinctions between sub-groups of asthmatic children. *J. Psychosom. Res.*, 1962, **6**, (4), 251–258.

Renaud, H., and Estess, F. Life history interviews with one hundred normal American males: "pathogenicity" of childhood. *Am. J. Orthopsychiat.*, 1961, **31**, 786–802.

Reynolds, M. M. Negativism of pre-school children. *Teach. Coll. Contrib. Educ.* #288, 1928.

Roberts, E. Thumb and finger sucking in relation to feeding in early infancy. *Am. J. Dis. Child.*, 1944, **68**, 7–8.

Robins, L. N. *Deviant children grown up.* London: E. and S. Livingstone, 1966.

Rogers, M. E., Lilienfield, A. M., and Pasamanick, B. *Prenatal and paranatal factors in the development of childhood behavior disorders.* Baltimore, Md.: Johns Hopkins University Press, 1955.

Rogerson, B. C. F., and Rogerson, C. H. Feeding in infancy and subsequent psychological difficulties. *J. ment. Sci.*, 1931, **85** (1), 1163–1182.

Rosen, B. M., Bahn, A. K., and Kramer, M. Demographic and diagnostic characteristics of psychiatric clinic outpatients in the U.S.A., 1961. *Am. J. Orthopsychiat.*, 1964, **24**, 455–467.

Rutter, M. *Children of sick parents.* London: Oxford University Press, 1966.

Rutter, M., Birch, H. G., Thomas, A., and Chess, S. Temperamental characteristics in infancy and the later development of behavior disorders. *Br. J. Psychiat.*, 1964, **110**, 651.

Rutter, M., and Graham, P. Psychiatric disorder in 10 and 11 year-old children. *Proc. R. Soc. Med.*, 1965, **59**, 382–387.

Rutter, M. E. Classification and categorization in child Psychiatry. *Int. J. Psychiat.*, 1967, **3**(3), 161–172.

Ryle, A., Pond, D., and Hamilton, M. The prevalence and patterns of psychologic disturbance in children of primary age. *J. child Psychol. Psychiat.*, 1965, **6**, 101–113.

Sarbin, T. R. Role theory. In G. Lindzey, (Ed.), *Handbook of social psychology.* Cambridge, Mass.: Addison-Wesley, 1954.

Shields, J. Personality differences and neurotic traits in normal school children. *Eugen. Rev.,* 1954, **45,** 213.

Sears, R. R., Whiting, J. W. M., Nowlis, V., and Sears, P. S. Some child rearing antecedents of aggression and dependency in young children. *Genet. Psychol. Monogr.,* 1953, **47,** 135–234.

Sewell, W. H., and Mussen, P. H. The effects of feeding, weaning, and scheduling procedures on childhood adjustment and the formation of oral symptoms. *Child Dev.,* 1952, **23,** 185–191.

Shepherd, M., Fisher, M., Stein, L., and Kessel, W. Psychiatric morbidity in an urban group practice. *Proc. R. Soc. Med.,* 1959, **52,** 269.

Shepherd, M., Cooper, A., Brown, A., and Kalton, G. Minor mental illness in London: some aspects of a general practice survey. *Br. Med. J.,* 1964, ii, 1359–1363.

Shepherd, M., Oppenheim, A. N., and Mitchell, S. Childhood behavior disorders and the child guidance clinic: an epidemiological study. *J. Psychol. Psychiat.,* 1966, **7,** 39–52.

Shirley, H. A behavior syndrome characterizing prematurely-born children. *Child Dev.,* 1939, **10,** 115–128.

Shouksmith, G., and Taylor, J. N. The effect of counseling on the achievement of high ability pupils. *Br. J. educ. Psychol.,* 1964, **24**(1), 51–57.

Slater, E. Psychotic and neurotic illness in twins. *M. R. C. Special Report Series* #238, 1958.

Slavson, S. R. *A textbook in analytic group psychotherapy.* New York: International Universities Press, 1964.

Spitz, R. A., Hospitalism. *Psychoanalytic Study of the Child.* Vol. I. New York: International Universities Press, 1945.

Srole, L., Langner, T. S., Michael, S. T., Opler, M. K., and Rennie, T. A. C. *Mental health in the metropolis.* New York: McGraw-Hill, 1962.

Stainbrook, E. Society and individual behavior. In B. Wolman, (Ed.), *Handbook of clinical psychology* New York: McGraw-Hill, 1965.

Stennet, R. G. Emotional handicap in the elementary years: phase or disease. *Am. J. Orthopsychiat.,* 1966, **36**(3), 444–449.

Stern, E. S. The Medea complex: the mother's homicidal wishes to her child. *J. ment. Sci.,* 1948, **94,** 321.

Stern, J. Developmental psychophysiology—a project in the making (Personal Communication). A longitudinal study of primary reaction patterns in children. *Compreh. Psychiat.,* 1968, **1,** 103.

Stott, D. H. Physical and mental handicaps following a disturbed pregnancy. *Lancet,* 1957, **1,** 1006–1012.

Stott, D. H. Infantile illness and subsequent mental and emotional development. *J. Genet. Psychol.,* 1959, **94,** 233–251.

Stott, D. H. Abnormal mothering as a cause of mental subnormality—I. A critique of some classic studies of maternal deprivation in the light of possible congenital factors. *J. child. Psychol. Psychiat.,* 1962, **3,** 79–91.

Stott, D. H. Congenital indications in delinquency. *Proc. R. Soc. Med.,* 1965, **58,** 703–706.

Strauss, A. A., and Lehtinen, L. E. *Psychopathology and education of the brain injured child.* New York: Grune and Stratton, 1947.

Stringer, L., and Glidewell, J. *Final report for early detection of emotional illness in school children.* Report to N.I.M.H., 1967.

Tanner, J. M. The morphological level of personality. *Proc. R. Soc. Med.,* 1947, **50,** 301–303.

Terman, L. M. Research on the diagnosis of pre-delinquent tendencies. *J. Delinq.*, 1925, **9**, 124–130.

Thomas, A., Birch, H. G., Chess, S., Hertzig, M. E., and Korn, S. *Behavioral individuality in early childhood.* New York: New York University Press, 1963.

Thomas, A., Birch, H. G., Chess, S., and Hertzig, M. E. A longitudinal study of primary reaction patterns in children. *Compreh. Psych.*, 1960, **1**, 103.

Van Ophuijsen, J. H. W. Primary conduct disturbances: their diagnosis and treatment. In N. D. C. Lewis, and B. L. Pacella, (Eds.), *Modern Trends in child psychiatry.*, New York: International Universities Press, 1945.

Waddington, C. H. *The strategy of genes.* New York: Macmillan, 1957.

Walker, R. N. Body build and behavior in young children. I. Body build and nursery school teachers' ratings. *Monogr. Soc. Res. Child. Dev.*, 1962, **27**(3), 1–94.

Walker, R. N. Body build and behavior in young children. II. Body build and parent's ratings. *Child Dev.*, 1963, **34** 1–23.

Walton, D. Experimental psychology and the treatment of a Ticquer. *J. child Psychol. Psychiat.*, 1961, **2**, 148–155.

Wenger, M. A. Study of the significance of measures of autonomic balance. *Psychosom. Med.*, 1947, **9**, 301.

Werner, H. The concept of development from a comparative and organismic point of view. In D. B., Harris, (Ed.), *Concept of development.* Minneapolis: University of Minnesota Press, 1957. Pp. 125–148.

Wertz, F. J. The fate of behavior disorders in adolescence. *Am. J. Orthopsychiat.*, 1962, **32**(3), 423–433.

Williams, C. D. The elimination of tantrum behavior by extinction procedures. *J. abnorm. soc. Psychol.*, 1959, **59**, 269.

Williams, E. J. Truancy in children referred to a clinic. *Ment. Hyg.*, 1947, **31**, 464–469.

Witkin, H. A., Dyk, R. B., Faterson, H. F., Goodenough, D. R., Karp, S. A. *Psychological differentiation.* New York: Wiley, 1962.

Witmer, H. Parental behavior as an index to the probable outcome of treatment in a child guidance clinic. *Am. J. Orthopsychiat.*, 1933, **3**, 431.

Witmer, H. A comparison of treatment results in various types of child guidance clinics. *Am. J. Orthopsychiat.*, 1935, **5**, 351–360.

Wittles, F. The super ego in our judgments of sex. *Int. J. Psychoanal.*, 1933, **14**, 335–340.

Wolf, E. Learning theory and psychoanalysis. *Br. J. med. Psychol.*, 1966, **39**(1), 1–10.

Wolff, S. Social and family background of pre-school children with behavior disorders attending a child guidance clinic. *J. child Psychol. Psychiat.*, 1961, **2**, 260–268.

Wolff, S. Symptomatology and outcome of preschool children with behavior disorders attending a child guidance clinic. *J. child Psychol. Psychiat.*, 1961, **2**, 269–276.

Wolff, S. Behavioral characteristics of primary school children referred to a psychiatric department. *Br. J. Psychiat.*, 1967, **113**(501) 885. (a)

Wolff, S. The contribution of obstetric complications to the etiology of behavior disorders in childhood. *J. child Psychol. Psychiat.*, 1967, **8**(1), 57–66. (b)

Wolman, B. *Contemporary theories and systems in psychology.* New York: Harper and Row, 1956.

Wooton, B. *Social science and social pathology.* London: Allen and Unwin, 1959.

Wynne, L., and Singer, M. Thought disorder and family relations of schizophrenics. II. A classification of forms of thinking. *Arch. gen. Psychiat.*, 1963, **9**, 199–206.

Yarrow, L. J. Separation from parents during early childhood. M. L. Hoffman, and L. W. Hoffman (Eds.), *Review of child development.* New York: Russell Sage, 1964.

Zax, M., Cowen, E. L., Izzo, L. D., and Trost, M. A. Identifying emotional disturbance in the school setting. *Am. J. Orthopsychiat.*, 1964, **24**, 447–454.

Zigler, E. Metatheoretical issues in developmental psychology. M. H. Marx, (Ed.), *Theories in contemporary psychology.* New York: Macmillan 1963.

29. Childhood Psychosis

WILLIAM GOLDFARB

The purpose of this chapter is to consider the present state of knowledge regarding childhood psychosis. Childhood refers to the period from infancy to prepubescence or approximately from birth to age 10. An unusually detailed and sober review of the subject has already been presented by Ekstein, Bryant, and Friedman (1958), who offered the most complete bibliography and evaluation of trends through the year 1956. Their review is still pertinent since the last 10 years of professional activity have concentrated on an elaboration and refinement of trends already manifest in child psychiatry in 1956. The bibliography of this chapter thus will not replicate in its entirety Ekstein's bibliography of the years preceding 1956. However, the work and consideration of the past 10 years will be represented very fully in the present bibliography and discussion.[1]

Such a survey leaves one with a burdensome sense of confusion. The disorders subsumed in the category of childhood psychosis are extremely heterogeneous. The criteria for diagnosis have not been uniform and precisely defined. Differing labels have been applied to the same or overlapping groups of children; for example, childhood schizophrenia (Bender, 1947), infantile autism (Kan-

ner, 1942), atypical development (Rank, 1949), organic psychosis or chronic brain damage (Knobloch and Pasamanick, 1962), or borderline psychosis (Ekstein and Wallerstein, 1957). Each of these designations represents a special point of view regarding diagnostic criteria, range of disorders included, etiology, treatment, and prognosis. Some of the labels, for example, childhood schizophrenia, are employed at times as general designations covering virtually all the psychotic conditions of childhood. At other times, the same label is used to designate a specific subgroup (Eisenberg, 1966) of childhood psychosis. Even the term "childhood psychosis" has varied meanings. Sometimes it is employed to cover the entire range of very severe childhood aberrations tagged by the preceding labels. At other times it is given a special meaning. For example, in one important report (Rutter, 1965) it is offered as an alternative designation for autism; and, on the other hand, the author proposes that the disorders referred to are totally separate from the adult schizophrenic reactions. It is therefore not surprising that the literature regarding childhood psychosis is replete with apparent contradictions.

The clinical descriptions are also highly diversified. Some case studies describe totally detached children, meager in adaptive equipment, devoid of language skills, and subnormal in intelligence. Others describe highly ideational children with complex defensive behavior—including phobic, obsessional, paranoid, and depressive reactions—and, at times, delusional formations. In some studies, many of the parents and relatives of schizophrenic children suffer from adult schizo-

[1] The present review of the literature used the major indices in psychiatry, psychology, child development (especially *Psychological Abstracts, Child Development Abstracts,* cumulative *Index Medicus*), digests of psychiatry, the annotated bibliographies of childhood psychosis (Goldfarb and Dorsen, 1956; Tilton, DeMyer, and Loew, 1966), and the periodicals and books in the English language which refer to childhood behavioral disorders.

phrenia (e.g., Bender and Grugett, 1956; Kaufman, Frank, Heims, Herrick, and Willer, 1959; Menolascino, 1965). In other studies, schizophrenia in the parents and relatives is infrequent or virtually nonexistent (Creak and Ini, 1960; Kanner, 1954; Rutter, 1965). Some studies have noted evidence of cerebral dysfunction (e.g., Goldfarb, 1961; Knobloch and Grant, 1961; Schoen and Yannet, 1960). Others find no evidence for such cerebral dysfunction in the group under investigation (e.g., Kanner, 1954). In one study greater depression of scores in verbal tests of intelligence than in nonverbal and spatial tests is described (Rutter, 1965). In another study, this test pattern is not observed (Goldfarb, 1961). Other contradictions will be described in the evaluative remarks to follow.

It will be possible, however, to find a way out of the perplexing morass of confusion and arrive at a firmer footing if one keeps in mind major methodologic questions and several guidelines for evaluating the information which is now available. These reflect convictions derived from empirical and now rather extended clinical and investigative experience. They may be summarized as follows:

1. Different labels may be referring to groups of children, which overlap in diagnosis and other characteristics, although similar labels may be referring to disparate groups of children. This problem can be avoided only if the reporter carefully defines his diagnostic criteria and describes his groups. It is to be noted that diagnostic criteria are frequently not offered or they are not uniform among studies.

2. The criteria are very broadly defined so that even when they are not overlapping they cause the inclusion in the samples under study of children who are highly diversified in behavioral characteristics and background. A need for finer subclassification of groups studied is indicated. (A basis for subclassification will be offered later in the present discussion.)

3. Each investigator studies and describes a specially selected sampling of psychotic children. The problem of generalizing arises and this problem is perhaps the most difficult to unravel.

One may safely presume that a sampling

of children who would be representative of the target universe of psychotic children is never achieved in the reported studies. The kind of psychotic child under surveillance is influenced by the therapeutic resources, the referring source, affiliation and intake criteria, and therapeutic philosophy of the treating agency, the community serviced, other community facilities for the care of the disturbed child, and many other factors. These factors may be difficult to pinpoint, but some illustrations suggest themselves immediately.

By its intake procedures and program requirements, each treatment setting filters selected varieties of children out of the total universe of psychotic children. Children in one treatment setting, therefore, may be very different from those in another setting. For example, the ages of children admitted to treatment differ at the various treatment installations. The children may be accepted for treatment in the nursery years, or early school period, or later. Age of admission to treatment, of course, reflects the statistics on age of onset. The general level of competence of the children under treatment may vary from setting to setting. Some hospitals accept children at every level of adaptive capacity, whereas other hospitals may accept children only if average or better in capacity. As will be seen, such selection by level of ego will reflect selectively the influence of a diversity of etiologic factors. Similarly, one setting may have a high ratio of children from broken families, while another may restrict admission to children from structurally intact families. In a more subtle fashion, the parents who are motivated to apply are influenced by the extent to which the treatment program desires participation by parents or excludes them.

Thus data reported in the literature undoubtedly reflect the character of the selection procedures of children under investigative observation in each treatment setting. In some studies, the average intellectual functioning of the sample of psychotic children is above normal (e.g., Bettelheim, 1955). In others, the average intellectual ratings of the children are far below normal (Goldfarb, 1961; Rutter, 1965). Even the cognitive patterns may reflect selection. For example, as noted, Rutter (1965) reports lower verbal than nonverbal functioning in a group of psychotic children, whereas Goldfarb (1961) reports lower nonverbal than verbal functioning in his group. It is therefore apparent that subclassification of the children and a suitable basis for describing the individual members of each sample are prerequisites if the findings from diverse experimental samples are to be either correlated or compared.

To assist in attaining a realistic overview of the current understanding of childhood psychosis it will also be helpful to have a historical perspective, since it casts light on differences among contemporary workers. A brief review of historical trends will thus be offered and the work of the major contributors in the English language will be noted. An effort will then be made to present an integrated discussion of childhood psychoses, including more detailed consideration of some mentioned in the historic overview. The discussion will touch on the following topics:

1. Classification of childhood psychoses.
2. Diagnosis; criteria.
3. Epidemiology.
4. Differential diagnosis.
5. Descriptive characteristics.
6. Etiology.
7. Treatment and course.

In order to integrate the total discussion, an approach to the diagnostic differentiation and subclassification will ultimately be presented. Though based on etiologic factors which are still best regarded as presumptive, such a subclassification has operational value in ordering observations of the children being observed.

HISTORICAL TRENDS

The concept of childhood psychosis is a recent one; and extensive interest in precise description and explanation is a twentieth-century phenomenon in child psychiatry. In point of time, it followed the formulation of the concept of adult psychosis. Indeed, it can be shown that the changing historical emphasis in the diagnosis of childhood psychosis, its treatment, and prognosis of its course, has always reflected the prevailing opinions regarding adult psychosis. A brief history of the changing status of the concept of childhood psychosis in child psychiatry will be summarized in order to underscore

the historical changes in meaning of the classification of psychosis in childhood. This historical interpretation will lean heavily on published reports by Bradley (1941), Potter (1933), Kanner (1942), Ekstein (Ekstein et al., 1958), and Eisenberg (1957). The earlier annotated bibliography by Goldfarb and Dorsen (1956) covering childhood psychosis through 1954, and the later one by Tilton, DeMyer, and Loew (1966) covering 1955 to 1964 also lend themselves readily to a historical analysis.

References to conditions comparable to psychosis can be found in the medical and psychiatric literature of the nineteenth century (Alexander, 1894, 1893; Ashby, 1905; Beach, 1898; Broadbent, 1878; Browne, 1859-60; Clevenger, 1883; Down, 1887; Esquirol, 1845; Ireland, 1896; Mills, 1898; Mitchell, 1870; Rush, 1812; Spitzka, 1890). Utilizing the clinical classifications current at that time, the authors described infantile "manias," "dementias," and "insanity." Like modern authors, they even referred to constitutional, psychological, and organic bases for these conditions; and, at times, they attempted to differentiate the "manias" from mental deficiency. However, the clinical descriptions were meager and it is apparent that there was very little knowledge or information about the course of these disorders. In the main, children now classified as psychotic would seem to have been absorbed into the larger, vaguely defined category of children with mental deficiency or deteriorating organic conditions.

In the first decade of this century attention to adult psychoses burgeoned sharply and great progress was made in their definition and classification. As noted, the major historical trends in the categorization and rationalization of adult psychiatric disorders were immediately reflected in the psychiatric considerations regarding childhood psychosis. Indeed, the very labels for classification of childhood psychosis as well as criteria for diagnosis were borrowed directly from the designations and descriptions of adult psychiatric entities. "Dementia praecocissima" (De-Sanctes, 1925) and "dementia infantilis" (Hulse, 1954) were undoubtedly derived from Kraepelin's (1919) "dementia praecox." Similarly, the diagnostic entity of "childhood schizophrenia" was an offshoot of Bleuler's

(1952) descriptions of the adult and adolescent schizophrenias. Beyond the labels, the substantive details of the theories pertaining to adult psychosis were quickly paralleled by postulates in the theories of childhood psychosis. The adult psychiatrists who most influenced child psychiatrists in their descriptions of childhood psychosis were those who were most significant in enhancing observation and classification of adult psychosis. The names that stand out most prominently are Kraepelin, Bleuler, Meyer, and Freud.

Kraepelin's contribution (1919) was to propose a variety of psychiatric syndromes in adulthood; for example, he described simple, hebephrenic, paranoid, and catatonic syndromes in dementia praecox on the basis of symptoms. He inferred that the four syndromes were expressions of a common diagnostic entity which he called "dementia praecox" since all presumably began in adolescence or early adult life and all involved mental deterioration. He proposed that the causes of all the disorders were cerebral degeneration or metabolic disorders; and he disapproved of psychological explanations of psychotic reactions.

Kraepelin was of major importance in encouraging careful, clinical observation and description. However, his adult descriptive categories, his overstress on symptoms, his blindness to the psychodynamic, intrapsychic, and psychosocial significance of symptoms, his total commitment to organic explanations, and his concept of inevitable dementia had a very restrictive influence on child psychiatry. His convictions tended to retard the search for psychological and social factors in serious childhood behavior disorders. They favored a nontherapeutic attitude and pessimism regarding outcome. During the early part of this century, when Kraepelin's influence was most prominent, study findings of the clinical course of psychotic children were characterized by dramatically poor clinical outcome in every case. This contrasted with the more hopeful outcome supported by statistics offered by child psychiatrists as therapeutic optimism grew (Eisenberg, 1966). Certainly, few workers today adhere to the concept of inevitable "dementia" or mental deterioration in all cases.

Bleuler's (1952) concept of schizophrenia and his criteria for diagnosing schizophrenic

reactions had a greater positive impact than Kraepelin on the developing classification of childhood psychosis. He disputed the notion of inevitable deterioration and placed greater stress on intrapsychic and adaptational features of psychotic manifestations. More specifically, he affirmed that the disorders included in the category of dementia praecox were not always characterized by deterioration; and that they also did not inevitably start in adolescence. He also stressed the notion that schizophrenia—his term—included a variety of disorders, and he preferred the plural designation, "the schizophrenias." He believed that the "splitting" or inner disharmony of feeling and thought which characterized the schizophrenias was produced by physical factors, but the clinical form was influenced by psychological factors. In attempting to give psychological meaning to the symptoms of schizophrenia he was guided by Freud's principles of intrapsychic dynamics and emotional determinism.

Bleuler specified the primary or key symptoms of schizophrenia, including (1) autism, that is, the excessive predominance of inner fantasy life over reality, (2) associative fragmentation and lack of continuity, (3) emotional disturbances and disharmony, and (4) marked emotional ambivalence. Secondary or accessory symptoms included (1) hallucinations, (2) delusions, (3) illusions, and (4) psychomotor aberrations as in catatonia.

In contrast to the limited value of Kraepelin's classification in childhood psychosis, Bleuler's criteria for psychosis were all found to be applicable to diagnosis of children by the early clinicians, for example, Potter (1933) and Bradley (1941), and are still reflected in modern diagnostic schemata. It is of major importance that Bleuler's emphasis on the determining role of intrapsychic dynamics in the symptoms of psychosis and his emphasis on the diversity of outcome and clinical course had a lasting impact on considerations of severe disturbance in childhood.

The current thought in regard to childhood psychosis has thus been more strongly therapeutic in intention and more perceptibly optimistic than in the past. The guiding notions of unconscious emotional determinism and of adaptation which have colored the observations and clinical descriptions of many important workers (e.g., Despert, 1947; Mahler, 1961; Rank, 1949) were derived from Freud's psychoanalytic system. An equally strong influence was Adolph Meyer's (1950-52) view of schizophrenia as a defective life accommodation which can be explained by the patient's life experiences. He held that the schizophrenic reactions are expressions of miscarried efforts to achieve order and balance in the face of diverse stresses and pressures on the individual. Meyer's emphasis on the adaptive significance of pathological symptoms and his argument against the "physical disease" concept of mental illness have strongly influenced considerations regarding childhood psychosis.

In their descriptions of dementia praecox and schizophrenia in adolescence and in adulthood, Kraepelin and Bleuler mentioned occasional onset in childhood. Kraepelin (1919) reported that 3.5% of his 1054 patients with dementia praecox had been under 10 years at time of onset. He suggested that certain forms of "idiocy" might represent early cases of dementia praecox. Bleuler (1952) reported that 5% of patients with adult schizophrenia showed onset of their difficulties early in childhood. It must be emphasized that these authors had little direct clinical experience with children. Their references to childhood personalities and circumstances predisposing to the abnormal personalities and reactions of the adolescent and adult periods were infrequent and retrospective in character.

Stimulated by the sharpening of classification of adults, however, psychiatrists began to search more directly for evidence of psychosis in children (DeSanctes, 1925; Hulse, 1954; Weygandt, 1915, 1933). Of course, they related their terminology and concepts to those that were current at the time, particularly Kraepelin's scheme for diagnosis of dementia praecox; and their statements were largely descriptive, seeing the disorders as degeneration of the central nervous system. Obviously, the cases described by these clinicians were loosely defined and included children who would now be included in the schizophrenic classification; others might now be classified in other categories, such as organic psychosis and mental deficiency.

The existence of a specific entity termed childhood schizophrenia was in fact questioned by many psychiatrists. Their doubts were augmented by their difficulty in distinguishing maturational immaturity from psychopathy in children. Since too little was known about the facts of normal child development, the definition of abnormality was not feasible. Certainly, the criteria for diagnosis of psychosis in adult life were not applicable to children. Nor could clear duplicates of the categories of adult psychosis, including the accepted Kraepelinian subdivisions of dementia praecox (simple, hebephrenic, paranoid, catatonic) and manic-depressive psychosis, be discerned in childhood. Clinical descriptions of conventional schizophrenic categories were reported but were strongly disputed. Examining these case reports today, it is likely that most investigators still question the suitability of a diagnosis such as hebephrenia or catatonia for classification of children before the period of adolescence.

In the third decade of this century, however, there was increasing acceptance of the diagnosis of childhood psychosis. Although there was a disposition to include psychotic children in the broader class of schizophrenics, special therapeutic services for psychotic children were organized and workers began to present systematic information including outcome (e.g., Kasanin and Kaufman, 1929).

The contemporary period which began in the 1930s has been characterized by a number of major trends. These trends refer to questions and issues of diagnosis, etiology, and treatment. The major questions of this period will be considered more fully throughout this report; but here again a historic perspective will enable the reader to evaluate developments.

Since the 1930s, all workers have been impressed with the necessity for diagnostic criteria which take into account the immaturity and special developmental aspects of childhood. A milestone in this regard was Potter's (1923) scheme for diagnosing childhood schizophrenia. His criteria were as follows:

1. A generalized retraction of interests from the environment.

2. Unrealistic thinking, feeling, acting.

3. Disturbances of thought, manifested through blocking, symbolization, condensa-

tion, perseveration, incoherence, and diminution, sometimes to the extent of mutism.

4. Defect in emotional rapport.

5. Diminution, rigidity, and distortion of affect.

6. Alterations of behavior with either an increase of motility, leading to incessant activity, or a diminution of motility, leading to complete immobility or bizarre behavior with a tendency to perseveration or stereotypy.

Potter strongly proposed that a typical schizophrenic reaction may appear long before the period of pubescence, but he recognized clearly the unique manner in which the mental and emotional immaturity of the child and his state of development affected his symptomatic expression. For example, he believed that their verbal limitations and mental concreteness explained the relative infrequency and simplicity of delusional reactions of psychotic children. Nevertheless the relationship between Potter's criteria for childhood schizophrenia and Bleuler's classical definition of the primary and secondary symptoms is patent.

In a more empirical spirit, Bradley and his colleagues at the Bradley Home asked themselves what characteristics do in fact distinguish children with "schizophrenic psychoses and schizoid personalities" (Bradley and Bowen, 1941). He described overt, objective symptoms found in four children with "actual schizophrenic psychosis and ten children with evidences of schizoid personality" without necessarily implying specific attributes of the sharply delineated personality types depicted by Bleuler and by Kraepelin. The 8 behavioral characteristics which distinguished these 14 children from 124 other children admitted for treatment to the Bradley Home were, in order of frequency:

1. Seclusiveness.

2. Irritability when seclusiveness was disturbed.

3. Daydreaming.

4. Bizarre behavior.

5. Diminution in number of personal interests.

6. Regressive nature of personal interests.

7. Sensitivity to comment and criticism.

8. Physical inactivity.

Bradley also commented that apathy and emotional blunting, characteristics of adult schizophrenia, were not prominent in the children. Following Bleuler's model of primary and secondary symptoms in schizophrenia, he was impressed with the primary significance of seclusiveness, bizarre behavior, and regression. Finally, he recommended that the diagnosis of schizophrenia should not be based only on the symptoms and that the course of the child's development and growth must also be considered in diagnosis.

Despert (1938) described 29 children admitted to the New York State Psychiatric Institute between 1930 and 1937. She defined schizophrenia as a "disease process in which the loss of affective contact with reality is coincident with or determined by the appearance of autistic thinking and accompanied by specific phenomena of regression and dissociation." This definition is not as detailed or even as precise as Potter's diagnostic criteria; but it adds the concept of a failure to achieve normal emotional relatedness to reality. Linked to this is Despert's reference to the children's anomalous speech, characterized by a dissociation between "language sign" and "language function"; that is, words are repeated echoically but they are not used to communicate meanings to others. Despert also referred to three types of onset: acute onset, insidious onset, and insidious onset followed by an acute episode. She stressed the importance of onset history in differentiating the descriptive picture, treatment response, and life course of the children. She was particularly impressed by the poor clinical prognosis in the event of acute onset of the disorder and anxiety.[2]

[2] This relationship between onset and outcome seems poorly supported by her data since all but 2 of the 29 children in Despert's group ultimately showed reduced level of functioning or marked deterioration. Indeed, the two cases of remission were children with disorders of insidious onset followed by an acute episode leading to admission to the hospital. Of interest in this regard is an unpublished study at the Ittleson Center, where a careful and systematic effort was made to define onset history of 48 psychotic children admitted between 1953 and 1963. Parents and collateral relatives were interviewed and observations of hospitals, doctors, and other professional observers were reviewed. Even so, it was extremely difficult to specify onset history.

Beginning in the 1940s there has been a large number of clinical investigators who have occupied themselves with clinical study, description, and treatment of psychotic children. Bender at Bellevue Hospital in New York City and Kanner at Johns Hopkins University have had the most impressive experience with psychotic children and their observations and speculations have had the most crucial impact on other workers. Major contributions have also been made by Mahler and Szurek. Because of their historic importance and their importance in stimulating the ideas and observations of other workers, the considerations of each of these workers will be summarized.

The two major students of childhood psychosis in the United States have undoubtedly been Lauretta Bender and Leo Kanner. Both have had the most extended experience with psychotic disorders in childhood and have had the opportunity to study their respective clinic populations with systematic attention to many facets of the problem. Both have also written the most precise descriptive criteria for diagnosis in this country, and have had the greatest influence on the definitions and observations of other workers.

Bender (1947, 1960) defines childhood schizophrenia as a "total psychobiological disorder in the regulation of maturation of all the basic behavior functions seen clinically in childhood. Thus it is a maturational lag with embryonic features as characterized by primitive (embryonic) plasticity in all patterned behavior in the autonomic or vegetative, perceptual, motor, intellectual, emotional and social areas."

Bender is quite conscious of the difficulties in differentiating childhood schizophrenia from other conditions. For example, children

___

In 47 of 48 cases, onset was insidious from the earliest days or weeks of life. In six of the children with insidious onsets, acute episodes were reported. Parental reports were considered quite unreliable since they often were unaware of bizarre manifestations in their children. In at least two cases where the parents had reported acute onset, candid movies documented pathological symptoms in children far before the dates of presumed acute onset reported by the parents. In the one case where it is almost certain that there was acute onset, the child's adaptive capacities did deteriorate sharply.

with diffuse encephalopathy or with disturbance in interpersonal relationships may experience anxiety to which they react by regressive motility and cognition, and social behavior with schizophrenic features. However, Bender presumes that in childhood schizophrenia there is a central core of psychosis. The concept of an "essential psychosis" is open to serious logical question. However, the notions of intrinsic physiological impairments and lesser adaptive competence and of resultant anxiety are helpful in explaining the behavior of the severely disordered children classified as psychotic or schizophrenic or by any other comparable label.

Bender has proposed that in every case, one may discern vasomotor disturbance, either in the direction of unresponsiveness or of excessive lability. Such disturbances are reflected in excessive flushing or pallor, or perspiration, or blueness of the extremities. She describes excessive febrile and "shock" reaction to infection or abnormally rapid recovery. Total pacing of autonomic response and recovery is presumably disordered in comparison to the normal child.

The daily rhythmic pattern of physiological responses is also disordered. Sleeping, eating, and elimination rhythms are abnormal. Growth abnormalities are to be seen; so that children are too obese or too thin, or too tall or too short. Menstruation in girls and puberty in boys may start at an abnormally young or abnormally advanced age.

Disturbances in patterned motility are particularly conspicuous. Incoordination, developmental delay in coordination, and motor insecurity are noteworthy. Bender first called attention to the significant residues of primitive motility and postural response in the children.

Certain postural responses are presented as "nearly specific" for childhood schizophrenia. For example, if the child stands with eyes closed and outstretched arms while the head is rotated on the neck by the examiner, the schizophrenic child turns his body so as to bring it in line with his head. This is the well known "whirling response" which is frequently seen in normal children below 6 years of age but very rarely in older children. Bender emphasizes that the whirling response in the schizophrenic children above 6 years of age is unlearned. It conforms with their intrinsic impulses to rotate and whirl in outward motility and even in their fantasies. Indeed it is presumed by Bender to be the key to many of their psychological problems, including their body fears, their defective engagement with outer reality, and their disorganized consciousness of time, space, and even personal identity. Related to these phenomena are the bodily dependence and physical compliance characteristic of schizophrenic children—qualities expressed in the way they lean on the adult and melt into the contours of any body they happen to contact. Bender proposes that the motor compliance represents the schizophrenic child's need for awareness of a stable, predictable center of gravity in the face of the inner disorganization and formlessness.

Physical impulsivity and discoordination are also reflected in darting behavior and facial grimacing; while the vague perception of the body seems to be a factor in the schizophrenic child's lack of concern with body secretions, body extensions, and clothes.

It is also clear that the deviant motor activity and the impaired body awareness are linked to the perceptual aberrations of the children. Very early in her case descriptions, Bender described the developmentally primitive visuomotor responses of schizophrenic children, including the tendency to verticalization of horizontal figures, the poor reproduction of visual images, the motor impulsivity, the vague differentiation of figure and ground. In addition to her general clinical descriptions, Bender demonstrated the value of test procedures using standard visual Gestalt figures and the drawing of the human figure to elucidate the schizophrenic child's disturbances in motility, perception, and body image.

Bender refers to three critical ages of onset: (1) the first 2 years of life, (2) from 3 to 4½ years, and (3) from 10 to 11½ years. In her experience, the most common age of onset is the period between 3 and 4½ years.[3]

Bender states explicitly, or at times implies,

that the symptoms she describes are noted in every case of diagnosed childhood schizophrenia and she accepts that some of these symptoms serve as criteria which are "near specific" for schizophrenia in childhood. Her convictions in this regard still need careful verification. Indeed, controlled systematic investigation (e.g., Goldfarb, 1961) would tend to contradict the universality of some of her proposed findings in schizophrenic children. Nevertheless, her clinical descriptions have been unsurpassed and have been of primary importance in stimulating investigation.

Bender believes that the tendency to childhood schizophrenia is genetically determined (Bender and Grugett, 1956). However, the clinical disorder results from a decompensation, often as a result of a physiological crisis which leads to brain damage or personality disintegration with the previously noted symptomatic disorders in personal identity, body image, personal relationships, orientation, language, and motility. In Bender's view, in the schizophrenia of early childhood, the precipitating crisis occurs in the paranatal period. Anxiety is the outstanding symptom, resulting from the clinical decompensation, and is responsible for a variety of secondary defensive manifestations. Bender (1960) thus further classifies the clinical expressions of childhood schizophrenia as follows:

1. Pseudo-defective type of child with autistic or regressive withdrawal. The child is retarded and most of all shows developmental arrest, poor homeostatic response, and biological regulation.

2. Pseudo-neurotic type, similar to Hoch and Polatin's (1949) adult pseudo-neurotic schizophrenia with phobic, obsessive-compulsive, hysterical, and anxious manifestations. The child often has good intelligence and active ideation, but is seriously disturbed in identity, body awareness, and temporal and spatial orientation. He may relate to others with explosive intensity.

3. Psychosomatic type, with visceral, respiratory, and allergic symptoms.

4. Pseudo-psychopathic type, with impulsivity and antisocial symptoms of late childhood.

5. Type characterized by frank psychotic episodes.

---

[3] This is not a universal experience and, for example, the most common age period of onset among Ittleson Center schizophrenic children is the first year.

6. Latent schizophrenia, which may never manifest itself or may appear symptom-free at certain times spontaneously, especially latency in girls or puberty in boys.

In follow-up reports of the schizophrenic children she treated at Bellevue Hospital, Bender (1953) notes that approximately two-thirds of the children were also diagnosed as schizophrenic in adolescence or adulthood. By implication, then, childhood schizophrenia is linked to adult schizophrenia, which itself is presumably determined genetically.

At the same time that Bender was developing her concepts of childhood schizophrenia, Kanner was taking note of a syndrome he termed "early infantile autism." In his first report (1942) he described a group of children who engaged with people and life circumstance in a manner far different from that of normal children. They withdrew from people and experience from the beginning of life and were presumably distinguished from schizophrenic children who withdrew from people after an initial period of engagement with them. In a series of reports, Kanner and Eisenberg continued to elaborate the symptoms of autistic children (Eisenberg and Kanner, 1956; Kanner, 1954, 1949), reported the characteristics of their families (Eisenberg, 1957b), and summarized a follow-up of a large group of carefully diagnosed children (Eisenberg, 1957a).

Kanner's criteria for the diagnosis of infantile autism are as follows:

1. Aloneness, extreme in degree and evident in earliest infancy. The babies do not respond with normal anticipatory gestures as the adults reach to pick them up and do not adapt to the bodies of those who hold them.

2. Impaired communication. Speech and language are not used for the purposes of communication. Often the children are entirely mute or, if speech is present, it is echolalic and does not convey meaning. Pronominal reversals and literalness are frequent; and affirmation is expressed by repetition rather than the use of the word "yes."

3. Obsessive insistence on the maintenance of sameness, with great anxiety in new and unfamiliar situations, and with repetitive ritualistic preoccupation.

4. Fascination for objects, in contrast to disinterest in people.

Kanner and Eisenberg have been persuaded that infantile autism represents a distinct diagnostic constellation. They differentiate infantile autism from schizophrenia on the basis of the very early onset in infancy of the autistic disorder, its course, and the familial background of the children designated as autistic. They also differentiate autism from mental deficiency since the autistic child presumably evidences segmental areas of capacity.

Recently, Rimland (1964) has recapitulated and publicized Kanner's descriptions of the syndrome of infantile autism. He has attempted to mobilize support for the view that infantile autism is a "unique psychosis" which is sharply differentiated from mental deficiency and childhood schizophrenia. However, in actual practice, Rimland's extensive criteria for differentiating infantile autism from childhood schizophrenia, which include those proposed by Kanner and Eisenberg, are not as precisely differentiating as he suggests. The child's characteristic "aloneness" and "preservation of sameness" from the earliest months of life remain the crucial features of the autistic child. Other Rimland criteria presumably differentiating the autistic child from the schizophrenic child, such as the autistic child's physical beauty and well formed body, his normal EEG, his excellent motor ability, the uniformly high intelligence and education of his parents, and the "idiot savant" spread of intellectual functions, are not confirmed by either clinical experience or the evidence of controlled experiment. Regarding etiology, Rimland postulates that the key dysfunction of infantile autism is cognitive and consists of the inability to relate new stimuli to remembered experience and to comprehend them. He speculates that this dysfunction is due to a defect in the reticular activating formation of the central nervous system, possibly as a result of hypoxia. His hypothesis regarding the role of the reticular activating system has not been supported by empirical investigation.

Bender's theory of childhood schizophrenia embodies a concept of a total integrative failure which is manifested in every variety of childhood disorder, including autism. Her propositions would thus tend to contradict the validity of a special subclass of childhood psychosis such as that of autism. Indeed, in her review of Kanner's concept of autism, Bender (1959) affirms that "autism is not synonymous with psychosis, nor does it indicate a specific type of mental illness." She views autistic behavior as a defensive response, secondary to a wide variety of more primary conditions such as schizophrenia, brain damage, emotional trauma, and emotional deprivation. Autistic responses thus represent a primitive phase of the normal developmental process which persist and have the significance of withdrawal in protection against the anxiety resulting from many varieties of impairment—genetic, cerebral, perceptual, and social. Anthony (1958) similarly notes the possibility of both a primary disposition to withdrawal and a secondary or defensive autistic reaction.

Bender's description of the defensive implication of the autistic symptom is convincing. However, it is a matter of interest that she herself avoids the adaptive and transactional significance of all the other symptoms of childhood schizophrenia. This applies even to those symptoms which one would be disposed to consider purely in terms of physiological deficit. Consider, for example, the phenomenon of whirling, as described by Bender or the related phenomenon of spontaneous circular motion. On entering the ward area of the in-patient children's service of a large city or state hospital, one is likely to see a sizable number of children moving in a circular fashion about the periphery of the large ward room and in total disengagement from other children.

In a visit to a well known children's service in a large state hospital, it was noted that two children were lying supine on the floor, two children were huddled on the window sill leaning on the protective screen, two were moving about the room, and, in the course of the afternoon, three children were observed to whirl on their own axis for very long periods. Only three children were involved with each other and the single ward attendant in a game of cards. Such aimless motility can obviously be induced by environmental monotony and formlessness; and vortical motion is rarely seen in residential centers in which there is deliberate planning for social and educational interaction throughout the day.

In the Henry Ittelson Center for Child Research which is a therapeutic center with a comprehensive program for psychotic children, the child's entire day is programmed and there is a constant consideration of the meaning and significance of each child's inclination to withdraw. Steps are then taken to make it unnecessary for the child to withdraw to achieve feelings of safety. Should a schizophrenic child be found lying on the floor or retreating into a corner or whirling in isolation, he becomes an immediate matter of staff concern. In the early days of the residential center, the large open grounds stimulated the children to run in vortical fashion around the main building. To counter this aimless rotation through the grounds, all areas were defined for specified purposes; such as the playground, the garden, the skating area and others as well. This put an end to the circular, boundless, aimless quality. In a similar fashion, the constant structuring and purposeful definition of time, space and program has eliminated all the usual kinds of detached motility.

In short, it should be noted that the entity "childhood schizophrenia" is an abstract construct applied to the data of natural observation; that the very name is historically recent; and that the perceptual, cognitive, and motor phenomena which serve as criteria reflect in part social, environmental, and emotional influences.

If Bender and Kanner have contributed most to the descriptive delineation of childhood psychoses, Margaret Mahler (1949, 1952, 1958, 1960, 1961; Mahler and Furer, 1960; Mahler, Furer, and Settlage, 1959; Mahler and Gosliner, 1955) has been most important in introducing a psychodynamic point of view into current considerations of these childhood conditions. In other words, she has proposed a series of intrapsychic events to explain the manifestations of childhood psychosis. Her theoretic propositions, derived from classical psychoanalysis, stress the crucial significance of disorders in identity formation and the differentiation of self from nonself and the central etiologic significance of disturbances in the relationship between mother and child. (She also accepts the probability of constitutional vulnerability in the psychotic child.)

Mahler hypothesizes that normal children take three steps in sequence as they move toward a clear, differentiated mental representation of themselves, distinct from the outer world. The first phase, which she terms the *normal autistic* phase, extends from birth to about 3 months. According to Mahler, in this phase, the infant presumably is aware of inner stimuli only and does not perceive objects outside his own body.[4] At about 3 months, the child enters the *symbiotic phase* of development. Here the child vaguely perceives that needs are satisfied by an external object, but the representation of the mother is not differentiated from the self-image. The infant's awareness of the person who satisfies his needs is blurred and, indeed, he is reacting to configurations of breast, face, and hands rather than a distinct unified image of mother. The third phase, termed the *separation-individuation phase*, coincides with the initial development of language and locomotion at 12-18 months. At this time, the baby begins to perceive his physical separateness and then the separateness of self, differentiated from the nonself. The mother presumably facilitates the development of the emergent purposeful functions by protecting the child against excessive stimulation and by assisting the child to organize stimuli which impinge on the child.

Mahler postulates that children diagnosed to be suffering with autistic psychosis have not grown beyond the normal autistic phase. The children fail to develop clearly articulated perceptions of the mother (and are unresponsive to her), of the self distinguished from the nonself, of the self differentiated from inanimate objects, of the inside and outside of their bodies. In the symbiotic psychosis, the children have presumably been unable to cope with the requirements of separation and individuation. In a state of panic over separation, they have remained fixed at or have regressed to a state in which they are psychologically one with the mother or, if the fear of psychological separation is severe

enough, they regress even further to the autistic state described earlier. Personal identity is absent and the child withdraws from social interaction.

On the basis of case study, Mahler suggests contributing factors such as excessive proprioceptive stimulation and painful illness, repeated psychological traumata, abnormal body closeness, and unpredictable mothering as in extreme maternal overstimulation followed by abandonment. Her concept of a breakdown in the system of reciprocal signalling necessary for constant interaction between mother and child is highly suggestive and parallels the findings of other workers in the area of communication (Goldfarb, Levy, and Myers, 1966).

Mahler's definitions of levels of identity and of affectional relationship are helpful in defining and giving meaning to the intrapsychic and interpersonal responses of psychotic children. They are thus advantageous in the design of therapeutic management. They are less useful in delineating clearly differentiated subclasses of childhood psychosis; moreover, few reports make profitable use of the distinction between autistic and symbiotic psychoses in systematic investigation.

Perhaps more than any other worker, Szurek (Boatman and Szurek, 1960) has striven for many years to confirm the hypothesis that the psychotic disorder is a consequence of emotional conflict and its resolution. He has depended largely on psychotherapy of the children and their parents to test his psychogenic hypothesis and to elucidate psychodynamic factors. Szurek and his colleagues have assumed that anxieties provoked by conflicted, ambivalent, or frightened parents distort the child's biological potentialities and may produce physiological aberrations. On the basis of these assumptions they have attempted to study and treat psychotic disorders by intensive psychotherapy.

As a result of these clinical discussions, psychiatry and associated disciplines showed a growing acceptance of the concept of childhood psychosis. Clinical observers also became increasingly aware that many children included in such diagnostic entities as mental deficiency, constitutional inferiority, psychopathic personality, and neurosis could more properly be included in the class of childhood

[4] Recent studies of young infants contradict Mahler's concept since they confirm the infant's awareness of visual stimuli.

psychosis. On the other hand, a spirit of uncertainty about the diagnosis of psychotic states in childhood persisted. Adequately precise and uniform criteria for distinguishing altered patterns of behavior from the normal range of child behavior were lacking. As a result, many workers continued to deny that the adult schizophrenias and psychoses had parallels in childhood. Certainly, diagnostic criteria based on alterations in behavior in the adult were not applicable to children whose adaptive functions were still in process of developmental change. Indeed, the group of workers in Boston, including Rank (1949), Putnam (1955), and their colleagues, entirely avoided the then current dispute over whether schizophrenia occurs in children by applying the term of "atypical" to very deviant children.

Some of the confusion about childhood psychosis may be dissipated if outstanding trends are distilled out of the very extensive discussions and literature. A number of key trends emerge in the diagnostic considerations of important workers. They may be summarized as follows:

1. Profound alterations in biological and psychological development, either in the form of regressions or of arrests, are noted by all observers. Fish, for example, in a series of studies (Fish, 1957, 1959, 1960b, 1961; Fish and Alpert, 1962), has focused on the deviations from standard norms of development which differentiated schizophrenic children from normal children. Her 10-year follow-up of children with deviations in consciousness, muscle tone, and motility in early infancy tended to confirm the link between these infantile disturbances and the perceptual and motor disturbances noted in older schizophrenic children.

2. All workers refer to the very global and total integrative failure demonstrated by schizophrenic children. The total personality is disordered. Anthony (1958) reflects the breadth of adaptive impairment in childhood psychosis when he proposes that the symptoms compose three areas of malfunctioning: "a. a psychological a-genesis leading to deficits in ego functioning. b. an a-cathexis, leading to difficulties in interpersonal relationships and displacement of affect on to things. c. an adualism, leading to a confusion of self and non-self and disturbances in the perception of the self."

3. Observers frequently refer to the highly variable and changing nature of the symptomatic expressions of schizophrenic children. Bender refers to the primitive plasticity in all integrative functions. Szurek (Boatman and Szurek, 1960), Ekstein (1966), and many others note the fluctuating, paradoxical nature of the behavior of the schizophrenic child. Certainly, in some of them, such behavioral fluctuation is dramatic. While a perplexing symptom, the behavioral fluctuation is also the major stimulus for therapeutic optimism and experimentation. In contrast to Bender's biological orientation and her concept of an inherited integrative failure implicit in her concept of plasticity, observers with greater therapeutic conviction are inclined to relate the adaptive fluctuation to social and interpersonal circumstance. Ekstein (1966), for example, links the behavioral regressions and progressive movements forward to the relationships of the psychotic child. The schizophrenic child with limited adaptive potentiality is easily frightened when he encounters stressful demands in relationship—demands which are beyond his capacity to cope with. His regressive behavior and fantasy are then viewed as defensive adjustments to avoid excessively painful anxiety.

4. All observers note a serious disturbance in emotional organization. Of unique significance is the absence of emotional engagement with all objects, both human and nonhuman. In other words, the child attends to the sensory and perceptual attributes of these objects rather than to their functional significance (Despert, 1938; Kanner, 1942). This, of course, is linked to the inability to perceive the essential living character of people.

5. A major advance in rationalizing the disorders subsumed by the diagnosis of childhood schizophrenia, or any of the other labels for childhood psychosis, is represented in the concept of ego aberration. Childhood schizophrenia is a label designating disturbance in the normal course of maturation of ego. Either as a result of arrest or regression, the essential qualities of normal ego are lacking. This concept derived from the psychoanalytic concept of the ego has been represented most explicitly in the case descriptions

and speculations of psychoanalytic reporters (Beres, 1955; Ekstein, 1966; Goldfarb, 1961; Mahler, 1949; Rank, 1949). Some of these observers refer to overall defects of ego. Such general defects of ego are implied in Szurek's descriptions of the paradoxical and contradictory character of the responses of schizophrenic children or in the previously noted references to the fluctuating and undifferentiated responses of schizophrenic children. Other observers describe impairments in specific aspects of ego. For example, Mahler has elaborated the various levels of arrest or regression seen in the normal course of development of affectional relationships. Indeed she proposes a subclassification of psychotic children on the basis of level and quality of relationship to others. In their descriptions of the atypical child, Rank and Putnam have focused essentially on evidences of disordered ego in the young child, with particular emphasis on defective communication and reality awareness. Beres' (1955) discussion of the specific facets of ego which are deficient in schizophrenic children is a significant clinical formulation because of its clarity and detail. The development of most important programs for the observation and elucidation of the impairments of schizophrenic children is largely derived from the psychoanalytic concept of ego; and, in a clinical research program such as that at the Ittleson Center, even more directly from the adaptational, psychodynamic position of Kardiner (1939) and Rado (1956). Indeed, as will be seen, the framework for our present discussion will be very strongly influenced by the adaptational position.

6. During the nineteenth century, psychotic conditions of childhood were generally explained by rather speculative references to an unstable or disordered nervous system, and to disordered heredity. Toward the end of the century there was a tentative recognition, however, of the influence of psychological and social factors in the symptomatic manifestations of psychosis. During the twentieth century, a variety of theories of the etiology of childhood psychosis have been propounded. These theories, of course, have been either biological and genetic or psychological and social in emphasis. Thus, as noted, some reporters have featured a genetic point of view (Bender and Grugett, 1956; Kallman and Roth, 1956); others have featured a psychodynamic bias (Boatman and Szurek, 1960; Despert, 1938; Mahler, 1949; Rank, 1949). Several authors have described children with definitive evidence of cerebral abnormality (DeSanctes, 1925; Hulse, 1954). Many authors, who have been impressed with psychological and social factors, have also presumed that the schizophrenic child was genetically or constitutionally vulnerable in the face of emotional stress (Goldfarb, 1961; Mahler, 1949; Rank, 1949).

A "single cause" explanation still holds strong attraction. However, there is a growing inclination to accept the concept of diverse etiologies, sometimes in combination, to explain the symptom patterns noted in childhood psychosis (Fabian and Holden, 1951; Goldfarb, 1961; Hirschberg and Bryant, 1954). If there has been a "breakthrough" in the study of etiology, it consists of the implementation of the concept of a multiplicity of factors, centered in the child and in the environment, to explain the adaptive accommodation of the child, which is then classified as psychosis.

CLASSIFICATION OF CHILDHOOD PSYCHOSES

Psychotic disorders refer to the most severe patterns of behavioral impairment. They include symptoms that refer to personality disintegration, failure to test reality correctly, and failure to achieve effective social and occupational relationships (*Diagnostic and Statistical Manual*, 1952). In the case of children, prepubescent in age, the symptoms reflect their developmental immaturity as well as the changeable character of their symptoms, so that the clinical picture in childhood may be quite different from that in adulthood. Nevertheless, in childhood as well as in adulthood, the functional impairment is profound, the personality is grossly disordered, highly regressive defenses are common, social behavior is often bizarre and socially unacceptable, reality testing is highly deficient, and the environment may be seriously distorted in the patient's understanding.

Empirically speaking, most child psychiatrists find it practical to approach the diagnostic differentiation of childhood psychoses within the general framework that has been developed for adults. For example, aware of the variety of disorders that may present themselves symptomatically as childhood psychosis, Eisenberg (1966) has recently proposed a classification which is noteworthy since it entails a consideration of etiological factors. His classification is based on two major divisions of childhood psychoses. Thus he distinguishes psychotic disorders caused by or associated with impairment of brain tissue function, where brain tissue pathology is demonstrable, from those psychotic disorders in which clearly defined structural changes in the brain have not as yet been demonstrated. He underscores the phrase "as yet" to indicate the tentative nature of the assignment of disorders to the latter division of psychoses.

In Eisenberg's classification, examples of psychoses linked to unequivocally demonstrable cerebral pathology are:

The toxic psychoses—caused by a very wide variety of toxic drugs and substances. Atropine, bromides, cortisone are examples of the many possible toxic agents.

Metabolic psychoses—caused by any of a variety of metabolic aberrations affecting the brain, such as pellagra, hypoglycemia, or amaurotic family idiocy.

Degenerative psychoses—caused by degenerative diseases such as Schilder's Disease. These degenerative diseases are very rare. However, there is evidence that some disorders ordinarily placed in the functional division of psychoses more properly belong in the subcategory of degenerative diseases. There is justification, for example, for considering the pathological possibility of degenerative cerebral disease in those cases included under the rubric of Heller's Disease (Hulse, 1954). In this syndrome, a normally developing child sharply deteriorates in many important functions, such as speech and self-care. Unequivocal neurological findings are often not present, but alterations in the cellular structure of the brain have been demonstrated in some cases (Benda, 1952). Even so, there is no definitive evidence of a specific or single entity in every clinical case.

Infectious psychoses—caused either by acute febrile encephalitic episodes or by more chronic inflammatory changes in the brain, as in childhood paresis.

Dysrhythmic psychoses—caused by cerebral dysrhythmic disturbances, and especially the episodic manifestations of psychomotor seizures.

Traumatic psychoses—caused by cerebral injury.

Neoplastic psychoses—caused by the injurious effects of cerebral tumor.

These psychoses which exist as a consequence of demonstrable brain damage can usually be diagnosed with ease by reference to history, neurological findings, and laboratory data. They are important to differentiate because they may require immediate medical attention. Even where the brain damage is chronic or not accessible to immediate rehabilitative effort, precise diagnosis is essential for realistic management.

On separating out the psychoses with demonstrable cerebral lesions, the psychoses which remain are those in which demonstrable and unequivocal tissue alterations have not as yet been demonstrated. It is most accurate to affirm that this remaining group of psychoses contains a very broad gamut of disorders in which etiology has not been established. The labels attached to them have been based on clinical description rather than a knowledge of cause. Although operationally separated from the demonstrable cases of cerebral impairment, they form a highly varied group of disorders in which organic features are by no means necessarily excluded. While confusing and ambiguous, this group of disorders represents the greatest proportion of psychotic disorders observed and treated in most psychiatric installations; thus the remainder of this chapter will concentrate on it.

The group of functional psychoses has never been satisfactorily subdivided. As noted, it even includes disorders that some workers would place in the division of organic disorders, for example, Heller's dementia infantilis. The most common diagnostic label for the entire group of functional childhood psychoses is childhood schizophrenia. On the other hand, other labels have been assigned to similar groups of children. Although some workers (Eisenberg, 1966; Hirschberg and Bryant, 1955) utilize these labels to designate specific conditions, such clinical specificity has by no means been demonstrated and is even unlikely. Indeed, any effort to subdivide psychoses using these diagnostic terms is not likely to arrive at nonoverlapping clinical subgroupings. For example, in his classification of functional psychoses, Eisenberg (1966) emphasizes two major subgroups: the infantile autistic psychoses, with onset in the first year, following Kanner (1949); and the schizophrenias which start after about 8 years of age and satisfy the diagnostic criteria for schizophrenia in the adult. He also includes in his category of functional psychoses those extremely rare disorders in which a presumably healthy child reflects the symptoms of a psychotic person with whom he has a close relationship (*folie-a-deux*) and equally rare cases of manic depressive psychosis (Anthony and Scott, 1960). Finally, in recognition of the opinions and authority of other workers, he includes a group of psychoses which he terms "psychoses associated with maturation failure." Although Eisenberg considers this last entity a doubtful one and unnecessary beyond those previously mentioned, it actually includes the descriptive syndromes most widely referred to in the literature, including Rank's (1955) atypical child syndrome, Szurek's childhood psychosis (Boatman and Szurek, 1960), Bender's (1941-42) childhood schizophrenia, psychosis on top of mental defect as described by Kraepelin (1919) and Weygandt (1915, 1933). If, for the moment, we exclude from consideration manic-depressive conditions which have not been observed before 12 years of age (Anthony and Scott, 1960), the very rare *folie-a-deux* conditions, and the schizophrenias in children whose symptoms occur after 8 years of age and resemble adult symptoms, we are left with the autistic psychoses and the psychoses associated with "maturation failure." Since the last subcategory is considered of doubtful necessity by Eisenberg, he is left with only one subcategory of psychosis in early childhood, infantile autistic psychosis. Practical clinical experience would suggest, however, that a large group of infantile psychoses are in need of categorization if they fall outside the strictly defined bounds of Kanner's infantile autism. This explains why a number of observers include an undifferentiated category of early childhood psychosis as well as infantile autism in their classification schemes (e.g., White, DeMeyer, and DeMeyer, 1964).

Eisenberg's differentiation of infantile autism and childhood schizophrenia is useful in stressing the significance of age of onset in subclassifying psychotic children. Linked to this is the differentiation of the earliest forms of infantile psychoses which are characterized by developmental arrest from the later childhood psychoses characterized by developmental regression. Numerous observers have made this differentiation (Despert, 1947; Mahler and Furer, 1960), and Anthony (1958) elaborates primary and secondary autistic reactions.

Any system of classification, such as Eisenberg's, which builds its diagnostic differentiations around the syndromes discussed earlier, is highly ambiguous in definition. In addition, as noted, in each of these presumably functional syndromes derived from observation of behavior, the factor of organic abnormality cannot be excluded with certainty, so that their inclusion in the functional psychoses is primarily a matter of convenience. Eisenberg, of course, is aware of these ambiguities. Even so, there is undoubted value in his primary division of psychotic disorders into those with identifiable disorders of the central nervous system and those in which such pathology has not been identified unequivocally.

DIAGNOSIS OF CHILDHOOD PSYCHOSIS

Until diagnostic uniformity is achieved, it will not be possible to arrive at a meaningful and reliable estimate of the prevalence of psychotic conditions in children and the impact of such conditions on the community. A significant effort to clarify and define "psychosis in childhood" was made by a British working group in 1960 (Creak, 1960a). This group preferred the term "schizophrenic syndrome in childhood" over the more general term "psychosis in childhood." The group report does not elaborate the basis for this preference, although it suggests that the term "psychosis" includes many disturbances in addition to the range of disorders noted in the functional psychoses. Although not totally warranted, the most popular designation for the functional psychoses has been "schizophrenia." The British working group of 13

clinicians defined 9 diagnostic criteria. Initially, these workers tried to confine themselves to observable clinical signs and behavior. However, they found it essential to
include some signs that frankly involve interpretations of behavior and others that refer
to developmental and historical data. The
clinician is likely to look with favor on this
kind of approach which presumes a degree
of intuitive organization of the complex data
of observation and history that must be dealt
with in diagnostic and therapeutic work with
children. Even so, the signs are sufficiently
precise and empirical to assure reliability of
appraisal. The "nine points" for diagnosing
the "schizophrenic" syndrome are as follows:

1. Gross and sustained *impairment of emotional relationships* with people. This includes
the more usual aloofness and the empty clinging (so-called symbiosis): also abnormal behavior towards other people as persons, such
as using them impersonally. Difficulty in mixing and playing with other children is often
outstanding and long-lasting.

2. *Apparent unawareness of his own personal identity* to a degree inappropriate to
his age. This may be seen in abnormal behaviour towards himself, such as posturing
or exploration and scrutiny of parts of his
body. Repeated self-directed aggression,
sometimes resulting in actual damage, may
be another aspect of his lack of integration
(see also point 5) as is also the confusion of
personal pronouns (see point 7).

3. *Pathological preoccupation with particular objects* or certain characteristics of them,
without regard to their accepted functions.

4. *Sustained resistance to change in the
environment* and a striving to maintain or
restore sameness. In some instances behaviour
appears to aim at producing a state of perceptual monotony.

5. *Abnormal perceptual experience* (in
the absence of discernible organic abnormality) is implied by excessive, diminished,
or unpredictable response to sensory stimuli
—for example, visual and auditory avoidance
(see also points 2 and 4), insensitivity to
pain and temperature.

6. Acute, excessive, and seemingly illogical
anxiety is a frequent phenomenon. This tends
to be precipitated by change, whether in
material environment or in routine, as well

as by temporary interruption of a symbiotic
attachment to persons or things (compare
points 3 and 4, and also 1 and 2).
(Apparently commonplace phenomena or
objects seem to become invested with ter-
rifying qualities. On the other hand, an
appropriate sense of fear in the face of
real danger may be lacking.)

7. *Speech* may have been lost or never
acquired, or may have failed to develop beyond a level appropriate to an earlier stage.
There may be confusion of personal pronouns (see point 2), echolalia, or other
mannerisms of use and diction. Though words
or phrases may be uttered, they may convey
no sense of ordinary communication.

8. *Distortion in motility patterns*—for example, (a) excess as in hyperkinesis, (b)
immobility as in catatonia, (c) bizarre postures, or ritualistic mannerisms, such as
rocking and spinning (themselves or objects).

9. *A background of serious retardation* in
which islets of normal, near normal, or exceptional intellectual function or skill may
appear.

These "nine points" or criteria are immediately comprehensible and acceptable within
the experience of psychiatrists who manage
severe childhood disorders of behavior. A
review at the Ittleson Center for Child Research of 48 children classified as psychotic
before the publication of the British group
demonstrated that all the major symptoms
of the children were encompassed in the nine
points. All the children showed five or more
of the nine points. All the children showed
four gross impairments including impairments
in human relationships (sign 1), defects in
personal identity (sign 2), excessive anxiety
provoked by change (sign 6), and speech
disturbance (sign 7). If speech disturbance
is restricted to the most extreme disorders
of communication such as implied in the
statement "Though words or phrases may
be uttered, they may convey no sense of ordinary communication," the sign of speech
disturbance is not found in all schizophrenic
children. However, careful evaluation of
speech and language by an expert speech
pathologist reveals finer shades of communication impairment in all the children.

Similarly, a review of 52 published reports which featured diagnostic symptoma-

tology in schizophrenia (Alanen, Arajarvi, and Viitamaki, 1964; Annell, 1963; E. F. Anthony, 1958; J. Anthony, 1958; Bender, 1941-42; Beves, 1955; Bergman and Escalona, 1949; Boatman and Szurek, 1960; Bradley and Bowen, 1941; Bruch, 1959; Cain and Heinz, 1961; Colbert and Koegler, 1958; DesLauriers, 1962; Despert, 1955, 1947, 1938; Eaton and Menolascino, 1967; Eisenberg, 1967, 1966; Eisenberg and Kanner, 1956; Ekstein, 1966; Elkisch, 1956; Escalona, 1948; Esman, 1960; Fish and Alpert, 1962; Fish, 1959; Goldberg and Soper, 1963; Goldfarb, 1964, 1963, 1958, 1956; Goldfarb and Mintz, 1961; Goldfarb, Braunstein, and Lorge, 1956; Kanner, 1942; Leach and Heath, 1956; Lohrenz, Levy, and David, 1962; Mahler, 1949; Menolascino, 1965; Norman, 1955, 1954; Potter, 1933; Pronovost, Wakstein, Wakstein, and Murphy, 1961; Putnam, 1955; Rank, 1955; Rimland, 1964; Schopler, 1965; Sable, 1955; Speers and Lansing, 1965; Starr, 1954; Stroh and Buick, 1964; Wolff and Chess, 1964; Yakovlev, Weinberger, and Chipman, 1948) indicated that all the behavioral symptoms described could be embodied in the nine points. (Bender's description of deviation in vasovegetative response was not included in this survey of key deviations in molar, "whole person" behavior.) It is safe to conclude, therefore, that there is an acceptable degree of agreement with regard to the British working party criteria for the diagnosis for the functional or for what has been called more frequently the schizophrenic forms of childhood psychosis.

It must be understood that no single symptom is diagnostic. Indeed, each of the symptoms may be found in other disorders such as brain damage without schizophrenic syndrome, although to a lesser degree than in diagnosed childhood schizophrenia (Creak, 1964). In practice, the diagnosis is made after a consideration of the total constellation of symptoms and behavioral characteristics.

Since the symptoms of childhood psychotic disorders represent a range of adaptive deficits, psychological tests which measure purposeful functions are useful in facilitating diagnosis, evaluating severity of impairments, and appraising change. All the well known psychological tests have been used, including tests of intelligence (Alanen et al., 1964;

Bergman, Heinz, and Marchand, 1951; Davids, 1958; DesLauriers and Halpern, 1947; Goldfarb, 1961; Pollack and Krieger, 1958; Wechsler and Jaros, 1965), conceptual response (Goldfarb, 1961; Halpern, 1966), perceptual and sensorimotor response (Bender and Keeler, 1952; Bender, 1949; Goldfarb, 1961), and projective tests (Baumler, 1957; Beck, Molish, and Sinclair, 1956; Beck, 1954; DesLauriers and Halpern, 1947; Lebowitz, Colbert, and Palmer, 1961; Piotrowski and Lewis, 1950). Among the projective tests, the Rorschach has been employed most widely and modified scoring systems have been developed to permit its systematic use in treatment and appraisal. In the latter regard, the most ambitious application of the Rorschach is that of Beck and Molish (Beck, 1954; Beck et al., 1956). They have applied the Q-technique to Rorschach judgments and have identified six patterns of schizophrenic maladjustment, of which two refer specifically to children. The use of psychological tests has been applied to the study of longitudinal progress of schizophrenic children in treatment. Other workers have developed tools for the observation of children in structured and semstructured play and of their spontaneous behavior (Loomis, 1960; Loomis, Hilgeman, and Meyer, 1957; Steisel, Weiland, Smith and Schulman, 1961; Steisel, Weiland Denny, Smith and Chaiken, 1960). The Oseretsky test and rail walking test have been used to test motor coordination; and standardized tests have been developed to study a broad gamut of neurological functions including sensory response, balance, postural and righting behavior, oculomotor behavior, and motor coordination (Goldfarb, 1961). From a diagnostic point of view, tests are extremely useful for purposes of refining diagnostic observations and making them more precise. As will be seen, psychological tests have also been the basis for most systematic studies of adaptive deficits in childhood psychosis.

EPIDEMIOLOGY

Once it had become recognized and accepted as a psychiatric entity, childhood psychosis became increasingly subject to report. Facilities for the care of childhood psychosis have risen sharply, including in-patient, day hospital, and out-patient clinical facilities.

Pressure for increasing such facilities continues to increase. It is a startling fact, therefore, that adequate data pertaining to incidence and prevalence are still lacking. In a major report summarizing the considerations of the outstanding workers in the area of childhood psychosis in the United States (Robinson, 1957), the data refer only to pressures and recommendations for service; relevant vital statistics regarding incidence and prevalence are not stated. It is obvious that accurate and systematic public planning will have to await such statistics.

The major hindrance to the accumulation of suitable field statistics is the absence of a widely accepted and uniform system of classification. The meager data now available, however, would suggest that childhood psychosis is a relatively rare condition. Hagnell's (1966) screening of an entire community, including 405 children, revealed that no child under 10 years had been hospitalized for psychiatric conditions during a 10-year period. In addition, Tizard (1966) reported an unpublished study by Lotter, O'Connor, and Wing in which the definition of the British working party as reported by Creak et al. (1961) was used to develop a questionnaire. The questionnaire was submitted to all Middlesex teachers of 8-, 9-, and 10-year-old children and the teachers were asked to note all children who showed the symptoms to a marked degree. The prevalence of psychosis in the 76,000 children surveyed is reported as 4 per 10,000. In all likelihood this statistic is reduced by the circumstance of school attendance—a circumstance which undoubtedly restricts the number of subnormal children who constitute an unknown but indisputably large proportion of psychotic children.

All studies of childhood psychosis confirm a considerably higher ratio of boys to girls (Bender and Grugett, 1956; Boatman and Szurek, 1960; Kallman and Roth, 1956; Kanner, 1954; Meyers and Goldfarb, 1962). For example, in Bender's group of 142 children admitted to Bellevue Hospital under 7 years of age between 1934 and 1951, the ratio of boys to girls was 2 to 1 (Bender and Grugett, 1956). In the same report Bender indicates that the ratio increased in favor of boys to 2.7 to 1, as the age of the schizophrenic child increased up to 12 years of age. In Kallmann and Roth's (1956) twin study, the 52 twin index cases showed more boys than girls in the proportion of 2.5 to 1. A study of 45 schizophrenic children at the Ittleson Center showed a boy to girl ratio of 2.7 to 1 (Meyers and Goldfarb, 1962). The latter study also showed that subgroups of schizophrenic children, differentiated by neurological study, vary in the proportion of boys to girls, so that variations in ratio of boys and girls which are reported in the literature may reflect selection influence and the selection of children in turn would seem to be linked to a variety of biological and social factors. In the Ittleson Center studies, for example, the "organic" subgroup of schizophrenic children had a higher proportion of boys to girls than did the "nonorganic" subgroup. On this basis, one might hypothesize that samples of schizophrenic children with higher ratio of boys to girls contain higher proportions of children with cerebral dysfunction than do samples of schizophrenic children with low ratio of boys to girls.

Similar considerations apply to data regarding order of birth, although the findings are not as clear. Several studies (Bender and Grugett, 1956; Kanner, 1954; Meyers and Goldfarb, 1962) have reported a high percentage of only or first-born children. Here, too, there may be a link between primigravity and cerebral dysfunction in schizophrenic children. The male predominance in brain-damaged children is a well known fact.

Systematic investigation of ethnic and cultural aspects of childhood psychosis are lacking. Bender (Bender and Grugett, 1956) reports a high proportion of Jewish children (about 50%) and a very low proportion of Negro children in her group of schizophrenic children in contrast to the nonpsychotic children on her ward service at Bellevue. She notes quite reasonably, however, that the Jewish community in New York City has had an advanced social service structure which encourages more Jewish parents to seek assistance. Beyond this, Jewish parents seemed attentively concerned about deviations in early childhood. Negro and Puerto Rican families were less inclined to make voluntary use of special community services and were less vigilant to schizophreniform deviations in early childhood. It is significant that whereas most admissions of schizophrenic children to Bender's inpatient service followed voluntary application by the parents, the bulk of the admissions of nonschizophrenic children on the ward service followed mandatory referrals by courts and social agencies.

Kanner (1954), too, records a "vast majority" of Anglo-Saxon and Jewish families in his study of families of autistic children. (Although not definite, Kanner implies a higher proportion of Anglo-Saxon and a lower proportion of Jewish families than Bender describes in her schizophrenic group. Twenty-seven percent of Kanner's autistic children as against about fifty percent of Bender's schizophrenic children were Jewish.) Here again, it is difficult to estimate the selection influence of undoubted social and cultural artifacts on the ethnic and cultural backgrounds of Kanner's sampling of autistic children.

The selective character of sampling in any study of psychotic children is immediately evident in a treatment and research installation for psychotic children such as the Ittleson Center. Here, too, the majority of families are Jewish. The program is available to all ethnic and cultural groups but it is administered by a Jewish social service agency. In New York City, where private child care facilities are under sectarian auspices, the welfare climate is still one in which children tend to be referred to the agencies administered by their own respective religious groups. This, for example, would tend to diminish the number of non-Jewish referrals to a Jewish agency.

Arbitrary social and environmental artifacts also undoubtedly influence other findings regarding education, occupation, and intelligence levels of the families of psychotic children under study. For example, at the Ittleson Center, admission has been on the basis of voluntary application by the parents. In addition, in accord with research needs, children have been selected from families with both parents living together. Similarly, the parents have had to agree to participate in the research program. This has eliminated cases of childhood psychosis in children from broken homes where legal neglect and dependency were characteristic. The requirements of voluntary application, structurally intact family, and willingness to participate

in research undoubtedly has biased the distribution of Ittleson Center families. On the basis of Hollingshead-Redlich ratings of social class, Ittleson Center families treated between 1956 and 1966 have included a greater proportion of families in the middle and upper social positions (classes 1 and 2) and a lesser proportion of families in the lower social positions (classes 4 and 5) than the Hollingshead-Redlich urban group (Goldfarb, 1967). The arbitrary selective impact of intake procedure on the kind of psychotic child and the kind of family treated at the Ittleson Center has become even clearer in recent years. In the more recent years, 1963-1966, Ittleson Center has been receiving a new variety of applications on behalf of their psychotic children from families in the lowest social and economic classes and from Negro and Puerto Rican families. This new flow of applications has been stimulated by the new community programs for alleviating the status of impoverished families and for overcoming the effects of poverty. Thus we are now seeing indisputable cases of serious ego deviation and psychosis, using our present diagnostic criteria, from social classes and cultural-ethnic groupings that had previously excluded themselves from the intake of treatment centers. Even now it is evident that these new families are more weakly motivated to seek the kind of treatment offered by these centers than previous families and are often merely complying passively with the recommendations of the "poverty" agencies.

Detailed consideration of this trend is offered to emphasize that older findings of social class, education, and intelligence of the families of psychotic children must be evaluated in the light of many selective factors. An example is found in Kanner's description of his families of autistic children. Virtually all his autistic children came from intelligent, sophisticated stock. Of 100 fathers, 96 were high school graduates, 74 were college graduates, and the majority were in the professional and business executive occupations. Similar trends were true of the mothers. Kanner remarks, "To this day, we have not encountered any one autistic child who came of unintelligent parents." It is difficult to state with certainty what selective factors could have been operating in addition to the fact of Kanner's university setting. It is possible to state, however, that treatment installations other than Kanner's, for example, the Ittleson Center, have treated children with conspicuous autistic features, as defined by Kanner, whose parents were unintelligent, uneducated, non-Jewish, and non-Anglo-Saxon. One can only conclude that the autistic children and the families studied and described so lucidly by Kanner represented a selected sampling of the total population of autistic children.

It has already been emphasized that there has been no systematic investigation of the correlations involving socioeconomic and cultural factors and characteristics of the parent samplings studied. Now it should be noted that there has not been sufficient or adequate investigation of the correlation between socioeconomic and cultural factors and the specific clinical attributes of children diagnosed as suffering from psychosis, schizophrenia, autism, symbiotic psychosis or any of the other class designations employed for these overlapping groups of children. Sanua (1967) has properly stressed the persistent need for assaying the linkage between sociocultural conditions in the backgrounds of diagnosed schizophrenic children and their symptomatic manifestations. He refers to Korn's (1963) study of Negro and Puerto Rican children who had been diagnosed as schizophrenic. Korn demonstrates that the predominant symptmatology in these psychotic children was aggressiveness and bizarre behavior. All had acquired speech and none could be described as autistic or symbiotic. This is of special interest since aggressiveness has not been an outstanding manifestation of the schizophrenic children in the Kanner and Bender samplings. Nor has it been observed as a common or central symptom of Ittlèson Center children, who have until recently been largely Jewish. However, recent admission to the Ittleson Center of schizophrenic children on referral from poverty agencies has introduced more Negro and Puerto Rican children; and they have indeed manifested a more central symptom of aggression and disturbance in impulse control. On the other hand, these Negro and Puerto Rican children at the Ittleson Center frequently do manifest strong autistic features and some possess all the attributes of Kanner's infantile autism. If we assume the accuracy of Korn's observation that none of the Puerto Rican and Negro children she described were autistic, then we must infer than an additional selective factor has been influencing the kind of Negro and Puerto Rican child admitted to Ittleson Center. Once again we are reminded of the necessity for intimate information about each child in any sampling of schizophrenic children if we wish to understand the meaning of the group data.

Kanner's reports of the intelligent, educated, professional "upper-class" families of children with infantile autism has strongly influenced current conceptions (Kallman and Roth, 1956; Kanner, 1954). Lowe (1964) has reported comparable findings for the families with "chronic undifferentiated schizophrenia." The parents of these children were more educated and had higher occupational status than parents of children with non-schizophrenic behavior disorders. On the other hand, Bender's families of children admitted to her very large city hospital in-patient service came from a different level of family background (Bender and Grugett, 1956). Although Kanner contrasted the families of his autistic children with those of the other nonpsychotic children in his psychiatric service, sampling bias was by no means controlled. Kanner's diagnostic assistance and guidance was sought after by intelligent, educated parents who were most likely to have heard of his special interest in autism; and it is doubtful that a similar social factor influenced the referral of other behavior disorders to his clinic.

The most recent report which has come to our attention is based on a statistical analysis of psychotic children admitted to the Children's Psychiatric Hospital of the University of Michigan Medical School between July 1961 and July 1963 (McDermott et al., 1967). Of the 676 children admitted, 76 (or 11.2%) were diagnosed to be suffering from psychosis. Only 23, however, were frankly psychotic, and 53 were borderline psychotic. Diagnoses of typical autistic or symbiotic psychoses were too rare to support any conclusions regarding social class. (There were five autistic psychoses, two symbiotic psychoses, and two autistic-symbiotic psychoses.) The most important conclusion was that there was no difference in incidence of psychosis and borderline psychosis among the five social class groups employed in the analysis (professional and executive, upper white collar, lower white collar, skilled laboring class, and unskilled laboring class.) The presence or absence of symptoms, including withdrawal and autism, hallucinations and delusions, affective disturbance, paranoid thinking, depression, phobias, obsessions, compulsions, and free-floating anxiety were also found not related to social class. However, "severe" autism and withdrawal were seen significantly most frequently in the professional-executive group and severe thought disturbance was seen most frequently in the professional-executive and skilled working-class groups. These findings would tend to support Kanner's description of infantile autism in upper-class sophisticated families. On the other hand, Kanner does not report a high incidence of working-class families.

But we are reminded by McDermott and his colleagues, whose experience is described in the University of Michigan report, of the small size of their sample, the likely bias of sampling, and the possible class bias of the medical diagnosticians. If one adds to this the uncertainty and imprecision of the evaluation of symptoms by severity, we are merely left with evidence that psychotic children may be found in all social classes. The relationship between the specific manifestations of childhood psychosis and social class will not be clarified till the complex problems of diagnosis, subclassification, and population sampling are solved.

DIFFERENTIAL DIAGNOSIS

The differential diagnosis of functional psychosis of childhood is a constant preoccupation in clinical practice and a frequent consideration in the literature. Efforts have been made to differentiate childhood psychosis from mental deficiency (Bakwin, 1950; Cassel, 1957; Eisenberg, 1966; Eveloff, 1960; Goldberg and Soper, 1963), epilepsy (Lilienfield, Pasamanick, and Rogers, 1955), aphasia (Rutter, 1965), brain damage (Bender, 1955; Goldfarb, 1961; Kennard, 1959; Pasamanick and Knobloch, 1961; Taft and Goldfarb, 1964), psychoneurosis (Despert, 1955), and responses to early psychological deprivation and discontinuity (Eveloff, 1960; Gold-

farb, 1949). Such efforts to differentiate childhood psychosis from the other conditions have not been very productive and enlightening for a variety of reasons:

1. The diagnosis of childhood psychosis is a symptomatic diagnosis. It must be clear by now that each of the diagnostic nine points noted above refers to a behavioral manifestation. That is to say the diagnosis of childhood psychosis is not an etiological diagnosis; and at the present time a diagnostic scheme based on cause is not likely to be universally acceptable because etiology remains an open question.

2. On the other hand, as E. F. Anthony (1958) has stressed very acutely, even the first 10 authentic cases will persuade the observer that many factors contribute to the child's deviant behavior.

3. The childhood behavior disorders which need to be differentiated from psychosis are often themselves diagnosed by symptom and frequently they too are imprecisely defined classes of deviation. For example, mental deficiency, like childhood psychosis, is a class enveloping many kinds of disorders and it is now known that subnormal intellectual functioning can be produced by a wide variety of physical, psychological, and environmental factors.

4. Comprehensive study of psychotic children reveals a very high incidence of all the preceding conditions which we presumably would want to differentiate from psychosis. For example, a very high incidence of mental subnormality—even very extreme subnormality—is described by virtually all observers of psychotic children. In addition, studies of mentally subnormal populations confirm a significant proportion of children with manifest symptoms of psychosis (Goldberg and Soper, 1963; Menolascino, 1965). Whether such children are included in the clinical universe of psychosis or that of mental deficiency is merely a matter of arbitrary observer preference.

It would seem most reasonable to conclude, therefore, that there is little profit in attempting clear, unequivocal differentiation of functional childhood psychosis from the other childhood behavior disorders, mentioned earlier. On the other hand, there is distinct value in defining the extent to which ego aberrations and deficiencies such as mental deficiency or language deficiency are manifested in childhood psychosis and the extent to which the symptoms of childhood psychosis reflect factors such as cerebral dysfunction, cerebral dysrhythmia, and environmental deficiencies.

DESCRIPTIVE CHARACTERISTICS

Most of our descriptive knowledge of psychotic children has come from individual case studies. In the main, these studies have represented clinical observations of psychotic children who were being cared for in a variety of psychiatric settings where there were varying degrees of therapeutic intention. Relative to the great interest in childhood psychosis and the very large number of case descriptions of psychotic children in the literature, there have been a restricted number of controlled investigations of the attributes and adaptive deficits of psychotic children. Their social relationships, their feelings as determinants of their behavioral styles, and their private lives are undoubtedly best studied within the context of comprehensive treatment and the extended therapeutic dialogue. In actual fact, the reports that grow out of psychotherapeutic observations feature the determining significance of vicissitudes in drive organization, inner fantasy, and especially object relationship and identity formation. However, these complex deviations in the organization of drives and in the internal integration of interpersonal responses—so difficult to assay experimentally and precisely —are nearly always paralleled by aberrations in purposeful function which are quantifiable and accessible to experimental assay. A broad range of adaptive functions has been studied including perception, cognition, motility, speech, and relational behavior. These studies have demonstrated failures in all areas of adaptive behavior, although the various experimental groups have differed in absolute level and pattern of impairment.

As previously mentioned, the variations in results have reflected variations in diagnosis, sampling, and assay technique. If this qualification is kept in mind, there is merit in demonstrating the level of capacity in a broad gamut of adaptive functions in the same group of psychotic children. This is particularly warranted if the individual members of the group have been studied intensively and can be characterized in regard to a number of pertinent variables which give depth and meaning to the behavioral findings.

A useful approach to the investigation of psychotic children is one which appraises their functions for contacting reality, for making generalizations about it and testing it, and for manipulating it in the service of survival, self-realization, and need gratification. Among these functions, embodied in the term "ego," are psychological processes such as perception, conceptualization, and psychomotor response. It is assumed that the child inherits his capacity for sending and perceiving, for ordering perceptual data into internal schemata, and for developing strategies for executing optimal adaptive maneuvers. It is also assumed that the child's potentialities for action and his awareness are modified by biologic needs and by very early and primary interpersonal experiences.

Viewed structurally, the ego may be defined as the self-directing and self-regulating aspect of the organism. It is the internal organizer which enables the organism to accommodate to an inner and outer world which is in a constant state of alteration and to cope with novelty and changing environmental requirements with appropriate strategies. The organizing function of the ego thus implies a continuous flow of perceptual input for purposes of regulating and guiding the child's actions and an ability to conceptualize and categorize the universal elements in complex and multiple experiences. On the basis of these monitoring and schematizing experiences, the child is able to achieve inner feelings of predictability and the continuity of the self and non-self.

Behavioral studies of psychotic children may thus be organized in accord with the following questions. What is known about the overall level of ego organization of the psychotic child? How intact is his sensory equipment? How well does he organize and give form to his sensory intake? How capably does he conceptualize and organize the flood of internal and external information for purposes of prediction and coordinated action in the face of environmental changes? How proficient and coordinated are his motor and executive responses? How well does he speak and communicate?

Sensory Functions

Frequently the histories of psychotic children arouse the suspicion of sensory loss. The possibility of deafness arises as a diagnostic issue with particular frequency. On the other hand, distressful, hypersensitive reactions to sensory stimulation have encouraged speculations of reduced sensory thresholds. Sensory thresholds have been measured, using the standard A-O charts at 20 feet for vision, pure tone audiometry at 500, 1000, 2000, and 4000 cycles per second for audition of frequencies in the speech range, and the Von Frey test for tactile thresholds (Goldfarb, 1961). These tests demonstrate clearly that psychotic and normal children do not differ in visual, auditory, and tactile acuity. Use of A-O color plates also confirms that psychotic children are not differentiated from normal in color vision (Goldfarb, 1961).

In contrast to their response to pure tone auditory thresholds, diagnosed schizophrenic children show higher thresholds for free-field speech stimuli than for pure tones (Hoberman and Goldfarb, 1963). This pattern of discrepancy between pure tone and speech thresholds is evidence that the phenomenon of "not-hearing," which is so characteristic of many psychotic children, is not a primary defect of sensory acuity. Rather it reflects altered attention to or integration of human speech by the children.

The peripheral sensory structures are thus ordinarily intact in psychotic children. Do they, however, perceive form and pattern on stimulation of a given sensory end organ? The answer to this question is of significance since it may be assumed that the harmonious execution of action sequences and the well articulated awareness of self as the organizer of intended action requires a constant and active organization of inner and outer cues.

A variety of tests have been employed to appraise the capacity to perceive configurational relationships. Table 1 summarizes a series of perceptual tests which have been utilized in the Ittleson Center program of observations. The tests include:

1. The esthesiometer test of threshold for discriminating two cutaneous stimuli presented simultaneously.
2. The Benton finger location test of the ability to localize the fingers of the hand which are touched.
3. The Gottschaldt test for locating a visual stimulus in a more complex field.
4. The Street figures test of perception of the whole when fragmented stimuli are presented.

The psychotic children are inferior to normals in each of these perceptual tests.

All investigations of perceptual response in psychotic children have confirmed the difficulties psychotic children have, as a group, with all variety of tests of perception and perceptual discrimination. For example, in Berkowitz's comparison of schizophrenic and nonschizophrenic patients in an in-patient service for children where a variety of psychophysical tests were used (Berkowitz, 1961), the schizophrenic children were in-

Table 1. Differences in Perceptual Tests between Normal and Schizophrenic Children; By Means

Function Tested or Rated	Test or Rating Technique	Units of Measurement	Means	
			Normal	Schizophrenic
Two-point discrimination	Esthesiometer	Mm. discriminated	13.3	22.1[a]
Finger location	Benton	Number correct	24.3	16.7[a]
Figure-ground discrimination	Gottschaldt	Number correct	7.0	3.1[a]
Configurational closure	Street	Number correct	7.0	4.9[a]

From Goldfarb (1961).

[a] Differences significant at .05 level.

ferior in three out of four tests of visual perception. Sensory inattention undoubtedly plays a part in these perceptual failures, although the failures are still shown by some of the children even after improvement in attention.

Fuller has studied directional orientation as manifested in the tendency to rotation in children's reproductions of visual designs (Fuller, 1963, 1965; Fuller and Chagnon, 1962). Schizophrenic children show a greater rotation effect than normals and nonschizophrenic emotionally disturbed children. Fuller speculates that the failures in directional orientation of schizophrenic children represent a lack of "cue utilization due to emotional excitation, arousal or disturbance." What is of interest in this theoretic formulation is the proposition that the schizophrenic child has available a lesser supply of visual cues for purposes of orientation in space or, perhaps, a tendency to misinterpret available cues. The schizophrenic child is therefore uniquely incapable of selecting pertinent cues for regulating the pertinence and appropriateness of his responses. On the other hand, one may speculate that his deficiencies in body awareness and body concept aggravate his problems in spatial orientation. Witkin (1962) has demonstrated quite conclusively that the normal child's separation of figure from ground in the outer world is paralleled by his capacity to perceive his own body as discrete from the total field which surrounds him. It has also been observed by clinicians that the schizophrenic child who is deficient in his conceptualization of his body as differentiated from his surroundings is disordered as well in his differentiation of external objects. In such clinical observation, a child who has difficulty in differentiating and articulating the right and left halves of his body is also disordered in his orientation to direction in outer space. Under these circumstances, the perceptual rotations of the schizophrenic child when he copies visual designs may reflect both deficient utilization of visual cues and the absence of an inner referent, that is, a stable body image.

Conceptual Functions

Impairments in the conceptual organization of perceptual experiences have been noted by all clinical observers of psychotic children (Bender, 1947; Goldfarb, 1964, 1963; Goldfarb and Mintz, 1961; Kanner, 1942; Norman, 1954). These failures in the meaningful organization and integration of experiences are reflected in deficiencies in the concepts of self, especially of the body, of the outer world, of time and space, and of other persons. They are also a key feature of the language disturbances of psychotic children and in all likelihood explain the unusual metaphoric tendencies, the idiosyncratic symbols, and oft-described syntactical errors such as pronominal reversals (Kanner, 1942, 1946). In highly concretistic fashion, the children are bound to the immediacy of each situation and have difficulty shifting to an abstract attitude.

The unusually concretistic orientation to experience of schizophrenic children has been confirmed by systematic and controlled observation and experiment. Norman (1954) observed the responses of schizophrenic children to a variety of objects. He was struck by their attention to the perceptual attributes of the objects, such as to the surface or color and their disregard of the function and utility of the objects. Schulman (1953) administered an object sorting test to schizophrenic children 7 to 14 years of age and compared their responses to those of a normal standardization group. The schizophrenic children showed more concretistic, less abstract levels of conceptualization. Although generalization should be limited because the population was small and its uniformity at each age very uncertain, the normal increase with age in frequency of abstract forms of conceptualization was not found in the schizophrenic group.

Friedman (1961) compared 20 white schizophrenic and nonschizophrenic boys of average intelligence in a color-form sorting test, an object sorting test, and two similarities tests. When compared with the nonschizophrenic boys, the schizophrenic boys showed greater inconsistency in abstract thinking, more vague and all-inclusive responses, more concretistic responses, and less capacity to shift from a concrete to an abstract orientation when helped. The schizophrenic children had less ability to learn the abstract attitude than did the normal chil-

Table 2. Differences in Conceptual Tests between Normal and Schizophrenic Children; By Means

Function Tested or Rated	Test or Rating Technique	Units of Measurement	Means	
			Normal	Schizophrenic
Directional discrimination	Right-left discrimination	Number correct	15.7	10.5[a]
Abstraction	Weigl	Sum credits	5.3	3.5[a]
Orientation to time, place, person	Orientation	Number correct	25.4	16.0[a]
Body representation	Human Figure Drawing (self)	Rank	234.3	118.8[a]
Intelligence	Wechsler Intell. Scale for Children	Verbal IQ	111.0	77.0[a]
		Performance IQ	104.7	70.5[a]
		Full IQ	108.8	72.4[a]

From Goldfarb (1961).
[a] Differences significant at .05 level.

dren whose first responses were also concretistic.

Some results using procedures for appraising capacity for abstraction and conceptualization are presented in Table 2. Included are a test for right-left discrimination, the Weigl test of categorization by form and color, an orientation test, and the human figure drawing test. All the tests demonstrate that schizophrenic children as a group have difficulties in a variety of tasks which call on ability for conceptual response. They have difficulty in directional response, categorization of objects by form and shape, orientation to time, place, and person, and the representation of the human body. These results parallel clinical findings which suggest a possible dynamic relationship between conscious thought and abstraction as a generic experience and the more personal and specific areas of awareness, that is, of time and space as dimensional abstractions and of the discrete body self as an entity which has duration in time and is anchored in space.

The best single measure of integrative functioning is the intelligence test. The intelligence quotient in an intelligence test such as the Wechsler Intelligence Scale for Children measures a child's intellectual functioning in relation to that of a normal standardization group. Obviously the intelligence quotient reflects more than inherent capacity for intellectual response alone. In the case of the psychotic child who is very deficient in

overall adaptive qualities such as attention, concentration, and persistence (Goldfarb, 1961), the IQ is best regarded as an excellent measure of ego competence at the time of assay. In Table 2, the psychotic children are shown to be inferior to normal children in verbal competence (verbal IQ), nonverbal competence (performance IQ), and in the measure of global competence which summates both verbal and nonverbal capacities (full IQ). In this group of schizophrenic children, 54% have full IQs below 75 and only 23% have full IQs of 90 or over. A majority of the psychotic children are thus seriously retarded and a relatively small proportion show average intellectual functioning.

Most studies of the intelligence of schizophrenic children have confirmed the generally low intellectual functioning of psychotic children. For example, Pollack (1967) has summarized 13 studies which include assays of intelligence of schizophrenic children. Mean IQ scores of the different samplings surveyed are at retarded levels and consistently below controls and at least one-third of the children have IQs below 70. Those reports included in Pollack's survey which refer to retest IQs have been interpreted to show IQ stability on retesting and correlations between first test and later retests are high. There is little doubt that low intellectual functioning is characteristic of most group studies. However, it is again necessary to point out that a broad range of IQ is characteristic and that a sizable number of psychotic children show superior IQs. In addition, the average level of each sample studied is affected by selective factors. Finally, a recent report (Goldfarb, Goldfarb, and Pollack, 1964) of changes in IQ of schizophrenic children while in in-patient treatment at the Ittleson Center demonstrates that sizable shifts in IQ can occur in the children.

The foregoing review has referred to failures in all aspects of behavior. Impairments in the reception and integration of incoming stimuli have been stressed by a number of workers, however. Such deficits in the processing of informational input are of key significance since they preclude proficient discriminative response, the definition of figures from background, anticipatory response, and the capacity to predict. Crucial symptoms of psychosis, such as impairment in body concepts, a more total impairment in self-awareness and in communication have been linked to primary perceptual failures (Goldfarb, 1963, 1964; Stroh and Buick, 1964). Indeed the failures in perceptual control and self-monitoring have been implicated in the disturbances of schizophrenic children in all action processes (Goldfarb, 1964).

Disturbances in the afferent phase of orientation among psychotic children have been viewed from a variety of vantage points, including observations of receptor preferences (Goldfarb, 1963, 1964, 1956; Schopler. 1965), the hierarchical organization of sensory systems (Hermelin ,1963), and intersensory integration (Birch and Walker, 1966).

Observation of psychotic children in natural life situations suggests an altered pattern of receptor behavior. Thus the children frequently avoid looking and listening and instead engage with the environment by touching, tasting, and smelling. This diminished investment in the distance receptors and preferential use of the proximal receptors contributes to the detached, isolated, bizarre impact of the children in clinical and social situations. The absence of eye-to-eye and vocal contact denies them very crucial techniques for social relationship. This deviation also precludes an overview and orientation to the global and configurational aspects of the nonhuman and human world, located at a distance from the child. In this sense it contributes to the psychotic child's deficits in

conceptual or abstract behavior, so fundamental to a capacity to predict and thereby to achieve a state of safety in a fluctuant world.

The avoidance of the distance receptors has been demonstrated experimentally in a variety of ways. Psychotic children, for example, are deficient in visual following behavior (Goldfarb, 1961). In response to a rotating drum with black and white lines, psychotic children show abnormally diminished nystagmic response. Optikinetic nystagmus requires attention to the visual stimulus and the absence of nystagmus response to the moving visual stimulus is interpreted to represent visual avoidance. On multiple, simultaneous, tactile stimulation, the normal child's perception of the multiple stimuli is improved when the eyes are open, whereas the perceptual response of psychotic children is not enhanced when they are permitted to use their eyes. Evidence for altered investment in the auditory sensory modality may be found in the delayed auditory feedback experiment. Here the delay in auditory feedback alters the speech of the normal child, whereas the schizophrenic child is less prone to vary from his usual pattern of speech. This has been interpreted to mean that the psychotic child is less disposed to use his hearing of his own voice as a basis for monitoring his vocal expression.

Schopler (1961) employed standardized situations for choosing between visual and tactual stimuli to compare schizophrenic children with normal children of the same age and with mental retardates of comparable mental age. Schizophrenic children were lower in visual preference than the normal children and retardates. The normals showed increasing visual preference with age. Schopler (1965) hypothesized that infantile autism may result from a deviant or disordered transition from near to distance receptor usage, presumably because of sensory deprivation. He proposed that the sensory deprivation itself is a consequence of constitutional inhibition of arousal functions of the central nervous system combined with maternal understimulation. Although this is still a speculative theory, he proposed treatment by stimulation and communication which would be based on the activity of the proximal receptors.

O'Connor and Hermelin have concerned themselves with detailed study of the hierarchical organization of sensory systems in the psychotic child (Hermelin and O'Connor, 1963, 1964, 1965; O'Connor and Hermelin, 1965) because this hierarchical organization determines which aspects of the environment are attended to, and which sensory configurations constitute figure and which constitute ground. In their concept of the hierarchical organization of sensory processes and of sensory dominance, they have proposed that in normal development of children interoceptive and visceral sensations are dominant in infants; gradually tactile and kinesthetic sensations predominate; they are followed by auditory and visual sensory systems. When a state of sensory development has been reached, the meaning rather than the modality of stimulation determines its place in the hierarchy of sensory organization. At this point, language and meaning direct the organization of sensory processes. In a series of comparisons of psychotic children in a mentally subnormal population and nonpsychotic normals and nonpsychotic subnormals of comparable performance IQ, Hermelin and O'Connor observed that the normal structural hierarchy of sensory responses was insufficiently developed in psychotic children. In addition, on presentation of paired combinations of light, sound, and touch stimuli, psychotic children as well as subnormal controls responded most readily to light stimuli; but, following this, the psychotic children were most responsive to touch stimuli and the controls to sound stimuli. O'Connor and Hermelin proposed that the failure to achieve auditory dominance may be a factor in the impaired speech of psychotic children. Changes in choice of sensory modality were affected equally in psychotic and subnormal groups by differential reward; and when stimulus intensity was varied, all children selected the most intense stimulus regardless of modality.

The apparent high threshold for perceiving visual and auditory stimuli in the absence of sensory defect which has been described in psychotic children is reflected in their failure to solve tasks of visual discrimination. There have been very few studies to delineate the aspects of stimulation that produce discriminative responses in psychotic children. Gillies (1965) demonstrated that objects which differed in shape, size, and color were easier to discriminate than stimuli which differed only in shape. Hermelin and O'Connor (Hermelin, 1963) showed that psychotic children and normal controls could be differentiated by discrimination tasks that could be solved by discrimination of differences in shape and directional orientation, whereas the two groups could not be differentiated by tasks that could be solved through the employment of kinesthetic, brightness, or size cues. Directional cues were particularly difficult for psychotic children to follow. This difficulty is undoubtedly influenced by the directional disorientation of psychotic children (Goldfarb, 1961). The impairment in utilization of shape differences and directional orientation in the process of visual discrimination is of interest since it has been proposed that these discriminations depend in large measure on learning and experience while brightness and size discrimination do not (Hebb, 1958). In contrast to their failure in visual discrimination, psychotic children do evidence capacity for discriminating configurations by touch.

Intensive clinical observation and treatment of psychotic children has tended to contradict the commonly held notion that psychotic children are totally impervious to stimulation. Rather, they would seem to be suffering from aberrations in sensory dominance and the hierarchical structuring of sensory processes, as noted earlier, and from a lack of techniques for schematizing and giving meaning to stimuli (Goldfarb, 1965). They are thus not isolated from experience. Rather, they orient themselves in aberrant fashion to stimulation and schematize those stimuli which do reach them in very ineffective fashion.

Clinical and experimental observations which confirm the social responsiveness of psychotic children are of pertinence in any efforts to explain the communication failures of psychotic children. The often described gamut of verbal disabilities range from total mutism to linguistic aberrations including excessive concreteness, echolalia, syntactical disturbances, and pronominal reversals. When they learn words, they remember and repeat them rather than use them for meaningful communication. All these deficits in communication have been attributed to social and emotional withdrawal (Kanner, 1942). Yet observation supports the conclusion that social responsiveness is not lacking. On the other hand, psychotic children do show deficits in sensory awareness and in patterning of experience which would in themselves impede the attainments of speech and communication. For example, in addition to the perceptual and conceptual deficits described previously, Hermelin and O'Connor (in press) have demonstrated deficient capacity for word patterning.

Birch and Hertzig (1967) have proposed that the fundamental mechanism of maladaptation in childhood schizophrenia is dissociation, which may be manifested in perception, cognition, and affect. To investigate the mode of interference in normal integrative behavior, Birch and his associates have studied the development of intersensory integration in normal and schizophrenic children. This investigation was based on the hypothetical proposition that an incomplete development of intersensory integration could lead to schizophrenic dissociation. The relationships among visual, haptic, and kinesthetic sensory modalities were studied by the method of paired comparisons, that is, the child compared a stimulus in one sensory modality with a stimulus in another sensory modality to judge whether the two stimuli were the same or different in pattern. The schizophrenic children showed many more errors in intersensory matching than did the normals. Birch concluded that schizophrenic children had a defect in the integration of multimodal inputs; further, in the light of other findings of disordered receptor preference and hierarchical relationships among sensory systems, he inferred a primary disorder in the afferent organization of behavior in the schizophrenic child. Presumably such afferent disturbance provided contradictory information to the child, who, in turn, attempted to solve the contradictions in input by sensory inhibition, perseverative behavior, total withdrawal, or disorganization of behavior. Birch's conclusions need to be viewed with caution inasmuch as the failures of the psychotic children might be a reflection of inattention rather than a genuine inability to integrate the different sense modalities.

In stressing the central dynamic significance of the psychotic child's deficiencies in receiving and processing sensory information, it is essential to recall that their adaptive failures are represented in some measure in all aspects of ego functioning. Thus, for example, there are failures in the central organization of perceptual information and in the motor and executive phase of behavior. What is of most significance is that the psychotic child is aware of and has intense feeling reactions to his ineptness in afferent, central coordinative, or efferent phases of adaptation. In response to both afferent and efferent failures, his defensive accommodations result in attributes which represent psychotic modes of response.

On the basis of intensive therapeutic contact with schizophrenic children, it has been proposed that a crucial consequence of the ego failures of psychotic children is the resultant inability to achieve a clear inner awareness of the self in action (Goldfarb, 1963). This involves deficiencies in the consciousness of self as sharply differentiated from the nonself, and an inability to attain a confident feeling of the permanence, intactness, and predictability of the self and the nonself. The child who does not derive from his own actions or from the responses of the outer world the stimuli he must have in order to monitor his behavior has difficulty achieving essential skills. Just as crucially, he does not attain a confident sense of pride in his own potentiality for self-fulfillment. Similarly, deficiencies in the central coordination and schematization of perceptions in the form of categorization and generalization preclude prediction and efficient execution. Finally, a primary difficulty in the motor or efferent phase of adaptive response will confirm the child's feelings of the uncertainty of his existence and thus will lead to overwhelming panic.

Speech

From the beginning of modern considerations regarding childhood psychosis, the diagnostic criteria have always included references to speech and language disturbance. For example, Bender (1941-42) referred very early to the deviations in language in schizophrenic children. Despert (1941), too, was struck by their disinclination to use vocal speech for purposes of communication. In his classical paper on infantile autism, Kanner (1946) elaborated the broad variety of speech disturbances he observed in infantile autism, including total mutism, echolalia, pronomial reversals, literalness and overconcreteness, metaphoric substitution and the use of analogy, and substituting parts for wholes or wholes for parts. Although Kanner was disposed to link these language disorders of autistic children to their social isolation, Scheerer and his co-workers (Scheerer, Rothman, and Goldstein, 1945) stressed the more essential significance of a defect in abstract attitude. Wolff and Chess (1945) have considered the most pronounced abnormality to be the tendency toward stereotypy and repetition. Others have been impressed by the metaphoric character of the communications and have utilized this concept in therapy by communicating within the child's metaphor (Ekstein, 1966; Ekstein and Wallerstein, 1957). Cunningham and Dixon (1961) elicited the speech of a 7-year-old autistic child in a standard situation and analyzed the vocal productions with reference to Piaget's suggestion for classification. This child's speech was like that of a 2½- to 3-year-old in variety of words and length of utterance. It was even more retarded in its monotonous repetitiveness, the infrequency of questions and giving of information, the incomplete sentences, the more frequent nouns, and the highly egocentric speech. In Weiland and Legg's (1964) study of speech form and of parts of speech employed in conversation, psychotic children employed more imperative verbs, more first person plural pronouns and fewer conjunctions than control children.

Clinically, the disorder in language has been employed to assay the severity of the more total impairment. Systematic study has confirmed the correlation between retardation in language and severity of clinical impairment (Wolff and Chess, 1965). Anthony (J. Anthony, 1958) has implemented this concept in his studies correlating language level and level of autistic withdrawal.

The level of speech as an indicator of clinical status was further confirmed by Eisenberg's (1956) observation that the autistic child's ability to communicate with speech by age 5 is significantly related to later adjustment in adolescence. In the event of a total impairment in language at the age of 5 years, adolescent adjustment was consistently very poor.

The clinical observations and studies of speech previously discussed have tended to focus on the lexical and syntactical aspects of speech. However, the communication of meaning and mood are highly dependent on the vocal and nonlexical aspects of speech. This applies particularly to the communication of the multiple levels of meaning and feeling which are communicated by speech and gesture. Schizophrenic children are deficient in denotative or referential communication but they would seem to be even more deficient in those aspects of speech which are the basis for connotative communication. Included among the latter aspects of speech are characteristics such as phonation, rhythm, and articulation. The assay of phonation refers to such elements of speech as volume, pitch, and voice quality; and rhythm refers to phrasing, fluency, stress, and intonation. Using the presumptive normal as a referent, schizophrenic children deviate significantly from normal in phonation, rhythm, and articulation (Goldfarb, 1961; Goldfarb, Braunstein, and Lorge, 1956).

Motor and Postural Behavior

Motor coordination and locomotor balance have been studied with a variety of tests, including the Heath Railwalking and Lincoln-Oseretsky Battery of tests. The psychotic children are consistently inferior to controls in these tests (Goldfarb, 1961).

Neurological Tests

In a sense, all the perceptual, cognitive, communication, and motor procedures which have already been mentioned assay neurological functions, since they refer to afferent, coordinative, and efferent phases of action systems. Also, the neurological test results to be described overlap with those which have already been summarized. They are being presented separately only because they represent standardized applications of classical neurological procedures for eliciting "soft" signs of neurological aberration. These neurological tests probe neurological integration as expressed in patterned behavior, and note deficiencies in motor coordination, muscle tone, gait, balance, and postural adjustment, and the integration (or extinction) of multiple and simultaneous sensory stimuli.

Such tests are of importance if one realizes that children with unequivocal localizing signs and other evidence of neurological disorders will most often have been referred to neurological clinics rather than to psychiatric clinics for study and treatment. Schizophrenic children in psychiatric installations are thus likely to manifest neurological signs which are equivocal; that is, specific pathological correlates of the signs have not been demonstrated. Bender first called attention to these signs and their dynamic significance in the personality development of diagnosed schizophrenic children (e.g., Bender, 1947 a). All reports confirm neurological abnormalities as manifested in gait disturbances, motor overflow, whirling, toe walking, deviations in vestibular reaction, and deviant postural and righting responses.

Relational Response

By definition, children who are diagnosed as psychotic, schizophrenic, or autistic manifest disorders in how they relate to others and express their attachments. It is not surprising therefore that in controlled studies using ratings of their social responses, they have generally been judged to be low in human responsiveness. For example, in a study by Schachter, Meyer and Loomis (1962), who compared schizophrenic children with normals and intellectual retardates, schizophrenic children showed abnormally severe impairment in relation with persons and things. Retardates resembled schizophrenic children in their disordered relations with things, but were like normal children in their relations with persons. In another study by the same group (Wright, Loomis, and Meyer, 1963), the schizophrenic children received low ratings in mutual trust and constructiveness and relatively high ratings in retentiveness, activity, and orality. Similarly, Steisel et al. (1960) used ratings to assay interaction and observed that normal children were as-signed higher social interaction scores than nonverbal psychotic children.

On the other hand, judgments of social interaction are very much influenced by the ability of the judger to empathize and communicate with the child. This, in turn, is influenced by the child's own techniques for expressing relationship and for communicating. Therefore the primary deviations of the schizophrenic child in perceptual interaction, in conceptualization, and in language act secondarily to increase the observer's sense of isolation from the child and thus to exaggerate the impression that the child himself is withdrawn and unresponsive. In intimate therapeutic experience in which an active effort is made to contact the child at his level of understanding and motivation, psychotic children are not by any means withdrawn in a total sense. Indeed, they seem hypervigilant to the environment and make repeated attempts to contact it and to understand it. The schizophrenic child's withdrawal itself often seems to be an active accommodation to an environment which has not found a means for bridging the gap of aberrant perceptual response and communication.

Experimental support for this clinical point of view has come from the careful studies of O'Connor and Hermelin (1963; Hermelin and O'Connor, 1963). Employing direct observation and quantification of approach and avoidance behavior in schizophrenic and control children with subnormal IQ, they demonstrated that schizophrenic children were not differentiated from controls in human response and approach behavior. Both groups showed equivalent amounts of exploratory and orientative responses toward stimuli. While schizophrenic children showed more self-generated behavior, the results cast doubt on the validity of that definition of childhood schizophrenia which features isolation from and unresponsiveness to the environment.

It is also true that psychotic children are highly responsive to experience and learning. Ferster (1961) has used Skinner's theoretic framework of operant conditioning to explain the development of autistic manifestations. Using the same framework, Ferster and De-Myer (1961) have described techniques for reinforcing desirable social behaviors. Seemingly under Ferster's influence, Lovaas and the group at the University of California (Lovaas, Freitag, Gold, and Kassara, 1965) have used the theoretic framework of operant conditioning to overcome undesirable traits in autistic children such as self-destructive behavior. Provided they possess sufficient intelligence, schizophrenic children in a therapeutic residence show average curves of educational achievement (Goldfarb and Pollack, 1964).

ETIOLOGY

The etiology of childhood psychosis is not established. The evidence in support of the current theories of cause is fragmentary, at best, and confounded by the present lack of diagnostic precision and uniformity. However, it is possible at this point to summarize the major hypotheses and to evaluate the "hard" findings in support of each theoretic position.

One hypothesis refers to a primary and intrinsic deficiency in the psychotic child. In this theoretic position, the child starts life as an atypical organism and his primary restrictions in adaptive capacities account sufficiently for the psychotic manifestations. Another hypothesis emphasizes the primary importance of the psychosocial environment. The unusual stress and influence of environment and particularly of interpersonal experience are viewed to be the primary factors causing the child to adapt in the aberrant fashion which we term psychotic. The third position proposes a transactional point of view in which each of the atypical traits or symptoms of the psychotic child is an end outcome of the unique interplay between the child's adaptive potentialities and predispositions and the specific enhancing or restricting qualities of the psychosocial environment. Evidence in support of each of these three theoretical positions will be noted.

Theories of Atypism

As summarized recently by Birch and Hertzig (1967), in order to confirm the point of view that the symptoms of childhood schizophrenia are manifestations of a "primarily atypical organism" investigators have sought two general bodies of evidence. One body of evidence is genetic and refers chiefly to concordance for psychosis among members of families of psychotic children. For purposes of convenience, biochemical studies are included in this category since atypical trends in endocrinological and enzymatic variations have been interpreted by some to support the concept of constitutional predisposition. However, even now it can be stated that the etiologic significance of biochemical variations actually remains uncertain in view of the lack of clinical diagnostic precision, the heterogeneity of children included in the universe of psychotic children, the dangers in interpreting causation in what is merely chemical-behavioral correlation. The other body of evidence in support of intrinsic deviancy refers to data which confirm primary dysfunction of the central nervous system and likelihood of damage to the central nervous system. The evidence includes somatic, historical, behavioral, and neurological findings.

It must be emphasized that the theoretic concepts of most serious workers have embodied notions of the primary vulnerability of all or at least some of the total universe of psychotic children. This applies to most of the observers who have had a special interest in emotional and interpersonal factors in psychosis, including clinical investigators such as Kanner (1954) or Mahler (Mahler, Furer, and Settlage, 1959), DeMeyer (White et al., 1964), Goldfarb (1961), and E. F. Anthony (1958), as well as those workers who hold the conviction that the primary genetic and/or physiological aberrations account sufficiently for the manifestations of childhood psychosis.

It is also to be noted that those theorists who have proposed that childhood psychosis is an early manifestation of the same genotype responsible for the symptoms of adult schizophrenia have tended to assume the genotype to be a sufficient cause of schizophrenic tendencies. Brain damage is thus viewed as a circumstance which merely precipitates the "schizophrenic process" in childhood. On the other hand, those who find evidence of damage to the brain in childhood psychosis may include some who feel that their findings have no bearing at all on the genetic hypothesis and that cerebral dysfunction, for whatever cause, is an important factor in itself in the elaboration of psychotic symptomatology in children.

Bender and her co-workers have argued most consistently for a genotype which is presumably responsible for both childhood schizophrenia and adult schizophrenia. She thus views childhood schizophrenia as an inherited encephalopathy which is diffuse in character and which interferes with normal biological, psychological, and social development. She has also found that in their developmental histories a majority of her group of children ultimately developed the symptoms of adult schizophrenia (Bender and Grugett, 1956), that as many as 43% of the mothers and 40% of the fathers were "mentally ill" (presumably schizophrenic); and in Bender's words, "Hereditary data on the schizophrenic children gave positive evidence in all the case records but one." Beyond instances of schizophrenia, the term "positive evidence" is not precisely defined. Certainly the data which Bender presents do not provide adequate tests of precisely formulated propositions regarding the schizophrenic genotype.

Other studies have reported prevalence of schizophrenia in the families. Generally speaking, they tend to support the finding of high prevalence of schizophrenia in the families, but there are wide quantitative variations in statistics among the various studies. Thus in a study of the parents of 45 early school age schizophrenic children at the Ittleson Center (Meyers and Goldfarb, 1962), 28% of the mothers, 13% of the fathers, and 8% of the siblings were classified as schizophrenic. In the Kallmann and Roth study (1956) of 52 twins and 50 singletons, the parental schizophrenia rate was 9% (or 12.5% if corrected for age differences). Kallmann does not present separate maternal and paternal rates since the data presumably do not show differences in schizophrenia rates between fathers and mothers.

Kanner's (1949) findings in his investigation of 100 children with infantile autism stand in dramatic contrast to the data offered by Bender and Grugett (1956), Meyers and Goldfarb (1962) and Kallmann and Roth (1956). Of the 100 parents studied by Kanner, only one parent gave evidence of a "major mental illness." In the entire group of 973 family members for whom data were available, including parents, siblings, grandparents, aunts, and uncles, there were 13 psychotic individuals, 2 alcoholics, 2 epileptics, and 2 mental defectives. Among the 131 siblings, 3 were diagnosed as autistic and 1 as schizoid. In Kanner's group, therefore, there would seem to be no correlation between early infantile autism and psychiatric disorders in the remainder of the family and in ancestry.

The contrast between Bender's data and Kanner's data has been interpreted to support the proposition that childhood schizophrenia and early infantile autism are different categories of behavioral disorder. Yet there is little doubt that Bender has included children with infantile autism comparable to those described by Kanner in her samplings of children with childhood schizophrenia; moreover, it can be stated unequivocally that a large proportion of the children in the Ittleson Center sample are characteristic examples of Kanner's cases of infantile autism.

There are other data variations that need explaining. For example, the parents of Bender's children contained more mothers and fathers with "mental illness" than noted in the Ittleson study, which in turn contained more parents with psychosis than noted by Kallmann and Roth. In addition, whereas fathers and mothers were apparently not differentiated significantly by Bender and Kallmann in regard to psychosis, there is considerably more psychosis in the mothers than in the fathers of the psychotic children at Ittleson Center.

We are thus reminded again that each investigator has been describing his own special segment of the larger universe of psychotic children. At best, data comparison is not feasible because of the differences among the studies in selection of children and in criteria for diagnosis of the children and the adults. For example, in the various studies mentioned, there were differences in the proportion of broken homes. The Ittleson Center study included no children from broken homes, whereas Kallmann reported that 34% of homes were broken and Bender stated that 23% of her families were disrupted by divorce or permanent separation. Further, in his investigation of twins, Kallmann attempted to achieve homogeneity in his group by eliminating from study all "very young children who presented the clinical picture of a psychosis with mental deficiency." In addition, he selected children in whom onset of disorder occurred after 7 years of age. He also regarded as the most crucial diagnostic criterion a distinct and conspicuous change in the behavior of a child who had previously developed normally. His group thus probably differed from Bender's population, which included psychotic children with divergent onset histories. Certainly Kallmann's group of children differed from the Ittleson sample, which consisted almost entirely of children with evidences of developmental deviation from the earliest months of life. Included in the Ittleson samples, too, were very large proportions of children with retarded mental functioning.

There were also differences among the investigators in their diagnoses of schizophrenia in the parents. Kanner refers merely to "major mental illness." Kallmann does not define his criteria for schizophrenia at all. He frequently employs the classification of "schizoid personality." This classification may include some included in the Ittleson study in the schizophrenic category, in Bender's designation of "ambulatory schizophrenia," and even in Kanner's cold, obsessional, mechanical parents.

The Ittleson Center study demonstrated a greater proportion of schizophrenic mothers than of schizophrenic fathers. This difference in data regarding maternal and paternal psychosis was not observed by Bender and by Kallmann. These findings may be explained by the differences in incidence of broken homes in the various groups under study. As noted, many of the homes of the Bender and Kallmann children were broken, whereas all the Ittleson homes were intact in formal structure. The selection of formally intact family units at Ittleson Center was arbitrary and by choice; but this selection procedure may have had the effect of filtering out the more disabled fathers. One might reason that the selection of intact families out of the total population of families of schizophrenic children had the effect of reducing the number of psychotic fathers relative to the total sampling of fathers of schizophrenic children, inasmuch as the fathers had to be stable enough to work and maintain the families. One might also speculate that the practical possibilities of a

family remaining intact are less affected by maternal psychosis than paternal psychosis, so that the higher ratio of psychotic mothers to psychotic fathers in intact families is understandable.

The most pertinent and careful study of the part played by the genetic factor in the development of "preadolescent schizophrenia" is Kallmann and Roth's (1956) study of 52 sets of twins and 50 singletons. The twins included 17 monozygotic and 35 dizygotic index pairs. As already observed, very young children who presented the clinical picture of a "psychosis with mental deficiency" were excluded. They also employed the diagnostic criterion of a definite change in the behavior of a child who had previously developed normally. The average age of onset was 8.8 years for male index cases and 11.1 years for female index cases. Of most interest are the differential concordance rates for two-egg and one-egg pairs with respect to schizophrenia and schizoid personality. Two-egg and one-egg co-twins of schizophrenic index cases differed in concordance for preadolescent schizophrenia (17.1 and 70.6%, respectively) and for adult schizophrenia (14.7 and 85.8%). As a test of the proposition that childhood schizophrenia is a childhood derivative of the same genotype responsible for adult schizophrenia, the above-noted twin concordance rates for children were compared with the twin concordance rates for adult schizophrenics reported by Kallmann in 1946. The earlier study was based on a study of 691 twin families. In the adult study, two-egg and one-egg co-twins differed respectively in concordance rates as follows: 10.3 and 69.0% without age correction and 14.7 and 85.8% with age correction. The differences between the two-egg and one-egg co-twins in both preadolescent and adult samples are statistically significant, whereas those between the preadolescent and adult samples are not. Nor were the preadolescent and adult groups significantly different in regard to schizophrenia rates for the parents (12.5 and 9.2%) and siblings (12.2 and 14.3%). Kallmann and Roth concluded that preadolescent schizophrenia is determined genetically to the same degree by the same "gene-specific deficiency state" as in adult schizophrenia.

In evaluating the Kallmann and Roth

investigation, one must keep in mind that their study of schizophrenic children referred to a small, very special sample of children. Thus this sample differed from the Ittleson (Meyers and Goldfarb, 1962), Bellevue (Bender and Grugett, 1956), and Hopkins (Kanner, 1954) samples, since the Kallmann-Roth sample contained children with relatively late age of onset and with higher intelligence. In addition, clear-cut, definable behavioral changes in behavior in a normally developing child, a circumstance which has been stressed by other workers as well (e.g., Eisenberg, 1966), is very rarely to be observed in young psychotic children. Bender's clinical observations of early maturational disorders in childhood schizophrenia, Fish's support of these clinical observations in her systematic and prospective studies of a group of babies, Kanner's exact clinical definitions of the infantile disorders of his group, and the uniform observation of developmental disorders from the earliest months of life in the psychotic group at the Ittleson Center would suggest the likelihood that Kallmann and Roth studied a group of children who were quite different from children who are ordinarily subsumed in the psychiatric categories of early childhood psychosis, childhood schizophrenia, or infantile autism. This conclusion is additionally supported by the fact that while Kallmann and Roth excluded mental deficiency, a majority of cases of childhood psychosis which have been tested systematically fall in the retarded ranges. Kallmann and Roth's study and conclusions, therefore, have very limited application to the range of children who are included in the psychotic universe by child psychiatrists.

In any case, even the studies of differential concordance rates for adult schizophrenia in dizygotic and monozygotic twins have come under critical review. For example, Kringlen (1966) studied schizophrenia in twins based on a study of all twins recorded in the Norwegian Birth Register from 1901 to 1930. In Kringlen's study of a sample of 342 pairs of twins, 35 to 64 years of age, where one or both of each twin pair had been hospitalized for "functional psychosis," the concordance figures ranged from 28 to 38% in monozygotic twins and from 5 to 14% in dizygotic twins. The concordance rates were thus significantly different from monozygotic and dizygotic twins; but the difference was considerably less than had been recorded in the older studies. These concordance rates do support a genetic factor in the etiology of schizophrenia, however, the genetic factor would seem to play a lesser role than had been assumed. Kringlen also demonstrated quite convincingly that the very high rates of twin concordance in the older studies resulted from errors in sampling and that the more representative the sampling, the lower the concordance rates.

Beyond the recent modification of concordance rates in the families of schizophrenic adults and especially in the different concordance rates of two-egg and one-egg twins, other considerations would make it hazardous to accept without question a specific genotype in itself sufficient to account for schizophrenia. For example, Birch and Hertzig have argued there is evidence that the risk of reproductive complication is greater for twins than for singleton pregnancies, and greater for monozygotic twins than for dizygotic twins. Twinning thus implies greater risk of injury to and aberrant development of the central nervous system. In this regard, Pollin's study of monozygotic twins discordant for schizophrenia (Pollin, Stabener, Mosher, and Tupin, 1966) is extremely important. Evidence of central nervous system dysfunction was very much higher in the schizophrenic members than in the nonschizophrenic members of the discordant twin pairs. Eight of the eleven psychotic members and only one of the nonpsychotic members showed neurological abnormality. Similarly, the schizophrenic members of the twin pairs were lighter than the nonschizophrenic members in birth weight. Indeed, in each twin pair, the schizophrenic member of the twin pair was lighter. Do concordance rates in twins reflect comparable risk of central nervous system trauma as much as genotypic agreement? As will be seen, this question is particularly pertinent in childhood schizophrenia where there is strong evidence in support of maldevelopment and damage to the central nervous system in a high percentage of the children.

Finally, as Kallmann and Roth themselves recognized, the role of the social influence of families with schizophrenic members may well be of significance in influencing the development of the psychotic children in these families. In the Ittleson Center study (Meyers and Goldfarb, 1962) participant observation of the families of schizophrenic children revealed that the families showed a broad range of adequacy in their psychosocial functioning. Some of the families seemed quite normal in functional adequacy. Psychosis in the parents and inadequate family functioning were linked.

Present findings, therefore, regarding the genetic factor in childhood psychosis are not possible to interpret unequivocally. Studies of concordance rates in early childhood psychosis still need to be done. In addition, these genetic studies will have to include the investigation of the functioning of the central nervous system of the children and of the psychosocial attributes of their families.

Theories of the genetic basis of psychosis assume that genetic variations are accompanied by enzymatic and metabolic variations. For this reason, the present reference to biochemical studies is now offered immediately after the discussion of genetics, although in actual fact any correlation between psychotic symptoms and biochemical findings is merely associative in import at best and does not necessarily have causative significance. The studies to which reference will be made do not offer unequivocal evidence of a definitive metabolic or biochemical error to account for all (or even a segment) of the attributes of psychotic children. Several disparate biochemical studies of these children have been made. Most findings are negative, however; where positive findings are noted, the link between the biochemical variations and the known psychological manifestations of childhood psychosis is not known.

Akerfeldt (1957) studied changes in the serum of adult mental patients and discovered that N, N-dimethyl-para-phenylenediamine hydrochloride was oxidized, most frequently within five minutes. This positive reaction was manifested when the normal yellow color was changed to red. In normal persons, the change took longer and changed to a lighter red tint. Akerfeldt found the reaction in 80% of the adult patients. These findings were confirmed by Abood (1957), who used para-phenylenidiamine as agent instead of N, N-dimethyl-para-phenylenediamine hydrochloride.

The chemical substances in the serum which have been implicated in the Akerfeldt reaction are ceruloplasmin, a copper containing oxidase enzyme, and ascorbic acid. Elevated levels of ceruloplasmin in the serum of patients with schizophrenia have thus been studied as a key factor in the Akerfeldt reaction, since speed of oxidation is proportionate to the level of ceruloplasmin, and increased speed of oxidation of epinephrine in patients with schizophrenia has been reported Leach and Heath, 1956).

Following Akerfeldt, a number of investigators studied ceruloplasm oxidase activity in diagnosed schizophrenic children and nonschizophrenic controls. Brown (1957) evaluated Akerfeldt serum reactions in 150 hospitalized nonpsychotic children and two identical twin girls with childhood schizophrenia. Nonpsychotic children showed 30% positive Akerfeldt reaction, 67% negative and 3% doubtful. The psychotic twins gave positive Akerfeldt reactions. These findings are obviously inconclusive.

Aparison and Drew (1958) studied the sera of seven schizophrenic children, six possibly schizophrenic children and ten children with nonschizophrenic psychiatric diagnosis. The Akerfeldt reaction did not differentiate schizophrenic and nonschizophrenic children.

Bakwin, Mosbach, and Bakwin (1958) used the Abood Technique to study ceruloplasmin activity in 45 schizophrenic children. No differences between schizophrenic and normal children were demonstrated. Later Bakwin (1961) reported determinations of serum copper levels in 91 schizophrenic children and 73 controls. Again, schizophrenic and nonschizophrenic children were not differentiated.

The concept of abnormal metabolites in the circulating blood has been tested in a variety of ways. Thus, in a gross test of this concept, an exchange transfusion was administered to a 5-year-old child with infantile autism (Freedman and Ginsberg, 1958). The results were quite negative since improvement was doubtful and behavioral regression was rapid.

Frohman and his co-workers (Frohman, Goodman, Beckett, Latham, Senf, and Gottlieb, 1962) studied the serum of 16 schizophrenic children and 14 nonschizophrenic children in in-patient care for serum influence on chicken erythrocyte effects on the lactate to pyruvate ratio (L/P ratio). Whereas serum of adult schizophrenics stimulated chicken erythrocytes to increase the L/P ratio, the sera of childhood schizophrenics and nonschizophrenic patients were not differentiated in regard to L/P effects. Like the Akerfeldt reaction, therefore, this is another example of a metabolic reaction which has been noted in adult schizophrenia and is not seen in childhood schizophrenia. It is of interest that a comparison of a group of adult schizophrenic patients who had an early history of manifestations of childhood psychosis and of another group of adult patients with more typical histories of onset demonstrated that the adults with histories of childhood schizophrenia were not different from the childhood schizophrenics and controls. In contrast, the adult schizophrenics with later, more usual onset histories increased the L/P ratio. Frohman suggests that this is evidence that childhood schizophrenia is an entirely different disorder from adult schizophrenia.

Adult studies of alteration in amino acid metabolism and in the metabolic pathways affecting serotonin levels have been duplicated in several studies of childhood psychosis. On the basis of the preconception that the biogenic indole-alkylamine, 5 hydroxytryptamine (5 HT or serotonin) has an important role in the functioning of brain neurones, there has been a search for evidence of abnormal 5-hydroxyindole metabolism. Sutton and Read (1958) studied an 18-month-old child with signs of infantile autism and noted decreased ability to convert tryptophane to urinary indole acids. Schain and Freedman (1961) also investigated alterations in the metabolic pathway of tryptophane (tryptophane → 5-hydroxytryptophane → 5-hydroxytryptamine → 5-hydroxyindoleacetic acid) in 23 children with diagnosis of infantile autism and in mentally retarded children matched with the autistics for age and sex. Consistently elevated 5-HT levels were found in 6 of the 23 infantile autistics. Severely retarded mental retardates had higher 5-HT levels than the mildly retarded. Sankar, Cates, Broer, and Sankar (1963) compared schizophrenic and nonschizophrenic children biochemically, and

showed that autistic children had higher red blood cell inorganic phosphate content, lower serotonin uptake by blood platelets, and higher plasma inorganic phosphate levels. Shaw, Lucas, and Rabinovitch (1959) compared schizophrenic and nonschizophrenic children in regard to the effects of tryptophane feeding on 5-H IAA excretion. No differences were found. Overall, therefore, the findings are not definitive and clear.

Syner and Shaw (1962) studied the effects of serum of childhood and adult schizophrenics on in vitro synthesis of glutamine and gamma-amino butyric acid. No differences were found among the two schizophrenic groups, a group of adults with personality disorders and a group of children with a variety of nonschizophrenic behavior disorders.

In spite of their potential significance in facilitating our understanding of childhood psychoses, it is obvious that very few biochemical studies of psychotic children have yielded unequivocally positive findings. They have tended to follow in the wake of the more comprehensive and more enthusiastic investigation of the matabolic and enzymatic alterations in adult schizophrenia; furthermore, important theoretic formulations stimulated primarily by empirical and clinical observations of psychotic children have not appeared. It is certain that this situation reflects in part the heterogeneity of the children subsumed in the class of children termed psychotic and the breadth of their behavioral manifestations. Nor is it entirely a hopeful procedure to apply uncritically to children the theoretic propositions and approaches found of use in studies of adult schizophrenics since the link between childhood and adult psychosis remains tenuous. Thus it is not surprising to learn that there are very few positive findings in those infrequent studies that have been attempted.

Where positive findings have been noted in studies of children, their significance is unclear; that is to say, the relationship between the biochemical findings of abnormality and the specific functional and behavioral alterations are not at all definable. This, too, is not surprising if one grasps that it is equally difficult to interpret the positive findings in the systematic chemical investigations of adults suffering from functional psychosis.

None of the hypotheses have been unequivocally confirmed; and the significance of the biochemical abnormalities which have been ascertained has been beclouded by such factors as the specific conditions of life of the patients under study (e.g., prolonged institutionalization, abnormal dietary variations of patients, infections, and even the very special effects of drug and other somatic therapies to which patients are so frequently submitted) (Kety, 1959a, 1966). Finally, it is sobering to grasp that barring a suitable theory combined with precisely pertinent and longitudinal biochemical as well as behavioral investigation, it is not possible to establish direction of cause. Implicitly or explicitly, biochemical abnormalities have usually been interpreted to reflect a genetic factor controlling the metabolic variations. Yet the correlation of biochemical and behavioral findings in itself does not establish whether the biochemical shifts have caused the behavioral alterations, or whether the biochemical shifts have followed the behavioral alterations, or whether both shifts have been merely coincidental without being causally related. An enormous amount of work in the biochemistry of childhood psychosis remains to be done.

Book, Nichtern, and Gruenberg (1963) performed cytogenetic analyses based on cellular cultures of tissues from skin biopsies of 10 schizophrenic children. They could detect no chromosomal abnormalities. The authors report that their findings confirm the findings of another group (Biesele et al., reported in Book et al., 1963) who noted normal karyotypes with 46 chromosomes in a cellular study using the blood culture technique. Current cytological techniques, therefore, do not support the notion of chromosomal abnormalities in childhood psychosis.

Evidence for central nervous system impairment in a proportion of psychotic children has come from many sources. These include studies of congenital stigmata, development, reproductive complications, neurological examination, electroencephalography, and perceptual and cognitive appraisal.

There have been occasional reports of "beautiful" children, anatomically well formed and functionally coordinated and graceful. Indeed, in one report (Rimland, 1964), such somatic attractiveness is even suggested as one criterion, presumably differentiating infantile autism from childhood schizophrenia. In actual fact such somatic differentiations of psychotic and normal children and among the presumed subgroups of psychotic children are quite speculative. What is perhaps more impressive in clinical practice is the frequent observation of anatomic abnormality. This has been confirmed in a study of anatomic stigmata of psychotic children and a normal control group of children (Goldfarb, 1967). The psychotic children showed a higher number of anatomic stigmata than did the normal children and more psychotic children manifested multiple stigmata.

Before the study of prenatal and perinatal complications in the reproductive histories of schizophrenic children had been investigated, such reproductive complications had been linked to a variety of psychiatric and psychological disorders in childhood (Kawi and Pasamanick, 1959; Knobloch and Pasamanick, 1962; Pasamanick and Knobloch, 1961; Pasamanick, Rogers, and Lilienfield, 1956; Pasamanick and Lilienfield, 1955). For example, histories of reproductive complication had been observed in children with childhood behavior disorders, mental deficiency, and reading disability more frequently than in other groups of matched children. In the past decade, there have been a significant number of studies of prenatal and perinatal complications in children with diagnosis of childhood schizophrenia. These studies (Goldfarb, 1961; Knobloch and Pasamanick, 1962; Knobloch and Grant, 1961; Osterkamp and Sands, 1962; Taft and Goldfarb, 1964; Terris, Lapouse, and Monk, 1964; Vorster, 1960; Zitrin, Ferber, and Cohen, 1964) carried on independently in different treatment installations have, in the main, supported each other. All demonstrate a higher incidence of prenatal and perinatal complications in children suffering from childhood psychosis than in control children. All these studies have been retrospective and subject to the errors of all retrospective studies. However, data derived from hospital records, which precluded the bias derived from a knowledge of the psychiatric diagnosis and the potential falsification of retrospective reporting, confirmed the findings which utilized information from the mothers (Taft and Goldfarb, 1964).

Developmental deviations suggestive of

dysfunction of the central nervous system have been noted by clinical observers. In her reports of schizophrenic children, Bender (1956) has repeatedly described atypical developmental patterns in schizophrenic children. Kanner's description (1942) of the failure of autistic children to respond during infancy with the preparatory anticipatory posture when reached for has been interpreted in terms of neurological abnormality as well as withdrawal from human contact.

Creak (1963) studied the development of 100 schizophrenic children in regard to important developmental landmarks in locomotor, sensorimotor, language, self-care, and social functions. Of these children, 46 showed normal development, 27 were uniformly delayed in all areas, and the balance demonstrated inconsistent growth combining delay and acceleration.

We have already described the universality of language disorders in psychotic children. Total absence of language or language delay or disordered development of language skills may be found in virtually all psychotic children (Goldfarb, 1961; Goldfarb et al., 1956). Although acute loss of language function has been recorded, it is more usual that the development of the capacity for communication in young psychotic children has not followed the normal course from the beginning of life.

Fish's (1957, 1959, 1960b, 1961; Fish and Alpert, 1962) investigations of the development of infants later found to be psychotic are of great importance. In her anticipatory as well as retrospective studies of the developmental course of schizophrenic children, she was impressed by very early deviation in muscle tone and in sensory responsiveness and by the irregular, fluctuant course of development in postural and locomotor response. Serious irregularities in early motor and postural development in the first two years of life were noted most frequently in children with most extreme cognitive deficiency (IQ below 70). These studies would support the proposition that defective integration of the central nervous system in the early years of life is a prominent feature of development in psychotic children.

Information elicited through the direct physical examination of the child in order to assay the intactness of his central nervous system is affected by a practical clinical trend.

As noted previously, children with manifest and unequivocal signs of neuropathology are likely to be referred to neurological services for diagnosis and treatment, whereas children in psychiatric services are not likely to show such obvious signs of impairment in the central nervous system. Thus clinical neurological examinations of psychotic children infrequently demonstrate the unequivocal signs of localized neurological impairment such as presence of abnormal reflexes, or alterations in normal reflexes, or asymmetrical failures in sensory and motor response. Obvious convulsive patterns are also not a usual complaint, although evidences of dysrhythmia and seizure trends frequently do emerge in the course of continued observation. However, impaired integrity of the central nervous system may be inferred from abnormalities and deficiencies in gait, posture, balance, motor coordination and control, muscle tone, and the integration of multiple and simultaneous sensory stimuli. Generally these deficiencies are best observed when the child is engaged in patterned activities such as walking, running, jumping, throwing, reaching, or performing delicate motor acts. These signs of defective neurological integrity are equivocal inasmuch as correlated cerebral pathology has not been demonstrated. However, they are noted in cases showing other unequivocal and localizing signs of neurological impairment. Similarly they are rarely seen in normal children (Goldfarb, 1967a, 1967b).

The importance of neurological impairments in influencing the feelings and fantasies of the psychotic child emerges in clinical introspective investigations such as are feasible in psychotherapy. The incoordination, the inability to integrate sensory stimuli, the motor overflow phenomena, the postural deficiencies all contribute to the psychotic child's failure in body concept and self-awareness. The children also suffer with feelings of intense distress and lack of pride, which accompany states of being in which the person does not achieve mastery and control of self.

Bender first described these "soft," that is, equivocal, neurological aberrations at length and also developed their dynamic role in inducing anxiety in schizophrenic children. Her suggestions for observing and evaluating postural behavior have been appraised by other observers (Goldfarb, 1961; Kramer, Rabkin, and Spitzer, 1958; Pollack and Krieger, 1958; Rachman and Berger, 1963; Silver and Gabriel, 1965). All the studies have offered evidence of deviant postural and righting reactions in schizophrenic children. However, such postural deviations are not as universal as implied in Bender's statements (Goldfarb, 1961; Kramer et al., 1958), nor are they entirely absent in nonschizophrenic groups. For example, in Kramer, Rabkin, and Spitzer's (1958) study of whirling in schizophrenic children, normal white children from middle-income families, and normal Negro children from lower-income families, schizophrenic children showed most frequent whirling. However, the Negro children showed more continual whirling than whites. Factors other than psychosis would seem to be influencing the postural reaction. In the Ittleson Center study, 65% of the children were diagnosed as suffering from neurological dysfunctions on the basis of the "soft" signs noted above.

The previously described restrictions in perceptual, perceptuomotor, and cognitive response of psychotic children have also been interpreted as evidence for dysfunction of the central nervous system. Thus the consistent findings of inferior intellect in psychotic children when they have been compared with normal children has been stressed (Pollack, in press). In addition, the unchanging character of the IQ, even when serious autistic reactions have been diminished, has been emphasized (Rutter, 1965). Also, the often-mentioned construct of "islets of intelligence" has been emphasized in clinical practice, although with little basis in fact, and in Rutter's (1965) opinion the unevenness chiefly reflects unusually impaired language functions in psychotic children.

Caution in interpreting these test findings must be exercised, inasmuch as low average findings in the groups of psychotic children which have been studied disguise the fact that a large proportion of psychotic children have normal intelligence test results. Similarly, a recent longitudinal study at the Ittleson Center confirms the finding that some psychotic children under therapeutic observation do indeed show dramatic rises in IQ. In addition, Rutter's observation of lower verbal than nonverbal IQ, presumed evidence

of aphasoid disturbances, is not substantiated in the Ittleson Center investigations.

In addition, Birch and Walker (1966) have demonstrated an interesting pattern of differences in perceptual and perceptuomotor response between diagnosed brain-damaged children and schizophrenic children. Thus both groups showed similar deficiency in building a block design on being presented with a visual model. However, on being asked to choose which of a number of constructions, including their own erroneous construction and a correct construction, resembled the model, the brain-damaged children were always able to choose the correct constructions. In contrast, the schizophrenic children tended to choose their own wrong constructions. Thus the brain-damaged children showed dissociation between perceptuomotor capacity and perceptual recognition, whereas schizophrenic children performed equally poorly in both perceptuomotor response and perceptual recognition. On the other hand, if the perceptual recognition test preceded the perceptuomotor test, the schizophrenic children were able to match the visual designs correctly. Thus the schizophrenic children were different from brain-damaged children in that the experience of prior failure in itself caused a disturbance of perceptual response. The psychotic child's deficiencies in perceptual, cognitive, and psychomotor abilities supports the hypothesis of dysfunction in the central nervous system in at least a sizable proportion of the children. On the other hand, it is also likely that the adaptive paths that culminate in perceptuomotor failure are different for brain-damaged children and psychotic children.

Studies of encephalographic records have also tended to support the likelihood of disturbances in functioning of the central nervous system in a high percentage of psychotic children. Kennard (1949) demonstrated more frequent abnormality in EEG records of hospitalized schizophrenic children than in normal members of their families. Among a group of severely disturbed children, the highest prevalence of abnormal records were manifested by schizophrenic children (Kennard, 1959). In addition, Kennard (1959) has related attributes of thought disturbance to abnormalities in the EEG.

White, DeMyer, and DeMyer (1964)

studied EEGs during promazine sedation of 58 schizophrenic children with autistic or symbiotic features, 44 children with chronic undifferentiated schizophrenia, 37 nonpsychotic children with pronounced behavior disorders characterized by "acting out" and impulsive manifestations, 10 children with neuroses, and 13 normal children. Apart from the neurotic children, the psychotic subgroups and the other psychiatric subgroups are not differentiated. However, EEG abnormalities were found in 51% of the 149 psychiatric patients while they were totally absent among the normal children.

Apart from evidences of convulsive disposition, the EEG tracings do not offer significant assistance in clinical subclassification of the children. Judgment of abnormality in EEG records in clinical practice is even more biased by a knowledge of the child's psychiatric diagnosis and symptoms than in the controlled studies such as that of White et al. Nevertheless, it would be safe to infer from all the evidence the existance of a high incidence of psychotic children with atypical electrical recordings. This inference receives support from clinically observable convulsive manifestations in a sizable number of psychotic children. Creak (1963), for example, noted that 12 of 100 schizophrenic children offered historical evidence of epilepsy. Bender (1959) too, has noted frequent convulsive disorders in adolescents diagnosed as schizophrenics in childhood.

Although still lacking in histopathological confirmation, the accumulated data from prenatal and perinatal histories, developmental courses, neurological histories and examinations, electroencephelography, and systematic studies of neurological functions, perception, and cognition provide rather indisputable evidence of impairment of the central nervous system. The disorders in the integration of neurological functions often occur very early in infancy and are thus first expressed in terms of sensory, perceptual, motor, and postural deviations and later in terms of the more complex cognitive and social failures and protective adjustments which are more usually viewed as the essential attributes of schizophrenic children.

On the other hand, these evidences of impaired integrity of the central nervous system are not found in all the children diagnosed as psychotic. Although it might be proposed that the failure to find neurological impairment in every case reflects the grossness of our present instruments, clinical experience would support the notion that emotional and psychosocial factors are implicated to a varying degree in the deviant adjustment of the children. Certainly not all brain-damaged children become psychotic, and, as elaborated and confirmed by Birch and Walker (1966), there are differences in the mechanisms involved in the failures of psychotic and brain-damaged children, although the failures of both groups of children may be similar in their final manifestations. We now turn, therefore, to a consideration of environmental and psychosocial factors.

Theories of Psychosocial Influence

The second general class of theories regarding the etiology of childhood psychosis embodies those hypotheses which maintain that environmental and especially interpersonal experiences are responsible for those attributes and behaviors which are termed psychotic. This class of theories has been supported by data from a number of sources, including case studies derived in large measure from psychotherapeutic contact with the psychotic children and their families, from psychological tests and interviews of the family members, from direct observation of the families as functional units, and more recently from clinical studies of family communication.

Until the last decade, the primary source of theories and observations of the families of psychotic children came out of direct therapeutic contact with the children and their parents. Studies of individual children in depth which utilize the techniques of psychotherapy do facilitate sensitive probing of intrapsychic processes and inner meanings and do bring to light in each case the role of social and interactional processes. Indeed, the case method would still seem to be the only comprehensive method we possess for studying transactionally the individual accommodations of the children to their own intrinsic limitations and potentialities, to the unique adaptive demands of the family, and to the reciprocal interplay between the child's own intrinsic dispositions and the extrinsic pressures and demands of the family environment. Psychotherapeutic engagement with psychotic children reminds one again and again that in circumstances in which the social and physical environment would seem to be influencing the outward responses of a psychotic child, a full comprehension of the child's responses entails a grasp of his inner fantasies and emotional responses.

Thus the case approach, which focuses on interpersonal and intrapsychic phenomena, has unsurpassed validity in explaining the individual under study. However, it lends itself easily to vagueness of definition and presumption; and it is particularly vulnerable to the influence of bias and preconception. Nor are these hazards corrected by the accumulation of inferences from many case records, which may merely result in a cumulative error.

Single trait descriptions of the parents on the basis of impressionistic inference from multiple case studies, for example, have not been productive. The definitions are ordinarily too vague and broadly inclusive. Usually, too, controls are not employed in these clinical investigations. Since the traits attributed to the parents of schizophrenic children are also to be found in other parents, the lack of controls precludes any possibility for inferring a link between parental traits and childhood psychosis. The hazards are not only represented in contradictions among observers; the same observer may present contradictory or at least incongruent descriptions. An example of these methodologic hazards may be found in the clinical reports of Despert. In one report Despert (1938) stated that 19 of 29 schizophrenic children had "aggressive, over-anxious, and over-solicitous mothers" and fathers who played a "subdued role." In a later report (Despert, 1951) she described emotional detachment and over-intellectualization in the mothers, characteristics which are quite different from oversolicitousness. Apart from the imprecision of the trait descriptions and the lack of controls, it is quite possible, as Sanua (1967) has cogently stressed, that the two groups of children came from families with different sociocultural backgrounds. The qualities of the two groups of mothers described by Despert may in fact have merely reflected the social and cultural qualities of their own class and ethical origins. If true, the observed

qualities would have little specific pathogenic significance.

The major clinical speculations are presented, therefore, to illustrate the kind of hypothesis that has been found useful in formulating the psychodynamics of each individual case and that has also influenced the hunches which are still to be confirmed by controlled study. There have been many individual case discussions, and reference will be made only to the speculations of several observers who have given evidence of applying the environmental-interpersonal conception to a large group of clinical cases and have strongly influenced the field.

The most straightforward and persistent effort to assay the psychogenic hypothesis through clinical-therapeutic observation is that described by Boatman and Szurek (1960). As a working hypothesis, Szurek and his associates at the Langley-Porter Neuropsychiatric Institute have proposed that the etiology of childhood schizophrenia is "entirely psychogenic." Psychotherapy has been used to "test" the more specific hypothesis that "the psychotic disorder is the result, in the form of conflict and its compromise solution, of the postnatal experience of each particular child early in life in interaction with significant adults who were themselves in conflict. . . ." Psychotic symptoms are seen to express an "almost all-pervasive, self-defeating circular conflict about (with repression of) basic sensual drives—conflict which results in the distortion of the drives and their frequent break-through as sado-masochistic behavior." The self-destructive resolutions of the child's conflicts result in distortions and impairments of learning. At the same time, Szurek and Boatman have noted few children whose maturational disorders were entirely determined "by physical and genetic-somatic factors."

Szurek's position on the etiology of childhood schizophrenia is useful as a working hypothesis if one's objective is to treat and modify the behavior of psychotic children; certainly it is helpful and reasonable to hold to a conviction of the immediate modifiability of psychotic children in any effort to alleviate their maladaptive responses. However, the concept that postnatal conflict and its resolution result in childhood psychosis requires careful definition and elaboration to avoid being overly simplistic. In some measure, semantic clarification is essential. For example, the phrase "conflict about (with repression of) basic sensual drives" implies intrapsychic emotional conflict between one portion of personality and another, for example, between instinctual drives and the ego, as defined by Freud in his descriptions of the neuroses. One needs to understand that the "conflicts" of psychotic children antedate in time those of children with neurotic behavior disorders and certainly those of normal children in the normal course of coping with the complexities of family existence. The "conflicts" of psychotic children refer rather to the elemental experience of babies in the course of the earliest perceptual encounters with the physical and nurturing world and are represented in fears which accompany such global experiences as separating and contacting or moving toward and moving away. There seems little doubt that faced with these hazardous experiences at a very early stage of life when the infantile adaptive capacities are very limited, the child resorts to the most immature forms of defensive behavior. At this point, the child shows manifestations which are termed "psychotic."

Mahler's clinical observations and speculations have been of great value in illuminating the interactions between the child and his mother with particular reference to their contribution to the child's differentiation of self. Although unequivocal symbiotic psychosis as defined by Mahler is rare, the psychodynamic features of extreme symbiotic reaction may be observed in the development of some psychotic children. The psychic fusion of the image of mother and the image of self is difficult to document although the verbalizations and productions would frequently tend to support this psychodynamic inference. There can be no doubt, however, that in some psychotic children, separation from the mother is accompanied by extreme panic far beyond the normal level of separation anxiety. Similarly, a protective fantasy of powerful control and absorption of the mother is frequently to be observed. Nor is the child who is so embroiled ever free of dread since movement toward or away from the nurturing person is fraught with danger.

Rank, Putnam, and their associates at the Putnam Clinic in Boston have also explored the emotional relationships between psychotic children of early preschool age, whom they have preferred to designate as "atypical," and their mothers (Putnam, 1955; Rank, 1949, 1955). Like Mahler, they have noted the part played by constitutional factors; but they have stressed the etiologic significance of early child-parent relationships and of early psychological traumata in childhood psychosis.

The role of the fathers was considered in Rank's delineation of pathogenic family influence, although the father's destructive impact presumably stemmed chiefly from his passivity in his relationships so that he did not counter or compensate for the more immediately negative influence of the mother. This contrasts with more recent clinical alertness to the father's strong responsibility for the crucial disorders of family organization that may be evident.

With obvious, though implicit stress on the primacy of the mother-child relationship, Rank described varieties of mothers who were incapable of performing their maternal function and of experiencing genuine gratification in fulfilling this function. Among these mothers were manifestly deviant and psychotic women. Rank also described a group of women who were adjusted outwardly and were even, on occasion, quite advanced in their educational and vocational attainments. They also worked very hard at the job of demonstrating their competence in the roles of wife and mother. However, they were putting on a show which belied their underlying emotional immaturity and "narcissism." In actual fact, they were devoid of genuine maternal drive and capacity for spontaneous affection for the children. Presumably, the mothers of "atypical" children themselves were often strongly ambivalent in their relationships to their own mothers and were thus restricted in their capacity to functional emotionally on behalf of their children.

Traumatic events presumably also contributed to the disorders of the "atypical" children. Specific traumata included births of siblings, separations from the parent, and physical illnesses.

In therapeutic work with the families of schizophrenic children, it is common experience to observe that the mothers lack full maternal feeling for their psychotic children.

At such times, it is impossible to determine whether the mother is expressing intense frustration and detachment in response to a child she is unable to contact or whether her restricted maternal drive preceded the birth of her deviant child. On occasion, the clinical evidence confirms narrowed or disordered maternal impulses before the birth of the psychotic child. Often, as Rank has suggested, the mother's own feelings of emotional deprivation impede the normal response of joy in mothering a baby. Or she may herself assume the helpless position of the infant in the family and thus resent the baby. Or she may overidentify with the baby and overindulge him so as to encourage arrest in ego growth. Occasionally, sexual conflict and reaction against the sexuality of the baby impedes maternal response. The specific psychodynamic features of each mother's failure to attain full maternal feeling thus varies from mother to mother. It is doubtful that a single psychodynamic paradigm accounts for all the varieties of restriction in maternal response that may be seen. In each case, the mother's inhibition in response to her child only can be clarified in a highly individualized fashion by a knowledge of her personal history and an extended intrapsychic exploration.

Impersonal, detached relationships between the psychotic child and his parents have been stressed by numerous observers. The outstanding statement in this regard has come from Kanner and Eisenberg (Eisenberg, 1957 b). They described the parents of children suffering with infantile autism as cold, obsessional, highly detached, and undemonstrative. All but about 10% showed this stereotype. In the main, they were also superior in intelligence and professional attainment. Eisenberg (1957 b), Kanner's close associate, in defining the syndrome of infantile autism, has reminded us of the importance of the father and, by implication, the entire family in the development of the autistic child. Thus he described the cold and very mechanical responses of about 85% of the fathers to their autistic children.

A recent review of case records of schizophrenic children at the Ittleson Center confirmed the Kanner parental stereotype in only 2 of 58 families of schizophrenic children. Similarly, as noted earlier, the Ittleson families were distributed among all social classes (Goldfarb, 1967 a). There is every reason for accepting Kanner's descriptions of his group of parents, and it would seem reasonable to conclude that his sampling of children differed from that of the Ittleson Center. There is also no reason for doubting the suggestion that parental lack of warmth is a factor encouraging the impairments in social response in some psychotic children.

With an eye on therapeutic application, Kaufman and his co-workers (Kaufman, Frank, Heims, Herrick, Rusir, and Willer, 1960; Kaufman et al., 1959) have classified parents of schizophrenic children using the information available in psychotherapy, psychological tests, and direct parent-child interaction. These workers presume a disturbed parent-child relationship in which the parents, because of their own emotional needs and defenses, encourage the psychotic child's behavior. The parents are classified into four groups, including pseudo-neurotic, somatic, pseudo-delinquent, and outwardly psychotic. The defensive manifestations of these groups of parents each in their own way presumably have a pathogenic influence and require specialized therapeutic management.

Although the therapeutic case study of individual children has been employed to support the theoretic concept that psychogenic and environmental factors are a sufficient cause of childhood psychosis, another point of view toward the case study which is less simplistic is helpful. The psychotic child's behavioral manifestations at any given moment in time are the result of both distant factors and of more immediate factors in his historical development. They reflect his own mode of adaptation to his own special history. As such, his adaptational accommodations cannot be understood apart from the highly individual interplay between himself and his environment. This meaningful albeit complex view of each child's developmental history can be described only by the case method. The method assumes biological variation in the expression of individual adaptive predisposition and potentiality and variation in psychosocial influence of the family; moreover, it strives to observe and rationalize the historical interplay between these individual and social processes. Each child manifests his own very unique adaptive history and, in this sense, his symptoms and behaviors can only be understood by the case method of study.

The case method also presumes that the children vary in their accessibility to environmental influence and their ability to cope with the normal range of psychological and physiological stress. Thus it may be presumed that some children suffer from conceptual deficiencies which impair their capacity to achieve inner mental patterns necessary for the attainment of an inner state of predictability and safety. Others, such as the hypersensitive children, first described by Bergman and Escalona (1949) and confirmed by numerous observations of others, are unable to cope with the ordinary range of perceptual input. On the other hand, the case method presumes that families vary in ability to enhance the children's development by responding to the behavior of the children in a way that would support ego growth and development.

In this framework, there is little point in classifying parents as adequate or inadequate apart from the child's behavior and requirements. The "adequate" parental response is that which is specifically contingent on the child's responses and is specifically designed to facilitate the desirable and to inhibit the undesirable forms of behavior. The normal parent may not understand how to contend with the child who is developing atypically and may be quite inadequate in his efforts to "normalize" the child. It is not surprising that, in the therapeutic encounter, the clinician finds little profit in labeling the parent "abnormal" or "normal" and generally concentrates on the details of the parents' interaction with the psychotic child. One can explain much of the child's behavior by this behavioral interplay without ever once considering diagnostic labels of the parents. This clinical approach to the psychotic child and his parents receives support from the systematic considerations of learning theorists who are able to illuminate much of a child's behavior by the responses of the environment. Ferster (1961), for example, has illustrated very acutely how the behavior of parents may reinforce autistic manifestations in the child. Nor does Ferster find it necessary to refer to more remote etiologic factors such as heredity or brain damage.

One approach to the evaluation of families, therefore, is to begin with the presumption that the families have not succeeded in enhancing the ego growth or, in some cases, in overcoming the primary ego deficits of the child termed psychotic. Beginning with this presumption, families have been described either as actively encouraging psychotic manifestations or as not responding in a manner necessary to facilitate ego growth totally and harmoniously.

An example of the latter type of behavior is embodied in the phrase "parental perplexity," which has been ascribed to parents of schizophrenic children (Goldfarb, Sibulkin, Behrens, and Jahoda, 1958). A more precise descriptive phrase perhaps would "parental paralysis," accompanied by an emotional response of bewilderment and perplexity. In this state of mind the parent is nonempathic, nongratifying, passive, and not inclined in his responses to assist the child in his construction of reality.

In clinical practice, judgments regarding the adequacy of the family as a determinant of the child's ability to find gratification and to grow in purposeful behavior are very much influenced by the bias of the observer. We have already described representative theories and observations of observers who offer psychodynamic and interpersonal explanations for the attributes of psychotic children. In contrast, observers with a strong bias for organic or hereditary explanations have been equally inclined to interpret their case findings regarding the families as evidence that the psychosocial climate of the families of psychotic children plays a very meager role in determining the aberrations of the children. Examples of the latter point of view are the influential reports of Bender and her colleagues (e.g., Bender and Grugett, 1956), Kallmann and Roth (1956), and, more recently, of Rutter (1965).

Bender and Grugett (1956) selected 30 case records of 142 schizophrenic children under 7 years of age. The selection was presumably "random," except that case records with inadequate data were excluded. The emotional climate of the families was judged on the basis of qualitative observations of family cohesion and stability, continuity of parents, observable adjustment to community expectations, interest in the child, relationships among family members, and consistency of attitudes. The validity of the judgments in each case is difficult to evaluate on the basis of Bender's reports, although she states "most" of the patients and families were known to the staff on a continuing basis. The ratings which summated globally the judgments of family climate and the approximate definitions which were offered in the body of Bender's discussion are as follows:

Negative:
> "Markedly deficient in emotional resources basic to the child's chance for satisfying his essential needs for affectional security."

Average:
> "More positive than negative influences."

Positive:
> "Impressively favorable home situations and parental attitudes."

Of these families, 8 offered a negative climate, 14 an average climate, and 8 a positive climate. Seven of the children came from families broken by divorce and separation. Bender and Grugett concluded that a considerable proportion of the families offered a "stable and supportive" background to the schizophrenic children. They contrasted this finding with the very deficient emotional climates of families of children with nonschizophrenic behavior disorders. Of the 30 nonschizophrenic children, 23 came from families which offered a negative emotional climate and an equal number did not have both parents at home.

Bender and Grugett's study has been quoted as evidence that environmental factors play no part in the development of childhood psychosis, whereas they do contribute significantly to the development of neurotic and delinquent behaviors. However, the study raises a number of methodologic questions. For example, the population represented by Bender's sample remains unclear. It differs, for example, from the Ittleson Center schizophrenic group where psychotic children from broken homes have been entirely excluded. Similarly, the rating of the children were not clearly independent of a knowledge of the source of the children. It is also difficult to be certain of the validity of the judgments of the emotional climate when the proportion of

families considered deficient in influence on the child (27%) was considerably less than the proportion of fathers (40%) and mothers (47%) who were diagnosed as schizophrenic.

Kallmann and Roth classified the families of the schizophrenic children in their investigations on the basis of more definable and tangible criteria than Bender and Grugett. Thus the home was classified as adequate if it was fair to good in socioeconomic position, if it was not disrupted by desertion, divorce, or separation, and if it was maintained by two well adjusted parents. The presence of one emotionally disturbed or socially inadequate parent was sufficient to classify a family as poor or inadequate. This study did not contain a control group of nonschizophrenic children of the same age and social position, thereby eliminating any possibility of linking deviation in family climate and childhood psychosis. Nevertheless, it is striking that in this study 71% of the families were described as inadequate. This proportion of inadequate homes is far above that noted by Bender and Grugett. Kallmann and Roth also noted that the ratio of adequate homes was reduced where there were cotwins and siblings diagnosed as schizoid and mentally retarded. Kallmann and Roth were impressed by the large proportion of normal siblings from inadequate homes and of schizoid siblings from adequate homes; they reasoned that the data contradict the direct correlation of adequacy of the home and normalcy of the child. As an alternative formula, they proposed a gene-specific vulnerability by schizophrenic children to stress and a nonspecific impairment of normal protective functions for coping with an unfavorable environment.

By Kallmann's definition of family adequacy, the great bulk of families of schizophrenic children are inadequate. As noted, this contradicts Bender's conclusions regarding the families of schizophrenic children. It is also striking that Kallmann and Roth themselves seemed to be unaware of the implications of these findings. They placed more emphasis on the lack of correlation between adjustment of the siblings and the adequacy of the homes, whereas it is likely that the narrow range in adequacy of the families and the concentration of the families in a classification of inadequacy precluded any likelihood of a high correlation between family adequacy and adjustment level of the siblings.

In his description of organic and emotional factors in early childhood psychosis, Rutter (1965) has stated rather firmly "There appears to be no reason to attribute the disorder to abnormal parental attitudes or behavior." However, in this statement he offered no firm data to support this contention for there is no evidence of systematic and detailed study of the families. Rutter's conclusion regarding the part the families played in the development of the children he was following was based on his observation that traumatic experiences had occurred among the children with brain damage as often as among the children without manifest brain damage; that many of the parents seemed normally adjusted, and where deviant they were quite inconsistent in behavior; and that the parents of the brain-damaged children often were abnormal.

To justify his position regarding the part played by the families, Rutter referred to evidence which had presumably been gathered previously by E. J. Anthony (1958) and his colleagues. In actual fact, a careful reading of Anthony's very thoughtful reports would tend to confirm a transactional position in which an interplay between the child's potentialities and the environmental capacity to meet the child's individual needs is held to account for the symptom of autism. Anthony proposes two types of autism. In primary autism, the child fails to emerge from the presumably normal infantile state of autism and has been unresponsive from the beginning. In secondary autism, the child emerges from the infantile, autistic state but then sinks back under stress and becomes unresponsive. In his investigations, Anthony demonstrated that the parents of both types of autistic children were quite different, although both groups of parents failed to meet the needs of their children. Thus an analysis of a section of a parental questionnaire dealing with self-criticism suggested that self-righteous mothers were predominantly in the primary group, whereas the mothers of children with secondary autistic reactions were confused and guilty. Examination of the mothers' mental status, in order to evaluate and classify qualitatively their ability to be in

"rapport" with their own children and the staff, indicated that 73% of the cold mothers belong to the primary group while 62% of the smothering mothers were in the secondary group. Rorschachs of the mothers showed that mothers of the children in the primary autistic category were more removed in social and emotional relationships than the mothers of children in the secondary autistic group (Bene, 1958). Presumably, a child who is unresponsive from the beginning remains so if the mother is also unresponsive. Similarly, in secondary autism, the child who is oversensitive withdraws defensively if his mother overstimulates or does not protect him from stimulation.[5]

The observation that the families vary in their functional adequacy as psychosocial environments for developing children has been confirmed by numerous observers. This diversity in family environment of psychotic children has been utilized as evidence for the conviction that childhood psychosis is not a consequence of emotional and interpersonal disorders, and that psychological influences are of secondary significance in the origin of psychotic manifestations. However, the line of inference is reasonable only within a theoretical framework which maintains that childhood psychosis is the outcome of a single cause. Obviously in a monocausal scheme the presence of both adequate and inadequate homes would contradict the significance of the family in childhood psychosis. However, in a multicausal theory in which the family environment is only one contributing factor, the poor homes might be a serious contributing factor for the maldevelopment of the psychotic children in these homes, while other factors, for example, cerebral dysfunction, would be more crucial in the case of psychotic children in the adequate homes. Evidence for this position will be presented in the summation of studies which have simultaneously evaluated both neurological and psychosocial factors in the same psychotic children.

The previously noted therapeutic investi-

[5] Compare Anthony's subdivision of autism with Goldfarb's findings that hypersensitive and hyposensitivity occur historically and even within brief intervals of time in the same child and his inference that hyposensitivity is the defensive reaction to hypersensitivity.

gations which favor the psychogenic hypothesis suffer from defects in precision of definition, controls, and objectivity of data. Similar criticisms may be leveled against a number of the studies which favor the genetic and organic hypotheses to explain childhood psychosis. In addition, the clinical investigations which have contradicted entirely the part that the families play in the development of psychotic children have been limited by the superficiality, the doubtful validity, and the unstated reliability of the estimates of family adequacy. In most cases, it is unclear from the reports whether genuine probing observation of the families preceded the ratings of the climate.

Therefore it would be useful to turn to a group of family investigations which have struggled consciously with problems of definition, sampling, controls, and independence of data.

Klebanoff (1959) used the Parental Attitude Research Instrument (PARI), a paper and pencil questionnaire to compare 15 mothers of hospitalized schizophrenic children, 15 mothers of hospitalized mentally retarded and brain-damaged children, and 26 mothers of normal children. Mothers of schizophrenic children showed less pathology in their stated attitudes than the mothers of brain-damaged and retarded children. (Mothers of the two deviant groups combined showed more pathological attitudes than the mothers of the normal children.) The data were interpreted to cast doubt on the theoretic proposition that maternal attitudes produce childhood psychosis. A major weakness of this questionnaire study, as of other questionnaire studies, is the tendency for questionnaires to elicit only those conscious answers which the subjects may feel are socially desirable. Actual behaviors and genuine emotional attitudes may be disguised.

The most significant trends in recent family studies therefore has been the direct study of the families as functional units and of the parents in interaction with the psychotic child, or the parents in interaction and communication with the investigator. Cross-sectional studies when the child is already schizophrenic cannot establish etiology. For operational reasons, designs for direct observations do, of course, presume that the quality of parent and parent-child interactions at the

moment of study replicates the interactions from the beginning of the psychotic child's life. Historical and therapeutic explorations have tended to support this presumption, although not with certainty. In studies including the psychotic child himself, it is difficult to tease apart the extent to which the parent is primarily responsible for the child's response or is merely responding to the disordered behavior of his psychotic child. Even so, if one can comfortably forgo considerations of primary etiology, it is always possible to observe whether the families' responses qualitatively enhance or minimize the abnormal responses of the children at the time of study. In addition, studies of the parents in interactional experiences in circumstances which exclude the psychotic child are revealing.

For the past 10 years at the Ittleson Center an effort has been made to evaluate the psychological climate of the families of psychotic children by direct participant observation. In a 3-hour period of participant observation, the observer focuses on interactions of the family members in their various roles, for example, mother and father as marital partners, mother and father as parents, and the family as an integrated functional unit. The observer then records a detailed report of the observations and rates the families' interactions in detail. Each of the ratings ranges from one pole in which the intersections are highly aberrant and pathological to the other pole in which the reactions are optimal for the family group and for the development of the child. Because of the intercorrelations among the ratings, the ratings are summed to yield a single score. Before initiating psychiatric treatment, the families have been studied routinely and independently of the clinical and psychiatric investigations. The summed score of family interaction is reliable and correlates significantly with other clinical judgments of parental behavior and with such specific dimensions as clarity of maternal communication (Goldfarb et al., 1966). An early study demonstrated that, on the average, the families of schizophrenic children were more aberrant in patterns of family interaction than families of preschool children treated for nonschizophrenic behavior disorders (Behrens and Goldfarb, 1958). Later studies, using control groups which were larger and consisted of average public school children, confirmed that the families of the psychotic children were more aberrant in patterns of interaction than the families of normal children (Goldfarb, 1961, 1962).

Meyers and Goldfarb (1961) used appraisals based on direct participant observations and on semistructured interviews of mothers to test the "parental perplexity" hypothesis. Mothers of schizophrenic children were more "perplexed" than mothers of normal children. In other words, the mothers of the psychotic children reacted to their children with greater uncertainty and indecisiveness than the mothers of normal children, less spontaneity and empathic response, less sensitivity to the child's needs, paralyzing bewilderment, and dramatic lack of control and authority. In contrast to the normal mothers, the mothers of the psychotic children were less inclined to guide, instruct, reinforce, and inhibit.

The Ittleson Center also has focused on maternal communication in appraising the interactions of schizophrenic children and their mothers (Goldfarb et al., 1966). Assuming that the mother's capacity to act as an effective reinforcer of her child's behavior is related to the clarity of her communications, errors in clarity of communication of the mothers were noted qualitatively and classified as follows:

1. Failure to stimulate the child's interest in active communication.

2. Failure to maintain the continuous flow of communication with the child.

3. Failure to reinforce normal and acceptable speech and communication in the children.

4. Active confounding of the child in regard to his construction of reality.

5. Missing or not responding to the child's cues.

6. Failure to cope with the child's unusual deviancies in communication.

Lennard, Beaulieu, and Embry (1965) studied behavior processes in families with a schizophrenic child by studying communication. Samples of communications among mother, father, and son in each of 10 families in which the son was diagnosed as psychotic and 7 control families with a normal son were analyzed quantitatively. Schizophrenic and control families differed in such variables as rate and volume of communication and in rates of intrusiveness. Thus in the schizophrenic families the father's number of communications was lower and the sons addressed less communication to the father and received less from him. In view of the common observation of mutual imperviousness in families with psychotic children, it is noteworthy that the schizophrenic child showed little success in spontaneous intrusion on two-person communication between the mother and father. Indeed, in the schizophrenic families, all three individual family members were more impervious than in the normal families to the communications of the others. As in the Ittleson Center studies, the impact of the obvious deviancy of the psychotic child and the degree to which the child's aberrant communications affected the attributes of the parents, for example, their imperviousness, is not clear. The same methodological problem applies to Lennard's observation that the mothers asked twice as many questions of the psychotic child as the mothers in the control group. That this is not merely a response to the unresponsive child is suggested by the observation that the mothers of the psychotic child also asked many more questions of the fathers than did the mothers of the control child. Lennard's interpretation of the findings in regard to intrusiveness, question asking, and personalization of communication is that the parents in the families of schizophrenic children are more discouraging of self-motivated behavior in their children than the parents of the control children.

In general, the quality of the analysis of the parents' communication patterns is limited by the observer's awareness of the source of the data. There is an inevitable contamination of the data by the obvious presence of the disturbed child, a condition which precludes total objectivity of judgment. Studies of maternal communication, therefore, in which the psychotic children do not participate and where it is not known to the observer which are the controls, are of value. In this regard, the studies of Singer and Wynne (1963), Rice, Kepecs, and Yahalom (1967), and Goldfarb, Goldfarb, and Scholl (1966) are noteworthy.

Singer and Wynne (1963) hypothesized that certain varieties of parental attention, communication, and relating to others are linked to the forms of mental disorder in their offspring. To test this proposition, they considered the responses of marital pairs as units in the Rorschach and Thematic Apperception Tests. Parents of autistic children were differentiated significantly from parents of childhood neurotics (of whom an equal number were acting-out and withdrawn children) and from parents of schizophrenics who had become ill in adolescence or adulthood. The parents of the child and adult groups may have differed in age and the differences in age may have influenced the test results. However, this factor is not considered explicitly by the authors and needs clarification. The parents of autistic children were differentiated from other parent groups in TAT by evidence of strong tendencies to disaffiliation, emotional distance, and lack of empathy. In contrast, parents of the adult schizophrenics showed more outstanding difficulties in focusing and sustaining attention. The TATs of the parents of the neurotic children were marked by other features and did not evidence the characteristic aberrations either of the parents of the autistic children or of the adult schizophrenics. In the Rorschach Tests, nearly all of the parents of adult schizophrenics evidenced serious thought disorders, while virtually none of the parents of the acting-out neurotic children had such thought disorders; the parents of schizophrenic children and of the withdrawn children were intermediate. (This finding was confirmed when level of perceptual development was appraised with Becker's method for scoring Rorschach genetic level.) Hostility, as manifested in Rorschach symbols, was rated higher in the parents of childhood schizophrenics than in the parents of adult schizophrenics. Parents of childhood schizophrenics were also more given to hostile initial responses than the other parent groups.

After eliminating all signs of identification in the samples of maternal communication, the speech of mothers of schizophrenic children at the Ittleson Center and of mothers of normal public school children were evaluated by a speech pathologist, who gave summed ratings based on evaluations of phonation, rhythm, and articulation (Goldfarb et al., 1966b). The speech of mothers of schizophrenic children was judged to be poorer than the speech of mothers of normal children; moreover, the mothers of the schizophrenic children were inferior to the mothers of normal children in ability to communicate meaning and mood.

Investigations of the families in regard to member interaction deal with extremely complex phenomena and the problems of definition and control are very difficult. Though such investigations have been going on in some centers for the past decade, they are still in an early phase of development. Slowly, however, reasonably consistent findings are emerging out of studies such as those referred to above, and they would cumulatively tend to support the hypothesis that the families of psychotic children as a whole are deviant and that their modes of interacting and communicating do not facilitate improved ego functioning in these children.

However, just as we have observed that not all psychotic children show signs of primary atypism and cerebral dysfunction, so it must be noted that not all families of psychotic children offer the children a deviant psychosocial and communication environment. This would tend to contradict a monocausal theory of the etiology of childhood psychosis. To complicate the picture, many psychotic children are contending simultaneously with the restraints placed on their development by both defects in cerebral integrity and disturbances in the psychosocial organization of their families. Such observations are rationalized most effectively by a multicausal theory of the origins of childhood psychosis.

In a multicausal theory of the etiology of the attributes of psychotic children, one might further propose that each psychotic child's adaptation reflects the influence of intrinsic defects in the child and of aberrations in the psychosocial climate of the family, that the two classes of disorder vary dimensionally from none to marked, and that the relative contributions of both classes of disorder to the psychotic child's manifestations vary along a continuum. Clinically, this would be demonstrated in the seriously brain-damaged child in a normal family, or in a somatically intact child reared in a highly deviant family, or in a neurologically impaired child in a highly deviant family.

When a group of psychotic children are classified by levels of neurological integrity, of family adequacy, and of adaptive competence, significant patterns of information emerge. Although degree of neurological impairment varies along a continuum, the crude division of psychotic children into those with evidence of neurological impairment ("organic") and those free of such evidence of neurological impairment ("nonorganic") has been valuable in ordering observations of psychotic children and their families. For example, in most tests of purposeful functions of normal children, organic psychotic children, and nonorganic psychotic children, a consistent gradient of capacity is observed. As a group, nonorganic psychotic children are superior to organic psychotic children (Goldfarb, 1961). In one study at the Ittleson Center, for instance, mean full IQs on the Wechsler Intelligence Scale for Children was 92 for nonorganic psychotic children and 62 for organic psychotic children. The majority of organic psychotic children are retarded in intellectual functioning, whereas the majority of the nonorganic children are average or higher. The most severely impaired children are virtually all in the organic segment of psychotic children.

In this study, nonorganic psychotic children are superior to the organic psychotic children in a broad range of functions, including perception, body orientation, discrimination of body cues, postural and righting functions, orientation, and psychomotor functions. Some aberrant responses which have been considered pathognomonic of schizophrenia are found chiefly in the organic subgroup and reflect impaired integrity of the central nervous system. This includes the whirling phenomena described by Bender, and the most extreme deviations in sensitivity to sensory stimuli. (The latter has been studied particularly in the auditory area, using a startle experiment.)

Organic and nonorganic psychotic children also differ in interactional character of their families, in psychiatric status of their parents, in clarity of communication of their mothers. Participant observation of the families as functional psychosocial units and appraisal of family adequacy with the Ittleson Center

Family Adequacy Scales demonstrate that the families of the organic psychotic children are closer to the normal in central tendency and range and that they are superior in interactional adequacy to the families of nonorganic psychotic children (Goldfarb, 1961). Virtually all the families of nonorganic psychotic children are deviant and contribute markedly to the disorders of the children, whereas the organic psychotic children are derived from all varieties of family including some that are highly deviant and contribute markedly to the deviancies of the children and some that are within the range of normal in psychosocial organization (Goldfarb et al., 1966c; Goldfarb, 1961, 1962). The organic subcluster of psychotic children also has a lower proportion of psychotic mothers than the nonorganic subcluster (Meyers and Goldfarb, 1962). As many as 44% of the mothers of the nonorganic subcluster of psychotic children have been diagnosed as schizophrenic in contrast to 21% of the organic subcluster. Fathers are not as significantly differentiated in mental status. In another study of clarity of maternal communication, the mothers of organic children show greater mean clarity of communication as well as a broader range of scores (Goldfarb et al., 1966c). All the evidence, therefore, supports the general inference that families of nonorganic psychotic children are more deviant than the families of organic psychotic children.

Although the studies are tentative and few, there is also evidence suggesting that the organic and nonorganic children show differing amounts and patterns of longitudinal change (Goldfarb, 1967a). The most impaired children, almost totally devoid of language and conceptual response, are found in the organic subcluster and show little growth and change even when concerted treatment and educational efforts are made. (This finding with regard to these most impaired children is very much in accord with Kanner and Eisenberg's findings [Eisenberg, 1956] with regard to autistic children who are mute at age 6 and Rutter's [1965] confirmatory findings. Rutter considered mutism a bad prognostic sign when combined with low intelligence.) Excluding this most impaired group of organic children, and even when matched with organic children in ego level at onset of treatment, nonorganic psychotic children show more growth in ego than organic children while in residential treatment (Goldfarb, 1967a). Where ego improvement is noted, the two clusters of psychotic children differ in patterns of change as well, as nonorganic children are more likely to show first signs of progress later in treatment than do the organic psychotic children. They also differ in responsiveness to day versus residential treatment (Goldfarb, Goldfarb, and Pollack, 1966). The organic children respond equally well to day and residential treatment, whereas nonorganic children would seem to respond more to the residential program.

THERAPEUTIC MANAGEMENT

Despite differences in theory regarding the etiology or etiologies of childhood psychosis, most programs of therapeutic management of psychotic children strive to organize the child's environment throughout the day in order to facilitate the development of the child's adaptive functions. This applies as much to those programs which question the role of direct psychotherapy in the treatment of psychotic children (Eisenberg, 1956; Rutter, 1966b) as it does to those programs whose conceptions have emerged out of the presumptions and convictions of psychoanalytic psychiatry (Boatman and Szurek, 1960; Despert, 1947; Goldfarb, 1965; Mahler and Furer, 1960; Rank, 1949). The value of the therapeutic environment is derived from the immediacy and its continuing and consistent responsiveness to all the pertinent behavioral manifestations of the psychotic child. In such an environment, attention focuses on every relational encounter with the psychotic child at the moment of the social interchange, and the responses of the adult environment are designed to diminish the confusion of the psychotic child and to enhance his adaptive efforts.

An organized, comprehensive, clinical program requires the cooperative efforts of many skills and disciplines, including psychiatrists, medical specialists (particularly neurologists), teachers, case workers, child care specialists, psychologists, and a variety of remedial specialists. In addition, varied therapeutic techniques are required, including milieu therapy, individual psychotherapy, specialized education and remedial education and chemotherapy.

A corrective point of view is most obviously implemented in the procedures of milieu therapy (Bettelheim, 1950, 1955, 1966; Goldfarb, 1965, in press; Noshpitz, 1962; Redl and Wineman, 1951; Robinson, 1957). The innumerable encounters with the psychotic child in the course of child care and schooling offer many opportunities for ego correction and rehabilitation. The adaptive significance and meaning of the child's behavior are considered in a highly individualized fashion and the adult responses are guided by the objective to improve the child's self-awareness and construction of reality. Enhancement of all ego functions of the child, for example, his capacity to communicate, have the ultimate purpose of improving the psychotic child's social relationships and human relatedness.

Milieu therapy refers to the planned design of a total environment guided by clear therapeutic objectives for each child. The milieu refers to every aspect of the climate surrounding the child, including such events as eating, sleeping, waking, recreation, dressing, and schooling and all the accompanying human interactions. For purposes of discussion only, specialized procedures such as direct individual psychotherapy and chemotherapy have been differentiated from milieu therapy. However, it is clear that all treatment modalities are profitable and need to be included in a comprehensive effort to assist the psychotic child.

Individual therapy refers to the intimate, reciprocating interchange between adult therapist and child in which the events are guided by a systematic theory of human behavior. It employs psychodynamic hypotheses based on concepts of behavior as motivated, adaptational, and interactional in significance, and oftimes outside the individual's conscious awareness. The discipline of individual treatment enables the therapist to infer the adaptational significance of the child's responses from the converging data of play therapy, verbal interchanges, and life observations.

It is important to grasp that individual therapy for the psychotic child is most feasible within the more general framework

of a realistic, intrusive, orderly, ego-enhanc-
ing social climate. Indeed it has seemed that
only under the circumstances of a clearly
articulated social environment does the psychotic child become aware of the conflictual
aspects of his very frightened, unhappy existence. In turn, the insights of individual
therapy deepen the understanding of those
who are more directly involved in the organization of the more total social environment.

It is also of interest that, very much like
milieu therapy, specialized developments in
individual therapy of psychotic children have
stressed the therapeutic objective of ego correction. Mahler (Mahler and Furer, 1960),
for example, has recommended a "corrective
symbiotic" experience in which the psychotic
child is helped to reexperience the symbiotic
phase of development directly with his mother
and then to replace this regressive relationship with a new, less ambivalent, more differentiated relationship. Alpert (Alpert and
Pfeiffer, 1964) also recommends a corrective
object relationship in which new adults, that
is, the therapist and teacher, compensate for
early maternal deprivation. DesLauriers
(1962) provides experiences which have the
objective of improving the psychotic child's
body awareness and psychological identity.
All three reporters, therefore, place key emphasis on actual experiences which enhance
ego growth and improve the child's repertoire of purposeful functions.

Treatment centers vary in their optimism
regarding the possibilities for change in the
families of psychotic children, and in their
implementation of family treatment. However, there is a growing disposition to offer
treatment to individual family members and
to families as units (Goldfarb, in press). The
treatment of families, including the child,
clarifies the more immediate link between
the style of family behavior, cognition and
communication, and related deficits in the
psychotic child; moreover, the treatment holds
promise for the improvement of the communication and relational responses of the entire
family.

Specialized derivatives of individual therapy and the therapeutic use of group processes have been utilized. For example, "group
therapy" of psychotic children has been utilized (Speers and Lansing, 1965). This would

seem to be a restricted variant of more comprehensive clinical programs for the treatment
of psychotic children. Similarly, joint therapy
of the parents as marital pairs, or of groups
of mothers and fathers has been employed.
As in family therapy, the objective is to
ameliorate familial conflicts and communication ambiguities which impede the clinical
progress of the psychotic child in the family.

Recently, too, the orderly application of
the principles of operant conditioning to improve the language, social behavior, and even
of self-mutilative behavior of severely disordered autistic children has been reported
(Ferster, 1961; Lovaas et al., 1965). The
systematic behavioral modifications confirm
what has actually always been known in clinical practice, that is, the educability of psychotic children. They also demonstrate the
value of learning techniques for modifying
symptoms and specified attributes. Operant
conditioning investigations have not as yet
shown that schedules of reinforcement are
able to effect the more total alterations necessary to achieve clinical and behavioral normality.

Chemotherapy is of value in some cases
for improving a psychotic child's accessibility
to stimulation and influence (Eisenberg, 1964;
Fish, 1960a; Nitchern, 1962). Drugs do not,
of course, in themselves undo old, learned responses or create new social or personal patterns. They are thus adjuvant techniques to
make the psychotic child more responsive to
the corrective influence of social processes
and are rarely sufficient in themselves to induce normal behavior. Nevertheless, they
may be helpful in reducing symptoms that
interfere with the psychotic child's engagement with his environment. For example,
they may be used to counteract extreme
apathy and withdrawal (trifluo-perazine),
anxiety, hyperactivity, and lack of impulse
control (chlorpromazine, diphenhydramine,
dextro-amphetamine).

Drugs, of course, are selected by the child
psychiatrist to alleviate specific symptoms,
such as those noted above, which may be
interfering with learning, social responses,
and psychotherapy. Careful medical supervision is essential since the effective range
varies from child to child and toxicity must
always be guarded against.

Other somatic procedures have been employed but have not established themselves as therapeutic procedures. For example, Bender (1947b) has utilized and recommends electroconvulsive therapy to stimulate the maturation of psychotic children and to reduce their anxiety. Her conclusions have been questioned by Clardy and Rumpf (1954). Neither the evaluations by Bender nor that of Clardy and Rumpf are free of data contamination, and the value of electroconvulsive therapy as a therapeutic procedure remains unsettled.

Bender and her colleagues (Bender, Faretra, and Cobrinik, 1963; Bender, Goldschmidt, and Sankar, 1961) have also utilized LSD-25 and UML-491 in the treatment of childhood schizophrenia. Behavioral improvement was noted. Freedman, Ebin, and Wilson (1962) employed LSD-25 with autistic children and were not hopeful regarding its treatment value. Nor have other drugs such as Marsilid (Freedman, 1958) or L-Glutavite (Levin and Impastato, 1961) established their value in treatment.

The essential therapeutic instrument for psychotic children, therefore, is the human being whose responses are designed to facilitate growth in impaired or arrested functions. Practical experience has indicated that corrective and socializing procedures must be applied for very long periods. Characteristically, the children and their families need assistance of diverse kinds throughout the psychotic child's childhood, including residential treatment, day hospital, out-patient service, and all varieties of remedial education.

Evaluative research to demonstrate the value of specific modalities of treatment is a rarity and there have been even fewer carefully controlled studies comparing the treatment response of treated and untreated children. Exceptions, perhaps, are the operant conditioning experiments (Ferster, 1961; Lovaas et al., 1965) and the occasional experiments in pharmacology (Fish, 1960a). In the absence of control groups of untreated children and suitable procedures for evaluation of change, it is impossible to either affirm or deny the part played by individual psychotherapy, milieu therapy, day hospitals, or residential treatment in the developmental improvements noted among a proportion of the children.

Eisenberg (1966) has summarized the result of follow-up of five studies including a total of 502 children made since 1940. Twenty-four percent of the children showed recovery. In the absence of treatment specification and evidence confirming the value of specific treatment methods, Eisenberg suggested that one may anticipate such recovery in a quarter of psychotic children in the natural course of their life histories and without specified treatment. Although 7 follow-up studies of 132 children before 1940 showed a recovery rate of only 7%, Eisenberg proposed that this reflected difference in diagnostic classification rather than in adequacy of treatment. This conclusion is supported by two major follow-up studies—Bender's (1953) study of her Bellevue series and the Kanner-Eisenberg (1955) study of the Hopkins' series of children with infantile autism. These studies of children who had received minimal or irregular psychotherapy indicated that about one-quarter eventually were adjusted in the community.

Although an imprecise estimate, these data would suggest that a treatment modality for psychotic children would have to show that significantly more than 25% of the children became normally adjusted after the treatment in order to be considered effective. The problem of evaluation, however, is not so simple. For example, in Brown's (1963) follow-up of children treated with individual therapy and specialized education in early childhood, there is a report of 36% improvement; however, Szurek and his group at Langley-Porter (Boatman and Szurek, 1960), who have been unquestionably sophisticated and zealous in their application of psychotherapy to their group of psychotic children and parents, report only 14% improvement. One is inevitably led to the conclusion that the differences in rate of improvement reported by various observers are more linked to differences in sampling than to differences in therapeutic management.

More specifically, severity of impairment is linked to the progress of the psychotic child. In a follow-up of 63 children with infantile autism, Eisenberg (1956) has reported that the presence or absence of functional language by age 5 years sharply distinguished two groups in adolescence. Of 30 children without speech by 5 years, only one child achieved a marginal social adjustment and even this child was subsequently hospitalized. In contrast, approximately half of the children with language were adjusting in the community and were at age level in school. Rutter (1965) suggested that the prognostic value of speech was due to the correlation of speech with intelligence. His data suggested that clinical improvement was more related to intellectual functioning than to language level. Improvement was more in the mute children with IQs above 50 than in those with IQ below 50. Of course, as previously noted, psychotic children tend to be impaired in all functions—both social and cognitive—and the IQ happens to be an excellent general indication of level of ego functioning. Studies at the Ittleson Center, for example, confirm that children with WISC Full IQs below 45 (comparable to Rutter's children with IQs below 50) are uneducable (Goldfarb and Pollack, 1964) and show no perceptible clinical progress in residential or day treatment (Goldfarb et al., 1966a).

Subclassification is obviously necessary if samplings of schizophrenic children at different treatment installations are to be compared. It is also fundamental in the delineation of the life course of schizophrenic children and in the evaluation of response to treatment. For example, employing a system of subclassification based on an appraisal of neurological integrity, of family interaction, and of severity of impairment, it has been possible to show that all the most impaired children, those who lack speech, are so low in intellectual functioning that they are unmeasurable and cannot discriminate important persons in their lives, are uneducable,

and avoid looking and listening, are to be found in the organic subcluster with evidences of neurological impairment. These children show no significant clinical progress in either residential or day treatment settings (Goldfarb, 1967a). It is also clear that the organic subcluster shows poorer progress in ego status than the nonorganic subcluster, even when carefully matched in ego status at the start of treatment (Goldfarb, 1967a). Finally, as already noted, there is suggestive evidence that the two subclusters of schizophrenic children show different response to such global programs of therapeutic management as day and residential treatments (Goldfarb et al., 1966a). While organic children in intact families respond equally well to day and residential treatment, children in the nonorganic subcluster appear to show more progress in residential programs. It would also seem that organic psychotic children who improve show upward changes very early in treatment, whereas the nonorganic children are more likely to manifest improvements in ego later in the treatment process. Indeed a majority of the nonorganic children in residential treatment do not begin to show perceptible alterations in adaptive competence until the second or even third year of the most comprehensive of the treatment programs.

This review of current progress in etiological understanding of childhood psychosis emphasizes that the primary requirement for scientific investigation and evaluative research is a meaningful subclassification of children who are presently included in the broad class of psychotic children.

References

Abood, L. G. Report given at first annual conference of the Brain Research Foundation, Chicago, Jan. 1953. *Scope Weekly*, 1957, **2.**

Akerfeldt, S. Oxidation of N, N-dimethyl-p-phenylenediamine by serum from patients with mental disease. *Science*, 1957, **125.**

Alanen, Y. O., Rekola, J. K., Stewen, A., Takala, K., and Tuovinen, M. On factors influencing the onset of schizophrenia in the light of a family study. 6th Int. Cong. Psychother., London, 1964.

Alanen, Y., Arajarvi, T., and Viitamaki, R. O. *Psychoses in childhood*. Copenhagen, Denmark: Munksgaard, 1964.

Alexander, H. C. B. Insanity in children. *Alien Neurol.*, 1894, **15**, 27–51. *Alien Neurol.*, 1893, **14**, 409–419. *J. Am. med. Ass.*, 1893, **21**, 511–519.

Alpert, A., and Pfeiffer, E. Treatment of an autistic child: introduction and theoretical discussion. *J. Am. Acad. Child Psychiat.*, 1964, **3**(4), 591–616.

Annell, A. L. The prognosis of psychotic syndromes in children. *Acta Psychiat. Scand.*, 1963, **39**, 235.

Anthony, E. J. An aetiological approach to the diagnosis of psychosis in childhood. *Z. Kinderpsychiat.*, 1958, **25**, 89–96.

Anthony, E. J. An experimental approach to the psychopathology of childhood. *Br. J. med. Psychol.*, 1958, **31**, 211–223.

Anthony, E. J., and Scott, P. Manic-depressive psychosis in childhood. *J. Psychol. Psychiat.*, 1960, **1**, 53–72.

Aparison, M. H., and Drew, A. L. N, N-dimethyl-p-phenylenediamine oxidation by serum from schizophrenic children. *Science*, 1958, **127**, 758.

Ashby, H. Some of the neuroses of early life. *Rep. Soc. Stud. Dis. Child.*, 1905, **5**, 251–267.

Bakwin, H. Psychologic aspects of pediatrics: childhood schizophrenia. *J. Pediat.*, 1950, **37**, 416–426.

Bakwin, R. M. Ceruloplasmin activity and copper levels in the serum of children with schizophrenia. *J. Am. Wom. Ass.*, 1961, **16**, 522–523.

Bakwin, R. M., Mosbach, E. H., and Bakwin, H. Ceruloplasmin activity in the serum of children with schizophrenia. *Pediatrics*, 1958, **22**, 905–909.

Baumler, Fr. Psychodiagnostische Untersuchungen bei einem 12-jahrigen schizophrenen Madchen: ein Beitrag zur Psychodiagnostik von Psychosen im Kindesalter. (A psychodiagnostic study of a 12-year-old schizophrenic girl: a contribution to the psychodiagnosis of childhood psychoses.) *Z. diag. Psychol.*, 1957, **5**, 114–122.

Beach, F. Insanity in children. *J. ment. Sci.*, 1898, **44**, 459–474.

Beck, S. J., Molish, H. B., and Sinclair, J. Current status of the Rorschach Test. Symposium, 1955, 3. Concerning researchers' thinking in schizophrenia research. *Am. J. Orthopsychiat.*, 1956, **26**, 728–800.

Beck, S. J. The six schizophrenias. *Res. Monogr. Orthopsychiat. Ass.*, 1954, **6**.

Behrens, M., and Goldfarb, W. A study of patterns of interaction of families of schizophrenic children in residential treatment. *Am. J. Orthopsychiat.*, 1958, **28**, 300–312.

Benda, C. E. *Developmental disorders of mentation.* New York: Grune & Stratton, 1952.

Bender, L. Childhood schizophrenia. *Nerv. Child*, 1941–42, **1**, 138–140.

Bender, L. Childhood schizophrenia: clinical study of one hundred schizophrenic children. *Am. J. Orthopsychiat.*, 1947, **17**, 40–56. (a)

Bender, L. One hundred cases of childhood schizophrenia treated with electric shock. *Trans. Am. Neurol. Ass.*, 1947, **72**, 165–169. (b)

Bender, L. Psychological principles of the Visual Motor Gestalt Test. *Trans. N.Y. Acad. Sci.*, 1949, **11**, 164–170.

Bender, L. Childhood schizophrenia. *Psychiat. Q.*, 1953, **27**, 663–681.

Bender, L. Twenty years of clinical research on schizophrenic children with special reference to those under six years of age. In G. Caplan, (Ed.), *Emotional problems of early childhood.* New York: Basic Books, 1955. Pp. 503–515.

Bender, L. Schizophrenia in childhood—its recognition, description, and treatment. *Am. J. Orthopsychiat.*, 1956, **26**, 499–506.

Bender, L. Autism in children with mental deficiency. *Am. J. ment. Defic.*, 1959, **63**(7), 81–86.

Bender, L. Treatment in early schizophrenia. *Progr. Psychother.*, 1960, **5**, 177–184.

Bender, L., Faretra, G., and Cobrinik, L. LSD and UML treatment of hospitalized disturbed children. *Recent adv. biol. Psychiat.*, 1963, **5**, 84–92.

Bender, L., Goldschmidt, L., and Sankar, S. D. V. Treatment of autistic schizophrenic children with LSD-25 and UML-491. *Recent adv. biol. Psychiat.*, 1961, **4**, 170–179.

Bender, L., and Grugett, A. A study of certain epidemiological factors in a group of children with childhood schizophrenia. *Am. J. Orthopsychiat.*, 1956, **26**, 131–145.

Bender, L., and Keeler, W. R. The body image of schizophrenic children following electroshock therapy. *Am. J. Orthopsychiat.*, 1952, **22**, 335–355.

Bene, E. A Rorschach investigation into the mothers of autistic children. *Br. J. med. Psychol.*, 1958, **31**, 226–227.

Beres, D. Ego deviations and the concept of schizophrenia. *Psychoan. Stud. Child*, 1955, **21**, 164–235.

Berg, I., Stark, G., and Jameson, S. Measurement of a stranger's influence on the behavior of young children with their mothers. *J. child Psychol. Psychiat.*, 1966, **7**(3/4), 243–250.

Bergman, M., Heinz, W., and Marchand, J. Schizophrenic reactions during childhood in mental defectives. *Psychiat. Q.*, 1951, **25**, 294–333.

Bergman, P., and Escalona, S. K. Unusual sensitivities in very young children. *Psychoanal. Stud. Child*, 1949, **3–4**, 333–352.

Berkowitz, P. H. Some psychological aspects of mental illness in children. *Genet. Psychol. Monogr.*, 1961, **63**, 103–148.

Bettelheim, B. *Love is not enough.* New York: Free Press, 1950.

Bettelheim, B. *Truants from life.* Glencoe, Ill.: Free Press, 1955.

Bettelheim, B. *The empty fortress.* New York: Macmillan, 1966.

Birch, H. G., and Hertzig, M. E. Etiology of schizophrenia: an overview of the relation of development to atypical behavior. Paper read at international Conference on Schizophrenia, Rochester, March 1967.

Birch, H. G., and Walker, H. A. Perceptual and perceptual-motor dissociation. *Archs. Gen. Psychiat.*, 1966, **14**(2), 113–118.

Bleuler, E. *Dementia praecox or the group of schizophrenias.* (Transl. by Joseph Zinkin.) New York: International Universities Press, 1952.

Boatman, M. J., and Szurek, S. A. A clinical study of childhood schizophrenia. In D. D. Jackson, (Ed.), *The etiology of schizophrenia.* New York: Basic Books, 1960. Pp. 389–440.

Book, J. A., Nichtern, S., and Gruenberg, E. Cytogenetical investigations in childhood schizophrenia. *Acta Psychiat. Scand.*, 1963, **39**, 309–323.

Bradley, C. *Schizophrenia in childhood.* New York: Macmillan, 1941.

Bradley, C., and Bowen, M. Amphetamine (benzedrine) therapy of children's behavior disorders. *Am. J. Orthopsychiat.*, 1941, **11**, 92–104. (a)

Bradley, C., and Bowen, M. Behavior characteristics of schizophrenic children. *Psych. Q.*, 1941, **15**, 296–315. (b)

Broadbent, W. H. Acute dementia in a child: recovery. *Med. Press Circ.*, 1878, **1**, 105–106.

Brown, B. F. Serum Akerfeldt for schizophrenia in children: preliminary reports. *J. Pediat.*, 1957, **51**, 46–48.

Brown, J. L. Follow up of children with atypical development (infantile psychosis). *Am. J. Orthopsychiat.*, 1963, **33**(5), 855–861.

Brown, R. I. The effects of varied environmental stimulation on the performance of subnormal children. *J. child Psychol. Psychiat.*, 1966, **7**, 251–261.

Browne, J. C. Psychical diseases of early life. *J. ment. Sci.*, 1859–60, **6**, 284–320.

Bruch, H. Studies in schizophrenia: the various developments in the approach to childhood schizophrenia. Psychotherapy with schizophrenics. *Acta Psychiat. Neurol. Scand.*, Kb., 1959, **34**, Suppl. 1130.

Bruch, H. Perceptual and conceptual disturbance in anorexia nervosa. *Psychom. Med.*, 1962, **24**(2), 187–194.

Cain, A. C., and Heinz, R. W. Interpretation within the metaphor. *Bull. Menninger Clin.*, 1961, **25**(6), 307–311.

Cassel, R. H. "Differentiation between the mental defective with psychosis and the childhood schizophrenic functioning as a mental defective. *Am. J. ment. Defic.*, 1957, **62**, 103–107.

Clardy, E. R., and Rumpf, E. M. Effect of electric shock treatment on children having schizophrenic manifestations. *Psych. Q.*, 1954, **28**, 616–623.

Clevenger, S. V. Insanity in children. *Am. J. neurol. Psychiat.*, 1883, **2**, 585–601.

Colbert, E. G., and Koegler, R. R. Toe walking in childhood schizophrenia. *J. Pediat.*, 1958, **53**, 219–220.

Creak, M. Childhood psychosis: a review of 100 cases. *Br. J. Psychiat.*, 1963, **109**, 84–89.

Creak, M. Schizophrenic syndrome in childhood. *Dev. Med. child Neurol*, 1964, **6**(5), 530.

Creak, M. Schizophrenic syndrome in childhood. Progress report of a working party. *Cerebral Palsy Bull.*, 1961, **3**, 501. (a)

Creak, M., et al. Schizophrenic syndrome in childhood: report of a working party. *Br. Med. J.*, 1961, **2**, 889–890. (b)

Creak, M., and Ini, S. Families of psychotic children. *J. child Psychol. Psychiat.*, 1960, **1**, 156–175.

Cunningham, A., and Dixon, C. A study of the language of an autistic child. *J. child Psychol. Psychiat.*, 1961, **2**, 193–202.

Davids, A. Intelligence in childhood schizophrenics, other emotionally disturbed children, and their mothers. *J. consult. Psychol.*, 1958, **22**, 159–163.

DesLauriers, A. *The experience of reality in childhood schizophrenia.* New York: International Universities Press, 1962.

DesLauriers, A., and Halpern, F. Psychological tests in childhood schizophrenia. *Am. J. Orthopsychiat.*, 1947, **17**, 57–67.

DeMyer, M. K., and Ferster, C. B. Teaching new social behavior to schizophrenic children. *J. Am. Acad. Child Psychiat.*, 1962, **1**(3), 443–461.

DeSanctes, S. La neuropsychiatria infantile. *Infanzia Anormale*, 1925, **18**, 633–661.

Despert, J. L. Schizophrenia in childhood. *Psychiat. Q.*, 1938, **12**, 366–371.

Despert, J. L. Thinking and motility disorder in a schizophrenic child. *Psychiat. Q.*, 1941, **15**, 522–536.

Despert, J. L. The early recognition of childhood schizophrenia. *Med. Clin. N. Amer.*, 1947, **31**, 680–687.

Despert, J. L. Psychotherapy in child schizophrenia. *Am. J. Psychiat.*, 1947, **104**, 36–43.

Despert, J. L. Some considerations relating to the genesis of autistic behavior in children. *Am. J. Orthopsychiat.*, 1951, **21**, 335–350.

Despert, J. L. Differential diagnosis between obsessive-compulsive neurosis and schizophrenia in children. In P. H. Hoch, and J. Zubin (Eds.), *Psychopathology of childhood.* New York: Grune & Stratton, 1955. Pp. 240–253.

Despert, J. L., and Sherwin, A. E. Further examination of diagnostic criteria in schizophrenic illness and psychoses of infancy and early childhood. *Am. J. Psychiat.*, 1958, **14**, 784–790.

Diagnostic and statistical manual: Mental disorders. Washington, D.C.: Amer. Psychiat. Assoc., 1952.

Down, J. L. *On some of the mental affections of childhood and youth: being the Lettsonian lectures delivered before the Medical Society of London in 1887.* London: Churchill, 1887.

Eaton, L., and Menolascino, M. D. Psychotic reactions of childhood. A follow-up study. *Am. J. Orthopsychiat.,* 1967, **37**, 521–529.

Eisenberg, L. The autistic child in adolescence. *Am. J. Psychiat.,* 1956, **112**, 607–613.

Eisenberg, L. The course of childhood schizophrenia. *A.M.A. Archs. Neurol. Psychiat.,* 1957, **78**, 69–83. (a)

Eisenberg, L. The fathers of autistic children. *Am. J. Orthopsychiat.,* 1957, **27**, 715–724. (b)

Eisenberg, L. Role of drugs in treating disturbed children. *Children,* 1964, **11**, 167–173.

Eisenberg, L. Psychotic disorders in childhood. In R. E. Cook (Ed.), *Biological basis of pediatric practice.* New York: McGraw-Hill, 1966.

Eisenberg, L. Psychotic disorders No. I: clinical features. In A. M. Freedman and H. I. Kaplan (Eds.), *Comprehensive textbook of psychiatry.* Baltimore, Md.: Williams and Wilkens, 1967. Pp. 1443–1448.

Eisenberg, L., and Kanner, L. Early autism—childhood schizophrenia symposium. *Am. J. Orthopsychiat.,* 1956, **26**, 556–564.

Ekstein, R. *Children of space and time, of action and impulse.* New York: Appleton-Century-Crofts, 1966.

Ekstein, R., Bryant, K., and Friedman, S. W. Childhood schizophrenia and allied conditions. In L. Bellak, and P. K. Benedict (Eds.), *Schizophrenia: a review of the syndrome.* New York: Logo Press, 1958. Pp. 555–593.

Ekstein, R., and Wallerstein, J. Choice of interpretation in the treatment of borderline and psychotic children. *Bull. Menninger Clin.,* 1957, **21**, 199–207.

Elkisch, P. The struggle for ego boundaries in a psychotic child. *Am. J. Psychother.,* 1956, **10**, 578–602.

Escalona, S. Some considerations regarding psychotherapy with psychotic children. *Bull. Menninger Clin.,* 1948, **12**, 126–134.

Esman, A. H. Childhood psychosis and childhood schizophrenia. *Am. J. Orthopsychiat.,* 1960, **30**, 391–396.

Esquirol, E. *Mental maladies. A treatise on sanity.* Philadelphia, Pa.: Lea and Blanchard, 1845. (Transl. by E. K. Hunt.)

Eveloff, H. H. The autistic child. *Archs. gen. Psychiat.,* 1960, **3**, 66–81.

Fabian, A. A., and Holden, A. Treatment of childhood schizophrenia in a child guidance clinic. *Am. J. Orthopsychiat.,* 1951, **21**, 571–583.

Ferster, C. B. Positive reinforcement and behavioral deficits of autistic children. *Child Dev.,* 1961, **32**, 437–456.

Ferster, C. B. Psychotherapy by machine communication in disorders of communication. *Res. Publ. Ass. res. nerv. ment. Dis.,* 1964, **12**, 317–333.

Ferster, C. B., and DeMyer, M. K. The development of performance in autistic children in an automatically controlled environment. *J. chron. Dis.,* 1961, **13**(4), 312–345.

Fish, B. The detection of schizophrenia in infancy. *J. nerv. Ment. Dis.,* 1957, **125**, 1–24.

Fish, B. Longitudinal observations on biological deviation in a schizophrenic infant. *Am. J. Psychiat.,* 1959, **116**(1), 25–31.

Fish, B. Drug therapy in psychiatry: psychological aspects. *Comp. Psychiat.,* 1960, **1**, 55–61. (a)

Fish, B. Involvements of the central nervous systems in infants with schizophrenia. *A.M.A. Archs. Neurol.,* 1960, **2**, 115–122. (b)

Fish, B. The study of motor development in infancy and its relationship to psychological functioning. *Am. J. Psychiat.*, 1961, **117**, 1113–1118.

Fish, B., and Alpert, M. Abnormal states of consciousness and muscle tone in infants born to schizophrenic mothers. *Am. J. Psychiat.*, 1962, **119**(5), 439–445.

Freeberg, N. E., and Payne, D. T. Parental influence of cognitive development in early childhood: a review. *Child Dev.*, 1967, **38**(1).

Freedman, A. M. Treatment of autistic schizophrenic children with Marsilid. *J. clin. exp. Psychopath.*, 1958, **19**(2), Suppl. 1, 138.

Freedman, A. M., Ebin, E. V., and Wilson, E. A. Autistic schizophrenic children —an experiment in the use of d-lysergic and diethylamide (LSD-25). *Archs. Gen. Psychiat.*, 1962, **6**, 203–213.

Freedman, A. M., and Ginsberg, V. Exchange transfusions in schizophrenic patients. *J. nerv. ment. Dis.*, 1958, **126**, 294–301.

Friedman, G. Conceptual thinking in schizophrenic children. *Genet. Psychol. Monogr.*, 1961, **63**, 149–196.

Frohman, C. E., Goodman, M., Beckett, P. G. S., Latham, L. K., Senf, R., and Gottlieb, J. S. The isolation of an active factor from serum of schizophrenic patients. *Ann. N. Y. Acad. Sci.*, 1962, **96**, 438–447.

Fry, W. F. The schizophrenic "who." *Psychoanal. Rev.*, 1962–63, **49**(4), 68–73.

Fuller, G. B. A further study on rotation: cross-validation. *J. clin. Psychol.*, 1963, **19**(1), 127–128.

Fuller, G. B. The objective measurement of perception in determining personality disorganization among children. *J. clin. Psychol.*, 1965, **2**(3), 305–307.

Fuller, G. B., and Chagnon, G. Factors influencing rotation in the Bender Gestalt performance of children. *J. proj. Tech.*, 1962, **26**, 36–46.

Gillies, S. Discrimination learning in psychotic children and subnormal controls. *Bull. Br. Psychol. Soc.*, 1965, **18**(59), 7A.

Goldberg, B., and Soper, H. H. Childhood psychosis or mental retardation: a diagnostic dilemma. I. Psychiatric and psychological aspects. *Cana. med. Ass. J.*, 1963, **89**, 1015–1019.

Goldfarb, W. Rorschach test differences between family-reared, institution-reared, and schizophrenic children. *Am. J. Orthopsychiat.*, 1949, **19**, 624–633.

Goldfarb, W. Receptor preferences in schizophrenic children. *A.M.A. Archs. neurol. Psychiat.*, 1956, **76**, 643–652.

Goldfarb, W. Pain reactions in a group of institutionalized schizophrenic children. *Am. J. Orthopsychiat.*, 1958, **28**, 777–785.

Goldfarb, W. *Childhood schizophrenia.* Cambridge, Mass.: Harvard University Press, 1961.

Goldfarb, W. Families of schizophrenic children. In L. C. Kolb et al. (Eds.), *Mental retardation.* (A series of Research Publ. ,A.R.N.M.D., #39.) Baltimore, Md.: Williams and Wilkens, 1962. Pp. 256–269.

Goldfarb, W. Self awareness in schizophrenic children. *Archs. gen. Psychiat.*, 1963, **8**(1), 47–60.

Goldfarb, W. An investigation of childhood schizophrenia. *Archs. gen. Psychiat.*, 1964, **11**(6), 620–634.

Goldfarb, W. Corrective socialization: a rationale for the treatment of schizophrenic children. (Saul Albert Memorial Lecture, McGill U.) *Can. Psychiat. Ass.*, 1965, **10**, 481–496.

Goldfarb, W. The subclassification of psychotic children: application to a study of longitudinal change. Presented at the Conference on Transmission of Schizophrenia, under the auspices of the Foundations' Fund for Research in Psychiatry, at Dorado Beach, Puerto Rico, June 26–July 1, 1967. (a)

Goldfarb, W. Factors in the development of schizophrenic children: an approach to subclassification. Report to First Rochester Conference on Schizophrenia, Rochester, March 1967. (b)

Goldfarb, W. Therapeutic management of schizophrenic children. In *Modern perspectives in international child psychiatry*. London. (In press.)

Goldfarb, W., Braunstein, P., and Lorge, I. A study of speech patterns in a group of schizophrenic children. *Am. J. Orthopsychiat.*, 1956, **26**, 544–555.

Goldfarb, W., and Dorsen, M. M. *Annotated bibliography of childhood schizophrenia and related disorders*. New York: Basic Books, 1956.

Goldfarb, W., Sibulkin, L., Behrens, M., and Jahoda, H. Parental perplexity and childhood confusion. In A. H. Esman (Ed.), *New frontiers in child guidance*. New York: International Universities Press, 1958. Pp. 157–170.

Goldfarb, W., and Mintz, I. The schizophrenic child's reactions to time and space. *Archs. gen. Psychiat.*, 1961, **5**, 535–543.

Goldfarb, W., Goldfarb, N., and Pollack, R. Changes in intelligence quotient of schizophrenic children during residential treatment. Presented at Am. Orthopsychiat. Assoc., March 1964.

Goldfarb, W., and Pollack, R. C. The childhood schizophrenic's response to schooling in a residential treatment center. In P. H. Hoch and J. Zubin (Eds.), *The evaluation of psychiatric treatment*. New York, Grune & Stratton, 1964. Pp. 221–246.

Goldfarb, W., Goldfarb, N., and Pollack, R. A three year comparison of day and residential treatments of schizophrenic children. *Archs. gen. Psychiat.*, 1966, **14**, 119–128. (a)

Goldfarb, W., Goldfarb, N., and Scholl, H. The speech of mothers of schizophrenic children. *Am. J. Psychiat.*, 1966, **122**, 1220–1227. (b)

Goldfarb, W., Levy, D. M., and Meyers, D. I. The verbal encounter between the schizophrenic child and his mother. In G. S. Goldman and D. Shapiro (Eds.), *Developments in psychoanalysis at Columbia University*. New York: Hafner Publishing Co., 1966. (c)

Hagnell, O. *A prospective study on the incidence of mental disorder*. Norstedts: Svenska Bokforlaget, 1966.

Halpern, E. Conceptual development in a schizophrenic boy. *J. Child Psychiat.*, 1966, **5**(1), 66–74.

Hamburger, A. *Psychopathologie des kindesalters*. Berlin: Springer, 1926. Pp. 780–808.

Hebb, D. O. *A textbook of psychology*. London: Saunders, 1958.

Hermelin, B. Response behavior of autistic children and subnormal controls. Paper for the XVII International Congress of Psychology, August 1963.

Hermelin, B., and O'Connor, N. The response and self-generated behavior of severely disturbed children and severely subnormal controls. *Br. J. soc. clin. Psychol.*, 1963, **2**(1), 37–43.

Hermelin, B., and O'Connor, N. Effects of sensory input and sensory dominance on severely disturbed, autistic children and on subnormal controls. *Br. J. Psychiat.*, 1964, **55**(2), 201–206.

Hermelin, B., and O'Connor, N. "Visual imperception in psychotic children." *Brit. J. Psychol.*, 1965, **56**(4), 455–460.

Hermelin, B., and O'Connor, N. Remembering of words by psychotic and subnormal children. *Br. J. Psychol.*, (In press).

Higgins, J. Effects of child rearing by schizophrenic mothers. *J. psychiat. Res.*, 1966, **4**(3), 153–167.

Hinton, G. G. Childhood psychosis or mental retardation: a diagnostic dilemma. II. Pediatric and neurological aspects. *Can. med. Ass. J.*, 1963, **89**, 1020–1024.

Hirschberg, J. C., and Bryant, K. H. Problems in the differential diagnosis of childhood schizophrenia. *Res. nerv. ment. Dis.*, 1954, **34**, 343–361.

Hirschberg, J. C., and Bryant, K. H. Problems in the differential diagnosis of childhood schizophrenia. *Res. nerv. ment. Dis.*, 1955, **34**, 454–461.

Hoberman, S. B., and Goldfarb, W. Speech reception thresholds in schizophrenic children. *J. Speech Hearing Res.*, 1963, **6**, 101–106.

Hoch, P. H., and Polatin, P. Pseudo-neurotic forms of schizophrenia. *Psychiat. Q.*, 1949, **23**, 248–276.

Hulse, W. C. Dementia infantilis. *J. nerv. ment. Dis.*, 1954, **319**, 471–477.

Ireland, W. W. Observations on mental affections in children, and allied neuroses. *Edinburgh Med. J.*, 1896, **42**, 326–330.

Jahoda, H., and Goldfarb, W. Use of a standard observation for the psychological evaluation of nonspeaking children. *Am. J. Orthopsychiat.*, 1957, **27**, 599–606.

Kallmann, F. J. Heredity-genetic theory, analysis of 691 twin index families. *Am. J. Psychiat.*, 1946, **103**, 309–322.

Kallmann, F. J., and Roth, B. Genetic aspects of preadolescent schizophrenia. *Am. J. Psychiat.*, 1956, **112**, 599–606.

Kanner, L. Autistic disturbances of affective contact. *Nerv. Child*, 1942, **2**, 217–250.

Kanner, L. Irrelevant and metaphorical language in early infantile autism. *Am. J. Psychiat.*, 1946, **103**, 242–246.

Kanner, L. Problems of nosology and psychodynamics of early infantile autism. *Am. J. Orthopsychiat.*, 1949, **19**, 416–426.

Kanner, L. To what extent is early infantile autism determined by constitutional inadequacies? *Ass. Res. nerv. ment. Dis., Proc. (1953)*, 1954, **33**, 378–385.

Kanner, L., and Eisenberg, L. Notes on the follow-up studies of autistic children. In P. H. Hoch and J. Zubin (Eds.), *Psychopathology of childhood*. New York: Grune & Stratton, 1955. Pp. 227–239.

Kardiner, A. *The individual and his society*. New York: Columbia University Press, 1939.

Kasanin, J., and Kaufman, M. R. A study of the functional psychoses in childhood. *Am. J. Psychiat.*, 1929, **9**, 307–384.

Katz, P. A. Verbal discrimination performance of disadvantaged children: stimulus and subject variables. *Child Dev.*, 1967, **38**(1).

Kaufman, I., Frank, T., Heims, L., Herrick, J., Rusir, D., and Willer, L. Treatment implications of a new classification of parents of schizophrenic children. *Am. J. Psychiat.*, 1960, **116**, 920–924.

Kaufman, I., Frank, T., Heims, L., Herrick, J., and Willer, L. Parents of schizophrenic children: Workshop, 1958: Four types of defense in mothers and fathers of schizophrenic children. *Am. J. Orthopsychiat.*, 1959, **29**, 460–472.

Kawi, A. A., and Pasamanick, B. Prenatal and paranatal factors in the development of childhood reading disorders. *Monogr. Soc. Res. Child Dev.*, 1959, **24**(4), 1–80.

Kennard, M. A. Interitance of electroencephalogram patterns in children with behavior disorders. *Psychosom. Med.*, 1949, **11**, 151–157.

Kennard, M. A. The characteristics of thought disturbance as related to electroencephalographic findings in children and adolescents. *Am. J. Psychiat.*, 1959, **115**, 911–921.

Kety, S. S. Biochemical theories of schizophrenia. Part I of a two part critical review of current theories and of the evidence used to support them. *Science*, 1959, **129**, 1528–1532. (a)

Kety, S. S. Biochemical theories of schizophrenia. Part II of a two part critical review of current theories and of the evidence used to support them. *Science,* 1959, **129**, 1590–1596. (b)

Kety, S. S. Current biochemical research in schizophrenia. In P. H. Hoch, and J. Zubin (Eds.), *Psychopathology of schizophrenia.* New York: Grune & Stratton, 1966.

Klebanoff, L. B. I. Parents of schizophrenic children: Workshop, 1958: Parental attitudes of mothers of schizophrenic, brain-injured and retarded, and normal children. *Am. J. Orthopsychiat.,* 1959, **29**, 445–454.

Knobloch, H., and Grant, D. K. Etiologic factors in "early infantile autism," and childhood schizophrenia. *Am. J. dis. Child.,* 1961, **102**, 535–536.

Knobloch, H., and Pasamanick, B. Etiologic factors in early infantile autism and childhood schizophrenia. Address at Tenth International Congress of Pediatrics, Lisbon, September 1962.

Korn, S. Family dynamics and childhood schizophrenia: a comparison of the family backgrounds of two low socioeconomic minority groups, one with schizophrenic children, the other with rheumatic fever children. Doctoral Dissertation, Yeshiva University Graduate School of Education, 1963.

Kraepelin, E. *Dementia praecox.* (Transl. by M. R. Barclay.) Edinburgh: Livingstone, 1919.

Kramer, Y., Rabkin, R., and Spitzer, R. L. Whirling as a clinical test in childhood schizophrenia. *J. Pediat.,* 1958, **52**(3), 295–303.

Kringlen, E. Schizophrenia in twins. An epidemiological study. *Psychiatry,* 1966, **29**(2).

Leach, B. E., and Heath, R. G. The in-vitro oxidation of epinephrine in plasma. *A.M.A. Archs. neurol. Psychiat.,* 1956, **76**, 444·

Lebowitz, M. H., Colbert, E. G. and Palmer, J O. Schizophrenia in children. *Am. J. dist. Child.,* 1961, **120**, 25–27.

Leitch, M. and Schaefer, S. A study of the Thematic Apperception Tests of psychotic children. *Am. J. Orthopsychiat.,* 1947, **17**, 337–342.

Lennard, H. L., Beaulieu, M. R., and Embrey, M. G. Interaction in families with a schizophrenic child. *Archs. gen. Psychiat.,* 1965, **12**(2), 166–183.

Levin, S., and Impastato, A. S. A pilot study of L-Glutavite in hospitalized "autistic" and "hyperactive" children. *Am. J. Psychiat.,* 1961, **118**, 459.

Lilienfeld, A. M., Pasamanick, B., and Rogers, R. Relationships between pregnancy experience and the development of certain neuropsychiatric disorders in childhood. *Am. J. Publ. Hlth.,* 1955, **55**, 637–642.

Lohrenz, J. G., Levy, L., and David, J. F. Schizophrenia or epilepsy? A problem in differential diagnosis. *Compreh. Psychiat.,* 1962, **3**(1), 54–62.

Loomis, E. A., Jr. Autistic and symbiotic syndromes in children. *Monogr. Soc. Res. Child Dev.,* 1960, **25**(3, Whole No. 77), 39–48.

Loomis, E. A., Jr., Hilgeman, L. M., and Meyer, L. Childhood psychosis: II. Play patterns as nonverbal indices of ego functions: a preliminary report. *Am. J. Orthopsychiat.,* 1957, **27**, 691–700.

Lovaas, O. I., Freitag, G., Gold, V. J., and Kassara, I. C. Experimental studies in childhood schizophrenia. Analysis of self-destructive behavior. *J. exp. child Psychol.,* 1965, **2**(1), 67–84.

Lowe, L. Families of children with early childhood schizophrenia. *Archs. gen. Psychiat.,* 1964, **14**.

Lutz, J. Über die schizophrenie un kindesalter, schweiz. *Archs. neurol. Psychiat.,* 1937, **390**, 335–372; 1937, **40**, 141–163.

Mahler, M. S. Remarks on psychoanalysis with psychotic children. *Q. J. child Behav.,* 1949, **1**, 18–21.

Mahler, M. S. On child psychosis and schizophrenia: autistic and symbiotic infantile psychoses. *Psychoanal. stud. Child,* 1952, **7**, 286–305.

Mahler, M. S. Autism and symbiosis: two extreme disturbances of identity. *Int. J. Psychoanal.*, 1958, **39**, (Parts II-IV), 1–7.

Mahler, M. S. Perceptual de-differentiation and psychotic "object relationship." *Int. J. Psychoanal.*, 1960, **41**(Parts IV-V), 548–553.

Mahler, M. S. On sadness and grief in infancy: loss and restoration of the symbiotic love object. *Psychoanal. stud. Child*, 1961, **16**, 332–351.

Mahler, M. S., and Furer, M. Observations on research regarding the "symbiotic syndrome" of infantile psychosis. *Psychoanal. Q.*, 1960, **29**, 317–327.

Mahler, M. S., Furer, M., and Settlage, C. F. Severe emotional disturbances in childhood: psychosis. In S. Arieti (Ed.), *American handbook of psychiatry.* New York: Basic Books, 1959. Pp. 816–839.

Mahler, M. S., and Gosliner, B. J. On symbiotic child psychosis: genetic, dynamic and restitutive aspects. *Psychoanal. stud. Child*, 1955, **10**, 195–214.

McDermott, J. F., et al. Social class and mental illness in children: the question of childhood psychosis. *Am. J. Orthopsychiat.*, 1967, **37**(3), 548–557.

Menolascino, F. Psychoses of childhood. Experiences of a mental retardation pilot project. *Am. J. ment. Defic.*, 1965, **70**(1), 83–92.

Metz, J. R. Conditioning generalized imitation in autistic children. *J. exp. child Psychol.*, 1965, **2**, 389–399.

Meyer, A. *The collected papers of Adolph Meyer.* Baltimore, Md.: Johns Hopkins Press, 1950–52.

Meyers, D. I., and Goldfarb, W. Studies of perplexity in mothers of schizophrenic children. *Am. J. Orthopsychiat.*, 1961, **31**, 551–564.

Meyers, D. I., and Goldfarb, W. Psychiatric appraisal of parents and siblings of schizophrenic children. *Am. J. Psychiat.*, 1962, **118**, 902–915.

Mills, C. K. Insanity in children. In L. Starr (Ed.), *An American textbook of the diseases of children.* (2nd ed.) Philadelphia, Pa.: Saunders, 1898.

Mitchell, A. Influence of diseases of early life on production of insanity. *Br. J. ment. Sci.*, 1870, **16**, 149–160.

Nichtern, S. Chemotherapy in child psychiatry. In A. J., Krakowski, and D. A. Santora (Eds.), *Child psychiatry and the general practitioner.* Springfield, Ill.: Thomas, 1962.

Norman, E. Reality relationships of schizophrenic children. *Br. J. med. Psychol.*, 1954, **27**, 126–141.

Norman, E. Affect and withdrawal in schizophrenic children. *Br. J. med. Psychoanal.*, 1955, **28**, 1–18.

Noshpitz, J. P. Notes on the theory of residential treatment. *J. child Psychiat.*, 1962, **1**(2), 284–296.

O'Connor, N., and Hermelin, B. Measures of distance and motility in psychotic children and severely subnormal controls. *Br. J. soc. clin. Psychol.*, 1963, **3**(1), 29–33.

O'Connor, N., and Hermelin, B. Sensory dominance in autistic imbecile children and controls. *Archs. gen. Psychiat.*, 1965, **12**, 99–103.

Osterkamp, A., and Sands, D. J. Early feeding and birth difficulties in childhood schizophrenia: a brief study. *J. genet. Psychol.*, 1962, **101**, 363–366.

Pasamanick, B., and Knobloch, H. Epidemiologic studies on the complications of pregnancy and the birth process. In G. Caplan (Ed.), *Prevention of mental disorders in children.* New York: Basic Books, 1961.

Pasamanick, B., and Lilienfeld, A. M. Association of maternal and fetal factors with the development of mental deficiency. *J. Am. med. Ass.*, 1955, **159**, 155–160.

Pasamanick, B., Rogers, M., and Lilienfeld, A. M. Pregnancy experience and the development of childhood behavior disorders. *Am. J. Psychiat.*, 1956, **112**, 613–618.

Piotrowski, Z. A., and Lewis, N. D. C. A case of stationary schizophrenia beginning in early childhood with remarks on certain aspects of children's Rorschach records. *Q. J. Child Behav.*, 1950, **2**, 115–139.

Pollack, M. Mental subnormality and childhood schizophrenia. In P. H. Hoch and J. Zubin (Eds.), *Psychopathology of mental development*. New York: Grune & Stratton, 1967.

Pollack, M., and Krieger, H. P. Oculomotor and postural patterns in schizophrenic children. *A.M.A. Archs. neurol. Psychiat.*, 1958, **79**, 720–726.

Pollin, W., Stabener, J. R., Mosher, L., and Tupin, J. Life history differences in identical twins discordant for schizophrenia. *Am. J. Orthopsychiat.*, 1966, **36**, 492–501.

Potter, H. W. Schizophrenia in children. *Am. J. Psychiat.*, 1933, **12**(6), 1253–1270.

Progress report of a working party. Schizophrenic syndrome in children. *Br. Med. J.*, 1961, **11**, 889–891.

Pronovost, W., Wakstein, M. P., Wakstein, N. J., and Murphy, A. T. The speech behavior and language comprehension of autistic children. *J. chron. Dis.*, 1961, **13**, 228–233.

Putnam, M. C. Some observations on psychosis in early childhood. In G. Caplan (Ed.), *Emotional problems of early childhood*. New York: Basic Books, 1955. Pp. 519–523.

Rachman, S., and Berger, M. Whirling and postural control in schizophrenic children. *J. child psychol. Psychiat.*, 1963, **4**, 137–155.

Rado, S. *Psychoanalysis of behavior*. New York: Grune & Stratton, 1956.

Rank, B. Adaptation of the psychoanalytic technique for the treatment of young children with atypical development. *Am. J. Orthopsychiat.*, 1949, **19**, 130–139.

Rank, B. Intensive study and treatment of preschool children who show marked personality deviations or "atypical development" and their parents. In G. Caplan (Ed.), *Emotional problems of early childhood*. New York: Basic Books, 1955.

Redl, F., and Wineman, D. *Children who hate*. New York: Free Press, 1951.

Rice, G., Kepecs, J. G., and Yahalom, I. Differences in communicative impact between mothers of psychotic and nonpsychotic children. *Am. J. Orthopsychiat.*, 1966, **36**, 529–543.

Rimland, B. *Infantile autism: the syndrome and its implications for a neural theory of behavior*. New York: Appleton-Century-Crofts, 1964.

Robinson, J. F. *Psychiatric inpatient treatment of children*. Amer. Psychiat. Assoc., 1957.

Rosenthal, D. The offspring of schizophrenic couples. *J. Psychiat. Res.*, 1966, **4**, 169–188.

Rush, B. *Medical inquiries and observations upon the diseases of the mind*. Philadelphia, Pa.: Kimber and Richardson, 1812.

Rutter, M. Classification and categorization in child psychiatry. *J. child psychol. Psychoanal.*, 1956, **6**(2), 71–83.

Rutter, M. The influence of organic and emotional factors on the origins, nature and outcome of childhood psychosis. *Dev. Med. child Neurol.*, 1965, **7**, 518–528.

Rutter, M. Behavioural and cognitive characteristics of a series of psychotic children. In J. Wing (Ed.), *Childhood autism: clinical, educational and social aspects*. London; Pergamon Press, 1966. (a)

Rutter, M. Prognosis: psychotic children in adolescence and early adult life. In J. Wing (Ed.). *Childhood autism: clinical, educational and social aspects*. London: Pergamon Press, 1966. (b)

Sankar, S. D. V., Cates, N., Broer, H. H., and Sankar, D. B. Biochemical parameters of childhood schizophrenia (autism) and growth. *Recent adv. biol. Psychiat.*, 1963, **5**, 176–183.

Sanua, V. D. The sociocultural aspects of childhood schizophrenia. In G. H. Zuk, and I. Boszormenyi-Nagy (Eds.), *Family therapy and disturbed families.* Palo Alto, Cal.: Science and Behavior Books, 1967.

Schachter, F., Meyer, L. R., and Loomis, E. A. Childhood schizophrenia and mental retardation: differential diagnosis before and after one year of psychotherapy. *Am. J. Orthopsychiat.*, 1962, **32**, 584–595.

Schain, R. J., and Freedman, D. X. Studies on 5-hydroxindole metabolism in autistic and other retarded children. *J. Pediat.*, 1961, **58**, 315.

Scheerer, M., Rothman, E., and Goldstein, K. A case of "idiot savant": an experimental study of personality organization. *Psychol. Monogr.*, 1945, **58**(4).

Schoen, R. J., and Yannet, H. Infantile autism: an analysis of 50 cases and a consideration of certain neurophysiologic concepts. *J. Pediat.*, 1960, **57**, 560–567.

Schopler, E. Early infantile autism and receptor processes. *Archs. gen. Psychiat.*, 1965, **13**(5), 327–335.

Schopler, E. Visual versus tactical receptor preference in normal and schizophrenic children. *J. abnorm. Psychol.*, 1966, **71**(2), 108–114.

Schulman, I. Concept formation in the schizophrenic child: a study of ego development. *J. clin. Psychol.*, 1953, **9**, 11–15.

Shaw, C. R., Lucas, J., and Rabinovitch, R. D. Effects of tryptophane loading on indole excretion. *Archs. gen. Psychiat.*, 1959, **1**, 366–370.

Silver, A., and Gabriel, H. P. The association of schizophrenia in childhood with primitive postural responses and decreased muscle tone. *Dev. med. child Neurol.*, 1964, **6**(5), 495.

Singer, M., and Wynne, L. C. Differentiating characteristics of the parents of childhood schizophrenics, childhood neurotics, and young adult schizophrenics. *Am. J. Psychiat.*, 1963, **120**(3), 234–243.

Soble, D. Some observations of childhood schizophrenia. *Psychiat. Q., Suppl.*, 1955, **29**, 272–290.

Speers, R. W., and Lansing, C. *Group therapy in child psychosis.* Chapel Hill: University of North Carolina Press, 1965.

Spitzka, E. D. Insanity. In J. M. Keating (Ed.), *Cyclopedia of the diseases of children.* Vol. 4. Philadelphia, Pa.: Lippincott, 1890, 1038–1053.

Starr, P. H. Psychoses in children: their origin and structure. *Psychoanal. Q.*, 1954, **23**, 544–565.

Steisel, I. M., Weiland, I. H., Smith, C. J., and Schulman, J. Interaction in nonverbal psychotic children II. Measuring by a differential diagnostic instrument. *Archs. gen. Psychiat.*, 1961, **5**, 141–145.

Steisel, I. M., Weiland, I. H., Denny, J. V., Smith, K., and Chaiken, N. Measuring interaction in non-verbal psychotic children. *Amer. J. Orthopsychiat.*, 1960, **30**, 405–411.

Stroh, G., and Buick, D. Perceptual development and childhood psychosis. *Br. J. Med. Psychol.*, 1964, **37**(4), 291–299.

Sutton, H. E., and Read, J. H. Abnormal amino acid metabolism in a case suggesting autism. *J. dis. Child*, 1958, **96**, 23–28.

Syner, F. H., and Shaw, C. R. Effect of schizophrenic serum on in vitro synthesis and gamma aminobutyric acid. *Comp. Psychiat.*, 1962, **3**, 309–313.

Taft, L. T., and Goldfarb, W. Prenatal and perinatal factors in childhood schizophrenia. *Dev. med. child Neurol.*, 1964, **6**(1), 32–43.

Terris, M., Lapouse, R., and Monk, M. A. The relations of prematurity and previous fetal loss to childhood schizophrenia. *Am. J. Psychiat.*, 1964, **121**, 476–481.

Tilton, J. R., DeMyer, M. K., and Loew, L. H. *Annotated bibliography on childhood schizophrenia.* New York: Grune & Stratton, 1966.

Tizard, J. Mental subnormality and child psychiatry. *J. child psychol. Psychiat.*, 1966, **7**, 1–15.

Vorster, D. An investigation into the part played by organic factors in childhood schizophrenia. *J. ment. Sci.*, 1960, **106**, 494–522.

Weakland, J. H., and Fry, W. F., Jr. Letters of mothers of schizophrenics. *Am. J. Orthopsychiat.*, 1962, **4**, 604–623.

Wechsler, D., and Jaros, E. Schizophrenic patterns on the WISC. *J. clin. Psychol.*, 1965, **21**(3), 288–291.

Weiland, I. H., and Legg, D. R. Formal speech characteristics as a diagnostic aid in childhood psychosis. *Am. J. Orthopsychiat.*, 1964, **34**, 91–94.

Weintraub, W., and Aronson, H. The application of verbal behavior analysis to the study of psychological defense mechanisms, IV: Speech pattern associated with depressive behavior. *J. nerv. ment. Dis.*, 1967, **144**(1).

Weygandt, W. Idiotic und imbezillitat. In G. Aschaffenberg (Ed.), *Handbook der psychiatrie.* Zweite Abt. Leipzig und Wien: Spezieller Teil, 1915.

Weygandt, W. Dementia praecocissima und dementia infantilis. *Med. Week,* 1933, 1053–1055.

White, P. T., DeMyer, W., and DeMyer, M. EEG abnormalities in early childhood schizophrenia: a double blind study of psychiatrically disturbed and normal children during promozene sedation. *Am. J. Psychiat.*, 1964, **120**, 950–958.

Witkin, H. et al. *Psychological differentiation.* New York: Wiley, 1962.

Wolff, S., and Chess, S. A behavioral study of schizophrenic children. *Acta Psychiat. Scand.,* 1964, **40**(4), 438–466.

Wolff, S., and Chess, S. Analysis of the language of fourteen schizophrenic children. *J. child psychol. Psychiat.*, 1965, **6**(1), 29–41.

Wright, D., Loomis, E., and Meyer, L. Observational Q-sort differences between schizophrenic, retarded and normal pre-school boys. *Child Dev.*, 1963, **34**(1), 169–185.

Yakovlev, P. I., Weinberger, M., and Chipman, C. E. Heller's syndrome as a pattern of schizophrenic behavior disturbance in early childhood. *Am. J. ment. Defic.*, 1948, **53**, 318–337.

Zitrin, A., Ferber, P., and Cohen, D. Pre- and paranatal factors in mental disorders in children. *J. nerv. ment. Dis.*, 1964, **139**, 357–361.

Name Index

Subject Index